Québec

Seventh Edition

Travel better, enjoy more

ULYSSES

Travel Guides

Research and Writing
Exploring
François Rémillard
Portrait
Benoit Prieur

Publisher
André Duchesne

Editor
Jacqueline Grekin

Production Assistance
Julie Brodeur
Pierre Daveluy
Annie Frenette
Séverine Giroux
Pierre Ledoux

Page Layout
Isabelle Lalonde

Computer Graphics
André Duchesne

Cartographer
Isabelle Lalonde

Artistic Director
Patrick Farei (Atoll)

Illustrations
Lorrette Pierson
Myriam Gagné
Marie-Annick Viatour

Photography
Cover Page
Patrick Escudero

Additional research and writing: Gabriel Audet, Caroline Béliveau, Julie Brodeur, Alexandre Chouinard, Daniel Desjardins, Alexandra Gilbert, Stéphane G. Marceau, Jacqueline Grekin, François Hénault, Judith Lefebvre, Claude Morneau, Yves Ouellet, Joël Pomerleau, Sylvie Rivard, Yves Séguin, Marcel Verreault.

Photography: *Architecture:* Guy Dagenais, Michel Gagné, Perry Mastrovito, Roger Michel, Roch Nadeau, Carlos Pineda, François Rémillard.
Nature: Michel Gagné, H. Hughes, Perry Mastrovito, Roch Nadeau, Sean O'Neill, Carlos Pineda, Philippe Renault, B. Terry.

Acknowledgements: Ulysses Travel Guides would like to thank the Associations Touristiques Régionales, in particular, Josée Lafleur (Association Touristique de l'Outaouais), Lina Racine (Association Touristique de Charlevoix), Josée Jacques (Tourisme Cantons-de-l'Est) and Manon Lefebvre (Association Touristique des Laurentides).

We gratefully acknowledge the financial support of the Government of Canada through the Book Publishing Industry Development Program (BPIDP) for our publishing activities. We would also like to thank the government of Québec for its SODEC income tax program for book publication.

Offices
CANADA: Ulysses Travel Guides, 4176 St. Denis Street, Montréal, Québec, H2W 2M5,
☎(514) 843-9447 or 1-877-542-7247, ⇌(514) 843-9448, info@ulysses.ca, www.ulyssesguides.com

EUROPE: Les Guides de Voyage Ulysse SARL, 127 rue Amelot, 75011 Paris, France, ☎01 43 38 89 50, ⇌01 43 38 89 52, voyage@ulysse.ca, www.ulyssesguides.com

U.S.A.: Ulysses Travel Guides, 305 Madison Avenue, Suite 1166, New York, NY 10165,
☎1-877-542-7247, info@ulysses.ca, www.ulyssesguides.com

Distributors
CANADA: Ulysses Books & Maps, 4176 St. Denis Street, Montréal, Québec, H2W 2M5,
☎(514) 843-9882, ext.2232, 800-748-9171, Fax: 514-843-9448, info@ulysses.ca, www.ulyssesguides.com

GREAT BRITAIN AND IRELAND: World Leisure Marketing, Unit 11, Newmarket Court, Newmartket Drive, Derby DE24 8NW, ☎1 332 57 37 37, Fax: 1 332 57 33 99, office@wlmsales.co.uk

SCANDINAVIA: Scanvik, Esplanaden 8B, 1263 Copenhagen K, DK, ☎(45) 33.12.77.66,
Fax: (45) 33.91.28.82

SWITZERLAND: OLF, P.O. Box 1061, CH-1701 Fribourg, ☎(026) 467.51.11, Fax: (026) 467.54.66

U.S.A.: BHB Distribution (a division of Weatherhill), 41 Monroe Turnpike, Trumbull, CT 06611,
☎1-800-437-7840 or (203) 459-5090, Fax: 1-800-557-5601 or (203) 459-5095

OTHER COUNTRIES: Ulysses Books & Maps, 4176 St. Denis Street, Montréal, Québec,
H2W 2M5, ☎(514) 843-9882, ext.2232, 800-748-9171, Fax: 514-843-9448, info@ulysses.ca,
www.ulyssesguides.com

Canadian Cataloguing-in-Publication Data (see p 4)
© May 2003, Ulysses Travel Guides.
All rights reserved
Printed in Canada
ISBN 2-89464-595-3

*Eastward, the view down the St. Lawrence towards the Gulf is
the finest of all, scarcely surpassed by anything in the world.
Your eye follows the range of lofty mountains until their
blue summits are blended and lost in the blue of the sky.*

Susanna Moodie, *Roughing it in the Bush* (1852)

National Library of Canada Cataloguing-in-Publication Data

Main entry under title:

Québec

(Ulysses travel guide)
Translation of: Le Québec
Includes index.

ISSN 1486-3502
ISBN 2-89464-595-3

1. Québec (Province) - Guidebooks. II. Series.

FC2907.Q4213   917.1404'4   C99-301663-4   F1052.7.Q4213

Write to Us

The information contained in this guide was correct at press time. However, mistakes can slip in, omissions are always possible, places can disappear, etc. The authors and publisher hereby disclaim any liability for loss or damage resulting from omissions or errors.

We value your comments, corrections and suggestions, as they help us to keep each guide up to date. The best contributions will be rewarded with a free book from Ulysses Travel Guides. All you have to do is write us at the following address and indicate which title you would be interested in receiving (see the list at the end of the guide).

Ulysses Travel Guides

4176 St. Denis Street
Montréal, Québec
Canada H2W 2M5

305 Madison Avenue
Suite 1166, New York
NY 10165

www.ulyssesguides.com
E-mail: *text@ulysses.ca*

Symbols

≡	Air conditioning
bkfst incl.	Breakfast included
⇌	Fax number
ℑ	Fireplace
⊙	Fitness centre
fb	Full board (lodging + 3 meals)
½b	Half board (lodging + 2 meals)
♿	Hotel with wheelchair access
K	Kitchenette
🐕	Pets allowed
≈	Pool
pb/sb	Both private and shared bathrooms*
sb	Shared bathroom*
ℝ	Refrigerator
ℜ	Restaurant
⌂	Sauna
✲	Spa
☎	Telephone number
🚢	Ulysses's favourite
®	Whirlpool

*Note that all establishments have private bathrooms unless otherwise indicated.

Attraction Classification

★	Interesting
★★	Worth a visit
★★★	Not to be missed

Hotel Classification

$	$50 or less
$$	$51 to $100
$$$	$101 to $150
$$$$	$151 to $200
$$$$$	more than $200

Unless otherwise indicated, the prices in the guide are
for one standard room, double occupancy in high season.

Restaurant Classification

$	$10 or less
$$	$11 to $20
$$$	$21 to $30
$$$$	more than $30

Unless otherwise indicated, the prices in the guide are for a
three-course evening meal for one person, not including drinks and tip.

All prices in this guide are in Canadian dollars.

Table of Contents

Table of contents *(continued)*

List of Maps

List of Maps *(continued)*

Map Symbols

🅱	Tourist information (permanent service)
🅿	Tourist information (seasonal service)
🏌	Golf course
▲	Campground
⛷	Downhill-ski centre
🏛	Museum
	Car ferry
	Passenger ferry
	Bus station
H	Hospital
P	Parking
❶	Sanctuary or monastery
✝	Church
⊠	Border post
	Lookout
	Métro station
	Steam train
	Whale-watching centre
⚓	Port or marina
	Pisciculture centre
	Train station
🚲	Bike path
	Ulysses Travel Bookshop
♠	Casino

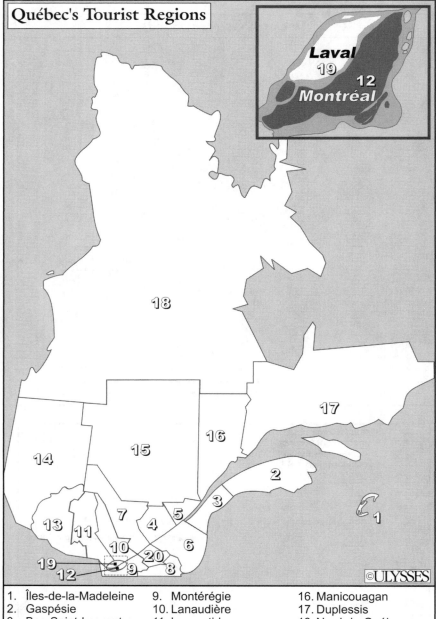

Québec's Tourist Regions

Laval
19
12
Montréal

1. Îles-de-la-Madeleine
2. Gaspésie
3. Bas-Saint-Laurent
4. Québec City Region
5. Charlevoix
6. Chaudière-Appalaches
7. Mauricie
8. Cantons-de-l'Est (Eastern Townships)
9. Montérégie
10. Lanaudière
11. Laurentides (Laurentians)
12. Montréal
13. Outaouais
14. Abitibi-Témiscamingue
15. Saguenay–Lac-Saint-Jean
16. Manicouagan
17. Duplessis
18. Nord-du-Québec (James Bay and Nunavik)
19. Laval
20. Centre-du-Québec

©ULYSSES

Portrait

Situated in the
extreme northeast of the North America, Québec is Canada's largest province.

It covers a surface area of 1,550,000 km², roughly equivalent to the size of France, Germany and the Iberian peninsula put together, or slightly larger than the state of Alaska. With the exception of certain southern regions, Québec is sparsely populated and is characterized by an expansive wilderness of lakes, rivers and forests. The province forms a huge northern peninsula, with James Bay and Hudson Bay to the west, Hudson Strait and Ungava Bay to the north, and the Gulf of St. Lawrence to the south. Québec also has very long land borders that it shares with Ontario to the west and southwest, with New Brunswick and the state of Maine to the southeast, with the states of New York, Vermont and New Hampshire to the south and with Labrador, part of the province of Newfoundland and Labrador, to the northeast.

Québec's borders changed several times prior to 1927, when the province was defined as we know it today. With Canadian Confederation in 1867, Québec occupied the territory previously known as Lower Canada, which corresponds to what is now south-

ern Québec. Soon, Québec expanded northward. By 1898, it included the region between Abitibi and the Rivière Eastmain, and in 1912, the province grew once again, when Nouveau Québec was added in the north. In 1927, London's Privy Council decided in favour of Newfoundland in its dispute with Québec over the immense territory of Labrador.

Geography

Québec's geography is dominated by the St. Lawrence River, the Appalachian Mountain range and the Canadian Shield, three of the most distinct geographical formations in North America. More

than a 1000km long, the St. Lawrence is the largest river leading to the Atlantic Ocean on the continent. The river has its source at the Great Lakes and is also fed by a number of major waterways, such as the Ottawa, the Richelieu, the Saguenay and the Manicouagan. Traditionally the primary route into the continent, the St. Lawrence played a central part in Québec's development. Even today, most of the province's population lives along the river, particularly in the Montréal region where nearly half Québec's population resides. To the south, near the U.S. border, the Appalachian mountains cross the St. Lawrence lowlands from southwestern Québec to the Gaspé peninsula. The hilly scenery of these regions is very similar to that of New England, although the mountains rarely exceed 1,000m in height. The remaining 80% of Québec's land mass is part of the Canadian Shield, a very old, heavily eroded mountain range extending over all of northern Québec. This region of the province has a tiny population and abundant natural resources, including vast forests and mighty rivers, some of which are used in the production of hydroelectric power.

Settling the Land

Traces of the seigneurial system used by the first colonists to settle the land can still be seen today in the St. Lawrence lowlands. Land was divided into long tracts running inland from the water. In order to give the maximum number of colonists access to the river, which was the only thoroughfare navigable by canoe in the summer and by sled in the winter. When all the land next to the river had been settled, another set of tracts was cleared along a road, called a *rang* (row), at the far end of the previously established tracts. Much of the land remains divided like this, and farmers still live as they would have years ago, working long, narrow fields. In certain other regions, close to the U.S. border, the first European settlers were British and they cleared the land according to a system of townships, which involved dividing the territory into squares. This system survives in some parts of the Cantons de l'Est (which means literally Eastern Townships), though it disappeared in many others with the massive influx of French settlers who imposed the seigneurial system.

Flora

As a result of climatic differences, the vegetation in northern Québec is sparse, while that in the south is quite lush (at least in the summer). Québec's flora can be divided into four zones from north to south: the tundra, the taiga, the boreal forest, and the deciduous forest.

The tundra occupies the northernmost reaches of Québec, principally along Hudson Bay and Ungava Bay. With a month-long growing season and severe winters when the ground is frozen several metres deep, vegetation in the tundra is limited to mosses, lichens and very small trees.

The taiga, an area of transition between the tundra and the boreal forest, covers more than a third of Québec and is characterized by sparse, very slow-growing trees such as spruce and larch.

Iris versicolor

The boreal forest covers a huge section of the province, from the edge of the taiga to the banks of the St. Lawrence in some regions. This is a very homogeneous zone made up of coniferous trees, primarily white pine, black pine, grey pine, balsam fir and larch. This forest is an important source of lumber and wood pulp.

The deciduous forest is in fact made up of coniferous and deciduous trees and covers the regions south of the St. Lawrence River to the U.S. border. Along with a variety of coniferous trees, this zone is rich in maple, birch, spruce and aspen.

Fauna

Québec's vast and varied wilderness boasts a richly diverse fauna. A multitude of animal species populates its immense forests, plains and arctic regions, and its seas, lakes and rivers are teeming with fish and aquatic animals. Refer to the colour section on Québec's wildlife, for more information.

History

By the time European settlers arrived in the New World, a mosaic of indigenous peoples had already been living on the continent for thousands of years. The ancestors of these people were nomads who began to cross the Bering Strait from northern Asia toward the end of the ice age, more than 12,000 years ago, and slowly populated the continent. Over the following millennia, as the glaciers receded, some of these groups began to settle in the northernmost parts of the continent, including the peninsula now known as Québec. A variety of native peoples, belonging to three language groups (Algonquian, Iroquoian and Inuit), were thus sharing the territory when the Europeans first began to explore North America. Established societies with very diverse ways of life occupied this vast region. For example, native peoples occupying in the valley of the St. Lawrence River lived primarily on fish, game, and food they grew themselves, while communities farther north depended mostly on meat gathered during hunting expeditions. All, however, made ample use of the canoe as a means of travelling along the "paths that walk", and maintained very close trade relations with the neighbouring nations. These societies, well-adapted to the rigours and distinctive features of the territory, were quickly marginalised with the onset of European colonization at the beginning of the 16th century.

New France

During his first exploration of the mouth of the St. Lawrence and the shores of what is now Newfoundland, the French explorer Jacques Cartier came into contact with fishermen from various parts of Europe. In fact, these waters were first explored by the Vikings sometime around the year 900, and were being visited regularly by European cod fishermen and whalers. However, Jacques Cartier's three voyages, which began in 1534, did represent an important step forward, as they established the first official contact between whites and the peoples and territory of this part of North America. On these expeditions, the Breton navigator sailed far up the St. Lawrence to the villages of Stadacona (now Québec City) and Hochelaga (on the island of Montréal). However, as Cartier's mandate from the king of France had been to find gold or a passage to Asia, his discoveries were considered unimportant and uninteresting. For several decades after this "failure," the French crown forgot about this distant, inhospitable place.

French interest in North America was rekindled when fur coats and hats became increasingly fashionable and therefore profitable in Europe. As the fur trade required a direct and constant link with local suppliers, a permanent presence in the New World was indispensable. Throughout the end of the 16th century, various

unsuccessful attempts at setting up trading posts on the Atlantic coast and in the interior of the continent were made. Finally, in 1608, under the leadership of Samuel de Champlain, the first permanent outpost was set up. Champlain and his men chose a location at the foot of a large cliff overlooking a considerable narrowing of the St. Lawrence. The collection of fortified buildings they constructed was named the Abitation de Québec (*kebec* is an Algonquian word meaning "where the river narrows"). During that first harsh winter in Québec, 20 of the 28 men posted there died of scurvy or malnutrition before ships carrying fresh supplies arrived in the spring of 1609. When Samuel de Champlain died on Christmas Day, 1635, there were about 300 pioneers living in New France.

Between 1627 and 1663, the Compagnies des Cents Associés held a monopoly on the fur trade and ensured the slow growth of the colony. Meanwhile, French religious orders became more and more interested in New France. The Récollets arrived first, in 1615; they were replaced by the Jesuits, who began arriving in 1632. Determined to convert the natives, the Jesuits settled deep in the

interior of the continent, near the shores of Georgian Bay, where they founded the Sainte-Marie-des-Huron mission. The Huron people, it can be assumed, put up with the presence of the Jesuits to maintain the trading arrangements they had established with the French. The mission was nevertheless abandoned after five Jesuits were killed during the Huron-Iroquois war of 1648-1649. This war was part of an extensive offensive campaign launched by the powerful Iroquois Five Nations between 1645 and 1655 and intended to wipe out all rival nations. The Huron, Pétun, Neutrals and Erie nations, each at least 10,000 strong, were almost completely annihilated within the space of 10 years. The offensive also threatened the existence of the French colony. In 1660 and 1661, Iroquois warriors mounted strikes all over New France, destroying crops and bringing about a decline in the fur trade. Louis the XIV, the king of France, decided to take the situation in hand. In 1663, he dissolved the Compagnies des Cents Associés and took on the responsibility of administering the colony himself, officially declaring New France, with its 3,000 settlers (or *habitants*), a French province.

Emigration to New France continued under the royal regime. Most people sent over were agricultural workers, though some also belonged to the military. In 1665, for example, the Carignan-Salières regiment was dispatched to the New World to fight the Iroquois. The Crown also took steps to encourage the natural growth of the population, which had theretofore been hindered by the lack of unmarried female immigrants. Between 1663 and 1673, 800 young women, known as the *filles du roi*, and each provided with a

JACQUES CARTIER
1534

dowry, were sent to find husbands in the New World. This period of the history of New France was also the glorious era of the *coureurs des bois*. Abandoning their land for the fur trade, these intrepid young men travelled into the heart of the continent to deal directly with native trappers. The primary occupation of most colonists, however, remained farming.

Society revolved around the seigneurial system. Land in New France was divided into seigneuries which in turn were divided into *rotures*. The long narrow lots running perpendicular to the rivers (most notably the St. Lawrence) gave everyone access to the water. Serfs were expected to pay an annual sum to their seigneur and to do certain tasks for them. Since the territory was so vast and so sparsely populated, however, colonists in New France enjoyed much higher profits once all their debts were paid than their counterparts in France.

The territorial claims made by the French in North America increased rapidly during this era as a result of expeditions made by religious orders, *coureurs des bois* and explorers, to whom we owe the discovery of most of the North American continent. New France reached its peak at the beginning of the 18th century. At this time, it had a monopoly on the North American fur trade, control of the St. Lawrence and was beginning to develop Louisiana. New France was thus able to contain the expansion of the more populous British colonies located between the Atlantic and the Appalachians. This changed following military defeat in Europe and the Treaty of Utrecht (1713) where France relinquished control of Hudson Bay, Newfoundland and Acadia to the British. France thereby lost a

large stake in the fur trade, as well as certain strategic military locations, all of which severely weakened its position in North America and marked the beginning of the end of New France. Over the following years, the stakes continued to mount. In 1755, British colonel Charles Lawrence took what he viewed as a preventive measure and ordered the deportation of the Acadians, French-speaking settlers living in what is now Nova Scotia. At least 7,000 Acadians, who had been considered British citizens since 1713, were displaced as a result of this directive. The fight for control of the colony came to an end several years later. Though Montréal was last to fall in 1760, it was the infamous battle of the Plains of Abraham a year before, where Montcalm's and Wolfe's troops met, that sealed the fate of New France with the loss of Québec City. At the time of the British conquest, the population of the colony had risen to 60,000. Of this number, 8,967 lived in Québec City, and 5,733 lived in Montréal.

British Rule

With the Treaty of Paris in 1763, French Canada, holdings east of the Mississippi and what remained of Acadia were officially ceded to England. For former subjects of the French crown, the first years under British rule were difficult ones. Territorial divisions dictated by the Royal Proclamation of 1763 denied the colony control of the fur trade, the most dynamic sector of its economy. In addition, the introduction of British civil law and the refusal to recognize the authority of the Pope put an end to both the seigneurial system and the Catholic hierarchy, the pillars on which French colonial society had been based. Finally, the Test Oath, required of anyone in a

high-ranking administrative position, discriminated against French Canadians, since it denied the transubstantiation of the Eucharist and the authority of the Pope. A large segment of the French elite returned to France while English merchants gradually took control of most businesses.

England, however, soon agreed to do away with the Royal Proclamation. To better resist the trend towards independence in its 13 colonies to the south, it sought to secure its place in Canada by gaining the favour of the population. In 1774, the Québec Act replaced the Royal Proclamation, introducing policies much more appropriate to a French Catholic colony.

The Canadian population remained French, until the end of the American Revolution when Canada experienced the arrival of a first big wave of Anglo-Saxon colonists. The new arrivals were Loyalists, Americans wishing to remain faithful to the British crown. Most moved to the Maritimes (formerly Acadia) and around Lake Ontario, but some also settled in regions inhabited strictly by francophones. With the arrival of these new colonists, British authorities passed the Constitution Act of 1791, which divided Canada into two provinces. Upper Canada, situated west of the Rivière Outaouais and mainly populated by anglophones, would be governed by British civil law. Lower Canada, which was mostly francophone, would be governed according to the French tradition of common law. In addition, the Act planted the seeds of a parliamentary system in Canada by creating a Legislative Assembly in each province.

Meanwhile, Napoleon's Continental System forced Britain to get its lumber from Canada.

From an economic standpoint, this was good for the colony. The development of a new industry was especially timely, as the fur trade, the original reason for the existence of the colony, was in steady decline. In 1821, the take-over of the Montréal-based Northwest Company by the Hudson's Bay Company marked the end of Montréal as the centre of the North American fur trade. Meanwhile, rural Québec suffered through an agricultural crisis caused by the exhaustion of farmlands and rapid population growth resulting from high birth rates among French-Canadian families, whose diet consisted almost entirely of pea soup and buckwheat pancakes (*galettes*).

These economic difficulties and the struggle for power between francophones and anglophones in Lower Canada combined to spark the Patriotes Rebellion of 1837 and 1838. The period of political conflict that fuelled the rebellion was initiated by the 1834 publication of the *92 Résolutions*, a scathing indictment of British colonial policy. The authors of the resolutions, a group of parliamentarians led by Louis-Joseph Papineau, decided to hold back from voting on the budget until Britain addressed their demands. Britain's response came in 1837 in the form of the *10 Resolutions*, written by Lord Russell, which categorically refused any compromise with their opponents in Lower Canada. In the fall of 1837, Montréal was the scene of violent clashes between the *Fils de la Liberté* (Sons of Liberty), made up of young French Canadians, and the Doric Club, comprised of Loyalists. Further confrontations occurred in the Richelieu valley region and in the county of Deux-Montagnes, where small insurgent groups stood up to the British army before being crushed. The following year, in an attempt to rekindle

the rebellion, a group of Patriotes met with the same fate in Napierville where they confronted 7,000 British troops. This time, however, colonial authorities sent a strong message to prospective rebels. In 1839, they hanged 12 Patriotes and deported many others.

When hostilities first broke out, London had sent an emissary, Lord Durham, to study the problems in the colonies. Expecting to find a population rebelling against colonial authority, Durham found instead two peoples, one French and one British in battle. The solution he later proposed in his report, known as the Durham Report, was radical. He suggested to authorities in Britain that gradual efforts should be made to assimilate French Canadians.

The Union Act, laid down by the British government in 1840, was largely based on the conclusions of the Durham Report. A new parliamentary system was introduced giving the two former colonies the same number of delegates, despite the fact that Lower Canada had a much larger population than Upper Canada. Financial responsibilities were also divided equally between the provinces, and English was made the sole official language. As armed insurrection had proven futile in the past, French Canada's political class sought to align itself with progressive anglophones in an attempt to resist these changes. Later, the struggle for responsible government became the central goal of this coalition.

The agricultural crisis, furthermore, remained as severe as ever in Lower Canada. Intensified by the constant arrival of immigrants and by the high birth rate, the situation resulted in a massive emigration of French Canadians to the United States. Between 1840

and 1850, 40,000 French Canadians left the country to seek employment in the factories of New England. To counteract this exodus, the Catholic Church and the government launched an extensive campaign to colonize outlying regions, such as Lac Saint-Jean. The harsh life in these newly settled regions, where colonists worked as farmers in the summer and lumberjacks in the winter, is poignantly depicted in Louis Hémon's novel *Maria Chapdelaine*. Nevertheless, the mass exodus from Québec did not stop until the beginning of the next century. It is estimated that about 750,000 French Canadians left the province between 1840 and 1930. From this point of view, the colonization campaign, which doubled the amount of farmland in Lower Canada, ended in failure. The swelling population of rural Québec was not effectively absorbed until several decades later with the start of industrialization.

The Canadian economy received a serious blow during this era when Britain abandoned its policy of mercantilism and preferential tariffs for its colonies. To cushion the effects of this change in British policy, United Canada signed a treaty in 1854, making it possible for certain goods to enter the United States without import duties. Canada's economy began to recover slightly but the treaty was revoked in 1866, under pressure from U.S. industrialists. - Resolving these economic difficulties was the impetus behind Canadian confederation in 1867.

Confederation

Under Canadian Confederation, Lower Canada became the Province of Québec. Three other provinces, Nova Scotia, New Brunswick, and

Ontario (formerly Upper Canada) joined the Confederation, which would eventually unite a vast territory stretching from the Atlantic to the Pacific Ocean. For French Canadians, this new political system reinforced their minority status, which began with the Union Act of 1840. The creation of two levels of government did, however, grant Québec jurisdiction over education, culture and civil law.

Confederation was slow to bring about positive economic change. The economy fluctuated for three decades before experiencing a real boom. The first years after Confederation did, however, see the development of local industry (thanks to the implementation of protective tariffs), the creation of a large, unified market and the development of the railway system across the territory. The industrial revolution that had begun in the mid-19th century picked up again in the 1880s. While Montréal remained the undisputed centre of this movement, it was felt in many smaller towns. The lumber industry, which had been one of the mainsprings of the economy during the 19th century, began exporting more cut wood than raw lumber, giving rise to a processing industry. Montréal was also the hub of the expanding railroad, leading the city to specialize in the production of rolling stock. The leather goods, clothing and food industries also enjoyed significant growth in Québec. This period of growth was also marked by the emergence of the brand-new textile industry, which would remain for many years Québec's flagship industry. Benefitting from a huge pool of unskilled labour, the textile industries initially employed mostly women and children.

This wave of industrialization accelerated the pace of urbanization and created a large and poor working class clustered near the factories. Montréal's working-class neighbourhoods were terribly unhealthy. Infant mortality in these areas was twice that of wealthy neighbourhoods.

Québec's cities were going through tremendous changes, and the situation in rural areas finally began to improve. Dairy production was gradually replacing subsistence farming, contributing to an improved standard of living among farmers.

In 1885, the tragic hanging of Louis Riel once again highlighted the opposition between Canada's two language groups: francophones and anglophones. Having led Métis and aboriginal rebels in the western part of the country, Riel, a French-speaking, Catholic Métis (a semi-nomadic group descended from French traders and Aboriginals) was found guilty of high treason and sentenced to death. French-Canadian public opinion was strongly in favour of a commuted sentence, while anglophones took the opposite view. The federal government under John A. Macdonald ultimately went ahead with the execution, and the reaction was quick and angry among the people of Québec.

The Golden Age of Economic Liberalism

With the beginning of the 20th century, a period of prodigious economic growth in Québec started and lasted until the Great Depression of the 1930s. Sharing the optimism and euphoria of Canadians, Prime Minister Wilfrid Laurier predicted that the 20th century would be Canada's.

Québec manufacturers profited during this period of growth. Thanks to new technology and new markets, the province's abundance of natural resources was the principal catalyst of this second wave of industrialization. Central to the new era was the production of electric power. With its numerous powerful rivers, Québec became a major producer of hydroelectric power in a matter of years. The resulting availability of affordable energy attracted industries with large electricity needs. Aluminum smelters and chemical plants were constructed in the vicinity of hydroelectric power stations. The mining industry also began to enjoy modest growth during this period with the development of asbestos mines in the Eastern Townships and copper, gold, zinc and silver mines in Abitibi. Above all, Québec's pulp and paper industry found huge markets in the United States, due to the depletion of U.S. forests and the rise of the popular press. To promote the development of processing industries in Québec, the exportation of logs was forbidden by the provincial government in 1910.

This new period of industrialization differed from the first one in several ways. Taking place largely outside the major cities, it led to an increase in urban growth in outlying regions. In some cases, cities sprang up in a matter of a few years. Unlike the manufacturing industries, the exploitation of natural resources required more qualified workers and a level of financing far beyond local means. Britain's stake in the economy, which up until now had been the largest, gave way to the triumphant rise of U.S. capitalism.

Despite rapid changes in Québec society (by 1921, half the population was living in urban centres), the church was still highly influential. With 85% of the overall population, including virtually all French Canadians as members, the Catholic Church was a major political force in the province. Because of the control it wielded over education, health care and social services, its authority was inescapable. The Catholic Church, moreover, did not hesitate to intervene in the political arena, often confronting politicians it considered to be too liberal.

When World War I began, the Canadian government gave its full support to Britain without hesitation. A significant number of French Canadians voluntarily enrolled in the army, although the percentage of volunteers per capita was far lower than that in other provinces. This lack of enthusiasm can doubtless be attributed both to Québec's long severed ties with France and, what is more important, to francophones' somewhat ambivalent feelings toward Britain. Canada soon set a goal of inducting 500,000 men. Since there were not enough volunteers, the government voted, in 1917, to introduce conscription. Reaction to this in Québec was violent and marked by fights, bombings and riots. In the end, conscription failed to appreciably increase the number of French Canadian recruits. Instead, it simply underlined once again the ongoing friction between English and French Canada.

The Great Depression

Between 1929 and 1945, two international-scale events, the Depression and World War II, greatly disrupted the country's political, economic and social progress. The Great Depression of the 1930s, originally viewed as a cyclical, temporary crisis, lengthened into a decade-long nightmare and put an end to Québec's rapid economic expansion. With Canada strongly dependent on foreign markets, the country as a whole was hard hit by the international stock market crash. Québec was unevenly affected. With its economy based to a large extent on exports, Montréal, along with towns dependent on the development of natural resources, took the hardest blows. The textile and food industries, which sold to the Canadian market, held up better during the first years of the Depression, before foundering, as well. The trend towards urbanization slowed as people began to view the countryside as a refuge where they could grow their own food. Poverty became more and more widespread, and unemployment levels reached 27% in 1933. Governments were at a loss in the face of this crisis, which they had expected to be short-lived. The Québec government started by introducing massive public works projects to provide jobs for the unemployed. As this proved insufficient, more direct help was gradually given. Very timidly put forward at first, since unemployment had always been considered a personal problem, these measures later helped many Quebecers. The federal government was also compelled to question the merits - of economic liberalism and to redefine the role of the state. Part of this trend included establishing the Bank of Canada in 1935, which permitted greater control over the monetary and financial system. However, it was not until the ensuing war years that a full-scale welfare state was created. In the meantime, the crisis led to the proliferation of political ideologies in Québec. The most popular of these, traditional nationalism, put great emphasis on values such as rural life, family, religion and language.

World War II

World War II began in 1939, and Canada became officially involved September 10th of that year. The Canadian economy received a much-needed boost as industry set out to modernize the country's military equipment and to meet the requirements of the Allies. Canada's close ties to Great Britain and the United States gave it an important diplomatic role, as indicated by the conferences held in Québec in 1943 and 1944. Early in the war, however, the problem of conscription surfaced again. While the federal government wanted to avoid the issue, mounting pressure from the country's anglophones forced a plebiscite on the issue. The results once again showed the division between francophones and anglophones: 80% of English Canadians voted in favour of conscription, while the same percentage of French Canadians were opposed to the idea. Mixed feelings toward Britain and France left French Canadians very reluctant to become involved in the fighting. However, they were forced to follow the will of the majority. In the end, 600,000 Canadians were recruited, 42,000 of whom died in action.

Québec was profoundly changed by the war. Its economy became much stronger and more diversified than before. As far as relations between Ottawa and Québec

City were concerned, the federal government's massive intervention during the war marked the beginning of its increased role in the economy and of the relative marginalization of provincial governments. In addition, the contact thousands of Quebecers had with European life and the jobs women held in the factories modified people's expectations. The winds of change were blowing, but were to come up against a serious obstacle: Premier Maurice Duplessis and his political allies.

1945-1960: The Duplessis Era

The end of World War II signalled a period of considerable economic growth, during which consumer demands repressed by the economic crisis and wartime rationing could finally be satisfied. Despite a few fluctuations, the economy performed spectacularly until 1957. However, this prosperity affected Québec's various social and ethnic groups unequally. Many workers, particularly non-unionized ones, continued to receive relatively low wages. Furthermore, the anglophone minority in Québec still enjoyed a far superior standard of living than the francophone majority. A francophone employee with the same skills and experience as an anglophone employee would routinely be paid less. With an economy largely controlled by English Canadians and Americans, French Canadians were held back. To some degree, francophones lived as second-class citizens in their own province.

Be that as it may, the economic growth encouraged a stable political environment, such that the leader of the Union Nationale party, Maurice Duplessis, remained in power as Premier of Qué-

bec from 1944 until he died in 1959. Duplessis's influence characterized this era, often referred to as *la grande noirceur*, or the great darkness. The Duplessis ideology was based on a sometimes paradoxical amalgam of traditional nationalism, conservatism and unbridled capitalism. He professed a respect for rural life, religion and authority, while at the same time provided major foreign business interests with highly favourable opportunities to exploit Québec's natural resources. In his mind, a cheap work force was one of those resources and it had to be preserved. To this end, he fought fiercely against unionization, not hesitating to use intimidation tactics when he felt it was necessary. These years were marked by many strikes but it was the asbestos strike of 1949 that most influenced the collective conscience. While Maurice Duplessis was the dominant personality of this period, his rule could only have been sustained through the tacit collaboration of much of the traditional and business elite, both francophone and anglophone. The church, seemingly at the height of its glory during these years, felt its authority weakening, which prompted it to support the Duplessis government in full measure.

Despite Duplessis's iron hand, opposing voices nonetheless emerged. The Liberal Party of Québec had difficulty getting organized, so opposition came mainly from outside the parliamentary structure. Artists and writers made their anger known by publishing the *Refus Global*, a bitter attack on the repressive atmosphere in Québec. The most organized opposition came from union leaders, journalists and the intellectual community. All these groups wanted modernization for Québec and endorsed the same neo-liberalist

economic credo favouring a strong welfare system. However, from quite early on, two different camps developed among these reformists. Certain individuals, such as Gérard Pelletier and Pierre Trudeau, believed modernization would result from a strong federal government, while neo-nationalists like André Laurendeau wanted change through a more powerful provincial government. These two groups, which quickly overshadowed traditionalism during the Quiet Revolution, would remain at odds with each other throughout modern Québec history.

The Quiet Revolution

In 1960, the Liberal Party under Jean Lesage was elected on a platform of change and stayed in power until 1966. This period, referred to as the Révolution Tranquille, or Quiet Revolution, was indeed marked by a veritable race for modernism. Over the course of just a few years, Québec caught up to the modern world. Control of education, health care and social services meant the provincial government played a bigger role in society. The church, thus stripped of its main spheres of influence, lost its authority and eventually its following, as dissatisfied Québec Catholics moved away from the church. State control of the production of hydroelectricity increased the provincial government's interests in the economy. Powerful economic reources thus permitted the government to establish itself, and French Canadians in general, in the business world. The great vitality brought to Québec society during the Quiet Revolution was symbolized by two events of international scope that took place in Montréal: Expo '67 and the 1976 Olympics.

Portrait

Important Dates in Québec's History

More than 12,000 years ago: Nomads from Northern Asia begin to cross the Bering Strait and gradually populate the Americas. With the melting of the glaciers, some of them settle on the peninsula now known as Québec: these are the ancestors of the Aboriginal people.

1534: Jacques Cartier, a navigator from Saint-Malo in Brittany, France, makes the first of three explorations of the Gulf and St. Lawrence River. These were the first official French expeditions to this territory.

1608: Samuel de Champlain and his men found Québec City, marking the beginning of a permanent French presence in North America.

1663: New France officially becomes a French province. Colonization continues.

1759: Québec City falls to British forces. Four years later, the King of France officially relinquishes all of New France, which now has a population of about 60,000 colonists of French origin.

1837-1838: The British army suppresses the Patriotes rebellion.

1840: Following the Durham Report, the Union Act seeks to create an English majority and eventually assimilate French Canadians.

1867: The Canadian Confederation is born. Four provinces, including Québec, sign the agreement. Six others eventually follow suit.

1914-1918: Canada participates in World War I. Anglophones and francophones disagree about conscription. Canada comes out of the conflict very divided.

1929-1939: The stock market crash and Great Depression hit Québec hard. In 1933, unemployment reaches 27%.

1939-1945: Canada participates in World War II. Once again, anglophones and francophones are divided on the issue of conscription.

1944-1959: Premier Maurice Duplessis leads Québec with a strong hand. This period is known as the "grande noirceur," or "great darkness."

1960: The Liberal Party is elected, marking the beginning of the Révolution Tranquille, or Quiet Revolution.

October 1970: A small terrorist group, the Front de Libération du Québec (FLQ), kidnaps a British diplomat and a Québec cabinet minister, igniting a serious political crisis.

November 1976: The Parti Québécois, a party favouring independence for Québec, wins the provincial election.

May 1980: A majority of the Québec population votes against holding negotiations aimed at Québec independence.

1982: The Canadian Constitution is repatriated without Québec's consent.

June 1990: The failure of the Meech Lake Accord on the Canadian Constitution is poorly accepted in Québec. Following this, opinion polls show that a majority of Quebecers are in favour of Québec sovereignty.

October 22, 1992: The federal government and the provinces organize a referendum on new constitutional offers. Considered unacceptable, these are rejected by a majority of Quebecers and Canadians.

October 30, 1995: The Parti Québecois government holds a referendum on Québec sovereignty: 49.4% of Quebecers vote "yes" to sovereignty and 50.6% vote "no."

The lively nature of Québec society in the 1960s engendered a number of new ideological movements, particularly on the left. The extreme was the Front de Libération du Québec (FLQ), a small group of radicals who wanted to "decolonize" Québec and launched a series of terrorist strikes in Montréal. In October 1970, the FLQ abducted James Cross, a British diplomat, and Jean Laporte, a Québec cabinet minister. The Canadian Prime Minister at the time, Pierre Elliot Trudeau, fearing a political uprising, called for the War Measures Act to be enforced. The Canadian army took to the streets of Montréal, thousands of searches were carried out and hundreds of innocent people temporarily imprisoned. Shortly afterward, Pierre Laporte was found dead. The crisis finally ended when the James Cross' kidnappers agreed to let him go in exchange for their safe conduct to Cuba. During this entire crisis, and long afterwards, Trudeau was severely criticized for invoking the War Measures Act. Some accused him of having done so mainly to quash the growing Québec independence movement.

The most significant political phenomenon in Québec between 1960 and 1980 was the rapid rise of moderate nationalism. Breaking with the traditionalism of the past, this new vision of nationalism championed a strong, open and modern Québec with increased powers for the provincial government, and, ultimately, political independence for the province. The nationalist forces rallied around René Lévesque, founder of the Mouvement Souveraineté-Association and then, in 1968, the Parti Québécois. After two elections, which saw only a handful of its representatives elected to Parliament, a stunning 1976 victory brought the

Parti Québécois to power. Right away, in 1977, the new government voted in a bill called Bill 101, that basically made French the sole official language in Québec. In response, many anglophones left the province, mainly for Ontario.

With a mandate to negotiate sovereignty for Québec, the party called a referendum in 1980. From the beginning, the referendum campaign revived the division between Québec sovereigntists and federalists. The struggle was intense and mobilized the entire population right up until the vote. Finally, after a campaign based on promises of a new style of federalism, the "No" (No to Sovereignty Association) side won out with 60% of the vote. Despite this loss, sovereigntists were consoled by how far their cause had come in only a few years. From a marginal trend in the 1960s, nationalism quickly proved itself to be a major political movement. The night of the defeat, Parti Québécois leader René Lévesque, charisma intact, vowed to his supporters that victory would be their's "next time."

Since 1980:
Breaks and Continuity

The independence movement and desire for self-determination amongst Quebecers engendered by the Quiet Revolution suffered a great setback with the loss of the referendum on sovereignty. For many, the 1980s began with a post-referendum depression, accentuated by a period of economic crisis in Canada unmatched since the 1930s. As the economy improved slightly over time, the unemployment rate remained very high and government spending resulted in a massive deficit. Like many other Western governments, Québec had to reassess the

policies of the past, though some feared that the new direction chosen would sacrifice the achievements of the Quiet Revolution.

The 1980s and early 1990s were a time of streamlining and one that saw the creation of global markets and the consolidation of large economic blocks. Canada and the United States signed the Free-Trade Agreement in 1989. The 1994 North American Free Trade Agreement (NAFTA) brought Mexico into this market, creating the largest tariff-free market in the world.

From a political standpoint, the question of Québec's political status surfaced again. In the early 1990s, the sovereigntist movement regained surprising momentum, spurred along by Quebecers' resentment at the failure in June 1990 of the Meech Lake Accord, an agreement aimed at reintegrating Québec into the "constitutional family" by giving it special status (see p 23). The governing bodies involved, in an attempt to resolve this impasse, called for a Canada-wide referendum on a new constitutional offer, held on October 26, 1992. The offer was flatly rejected everywhere in Canada, but for differing reasons. The federal election of October 25, 1993, saw the sovereigntist Bloc Québécois win two-thirds of the ridings in Québec and form the official opposition in the Canadian Parliament. The next year, the Parti Québecois was elected in Québec; high on its agenda was the holding of a referendum on the sovereignty of Québec.

Less than one year after its election, the Parti Québecois, launched a referendum campaign, as promised, for the sovereignty of Québec. As with the first referendum, 15 years earlier in 1980, the Québec population was very

Municipal Mergers

In 2001, the Québec government passed a law requiring most of Québec's municipalities to merge with their neighbours in order to create larger regional entities. On January 1, 2002, several towns and villages lost their official name and became part of a bigger city. The city of Montréal, for example, now includes all the towns on the island of Montréal, and in Québec City, the towns that made up the former Communauté urbaine de Québec are now part of

Québec City itself. The mergers involved plenty of hiccups, and the process is far from being complete. This is why we have decided, for the time being, not to modify most town names in this guide. In most towns that must be renamed, the choice of a new name is much cause for debate, and we believe that it is still too soon to use place names that will actually take years to be adopted. Nevertheless, you will have no trouble finding your way around the province of Québec.

divided on the issue. This time, however, the results were unbelievably close. The suspense lasted right until the last ballot was counted on referendum night, October 30, 1995. The results told of a population divided: 49.4% of Quebecers voted "yes" to Québec sovereignty and 50.6% voted "no". The profound question of Québec's political status thus remained unresolved following this referendum, which in effect only served to underline the division that exists within the population. In recent years, opinion polls have indicated that Quebecers are more interested in discussing other matters of public policy, like the economy and the environment, yet the "national question" will likely remain an issue in Québec politics for the foreseeable future.

Politics

The British North America Act is the constitutional document on which Canadian Confederation is based. It creates a division of powers between the levels of government. In addition to a central government based in Ottawa, therefore, each of the 10 Canadian provinces has a government with the power to legislate in certain domains. The constitutional conflict between Québec and the Canadian government is largely a product of disagreements over precisely how these powers should be divided.

Based on the British model, Canada's and Québec's political systems give legislative power to a parliament elected by universal suffrage. In Québec, the Parliament is called the Assemblée Nationale. It has 125 seats, each repre-

senting a riding in the province. In Ottawa, power belongs to the House of Commons, with members from regions across the country. The federal government also has an Upper Chamber, the Senate. This institution has gradually had all its real power reduced and its future is now unclear. In an election, the party with the most elected representatives forms the government. These elections are held about every four years and function according to the single-ballot majority system. This kind of system generally leaves room for only two major political parties. It also, however, has the advantage of ensuring great stability between each election, while making it possible to identify each member of Parliament with a particular riding.

Federal Politics

At the federal level, two parties, the Liberal Party and the Conservative Party, have each governed the country at various times since Confederation in 1867. Quebecers and French-speaking Canadians in general have, until recently, strongly supported the Liberal Party. The first three French-speaking Prime Ministers of Canada, moreover, represented this party. The Conservative Party, long associated with British imperialism and with the implementation of conscription in 1917, has traditionally made little room for francophones. Recently, the Conservative Party has shown signs of greater openness. In 1984, the party was thus voted into power in a federal election, and retained that power in the next election in 1988, with tremendous support from Québec. They were, however, defeated by the Liberal Party in the election of October 25, 1993, which placed Jean Chrétien at the head of Canadian government. This election led to a spectacular rearrangement of Canada's political map and signalled the rise of two new federal political parties: the Reform Party and the Bloc Québécois. The Reform Party, a populist right-wing party, elected 52 members of parliament, almost exclusively from Western Canada. The Bloc Québécois won 54 seats, or more than two thirds of the seats in Québec. Born out of the Meech Lake fiasco, the Bloc Québécois's goal is to promote Québec sovereignty at the federal level. Meanwhile, the Progressive Conservative Party, in power up until then, and the New Democratic Party, the eternal third-place finishers on the federal scene, were virtually wiped off the political map.

The results of the 1993 federal election were confirmed during the most recent election in the spring of 1997. The Liberal Party was re-elected, though with a smaller majority despite massive support from Ontario, the most populous Canadian province. The Reform Party was once again the big winner in the West, claiming even more seats than in the previous election and ousting the Bloc Québécois from official opposition status. The Bloc's performance was not as strong as in 1993; however they won 45 of the 75 seats in Québec. As for the Progressive Conservatives and the New Democrats, they regained some of their former strengths thanks to voters in Atlantic Canada. The Canadian political map has never been so complex. The Liberal Party's inability to gain much support outside of Ontario, Reform's performance in the West and the large contingent of Bloc Québécois members of parliament certainly puts in question the idea of a Canadian consensus.

Provincial Politics

Two political parties dominate Québec politics: the Parti Québécois (PQ) and the Parti Libéral du Québec (PLQ). In April 2003, the Liberal party, led by Jean Charest, defeated the PQ, which had held power since 1994. The PQ, a relatively young party, previously led the provincial government from 1976 to 1985, with the charismatic René Lévesque at the head. The Liberal victory promises to change the playing field when it comes to the major source of disagreement between these two parties: the political status of Québec. Since it was founded, the PQ has pursued the objective of gaining political sovereignty for Québec. The Liberal Party, on the other hand, has sought more power for the provincial government, though it remains loyal to the Canadian federalist system.

A third party, the Action démocratique du Québec (ADQ), led by Mario Dumont, is now on the scene. Despite some major victories in a 2002 bi-election, its performance in the 2003 election was less impressive.

Federal-Provincial Relations

Over the course of the last 40 years, federal-provincial relations and the conflicts between federalists and Québec sovereigntists, has dominated politics in Canada. This ongoing dispute continues to fuel public debate. Since the Quiet Revolution, successive Québec governments have all considered themselves representatives of a distinct society, demanding special status for Québec and greater independence from the federal government. Faced with the prospect of Québec

autonomy, the federal government has resisted vigorously, arguing that there is only one Canada and that Québec is one province like the others. During this same 30-year period, the federal government was attempting to repatriate the Canadian constitution in London, a task that requires the support of the provinces. While Québec did not oppose the repatriation of the constitution, it decided that such a development could be an opportunity to bring about a major revision of its place in the country and an increase of its powers. However, the province's demands were never met by the federal government, and Québec, long supported by other provinces, responded by blocking the repatriation of the Constitution at the federal-provincial conferences of 1964 and 1971.

The Referendum of 1980

The stakes were much higher once the Parti Québécois took power in 1976. This party, whose reason for being was the creation of a sovereign Québec, worried the federal government and Québec's federalist forces. In 1980, the PQ decided to hold a referendum on sovereignty, asking Quebecers to give the party a mandate to negotiate a sovereignty-association with the rest of the country. The referendum campaign that followed was a showdown between federalist forces, represented by the Liberal Party of Québec and the Canadian government, and sovereigntist forces, represented by the Parti Québécois.

This clash of the two main views that had defined the contemporary political scene in Québec also took on the appearance of a fight to the finish between two men: Pierre Elliot Trudeau and

René Lévesque. After a long battle, marked by a good deal of demagoguery, the campaign concluded on May, 20, 1980, with 60% of Quebecers voting against the negotiation of sovereignty association. Taking into account the anglophone vote, the results showed that the francophone population was about evenly split on the issue. The vote came as a serious jolt to those who had dreamed of an independent state with a francophone majority in North America. On referendum day 1980, a majority of Quebecers decided to give federalism another chance and placed their future in Pierre Elliot Trudeau's hands. Trudeau, without being very specific about what he meant, promised that voting No in the referendum meant voting Yes to a new Canada.

Quebecers were quick to discover, however, that Trudeau's new federalism did not address their province's traditional demands. In November of 1981, Trudeau called a federal-provincial conference with the goal of repatriating the Constitution. Québec, with the support of certain other provinces, intended to block the federal project, but a spectacular turnaround occurred in a late-night meeting to which Québec was not invited. Following this event, which became known as the "night of the long knives", the federal government imposed a new constitutional pact on Québec in 1982, knowing full well that the Québec National Assembly was fiercely opposed to signing it. Not only were Québec's language laws placed in jeopardy and provincial powers not increased, but the new constitutional pact also removed the Québec government's veto right on all constitutional amendments. Having won the referendum victory, the federalists thus attempted to silence Québec's separatist impulses once and for all.

From Meech Lake to Charlottetown

After a break of several years, the constitutional saga entered a new and tumultuous era with the elections of Brian Mulroney in Ottawa (1984) and the Liberal Party led by Robert Bourassa in Québec (1985). Bringing Québec back into the constitutional fold with "honour and enthusiasm" became a priority for the new Canadian Prime Minister. In 1987, the federal government and the 10 provinces drew up an agreement, known as the Meech Lake Accord, which called for constitutional changes in response to a minimum of Québec's traditional demands. To become official, the Accord had to be ratified by the Legislative Assemblies of the 10 provinces before June 24, 1990. This seemed simple enough. However, the situation turned into a monumental fiasco when certain provincial premiers were elected out of office and replaced by opponents of the deal, when the Premier of Newfoundland changed his mind on the matter, and when public opinion in English Canada turned against the agreement, considered too advantageous to Québec. After a number of hopeless attempts to save it, what was to have been a "great national reconciliation" ended in resounding failure. By coincidence, June 24, the day the Meech Lake Accord failed to win approval, is Québec's national holiday, Saint-Jean-Baptiste Day. Hundreds of thousands of frustrated Quebecers took to the streets that day. In an attempt to avert a major swing towards sovereignty, Premier Bourassa resolved to present the federal government with an ultimatum. He announced that a referendum would be held before October 26, 1992, either on an acceptable federalist offer or on the proposition of sovereignty for Québec. Until the last moment, Robert Bourassa truly believed the other provinces and the federal government would produce, for the first time in the recent history of the country, an agreement responding to the demands of a majority of Quebecers.

However, as the referendum date came near and it became clear that this was not going to happen, he put aside his threats and once again entered into negotiations with the other provinces and the federal government. A general agreement, the Charlottetown Accord, was thrown together in a few days. This was presented not only as a response to Québec's aspirations, but also to those of the other Canadian provinces and Canada's aboriginal peoples. To be ratified, however, this agreement had to be accepted by a majority of the population of each province. October 26, 1992, the date originally planned for a provincial referendum on Québec's future, was kept as the date for this Canada-wide referendum. Bourassa promised to succeed in "selling" the package to the people of Québec. However, from the beginning, a majority of Quebecers were fiercely opposed to the deal and Bourassa even lost the support of certain militants within his own party. The rejection of the agreement by Quebecers was therefore no surprise. It was rejected by a number of other provinces, as well, though for completely opposite reasons. The matter of Québec's political status thus remained unresolved.

No: 50.6%
Yes: 49.4%

Tired of the endless discussions throughout Canada on

Portrait

the Québec issue, Quebecers were anxious for the situation to be resolved. The opportunity presented itself with the 1993 federal election. With the election of the Bloc Québécois as official opposition in the Canadian Parliament, sovereigntist Quebecers could now show their support for Québec sovereignty at the federal level. In the beginning, the Bloc only expected a small showing, enough to make the sovereigntist case in Ottawa, the federal capital, but what occurred was a veritable landslide in Québec. The party won two thirds of the province's ridings and became the official opposition in Ottawa. The following year, the Québec population was called upon to elect a new provincial government, and it chose the Parti Québécois, the principal proponent of Québec sovereignty for the last quarter century. And so, with a strong sovereigntist force in the Canadian Parliament and the Parti Québécois at the head of the Québec government, Quebecers would once again be given a choice between sovereignty and Canadian federalism.

After a few months a referendum was set for October 30, 1995. Fifteen years after the 1980 referendum, federalists and sovereigntists once again found themselves engaged in the campaign of their lives, one whose outcome would determine the nature of Québec's political status. From the start of the campaign, both sides realized that the population was divided. No one could have predicted such a close race, however. The night of the referendum, every single ballot had to be counted before the results were known: 50.6% of Quebecers voted no to sovereignty while 49.4% voted yes. A mere 28,000 votes separated the two options; Québec was literally split right down the middle. Although

the leaders of the sovereignty movement announced on the night of the vote that another referendum would be called very soon, the movement seems to have lost its momentum and the recent victory of the Liberals, for whom sovereignty is not a goal, precludes the possibility of another referendum in the immediate future.

The Economy

Long avoided by a majority of francophones, the world of business now occupies a particularly important place within Québec society. Since the 1960s, it has become a vehicle through which francophones have sought to take control of their own destiny, something that represents a significant social change. Until the Quiet Revolution, French students usually studied law or medicine or joined the clergy. The business world, seen as shallow and controlled by anglophones, was also largely inaccessible. Francophones' attitudes have changed drastically in the last 30 years: indifference has given away to a clear desire for direct involvement in Québec's economy. Today, a large proportion of students in the province study business administration. In fact, Québec is now turning out more graduates in this field than any other province. Media attention on the success of Québec entrepreneurs has helped to fuel this trend. The increased business

activity among francophones has overshadowed Anglo-Canadian and U.S. interests in the province. Over the last few years, there has been a reduction of a foreign presence, particularly from the United States, in the Québec economy. This is explained by many factors, including a climate of political uncertainty, the energy of local entrepreneurs, federal laws controlling investments by outsiders and the decline in certain sectors controlled by U.S. investors. However, the impact of the 1989 Free Trade Agreement between Canada and the United States and of the 1994 agreement that included Mexico in that market may reverse this trend.

The Government's Role

As in many western countries, government influence over business has been reduced over the past 10 years. Despite this trend, the government remains, in many ways, an important player in the development of the economy. In fact, it is now the largest employer in Québec, boasting many highly qualified management-level employees, as well as being active in stimulating the economy. The expansion of Hydro-Québec is a good example of the Québec government's successful intervention in business. From the time of Premier Jean Lesage, Hydro-Québec has had an almost exclusive monopoly on the production and distribu-

Barrage Daniel-Johnson

tion of hydroelectricity in Québec. This vital public enterprise, through the great sweep of its activities, has propelled the success of many private businesses in Québec. Certain engineering firms also owe their growth, in Québec and beyond, to experience gained through participation in the construction of Hydro-Québec's immense hydroelectric projects. The Québec government has also had at its disposal over the last few decades a number of powerful investment tools for economic development, the most famous being the Caisse de Dépot et de Placement. This institution, which manages capital from the retirement funds of a huge number of Québec workers, has become a financial giant. While making only modest investments in its first few years, the Caisse de Dépot et de Placement began to provide massive support for Québec businesses after the Parti Québécois came to power in 1976.

Today, the CDPQ has one of the biggest stock portfolios in Canada. Presently, the concern exists that too much public intervention can be bad for an economy, but in a small economy like Québec's, the need for strong state involvement is generally agreed on.

Québec's Economic Future

Québec's economy is going through a period of great change, largely resulting from a move away from industrialization, as is seen in many Western countries. The effects have been a diversification of the economy, a reduction in mining and the decline of certain traditional industries. At the same time, there has been growth in several new and promising sectors.
Because of its abundance of affordable electric power, Québec has become the

world's third-largest producer of molten aluminium and is an important centre for the processing of other metals. Also, industries creating finished products in the fields of transportation, machinery and electrical appliances are important to Québec's economy. The Bombarbier company, for example, which began as a family snowmobile business, has expanded to become a major producer of rail and air transport products.

Despite recent trends, natural resources remain a key asset for Québec. By harnessing certain powerful rivers in northern Québec, Hydro-Québec produces a colossal amount of electrical power, 25,600 MW. Forest industries continue to have a significant place in Québec's economy, providing 100,000 jobs, and representing 10% of the GDP. Lastly, the decline in the metal market around the world has resulted in a decrease in the once profitable mining of iron, asbestos, copper and zinc. Only gold production, with an annual total of 52,000 tonnes, has increased.

The recent restructuring of Québec's economy did not occur without some adverse consequences. Over the last years, the unemployment rate in the province has consistently hovered around 10%. A shortage of jobs has hit certain parts of Montréal and a number of outlying regions particularly hard. In addition, the middle class has experienced an increasingly lower standard of living, while the rich have become richer. The progress made since the Quiet Revolution, particularly regarding the domination of the Québec economy by Quebecers, is significant, but Québec faces many other important challenges before its economy can guarantee the development of a more harmonious society.

Population

As is the case in the rest of America, the people of Québec have a diverse ancestry. The aboriginal peoples were joined by French colonists in the 16th century, the descendants of whom represent a majority of the current population. Over the last two centuries, Québec has experienced waves of immigration from all over the world, particularly from Britain and the United States. The 1996 census put Québec's population at over 7 million.

Aboriginal Peoples

The original inhabitants of Québec, the Inuit and 10 other First Nations (formerly known as Indians), now represent less than one percent of Québec's total population. The ancestors of these peoples began to cross the Bering Straight from Northern Asia more than 12,000 years ago and moved into the region which would come to be known as Québec in successive waves several thousand years later. When Jacques Cartier "discovered" the region around the Gulf of St. Lawrence in the name of François I, the King of France, the area had already been home to a number of civilizations for thousands of years. During that period, the territory was populated by a complex mosaic of indigenous cultures, each with its own language, way of life and religious practices. With lifestyles adapted to climate and to the particularities of the landscape, northern populations survived by hunting and fishing, while the peoples of the St. Lawrence valley grew much of their food. The Aboriginal population of Québec did not have a written language. Their history comes to us through oral tradition,

Aboriginal Art

Aboriginal works of art were once considered anthropological specimens and collected almost exclusively by ethnological museums. It was only in the latter 20th century that they gradually obtained the status of "art." Since First Nations did not traditionally disassociate art from everyday objects, their work did not measure up to the canons of conventional European art. It was only after many struggles, some of which have yet to be won, that Aboriginal works were introduced into art museums. Canadians have showed an increased interest in Aboriginal art since the 1960s and 1970s, with over 100 Canadian museums today displaying various collections. While artistic practices vary greatly from region to region, the differences between First Nations and Inuit art are the most marked.

Inuit art is very popular in Canada; it is regularly exhibited in museums and appreciated by numerous collectors. Cooperatives were formed in the 1950s to promote and disseminate the arts of the Far North, a major turning point in

the history of Inuit art. Before this time, the objects created were small: toys, tools and sacred amulets. Near the end of the 1940s, however, sculptures began to appear as they do today, sometimes reaching 1m in height and assuming a variety of shapes and colours. These sculptures were made of bone, ivory, caribou tines and, occasionally, antler or wood. The most popular material, however, remains stone, which has been sculpted by the Inuit for millennia. Also known as "soapstone," this rock comes from the steatite family and its colour varies between grey, green and black; the darker it is, the denser it is. Stonecut printing is a recent practice that has become popular due to the simplicity of the lines and the quality of the product. Some Inuit art forms are practised exclusively by women, such as basketry, dollmaking, sewing, embroidery and beadwork, as well as hide and leather work.

The Inuit call their art *sananquaq*, which means "small portrayal of reality." For the artists, who are often hunters and

fishers, the best works are those that faithfully capture human or animal movement. Sculptures, like carvings, tell stories that are part of a heritage passed down through the oral tradition: myths and legends, dreams, the forces of nature, relationships between people and animals and the work of daily life. Themes and styles vary from one region to another.

First Nations people produce fewer sculptures than their northern neighbours, except for those on the West Coast, a region renowned for its totemic art. While those in eastern and northern Canada preferred creating very small items, perhaps because most First Nations peoples were nomadic, it was quite the opposite for those on the Pacific coast. Their totems, which represented the lineage of different tribes, could reach heights of 20 to 25m. The motifs were inspired by the spirit world, the animal world, as well as from mythology. Totemic culture has existed for thousands of years, but the only totems we now see are those preserved in museums or in parks. The oldest of them is about 300 years old. Generally speaking, the works of First Nations artists were made with materials such as wood, leather or cloth. They also created many three-dimensional works (masks, dream catchers, decorated objects), silk-screen prints and works on paper.

Many First Nations and Inuit artists have adopted contemporary materials and practices such as video, installation work, performance or new technologies. Contemporary Aboriginal art, present throughout Canada, is laden with political innuendo.

from explorers' journals and anthropological research.

With the arrival of the first European colonists in the 16th century, these ancient civilizations went into decline. Unlike the European conquest of certain other regions in the Americas, clashes between colonists and Aboriginals are not common to Québec history. The low population density of the vast territory allowed the first settlers to establish their small colonies without directly challenging the indigenous population, which for a long time were numerous.

However, the First Nations of Québec did suffer enormously during the first years of European colonization with the introduction of certain illnesses, such as influenza, measles and tuberculosis. In some areas, nearly half the Aboriginal population was wiped out as a result of these diseases.

Further devastation resulted as Aboriginal peoples engaged in bloody warfare against each other (using firearms provided by colonists) for control of the fur trade, a business introduced by the Europeans. Between 1645 and 1655, the Iroquois Confederacy nearly wiped out other Aboriginal peoples. The destruction of Aboriginal civilizations contin-

ued with territorial losses to the unrelenting spread of colonization. While the Aboriginals of Québec were rarely the target of European military aggression, they were nevertheless soon overpowered by the colonists.

There are roughly 74,000 Aboriginals presently living in Québec, three quarters of whom live in small communities scattered across the province. Though some of these groups live in areas where they can hunt and fish, in most cases traditional lifestyles have not survived. With the loss of their culture and the resulting sense of alienation, Aboriginals endure major social problems.

In recent years, however, Aboriginals living in Québec have managed to attract increased attention from the media, leading to a sensitization on the part of government and the rest of the population to their issues. Aboriginal land claims and issues of self-government have attracted significant attention, particularly during the summer of 1990, when, for two months, armed Mohawks barricaded one of the main bridges connecting Montréal to the south shore of the St. Lawrence. The incident forced native concerns to the forefront.

Two years later, an important step was taken with a project to reform the Canadian constitution to include a provision for native self-government. While a majority of Quebecers and Canadians voted against this constitutional reform package, called the Charlottetown Accord, on October 26, 1992, they did so in response to other, unrelated provisions. In fact, native claims enjoy strong support throughout the country.

Québec's 11 First Nations are part of three distinct cultural families. The Abenaki, Algonquin, Attikamek, Cree, Malecite, Micmac, Montagnais, and Naskapi are all part of the Algonquian culture, while the Wendat-Huron and the Mohawk are Iroquoian. The Inuit, for their part form a culture entirely their own. The following is a brief description of each of Québec's 11 First Nations, in alphabetical order.

Originally occupying the region that is now New England, where many still live, the **Waban Aki (Abenaki)** settled first in Sillery (near Québec City) around 1675, then in 1684 next to falls of the Rivière Chaudière. The Waban Aki (Abenaki) had close ties with the French colonists, and shared many of their ancestral skills with them, including it seems the art of making maple syrup. During the colonial wars the Waban Aki sided with the French and also participated in the defence of the colony against British invaders, who were established to the south. In 1700, a group of them settled permanently in Odanak, a village that was later sacked during the British conquest in 1759. Today, there are two Waban Aki villages in Québec – Odanak and Wôlinak – located on the south shore of the St. Lawrence between the cities of Sorel and Bécancour. Of the 1,600 Waban Aki living in Québec, about 350 live in one of the two villages. The baskets woven of hay and ash, for which the Waban Aki are famous, are still made in these villages; however most Waban Aki work in the neighbouring cities or elsewhere in Québec. The Waban Aki language has practically disappeared.

Having lived in more or less remote areas away from the city centres, the **Anishnabe (Algonquin)** were able to preserve their nomadic way of life, living off the land, hunting, fishing and gathering. The traditional activities of the Algonquin were upset with the arrival of lumberjacks and prospectors to the Abitibi region in the middle of the 19th century. Their way of life thus became less nomadic. In Québec, there are approximately 6,500 Anishnabe, 4,000 of which live in the communities of Grand-Lac-Victoria, Lac-Rapide and Maniwaki, in the Outaouais region, and Hunter's Point, Kebaowek, Lac-Simon, Pikogan, Témiscaming and Winneway, in Abitibi-Témiscamingue. The Anishnabe language is still used in most of these communities.

Almost completely decimated during the 17th century as a result of epidemics and Iroquois wars, the **Attikamekw** took refuge with the Cree or Montagnais peoples before integrating with a group from

Lake Superior known as the O'pimittish Ininivac, who later settled in the Haute-Mauricie. The 4,000 Attikamekw in Québec still live in this region, mainly in the villages of Manouane, Weymontachie and Obedjiwan. The Attikamekw have remained close to nature – working in forestry and advocating the development of resources while preserving the balance of nature. The Attikamekw language which is similar to Montagnais, is still spoken by the populations of all three communities.

Remarkably well adapted to the land and the rigours of the climate, the **Ndooheenoo (Cree)** have lived in Northern Québec for about the last 5,000 years. Despite their remote isolation, the Ndooheenoo came into regular contact with Europeans very early. From the 17th century on, fur-trading with non-native merchants constituted one of the principal economic activities of the Ndooheenoo nation. The decline in the fur-trade and the Canadian and Québec governments' increased interest in the development of Québec's far north, starting in the 1950s, have had a profound effect on the interaction between the Ndooheenoo and their environment. However, it was the signing in 1975 of the James Bay and Northern Québec

Agreement, by the governments of Québec and Canada that really changed the Ndooheenoo way of life. This signing allowed Hydro-Québec to construct hydroelectric dams on some of the most powerful rivers of the region; in exchange the Ndooheenoo were given $225 million, ownership of $13,696km^2$ and exclusive hunting and fishing rights in a territory measuring $151,580km^2$. The Agreement provided the Ndooheenoo with the resources to take an active part in the economic development of their region, as shown by the number of dynamic enterprises undertaken by this nation in the last 10 years. The 10,500 Ndooheenoo (Cree) of Québec today live in nine villages: Waskaganish, Eastmain, Wemindji and Chisasibi, on the shores of James Bay; Whapmagoostui, near Hudson Bay; Nemiscau, Waswanipi and Mistissini, in the interior; and Oujé-Bougoumou, near the city of Chibougamau. The Ndooheenoo language is still used by most of the population.

The **Inuit**, sometimes still erroneously called Eskimo, have lived for about 4,500 years in the extreme north of Québec, in a region known in Inuktitut as Nunavik, which means "land to live off." Right up to the beginning of the 20th century, the Inuit still lived as their ancestors had, hunting with traditional weapons and living in igloos. The adaptation to a more modern lifestyle only occurred in the last few decades, and is still very new.

Inuit woman and baby

Like the Cree, the Inuit also signed the James Bay and Northern Québec Agreement. Among other things, this convention granted the Inuit a greater degree of independence and self-government. They administer most of the services in Nunavik, and will eventually receive a regional government. The monetary compensation received by the Inuit is managed by the Société Makivik, and provides the Inuit with the tools necessary to play a larger role in the economic development of their region. In fact, thanks to Société Makivik, the Inuit of Québec are the owners of Air Inuit and First Air airline companies, which play a dominant role in air transport in Northern Canada. The 6,850 Inuit in Québec live in 14 villages located on the shores of Hudson Bay (Kuujjuarapik, Umiujaq, Inukjuak, Payungnituk, Akulivik), Hudson Strait (Ivujivik, Salluit, Kangiqsujjuaq, Quaqtag) and Ungava Bay (Kangirsuk, Aupaluk, Tasiujaq, Kuujjuaq and Kangiqsualujjuaq). A few dozen Inuit live in Chisasibi. The language of the Inuit, Inuktitut, is used in these communities. In Inuit schools it is the only language of instruction from kindergarten to third grade. Even though the Inuit have adopted a more modern lifestyle, their ancestral culture and values remain significant.

Scattered across the territory the **Welustuk (Malecite)**, who were for a long time known as Etchemins, number only about 270 in Québec. They are also the only Aboriginal nation that does not have their own village. However, in 1827 the government created the first native reserve for them, on the shores of the Rivière Verte, in the Bas-St-Laurent region. The reserve was eventually bought back by the government because the Welustuk hardly ever used it

and preferred to remain nomadic. In the end the Welustuk never settled down in one community, and were eventually integrated into neighbouring white communities. Even though the language is no longer spoken and no village exists, the Welustuk have had a chief and band-council since 1987.

Aboriginal basket

The **Mi'kmaq (Micmac)**, who number just under 4,000 in Québec, settled in the Gaspésie region and formed the villages of Restigouche and Gesgapegiag, or lived with non-natives in Gaspé and the surroundings. Definitely one of the first Aboriginal nations, if not the first, to come into contact with Europeans, the MïgMaqs were living on the shores of the St. Lawrence and the coast of the Atlantic Ocean when the colonists arrived. Known as accomplished seamen, the MïgMaq also established temporary and permanent camps on various islands in the Gulf of St. Lawrence. With the economic development of the region, many Micmac became lumberjacks and labourers. A considerable number of MïgMaq still speak the language, which is now taught in the two community schools.

When the Europeans arrived, the **Kanien'Kahaka (Mohawks)** formed one of the five Iroquois nations of the powerful Five-Nation Confederation, which was at the heart of the

fur-trade war in the 17th century. Despite their association with this sophisticated political system, the Kanien'Kahaka were still very independent and ambitious. Later, after they had become more sedentary, many became very skilled craftsmen, particularly as specialized steel workers. The Kanien'Kahaka have an international reputation, even today, as expert craftsmen with steel on skyscrapers and bridges. Numbering around 12,000, the Kanien'Kahaka are the largest group of Aboriginals in Québec. They live mainly in three villages: Kahnawake, located close to Montréal, on the south shore of the St. Lawrence; Akwesasne, in the southwest corner of the province, overlapping the borders of Québec, Ontario and the state of New York; Kanesatake, about 50km west of Montréal on the shores of the Lac des Deux-Montagnes. Recall that land-claims by the Kanesatake Kanien'Kahaka were at the centre of a crisis during the summer of 1990. Though many Kanien'Kahaka have adapted to modern North American culture, others still live according to their ancestral teachings, based on the Great Law of Peace. Kanien'Kahaka society is traditionally matriarchal, as such the clan mothers choose the chief. The Kanien'Kahaka (Mohawk) language is still spoken by several members of the communities.

Isolated across the vast regions of the Côte-Nord and the Basse-Côte-Nord, the **Innus (Montagnais)** lived essentially by hunting, fishing, gathering and by the fur-trade up until the beginning of the 20th century. The arrival of the mining and forestry industries, as well as the construction of hydroelectric dams, completely disrupted their way of life. Their culture remains nevertheless very vibrant, and the Innuat language is still spoken in most communities, especially the more isolated ones. The musical group Kashtin, from Uashat-Maliotenam, whose success in Europe and America, is proof positive of the vital culture of this nation, as is the recent publication of the first Montagnais-French dictionary. In number the 12,000 Innuat form the second largest Aboriginal nation in Québec. They live in seven communities: Les Escoumins, Betsiamites, Uashat-Maliotenam in the Côte-Nord; Mingan, Natashquan, La Romaine and Pakuashipi in the Basse-Côte-Nord; Mashteulatsh in Lac-Saint-Jean, and Matimekosh near Schefferville.

The **Naskapi** nation has only one village in Canada—Kawawachikamach—founded in 1984 and located in northern Québec, a few kilometres from Schefferville. In accordance with the Northeastern Québec Agreement, the 475 Naskapis of Kawawachikamach own 285km^2 of territory and have exclusive hunting, fishing and trapping rights in a 4,144km^2 territory. The Naskapis, who have only recently embraced modern culture, still hunt caribou, whose flesh and fur allow them to survive the harsh conditions of the arctic tundra. The Naskapi language is still spoken by the entire population.

When the first French colonists arrived the **Wendat-Huron** inhabited about 20 large villages in southeastern Ontario on the shores of Georgian Bay. Besides being excellent farmers they controlled an extensive commercial empire, which stretched from the Great Lakes to the Rivière Saguenay and Hudson Bay, and quite naturally became the main trading partners of the French merchants in the early years of colonization. How-

ever, this economically profitable relationship did not last, for within a few years the Wendat-Huron population was decimated, first by epidemics in 1634 and 1639, and then by repeated Iroquois attacks starting in 1640. In 1649 the remaining 300 Wendat-Hurons took refuge on the outskirts of Québec City, then settled on Île d'Orléans in 1657, then finally near the Rivière Saint-Charles in 1697, where the village of Wendake now sits. Located near Loretteville, this economically flourishing community is the only Wendat-Huron village in Québec. Of the approximate 2,500 Wendat-Hurons who live in Québec, about 950 live in Wendake. Some of the goods produced in Wendake, such as the moccasins, canoes and snowshoes, are known worldwide. The Huron language is no longer used in Québec.

Francophones

A large percentage of Québec's francophones are descendants of the original French colonists who arrived in the country gradually between 1608 and 1759. By 1663 there were only 3,000 settlers in New France. With an increased number of immigrants arriving and settlers starting families, the population of Québec stood at about 60,000 at the time of the British conquest in 1759. The settlers were mostly farmers from western France.

Today, after just over two centuries, the descendants of these 60,000 French-Canadians number in the millions, seven million of whom still live in Canada. Some interesting comparisons have been made between Québec's sharp rate of population growth and the growth rates seen elsewhere between 1760 and 1960. For example, while the population of the world during this same

200-year period grew three times, and the population of Europe grew five times, the population of francophone Canada grew 80 times. This statistic is particularly surprising given that immigration from France had dwindled to almost nothing and that there were very few marriages between British and French families (with the exception of a number of Irish-French unions). In addition, between 1840 and 1930, about 900,000 Quebecers, most of them francophone, left Canada for the United States. This phenomenal growth of Canada's French population resulted largely from a remarkably high birth rate. Indeed, for a long time, French-Canadian women had an average of eight children. Families of 15 or 20 children were not unusual. This trend can be attributed to the influence of the Catholic church, which sought to counterbalance the growth of the Protestant church in Canada. Interestingly, francophone Quebecers now have one of the lowest birth rates in the world, similar to that found in Germany and other Western European countries.

The French majority in Québec had long been deprived of control over the economy of the province. In 1960, francophones earned an average 66% of what anglophones did. With the Quiet Revolution, francophones began to take control of their economy. At the same time, they stopped thinking of themselves as French-Canadians and began to define themselves as Quebecois. Québec's total population, 82% of which is francophone, is characterized by an increasing number of immigrants.

Anglophones

Anglophones were for a long time stereotyped as Protestant

Glossary of Unique Québecois Expressions

achaler: to bother someone

blonde: a girlfriend

breuvage: in general, all non-alcoholic beverages

carosse: an airport or store cart

cenne: a penny

c'est pas pire: an expression warning of the banality of a situation or thing; also means: that's not too bad (according to the tone of voice)

char: automobile

chum: friend, buddy, boyfriend; ex: *mon chum* for a male friend and *ma chumme* for a female friend

dépanneur: a convenience store, (to be *en panne* means out of order, not working)

dispendieux: something that is expensive; ex: a car that is *dispendieuse*

donner un bec: to give a friendly kiss, the word bec means "mouth" or "beak" in a figurative sense; ex: *se sucrer le bec* = to eat sweets

être tanné: to have enough of a situation, at the end of one's rope

jaser: to chat

le fun: a good time, to be good or great or fun

liqueur: a flavoured, non-alcoholic drink, a soft drink

niaiseux: a stupid person or situation; ex: a person who is "*niaiseuse*," *une situation niaiseuse*

plate: used to describe an unpleasant situation; ex: missing the bus, *c'est plate*!

piastre: (pronounced "piasse"): dollar

se tasser: to make room for somebody, to move over.

and rich. In reality, Anglo-Quebecers have always been a diversified group. While anglophones may have been paid more on average, there have always been anglophones in every socio-economic group. The integration of anglophone immigrants from many backgrounds into Québec society has created a particularly heterogenous minority.

The first anglophone settlers arrived in Québec after the Conquest of 1759. Most were merchants and they represented a small fraction of the total population. A second wave of English-speaking immigrants arrived from the United States between 1783 and the beginning of the 19th century. Of this group, many were British Loyalists and others were simply farmers looking for land. Throughout the 19th century, immigrants from the British Isles arrived in Québec in great numbers. These British, Scottish and Irish arrivals, who were often dispossessed in their own country or the victims of famine, generally settled in the Eastern Townships, the Outaouais region or in Montréal. The declining number of immigrants from Great Britain at the end of the 19th century has been made up for by the integration of newcomers from a variety of other places. Immigrants from countries other than France or Great Britain have generally preferred to adopt the English language, feeling that this was necessary for economic success.

For the same reason, a number of francophones have become assimilated into Québec's anglophone culture. A breakdown of the anglophone population according to origin shows that 60% of the population have British origins, 15% have French origins, 8% have Jewish origins and 3% have Italian origins.

English-speaking Quebecers currently represent just over 10% of the total population of the province. Three quarters of this group lives in Montréal, most in the west end of the city. They have their own institutions (schools, universities, hospitals, media), which function just as francophone institutions do.

Anglophones represent a fairly large economic force, though unlike several decades ago, they no longer dominate Québec's economy. The rise of the independence movement, Québec francophones's increasing role in the economy and the creation of linguistic laws aimed at protecting the French language have shaken up the anglophone community. Though many have simply left the province, the majority has stayed and adapted. For example, 60% of anglophones surveyed say that they can speak French. This demonstrates a marked increase. Francophones and anglophones may differ on certain issues, but

anglophones generally feel a profound attachment to Québec and particularly to Montréal, a city they played a major role in building.

Quebecers of Other Ethnic Origins

Immigrants from elsewhere besides France, Great Britain and the United States really only started to arrive at the beginning of the 20th century. In the first part of the century, before the economic crisis of the 1930s and World War II put a stop to immigration to Québec, most new arrivals were of Jewish and Italian descent. During the era of post-war prosperity, immigrants began to come in even greater numbers than before. Most originated in Southern and Eastern Europe. Starting in the 1960s, Québec began to see the arrival of immigrants from every continent. The greatest number came from Indochina and Haiti. At present, Quebecers of Italian, Jewish and Greek origin represent the largest ethnic minorities.

Even though these new arrivals tended to preserve their own culture as much as possible, they eventually adopted either the English or the French language, and were then integrated into that particular community. This integration was until recently the source of significant social tensions. Not so long ago immigrants for the most part were assimilated into the anglophone community, which threatened to completely reverse the linguistic balance, and therefore create a split within Québec's population between francophones and the rest of the population, known as allophones. Promoted in 1977, Bill 101, was intended to remedy this situation, by encouraging immigrants to integrate into the language of the majority by

forcing new arrivals into French schools. However, following pressures by the anglophone community in Québec and the rest of Canada, the law gradually lost its authority.

Architecture

The 17th and 18th Centuries

A Vast Territory to Defend and Develop

During the Age of Enlightenment, the immense French territory in America was something to behold. In 1750, New France stretched from Acadia to the estuary of the Mississippi and from the foothills of the Appalachians to those of the Rockies. Explorers and soldiers who forged these unknown territories were usually content just to bury plaques of tin or terracotta in significant places (promontories, river mouths), claiming them for the King of France. Sometimes a small fort was erected to defend a critical pass. These buildings occasionally gave rise to villages, which years later grew into the large cities of the American Midwest like Detroit or Pittsburgh. The hinterland remained for the most part untouched. This was native territory, visited sporadically by white fur trappers, and Jesuit missionaries. The population of French origin, which reached about 65,000 souls in 1759, was concentrated in the valley of the St. Lawrence between Tadoussac and Montréal. Close to a quarter of this total lived in the three towns that lined the river (Québec City: pop. 8,400, Trois-Rivières: pop. 650 and Montréal: pop. 5,200), this represented a higher proportion of urban population than in France at the same time (22% in

Canada compared to only 17% in France)!

The feeling of insecurity on the part of inhabitants as well as the King's desire to protect his colony, led the citizens of the towns and villages of New France to surround their settlements with fortified enclosures made of stone or wood, designed according to the principles of Vauban, military engineer of Louis XIV. These strongholds, financially supported by the Crown, were completed by a network of forts intended to slow the advancement of the enemy. Their walls had to be designed to withstand both the surprise attacks by hostile native tribes and the British Army, who were arriving by sea in warships equipped with heavy artillery weapons. By the end of the French Regime, Montréal and Québec City were both typical French provincial towns well-protected within their walls. Inside, the streets were lined with churches whose steeples reached above the walls, convents, colleges, hospitals and a few aristocratic and bourgeois homes surrounded by French gardens. Added to that would be a *place d'armes* (parade ground) and a market square.

For a long time the rivers, in particular the St. Lawrence, were the roads of New France. These water-ways became punctuated by portage routes, which often developed into tiny hamlets with little else besides an inn and a chapel. It was not until 1734 that a land route suitable for vehicles between Montréal and Québec City was opened. The Chemin du Roy (more or less present-day Route 138), as it was called, was

only passable in summer, during the winter the frozen river once again became the main thoroughfare. In 1750, the trip from Québec City to Montréal along the Chemin du Roy took five days.

The banks of the St. Lawrence River and Rivière Richelieu were slowly cleared and farmed. The King of France, who had chosen the seigneurial system to develop Canada, conceded long rectangles of land, perpendicular to the water, to individuals and religious communities, who in exchange kept hearth and home and recruited new colonists. These new colonists in turn promised to pay the *cens* (tax) and swear *foi et hommage* (faith and homage) to their seigneur.

Under the French Regime, few seigneurs actually fulfilled their obligations, finding their land too isolated and exposed to Iroquois and British attacks, while others used their land as hunting grounds or for speculation. It was not until the end of the 18th century that most of the seigneuries granted between 1626 and 1758 were actually cleared and planted.

The seigneuries were developed according to a strict model, which shaped the countryside of the valley of the St. Lawrence River and that of the Richelieu. Close to the

river that supplied the seigneury would sit the seigneur's *domaine*, which included the manor house and wind or water mill, intended to grind the grains harvested by the workers into flour. The *commune*, a common pasture land, was also located on the river bank. A small village would be located to the side, generally including a simple church and five or six stone or wooden houses. The rest of the seigneury consisted of long narrow strips of land, laid out in successive rows, called *rangs*, and conceded to the colonists parcel by parcel as the number of families grew. Each strip was linked one to the other by *côtes*, roads bordering the narrow edge of the land concessions, and by *montées*, which traversed the seigneury perpendicularly to the *rangs* and the *côtes*. The seigneurial system was abolished in 1854; however, the division of land in *rangs* is still visible today.

French Architecture Adapted for the Québec Context

Of the enemies to do battle with, the cold was without a doubt the most dreaded. After rather difficult and often tragic beginnings, during which some colonists froze to death because their only shelter was a rickety wooden cabin with paper windows, French architecture slowly adapted to the long winters. It had to overcome the shortage of skilled workers, in particular stone-cutters, as well as the lack of the necessary materials on the local market, like glass for the windows and slate for the roofs, which otherwise had to be shipped in at great expense. As such, the architecture of the French Regime is an architecture of colonization, pure and economic, where each element has a specific function, essential to the well-being of the inhabitants.

Martello tower

The French Regime house consisted of a modest rubble-stone rectangle squared off by two chimneys, and topped with a double-sloped roof covered with cedar shingles. Openings in the walls were few and far between and filled with small casement windows, since larger pieces of glass did not usually survive the ocean passage. The door was made of moulded panels. The interior remained rustic, since the priority was heating. The number of rooms was limited to the number of chimneys, since each room had to be heated. Starting in 1740, several buildings were equipped with cast iron stoves, forged at the Saint-Maurice ironworks. Occasionally, stone sinks and built-in cupboards were found, and even more rarely, Louis XV-style panelling. Seigneurial manors were architecturally similar to the houses of prosperous farms. There were exceptions, particularly with busy seigneurs or with religious communities where the manor also served as a convent. These manors took on the allure of veritable castles, the most famous being the Château de Longueuil, which no longer exists.

The architecture of the towns varied little from that of the country. The first priority remained, of course, the eternal battle with the cold. Added to this however was the prevention of fires, which could easily result in tragedy in the absence of an effective fire-fighting system. Two edicts written by New France Intendants in 1721 and in 1727 pertained to construction inside the town walls. Wooden houses with mansard roofs and their dangerous wooden shingles, were forbidden; all buildings had to be made of stone and be equipped with fire-break walls; attic floors had to be covered with terracotta tiles. Those who could not afford to obey such strict standards built up

small communities outside the walls. Few examples remain of these wood houses, whose architecture was sober and functional.

Certain buildings were always more sophisticated. As expected in this colony settled by a devout society, the churches and chapels were the most elaborate. Some were even adorned with beautiful baroque façades of cut stone. Even more important though were the bright interiors, decorated with numerous Louis-XIV- and Louis-XV-style wood embellishments, painted white and gold leafed, which appeared in the first half of the 18th century. Most of the churches and chapels in the cities therefore were built with respect to classic French urban perspectives. Unfortunately, these perspectives were eliminated during the 19th century to ease traffic circulation. In the cities you might come upon *hôtels particuliers* with yards and gardens, more prominent however were three- and four-storey buildings, occupied by businesses and built close to the street. These occasionally included a workshop and stone-vaulted basements for storing merchandise. A few beautiful examples of these basements can be found surrounding the Place Royale de Québec (see p 319).

After the Conquest

New France was devastated by the Seven Years' War, leaving many of its most beautiful buildings in ruins. What the British conquest of 1760 did not succeed in destroying, the American invasion of 1775 and the War of 1812 did. Despite the political turmoil, however, the architectural vocabulary remained the same up until the end of the 18th century because the British population was too small to have an impact, and all the businessmen and labourers

remained essentially French Canadian. The English Palladian style of architecture, influenced by the work of Andreo Palladio in Italy, was only visible after 1780 following the construction of a few homes for British dignitaries and high-ranking military officers posted in Québec City.

The 19th Century

The Evolution of a Tradition

The combination of the French Regime and Palladian architectural styles, as well as the Regency trend, formed the basis of traditional Québec architecture, which reached its peak in the 19th century. It differed from the style of the previous century mainly by a lengthening of the drip moulding, which extended out to cover the long balcony across the front of the house. The elaborate and gabled drip mouldings of Regency cottages, inspired by Oriental architecture, found a new function here. The balconies served as a halfway point between inside and outside, and as a place to relax in the summer. They also prevented snow from blocking windows and doors in the winter. Other particularly useful innovations of note were the decreased slope of the roofs, which avoided the inevitable wall of snow that would come falling down each time an unlucky inhabitant stepped outside, the raising of the masonry brick foundation to separate the house from the ground, and the installation of chimneys against the walls instead of in the middle, thereby creating a better distribution of heat.

The windows remained French, but became more numerous and the number of panes decreased from 12 to 6; a storm window was added in the winter and a screen in the summer for the maximum comfort of those inside. Around 1820, the summer kitchen was introduced, a sort of lean-to positioned on the north side of the house, therefore exposed to cold winds. This room was cooler in summer and closed in winter. It was used to store perishables, while at the same time protecting the main house from chilly winter winds. Eventually, the shingle roof was replaced by sheet metal, a material that is both resistant and inflammable and which was used also on steeples and churches.

Churches also benefited from the contribution of Palladianism, thanks mostly to the Baillargé family from Québec City, who revolutionized the art of building churches in Québec. This dynasty of architects added Palladian windows and pediments to the façades. They also added Louis XVI elements to the liturgical furniture. At the other end of the scale, Louis-Amable Quévillon (1749-1823) assembled every sumptuous element of the French Regime to create his highly decorated diamond-and-star-patterned ceilings.

The population of the villages of Québec was growing rapidly, leading to the enlargement or replacement of several churches of the French Regime. The Catholic nuns built convents and colleges for the education of boys and girls. In every region a new class of professionals including notaries, lawyers and doctors were building large homes. Traditional Québec villages established in this era differed from Ontarian and American villages; they consisted of country-style homes located very close together, so close they were almost duplexes;

commercial buildings were rare, so boutiques and stores were located in buildings that resembled the residential dwellings. This style is explained by the townspeople's fear of fire (most of these village homes were made of wood), and by the Catholic Church's negative attitude towards the expansion of commerce.

American and British Immigration

Following the signing of the Treaty of Versailles in 1783, recognizing the independence of the United States, a number of Americans loyal to the crown of England took refuge in what remained of British North America, namely Canada. They brought with them a decidedly Georgian style of architecture from New England, characterized by the use of red brick, and white wooden accents. These new arrivals settled in areas left vacant by the French Regime, which the British colonial government divided into townships in the first half of the 19th century. Most of these townships are located in the Eastern Townships (see p 181) and the Outaouais (Ottawa Valley) regions (see p 254).

Québec City and Montréal also received a large number of Scottish and Irish immigrants between 1800 and 1850. They brought with them the severe but elegant neoclassical style of architecture, such as is seen in Dublin and in Glasgow. As a result, cut stone definitively replaced rubble stone around 1810. Sash windows and columned porticoes became more common in urban settings, as did all manner of Greek-and ancient Roman-inspired architectural styles (pediments, Tuscan pilasters, parapets with palmettes). The first democratically elected municipal governments undertook the lighting and paving of the streets. This was also the era of large-scale engineering projects such as the dredging of the Canal de Lachine (1821-1825) and the appearance of shipyards larger than any ever seen before. This bustle of economic activity also attracted the rural French-Canadian population to the cities, such that the population of Montréal surpassed that of Québec City around 1830, and reached the 100,000 mark in 1860.

The Reign of Historicism

The building of the Protestant orphanage in Québec City in 1823, and in particular that of the Église Notre-Dame in Montréal between 1824 and 1829, both of which are Gothic Revival, announced the arrival of historicism in Québec architecture. Originally quite marginal, historicism would come to dominate the skyline of Québec's cities and towns in the second half of the 19th century. It is defined by the use of decorative elements taken from different architectural epochs in history, which were popularized thanks to archeological discoveries, the invention of photography, and the popularity of historical novels across the world.

An array of architectural styles influenced by ancient trends appeared almost simultaneously just before, and during, the reign of Queen Victoria (1837-1901), which explains why all these styles, so different from one another, are all united under the simplified architectural term "Victorian." America being sufficiently removed from the Middle Ages and the Renaissance, was not affected by the pastiche elements that for so long influenced Europe. As such, North-American Victorian architecture was altogether new. It employed a backward-looking style, that was meaningful only to North Americans.

The Gothic Revival style, with its pointed arches, pinnacles and battlements, was for a long time reserved for churches, since the Middle Ages, from which it originated, was a period of great religious fervour. Similarly, the Renaissance Revival style was favoured by the bourgeois class for the building of sumptuous residences, since the Italian Renaissance corresponded to the birth of a powerful middle class. The Second Empire style is associated with Napoleon III's refinement of Paris. The mansard roofs, covered in slate, were used repeatedly in Québec residential architecture and in a whole series of public buildings. Their popularity is a result of the French heritage of Québec society, but also the vogue of the style throughout North America between 1865 and 1900. Also not to be forgotten are the Romanesque Revival style characterized by compound arches and short squat columns, the Queen Anne style, used in the suburbs of the new middle class, and in

particular the Château Style, a mixture of the architecture of Scottish manors and Loire châteaux, which became, over the years, a sort of Canadian "National Style."

Victor Bourgeau (in the region of Montréal) and Joseph Ferdinand Peachy (in the region of Québec City), showed their talents well in the building of innumerable historicistic parochial churches, of different styles from economical to elaborate. Bourgeau originally worked with a neoclassical vocabulary, as much a product of Brit John Ostell as the church architecture of the French Regime, before gradually turning towards Gothic Revival, and then Romanesque Revival. Peachy left his mark through a series of Renaissance Revival and Second Empire works.

Industrialization and Comfort

The Victorian era might seem contradictory, since while it looked backward in terms of its architectural style, it looked decidedly forward when it came to comfort. As such, the technological innovations that made life much more agreeable are often overlooked: running water, automatic hot water heaters, more washrooms, central heating, telephones and electricity. Among the permanent changes to the buildings that are of note were the popularity of bay windows, bow-windows and box-windows, as well as the use of flat roofs covered with tar and pebbles, which retained the snow until it melted creating a natural insulator. Some of the more complex roofs belonging to religious and public buildings were covered with richly ornamented copper, which over the years acquired a rich green hue as a result of oxidation (verdigris).

In the second half of the 19th century, the railroad finally linked the major centres effectively. The railway also led to the development of land north of the St. Lawrence (Saguenay–Lac-Saint-Jean, Laurentians and Témiscamingue) thereby helping French-Canadian farmers extend the boundary of settled land in Québec. The Industrial Revolution transformed the cities into manufacturing centres for primary goods. Workers' neighbourhoods sprouted like weeds around the factories, well-serviced by a network of tramways, originally horse-drawn (1861), then electrified (1892). The cities of Montréal and Québec City became bustling and business-oriented. Large stores, theatres, bank and insurance company headquarters opened their doors, attracting even more workers. Meanwhile, the rest of Québec, essentially agriculturally oriented, was still anchored in tradition, and would remain relatively isolated up until the middle of the 20th century.

The 20th Century

The Standard Urban Dwelling

The record birth rate in rural Québec around 1900, where families with 12 children were common, began to overburden the land. New regions such as Abitibi were opened up for settlement by the clergy, yet the attraction of the city proved insurmountable, despite the meagre wages. These uprooted workers longed for aspects of their country homes in the city: galleries and balconies, numerous well-lit rooms, a lot of storage space, which might also serve as henhouse or stables if necessary. It all had to be inexpensive to heat and relatively easy to maintain. Thus, the Montréal-style dwelling was born!

Its exterior staircases, which wound their way tightly to the second floor in the limited space between the sidewalk and balcony, avoided the need to heat an interior stairwell. The balconies were reminiscent of rural galleries, leading directly into the homes (one or two per floor), which each had their own exterior entrance. Between 1900 and 1930, thousands of these duplexes, triplexes, quadruplexes, and quintuplexes were built along Montréal's straight streets. These two- and three-storey buildings, with wooden frames and built on top of each other, were covered either with local limestone, or brick. Even though the dwelling was supposed to be economical, each one was adorned with a decorative cornice or parapet, balconies with Tuscan columns and beautiful *art nouveau* inspired stained-glass windows.

During the same era, a whole series of one-industry towns (paper or mining) were being born across Québec. These urban areas were created by the industries, and therefore equipped with a precise urban plan from the beginning. This included a well-designed public and residential architecture, renowned architectural works, modelled after English city-gardens.

Back to Basics

The École des Beaux-Arts de Paris, whose teachings engendered rigorous principles of architectural composition (symmetry, monumentalism), as well as a blend of French classicism, received a positive response among enlightened French-Canadians at the beginning of the 20th century. They sought to make a torch of the Beaux-Arts style, signalling the French presence in America. The twin columns,

wrought-iron balconies supported by stone brackets and decorated railings were also found in the wealthy Anglo-Saxon neighbourhoods, for whom the Beaux-Arts style represented the tradition of Parisian refinement.

This timid back-to-basics movement on the part of French Canadians, took on much larger proportions with the descendants of English and Scottish merchants, making pilgrimages back across the Atlantic to rediscover the ruins of such and such Welsh Manor, or such and such Scottish farm-house that grandfather grew up in. The British Arts and Crafts Movement found among these people enthusiasts of Herefordshire tiles, Elizabethan wainscotting, and Tudor chimneys. These people, who were sensitized to Great Britain's rural architecture and planned to reproduce it in Québec, were ironically the first to attempt to save some of the rural architecture of the French Regime, which was in sad decline in 1920. At the beginning of the 1930s, some new buildings inspired by New France styling were being constructed. The Quiet Revolution during the 1960s fortunately awakened a larger portion of the population to the importance of the traditions of their French heritage. It was the beginning of an era of painstaking restoration. However, while a part of the heritage was put on a pedestal, another part, that of the 19th century, was shoved off by the wrecking ball! The destruction went on until the 1980s. Efforts continue today to stave off the deterioration caused by the massive wave of demolition whose results have been compared to those of a military bombardment, and which left vacant lots scattered across the cities.

North American Influence

The favourable contacts that Québec architects and artists maintained with their colleagues in Paris, Brussels and London, did not deter them from opting out for America at the beginning of the 20th century. And so the first skyscrapers pierced the Montréal sky in 1928, following the definitive repeal of a ruling limiting the height of buildings to 10 storeys. Celebrated architects from the United States designed many of Montréal's towers, giving the downtown core its present, decidedly North-American skyline. The geometric and aerodynamic French Art-Deco style, of which there are several examples in all regions of Québec, was replaced by Modern American architecture following the Second World War. Expo '67 presented the perfect opportunity to provide Montréal and the whole province with bold, representative examples of international architecture.

The Quiet Revolution of the 1960s corresponds to a massive expansion of the suburbs and the construction of major public infrastructures. Since then, new highways crisscross Québec; huge schools, hospitals, cultural centres, and museums opened in towns where before there was only a church and a convent. Northern Québec received considerably more attention with the construction of major hydroelectric complexes. Cities underwent radical transformations in these respects: construction of the métro (subway system) in Montréal, vast modern government complexes in Québec City, etc.

At the beginning of the 1980s, the weariness resulting from the *ad nauseam* repetition of the same formulas put forward by the modernists, provoked a return to the styles of the past by way of post-modernism, which freely combines reflective glass and polished granite in compositions that echo Art Deco and neoclassicism. The 1990s for their own part present two opposing ideas: the culmination of post-modernism, in the form of a Romantic architecture, and the search for a new ultra-modern style of architecture, making use of new materials, computers and electronics.

The Arts

The aspirations and the concerns of a society are reflected in the work of its artists. For a long time, artistic expression in Québec presented an image of a people constantly on the defensive, tormented by an unsatisfactory present situation and filled with doubt over the future. However, after World War II, and particularly after the Quiet Revolution, Québec culture evolved and became more affirming. Open to outside influences, and often very innovative, Québec culture is now remarkably vital.

Québec Literature in French

Literary output in Québec began with the writings of early explorers, like Jacques Cartier, and members of religious communities. These manuscripts were usually intended to describe the New World to authorities back in France. The lifestyles of the Aboriginals, the geography of the region and the beginnings of colonization were the topics most often covered by authors of the period, such as Père Sagard (*Le Grand Voyage au Pays Hurons*, 1632) and Baron de La Hontan (*Nouveaux Voyages en Amérique Septentrionale*, 1703).

The oral tradition dominated literature during 18th century and the beginning of the 19th century. Later, the legends that had been passed down over generations, involving such things as ghosts, werewolves and pacts with the devil, were put down in writing. It was not until the end of the 19th century that Québec produced a more advanced literary movement. Most of the literary output of this period dealt with the theme of survival and reflected nationalist, religious and conservative values. The romanticization of life in the country, far from the temptations of the city, was a common element. Glorifying the past, particularly the period of French rule, was another common theme in the literature of the time. With the exception of certain works, most of the novels from this period are only of socio-historic interest.

Traditionalism continued to profoundly influence literary creation until 1930, when certain new literary movements began to emerge. The École Littéraire de Montréal (Montréal Literary School), and particularly the works of the poet Émile Nelligan, who was inspired by Baudelaire, Rimbaud, Verlaine and Rodenbach, stood in contrast to the prevailing style of the time. Nelligan, who remains a mythical figure, wrote poetry at a very young age, before lapsing into mental illness. Rural life remained an important ingredient of Québec fiction during this period, though certain authors began to put country life in a different light. Louis Hémon, in *Maria Chapdelaine* (1916), presented rural life more realistically, while Albert Laberge (*La Scouine*, 1918) presented the mediocrity of a country existence.

During the Great Depression and World War II, Québec literature began to reflect

modernism. Literature with a rural setting, which continued to dominate, gradually began to incorporate themes of alienation. Another major step was taken when cities, where most of Québec's population actually lived, began to be used as settings in francophone fiction, in books such as *Bonheur d'Occasion* (*The Tin Flute* 1945), by Franco-Manitoban Gabrielle Roy.

Modernism became a particularly strong literary force with the end of the war, despite Maurice Duplessis's repressive administration. Two genres of fiction dominated during this period: the urban novel and the psychological novel. Québec poetry entered a golden era distinguished by the work of a multitude of writers such as Gaston Miron, Alain Grandbois, Anne Hébert, Rina Lasnier and Claude Gauvreau. This era essentially saw the birth of Québec theatre, as well. With regard to essay writing, the *Refus Global* (1948), signed by a group of painters, was the most incisive of many diatribes critical of the Duplessis administration.

Québec writers gained greater prominence with the political and social vitality brought about by the Quiet Revolution in the 1960s. A great number of political essays, such as *Nègres Blancs d'Amérique* (1968), by Pierre Vallières, reflected an era of reappraisal, conflict and cultural upheaval. Through the plays of Marcel Dubé and those of rising talents such as Michel Tremblay, Québec theatre truly came into its own during this period. The use by novelists, poets and dramatists of idiomatic French-Canadian speech, called *joual*, was an important literary breakthrough of the time.

Contemporary literature is rich and diversified. Writers, such as Victor-Lévy Beaulieu,

Jacques Godbout, Alice Parizeau, Roch Carrier, Jacques Poulin, Louis Caron, Yves Beauchemin, Suzanne Jacob and, more recently, Louis Hamelin, Robert Lalonde, Gaetan Soucy, Christian Mistral, Dany Laferrière, Ying Chen, Sergio Kokis, Denise Bombardier, Arlette Cousture and Marie Laberge have joined the ranks of previously established authors.

Québec Literature in English

Québec's English-language literary soul is located in Montréal and its best-known author was Mordecai Richler (1931-2001), whose sharply comic prose, as salty as smoked meat on rye, depicts life in the cold-water flats and Kosher delis of mid-town Montréal in the 1950s. Novels such as *The Apprenticeship of Duddy Krantz* (1959), *The Street* (1969) and *St. Urbain's Horseman* (1971) portray a neighbourhood whose face is now changed but still recognizable on certain corners, such as Clark and Fairmount. Richler was also a frequent contributor to the *New Yorker*, with his crusty and controversial accounts of Québec politics.

Other well-known literary voices of English-Montréal include poet Irving Layton, gravel-throated crooner/poet Leonard Cohen, novelist and essayist Hugh MacLennan and poet and novelist Mavis Gallant. On the stage, playwright David Fennario's *Balconville* (1979), which examines the lives of middle-class anglophones and francophones in Montréal, is one of the city's best-known works in English.

Montreal's latest literary star is writer Yann Martel. Born in Spain in 1963 to diplomat parents, Martel won the prestigious Booker Prize in 2002 for his novel *Life of Pi*, a fish tale of a story about a teenaged Indian boy shipwrecked on a lifeboat with a Bengal tiger.

Theatre

Québec theatre made a name for itself in the 1980s, with the staging of numerous big productions, several of which incorporated different forms of artistic expression (dance, singing, video). As a result, many small theatres sprang up in Montréal. Among Québec's brightest stars in contemporary theatre are the troupe Carbone 14, and directors André Brassard, Robert Lepage, Lorraine Pintal, René-Richard Cyr, and the authors René-Daniel Dubois, Michel-Marc Bouchard, Jean-Pierre Ronfard and Wajdi Mouhawad.

Music and Song

Music entered a modern era in Québec after World War II. In 1961, Québec hosted an international festival of *musique actuelle* (experimental music). Also in the 1960s, large orchestras, most notably the Orchestre Symphonique de Montréal (OSM), began to attract bigger crowds.

Several important music festivals are held throughout Québec, including the festival of *musique actuelle* in Victoriaville and the summer festival in the Lanaudière region.

The popular song, which has always been important to Québec folk culture, gained further popularity after World War I with the rise of radio and the improved quality of music recordings. The greatest success was known by La Bolduc (Marie Travers), who sang popular songs in idiomatic French. In the 1950s, the prevailing popular music trend involved adapting American songs or reinterpreting songs from France. As a result, certain talented Québec song writers working at the time, like Raymond Lévesque and Félix Leclerc, were virtually ignored until the 1960s.

With the Quiet Revolution, song writing in Québec entered a new and vital era. Singers like Claude Leveillé, Jean-Pierre Ferland, Gilles Vigneault and Claude Gauthier won over crowds with nationalist and culturally significant lyrics. In 1968, Robert Charlebois made an important contribution to the Québec music scene by producing the first French-language rock album.

Currently, established performers like Plume Latraverse, Michel Rivard, Diane Dufresne, Pauline Julien, Ginette Reno, Jim Corcoran, Claude Dubois, Richard Séguin, Paul Piché and Marjo are joined by newcomers like Jean Leloup, Richard Desjardins, Daniel Bélanger, Dan Bigras, Bruno Pelletier, Kevin Parent, Lynda Lemay, Luce Dufault, Daniel Boucher, Isabelle Boulay and the band La Chicane. The most well known name these days is Céline Dion, who sings in both French and English. Her amazing voice has made her *the* pop diva around the world. There is also the particular achievement of songwriter Luc Plamondon and his participation in the production of *Starmania* and *Notre-Dame de Paris*. In addition, certain non-francophone artists, like Leonard Cohen, Corey Hart, and Bran Van 3000, enjoy and have enjoyed a strong international reputation.

Visual Arts

Visual art in Québec through most of the 19th century

displayed a rather antiquated aesthetic. With the support of major art collectors in Montréal, Québec artists began to experiment somewhat towards the end of the 19th century and the beginning of the 20th century. Landscape artists, including Lucius R. O'Brien, achieved a certain success during this period. The Barbizon school, characterized by representations of rural life, was also influential. Inspired by the La Haye school, painters like Edmund Morris began to introduce a suggestion of subjectivism into their work.

The works of Ozias Leduc, which were influenced by Symbolism, began to show a tendency towards the subjective interpretation of reality, as did the sculptures of Alfred Laliberté at the beginning of the 20th century. Some works completed around this time exhibit a certain receptiveness of European styles, among them the paintings of Suzor-Côté. It is however, in the work of James Wilson Morrice, who was inspired by Matisse, that the influence of the European School is most explicitly detectable. Morrice, who died in 1924, is considered by most as the forerunner of modern art in Québec. It would, however, take several years, marked notably by the work of landscape and urban artist Marc-Aurèle Fortin, before the visual arts in Québec were in line with contemporary trends.

Québec modern art began to affirm itself during World War II thanks to the leaders of the movement, Alfred Pellan and Paul-Émile Borduas. In the 1950s, two major trends developed in Québec's art community. The most significant of these involved nonfigurative works, of which

there were two general categories: abstract expressionism, as seen in the works of Marcelle Ferron, Marcel Barbeau, Pierre Gauvreau and Jean-Paul Riopelle, and geometric abstraction, represented by artists such as Jean-Paul Jérôme, Fernand Toupin, Louis Belzile and Redolphe de Repentigny. The other major trend in art was a new wave of figurative painting by artists like Jean Dallaire and Jean-Paul Lemieux.

Post-war trends continued into the 1960s. The emergence of new painters, such as Guido Molinari, Claude Tousignant and Yves Gaucher brought increased attention to the geometric abstraction style. Engraving and printmaking became more common mediums of expression, art "happenings" were frequent and artists began to be asked to provide work for public places. Styles and influences diversified greatly in the early 1970s, resulting in the eclectic art scene found in Québec today.

Cinema

While some full-length films were made earlier, the birth of Québec cinema really did not occur until after World War II. Between 1947 and 1953, independent producers brought a number of literary adaptations to the screen, including *Un Homme et Son Péché* (1948), *Seraphin* (1949), *La Petite Aurore l'Enfant Martyre* (1951) and *Tit-Coq* (1952). However, the arrival of television in the early 1950s resulted in a 10-year period of stagnation for the Québec film industry.

A cinematic renaissance during the 1960s occurred largely

thanks to the support of the National Film Board (NFB-ONF). With documentaries and realistic films, directors focused primarily on a critique of Québec society. Later, the full-length feature film dominated with the success of certain directors like Claude Jutra (*Mon Oncle Antoine*, 1971), Jean-Claude Lord (*Les Colombes*, 1972), Gilles Carle (*La Vraie Nature de Bernadette*, 1972), Michel Brault (*Les Ordres*, 1974), Jean Beaudin (*J.A. Martin Photographe*, 1977) and Frank Mankiewicz (*Les Bons Débarras*, 1979). The NFB-ONF and other government agencies provided most of the funding for these largely uncommercial works.

Import feature films of recent years include those of Denys Arcand (*Le déclin de l'Empire américain*, 1986, *Jésus de Montréal*, 1989, and *Stardom*, 2000, all available in English), Jean-Claude Lauzon (*Un zoo la nuit*, 1987, and *Léolo*, 1992), Léa Pool (*À corps perdu*, 1988), Jean Beaudin (*Being at Home With Claude*, 1992) and François Girard (*The Red Violon*, 1998). Director Frédérick Back won an Academy Award in 1982 for *Crac!* and another one in 1988 for his superbly animated film, *The Man who Planted Trees*.

Daniel Langlois has also made significant contributions to Québec cinema. A key player in the film industry, he has been very involved in the development of film centres and festivals. He founded Softimage, which designs special effects software that has been used in several well-known feature-length films in the past several years. He has also opened up a new cinema complex in Montréal called Ex-Centris (see p 140).

Practical Information

Information in this

chapter will help you to plan your trip to Québec.

It contains important details on entrance formalities, getting here, getting around, as well as other useful information for visitors. We also explain how to use this guide. We wish you happy travels in Québec!

Entrance Formalities

Passports

A valid passport is usually sufficient for most visitors planning to stay less than three months in Canada. U.S. citizens do not need a passport, but it is, however, a good form of identification. US citizens and citizens of Western Europe do not need a visa. For a complete list of countries whose citizens require a visa, see the **Canadian Citizenship and Immigration** Web site (*www.cic.gc.ca*) or contact the Canadian embassy or consulate nearest you.

Extended Visits

Visitors must submit a request to extend their visit **in writing** and **before** the expiration of their visa (the date is usually written in your passport) to an Immigration Canada office. To make a request, you must have a valid passport, a return ticket, proof of sufficient funds to cover the stay, as well as the $75 non-refundable filing-

fee. In some cases (work, study), however, the request must be made **before** arriving in Canada.

Customs

If you are bringing gifts into Canada, remember that certain restrictions apply:

Smokers (legal age is 18) can bring in a maximum of 200 cigarettes, 50 cigars, 200g of tobacco, and 200 tobacco sticks.

For **wine,** the limit is 1.5 litres; for **liquor,** 1.14 litres. The limit for beer is 24 355ml cans or 341ml bottles. The legal drinking age in Quebec is 18 years.

For more information on Canadian customs regulations, contact the **Canada Customs and Revenue Agency** (☎800-

461-9999 *within Canada,* ☎204-983-3500 *or 506-636-5067 outside Canada,* www.ccra-adrc.gc.ca)

There are very strict rules regarding the importation of **plants**, **flowers**, **food** and other **vegetation**; it is therefore not advisable to bring any of these types of products into the country. If it is absolutely necessary, contact the Customs-Agriculture service of the Canadian embassy **before** leaving.

If you are travelling with **pets**, you will need a health certificate (available from your veterinarian), as well as a rabies vaccination certificate. Remember that the vaccination must be carried out **at least** 30 days **before** your departure and should not have been administered more than one year ago.

Tax reimbursements for visitors: it is possible to get reimbursed for the tax paid on purchases made while in Québec (see p 51).

Embassies and Consulates

For a complete list of Canadian embassies and consulates abroad, consult the following Government of Canada Web site: *www.dfait-maeci.gc.ca*.

Abroad

DENMARK
Canadian Embassy
Kr. Bernikowsgade 1,
1105 Copenhagen K
☎*(45) 12.22.99*
≈*(45) 14.05.85*

GERMANY
Canadian Consulate General
Internationales Handelszentrum
Friedrichstrasse 95, 23rd floor
10117 Berlin
☎*(30) 261.11.61*
≈*(30) 262.92.06*

GREAT BRITAIN
Canada High Commission
Macdonald House
One Grosvenor Square
London, W1X 0AB
☎*(171) 258-6600*
≈*(171) 258-6384*

NETHERLANDS
Canadian Embassy
Parkstraat 25, 2514JD, The Hague
☎*(70) 361-4111*
≈*(70) 365-6283*

SWEDEN
Canadian Embassy
Tegelbacken 4, 7th floor, Stockholm
☎*(8) 613-9900*
≈*(8) 24.24.91*

UNITED STATES
Canadian Embassy
501 Pennsylvania Ave. NW
Washington, DC, 20001
☎*(202) 682-1740*
≈*(202) 682-7726*

Canadian Consulates General:

1175 Peachtree St. NE
100 Colony Square, Suite 1700,
Atlanta, Georgia, 30361-6205
☎*(404) 532-2000*
≈*(404) 532-2050*

Three Copley Place, Suite 400
Boston, Massachusetts, 02116
☎*(617) 262-3760*
≈*(617) 262-3415*

Two Prudential Plaza, 180 N
Stetson Ave., Suite 2400, Chicago,
Illinois, 60601
☎*(312) 616-1860*
≈*(312) 616-1877*

St. Paul Place, Suite 1700,
750 N. St. Paul St., Dallas, Texas,
75201-3247
☎*(214) 922-9806*
≈*(214) 922-9815*

600 Renaissance Center, Suite 1100
Detroit, Michigan, 48234-1798
☎*(313) 567-2085*
≈*(313) 567-2164*

550 South Hope St., 9th floor
Los Angeles, California, 90071-2327
☎*(213) 346-2700*
≈*(213) 620-8827*

Suite 900, 701 Fourth Ave. S
Minneapolis, Minnesota,
55415-1899
☎*(612) 333-4641*
≈*(612) 332-4061*

1251 Avenue of the Americas,
Concourse Level, New York, NY
10020-1175
☎*(212) 596-1628*
≈*(212) 596-1666/1790*

3000 HSBC Center, Buffalo, NY
14203-2884.
☎*(716) 858-9500*
≈*(716) 852-4340*

412 Plaza 600, Sixth and
Stewart sts., Seattle, Washington
98101-1286
☎*(206) 442-1777*
≈*(206) 443-9662*

In Montréal

DENMARK
1 Place-Ville-Marie, 35th floor
H3B 4M4
☎*(514) 871-8977*

GERMANY
1250 Boulevard René-Lévesque
Ouest, Suite 4315, H3B 4X1
☎*(514) 931-2277*

GREAT BRITAIN
1000 de la Gauchetière Ouest
Suite 901, H3B 3A7
☎*(514) 866-5863*

NETHERLANDS
1002 Rue Sherbrooke Ouest
Suite 2201, H3A 3L6
☎*(514) 849-4247*
≈*(514) 849-8260*

SWEDEN
8400 Boulevard Décarie, H4P 2N2
☎*(514) 345-2727*

UNITED STATES
Place Félix-Martin
1155 Rue Saint-Alexandre
☎*(514) 398-9695*
≈*(514) 398-9748*
Mailing address:
C.P. 65 Station Desjardins Montréal,
H5B 1G1

Tourist Information

Québec is divided into 20 tourist regions. Each region has its own regional tourist association, called the Associations Touristiques Régionales or ATR, responsible for the distribution of information on the region. Basic information guides are published for each tourist region and are available free of charge from these associations and offices (addresses are provided in the respective chapter), or from the Délégations Générales du Québec outside of Québec. In Montréal, Québec City, and Laval, tourist information is available from provincial tourism offices.

Official Tourist Information

By telephone, Internet or mail:

Tourisme Québec
CP 979, Montréal
H3C 2W3
☎*877-266-5687*
www.tourisme.gouv.qc.ca
www.bonjourquebec.com

In Montréal:

For detailed information, maps, flyers or accommodation information for Montréal and other tourist regions of Québec:

Centre Infotouriste
1001 Rue du Square-Dorchester
(métro Peel)
☎/≈*(514) 393-1072*
☎*800-665-1528*

In Québec City

Centre Infotouriste de Québec
12 Rue Sainte-Anne, Québec
G1R 3X2
☎*(418) 694-1602*
☎*800-665-1528*

Centre d'Information de l'Office du Tourisme et des Congrès de la région de Québec
835 Avenue Wildfrid Laurier, Québec
G1R 2L3
☎*(418) 649-2608*
≈*(418) 522-0803*

Guidebooks and Maps

There are various specialized guidebooks and maps that might prove very useful for visitors seeking more information on certain aspects of Québec. Note that most of these are in French. Guides for specific regions include *Gaspésie–Bas-Saint-Laurent–Îles de la Madeleine*; *Charlevoix, Saguenay-Lac-Saint-Jean*; *Côte-Nord*; *Abitibi–Grand Nord* (Guides de Voyage Ulysse, available in French only), *Québec City* and *Montréal* (Ulysses Travel Guides). And for outdoor enthusiasts: *Le Québec cyclable* (Guides de Voyage Ulysse; a French-language guide to the bicycle trails in Québec) and *Hiking in Québec* (Ulysses Travel Guides). For information on accommodations: *Inns and Bed and Breakfasts in Québec* (Ulysses Travel Guides).

Ulysses Travel Bookshop
4176 Rue Saint-Denis
(Métro Mont-Royal)
☎*(514) 843-9447*

560 Président-Kennedy
(Métro McGill)
☎*(514) 843-7222*

Airports

There are two major airports in the province of Québec: **Dorval** and **Mirabel**. A third one, in **Québec City**, is much smaller and serves only a limited number of destinations, although it does receive some international flights. The Dorval and Québec City airports are intended for international and domestic flights, whereas Mirabel Airport handles only chartered flights.

The Mont-Tremblant ski resort (see p 238) has an international airport that handles flights from the United States and Toronto.

Dorval International Airport

Location

Dorval airport is located approximately 20km from downtown Montréal, and is 20min by car. To get downtown from here, take Aut. 20 E. to the junction of Aut. 720 (the Ville-Marie), follow signs for "Centre-ville, Vieux-Montréal."

Information

For information regarding airport services (arrivals, departures, other information), an information counter is open from 6am to 10pm seven days a week: ☎*(514) 394-7377*, *www.admtl.com*

Buses

Dorval to Downtown Montréal:

La Québécoise *($11 one way, $19.75 return; every 30min from 7am to 1am;* ☎*931-9002)* provide bus service from the airport to downtown. The bus stops at the Aérogare Centre-ville *(777 De La Gauchetière, corner University)*, and the bus terminal *(505 Boul. de Maisonneuve Est, Berri-UQAM métro)*.

Downtown to Dorval: The same service (see above) is available every 30min from 3:30am to 11pm.

Dorval to Mirabel: The same bus company provides transportation between Montréal's two international airports *(the schedule varies; service is free for passengers in transit within 15hrs; $18 one way, $28 return;* ☎*418-520-2916)*.

You can also use public transportation to get downtown. From the airport, take bus no. 204 east until the Dorval bus terminal. From there, take bus no. 211 east until its terminal at Lionel-Groulx métro station. Information: ☎*288-6287*.

Dorval to Québec City: The bus company La Québécoise provides direct service *($53 one way; every day 7am to 1am every 30min;* ☎*631-1856)*.

Car Rentals

The major car rental companies have offices at the airport.

Practical Information

Taxis

Taxi service is offered from 6am until the last flight. The rate is $28 plus $1 airport tax for trips between Dorval and downtown Montréal. All taxis serving Dorval Airport are supposed to accept credit cards.

Limousines

Fixed rate (*$47.70*) to downtown. For information: ☎*(514) 633-3019*.

Foreign Exchange

ICE Currency EXchange counter is open from 5:30am to 9pm, but a commission is charged. Better exchange rates are available in downtown Montréal (see p 77).

Taxes

Everyone leaving Dorval International Airport (except those in transit) must pay a $15 Airport Improvement Fee. There are several counters and machines selling these tickets on the departure level.

Lost and Found

☎*(514) 636-0499*

Mirabel International Airport

Location

This airport is located approximately 50km north of Montréal, in Mirabel. To reach downtown Montréal from Mirabel, follow the Autoroute des Laurentides S. (Aut. 15) until it intersects with Autoroute Métropolitaine E. (Aut. 40), which you follow for a few kilometres, then continue once again on the 15 S. (here, called Autoroute Décarie) until Autoroute Ville-Marie (Aut. 720). Follow the signs for "Centre-ville, Vieux-Montréal." The trip takes 40 to 60min.

Information

For information concerning airport services (arrivals and departures), an information counter is set up for visitors (*Mon-Thu, and Sat 11am to 11pm, Fri 11am to midnight, Sun 5am to midnight;* ☎*450-394-7377 or 800-465-1213, www. admtl.com*).

Bus

Mirabel to downtown Montréal:

La Québécoise
☎*(514) 931-9002*
www.autobus.qc.ca
Departure: schedule varies according to flight arrivals and departures
Cost: $20 one-way, $30 return
The bus stops at the train station (*777 De La Gauchetière, corner University*), and the Station Centrale (bus terminal) (*505 Boulevard De Maisonneuve Est, Métro Berri-UQAM*).

Downtown to Mirabel:

See above.

Mirabel to Dorval:

La Québécoise
☎*(514) 931-9002*
www.autobus.qc.ca
Departure: schedule varies according to arrivals and departures
Cost: $18 one-way, $28 return, free for passengers with transfers in under 15 hours.

Limousine

Limousine service is provided by **Limousines Montréal** (*$135;* ☎*514-333-5466*).

Taxis

At Mirabel, services are more limited and expensive (*around $70*) than at Dorval airport, given the distance between Mirabel and downtown Montréal. The shuttle service

is more advantageous in this case.

Car Rentals

All the large car-rental companies have offices at the airport.

Foreign Exchange

ICE Currency Exchange is open during flight arrivals and departures, but they charge a commission. Better exchange rates are available in downtown Montréal. This establishment, however, has various automatic teller machines to exchange more common currencies.

Taxes

Everyone leaving Mirabel International Airport (except those in transit) must pay a $15 Airport Improvement Fee. There are several counters and machines selling these tickets on the departure level.

Lost and Found

☎*(450) 476-3010*

Jean-Lesage Airport (Québec City)

Location

Though small, Québec City's airport handles international flights. It is located on the periphery of Sainte-Foy and L'Ancienne-Lorette. To get there from Vieux-Québec, take Boulevard Laurier heading west to Autoroute Henri-IV (Aut. 40 N). From there, take Boulevard Hamel going west and follow it until the Route de l'Aéroport.

500 Rue Principale, Sainte-Foy
☎*(418) 640-2700*
www.aeroportdequebec.com

Taxis

A taxi from the airport to Vieux-Québec costs $24.50, $11 to Sainte-Foy. Some cars can carry as many as six passengers.

Car Rentals

Various car rental agencies are located at the airport.

Foreign Exchange

The **Travelex** company (☎418-877-5768) foreign exchange office is open during flight arrivals and departures.

Taxes

Everyone leaving Jean- Lesage Airport (except those in transit) must pay a $15 Airport Improvement Fee. There are several counters and machines selling these tickets on the departure level.

Lost and Found

☎*(418) 640-2600*

Getting There and Getting Around

By Car

Good road conditions and cheaper oil prices than in other parts of the world make driving an ideal way to travel all over Québec. Excellent road and regional maps published in Québec can be found in bookstores and in tourist information centres.

Things to Consider

Driver's License: As a general rule, foreign driver's licenses are valid for six months from the arrival date in Canada.

Winter Driving: Although roads are generally in good condition, the dangers brought on by drastic climatic conditions must be taken into consideration. Roads are often transformed into virtual skating rinks by black ice. Wind is also a factor, causing blowing

snow, and reducing visibility to almost nil. All these factors, which Quebecers are used to, require prudent driving. If you plan on driving through remote areas, be sure to bring along a blanket and some supplies should your car break down.

Driving and the Highway Code: Turning right on a red light was **forbidden** in Québec until very recently. It is now permitted everywhere in the province (unless otherwise indicated) **except on the island of Montréal**. Priority to the right is the law here; however, it is not always observed, so pay attention. Signs marked "Arrêt" or "Stop" against a red background must always be respected. Come to a complete stop even if there is no apparent danger.

When a school bus (usually yellow) has stopped and has its signals flashing, you must come to a complete stop, no matter what direction you are travelling in. Failing to stop at the flashing signals is considered a serious offense and carries a heavy penalty. Wearing seatbelts in the front and back seats is compulsory at all times.

Pay attention to reserved bus lanes! They are marked by a large white diamond and signs clearly indicating the hours you cannot drive in these lanes, except when making a right turn.

There are no tolls on Québec highways (*autoroutes*), and the speed limit on them is 100km/h. The speed limit on secondary highways is 90km/h, and 50km/h in urban areas.

Gas Stations: Gasoline prices are less expensive than in Europe. However, due to hidden taxes, gas prices in Québec are considerably higher than those in the United States and in Western

Canada. Some gas stations (especially in the downtown areas) might ask for payment in advance as a security measure, especially after 11pm.

Car Rentals

Many travel agencies have agreements with the major car-rental companies (Avis, Budget, Hertz, etc.) and offer good values; contracts often include added bonuses (reduced ticket prices for shows, etc.). Package deals are usually a good deal. However, if you cannot get a package, it is cheaper to rent your car here than it is from abroad.

One good way to save on rental costs and meet local Quebecers is through a group of car poolers known as ALLO-STOP (see p 49), where rides are organized and costs are shared.

When renting a car, find out if:

The contract includes unlimited kilometres and if the insurance offered provides full coverage (accident, property damage, hospital costs for you and passengers, theft).

Attention:

To rent a car in Québec, you must be at least 21 years of age and have had a driver's license for **at least** one year. If you are between 21 and 25, certain companies (for example Avis, Thrifty, Budget) will ask for a $500 deposit, and in some cases they will also charge an extra sum for each day you rent the car. These conditions do not apply for those over 25 years of age.

A credit card is extremely useful for the deposit to avoid tying up large sums of money, and in some cases (gold cards) can cover the insurance.

Most rental cars have an automatic transmission; however, you can request a car with a

Practical Information

manual shift. Child safety seats cost extra.

Renting an RV (Motorhome, Camper-Trailer or Caravan)

Although this is a fairly expensive way to get around, Rvs are an excellent way to discover the great outdoors. As with the car rental, however, a package deal organized through a travel agency is the most economical means of renting this type of vehicle. Your travel agent can provide you with more information.

Because of high demand and the short camping season, it is necessary to reserve early to get a good choice of trailers. When planning a summer holiday, it is best to reserve by January or February at the latest.

Remember to examine the insurance coverage carefully, as these vehicles are very expensive. Make sure the kitchen utensils and the bedding are included in the rental price.

Here is a helpful address if you decide to rent on the spot. There are many other companies listed in the Yellow Pages phone book under the heading *Véhicules Récréatifs* (recreation vehicles).

Cruise Canada
☎*(514) 628-7093*

Accidents and Emergencies

In case of serious accident, fire or other emergency, dial *911* or *0*.

If you run into trouble on the highway, pull onto the shoulder of the road and turn the hazard lights on. If it is a rental car, contact the rental company as soon as possible. Always file an accident report. If a disagreement arises over

who was at fault in an accident, ask for police help.

If you are planning a long trip and decide to buy a car, it is a good idea to become a member of the Canadian Automobile Association, or C.A.A., which can offer help throughout Québec and Canada. If you are a member in your home country of an equivalent association (U.S.A.: American Automobile Association; Great-Britain: Automobile Association; Australia: Australian Automobile Association), you have the right to some free services. For further information, contact your association or the C.A.A. in Montréal:

C.A.A.
1180 Drummond, H3G 2R7
☎*(514) 861-7111*

By Bus

While a car may be the easiest way to get around, buses are relatively cheap and provide access to most of Québec. With the exception of city buses, which are government run, long-distance bus companies are privately run. The following companies cover Québec:

Greyhound
☎*800-661-8747*
www.greyhound.ca
Covers all of Western Canada to Montréal.

Orléans Express
☎*(514) 842-2281*
www.orleansexpress.com
The main company in Québec.

Smoking is prohibited on buses and pets are not allowed. In general, children under five travel free of charge and people aged 60 and over get significant discounts.

Travel Times from Montréal by Bus

Québec City
3hrs

Saint-Jovite
2hrs

Saint-Sauveur
1hr 30min

Val-David, Sainte-Agathe
1hr 50min

Sherbrooke
2hrs 10min

Trois-Rivières
1h 30min

Rimouski
7hrs

Toronto
7hrs

Ottawa
2hrs 20min

Gaspé
15hrs

Bus Stations

Montréal
Station Centrale, 505 Boulevard de Maisonneuve Est, corner Berri (Berri-UQAM métro)
☎*(514) 842-2281*

Québec City
Gare du Palais, 320 Rue Abraham-Martin
☎*(418) 525-3000*

Sainte-Foy
3001 Chemin des Quatre-Bourgeois
☎*(418) 650-0087*

Bus Tours

Some companies also offer package deals on excursions of a day or more, which (depending on the length of the tour) include accommodation and guided tours. There is quite a variety of tours available, too many to list here.

For further information on these tours, contact the

Table of distances (km)
Via the shortest route

© ULYSSES

	Baie-Comeau	Boston (Mass.)	Charlottetown (P.E.I.)	Chibougamau	Chicoutimi	Gaspé	Halifax (N.S.)	Hull	Montréal	New York (N.Y.)	Niagara Falls (Ont.)	Québec City	Rouyn-Noranda	Sherbrooke	Toronto (Ont.)
Boston (Mass.)	1040														
Charlottetown (P.E.I.)	724	1081													
Chibougamau	679	1152	1347												
Chicoutimi	316	849	992	363											
Gaspé	337	1247	867	1039	649										
Halifax (N.S.)	807	1165	265	1430	1076	952									
Hull	869	701	1404	725	662	1124	1488								
Montréal	676	512	1194	700	464	930	1290	207							
New York (N.Y.)	1239	352	1421	1308	1045	1550	1508	814	608						
Niagara Falls (Ont.)	1334	767	1836	1298	1126	1590	1919	543	670	685					
Québec City	422	648	984	515	211	700	1056	451	253	834	925				
Rouyn-Noranda	1304	1136	1833	493	831	1559	1916	536	638	1246	858	877			
Sherbrooke	662	426	1187	724	451	915	1271	347	147	657	827	240	782		
Toronto (Ont.)	1224	906	1746	1124	1000	1476	1828	399	546	823	141	802	606	693	
Trois-Rivières	545	566	1089	574	338	808	1173	331	142	750	814	130	747	158	688

Example: The distance between Québec City and Chicoutimi is 211 km.

Centre Infotouriste in Montréal or in Québec City.

By Train

Travelling by train can be very interesting, particularly when covering great distances, as they provide an excellent level of comfort. **Via Rail Canada** is the main passenger railway company in Canada.

Via Rail
☎**888-842-7245**
www.viarail.ca

The **Québec North Shore & Labrador Railway Company** *(☎418-962-9411)* only serves two lines in the northeast: Sept-Îles to Schefferville (once a week) and Sept-Îles to Labrador City (twice a week).

By Boat

There is an almost endless list of possible cruises and boating excursions available throughout Québec. River boat trips on what are known as *bateau mouche* (sightseeing boats) are also available. In some cases, naturalists are on board to give interesting presentations on the ecosystem of the area, providing insights into the flora and fauna. Although many options are offered, some deserve mention:

From Montréal

For thrill-seekers who don't mind a bumpy and wet ride, try going down the Rapides de Lachine.

Cruise around the Îles de Boucherville. Take a night cruise and enjoy a stunning view of the Montréal skyline.

From Québec

Tour of Île d'Orléans.

Saguenay

Sightseeing trip to the Saguenay fjord. This is the only navigable fjord in North America; it is as deep as 275m in some places.

On the St. Lawrence

Whale-watching excursions in zodiacs, guided cruises around Montréal and Québec City, dinner cruises, and long cruises between Montréal and Québec City) are offered by **Croisières AML** *(124 Rue Saint-Pierre, Québec, ☎418-692-1159 or 800-563-4643, ≈692-0845, www. croisieresaml.com).*

The North Shore

Nordik Express (☎418-723-8787): trips along the Côte-Nord from Sept-Îles to Blanc-Sablon, passing by Île d'Anticosti, as well as through 12 towns accessible only by boat.

The Îles-de-la-Madeleine

Sightseeing trips around the islands.

CTMA Vacancier
☎**986-3278 or 888-986-3278**
This weekly sightseeing cruise departs Montréal Fridays at noon and arrives on the islands Sundays at noon, with whale-watching and other stops scheduled along the way. The return trip to Montréal arrives Tuesday evening.

Québec City

The *M/S Jacques-Cartier* is a cruise ship that holds up to 400 passengers. Excursions are offered on several navigable rivers in Québec: the Outaouais, the St. Lawrence, the Richelieu and the Saguenay. Although its port of registry is located at Trois-Rivières, the *M/S Jacques Cartier* offers cruises from various cities in the province.

For reservations call ☎*(819) 375-3000* or *800-567-3737*, ≈*(819) 375-1975*, or visit *http://croisieres. qc.ca.*

Pleasure Boating

For pleasure-boating enthusiasts, the **Fédération de Voile du Québec** *(☎514-252-3097)* publishes the *Guide Nautique du Saint-Laurent* in French, which describes the various marinas and the different services offered on site. Always bring along warm clothing, even in summer, as it can get cool on the open water.

By Ferry

Ferries cross the St. Lawrence River and other waterways at several points. Given their large number and frequent timetable changes, we cannot list them all. For further information, check the "Finding Your Way Around" section of the guide on the region you want to visit. Ask beforehand if you plan on bringing your car on the ferry, as not all ferries can accommodate automobiles.

By Plane

Flying is by far the most expensive mode of transportation; however, some airline companies, especially the regional ones, regularly offer special rates (off season, short stays). Once again, it is wise to shop around and compare prices.

Air Canada
☎**888-247-2262**
www.aircanada.ca
Air Canada, Canada's national airline, provides regular flights between Montréal and major cities in the United States and Europe, as well as within Canada.

In addition to Air Canada, international carriers serving Montréal include:

KLM
www.flyklm.com

British Airways
www.british-airways.com

Air France
www.airfrance.com

Iberia
www.iberia.com

From the United States, American Airlines, Delta Airlines, Northwest Airlines, United Airlines, Air Canada and their affiliates offer daily direct or connecting flights to Montréal.

In recent years, Canada has seen a burgeoning of low-cost and charter airlines that provide flights between Montréal and other Canadian cities.

Tango (☎*800-315-1390 www.flytango.com*), a subsidiary of Air Canada, provides flights between Montréal and other Canadian cities with fewer frills and restrictions than traditional Air Canada flights.

Air travel within Québec is provided by **Air Canada Jazz**, a subsidiary of Air Canada that links Montréal and Québec City with many destinations, such as Baie-Comeau, Sept-Îles, Gaspé and Îles-de-la-Madeleine.

During the high season (May-Sep), the charter company **Air Transat** (☎*866-847-1919, www.air transat.com*) offers flights.

WestJet (☎*888-937-8538 or 800-538-5696, www.westjet. com*) offers connections between Québec and British Columbia, Alberta, Saskatchewan, Manitoba, Ontario and New Brunswick.

Another newcomer is **Jetsgo** (☎*866-448-5888, www.jetsgo. net*), which links Montréal with Toronto as well as the east and west coasts of Canada.

Québec's Far North

Two companies, owned and operated by native communities, provide regular flights to Québec's far north:

Air Creebec
☎*(819) 825-8355*
⇌*(819) 825-0885*
Reservations:
☎*800-567-6567*
www.aircreebec.ca
Air Creebec serves Chibougamau, Chisasibi, Roberval and Wemindji, among others. Flights depart from Val-d'Or or Montréal.

First Air
☎*800-267-1247*
Air Inuit
☎*800-361-2965*
First Air and Air Inuit serve Inukjuak, Kuujjuarapik, Ivujivik, among others.

By Seaplane

Not the most conventional means of transportation, a seaplane is perhaps the most exciting to get an overview of a region or city. For visitors on a tight schedule, it is an ideal way of seeing the massive James Bay hydro-electric complexes, or of reaching the First Nations reserves and outfitters for short fishing or hunting trips. Flights over Montréal and the surrounding area, as well as Saguenay, Lac-Saint-Jean, Charlevoix, Québec City and the Laurentians, are also available. In fact, this service is offered in most tourist regions. As schedules change often, it is best to get information on departure times directly from the company.

By Bicycle

Bicycling is very popular in Québec, especially in the cities like Montréal. Bicycle paths have been set up so that cyclists can get around easily and safely, but caution is always recommended, even on these paths. Bicycle touring is possible throughout Québec.

Hitchhiking and Ride Sharing

There are two types: "free" hitchhiking, which is prohibited on highways, and "organized" hitchhiking with a group called **Allo-Stop** *(www.allostop. com)*. "Free" hitchhiking is more common, especially during the summer, and easier to do outside the large city centres, but is not particularly safe.

"Organized" hitchhiking, or ridesharing, with Allo-Stop, works very well in all seasons. This reputed company pairs drivers who want to share their car for a small payment with passengers needing a ride. A membership card is required and costs $6 for a passenger and $7 for a driver per year. The driver receives part (approximately 60%) of the fees paid by the passengers. Destinations include virtually everywhere in the province of Québec.

Examples of ALLO-STOP prices:

Montréal-Québec
$15

Montréal-Saguenay
$30

Montréal-Tadoussac
$30

Children under five cannot travel with Allo-Stop because of a regulation requiring the use of child safety-seats. Not all drivers accept smokers, and not all passengers want to be exposed to smoke, so check on this ahead of time.

Practical Information

For registration and information:

Allo-Stop Montréal
4317 Rue Saint-Denis
☎*(514) 985-3032*

Allo-Stop Québec
665 Rue Saint-Jean
☎*(418) 522-0056*
2360 Chemin Ste-Foy
☎*(418) 522-0056*

Allo-Stop Chicoutimi
☎*(418) 695-2322*

Allo-Stop Jonquière
2370 St-Dominique
☎*(418) 695-2322*

Allo-Stop Rimouski
106 Rue St-Germain
☎*(418) 723-5248*

Allo-Stop Sherbrooke
1204 King O.
☎*(819) 821-3637*

Money and Banking

Most banks exchange U.S. and European currency but almost all will charge commission. There are exchange offices that have longer hours, and some don't take commission. Remember to ask about fees and compare rates.

Currency

The monetary unit is the dollar ($), which is divided into cents (¢). One dollar = 100 cents.

Bills come in 5-, 10-, 20-, 50-, 100-, 500- and 1000-dollar denominations, and coins come in 1- (pennies), 5- (nickels), 10- (dimes), 25-cent pieces (quarters), and in 1-dollar (loonies) and 2-dollar coins (twoonies).

In Québec, Francophones sometimes speak of "*piastres*" and "*sous*" which are dollars and cents respectively.

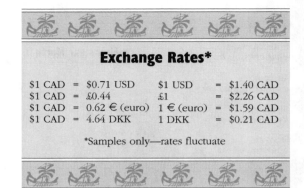

Exchange Rates*

$1 CAD	=	$0.71 USD	$1 USD	= $1.40 CAD
$1 CAD	=	£0.44	£1	= $2.26 CAD
$1 CAD	=	0.62 € (euro)	1 € (euro)	= $1.59 CAD
$1 CAD	=	4.64 DKK	1 DKK	= $0.21 CAD

*Samples only—rates fluctuate

Traveller's Cheques

Remember that Canadian dollars are different from U.S. dollars. If you do not plan on travelling to the United States on the same trip, it is best to get your traveller's cheques in Canadian dollars. Traveller's cheques are accepted in most large stores and hotels, however it is easier and to your advantage to change your cheques at an exchange office.

Credit Cards

Most major credit cards are accepted at stores, restaurants and hotels. While the main advantage of credit cards is that they allow visitors to avoid carrying large sums of money, using a credit card makes leaving a deposit for car rental much easier. Also some cards, gold cards for example, automatically insure you when you rent a car. In addition, the exchange rate with a credit card is generally better. The most commonly accepted credit cards are Visa, MasterCard, and (less so) American Express.

Credit cards offer a chance to avoid service charges when exchanging money. By overpaying your credit card (to avoid interest charges), you can then withdraw against it.

You can thus avoid carrying large amounts of money or traveller's cheques. Withdrawals can be made directly from an automatic teller if you have a personal identification number for your card.

Banks

Banks can be found almost everywhere and most offer the standard services for tourists. Remember to ask about any commission fees before beginning any transactions. Most bank branches have automated teller machines (ATMs), which generally accept foreign bank cards so you can withdraw directly from your account at home for a modest fee. Long-term visitors are permitted to open a bank account in Canada, provided they have two pieces of identification.

Automated Teller Machines (ATMs)

Several banks offer ATM service for cash withdrawals. Most are members of the Cirrus and Plus networks, which allow visitors to make direct withdrawals from their personal accounts. You can use your card as you do normally—you'll be given Canadian dollars with a receipt, and the equivalent amount will be debited from your account. All this will take no more time that it would at your own bank! That said, the network can sometimes experience communication problems that will prevent you from obtaining money. If your transaction is refused by the ATM at one bank, try another bank where you might have better luck. In any case, take precautions so that you do not find yourself empty-handed.

Taxes and Tipping

Taxes

The ticket price on items usually **does not include tax**. There are two taxes, the GST (federal Goods and Services Tax, TPS in French) of 7% and the PST (provincial sales tax, TVQ in French) at 7.5% on goods and on services. They are cumulative, therefore you must add 14.59 % in taxes to the price of most items and to restaurant and hotel prices. There is an additional tax on hotel rooms. See the "Accommodations" section on p 54 for more details.

There are some exceptions to this taxation system, such as books, which are only taxed 7% and food (except for ready-made meals), which is not taxed at all.

Tax Refunds for Non-Residents

Non-residents can be refunded for the GST paid on purchases made while in Canada. To obtain a refund, it is important to keep your receipts. It is important to note that to be eligible, your purchases must total at least $200. For further information, call ☎*800-668-4748* (within Canada) or *(902) 432-5608* (outside Canada) or visit *www.ccra-adrc.gc.ca/ visitors*.

Since April 2001, visitors must have their exported goods inspected and receipts validated by Canada Customs as they leave Canada at the Customs Information Centre in Dorval or Mirabel airports or at any land border. The refund can then be claimed either by mail or at participating duty-free stores at land-border crossings.

Note that the TVQ is no longer eligible for refund.

Note that there are private companies that will claim and receive the refund on your behalf, but you will pay a service charge for the privilege. Better to deal directly with Canada Customs, as there is no charge involved.

Tipping

In general, tipping applies to all table service in restaurants and to both table and bar service in bars and nightclubs (no tipping in fast-food restaurants). The tip is usually about 15% of the bill before taxes, but varies, of course, depending on the quality of service.

Tipping is also standard in taxis (approximately 10% of the fare) and hair salons (10-15%). A $1 to $3 tip is usually given for valet parking, regardless of whether or not you pay a parking fee. In deluxe hotels, housekeeping staff should be tipped approximately $5 to $10 per day, although $2 to $3 per day is fine in a less swanky hotel. As for bell hops, the tip is sometimes included in the hotel rate, (particularly for large groups travelling together), but if it is not, $3 to $5 per bag is appropriate.

Telecommunications

Local area codes are clearly indicated in the "Practical Infor-

mation" section of every chapter. Dialling these codes is unnecessary if the call is local. For long-distance calls, dial *1* for the United States and Canada, followed by the appropriate area code and the subscriber's number. The same goes for a fax. Phone numbers preceded by *800*, *877*, *866* or *888* are toll-free from Canada, and often from the US, as well. To contact an operator, dial *0*.

Considerably less expensive than in Europe, public phones are scattered throughout the city, easy to use and some even accept credit cards. Local calls cost $0.25 for unlimited time. For long distance calls, equip yourselves with quarters ($0.25 coins), or purchase a $10, $15 or $20 Smart Card ("La Puce"), on sale at newsstands in convenience stores, or at Bell Téléboutiques. For example, a call from Montréal to Québec City will cost $2.50 for the first 3min and $0.38 for every additional minute. Calling from a private residence will cost even less. Paying by credit card or with the prepaid "HELLO!" card is also possible, but be advised that they are considerably more expensive.

When calling abroad you can use a local operator and pay local phone rates. First dial *011* then the international country code and then the phone number:

AUSTRALIA	*61*
BELGIUM	*32*
GERMANY	*49*
IRELAND	*353*
ITALY	*39*
NETHERLANDS	*31*
NEW ZEALAND	*64*
SPAIN	*34*
SWITZERLAND	*41*
UNITED KINGDOM	*44*

To call Great Britian, dial *011* + *44* + the area code (London *171* or *181*) + the number you are trying to reach. The same goes for Australia,

New Zealand and most European countries.

Another way to call abroad is by using the direct access numbers below to contact an operator in your home country.

UNITED STATES
AT&T
☎*800-CALL-ATT*
MCI
☎*800-888-8000*

British Telecom Direct
☎*800-408-6420*
☎*363-4144*

Business Hours and Holidays

Business Hours

Stores

The law respecting business hours allows stores to be open the following hours:

• Monday to Wednesday from 8am to 9pm; though most stores open at 10am and close at 6pm

• Thursday and Friday from 8am to 9pm; though most open at 10am

• Saturday from 8am to 5pm; though most open at 10am

• Sunday from 8am to 5pm; most open at noon. Not all stores open on Sundays.

Dépanneurs (convenience stores that sell food) are found throughout Québec and are open later, sometimes 24hrs a day.

Banks

Banks are open Monday to Friday from 10am to 3pm. Most are open on Thursdays and Fridays, until 6pm or even 8pm. Automatic teller machines operate 24hrs a day.

Post Offices

Large post offices are open from 9am to 5pm. There are several smaller post offices throughout Québec, located in shopping malls, *dépanneurs*, and even pharmacies; they are open much later than the larger ones.

Holidays

Here is a list of public holidays in Québec. Most government offices and banks are closed on these days.

January 1st and 2nd
(*New Year and the day after*)

Easter Monday

3rd Monday in May
(*Jour des Patriotes* or *Victoria's Day*)

June 24
(*Saint-Jean-Baptiste Day,*
Québec's national holiday)

July 1st
(*Canada Day*)

1st Monday in September
(*Labour Day*)

2nd Monday in October
(*Thanksgiving*)

November 11
(*Remembrance Day; only*
banks and federal govern-
ment services are closed)

December 25 and 26
(*Christmas and Boxing Day*)

Time Difference

Québec is 6hrs behind continental Europe and 3hrs ahead of the North American west coast. The entire province of Québec (save for the Îles de la Madeleine, which are an hour ahead) operates on Eastern Standard Time. Keep in mind that there are several time zones across Canada. Daylight

Savings Time (+1hr) starts the first Sunday in April and finishes the last Sunday in October (-1hr).

www.meteomedia.com

Climate and Clothing

Climate

Québec's seasonal extremes set the province apart from much of the world. Temperatures can rise above 30°C in summer and drop to -25°C in winter. Visiting Québec during the two "main" seasons (summer and winter) is like having visited two totally different countries, with the seasons influencing not only the scenery, but the lifestyles and behaviour of the province's residents.

Winter

"*Mon pays ce n'est pas un*
pays, c'est l'hiver..."

("My country is not a country, it's winter")

– Gilles Vigneault

Mid-November to the end of March is the best time for skiing, snowmobiling, skating, snowshoeing and other winter sports. In general, there are five or six large snow storms per winter. Howling wind often makes the temperatures bitterly cold, causing "drifting snow" (very fine snow that is blown by the wind). One bright spot is that though it may be freezing, Québec gets more hours of winter sunshine than Europe.

Spring

Spring is short, lasting roughly from the end of March to the end of May, and heralded by the arrival of "slush," a mixture of melted snow and mud. As the snow disappears, long-buried plants and grass, yellowed by frost and mud, come to life again. Nature's welcomed reawakening is spectacular.

Summer

Summer in Québec blossoms from the end of May to the end of August and may surprise some who think of Québec as a land of snow and igloos. The heat can be quite extreme and often seems much hotter because of the accompanying humidity. The vegetation becomes lush, and don't be surprised to see some rather exotic-looking red and green peppers growing in window boxes—the temperature is almost high enough to fool you into thinking you are in Mexico! City streets are decorated with flowers, and restaurant terraces are always full. It is also the season when many different festivals are held all across Québec (see the "Festivals and Events" section p 59).

Fall

The fall colours can last from September to November. Maple trees form one of the most beautiful living pictures on the North American continent. Leaves are transformed into a kaleidoscope of colours from bright green to scarlet red, to golden yellow. Temperatures will stay warm for a while, but eventually the days and especially the nights will become quite cold.

Indian Summer

This relatively short period (only a few days) during the late fall are like summer's triumphant return! Referred to as Indian Summer, it is in fact the result of warm air currents from the Gulf of Mexico. This time of the year is called Indian Summer because it represented the last hunt before winter. Aboriginals took ad-

vantage of the warm weather to stock up on provisions before the cold weather arrived.

Health

Vaccinations are not necessary for people coming from Europe, the United States and Australia. On the other hand, it is strongly suggested, particularly for medium or long-term stays, that visitors take out health and accident insurance. There are different types, so it is best to shop around. Bring along all medication, especially prescription drugs. Unless otherwise stated, the water is drinkable throughout Québec.

In the winter, moisturizing lotion and lip balm are useful for people with sensitive skin, since the air in many buildings is very dry.

During the summer, always protect yourself against sunburn. It is often hard to feel your skin getting burned by the sun on windy days. Do not forget to apply sun screen!

Security

Violence is far less prevalent in Québec than in the United States. A genuine non-violence policy is advocated throughout the province.

Visitors who take the same precautions they would at home have no need to be overly worried about personal security. In case of an emergency, call *911*.

Travellers with Disabilities

Kéroul, an association that specializes in tourism for people with disabilities, publishes a guide called *Accessible Québec*

($10), which lists hotels, attractions and restaurants that are accessible to people with disabilities throughout the province. These places are listed by tourist region.

Kéroul
4545 Avenue Pierre-De Coubertin
C.P. 1000, Succursale M
Montréal, H1V 3R2
☎*(514) 252-3104*
⇌*(514) 254-0766*
www.keroul.qc.ca

Most of the regions also have associations that organize leisure and sports activities for people with disabilities. Contact the following organization for the addresses of these associations:

Association Québécoise de Loisir pour Personnes Handicapées
4545 Avenue Pierre-De Coubertin
C.P.1000, Succursale M
Montréal, H1V 3R2
☎*(514) 252-3144*
⇌*(514) 252-8360*
www.aqlph.qc.ca

Senior Citizens

Seniors who would like to meet people their age can do so through the organization listed below. It provides information about activities and local clubs throughout Québec:

Fédération de l'Âge d'Or du Québec
4545 Avenue Pierre-De Coubertin
C.P. 1000, Succursale M
Montréal, H1V 3R2
☎*(514) 252-3017*
⇌*(514) 252-3154*

Reduced transportation fares and entertainment tickets are often made available to seniors. Do not hesitate to ask.

Children

Children in Québec are treated like royalty. Facilities

are available almost everywhere you go, whether it be transportation or leisure activities. Generally, children under five travel for free, and those under 12 are eligible for fare reductions. The same rules apply for various leisure activities and shows. Find out before you purchase tickets. High chairs and children's menus are available in many restaurants, while a few of the larger stores provide a babysitting service while parents shop.

Exploring

Every chapter in this guide leads you through one or more of Québec's tourist regions. The name of each attraction is followed by its address and phone number. The prices indicated are admission fees for one adult. It is best to inquire, because most attractions offer discounts for children, students, senior citizens and families. Some attractions are only open during the summer, but may welcome groups upon request in the off-season.

Attractions are classified according to a star-rating system, so you can spot the must-sees at a glance.

★	Interesting
★★	Worth a visit
★★★	Not to be missed

Accommodations

A wide choice of accommodations to fit every budget is available in most regions of Québec. Most places are very comfortable and can offer a number of extra services. Prices vary according to the type of accommodation, but remember to add the 7% GST (federal Goods and Services Tax) and the 7.5% provincial tax. The GST is refund-

able to non-residents (see p 51). A specific tax on accommodation rates in Québec, called Taxe Spécifique sur l'Hébergement, was introduced to support the tourist infrastructures of all regions. Visitors will thus incur this $2/night tax (regardless of the total of your bill) in establishments in Montreal and Laval.

Tourism Québec, in collaboration with the *Corporation des Services aux Établissements Touristiques Québécois*, has set up a new system for classifying lodging in Québec.

The classification, which ranges from one to five stars, complies with international standards and provides visitors with a point of reference from which to judge the quality of the hotel. This system assesses the amenities and services available in the establishment by means of an objective point scale–the more amenities and services available, the more points awarded. The listed accommodations bear a plaque with *Hébergement Québec* inscribed on it.

Under the "Accommodations" headings of this guide, the quality of the lodgings is not defined according to the standards of Tourism Québec, but rather to the authors' judgement, taking into account such factors as the quality of service, decor, location and value.

When reserving in advance, which is strongly recommended during the summer months, a credit card is indispensable for the deposit, as payment for the first night is often required in advance.

There is a reservation service in the Montréal and Québec City (summer only) tourist information centres. It is called **Hospitalité Canada** (*www.hospitality-canada. com*), and takes care of visi-

tors' hotel reservations for free:

Centre Infotouriste de Montréal
1001 Rue du Square-Dorchester
Montréal, Québec, H3B 4V4
☎/≈*(514) 393-1072*
☎*800-665-1528*

Centre Infotouriste de Québec
12 Rue Sainte-Anne, Québec, G1R 3X2
☎*(418) 694-1602*
☎*800-665-1528*

Prices and Symbols

All the prices mentioned in this guide apply to a **standard room for two people in peak season**. Prices are indicated with the following symbols:

$	$50 or less
$$	$51 to $100
$$$	$101 to $150
$$$$	$151 to $200
$$$$$	more than $200

The actual cost to guests is often lower than the prices quoted here, particularly for travel during the off-peak season. Also, many hotels and inns offer considerable discounts to employees of corporations or members of automobile clubs (CAA, AAA). Be sure to ask about corporate rate and other discounts, as they are often very easy to obtain.

The various services offered by each establishment are indicated with a small symbol, which is explained in the legend in the opening pages of this guidebook. By no means is this an exhaustive list of what the establishment offers, but rather the services we consider to be the most important.

Please note that the presence of a symbol does not mean that all the rooms have this service; you sometimes have to pay extra to get, for example, a whirlpool tub. And likewise, if the symbol is not attached to an establishment, it means that the establishment cannot offer you this service. Please note that unless otherwise indicated, all lodgings in this guide offer private bathrooms.

The Ulysses Boat

The Ulysses boat pictogram appears next to our favourite accommodations. While every establishment recommended in this guide was included because of its high quality and/or uniqueness, as well as its high value, every once in a while we come across an establishment that absolutely wows us. These, our favourite establishments, are awarded a Ulysses boat. You'll find boats in all price categories: next to exclusive, high-price establishments, as well as budget ones. Regardless of the price, each of these establishments offers the most for your money. Look for them first!

Hotels

There are countless hotels across Québec, and they range from modest to luxurious. Most hotel rooms come equipped with a private bathroom. The prices we have listed are rack rates in the high season. In the majority of establishments, however, a whole slew of discounts, up to 50% in some cases, is possible. Weekend rates are often lower when a hotel's clientele is mostly business people. There are also corporate rates, rates for auto-club members, and seniors discounts to take advantage of. Be sure to ask about package deals, promotions and discounts when reserving.

Bed and Breakfasts

Bed and breakfasts are well distributed throughout most of Québec, and besides the obvious price advantage is their unique family atmosphere. They also provide the opportunity to appreciate a regional architecture and cultural exchange, many of the small houses are quite picturesque. Credit cards are not always accepted in bed and breakfasts. Prices for a room also include breakfast. Unlike hotels, rooms in private homes do not always have private bathrooms.

In Québec, bed and breakfasts are known as *gîtes touristiques* or *Gîtes et Auberges du Passant*. The latter term refers to bed and breakfasts that are members of the Fédération des Agricotours du Québec and that they conform to their regulations and standards. Each year, the Fédération, in collaboration with Ulysses Travel Guides, produces the guide *Inns and Bed & Breakfasts in Québec*, which describes bed and breakfasts, farm-stays and country-style dining, as well as country and city houses for rent, in every region of the province.

Motels

There are many motels throughout the province, but they tend to be cheaper and lacking in atmosphere. They are particularly useful when pressed for time.

Youth Hostels

Youth hostel addresses are listed in the "Accommodations" section for the cities in which they are located.

For more information, contact:

Tourisme Jeunesse
☎(514) 252-3117
☎800-461-8585
≈(514) 252-3119
www.tourismej.qc.ca

University Residences

Due to certain restrictions, this can be a complicated alternative. Residences are only available during the summer (mid-May to mid-August); reservations must be made several months in advance, usually by paying the first night with a credit card.

This type of accommodation, however, is less costly than the "traditional" alternatives, and making the effort to reserve early can be worthwhile. Visitors with valid student cards can expect to pay approximately $20 plus tax, while non students can expect to pay around $33. Bedding is included in the price, and there is usually a cafeteria in the building (meals are not included in the price).

Spas

Spas, known as *relais santé*, are becoming increasingly popular. Professionals provide treatments such as hydrotherapy, massage therapy and beauty care in establishments that differ according to their various menus, activities and services. For more information, or to choose the spas that best suits your needs:

Relais Santé Spa Association
☎800-788-7594
www.relais-sante.com

Staying in Aboriginal Communities

The opportunities for staying in First Nations communities

are limited but are becoming more popular. As the reserves are managed by Aboriginal groups, in some cases it is necessary to obtain authorization from the band council to visit.

Camping

Next to being put up by friends, camping is the most inexpensive form of accommodation. Unfortunately, unless you have winter-camping gear, camping is limited to a short period of the year, from June to August. Services provided by campgrounds can vary considerably. Campsites can be either private or publicly owned. The prices listed in this guide apply to campsites without hookups for campers, and vary depending on additional services. Take note that campgrounds are not subject to the accommodation tax.

The Conseil du Développement du Camping au Québec, in collaboration with the Fédération Québécoise de Camping et Caravaning, publishes an annual guide entitled *Camping-Caravaning*, which lists 300 campgrounds and their services. It is available for free from the regional tourist associations or from the Fédération Québécoise de Camping et Caravaning.

Fédération Québécoise de Camping et Caravaning
4545 Avenue Pierre-De Coubertin, C.P. 1000, Succursale M, Montréal, H1V 3R2
☎*(514) 252-3003*
☎*866-237-3722*
⇒*(514) 254-0694*
www.campingquebec.com

Restaurants

Though you may have learned differently in your French classes, Quebecers refer to breakfast as *déjeuner*, lunch as

dîner, and dinner as *souper*. Many restaurants offer a "daily special" (called *spécial du jour*), a complete meal for one price, which is usually less expensive than ordering individual items from the à-la-carte menu. Served only at lunch, the price usually includes a choice of appetizers and main dishes, plus coffee and sometimes dessert. In the evenings, a table d'hôte (same formula, but slightly more expensive) is also an attractive possibility.

Prices in this guide refer to the evening table d'hôte for one person, or an equivalent meal in including appetizer, main course and dessert, before taxes and tip (See "Taxes and Tipping", p 51).

$	$10 or less
$$	$11 to $20
$$$	$21 to $30
$$$$	more than $30

The Ulysses Boat

The Ulysses boat pictogram appears next to our favourite restaurants. For more information, see p 55.

"Bring Your Own Wine" Restaurants

Québec has restaurants where you can bring your own wine. This is because in order to sell alcohol, a restaurant must have an alcohol permit, which is very expensive. Restaurants who want to offer their clientele a less expensive menu opt for a special type of permit that allows their patrons to bring their own bottle of wine. In most cases, a sign in the restaurant window indicates whether alcohol can be purchased on the premises (*permis d'alcool*) or if you

should bring your own (*apportez votre vin*). Besides the alcohol permit, there is also a bar permit. Restaurants with only the alcohol permit can sell alcohol, beer and wine, but only if they are accompanied by a meal. Restaurants with both permits can sell you just a drink, even if you do not order a meal.

Cafés

Many people in Québec are *espresso* connoisseurs. Numerous little restaurants with a relaxed, convivial atmosphere also serve as cafés. Every city has some, especially Montréal and Québec, and several are institutions in certain parts of the city. Coffee reigns supreme in these places, but good, small meals are also served such as soups, salads or *croques-monsieur*, and, of course, croissants and desserts!

Sugar Shack or Cabane à sucre

Called "sugaring-off" at the "sugar-shack" in English, this is a true Québécois tradition. Sap begins to rise in the trees at the beginning of the spring thaw. Taps are inserted in the maple trees in order to retrieve the sap. After a rather involved boiling process, the sap is transformed into a sugary syrup known as maple syrup. In the early spring, Quebecers from across the province venture off into the countryside (to the maple groves) to spend the day at the sugar shack, dining on such specialties as eggs with maple syrup and deep-fried lard (called *oreilles de crisse*). After this, it is time for *la tire*, hot maple syrup which is poured on snow, hardening into a delicious toffee that you roll onto a stick and enjoy!

Sugar shack

Bars and Nightclubs

Most pub-style bars do not charge a cover (although in winter there is usually a mandatory coat-check). Expect to pay a few dollars to get into nightclubs and shows on weekends. Québec nightlife is particularly lively, and it doesn't hurt that the sale of alcohol continues until 3am. Some bars remain open past this hour but serve only soft drinks. Drinking establishments that only have a tavern or brasserie permit must close at midnight. In small towns, restaurants also frequently serve as bars. Those seeking entertainment come nightfall should therefore consult the "Restaurant" sections in every chapter, as well as the "Entertainment" section.

Happy Hour

Bars in downtown areas offer two-for-one specials during *Heures Joyeuses* or *cinq à sept* (usually from 5pm to 7pm). During these hours you can buy two beers for the price of one, or drinks are offered at a reduced price. Some snack bars and dessert places also offer the same discounts. A

Québec law prohibits the advertising of these specials, so if you are interested, ask your waiter or waitress.

Wine, Beer and Alcohol

In Québec, the provincial government is responsible for regulating alcohol, sold in liquor stores known as Société des Alcool du Québec (SAQ). If you wish to purchase wine, imported beer or hard liquor, you must go to a branch of the SAQ. Some, known as "Sélection," offer a more varied and specialized selection of wines and spirits. SAQ outlets can be found throughout the city, but their opening hours are fairly limited, with the exception of so-called "Express" branches, open later but offering a more limited choice. As a general rule, their opening hours are the same as those of stores. Convenience and grocery stores are authorized to sell Canadian beer and a few wines, but the choice is slim and the quality of wines mediocre.

You must be at least 18 years old to purchase alcohol, the sale of which is not permitted after 11pm.

Beer

Two huge breweries share the largest part of the beer market in Québec: Labatt and Molson-O'Keefe. They each produce different types of beer, mostly lager, with varying levels of alcohol. In bars, restaurants, and nightclubs, draft beer is cheaper than bottled beer.

Besides these large breweries, some interesting independent micro-breweries have developed in the past few years. The variety and taste of these beers make them quite popular in Québec. However, because they are micro-brews, they are not available everywhere. Here are a few of Québec's micro-brewery beers: Unibroue (Maudite, Blanche de Chambly and Fin du Monde), McAuslan (Griffon, St-Ambroise), Le Cheval Blanc (Cap Tourmente, Berlue), Les Brasseurs du Nord (Boréale) and GMT (Belle Gueule).

Wine

Québec produces a small variety of wines, mostly white. Grapes are grown in the Eastern Townships region. Tours (see p 185) of the area can help you discover this beautiful region. Apple cider is also produced in Québec, mostly in the Montérégie Region.

Gay and Lesbian Life

In 1977, Québec became the second political entity in the world, after Holland, to include in its charter of rights the non-discrimination clause on the basis of sexual orientation. Quebecers' attitudes towards homosexuality are, in general, open and tolerant. Montréal and Québec City offer many services to the gay and lesbian community. In Montréal, most of these services are concentrated in the part of town known as **The Village**, located on Rue Sainte-Catherine, between Amherst and Papineau streets, as well as on the surrounding streets. The gay village in Québec City is found on Rue Saint-Jean-Baptiste, outside the walls of the old city. Below is a list of a few of the available services.

The following telephone line provides details on the activities in the city: **Gai Écoute** (*listening and information 11h à 3h;* ☎ *514-866-0103 or 888-505-1010*).

The **Centre Communautaire des Gais et Lesbiennes** (*2075 Rue Plessis*, ☎ *514-528-8424*) organizes various activities, such as dances, language courses, music lessons, etc.

The **Défilé de la Fierté Gaie et Lesbienne** (The Pride Parade) takes place on the first weekend in August on Rue Sainte-Catherine and ends with various performances (*information: Divers Cité, 4067 Boulevard St-Laurent;* ☎ *285-4011*).

Several free magazines containing information concerning the gay and lesbian communities are available in bars and other establishments serving the gay and lesbian communities: *RG*, *Fugues* and *Orientations*, *Être Montréal*, and *Entre-elles*.

Advice for Smokers

Cigarette smoking is considered taboo and is being prohibited in more and more public places:

- in shopping centres
- in buses and métros
- in government offices

Since December 1999, smoking sections in most public places (restaurants, cafés) must be closed off. Cigarettes are still sold in most places though (bars, grocery and convenience stores, and newspaper and magazine shops).

Shopping

What to Buy?

Electronics

Montréal is a major centre for telecommunications, therefore it might be a good idea to buy some gadgets such as answering machines, fax machines or cordless telephones and cellular phones. However, be aware that these devices may require a special adaptor for use in your home country. Importing these items may be illegal in certain European countries.

Compact Discs

Compact discs are much less expensive than in Europe, however, they may be more expensive than in the United States.

Books

Books by Québec Francophone authors are ideal purchases for those interested in the Francophone culture. English-language Quebecers and Canadian literature is easier to find here than elsewhere in the world. In addition, American books are sold in the English bookstores throughout the province at better prices than in Europe. A wide selection of French-language books is available.

Furs and Leather

Clothes made from animal skins are of very good quality and their prices are relatively low. Approximately 80% of

fur items sold in Canada are made in the "fur area" of Montréal.

Maple Syrup

There are many varieties of maple syrup. Some are thicker and more syrupy than others, some are dark and some are light in colour, and some have more sugar than others; in any case, it would be sinful to pass up a chance to at least try a few!

Blueberry Wine

This wine is made from blueberries and is available in most stores of the Sociéte des Alcools du Québec (SAQ, liquor stores).

Local Wine

Local wines are available in the Eastern Townships.

Dandelion Wine

This dry white wine made from dandelion flowers is available in the Beauce region.

Mead

A honey wine, mead is produced in *hydromelleries* in certain parts of Québec, including Mirabel, just north of Montréal.

Apple Cider

Made in the Montérégie region, along with many other apple-based products (vinegar, butter, alcohol, etc.).

Liqueurs

Many different liqueurs are produced locally. Try the famous peach schnapps and "Caribou," a very strong grain liqueur.

Local Arts & Crafts

These consist of paintings, sculptures, woodwork, ceramics, coppered enamel and weaving.

Aboriginal Arts & Crafts

There are beautiful Aboriginal sculptures made from different types of stone that are generally quite expensive. Make sure the sculpture is authentic by asking for a certificate of authenticity issued by the Canadian government. Good quality imitations are widely available and are much less expensive.

Festivals and Events

Québec's colourful history and distinct, culturally diverse population are well represented by a variety of cultural activities each year. Given the impressive number (approximately 250) of festivals, annual expositions, exhibitions, fairs, gatherings and other events, it is impossible to list them all. We have, however, selected a few of the highlights, which are described in the "Entertainment" sections of each chapter, and in the section below. The *Bottin des Fêtes et Festivals du Québec,* published by the Festivals et Événements Québec (☎ 514-252-3037 or 800-361-7688), provides a complete listing and is available in magazine stores.

Calendar of Events

February

Montréal
La Fête des Neiges
(winter festival)

Hull - Ottawa (Outaouais)
Winterlude

Québec City
Québec Winter Carnival

**Chicoutimi
(Saguenay–Lac-Saint-Jean)**
Le Carnaval-Souvenir de
Chicoutimi

May

**Plessisville
(Centre-du-Québec)**
Le Festival de l'érable de
Plessisville (maple festival)

**Victoriaville
(Centre-du-Québec)**
Le Festival international de
musique actuelle de
Victoriaville (Victoriaville New
Music International Festival)

June

Montréal
International Fireworks Competition
Canadian Grand Prix

**Saint-Jean-Port-Joli
(Chaudière-Appalaches)**
Internationale de la Sculpture
(International Sculpture Festival)

Matane (Gaspésie)
Le Festival de la Crevette
(shrimp festival)

Tadoussac (Manicouagan)
Le Festival de la Chanson de
Tadoussac (song festival)

July

Montréal
International Fireworks Competition
Montreal International Jazz
Festival (begins end June)
Just for Laughs Comedy Festival
Francofolies
(French music festival)

Kahnawake (Montérégie)
Pow Wow

Saint-Hyacinthe (Montérégie)
L'Exposition régionale agricole
de Saint-Hyacinthe
(Regional Agricultural Fair)

Sorel (Montérégie)
Le Festival de la Gibelotte de
Sorel
("gibelotte," fish stew festival)

**Salaberry-de-Valleyfield
(Montérégie)**
Valleyfield International Regatta

Magog (Eastern Townships)
La Traversée internationale du
lac Memphrémagog (Lake
Memphrémagog International
Swimming Marathon)

Orford (Eastern Townships)
Orford Festival

Joliette (Lanaudière)
Lanaudière International Festival

Hull - Ottawa (Outaouais)
Ottawa and Hull International
Jazz Festival

**Drummondville
(Centre-du-Québec)**
World Folklore Festival

Québec City
Québec City Summer Festival

**Beauport
(Area around Québec City)**
Les Grands feux Loto-Québec
(musical fireworks show)

**Saint-Jean-Chrysostome
(Chaudière-Appalaches)**
Le Festivent

Mont-Saint-Pierre (Gaspésie)
La Fête du Vol Libre (handgliding event)

Saint-Irénée (Charlevoix)
Le Festival international du
Domaine Forget

Roberval (Saguenay–Lac-Saint-Jean)
La Traversée internationale du
lac Saint-Jean (swimming marathon)

August

Montréal
World Film Festival (WFF)
Divers-cité (GayPride) parade.

Chambly
La Fête de Saint-Louis
La Fête Bières et Saveurs

Saint-Jean-sur-Richelieu (Montérégie)
Le Festival des montgolfières (hot-air balloon festival)

Orford (Eastern Townships)
Orford Festival

Mont-Tremblant (Laurentians)
Le Festival de Blues de Mont-Tremblant (blues festival)
Le Festival de la Musique (music festival)

Trois-Rivières (Mauricie)
Grand Prix Automobile

Québec City
Expo-Québec
Plein Art ("fresh art")

Beauport (Area around Québec City)
Les Grands feux Loto-Québec (musical fireworks show)

Montmagny (Chaudière-Appalaches)
World Accordion Jamboree

Île du Havre Aubert (Îles-de-la-Madeleine)
Sand Castle Competition

Saint-Irénée (Charlevoix)
Le Festival international du Domaine Forget

Baie-Saint-Paul (Charlevoix)
Symposium of Young Canadian Painters

September

Granby (Eastern Townships)
Le Festival de la chanson de Granby (song festival)

Saint-Donat (Lanaudière)
Autumn Colours Weekend

Laurentians
Le Festival des Couleurs (autumn colours festival)

Val-Morin (Laurentians)
Les couleurs en vélo (cycling event)

Gatineau (Outaouais)
Hot Air Balloon Festival

Saint-Tite (Mauricie)
Western Festival

Rimouski (Bas-Saint-Laurent)
Le Festi-Jazz (jazz fest)
Le Carrousel international du film de Rimouski (film festival)

Baie-Saint-Paul (Charlevoix)
Rêves d'automne (Autumn Dreams)

October

Montréal
Montreal International Festival of Cinema and New Media

Laurentians
Le Festival des couleurs (autumn colours festival)

Rouyn-Noranda (Abitibi-Témiscamingue)
Le Festival du cinéma international en Abitibi-Témiscamingue (international film festival)

Trois-Rivières (Mauricie)
International Poetry Festival

Montmagny (Chaudière-Appalaches)
Le Festival de l'Oie Blanche (Snow Goose Festival)

November

Saint-Denis (Montérégie)
La Fête des Patriotes

Work and Study

Studying in Québec

To study in Québec, individuals from outside Canada must first obtain a CAQ (Certificat d'Acceptation du Québec) issued by the Ministère des Communautés Culturelles et de l'Immigration du Québec, as well as a federal permit allowing an extended visit.

To obtain these documents, you must **first** be registered at a college or university for at least six months, with a minimum of 24hrs of classes per week. You must also provide proof of financial resources necessary to pay your living expenses and tuition. Moreover, you must have medical and hospitalization insurance and a medical exam may be required.

Student Employment

If you have obtained a residence permit to study in Québec, you have the right to work under certain conditions. Working on campus as a research assistant, or work providing experience in your field of study, are just some of the possibilities offered to students.

Spouses of students admitted as visitors can also work for the duration of the student's stay. The laws, however, change regularly, so it is best to obtain information from the Délégation Générale du Québec or the Canadian consulate of your home country (see p 42).

Temporary Work

All the paperwork must be done from your home country. Your Canadian employer must make a request at a Canada Employment Centre. If the job offer is deemed admissible, you will have to appear before a member of the Québec delegation who will evaluate your abilities, and inform you as to the next steps to take.

Remember that if you have not received a working visa, it is against the law to work in the country. Also, the work permit is valid only for the job and the employer with which you applied, and were accepted, and only for the duration of this job.

Caution: authorization to work in Québec does **not** mean that you can stay on as an immigrant.

Au Pair Work

As with other temporary work, a request for a permit must be made by the employer, and is only valid for this job. The employee must reside with the employer.

Seasonal Work

This type of work is concentrated in the agricultural field and varies from apple-picking to agricultural training courses. Obtaining a work visa beforehand is required. Contact the Canadian embassy or consulate in your home country for additional information.

Pets

Dogs on a leash are permitted in most public parks in cities. Québec's provincial parks, however, are definitely not pet-friendly (domestic animals are prohibited) and pets are not particularly welcome at federal parks in Québec, either (although Forillon National Park is a pleasant surprise in this regard—dogs are permitted on beaches and hiking trails). Small pets are allowed on the public transportation systems in cities, as long as they are in a cage or small enough to remain in the arms of the owner. Pets are generally not allowed in stores; nor in restaurants, although some establishments with terraces permit pets. Seeing Eye dogs are not subject to such restrictions.

Québec Cuisine

Although many restaurant dishes are similar to those served in the rest of Canada or the United States, some of them are prepared in a typi-

cally Québécois way. These unique dishes should definitely be tasted:

La soupe aux pois
pea soup

La tourtière
meat pie

Le pâté chinois
(also known as shepherd's pie) layered pie consisting of ground beef, potatoes, and corn

Les cretons
a type of pâté of ground pork cooked with onions in fat

Le jambon au sirop d'érable
ham with maple syrup

Les fèves au lard
baked beans

Le ragoût de pattes de cochon
pigs' feet stew

Le cipaille
layered pie with different types of meat

La tarte aux pacanes
pecan pie

La tarte au sucre
sugar pie

La tarte aux bleuets
blueberry pie

Le sucre à la crème
rich maple-syrup fudge

In the country, you may also have the opportunity to enjoy some exceptional regional specialties like venison, hare, beaver, Atlantic salmon, Arctic char and Abitibi caviar.

The Corporation de la Cuisine Régionale au Québec has been promoting Québec regional cuisine ever since the organization's establishment in 1993. In 1999, in collaboration with Ulysses Travel Guides, they published *La Cuisine Régionale au Québec*, a French-language guide to restaurants and producers

who have helped promote this cuisine throughout Québec.

The Language of Québec

Language is a hot issue in Québec. Quebecers are very proud of their unique version of French and have struggled long and hard to preserve it while surrounded on all sides by English. The accent and vocabulary are different from European French, and can be surprising at first, but have a charm all their own.

French or English?

When writing a guide to a place where the use and preservation of language are a part of daily life, certain decisions have to be made. We have tried to keep our combined use of English and French consistent throughout the guide. The official language in Québec is French, so when listing attractions and addresses, we have kept the titles in French, except with federal sites, which have official names in both languages, and with certain sites, in Montréal and the Eastern Townships, for example, which have two names as well. This will allow readers to make the connection between the guide and the signs they will be seeing. The terms used in these titles are in the glossary at the end of the guide, but we are confident that after a couple of days, you will not even need to check!

English style has been used in the text itself to preserve readability. In areas such as Montréal, Ottawa-Hull, and the Eastern Townships, visitors will hear English almost as much as French. English-speaking visitors to these areas will often be able to take a break from practising their

French, if they want. Just remember, a valiant effort and a sincere smile go a long way! A complete list of all the local expressions would be too long to include in this guide. Travellers interested in knowing a bit more on the subject can refer to the *Canadian French for Better Travel* conversation guide, published by Ulysses Travel Guides.

Learning French

Travellers hoping to learn the language of Molière while in Québec can either absorb it as they go, or might prefer to take French lessons. In-depth courses are offered at Cégeps and universities, while private schools usually offer more courses of varying lengths and difficulties. Here are a few schools to check out:

Centre Linguista
☎**(514) 397-1736**

Language Studies Canada
☎**(514) 499-9911**

Berlitz Language Centre
☎**(514) 288-3111**

Université Laval in Québec City and Université de Montréal in Montréal offer undergraduate French language courses for non-Francophones. The École des Langues Vivantes (☎*418-656-2321*, ⇒*418-656-7018*, *elv@elv.ulaval.ca*) also offers intensive summer courses.

Miscellaneous

Drugs

Recreational drugs are against the law and not tolerated (even "soft" drugs). Anyone caught with drugs in their possession risks severe consequences.

Electricity

Voltage is 110 volts throughout Canada, the same as in the United States. Electricity plugs have two parallel, flat pins. Adaptors are available here.

Folklore

Québec's rich folklore offers an interesting insight into the history and culture of the province. The organization below regroups various regional committees aimed at the pres-ervation and development of folklore. Several activities are organized depending on the seasons and locations. For more information:

Association Québécoise des Loisirs Folkloriques
4545 Avenue Pierre-De Coubertin
C.P. 1000, Succursale M
Montréal, H1V 3R2
☎**(514) 252-3022**
www.quebecfolklore.qc.ca

Laundromats

Laundromats and dry cleaners are found almost everywhere in urban areas. In most cases, detergent is sold on site. Although change machines are sometimes provided, it is best to bring plenty of coins with you.

Museums

Most museums charge admission; however, permanent exhibits at some museums are free on Wednesday evenings from 6pm to 9pm, while reductions are offered for temporary exhibits. Reduced prices are available for seniors, children, and students. Call the museum for further details.

Newspapers

International newspapers can easily be found in the cities. The major Québec newspapers are: in French *Le Devoir*, *La Presse*, *Le Journal de Montréal* from Montréal and *Le Soleil*, from Québec City; and in English *The Gazette* from Montréal. Four free weekly newspapers—*Voir* (in French – also Outaouais region and Québec City editions, *www.voir.ca*), *Ici* (French), the *Mirror* and *Hour*—are published in Montréal with information on restaurants, entertainment and other cultural activities.

Religion

Almost all religions are represented. Unlike English Canada, the majority of the Québec population is Catholic, although most Quebecers are not practising.

Weather

For road conditions:
☎**(514) 284-2363 or 877-393-2363**

For weather forecasts:
☎**(514) 283-3010**
www.meteomedia.com

Outdoors

Québec's wide-open
spaces and spectacular countryside make it
ideal for all types of outdoor activities.

This chapter outlines the various outdoor activities practised in Québec. However, what follows is in no way a complete list of the multitude of choices available to visitors in each region. For each activity or sport, the basic information needed to organize an outing is given, along with the address of the specific federation or organization in charge of the activity. Refer to the specific regional chapter to find out which activities can be done where. For clarity we have categorized the activities as either winter or summer recreation.

Le Regroupement Loisir Québec

This private non-profit organization groups together more than 100 provincial organizations (federations, movements, associations) responsible for the promotion of various sports or activities. Its goal is to provide these organizations with the financial and technical support they need. Most of the organization's offices are located in Montréal's Olympic Stadium.
Regroupement Loisir Québec
4545 Avenue Pierre-De Coubertin
C.P. 1000, Succursale M
Montréal, H1V 3R2
☎(514) 252-3126

Parks and Reserves

Throughout Québec there are national parks administered by the federal government, and provincial parks administered by the Québec government. To make matters more confusing, since 2001, Québec's provincial parks are officially known as *parcs nationaux*, or national parks. For clarity, note that in this guidebook, the term "national park" refers to parks administered by the federal government. Most of the parks offer a variety of services and facilities: information centres, maps, nature interpretation programs, guides and camping. Since

these services often depend on the season and are not available in all parks, it is best to check with the park offices ahead of time. It is possible to reserve campsites (except backwood sites), shelters and chalets (in provincial parks). Note that reservation policies for campsites in national parks vary from one to the other. Check with the park concerned or with Park Canada (see above).

In most parks, networks of marked trails, many kilometres in length, traverse the area, permitting amateurs and experts alike to take advantage of the activities offered: hiking, canoeing, cross-country skiing and even snowmobiling. Backwood campsites and shelters are set up along the trails in some parks. Some of the backwood sites are quite

Sépaq Admission Fee

An admission fee is charged in all parks and wildlife reserves managed by Sépaq (Société des Établissements de Plein Air du Québec), which includes most natural reserves in Québec. This fee is the same for all parks ($3.50 per adult) and gives access to the park for the entire day. Annual passes are also available, either for the entire network of parks ($30) or for one park that you wish to visit at your leisure ($16.50). Note that this admission fee is included in the rental price of shelters, cabins and campsites.

basic, without even running water, so come well-prepared. Some trails lead deep into forests far from civilization, so it is advisable to stick to the marked trails. Maps with the various trails, campsites and shelters are very helpful and available for most parks.

National Parks

There are four national parks in the province of Québec: Forillon National Park in the Gaspésie region, La Mauricie National Park in the Mauricie region, Mingan Archipelago National Park Reserve in the Duplessis region and the Saguenay–Saint-Laurent Marine Park. Beside these parks, the Canadian Parks Service also runs various National Historic Sites.

More information is available on these parks by contacting Parks Canada headquarters:

Parks Canada
25 Rue Eddy, Hull
☎*888-733-8888*
www.parkscanada.gc.ca

Provincial Parks

There are 22 provincial parks in Québec, which can be geared toward conservation or recreation. While hunting is prohibited, fishing is permitted in some parks—a license is required.

Société de la Faune et des Parcs
☎*800-561-1616*
www.fapaq.gouv.qc.ca

The Société des Établissements de Plein Air du Québec (Sépaq) manages around 50 outdoor establishments in Québec. Sépaq's goal is to promote these sites while ensuring the conservation and preservation of their natural resources. For more information about the outdoor activities offered by Sépaq, as well as their sites, contact them at:

Sépaq
801 Chemin St-Louis, Bureau 180 Québec, G1S 1C1
☎*(418) 686-4875*
≈*(418) 686-6160*
www.sepaq.com

For reservations:
☎*(418) 890-6527*
☎*800-665-6527*
inforeservation@sepaq.com

Réserves Fauniques

Réserves Fauniques (provincial wildlife reserves) cover larger areas than the other parks. Organized fishing and hunting are permitted here. Québec has many provincial wildlife reserves, such as La Vérendrye, Saint-Maurice, Laurentides, Portneuf, Mastigouche, Rouge-Matawin, Papineau-Labelle and Chic-Chocs. They are also administered by Sépaq (see above). Sépaq distributes a yearly French-language publication called *Activités Services*, which outlines the activities and services offered in the parks and wildlife reserves of the province of Québec.

ZECs and Outfitters

The Zones d'Exploitation Contrôlée (ZEC), or controlled development zones, are also Québec government property. Unlike parks and wildlife reserves, they are not generally set up for visitors, but hunting and fishing are practised here. Outfitters, called *pourvoiries* in Québec, are private establishments specially set up for hunting and fishing. Some just have rustic huts and others luxurious inns with fancy restaurants.

Jardins du Québec

The province of Québec has wonderful gardens where it's a pleasure to discover landscapes of unparalleled beauty. Along with historic buildings, artwork and ancestral traditions, gardens are considered an integral part of Québec's heritage.

In 1989, the Association des Jardins du Québec brought together the great gardens of Québec to promote ornamental horticulture and to let nature lovers familiarize themselves with it. This association, in collaboration with Tourisme Québec, has also created a pamphlet describing the province's main gardens, as well as their location. So take a walk on these "garden paths"!

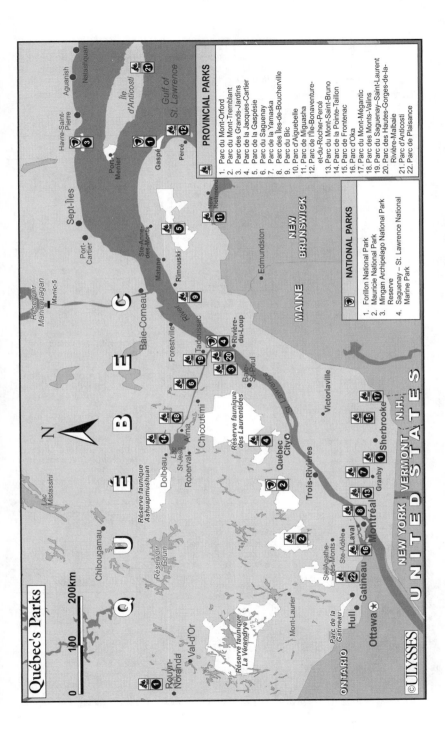

Québec's Parks

PROVINCIAL PARKS

1. Parc du Mont-Orford
2. Parc du Mont-Tremblant
3. Parc des Grands-Jardins
4. Parc de la Jacques-Cartier
5. Parc de la Gaspésie
6. Parc du Saguenay
7. Parc de la Yamaska
8. Parc des Îles-de-Boucherville
9. Parc du Bic
10. Parc d'Aiguebelle
11. Parc de Miguasha
12. Parc de l'Île-Bonaventure-et-du-Rocher-Percé
13. Parc du Mont-Saint-Bruno
14. Parc de la Pointe-Taillon
15. Parc de Frontenac
16. Parc d'Oka
17. Parc du Mont-Mégantic
18. Parc des Monts-Valins
19. Parc du Saguenay–Saint-Laurent
20. Parc des Hautes-Gorges-de-la-Rivière-Malbaie
21. Parc d'Anticosti
22. Parc de Plaisance

NATIONAL PARKS

1. Forillon National Park
2. Mauricie National Park
3. Mingan Archipelago National Park Reserve
4. Saguenay – St. Lawrence National Marine Park

© ULYSSES

Summer Activities

As soon as the temperature inches above 0°C and the ice starts to melt, Quebecers and visitors alike start to look forward to days in the country. While your choice of clothing will vary with the season, do not forget that evenings and nights are often quite chilly (except in July and August). In certain regions of the province, regardless of the temperature, a long-sleeved shirt is indispensable unless you want to serve yourself as dinner to the mosquitoes and black flies. If you plan on venturing into the woods in June, bring insect repellent and use it!

Hiking

Hiking is accessible to all and is practised all over Québec. Many parks have hiking trails of varying length and difficulty. A few have longer trails that head deep into the wilderness for 20 to 40km. Respect the trail markings and always leave well prepared when you follow these trails. Maps that show the trails, campsites and shelters are available. Reservations for shelters in wildlife reserves as well as those in Parc de la Gaspésie and Parc de la Jacques-Cartier can be made starting in May by calling

☎800-665-6527 or ☎(418) 890-6527 or by faxing ☏(418) 528-6025.

An excellent guide called *Hiking in Québec* (Ulysses Travel Guides) is available in bookstores and camping stores. A hiking guide with something for everyone, it suggests various trails and trips, and classifies them according to their length and level of difficulty. The Fédération Québécoise de la Marche (Québec Hiking Federation) (☎514-252-3157), promotes hiking, snowshoeing and city walking, and can also provide information.

Cycling

Exploring by bike is one of the most rewarding ways of discovering the diverse regions of Québec. There is quite a variety of publications to help organize your two-wheeled excursions. Ulysses Travel Guides publishes two French language guides: *Le Québec Cyclable* and *Cyclotourisme au Québec*, which list short and long bikepaths in Québec.

Mountain-bike trails have been cleared in most of the parks. Check with the information desk of the particular park.

The Centre Infotouriste in Montréal distributes free-of-charge a complete map of the bike-paths of Montreal. Cycling these paths is an exciting way to get to know Montréal in the summer. If you have time, use the map to tour the whole island!

Many bike shops have bikes for rent. Check with Vélo-Québec or the local tourist office to locate a place; otherwise look in the *Yellow Pages* under "*Bicyclettes-Location*" or "Bicycle-Rental". Insurance is a good idea. Some

places also include theft insurance in the rental fee, but be sure to check this when you rent.

Canoeing

Québec's vast territory is dotted with a multitude of lakes and rivers, making it a canoe enthusiast's dream. Many of the parks and Réserves Fauniques are departure points for canoe trips of one or more days. For longer trips, backwoods campsites are available for canoeists. Maps of the canoe trips and trails, as well as canoe-rental services, are available at park information centres. River rafting is most popular in the springtime, when water levels are highest after the spring thaw.

An excellent map, *Les Parcours Canotables du Québec*, (Canoe Trips of Québec) is available in travel bookstores. A series of map-guides for rivers (up to 125 different maps) is available, as is a guide for beginners called *Guide Canot-Camping*, available only in French. For information, contact the Fédération Québécoise du Canot et du Kayak, which is part of the Regroupement Loisir Québec (☎514-252-3001).

Beaches

The shores of Québec's rivers and countless lakes are lined with everything from fine white sand to pebbles to boulders. You should not have any trouble finding one that suits your sport or style of sunbathing. Unfortunately, swimming in the waters around the island of Montréal

Respect the Forest!

As a hiker, it is important to realize your role in preserving and respecting the fragility of the ecosystem and to comprehend your impact on your surroundings. Here are a few guidelines:

First of all, stay on the trails even if they are covered in snow or mud in order to protect the ground vegetation and avoid widening the trail.

Unless you're heading off on a long trek, wear lightweight hiking boots, as they do less damage to vegetation. When in a group in alpine regions, spread out and walk on rocks as much as possible to avoid damaging vegetation.

It is just as important to protect waterways,

bodies of water and the ground water when in mountainous regions. When digging back-country latrines, place them at least 30 metres from all water sources, and cover everything (paper included) with earth.

Never wash yourself in lakes or streams.

At campsites dispose of waste water only in designated areas.

The water is not always potable and therefore should be boiled for at least 10 minutes before drinking.

Never leave any garbage behind. Bags for this are provided at Parks Canada offices.

Certain types of flowers are endangered, so do not pick anything.

Leave everything as you find it so that those that follow can enjoy the beauty of nature as you did.

For safety reasons, always keep your dog on a leash, or leave it at home. Dogs that roam free have a tendency to wander off and chase wild animals. They have even been known to chase down bears and then take refuge with their masters. Warning: dogs are not allowed in the Parcs Québec network and are severely restricted in most federal parks. Inquire before your arrival.

Outdoors

is no longer possible because of the pollution in the St. Lawrence and the Rivière des Prairies.

The city does, however, run a public beach on Île-Notre-Dame, where you can splash about in filtered river water. Beware though—this place is very popular and access is limited, so get there early!

Nudism

Nudism is practised in certain areas of Québec. The Nudist Federation, Fédération Québécoise de Naturisme, promotes these activities. Besides publishing a magazine called *Au Naturel*, the federation puts out a guide each summer and organizes activities in the winter (under wraps, of course!). Members of the

International Federation of - Nudists have certain privileges when they present their IFN card. For information, contact the federation itself or the Regroupement Loisir Québec (☎514-252-3014).

Pleasure Boating

La Fédération de Voile du Québec (Québec Sailing Federation) is an organization of clubs, schools and associations involved in sailing and pleasure boating. The federation offers courses and a data base of important information. In addition to the *Annuaire de la Voile* a French language listing of clubs and schools, they publish a seasonal bilingual periodical, *Le Bulletin Voile Québec*. For information, check with the federation itself, which is part of the Regroupement Loisir Québec (☎514-252-3097). The *Guide des Marinas du Québec*, in French, which lists the facilities in every marina in the province, is available in bookstores and boating supply stores and could also prove useful.

Waterskiing

La Fédération Québécoise de Ski Nautique (Québec Federation of Waterskiing) provides information, guide-books and lessons. It also publishes a French-language newsletter called *Ski Nautique Québec*. For information, contact the federation through the Regroupement Loisir Québec (☎514-252-3092).

Hunting and Fishing

Hunting and fishing are both strictly regulated. Given the complexity of the regulations, it is a good idea to check with the **Société de la Faune et des Parcs** (☎800-561-1616, *www.fapaq.gouv.qc.ca*). Free bilingual brochures containing the essentials about the hunting and fishing regulations and restrictions are available.

As a general rule, the following applies:

A Québec permit is required to hunt or fish. Permits are available in most sporting

stores and from outfitters. Hunting of migratory birds is only permitted with a federal permit, which can be purchased in any post office. A certificate to bear fire-arms or a permit by the province or country of origin is required when requesting this type of permit.

A permit to hunt moose is limited to a specific zone defined by the government. Permits are issued depending on the hunting zone, time of year, the species and the existing quotas. It is a good idea to obtain your permit well in advance, since there are numerous restrictions.

Fishing and hunting seasons are established by the province and must be respected at all times. The season depends on the type of game: deer is usually at the beginning of November; moose from mid-September to mid-October; caribou in summer or winter, depending on the zone; bear from mid-September to mid-November; partridge from mid-September to the end of December; hare from mid-September to March. While hunting, always wear an orange fluorescent singlet. Hunting at night is not permitted. For the purpose of conservation, the number of game is limited, and protected species cannot be hunted. All hunters must declare their kill at one of the registration centres (most of which are located on access roads to the hunting zones) within 48 hours of leaving the zone.

Hunting and fishing are permitted in the wildlife reserves and parks according to certain rules.

Humpback whale

Reservations are required for access to waterways. For more information, check directly with the park or reserve office where you plan to hunt or fish.

Birdwatching

In addition to the national and provincial parks, there are many other interesting birdwatching spots throughout Quebec. We recommend two interesting guides:

Les Meilleurs Sites d'Observation des Oiseaux du Québec, published by Éditions Québec-Science.

Peterson's Field Guide: All the Birds of Eastern and Central North America, published by Houghton Mifflin.

Whale-watching

The St. Lawrence is teeming with diverse marine life. A large part of it is made up of numerous marine mammals, including many species of whales (belugas, finback whales and blue whales). Whale-watching expeditions are popular in the tourist regions of Charlevoix, Saguenay–Lac-Saint-Jean, Bas-Saint-Laurent, Manicouagan, Duplessis and the Gaspésie. For more information, refer to the chapter in the guide covering the corresponding region.

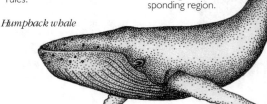

Golf

Groomed golf courses exist in all corners of Québec. A map called *Le Golf au Québec,* as well as the *Guide Maxi-Golf,* should provide all the teeing-off information necessary. Both are available in travel bookstores and at the Centre Infotouriste in Montréal and in Québec City.

Horseback Riding

Many horse stables offer lessons or trail rides. Some even organize longer trips of more than one day. Both types of riding, English and Western, are available depending on the stable. As the two styles are very different, check which one is offered when making reservations. Some provincial parks have horseback-riding trails.

Québec à Cheval (Québec on horseback) is an organization that promotes horseback riding. They distribute an annual French publication free-of-charge called *Découvrir le Québec à Cheval* (Discovering Québec on Horseback). Courses are also offered. For more information, check with Québec à Cheval, which is part of the Regroupement Loisir Québec (☎450-434-1433).

Scuba Diving

Most of the regions of Québec offer dive sites, and there are at least 200 diving centres, schools or clubs. For more complete information on diving in Québec, contact the Fédération Québécoise des Activités Subaquatiques (Québec Federation of Underwater Activities) (☎514-252-3009).

Climbing

Climbing enthusiasts can practise their sport in summer and in winter, when there are ice walls for climbers of all levels. Adequate and reliable equipment (often rented on site) and a firm grasp of the basic techniques are crucial to this sport. Some climbing centres offer beginners' courses.

For information concerning ice and rock climbing activities, beginner courses and more advanced courses, contact the Fédération Québécoise de la Montagne, also part of the Regroupement Loisir Québec (☎514-252-3004). A French language magazine called *Le Mousqueton,* (The Karabiner), is available free of charge from the Regroupement.

Hang-gliding and Paragliding

Hang-gliding has been practised in Québec since the 1970s. The mountains and cliffs most conducive to this sport are located in the regions of Gaspésie, Charlevoix, the Appalachians and Laurentides. Paragliding is a relatively new sport in Québec.

These sports are dangerous and can only be attempted after following a course given by an accredited instructor. For more information, contact the Association Québécoise de Vol Libre (The Québec Association of Hang-gliding and Paragliding) (☎514-890-5276).

Winter Activities

A road map called *Sports d'Hiver Québec* (Québec Winter Sports) outlines the various winter sports practiced in Québec. It contains a list of facilities organized by location and sport, as well as directions on how to get there. This map is available in most travel bookstores and at the Centre Infotouriste in Montréal and in Québec City. The Minister of Tourism also publishes a brochure describing various winter sports and activities.

Downhill Skiing

There are many downhill-ski centres in Québec. Some of these have lighting systems and offer night skiing. Hotels located near the ski hills often offer package-deals including accommodations, meals and lift tickets. Check when reserving your room.

Lift tickets are very expensive; in an effort to accommodate all types of skiers, most centres offer half-day, whole-day and night passes. Some centres have even started offering skiing by the hour.

Cross-country Skiing

There are many parks and ski centres with well-kept cross-country trails. In most ski centres you can rent equipment by the day. Many places offer longer trails, with shelters alongside them offering accommodations for skiers. To ensure a spot in a shelter, reservations are required. Call ☎800-665-6527 or ☎(418) 890-6527 from mid-October on. For skiers on longer trails, some ski centres offer a service that delivers food to the shelter by snowmobile.

Snowshoeing

Reinvented today as a leisure pastime, the snowshoe was first invented by Aboriginals as a means of transportation on deep snow. There is no association in Québec for enthusiasts of this sport, which is mainly practised in cross-country ski-centres.

Snowmobiling

Now this is a popular Québec sport! It was, after all, a Quebecer named Joseph-Armand Bombardier who invented the snowmobile, thereby giving life to one of the most important industries in Québec, now involved in the building of airplanes and railway materials.

A network of more than 26,000km of cleared snowmobile trails criss-crosses Québec. Trails cross diverse regions and lead adventurers into the heart of the wilderness. Along the trails are all the necessities for snowmobiling: repair services, heated sheds, fuel, and food services. It is possible to rent a snowmobile and the necessary equipment in certain snowmobiling centres. The magazine *Motoneige Québec* is sold at newspaper stands. A map called *Sentiers de Motoneige à Travers le Québec* (Snowmobile Trails

Across Quebec) is also available. It indicates the location of trails, service centres, and towns where equipment can be rented.

To use the trail, you must have the registration paper for your vehicle and a membership card. The membership card is available from the Fédération des Clubs de Motoneigistes. No-fault insurance is strongly recommended.

Certain safety rules apply. A helmet is mandatory and driving on public roads is forbidden unless the trail follows it. Headlights and brake lights must be lit at all times. The speed-limit is 60km/h. It is preferable to ride in groups. Lastly, always stick to cleared trails.

For information, contact the Fédération des Clubs de Motoneigistes du Québec, part of the Regroupement Loisir Québec (☎514-252-3076).

Dogsledding

Used by the Inuit for transportation in the past, today dogsledding has become a respected sporting activity. Competitive events abound in northern countries all over the world. In recent years, tourist centres have started offering dogsledding trips lasting anywhere from a few hours to a few days. In the latter case, the tour organizer provides the necessary equipment and shelter. In general, you can expect to cover 30km to 60km per day, and this sport is more demanding than it looks, so good physical fitness is essential for long trips. Centres that offer dogsled trips

are listed throughout the guide.

Skating

Most municipalities have public skating rinks set up in parks, on rivers or lakes. Some places have rental services and even a little hut where you and your skates can warm up.

Ice-fishing

This sport has become more and more popular in recent years. The basic idea, as the name suggests, is to fish through the ice. A small wooden shack built on the ice keeps you warm during the long hours of waiting for the big one! The main regions for this sport are the Eastern Townships, Mauricie, Centre-du-Québec, and Saguenay–Lac-Saint-Jean regions. This guide mentions various spots for ice-fishing.

Montréal

A city of paradoxes

at the crossroads of America and Europe, with a soul both Latin and northern, Montréal holds nothing back.

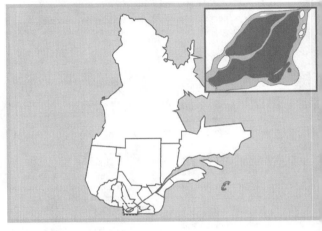

It succeeds in delighting American tourists with its "European" charm, but also manages to surprise overseas travellers with its haphazard character and nonchalance. Montréal is an enchanting city to visit, an exhilarating place to discover; it is generous, friendly and not at all mundane. And, when it comes time to celebrate jazz, film, comedy, St. Patrick's Day or Saint-Jean-Baptiste Day, hundreds of thousands of people flood into the streets, turning events into festive public gatherings.

This festive spirit lasts all year in the city's countless cafés, nightclubs and bars, which are constantly packed by a joyful, urban crowd. While Montrealers know how to party, they also enjoy celebrating the arts. With French and North American influences, as well as the vitality of new arrivals, Montréal is an international city and the primary centre of culture in Québec. The abundance of high quality work produced here, most notably in the fields of theatre, fashion, literature and music, attests to the dynamism and creativity of the local population. The city has also earned an enviable reputation

among foodies; many believe that one can eat better in Montréal than anywhere else in North America.

Montréal's richly varied urban landscape illustrates the different stages of the city's evolution. The oldest buildings in Vieux-Montréal, or Old Montréal, predate the glass skyscrapers downtown by a period of over three centuries, during which the city was in constant expansion. The splendour of Montréal's countless churches, the neoclassical facades of the banks along Rue Saint-Jacques, the flat-roofed little houses in the working-class neighbourhoods and the sumptuous residences

of the "Golden Square Mile" all bear witness, like so much else here, to the city's recent and not-so-recent history. Montréal's important role, both past and present, as the province's main centre of artistic and intellectual activity, and as a large industrial, financial, commercial and port city, is eloquently reflected in its rich architectural heritage.

Though its towering glass and concrete skyline gives it the appearance of a big North American city, Montréal is above all a city of narrow streets, of neighbourhoods, each with its own church, handful of businesses, corner delicatessen, brasserie or tavern. Over the years, the city has also been shaped by an increasingly cosmopolitan population. The division between the east and west (between French-speakers and English-speakers, respectively) still exists to a certain degree, although it no longer stirs up the same feelings. The "two solitudes" have developed a greater respect for one another, and in spite of all their differences, appreciate the distinct advantages of living in this Québec metropolis.

Over the past century, immigrants from all over the world have joined these two main elements of Montreal society. Some of these minorities, notably the Italians, Greeks, Jews, Asians and Portuguese, have established communities in specific areas and have preserved certain aspects of their particular cultures. The great diversity of these neighbourhoods and their inhabitants help give Montréal a unique charm and a character that is markedly different from that of the rest of Québec.

A Brief History of Montréal

During his second voyage to North America in 1535, Jacques Cartier sailed up the St. Lawrence River to Montréal, explored the shores of the island and climbed Mont Royal. While Cartier may not have been the first European to visit the island, which is located at the confluence of two rivers now known as the St. Lawrence and the Ottawa, he was nevertheless the first

to report its existence. In those days, the Aboriginals referred to it as Hochelaga. At the time of Cartier's arrival, a large fortified town populated by about 1,000 Iroquois stretched across the slopes of Mont Royal. This town was evidently destroyed or abandoned a few years later, since when the great explorer Samuel de Champlain, founder of Québec City, came here in 1611, he found no trace of it. He did note, however, that the island would make a very good spot for a trading post.

It was not the fur trade, however, that gave rise to the founding of Montréal. Originally named Ville-Marie, the city was established by a group of devout French citizens who came here in hopes of converting the Aboriginal people to Christianity. Under the direction of Paul de Chomedey, Sieur de Maisonneuve, 50 men and four women, including Jeanne Mance, founded Ville-Marie on May 18, 1642. Their plans soon came up against Iroquois opposition, however—so much so that until the signing of a peace treaty in 1701, the French and the Iroquois engaged in such constant conflict that the very existence of the settlement was threatened on a number of occasions.

Although Montréal was originally founded for the "glory of Christianity," merchants quickly replaced members of religious orders and other bearers of the "word." The numerous waterways leading deep into the hinterland provided easy access to rich hunting grounds. Montréal soon became an important business hub, and remained the main fur-trading centre in North America for nearly 150 years. The city also served as the starting point for the *coureurs des bois* (trappers) and explorers who set out to discover the vast territory stretching

from Louisiana to Hudson Bay.

After the British army took Montréal in 1760, the Scots took over the fur trade from the French. The city became the metropolis of the country during the 1820s, when its population surpassed that of Québec City. From that point on, Montréal underwent rapid changes; thousands of immigrants from the British Isles settled in the city, or simply passed through it on their way to other regions in North America. For a certain period of time, before the industrialization of the mid-19th century began attracting a continual influx of people from the Québec countryside, there was even a British majority here.

By the turn of the 20th century, Montréal had become a major industrial city, whose upper-class residents controlled 70% of the wealth in Canada. The industrial revolution had also generated a large working class, composed mainly of French Canadians and Irish, who lived in wretched conditions. Meanwhile, immigrants from outside Great Britain—particularly Jews from Eastern Europe, Germans and Italians—began to pour into the city, which was beginning to take on a cosmopolitan character.

During the 20th century, Montréal grew continually, swallowing up neighbouring towns and villages due to the steady influx of both rural Quebecers and immigrants. Starting in the 1950s, the city even began spreading beyond the island itself, turning the adjacent countryside into a suburban zone. Its economic centre gradually shifted from Old Montréal to the area around Boulevard Dorchester (now Boulevard René-Lévesque), where glass and concrete skyscrapers have since sprouted up.

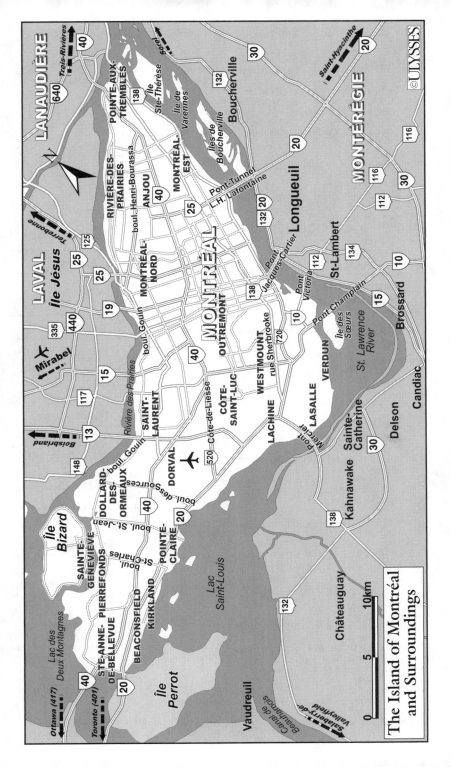

The Island of Montréal and Surroundings

In the 1960s and 1970s, Mayor Jean Drapeau, who has often been accused of megalomania, strengthened "his" city's international reputation by bringing about the construction of a subway (métro) system in 1966, and by organizing large-scale events. Montréal hosted the 1967 World Fair (Expo '67), the 1976 Summer Olympics and the 1980 Floralies Internationales. Montrealers celebrated the 350th anniversary of their city in 1992.

Finding Your Way Around

Until recently, there were 28 municipalities on the island of Montréal, which measures 32km by 16km at its widest. Since January 1, 2002, following a law passed by the Government of Québec, all of these municipalities have merged and now form the City of Montréal, which has a population of 1.81 million people. When the greater Montréal communities of the Rive-Sud (South Shore), Laval and the Rive-Nord (North Shore) are added, Montréal's total population approches 3.5 million inhabitants. Downtown runs along the St. Lawrence River, south of Mont Royal (234m), which is one of the 10 hills of the Montérégie region.

The following nine walking tours crisscross Montréal and Laval: **Tour A: Vieux-Montréal ★★★** (see p 77), **Tour B: Downtown ★★★** (see p 88), **Tour C: Shaughnessy Village ★★** (see p 97), **Tour D: Mont Royal and Westmount ★★** (see p 100), **Tour E: Maisonneuve ★★** (see p 105), **Tour F: Île Sainte-Hélène and Île Notre-Dame ★★** (see p 109), **Tour**

G: Quartier Latin ★★ (see p 112), **Tour H: Plateau Mont-Royal ★** (see p 116), and **Tour I: Laval** (see p 119). For more Montréal tours, please see the Ulysses Travel Guide *Montréal*.

By Car

There are two possible routes from Québec City. The first is via Aut. 20 W. to the Pont Champlain, then follow Aut. 10 straight into the centre of town. The other route is via Aut. 40 W. to Aut. 15, and follow the signs for downtown, *centre-ville*.

Visitors arriving from Ottawa should take Aut. 40 E. to Aut. 15, then follow the signs for downtown, while those arriving from Toronto should take Aut. 20 E. onto the island, then follow the signs for downtown via Aut. 720.

Visitors arriving from the United States on Aut. 10 (Autoroute des Cantons de l'Est) or Aut. 15 will enter Montréal by way of the Pont Champlain and Aut. 10.

Several bridges connect Montréal to **Laval**, including Pont Lachapell (Gouin Ouest and Boulevard Laurentian), Pont Viau (Gouin and Lajeunesse, métro Henri-Bourassa), Pont Louis-Bisson (the easternmost bridge on Goiuin Ouest) and finally, Pont Pie-IX (Gouin and Boulevard Pie-IX).

Car Rentals

Avis
1225 rue Metcalfe
☎*866-2847*
505 boulevard De Maisonneuve Est
☎*288-9934*

Budget
1240 rue Guy
☎*937-9121*
895 rue De La Gauchetière Ouest
☎*866-7675*

Discount
607 boulevard De Maisonneuve O.
☎*286-1554*

Hertz
1073 rue Drummond
☎*938-1717*
1475 rue Aylmer
☎*842-8537*

National
1200 rue Stanley
☎*878-2771*

Via Route
1255 rue Mackay
☎*871-1166*

Airports

Mirabel Airport: see p 44
Dorval Airport: see p 43

Bus Station

Station Centrale
505 Boulevard de Maisonneuve Est
(métro Berri-UQAM)
☎*(514) 842-2281*

Train Station

Gare Centrale
895 Rue de la Gauchetière Ouest
(métro Bonaventure)
☎*(514) 871-7765*
☎*800-361-5390 (from Québec)*
☎*800-561-8630 (elsewhere in Canada)*

Public Transportation

Montréal's métro (subway) and bus network covers the entire metropolitan region. A pass entitling the holder to unlimited use of the public transportation services for one month costs $52 and is on sale at the beginning of the month only. Tourist cards, valid for one day (*$7*) or three consecutive days (*$14*) also entitle the holder to unlimited use of the public transportation services. For shorter stays or less moving about, visitors

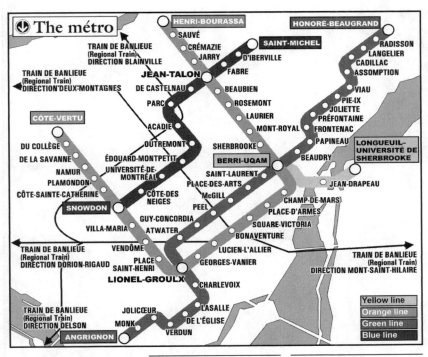

The métro

HENRI-BOURASSA
HONORÉ-BEAUGRAND
SAUVÉ
TRAIN DE BANLIEUE (Regional Train) DIRECTION BLAINVILLE
CRÉMAZIE
SAINT-MICHEL
RADISSON
LANGELIER
CADILLAC
ASSOMPTION
JARRY
D'IBERVILLE
TRAIN DE BANLIEUE (Regional Train) DIRECTION DEUX-MONTAGNES
JEAN-TALON
FABRE
DE CASTELNAU
BEAUBIEN
VIAU
PARC
ROSEMONT
PIE-IX
JOLIETTE
ACADIE
LAURIER
PRÉFONTAINE
CÔTE-VERTU
OUTREMONT
MONT-ROYAL
FRONTENAC
DU COLLÈGE
ÉDOUARD-MONTPETIT
SHERBROOKE
PAPINEAU
LONGUEUIL-UNIVERSITÉ DE SHERBROOKE
DE LA SAVANNE
UNIVERSITÉ-DE-MONTRÉAL
BERRI-UQAM
BEAUDRY
NAMUR
SAINT-LAURENT
PLAMONDON
PLACE-DES-ARTS
JEAN-DRAPEAU
CÔTE-SAINTE-CATHERINE
CÔTE-DES-NEIGES
McGILL
SNOWDON
PEEL
CHAMP-DE-MARS
GUY-CONCORDIA
PLACE-D'ARMES
VILLA-MARIA
ATWATER
SQUARE-VICTORIA
BONAVENTURE
TRAIN DE BANLIEUE (Regional Train) DIRECTION DORION-RIGAUD
VENDÔME
LUCIEN-L'ALLIER
PLACE SAINT-HENRI
GEORGES-VANIER
TRAIN DE BANLIEUE (Regional Train) DIRECTION MONT-SAINT-HILAIRE
LIONEL-GROULX
CHARLEVOIX
TRAIN DE BANLIEUE (Regional Train) DIRECTION DELSON
JOLICŒUR
L'ASALLE
MONK
DE L'ÉGLISE
ANGRIGNON
VERDUN

Yellow line
Orange line
Green line
Blue line

can purchase six tickets for $9.50, or single tickets at $2.25 each. Children and seniors benefit from reduced fares. Tickets and passes can be purchased at all métro stations and some pharmacies and convenience stores. **Take note that bus drivers do not sell tickets and do not give change.**

For more information on the public transportation system, call:
STM
☎*(514) 288-6287*
(A-U-T-O-B-U-S)
www.stm.info

Laval
10765 Rue Lajeunesse
at the corner of Henri-Bourassa
Boulevard and Lajeunesse Street
(Henri Bourassa métro Station)
☎*(514) 688-6520*

Taxis

Co-op Taxi:
☎*(514) 725-9885*
Diamond: ☎*(514) 273-6331*
Taxi LaSalle: ☎*(514) 277-2552*

Practical Information

Area code: *514*, except for Laval, which is *450*

Tourist Information

Centre Infotouriste
1001 Rue du Square-Dorchester
(Peel métro station)
☎*(514) 873-2015*
www.tourisme-montreal.org
The centre is open from 8:30am to 7:30pm, every day during summer, and from 9am to 6pm every day from September to June.

Bureau du Vieux-Montréal
174 rue Notre-Dame Est
métro Champ-de-Mars
☎*874-1696*
This small tourist booth provides information only on Montréal.

Laval
2900 Boulevard Saint-Martin Ouest
Chomedey
☎*(514) 682-5522*

Montréal

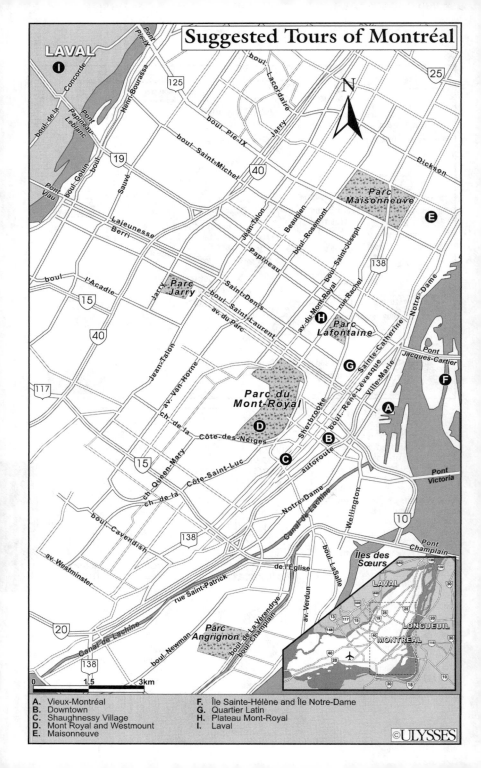

Suggested Tours of Montréal

A. Vieux-Montréal
B. Downtown
C. Shaughnessy Village
D. Mont Royal and Westmount
E. Maisonneuve
F. Île Sainte-Hélène and Île Notre-Dame
G. Quartier Latin
H. Plateau Mont-Royal
I. Laval

©ULYSSES

Foreign Exchange

A number of downtown banks offer currency exchange services. In most cases, there is a service charge. Foreign exchange offices don't always charge a fee, so it is best to inquire beforehand. Most banks are able to exchange U.S. currency.

Banque Nationale du Canada
1140 rue Sherbrooke Ouest
☎281-9640
895 rue De La Gauchetière Ouest
☎394-5555
www.bnc.ca

Automatic teller machines that exchange foreign currency are available in Complexe Desjardins (on Sainte-Catherine Ouest, between Jeanne-Mance and Saint-Urbain). They are open from 6am to 2am. These machines can provide Canadian funds in exchange for various foreign currencies, or the reverse. There are similar machines at Mirabel Airport.

Post Offices

1250 rue University
☎846-5401

1695 rue Ste-Catherine Est
☎522-3220

Exploring

Tour A: Vieux–Montréal

In the 18th century, Montréal, like Québec City, was surrounded by stone fortifications. Between 1801 and 1817, these ramparts were demolished due to the efforts of local merchants, who saw

them as an obstacle to the city's development. The network of old streets, compressed after nearly a century of confinement, nevertheless remained in place. Today's Vieux-Montréal, or Old Montréal, thus corresponds quite closely to the area covered by the fortified city.

During the 19th century, this area became the hub of commercial and financial activity in Canada. Banks and insurance companies built sumptuous head offices here, leading to the demolition of almost all buildings erected under the French Regime. The area was later abandoned for nearly 40 years in favour of the modern downtown area of today. Finally, the long process of putting new life into Old Montréal got underway during the preparations for Expo '67, and it continues today with numerous conversion and restoration projects. This revitalization has even gotten a second wind since the late 1990s. In fact, several high-end hotels have been established in historic buildings, while many Montrealers have rejuvenated the neighbourhood by making it their home. In addition, the new Cité du Multimédia now occupies a large sector southwest of the district; this redevelopment project in the southwest of Old Montréal attracted firms specializing in information technology and multimedia, bringing new life to this neighbourhood and filling its streets with young professionals.

The tour begins at the west end of Old Montréal, on Rue McGill, which marks the site of the surrounding wall that once separated the city from the Faubourg des Récollets (Square-Victoria métro). Visitors will notice a considerable difference between the urban fabric of the modern downtown area behind them, with its wide boulevards lined with glass and steel skyscrapers, and the old part of the city, whose narrow, compact streets are crowded with stone buildings.

The **Tour de la Bourse** ★ *(Place de la Bourse, Square-Victoria métro, ☎871-2424)*, or the stock exchange tower, dominates the surroundings. It was erected in 1964 according to a design by the famous Italian engineers Luigi Moretti and Pier Luigi Nervi, to whom we owe the Palazzo dello Sport (sports stadium) in Rome and the Exhibition Centre in Turin.

The elegant 47-storey black tower houses the offices and trading floor of the exchange. It is one of many buildings in this city designed by foreign talents. Its construction was intended to breathe new life into the business section of the old city, which was deserted after the stock market crash of 1929 in favour of the area around Square Dorchester. According to the initial plan, there were supposed to be two, or even three, identical towers.

In the 19th century, **Square Victoria** was a Victorian garden surrounded by Second Empire and Renaissance Revival stores and office buildings. Only the narrow building at 751 Rue McGill survives from that era. On the south side of Rue Saint-Antoine, visitors will find a **statue of Queen Victoria**, executed in 1872 by English sculptor Marshall Wood. An authentic Art Nouveau **Parisian métro railing**, designed by Hector Guimard in 1900 and given to the City of Montréal by the City of Paris for Expo '67, was installed at one of the entrances to the Square-Victoria métro station.

The headquarters of the two organizations that control international civil aviation, IATA (the International Air Transport Association) and ICOA

Montréal

(the International Civil Aviation Organization) are located in Montréal. The latter is a United Nations organization that was founded in 1947 and is located in the **Maison de l'OACI** *(at the corner of University and St-Antoine Ouest)*, which houses the delegations of its 183 member countries. The back of the building, which has been connected to the Cité Internationale de Montréal, is visible from Square Victoria. Completed in 1996, it was designed by architect Ken London, who was inspired somewhat by Scandinavian architecture of the 1930s.

Enter the covered passageway of the Centre de Commerce Mondial.

World trade centres are exchange organizations intended to promote international trade. Montréal's **Centre de Commerce Mondial / World Trade Centre** ★ *(Rue McGill,*

Square-Victoria métro), completed in 1991, is a new structure hidden behind an entire block of old façades. An impressive glassed-in passageway stretches 180m through the centre of the building, along a portion of the Ruelle des Fortifications, a lane marking the former location of the northern wall of the fortified city. Alongside the passageway, visitors will find a fountain and an elegant stone stairway, which provide the setting for a statue of Amphitirite, Poseidon's wife, taken from the municipal fountain in Saint-Mihiel-de-la-Meuse, France. This work dates back to the mid-18th century; it was executed by Barthélémy Guibal, a sculptor from Nîmes, France, who also designed the fountains gracing Place Stanislas in Nancy, France.

Climb the stairway, then walk along the passageway to the modest entrance of the lobby of the Hôtel Inter-Continental.

Turn right onto the footbridge leading to the Nordheimer building.

This edifice was restored in order to accommodate the hotel's reception halls, which are linked to the trade centre. Erected in 1888, the building originally housed a piano store and a small concert hall where many great artists performed, including Maurice Ravel and Sarah Bernhardt. The interior, with its combination of dark woodwork, moulded plaster and mosaics, is typical of the late 19th century, characterized by exuberant eclecticism and lively polychromy. The façade, on Rue Saint-Jacques, combines Romanesque Revival elements, as adapted by American architect Henry Hobson Richardson, with elements from the Chicago School, notably the many-windowed metallic roof.

Exit via 363 Rue Saint-Jacques.

● ATTRACTIONS

1.	Tour de la Bourse	13.	Musée d'Archéologie et d'Histoire de Montréal / Montréal Museum of Archaeology and History and the Pointe-à-Callière
2.	Square Victoria		
3.	Maison de l'OACI		
4.	Centre de Commerce Mondial / World Trade Centre		
		14.	Place D'Youville
5.	Banque Royale / Royal Bank	15.	Hôpital Général des Sœurs Grises
6.	Banque Molson / Molson Bank	16.	Musée Marc-Aurèle-Fortin
		17.	Vieux-Port de Montréal / Old Port
7.	Place d'Armes	18.	Le Bateau-Mouche
8.	Banque de Montréal / Bank of Montréal	19.	Canal de Lachine / Lachine Canal
9.	Basilique Notre-Dame	20.	Centre des Sciences de Montréal
10.	Vieux Séminaire		
11.	Cours Le Royer	21.	Auberge Saint-Gabriel
12.	Place Royale		

22.	Palais de Justice	
23.	Édifice Ernest-Cormier	
24.	Vieux Palais de Justice	
25.	Place Jacques-Cartier	
26.	Hôtel de ville	
27.	Château Ramezay	
28.	Sir-George-Étienne-Cartier National Historic Site	
29.	Gare Viger	
30.	Gare Dalhousie	
31.	Chapelle Notre-Dame-de-Bonsecours	
32.	Maison Papineau	
33.	Marché Bonsecours	
34.	Tour de l'Horloge	

◯ ACCOMMODATIONS

1.	Auberge Alternative	6.	Hôtel Inter-Continental Montréal	12.	St-Paul Hotel (R)
2.	Auberge Bonaparte (R)			13.	XIX Siècle
3.	Auberge du Vieux-Port	7.	Hôtel Nelligan		
4.	Hostellerie et Restaurant Pierre du Calvet 1725 (R)	8.	Hôtel Place d'Armes		
		9.	Le Saint-James	(R) establishment with restaurant (see description)	
5.	Hôtel Gault	10.	Le Saint-Sulpice		
		11.	Passants du SansSoucy		

● RESTAURANTS

1.	Bio Train	5.	Gibby's	9.	Soto
2.	Chez Better	6.	La Gargote	10.	Stash's Café Bazar
3.	Chez Delmo	7.	Le Petit Moulinsart	11.	Titanic
4.	Chez Queux	8.	Modavie	12.	Vieux Saint-Gabriel

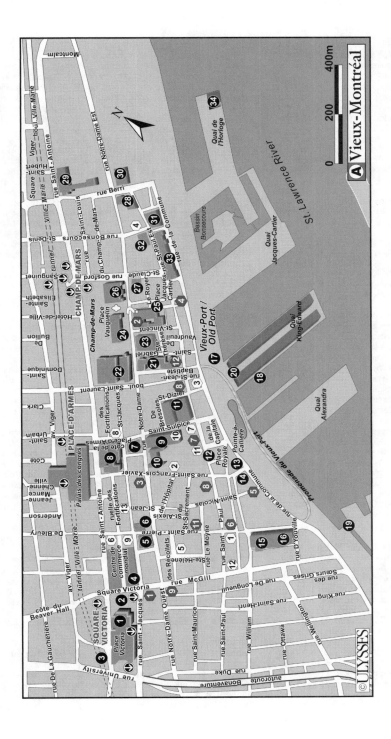

A Vieux-Montréal

Rue Saint-Jacques was the main artery of Canadian high finance for over a century. This role is reflected in its rich and varied architecture, which serves as a veritable encyclopedia of styles from 1830 to 1930. In those years, the banks, insurance companies and department stores, as well as the nation's railway and shipping companies, were largely controlled by Montrealers of Scottish extraction, who had come to the colonies to make their fortune.

Begun in 1928 according to plans by New York skyscraper specialists York and Sawyer, the former head office of the **Banque Royale / Royal Bank ★★** *(360 Rue St-Jacques, Square-Victoria métro)*, was one of the last buildings erected during this era of prosperity. The 22-storey tower has a base inspired by Florentine palazzos, which corresponds to the scale of the neighbouring buildings. Inside the edifice, visitors can admire the high ceilings of this "temple of finances built at a time when banks needed impressive buildings to win customers' confidence. The walls of the great hall are emblazoned with the heraldic insignia of eight of the 10 Canadian provinces, as well as those of Montréal (St. George's Cross) and Halifax (a yellow bird), where the bank was founded in 1861.

The **Banque Molson / Molson Bank ★** *(288 Rue St-Jacques, Square-Victoria métro)*, was founded in 1854 by the Molson family, famous for the brewery established by their ancestor, John Molson (1763-1836), in 1786. The Molson Bank, like other banks at the time, even printed its own paper money—an indication of the power wielded by its owners, who contributed greatly to the city's development. The head office of the family business looks more like

a patrician residence than an anonymous bank. Completed in 1866, it is one of the earliest examples of the Second Empire, or Napoleon III, style to have been erected in Canada. This French style, modelled on the Louvre and the Paris Opera, was extremely popular in North America between 1865 and 1890. Above the entrance, visitors will see the sandstone carvings of the heads of William Molson and two of his children. The Molson Bank merged with the Bank of Montréal in 1925.

Walk along Rue Saint-Jacques; you'll soon come to - Place d'Armes.

Under the French Regime, **Place d'Armes ★★** *(Place-d'Armes métro)* was the heart of the city. Used for military manoeuvres and religious processions, the square was also the location of the Gadoys well, the city's main source of potable water. In 1847, the square was transformed into a lovely, fenced-in Victorian garden, which was destroyed at the beginning of the 20th century in order to make room for a tramway terminal. In the meantime, a **monument to Maisonneuve** was erected in 1895. Executed by sculptor Philippe Hébert, it shows the founder of Montréal, Paul de Chomedey, Sieur de Maisonneuve, surrounded by prominent figures from the city's early history, namely Jeanne Mance, founder of the Hôtel-Dieu (hospital), Lambert Closse, along with his dog Pilote, and Charles Lemoyne, head of a family of famous explorers. An Iroquois warrior completes the tableau.

The square, which is in fact shaped more like a trapezoid, is surrounded by several noteworthy buildings. The **Banque de Montréal / Bank of Montréal ★★** *(119 Rue St-Jacques, Place-d'Armes*

métro), founded in 1817 by a group of merchants, is the country's oldest banking institution. Its present head office takes up an entire block on the north side of Place d'Armes. A magnificent building by John Wells, built in 1847 and modelled after the Roman Pantheon, it occupies the place of honour in the centre of the block, and offers customer banking. Its Corinthian portico is a monument to the commercial power of the Scottish merchants who founded the institution. The capitals of the columns, severely damaged by pollution, were replaced in 1970 with aluminum replicas. The pediment includes a bas-relief depicting the bank's coat of arms carved out of Binney stone in Scotland by Her Majesty's sculptor, Sir John Steele.

The interior was almost entirely redone in 1904-05, according to plans by celebrated New York architects McKim, Mead and White (Boston Library, Columbia University in New York City). On this occasion, the bank was endowed with a splendid banking hall, designed in the style of a Roman basilica, with green syenite columns, gilded bronze ornamentation and beige marble counters. A small **Numismatic Museum** *(free admission; Mon-Fri 9am to 5pm)*, located in the lobby of the more recent building, displays bills from different eras, as well as an amusing collection of mechanical piggy banks. Across from the museum, visitors will find four bas-reliefs carved out of an artificial stone called *coade*, which once graced the façade of the bank's original head office. These were executed in 1819, after drawings by English sculptor John Bacon.

The surprising red sandstone tower at number 511 Place d'Armes was erected in 1888 for the New York Life Insurance Company according to a design by architects Babb,

Cook and Willard. Although it only has eight floors, it is regarded as Montréal's first skyscraper. The stone used for the facing was imported from Scotland. At the time, this type of stone was transported in the holds of ships, where it served as ballast until it was sold to building contractors at the pier. The edifice next door (507 Place-d'Armes) is adorned with beautiful Art Deco details. It was one of the first buildings over 10 stories to be erected in Montréal after a regulation restricting the height of structures was repealed in 1927.

On the south side of Place d'Armes, visitors will find the Basilique Notre-Dame and the Vieux Séminaire, which are described below.

In 1663, the seigneury of the island of Montréal was acquired by the Sulpicians from Paris, who remained its undisputed masters up until the British Conquest of 1760. In addition to distributing land to colonists and laying out the city's first streets, the Sulpicians were responsible for the construction of a large number of buildings, including Montréal's first parish church (1673). Dedicated to *Notre Dame* (Our Lady), this church had a beautiful Baroque façade, which faced straight down the centre of the street of the same name, creating a pleasant perspective characteristic of classical French town-planning.

At the beginning of the 19th century, however, this rustic little church cut a sorry figure when compared to the Anglican cathedral on Rue Notre-Dame and the new Catholic cathedral on Rue Saint-Denis, neither of which remains today. The Sulpicians therefore decided to surpass their rivals once and for all. In 1823, to the great displeasure of local architects, they commissioned New York architect James O'Donnell, who came from an Irish Protestant background, to design the largest and most original church north of Mexico.

Basilique Notre-Dame ★ ★ ★ *(\$2; 110 Rue Notre-Dame Ouest, Place-d'Armes métro, ☎842-2925),* built between 1824 and 1829, is a true North American masterpiece of Gothic Revival architecture. It should be seen not as a replica of a European cathedral, but rather as a fundamentally neoclassical structure characteristic of the Industrial Revolution, complemented by a medieval-style decor which foreshadowed the historicism of the Victorian era. These elements make the building remarkable.

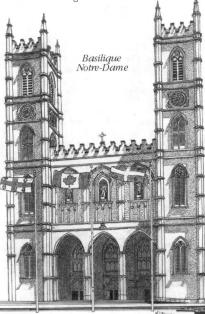

Basilique Notre-Dame

O'Donnell was so pleased with his work that he converted to Catholicism before dying so that he could be buried under the church. Between 1874 and 1880, the original interior, considered too austere, was replaced by the fabulous polychromatic decorations found today. Executed by Victor Bourgeau, then the leading architect of religious buildings in the Montréal region, along with about 50 artists, it is made entirely of wood, painted and gilded with gold leaf. Particularly noteworthy features include the baptistery, decorated with frescoes by Ozias Leduc, and the powerful electro-pneumatic Casavant organ with its 5,772 pipes, often used during the numerous concerts given at the basilica. Lastly, there are the stained-glass windows by Francis Chigot, a master glass artist from France, which depict various episodes in the history of Montréal. They were installed in honour of the church's centennial.

To the right of the chancel, a passage leads to the Chapelle du Sacré-Cœur (Sacred Heart Chapel), added to the back of the church in 1888. Nicknamed the Chapelle des Mariages (Wedding Chapel) because of the countless nuptials held there every year, it was seriously damaged by fire in 1978. The spiral staircases and the side galleries are all that remain of the exuberant, Spanish-style Gothic Revival decor of the original. The architects Jodoin, Lamarre and Pratte decided to tie these vestiges in with a modern design, completed in 1981, and included a lovely sectioned vault with skylights, a large bronze reredos by Charles Daudelin and a Guilbault-Thérien mechanical organ. To the right, on the way out of the chapel, visitors will find the small **Musée de la Basilique**, a museum displaying various treasures, including embroidered liturgical clothing as well as the episcopal throne and personal effects of Monseigneur de Pontbriand, the last bishop of New France.

The **Vieux Séminaire** ★ *(116 Rue Notre-Dame Ouest, Place-d'Armes métro)*, or old seminary, was built in 1683 in the style of a Parisian *hôtel particulier*, with a courtyard in front and a garden in back. It is the oldest building in the city. For more than three centuries, it has been occupied by Sulpician priests, who, under the French Regime, used it as a manor from which they managed their vast seigneury. At the time of the building's construction, Montréal had barely 500 inhabitants and was constantly being terrorized by Iroquois attacks. Under those circumstances, the seminary, albeit modest in appearance, represented a precious haven of European civilization in the middle of the wilderness. The public clock at the top of the façade, installed in 1701, may be the oldest one of its kind in the Americas.

Take Rue Saint-Sulpice, which runs alongside the basilica.

The immense warehouses of the **Cours Le Royer** ★ *(Rue St-Sulpice, Place-d'Armes métro)* belonged to the *religieuses hospitalières* of Saint-Joseph. These nursing sisters of Saint-Joseph rented them out to importers. Designed between 1860 and 1871 by Michel Laurent and Victor Bourgeau, who seldom worked on commercial structures, they are located on the site of Montréal's first Hôtel-

Dieu (hospital), founded by Jeanne Mance in 1643. The warehouses, covering a total of 43,000m², were converted into apartments and offices between 1977 and 1986. The small Rue Le Royer was excavated to make room for an underground parking lot, now covered by a pleasant pedestrian mall.

Montréal Museum of Archaeology and History

Turn right on Rue Saint-Paul, towards Place Royale, which lies on the left-hand side of the street.

Montréal's oldest public square, **Place Royale**, dates back to 1657. Originally a market square, it later became a pretty Victorian garden surrounded by a cast-iron fence. In 1991, it was raised in order to make room for an archaeological observation site. It now links the Musée d'Archéologie de Montréal to the **Maison de l'ancienne Douane**, the old customs house, on the north side. The latter is a lovely example of British neoclassical architecture transplanted into a Canadian setting. The building's austere lines, accentuated by the facing, made of local grey stone, are offset by the appropriate proportions and simplified references to antiquity. The old customs house was built in 1836 according to drawings by John Ostell, who had just arrived in Montréal. It

is now an integral part of the museum.

The **Musée d'Archéologie et d'Histoire de Montréal / Montréal Museum of Archaeology and History** ★ ★ *($9.50; Sep to Jun Tue-Fri 10am to 5pm, Sat and Sun 11am to 5pm; Jul and Aug Mon-Fri 10am to 6pm, Sat and Sun 11am to 6pm; 350 Place Royale, Pointe-à-Callière, Place-d'Armes métro, ☎872-9150)* lies on the exact site where Montréal was founded on May 18, 1642, the **Pointe-à-Callière**. The Rivière Saint-Pierre used to flow alongside the area now occupied by Place d'Youville, while the muddy banks of the St. Lawrence reached almost as far as the present-day Rue de la Commune. The first colonists built Fort Ville-Marie out of earth and wooden posts on the isolated point of land created by these two bodies of water. Threatened by Iroquois flotillas and flooding, the leaders of the colony soon decided to establish the town on Coteau Saint-Louis, the hill now bisected by Rue Notre-Dame. The site of the fort was then occupied by a cemetery and the château of Governor de Callière, hence the name.

The museum uses the most advanced techniques available to provide visitors with a survey of the city's history. Attractions include a multimedia presentation, a visit to the vestiges discovered on the site, excellent models illustrating the stages of Place Royale's development, holograms and thematic exhibitions. Designed by architect Dan Hanganu, the museum was erected in 1992, the city's 350th anniversary.

Head towards Place d'Youville, to the right of the museum.

Stretching from Place Royale to Rue McGill, **Place d'Youville** owes its elongated shape to its location on top of the bed of the Rivière Saint-Pierre, which was canalized in 1832.

In the heart of Place d'Youville stands the former fire station no. 3, one of Québec's rare examples of Flemish-inspired architecture. The station is now home to the **Centre d'histoire de Montréal** (*$4.50; May to Sep Tue-Sun 10am to 5pm, Sep to May Wed-Sun 10am to 5pm; 335 Place d'Youville, ☎872-3207*), which was recently entirely renovated. A lovely exhibit showcasing various objects relating Montréal's history is presented on the first two floors. Thanks to lively presentations, visitors can follow the city's evolution and learn about significant events such as Expo '67, discover daily life in various eras, hear about major strikes in the city and see how several heritage buildings were demolished. The sound effects, among other things, play a particularly important role, as you can hear taped testimonies of Montrealers of various origins talking about their city. On the top floor are temporary exhibits as well as a glassed-in overpass from which you can admire Old Montréal.

Turn left on Rue Saint-Pierre.

The Sœurs de la Charité (Sisters of Charity) are better known as the Sœurs Grises (Grey Nuns), a nickname given to them because they were falsely accused of selling alcohol to the natives and thus getting them tipsy (in French, *gris* means both grey and tipsy). In 1747, the founder of the community, Saint Marguerite d'Youville, took charge of the former Hôpital des Frères Charon, established in 1693, and transformed it into the **Hôpital Général des Sœurs Grises** ★ (*138 Rue St-Pierre,*

Square-Victoria métro), a shelter for the city's homeless children. The west wing and the ruins of the chapel are all that remain of this complex built during the 17th and 18th centuries in the shape of an *H*. The other part, which made up another of the old city's classical perspectives, was torn open when Rue Saint-Pierre was extended through the middle of the chapel. The right transept and part of the apse, visible on the right, have been reinforced in order to accommodate a work of art representing the text of the congregation's letters patent.

The small **Musée Marc-Aurèle-Fortin** (*$5; Tue-Sun 11am to 5pm; 118 Rue St-Pierre, Square-Victoria métro, ☎845-6108*), which has only a few rooms, is entirely dedicated to the work of Marc-Aurèle Fortin. Using his own unique style, Fortin painted picturesque Québec scenes. Paintings executed on a black background and majestic trees are just a couple of his trademarks. The museum has some lovely pieces.

Head across Rue de la Commune to the Promenade du Vieux-Port, which runs alongside the St. Lawrence.

The Port of Montréal is the largest inland port on the continent. It stretches 25km along the St. Lawrence, from Cité du Havre to the refineries in the east end. The **Vieux-Port de Montréal / Old Port** ★ ★ (*Place-d'Armes or Champs-de-Mars métro*) corresponds to the historic portion of the port, located in front of the old city. Abandoned because of its obsolescence, it was revamped between 1983 and 1992, following the example of various other centrally located North American ports.

The old port encompasses a pleasant park, laid out on the embankments and coupled with a promenade, which runs

alongside the piers or *quai*, offering a "window" on the river and the few shipping activities that have fortunately been maintained.

The layout accents the view of the water, the downtown area and Rue de la Commune, whose wall of neoclassical, grey-stone warehouses stands before the city, one of the only examples of so-called "waterfront planning" in North America. From the port, visitors can set off on an excursion on the river and the Lachine Canal aboard **Le Bateau Mouche** (*$23; mid-May to mid-Oct, departures every day at 10am, noon, 2pm, 4pm; Quai Jacques-Cartier, ☎849-9952*), whose glass roof enables passengers to fully appreciate the beauty of the surroundings. These guided tours last 1.5hrs. At night, you can also enjoy a supper and a dance on the boat.

The **navettes fluviales**, or river shuttles, (*☎281-8000*) ferry passengers to Île Sainte-Hélène (*$3.45*) and Longueuil (*$4*), offering a spectacular view of the old port and Old Montréal along the way.

On the right, directly in line with Rue McGill, visitors will find the mouth of the **Canal de Lachine / Lachine Canal**, inaugurated in 1825. This waterway made it possible to bypass the formidable rapids, known as the Rapides de Lachine, upriver from Montréal, thus providing access to the Great Lakes and the American Midwest. The canal also became the cradle of the industrial revolution in Canada, since the spinning and flour-mills were able to harness its power, as well as a direct means of taking in supplies and sending out shipments (from the boat to the factory and vice versa). Closed in 1959 when the seaway was opened, the canal was turned over to the Canadian Parks Service. A bicycle path now

Montréal

runs alongside it, continuing on to the *vieux-port* or old port.

The locks, restored in 1991, lie adjacent to a park and a boldly designed lock-keeper's house. Behind the locks stands the last of the old port's towering **grain silos**. Erected in 1905, this reinforced concrete structure excited the admiration of Walter Gropius and Le Corbusier when they came here on a study trip. It is now illuminated as if it were a monument. In front, visitors will see the strange pile of cubes that form Habitat '67 (see p 109) on the right, and the **Gare Maritime Iberville** (☎496-7678), the harbour station for liners cruising the St. Lawrence, on the left.

The **Centre des sciences de Montréal** ★ (*$10; every day May to Oct 10am to 6pm, Oct to May Tue-Sun 10am to 6pm; quai King-Edward, Place-d'Armes métro, ☎496-4724 or 877-496-4724*), an interactive science-and-entertainment complex occupying a modern building, invites you to discover the secrets of the world of science and technology while having a great time. The centre features three interactive exhibition halls where participants can take part in science experiments, games of skill and several cultural and educational activities. The centre also boasts a 2-D and 3-D **IMAX** theatre and the Immersion Interactive Cinema.

Walk along the promenade to **Boulevard Saint-Laurent**, one of the city's main arteries, which serves as the dividing line between east and west not only as far as place names and addresses are concerned, but also from a linguistic point of view. Traditionally, there has always been a higher concentration of English-speakers in the western part of the city, and French-speakers in the eastern part, while ethnic minorities of all different origins are concentrated along Boulevard Saint-Laurent.

Head up Boulevard Saint-Laurent to Rue Saint-Paul. Turn right, then left on to a narrow street named Rue Saint-Gabriel.

It was on this street that Richard Dulong opened an inn in 1754. Today, the **Auberge Saint-Gabriel** (*426 Rue St-Gabriel, Place-d'Armes, ☎878-3561*), the oldest operating Canadian inn, is a restaurant (see p 130). It occupies a group of 18th-century buildings with sturdy fieldstone walls.

Turn right on Rue Notre-Dame.

Having passed through the financial and warehouse districts, visitors now enter an area dominated by civic and legal institutions; no fewer than three courthouses lie clustered along Rue Notre-Dame. Inaugurated in 1971, the massive new **Palais de Justice** (*1 Rue Notre-Dame Est, Champs-de-Mars métro*), or courthouse, dwarfs the surroundings. A sculpture by Charles Daudelin entitled *Allegrocube* lies on its steps. A mechanism makes it possible to open and close this stylized "hand of justice."

From the time it was inaugurated in 1926 until it closed in 1970, the **Édifice Ernest-Cormier** ★ (*100 Rue Notre-Dame Est, Champs-de-Mars métro*) was used for criminal proceedings. The former courthouse was converted into a conservatory and was named after its architect, the illustrious Ernest Cormier, who also designed the main pavilion of the Université de Montréal and the doors of the United Nations Headquarters in New York City. The courthouse is graced with outstanding bronze sconces, cast in Paris at the workshops of Edgar Brandt. Their installation in 1925 ushered in the Art Deco style in Canada. The main hall, faced with travertine and topped by three dome-shaped skylights, is worth a quick visit.

The **Vieux Palais de Justice** ★ (*155 Rue Notre-Dame Est, Champs-de-Mars métro*), the oldest courthouse in Montréal, was built between 1849 and 1856, according to a design by John Ostell and Henri-Maurice Perrault, on the site of the first courthouse, which was erected in 1800. It is another fine example of Canadian neoclassical architecture. After the courts were divided in 1926, the old Palais was used for civil cases, judged according to the Napoleonic Code. Since the opening of the new Palais to its left, the old Palais has been converted into an annex of the city hall, located to the right.

Place Jacques-Cartier ★ (*Champs-de-Mars métro*) was laid out on the site once occupied by the Château de Vaudreuil, which burned down in 1803. The former Montréal residence of the governor of New France was without question the most elegant private home in the city. Designed by engineer Gaspard Chaussegros de Léry in 1723, it had a horseshoe-shaped staircase leading up to a handsome cut-stone portal, two projecting pavilions (one on each side of the main part of the building), and a formal garden that extended as far as Rue Notre-Dame. After the fire, the property was purchased by local merchants, who decided to give the government a small strip of land, on the condition that a public market be established there, thus increasing the value of the adjacent property, which

Hôtel de ville

remained in private hands. This explains Place Jacques-Cartier's oblong shape.

Merchants of British descent sought various means of ensuring their visibility and publicly expressing their patriotism in Montréal. They quickly formed a much larger community in Montréal than in Québec City, where the government and military headquarters were located. In 1809, they were the first in the world to erect a monument to Admiral Horatio Nelson, who defeated the combined French and Spanish fleets in the Battle of Trafalgar. Supposedly, they even got the French Canadian merchants drunk in order to extort a financial contribution from them for the project. The base of the **Colonne Nelson**, or the Nelson Column, was designed and executed in London, according to plans by architect Robert Mitchell. It is decorated with bas-reliefs depicting the exploits of the famous Admiral at Abukir, Copenhagen, and of course Trafalgar. The statue of Nelson at the top was originally made of an artificial type of stone, but after being damaged time and time again by protestors, it was finally replaced by a fibre-glass replica

in 1981. The column is the oldest extant monument in Montréal. At the other end of Place Jacques-Cartier, visitors will see the **Quai Jacques-Cartier** and the river, while **Rue Saint-Amable** lies tucked away on the right, at the halfway mark. During summer, artists and artisans gather on this little street, selling jewellery, drawings, etchings and caricatures.

Under the French Regime, Montréal, following the example of Québec City and Trois-Rivières, had its own governor, not to be confused with the governor of New France as a whole. The situation was the same under the English Regime. It wasn't until 1833 that the first elected mayor, Jacques Viger, took control of the city. This man, who was passionately interested in history, gave Montréal its motto *(Concordia Salus)* and coat of arms, composed of the four symbols of the "founding" peoples, namely the French *fleur-de-lys*, the Irish clover, the Scottish thistle and the English rose, all linked together by the Canadian beaver.

After occupying a number of inadequate buildings for decades (a notable example was the Hayes aqueduct, an edifice

containing an immense reservoir of water, which cracked one day while a meeting was being held in the council chamber immediately below; it's easy to imagine what happened next), the municipal administration finally moved into its present home in 1878. The **hôtel de ville ★** *(275 Rue Notre-Dame Est, Champs-de-Mars métro)*, or city hall, is a fine example of the Second Empire, or Napoleon III, style, is the work of Henri-Maurice Perrault, who also designed the neighbouring courthouse. In 1922, a fire (yet another!) destroyed the interior and roof of the building, later restored in 1926, after the model of the city hall in Tours, France. Exhibitions are occasionally presented in the main hall, which is accessible via the main entrance. Visitors may also be interested to know that it was from the balcony of the city hall that France's General de Gaulle cried out his famous *"Vive le Québec libre!"* ("Freedom for Québec!") in 1967, to the great delight of the crowd gathered in front of the building.

Head to the rear of the Hôtel de Ville, by way of the pretty **Place Vauquelin**, *the continuation of Place Jacques-Cartier.*

The statue of Admiral Jean Vauquelin, defender of Louisbourg at the end of the French Regime, was probably put here to counterbalance the monument to Nelson, a symbol of British control over Canada. Go down the staircase leading to the **Champ-de-Mars**, modified in 1991 in order to reveal some vestiges of the fortifications that once surrounded Montréal. Gaspard Chaussegros de Léry designed Montréal's ramparts, erected between 1717 and 1745, as well as those of Québec City. The walls of Montréal, however, never saw war, as the city's com-

Montréal

mercial calling and its location ruled out such rash acts. The large, tree-lined lawns are reminders of the Champ-de-Mars's former vocation as a parade ground for military manoeuvres up until 1924. A view of the downtown area's skyscrapers opens up through the clearing.

Head back to Rue Notre-Dame.

The humblest of all the "châteaux" built in Montréal, the **Château Ramezay** ★ ★ *($6; summer, every day 10am to 6pm; rest of the year, Tue-Sun 10am to 4:30pm; 280 Rue Notre-Dame Est, Champs-de-Mars métro, ☎861-3708)* is the only one still standing. It was built in 1705 for the governor of Montréal, Claude de Ramezay, and his family. In 1745, it fell into the hands of the Compagnie des Indes Occidentales (The French West Indies Company), which made it its North American headquarters. Precious Canadian furs were stored in its vaults awaiting shipment to France. After the conquest (1760), the British occupied the house, before being temporarily removed by American insurgents who wanted Québec to join the nascent United States. Benjamin Franklin even came to stay at the château for a few months in 1775, in an attempt to convince Montrealers to become American citizens.

In 1896, after serving as the first building of the Montréal branch of the Université Laval in Québec City, the château was converted into a museum, under the patronage of the Société d'Histoire et de Numismatique de Montréal (Montréal Numismatic and Antiquarian Society), founded by Jacques Viger. Visitors will still find a rich collection of furniture, clothing and everyday objects from the 18th and 19th centuries here, as well as

many Aboriginal artefacts. The Salle de Nantes is decorated with beautiful Louis XV-style mahogany panelling, designed by Germain Boffrand and imported from the Nantes office of the Compagnie des Indes (circa 1750).

Walk along Rue Notre-Dame to Rue Berri.

At the corner of Rue Berri lies the **Sir George-Étienne-Cartier National Historic Site** ★ *($4; early Sep to late Dec and early Apr to late May, Wed-Sun 10am to noon and 1pm to 5pm; late May to early Sept 10am to 6pm; closed Jan to Mar; 458 Rue Notre-Dame Est, Champs-de-Mars métro ☎283-2282),* composed of twin houses inhabited successively by George-Étienne Cartier, one of the Fathers of Canadian Confederation. Inside, visitors will find a reconstructed mid-19th-century French Canadian bourgeois home. In summer and at Christmas time, the "museum theatre" invites you to its interactive reconstruction of a formal bourgeois sitting room. Interesting educational soundtracks accompany the tour and add a touch of authenticity to the site. The neighbouring building, at number 452, is the former **Cathédrale Schismatique Grecque Saint-Nicolas**, built around 1910 in the Romanesque-Byzantine Revival style.

Rue Berri marks the eastern border of Old Montréal, and thus the fortified city of the French Regime, beyond which extended the Faubourg Québec, excavated in the 19th century to make way for railroad lines, which explains the sharp difference in height between the hill known as Coteau Saint-Louis and the Viger and Dalhousie stations. **Gare Viger**, visible on the left, was inaugurated by Canadian Pacific in 1895 in order to serve the eastern part of the

country. Its resemblance to the Château Frontenac in Québec City is not merely coincidental; both buildings were designed for the same railroad company and by the same architect, an American named Bruce Price. The Château-style station, closed in 1935, also included a prestigious hotel and large stained-glass train shed that has since been destroyed.

Smaller **Gare Dalhousie**, located near the Maison Cartier *(514 Rue Notre-Dame, Champs-de-Mars métro),* was the first railway station built by Canadian Pacific, a company established for the purpose of building a Canadian transcontinental railroad.

The station was the starting point of the first transcontinental train headed for Vancouver on June 28, 1886. Canadian Pacific seems to have had a weakness for foreign architects, since it was Thomas C. Sorby, Director of Public Works in England, who drew up the plans for this humble structure.

Today, it is used by the École Nationale du Cirque (the National Circus School). From the top of Rue Notre-Dame, the port's former refrigerated warehouse, made of brown brick, is visible, as well as Île Sainte-Hélène, in the middle of the river. This island, along with Île Notre-Dame, was the site of the Expo '67.

Turn right on Rue Berri, and right again on Rue Saint-Paul, which offers a lovely view of the dome of the Marché Bonsecours. Continue straight ahead to Chapelle Notre-Dame-de-Bonsecours.

This site was originally occupied by another chapel, built in 1657 upon the recommendation of Saint Marguerite Bourgeoys, founder of the congregation of Notre-Dame.

The present **Chapelle Notre-Dame-de-Bonsecours** ★ *(400 Rue St-Paul Est, Champs-de-Mars métro)* dates back to 1771, when the Sulpicians wanted to establish a branch of the main parish in the eastern part of the fortified city. In 1890, the chapel was modified to suit contemporary tastes, and the present stone façade was added, along with the "aerial" chapel looking out on the port. Parishioners asked God's blessing on ships and their crews bound for Europe from this chapel.

The interior, redone at the same time, contains a large number of votive offerings from sailors saved from shipwrecks. Some are in the form of model ships, hung from the ceiling of the nave.

Between 1996 and 1998, excavations below the chapel's nave uncovered several artifacts, including some dating from the colony's early days. Today, the **Musée Marguerite-Bourgeoys** ★ *($6; May to Oct every day 10am to 5pm, Nov to mid-Jan every day 11am to 3:30pm, mid-Mar to late Apr 11am to 5pm, closed mid-Jan to mid-Mar; 400 Rue St-Paul Est, ☎282-8670)* displays these interesting archaeological finds. But there is even more to explore: adjoining the Notre-Dame-de-Bon-Secours chapel, it leads from the top of the tower, where the view is breathtaking, to the depths of the crypt, where the old stones tell their own story. Learn about the life of Marguerite Bourgeoys, a pioneer of education in Québec, admire her portrait and discover the mystery surrounding her. In summer, from Thursday to Sunday, a play is presented twice a day in the crypt (in English at 1:30pm and in French at 3:30pm). Four actors retell the history of the chapel and the colony by bringing to life a wide array of historic figures.

The **Maison Pierre-du-Calvet**, at the corner of Rue Bonsecours *(number 401)*, is representative of 18th-century French urban architecture adapted to the local setting, with thick walls made of fieldstone embedded in mortar, storm windows doubling the casement windows with their little squares of glass imported from France, and high firebreak walls, then required by local regulations as a means of limiting the spread of fire from one building to the next. The building houses one of the best inns in Montréal: **L'Hostellerie et Restaurant Pierre du Calvet 1725** (see p 124 and p 130).

A little higher on Rue Bonsecours, visitors will find the **Maison Papineau** *(440 Rue Bonsecours, Champs-de-Mars métro)* inhabited long ago by Louis-Joseph Papineau (1786-1871), lawyer, politician and head of the French Canadian nationalist movement up until the insurrection of 1837. Built in 1785 and covered with a wooden facing made to look like cut stone, it was one of the first buildings in Old Montréal to be restored (1962).

The **Marché Bonsecours** ★ ★ *(350 Rue St-Paul Est)* was erected between 1845 and 1850. The lovely grey stone neoclassical edifice with sash windows is on **Rue Saint-Paul**, for many years Montréal's main commercial artery. The building is adorned with a portico supported by cast iron columns moulded in England, and topped by a silvery dome, which for many years served as the symbol of the city at the entrance to the port. The public market, closed since the early 1960s following the advent of the supermarket, was transformed into municipal offices, then an exhibition hall before finally reopening partially in 1996.

It now presents an exhibition and is host to arts and crafts shops. The building originally housed both the city hall and a concert hall upstairs. The market's old storehouses, recently renovated, can be seen on Rue Saint-Paul. From the large balcony on Rue de la Commune you can see the partially reconstructed Bonsecours dock, where paddle-wheelers, full of farmers who came to the city to sell their produce, used to moor.

Walk to Place Jacques-Cartier, then turn left, toward the old port.

At the southern end of Place Jacques-Cartier rise the multiple metallic points of the **Pavillon Jacques-Cartier**. Inside you'll find a cafeteria and terrace-bar, as well as a promenade extending all the way to the southeastern edge of the pier upon which the pavilion stands.

The **Tour de l'Horloge** ★ *(at the end of the Quai de l'Horloge; May to Oct)* is visible to the east from the end of Quai Jacques-Cartier. Painted a pale yellow, the structure is actually a monument erected in 1922 in memory of merchant marine sailors who died during WWI. It was inaugurated by the Prince of Wales (who became Edward VIII) during one of his many visits to Montréal. An observatory at the top of the tower provides a clear view of Île Sainte-Hélène, the Jacques-Cartier bridge and the eastern part of Old Montréal. Standing on Place Belvédère at the base of the tower, one has the impression of standing on the deck of ship as it glides slowly down the St. Lawrence and out to the Atlantic Ocean.

To return to the métro, walk back up Place Jacques-Cartier, cross Rue Notre-Dame, Place Vauquelin and finally Champ-de-Mars, to the station of the same name.

Montréal

Tour B: Downtown

The downtown skyscrapers give Montréal a typically North American look. Nevertheless, unlike most other cities on the continent, there is a certain Latin spirit here, which seeps in between the towering buildings, livening up this part of Montréal both day and night. Bars, cafés, department stores, shops and head offices, along with two universities and numerous colleges, all lie clustered within a limited area at the foot of Mont Royal.

At the beginning of the 20th century, Montréal's central business district gradually shifted from the old city to what was up until then a posh residential neighbourhood known as The Golden Square Mile, inhabited by upper-class Canadians. Wide arterial streets such as Boulevard René-Lévesque (then known as Dorchester Street) were then lined with palatial residences surrounded by shady gardens. The city centre underwent a radical transformation in a very short time (1960-1967), marked by the construction of Place Ville-Marie, the métro, the underground city, Place des Arts, and various other infrastructures which still exert an influence on the area's development.

Walk up on Rue Guy from the exit of the Guy-Concordia métro station, then turn right on Rue Sherbrooke.

In addition to being invaded by the business world, the Golden Square Mile also underwent profound social changes that altered its character: the exodus of the Scottish population, the shortage of servants, income taxes, World War I, during which the sons of many of these families were killed, and above all the stock market crash of 1929, which ruined many businessmen. Consequently, numerous mansions were demolished and the remaining population had to adjust to more modest living conditions. **The Linton ★** *(1509 Rue Sherbrooke Ouest, Guy-Concordia métro)*, a prestigious apartment building erected in 1907, provided an interesting alternative. It was built on the grounds of the house of the same name still visible in the back, on little Rue Simpson. The façade of the Linton is adorned with lavish Beaux-Arts details made of terracotta and a beautiful cast-iron marquee.

The lovely presbyterian **Church of St. Andrew and St. Paul ★★** *(at the corner of Rue Redpath, Guy-Concordia métro)* was one of the most important institutions of the Scottish elite in Montréal. Built in 1932 according to plans by architect Harold Lea Fetherstonaugh as the community's third place of worship, it illustrates the endurance of the medieval style in religious architecture. The stone interior is graced with magnificent commemorative stained-glass windows. Those along the aisles came from the second church and are for the most part significant British pieces, such as the windows of Andrew Allan and his wife, produced by the workshop of William Morris after sketches by the famous English Pre-Raphaelite painter, Edward Burne-Jones. The

Scottish-Canadian Black Watch Regiment has been affiliated with the church ever since it was created in 1862.

The **Musée des Beaux-Arts de Montréal / Montreal Museum of Fine Arts** *(free admission for the permanent collection; $12 for temporary exhibitions, half-price Wed 5:30pm to 9pm; open Wed-Sun 11am to 6pm, Wed until 9pm; 1380 Sherbrooke O., Guy-Concordia métro, ☎285-2000)*, Montréal's Museum of Fine Arts is the oldest and largest museum in Québec. It was founded in 1860 by the Art Association of Montréal, a group of Anglo-Saxon art lovers.

The Pavillon Beniah-Gibb, on the north side of Rue Sherbrooke *(1379 Rue Sherbrooke Ouest)*, opened its doors in 1912. Its facade, made of white Vermont marble, is the work of the Scottish merchants' favourite architects, the prolific Edward and William Sutherland Maxwell. The building became too small for the museum's collection and was enlarged towards the back on three different occasions. Finally, in 1991, architect Moshe Safdie designed the Pavillon Jean-Noël-Desmarais, just opposite on the south side of Rue Sherbrooke. This new wing includes the red brick facade of a former apartment building and is linked to the original building by tunnels under

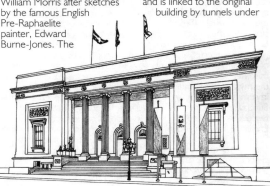

Montreal Museum of Fine Arts

Rue Sherbrooke. The museum's main entrance is now in the new wing, at the corner of Rue Crescent.

The small **Musée des Arts Décoratifs de Montréal / Museum of Decorative Arts** ★ moved to the the Pavillon Jean-Noël-Desmarais of the Montreal Museum of Fine Arts in 1997 and it is now part of the museum's permanent collection. Its new location was designed by architect Frank Gehry, and the white walls combined with the wood floor make the place seem more spacious, fully accentuating the works on display. The museum hosts temporary exhibitions of pieces by designers from here and abroad. The museum's permanent collection is made up of furniture and decorative objects in the International Style (from 1935 on) donated by Liliane and David Stewart.

Erected in 1892, the **Erskine & American United Church** ★ *(at the corner of Avenue du Musée)* is an excellent example of the Romanesque Revival style as interpreted by American architect Henry Hobson Richardson. The textured sandstone, large arches flanked by either squat or disproportionately elongated columns, and sequences of small, arched openings are typical of the style. The auditorium-shaped interior was remodelled in the style of the Chicago School in 1937. The lower chapel (along Avenue du Musée), contains lovely, brilliantly coloured, Tiffany stained-glass windows.

Rue Crescent ★ *(Guy-Concordia métro)*, located immediately east of the museum, has a split personality. To the north of Boulevard de Maisonneuve, the street is lined with old row houses, which now accommodate antique shops and luxury boutiques, while to the south, it is crowded with night clubs,

restaurants and bars, most with sunny terraces lining the sidewalks. For many years, Rue Crescent was known as the English counterpart of Rue Saint-Denis. Though it is still a favourite among American visitors, its clientele is more diversified now.

A symbol of its era, **Le Château** ★ *(1321 Rue Sherbrooke Ouest, Guy-Concordia métro)*, a handsome Château-style building, was erected in 1925 for a French Canadian businessman by the name of Pamphile du Tremblay, owner of the French-language newspaper *La Presse*. Architects Ross and Macdonald designed what was at the time the largest apartment building in Canada. The Royal Institute awarded these architects a prize for the design of the fashionable **Holt Renfrew** *(1300 Rue Sherbrooke Ouest)* store which stands across the street in 1937. With its rounded, horizontal lines, the store is a fine example of the Streamlined Art Deco style.

The last of Montréal's old hotels, the **Ritz-Carlton** ★ *(1228 Rue Sherbrooke Ouest, Guy-Concordia or Peel métro)* was inaugurated in 1911 by César Ritz himself. For many years, it was the favourite gathering place of the Montréal bourgeoisie. Some people even stayed here year-round, living a life of luxury among the drawing rooms, garden and ballroom. The building was designed by Warren and Wetmore of New York City, the well-known architects of Grand Central Station on New York's Park Avenue. Many celebrities have stayed at this sophisticated luxury hotel over the years, including Richard Burton and Elizabeth Taylor, who were married here in 1964.

Continue along Rue Sherbrooke to the entrance of Maison Alcan. Three note-

worthy buildings lie across the street. **Maison Baxter** *(1201 Rue Sherbrooke Ouest, Peel métro)*, on the left, boasts a beautiful stairway. **Maison Forget** *(1195 Rue Sherbrooke Ouest, Peel métro)*, in the centre, was built in 1882 for Louis-Joseph Forget, one of the only French Canadian magnates to live in this neighbourhood during the 19th century. The building on the right is the **Mount Royal Club**, a private club frequented essentially by business people. Built in 1905, it is the work of Stanford White of the famous New York firm McKim, Mead and White, architects of the head office of the Bank of Montréal on Place d'Armes (see p 80).

Maison Alcan ★ *(1188 Rue Sherbrooke Ouest, Peel métro)*, head office of the Alcan aluminum company, is a fine example of historical preservation and inventive urban restructuring. Five buildings along Rue Sherbrooke, including the lovely **Maison Atholstan** *(1172 Rue Sherbrooke Ouest)*, the first Beaux-Arts–style structure erected in Montréal (1894), have been carefully restored and joined in the back to an atrium, which is linked to a modern aluminum building. The garden running along the south wall of the modern part provides a little-known passageway between Rue Drummond and Rue Stanley.

Enter the atrium through the Sherbrooke entrance, which used to lead into the lobby of the Berkeley Hotel. Exit through the garden, go to the left and head south on Rue Stanley. Turn left on Boulevard de Maisonneuve, then right on Rue Peel.

Montréal has the most extensive **underground city** in the world. Greatly appreciated in bad weather, it provides access to more than 2,000 shops and restaurants, as well

Montréal

as movie theatres, apartment and office buildings, hotels, parking lots, the train station, the bus station, Place des Arts and even the Université du Québec à Montréal (UQAM) via tunnels, atriums and indoor plazas.

Les **Cours Mont-Royal** ★★ *(1455 Rue Peel, Peel métro)* are duly linked to this sprawling network, which centres around the various métro stations. A multi-purpose complex, Les Cours consists of four levels of stores, offices and apartments laid out inside the former Mount Royal Hotel. With its 1,100 rooms, this Jazz Age palace, inaugurated in 1922, was the largest hotel in the British Empire. Aside from the exterior, all that was preserved during the 1987 remodelling was a portion of the ceiling of the lobby, from which the former chandelier of the Monte Carlo casino is suspended. The four 10-story *cours* (inner courts) are defi-

nitely worth a visit, as is a stroll through what may be the best-designed shopping centre in the downtown area. The building that looks like a small Scottish manor across the street is in fact the head office of the Seagram Company (Barton & Guestier wines).

Head south on Rue Peel to Square Dorchester.

At Montreal's tourist office, the **Centre Infotouriste** *(1001 Rue du Square-Dorchester, Peel métro)*, visitors will find representatives from a number of tourist-related enterprises, such as tourist information offices, Greyhound bus company, the Le Réseau hotel-reservation service and Ulysses Travel Bookshop.

From 1799 to 1854, **Square Dorchester** ★ *(Peel métro)* was occupied by Montréal's Catholic cemetery, which was then moved to Mont Royal, where it is still located. In

1872, the city turned the free space into two squares, one on either side of Dorchester Street (now Boulevard René-Lévesque). The northern portion is called Square Dorchester, while the southern part was renamed Place du Canada to commemorate the 100th anniversary of Confederation (1967).

A number of monuments adorn Square Dorchester. In the centre, there is an equestrian statue dedicated to Canadian soldiers who died during the Boer War in South Africa, while around the perimeter stand a handsome statue of Scottish poet Robert Burns styled after Bartholdi's Roaring Lion and donated by the Sun Life insurance company, and Émile Brunet's monument to Sir Wilfrid Laurier, Prime Minister of Canada from 1896 to 1911. The square also serves as the starting point for guided bus tours.

● **ATTRACTIONS**

1.	The Linton	13.	Place du Canada	26.	Centre Eaton
2.	Church of St. Andrew and St. Paul	14.	St. George's Anglican Church	27.	Christ Church Cathedral
3.	Musée des Beaux-Arts de Montréal / Montréal Museum of Fine Arts	15.	Tour IBM-Marathon	28.	Square Phillips
		16.	Gare Windsor / Windsor Station	29.	La Baie / The Bay
				30.	St. James United Church
4.	Erskine & American United Church	17.	Centre Bell / Bell Centre	31.	Église du Gesù
		18.	Marriott Château Champlain	32.	St. Patrick's Basilica
5.	Rue Crescent	19.	Planétarium de Montréal	33.	Musée d'Art Contemporain de Montréal
6.	Le Château	20.	1000 de la Gauchetière		
7.	Maison Alcan	21.	Cathédrale Marie-Reine-du-Monde	34.	Place des Arts
8.	Cours Mont-Royal			35.	Complexe Desjardins
9.	Centre Infotouriste	22.	Place Bonaventure	36.	Monument National
10.	Square Dorchester	23.	Place Ville-Marie	37.	Chinatown
11.	Windsor	24.	Place Montréal Trust	38.	Palais des Congrès de Montréal
12.	Édifice Sun Life	25.	Tour BNP		

○ **ACCOMMODATIONS**

1.	Auberge de Jeunesse	7.	Hôtel du Nouveau Forum	14.	Manoir Ambrose
2.	Château Versailles	8.	Hôtel Le Germain	15.	McGill University
3.	Fairmont The Queen Elizabeth	9.	Hôtel Renaissance Montréal	16.	Novotel Montréal Centre
		10.	Hôtel Wyndham Montréal	17.	Ritz-Carlton (R)
4.	Hilton Montréal Bonaventure	11.	L'Abri du Voyageur		
5.	Hôtel Casa Bella	12.	Le Centre Sheraton	(R) establishment with restaurant (see description)
6.	Hôtel de la Montagne (R)	13.	Loews Hôtel Vogue		

● **RESTAURANTS**

1.	Altitude 737	8.	Jardin Sakura	15.	Marché Mövenpick
2.	Ben's Delicatessen	9.	Julien	16.	Mr Ma
3.	Biddle's Jazz and Ribs	10.	L'Actuel	17.	Parchemin
4.	Brûlerie Saint-Denis	11.	Le Commensal	18.	Piment Rouge
5.	Café du Nouveau Monde	12.	Le Paris	19.	Troïka
6.	Chez Georges	13.	Les Caprices de Nicolas	20.	Wienstein 'n' Gavino's Pasta Bar Factory Co.
7.	Desjardins Sea Food	14.	Mangia		

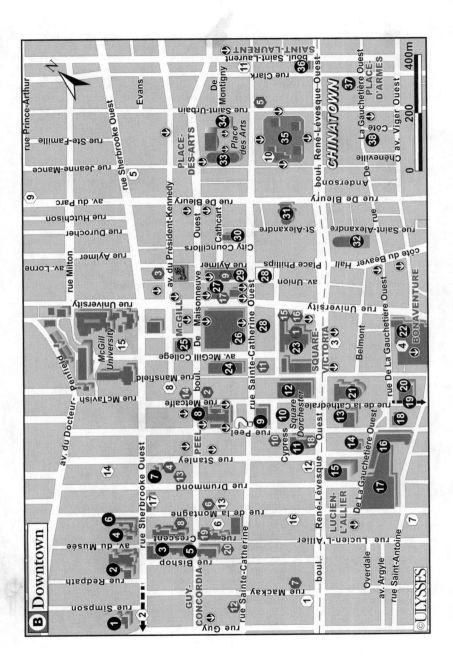

The **Windsor** ★ *(1170 Rue Peel, Peel métro)*, the hotel where members of the royal family used to stay during their visits to Canada, no longer exists. The prestigious Second Empire–style edifice, built in 1878 by architect W. W. Boyington of Chicago, was claimed by fire in 1957. All that remains of it is an annex erected in 1906, which was converted into an office building in 1986. The ballrooms and lovely Peacock Alley have, however, been preserved. An impressive atrium, visible from the upper floors, has been constructed for the building's tenants. The handsome **Tour CIBC**, designed by Peter Dickinson (1962), stands on the site of the old hotel. Its walls are faced with green slate, which blends harmoniously with the dominant colours of the buildings around the square, the greyish beige of stone and the green of oxidized copper.

The **Édifice Sun Life** ★ ★ *(1155 Rue Metcalfe, Peel métro)*, erected between 1913 and 1933 for the powerful Sun Life insurance company, was for many years the largest building in the British Empire. It was in this "fortress" of the Anglo-Saxon establishment, with its colonnades reminiscent of ancient mythology, that the British Crown Jewels were hidden during World War II. In 1977, the company's head office was moved to Toronto, in protest against provincial language laws excluding English. Fortunately, the chimes that ring at 5pm every day are still in place and remain an integral part of the neighbourhood's spirit.

Place du Canada ★ *(Bonaventure métro)*, the southern portion of Square Dorchester, is the setting for the annual Remembrance Day ceremony (November 11th), which honours Canadian soldiers killed in the two World Wars and in the Korean War. Veterans reunite around the War Memorial, which occupies the place of honour in the centre of the square. A more imposing monument to Sir John A. Macdonald, Canada's first Prime Minister, elected in 1867, stands alongside Boulevard René-Lévesque.

A number of churches clustered around Square Dorchester before it was even laid out in 1872. Unfortunately, only two of the eight churches built in the area between 1865 and 1875 have survived. One of these is the beautiful Gothic Revival–style **St. George's Anglican Church** ★ ★ *(at the corner of Rue de la Gauchetière and Rue Peel, Bonaventure métro)*. Its delicately sculpted sandstone exterior conceals an interior covered with lovely, dark woodwork. Particularly noteworthy are the remarkable ceiling, with its exposed framework, the woodwork in the chancel, and the tapestry from Westminster Abbey, used during the coronation of Elizabeth II.

The elegant 47-storey **Tour IBM-Marathon** ★ *(1250 Boulevard René-Lévesque Ouest, Bonaventure métro)*, forming part of the backdrop of St. George's, was completed in 1991 according to a design by the famous New York architects Kohn, Pedersen and Fox. Its winter bamboo garden is open to the public.

In 1887, the head of Canadian Pacific, William Cornelius Van Horne, asked his New York friend Bruce Price (1845-1903) to draw up the plans for **Gare Windsor / Windsor Station** ★ *(at the corner of Rue de la Gauchetière and Rue Peel, Bonaventure métro)*, a modern train station that would serve as the terminus of the transcontinental railroad, completed the previous year. At the time, Price was one of the most prominent architects in the eastern United States, where he worked on residential projects for high-society clients, as well as skyscrapers like the American Surety Building in Manhattan. Later, he was put in charge of building the Château Frontenac in Québec City, thus establishing the Château style in Canada.

Massive-looking Gare Windsor, with its corner buttresses, Roman arches outlined in the stone, and series of arcades, is Montréal's best example of the Romanesque Revival style as interpreted by American architect Henry Hobson Richardson. Its construction established the city as the country's railway centre and initiated the shift of commercial and financial activity from the old town to the Golden Square Mile. Abandoned in favour of the Gare Centrale after World War II, Windsor Station was used only for commuter trains up until 1993. Today, the Gare Windsor houses many stores and offices.

The **Centre Bell / Bell Centre** *(1250 Rue de la Gauchetière Ouest, Bonaventure métro)*, built on the platforms of Windsor Station, now blocks all train access to the venerable old station. Opened in 1996 (when it was called the Molson Center), this immense oddly shaped building succeeds the Forum on Sainte-Catherine as the home ice of the National Hockey League's Montréal Canadiens. The amphitheatre can seat 21,247 people and boasts 138 glassed-in private boxes sold to Montréal companies for hefty sums. The National Hockey League's regular season runs from October to April, and the play-offs can carry on into June. Big-name musical acts perform at the centre.

Guided tours *($8; English tour at 11:15am and*

2:45pm, 75 min; ☎*989-2841)* of the centre are available. These include, when possible, a visit to the Canadiens' dressing room and a chance to see the team practise.

Built in 1966, the **Marriott Château Champlain ★** *(1 Place du Canada, Bonaventure métro)*, nicknamed the "cheese grater" by Montrealers due to its many arched, convex openings, was designed by Québec architects Jean-Paul Pothier and Roger D'Astou. The latter is a disciple of American architect Frank Lloyd Wright, with whom he studied for several years. The hotel is not unlike some of the master's late works, characterized by rounded, fluid lines.

The **Planétarium de Montréal ★** *($6.50; Jun to Sep, every day 1:15pm to 3:45pm and 8:30pm; early Sep to late Jun, Tue-Sun, 1:15pm to 3:45pm, Thu-Sun 8:30; presentations last 45min; 1000 Rue St-Jacques Ouest, Bonaventure métro,* ☎*872-4530)* projects astronomy films onto a 20m hemispheric dome. The universe and its mysteries are explained in a way that makes this marvellous, often poorly understood world accessible to all. Guest lecturers provide commentaries on the presentations.

Tour **1000 de la Gauchetière** *(1000 Rue de la Gauchetière, Bonaventure métro)*, a 51-storey skyscraper, was completed in 1992. It houses the terminus for buses linking Montréal to the South Shore, as well as the **Amphithéâtre Bell** an indoor skating rink open year-round *($5, skate rentals $4.50; schedule changes frequently, call* ☎*395-0555)*. The architects wanted to set the building apart from its neighbours by crowning it with a copper-covered point. Its total height is the maximum allowed by the city, namely the height of

Mont Royal. The ultimate symbol of Montréal, the mountain may be not surpassed under any circumstances.

Cathédrale Marie-Reine-du-Monde ★★ *(Boulevard René-Lévesque Ouest at the corner of Mansfield, Bonaventure métro)* is the seat of the archdiocese of Montréal and a reminder of the tremendous power wielded by the clergy up until the Quiet Revolution. It is exactly one third the size of St. Peter's in Rome. In 1852, a terrible fire destroyed the Catholic cathedral on Rue Saint-Denis. The ambitious Monseigneur Ignace Bourget (1799-1885), who was bishop of Montréal at the time, seized the opportunity to work out a grandiose scheme to outshine the Sulpicians' Basilique Notre-Dame and ensure the supremacy of the Catholic Church in Montréal. What could accomplish these goals better than a replica of Rome's St. Peter's, right in the middle of the Protestant neighbourhood?

Despite reservations on the part of architect Victor Bourgeau, the plan was carried out. The bishop even sent Bourgeau to Rome to measure the venerable building. Construction began in 1870 and was finally completed in 1894. Copper statues of the 13 patron saints of Montréal's parishes were installed in 1900.

Modernized during the 1950s, the interior of the cathedral is no longer as harmonious as it once was. Nevertheless, there is a lovely replica of Bernini's baldaquin, executed by sculptor Victor Vincent. The bishops and archbishops of Montréal are interred in the mortuary chapel on the left, where the place of honour is occupied by the recumbent statue of Monseigneur Bourget. A monument outside

reminds visitors yet again of this individual, who did so much to strengthen the bonds between France and Canada.

An immense, grooved concrete block with no façade, **Place Bonaventure ★** *(1 Place Bonaventure, Bonaventure métro)*, which was completed in 1966, is one of the most revolutionary works of modern architecture of its time. Designed by Montrealer Raymond Affleck, it is a multi-purpose complex built on top of the railway lines leading into the Gare Centrale. It contains a parking area, a two-level shopping centre linked to the métro and the underground city, two large exhibition halls, wholesalers, offices, and an intimate 400-room hotel laid out around a charming hanging garden, worth a short visit.

Place Bonaventure is linked to the métro station of the same name, designed by architect Victor Prus (1964). With its brown-brick facing and bare concrete vaults, the station looks like an early Christian basilica. The **Montréal métro** system has a total of 65 stations divided up among four lines used by trains running on rubber wheels (see map of métro, at the beginning of this chapter). Each station has a different design, some very elaborate.

A railway tunnel leading under Mont Royal to the downtown area was built in 1913. The tracks ran under Avenue McGill College, then multiplied at the bottom of a deep trench, which stretched between Rue Mansfield and Rue University. In 1938, the subterranean **Gare Centrale** was built, marking the true starting point of the underground city. Camouflaged since 1957 by the **Hôtel Reine-Elizabeth**, the Queen Elizabeth Hotel, it has an interesting, Streamlined Art Deco waiting hall.

Montréal

Place Ville-Marie ★ ★ ★
(1 Place Ville-Marie, Bona-
venture métro), was erected
above the northern part of the
formerly open-air trench in
1959. The famous Chinese-
American architect Ieoh Ming
Pei (Louvre Pyramid, Paris;
East Building of the National
Gallery, Washington, D.C.)
designed the multipurpose
complex built over the railway
tracks and containing vast
shopping arcades now linked
to most of the surrounding
edifices. It also encompasses a
number of office buildings,
including the famous cruciform
aluminum tower, whose un-
usual shape enables natural
light to penetrate all the way
into the centre of the structure, while at the same time
symbolizing Montréal, a Catholic city dedicated to the Virgin
Mary.

In the middle of the public
area, a granite compass card
indicates true north, while
Avenue McGill College, which
leads straight toward the
mountain, indicates "north" as
perceived by Montrealers in
their everyday life. This artery,
lined with multicoloured skyscrapers, was still a narrow
residential street in 1950. It
now offers a wide view of
Mont Royal, crowned by a
metallic cross erected in
1927 to commemorate the
gesture of Paul Chomedey de
Maisonneuve, founder of
Montréal, who climbed the
mountain in January 1643 and
placed a wooden cross at its
summit to thank the Virgin
Mary for having spared Fort
Ville-Marie from a devastating
flood.

Cross Place Ville-Marie and
take Avenue McGill College.

Avenue McGill College was
widened and entirely redesigned during the 1980s.
Walking along it, visitors will
see several examples of eclectic, polychromatic postmodern
architecture composed largely
of granite and reflective glass.

Place Montréal Trust *(at the*
corner of Rue Ste-Catherine,
McGill métro) is one of a
number of Montréal shopping
centres topped by an office
building and linked to the
underground city and the
métro by corridors and private
plazas.

The **Tour BNP ★** *(1981 Ave-*
nue McGill College, McGill
métro), certainly the best
designed building on Avenue
McGill College, was built for
the Banque Nationale de Paris
in 1981, by the architectural
firm Webb, Zerafa, Menkès,
Housden Partnership (Tour
Elf-Aquitaine, Paris; Royal
Bank, Toronto). Its bluish glass
walls set off a sculpture entitled *La Foule Illuminée* (The
Illuminated Crowd), by the
Franco-British artist Raymond
Mason.

Return to Rue Sainte-
Catherine Ouest.

Rue Sainte-Catherine is
Montréal's main commercial
artery. It stretches 15km,
changing in appearance several times along the way.
Around 1870, it was still
lined with row houses; by
1920, however, it had al-
ready become an integral
part of life in Montréal. Since
the 1960s, a num-
ber of shopping
centres linking
the street to
the adjacent
métro lines
have
sprouted up

among the local businesses.
The **Centre Eaton** *(Rue Ste-*
Catherine Ouest, McGill
métro) is the most recent of
these. It is composed of a
long, old-fashioned gallery
lined with five levels of shops,
restaurants and movie theatres, and is it's now linked to
Place Ville-Marie by a pedestrian tunnel.

The **Eaton** department store
(677 Rue Ste-Catherine Ouest,
McGill métro), one of the
largest department stores on
Ste-Catherine and an institution across Canada, went
bankrupt and had to close its
doors in 1999. The imposing
nine-storey building now
houses another department
store, Les Ailes de la Mode. Its
magnificent Art Deco dining
room on the 9th floor, designed by Jacques Carlu and
completed in 1931, is a historic monument, but not
currently open to the public.

The first Anglican cathedral in
Montréal stood on Rue
Notre-Dame, not far from
Place d'Armes. After a fire
in 1856, **Christ Church**
Cathedral ★ ★ *(at the*
corner of Rue University,
McGill métro) was relo-
cated nearer the commu-
nity it served, in the heart
of the nascent
Golden
Square Mile.
Using the
cathedral of
his home-
town,
Salisbury,

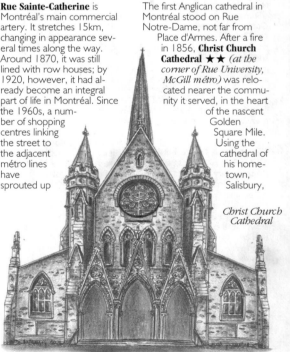

Christ Church
Cathedral

as his model, architect Frank Wills designed a flamboyant structure, with a single steeple rising above the transepts. The plain interior contrasts with the rich ornamentation of the Catholic churches included in this walking tour. A few beautiful stained-glass windows from the workshops of William Morris provide the only bit of colour.

The steeple's stone spire was destroyed in 1927 and replaced by an aluminum replica; otherwise, it would have eventually caused the building to sink. The problem, linked to the instability of the foundation, was not resolved, however, until a shopping centre, the Promenades de la Cathédrale, was constructed under the building in 1987. Christ Church Anglican Cathedral thus rests on the roof of a shopping mall. On the same occasion, a postmodern glass skyscraper topped by a "crown of thorns" was erected behind the cathedral. There is a pleasant little garden at its base.

It was around **Square Phillips** ★ *(at the corner of Rue Union, on either side of Rue Ste-Catherine, McGill métro)* that the first stores appeared along Rue Sainte-Catherine, which was once strictly residential.

Henry Morgan moved Morgan's Colonial House, now **La Baie / the Bay**, *(McGill métro)* here after the floods of 1886 in the old city. Henry Birks, descendant of a long line of English jewellers, arrived soon after, establishing his famous shop in a handsome beige sandstone building on the west side of the square. In 1914, a monument to King Edward VII, sculpted by Philippe Hébert, was erected in the centre of Square Phillips. Downtown shoppers and employees alike enjoy relaxing here.

A former Methodist church designed in the shape of an auditorium, **St. James United Church** *(463 Rue Ste-Catherine Ouest, McGill métro)* originally had a complete façade looking out onto a garden. In 1926, in an effort to counter the decrease in its revenue, the community built a group of stores and offices along the front of the building on Rue Sainte-Catherine, leaving only a narrow passageway into the church. Visitors can still see the two Gothic Revival– style steeples set back from Rue Sainte-Catherine.

Turn right on Rue de Bleury.

After a 40-year absence, the Jesuits returned to Montréal in 1842 at Monseigneur Ignace Bourget's invitation. Six years later, they founded Collège Sainte-Marie, where several generations of boys would receive an outstanding education. **Église du Gesù** ★ ★ *(1202 Rue de Bleury, Place-des-Arts métro)* was originally designed as the college chapel. The grandiose project begun in 1864 according to plans drawn up by architect Patrick C. Keely of Brooklyn, New York, was never completed, due to lack of funds. Consequently, the church's Renaissance Revival–style towers remain unfinished. The *trompe-l'œil* decor inside was executed by artist Damien Müller. Of particular interest are the seven main altars and surrounding parquetry, all fine examples of cabinet work. The large paintings hanging from the walls were commissioned from the Gagliardi brothers of Rome. The Jesuit college, erected to the south of the church, was demolished in 1975, but the church was fortunately saved, and then restored in 1983.

Visitors can take a short side-trip to St. Patrick's Basilica. To do so, head south on Rue de Bleury. Turn right on Boulevard René-Lévesque, then left

on little Rue Saint-Alexandre. Enter the church through one of the side entrances.

Fleeing misery and potato blight, a large number of Irish immigrants came to Montréal between 1820 and 1860, and helped construct the Lachine Canal and the Victoria bridge. **St. Patrick's Basilica** ★ ★ *(460 Boul. René- lévesque O., Place-des-Arts métro)*, was thus built to meet a pressing new demand for a church to serve the Irish Catholic community. When it was inaugurated in 1847, St. Patrick's dominated the city below. Today, it is well hidden by the skyscrapers of the business centre. Architect Pierre-Louis Morin and Père Félix Martin, the Jesuit superior, designed the plans for the edifice, built in the Gothic Revival style favoured by the Sulpicians, who financed the project. One of the many paradoxes surrounding St. Patrick's is that it is more representative of French than Anglo-Saxon Gothic architecture. The high, newly restored interior is spectacular in pale green, pink and gold. Each of the pine columns that divide the nave into three sections is a whole tree trunk, carved in one piece. The entire roof was recently redone and its brilliant copper has not yet dulled to green. Even a brief visit will leave you speechless.

Head back to Rue Sainte-Catherine Ouest.

Formerly located at Cité du Havre, the **Musée d'Art Contemporain de Montréal** ★ ★ *($6; free admission Wed 6pm to 9pm; Tue-Sun 11am to 6pm; 185 Rue Ste-Catherine Ouest, at the corner of Rue Jeanne-Mance, Place-des-Arts métro, ☎847-6226)*, Montréal's modern art museum, was moved to this site in 1992. The long, low building, erected on top of the Place des Arts parking lot, contains eight rooms,

Montréal

where post-1940 works of art from both Québec and abroad are exhibited. The interior, which has a decidedly better design than the exterior, is laid out around a circular hall. On the lower level, an amusing metal sculpture by Pierre Granche entitled *Comme si le temps... de la rue* (As if time... from the street), shows Montréal's network of streets crowded with helmeted birds, in a sort of semicircular theatre.

During the rush of the Quiet Revolution, the government of Québec, inspired by cultural complexes like New York's Lincoln Center, built **Place des Arts** ★ *(175 rue Ste-Catherine Ouest, Place-des-Arts métro)*, a collection of five halls for the performing arts. Salle Wilfrid Pelletier, in the centre, was inaugurated in 1963 (2,982 seats). It accommodates both the Montreal Symphony Orchestra and the Opéra de Montréal. The cube-shaped Théâtre Maisonneuve, on the right, contains three theatres, Théâtre Maisonneuve (1,460 seats), Théâtre Jean-Duceppe (755 seats) and the intimate little Café de la Place (138 seats). The Cinquième Salle (350 seats) was built in 1992 in the course of the construction of the Musée d'Art Contemporain. Place des Arts is linked to the governmental section of the underground city, which stretches from the Palais des Congrès convention centre to Avenue du Président-Kennedy. Developed by the various levels of government, this portion of the underground network distinguishes itself from the private section, cen-

tred around Place Ville-Marie, farther west.

Since 1976, the head office of the Fédération des Caisses Populaires Desjardins, the credit union, has been located in the vast **Complexe Desjardins** ★ *(Rue Ste-Catherine Ouest, Place-des-Arts métro)*, which houses a large number of government offices as well. The building's large atrium surrounded by shops is very popular during the winter months. A variety of shows are presented in this space, also used for recording television programmes.

Chinatown gate

The tour now leaves the former Golden Square Mile and enters the area around **Boulevard Saint-Laurent**. At the end of the 18th century, the Faubourg Saint-Laurent grew up along the street of the same name, which led inland from the river. In 1792, the city was officially divided into east and west sections, with this artery marking the boundary. Then, in the early 20th century, the

addresses of east-west streets were reassigned so that they all began at Boulevard Saint-Laurent. Meanwhile, around 1880, French Canadian high society came up with the idea of turning the boulevard into the "Champs-Élysées" of Montréal.

The west side was destroyed in order to make the street wider and to reconstruct new buildings in Richardson's Romanesque Revival style, which was in fashion at the end of the 19th century. Populated by the successive waves of immigrants, who arrived at the port, Boulevard Saint-Laurent never attained the heights of glory anticipated by its developers. The section between Boulevard René-Lévesque and Boulevard de Maisonneuve did, however, become the hub of Montréal nightlife in the early 20th century. The city's big theatres, like the Français, where Sarah Bernhardt performed, were located around here. During the Prohibition era (1919-1930), the area became run-down. Every week, thousands of Americans came here to frequent the cabarets and brothels, which abounded in this neighbourhood up until the end of the 1950s.

Turn right on Boulevard Saint-Laurent.

Erected in 1893 for the Société Saint-Jean-Baptiste, which is devoted to protecting the rights of French-speakers, the **Monument National** ★ *(1182 Boulevard St-Laurent, Saint-Laurent métro)* was intended to be a cultural centre dedicated to the French Canadian cause. It offered business courses, became the favourite platform of political orators and presented shows of a religious nature. However, during the 1940s, it also hosted cabaret shows and plays, launching the careers of a number of Québec performers, including Olivier Guimond Senior and Junior. The building was sold to the National Theatre School of Canada in 1971. As Canada's oldest theatre, it was artfully restored for its 100th anniversary.

Cross Boulevard René-Lévesque, then turn right on Rue de la Gauchetière.

Montréal's **Chinatown ★** *(Rue de la Gauchetière, Place-d'Armes métro)* may be rather small, but it is nonetheless a pleasant place to walk around. A large number of the Chinese who came to Canada to help build the transcontinental railroad, completed in 1886, settled here at the end of the 19th century. Though they no longer live in the neighbourhood, they still come here on weekends to stroll about and stock up on traditional products. Rue de la Gauchetière has been converted into a pedestrian street lined with restaurants and framed by lovely Chinese-style gates.

To the west of Rue Saint-Urbain lies Montreal's convention centre, the **Palais des Congrès de Montréal** *(201 Rue Viger Ouest, Place-d'Armes métro, ☎871-3170)*, a forbidding mass of concrete erected over the Aut. Ville-Marie highway, which contributes to the isolation of the old city from downtown. A small entrance on Rue de La Gauchetière leads into the long, windowed main hall in the centre. The conference rooms (16,700m²) can hold up to 5000 convention-goers at a time. The centre is undergoing a major renovation and expansion.

To return to the starting point of the tour, walk back up Boulevard Saint-Laurent to the Saint-Laurent métro station (at the corner of Boulevard de Maisonneuve). Take the métro west to the Guy-Concordia station.

Tour C: Shaughnessy Village

When the Sulpicians took possession of the island of Montréal in 1663, they kept a portion of the best land for themselves, then set up a farm and a native village there in 1676. Following a fire, the native village was relocated several times before being permanently established in Oka. A part of the farm, corresponding to the area now known as Westmount, was then granted to French settlers. The Sulpicians planted an orchard and a vineyard on the remaining portion. Starting around 1870, the land was separated into lots. Part of it was used for the construction of mansions, while large plots were awarded to Catholic communities allied with the Sulpicians. It was at this time that Shaughnessy House was built—hence the name of the neighbourhood. During the 1970s, the number of local inhabitants increased considerably, making Shaughnessy Village the most densely populated area in Québec.

From Rue Guy (Guy-Concordia métro) turn left on Rue Sherbrooke.

Masonic lodges, which had already existed in New France, increased in scale with British immigration. These associations of free-thinkers were not favoured by the Canadian clergy, who denounced their liberal views. Ironically, the **Masonic Temple ★** *(1850 Rue Sherbrooke Ouest, Guy-Con-*

cordia métro), one of Montréal's Scottish lodges, stands opposite the Grand Séminaire, where Catholic priests are trained. The edifice, built in 1928, enhances the secret, mystical character of Freemasonry with its impenetrable, windowless façade, equipped with antique vessels and double-headed lamps.

The Sulpicians' farmhouse was surrounded by a wall linked to four stone corner towers, earning it the name Fort des Messieurs. The house was destroyed when the **Grand Séminaire ★★** (1854-1860) *(2065 Rue Sherbrooke Ouest, Guy-Concordia métro)* was built, but two towers, erected in the 17th century according to plans by François Vachon de Belmont, superior of the Montréal Sulpicians, can still be found in the institution's shady gardens. It was in one of these that Saint Marguerite Bourgeoys taught young native girls. Around 1880, the long neoclassical buildings of the Grand Séminaire, designed by architect John Ostell, were topped by a mansard roof by Henri-Maurice Perrault. Information panels on Rue Sherbrooke, directly in line with Rue du Fort, provide precise details about the farm buildings.

It is well worth entering the Seminary to see the lovely Romanesque Revival–style chapel, designed by Jean Omer Marchand in 1905. The ceiling beams are made of cedar from British Columbia, while the walls are covered with stones from Caen. The 80m-wide nave is lined with 300 hand-carved oak pews. Sulpicians who have died in Montréal since the 18th century are interred beneath it. The Sulpician order was founded in Paris by Jean-Jacques Olier in 1641, and its main church is the Saint-Sulpice in Paris, which stands on the square of the same name.

Montréal

The Congrégation de Notre-Dame, founded by Saint Marguerite Bourgeoys in 1671, owned a convent and a school in Old Montréal. Reconstructed in the 18th century, these buildings were expropriated by the city at the beginning of the 20th century as part of a plan to extend Boulevard Saint-Laurent all the way to the port. The nuns had to leave the premises and settle into a new convent. The congregation thus arranged for a convent to be built on Rue Sherbrooke, according to a design by Jean Omer Marchand (1873-1936), the first French Canadian architect to graduate from the École des Beaux-Arts in Paris. The immense complex now bears witness to the vitality of religious communities in Québec before the Quiet Revolution of 1960.

The decline of religious practices and lack of new vocations forced the community to move into more modest buildings. **Dawson College ★** (*3040 Rue Sherbrooke Ouest, Atwater métro*), an English-language college or CÉGEP (*collège d'enseignement général et professionnel*), has been located in the original convent since 1987.

The yellow-brick building, set on luxuriant grounds, is probably the most beautiful CÉGEP in Québec. It is now directly linked to the subway and underground city. The Romanesque Revival-style chapel in the centre has an elongated copper dome reminiscent of Byzantine architecture. It now serves as a library and has been barely altered.

Head south on Avenue Atwater, then turn left on Rue Sainte-Catherine Ouest. Pass by the old Montreal Forum now converted into a huge cinema complex.

On Avenue Atwater, stands **Place Alexis-Nihon**, a multi-purpose complex containing a shopping mall, offices and apartments that is linked to the underground city. **Square Cabot** used to be the terminal for all buses serving the western part of the city.

Turn right on Rue Lambert-Closse, then left on Rue Tupper.

Between 1965 and 1975, Shaughnessy Village witnessed a massive wave of demolition. A great many Victorian row houses were replaced by highrises, whose rudimentary designs, characterized by an endless repetition of identical glass or concrete balconies, are often referred to as "chicken coops." **Avenue Seymour ★** is one of the only streets in the area to have escaped this wave, which has now been curbed. Here, visitors will find charming houses made of brick and grey stone, with Queen Anne, Second Empire or Romanesque Revival details.

Turn right on Rue Fort and then left on small Rue Baile (watch out for the fast-moving traffic heading to the highway on-ramp). Follow the path east alongside the CCA to reach René-Lévesque.

Founded in 1979 by Phyllis Lambert, the **Centre Canadien d'Architecture / Canadian Centre for Architecture ★★★** (*$6, free Thu 5:30pm to 8pm; Oct to Jun Wed-Sun 11am to 6pm; 1920 Rue Baile, Guy-Concordia métro, ☎939-7026*), is both a museum and a centre for the study of world architecture. Its collections of plans, drawings, models, books and photographs are the most important of their kind in the entire world. The Centre, erected between 1985 and 1989, has six exhibition rooms, a bookstore, a library, a 217-seat auditorium and a wing specially designed for researchers, as well as vaults and restoration laboratories. The main building, shaped like a *U*, was designed by Peter Rose, with the help of Phyllis Lambert. It is covered with grey limestone from the Saint-Marc quarries near Québec City. This material, which used to be extracted from the Plateau Mont-Royal and Rosemont quarries in Montréal, adorns the façades of many of the city's houses.

The centre surrounds the **Maison Shaughnessy ★**, whose façade looks out onto Boulevard René-Lévesque Ouest. This house is in fact a pair of residences, built in 1874 according to a design by architect William Tutin Thomas. It is representative of the mansions that once lined Boulevard René-Lévesque (formerly Boulevard Dorchester). In 1974, it was at the centre of an effort to salvage the neighbourhood, which had been torn down in a number of places. The house, itself threatened with demolition, was purchased at the last moment by Phyllis Lambert. She set up the offices and reception rooms of the Canadian Centre for Architecture inside. The building was named after Sir Thomas Shaughnessy, a former president of the Canadian Pacific Railway Company, who lived in the house for several decades. Neighbourhood residents who formed an association, subsequently chose to name the entire area after him.

Walk along Boulevard René-Lévesque and turn left on Rue Saint-Mathieu.

The amusing **architecture garden**, by artist Melvin Charney, lies across from Shaughnessy House between two highway on-ramps. It illustrates the different stages of the neighbourhood's development using a portion of the Sulpicians' orchard on the left, stone lines to indicate borders

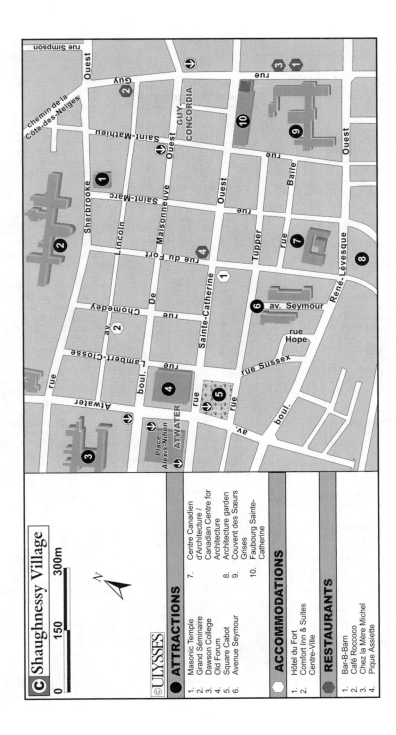

Shaughnessy Village

© ULYSSES

0   150   300m
N

● ATTRACTIONS

1. Masonic Temple
2. Grand Séminaire
3. Dawson College
4. Old Forum
5. Square Cabot
6. Avenue Seymour
7. Centre Canadien d'Architecture / Canadian Centre for Architecture
8. Architecture garden
9. Couvent des Sœurs Grises
10. Faubourg Sainte-Catherine

⬡ ACCOMMODATIONS

1. Hôtel du Fort
2. Comfort Inn & Suites Centre-Ville

◆ RESTAURANTS

1. Bar-B-Barn
2. Café Roccoco
3. Chez la Mère Michel
4. Pique Assiette

of 19th-century properties and rose bushes reminiscent of the gardens of those houses. A promenade along the cliff that once separated the wealthy neighbourhood from the working-class sector below offers a view of the lower part of the city (Little Burgundy, Saint-Henri, Verdun) and the St. Lawrence River. Some of the highlights of this panorama are represented in a stylized manner, atop concrete posts.

Like the Congrégation de Notre-Dame, the Sœurs Grises had to relocate their convent and hospital, which used to be situated on Rue Saint-Pierre in Old Montréal (see p 83). They obtained part the Sulpicians' farm, where a vast convent, designed by Victor Bourgeau, was erected between 1869 and 1874. The **Couvent des Sœurs Grises** ★★ *(1185 Rue St-Mathieu, Guy-Concordia métro)*, located in the Centre Marguerite d'Youville, is the product of an architectural tradition developed over the centuries in Québec. The chapel alone reveals a foreign influence, namely the Romanesque Revival style favoured by the Sulpicians, as opposed to the Renaissance and Baroque Revival styles preferred by the church.

Turn right on Rue Sainte-Catherine Ouest.

At the **Faubourg Sainte-Catherine** ★ *(1616 Rue Ste-Catherine Ouest, Guy-Concordia métro)*, a large converted, glass-roofed garage, visitors will find movie theatres, a market made up of small specialty shops selling local and imported products, and a fast-food area.

To return to the Guy-Concordia métro station, head north on Rue Guy.

Tour D: Mont Royal and Westmount

Montréal's central neighbourhoods were built around **Mount Royal** (Mont Royal in French), an important landmark in the cityscape. Known simply as "the mountain" by anglophone Montrealers, this squat mass, measuring 234m at its highest point, is composed of intrusive rock. It is in fact one of the seven hills of the St. Lawrence plain in the Montérégie region. A "green lung" rising up at the far end of downtown streets, it exerts a positive influence on Montrealers, who, as a result, never totally lose touch with nature. The mountain actually has three summits; the first is occupied by Parc du Mont-Royal, the second by the Université de Montréal, and the third by Westmount, a wealthy neighbourhood with lovely English-style homes which, up until recently, was an independent city. In addition to these areas, there are the Catholic, Protestant and Jewish cemeteries, which, considered as a whole, form the largest necropolis in North America.

To reach the starting point of the tour, take bus no.11 from the Mont-Royal métro station, located on the Plateau Mont-Royal, and get off at the Belvédère Camillien-Houde.

From the **Belvédère Camillien-Houde** ★★ *(Voie Camillien-Houde)*, a lovely scenic lookout, visitors can look out over the entire eastern portion of Montréal. The Plateau Mont-Royal lies in the foreground, a uniform mass of duplexes and triplexes, pierced in a few places by the oxidized copper bell towers of parish churches, while the Rosemont and Maisonneuve districts lie in the background, with the Olympic Stadium

towering over them. In clear weather, the oil refineries in the east end can be seen in the distance.

The St. Lawrence River, visible on the right, is only 1.5km wide at its narrowest point. The Belvédère Camillien-Houde is Montréal's version of Inspiration Point and a favourite gathering place of sweethearts with cars.

Climb the staircase at the south end of the parking lot, and follow Chemin Olmsted on the left, which leads to the chalet and main lookout. You will pass the mountain's cross on the way.

Pressured by the residents of the Golden Square Mile, who saw their favourite playground being deforested by various firewood companies, the City of Montréal created **Parc du Mont-Royal / Mount Royal Park** ★★★ in 1870. Frederick Law Olmsted (1822-1903), the celebrated designer of New York's Central Park, was commissioned to design the park. He decided to preserve the site's natural character, limiting himself to a few lookout points linked by winding paths. Inaugurated in 1876, the park, which covers 101ha on the southern part of the mountain, is cherished by Montrealers as a place to enjoy the fresh air (see also p 121).

The **Chalet du Mont Royal** ★★★ *(every day 8:30am to 9pm; Parc du Mont-Royal, ☎872-3911)*, located in the centre of the park, was designed by Aristide Beaugrand-Champagne in 1932 as a replacement for the original structure, which was about to collapse. During the 1930s and 1940s, big bands gave moonlit concerts on the steps of the building. The interior is decorated with remounted paintings depicting scenes from Canadian history. They were commissioned

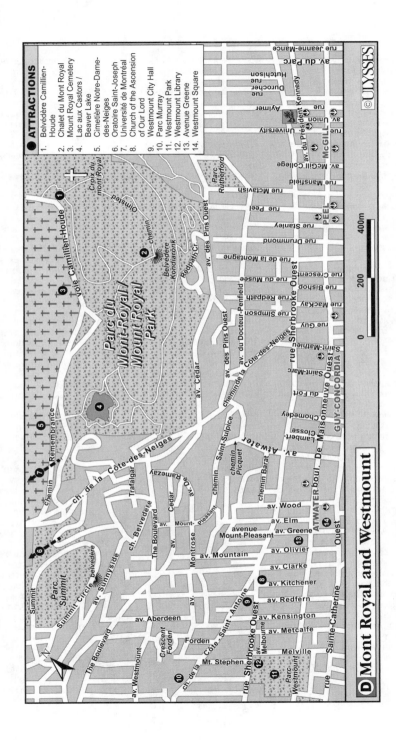

ATTRACTIONS

1. Belvédère Camillien-Houde
2. Chalet du Mont Royal
3. Mount Royal Cemetery
4. Lac aux Castors / Beaver Lake
5. Cimetière Notre-Dame-des-Neiges
6. Oratoire Saint-Joseph
7. Université de Montréal
8. Church of the Ascension of Our Lord
9. Westmount City Hall
10. Parc Murray
11. Westmount Park
12. Westmount Library
13. Avenue Greene
14. Westmount Square

D Mont Royal and Westmount

© ULYSSES

from some of Québec's great painters, such as Marc-Aurèle Fortin and Paul-Émile Borduas. Nevertheless, people go to the chalet mainly to stroll along the lookout and take in the exceptional view of downtown from the **belvédère Kondiaronk**, best in the late afternoon and in the evening, when the skyscrapers light up the darkening sky.

Take the gravel road leading to the parking lot of the chalet and Voie Camillien-Houde. One of the entrances to the Mount Royal Cemetery lies on the right.

The **Mount Royal Cemetery** ★★ (*Voie Camilien Houde*) is a Protestant cemetery that ranks among the most beautiful spots in the city. Designed as an Eden for the living visiting the deceased, it is laid out like a landscape garden in an isolated valley, giving visitors the impression that they are a thousand miles from the city, though they are in fact right in the centre of it. The wide variety of hardwood and fruit trees attract species of birds found nowhere else in Québec. Founded by the Anglican, Presbyterian, Unitarian and Baptist churches, the cemetery opened in 1852. Some of its monuments are true works of art, executed by celebrated artists. The families and eminent personalities buried here include the Molson brewers, who have the most impressive and imposing mausoleum, shipowner Sir Hugh Allan, and numerous other figures from the footnotes and headlines of history, such as Anna Leonowens, governess of the King of Siam in the 19th century and inspiration for the play *The King and I*.

Oratoire Saint-Joseph

On the left, on the way to Lac aux Castors, visitors will see the last of the mountain's former farmhouses, **Maison Smith**, headquarters of the *Amis de la montagne* (friends of the mountains) association.

Continue along Voie Camillien Houde, then head west on Chemin Remembrance. Take the road leading to Lac aux Castors (see map).

Small **Lac aux Castors / Beaver Lake** (*alongside Chemin Remembrance*), was created in 1958 in what used to be a swamp. In winter, it becomes a pleasant skating rink. This part of the park also has grassy areas and a sculpture garden. It is laid out in a more conventional manner than the rest, violating Olmsted's purist directives.

The **Cimetière Notre-Dame-des-Neiges** ★★, Montréal's largest cemetery, is a veritable city of the dead, as more than a million people have been buried here since it opened in 1854. It replaced the cemetery in Square Dominion, which was deemed too close to the neighbouring houses.

Unlike the Protestant cemetery, it has a conspicuously religious character, clearly identifying it with the Catholic faith. Accordingly, two heavenly angels flanking a crucifix greet visitors at the main entrance on Chemin de la Côte-des-Neiges. The "two solitudes" (Canadians of French Catholic and Anglo-Saxon Protestant extraction) thus remain separated even in death. The tombstones read like a who's-who in the fields of business, arts, politics and science in Québec. An obelisk dedicated to the Patriotes of the rebellion of 1837-38 and numerous monuments executed by renowned sculptors lie scattered alongside the 55km of roads and paths that crisscross the cemetery.

Both the cemetery and the roads leading to it offer a number of views of the **Oratoire Saint-Joseph** ★★ (*free admission; every day 6:30am to 9:30pm; 3800 Chemin Queen Mary, ☎733-8211*). The enormous building topped by a copper dome, the second-largest dome in the world after that of St. Peter's in Rome, stands on a hillside, accentuating its mystical aura. From the gate at the entrance, there are over 300 steps to climb to reach the oratory. Small buses are also available for worshippers who do not want to climb the steps. The oratory was built between 1924 and 1956, thanks to the efforts of the blessed Frère André, porter of Collège Notre-Dame (across the street), to whom many miracles are attributed. A veritable religious complex, the oratory is dedicated to both Saint Joseph and its humble creator. It includes the lower and upper basilicas, the crypt of Frère André and two museums, one dedicated to Frère André's life, the other to sacred art.

Visitors will also find the porter's first chapel, built in 1910, a cafeteria, a hostelry and a store selling devotional articles. The oratory is one of the most important centres of worship and pilgrimage in North America. Each year, it attracts some 2,000,000 visitors. The building's neoclassical exterior was designed by Dalbé Viau and Alphonse Venne, while the essentially modern interior is the work of Lucien Parent and French Benedictine monk Dom Paul Bellot, the author from Saint-Benoît-du-Lac in the Cantons de l'Est, or Eastern Townships. It is well worth visiting the upper basilica to see the stained-glass windows by Marius Plamondon, the altar and crucifix by Henri Charlier, and the astonishing gilded chapel at the back. The oratory has an imposing Beckerath-style organ, which can be heard on Wednesday evenings during the summer. Outside, visitors can also see the chimes, made by Paccard et Frères and originally intended for the Eiffel Tower, as well as the beautiful Chemin de Croix (Way of the Cross) by Louis Parent and Ercolo Barbieri, in the gardens on the side of the mountain. Measuring 263m, the oratory's observatory, which commands a sweeping view of the entire city, is the highest point on the island.

Aiming to preserve its monopoly on French-language university education in Québec, after many attempts, Québec City's Université Laval finally opened a branch of its institution in the Château Ramezay (see p 86). A few years later, it moved to Rue Saint-Denis, giving birth to the Quartier Latin (see p 112).

The **Université de Montréal** ★ *(2900 Boulevard Édouard-Montpetit)* finally became autonomous in 1920, enabling its directors to develop grandiose plans. Ernest Cormier (1885-1980) was approached about designing a campus on the north side of Mont Royal. The architect, a graduate of the École des Beaux-Arts in Paris, was one of the first to acquaint North Americans with the Art Deco style.

The plans for the main building evolved into a refined, symmetrical Art Deco structure faced with pale-yellow bricks and topped by a central tower, visible from Chemin Remembrance and Cimetière Notre-Dame-des-Neiges. Begun in 1929, construction on the building was interrupted by the Stock Market Crash, and it wasn't until 1943 that the first students entered the main building on the mountain. Since then, a whole host of pavilions has been added, making the Université de Montréal the second-largest French-language university in the world, with a student body of over 58,000. Since the entrance to the university is somewhat removed from the present route, a visit to the campus constitutes an additional excursion that takes about an hour.

The École Polytechnique of the Université de Montréal, which is also located on Mont Royal, was the scene of a tragedy that marked the city and all of Canada. On December 6, 1989, 14 female students were murdered in cold blood inside the École Polytechnique by a crazed misogynist who targeted the women at the school. To keep the memory of these women, and that of all female victims of violence, alive, the **Place du 6-décembre-1989** *(corner Decelles and Queen-Mary)* was erected on December 6, 1999, to com-

memorate the 10th anniversary of the massacre. There, artist Rose-Marie Goulet erected her *Nef pour quatorze reines* (Nave for Fourteen Queens), inscribed with the names of the victims of the Polytechnique massacre.

*Back on the mountain, follow the trails through Parc du Mont-Royal to the exit leading to **Westmount** (see map).*

This wealthy residential neighbourhood of 20,200 inhabitants was an independent city before (reluctantly) joining the City of Montréal. It has long been regarded as the bastion of the Anglo-Saxon elite in Québec. After the Golden Square Mile was invaded by the business centre, Westmount assumed its role. Its shady, winding roads on the southwest side of the mountain are lined with Neo-Tudor and Neo-Georgian residences, most of which were built between 1910 and 1930. Upper Westmount offers some lovely views of the city below.

Take The Boulevard to Avenue Clarke (near the small triangular park), then turn left to reach Rue Sherbrooke Ouest.

Erected in 1928, Westmount's English Catholic church, The **Church of the Ascension of Our Lord** ★ *(corner Avenue Kitchener, Atwater métro)* is evidence of the staying power of the Gothic Revival style in North American architecture and the historical accuracy, ever more apparent in the 20th century, of buildings patterned after ancient models. With its rough stone facing, elongated lines and delicate sculptures, it looks like an authentic church from a 14th-century English village.

Westmount is like a piece of Great Britain in North America. Its **City Hall** ★ *(4333 Rue Sherbrooke Ouest)* was built in the Neo-Tudor style, inspired by the architecture of the age of Henry VIII and Elizabeth I, which was regarded during the 1920s as the national style of England because it originated from the British Isles. The style is characterized in part by horizontal openings with multiple stone transoms, bay windows and flattened arches. The impeccable green of a lawn-bowling club lies at the back, frequented by members wearing their regulation whites.

Take Chemin de la Côte-Saint-Antoine to Parc Murray.

In Québec, the term *côte*, which translates literally as "hill," usually has nothing to do with the slope of the land, but is a leftover division of the seigneurial system of New France. The roads linking one farm to the next ran along the tops of the long rectangles of land distributed to colonists. As a result, these plots of land gradually became known as *côtes*, from the French word for "side," *côté*. Côte Saint-Antoine is one of the oldest roads on the island of Montréal. Laid out in 1684 by the Sulpicians on a former native trail, it is lined with some of Westmount's oldest houses. At the corner of Avenue Forden is a **milestone** dating back to the 17th century, discreetly identified by the pattern of the sidewalk, which radiates out from it. This is all that remains of the system of road signs developed by the Sulpicians for their seigneury on the island of Montréal.

For those who would like to immerse themselves in a Mid-Atlantic atmosphere, a blend of England and America, **Parc Murray** *(north of Avenue Mount Stephen)* offers the perfect combination: a football field and tennis courts in a country setting. Here, visitors will find the remains of a natural grouping of acacias, an extremely rare species at this latitude, due to the harsh climate. The trees' presence is an indication that this area has the mildest climate in Québec. This mildness is a result of both the southwest slant of the land and the warm air coming from the nearby Lachine rapids.

Go down Avenue Mount Stephen to return to Rue Sherbrooke Ouest.

Westmount Park ★ was laid out on swampy land in 1895. Four years later, Québec's first public library, the **Westmount Library** *(4575 Rue Sherbrooke Ouest)* was erected on the same site. Up until then, religious communities had been the only ones to develop this type of cultural facility, and the province was therefore somewhat behind in this area. The red-brick building is the product of the trends toward eclecticism, picturesqueness and polychromy that characterized the last two decades of the 19th century.

From the park, head east on Avenue Melbourne, where there are some fine examples of Queen Anne–style houses. Turn right on Avenue Metcalfe, then left on Boulevard de Maisonneuve Ouest.

At the corner of Avenue Clarke stands **Église Saint-Léon ★**, the only French-language Catholic parish in Westmount. The sober, elegant Romanesque Revival façade conceals an exceptionally rich interior décor begun in 1928 by artist Guido Nincheri, who also painted the frescoes in **Château Dufresne** (see p 106). Nincheri was provided with a large sum of money to decorate the church using no substitutes and no tricks. Accordingly, the floor and the base of the walls are covered with the most beautiful Italian and French marble available, while the upper portion of the nave is made of Savonnières stone and the chancel, of the most precious Honduran walnut, hand-carved by Alviero Marchi. The complex stained-glass windows depict various scenes from the life of Jesus Christ, including a few personages from the time of the church's construction, whom visitors will be amused to discover among the Biblical figures. Finally, the entire Christian pantheon is represented in the chancel and on the vault in vibrantly coloured frescoes, executed in the traditional manner using an egg-wash. This technique (used, notably, by Michelangelo) consists of making pigment stick to a wet surface with a coating made of egg, which becomes very hard and resistant when dry.

Continue along Boulevard de Maisonneuve, which leads through the former French section of Westmount before intersecting with Avenue Greene.

On **Avenue Greene**, a small street with a typically English-Canadian character, visitors will find several of Westmount's fashionable shops. In addition to service-oriented businesses, there are art galleries, antique shops and bookstores filled with lovely things.

Architect Ludwig Mies van der Rohe (1886-1969), one of the leading masters of the modernist movement and the head of Bauhaus in Germany, designed **Westmount Square ★★** *(at the corner of Avenue Wood and Boulevard de Maisonneuve Ouest, Atwater métro)* in 1964. The complex is typical of the architect's North American work, characterized by the use of black metal and tinted glass. It includes an underground shopping centre topped by three towers containing offices and apartments. The public areas were originally covered with veined white travertine, one of Mies's favourite materials, which was replaced by a layer of granite, more resistant to the harsh climatic effects of freezing and thawing.

An underground corridor leads from Westmount Square to the Atwater métro station.

Tour E: Maisonneuve

In 1883, the city of Maisonneuve was founded in eastern Montréal by farmers and French Canadian merchants; port facilities expanded into the area and the city's development picked up. Then, in 1918, the formerly autonomous city was annexed to Montréal, becoming one of its major working-class neighbourhoods, with a 90% francophone population. In the course of its history, Maisonneuve has been profoundly influenced by men with grand ideas, who wanted to make this part of the province a place where people could thrive together.

Upon taking office at the Maisonneuve town hall in 1910, brothers Marius and Oscar Dufresne instituted a rather ambitious policy of building prestigious Beaux-Arts–style public buildings intended to make "their" city a model of development for French Québec. Then, in 1931, Frère Marie-Victorin founded Montréal's Jardin Botanique (botanical garden) in Maisonneuve; today, it is the second-largest in the world. The last major episode in the area's history was in 1971, when Mayor Jean Drapeau initiated construction on the immense sports complex used for the 1976 Olympic Games.

From the Pie-IX métro station, climb the hill leading to the corner of Rue Sherbrooke Est.

The **Jardin Botanique, Maison de l'Arbre** and **Insectarium** ★★★ *(admission to the greenhouses and Insectarium, $10, $7 in low season, combined ticket for the Biôdome and the Tour Olympique (Olympic Tower) $24 valid for 2 days; May to Sep, every day 9am to 7pm; Sep to May 9am to 5pm; 4101 Rue Sherbrooke Est, métro Pie-IX, ☎872-1400)* are located on the same site. The Jardin Botanique de Montréal, covering an area of 73ha, was begun during the economic crisis of the 1930s on the site of Mont-de-La-Salle, home base of the brothers of the Écoles Chrétiennes, by frère Marie-Victorin, a well-known Québécois botanist. Behind the Art Deco building occupied by the Université de Montréal's institute of biology, visitors will find a stretch of 10 connected greenhouses open year-round, which shelter, most notably, a precious collection of orchids and the largest grouping of bonsais and *penjings* outside of Asia. The latter includes the famous Wu collection, given to the garden by master Wu Yee-Sun of Hong Kong in 1984.

Thirty outdoor gardens, open from spring through autumn, and designed to educate and amaze visitors, stretch to the north and west of the greenhouses. Particularly noteworthy are a beautiful rosary, the Japanese garden and its *sukiya*-style tea pavilion, as well as the very beautiful Chinese Lac de Rêve, or Jardin de Chine, garden, whose pavilions were designed by artisans who came here from China specifically for the task. Since Montréal is twinned with Shanghai, it was deemed appropriate that it should have the largest such garden outside of Asia. During late-summer nights, the

Chinese Garden is decorated with hundreds of Chinese lanterns that create a wonderful fairytale-like setting of light and flowers.

Another must-see is the **First Nations Garden**. It is the result of efforts by several contributors, both Aboriginal and non-Aboriginal, including Brother Marie-Victorin, who was hoping to integrate a garden of medicinal plants used by Aboriginal communities. His achievement allows the uninitiated to familiarize themselves with the Aboriginal world, especially their use of plants. Among other things, here you will learn the many ways that the Huron-Wendat and Mohawk peoples use corn. Québec's 11 First Nations are represented in their natural habitat zones: deciduous forest, coniferous forest and the Arctic zone. An exhibition pavilion completes the tour.

The northern part of the botanical garden is occupied by an arboretum. The **Maison de l'Arbre**, literally the "tree house," was established in this area to educate people about the life of a tree. The interactive, permanent exhibit is actually set up in an old tree trunk. There are displays on the yellow birch, Québec's emblematic tree. The building's structure, consisting of different types of wooden beams, reminds us how leafy forests really are. Note the play of light and shade from the frame onto the large white wall, meant to resemble trunks and branches. The terrace in the back is an ideal spot from which to contemplate the arboretum's pond; it also leads to a charming little bonsai garden. To reach the Maison de l'Arbre, climb on board the *Balade*, the shuttle that regularly tours the garden, or use the garden's northern entrance located on Boulevard Rosemont.

Montréal

The **Insectarium** (☎872-8753) is located to the east of the greenhouses. This innovative, living museum invites visitors to discover the fascinating world of insects. Watch for the various activities organized throughout the year. You could, for instance, sample edible insects, if you're so inclined.

Return to Boulevard Pie-IX.

The **Château Dufresne** ★★ (2929 Rue Jeanne-d'Arc, Pie-IX métro) is in fact two 22-room private mansions behind the same façade, built in 1916 for brothers Marius and Oscar Dufresne, shoe-manufacturers and authors of a grandiose plan to develop Maisonneuve. The plan was abandoned after the onset of World War I, causing the municipality to go bankrupt. Their home, designed by Marius Dufresne and Parisian architect Jules Renard, was supposed to be the nucleus of a residential upper-class neighbourhood, which never materialized. It is one of the best examples of Beaux-Arts architecture in Montréal. The Château Dufresne now houses temporary exhibitions as well as a collection of furniture and decorative objects.

Go back downhill on Boulevard Pie-IX, then turn left on Avenue Pierre-de-Coubertin.

Jean Drapeau was mayor of Montréal from 1954 to 1957, and from 1960 to 1986. He dreamed of great things for "his" city. Endowed with exceptional powers of persuasion and unfailing determination, he saw a number of important projects through to a successful conclusion, including the construction of Place des Arts, the métro, Expo '67

and, of course, the 1976 Summer Olympics.

For this last international event, however, it was necessary to equip the city with the appropriate facilities. In spite of the controversy this caused, the city sought out a Parisian visionary to design something completely original. A billion dollars later, the major work of architect Roger Taillibert, who also designed the stadium of the Parc des Princes in Paris, stunned everyone with its curving, organic concrete shapes. The **Stade Olympique** ★★★ (*$5.25, package with tour and funicular $10.25; guided tours in French at 11am and 2pm, and in English at 12:40pm and 3:40pm; 4141 Avenue Pierre-de-Coubertin,* ☎252-8687) is also known as the Olympic Stadium and the "Big O." The 56,000-seat oval stadium is covered with a kevlar roof supported by cables stretching from the 190m leaning tower. In the distance, visitors will see the two pyramidal shaped

Stade Olympique

towers of the **Olympic Village**, where the athletes were housed in 1976. Each year, the stadium hosts different events. From April to September, Montréal's National League baseball team, the Expos, plays its home games here.

The stadium's tower, which is the tallest leaning tower in the world, was rebaptised the **Tour de Montréal**. A funicular (*$9; every day 10am to 5pm*) climbs the structure to an

interior observation deck which commands a view of the eastern part of Montreal. Exhibits on the Olympics are presented on the upper levels and there is also a rest area with a bar. The foot of the tower houses the swimming pools of the Olympic Complex and a cinema, while the former cycling track, known as the Vélodrome, located nearby, has been converted into an artificial habitat for plants and animals called the **Biodôme** ★★★ (*$10; every day 9am to 5pm; 4777 Avenue Pierre de Coubertin, Viau métro,* ☎868-3000). This new type of museum, associated with the Jardin Botanique, contains four very different ecosystems—the Tropical Rainforest, the Laurentian Forest, the St. Lawrence Marine Ecosystem and the Polar World—within a space of 10,000m². These are complete micro-climates, including plants, mammals and free-flying birds, and close to real climatic conditions. Remember to dress for both tropical and polar conditions!

Ice hockey holds a special place in the hearts of Quebecers. Many consider Maurice "the Rocket" Richard (1921-2000) the greatest hockey player of all time. **L'Univers Maurice "Rocket" Richard** (*free admission; Tue-Sun noon to 8pm; 2800 Rue Viau,* ☎251-9930, *Viau métro*) is a small museum in his honour. Located in the arena that carries his name, next to the Olympic facilities, the museum contains equipment, trophies and other significant memorabilia that once belonged to this hero of hockey who played for the Canadiens from 1942 to 1960. The museum also has a small boutique with hockey paraphernalia.

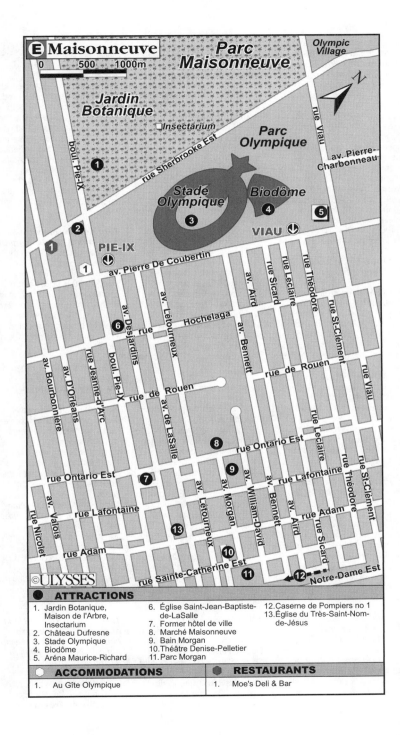

E Maisonneuve

0   500   1000m

Parc Maisonneuve

Olympic Village

Jardin Botanique

☐Insectarium

rue Sherbrooke Est

Parc Olympique

boul. Pie-IX

Stade Olympique

Biodôme

VIAU

rue Viau

av. Pierre-Charbonneau

PIE-IX

av. Pierre De Coubertin

av. Aird

rue Sicard

rue Leclaire

rue Théodore

rue St-Clément

rue Viau

av. Desjardins

rue Létourneux

rue Hochelaga

av. Bennett

rue de Rouen

av. Bourbonnière

av. D'Orléans

av. Jeanne-d'Arc

boul. Pie-IX

rue de Rouen

av. de LaSalle

rue Leclaire

rue St-Clément

rue Ontario Est

rue Lafontaine

av. Valois

rue Nicolet

rue Ontario Est

rue Lafontaine

av. Létourneux

av. Morgan

av. William-David

av. Bennett

av. Aird

rue Théodore

rue Sicard

rue St-Clément

rue Adam

rue Adam

rue Sainte-Catherine Est

Notre-Dame Est

©ULYSSES

● ATTRACTIONS

1. Jardin Botanique, Maison de l'Arbre, Insectarium
2. Château Dufresne
3. Stade Olympique
4. Biodôme
5. Aréna Maurice-Richard
6. Église Saint-Jean-Baptiste-de-LaSalle
7. Former hôtel de ville
8. Marché Maisonneuve
9. Bain Morgan
10. Théâtre Denise-Pelletier
11. Parc Morgan
12. Caserne de Pompiers no 1
13. Église du Très-Saint-Nom-de-Jésus

○ ACCOMMODATIONS	● RESTAURANTS
1. Au Gîte Olympique	1. Moe's Deli & Bar

As for the **Aréna Maurice-Richard** *(2800 Rue Viau, Viau métro,* ☎*872-6666,)*, it precedes the Olympic Village, with which it is now affiliated, by 20 years. Its rink is the only one in Eastern Canada whose area respects international norms. Canada's Olympic speed-skating team practises here, as do several figure-skating champions. A statue of Maurice Richard has stood in front of the entrance to the arena since 1998. Measuring 2.5m in height and cast at the Atelier du Bronze Inverness, it is the work of sculptors Annick Bourgeau and Jules Lasalle.

Return to Boulevard Pie-IX and head south.

Église Saint-Jean-Baptiste-de-LaSalle *(corner of Rue Hochelaga, Pie-IX métro)* was built in 1964 within the context of the Vatican II liturgical revival. In an effort to maintain its following, members of the Catholic clergy cast aside traditions and introduced an audacious style of architecture, which still, however, did not advance their goal. The evocative mitre-like exterior conceals a depressing interior made of bare concrete, which looks like it is falling onto the congregation.

Continue south on Boulevard Pie-IX, then turn left on Rue Ontario.

In 1911, the Dufresne administration kicked off its policy of grandeur by building the **hôtel de ville ★** *(4120 Rue Ontario Est)*, a city hall designed by architect Cajetan Dufort. From 1926 to 1967, the building was occupied by the Institut du Radium, which specialized in cancer research. Since 1981, the edifice has served as the Maison de la Culture Maisonneuve, one of the City of Montréal's neighbourhood cultural centres. On the second floor, a 1915 bird's-eye-view drawing of Maisonneuve shows the prestigious buildings as they stood back then, as well as those that remained only on paper.

Built directly in line with Avenue Morgan in 1914, the **Marché Maisonneuve ★** *(4445 rue Ontario Est,* ☎*937-7754)* is one of Montréal's most pleasant public markets. Since 1995, it has occupied a much newer building than the one next door where it was once set. The Marché Maisonneuve is in keeping with a concept of urban design inherited from the teachings of the École des Beaux-Arts in Paris, known as the City Beautiful movement in North America. It is a mixture of parks, classical perspectives and civic and sanitary facilities. Designed by Cajetan Dufort, the market Dufresne's most ambitious project. The centre of **Place du Marché** is adorned with an important work by sculptor Alfred Laliberté, entitled *La Fermière* (The Woman Farmer).

Follow Avenue Morgan.

Although it is small, the **Bain Morgan ★** *(1875 Avenue Morgan)*, a bath house, has an imposing appearance due to its Beaux-Arts elements—a monumental staircase, twin columns, a balustrade on the top and sculptures by Maurice Dubert from France. A bronze entitled *Les Petits Baigneurs* (The Little Bathers) is another piece by Alfred Laliberté. Originally, people came to the public baths not only to relax and enjoy the water, but also to wash, since not all houses in working-class neighbourhoods such as this were equipped with bathrooms.

In 1977, the former Cinéma Granada was converted into a theatre and renamed **Théâtre Denise Pelletier** *(4353 Rue Ste-Catherine Est)* after one of the great actresses of the Quiet Revolution, who died prematurely. The terra cotta façade is decorated in the Italian Renaissance style. The original interior (1928), designed by Emmanuel Briffa, is of the atmospheric type and has been partially preserved. Above the colonnade of the mythical palace encircling the room is a black vault that used to be studded with thousands of stars, making the audience feel as if they were attending an outdoor presentation. A projector was used to create images of moving clouds and even airplanes flying through the night.

Parc Morgan *(at the southernmost end of Avenue Morgan)* was laid out in 1933 on the site of the country house belonging to Henry Morgan, owner of the stores of the same name. From the cottage in the centre there is an interesting perspective on the Marché Maisonneuve silhouetted by the enormous Olympic Stadium.

Follow Rue Sainte-Catherine Est west to Avenue Létourneux, and turn left.

Maisonneuve boasted two firehouses, one of which had an altogether original design by Marius Dufresne. He was trained as an engineer and businessman, but he also took a great interest in architecture. Impressed by the work of Frank Lloyd Wright, he designed the **Caserne de Pompiers no 1 ★** *(on the south side of Rue Notre-Dame)*, or fire station, as an adaptation of the Unity Temple (1906) in Oak Park, on the outskirts of Chicago. The building was therefore one of the first works of modern architecture erected in Canada.

Turn right on Avenue Desjardins. Due to the unstable ground in this part of the city, some of the houses tilt to an alarming degree.

Behind the somewhat drab Romanesque Revival façade of the **Église du Très-Saint-**

Nom-de-Jésus ★ *(at the corner of Rue Adam)*, built in 1906, visitors will discover a rich, polychromatic decor, created in part by artist Guido Nincheri, whose studio was located in Maisonneuve. Particularly noteworthy are the large organs built by the Casavant brothers, divided up between the rear jube and the chancel—very unusual in a Catholic church. Because this building stands on the same shifting ground as the neighbouring houses, its vault is supported by metal shafts.

Tour F:
Île Sainte-Hélène and
Île Notre-Dame

When Samuel de Champlain reached the island of Montréal in 1611, he found a small rocky archipelago located in front of it. He named the largest of these islands in the channel after his wife, Hélène Boulé. **Île Sainte-Hélène** later became part of the seigneury of Longueuil. Around 1720, the Baroness of Longueuil chose the island as the site for a country house surrounded by a garden. It is also worth noting that in 1760, the island was the last foothold of French troops in New France, commanded by Chevalier François de Lévis. Recognizing Île Saint-Hélène's strategic importance, the British army built a fort on the eastern part of the island at the beginning of the 19th century. The threat of armed conflict with the United States having diminished, the Canadian government rented Île Sainte-Hélène to the City of Montréal in 1874, at which time the island was turned into a park and linked to Old Montréal by ferry and, from 1930 on, by the Jacques-Cartier bridge.

In the early 1960s, Montréal was chosen as the location of the 1967 World's Fair (Expo '67). The city wanted to set up the event on a large, attractive site near the downtown area; a site such as this, however, did not exist. It was thus necessary to build one: using soil excavated during the construction of the métro tunnel, Île Notre-Dame was created, doubling the area of Île Sainte-Hélène. From April to November 1967, 45-million visitors passed through Cité du Havre, the gateway to the fairground, and crisscrossed both islands. Expo, as Montrealers still refer to it, was more than a jumble of assorted objects; it was Montréal's awakening, during which the city opened itself to the world, and visitors from all over discovered a new art of living, including mini-skirts, colour television, hippies, flower power and protest rock.

It is not easy to reach Cité du Havre from downtown. The best way is to take Rue Mill, then Chemin des Moulins, which runs under Aut. Bonaventure to Avenue Pierre-Dupuy. This last road leads to Pont de la Concorde and then over the St. Lawrence to the islands. It is also possible to take bus number 168 from the McGill métro station.

The **Tropique Nord, Habitat '67** and the **Parc de la Cité du Havre ★ ★** were all built on a spit of land created to protect the port of Montréal from ice and currents. This point of land also offers some lovely views of the city and the water. The administrative offices of the port are located at the entrance to the area, along with a group of buildings that once housed the Expo-Théâtre and Musée d'Art Contemporain (see p 95). A little farther on, visitors will spot the large glass wall of the Tropique Nord, a residential complex composed of apartments with a view of the outdoors on one side, and an interior tropical garden on the other.

Next, visitors will see Habitat '67, an experimental housing development built for Expo '67 in order to illustrate construction techniques using prefabricated concrete slabs, and to herald a new art of living. The architect, Moshe Safdie, was only 23 years old when he drew up the plans. Habitat '67 looks like a gigantic cluster of cubes, each containing one or two rooms. The apartments are as highly prized as ever and are lived in by a number of notable Quebecers.

At the Parc de la Cité du Havre, visitors will find 12 panels containing a brief description of the history of the St. Lawrence River. A section of the bicycle path leading to Île Notre-Dame and Île Sainte-Hélène passes through the park.

Cross Pont de la Concorde.

Parc Jean-Drapeau ★ ★ *(Jean-Drapeau métro)* lies on Île Sainte- Hélène, which originally covered an area of 50ha but was enlarged to over 120ha for Expo '67. The original portion corresponds to the raised area studded with boulders made of breccia. Peculiar to the island, breccia is a very hard, ferrous stone that takes on an orange colour when exposed to air for a long time. In 1992, the western part of the island was transformed into a vast open-air amphitheatre, where large-scale shows are presented. In this lovely riverside park, visitors will find *L'Homme* ("Humankind"), a large metal sculpture by Alexandre Calder, created for Expo '67.

A little farther, close to the entrance to the Jean-Drapeau métro station, is a work by the Mexican artist Sebastian entitled *La porte de l'amitié* (The Door to Friendship). This

Montréal

sculpture was given to the City of Montréal by Mexico City in 1992 and erected on this site three years later to commemorate the signing of the free-trade agreement between Canada, the United States and Mexico (NAFTA).

Follow the trails leading toward the heart of the island.

The pool house, faced with breccia stone, and outdoor swimming pools, built during the Great Depression of the 1930s, lie at the edge of the original park. This island, with its varied contours, is dominated by the **Tour Lévis**, a simple water tower built in 1936, which looks like a dungeon, and by the blockhouse, a wooden observation post erected in 1849.

Follow the signs for the Fort de l'île Sainte-Hélène.

After the War of 1812 between the United States and Great Britain, the **Fort de l'Île Sainte-Hélène ★ ★** *(Jean-Drapeau métro)* was built so that Montréal could be properly defended if ever a new conflict were to erupt. The construction, supervised by military engineer Elias Walker Durnford, was completed in 1825. Built of breccia stone, the fort is in the shape of a jagged *U*, surrounding a drill ground, used today by the Compagnie Franche de la Marine and the 78th Regiment of the Fraser Highlanders as a parade ground. These two costumed mock regiments delight visitors by reviving Canada's French and Scottish military traditions. The drill ground also offers a lovely view of both the port and **Pont Jacques-Cartier**, inaugurated in 1930, which straddles the island, separating the park from La Ronde.

The arsenal is now occupied by the **Musée Stewart ★ ★** *($6; May to Labour Day, every day 10am to 6pm;*

Labour Day to May, Wed-Mon 10am to 5pm; ☎*861-6701),* which is dedicated to colonial history and the exploration of the New-World. The museum exhibits objects from past centuries, including interesting collections of maps, firearms, and scientific and navigational instruments collected by Montréal industrialist David Stewart and his wife Liliane. Staff dressed as historic figures guide visitors.

The vaults of the former barracks now house **Le Festin des Gouverneurs**, a restaurant geared mainly toward large groups. Each evening, it recreates the atmosphere of a New France feast (see p 134).

La Ronde ★ *($32; schedule* ☎*397-7777; Jean-Drapeau métro;* ☎*872-7044),* an amusement park set up for Expo '67 on the former Île Ronde, opens its doors to both the young and the not-so-young every summer. For Montrealers, an annual trip to La Ronde has almost become a pilgrimage. An international fireworks competition is held here twice a week during the months of June and July.

Head toward the Biosphere on the road that runs along the south shore of the island.

Built in 1938 as a sports pavilion, the **Restaurant Hélène-de-Champlain ★** was inspired by the architecture of New France and is thus reminiscent of the summer house of the Baroness of Longueuil, once located in the area. Behind the restaurant is a lovely rose garden planted for Expo '67, which embellishes the view from the dining room. The **former military cemetery** of the British garrison stationed on Île Sainte-Hélène from 1828 to 1870 lies in front of the building. Most of the original tombstones have disappeared. A commemorative monument,

erected in 1937, stands in their place.

Very few of the pavilions built for Expo '67 have survived the destructive effects of the weather and the changes in the islands' roles. One that has is the former American pavilion, a veritable monument to modern architecture. The first complete geodesic dome to be taken beyond the stage of a model, it was created by the celebrated engineer Richard Buckminster Fuller (1895-1983). **The Biosphere ★ ★** *($8.50; late Jun to early Sep every day 10am to 6pm; early Sep to late Jun, Wed-Mon, 10am to 5pm; Jean-Drapeau métro,* ☎*283-5000),* built of tubular aluminum and measuring 80m in diameter, unfortunately lost its translucent acrylic skin in a fire back in 1978. An environmental interpretive centre on the St. Lawrence River, the Great Lakes and the different Canadian ecosystems is now located in the dome. The permanent exhibit aims to sensitize the public on issues of sustainable development and the conservation of water as a precious resource. There are four interactive galleries with giant screens and hands-on displays to explore and delight in. A terrace restaurant with a panoramic view of the islands completes the museum.

Cross over to Île Notre-Dame on the Pont du Cosmos.

Île Notre-Dame emerged from the waters of the St. Lawrence in just 10 months, with the help of 15-million tons of rock and soil transported here from the métro construction site. Because it is an artificial island, its creators were able to give it a fanciful shape by playing with both soil and water. The island is therefore traversed by pleasant **canals and gardens ★ ★** *(Jean-Drapeau métro and bus no.167),* laid out for the 1980 Floralies Internationales,

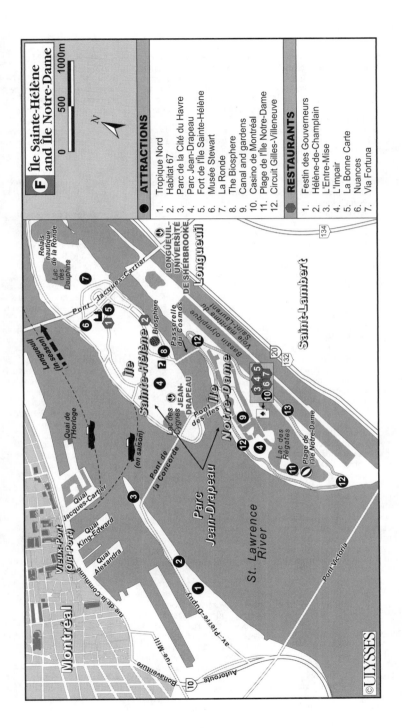

Île Sainte-Hélène and Île Notre-Dame

N 0 500 1000m

ATTRACTIONS

1. Tropique Nord
2. Habitat 67
3. Parc de la Cité du Havre
4. Parc Jean-Drapeau
5. Fort de l'île Sainte-Hélène
6. Musée Stewart
7. La Ronde
8. The Biosphere
9. Canal and gardens
10. Casino de Montréal
11. Plage de l'île Notre-Dame
12. Circuit Gilles-Villeneuve

RESTAURANTS

1. Festin des Gouverneurs
2. Hélène-de-Champlain
3. L'Entre-Mise
4. L'Impair
5. La Bonne Carte
6. Nuances
7. Via Fortuna

© ULYSSES

an international flower show. Boats are available for rent, enabling visitors to ply the canals and admire the flowers mirrored in their waters.

Casino de Montréal ★ *(free admission, parking and coat check; every day 24hrs; Jean-Drapeau métro, bus no.167;* ☎*392-2746)* occupies the former French and Québec pavilions of Expo '67. The main building corresponds to the old **French Pavilion ★**, an aluminum structure designed by architect Jean Faugeron. It was renovated in 1993 at a cost of $92.4 million in order to accommodate the casino. The upper galleries offer some lovely views of downtown Montréal and the St. Lawrence Seaway.

Immediately to the west of the former French pavilion, the building shaped like a truncated pyramid is the former **Québec pavilion ★** *(every day 9am to 3am)*. It was incorporated into the Casino after being raised and recovered with gold-tinted glass in 1996.

Visitors will find all sorts of things to do at the casino, and all this in a very festive atmosphere; some 15,000 people visit the casino each day. With 2,700 slot machines and 107 gaming tables, this is one of the 10 largest casinos in the world. This is also a popular spot thanks to its bars and cabaret, along with its four restaurants, including **Nuances** (see p 134), which is rated as one of the best in Canada. Entrance is reserved for those 18 and over.

Nearby, visitors will find the entrance to the **Plage de l'Île Notre-Dame** *($7.50; late Jun to late Aug, every day 10am to 7pm;* ☎*872-6120)*, a beach enabling Montrealers to lounge on real sand right in the middle of the St. Lawrence. A natural filtering system keeps the water in the small lake clean, with no need for chemical additives. The number of swimmers allowed on the beach is strictly regulated, however, so as not to disrupt the balance of the system.

There are other recreational facilities here as well, namely the **Olympic Basin** created for the rowing competitions of the 1976 Olympics and the **Circuit Gilles-Villeneuve** *(Jean-Drapeau métro and bus no.167)*, where Formula One drivers compete every year in the Grand Prix Player's du Canada, part of the international racing circuit.

To return to downtown Montréal, take the métro from the Jean-Drapeau station.

Tour G: Quartier Latin

People come to the Quartier Latin, a university neighbourhood centred around Rue Saint-Denis, for its theatres, cinemas and countless outdoor cafés, which offer a glimpse of its heterogeneous crowd of students and revellers. The area's origins date back to 1823, when Montréal's first Catholic cathedral, Église Saint-Jacques, opened on Rue Saint-Denis. This prestigious edifice quickly attracted the cream of French Canadian society—mainly old noble families who had remained in Canada after the Conquest—to the area.

In 1852, a fire ravaged the neighbourhood, destroying the cathedral and Monseigneur Bourget's bishop's palace in the process. Painfully reconstructed in the second half of the 19th century, the area remained residential until the Université de Montréal was established here in 1893, marking the beginning of a period of cultural turmoil that would eventually lead to the Quiet Revolution of the 1960s. The Université du Québec, founded in 1974, has since taken over from the Université de Montréal, the latter now located on the north side of Mont Royal. The presence of the university has ensured the quarter's prosperity.

This tour starts at the west exit of the Sherbrooke métro station.

The **Institut de Tourisme et d'Hôtellerie du Québec** *(3535 Rue St-Denis, Sherbrooke métro)*, a school devoted to the tourism and hotel industries, ironically occupies what many people consider the ugliest building in Montréal. Set on the east side of Square Saint-Louis, on Rue Saint-Denis, it is part of an uninspiring group of buildings designed between 1972 and 1976, on the eve of the Olympics. The institute's courses in cooking, tourism and hotel management are nevertheless excellent.

Cross Rue Saint-Denis to Square Saint-Louis.

After the great fire of 1852, a reservoir was built at the top of the hill known as Côte-à-Barron. In 1879, it was dismantled and the site was converted into a park by the name of **Square Saint-Louis ★★** *(Sherbrooke métro)*. Developers built beautiful Second Empire– style homes around the square, making it the nucleus of the French Canadian bourgeois neighbourhood. These groups of houses give the area a certain harmonious quality rarely found in Montréal's urban landscape. **Rue Prince-Arthur** extends west from the square. In the 1960s, this pedestrian street (between Boulevard Saint-Laurent and Avenue Laval) was the centre of the counterculture and the hippie movement in Montréal.

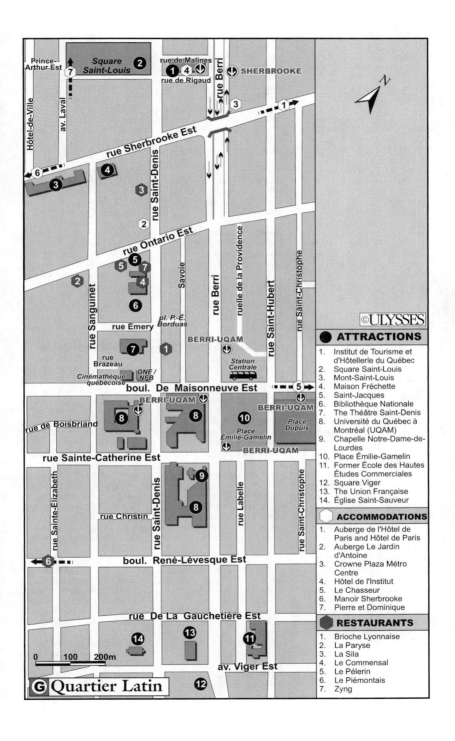

G Quartier Latin

©ULYSSES

● ATTRACTIONS
1. Institut de Tourisme et d'Hôtellerie du Québec
2. Square Saint-Louis
3. Mont-Saint-Louis
4. Maison Fréchette
5. Saint-Jacques
6. Bibliothèque Nationale
7. The Théâtre Saint-Denis
8. Université du Québec à Montréal (UQAM)
9. Chapelle Notre-Dame-de-Lourdes
10. Place Émilie-Gamelin
11. Former École des Hautes Études Commerciales
12. Square Viger
13. The Union Française
14. Église Saint-Sauveur

⬡ ACCOMMODATIONS
1. Auberge de l'Hôtel de Paris and Hôtel de Paris
2. Auberge Le Jardin d'Antoine
3. Crowne Plaza Métro Centre
4. Hôtel de l'Institut
5. Le Chasseur
6. Manoir Sherbrooke
7. Pierre et Dominique

⬡ RESTAURANTS
1. Brioche Lyonnaise
2. La Paryse
3. La Sila
4. Le Commensal
5. Le Pélerin
6. Le Piémontais
7. Zyng

Today, it is lined with numerous restaurants and terraces. On summer evenings, street performers liven up the atmosphere.

Turn left onto **Avenue Laval**, one of the only streets in the city where the Belle Époque atmosphere is still very tangible. Abandoned by the French Canadian bourgeoisie from 1920 on, the houses were converted into rooming houses before attracting the attention of local artists, who began restoring them one by one. Poet Émile Nelligan (1879-1941) lived at number 3688 with his family at the turn of the 20th-century. The Union des Écrivains Québécois (Québec Writers' Association) occupies number 3492, the former home of film-maker Claude Jutra, who directed such films as *Mon Oncle Antoine* (Uncle Antoine). A number of other artists, including singer Pauline Julien and her late husband the poet and politician Gérald Godin, writers Michel Tremblay and Yves Navarre and pianist André Gagnon, live or have lived in the area around Square Saint-Louis and Avenue Laval.

Mont-Saint-Louis ★
(244 Rue Sherbrooke Est, Sherbrooke métro), a former boys' school run by the brothers of the Écoles Chrétiennes, was built facing straight up Avenue Laval in 1887. The long façade punctuated with pavilions, grey stone walls, openings with segmental arches and mansard roof make this building one of the most characteristic examples of the Second Empire style as adapted to suit Montréal's big institutions. The school closed its doors in 1970, and the edifice was converted into an apartment building in 1987, at which time an unobtrusive parking lot was built under the garden.

Journalist, poet and Member of Parliament Louis Fréchette (1839-1908) lived in the **Maison Fréchette** *(306 Rue Sherbrooke Est, Sherbrooke métro)* a Second Empire–style house. Sarah Bernhardt stayed here on several occasions during her North American tours.

Turn right on Rue Saint-Denis and walk down "Côte-à-Barron" toward the Université du Québec à Montréal.

Montée du Zouave, the hill on the right known today as *Terrasse Saint-Denis*, was the favourite meeting place of Québec's poets and writers a century ago. The group of houses was built on the site of the home of Sieur de Montigny, a proud papal Zouave.

Montréal architect Joseph-Arthur Godin was one of the precursors of modern architecture in North America. In 1914, he began construction on three apartment buildings with visible reinforced concrete frames in the Quartier Latin area. One of these is the **Saint-Jacques ★** *(1704 Rue St-Denis, Berri-UQAM métro)*. Godin blended this avant-garde concept with subtle Art-Nouveau curves, giving the buildings a light, graceful appearance. The venture was a commercial failure, however, leading Godin to bankruptcy and ending his career as an architect.

The **Bibliothèque Nationale ★** *(1700 Rue St-Denis, Berri-UQAM métro)*, the national library, was originally built for the Sulpicians, who looked unfavourably upon the construction of a public library on Rue Sherbrooke (see p 118). Even though many works were still on the *Index*, and thus forbidden reading for the clergy, the new library was seen as unfair competition. Known in the past as

Bibliothèque Saint-Sulpice, this branch of the Bibliothèque Nationale du Québec was designed in the Beaux-Arts style by architect Eugène Payette in 1914. This style, a synthesis of classicism and French Renaissance architecture, was taught at the École des Beaux-Arts in Paris, hence its name in North America. The interior is graced with lovely stained-glass windows created by Henri Perdriau in 1915. The Bibliothèque Nationale is set to move, however, to a brand-new building, currently under construction, at the corner of Rue Berri and Boulevard de Maisonneuve. The new library should be inaugurated in late 2003. It will house the collections of the former Bibliothèque Nationale and of the Bibliothèque Centrale de Montréal, all under one roof.

The Théâtre Saint-Denis
(1594 Rue St-Denis, Berri-UQAM métro, ☎790-1111) is made up of two theatres, among the most popular in the city. During summer, the Festival Juste pour Rire, also known as the Just for Laughs Festival, is presented here. The theatre opened in 1914, and has since welcomed big names in show business from the world over. Modernized several times over the years, it was completely renovated yet again in 1989. As visitors can see, the top of the original theatre is higher than the recently added pink-granite façade.

The offices of the **Office National du Film du Canada (ONF) / National Film Board of Canada (NFB)** are located at the corner of Boulevard de Maisonneuve. The ONF-NFB has the world's only **cinérobothèque** *($5/2hrs; Tue-Sun noon to 9pm; ☎496-6887)*, enabling about 100 people to watch different films at once. The complex also has a movie theatre *($5/2hrs; $3/1hr; every day, monthly* schedule) where various documentaries and movies are screened and where it is possible to rent all the movies from the ONF archives. Film buffs can also visit the **Cinémathèque Québécoise** *(exhibits $5, films and exhibits $7.50, Wed free admission from 6pm to 8:30pm; Wed 3pm to 8:30pm, Thu-Sun 3pm to 6pm; 335 Boulevard de Maisonneuve Est;* ☎*842-9768),* a little further west, which has a collection of 25,000 Canadian, Québec and foreign films, as well as hundreds of pieces of equipment dating back to the early history of film. The Cinémathèque recently reopened after extensive renovations. UQAM's new concert hall, **Salle Pierre-Mercure**, is across the street.

Unlike most North American universities, with buildings contained within a specific campus, the campus of the **Université du Québec à Montréal (UQAM)** ★ *(Berri-UQAM métro)* is integrated into the city fabric like French and German universities built during the Renaissance. It is also linked to the underground city and the métro. The university is located on the site once occupied by the buildings of the Université de Montréal and the Église Saint-Jacques, which was reconstructed after the fire of 1852. Only the wall of the right transept and the Gothic Revival steeple were integrated into Pavillon Judith-Jasmin (1979), and these elements have since become the symbol of the university. UQAM is part of the Université du Québec, founded in 1969 and established in cities across the province. Every year, over 40,000 students attend this flourishing institution of higher learning.

Turn left on Rue Sainte-Catherine Est.

Artist Napoléon Bourassa lived in a large house on Rue Saint-Denis. **Chapelle Notre-Dame-de-Lourdes** ★ *(430 Rue Ste-Catherine Est, Berri-UQAM métro),* erected in 1876, was his greatest achievement. It was commissioned by the Sulpicians, who wanted to secure their presence in this part of the city. Its Roman-Byzantine style is in some way a summary of its author's travels. The little chapel's recently restored interior, adorned with Bourassa's vibrantly coloured frescoes, is a must-see.

Place Émilie-Gamelin ★ *(at the corner of Rue Berri and Rue Ste-Catherine, Berri-UQAM métro),* laid out in 1992 for Montréal's 350th anniversary, is the city's newest large public space. In 1994, the area along Rue Sainte-Catherine was renamed **Esplanade Émilie-Gamelin**, while the northern section was renamed **Place du Quartier Latin**. At the far end, visitors will find some curious metal sculptures by Melvin Charney, who also designed the garden of the Canadian Centre for Architecture (see p 98). Across the street lies the bus terminal (Station Centrale), built on top of the Berri-UQAM métro station, where three of the city's four metro lines converge. To the east, the Galeries Dupuis and the Atriums, two shopping centres containing a total of about 100 stores, are located on the site of the former Dupuis Frères department store. A few businesses dear to Montrealers, such as the Archambault record shop, still grace Rue Sainte-Catherine Est. The part of this street between Rue Saint-Hubert and Avenue Papineau is regarded as Montréal's Gay Village because it is lined with a large number of bars, danceclubs and specialty shops frequented mainly by gay men and lesbians.

Turn right on Rue Saint-Hubert, then right again on Avenue Viger.

A symbol of the social ascent of a certain class of French Canadian businessmen in the early 20th century, the former business school, the **École des Hautes Études Commerciales** ★ *(535 Avenue Viger, Berri-UQAM or Champs-de-Mars métro),* profoundly altered Montréal's managerial and financial circles. Prior to the school's existence, these circles were dominated by Canadians of British extraction. This imposing building's very Parisian Beaux-Arts architecture (1908), characterized by twin columns, balustrades, a monumental staircase and sculptures, bears witness to the Francophile leaning of those who built it. In 1970, this business school, known as HEC, joined the campus of the Université de Montréal on the north side of Mont Royal.

Before moving to the Square Saint-Louis area around 1880, members of the French Canadian bourgeoisie settled around **Square Viger** *(Avenue Viger, Berri-UQAM or Champs-de-Mars métro)* during the 1850s. Marred by the underground construction of Aut. Ville-Marie (1977-79), the square was redesigned in three sections by as many artists, who opted for an elaborate design, as opposed to the sober style of the original 19th-century square. In the background, visitors will see the castle-like former Gare Viger (see p 86).

The Union Française *(429 Avenue Viger Est, Berri-UQAM or Champs-de-Mars métro),* Montréal's French cultural association, has occupied this old, aristocratic residence since 1909. Lectures and exhibitions on France and its various regions are held here. Every year, Bastille Day (July 14) is celebrated in Square Viger, across the street. The

Montréal

house, attributed to architect Henri-Maurice Perrault, was built in 1867 for shipowner Jacques-Félix Sincennes, founder of the Richelieu and Ontario Navigation Company. It is one of the oldest examples of Second Empire architecture in Montréal.

At the corner of Rue Saint-Denis is the **Église Saint-Sauveur** *(329 Avenue Viger, Berri-UQAM or Champs-de-Mars métro)*, a Gothic Revival church built in 1865, according to a design by architects Lawford and Nelson. From 1922 to 1995, it was the seat of Montréal's Syrian Catholic community. The church has a semicircular chancel, adorned with lovely stained-glass windows by artist Guido Nincheri.

Tour H: Plateau Mont-Royal

If there is one neighbourhood typical of Montréal, it is definitely the Plateau Mont-Royal. Thrown into the spotlight by writer Michel Tremblay, one of its illustrious sons, the "Plateau," as its inhabitants refer to it, is a neighbourhood of penniless intellectuals, young

professionals and old Francophone working-class families. Its long streets are lined with duplexes and triplexes adorned with amusingly contorted exterior staircases leading up to the long, narrow apartments that are so typical of Montréal.

Flower-decked balconies made of wood or wrought iron provide box-seats for the spectacle on the street below. The Plateau is bounded by the mountain to the west, the Canadian Pacific railway tracks to the north and east, and Rue Sherbrooke to the south. It is traversed by a few major streets lined with cafés and theatres, such as Rue Saint-Denis and Avenue Papineau, but is a tranquil area on the whole. A stroll through this area is a must for visitors who want to grasp the spirit of Montréal.

This tour starts at the exit of the Mont-Royal métro station. Turn right on Avenue du Mont-Royal, the neighbourhood's main commercial artery.

The **Monastère des Pères du Très-Saint-Sacrement ★** *(500 Avenue du Mont-Royal Est, Mont-Royal métro)* and its church, Église Notre-Dame-

du-Très-Saint-Sacrement, were built at the end of the 19th century for the community of priests (*Père* is the French word for Father) of the same name. The somewhat austere façade of the church conceals an extremely colourful interior with an Italian-style decor designed by Jean-Zéphirin Resther. This sanctuary, dedicated to the "eternal Exhibition and Adoration of the Eucharist," is open for prayer and contemplation every day of the week. Baroque music concerts are occasionally presented here.

Continue heading east on **Avenue du Mont-Royal Est**, blending in with the neighbourhood's widely varied inhabitants on their way in and out of an assortment of businesses, ranging from chic pastry shops to shops selling knick-knacks for a dollar and used records and books.

Turn right on Rue Fabre for some good examples of Montréal-style housing. Built between 1900 and 1925, the houses contain between two and five apartments, all with private entrances from outside. Decorative details vary from one building to the next. Visitors will see Art Nouveau stained glass, parapets,

● ATTRACTIONS

1. Monastère des Pères du Très-Saint-Sacrement	4. Place Charles-de-Gaulle
2. Parc Lafontaine	5. Former Institut des Sourdes-Muettes
3. Église de l'Immaculée-Conception	6. Église Saint-Jean-Baptiste

○ ACCOMMODATIONS

1. Auberge de la Fontaine	3. Gîte du Parc Lafontaine
2. B & B Bienvenue	4. Vacances Canada 4 Saisons

● RESTAURANTS

1. Aux 2 Marie	12. Côté Soleil	23. Lélé da Cuca
2. Beauty's	13. Fruit Folie	24. Misto
3. Bières & Compagnie	14. Khyber Pass	25. Moishe's Steak House
4. Binerie Mont-Royal	15. L'Anecdote	26. Ouzeri
5. Brûlerie Saint-Denis	16. L'Express	27. Psarotaverna du Symposium
6. Cactus	17. La Gaudriole	28. Schwartz's Montréal Hebrew
7. Café Cherrier	18. La Raclette	Delicatessen
8. Café El Dorado	19. Laloux	29. Tampopo
9. Café Rico	20. Le 917	30. Toqué
10. Chu Chai	21. Le Piton de la Fournaise	31. Vents du Sud
11. Continental	22. Le P'tit Plateau	

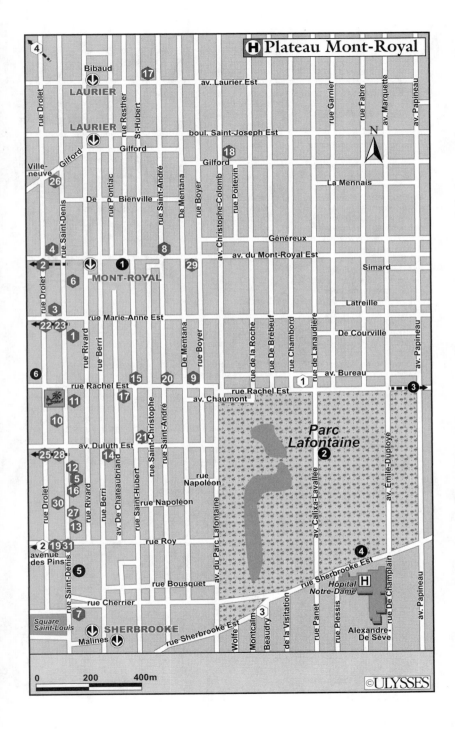

cornices made of brick or sheet metal, balconies with Tuscan columns, and ornamental ironwork shaped in ringlets and cables.

Turn left on Rue Rachel Est.

At the end of Rue Fabre, visitors will find **Parc Lafontaine** *(Sherbrooke métro)*, the Plateau's main green space, laid out in 1908 on the site of an old military shooting range. Monuments to Sir Louis-Hippolyte Lafontaine, Félix Leclerc and Dollard des Ormeaux have been erected here. The park covers an area of 40ha and is embellished with two artificial lakes and shady paths for pedestrians and cyclists. There are tennis courts and bowling greens for summer sports enthusiasts, and in the winter the frozen lakes form a large rink, which is illuminated at night. The Théâtre de Verdure (outdoor theatre) is also located here. Every weekend, the park is crowded with people from the neighbourhood, who come here to make the most of beautiful sunny or snowy days.

The parish churches on Plateau Mont-Royal, designed to accommodate large French Canadian working-class families, are enormous. The Romanesque Revival **Église de l'Immaculée-Conception** *(at the corner of Avenue Papineau, Sherbrooke or Mont-Royal métro)*, designed by Émile Tanguay, was built in 1895. The interior, decorated with plaster statues and remounted paintings, is typical of that period. The stained-glass windows come from the Maison Vermont in France.

Turn right on Avenue Papineau and right again on Rue Sherbrooke Est.

An obelisk dedicated to General de Gaulle, by French artist Olivier Debré, towers over the long **Place Charles-de-Gaulle** *(at the corner of Avenue Émile-Duployé, Sherbrooke métro)*, located alongside Rue Sherbrooke. The monument, made of blue granite from the quarries of Saint-Michel-de-Montjoie in Normandy, stands 17m high. It was given to the City of Montréal by the City of Paris in 1992, on the occasion of Montréal's 350th anniversary.

Hôpital Notre-Dame, one of the city's major hospitals, lies across the street. The attractive **École Le Plateau** (1930) is located a little further west, at 3700 Avenue Calixa-Lavallée. This Art Deco building, designed by architects Perrault and Gadbois, also houses the hall used by the Montréal Symphony Orchestra in its early days. A trail to the north of the school provides access to the lakes in Parc Lafontaine.

Back on Rue Sherbrooke Est, visitors will find the **Bibliothèque Centrale de Montréal** *(1210 Rue Sherbrooke Est)*, the city's public library, inaugurated in 1917 by Maréchal Joffre. Even back in the early 20th century, the edifice was of modest size, given the number of people it was intended to serve, a result of the clergy's reservations about a non-religious library opening in Montréal. Today, fortunately, the library has a network of 27 neighbourhood branches. Inside, an entire room is devoted to the genealogy of French Canadian families (Salle Gagnon, in the basement). When the new Bibliothèque Nationale moves to a brand-new building, currently under construction, at the corner of Rue Berri and Boulevard de Maisonneuve, in late 2003, it will house the collections of the former Bibliothèque Nationale and of the Bibliothèque Centrale de Montréal, all under one roof.

The monument to Sir Louis-Hippolyte Lafontaine (1807-1864), after whom the park was named, is located across the street. Regarded as the father of responsible government in Canada, Lafontaine was also one of the main defenders of the French language in the country's institutions.

Take Rue Cherrier, which branches off from Rue Sherbrooke Est across from the monument.

Rue Cherrier, along with Square Saint-Louis, located at its west end, once formed the nucleus of the French Canadian bourgeois neighbourhood. At number 840, visitors will find the **Agora de la Danse**, where the studios of a variety of dance companies are located. The red-brick building, completed in 1919, originally served as the Palestre Nationale, a sports centre for neighbourhood youth and the scene of many tumultuous public gatherings during the 1930s.

Turn right on Rue Saint-Hubert, lined with fine examples of vernacular architecture. Turn left on Rue Roy to see Église Saint-Louis-de-France, built in 1936 as a replacement for the original church, destroyed by fire in 1933.

At the corner of **Rue Saint-Denis** stands the former **Institut des Sourdes-Muettes** (*3725 Rue St-Denis, Sherbrooke métro*), a large, grey-stone building made up of numerous wings and erected in stages between 1881 and 1900.

Built in the Second Empire style, it covers an entire block and is typical of institutional architecture of that period in Québec. It once took in the region's deafs. The strange chapel with cast-iron columns, as well as the sacristy, with its tall wardrobes and surprising spiral staircase, may be visited upon request from the entrance on Rue Berri.

Head north on Rue Saint-Denis.

Between Boulevard De Maisonneuve, to the south, and Boulevard Saint-Joseph, to the north, this long artery is lined with numerous outdoor cafés and beautiful shops, established inside Second Empire–style residences built during the second half of the 19th century. Visitors will also find many bookstores, tea rooms and restaurants that have become veritable Montréal institutions over the years.

Take a brief detour left onto Rue Rachel Est in order to see Église Saint-Jean-Baptiste and the institutional buildings around it.

Église Saint-Jean-Baptiste ★★ (*309 Rue Ra-*

chel Est, Mont-Royal métro), dedicated to the patron saint of French Canadians, is a gigantic symbol of the solid faith of the Catholic working-class inhabitants of the Plateau Mont-Royal at the turn of the 20th century, who, despite their poverty and large families, managed to amass considerable amounts of money for the construction of sumptuous churches. The exterior was built in 1901, according to a design by architect Émile Vanier. The interior was re-done after a fire, and is now a veritable Baroque Revival masterpiece designed by Casimir Saint-Jean that is not to be missed. The pink-marble and gilded wood baldaquin in the chancel (1915) shelters the altar, which is made of white Italian marble and faces the large Casavant organs— among the most powerful in the city—in the jube. Concerts are frequently given at this church. It can seat up to 3,000 people.

Collège Rachel, built in 1876 in the Second Empire style, stands across the street from the church. Finally, west of Avenue Henri-Julien, visitors will find the former **Hospice Auclair** (1894), with its semi-circular entrance on Rue Rachel. On Rue Drolet, south of Rue Rachel, there are several good examples of the working-class architecture of the 1870s and 1880s on the Plateau, before the advent of vernacular housing, such as the duplexes and triplexes with exterior staircases like those found on Rue Fabre.

Go back to Rue Saint-Denis and continue walking north to Avenue du Mont-Royal. Turn right to return to the Mont-Royal métro station.

Tour I: Laval

Laval, Québec's second-largest city, is located on a large island north of Montréal called

Île Jésus. The island is surrounded by three bodies of water, Lac des Deux-Montagnes to the east, Rivière des Prairies to the south and Rivière des Mille-Îles to the north. French settlers were attracted to Île Jésus very early on by its fertile soil. Saint-François-de-Sales, the first village on Île Jésus, was founded in 1706 after a peace treaty with the Aboriginal people was signed. Laval is now a residential and industrial suburb, but it has managed to preserve some of its architectural heritage and farmland, and also has set aside several large spaces for outdoor activities. Laval is easily accessible from Montréal by car (see p 74).

The **Cosmodôme ★** (*$11.50; late Jun to early Sep, every day 10am to 6pm; early Sep to late Jun, Tue-Sun 10am to 6pm; 2150 Aut. 15, St-Martin Ouest Exit, ☎978-3600*) is a space museum. A tour of the premises starts with a fascinating multimedia presentation on the history of the discovery of outer space. The second part is devoted to means of space travel and explains the laws of physics that govern life in outer space using all sorts of high-tech interactive displays. The third part deals with telecommunications and the "global village"; the fourth, devoted to Earth, explains the principal terrestrial phenomena, such as the changing of the seasons and geology. Section five contains the museum's *pièce de résistance*, a piece of lunar rock. This sample was donated by NASA, thus granting this Laval museum international recognition. A look at the solar system winds things up; there are scale reproductions of all the planets, showing how very small Earth is when compared to the solar system as a whole. The Cosmodôme offers budding astronauts a space camp (*half-day to 6 days; ☎800-565-2267*). In addition to taking part in a host of science

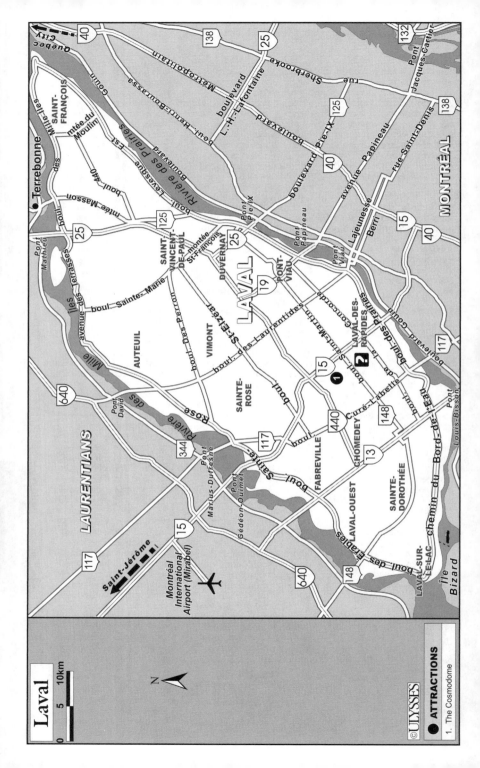

Laval

0   5   10km

N

© ULYSSES

ATTRACTIONS

● 1. The Cosmodome

workshops and activities, "young recruits" will also get the chance to go on a space mission and train on NASA simulators.

Parks

The island of Montréal is dotted with parks where visitors can enjoy all sorts of activities. **Parc Angrignon** (*3400 Boulevard des Trinitaires*), **Parc Lafontaine** (see p 118), **Parc du Mont-Royal** (see below), **Parc Jeanne-Mance** (*Avenue de l'Esplanade, between Avenue du Mont-Royal and rue Duluth*) and **Parc René-Lévesque** (*at the west end of the Lachine canal*) are all very pleasant places to relax in a peaceful atmosphere. Year-round, Montrealers take advantage of these small islands of greenery to unwind far from the urban tumult, while remaining right in the heart of the city. Following are the other popular parks:

Tour D: Mount-Royal and Westmount

All year-round, Montrealers flock to **Parc du Mont-Royal**, a huge green expanse in the middle of the city, to enjoy a wide range of athletic activities. During summer, footpaths and mountain-bike trails are open. Bird feeders have been set up along one trail for bird-watchers. During winter, the paths serve as cross-country ski trails, leading across the snowy slopes of the mountain, and Lac aux Castors becomes a big, beautiful skating rink, where people of all ages come to enjoy themselves.

Tour F: Île Sainte-Hélène and Île Notre-Dame

Parc Jean-Drapeau (☎872-6120) encompasses both Île Sainte-Hélène and Île Notre-Dame. Montrealers flock here on sunny summer days to enjoy the beach and the swimming pools. Footpaths and bicycle trails crisscross the park. In wintertime, a whole host of activities is organized here, including cross-country skiing (14km), tobogganing, ice fishing and skating on the 2km-long Olympic rowing basin.

Tour I: Laval

Parc de la Rivière-des-Mille-Îles (*345 Boulevard Ste-Rose*, ☎622-1020) is a beautiful place to stop. The archipelago's plants and wildlife are accessible along several paths. You can also enjoy several activities like kayaking and pedal-boating. Equipment can be rented on site. The park is popular amongst hikers and cross-country skiers. This is a series of short paths on various islands. The hike includes observation points that reveal this self-contained environment.

Outdoor Activities

Cycling

Cyclists will be thrilled to discover nearly 400km of interesting bicycle paths that traverse the island of Montréal. A map of the paths

is available at tourist information offices, or visitors can purchase *Biking Montréal*, published by Ulysses Travel Guides. Except during rush hour, bicycles can be taken on the métro.

The area around the **Lachine Canal** has been redesigned in an effort to highlight this communication route during the 19th and early 20th centuries (see p 83). A pleasant bike path was laid out alongside the canal. Very popular with Montrealers, especially on Sundays, the path leads to **Parc René-Lévesque**, a narrow strip of land jutting out into Lac Saint-Louis that offers splendid views of the lake and surroundings. There are benches and picnic tables in the park and plenty of seagulls to keep you company. The path leads around the park, returning beside the river and the Lachine Rapids. Many birds frequent this side of the park, and if you are lucky you might see some great blue herons.

Île Notre-Dame and **Île Sainte-Hélène** are accessible from Old Montreal. The path runs through an industrial area, then through the Cité du Havre before reaching the islands (cyclists can cross the river on the Pont de la Concorde). It is easy to ride from one island to the other. The islands are well maintained and are a great place to relax, stroll and admire Montréal's skyline.

Bicycle Rentals

La Cordée
2159 Rue Ste-Catherine Est, Papineau métro
☎524-1106
$18 to $35 for a full day (a $250 to $300 deposit is required).

Montréal

Rafting

**Les Descentes sur
le Saint-Laurent**
early May to late Oct;
8912 boul. Lasalle
☎*767-2230 or 800-324-7238*
Les Descentes sur le Saint-Laurent offers various types of river rides in inflatable boats down the Lachine Rapids, and the office is located only minutes from downtown. Along with the river ride, there is a presentation on the history and ecology of the rapids and the bird sanctuary on Île aux Hérons. A shuttle service is offered free of charge from the Centre Infotouriste.

Skating

Ice-skating has not lost any of its popularity in Montréal. This sport is inexpensive and requires minimal equipment and technique.

During the winter, a number of public skating rinks are set up. Among the nicest ones are:

Lac aux Castors
Parc du Mont-Royal

Parc Lafontaine
between Sherbrooke and Rachel, and Papineau and Lafontaine

Vieux-Port
333 Rue de la Commune Ouest
☎*496-PORT*

Parc Maisonneuve
4601 Rue Sherbrooke Ouest
☎*872-5558*

Parc des Îles
on the Olympic rowing basin on Île Notre-Dame
This rink is the longest in Montréal, at 1.6km.

Amphithéatre Bell
$5
1000 Rue De La Gauchetière Ouest
☎*395-0555*
The Amphithéatre Bell, located in 1000 de la Gauchetière (the tallest office building in Montréal), houses a large skating rink with a surface area of 900m². The rink is surrounded by food stands and rest areas, and overlooked by a mezzanine. Above the skating rink is a superb glass dome that lets the sun shine in. Ice skates can be rented at the rink for $4.

Adventure Packages

If you are travelling to Montréal and long for the outdoors, why not take part in one of the activities offered by **Globe-Trotteur Aventure Canada** *(4764 Papineau,* ☎*849-8768 or 888-598-7688)?* This young company offers many winter and summer tour packages, such as horseback riding, canoeing, camping and snowmobiling in different regions around Montréal. These packages include transportation and equipment rental, which can be quite useful for travellers. An experienced guide will accompany you during these tours, which can last from half a day to 24 days. In summer, a fixed activity schedule will help you better plan your expeditions.

Accommodations

Travellers will discover a large variety of comfortable lodgings in all categories in Montréal. Rates vary greatly from one season to the next. They are much higher during the summer, but usually lower on the weekends than during the week. Remember that the weeks of the Grand Prix (June) and of the Jazz Festival (end Jun to beg. Jul) are the busiest of the year; we recommend making reservations well in advance if you plan to be in Montréal during these events. In the off-season, it is often possible to obtain better rates than the ones quoted in this guide.

In Montréal's Infotouriste information centre, there is a service which makes hotel reservations free of charge:

Hospitalité Canada
1001 Rue du Square-Dorchester
Montréal H3B 4V4
☎*393-9049 or 800-665-1528*

The **Fédération des Agricotours** *(☎252-3138)* publishes an annual guide entitled *Inns and Bed & Breakfasts in Québec*, which lists the names and telephone numbers of all of its members who provide rooms for travellers. The rooms offered have been selected according to the federation's standards of quality. They are also fairly economical. The guide is available in bookstores.

Réseau de Gîte Montréal Centre-ville
$$
3458 Avenue Laval
☎*289-9749 or 800-267-5180*
≈*287-7386*
Gîte Montréal is an association of nearly 100 bed & breakfasts *(gîtes)*, mostly Victorian houses in the Latin Quarter. In order to make sure that all rooms offered are comfortable, the organization visits each one. Reservations required.

Relais Montréal Hospitalité
3977 Avenue Laval
☎*287-9635 or 800-363-9635*
≈*287-1007*
About 30 bed and breakfasts are also registered with the Relais Montréal Hospitalité. All have been carefully inspected, and the rooms are clean and

comfortable. The establishments are located throughout Montreal, though many are on on Rue Laval.

Tour A: Vieux-Montréal

Auberge Alternative
$ per person in the dormitory
$$ for two people in the rooms
sb, ☎, *K*
358 Rue St-Pierre
☎282-8069
www.auberge-alternative.qc.ca
Located in Old Montreal, the Auberge Alternative is run by a young couple in a renovated building dating from 1875. The 34 beds in the rooms and dormitories are rudimentary but comfortable, and the bathrooms are very clean. Brightly coloured walls, lots of space and a large common room and kitchen with stone walls and old wooden floors complete the facilities. Guests have laundry machines at their disposal. Twenty-four hour access.

🌴 Passants du Sans-Soucy
$$$ bkfst incl.
≡, ⊛
171 Rue St-Paul Ouest
☎842-2634
≈842-2912
Passants du Sans-Soucy is an extremely pleasant inn set in the heart of the old city, whose charming rooms are furnished with antiques. Built in 1723, the building was renovated about 10 years ago. Reservations required.

🌴 Auberge du Vieux-Port
$$$$ bkfst incl.
≡, *K*, ℜ, ⊛
97 Rue de la Commune E.
☎876-0081 or 888-660-7678
≈876-8923
www.aubergeduvieuxport.com
The Auberge du Vieux-Port stands right in front of the Old Port. Opened in 1996, this place is a real gem. It occupies a historic building dating from

1882, whose stone walls have been left exposed in the chic, attractively decorated lobby. All the rooms have been decorated so as to pay homage to the past, with outstanding results. Each has a telephone with voice mail. There is a French restaurant in the basement, where you can see a segment of the fortifications of the old city. No smoking in the rooms.

Auberge Bonaparte
$$$$ bkfst incl.
⊛, ≡, ℜ
447 Rue St-François-Xavier
☎844-1448
≈844-0272
www.bonaparte.ca
Well known for its delicious French cuisine (see p 130), Bonapart restaurant now has offers a 30-room inn on its upper floors. They are all quite comfortable and feature a lovely decor, although the beds don't look quite as inviting as they should. The rooms at the rear of the building, which dates from 1886, overlook the Jardin des Sulpiciens, behind the Notre-Dame basilica. Breakfast is served at the restaurant.

XIXe Siècle
$$$$ bkfst incl.
⊛, ≡
262 Rue St-Jacques Ouest,
☎985-0019
≈985-0059
www.hotelxixsiecle.com
Located in a Second Empire former bank building, the XIXe (dix-neufième) Siècle (19th century) hotel combines the charm of the 19th century with modern amenities. Its rooms are spacious, a quality emphasized by their high ceilings and large windows. Warm colours, stylish furnishings, lovely fabrics and beautiful bathrooms provide a comfortable, cozy decor. The breakfast room is decorated in harmonious black and white tones, while the lobby welcomes guests with armchairs and a collection of books.

Hôtel Place d'Armes
$$$$bkfst incl.
⊛, ≡, ℜ, ⊘
☎701 Côte de la Place d'Armes
☎842-1887 or 888-450-1887
≈842-6469
www.hotelplacedarmes.com
One of the first boutique hotels to have taken over Old Montréal was the Hôtel Place d'Armes. It stands at the corner of the square of the same name, which also faces the magnificent Notre-Dame Basilica. Some of the rooms offer a lovely view of the basilica while others overlook the city, on the opposite side. And if you get tired of the outdoor panorama, you can always admire the interior scene, which is just as attractive. Dark wood and cream tones give the decor a gorgeous, classical look, and some rooms even have a brick wall. Equipped with CD players, high-speed Internet access and modern bathrooms, all are comfortable and practical. In addition to breakfast in the morning, wine and cheese are offered in the lobby before dinner.

🌴 Hôtel Inter-Continental Montréal
$$$$-$$$$$
≈, ⊘, ℜ, △, ≡, ⅄, 🐾
360 Rue St-Antoine Ouest
☎987-9900 or 800-327-0200
≈847-8730
www.montreal.interconti.com
Except for one of its wings, this hotel, located on the edge of Old Montreal, is a fairly new building (1991) that is linked to the Centre de Commerce Mondial (World Trade Centre) and several shops. The Palais des Congrès (convention centre) is right nearby. The hotel has an original look, due to its turret with multiple windows, where the living rooms of the suites are located. The rooms are tastefully decorated with simple furniture. Each one is equipped with a spacious bathroom, among other nice

Montréal

touches. Guests are courteously and attentively welcomed. Business people will enjoy all the necessary services, such as computer hookups, fax machines and photocopiers.

St-Paul Hotel
$$$$$
≡, ⊘, ℜ
355 Rue McGill
☎*380-2222 or 866-380-2202*
⇌*380-2200*
www.hotelstpaul.com
The St-Paul Hotel's 96 rooms and 24 suites are housed in a superb historic building that has been entirely renovated. Consequently, the interior decor is very modern, and various materials blend harmoniously to create a stunning effect. With alabaster and fire, fur and vinyl, black tiling and cream-coloured fabrics, each room has been created with utmost care. The result is an audacious and avant-garde design, making it a unique place where wealthy, fashionable guests can get together. Despite the bold decor, some of the spaces are quite warm and inviting. For example, in some rooms, the bed area is delimited by a curtain that lends a cozy effect. The hotel's restaurant, Cube (see p 130), is already internationally renowned.

Hostellerie et Restaurant Pierre du Calvet 1725
$$$$$ bkfst incl.
ℜ, ≡, ℜ
405 Rue Bonsecours
Champ-de-Mars métro
☎*282-1725*
⇌*282-0456*
www.pierreducalvet.ca
This is one of Montréal's oldest homes, discretely tucked away at the intersection of Bonsecours and Saint-Paul streets. It has recently been entirely renovated, as have many other older houses in the neighbourhood. The rooms, each different from the next and each with its own fireplace, exude a refined

charm, with lovely antique wood panelling accentuated by stained glass and beautiful antiques. Moreover, the bathrooms are tiled in Italian marble. A pretty indoor courtyard and day room allow guests to escape from the crowds. Breakfast is served in a lovely Victorian dining room. The service is attentive and meticulous. In short, this inn, located in the heart of the city's historic district, is a real gem that will make your stay absolutely unforgettable.

Hôtel Nelligan
$$$$$ bkfst incl.
≡, ℜ, ℜ, ⊘, ⊛
106 Rue St-Paul Ouest
☎*788-2040 or 877-788-2040*
⇌*788-2041*
www.hotelnelligan.com
It's anyone's guess what the famous poet would have thought of the luxury hotel bearing his name, but one thing's for sure: this place is something else! Recently opened in Old Montréal, this boutique hotel boasts 60 all-equipped, very comfortable rooms and suites. The establishment belongs to a family that owns many others in the neighbourhood and, as such, has the know-how to make a place special. Between the lobby and the restaurant is a lovely inner courtyard where breakfast is served. Some of the rooms overlook the courtyard, which, despite the lack of view, makes for a quieter environment. The rooms are attractive, with stone and/or brick walls, wood blinds, modern bathrooms (some of which feature a double whirlpool) and down-filled duvets. Wine and cheese are served in the courtyard from 5pm to 7pm, next to an inviting reading nook. In fact, the poetry theme is found throughout the hotel; for instance, the rooms are decorated with canvases on which Nelligan's poems have been handwritten.

Le Saint-Sulpice
$$$$$
≡, ℜ, ⅋, ℜ, ⊘, K
414 Rue St-Sulpice
☎*288-1000 or 877-SULPICE*
⇌*288-0077*
www.concorde-hotels.com
Enter the huge lobby of the Saint-Sulpice hotel and discover a world of luxury and comfort with a touch of Old Montréal. Throughout the establishment, decorative elements remind guests that the site is steeped in history: amber and mahogany woodwork, stone walls, rugs with *fleur de lys* motifs, fireplace, etc. After all, the Sulpicians played a major role in the city's history! In fact, their basilica and seminary are located next door to the hotel, whose courtyard features a fountain and offers direct access to the beautiful Jardin des Sulpiciens. Because it is an all-suite hotel, you will have enough room to move around and a kitchenette to boot. You can also rent apartments (condos) for longer stays. Best of all, some of the suites have a balcony or a roof patio.

Hôtel Gault
$$$$$ bkfst incl.
≡, ⊘
449 Rue Ste-Hélène (at Ave des Récollets)
☎*904-1616 or 866-904-1616*
⇌*904-1717*
www.hotelgault.com
Opened in June 2002, Hôtel Gault is a small, 30-room hotel reminiscent of a private mansion…one could get used to living here! It features designer furnishings and accessories that were created especially for its innovative decor. The lobby features large windows that give an impression of space, and there is a cozy reading nook at the rear. Breakfast is served communal style at a large table. All the rooms, occupying four floors, are decorated by theme. Each is unique, though all share a similar contemporary style. With the exception of the lofts, the rooms are not very

big, but the space is well designed and very comfortable. The lovely, modern bathrooms are equipped with old-fashioned tubs, a heated floor and all the amenities to pamper yourself. Some rooms have a patio and all windows open onto the street and the pretty flower boxes that enhance the facade.

Le Saint-James
$$$$$
≡, ⊛
355 Rue St-Jacques
☎*841-3111 or 866-841-3111*
⇀*841-1232*
www.hotellestjames.com
A magnificent hotel that exudes luxury, Le Saint-James opened in the spring of 2002 and is the delight of a well-off clientele who wishes to explore Montréal while enjoying a comfortable stay in a sumptuous, refined environment. Fittingly, it stands in the very heart of Montréal's former business district, in a gorgeous building that has seen many a financial transaction and, in the past few years, has undergone major renovations. While its designers were busy restoring this building's former lustre and adding modern amenities, a team of specialists was scouring Europe, the Far East and the rest of the planet handpicking furnishings and art work. Antiques, paintings, sculptures and furnishings now richly decorate the hotel's lobby, hallways, rooms and suites. The result will please even the most demanding guest! The building's architecture, with its friezes and mouldings, is accentuated by the decor's warmth and richness, as well as top-quality services and amenities.

Tour B: Downtown

Auberge de Jeunesse
$
≡, K
1030 Rue Mackay
☎*843-3317*
www.hostellingmontreal.com
This youth hostel, located a stone's throw from the downtown area, offers 250 beds in rooms for four to 10 people as well as about 15 private rooms. All rooms features private bathrooms. This hotel is one of the cheapest in Montréal. Guests have the use of a washer and dryer, as well as a kitchen, a luggage checkroom, a pool table and a TV room. This is a non-smoking hostel.

McGill University
$
sb, K, ℝ
mid-May to mid-Aug
3935 University, McGill métro
☎*398-6367*
⇀*398-4854*
There are about 1,100 rooms, each containing one or two beds, in the six residence halls of McGill University. The rooms are small, but each has a large chest of drawers and a desk, and some offer a magnificent view of Mont Royal. Most are equipped with a miniature refrigerator, and all the windows open. There are two kitchenettes and two large bathrooms on each floor. For an additional charge, guests can use the university pool, gym and tennis courts.

L'Abri du Voyageur
$-$$
sb, ≡
9 Rue Ste-Catherine Ouest
☎*849-2922*
www.abri-voyageur.ca
This is the perfect hotel for young travellers. It is located on bustling Rue Sainte-Catherine, almost at the corner of Boulevard Saint-Laurent, right in the heart of Montréal's nightlife! There are only four bathrooms in the

two-storey hotel, but all of the rooms have sinks. The rooms are simple and clean, and the welcome is friendly.

Manoir Ambrose
$$ bkfst incl.
pb/sb, ≡
3422 Rue Stanley
☎*288-6922*
www.manoirambrose.com
Manoir Ambrose is set in two big, beautiful Victorian stone houses, side by side on a peaceful street. It has several little rooms scattered all over the house. The outdated décor will amuse some guests, but the rooms are well-kept and the service is friendly. Laundry service for a fee (*$5*).

Hôtel du Nouveau Forum
$$ bkfst incl.
pb/sb, ≡, ℜ
1320 Rue St-Antoine Ouest
☎*989-0300 or 888-989-0300*
⇀*931-3090*
www.nouveau-forum.com
Located right next to the Bell Centre and not far from Old Montreal, the Hôtel du Nouveau Forum has about 40 small, modest but decent rooms. It occupies a historic store house that has been renovated inside and out. Fortunately, the friendly staff add a little warmth to the rather sterile atmosphere of the hallways and the dining room, where a very hearty breakfast is served. There is a public telephone on each floor, and guests can communicate with the reception desk by intercom. The rooms do not have bathtubs.

Hotel Casa Bella
$$ bkfst incl.
pb/sb, ≡
264 Rue Sherbrooke Ouest
☎*849-2777 or 888-453-2777*
⇀*849-3650*
www.hotelcasabella.com
Located near Place des Arts on Rue Sherbrooke beside an abandoned lot, Hotel Casa Bella is a charming hotel set in a century home. The rooms are pretty and reflect the care that has gone into decorating

Montréal

them. There is free laundry service and free parking. The friendly welcome makes guests feel quickly at ease. Good value for the money.

Hôtel de la Montagne
$$$
⊛, ℜ, ≈, ≡
1430 Rue de la Montagne
☎288-5656 or 800-361-6262
⇄288-9658
www.hoteldela
montagne.com
Besides its 135 rooms spread over 19 floors, the Hôtel de la Montagne also has a pool, an excellent restaurant and a bar, as well as friendly and courteous staff. The pool is outside, on the roof, and is only open in the summer.

Hôtel Renaissance Montréal
$$$
ℜ, ⊛, ≈, ⊘, ≡, △, 🐾, ᴄ.
3625 Avenue du Parc
☎288-6666 or 800-363-0735
⇄288-2469
www.renaissancehotels.com
Both tourists and business people stay in these fully equipped rooms. The hotel has a new fitness centre, and guests have access to the pool at the Université de Montréal's athletic centre. There is a coffee maker in each room.

Château Versailles
$$$$ bkfst incl.
ℜ, ⊛, △, ⊘, ≡, ℑ
1659 Rue Sherbrooke Ouest
☎933-8311 or 888-933-8111
⇄933-6867
www.versailleshotels.com
The Château Versailles reopened in 2000 after major renovations. It was converted into a charming boutique hotel whose 65 rooms have preserved some of the old building's elements, such as mouldings, fireplaces and light fixtures, combined with Victorian and modern accessories. The result is a lovely, relaxing atmosphere.

Hôtel Wyndham Montréal
$$$$ bkfst incl.
≈, △, ⊘, ℜ, ≡
1255 rue Jeanne-Mance
☎285-1450 or 800-361-8234
⇄285-1243
www.wyndham.com
The Wyndham Montréal is part of Complexe Desjardins. Consequently, there is a series of shops, movie theatres and restaurants on the main floor. Located a step away from Place des Arts and the Musée d'Art Contemporain, the hotel has a prime downtown location right next to all the action of the summer Jazz Festival along Rue Ste-Catherine. The large, comfortable rooms live up to one's expectations of a hotel of this category.

Novotel Montréal Centre
$$$$
⊘, △, ℜ, ≡, ᴄ., ⊛
1180 Rue de la Montagne
☎861-6000 or 800-221-4542
⇄861-0992
www.novotel.com
Novotel is a French hotel chain. The pleasant rooms in its downtown Montréal hotel are equipped with numerous extras, including a large desk and outlets for computers. Special packages are available for guests travelling with children. The emphasis seems to be on security, as there is no access to the upper floors after 10pm without your room key. No-smoking rooms.

Hilton Montréal Bonaventure
$$$$
≈, ⊘, ℜ, ≡, ᴄ., 🐾
1 Place Bonaventure
☎878-2332 or 800-267-2575
www.hiltonmontreal.com
Guests of the Hilton Montréal Bonaventure, located on the boundary between downtown and Old Montreal, enjoy a number of little extras that make this hotel a perfect place to relax. The rooms are decorated in a simple manner, without a hint of extravagance. The hotel has a heated outdoor swimming pool, where guests can swim all year-

round, as well as a lovely garden and access to the underground city (see p 142).

Le Centre Sheraton
$$$$$
≈, ⊘, △, ℜ, ≡, ⊛, ᴄ.
1201 Boulevard René-Lévesque
☎878-2000 or 800-325-3535
⇄878-3958
Standing over 30 stories high, this giant has 825 attractive rooms. A number of little extras (coffee makers, hair dryers, irons and ironing boards, non-smoking floors) add to their comfort. Some rooms are equipped for business people with fax machines, modem hook-ups, voice mailboxes, etc. Take some time to admire the beautiful lobby, decorated with picture windows and tropical plants.

Fairmont The Queen Elizabeth
$$$$$
⊛, ≈, ℜ, ⊘, ᴄ., ≡
900 Boulevard René-Lévesque Ouest
☎861-3511 or 800-441-1414
⇄954-2256
www.fairmont.com
Fairmont The Queen Elizabeth is one Montréal hotel that has set itself apart over the years. Its lobby, decorated with fine wood panelling, is magnificent. Visitors will find a number of shops on the main floor. Two of the hotel's floors, designated "Entrée Or," boast luxurious suites and are like a hotel within the hotel. Numerous renovations were completed in 1996. The hotel advantageously located in the heart of downtown, and its underground corridors, furthermore, provide easy access to the train station and the underground city.

Ritz-Carlton
$$$$$
⊘, ℜ, ≡, ⊛, ℑ
1228 Rue Sherbrooke Ouest
☎842-4212 or 800-363-0366
⇄842-4907
www.ritzcarlton.com
The Ritz-Carlton opened in 1912 and has been renovated

over the years in order to continue offering its clientele exceptional comfort; it has managed, however, to preserve its original elegance. The rooms are decorated with superb antique furniture. The marble bathrooms, moreover, add to the charm of this outstanding establishment.

Loews Hôtel Vogue
$$$$$
⊛, ⊘, ℜ, ≡
1425 Rue de la Montagne
☎*285-5555 or 800-465-6654*
⇄*849-8903*
www.loewshotels.com
At first sight, the Loews Hôtel Vogue, a glass and concrete building with no ornamentation, looks bare. The lobby, however, embellished with warm-coloured woodwork, gives a more accurate idea of the luxury and elegance of this establishment. The large rooms, with their elegant furniture, reveal the comfort of this hotel. Each room has a whirlpool bath and two suites have saunas.

Hôtel Le Germain
$$$$$
⊘, ≡, ℜ, 🐾
2050 Rue Mansfield
☎*849-2050 or 877-333-2050*
⇄*849-1437*
www.hotelboutique.com
Right in the heart of downtown Montréal stands a former office tower that was converted into a hotel: Hôtel Le Germain. This establishment is part of the new trend of boutique hotels, where service is personalized and special care is given to decor. Each room has been carefully designed in a minimalist style of earth and cream tones, mahogany or rattan furnishings and fabulous accessories. The overall effect is inducive to total relaxation. The building's first vocation as an office building is not forgotten, however;

it is found in various architectural details (concrete ceilings, for example) and in the hotel's more functional aspects (Internet-equipped desks and ergonomic chairs). Although the corner rooms have great windows, the best view can be enjoyed at the hotel restaurant, with an entire wall of windoww overlooking Rue Président-Kennedy.

Tour C: Shaughnessy Village

Hôtel du Fort
$$$
⊘, ≡, ℝ, *K*
1390 Rue du Fort, Atwater métro
☎*938-8333 or 800-565-6333*
www.hoteldufort.com
The Hôtel du Fort offers comfort, security and personalized service. All 127 rooms have kitchenettes equipped with microwave ovens, refrigerators, coffee makers, as well as hair dryers and mini-bars. The deluxe rooms and suites also have modem hook-ups. All the windows in the rooms open.

Tour E: Maisonneuve

Au Gîte Olympique
$$ bkfst incl.
P2752 Boulevard Pie-IX
☎*254-5423 or 888-254-5423*
⇄*254-4753*
www.dsuper.net/~olympic
Although it is located on very busy Boulevard Pie-IX, Gîte Olympique offers five quiet rooms and a great view of the Olympic Stadium. There are two sitting rooms where guests can relax or meet other travellers. In summer, breakfast is served on a large rear terrace. Located two steps from the Pie-IX métro station and the main attractions of the eastern part of the city.

Tour G: Quartier Latin

Auberge de l'Hôtel de Paris
$
sb
901 Rue Sherbrooke Est, Sherbrooke métro
☎*522-6861 or 800-567-7217*
⇄*522-1387*
www.hotel-montreal.com
In 1995, the Hôtel de Paris (see p 128) opened the Auberge de l'Hôtel de Paris, a house across the street with 10 spacious rooms and a 40-bed hostel divided into dormitories for four, eight or 14 people. A blanket, sheets and a pillow are provided. The common kitchen is small but has everything you'll need to prepare meals, and there's an outdoor seating area with an attractive view. The place has four showers and toilets, and there's a laundromat right nearby. No curfew.

Pierre et Dominique
$$ bkfst incl.
sb
271 Square St-Louis
☎*286-0307*
www.pierdom.qc.ca
Square Saint-Louis (see p 112) is a pleasant park surrounded by beautiful Victorian houses. This private home stands out for its extremely comfortable and tastefully decorated rooms. Non-smoking.

Le Chasseur
$$ bkfst incl.
sb/pb, ≡
1567 Rue St-André
☎*521-2238 or 800-451-2238*
Not too far from the gay village, this B&B offers tastefully decorated rooms and service with a smile. In the summer, the terrace provides a welcome escape from the bustle of the city and a chance to relax.

Montréal

Hôtel de Paris
$$
≡, K, ℜ, 🐕
901 Rue Sherbrooke Est, Sherbrooke métro
☎*522-6861 or 800-567-7217*
≈*522-1387*
www.hotel-montreal.com
A lovely house built in 1870, the Hôtel de Paris has 39 rooms. Recently renovated, the house has retained its distinctive character, thanks to the magnificent woodwork in the entryway. The rooms are comfortable.

Manoir Sherbrooke
$$-$$$ bkfst incl.
pb/sb, ⊛, ≡
157 Rue Sherbrooke Est
☎*285-0895 or 800-203-5485*
≈*284-1126*
The Hôtel Armor-Manoir Sherbrooke is an old stone house. The rooms are modest, while the staff are polite and efficient.

Auberge le Jardin d'Antoine
$$$ bkfst incl.
≡, ⊛
2024 Rue St-Denis
☎*843-4506 or 800-361-4506*
≈*281-1491*
www.hotel-jardin-antoine.qc.ca
The three-storey Jardin d'Antoine has about 25 carefully decorated rooms, some with exposed brick walls and hardwood floors. Many comfortable, well-equipped suites are also available. The back garden is rather small, but the balconies are adorned with flower baskets and the effect is very attractive.

Hôtel de l'Institut
$$$ bkfst incl.
≡, ℜ, ⚷
3535 Rue St-Denis, Sherbrooke métro
☎*282-5120 or 800-361-5111*
≈*873-9893*
www.hotel.ithq.qc.ca
The Hôtel de l'Institut occupies the upper floors of the Institut de Tourisme et d'Hôtellerie du Québec (ITHQ), a renowned postsecondary college devoted to

the hospitality industry. The hotel is run by students enrolled in practical classes at the ITHQ or who are undergoing on-the-job training there. Their work is closely monitored by the professors charged with grooming them for the finest hotels in the world; the result is very comfortable rooms and quality service, including full concierge service. The hotel is located right on Rue Saint-Denis, with its scores of restaurant terraces, shops and cafés, and right near the pedestrian mall on Rue Prince-Arthur, which is packed with restaurants and cafés.

Crowne Plaza Métro Centre
$$$$
ℜ, ☺, ≈, ⊛, ≡, ⌂, 🐕
505 Rue Sherbrooke Est, Sherbrooke métro
☎*842-8581 or 800-561-4644*
≈*842-8910*
www.crowneplaza-montreal.com
The 318 spacious rooms of the Crowne Plaza Métro Centre have a modern decor and are all equipped with coffee makers, colour televisions and two telephones. The hotel is located right near the Quartier Latin, steps away from numerous restaurants, bars and shops. It offers a number of services for business people, including voice mail and a secretarial service.

Tour H:
Plateau Mont-Royal

Vacances Canada 4 Saisons
$
sb
Collège Français, 5155 de Gaspé, Laurier métro
☎*270-4459*
≈*278-7508*
Unlike those in the university residences, the rooms at Vacances Canada 4 Saisons are available year-round (550 beds in summer, 220 in winter). In addition, studios with private baths and kitchenettes

may be rented for $300 a month (all included).

Gîte du Parc Lafontaine
$-$$ bkfst incl.
Jun to late Aug
sb, K
1250 Rue Sherbrooke Est
☎*522-3910 or 877-350-4483*
www.hostelmontreal.com
This century-old rooming house provides guests with furnished rooms, a kitchen, a living room, a small laundry room, a terrace and a warm welcome. The hostel is ideally located next to Parc Lafontaine and close to Rue Saint-Denis.

🌴 **B & B Bienvenue**
$$ bkfst incl.
pb/sb
3950 Avenue Laval
☎*844-5897 or 800-227-5897*
≈*844-5894*
www.bienvenuebb.com
The B & B Bienvenue is just two steps south of Rue Duluth. Located on a lovely quiet street, this establishment offers eight small but charmingly decorated rooms with large beds. This well-established bed and breakfast occupies a very pretty, well-maintained house with a peaceful, friendly atmosphere. A very generous breakfast is served in the pleasant dining room.

🌴 **Auberge de la Fontaine**
$$$ bkfst incl.
⊛, ≡, ℝ, ⚷
1301 Rue Rachel Est
☎*597-0166*
≈*597-0496*
www.aubergedela fontaine.com
The Auberge de la Fontaine lies opposite lovely Parc Lafontaine. Designed with a great deal of care, it has a lot of style. A feeling of peace and relaxation emanates from the rooms, all of which are attractively decorated. Guests are offered a complimentary snack during the day. All these features have made this a popular place—so much so that it is best to make reservations.

Near the Airports

Mirabel International Airport

Château de l'Aéroport-Mirabel
$$$
≈, △, ☯, ℜ, ≡ 占
12555 Rue Commerce
☎*476-1611 or 800-361-0924*
⟜*476-0873*
www.chateaumirabel.com
Directly accessible from the airport, this hotel was built to accommodate travellers with early morning flights. Unlike its downtown cousins, this hotel's high season is from November to May. The rooms are very functional and comfortable.

Dorval International Airport

Best Western Aéroport de Montréal
$$-$$$ bkfst incl.
☯, △, ≈, ℜ, ⊛
13000 Chemin Côte-de-Liesse
☎*631-4811 or 800-361-2254*
⟜*631-7305*
www.bwdorval.com
The rooms in the Best Western Aéroport de Montréal are pleasant and affordable. The hotel also offers an interesting service: after spending the night here, guests can park their car here for up to three weeks, free of charge. Free airport shuttle service available.

Hilton Montréal Aéroport
$$$ bkfst incl.
☯, ≈, △, ℜ, ≡, 🐾, 占, ℝ
12505 Côte-de-Liesse
☎*631-2411 or 800-567-2411*
⟜*631-0192*
This Hilton has pleasant rooms but the main advantage is its proximity to the airport.

Restaurants

Montréal's reputation as far as food is concerned is enviable, to say the least; it is also well-deserved. The culinary traditions of countries around the world are represented here by restaurants in every price range. The best thing is that no matter what your budget, a memorable meal is always possible! The following descriptions are grouped according to location, in the same order as the tours to make it easier for visitors to find those hidden treasures while they are exploring a particular area.

Tour A: Vieux-Montréal

Bio Train
$
Mon-Fri 5am to 5pm
410 Rue St-Jacques
☎*842-9184*
For health food, Bio Train is a favourite self-serve restaurant. Things move very quickly at lunchtime.

Titanic
$
Mon-Fri 9am to 4:30pm
445 Rue St-Pierre
☎*849-0894*
Titanic is a very busy lunch spot located in a semi-basement. It offers a multitude of baguette sandwiches and Mediterranean-style salads, feta and other cheeses, smoked fish, *pâtés*, marinated vegetables... Delicious!

Chez Delmo
$$
Tue-Sat
211 Rue Notre-Dame Ouest
☎*849-4061*
The specialty of Chez Delmo is fish and seafood. The outstanding *bouillabaisse* is not to be missed. The first room, with its two long oyster bars, is the most pleasant one.

La Gargote
$$
351 Place D'Youville
☎*844-1428*
La Gargote is not what you would expect from its name, which means "a cheap place to eat" in French. Rather, it is a small French restaurant that attracts a regular clientele and curious newcomers. The decor is inviting, the cuisine tasty, and the prices affordable.

Chez Better
$
160 Notre-Dame Est
☎*861-2617*
The menu at Chez Better, a chain of restaurants, consists mainly of German sausages, French fries and sauerkraut. While the layout varies from one location to the next, the atmosphere is always relaxed. This particular branch occupies an old house from the French Regime.

Stash's Café Bazar
$$
200 Rue St-Paul Ouest
☎*845-6611*
This charming little Polish restaurant with a simple, cozy decor, is the ideal choice for delicious cheese-stuffed pirogies, sausage and sauerkraut. The vodka is also excellent.

✗🐾 Le Petit Moulinsart
$$
noon to 3pm and 5pm to 11pm
139 Rue St-Paul Ouest
☎*843-7432*
Le Petit Moulinsart is a friendly Belgian bistro that could easily pass for a small museum devoted to the characters of the *Tintin* comic books by Georges Rémi, a.k.a. Hergé. All sorts of objects and posters related to the *Tintin* books decorate the walls, menus and tables of the establishment. Service is friendly, but slow. Besides the traditional dish of mussels and French fries, don't miss Colonel Sponz's sorbet

and Capitaine Haddock's salad.

Modavie
$$-$$$
1 Rue St-Paul Ouest
☎287-9582
You will recognize Modavie, at the corner of Boulevard Saint-Laurent by the awning above its windows. Its beautiful decor, both modern and antique, creates a soothing atmosphere. Mediterranean-style meat, pasta and fish dishes are served.

Le Bonaparte
$$$
443 Rue St-François-Xavier
☎844-4368
The varied menu of the French restaurant Bonaparte always includes some delicious surprises. Guests can savour them in one of the establishment's three rooms, all richly decorated in the Empire style. The largest offers the warmth of a fireplace in winter, while another, named La Serre ("the greenhouse"), reveals a subdued ambiance, thanks to its many potted plants.

Soto
$$$
500 Rue McGill
☎864-5115
In a large space within one of Rue McGill's beautiful late-19th-century buildings, Soto serves top-notch Japanese fare befittingly presented as a feast for the eyes, which serves to prepare you for the treat awaiting your palate. Lunch specials allow you to sample a range of sushi, maki, sashimi or tempura dishes without inflating the bill. The food is pricier at night, but is there any such thing as good, low-priced Japanese cuisine?

Vieux Saint-Gabriel
$$$
Closed on Sun, dinner only on Sat
426 Rue St-Gabriel
☎878-3561
The attraction of the Vieux Saint-Gabriel lies above all in its enchanting decor reminiscent of the first years of New France; the restaurant is set in an old house that served as an inn in 1754 (see p 84). The French and Italian selections from the somewhat predictable menu are adequate.

Gibby's
$$$-$$$$
dinner only
298 Place d'Youville
☎282-1837
Gibby's is located in a lovely, renovated old stable and its menu offers generous servings of beef or veal steaks served at antique wooden tables set around a glowing fire and surrounded by low brick and stone walls. In the summer months, patrons can eat comfortably outdoors in a large inner courtyard. All in all, an extraordinary decor, which is reflected in the rather high prices. Vegetarians beware.

Chez Queux
$$$-$$$$
158 Rue St-Paul
☎866-5194
Ideally located in Old Montreal and overlooking Place Jacques-Cartier, Chez Queux serves classic French cuisine in the finest tradition. Refined service in an elegant setting guarantee a positive culinary experience.

Cube
$$$$
355 Rue McGill
☎876-2823
Cube, located in the St-Paul Hotel (see p 124), invites you to meet its famous chef, Claude Pelletier, who will take you on a colourful, flavour-filled adventure. The restaurant has been very popular since it opened in the summer of 2001. Montréal's

trendsetters come here often, not only for the exceptional cuisine but also to see and be seen. Like the hotel, the decor is stunning, composed of various materials that create unexpected results. On the second floor, the Bar Cru serves raw treats such as tartares and carpaccio in a lounge-style ambiance. Definitely one of the hippest places in town.

🏛 Hostellerie et Restaurant Pierre du Calvet 1725
$$$$
Tue-Sat
401 Rue Bonsecours
☎282-1725
The old jewel among Montréal restaurants, the Filles du Roi restaurant has given way to a magnificent inn (see p 124) boasting one of the best dining rooms in the city. The establishment is particularly recommended for its delicious and imaginative French cuisine. Its menu, based on game, poultry, fish and beef, changes every two weeks. The elegant surroundings, antiques, ornamental plants and discrete service further add to the pleasure of an evening meal here.

Tour B: Downtown

Ben's Delicatessen
$
900 Boul. de Maisonneuve Ouest
☎844-1000
A century ago, a Lithuanian immigrant modified a recipe from his native country to suit the needs of workers, and thus introduced the smoked meat sandwich to Montréal, and in the process created Ben's Delicatessen. Over the years, the restaurant has become a Montréal institution, attracting a motley crowd from 7am to 4am. This is where people come when the bars close! The worn, Formica tables and yellowed photographs give the restaurant an austere appearance that's part of its charm.

Brûlerie Saint-Denis
$
2100 Rue Stanley, in the Maison Alcan
☎**985-9159**
The Brûlerie Saint-Denis serves the same delicious coffee blends, simple meals and sinful desserts as the other two Brûleries. Though the coffee is not roasted on the premises, it does come fresh from the roasters on St-Denis (see also p 135).

Biddle's Jazz and Ribs
$-$$
2060 rue Aylmer
☎**842-8656**
A jazz institution in Montreal, Biddle's was run by Montreal's jazzman extraordinaire Charlie Biddle until his passing in 2003. Biddle's remains the spot to hear live jazz, and attracts a crowd of business people and jazz lovers, who chow down on ribs and chicken wings while enjoying music played at a volume that still allows dinner conversation. A seat on the patio is a pleasure in the all-too-brief summer season.

Mangia
$-$$
1101 Boulevard De Maisonneuve Ouest
☎**848-7001**
Mangia is a counter-shop and one of the few places in downtown Montréal where you'll find good, reasonably priced meals to enjoy in an attractive atmosphere or to go. Salads and pasta dishes, each more enticing than the last, are sold by weight, and sandwiches and more elaborate meals like steak with bell peppers are also on the menu.

Marché Mövenpick
$-$$
Place Ville-Marie
☎**861-8181**
Marché Mövenpick is a unique market/cafeteria-restaurant concept. You have to show every chef a card on which he will note your choices so you can pay for them on your way

out. There are stalls for many different kinds of food from around the world made with the freshest ingredients and in every price range. Just order something and get your passport stamped. The food is excellent (considering that it's fast food) and includes Asian soups, Indonesian *bami goreng* and custom-made pizzas; there is also fish, seafood, steak, soup, salad, dessert and juice counters, a pub, a bar—even a French bistro serving the finest wines and steak tartare! The place can sometimes be a zoo and seats hard to find. The Swiss chain is currently expanding in North America.

Le Commensal
$-$$
1204 McGill College
☎**871-1480**
Le Commensal is a buffet-style vegetarian restaurant. The food is sold by weight. Le Commensal is open every day until 11pm. The inviting, modern decor and big windows looking out on the downtown streets make it a pleasant place to be (see p 134).

Café du Nouveau Monde
$$
84 Rue Ste-Catherine Ouest
☎**866-8668**
The Café du Nouveau Monde is a lovely addition to this section of town. Sip a glass of wine or a coffee, or sample a dessert in the deconstructionist decor of the ground-floor dining room, or have a good meal upstairs in the atmosphere of a Parisian brasserie. The menu matches the decor: classic French bistro cuisine. Impeccable service, beautiful presentation and excellent food.

Jardin Sakura
$$
2114 Rue de la Montagne
☎**288-9122**
With a name like Jardin Sakura, diners might expect a more refined decor ("*Sakura*"

is the beautiful flower on Japanese cherry trees). The menu offers decent Japanese cuisine, though the sushi is not always a success. The service is very attentive.

Le Paris
$$
1812 Rue Ste-Catherine Ouest
☎**937-4898**
If you like *boudin, foie de veau* or mackerel in white wine, Le Paris is the place to enjoy such French delicacies in a friendly and relaxed ambiance. As for the décor, well, it hasn't changed in years. The wine list is, however, quite respectable and up to date.

⅄ L'Actuel
$$-$$$
Mon-Sat
1194 Rue Peel
☎**866-1537**
L'Actuel, the most authentic Belgian restaurant in Montréal, is always full for lunch and dinner. It has two large, fairly noisy and very lively dining rooms, where affable waiters hurry about among the clientele of business people. The restaurant serves mussels, of course, as well as a number of other specialties.

Wienstein 'n' Gavino's Pasta Bar Factory Co.
$$-$$$
1434 Rue Crescent
☎**288-2231**
Wienstein 'n' Gavino's Pasta Bar Factory Co. occupies a modern building that visitors and locals alike might swear had been part of the streetscape for years. The look is just as effective inside, where exposed brick walls, bright yet weathered Mediterranean floor tiles and ventilation ducts in the rafters give the place the feel of an old warehouse. Everything is on display here, in particular the feverish activity in the kitchen on the upper level. Each table receives a loaf of fresh French bread along with olive oil for dipping and roasted garlic for spreading. Among the menu

Montréal

offerings, the pizzas are decent, if a little bland, but the pasta dishes are delicious, especially the Gorgonzola with dill. Red snapper in foil is another delectable treat.

Altitude 737
$$-$$$
Thu-Sat from 5pm
1 Place Ville-Marie
☎*397-0737*
Located on the 42nd floor of Place Ville-Marie, Altitude 737 boasts large windows allowing for an unobstructed view of Montréal and its surroundings. As for the menu, it offers various French-inspired dishes. Be warned that the prices here are as high as the restaurant is.

Chez Georges
$$-$$$
1415 Rue de la Montagne
☎*288-6181*
Chez George serves traditional and delicious French cuisine. Attentive and efficient service. This is a prized meeting place for the area's business people.

Parchemin
$$$
Mon-Sat
1333 Rue University
☎*844-1619*
Occupying the former rectory of the Christ Church Cathedral, the Parchemin is distinguished by its stylish decor and velvety atmosphere. Guests enjoy carefully prepared French cuisine, suitable for the finest of palates. The four-course table d'hôte, with its wide range of choices, is an excellent choice.

Julien
$$$
Mon-Sat
1191 Rue Union
☎*871-1581*
Julien is a Montréal institution, thanks largely to its *bavette à l'échalote* or steak with shallots, which is one of the best in the city. But it isn't just the *bavette* that attracts patrons, as each dish is more succulent

than the last. For that matter, everything here is impeccable, from the service to the décor and the wine list.

Mr. Ma
$$$
1 Place Ville-Marie (corner Cathcart and Mansfield)
☎*866-8000*
With two dining rooms, one that lets natural light in during the day, Mr. Ma makes Szechuan cuisine that is nothing extraordinary but offers good value, especially for the downtown area. The seafood dishes are a good choice.

Troïka
$$$
2171 Rue Crescent
☎*849-9333*
Troïka epitomizes a typical Russian restaurant. Hanging tapestries, mementos, dark and intimate corners and live accordion music conjure up images of the old country. The food is authentic and excellent.

Desjardins Sea Food
$$$-$$$$
1175 Rue Mackay
☎*866-9741*
Desjardins Sea Food has long been one of the best seafood restaurants in Montréal. Everything is fresh and delicious and served in a refined atmosphere with plush decor where wall-to-wall carpeting, white napkins, flowers and crystal set the tone. You can have a wonderful meal here in a peaceful setting right in middle of downtown, surrounded by big bay windows that let in a lot of light, and comfortably seated in padded high-backed chairs. Professional service, and though prices are on the high side, the value is excellent.

Jardin du Ritz
$$$$
1228 Rue Sherbrooke Ouest
☎*842-4212*
The Jardin du Ritz is the perfect escape from the summer heat and the constant fast pace of downtown. Classic French

cuisine is featured on the menu, with tea served on a patio surrounded by flowers and greenery, next to the pond with its splashing ducks. Only open during the summer months, the Jardin is an extension of the hotel's other restaurant, Le Café de Paris (see below).

Café de Paris
$$$$
1228 Sherbrooke Ouest
☎*842-4212*
The Café de Paris is the renowned restaurant at the magnificent Ritz-Carlton Hotel (see p 126). Its sumptuous blue-and-ochre decor is absolutely beautiful. The carefully thought-out menu is delicious.

Les Caprices de Nicolas
$$$$
2072 Rue Drummond
☎*282-9790*
Les Caprices de Nicolas is one of the very best restaurants in Montréal, with highly innovative and very sophisticated French cuisine. There is an interesting arrangement whereby, for the price of a bottle of wine, you can sample different wines by the glass to accompany every course of the meal. The service is friendly and impeccable, and the décor is an indoor garden.

Le Lutétia
$$$$
Tue-Sat
1430 Rue de la Montagne
☎*288-5656*
The chic Victorian décor on display at the restaurant at Hotel de la Montagne, Le Lutétia, cannot fail to impress, nor can its menu, with all the classics of French cuisine: lamb chops, rib steak and filet mignon.

Piment Rouge
$$$$
1170 Rue Peel
☎*866-7816*
Piment Rouge prepares delicious Chinese and Szechuanese specialties, served in a pleasant setting. A

visit to this restaurant guarantees a satisfied palate. The service is efficient and friendly.

Tour C: Shaughnessy Village

Bar-B-Barn
$-$$
1201 Rue Guy
☎**931-3811**
The Bar-B-Barn serves sweet, delicious pork ribs cooked just right. The food is hardly refined, especially seeing as you have to eat it with your hands, but it appeals to many Montrealers. Those planning to come here on the weekend should prepare to be patient, since there is often a long wait.

Pique Assiette
$-$$
2051 Rue Ste-Catherine Ouest
☎**932-7141**
Pique Assiette has an Indian-style décor and a quiet atmosphere. The lunchtime Indian buffet is well worth the trip. The menu focuses on excellent curries and Tandoori specialties. Guests can have as much *nan* bread as they please. Anyone with a weak stomach should stay away, however because the food is very spicy. English beer washes these dishes down nicely.

Café Roccoco
$$
1650 Ave. Lincoln
☎**938-2121**
Café Roccoco is a charming little Hungarian restaurant mostly frequented by a Magyar-speaking clientele. The food is decent and served with lots of paprika. The pink and scarlet drapes and tablecloths give this place a cute Eastern European décor that would be made even more romantic with candles on each table. Excellent selection of cakes.

🐾 Chez la Mère Michel
$$$-$$$$
Closed Sat, Sun, Mon noon
1209 Rue Guy
☎**934-0473**
Considered by many to be one of Montréal's best restaurants, Chez la Mère Michel is the definition of fine French dining. Inside a lovely old house on Rue Guy are three exquisitely decorated, intimate dining rooms. Banquettes and chairs covered in richly printed fabrics welcome patrons to their elegantly set tables, and a cozy fireplace and profusion of plants set the mood. Chef Micheline creates delightful French regional specialties and an alternating five-course seasonal table d'hôte menu with market-fresh ingredients. The service is friendly and attentive. The wine cellar has some of the finest bottles in the city.

Westmount (Tour D), Notre-Dame-de-Grâce and Côte-des-Neiges

Pizzafiore
$
3518 Lacombe
☎**735-1555**
Upon entering Pizzafiore, visitors will see the cook standing beside the wood-burning pizza oven. He makes pizza for every taste, with every different kind of sauce, topped with the widest range of ingredients imaginable. This pleasant restaurant is often filled with locals and people from Université de Montréal.

Aux Deux Gauloises
$$
5195 Chemin de la Côte-des-Neiges
☎**737-5755**
The kitchen of this French restaurant churns out a wide variety of crêpes, each more delicious than the last. Pleasant ambiance and friendly service.

La Louisiane
$$-$$$
Tue-Sun dinner only
5850 Rue Sherbrooke Ouest
☎**369-3073**
A meal at La Louisiane is like a trip to the Bayou. You can start with a plate of authentic hush puppies, continue with something spicy like crayfish *étouffée* or shrimp magnolia and finish up with an order of heavenly bananas Foster. Huge paintings of New Orleans street scenes adorn the walls and the sounds of jazz filling the air complete the mood. Still a fashionable spot years after the Cajun cuisine trend was all the rage.

Kaizen
$$$$
4120 Rue Ste-Catherine O.
☎**932-5654**
Kaizen serves all the classics from the land of the rising sun. The prices are high but the portions are gargantuan! The staff won't even mind if you share your plate.

Circuit E: Maisonneuve

Moe's Deli & Bar
$$
3950 Rue Sherbrooke Est
☎**253-6637**
Moe's Deli & Bar is particularly prized for its "happy hour," which fills up the bar; the restaurant is often just as crowded, however. The menu is extremely varied though we would recommend the salads, sandwiches and grilled specialties over most other menu items. Tempting dessert choices are available as well. The music is loud, the atmosphere, lively and the decor, reminiscent of an English pub. The Olympic Stadium is just a few steps away.

Montréal

Tour F:
Île Sainte-Hélène
and Île Notre-Dame

🍴 Hélène de Champlain
$$$
☎**395-2424**
Located on Île Sainte-Hélène, Hélène de Champlain lies in an enchanting setting, without question one of the loveliest in Montréal. The large dining room, with its fireplace and view of the city and the river, is extremely pleasant. Each corner has its own unique charm, overlooking the ever-changing surrounding landscape. Though the restaurant does not serve the fanciest of gastronomic cuisine, the food is very good. The service is courteous and attentive.

Festin des Gouverneurs
$$$$
☎**879-1141**
Festin des Gouverneurs creates feasts like those prepared in New France at the beginning of colonization. Characters in period costumes and traditional Québec dishes bring patrons back in time to these celebrations. The restaurant only serves groups and reservations are required.

🍴 Nuances
$$$$
dinner only
Casino de Montréal, Île Notre-Dame
☎**392-2708**
☎**800-665-2274 ext 4322**
On the fifth floor of Montréal's Casino, Nuances is one of the best dining establishments in the city, perhaps even the country. Refined and imaginative cuisine is served in a décor bathed in mahogany, brass, leather and views of the city lights. Of particular note on the menu are the creamy lobster *brandade* in flaky pastry (*brandade crémeuse de homard en millefeuille*), brochette of grilled quail (*brochette de caille grillée*), roast cutlet of duck (*magret de canard rôti*), tenderloin of

Québec lamb (*longe d'agneau du Québec*) or striped polenta with grilled tuna (*polenta rayée entourée d'une grillade mi-cuite de thon*). The delectable desserts are each exquisitely presented. The plush and classic ambiance of this award-winning restaurant is perfect for business meals and special occasions. The casino also has four less expensive restaurants: **Via Fortuna ($$)**, an Italian restaurant, **L'Impair ($)**, a buffet, **La Bonne Carte ($$)**, a buffet with *à la carte* service and **L'Entre-Mise ($)**, a snack bar.

Tour G: Quartier Latin

Brioche Lyonnaise
$
1593 Rue St-Denis
☎**842-7017**
Brioche Lyonnaise is a pastry shop and café offering an extremely wide selection of pastries, cakes and sweetmeats, all the more appealing because everything really is as delicious as it looks!

La Paryse
$
302 Rue Ontario E.
☎**842-2040**
In a 1950s-style décor, La Paryse is regularly frequented by students, and by looking at its menu, you will understand why: delicious hamburgers and home fries are served in generous portions.

Le Pèlerin
$
330 Rue Ontario Est
☎**845-0909**
Located near Rue Saint-Denis, Le Pèlerin is a pleasant, unpretentious café. The wooden furniture, made to look like mahogany, and the works of modern art on exhibit create a friendly atmosphere that attracts a diverse clientele. This is the perfect place to grab a bite and chat with a friend. The service is attentive and friendly.

Le Commensal
$-$$
1720 Rue St-Denis
☎**845-2627**
This well-known vegetarian restaurant offers a self-serve, buffet-style array of tasty, healthy dishes sold by weight. Its large bay windows in the front, brick walls and different levels lack warmth, but the fare is good and the atmosphere is relaxed.

Zyng
$-$$
1748 Rue St-Denis
☎**284-2016**
1254 Rue Ste-Catherine Est
☎**522-9964**
1371 Ave. du Mont-Royal Est
☎**523-8883**
This branch of the Toronto chain of friendly noodle and *dim sum* restaurants brings flair to this overly commercial part of St-Denis. The flavours of China, Japan, Thailand, Korea and Vietnam meet and mix here, creating very original dishes.

Le Piémontais
$$
Mon-Sat
1145-A Rue de Bullion
☎**861-8122**
All true lovers of Italian cuisine know and adore this restaurant. The dining room is narrow and the tables are close together, making this place very noisy, but the soft, primarily pink décor, the kind, good humoured and efficient staff, and the works of culinary art on the menu make dining here an unforgettable experience.

La Sila
$$$-$$$$
2040 Rue St-Denis
☎**844-5083**
La Sila serves traditional Italian cuisine in an elegant setting, which includes an inviting bar and an outdoor terrace for warm summer evenings. Fresh pastas cooked just right are topped with flawless sauces. The wine list boasts

the finest Italian vintages. Free parking.

Tour H: Plateau Mont-Royal

Aux 2 Marie
$
4329 Rue St-Denis
☎*844-7246*
Locals hang out at this small charming café. Besides an impressive selection of coffees roasted on the premises, they also serve excellent and unpretentious meals at affordable prices.

L'Anecdote
$
801 Rue Rachel Est
☎*526-7967*
Serves hamburgers and vegetarian club sandwiches made with quality ingredients. The place has a 1950s-style décor, with movie posters and old Coke ads on the walls.

Binerie Mont-Royal
$
367 Avenue Mont-Royal Est
☎*285-9078*
With its décor made up of four tables and a counter, the Binerie Mont-Royal looks like a modest little neighbourhood restaurant. It is known for its specialty, baked beans (*fèves au lard or "binnes"*) and also as the backdrop of Yves Beauchemin's novel, *Le Matou* (*The Alley Cat*).

Brûlerie Saint-Denis
$
3967 Rue St-Denis
☎*286-9158*
The Brûlerie imports its coffees from all over the world and offers one of the widest selections in Montréal. The coffee is roasted on the premises, filling the place with a very distinctive aroma. The menu offers light meals and desserts (see also p 131).

Café Rico
$
969 Rue Rachel E.
☎*529-1321*
Café Rico is a small coffee-roasting joint whose policy is to use fair-trade coffee exclusively. So why not drop by this charming café, with its casual decor consisting of a few tables, a hammock and plants, to savour its delicious blends? As an accompaniment, you'll have to make do with a simple sandwich or biscuit, but in compensation, you can linger for hours in this convivial setting that serves as a gathering place for a fair share of java junkies.

Fruit Folie
$
3817 Rue St-Denis
☎*840-9011*
Patrons flock to Fruit Folie for its spectacular breakfasts, which are not only delicious but also very affordable. You'll simply go crazy (*"folie"*) for their fruit-filled plates! The restaurant opens every day at 7am, but if you sleep in on Sundays and only arrive after 11am, expect to wait in line; this is especially so if you have your heart set on a table on the terrace. Fruit Folie also serves simple dishes such as pasta and salads for lunch and dinner.

Schwartz's Montréal Hebrew Delicatessen
$
3895 Boulevard St-Laurent
☎*842-4813*
Montréal is famous for its smoked meat and, according to many people, the best can be found at Schwartz's Montréal Hebrew Delicatessen. Patrons come here for a sandwich on the go and to rub elbows with carnivorous connoisseurs who often travel a long ways for this delicacy. The small establishment is not exactly welcoming, but authenticity is guaranteed.

Lélé da Cuca
$-$$
dinner only
bring your own wine
70 Rue Marie-Anne Est
☎*849-6649*
This tiny restaurant serves Mexican and Brazilian dishes. It can only accommodate about 30 people, but exudes a relaxed and laid-back ambience.

Tampopo
$-$$
4449 Rue Mentana
☎*526-0001*
Tampopo's tiny space is a constant beehive of activity. A multitude of people from the Plateau and beyond come here at practically all hours of the day to chow down on good Asian food. Bountiful Tonkinese soups share menu space with a series of noodle dishes. Behind the counter, cooks sauté vegetables, meat and seafood done to a turn in huge woks. Take a seat on a small stool at the counter or on a floor mat at one of three low tables and be sure to savour the Oriental-style decor as well!

Le 917
$$
dinner only
bring your own wine
917 Rue Rachel Est
☎*524-0094*
For quality French cuisine at reasonable prices, try Le 917. The large mirrors on the walls, the close-set tables and the waiters in aprons create a bistro atmosphere that perfectly matches the cuisine. Giblets, kidneys and calf sweetbread are particularly well prepared here, and will melt in your mouth!

Beauty's
$$
93 Avenue du Mont-Royal Ouest
☎*849-8883*
Beauty's is known for its hearty, delicious brunches. The place is often crowded on weekend mornings. It is only

Montréal

...for breakfast, lunch and brunch.

Bières & Compagnie
$$
4350 Rue St-Denis
☎844-0394
Let yourself be seduced by an excellent meal: sausages, grilled dishes, mussels, ostrich, bison and caribou burgers. Add to this one of the establishment's 115 local and imported beers, and you have everything you need to fully enjoy the musical ambiance this place has to offer.

Cactus
$$
4461 Rue St-Denis
☎849-0349
Cactus prepares refined Mexican food. Though servings are small, the ambiance is cozy and very pleasant. The restaurant's little terrace is very popular during the summer.

Café El Dorado
$$
921 Avenue du Mont-Royal Est
☎278-3333
Locals in the know head over to Café El Dorado for a coffee or a bite in its spectacular, curvilinear decor.

 ## Chu Chai
$$
4088 Rue St-Denis
☎843-4194
Chu Chai deserves praise for breaking the monotony and daring to be innovative. The Thai vegetarian menu is quite a surprise: vegetarian shrimp, vegetarian fish, and even vegetarian beef and pork. The resemblance to the real thing is so extraordinary that you will spend the evening wondering how they do it! The chef affirms that they really are made of vegetable-based products like seitan and wheat. The delicious results delight the clientele that squeezes into the modest dining room or onto the terrace. They have inexpensive lunch specials. Next door is Chu Chai's little sister, **Chu Chai Express**,

which offers take-out meals are ready-made delicacies to enjoy in tasteful, relaxing surroundings. You can bring your own wine.

 ## Côté Soleil
$$
closed Mon in winter
3979 Rue St-Denis
☎282-8037
Coté Soléil offers consistently fresh items from a menu that changes every day and never misses the mark. Excellent, occasionally inventive French cuisine is served at prices so affordable that this is probably the best value in the neighbourhood. The service is attentive and always friendly. There is a pleasant sidewalk terrace, and the décor is simple but inviting. The service is attentive and friendly, and the setting, although simple, is quite warm. In summer, there are two sunny terraces: one on the busy street and the other in the lovely garden.

La Gaudriole
$$
825 Avenue Laurier Est
☎276-1580
La Gaudriole is in cramped and somewhat uncomfortable quarters, but serves excellent "hybrid" French cuisine, which incorporates flavours from around the world. The menu is constantly changing, so the ingredients are always fresh, allowing chef Marc Vézina's creativity to shine through.

Ouzeri
$$
4690 Rue St-Denis
☎845-1336
Ouzeri set out on a mission to offer its clientele refined Mediterranean cuisine, and succeeded. The food is excellent, and the menu includes several surprises, such as vegetarian moussaka and scallops with melted cheese. With its high ceilings and long windows, this is a pleasant place where you'll be tempted to linger on and on, especially when the Greek

music sets your mind wandering.

Vents du Sud
$$
bring your own wine
323 Rue Roy Est
☎281-9913
These "southern winds" are warm, gentle and carry a thousand and one mouth-watering aromas. In the depths of winter, when you've had enough of the cold and need a good, hearty meal, head to this little Basque restaurant. Basque cuisine, dominated by tomatoes, red peppers and onion, is hearty and tasty. And if you're still in need of warming up at the end of the meal, the ebullient owner will be happy to explain how to play pelota.

Khyber Pass
$$
bring your own wine
506 Avenue Duluth Est
☎849-1775
Exotic and inviting, Khyber Pass restaurant offers traditional Afghani cuisine featuring a cornucopia of surprising, delicious flavours. For starters, the morsels of pumpkin covered with a yoghurt, mint and garlic sauce, and the boiled ravioli smothered in a tomato-lentil sauce are especially delectable. This savoury adventure continues with a selection of grilled lamb, beef and chicken dishes, prepared with a marinade that blends perfectly with the fragrant rice. Attentive service and outdoor dining in summer.

Café Cherrier
$$-$$$
3635 Rue St-Denis
☎843-4308
The meeting place *par excellence* of many fortyish professionals, the terrace and dining room of Café Cherrier are always packed. The atmosphere is reminiscent of a French *brasserie*, highly animated and busy, which can lead to fortuitous meetings. The menu features bistro-type

meals that are generally quite tasty, but the service can be uneven.

 Continental
$$-$$$
dinner only
4169 St-Denis
☎845-6842
The staging is very subtle at the Continental. Some evenings, the restaurant is positively charming, with its attentive, courteous staff, stylish clientele and modern 1950s-style décor. The varied menu ranks among the best in Montréal and includes a few surprises, such as veal kidneys with thyme and crunchy Asian noodles. The cuisine can be sublime, and the presentation is always excellent.

 Laloux
$$-$$$
Sat and Sun dinner only
250 Avenue des Pins Est
☎287-9127
Occupying a superb residence, Laloux resembles a chic and elegant Parisian-style bistro. People come here to enjoy nouvelle cuisine of consistently high quality, which is one of the best in Montréal. A reasonably priced *menu théâtre*, which includes three light courses, is offered.

Misto
$$-$$$
929 Avenue Mont-Royal Est
☎526-5043
Misto is an Italian restaurant patronized by a hip clientele, who come here to savour delicious and imaginative Italian cooking. The décor features exposed brick walls and shades of green, and the noisy atmosphere and crowded tables only add to the ambiance and the attentive and friendly service.

La Raclette
$$-$$$
bring your own wine
1059 Rue Gilford
☎524-8118
La Raclette is a popular neighbourhood restaurant on warm

summer evenings, thanks to its attractive terrace. Menu choices like raclette (of course), salmon with *Meaux* mustard and cherry clafoutis are some of the other draws. Those with a hearty appetite can opt for the *menu dégustation*, which includes appetizer, soup, main dish, dessert and coffee.

Moishe's Steak House
$$$
dinner only
3961 Boulevard St-Laurent
☎845-3509
Moishe's serves what are without a doubt the best steaks in town. The secret of this deliciously tender meat lies in the aging process. One of the specialties is chopped liver and fried onions.

Le P'tit Plateau
$$$
Tue-Sat
bring your own wine
330 Rue Marie-Anne Est
☎282-6342
A neighbourhood restaurant, Le P'tit Plateau offers a family atmosphere and attentive service. Simple and unpretentious cuisine.

L'Express
$$$
3927 Rue St-Denis
☎845-5333
A yuppie gathering place during the mid-1980s, L'Express is still highly rated for its locomotive dining-car decor and lively Parisian bistro atmosphere, which few restaurants have managed to recreate. In addition to the consistently appealing menu, the above-mentioned factors have earned this restaurant a solid reputation over the years.

Psarotaverna du Symposium
$$$
3829 Rue St-Denis
☎842-0867
The blue and white decor and warm island spirit of the service at La Psarotaverna du Symposium transports guests instantly to the Aegean Sea.

Fish (sea bream) and seafood are the specialties here. Try the delicious moussaka and *saganaki*. For dessert, make sure to sample the delicious, milk-based *galatoboureco*.

Le Piton de la Fournaise
$$$
bring your own wine
835 Avenue Duluth Est
☎526-3936
Tiny and charming, Le Piton de la Fournaise sparkles with life and is a treat for the senses. Here, you can sample ingeniously prepared cuisine from Reunion island that is full of surprises, thanks to its aromas, spices and textures. In order to fully enjoy a meal here, it's best to come unhurried and make a night of it.

 Toqué
$$$$
3842 Rue St-Denis
☎499-2084
If you're looking for a new culinary experience, Toqué is without a doubt the place to go in Montréal. Chef Normand Laprise insists on having the freshest ingredients and prepares and serves dishes with great care. And then there are the desserts, which are veritable modern sculptures. The service is exceptional, the wine list good, the new decor elegant, and the high prices do not seem to deter anyone. One of the most original dining establishments in Montréal.

Entertainment

Bars and Nightclubs

From sundown until early morning, Montréal is alive with the sometimes boisterous, other times more romantic

Montréal

rhythm of its bars. Crowded with people of all ages, there are bars designed to suit everyone's tastes, from the sidewalk bars along Rue Saint-Denis to the underground bars of Boulevard Saint-Laurent; from the crowded clubs on Rue Crescent to the gay bars in the "Village"; there are whole other worlds to discover.

L'Air du Temps Jazz
194 Rue St-Paul Ouest
☎842-2003
L'Air du Temps ranks among the most famous jazz bars in Montréal. Located in the heart of Old Montréal, it has a fantastic interior décor with scores of antiques. As the place is often packed, it is a good idea to arrive early to get a decent seat. The cover charge varies according to the show. Call for information on upcoming acts.

Le Balattou
4372 Boulevard St-Laurent
☎845-5447
Dark, smoky, jam-packed, hot, hectic and noisy, Le Balattou is without a doubt the most popular African nightclub in Montréal. Shows are presented only during the week, when the cost of admission varies.

Belmont sur le Boulevard
4483 Boulevard St-Laurent, corner of Avenue Mont-Royal
☎845-8443
A clientele composed mainly of junior executives crowds into the Belmont sur le Boulevard. On weekends, the place is literally overrun with customers.

Bily Kun
354 Rue Mont-Royal Est
☎845-5392
The second bar opened by the "Cheval Blanc" microbrewery, Bily Kun offers a wide selection of beers, including the excellent and reasonable house brand. With an original décor of mounted ostrich necks, this place has a friendly and very lively atmo-

sphere and is always packed. Live jazz Sundays and Fridays.

Café Campus
57 Prince Arthur E.
☎844-1010
Forced to move from its location in front of the Université de Montréal, Café Campus has settled into a large place on Rue Prince Arthur. Over the years, it has become a Montréal institution. The décor is still quite plain. Good musicians frequently perform here.

Café Sarajevo
2080 Clark
☎284-5629
Café Sarajevo hosts gypsy bands on Thursdays, Fridays and Saturdays, and jazz musicians the rest of the week. The crowd is a mix of bohemian students and, of course, Yugoslavians, and the decor is straight out of a bar in that country. While sipping a beer or a glass of red Hungarian wine, why not try some Balkan specialities, such as *bourek* (meat and filo pastry roll), *pleckavica* (hamburger) and *cevapcici* (meatballs) served with *ajvar* (red pepper spread). There is a patio out back that is pleasant during the summer. Meet Osman, the charismatic owner, who bears an uncanny resemblance to Sean Connery! Closed Mondays. Cover charge later in the evening for performances.

Le Cheval Blanc
809 Rue Ontario Est
☎522-0211
Le Cheval Blanc is a Montréal tavern and micro-brewery that does not appear to have been renovated since the 1940s; hence its unique style! Excellent beers are brewed on the premises.

Les Deux Pierrots
104 Rue St-Paul Ouest
☎861-1270
A noisy, enthusiastic crowd is drawn to Aux Deux Pierrots to sing along with Québec variety singers. During sum-

mer, there is a pleasant outdoor terrace.

Diable Vert
4557 Rue St-Denis
☎849-5888
The Diable Vert is the place to go to let loose on a large dance floor. Because it is very popular with students, there might be a lineup. Cover charge is $2 (including coatcheck) on Wednesday and Thursday nights and $3 on Friday and Saturday nights.

Dogue
4177 Rue St-Denis
☎845-8717
The Dogue is the ideal place to dance, dance, dance! The music, which ranges from Elvis classics to the latest Rage Against the Machine hit, gratifies a rather young, high-spirited crowd thirsting for cheap beer. There are two pool tables, which are a bit in the way, but keep the pool sharks entertained. The place is jampacked seven days a week, so you are strongly advised to get here early.

Les Foufounes Électriques
87 Rue Ste-Catherine Est
☎844-5539
Les Foufounes Électriques is a fantastic, one-of-a-kind bar/dance club/pick-up joint. The best bar in Québec for dancing to alternative music, it attracts a motley crowd of young Montrealers, ranging from punks to medical students. The decor, consisting of graffiti and strange sculptures, is wacky, to say the least. Don't come here for a quiet night.

Hurley's Irish Pub
1225 Rue Crescent
☎861-4111
Discreetly tucked away south of Rue Sainte-Catherine among the innumerable Crescent Street restaurants and bars, Hurley's Irish Pub succeeds in recreating an atmosphere worthy of traditional Irish pubs, thanks largely to the

excellent amateur Irish folk musicians and the world-famous Guinness.

Île Noire Pub
342 Rue Ontario Est
☎982-0866
The Île Noire is a beautiful bar in the purest Scottish tradition. The abundance of precious wood used for the décor gives the place a cozy charm and sophisticated atmosphere. The knowledgeable staff guide guests through the impressive list of whiskeys. The bar also has a good selection of imported draught beer. Unfortunately, the prices are high.

Jello Bar
151 Rue Ontario Est
☎285-2621
Jello Bar is strewn with an unusual mix of furniture and knick-knacks straight out of the suburban living rooms of the 1960s and 1970s. The bar serves a selection of 32 different martini cocktails to be sipped to the mellow sounds of jazz or blues. Great musical acts are regularly booked.

The Loft
1405 Boulevard Saint-Laurent
The Loft, with its austere techno interior accented in mauve and alternative music, attracts a varied clientele between the ages of 18 and 30. Interesting exhibits are occasionally presented. Pool tables provide some diversion, and the roof-top terrace is pleasant.

Newtown
1476 Rue Crescent
☎284-6555
Owned by Québec's favourite Formula 1 driver, Jacques Villeneuve, Newtown draws crowds of patrons who feel the urge to see and be seen while dining in the beautiful restaurant, dancing at the nightclub or having a drink in the lush ambiance of the lounge in this huge, splendidly designed complex.

P'tit Bar
3451 Rue St-Denis
☎281-9124
Right opposite Square Saint-Louis, the P'tit Bar is the perfect place to discuss literature, philosophy, photography, etc. The former hangout of the late Gérald Godin, a celebrated Québec poet, this place will appeal to fans of French music. Photo exhibits make up the sober decor.

Saint-Sulpice
1682 Rue St-Denis
☎844-9458
The Saint-Sulpice occupies all three floors of an old house and is tastefully decorated. Its front and rear terraces are perfect places to make the most of summer evenings.

Sherlock's
1010 Rue Ste-Catherine Ouest
☎878-0088
Sherlock's has a very lovely décor, reminiscent of an English pub, including busts of Sherlock Holmes. It is also very big and very popular! Everything, however, is quite expensive, and the restaurant is not recommended. About 15 pool tables are also at the disposal of customers.

Sir Winston Churchill Pub
1459 Rue Crescent
☎288-3814
An English-style bar, the Sir Winston Churchill attracts crowds of singles who come here to cruise and meet people. It has pool tables and a dance floor.

Swimming
3643 Boulevard St-Laurent
☎282-7665
The entrance to Swimming leads through the dilapidated vestibule of a building dating back to a century ago or so, making the view from the third floor of this gigantic pool room even more striking. The large rectangular bar and endless rows of pool tables and players are surrounded by glazed concrete columns, deliberately emphasized and

topped by strange polyhedrons. The old tin ceiling is a reminder of both the industrial city of the early 20th century and the building's original purpose.

Thursday's
1449 Rue Crescent
☎288-5656
Thursday's bar is very popular, especially among the city's English-speaking population. It is a favourite meeting place for business people and professionals.

Upstairs Jazz Club
1254 Rue Mackay
☎931-6808
Located in the heart of downtown Montréal, Upstairs hosts jazz and blues shows seven days a week. During summer, the walled terrace behind the bar is a wonderful place to take in the sunset.

The Old Dublin Pub
1219A Rue University
☎861-4448
An Irish pub with live Celtic music and an impressive selection of draught beer, the Old Dublin is a Montréal institution and one of the first of the now-ubiquitous genre in the city.

Whisky Café
5800 Boulevard St-Laurent
☎278-2646
The Whisky Café is so conscientiously decorated that even the men's bathrooms are a strange tourist attraction. The warm colours used in a modern setting, the tall columns covered with woodwork and pre-1950s-style chairs all create a sense of comfort and elegance. The well-off, well-bred clientele is mainly gilded youth between the ages of 20 and 35.

Zinc Café Bar Montréal
1148 Avenue Mont-Royal Est
☎523-5432
Looking for a good place to talk about everything and nothing while enjoying a *picon bière*? The Zinc Café Bar is an

Montréal

inviting place that serves a variety of unusual drinks.

Gay Bars and Nightclubs

Cabaret l'Entre-Peau
1115 Rue Ste-Catherine Est
☎*525-7566*
Cabaret l'Entre-Peau puts on transvestite shows. The place attracts a lively, mixed clientele.

Sky Pub and Sky Club
1474 Rue Ste-Catherine Est
☎*529-6969*
Sky Pub, the busiest gay bar in Montréal, boasts a refined, cozy and elegant decor. A profusion of wood and in-spired lighting have made this place popular since its opening. The loud and uninspired music, however, leaves a bit to be desired. In the summer there is people-watching on the terrace facing Sainte-Catherine. With its three or four dance floors that each play a different type of music (alternative, commercial, techno, retro, etc.), the two-storey club rivals Unity as Montréal's largest gay club. Obviously, in such an immense place, there is more than one atmosphere. The crowd is mostly young and the cover charge changes frequently.

Theatres and Concert Halls

Montréal has a distinct cultural scene. All year round, there are shows and exhibitions, that enable Montrealers to discover different aspects of the arts. Accordingly, shows and films from all over the world, exhibitions of all different styles of art, and festivals for all tastes and ages are presented here. The free weekly newspapers *Voir, Ici, The Mirror* and *Hour* review the main events taking place in Montréal.

Prices vary greatly from one theatre to the next. Most of the time, however, there are discount rates for children, students and seniors.

Place des Arts
260 Boulevard de Maisonneuve Ouest
Place-des-Arts métro
☎*285-4200*
☎*842-2112 (for the box office)*
The complex contains five performance spaces: Salle Wilfrid-Pelletier, Théâtre Maisonneuve, Théâtre Jean-Duceppe, Théâtre du Café de la Place and the Cinquième Salle, opened in 1992. The **Orchestre Symphonique de Montréal** (☎*842-2112*), **I Musici Chamber Orchestra** (☎*982-6037*) and **Grands Ballets Canadiens** (☎*849-0269*) perform in the main hall.

Spectrum
318 Rue Ste-Catherine Ouest
☎*861-5851*
Place-des-Arts métro
Shows usually begin around 11pm. Count on at least $10 to get in. Shows after 11pm are usually free during the Jazz Festival.

Théâtre Saint-Denis
1594 Rue St-Denis
Berri-UQAM métro
☎*849-4211*

Ticket Sales

There are three major ticket agencies in Montréal that sell tickets for shows, concerts and other events over the telephone. Service charges, which vary according to the show, are added to the price of the ticket. Credit cards are accepted.

Admission
☎*790-1245*
☎*800-361-4595*

Tel-spec
☎*790-1111*

Movie Theatres

Montréal has many movie theatres in downtown. Special rates are offered on Tuesdays and for matinees.

The following show films in French:

Le Parisien
480 Rue Ste-Catherine Ouest
McGill métro
☎*866-0111*

Le Quartier Latin
305 Rue Émery, corner of St-Denis
Berri-UQAM métro
☎*849-4422*

The following show films in English:

Centre Eaton
705 Rue Ste-Catherine Ouest
McGill métro
☎*866-0111*

Paramount
977 rue Ste-Catherine Ouest
Peel métro
☎*842-5828*

The following are repertory theatres:

La Cinémathèque Québécoise
335 Boulevard de Maisonneuve Est
Berri-UQAM métro
☎*842-9763*
shows films in French

Cinéma du Parc
3516 Avenue Du Parc
☎*281-1900*
The Cinéma du Parc is *the* place to see international, indie and cult flicks.

Ex-Centris
3536 Boulevard St. Laurent
☎*847-3536*
French and English

Impérial
1430 Rue de Bleury
☎*848-0300*
Place-des-Arts métro
This is the oldest movie theatre in Montréal, and by far the

most beautiful. Currently closed for renovations.

Le Cinéma IMAX
at the Vieux-Port de Montréal, on Rue de la Commune, corner of Boulevard St-Laurent
☎**496-4629**
Films are presented on a giant screen.

Office National du Film (National Film Board)
1564 Rue St-Denis
☎**496-6895**
A *cinérobothèque* allows several people to watch NFB films at once. A robot, the only one like it in the world, loads each machine. The complex is dedicated to Québec and Canadian cinema.

Festivals

During summer, festival fever takes hold of Montréal. From May to September, the city hosts a whole series of festivals, each with a different theme. One thing is certain: there is something for everyone. As the summer season draws to a close, the events become less frequent.

The **Tour de l'Île** *(www.velo. qc.ca/tour)* usually takes place in June. The event can accommodate a maximum of 45,000 cyclists, who ride together for some 65km around the island of Montréal. Registration begins in April, and costs $22 for adults and $10 for children (7 to 14 years old) and senior citizens. Registration forms are available at Canadian Tire stores (in Québec) and from **Tour de l'Île de Montréal** *(1251 Rue Rachel Est, ☎521-8687).*

Mid-June is marked by an international event that captivates a large number of fans from all over North America: the **Grand Prix Air Canada** *(to reserve seats, call ☎350-0000,*

www.grandprix. ca), which takes place at the Circuit Gilles Villeneuve on Île Notre-Dame. This is without question one of the most popular events of the summer. During these three days, it is possible to attend a variety of car races, including the roaring, spectacular Formula One competition.

The **Concours International d'Art Pyrotechnique (International Fireworks Competition)** *(☎397-2000; www.montreal feux.com)* starts around mid-June and ends in late July. The world's top pyrotechnists present high-quality pyro-musical shows every Saturday in June and every Sunday in July. Montrealers crowd to La Ronde amusement park *(tickets cost $29 or $38; call ☎ 790-1245),* on the Pont Jacques-Cartier or alongside the river (both at no cost) to admire the spectacular blossoms of flame that colour the sky above the city and last for over half an hour.

During the **Festival International de Jazz de Montréal** *(☎871-1881),* hundreds of shows set to the rhythm of jazz and its variations are presented on stages erected around Place des Arts. From late June to early July, this part of the city and a fair number of theatres are buzzing with activity. The event offers people an opportunity to take to the streets and be carried away by the festive atmosphere of the fantastic, free outdoor shows that attract Montrealers and visitors in large numbers.

Humour and creativity are highlighted during the **Festival Juste pour Rire (Just for Laughs Festival)** *(☎790-4242),* which is held from mid-July to late July. Theatres host comedians from a variety of countries for the occasion. Théâtre Saint-Denis presents shows consisting of short performances by a number of

different comedians. Outdoor activities take place in the Quartier-Latin, on Rue Saint-Denis south of Rue Sherbrooke, which is closed to traffic.

The **FrancoFolies** *(☎523-3378, www.francofolies.com)* are organized to promote French-language music and song. During late-July, artists from francophone countries (Europe, Africa, French Antilles, Québec and French Canada) perform, providing spectators with a unique glimpse of the French-speaking world's musical talent.

At the end of the summer, the **Festival International des Films du Monde (World Film Festival)** *(☎848-3883, www.ffm-montreal.org)* takes over various Montréal movie theatres. During this competition, films from different countries are presented to Montréal audiences. At the end of the competition, prizes are awarded to the best films. The most prestigious category is the Grand Prix des Amériques. During the festival, films are shown from 9am to midnight, to the delight of movie-goers across the city. An outdoor screening takes place at Place des Arts every night during the festival. Outdoor shows are also presented at the Place des Arts.

Held in mid-October at the Ex-Centris complex, the **Montreal International Festival of New Cinema and New Media** *(☎847-9272, www.fcmm.com)* aims to promote and develop *cinéma d'auteur* and digital creation.

Winter's cold does not preclude the festival spirit; it merely provides an opportunity to organize another festival in Montréal, this time to celebrate the pleasures and activities of this frosty season! The **Fête des Neiges de Montréal** *(☎872-6120, www.fetedesneiges.com)* takes

Montréal

place on Île Notre-Dame, from the end of January to mid-February. Skating rinks and giant toboggans are available for the enjoyment of Montréal families. The snow-sculpture competition also attracts a number of curious onlookers.

Spectator Sports

Centre Bell
1250 Rue de la Gauchetière
☎989-2841
In the fall, the hockey games of the famous Montreal Canadiens hockey team start in the Centre Bell. There are 42 games during the regular season followed by the play-offs, semi-finals and the Stanley Cup.

Stade Olympique
4141 Avenue Pierre-de-Courbertin
☎252-4679
Spring signals the beginning of baseball season. The Expos play against the various teams of the National Baseball League at the Olympic Stadium.

Shopping

Whether it be original Québec creations or imported articles, Montréal's shops sell all sorts of merchandise, each item more interesting than the last. To assist you in your shopping, we have prepared a list of shops with exceptionally high-quality, original or inexpensive products.

The Underground City

The 1962 construction of Place Ville-Marie, with its underground shopping mall, marked the origins of what is known today as the underground city. The development of this "city under the city" was accelerated by the construction of the métro system, or subway, which opened in 1966. Soon, many downtown businesses and office buildings, as well as a few hotels, were strategically linked to the underground pedestrian network and, by extension, to the métro.

Today, the underground city, now the largest in the world, has five distinct sections. The first lies at the very heart of the métro system, around the Berri-UQAM station, and is connected to the Université du Québec à Montréal (UQAM), the Galeries Dupuis and the bus station. The second stretches between the Place-des-Arts and Place-d'Armes stations, and is linked to Place des Arts, the Musée d'Art Contemporain, Complexe Desjardins, Complexe Guy Favreau and the Palais des Congrès, forming an exceptional cultural ensemble. The third, at the Square-Victoria station, serves the business centre. The fourth, which is the busiest and most important one, encompasses the McGill, Peel and Bonaventure stations. It includes the Bay department store; the Promenades de la Cathédrale, Place Montréal Trust and Cours Mont-Royal shopping centres, as well as Place Bonaventure, 1000 de la Gauchetière, the train station and Place Ville-Marie. The fifth and final area is located in the commercial section around the Atwater station; it is linked to Westmount Square, Dawson College and Place Alexis Nihon.

Shopping Malls and Department Stores

Several downtown shopping centres and department stores offer a good selection of clothing by well-known fashion designers, including Jean-Claude Chacok, Cacharel, Guy Laroche, Lily Simon, Adrienne Vittadini, Mondi, Ralph Lauren and many others.

The Bay
Square Phillips
on Rue Ste-Catherine Ouest
☎281-4422

Ogilvy
1307 Rue Ste-Catherine Ouest
☎842-7711

Westmount Square
4 Westmount Square
☎932-0211

Simons
977 Ste-Catherine O.
☎282-1840

Les Ailes de la Mode
677 Rue Ste. Catherine O
☎282-4537

Québec Designers

Revenge
3852 Rue St-Denis
☎843-4379
Not every inspired creation comes from Paris. Revenge sells lovingly crafted originals and accessories created by talented Quebec designers for both men and women.

Jeans

All kinds of jeans are available in Montreal, often at lower prices than in Europe.

Levi's
705 Rue Ste-Catherine Ouest, in the Centre Eaton
☎286-1574
1241 Rue Ste-Catherine Ouest
☎288-8199

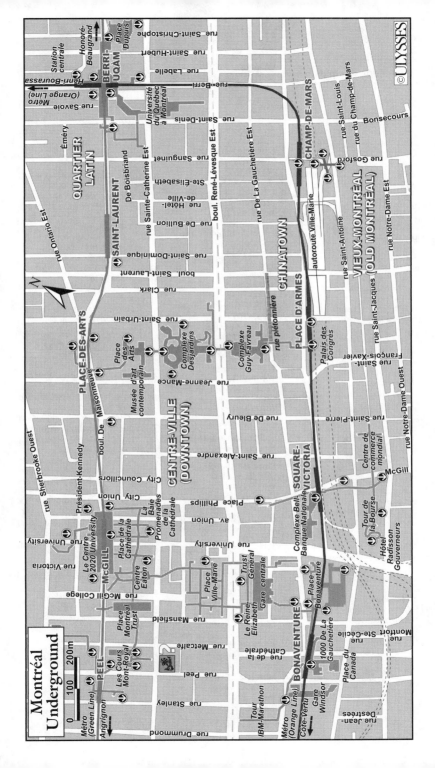

Outdoor Equipment

La Cordée
2159 Rue Ste-Catherine Est
☎*524-1106*
La Cordée opened in 1953 to outfit the Boy Scouts and Girl Guides of Québec. Now they serve just about anyone who wants the best quality outdoor equipment. Renovated and expanded in 1997, the store is the largest of its kind in Montréal, and its layout and design make it a very pleasant place to shop.

Kanuk
485 Rue Rachel Est
☎*527-4494*
Kanuk manufactures popular winter outerwear. You can buy their merchandise at their huge outlet, located right above the factory. Kanuk winter coats come in various styles and are extremely warm. Keep an eye out for their seasonal sales, which draw crowds.

Bookstores

Montréal has both French and English bookstores. Books from Québec, Canada and the United States are available at reasonable prices. Books from Europe are slightly more expensive because of import costs. Anyone interested in Québécois literature will find a large selection in Montréal stores.

General

Archambault
500 Rue Ste-Catherine Est
☎*849-6201*

Champigny
4380 Rue St-Denis
☎*844-2587*
5219 Chemin de la Côte-des-Neiges
☎*844-2587*

Chapter's
1171 Rue Ste-Catherine Ouest
☎*849-8825*

Indigo
Place Montréal Trust
☎*281-5549*

Librairie Gallimard
3700 Boulevard St-Laurent
☎*499-2012*

Librairie Paragraphe
2220 McGill College
☎*845-5811*

Librairie Renaud-Bray
5252 Chemin de la Côte-des-Neiges
☎*342-1515*
4301 Rue St-Denis
☎*499-3656*
5117 Avenue du Parc
☎*276-7651*
1474 Rue Peel
☎*287-1011*
1376 Rue Ste-Catherine Ouest
☎*876-9119*

Coles
Place Ville-Marie
☎*861-1736*
Promenades de la Cathédrale
625 Rue Ste-Catherine Ouest
☎*289-8737*

Specialty Bookstores

Librairie Allemande
3488 Chemin de la Côte-des-Neiges
☎*933-1919*
German books.

Librairie Boule de Neige
4433 Rue St-Denis
☎*849-0959*
Esoteric and New Age books.

Librairie C.E.C. Michel Fortin
3714 Rue St-Denis
☎*849-5719*
Education and languages.

Librairie Olivieri
5219 Chemin de la Côte-des-Neiges
☎*739-3639*
Foreign literature, science, art.

Librairie Olivieri
185 Rue Ste-Catherine Ouest
☎*847-6903*
Contemporary art books.

Librairie Ulysse
4176 Rue St-Denis
☎*843-9447*
560 Avenue du Président-Kennedy
☎*843-7222*
Travel guides.

Music

The following megastores have the largest selection of compact discs of all musical genres at the lowest prices:

Archambault Musique
500 Rue Ste-Catherine Est
☎*849-6201*
Place des Arts
175 Rue Ste-Catherine Ouest
☎*281-0367*

HMV
1020 Rue Ste-Catherine Ouest
☎*875-0765*

Québec Crafts

Québec art is produced by artists from many cultures: French and English Canadian, Mohawk, Cree, Inuit, and others. Each year in December at **Place Bonaventure** (*901 Rue de La Gauchetière Ouest*), these artists display and sell their work in a giant exposition hall; this event is called "**Le Salon des métiers d'art du Québec**." If you miss the show, **Le Rouet** (*136 St-Paul Est*, ☎*875-2333; 1500 Avenue McGill College*, ☎*843-5235*) sells sculptures, pottery and ceramics by several Québec artists.

Guilde Canadienne des Métier d'Art
1460 Rue Sherbrooke Ouest
☎*849-6091*
Guilde Canadienne des Métier d'Art has a shop that sells hand-crafted Canadian objects. As well, there are two small galleries that deal in Inuit and other native art.

Bonsecours Market
390 Rue St-Paul Est
The Bonsecours Market is the place to shop for crafts or

exclusive designer items. Among the galeries to visit, keep in mind the Galerie des Métiers d'Art du Québec and the Galerie de l'Institut de Design Montréal.

Bagels

How can you speak of Montréal bakeries without mentioning bagels?! Montréal is famous internationally for these kosher little breads, and they are probably the best bagels in the world. Whether this is true or not, they are certainly delicious and much loved. Many bakeries, especially in Outremont and Mile-End, make several varieties of them in a wood-burning oven. Among these are the famous **Fairmount Bagel Bakery** *(74 Fairmount O.,* ☎ *277-0667)*, open 24hrs, and the **Bagel Shop** *(158 St-Viateur O.,* ☎ *270-2972).*

Specialty Grocers

The **Première Moisson** bakery cannot really be called a craft bakery because it is a chain of shops. However, each one prepares fresh delicious baked goods daily, straight from, if you please, a wood-burning oven! The whole-wheat baguettes are the best in the city. Meats, cakes, chocolates and delicious ready-made dishes are also sold here. Première Moisson also has stores in Montréal's three public markets, as well as the Gare Centrale and 1271 Bernard Ouest.

Fromagerie Hamel
220, rue Jean-Talon E.
☎*272-1161*
There is a panoply of little shops worth mentioning around the Jean-Talon Market. One of these is

Fromagerie Hamel, one the best cheese shops in the city, which is known for the fine quality and wide selection of its products, as well as its excellent service. Definitely sample their cheeses if offered. Despite the lineup, the staff always sees to customers' every need.

La Queue de Cochon
1328, av. Laurier E.
☎*527-2252*
6400 Rue St-Hubert
☎*527-2252*
Fine gourmets will definitely like the excellent products at La Queue de Cochon, a small craft-style *charcuterie* (butcher shop). A variety of terrines and sausages such as *boudin blanc* and *boudin noir* (white-pudding and blood-pudding sausages), as well as several prepared dishes, are available here. Pork products are obviously the speciality here, and after the owner (from Vendée, France) and his family tell you all about them, you won't want to leave without buying something!

Gift Shops

Montréal's museum gift shops are almost like museums in themselves. They sell various reproductions lovely enough to embellish any home. Here are two to remember:

Boutique du Musée d'Art Contemporain
185 Rue Ste-Catherine Ouest
☎*847-6226*

Boutique du Musée des Beaux-Arts de Montréal
1390 Rue Sherbrooke Ouest
☎*285-1600*

However, there are many other places with great gift ideas:

Céramique
4201B, Rue St-Denis
☎*848-1119*
95 rue de la Commune E.
☎*868-1611*
If you are looking for an original gift, at the Céramique art-café you can paint a clay object yourself while comfortably seated and enjoying a light meal or a drink. The experienced staff is there to help you. This is probably the most personalized gift you can get!

Franc Jeu
4152 Rue St-Denis
☎*849-9253*
Pinocchio and Capucine, Babar and Milou will delight children at Franc Jeu, which has a vast assortment of toys for all ages, from babies to those enjoying their second chilhood...

Valet de Coeur
4408 Rue St-Denis
☎*499-9970*
Playing is not only for children, and Valet de Coeur has games for everyone, from three-dimensional puzzles, Chinese checkers and chess sets to a variety of parlour games.

Jewellery Stores

Birks
1240 Square Phillips
☎*397-2511*
A veritable Montréal institution, Birks has beautiful jewellery, such as diamond engagement rings, wedding bands and anniversary gifts. The elegant shop is worth a look in itself.

For designer jewellery, take a peek at **Kyose** *(Cours Mont-Royal, Rue Ste-Catherine Ouest,* ☎*849-6552)* or **Oz Bijoux** *(3915 Rue St-Denis,* ☎*845-9568).*

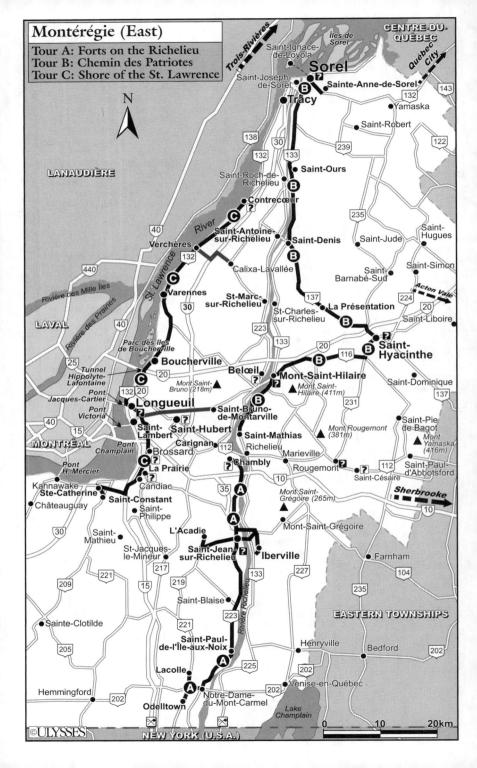

Montérégie

The six hills

in Montérégie, Mont Saint-Bruno, Mont Saint-Hilaire, Mont Yamaska, Mont Rigaud, Mont Saint-Grégoire and Mont Rougemont, are the only large hills in this otherwise flat region.

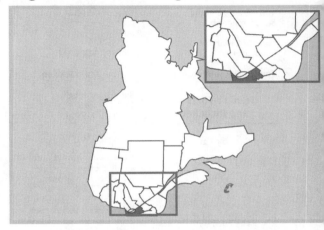

The hills, which do not rise much over 500m, are spread out and were long considered ancient volcanoes. Actually, they are metamorphic rocks that did not break through the upper layer of the earth's crust and became visible as the neighbouring land eroded over a long period of time.

The Montérégie area is a beautiful plain, rich in history and agriculture, located between Ontario, New England and the foothills of the Appalachians in the Eastern Townships. Located just south of Montréal, with many natural transportation routes, such as the majestic Rivière Richelieu, Montérégie has always played an important military and strategic role. The many fortifications that can now be visited in the area were once outposts that served to protect the colony from the Iroquois, the British and the Americans. It was also in Montérégie that the United States experienced its first military defeat, in 1812. It was here, too, in Saint-Charles-sur-Richelieu and

Saint-Denis, that the Patriotes (French for patriots, those who supported Papineau in the Rebellion of Lower Canada) and the British confronted each other, during the 1837-1838 rebellion.

Although the towns surrounding the island of Montréal have become the southern suburbs of this large city, most of Montérégie has managed to preserve its pastoral charm. Medium-sized towns such as Saint-Jean-sur-Richelieu and Saint-Hyacinthe (farm produce capital of Québec) continue to preserve their own institutions and identities, while a large part of the region's economy is still connected to agriculture and

livestock. To visit Montérégie is to explore the superb Vallée du Richelieu, to experience the area's rich historical heritage and to breathe the fresh country air. Apple picking in the Rougemont orchards is also very popular during the fall.

Finding Your Way Around

From the island of Montréal, the bridges across the St. Lawrence River lead to Montérégie. There are two distinct parts of this region: the Rive-Sud (south shore), a large plain punctuated by rivers south and east of Montréal, and the western point of the mainland leading from the Ontario border to the island of Montréal, bordered by Lac Saint-François and the Ottawa River. Five tours are outlined:

Tour A: Forts on the Richelieu ★★

Tour B: Chemin des Patriotes ★★

Tour C: Shore of the St. Lawrence ★

Tour D: Vaudreuil-Soulanges ★

Tour E: The Southwest ★

Tour A: Forts on the Richelieu

By Car

From Montréal, take the Champlain Bridge (Pont Champlain), then Aut. 10 to Chambly, on the western shore of the Rivière Richelieu, to the Boulevard Fréchette exit. From Chambly, take Rte. 223 S., then follow Rte. 202 and 221 to complete the tour.

By Ferry

Saint-Paul-de-l'Île-aux-Noix – Île-aux-Noix
mid-May to mid-Nov
☎*(450) 291-5700*

Bus Station

Saint-Jean-sur-Richelieu
600 Boulevard Pierre-Caisse
☎*(450) 359-6024*

Tour B: Chemin des Patriotes

By Car

From Montréal, take the Champlain Bridge (Pont Champlain), then Aut. 10 across the Rivière Richelieu, then take Rte. 133 N., also called "Chemin des patriotes."

Drive along the eastern shore of the Richelieu, from St-Mathias to Mont-St-Hilaire. From here, take Rte. 116 and then Rte. 231 to St-Hyacinthe. From here, Rte. 137 N. leads to St-Denis and Rte. 133 to Sorel.

Bus Station

Saint-Hyacinthe
1330 Rue Calixa-Lavallée
☎*(450) 773-3287*

Sorel
191 Rue du Roi
☎*(450) 743-4411*

Train Station

Saint-Hyacinthe
1450 Rue Sicotte
☎*800-361-5390*

By Ferry

Saint-Denis – Saint-Antoine-sur-Richelieu
mid-May to mid-Nov
☎*(450) 787-2759*

Saint-Marc-sur-Richelieu – Saint-Charles-sur-Richelieu
mid-May to mid-Nov
☎*(450) 584-2813*

Saint-Roch-de-Richelieu – Saint-Ours
mid-May to mid-Nov
☎*(450) 785-2161*

Sorel – Saint-Ignace-de-Loyola
year-round
☎*(450) 743-3258 or 836-4600*

Tour C: Shore of the St. Lawrence

By Car

From Montréal, take the Mercier Bridge toward La Prairie, then Rte. 132 E., the main road for this tour. When you reach Ste-Catherine, drive along the river until Contrecœur. You can also make a detour to St-Bruno and Calixa-Lavallée.

Bus Station

Longueuil
120 Place Charles-Lemoyne
☎*(450) 670-3422*

Longueuil
STRSM (*Metro and bus terminal, Longueuil–Université-de-Sherbrooke station*)
100 Place Charles-Lemoyne
☎*(450) 463-0131*

By Ferry

Longueuil – Île Charron
mid-May to early Oct
☎*(450) 442-9575*

River shuttle Longueuil – Montréal
mid-May to early Oct
☎*(514) 281-8000*

Tour D: Vaudreuil-Soulanges

By Car

From Montréal, take Aut. 20 W. to Vaudreuil-Dorion, the start of the tour. By taking Rte. 342, you can reach Como, Hudson, Rigaud and Pointe-Fortune. Take either Rte. 342 or Aut. 40 to Rte. 201 to Coteau-du-Lac. From here, head east along the St. Lawrence River to Pointe-des-Cascades, then north to Île Perrot.

By Ferry

Hudson – Oka
mid-May to mid-Nov
☎*(450) 458-4732*

Tour E: The Southwest

By Car

From Montréal, cross the Mercier Bridge and take Rte. 138 to the intersection of Rte. 132. Take Rte. 132 to St-Timothée (Salaberry-de-

Valleyfield is a few kilometres further). Then go south on Rte. 132, cross the Canal de Beaharnois, and continue to Rivière Châteauguay. Drive south along the river to Ormstown, from where Rte. 201 follows Rte. 202 and will lead you through to the end of the tour.

Practical Information

The area code for Montérégie is **450**, except for Île Perrot, which is **514**.

Tourist Information

Regional Office

Association Touristique Régionale de la Montérégie
11 ch. Marieville, Rougemont
J0L 1M0
☎*(450) 469-0069*
☎*866-469-0069*
☎*(514) 990-4600*
≈*(450) 469-1139*
www.tourisme-monteregie.qc.ca

Tour A: Forts on the Richelieu

Saint-Jean-sur-Richelieu
31 Rue Frontenac, J3B 7X2
☎*542-9090*
☎*888-781-9999*
≈*542-9091*

Tour B: Chemin des Patriotes

Mont-Saint-Hilaire
1080 Chemin des Patriotes Nord, J3H 5W1
☎*536-0395*
☎*888-736-0395*
≈*536-3147*
www.vallee-du-richelieu.ca

Saint-Hyacinthe
Parc des Patriotes, 2090 Rue Cherrier, J2S 8R3
☎*774-7276*
☎*800-849-7276*
≈*774-9000*
www.tourismesainthyacinthe.qc.ca

Sorel-Tracy
92 Chemin des Patriotes, J3P 2K7
☎*746-9441*
☎*800-474-9441*
≈*746-0447*

Tour C: Shore of the St. Lawrence

Longueuil
205 Chemin Chambly, J4H 3L3
☎*670-7293*
≈*670-5887*
www.gensdaffaires.longueuil.qc.ca

Tour D: Vaudreuil-Soulanges

Vaudreuil-Dorion
seasonal office
331 Rue Saint-Charles (Maison Valois)
☎*424-8620*

Tour E: The Southwest

Salaberry-de-Valleyfield
980 Boulevard Mgr-Langlois, J6S 5X6
☎*377-7676*
☎*800-378-7648*
≈*377-3727*
www.tourisme-suroit.qc.ca

Kahnawake
C.P. 720, Kahnawake, J0L 1B0
☎*632-7500*
≈*638-5958*
www.kahnawake.com/tourism

Exploring

Tour A: Forts on the Richelieu

Duration of tour: two days

This tour goes from Chambly all the way to the U.S. border and gives visitors the opportu-

Names of New Merged Cities

Saint-Jean-sur-Richelieu
Merger of Saint-Jean-sur-Richelieu, Saint-Luc, Iberville, Saint-Athanase and L'Acadie.

Lacolle
Merger of Lacolle and Notre-Dame-du-Mont-Carmel.

Saint-Hyacinthe
Merger of Saint-Hyacinthe, the city and the parish of Sainte-Rosalie, Saint-Hyacinthe-le-Confesseur, Saint-Thomas-d'Aquin and Notre-Dame-de-Saint-Hyacinthe.

Longueuil
Merger of Boucherville, Brossard, Greenfield Park, LeMoyne, Longueuil, Saint-Bruno-de-Montarville, Saint-Hubert and Saint-Lambert.

Salaberry-de-Valleyfield
Merger of Salaberry-de-Valleyfield, Saint-Timothée and Grande-Île.

Beauharnois
Fusion de Beauhar-nois, Maple Grove and Melocheville.

nity to explore the defence network built along the Rivière Richelieu under the French Regime, which was reinforced following the British Conquest. This string of forts served to control access to the Richelieu, which, for a long time, was the main communication route between Montréal, New England and New York, via Lake Champlain and the Hudson River.

★★
**Chambly
(pop. 20,000)**

The town of Chambly occupies a privileged site alongside the Richelieu. The river widens here to form the Bassin de Chambly at the end of the rapids, which once hindered navigation on the river and made the area a key element in New France's defence system.

In 1665, the Carignan-Salières regiment, under the command of Captain Jacques de Chambly, built the first pile fort to drive back the Iroquois, who made frequent incursions into Montréal from the Mohawk River. In 1672, the captain was granted a seigneury in his name for services rendered to the colony.

The town that gradually formed around the fort flourished during the War of 1812, while a sizeable British garrison was stationed there. Then, in 1843, the Canal de Chambly opened, allowing boats to bypass the Richelieu Rapids and thereby facilitating commerce between Canada and the United States. Many transportation and import-export companies opened in the area at this time. Today, Chambly is both a suburb of Montréal and a getaway and leisure spot.

Follow Avenue Bourgogne to the narrow **Rue Richelieu ★**, which leads to the fort. Travel along the Parc des Rapides, where the Barrage de Chambly can be admired from up close. Imposing homes built in the first half of the 19th century line both sides of the road.

The comfortable palladian-style house known as **Maison John-Yule** *(27 Rue Richelieu)* was built in 1816. John Yule, of Scottish descent, emigrated to Canada with his brother William in the late 18th century. A few years later, William became seigneur of Chambly. John Yule prospered from his local flour and carding mills.

The **Atelier du Peintre Maurice Cullen** *(28 Rue Richelieu)* was built in 1920 on the foundations of William Yule's seigneurial manor. The house served as a studio for Canadian painter Maurice Cullen (1866-1934).

Colonel Charles-Michel d'Irumberry de Salaberry is known for his decisive victory over the American Army during the War of 1812-1814. Salaberry and his wife, Julie Hertel de Rouville, were descendants of French nobility who chose to stay in Canada despite the British Conquest of 1760. They moved into the **Manoir de Salaberry** *(18 Rue Richelieu)*, built around 1814, in order to govern the seigneury of Chambly, one third of which belonged to them at that time. The Manoir de Salaberry is one of the most elegant properties in the region, mixing French and Palladian architectural styles.

Following the War of 1812, several military infrastructures were built in the vicinity of Fort Chambly. Many have since been demolished, while others have been renovated. This is the case with the **Maison Ducharme** *(10 Rue Richelieu)*, a former soldiers' barracks, built in 1814 and transformed into a residence at the end of the 19th century.

The former **Corps de Garde (guardhouse)** *(8 Rue Richelieu)*, built in 1814, is next to the Maison Ducharme to the north. It is adorned with a wooden Palladian-style portico, the only element that truly distinguishes it from French Regime architecture. It houses an exhibit on the British presence in Chambly. At the end of Rue Richelieu, the Fort de Chambly can be seen in the middle of a park.

Turn left on Rue du Parc, and take Avenue Bourgogne to the right.

Many British people, civilian and military, as well as American Loyalists, settled in Chambly during the first half of the 19th century. The **St. Stephen Anglican Church ★** *(2004 Avenue Bourgogne)* was built in 1820 to serve this community, as well as the fort's garrison. The exterior, designed by local entrepreneur François Valade, is reminiscent of the Catholic churches of that era.

Fort Chambly National Historic Site ★★★ *($5; mid-May to late Jun 10am to 5pm, late Jun to early Sep 10am to 6pm, early Sep to mid-Oct week-ends; 2 Rue De Richelieu, ☎658-1585)* is the largest remaining fortification of the French Regime. It was built between 1709 and 1711 according to plans drawn by engineer Josué Boisberthelot de Beaucours at the request of the marquis of Vaudreuil. The fort, defended by the Compagnies Franches de la Marine, had to protect New France against a possible British invasion. It replaced the four pile forts that had occupied this site since 1665.

The military complex is located in a spectacular setting along the Bassin de Chambly, where the rapids begin. It is a rectangular building of rubble stone, with fortified bastions and completed by small

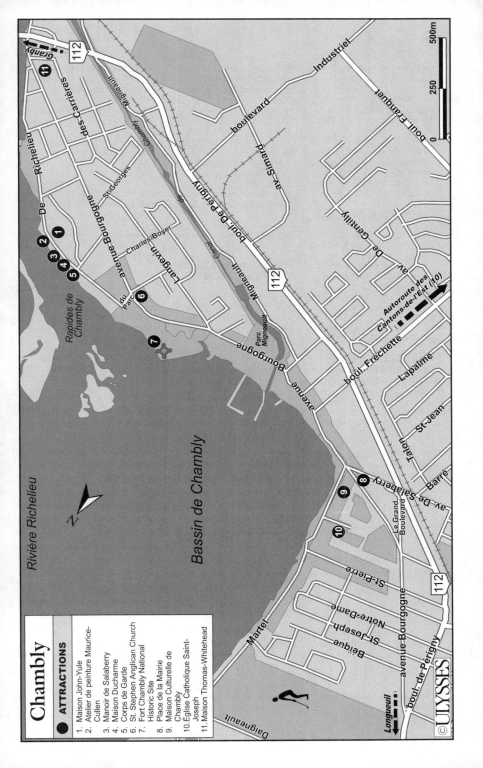

Chambly

ATTRACTIONS

1. Maison John-Yule
2. Atelier de peinture Maurice-Cullen
3. Manoir de Salaberry
4. Maison Ducharme
5. Corps de Garde
6. St. Stephen Anglican Church
7. Fort Chambly National Historic Site
8. Place de la Mairie
9. Maison Culturelle de Chambly
10. Église Catholique Saint-Joseph
11. Maison Thomas-Whitehead

© ULYSSES

wooden watchtowers. The interior of the fort houses an interesting interpretation centre describing the strategic importance of the Rivière Richelieu throughout history, the activities of the French garrison, the peopling of the Chambly seigneury and numerous objects found during archaeological digs, providing insight into the daily life of the inhabitants.

The **Place de la Mairie**, built in 1912, can be found at the intersection of Avenue Bourgogne and Rue Martel. In front of it stands a bronze statue by Louis-Philippe Hébert, commemorating the hero of the battle of Châteauguay, Charles-Michel d'Irumberry de Salaberry.

Take Rue Martel, which runs along the Bassin de Chambly.

The **Maison Culturelle de Chambly** (*56 Rue Martel*), Chambly's community centre, is located in this former convent of the Congrégation de Notre-Dame, erected in 1885. The building, with its two-sided roof and long wooden gallery, is typical of the convents that sit imposingly in the heart of most Québec cities and towns.

The **Église Catholique Saint-Joseph** (*164 Rue Martel*) was built in 1881 from the remains of the walls of the first church (1784) after it was seriously damaged by fire. In front of the church is the last known piece of artwork by sculptor Louis-Philippe Hébert, the statue of parish priest Migneault.

Return to Rue Martel, then take Avenue Bourgogne toward Saint-Jean-sur-Richelieu.

When leaving Chambly, you'll spot a blue wooden house. The **Maison Thomas-Whitehead** (*2592 Avenue Bourgogne*) was built in 1815

for an employee of the fort barracks. Few of these wooden houses, once very popular in villages and suburbs of large cities, survived the many fires that ravaged Québec during the 19th century. A 1934 painting by Robert Pilot showing the Thomas-Whitehead home in winter (*The Blue House*, Musée des Beaux-Arts de Montréal) served as a reference during its restoration in 1985.

Follow Rte. 223 South to Saint-Jean-sur-Richelieu.

★
Saint-Jean-sur-Richelieu (pop. 37,850)

This industrial city was, for a long time, an important gateway into Canada from the United States, as well as an essential rest stop on the road from Montréal. Three features made this city important: its port on the Richelieu, active from the end of the 18th century onwards; its railway, the first in Canada, which linked the town to La Prairie as of 1836; and the opening of the Canal de Chambly in 1843. In the mid-19th century, many businesses in Saint-Jean-sur-Richelieu related to or dependent on these transportation routes prospered, such as pottery and earthenware manufacturers (teapots, jugs and plates were to become the region's specialties). The city's architecture reflects its industrial past, with its factories, commercial buildings, working-class areas and beautiful Victorian homes.

Saint-Jean's roots, however, are much older. It developed around Fort Saint-Jean, built in 1666. In 1775, it was attacked many times by the American rebel army, which finally had to beat a retreat upon the arrival of British troops. The fort has been rebuilt many times and is now home to the Collège Militaire Royal de Saint-Jean.

Take **Rue Richelieu**, the main commercial road, into Saint-Jean. The street was devastated by fire on two occasions during the course of its history. It was rebuilt immediately after the last fire in 1876, giving it an architectural homogeneity unusual in Québec.

With the exception of the Musée du Fort Saint-Jean, the city's tourist attractions are located in a limited area that can be covered on foot from Rue Richelieu. Return to Rue Saint-Jacques and continue to the corner of Rue de Longueuil.

The body of the **Cathédrale Saint-Jean-L'Évangéliste** (*corner Saint-Jacques and Longueuil*) dates back to 1827, but the exterior was completely redone in 1861, when the facade and the chevet were switched. The current facade, with its copper bell, dates from the early 20th century.

The neoclassical **Palais de Justice** is located at the north end of Rue de Longueuil, and was built in 1854 in a grey limestone that was very popular at the time. Take Rue de Longueuil south to Place du Marché.

The **Musée du Haut-Richelieu** ★ (*$4; late Jun to early Sep every day 9:30am to 5pm; early Sep to late Jun, Tue-Sun 9:30am to 5pm; 182 Rue Jacques-Cartier Nord, ☎347-0649*) is located inside the former public market, built in 1859. Apart from various objects relating to the history of *Haut-Richelieu*, the upper-Richelieu, the museum holds an interesting collection of pottery and earthenware produced in the region during the 19th century, including beautiful pieces from the Farrar and St. Johns Stone Chinaware companies.

The construction date of the bourgeois building, the **Maison**

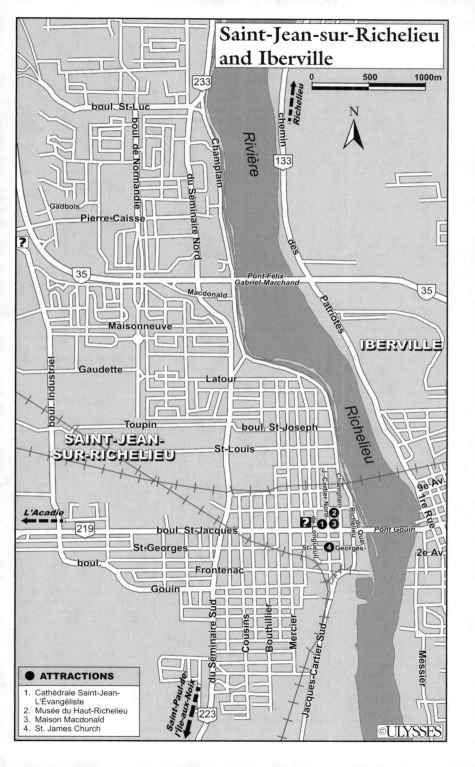

Saint-Jean-sur-Richelieu and Iberville

0   500   1000m

N

boul. St-Luc

boul. de Normandie

du Séminaire Nord

Champlain

233

Rivière

chemin Richelieu

133

35

Gadbois
Pierre-Caisse

Macdonald

Pont Félix-
Gabriel-Marchand

des Patriotes

35

Maisonneuve

IBERVILLE

Gaudette

Latour

boul. Industriel

Richelieu

Toupin

boul. St-Joseph

SAINT-JEAN-
SUR-RICHELIEU

St-Louis

Champlain

9e Av.

J.-Cartier Nord

1re Rue

L'Acadie

219

boul. St-Jacques

2 ❷
1 ❶ ❸ 3

du Quai
de Longueuil

Pont Gouin

St-Georges

❼

St-   ❹   Georges

2e Av.

boul.

Frontenac

Gouin

du Séminaire Sud

Cousins

Bouthillier

Mercier

Jacques-Cartier Sud

Messier

Saint-Paul-de-
l'Île-aux-Noix

223

● ATTRACTIONS

1. Cathédrale Saint-Jean-
   L'Évangéliste
2. Musée du Haut-Richelieu
3. Maison Macdonald
4. St. James Church

©ULYSSES

Macdonald *(166 Rue Jacques-Cartier Nord)*, is not known, but it appeared on maps for the first time in 1841. What is known, however, is that its current design is the result of the addition of a mansard roof and Second Empire styling around 1875. At that time, the house belonged to Duncan Macdonald, owner of the St. Johns Stone Chinaware Company. He held many receptions here until the collapse of his business.

The **St. James Church** *(corner Jacques-Cartier and Saint-Georges)*, built in 1817, is one of the oldest Anglican churches in Montérégie. Its American-inspired architecture reminds us that, during this period, Saint-Jean was home to a large community of Loyalist refugees from the United States.

A visit to Saint-Jean-sur-Richelieu can be completed with a walk along the river, on the strip of land that demarcates the mouth of the Canal de Chambly.

Iberville
(pop. 9,880)

Across from Saint-Jean, on the other bank of the Richelieu, is Iberville, accessible via the Pont Gouin bridge. The land that makes up the municipality, once known as Mille Roches, was granted to brothers Charles and Clément Sabrevois de Bleury in 1733. In 1770, following the Conquest, the French owners withdrew, and the seigneury passed into the hands of Gabriel Christie and Moses Hazen. In 1815, the village of Christieville came into being. The village was the beginning of the municipality of Iberville, a tranquil community that is home to many who work or study in Saint-Jean.

This optional excursion begins at the exit from the Pont Gouin. Turn left on 1re Rue, which runs along the Richelieu.

The Saint-Athanase-de-Bleury Catholic parish, founded in 1822, built **Église Saint-Athanase** *(1re Rue)*, their third church, in 1914. The presbytery, however, dates back to 1836. There is a panoramic view of Saint-Jean-sur-Richelieu from the front steps of the church.

In 1835, William Plenderleath Christie inherited the family seigneury. During the same year, he began construction on the imposing **Manoir Christie ★** *(375 1re Rue)*, done in Georgian style and visible through the trees. It is a large stone house, whose roof is topped with an elegant lantern. The Christies only lived in their Iberville property sporadically, as they found themselves in London, then in Bath. Their former home remains one of the most evocative of the seigneurial regime *(not open to visitors)*.

Return toward Saint-Jean-sur-Richelieu by the Pont Gouin bridge then take Rue Saint-Jacques to the junction with Rte. 219 S. Follow the directions toward L'Acadie. Temporarily inland from the Richelieu shore, this other optional excursion takes you to one of the area's most charming villages.

★
L'Acadie
(pop. 5,300)

During the Seven Years War between France and England, Acadia (part of present-day Nova Scotia and New Brunswick) was conquered, and in 1755, the Acadians, who owned the best properties, were deported to faraway lands. Between 1764 and 1768, some of them returned from exile and established themselves on the shore of Petite Rivière. They formed "Petite Acadie," which later became the village of L'Acadie. In the early 19th century, a contingent of Swiss families joined the community, settling in the locality of Grande-Ligne.

In L'Acadie, the **Église Sainte-Marguerite-de-Blairfindie ★★** *(308 Chemin du Clocher)*, the presbytery and the old school are some of the most picturesque and best-kept institutional buildings in the Montérégie area. The Catholic parish of Sainte-Marguerite was canonically constituted in 1784, but it wasn't until 1801 that the present-day stone church was completed. With its Latin-cross style, twin lantern bell-tower and windows built according to the precepts of Father Conefroy, the church is a fine example of traditional Québec architecture. Note the covered passageway (1822), which shelters churchgoers from bad weather as they walk from the presbytery to the church.

The lovely wood Louis-XV-style interior decor was completed between 1802 and 1809 under the supervision of Jean-Georges Finsterer, a local artisan. In addition, the church features several paintings, including *Marie au tombeau* and *Saint René*, by Louis Dulongpré (circa 1802). The cemetery features another interesting work, a Madonna and Infant Jesus by sculptor Philippe Hébert (Monument Roy, 1897).

Several years ago, a certain Mr. Bertrand acquired the hobby of reconditioning old farm equipment. What was at first simply a hobby soon became a passion. Faced with the problem of storing his large collection of machines, he decided to buy a small farmhouse on the banks of Rivière l'Acadie. This is how the **Musée René Bertrand** *($6, late Jun to early Sep, every day 10am to 5pm, Sep and Oct, Sat and Sun 1pm to*

5pm; 2864 Rte. 219, ☎346-1630) was born. In addition to numerous ploughing implements, there is a large collection of antique objects that will stir the memories of the older generation and arouse the curiosity of the younger one. There's a small amusement park that offers tractor rides, an excellent little restaurant that serves dishes made with old recipes, as well as a picnic area.

Saint-Paul-de-l'Île-aux-Noix (pop. 1,950)

This village is known for its fort, built on Île aux Noix (literally, island of nuts) in the middle of the Richelieu. Farmer Pierre Joudernet was the first occupant of the island, and he payed his seigneurial rent in the form of a bag of nuts, hence the island's name. Towards the end of the French Regime, the island became strategically important because of its proximity to Lake Champlain and the American colonies. The French began to fortify the island in 1759, but had such poor resources that the fort was taken by the British without difficulty. In 1775, the island became the headquarters for the American revolutionary forces, who attempted to invade Canada. Then, during the War of 1812, the reconstructed fort served as a base for the attack on Plattsburg (New York State) by the British.

Visitors must leave their cars at the information centre (61e Avenue) to take the ferry to the island.

Fort-Lennox National Historic Site ★★ *($5.75; mid-May to late Jun, Mon-Fri 10am to 5pm, Sat and Sun 10am to 6pm; late Jun to early Sep, Mon-Sun 10am to 6pm, early Sep to early Oct Sat and Sun 10am to 6pm, by reservation during the week; 1 61st Avenue, ☎291-5700)* takes up

two-thirds of Île aux Noix and significantly alters its face. It was built on the ruins of previous forts between 1819 and 1829 by the British, prompting the construction of Fort Montgomery by the Americans just south of the border. Behind the wall of earth and surrounded by large ditches are a powder keg, two warehouses, the guardhouse, the officers' residences, two barracks and 19 blockhouses. This charming cut-stone ensemble by engineer Gother Mann is a good example of the colonial neoclassical architecture style of the British Empire.

Return to Rte. 223 S. toward Lacolle.

Saint-Bernard-de-Lacolle

The two-storey **Blockhaus de Lacolle ★** *(free admission; late May to late Aug every day 10am to 5:30pm; early Sep to early Oct Sat and Sun 10am to 5:30pm; 1 Rue Principale, ☎246-3227)*, a squared wooden building with loopholes, is found at the southernmost point of the Saint-Paul-de-l'Île-aux-Noix municipality. It dates back to 1782, making it one of the oldest wooden structures in Montérégie. It is also one of the few buildings of this type to survive in Québec.

From here, it is only about 10km to the American border. Although Canada-U.S. relations have been very cordial for many decades now, this was not always the case. In the late 18th century, the blockhouse acted as a sentry at the forefront of the Richelieu's defence system. The occupants had to warn soldiers in neighbouring forts of the imminent arrival of troops from the other side of the border.

Turn right on Rte. 202 W. to

connect with Aut. 15 N. Two short optional excursions can be taken to the village of Lacolle (Rte. 221 N.) and the Église d'Odelltown in Notre-Dame-du-Mont-Carmel (Rte. 221 S.).

Lacolle (pop. 1,400)

Lacolle was once part of the Beaujeu seigneury, property of Daniel Hyacinthe Liénard de Beaujeu. During the American Revolution, a few Dutch families living in northern New York State came to settle in the region, which explains the many Dutch-style red-brick homes.

Behind the village is the former Napierville Junction Railway station (Canadian National), the **Gare de Lacolle**, built in 1930 in the style of a French provincial manor. As the first stop on the Canadian side of the border, the station became more important than the size of the town might have merited.

Odelltown

This small hamlet with only a few dozen inhabitants is now part of the Notre-Dame-du-Mont-Carmel municipality.

Odelltown was the scene of a decisive episode during the rebellion of 1837-38, when the Patriotes, who took refuge in the nearby United States, attempted to make a breakthrough by taking the region of Lacolle by storm. They

Blockhaus de Lacolle

W. Parson

declared the area the *République du Bas-Canada* (Republic of Lower Canada). This lasted only seven days, however, since the Patriotes were forced to retreat when faced with the arrival of British troops commanded by Colborne. The Patriotes attacked the Loyalist community of Odelltown before recrossing the border. The inhabitants of the hamlet, who took refuge in their church, defended themselves fiercely until the arrival of the troops.

The many Dutch Loyalist families who settled in the area became Methodists upon their arrival in Canada. The small Methodist **Odelltown Church** *(243 Rte. 221)* was built in 1823, making it one of the oldest Methodist churches in Québec.

Return to Rte. 202 W., which leads to Hwy. 15 N., toward Montréal.

Tour B: Chemin des Patriotes

Duration of tour: three days

The Vallée du Richelieu was the second area of settlement in New France, after the banks of the St. Lawrence, and many traces remain of the former seigneuries granted along the river in the 17th and 18th centuries. In the early 19th century, it was one of the most populous regions in Québec, and as such, the aftershocks of the 1837-1838 armed rebellion were keenly felt in the area. Meaningful testimonies of these events, among the most tragic in the history of Québec, are numerous throughout the valley.

Saint-Mathias (pop. 3,750)

This municipality, once an important port on the

Richelieu, is now a quiet residential suburb. There are beautiful homes and a church with one of the most interesting interiors in the region.

Saint-Mathias was the site of significant events during the American War of Independence, as Ethan Allen and his Green Mountain Boys from Vermont took over the village in order to convince the inhabitants to join the United States. Saint-Mathias experienced a new period of intense activity during the 1837-38 rebellion, when the Patriotes' militia established their headquarters here.

The **Magasin Franchère** *(254 Chemin des Patriotes)* is the only remaining evidence of commercial activity in Saint-Mathias during the 19th century. The store was built in 1822 for brothers Joseph and Timothée Franchère. Timothée was jailed in 1838 for participating in the rebellion. The store originally housed two apartments where many *Patriote* meetings took place.

Noted for its outstanding interior decor and its stone cemetery enclosure, the **Église Saint-Mathias ★★** *(279 Chemin des Patriotes)* also boasts a charming

exterior that reflects traditional Québec architecture. It was built in 1784 by mason François Châteauneuf.

Continue heading north along Chemin des Patriotes. The silhouette of Mont Saint-Hilaire, the highest hill in Montérégie (411m), comes into view as you approach.

★ Mont-Saint-Hilaire (pop. 13,000)

This small town, located at the foot of Mont Saint-Hilaire, was originally part of the seigneury of Rouville, granted to Jean-Baptiste Hertel in 1694. It remained in the hands of the Hertel family until 1844, when it was sold to Major Thomas Edmund Campbell, secretary to the British governor, who ran an experimental farm that remained in operation until 1942.

Mont-Saint-Hilaire has two urban centres, one along the Richelieu, where the parish church is located, and the other on the southeast side of the mountain, which enjoys a mild microclimate and is home to orchards and maple groves.

Though recently scarred by the addition of parking lots and an ostentatious gate, the

Manoir Rouville-Campbell

Manoir Rouville-Campbell ★
(125 Chemin des Patriotes Sud) remains one of the most magnificent manor houses in Québec. It was built in 1854 by British architect Frederick Lawford, who also contributed to the interior decor of the Église de Saint-Hilaire. During the 1980s, the house and the stables were transformed into an inn (see p 176). Facing the Manoir Rouville-Campbell, stands Mont-Saint-Hilaire's **Monument aux Patriotes**.

The façade of the **Église Saint-Hilaire ★★** *(260 Chemin des Patriotes Nord)* was originally supposed to have two towers topped with spires. As a result of internal arguments, only the bases of the towers were erected in 1830, and a steeple, placed in the centre of the facade, was later installed. The interior decor, done in the Gothic Revival style, was completed over a long period of time, between 1838 and 1928. The masterpiece of this interior is the work of painter Ozias Leduc (1864-1955), and was completed at the end of the 19th century.

The presbytery (1798) is north of the church, while the **Couvent des Sœurs des Saints Noms de Jésus et de Marie**, with its odd rounded wing, is located behind the church. From the square of the Église Saint-Hilaire, visitors can see the Église de Saint-Mathieu-de-Belœil on the other side of the Richelieu.

The **Musée d'Art de Mont-Saint-Hilaire ★** *($4; Tue 10am to 8:30pm, Wed-Sat 10am to 5pm, Sun 1pm to 5pm; 150 Rue du Centre-Civique, ☎536-3033)* promotes the development of contemporary visual arts and highlights the works of famous artists who have lived in Mont-Saint-Hilaire including Ozias Leduc, Paul-Émile Borduas and Jordi Bonet.

Follow Rte. 133 N. Turn right onto Rte. 116 E. (follow the directions for the Centre de Conservation de la Nature du Mont Saint-Hilaire). Take Rue Fortier to the right, which turns into Chemin Ozias-Leduc. Finally, turn left onto the Chemin de la Montagne, then again on Chemin des Moulins. The pretty Chemin de la Montagne is lined with apple orchards. The owners sell apples, juice, cider, and apple sauce in September and October at small roadside stands.

The **Centre de Conservation de la Nature du Mont Saint-Hilaire ★★** (see p 173).

The tour leaves the Vallée du Richelieu for a short while in order to pass through Saint-Hyacinthe, known as the "farm-produce capital of Québec." To get there, return to Rte. 116 E. for approximately 20km. Enter the city by Rue Girouard, passing under the **Porte des Anciens Maires**, *a medieval-style monument located along the Rivière Yamaska.*

★★
Saint-Hyacinthe
(pop. 39,350)

Saint-Hyacinthe's main attraction is the vitality of the city and its inhabitants. The city is divided into the upper part of town, which is more administrative, religious and middle-class, and the lower part of town, more working-class and commercial. Rarely in rural Québec have the liveliness of a town centre and the monuments that dominate its landscape been so successfully preserved as here. It is best to explore downtown Saint-Hyacinthe on foot.

Saint-Hyacinthe was settled in the late 18th century, around the mills on the Rivière Yamaska and the estate of Jacques-Hyacinthe Delorme, seigneur of Maska. The surrounding fertile soil helped the town expand rapidly, attracting several religious institutions, businesses and industries. The processing and distribution of agricultural products still plays a leading role in the town's economy. Saint-Hyacinthe also has the only French-language veterinary medicine program in North America, as well as farm-produce research and insemination institutes. A large regional agricultural fair is held here every July.

The town also specializes in the construction of large pipe organs. The Casavant brothers set up their famous organ factory outside the city in 1879 *(900 Rue Girouard Est)*. Approximately 15 electro-pneumatic organs are made here every year and are installed throughout the world by the house experts. Guided tours are sometimes organized. Guilbault-Thérien organ-builders have been building mechanical traction organs since 1946, according to 18th-century French and German models *(2430 Rue Crevier)*. Saint-Hyacinthe also has a music bookstore dedicated solely to the organ and the harpsichord *(Ex Arte, 12790 Rue Yamaska)*.

Rue Girouard Ouest ★ is the main street in the upper part of Saint-Hyacinthe. This opulent residential neighbourhood reflects the success of local entrepreneurs. It lies between the gates known as the Portes des Anciens Maires, erected in 1927 to honour the memory of the 11 first magistrates of the city, and the Église Notre-Dame-du-Rosaire. Examples of Victorian architecture abound here, such as the house at number 2790, designed in the Queen Anne style, distinguished by its turret and setting-sun-motif carved into the central gable.

The large white house at number 2500, decorated with dormer windows and a bell

Montérégie

turret (circa 1860), is the original part of the **Monastère du Précieux-Sang**, which houses a community of nuns. The monastery, enlarged many times, has red-and-white brick wings that contrast oddly with the style of the building.

The two rusticated-stone buildings that for many years housed the Saint-Hyacinthe **Bureau de Poste** (post office) *(1915 Rue Girouard Ouest)*, as well as the former **Douane** *(1995 Rue Girouard Ouest)*, or customs house, are two of the rare buildings of this type to have survived the wave of modernization that took place during the 1960s. The buildings are now used for offices and housing.

The **Cathédrale Saint-Hyacinthe-le-Confesseur** ★ *(1900 Rue Girouard Ouest)* is a squat building despite its 50m-high spires. It was built in 1880 and modified in 1906 according to designs by Montréal architects Perrault and Venne. They contributed the Romanesque Revival style and interesting rococo interior, reminiscent of some of the subway stations in Moscow.

Continue along Rue Girouard heading east.

The **Parc Casimir-Dessaulles** *(Rue Girouard Ouest at the corner of Avenue du Palais)*, named after an important mayor of Saint-Hyacinthe, was laid-out in 1876 on the ruins of the seigneurial estate. It quickly became the favourite place of the local bourgeois class, who had many imposing homes built near here. Today, it hosts various outdoor activities (contests, concerts, etc.). To the east is the city hall or **Hôtel de Ville** *(700 Avenue de l'Hôtel-de-Ville)*, located in the former Hôtel Yamaska, remodelled and enlarged in 1923, and to the north is the

new **Palais de Justice** (courthouse).

Go to the lower part of town via Avenue Mondor. Turn right on Rue des Cascades Ouest.

Rue des Cascades ★ is the main commercial artery in Saint-Hyacinthe. It fell victim to fire in 1876, but was quickly rebuilt. The street is lined with many pleasant shops and cafés. The **Place du Marché**, demarcated in 1796 by the seigneur of Maska, can be found at number 1555. The market building (1877) remains the real heart of town, as agriculture is still the largest industry here.

The **Allée du Marché**, west of Place du Marché, is a modern reconstruction built after a devastating fire in 1970, which destroyed several dozen buildings between Rue Saint-François and Rue Sainte-Anne. Architects Courchesne and Bergeron created a multipurpose group of buildings linked by a pedestrian walkway, helping to revitalize the downtown area.

A testimony to the 19th century, the **Marché de Saint-Hyacinthe** *(1555 Rue des Cascades Ouest)* is the oldest market in Québec and the symbol of the city's farm-producing industry. Market-gardeners bring their produce here in the summer and, inside, there are some specialty shops that are open year round.

Expression *(year round, Tue-Fri 10am to 5pm, Wed to 9pm, Sat and Sun 1pm to 5pm; 495 Rue St-Simon, 3rd floor, ☎773-4209)*, an organization whose mission is to promote contemporary art, is located above the Marché Central de Saint Hyacinthe. The gallery, considered one of the most beautiful in Québec, hosts approximately 10 exhibitions each year.

Originally created for scholastic purposes (a practice site for landscape management students of the Institut Agroalimentaire is just across the street), the **Jardin Daniel-A.- Séguin** ★ *($7; mid-Jun to early Sep, every day 10am to 5pm; 3215 Rue Sicotte, ☎778-6504, ext. 215, or 778-0372)*, has been open to the public since 1995. With the help of guided tours, information panels and workshops, amateur horticulturalists can improve their knowledge to better tend their own gardens.

Continue on Rue Sicotte to Boulevard Choquette, turn left. On Choquette go to Boulevard Casavant Ouest and turn right. Continue to Boulevard Laframboise (Rte. 137), turn left and head to La Présentation and Saint-Denis.

La Présentation (pop. 1,855)

The beautiful church in this modest village was built shortly after the La Présentation parish was created, following the division of part of Saint-Hyacinthe in 1804.

The **Église de La Présentation** ★★ *(551 Chemin de L'Église)* is unique among other temples built in Montérégie during the same era because of its finely sculpted stone facade, completed in 1819. Note the inscriptions written in Old French above the entrances. The vast presbytery, hidden in the greenery, as well as the modest sexton house, complete this landscape typical of Québec rural parishes.

Follow Rte. 137 N. to Saint-Denis. Turn left on Chemin des Patriotes, which runs along the Richelieu (Rte. 133 S.).

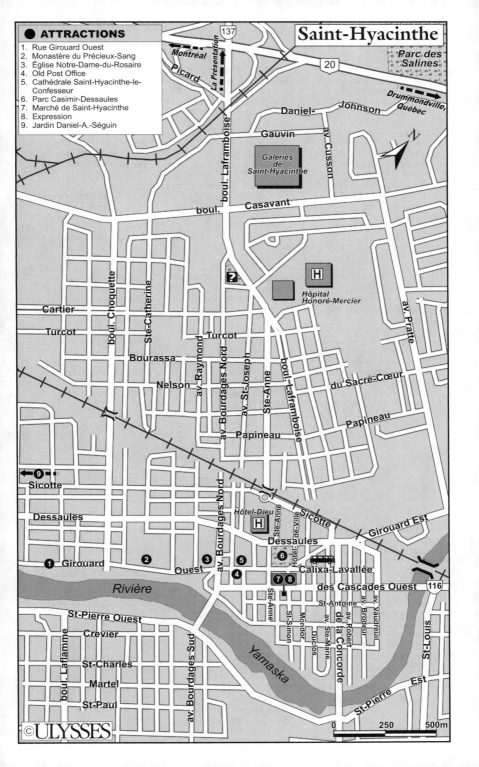

Saint-Hyacinthe

● ATTRACTIONS

1. Rue Girouard Ouest
2. Monastère du Précieux-Sang
3. Église Notre-Dame-du-Rosaire
4. Old Post Office
5. Cathédrale Saint-Hyacinthe-le-Confesseur
6. Parc Casimir-Dessaules
7. Marché de Saint-Hyacinthe
8. Expression
9. Jardin Daniel-A.-Séguin

Parc des Salines

Montréal

Drummondville, Québec

Picard

La Présentation

boul. Laframboise

Daniel-Gauvin

Johnson

av. Cusson

Galeries de Saint-Hyacinthe

boul. Casavant

H Hôpital Honoré-Mercier

Cartier

Turcot

boul. Choquette

Ste-Catherine

Turcot

av. Raymond

av. Bourdages-Nord

av. St-Joseph

Ste-Anne

boul. Laframboise

av. Pratte

du Sacré-Cœur

Bourassa

Nelson

Papineau

Papineau

Sicotte

Dessaules

Hôtel-Dieu **H**

Ste-Anne

Sicotte

Girouard Est

① Girouard

②

③

④

⑤

Ouest

av. Bourdages-Nord

Dessaules

⑥

Hôtel-de-Ville

Calixa-Lavallée

des Cascades Ouest

St-Antoine

av. Vaudreuil

av. Brodeur

⑦ **⑧**

Ste-Anne

St-Simon

Mondor

Duclos

av. Ste-Marie

av. Robert

de la Concorde

Rivière

St-Pierre Ouest

Crevier

boul. Laflamme

St-Charles

Martel

St-Paul

av. Bourdages-Sud

Yamaska

St-Pierre Est

St-Louis

© ULYSSES

0   250   500m

★
Saint-Denis
(pop. 2,110)

Throughout the 1830s, Saint-Denis was home to large political gatherings as well as the headquarters of the *Fils de la Liberté* (Sons of Freedom), a group of young French Canadians who wanted Lower Canada (Québec) to become an independent country. But even more important, Saint-Denis was the site of the only Patriotes victory over the British during the 1837-38 rebellion. On November 23, 1837, General Gore's troops were forced to withdraw to Sorel after a fierce battle against the Patriotes, who were poorly equipped but determined to defeat the enemy. The British troops took revenge a few weeks later, however, by surprising the inhabitants while they slept, pillaging and burning the houses, businesses and industries of Saint-Denis.

The town of Saint-Denis, founded in 1758, experienced an intense period of industrialization in the early 19th century. Canada's largest hat industry was located here, which produced the famous beaver pelt top hats worn by men throughout Europe and America. Other local industries in Saint-Denis included pottery and earthenware. The repression that followed the rebellion put an end to this economic expansion, and from then on, the town became a small agricultural village.

A monument was unveiled in 1913 in **Parc des Patriotes** to honour the memory of the Saint-Denis Patriotes. It is located in the middle of the square that was known as Place Royale before becoming Place du Marché, a market place, and then a public park in the early 20th century.

The **Maison Nationale des Patriotes** ★ *($5; May to Sep, every day 10am to 5pm; Nov, Tue-Fri 10am to 5pm; 610 Chemin des Patriotes, ☎787-3623).* To the south of the park stands a former stone inn built for Jean-Baptiste Mâsse in 1810. The building's irregular shape is characteristic of urban homes of the late 18th century (firebreak walls with corbels, veranda on the main floor, optimum usage of the land). It is one of the rare examples of this type found outside of Montréal and Québec City.

Since 1988, the building has housed an informative interpretation centre dealing with the 1837-38 rebellion and the history of the Patriotes. The main battles of the rebellion are described, as are the causes of these revolts, which had a great impact on the Richelieu region and the entire province of Québec. Two interesting festivals take place here: the **Fête du Vieux Marché** *(mid-Aug, Parc des Patriotes, ☎787-2401 or 787-3229),* a re-creation of an old public market with approximately 100 craftspeople in historical costume, who visitors get to see at work; and the **Fête des Patriotes** *(3rd Sun of Nov; ☎450-787-3623),* a popular gathering in commemoration of the 1837 Patriotes victory.

Across from the church stands the **Maison Cherrier** *(639 Chemin des Patriotes),* a comfortable home that François Cherrier, parish priest of Saint-Denis from 1763 to 1809, had built when he retired. He unfortunately did not have the opportunity to enjoy it, as he passed away before the roof was completed in 1810.

Return to Rte. 133 North *(Chemin des Patriotes)* heading toward Saint-Ours. The site of the 1837 battle at Saint-Denis is located near Rue

Phaneuf, at the edge of town. The Maison Pagé at 553 Chemin des Patriotes was the scene of the first skirmishes between the Patriotes and the British troops. Six wounded British soldiers were treated by the young Dormicour women at the **Maison Dormicour** *(549 Chemin des Patriotes).*

Saint-Ours
(pop. 1,620)

Descendants of the Saint-Ours seigneurs still inhabit the seigneurial manor on land granted by Louis XIV in 1672 to their ancestor Pierre de Saint-Ours, captain in the Carignan-Salières regiment. The small village that neighbours the seigneur's house was once an active port on the Richelieu. The only surviving reminder of this activity is the lock, rebuilt in 1933.

The **Écluse de Saint-Ours** *($1.50; mid-May to mid-Oct; 2930 Chemin des Patriotes, ☎447-4888).* For a long time, the Richelieu was a vital communication route between Montréal and New York, via Lake Champlain and the Hudson river. The river was held in awe until the beginning of the 19th century because it allowed the enemy to enter Québec territory. However, with long-lasting peace between Great Britain and the United States achieved following the War of 1812, the Richelieu became an important trade link between Canada and the United States. The first lock, built in 1849, was refurbished in the 20th century. Today, picnic tables and lookouts add to the site.

The **Manoir de Saint-Ours** *(2500 Rue de l'Immaculée-Conception)* stands amidst a wooded area on the outskirts of town, and is sometimes hard to see in the summer. A bust of Pierre de Saint-Ours stands on the side of the road and is the only indication of the manor's presence. Essentially, it is a quarried-stone house surrounded by a large wooden gallery with views of the garden and Richelieu Valley. The manor was built in 1792 for Charles de Saint-Ours, fourth seigneur of the property, and was modified in the current style in 1870.

Continue along Rte. 133 N. (Chemin des Patriotes) to Sorel, where it turns into Chemin Saint-Ours, then into Rue de la Reine.

Sorel
(pop. 25,000)

In Sorel, the Richelieu flows into the St. Lawrence. Heavy industry and naval construction are still the town's main economic activities. It got its name from Pierre de Saurel, captain of the Carignan-Salières regiment, to whom the land was granted in 1672. The town itself owes its current layout to British governor Frederick Haldimand, who wanted to make a model town populated by the British. He tried to attract American Loyalists to Sorel (once named William-Henry) in several different ways. First, the town joined the Domaine Royal in 1781, then adopted a checkerboard plan in 1783 when the streets were named in honour of members of the British royal family at that time (Augusta, Charlotte, George, etc.), and an Anglican mission was opened in 1784. Despite all this, his plan was a resounding failure.

During the 1860s, Sorel experienced phenomenal growth with the opening of several naval building sites that are still in operation. At the same time, the town adopted its original name, but changed the spelling.

The white stucco **Maison des Gouverneurs** *(90 Chemin Saint-Ours)* was built in 1781 to accommodate the Bruns-

wick regiment's major, who was stationed in Sorel to counter the threat of an American invasion. The regiment, made up of German and Swiss mercenaries, was under the command of General von Riedesel, who immediately enlarged the house to make it more comfortable. For Christmas 1781, Riedesel and his family set up the first Christmas tree in America, in the Maison des Gouverneurs. A sculpture in the shape of a Christmas tree now stands in front of the home to commemorate the event.

From 1784 to 1860, the house served as a summer residence for the Governor Generals of Canada. During these years, it accommodated many famous people such as Lord Dorchester, the Duke of Kent (father of Queen Victoria) and Prince William-Henry (future William IV).

Continue along Rue de la Reine toward the downtown area.

The **Carré Royal** *(corner Charlotte and de la Reine)* is a pleasant green space in the centre of Sorel, incorrectly named "Carré Royal," an improper translation of the Royal Square. It was demarcated in 1791 and landscaped along the lines of the British Union Jack.

To the east of the square is the Anglican **Christ Church** *(79 Rue du Prince)* and its presbytery, built in the Gothic Revival style in 1842. The Sorel mission, whose foundation dates back to 1784, is the dean of the Anglican churches of Québec. For a long time, it was placed under the patronage of the Crown, which meant that its minister was named directly by the British sovereign.

The **Place du Marché** *(at the end of Rue de la Reine)* includes the original market

(rebuilt in 1937 in the Art Deco style) in its centre, and several interesting shops and cafés on the periphery. The neighbourhood has a strange port atmosphere, with cranes, sheds and ships. The Richelieu and the St. Lawrence are visible from several lookout points between these buildings, as well as to the east, from a park located along Rue Augusta.

The Sorel Catholic parish was created in 1678 by Monseigneur de Laval. Construction of the **Église Saint-Pierre ★** *(170 Rue George)* began in 1826, but the building has been considerably modified over the years. Among the original elements are the cutstone portals of the facade and, inside, the division of the nave into three vessels, supported by beautiful Corinthian pillars, an unusual sight during this era. Also of interest are the choir stalls, taken from the old Église Notre-Dame in Montréal, demolished in 1830.

An optional excursion is possible to Sainte-Anne and the islands of Sorel to explore the Pays du Survenant (named after a novel). From Rue George, take Boulevard Fiset south. Turn left onto Rue de l'Hôtel-Dieu, which becomes Rue de la Rive. Take Chemin du Chenal-du-Moine through Sainte-Anne-de-Sorel.

★
Sainte-Anne-de-Sorel
(pop. 2,800)

This village is more oriented towards hunting and fishing than other communities in Montérégie because of its proximity to the Sorel islands. Writer Germaine Guèvremont (1893-1968), who lived on one of these islands, introduced this archipelago, located in the middle of the St. Lawrence, to the literary world in her novel *Le Survenant*.

Montérégie

The best way to explore the **Îles de Sorel** ★ is by taking one of the cruise boats that cross the archipelago of approximately 20 islands *(two types of cruises are offered: Croisière des Îles de Sorel, 1665 Chemin du Chenal-du-Moine, and excursions et expéditions en canot, ☎743-7227 or 800-361-6420).* The hour-and-a-half-long cruises begin at the Chenal du Moine. This large waterway was named in the 17th century following the discovery of the frozen body of a Recollet monk *(moine)* who had been travelling from Trois-Rivières to Sorel along the channel *(chenal).*

The islands are an excellent place to observe aquatic birds, especially during the spring and fall. A few houses on piles with individual piers dot the flat landscape, which offers views of the vast expanse of Lac Saint-Pierre downstream. There are two restaurants at the end of the Île d'Embarras (accessible by car) that serve *gibelotte,* a fish fricassee typical of this region.

Return to Sorel. To reach Montréal, take Rue de l'Hôtel-Dieu heading west. Turn left on Rue du Roi, then right onto Chemin Saint-Ours which leads to Aut. 30; follow it to Montréal.

Tour C: Shore of the St. Lawrence

Duration of tour: two days

The shores of the St. Lawrence surrounding the island of Montreal have become bedroom communities of the metropolis. Once farming villages or small industrial towns, they have experienced tremendous growth over the past 40 years, with the exodus of urban populations to the suburbs. In some cases, these towns have preserved their interesting urban cores where churches, museums and old houses can be found. Throughout this tour, Montréal looms across the river and can be admired from many different perspectives.

Saint-Constant (pop. 22,000)

This municipality has a large railway museum, the Musée Ferroviaire Canadien, as well as an ecomuseum, considered a forerunner in its field.

The **Musée Ferroviaire Canadien** ★★ *($12; late Jun to early Sep every day 10am to 6pm, Sep and Oct week-ends; 110 Rue Saint-Pierre, ☎632-2410)* displays an impressive collection of railway memorabilia, locomotives, freight cars, and maintenance vehicles. The famous *Dorchester* locomotive, put into service in 1836 on the country's first railway, between Saint-Jean-sur-Richelieu and La Prairie, is worth noting, as are many luxurious passenger cars of the 19th century that belonged to Canadian Pacific. Also on display are foreign locomotives such as the powerful *Châteaubriand* from the SNCF (French Railway System), put into service in 1884.

The **Écomusée de Saint-Constant** *($3; early May to early Sep, Tue-Fri 9am to 5pm, Sat and Sun 10am to 7pm; by appointment; 66 Rue Maçon, ☎632-3656)* is more of a an environmental-awareness centre for the local population than a museum for the general public. However, visitors interested in the traditional tools, work, local customs, genealogy and ecology of the region will find plenty of interesting information.

Return toward Sainte-Catherine. Take Boulevard Marie-Victorin east. You will travel along the seaway and cross

the town of **Candiac** *before reaching La Prairie. Take Boulevard Salaberry, and turn left onto Rue Desjardins, which turns into Rue Saint-Laurent in Vieux-La Prairie. Turn left on Chemin de Saint-Jean.*

★ La Prairie (pop. 18,800)

The seigneury of La Prairie was granted to the Jesuits in 1647, who turned the land into a retreat for their missionaries and a village for converted Iroquois. More and more French settlers began populating the surrounding area, forcing the Jesuits to move their mission in order to shield their protégés from the bad influence of Europeans. La Prairie's strategic location led the authorities to fortify the village in 1684. Very little remains today of the stone-and-wood enclosure that was dismantled by the Americans during the 1775 invasion.

La Prairie experienced a new era of prosperity in the early 19th century when it became an important link in the transportation route that brought merchandise to the United States, and in particular to the American port of Portland, Maine; which is ice-free during the winters. A pier was built in 1835, where steamships linking the South Shore to Montréal docked. The following year saw the inauguration of Canada's first railway, linking Saint-Jean-sur-Richelieu to La Prairie. Unfortunately, a fire started in a locomotive in 1864 destroyed the village and obliterated almost all traces of the French Regime buildings. The event put an end to a promising future. However, the economy recovered with the opening of the brickyards, and of a new working-class neighbourhood established in 1880 in the Rue Sainte-Rose area. It was called *Fort Neuf* (new fort), to distinguish it from the old fortified village.

It is best to visit Vieux-La Prairie on foot, given the narrowness of the streets and the small size of the historic district. There is parking on Chemin de Saint-Jean near the Église de la Nativité de la Sainte Vierge.

La Prairie's first church, built in 1687, is long gone. Construction of the **Église de la Nativité de la Sainte Vierge** ★ *(155 Chemin de Saint-Jean)* began in 1840. It has a high neoclassical facade designed by architect Victor Bourgeau, and is topped with an elegant peristyle steeple that dominates the surrounding area.

The corner building across from the church *(120 Chemin de Saint-Jean)* and the **Maison Aubin** *(150 Chemin de Saint-Jean)*, built in 1824, are good examples of the persistence of French Regime architecture following the British Conquest of 1760.

An interpretive trail across from the church leads behind the old market building (1863). In addition to the market, this brick building originally housed the fire department on the main floor and a theatre upstairs. An interesting museum dealing with the history of La Prairie, the **Musée du Vieux-Marché** *(free admission; Mon-Fri 9am to 5pm, Sat and sun 1pm to 5pm; 249 Rue Sainte-Marie, ☎659-1393)*, now occupies the building.

The streets of Vieux-La Prairie ★★ have an urban character rarely found in Québec villages during the 19th century. Several houses were carefully restored after the Québec government declared the area a historic district in 1975. A stroll along Saint-Ignace, Sainte-Marie, Saint-Jacques and Saint-Georges

streets reveals this distinctive flavour. Some of the wood houses are reminiscent of those once found in Montréal districts *(240 and 274 Rue Saint-Jacques)*. Other homes draw their inspiration from French Regime architecture (two-sided roofs, firebreak walls, dormer windows), except for the fact that they are partially or totally built of brick instead of stone *(234 and 237 Rue Saint-Ignace, 166 Rue Saint-Georges)*. Lastly, the stone house covered with wood at number 238 Rue Saint-Ignace is the only surviving testimony of the French Regime in Vieux-La Prairie.

Return to Chemin de Saint-Jean.

At the end of the streets on the left is a square with a bandstand and a plaque commemorating the battle of La Prairie (1691), which pitted French settlers against Aboriginal peoples, who were loyal to the British army. The square, known as Square Foch and then Square La Mennais, once directly overlooked the river. The soft sound of lapping waves was drowned out in 1960 by the sound of traffic on a six-lane highway built between the village and the seaway.

Return to Chemin de Saint-Jean, but take it in the opposite direction. Turn right onto Rue Saint-Laurent, then right again onto Rue Saint-Henri. Take Aut. 15 (Rte. 132), which passes through Brossard before reaching Saint-Lambert (exit Boulevard Simard). Turn left onto Chemin Riverside (also called Riverside Drive).

Saint-Lambert (pop. 22,000)

The development of Saint-Lambert was closely linked to the construction of the Victoria Bridge during the 19th cen-

tury. The railway attracted a large anglophone community, which imparted a British flavour to the town. There are a few old farm houses along the St. Lawrence that have been well restored by their owners. Unfortunately, Saint-Lambert lost much of its charm when the highway was built, separating the town from the river.

The **Victoria Bridge** ★ is the oldest bridge linking the island of Montréal to the mainland. It was built with difficulty by hundreds of Irish and French Canadian workers between 1854 and 1860 for the Grand Trunk railway company. It started out as a tubular bridge, designed by famous British engineer Robert Stephenson, known for the Menai Strait bridge in Wales. He is the son of George Stephenson, inventor of steam traction on railways. The bridge has since been modified several times, mainly to allow for automobile traffic. The only remaining original structures are the pointed pillars, for breaking up the ice. The bridge's 2,742m length was exceptional for the time—journalists called it the eighth wonder of the world!

The **Écluse de Saint-Lambert** ★ *(free admission; mid-Apr to late Sep, every day sunrise to sunset; at the trunk road of Boulevard Sir-Wilfrid-Laurier)* locks are the gateway to the seaway, which begins here and ends 3,800km downstream, at the tip of the Great Lakes. The seaway allows ships to bypass the natural obstacles posed by the St. Lawrence and to provide a direct route to the centre of the continent. Its opening in 1959 led to the closing of the Canal de Lachine and contributed to the economic decline of southwestern Montréal. The sophisticated mechanisms and the view of Montréal make the locks at Saint-Lambert the most interesting of the Montérégie locks.

The **Musée Marsil** *($2; Tue-Fri 10am to 5pm, Sat and Sun 11am to 5pm; 349 Chemin Riverside, ☎923-6601)* presents temporary art and history exhibits, as well as an interesting collection of costumes and textiles. It is located in the Marsil house, whose stone foundation probably dates back to 1750.

Similar houses can still be seen along Chemin Riverside, buried amongst suburban cottages. At number 405, the **Maison Auclair** (circa 1750), has undergone fewer changes than the Maison Marsil, and better illustrates the humble rural architecture of the French Regime. The **Maison Mercille**, at number 789 (circa 1775), is more imposing than its neighbours of the same era. The dairy adjoining the main building has a window protected by rather ominous-looking bars called *étripe-chats* (cat-gut) in French.

An optional excursion to the municipality of Saint-Bruno-de-Montarville further inland explores Mont Saint-Bruno, one of Montérégie's hills. To get there, take Boulevard Sir-Wilfrid-Laurier and turn left onto Chemin de la Rabastalière. If you do not want to take this excursion, continue toward Longueuil on Chemin Riverside, which turns into Rue Saint-Charles Ouest. One kilometre before arriving downtown, the road runs through overpasses leading to the Pont Jacques-Cartier, as well as a neighbourhood of modern highrises grouped around the Longueuil métro station.

Parc du Mont-Saint-Bruno ★
(330 Chemin des 25 Est), see p 174.

★
**Longueuil
(pop. 137,100)**

Since 2002, the new merged city of Longueuil comprises eight former municipalities: Boucherville, Brossard, Greenfield Park, Saint-Bruno-de-Montarville, Saint-Hubert, Saint-Lambert, Le Moyne and the old city of Longueuil (now known as Vieux-Longueuil). The total population of the new city is 385,000.

Located across from Montréal, Longueuil is the most populous city in Montérégie. It once belonged to the Longueuil seigneury, granted to Charles Le Moyne (1624-1685) in 1657. He headed a dynasty that played a key role in developing New France. Many of his 14 children are famous, such as Pierre Le Moyne d'Iberville (1661-1706), first governor of Louisiana, Jean-Baptiste Le Moyne de Bienville (1680-1768), founder of New Orleans, and Antoine Le Moyne de Châteauguay (1683-1747), governor of Guyana.

His eldest son, Charles Le Moyne de Longueuil, inherited the seigneury upon the death of his father. Between 1685 and 1690, he had a fortified castle built on the site of the current Église Saint-Antoine-de-Padoue. The castle had four corner towers, a church and many wings. In 1700, Longueuil was raised to the rank of baron by Louis XIV, the only such case in the history of New France. The baron of Longueuil saw to the development of his land, which continued to expand until it reached the banks of the Richelieu.

Longueuil experienced continuous growth during the 19th century with the introduction of the railway (1846) and the arrival of many summer vacationers who built beautiful villas along the river banks. At the beginning of the 20th century, the town welcomed a small Pratt and Whitney factory, which created an important industrial centre specializing in engineering and airplane technology. The construction of the Jacques-Cartier Bridge between Montréal and the south shore, inaugurated during the 1930s, made Longueuil one of Montréal's first suburbs. Many examples of cottages built between the two world wars can still be seen south of Rue Saint-Charles. Today, the embankments of the nearby seaway and the lakeside highway deprive Longueuil of all direct contact with water. The town remedied the situation by setting up a marina and a cycling path along the river, both accessible by footbridges.

Rue Saint-Charles is Longueuil's main commercial artery. Many pleasant cafés and restaurants can be found east of the **town hall** *(300 Rue Saint-Charles Ouest)*. Near the Catholic church, the former **Foyer Saint-Antoine des Sœurs Grises**, designed in 1877 by Victor Bourgeau, now houses artistic and social organizations.

The site of the **Église Saint-Antoine-de-Padoue** ★ ★ *(Rue Saint-Charles, at the corner of Chemin de Chambly)* was once occupied by a 17th-century castle known as the Château de Longueuil. After being besieged by American rebels during the 1775 invasion, it was requisitioned by the British army. A fire broke out while a garrison was stationed here, in 1792, destroying a good part of the building. In 1810, the ruins were used as a quarry during the building of a second Catholic church. A few years later, Rue Saint-Charles was built right through the rest of the site, forcing the complete destruction of this unique North American building. Archaeological excavations took place during the 1970s, tracing the castle's exact site and unearthing part of its foundations, visible to the east of the church.

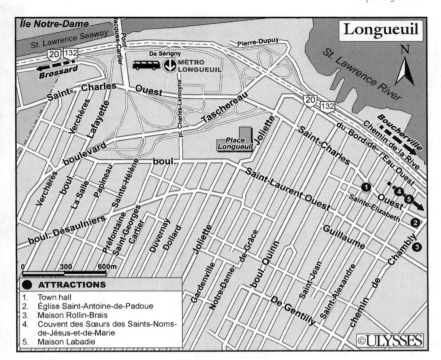

ATTRACTIONS

1. Town hall
2. Église Saint-Antoine-de-Padoue
3. Maison Rollin-Brais
4. Couvent des Sœurs des Saints-Noms-de-Jésus-et-de-Marie
5. Maison Labadie

The 1810 church was demolished in 1884 to make room for the present building, the largest church in Montérégie. The exterior is inspired by flamboyant Gothic art, but remains close to Victorian eclecticism.

The Longueuil tourist information centre is located in the **Maison Rollin-Brais** *(205 Chemin de Chambly)*, an 18th-century stone house. Throughout its history, the house has accommodated an inn and a forge. The imposing building at number 225 once housed the Collège de Longueuil. Straight down Chemin de Chambly is an interesting view of the leaning tower of Montréal's Olympic Stadium.

The **Couvent des Sœurs des Saints-Noms-de-Jésus-et-de-Marie** ★ *(tours by appointment; 80 Rue Saint-Charles*

Est, ☎*651-8104)*, has been beautifully restored and is still inhabited by the Saints-Noms-de-Jésus-et-de-Marie nuns, a religious community founded in Longueuil in 1843 by the blessed Mother Marie-Rose. The building includes a residence built in 1769, but the main construction work was carried out between 1844 and 1851.

East of the convent is the **Maison Labadie**, built in 1812 on land that was once part of the seigneurial estate *(90 Rue Saint-Charles Est)*. The Saints-Noms-de-Jésus-et-de-Marie religious order devoted to the education of young girls was founded in this house. The neighbouring house *(100 Rue Saint-Charles Est)* was built in 1749.

Continue heading east towards Boucherville along Rue Saint-Charles Est, which turns

into Boulevard Marie-Victorin. Breathtaking views of the port of Montréal can be seen along the way.

★
**Boucherville
(pop. 36,200)**

Unlike many seigneuries in New France that were granted to servicemen or tradesmen, the Boucherville seigneury was handed over by Intendant Talon to a settler from Trois-Rivières, Pierre Boucher, in 1672. Rather than speculate or use it as a hunting reserve, Boucher made sustained efforts to develop his seigneury, an act that earned him a title of nobility from the king. By the end of the 17th century, Boucherville already consisted of a fortified village, a couple of mills and a church. Few buildings of this period survived the major fire in 1843

Montérégie

which destroyed a large part of the town.

The seigneury of Boucherville remained in the hands of the Boucher family until the abolition of the seigneurial regime in 1854. More recently, residents of this municipality fought successfully to have Aut. 15 skirt around the old village and run further inland, thereby preserving the beauty and tranquillity found by the water's edge.

Parc des Îles-de-Boucherville, see p 174.

Like its two neighbours, the **Maison Louis-Hippolyte-Lafontaine** *(free admission; Thu and Fri 7pm to 9pm, Sat and Sun 1pm to 5pm; 314 Boulevard Marie-Victorin,* ☎ *449-8347)* was moved to the Parc de la Brocquerie in 1964. It had previously been located in the heart of the village of Boucherville. Louis-Hippolyte Lafontaine, an ardent defender of French Canadians and Prime Minister of United Canada in 1842 and from 1848 to 1850, grew up here. The building, whose construction dates back to 1766, now houses an exhibition centre with a section dedicated to the house's history. The park was once part of the Sabrevois de Bleury family estate, and surrounded the La Brocquerie villa, which was built around 1735 but unfortunately destroyed by fire in 1971.

The **Manoir de Boucherville** ★ *(468 Boulevard Marie-Victorin)* is one of the rare stone manors dating back to the French Regime to have survived in the Montréal area. The large stone house was built in 1741 for François-Pierre Boucher, the third seigneur of Boucherville. The Boucher family lived in the manor until the end of the 19th century. Especially interesting are the purely decora-

tive firebreak walls that slope slightly steeper than the roof.

The harmonious ensemble of the **Église Sainte-Famille** ★ ★ *(560 Boulevard Marie-Victorin)*, the convent (1890) and the presbytery (1896), surrounds a public square, created during the 17th century. The church is an important piece of vernacular architectural work in Québec. It was built in 1801, according to plans by parish priest Pierre Conefroy. He was not content with sketching the outlines, so he drew up a detailed plan. Thus, the Boucherville church, with three portals at the front and its large Latin-cross layout, served as a model for religious architecture in Québec villages up until 1830. Damaged by fire in 1843, it was restored the same year.

★
Varennes
(pop. 15,800)

This town has always been a small, isolated agricultural community, specializing in market gardening. Since the 1950s however, many chemical and petroleum industries have moved in just east of the old part of town. Hydro-Québec also opened a research centre here in 1967, known as IREQ.

Located at the entrance to the old village, the wooden **Calvary** *(2511 Rue Sainte-Anne)* is one of the oldest monuments of this type to survive in Québec. In 1829 the current cross replaced the 18th-century cross, though some of the original statues were salvaged.

The **Basilique** and **Chapelles Votives** ★ *(Rue Sainte-Anne)*. The votive chapels serve mainly as altars of repose during Corpus Christi processions. At one time, many of them lined the roads of Québec, but several disappeared following a decline in religion. The chapels in

Varennes are still visited by pilgrims, and are open for worship during the summer. The oldest one, in neoclassical style, was built in 1832 to replace a building from the early 18th century. The second one was erected in 1862 according to plans by Victor Bourgeau in the Gothic Revival style, identifiable by its spire and its pointed arches. It has very elaborate ornamentation for this type of building. The vast Romanesque Revival–style church that dominates the village was elevated to the rank of minor basilica by Rome in 1993. Beyond its high facade with two steeples, visitors will discover a richly decorated interior. Many traditional Québec houses can be seen along **Rue Sainte-Anne**, in pleasant surroundings facing the river.

Verchères
(pop. 5,125)

In 1692, heroine Madeleine de Verchères took charge of the pile fort and village, defending it against Iroquois attacks from all sides. News of her brilliant victory resonated throughout the colony and lifted the settlers' spirits during a time of war and food shortages. Afterward, the town of Verchères developed slowly, following the ups and downs of the harvest. However, like Varennes, it has experienced massive industrialization over the past few decades.

Up until the mid-19th century, Verchères boasted seven mills *(moulins)* to grind its grain. Today, only two remain, including the **mill** on Rue Madeleine, built in 1730, and transformed by the municipality into an exhibition centre. It served as a lighthouse from 1913 to 1949, which explains its appearance.

The imposing **Monument à la Mémoire de Madeleine de Verchères**, cast in bronze by Louis-Philippe Hébert, stands proudly facing the river beside the mill, commemorating this figure. The statue is a testimony to the feelings of Verchères residents for this frail but courageous adolescent of the 17th century who has become an almost mythic figure over the years.

The **Église Saint-François-Xavier** *(Rue Madeleine)* was built in 1787 on the site of the first church (1724). The facade was updated in the late 19th century, giving it a Romanesque Revival style. The interior, decorated by Louis-Amable Quévillon, is more interesting, including the flat-bottomed chancel with a flat backdrop and adorned with a triumphal arch (1808), as well as French paintings from the 18th century, sold off by Parisian churches during the French Revolution.

Contrecœur (pop. 5,900)

Steel industry giants Sidbec-Dosco and Stelco, haunt the landscape of this town located in the heart of the "steel region." The downtown area has luckily managed to preserve some interesting rural buildings.

Maison Lenoblet-du-Plessis *(free admission; late Jun to late Aug, every day 10am to 7pm; 4752 Boulevard Marie-Victorin, ☎587-5750 or 587-5988).* This 1794 house was extensively transformed in the late 19th century to give it a Victorian feeling. For a long time it belonged to lawyer Alexis Le Noblet-Duplessis (1780-1840). He welcomed Patriotes during many secret meetings, which led to the armed rebellion of 1837-38. The insurrection was very active in the Richelieu Valley, located not far from the rear guard post of Contrecœur.

Today the house is municipal property and accommodates a museum that retraces the history of both the building and the town. It is located in the middle of the pretty **Parc Cartier-Richard**, where a walkway and lookout provide great views of the St. Lawrence.

To reach Montréal, take Aut. 30, then head towards the Pont-Tunnel Louis-Hippolyte-Lafontaine, Pont Jacques-Cartier or Pont Champlain. On the way, you can stop at the Hydro-Québec Électrium, located inside the city limits of Sainte-Julie (Exit 128).

The **Électrium d'Hydro-Québec** ★ *(free admission; early Jun to late Aug, every day 9:30am to 4pm; rest of the year, Mon-Fri 9:30am to 4pm and Sun 1pm to 4pm; Aut. 30, exit 128; ☎658-8977 or 800-267-4558)* is especially interesting for younger visitors. It offers computer games, as well as examples of the various uses for electricity.

Tour D: Vaudreuil-Soulanges

Duration of tour: one day

This region forms a triangular point of land isolated from the rest of Montérégie. It is demarcated to the west by the Ontario border, to the north and east by the Ottawa River and the beautiful Lac des Deux-Montagnes and Lac Saint-Louis, both areas known for excellent water sports, and lastly, to the south, by the St. Lawrence, which widens here to form Lac Saint-François. Don't be surprised if you hear the name Suroît mentioned—the region is sometimes referred to by this name for a wind from the southwest. Visitors can see beautiful properties in the distant Montréal suburbs, as well as many lakeside landscapes.

Vaudreuil-Dorion (pop. 20,000)

The western tip of the region was once part of the network of old seigneuries under the French Regime. As a result, it was considered part of Québec, rather than the neighbouring province of Ontario during the creation of Upper and Lower Canada (1791). The seigneuries of Vaudreuil and of Soulanges, granted in 1702, developed with difficulty, since they were located upstream from the impassable Lachine Rapids. Thus, despite its proximity to Montréal, the area was sparsely populated until the end of the 18th century. **Dorion**, once an integral part of the Vaudreuil seigneury, developed with the help of tradesmen of German descent. The seigneury of **Vaudreuil** was granted to François de Rigaud, marquis of Vaudreuil, in the early 18th century. As governor of Montréal, he was too busy to run his seigneury. He sold it along with his estate on Rue Saint-Paul to Michel Chartier de Lotbinière before leaving for France in 1763. Lotbinière worked hard to develop the estate. Through marriage, the seigneury passed into the hands of Robert Unwin Harwood, who attracted British settlers to the region. They settled mostly in the villages of Como and Hudson, which have retained a certain British flavour. Dorion and Vaudreuil merged to become one municipality in 1996.

The **Maison Trestler** ★ *($3.50; Mon-Fri 9am to 5pm, Sun 1pm to 4pm; concerts Wed 8pm in summer; 85 Chemin de la Commune, ☎455-6290)* is ideally located on the shores of Lac des Deux-Montagnes. This unusual stone house is 44m long and was built in stages between 1798 and 1806. The owner of the house, Jean-Joseph Trestler, a mercenary in the Hesse-Hanau regiment, arrived in Canada in 1776. Ten years later, he settled in Dorion and became involved in the fur trade. In 1976 the house was partially converted into a cultural centre by the current owners. Concerts and conferences are now held here.

Return to Boulevard Saint-Henri. Turn right in the direction of Vaudreuil, where the road turns into Boulevard Roche.

Built between 1783 and 1789, the **Église Saint-Michel ★★** *(414 Avenue St-Charles)* was given a new Gothic Revival-style facade in 1856 in an effort to modernize it. The Latin cross layout and apse with cut-off corners are similar to the first churches of the French Regime. The most complete collection of liturgical furniture sculpted by Philippe Liébert in the 18th century (pulpit, high altar, candelabra, statues) is located inside. Also of particular note, because they were eliminated from most other Québec churches during the restorations that took place in the 1960s, are the seigneurial bench and the polychromatic decor painted in trompe-l'œil by F. E. Meloche in 1883. Other interesting elements include the 1871 organ and the striking paintings, including one entitled *Saint Louis*, painted in 1792 by Louis-Chrétien de Heer.

The **Musée Régional de Vaudreuil-Soulanges ★** *($3; Mon-Fri 9:30am to 4:30pm, Tue also 7pm to 9:30pm, Sat and Sun 1pm to 4:30pm; 431 Avenue St-Charles, ☎455-2092),* founded in 1953, is one of Québec's oldest regional museums, and a testimony to Vaudreuil's cultural vitality at the time. It is located in the former Collège Saint-Michel (1857), once run by the clerics of Saint-Viateur. The beautiful building, covered with a mansard roof,

houses collections of everyday items, craft tools from the 18th and 19th century, as well as interesting religious art, antique paintings and carvings.

Como

Visitors to this charming village can enjoy beautiful views of Oka (see p 230), located on the other side of the lake. A ferry links Oka to Como.

★
Hudson
(pop. 5,250)

Hudson is a lovely, mostly English-speaking town. The well-off residents live in comfortable homes, both modern and old. Many enjoy the rural landscape and then commute to work in downtown Montréal by commuter train (Rigaud-Montréal) during the week. In the summer, residents of this lakeside community practise their favourite water sports on Lac des Deux-Montagnes. Whatever the season, exploring this small town with its many shops, charming little restaurants and small, tree-lined streets, is a pleasure.

The **St. James of Hudson Anglican Church** was founded in 1841 at the instigation of Seigneur Harwood de Vaudreuil. The structure is a good example of a stone Gothic Revival village church.

On Saturdays from Spring to the end of October, don't miss **Finnegan's Market** *(775 Main Road, ☎458-4377),* an animated market in a mostly outdoor setting. Antiques, crafts, and plants are among the items on offer—a real "country-style" market, rather than a flea market.

Rigaud
(pop. 6,280)

The sons of the Marquis of Vaudreuil were granted the Rigaud seigneury in 1732.

However, the village did not develop until after the arrival of the clerics of Saint-Viateur, who opened **Collège Bourget** in 1850. In addition to its educational vocation, Rigaud welcomes pilgrims to its hilltop sanctuary.

Follow Rue Saint-Jean-Baptiste (Rte. 342). Turn left onto Rue Saint-Pierre. Follow the directions to the sanctuary.

The **Sanctuaire Notre-Dame-de-Lourdes ★** *(early May to late Sep, every day 9am to 5pm; 20 Rue de Lourdes, ☎451-4631 or 451-0655).* Suffering from illness in 1874, Brother Ludger Pauzé carved a small hole in a rock and placed a statuette of the Virgin Mary there as a demonstration on his faith. And so, worship of Mary began in Rigaud. First, an eight-sided chapel, from which visitors can enjoy a beautiful view of the region, was built in 1887. Later, various additions were made so outdoor celebrations could be organized for large crowds. These included a new chapel, where mass has been celebrated since 1954. Not far from the sanctuary is a strange pile of stones left on this site after the ebb of the Champlain Sea during glaciation. Legend has it that this bed of stones was once a potato field. God, appalled to see its owner working on a Sunday, changed it to a field of stones now known as "devil's field."

Return to Aut. 40 E. until Exit 17. Follow Rte. 201 S. passing through Saint-Clet to arrive in Coteau-du-Lac, located on the edge of the St. Lawrence. Turn right onto Chemin du Fleuve.

★
Coteau-du-Lac
(pop. 5,400)

A narrowing of the river combined with a series of rapids makes sailing impossible here. The St. Lawrence reaches its

The Seasons in Québec

Québec folksinger Gilles Vigneault said it best: "Mon pays ce n'est pas un pays, c'est l'hiver" (my country is not a country, it is winter). Though this long, cold season is so closely associated with Québec, all four seasons leave their mark on the province: the cold freezes waterfalls into walls of ice in winter, waters rise and the plants come to life with the spring thaw, bright sun and sometimes unbearable heat waves last through the summer until Indian summer, the final hurrah before the brilliant spectacle of the fall colours. Quebecers have learned to make the most of the many incarnations of their home, heading to the mountains, forests, lakes and mighty rivers no matter what the season...

Félix Leclerc, a beloved Québecois folksinger, honoured the simple pleasures of spring in *L'hymne au printemps:* the calls of frogs and robins herald the arrival of spring: tiny buds on trees and bushes slowly grow into leaves and flowers, dandelions blanket the fields and the fresh smell of the earth returns to the air...

The St. Lawrence lowlands still bear the stamp of the old French seigneurial system, which divided the land into long, narrow rectangular plots in order to give the greatest number of colonists possible access to the waterways. Beyond the farmhouses lined up along the *rangs* (country roads), the fields run on as far as the eye can see.

A fisher's life is a hard one, requiring backbreaking work, endurance and patience. The bounty of those fishing in the Gulf of St. Lawrence includes crab, shrimp, scallops, turbot, halibut, herring and mackerel.

Québec is very rich in wildlife. Those who quietly explore the country's parks and other rural areas may be delighted to encounter anything from racoons to moose, the latter often found near bodies of water, as pictured here.

The remote and mysterious Îles-de-la-Madeleine (Magdalen Islands) have been sculpted by the wind and the sea.

Land of lakes and rivers, Québec is a choice spot for a slew of water sports: canoeing, kayaking, sailing, windsurfing, fishing, rafting...and the list goes on.

Country house, summer cottage or lakefront chalet...call it what you will, it is the dream of many an urban dweller in this province. What better way to pass the summer than out in the country, far from the heat and humidity of the city?

When fall arrives, the forests of Québec ignite with colour. This blaze of red, orange and gold transforms the countryside and is best experienced during those last warm days of Indian summer.

As soon as the waterways and lake freeze over, the shacks go up, the hole in the ice is drilled and the ice fishing, *pêche blanche,* season begins.

These two huskies and their team members lead the way to adventure across Québec's winter landscape. Several companies have revived this traditional Inuit mode of transportation and today make it available to the public.

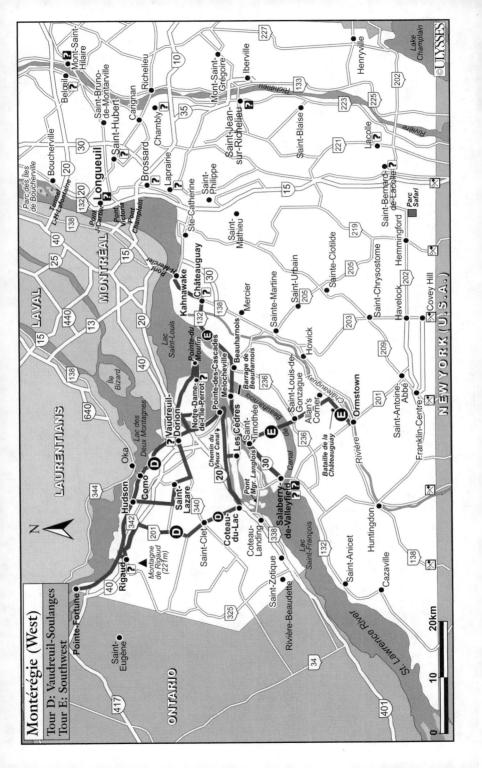

lowest level after a change in altitude of 25m over just 12.8km. Coteau-du-Lac therefore became a rallying and portage point even before the arrival of the Europeans. Many vestiges of Aboriginal civilization have been found here, namely three skeletons including 6,000 years old. At the end of the French Regime (1759), authorities set up a sort of channel at the end of a small point, a simple reinforced dyke made with piles of rocks and parallel to the shore. Through this first canal, boatmen pulled flat-bottomed boats filled with furs. In 1779, the British constructed the first lock in North America here. A fort built by military engineer William Twiss was added to the canal in 1812.

Relics of the British and French canals can be seen from the **Coteau-du-Lac National Historic Site ★** *($4; mid-May to early Sep, Wed-Sun 10am to 5pm; early Sep to mid-Oct, weekends 10am to 5pm; 308A Chemin du Fleuve, ☎763-5631)* as can ruins of the fort erected to defend this important passageway. Visitors first reach the welcome centre, where an instructive model fort recreates the area at the peak of its activity. Then, a trail through the site provides a closer look at the ruins of the facilities, as well as an outdoor reconstruction of the blockhouse, built by the British at the end of the point. There is also a beautiful view of the St. Lawrence rapids from here.

Return to Chemin du Fleuve heading east (towards Les Cèdres and Pointe-des-Cascades). Three kilometres from Coteau-du-Lac, a hydroelectric power station designed to resemble a German castle can be seen to the left, set back from the road; it has now been transformed into a residence (not open to the public). This rare building, erected in 1899, supplied

electricity to the Canal de Soulanges facility. The canal stretches along the north bank of the river between Coteau-Landing and Pointe-des-Cascades. Québec sculptor Armand Vaillancourt had his workshop here for many years.

Follow Chemin du Fleuve to Pointe-des-Cascades. Turn left onto Rue Centrale, then make an immediate right onto Chemin du Canal.

Pointe-des-Cascades (pop. 950)

Located at the mouth of the Ottawa River, this town owes its existence to the Canal de Soulanges, which is now closed. Pointe-des-Cascades was visited as early as 1684 by the Baron of Lahontan, while a bloody war between the French and the Iroquois raged in the area. The first channel was set up by the French in 1749, followed by a small lock in 1805, named Canal Cascades. This canal and the Canal de Coteau-du-Lac were replaced by the first Canal de Beauharnois, which opened in 1845 on the south side of the St. Lawrence. The Canal de Soulanges, set up on the site of the Canal Cascades, succeeded the Canal de Beauharnois in 1899; it ceased operating when the St. Lawrence Seaway opened (current Canal de Beauharnois) in 1959.

The **Théâtre des Cascades ★** *(at the eastern trunk road of Chemin du Canal; ☎455-8855 or 866-494-8855)*, a summer theatre in a lumber warehouse now occupies the former command station of the Canal de Soulanges. Beautiful brick buildings designed by engineer Thomas Monroe in 1900 can be seen throughout the site, as can two lighthouses and three of the five locks. There are also lovely views of the Ottawa River, Lac Saint-

Louis and Île Perrot from the entrance of the canal. There is also a campground on site.

Return to Rue Centrale. Turn right onto Rte. 338 E., then right again onto Aut. 20. Cross the bridge over the Ottawa River to Île Perrot (Exit Boulevard Don-Quichotte). Follow Boulevard Perrot and turn left onto Boulevard Don-Quichotte.

Île-Perrot (pop. 1,000)

In 1672 the seigneury of Île Perrot was granted to the governor of Montréal, François-Marie Perrot, who set up a fur-trading post at the fief of Brucy. The seigneury then passed into the hands of Charles Le Moyne, before being sold in 1703 to Joseph Trottier Desruisseaux, who set up a farm on the point near the mill. His widow began construction of Île Perrot's first church in 1740. Because it is closer to Montréal and not cut off by the rapids that hamper river traffic, the seigneury of Île Perrot experienced more extensive development than other lands in the area granted under the French Regime.

The **Parc Historique de la Pointe-du-Moulin ★** *(free admission; mid-May to late Aug, every day 9am to 5pm; late Aug to mid-Oct, weekends; 2500 Boulevard Don-Quichotte, ☎514-453-5936)*. Beyond the modern reception area, visitors can reach the wooded park, which on clear days provides beautiful views of downtown Montréal across Lac Saint-Louis. The windmill, built in 1708, and the miller's house are located at the end of the point. Guides explain how the mill works (it is still in working order today), and the history of the area. A heritage information centre and picnic areas are also set up on site.

Return to Boulevard Perrot. Turn left, then left again onto Rue de l'Église.

The **Église Sainte-Jeanne-de-Chantal** ★ ★ *(1 Rue de l'Église)* is often described as the perfect example of a French Canadian church in the Montréal region. In fact, its modest dimensions, reminiscent of the first churches of the French Regime, as well as its interior decor in the Louis XV and Louis XVI styles, make the church an excellent example of traditional Québec architecture. The building was completed in 1786, and embellished between 1812 and 1830 under the direction of Joseph Turcault and Louis-Xavier Leprohon. A commemorative chapel, with its back to the river, was built in 1953, using the stones from the first church of Pointe-du-Moulin (1753). The chapel walls contain the Intendant Hocquart's plaque, which gave the seigneur of Île Perrot permission to establish a parish on this land (1740), as well as strange red sandstone mascarons (masks) brought over from France around 1945 by Colonel Roger Maillet. The chapel towers above a terraced cemetery, which is unique in Québec.

Parc Historique de la Pointe-du-Moulin

M. Pierson

Return to Montréal on Aut. 20.

Tour E: The Southwest

Duration of tour: 1½ days

This tour covers the southwestern part of Montérégie. It winds through the region along the shores of Lac Saint-Louis, through the foothills of the Appalachians along the New York State border and into the valley of the Rivière Châteauguay. The southwest is an agricultural region, perfect for autumn strolls, fruit-picking and market-going. The old seigneuries established along the lake and the Rivière Chateauguay are mostly French-speaking, while the townships that developed in the interior at the beginning of the 19th century are still mostly English-speaking.

Kahnawake
(pop. 6,200)

In 1667, the Jesuits set up a mission for the converted Iroquois at La Prairie. After moving four times, the mission settled permanently in Sault-Saint-Louis in 1716. The Saint-François-Xavier mission has now become Kahnawake, a name that means "where the rapids are." Over the years, Iroquois Mohawks from the State of New York joined the mission's first inhabitants, so that English is now the first language on the reserve, even though most inhabitants still use the French names given to them by the Jesuits. In 1990, Mohawk Warriors demonstrated by blocking the Mercier Bridge (Pont Mercier) for months in a show of support for the demands made by the Mohawks of Kanesatake (Oka). Tension between Québec authorities and the Mohawks still exists in the area sur-

rounding the reserve, but visitors need not worry as they are generally warmly welcomed in Kahnawake.

The **Enceinte**, **Musée** and **Église Saint-François-Xavier** ★ ★ *(Main St.)*, or the Saint-François-Xavier wall, museum and church. Villages and missions were required under the French Regime to surround themselves with fortifications. Very few of these walls have survived. The wall of the Kahnawake mission, still partially standing, is the kind of ruin rarely found north of Mexico. It was built in 1720 according to plans of the King's engineer, Gaspard Chaussegros de Léry, to protect the church and the Jesuit convent, built in 1717. The guardroom, powder magazine and officers' residences (1754) are also still standing. From the platform behind the Jesuit convent, visitors can enjoy spectacular views of the seaway, Lachine and Montréal.

The church was modified in 1845 according to the plans of Jesuit Félix Martin, and redecorated by Vincent Chartrand (1845-47), who also made some of the furniture. Guido Nincheri designed the polychromatic vaulted ceiling in the 20th century. Also found here is the tomb of Kateri Tekakwitha, a young Aboriginal. The convent houses the museum of the Saint-François-Xavier mission, where visitors can see some of the objects that belonged to the Jesuits, who still lead the parish. The village around the church offers one of the largest concentrations of fieldstone in Québec. However, like the fortified walls, these homes are not shown off to their full advantage; many of them have been defaced, covered up with more modern materials, or simply abandoned.

Take Chemin Saint-Bernard towards Châteauguay (near the metallic cross and the school). *Turn left onto Chemin Christ-Roi (after the water purification plant), then right onto Rue Dupont. Turn left onto Boulevard Salaberry Nord, follow the Rivière Châteauguay until the Pont Laberge. Cross the bridge to get to the Église Saint-Joachim. Turn right onto Boulevard Youville behind the church, where the parking lot is located.*

Châteauguay (pop. 42,200)

The Châteauguay seigneury was granted to Charles Le Moyne in 1673. He immediately had Château de Guay built on Île Saint-Bernard, at the mouth of the Rivière Châteauguay. One hundred years later, a village stood out around the Église Saint-Joachim. The roads and boulevards that run along the river and Lac Saint-Louis are still dotted with pretty farmhouses built between 1780 and 1840, when the seigneury belonged to the Sœurs Grises (the Grey Nuns). The municipality has developed considerably since 1950, making it a large component of the Montréal suburbs.

When the first church in Châteauguay was built in 1735, it was the westernmost parish on the south shore of the St. Lawrence. Work on the present **Église Saint-Joachim ★ ★** *(1 Boulevard Youville)* began in 1775 in order to better serve a growing number of parishioners. The **Hôtel de Ville** neighbours the church to the north. It is located in the former convent of the Congrégation de Notre-Dame (1886).

Continue along Boulevard Youville and travel along the river to Lac Saint-Louis.

Route de Léry ★ *(Chemin du Lac-Saint-Louis).* **Île Saint-Bernard**, which still belongs to the Sœurs Grises, can be seen

on the right; it is not open to visitors. The large stone house sitting on the shore is the seigneurial estate, the **Manoir d'Youville**, built by the nuns in 1774 on the site of the Château de Guay.

Chemin du Lac-Saint-Louis joins up with Rte. 132 W. at Maple Grove. Follow this road toward Beauharnois.

Beauharnois (pop. 6,665)

The seigneury of Villechauve was granted to the Marquis of Beauharnois, 15th governor of New France, in 1729. At the end of the 18th century, tradesman Alexander Ellice announced his intention to purchase it. He then had a saw mill built on the Rivière Saint-Louis, vestiges of which still remain. In 1863, the Kilgour family opened a large furniture factory in Beauharnois, turning the village into a small industrial city. The large brick buildings still dominate the river's west bank. Today, Beauharnois is known mostly for its hydro-electric power plant, the third-largest in Québec.

The **Église Saint-Clément ★** *(at the top of the hill on Chemin Saint-Louis)* is very picturesque when seen from the Rivière Saint-Louis. Its Romanesque Revival–style facade, attributed to Victor Bourgeau, is built in front of a simple nave, completed in 1845.

Melocheville (pop. 2,366)

The locks that control the Beauharnois canal and hydro-electric station (the third-most important in Québec) are located here.

The **Centrale Hydroélectrique de Beauharnois ★ ★** *(free admission; mid-May to early Sep, every day; tours at 9:30am, 11:15am, 1pm,*

2:45pm; 80 Boulevard Edgar-Hébert, ☎800-365-5229) was once the jewel of the large Montréal Light, Heat and Power Electric Company, owned by the uncompromising Sir Herbert Holt. Built in stages between 1929 and 1956, the power plant is a sprawling 864m long. The electricity produced in Beauharnois is distributed throughout Québec and to the United States during the summer, when local demands are not as high. The power plant now belongs to Hydro-Québec. It is open to visitors; guided tours include the very long turbine room, as well as the computers used in the control room.

Rte. 132 runs in front of the power plant before disappearing under the Canal de Beauharnois, opened in 1959. It is the last in a series of canals set up along the St. Lawrence. The canals are used to bypass the many rapids found in the area, and resolve the navigational problem posed by a 25m drop between Lac Saint-Louis and Lac Saint-François.

The **Parc Archéologique de la Pointe-du-Buisson ★** *($4; mid-May to early Sep, Mon-Fri 10am to 5pm, Sat and Sun 10am to 6pm; mid-Sep to mid-Oct, Sat and Sun noon to 5pm; 333 Rue Edmond, ☎429-7857).* The Buisson headland was inhabited sporadically for thousands of years by Aboriginals, leaving the area rich with artifacts (arrowheads, cooking pots, harpoons, etc). During the summer, different areas of the archaeological park can be visited, such as the excavation site, active since 1977, the information centre and the reconstructed prehistoric fishing camp. Nature paths and picnic areas are also available

The **Parc Régional des Îles de Saint-Timothée**, see p 174.

Take Aut. 30 E. to Salaberry-de-Valleyfield.

Salaberry-de-Valleyfield (pop. 26,970)

This industrial city came into being in 1845 around a saw and paper mill purchased a few years later by the Montréal Cotton Company. This growing industry led to an era of prosperity in the late 19th century in Salaberry-de-Valleyfield, making it one of Québec's main cities at the time. The old commercial and institutional centre on Rue Victoria recalls this prosperous period, and gives the city more of an urban atmosphere than Châteauguay, whose population is higher. The city is cut in half by the old Canal de Beauharnois, in operation from 1845 to 1900 (not to be confused with the current Canal de Beauharnois located to the south of the city).

A diocese since 1892, Salaberry-de-Valleyfield was graced with the current **Cathédrale Sainte-Cécile ★** *(31 Rue de la Fabrique)* in 1934, following a fire in the previous church. The cathedral is a colossal piece of work. Architect Henri Labelle designed it in the late Gothic Revival style, narrower and closer to the historical models, added with elements of Art Deco. The facade is adorned with a statue of Sainte Cécile, patron saint of musicians, and the bronze entrance doors are decorated with many bas-reliefs done by Albert Gilles, depicting the life of Jesus.

The Pont Monseigneur-Langlois, west of Salaberry-de-Valleyfield, connects the Southwest tour to the Vaudreuil-Soulanges tour. To continue on the Southwest tour, return to Saint-Timothée. Turn right and head towards the Village of Saint-Louis-de-Gonzague to get to the banks of the Rivière Châteauguay.

Allan's Corner (pop. 120)

The **Battle of the Châteauguay National Historic Site ★** *($4; mid-May to late Aug, Wed-Sun 10am to 5pm; late Aug to mid-Oct, Sat and Sun 10am to 5pm; closed on holidays except Jul 1st; 2371 Chemin Rivière-Châteauguay Nord, ☎829-2003)* is also called the Lieu Historique National de la Bataille de la Châteauguay. During the U.S. War of Independence (1775-76), the Americans attempted their first take-over of Canada, a British colony since 1760. They were forced back by the majority French population. In 1812-13, the Americans tried once again to take over Canada. This time, it was loyalty to the Crown of England and the decisive battle of Châteauguay that bungled the Americans' attempt. In October 1813, the 2,000 troops of U.S. General Hampton gathered at the border. They entered Canadian territory during the night along the Rivière Châteauguay. But Charles Michel d'Irumberry de Salaberry, seigneur of Chambly, was waiting for them along with 300 militiamen and a few dozen Aboriginals. On October 26, the battle began. Salaberry's tactics got the better of the Americans, who retreated, putting an end to a series of conflicts and inaugurating a lasting friendship between the two countries.

There is an **interpretive centre** near the battlefield, where a model of the site, uniforms and artifacts unearthed during excavations are on display.

Travel along the Rivière Châteauguay until Ormstown.

★ Ormstown (pop. 1,575)

Founded by British settlers, Ormstown was named in honour of one of the sons of Seigneur Alexander Ellice de Beauharnois. It is, without a doubt, one of the prettiest villages of Montérégie. Many churches of various denominations are found here, such as the stone **St. James Anglican Church** (1837). Note the colourful homes on the west shore, with their red bricks, white wooden accents, and green (or black) shutters. Ormstown specializes in horse-breeding. There is a **racetrack** here, as well as a few riding schools (breeding and boarding), owned by long-standing families of British origin.

Parks

Tour B: Chemin des Patriotes

Situated on the upper half of Mont Saint-Hilaire the **Centre de la Nature du Mont-Saint-Hilaire ★★** *($4; every day 8am until one hour before sundown; 422 Chemin des Moulins, Mont-Saint-Hilaire, ☎467-1755)*, is a former estate that brigadier Andrew Hamilton Gault passed on to Montréal's McGill University in 1958. Scientific research is conducted at this nature conservation centre and recreational activities (hiking, cross-country skiing) are permitted throughout the year on half of the estate, which covers 11km². The Centre was also recognized as a Biosphere Reserve by UNESCO in 1978 for its virgin forest. An information centre on the formation of the Montérégie hills and a garden of indigenous plants can be found at the park's entrance.

Small Lac Hertel, visited by migrating birds, is located at the bottom of a valley. The surrounding peaks are criss-crossed by a 24km-long net-work of paths. One of these peaks, called Pain du Sucre or Sugarloaf, offers an excep-tional panoramic view of the Richelieu valley. On clear days, visitors can also see Montréal to the west (before noon) and the Appalachians to the southeast (during the afternoon).

Tour C: Shore of the St. Lawrence

Parc du Mont-Saint-Bruno ★ *($3.50 parking included; every day 8am until sun-down; 330 Chemin des 25 Est, St-Bruno-de-Montarville,* ☎*653-7544)* was once a holiday resort frequented by upper-class, English-speaking Montrealers. Many families, such as the Birks, the Drummonds and the Merediths, had beautiful second homes built here in what is now a park. There are two lakes at the top of the mountain, Lac Seigneurial and Lac du Moulin, next to a 19th-century water mill. The park is a pleasant place to walk and relax. Self-guided trails and guided walks help familiarize visitors with the park. Cross-country skiing is possible during the winter, with almost 27km of trails set up and small heated cabins along the way.

To get to the **Parc des Îles-de-Boucherville** *(year-round, every day 8am to sundown; 55 Île Sainte-Marguerite, Boucherville,* ☎*928-5088),* take Aut. 20, Exit 89, or take the ferry from Longueuil *(Promenade René-Lévesque).* Some of the islands are still farmland, but the archipelago, linked by cable-ferries, is accessible to visitors. The park is devoted to outdoor activi-

ties, mainly cycling and hiking in the summer. There is also a golf course and a picnic area frequented by birds of all kinds; the park is a favourite among ornithologists. You can also get a completely different perspective on the park by exploring it in a canoe; there are four tours totalling 28km.

Tour D: Vaudreuil-Soulanges

Take Rte. 132 W. and follow the signs starting at St-Anicet to **Lac Saint-François National Wildlife Area** ★ ★ *(free admission; Chemin de la Pointe-Fraser Dundee,* ☎*370-6954),* also called Réserve Nationale de Faune du Lac St-François. On the south shore of the St. Lawrence River, this park is a wetland recognized by the Ramsar Convention (a world wide list of protected sites). Visitors can observe 220 species of birds, 600 plants and over 40 species of mam-mals. From May to October, excursions in Rabaska canoes and hikes, both with guides, are offered.

Tour E: The Southwest

On the banks of the St. Law-rence, close to the town of Salaberry-de-Valleyfield, is the tourist-recreation complex on the **beach** of the **Parc Régional des Îles de Saint-Timothée** *($7; mid-Jun to early Sep Mon-Fri 10am to 5pm, Sat and Sun 10am to 7pm; Jul every day 10am to 7pm; 240 Rue St-Laurent,* ☎*377-1117).* Popular for a number of years, this spot offers all sorts of activities: swimming, in-line skating, kayaking lessons, a volleyball competition, canoe and pedal-boat rental, etc. It's an inter-esting place for families and groups but not recommended for those seeking peace and quiet.

Outdoor Activities

Hiking

The Montérégie region in-cludes six hills that were, for a long time, thought to be old volcanos. They actually consist of metamorphic rock that didn't break the surface of the earth's crust. These hills are great for day hikers, and most are accessible from the high-ways. Here are some of the best places:

Parc des Îles-de-Boucherville *(55 Île Ste-Marguerite, Louis-Hyppolite-Lafontaine tunnel, Exit 89,* ☎*928-5088),* located on an island in the middle of the St. Lawrence River, has a lot to offer in terms of flora and fauna. Over 170 species of fish and 40 species of birds have been spotted here.

Parc du Mont-Saint-Bruno *(330 Chemin des 25 Est,* ☎*653-7544),* nestled in the middle of the charming munic-ipality of Saint-Bruno, offers a network of pleasant trails that lead to a number of lakes. Many picnic and rest areas have been set up to accom-modate hikers.

The **Centre de la Nature du Mont-Saint-Hilaire** *(422 Chemin des Moulins,* ☎*467-1755)* is 400m high, has many trails that offer great hiking possibilities, and rewards your efforts with fantastic views, notably along the Pain de Sucre trail.

The **Étangs Garand** *(834 Route 104,* ☎*346-8580),* in Saint-Grégoire, offers won-derful hiking in maple groves and orchards.

Lac-Saint-François National Wildlife Area (☎370-6954), also called Réserve Nationale de Faune du Lac Saint-François, on the south shore of the St. Lawrence close to Salaberry-de-Valleyfield, is not to be missed. The marsh environment, canals and ponds are home to unique vegetation and wildlife; certain species aren't found anywhere else in the country.

Cycling

Cycling has become much more popular over the last few years. For this reason, Montérégie, along with the Eastern Townships, established an amazing network of bicycle trails. The **Montérégiade** trail, inaugurated in 1993, links the two regions and is the first step in the creation of a far-reaching corridor, which, when complete, will extend to the Appalachian Trail in Maine.

Here are a few other suggestions for paths in the region:

Tour A: Forts on the Richelieu

Canal de Chambly (*1840 Avenue Bourgogne*, ☎447-8888; *39km from Chambly to St-Jean*). While riding alongside the historic Chambly Canal and Richelieu River, you'll see lock-keepers at work, daysailors and magnificent views of the Richelieu. If you're lucky, you might even spot a mallard or a heron.

The **Circuits des Pommes** (☎469-0069; *49km*), which means apple route, could not have a more appropriate name. The wonderful thing about this trail is the many tasty, refreshing discoveries that can be made all along the way; they also provide great excuses to catch your breath.

Be careful about wine and cider sampling: drinking and driving do not go well together.

Circuit de Covey Hill (☎469-0069; *90.7km*), a route shared with motor vehicles, loops through the lovely Covey Hill valley and crosses fields, orchards and charming little towns. Residents say that the area benefits from a microclimate; the sun shines more here than anywhere else in Québec.

Fruit Picking

Fruit picking! What better way to pass the time than outdoors and in fine company? It's also economical since you can stock up on your favourite fruits at unbeatable prices. The towns of Mont-Saint-Hilaire, Rougemont and Mont-Saint-Grégoire are famous for their apples. Be aware, however, that in season (*weekends in Sep and Oct*), traffic on the small roads, especially in the Mont-Saint-Hilaire area, is a nightmare. If you can, go during the week.

Kayaking

Tour A: Forts on the Richelieu

Kayak et cetera (*1577 Avenue Bourgogne, Chambly, behind the Maison Culturelle*, ☎658-2031) offers kayak and canoe rentals. Classes are available for young people, 12 years old and up, and for adults of all levels.

Cross-country Skiing

Although Montérégie is obviously neither the Laurentians nor the Eastern Townships, there is still a good network of cross-country ski trails here. It is close to the city and the trails are easier. The following parks have trails:

Centre de la Nature du Mont-Saint-Hilaire (*$4; 422 Chemin des Moulins*, ☎467-1755; *3 trails, 10km*)

Parc du Mont-Saint-Bruno (*$10.50 including access to the park; rental; 330 Chemin des 25 Est, Saint-Bruno*, ☎653-7544; *9 trails, 35km*)

Base de Plein-Air des Cèdres (*$7; rental; 1677 Chemin St-Dominique, Les Cèdres*, ☎452-4736 or 452-2434; *50km*)

Accommodations

Tour A: Forts on the Richelieu

Chambly

Auberge L'air du Temps
$$
124 Rue Martel
☎658-1642
☎888-658-1642
≈658-2830
www.airdutemps.qc.ca
This charming house right across from Bassin de Chambly has been tastefully decorated despite the slight overabundance of pastels. There is one large guest room on the ground floor and four others in the old attic. Friendly reception.

Maison Ducharme

$$

≈

10 Rue De Richelieu
☎*447-1220*
⇋*447-1018*
This pleasant B&B occupies a 19th-century barracks (see p 150), right near Fort Chambly. Tastefully decorated, the house is steeped in the antique luxury of another era, when people took the time to make every detail in their home immaculate. A lovely English garden and pool add to this large property next to the Rivière Richelieu rapids.

Saint-Jean-sur-Richelieu

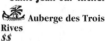 **Auberge des Trois Rives**

$$

≡, ℜ

297 Rue Richelieu
☎*358-8077*
Auberge des Trois Rives is a pleasant B&B in a rustic home. A restaurant and a terrace offer a lovely view of the water. There are 10 modestly decorated but comfortable rooms spread over two floors. Take note that prices may be higher during the hot-air balloon festival.

Relais Gouverneur

$$$-$$$$

≡, ≈, ℝ, ℜ, △

725 Boulevard du Séminaire
☎*348-7376 or 800-667-3815*
⇋*348-9778*
www.aubergebarris.com
The Relais Gouverneurs Saint-Jean-sur-Richelieu stands at the entrance to the city, along the Rivière Richelieu. The rooms are spacious and bright. Facilities include an indoor swimming pool, a bar and a non-smoking floor. Service is courteous.

Tour B: Chemin des Patriotes

Beloeil

Hostellerie Rive Gauche

$$$

≡, ℑ, ℜ, ⊛

1810 Boulevard Richelieu
☎*467-4477 or 888-608-6565*
⇋*467-0525*
hostellerierivegauche.com
Hôtellerie Rive Gauche is located off Aut. 20 (Exit 112), along the shore of the Rivière Richelieu. This inn has 22 rooms decorated in warm tones and linens, and offers a view of the water. Two tennis courts and a cozy dining room are available for guests.

Mont-Saint-Hilaire

Auberge Montagnard

$$-$$$

≡, 🐾, ≈, ℜ, ⊛

439 Boulevard Laurier
☎*467-0201 or 800-363-9109*
⇋*467-0628*
Auberge Montagnard is located on a noisy boulevard across from Mont Saint-Hilaire. It offers old-fashioned but comfortable rooms, with a friendly staff.

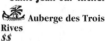 **Manoir Rouville-Campbell**

$$$$

≡, ≈, ℜ

125 Chemin des Patriotes
☎*446-6060 or 800-714-1214*
⇋*446-4878*
www.manoirrouville campbell.com
Manoir Rouville Campbell has a mystical air about it; as you enter the manor it's as though time has stopped or even gone back a century. This place, now 200 years old, has seen many chapters of Québec history unfold. It was converted into a luxury hotel in 1987 and is now owned by Québec comedian Yvon Deschamps. The dining room, bar and gardens overlooking the Rivière Richelieu complement this lordly manor.

Saint-Hyacinthe

Hôtel des Seigneurs

$$$$

≡, ⊙, 🐾, ≈, ℝ, ℜ, ⊛

1200 Rue Daniel-Johnson Ouest
☎*774-3810 or 866-734-4638*
⇋*774-6955*
www.hoteldesseigneurs.com
Located by the highway, the Hôtel des Seigneurs offers attractive rooms and many services to ensure its guests a pleasant stay. Tennis and squash courts are available, and the peaceful lobby is decorated with plants and a fountain.

Saint-Marc-sur-Richelieu

Auberge Handfield

$$-$$$

≡, ℑ, ⊙, 🐾, ≈, ℜ, △, ☻, ⊛

555 Boulevard Richelieu
☎*584-2226*
⇋*584-3650*
www.aubergehandfield.com
Located in a beautiful home across from the Richelieu, Auberge Handfield is a true escape. It offers its guests many amenities and services, including the *Escale* boat-theatre. The garden is well kept and offers a great view. The rooms are modest, but nevertheless comfortable.

 Hostellerie Les Trois Tilleuls

$$$-$$$$

≡, ℑ, ⊙, ≈, ℝ, ℜ, △, ☻, ⊛

290 Boulevard Richelieu
☎*856-7787 or 800-263-2230*
⇋*584-3146*
Hostellerie les Trois Tilleuls belongs to the prestigious Relais et Châteaux association. Built next to the Rivière Richelieu, it enjoys a tranquil rural setting. The name of the establishment comes from the three grand linden trees, called *tilleul* in French, which shade the property. The rooms are decorated with rustic furniture and each has a balcony overlooking the river. Outside, guests have access to gardens, a lookout and a heated pool.

Tour D: Vaudreuil-Soulanges

Vaudreuil-Dorion

Château Vaudreuil Suite Hôtel
$$$$$
≡, ℑ, ⊘, ≈, ℜ, △, ⊛
21700 Transcanadienne
☎*455-0955*
☎*800-363-7896*
⇔*455-6617*
www.chateau-vaudreuil.com
Located on Lac des Deux-Montagnes, this modern, imposing-looking hotel, which has very comfortable rooms, is a good choice in this region.

Hudson

Auberge Willow Place
$$ bkfst incl.
≡, ℜ
208 Main Road
☎*458-7006*
⇔*458-4615*
willowplaceinn.com
Auberge Willow Place is pleasantly located on the shores of Lac des Deux-Montagnes. Old-fashioned charm and a grand yet mellow British-style atmosphere.

Restaurants

Tour A: Forts on the Richelieu

Carignan

 **Au Tournant de la Rivière**
$$$$
Wed-Sun
5070 Rue De Salaberry
☎*658-7372*
Au Tournant de la Rivière has a critically acclaimed gourmet menu. In business for more than 20 years, the establishment's succulent French cuisine has helped it maintain its standing among the best restaurants in Québec. A must for gourmet palates.

Chambly

Chez Marius
$-$$
1737 Bourgogne
☎*658-6092*
The Chez Marius snack bar is a local favourite. While savouring a delicious hamburger and poutine combo, you can look at old photographs documenting the history of the restaurant, as well as that of Chambly. During summer, you can eat outdoors on the riverside terrace.

Crêperie du Fort Chambly
$$-$$$
1717 Bourgogne
☎*447-7474*
Crêperie du Fort Chambly, on the edge of Bassin de Chambly, occupies a wooden house that recalls the sea. They serve crêpes, of course, but also cheese fondues. Waterfront terrace and friendly service. Brunch on Sundays.

La Maison Bleue
$$$-$$$$
Tue-Sun
2592 Bourgogne
☎*447-1112*
What was once the large, wood-framed home of Thomas Whitehead (see p 152) now houses a luxurious restaurant with a country feel: large fireplaces, creaky floors and antiques. Upstairs, private rooms can be reserved, except in summer, for family gatherings or business meetings. Classic French cuisine and a warm reception.

Richelieu

Aux Chutes du Richelieu
$$$-$$$$
Wed-Sun
486 1re Rue
☎*658-6689*
Aux Chutes du Richelieu prepares excellent French and Italian cuisine. Their crêpes Suzette are truly sinful. What's more, you can admire the Richelieu falls while you eat.

Saint-Jean-sur-Richelieu

 Manneken Pis
$
320 Rue De Champlain
☎*348-3254*
With a name like that, Belgian waffles are sure to be nearby—and what delicious waffles they are, with such fine chocolate! The coffees, roasted on site, are also excellent. A pleasant terrace faces a little marina. They also serve bread with various spreads, and salads.

Le Samuel II
$$-$$$
291 Rue Richelieu
☎*347-4353*
Much loved by locals, Le Samuel II has always had a faithful following of connoisseurs. Large bay windows overlooking the canal offer a view of the boats going by. Always a delight.

Chez Noeser
$$$$
Thu-Sun
bring your own wine
236 Rue De Champlain
☎*346-0811*
A few years ago, Denis and Ginette Noeser left Montréal and their Rue Saint-Denis restaurant to settle in Saint-Jean-sur-Richelieu. Their latest restaurant offers particularly courteous service and delicious classic French cuisine. There is a terrace during the summer months.

Montérégie

Lacolle

Brochetterie Pharos
$$
7 Rue de l'Église
☎246-3897
Brochetterie Pharos would be a Greek restaurant like any other were it not located in a church—a sign of the changing times in Québec, where many churches are being turned into restaurants, luxury apartments, condos and other businesses.

Tour B: Chemin des Patriotes

Saint-Bruno-de-Montarville

La Rabastalière
$$$
Tue-Sun
125 de la Rabastalière
☎461-0173
La Rabastalière occupies a warm, century-old home; the restaurant offers classic French cuisine plus a gourmet six-course menu that varies each week. There is a sunroom for quiet meals. The staff is friendly and the food excellent.

Saint-Hyacinthe

L'Auvergne
$$$
Tue-Sun
1475 Rue des Cascades Ouest
☎774-1881
L'Auvergne has long offered one of the best French cuisines in the region in its two small dining rooms. Brunch is served on Sundays from 10am.

Beloeil

Le Trait d'Union
$-$$
919 Boulevard Wilfrid-Laurier
☎446-5740
Le Trait d'Union is an unpretentious, hip little bistro where local residents come to meet. With its relaxed atmosphere and charming terrace, you're sure to have a pleasant time. They serve healthy little dishes

at affordable prices. Open for breakfast on weekends.

Crêperie du Vieux-Beloeil
$$
Tue-Sun
940 Boulevard Richelieu
☎464-1726
The Crêperie du Vieux-Beloeil offers generous portions of their house crêpes, made of white flour or buckwheat, and served with seafood, ham or cheese.

Restaurant Ostéria
$$
914 Boulevard Wilfrid-Laurier
☎464-7491
L'Ostéria, located in the old part of town, is a charming little restaurant that serves fine Italian cuisine, veal and game, as well as copious Sunday brunches. The adjoining terrace is inviting, and they offer a children's menu.

Danvito
$$$-$$$$
Mon-Sat
154 Boulevard Wilfrid-Laurier
☎464-5166
Hidden in Beloeil's commercial district, Danvito attracts a business clientele with its fine Italian cuisine and Mediterranean character. They serve the traditional spaghetti *carbonara* and a succulent *manicotti fiorentina*. The decor is simple and airy.

Saint-Marc-sur-Richelieu

Auberge Handfield
$$$-$$$$
555 Boulevard Richelieu
☎584-2226
Auberge Handfield houses a large dining room decorated with wood beams. The country atmosphere and delicious Québec cuisine complement each other. In the spring you can also sample sweets from the sugar shack.

Hostellerie Les Trois Tilleuls
$$$$
290 Boulevard Richelieu
☎856-7787
☎800-263-2230
The restaurant in the Hostellerie des Trois Tilleuls serves up some gems of fine French gastronomy. The artfully prepared menu offers traditional and sophisticated meals, and the dining room has a nice view of the river. The beautiful terrace is open to guests during the summer.

Le Champagne
$$$$
Wed-Sat
1000 Chemin du Rivage
☎787-2966
Le Champagne looks like an old Moroccan castle. The interior is magnificently decorated with panelling, while the tables are set with silverware, fine glassware, signed dishes and embroidered tablecloths. Delicious French cuisine. Reservations required.

Tour C: Shore of the St. Lawrence

Saint-Lambert

Café-Passion
$
476 Rue Victoria
☎671-1405
Café-Passion, located in the heart of Saint-Lambert, has quite a following. Although it is a pleasant place, the food does not quite live up to all the fuss. The decor is trendy and the food somewhat bland. Nevertheless, it's an acceptable choice for an inexpensive meal.

Au Vrai Chablis
$$$-$$$$
Tue-Sat
52 Rue Aberdeen
☎465-2795
The food-service professionals here invite you to partake of a fabulous fine-dining experience. The menu changes daily and lists French specialties,

superbly prepared by renowned chef Bernard Jacquin.

Longueuil

Charcuterie du Vieux-Longueuil
$
193 Rue St-Charles Ouest
☎670-0643
For a good sandwich, the Charcuterie du Vieux Longueuil is an excellent choice, despite the slightly rushed service.

Restaurant l'Incrédule
$$-$$$
288 Rue St-Charles Ouest
☎674-0946
L'Incrédule offers an interesting choice of bistro-style meals, as well as an excellent selection of imported beer, scotch and port.

Saint-Hubert

Bistro des Bières Belges
$-$$
2088 De Montcalm
☎465-0669
The Bistro des Bières Belges, as its alliterative name reveals, has a selection of about 60 Belgian beers. The menu is also in the Flemish tradition. Reservations required on the weekend.

Tour D: Vaudreuil-Soulanges

Rigaud

Sucrerie de la Montagne
$$$$
300 rang St-Georges
☎451-5204
The Sucrerie de la Montagne is practically an attraction in itself. It serves traditional sugaring-off dishes, such as those perennial favourites *oreilles de Christ* (literally Christ's ears, but actually deep-fried lard) and *œufs dans le sirop* (eggs in syrup). A folk group livens up the atmosphere with rigadoons and quadrille tunes. Open year-round.

Hudson

Clémentine
$$-$$$
398 Rue Principale
☎458-8181
Chez Clémentine is easily one of the finest restaurants in Québec. A member of Toques Blanches Internationales, this small restaurant, located in a magnificent little country house in the heart of town, serves innovative cuisine. The service is courteous and friendly.

Auberge Willow Place
$$$
208 Main Road
☎458-7006
On the shores of Lac des Deux-Montagnes, Auberge Willow Place serves steaks and grilled specialties. With its English-style decor and cozy atmosphere, this place is irresistible. Courteous young staff and a lovely lakefront location add to its charm.

Entertainment

Bars and Nightclubs

Saint-Bruno-de-Montarville

Bar 1250
1250 Roberval
☎653-1900
Bar 1250, equipped with three pool tables, attracts a young, unpretentious clientele. The preference is for good old rock 'n' roll on Wednesdays and Thursdays, and Top-40 hits on the Fridays and weekends.

Chambly

Bistro Le Vieux Bourgogne
1718 Avenue Bourgogne
☎447-9306
Bistro Le Vieux Bourgogne attracts a young crowd with traditional French and Québec tunes.

Saint-Mathias

Super 9
9 Rue Dufour
☎658-5170
It's not every day that you come across a danceclub in an old barn, and this one has been a popular weekend spot for young people from all over the region for many generations. Essentially, this place is a typical, small-town club with lasers, sports cars and all the other hoopla. Nonetheless, there's no lack of ambiance here.

Saint-Hyacinthe

Le Bilboquet
1850 Rue des Cascades Ouest
☎771-6900
Le Bilboquet is a comfortable spot. It's a microbrewery (they brew Métayer Blonde, Brune and Rousse), a fun place for a meal with friends, and also a centre for the promotion of the arts. They invite musicians to play, decorate the premises with works by local artists, present plays and poetry readings and host literary discussions.

Theatre

Upton

Unique in North America, the concept of **Théâtre de la Dame de Coeur** *(Jun to early Sep Wed-Sun; 611 Rang de la Carrière, ☎549-5828)* is sure to fascinate young and old alike. Located in a magnificent historic site, the "Queen of Hearts" puts on terrific

Montérégie

marionette shows complete with striking visual effects. The outdoor theatre has an immense roof and pivoting seats that are heated on chilly evenings.

Festivals and Cultural Events

Saint-Jean-sur-Richelieu

The **Festival de Montgolfières** *(2nd week of Aug;* ☎*347-9555, www.montgolfieres. com)*, a hot-air-balloon festival, fills the sky over Saint-Jean-sur-Richelieu with approximately 100 multicoloured hot-air balloons. Departures take place every day from 6am to 6pm, weather permitting. Exhibitions and shows make up some of the other activities that take place during the festival.

Chambly

The **Fête de Saint-Louis** *(late Aug;* ☎*658-1585)* at Fort Chambly recreates old military encampments and an old-style market. Military manoeuvres by the Compagnie Franche de la Marine are part of the show. Restaurants in the area prepare special colonial-style menus.

Chambly is home to Unibroue, one of the biggest craft breweries in the province. The brewery organizes the **Fête Bières et Saveurs** *(late Aug and early Sep;* ☎*658-7310)*, a beer festival. The popularity of this event has exceeded all expectations, with attendance rising year after year. Beers from all over the world can be sampled at Fort Chambly.

Saint-Denis

The **Fête des Patriotes** *(3rd Sun in Nov;* ☎ *787-3623)* is a popular gathering that takes place in Saint-Denis to commemorate the only Patriotes' victory, November 23rd 1837.

Salaberry-de-Valleyfield

Salaberry-de-Valleyfield hosts the **Régates Internationales de Salaberry-de-Valleyfield** *(1st week end of Jul;* ☎*371-6144 or 888-371-6144)*. The competition involves several categories of hydroplane races, with speeds reaching 240km/h. The regattas always attract a large number of visitors.

Kahnawake

Various traditional Aboriginal events (dances, songs, etc.) are organized as part of the **Pow Wow** *(2nd week end of Jul;* ☎*632-8667)*, held in Kahnawake every year during the second weekend of July. Most of the activities are held on Île Kateri Tekakwitha.

Shopping

Mont-Saint-Grégoire

Les Jardins de Versailles *(late Jun to mid-Oct, every day 10am to 5pm, mid-Oct to late Jun, Wed-Sun 10am to 5pm; 399 Rang Versailles, Route 227,* ☎*346-6775)* specializes in beautiful dried-flower arrangements. Workshops are offered.

La Maison sous les Arbres *(2024 Route 133 Sud,* ☎*347-1639)*. Imagine an art gallery set up in a private home; you can shop for your bathroom articles in the bathroom, kitchen articles in the kitchen, and so on. Great for people who love to poke around in other people's houses.

Vignoble Dietrich-Jooss *(year- round, Tue-Sun 10am* to 5pm; 407 Grande Ligne, ☎*347-6857)*. Friendly owners Victor, Christiane and their daughter Stéphanie, originally from Alsace, have owned this vineyard since 1986 and their wines have already earned dozens of prizes in various prestigious international competitions. Connoisseurs consider the white *cuvé spécial* to be the most Alsatian in character. Wine tasting available.

Hudson

Finnigan's Market *(shop Sun 11am to 5pm; public market May to Nov, Sat only, 9am to 4pm; 775 Rue Principale,* ☎*458-4377)*. This famous outdoor antique market also has loads of other great finds and is one place in the region not to be missed. It's a joy to wander around all these treasures. A hot spot for collectors!

Saint-Antoine-Abbé

Vins Mustier Gerzer, Hydromel *(year-round, 3299 Rte. 209,* ☎*826-4609)*. Light and fresh, mead is the perfect drink for those wonderful summer days, and Vins Mustier, in the splendid St-Antoine-Abbé region, is an expert in the field. This place is also devoted to bee-keeping and offers a wide variety of honey-based products. Sampling available.

Otterburn Park

The **Chocolaterie La Cabosse d'Or** *(summer, every day 9am to 10pm; rest of the year, Sat-Wed 9am to 6pm, Thu and Fri 9am to 9pm; 973 Chemin Ozias-Leduc,* ☎*464-6937)* has earned its reputation not only for selling Belgian chocolate of the finest quality but also for its enchanting fairy-tale ambiance. It's a splendid house with a shop, a terrace and a tearoom. The hostesses greet you with a smile.

The Eastern Townships

This is a beautiful
region in the Appalachian foothills, in the southern-most part of Québec.

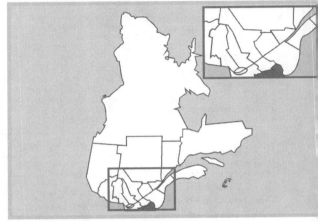

The rich architectural heritage and mountainous countryside give Les Cantons d'Est (the Eastern Townships) a distinctive character reminiscent in many ways of New England.

Picturesque villages marked by what is often typically English architecture lie nestled between mountains with rounded summits and lovely little valleys.

As may be gathered from many place names, such as Massawippi and Coaticook, this vast region was originally explored and inhabited by the Abenaki First Nation. Later, when New France came under British control and the United States declared its independence, many American colonists still loyal to the British monarchy (known as Loyalists) settled in the Eastern Townships. Throughout the 19th century, these settlers were followed by waves of immigrants from the British Isles, mainly Ireland, and French colonists from the overpopulated St. Lawrence lowlands. Though the local population is now over 90% French-speaking, the area still bears obvious traces of its British past, most notably in its

architecture. Many towns and villages are graced with majestic Anglican churches surrounded by beautiful 19th-century Victorian or vernacular American-style homes. The Townships are still home to a handful of prestigious English institutions, like Bishop's University in Lennoxville.

Though dairy farms still grace the countryside, the Eastern Townships is now a dynamic region with two universities and a number of high technology enterprises. Located about an hour's drive from Montréal, this is cottage country and vacation land for many. The mountains are great for winter skiing, and the lakes and rivers perfect for

summer water sports. But visitors also come to the Eastern Townships for its fine food and wineries, or simply to take part in one of its various festivals or family activities.

In terms of territorial division, the townships (*cantons*) are different from seigneuries. Not only are they more or less square, rather than oblong, but their administrative system was based on a British model. Instead of being granted to a single individual, a township was established at the request of the community wishing to settle there. Most were founded in the 19th century, filling spaces left vacant by the French seigneurial system, usually mountainous sites removed from the already populated banks of the St. Lawrence and its tributaries, which at the time were the colony's main transportation routes. Nowhere in Québec was this means of populating the territory more widespread that in the Eastern Townships.

In 1966, following the division of Québec into administrative regions, the Eastern Townships region took on the name "Estrie." Thirty years later, however, the region's tourist association decided to return to the original appellation. For that matter, the local populace's deep attachment to the area was such that the original name had never been abandoned in the first place. Consequently, "Eastern Townships" now denotes the region's important touristic vocation while "Estrie" refers to the administrative region.

Finding Your Way Around

Located southeast of Montréal, the Eastern Townships region is in competition with the Laurentians, to the northwest, for the honour of being Montréalers' favourite "playground." The three tours below will help you explore the Eastern Townships: **Tour A: The Orchards ★**, **Tour B: The Lakes ★★★** and **Tour C: The Back Country ★**.

Tour A: The Orchards

By Car

From Montréal, cross the Champlain bridge and the Autoroute des Cantons de l'Est (Aut. 10) to Exit 29, then head south on the 133. Near Philipsburg and the U.S. border, keep left in order to turn onto the small road leading to Saint-Armand-Ouest and Frelighsburg. Rte. 213 takes over until you reach Dunham, where you can either turn left on Rte. 202 to go to Mystic or head north on Rte. 202, then Rte. 241, to reach Waterloo. From there, Rte. 112 leads to Rougemont via Granby, while Rte. 220 meets Rte. 243, towards Valcourt.

Tour B: The Lakes

By Car

From Montréal, take the Autoroute des Cantons de l'Est (Aut.. 10) to Exit 90, then head south on Rte. 243. Make sure to turn left towards Knowlton in order to follow the eastern shore of Lac Brome. In Knowlton, Rte. 104 leads to the intersection with Rte. 215. Turn left towards Brome and Sutton. By following Rte. 139 then Rte. 243 from here, you will reach Bolton Sud, where you can pick up Rte. 245 to Saint-Benoît-du-Lac. By continuing around the northern tip of Lac Memphrémagog on Rte. 247, you will end up in Rock Island. The last portion of the tour follows Rte. 143, with a detour on Rte. 141 to Coaticook, and then Rte. 208 to Sherbrooke.

Bus Stations

Sutton
28 Rue Principale (Esso station)
☎*(450) 538-2452*

Magog-Orford
67 Rue Sherbrooke (Terminus Café)
☎*(819) 843-4617*

Sherbrooke
20 Rue King Ouest
☎*(819) 569-3656*

Tour C: The Back Country

By Car

From Sherbrooke, take Rte. 108 to Birchton. From Cookshire, follow Rte. 212 to St-Augustin-de- Woburn. From here head north on Rte. 161 along the eastern shore of Lac Memphrémagog to Ham-Nord from where Rte. 216 and then Rte. 255 lead to Danville.

Bus Station

Lac-Mégantic
6630 Rue Salaberry (Dépanneur Fatima)
☎*(819) 583-0112*

Practical Information

There are two area codes in the Eastern Townships; **819** and **450**. To avoid confusion, the area codes have been included in this chapter.

Tourist Information

Regional Office

Tourisme Cantons de l'Est
20 Rue Don-Bosco S., Sherbrooke
J1L 1W4
☎*(819) 820-2020*
☎*800-355-5755*
≈*(819) 566-4445*
www.tourismecantons.qc.ca

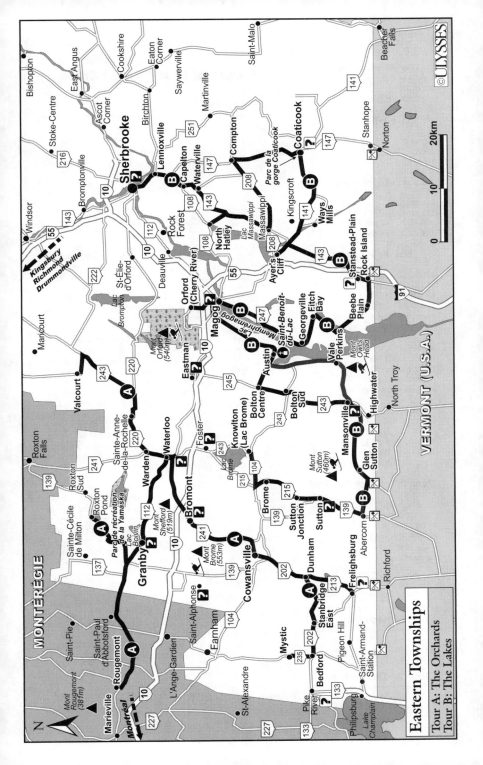

Tour A: The Orchards

Bromont
15 Boulevard Bromont, J2L 2K4
☎*(450) 534-2006*
☎*877-276-6668*

Granby
650 Rue Principale, J2G 8L4
☎*(450) 372-7273*
☎*800-567-7273*
www.granby-bromont.com

Rougemont
11 Chemin Marieville, J0L 1M0
☎*(450) 469-0069*
☎*866-469-0069*

Tour B: The Lakes

Magog
55 Rue Cabana, J1X 2C4
☎*(819) 843-2744*
☎*800-267-2744*
www.tourisme-
membremagog. com

Sherbrooke
3010 Rue King Ouest, J1L 1Y7
☎*(819) 821-1919*
☎*800-561-8331*
www.sdes.ca/tourisme

Sutton
1049, 11-B Rue Principale Sud
CP 1049, J0E 2K0
☎*(450) 538-8455*
☎*800-565-8455*
www.sutton-info.qc.ca

Tour C: The Back Country

Lac-Mégantic
3295 Rue Laval N., G6B 1A5
☎*(819) 583-5515*
☎*800-363-5515*
www.tourisme-
megantic.com

Exploring

Tour A: The Orchards

Duration of tour: one day

Names of New Merged Cities

Cookshire–Eaton
Merger of Cookshire, Eaton, Newport and Sawyerville.

Eastman
Merger of Stukely and Eastman.

Sutton
Merger of the city and the township of Sutton.

Sherbrooke
Merger of Sherbrooke, Rock Forest, Fleurimont, Bromptonville (parts of), Lennoxville, Deauville, Stoke (parts of) and Saint-Élie-d'Orford (parts of).

There are three clusters of orchards in the countryside surrounding Montréal, one in the Saint-Joseph-du-Lac region, another in the Saint-Antoine-Abbé region, and a third, which is both larger and more spread out, in the western part of the Eastern Townships. In recent years, vineyards have grown up alongside the traditional apple orchards, turning a part of this tour into a sort of miniature wine route. In the fall, city dwellers come here on Sundays to admire the brilliant foliage, watch the grape harvest and pick their own MacIntosh apples in one of the many pick-your-own orchards. Apple growers also sell their products (apple butter, cider, juice, pies) by the side of the road, while viticulturists (wine growers) offer guided tours of their properties, and provide visitors with an opportunity to taste and purchase their wine.

★
**Frelighsburg
(pop. 1,050)**

Eastern Townships' architecture differs from that of the rest of Québec, due to its Anglo-American origins, which account for the frequent use of red brick and white clapboard and the predominance of sash windows, composed of two vertically sliding panels. In houses built prior to 1860,

the window panes are usually separated into little squares (three or four squares wide and four to eight squares high), while windows in the more recent Victorian houses contain large, undivided plates of glass.

The charming village of Frelighsburg grew up around its stone **mill** (*private, no visitors allowed; 12 Rte. 237 N.*), built in 1790 by two Loyalist pioneers. In 1839, the structure was enlarged by its new owner, Abram Freligh of New York State, for whom the village was named. The mill, which was converted into a residence in 1967, is visible through the trees on the left.

Frelighsburg's **Anglican Church** ★ is very well situated atop a hill overlooking the village. Both its oblong structure and its steeple, which is at the side of the nave and marks the main entrance, are uncommon architectural features in the Eastern Townships. The church was built in 1884 in the Gothic Revival style advocated by the Church of England. Its red brick walls, yellow brick casings and slate roof create a polychromatic effect not unlike that of village churches in Ontario.

Take Rte. 213 N. toward Dunham.

★
Dunham
(pop. 3,400)

Traditionally, a single, somewhat imposing church lies at the centre of towns founded by Catholic French Canadians. As villages in the Eastern Townships are often inhabited by Anglicans, Presbyterians, Methodists, Baptists and Lutherans, little churches of various denominations abound. Accordingly, a number of churches are sprinkled among the well-kept residences lining Dunham's main street (*Rue Principale*). The oldest township in Lower Canada, Dunham is home to some of the first houses ever built in the Eastern Townships. **All Saints Anglican Church**, built of stone between 1847 and 1851, looks straight down the center of Rte. 202, known as the wine route.

Turn left on Rte. 202 W. to start the wine route. It is also possible to visit Stanbridge East, Bedford and Mystic from this road. Afterward, continue on the 213 N. towards Cowansville.

★
The Wine Route

European visitors might consider it quite presumptuous to call the road between Dunham and Stanbridge East (*Rte. 202 W.*) the "Wine Route," (indicated by blue road signs from Autoroute 10) but the concentration of vineyards in this region is unique in the province, and Québec's attempts at wine-making have been so surprisingly successful that people have been swept away by their enthusiasm. There are no châteaux or distinguished old counts here, only growers who sometimes have to go as far as renting helicopters to save their vines from freezing. The rotor blades cause the air to circulate, preventing frost from forming on the ground during

crucial periods in May. The region is, however, blessed with a microclimate and soil favourable for grape growing (slate). Most of the local wines are sold only at the vineyards where they are produced.

You can visit the **L'Orpailleur** (*1086 Rte. 202, ☎450-295-2763*) winery, whose products include a dry white wine and Apéridor, an apéritif similar to Pineau des Charentes. They also produce a delicious fortified white wine called La Marquise, La Part des Anges, a white wine and brandy mixture with a nutty flavour, as well as a highly acclaimed ice wine.

The **Domaine des Côtes d'Ardoises** (*879 Route 202, ☎450-295-2020*) is one of the few Québec vineyards that produces red wine. Here, as at other wineries, the owner will give you a warm welcome.

Les Blancs Coteaux (*1046 Chemin Bruce, Route 202, ☎450-295-3503*) not only makes quality wine but also has a lovely craft shop.

★
Stanbridge East
(pop. 860)

This charming village is known mainly for its regional museum. Along its shady streets, visitors can also see large houses surrounded by gardens. **St. James the Apostle** (circa 1880), an Anglican church made of multicoloured brick, is particularly noteworthy, as its cruciform structure is somewhat unusual in Québec.

The **Musée Missisquoi ★** (*$3.50; late May to mid-Oct, every day 10am to 5pm; 2 River St., ☎450-248-3153*) is devoted to preserving the region's essentially Loyalist heritage. The 12,000 objects displayed are housed in three period buildings, the **Cornell Mill** (1832), **Bill's Barn**, which

houses antique cars and ploughing implements, and the **Magasin Général Hodge**, a general store whose counters date back to the beginning of the 20th century.

Continue on Rte. 202 W. to Bedford.

Bedford
(pop. 2,750)

Another little town with American and Loyalist characteristics, Bedford is renowned for its grey and green slate extracted from surrounding quarries. Visitors can see lovely red-brick houses surrounded by greenery, most built during the second half of the 19th century, as well as the pretty **St. James Anglican Church** (circa 1840), also made of brick. The **Pont des Rivières**, to the northwest, is a 41m covered bridge, built in 1884. One of a few rare examples of wooden Howe-style bridges to be found in Québec, it is characterized by girders assembled in the shape of a cross.

If you are interested in the local architecture, pick up a copy of the *Bedford Historic Esplanade Heritage Tour*, a pamphlet that outlines a tour of 10 impressive 19th- and early 20th-century buildings in and around Bedford (*available at 1 rue Principale Mon-Fri 9am to 4:30pm*) or from Restaurant L'Interlude, (*48 rue Principale*). Bicycles are available free of charge at the latter location, for those who would like to follow the tour on two wheels).

To get to Mystic, turn right on Rte. 235 N. The village is located off the main road.

★
Mystic

Mystic is like a little piece of New England in Québec. Its population is still mainly anglophone.

Blink, and the village is gone: its central focus is the dodecagonal (12-sided) Walbridge Barn, built by American industrialist A.S. Walbridge around 1885. Unfortunately, the barn and its surrounding 40ha domain are not open for visits.

You can, however, visit the old general store. Built around 1860, the pink clapboard building is now a chocolatier known as **L'Oeuf** (229 Chemin Mystic; ☎450-248-7529). Chocoholic or not, step inside, as the interior has been well preserved. Adjoining the chocolatier is a restaurant and inn of the same name.

Head back towards Dunham to continue the main tour.

Cowansville
(pop. 12,100)

Another Loyalist community, Cowansville has lovely Victorian homes made of wood and brick, as well as a few interesting public and commercial buildings, which bear witness to the town's prosperous past. Especially interesting is the former **Eastern Townships Bank** (225 Rue Principale), built in 1889, which has been converted into a community centre. The edifice's mansard roof is characteristic of the Second Empire style, which was popular both among the English and French. Not far away lies the small, Anglican **Trinity Church**, a Gothic Revival structure erected in 1854, and surrounded by a cemetery.

Take Rte. 241 N., located east of Cowansville.

Bromont
(pop. 5,500)

Developed in the 1960s, Bromont has become a favourite vacation area among Montréalers. It is renowned for its downhill ski resort, its

sports facilities, and also for having hosted the 1976 Olympic equestrian competitions.

Visiting the **Musée du Chocolat** (*$1.25; Jun to Oct, Mon-Fri 10am to 6pm, Sat and Sun 9am to 5:30pm; Nov to May, Mon-Fri 10am to 6pm, Sat and Sun 9am to 5:30pm; 679 Rue Shefford, ☎450-534-3893*) is a golden opportunity for gourmands with discriminating palates to indulge in sinfully delicious chocolate. The museum presents the history of chocolate since the arrival of the Spanish in South America, the process of changing cocoa beans into powder and a few art works featuring... chocolate, of course! If your taste buds become overly sated, you can purchase all kinds of delicious sweets made right on the premises. Light meals are also served here.

The **Centre Équestre**, riding school, see p 199.

The **Station de Ski Bromont**, ski resort, see p 200.

From here, visitors can make an optional detour to Valcourt, the village where Joseph-Armand Bombardier developed and began marketing the snowmobile.

To get there, take Rte. 241 to Warden. Turn right on Rte. 220, in the direction of Sainte-Anne-de-la-Rochelle, then left on Rte. 243, and follow the signs for Valcourt.

Valcourt
(pop. 3,400)

Bombardier was not the only mechanic in Québec to develop a motor vehicle for use on snow-covered surfaces. Residents had to come up with something, since many roads in the province were not cleared of snow until the beginning of the 1950s. As automobiles were, for all practical purposes, somewhat

unreliable, people had to depend on the same means of transportation as their ancestors, namely, the horse-drawn sleigh. Bombardier, however, was the only individual to make a profit from his invention, most notably because of a lucrative contract with the army during World War II. Though the company later diversified and underwent considerable expansion, it never left the village of Valcourt—which is to this day the site of its head office.

The **Musée J.-Armand-Bombardier** ★ (*$5; early May to early Sep every day 10am to 5pm, early Sep to early May every day 10am to 5pm; 1001 Avenue Joseph-Armand-Bombardier; ☎450-532-5300*) is a museum that traces the development of the snowmobile, and explains how Bombardier's invention was marketed all over the world. Different prototypes are displayed, along with a few examples of various snowmobiles produced since 1960. Group tours of the factory are also available.

From Waterloo, take Rte. 112 W. to Granby.

Granby
(pop. 45,200)

A few kilometres from the verdant Parc de la Yamaska, Granby, the "princess of the Eastern Townships," basks in the fresh air of the surrounding countryside. In addition to its Victorian homes, this city boasts grand avenues and parks graced with fountains and sculptures. Transected by the Yamaska Nord river, it is also the point where the Montérégiade and Estriade bicycle trails converge. The city's youth and dynamism are reflected in its multiple festivals, notably the Festival International de la Chanson, an international festival of song that has exposed the French-speaking world to a number of excellent performers.

Visitors to the **Granby Zoo** ★ ★ *($23.45; end May to end Aug, every day 10am to 7pm; beg Sep to mid-Oct Sat and Sun 10am to 6pm; take Exit 68 or 74 from Aut. 10 and follow the signs; 525 Rue St-Hubert,* ☎*450-472-6290 or 877-472-6290)* can see some 175 animal species, mainly from North America and Africa. This is an old-style zoo, so most of the animals are in cages and there are few areas where they can roam freely. It is nevertheless an interesting place to visit, particularly for young children. The admission fee provides access to the Amazoo, a water park, that was recently added to the site.

The **Parc de la Yamaska**, see p 197.

The **Centre d'Interprétation de la Nature du Lac Boivin**, see p 197.

Continue on Route 112 W. towards Rougemont.

Rougemont (pop. 2,500)

Though it is located outside of the Eastern Townships tourist area, Rougemont attracts visitors because of its status as Québec's apple capital. The village lies at the base of the smallest hill in the Montérégie region, Mont Rougemont.

The **Cidrerie Artisanale Michel Jodoin** *(free admission; Mon-Fri 9am to 5pm, Sat and Sun 10am to 4pm; 1130 Rang de la Petite Caroline,* ☎*450-469-2676)*, produces high-quality hard ciders and lovely sparkling apple juice. The secret lies in the aging process, which takes place in oak barrels, with delicious results. Visitors have the opportunity to taste, and of course buy, the various

products produced on site, as well as tour the facility.

This is the end of the Orchards Tour. To return to Montréal, take Rte. 112 W. until it intersects with Rte. 227 S., then turn left to reach Aut. 10. To reach Tour B, continue eastward on Route 112 until Waterloo. From there, turn right and take Route 220 South until Knowlton.

Tour B : The Lakes

Duration of tour: two days

This tour winds around the three most popular lakes in the Eastern Townships and includes sweeping views, charming villages, and friendly inns. It is an ideal excursion just a short distance from Montréal. In the summer, visitors can enjoy a variety of water sports, go rock-climbing, hiking, skiing or snowshoeing.

★ ★ Knowlton (pop. 5,100)

When the Townships are compared to New England, Knowlton is often given as an example. Quaint shops and restaurants welcome visitors strolling through this well-to-do little village. In contrast to traditional French-Canadian villages, where the accent is on the parish church and its presbytery, civic buildings are the highlight in Knowlton. A notable example is the **Old Courthouse** (*15 Rue St. Paul*), designed in the Greek Revival style by Timothy E. Chamberlain and built in 1859. The building is now home to the Brome County Historical Society. All around, visitors will see examples of Loyalist architecture, characterized by red brick, white trim and dark-green shutters. Pick up a copy

of the *Historic Walking Tour* brochure at Auberge Knowlton or Restaurant Le Relais (see p 208), for more information on Knowlton's many historic buildings.

Knowlton is known as a centre for duck production and the meat is featured on the menus of local inns and restaurants when in season.

Lac Brome ★ is popular among windsurfers, who can use a parking lot and a little beach on the side of the road near Knowlton.

The **Brome County Museum** ★ *($3.50; mid-May to mid-Sep, Mon-Sat 10am to 4:30pm, Sun 11am to 4:30pm; 130 Rue Lakeside;* ☎*450-243-6782)*, the historical museum of Brome County, occupies five Loyalist buildings and traces the lives and history of the region's inhabitants. In addition to the usual furniture and photographs, visitors can see a reconstructed general store, a 19th-century court of justice and, what's more unusual, a collection of military equipment, including a World War I airplane.

The village of Knowlton is now part of the municipality of Lac-Brome, which encircles the lake. To reach Sutton, turn right onto Rte. 104 W. at the end of Chemin Lakeside, and then left onto Rte. 215 S. in the direction of Brome and Sutton Junction.

★ Sutton (pop. 3,350)

Sutton, which is located at the base of the mountain of the same name, is one of the major winter resorts in the Eastern Townships. The area also has several well-designed golf courses. Among the local houses of worship, the Gothic Revival Anglican **Grace Church**, built out of stone in

1850, is the most noteworthy. Unfortunately, though, its steeple no longer has its pointed arch.

Take Rte. 139 S. towards the tiny village of Abercorn, located less than 3km from the U.S. border (Vermont). From there, turn left on the secondary road that runs along the beautiful valley of the Rivière Missisquoi and passes through Glen Sutton, Highwater and Mansonville before reaching Vale Perkins.

Mont Sutton ★, see p 200.

Vale Perkins

From Vale Perkins, **Owl's Head** is visible on the right. A charming little Ukrainian chapel lies further along. The scenic road then runs alongside **Sugar Loaf** and **Mont Éléphant**. Near the latter, there are heaps of stones known as cairns, as well as a large flat stone engraved with hieroglyphics of enigmatic origins. Some people associate these archaeological relics with the Loyalist colonists, while others attribute them to the local Aboriginals, and still others, believe it or not, to the Phoenicians who, it would seem, left their mark in the very distant past. From the top of the hill overlooking **Knowlton's Landing**, there is a delightful view of **Lac Memphrémagog**, the pride of the Eastern Townships. The little village at the foot of the hill is where vacationing Montréalers used to board the ferryboat to go to the eastern shore of the lake.

Owl's Head ★, see p 200.

★★
Lac Memphrémagog

Lac Memphrémagog, which is 44.5km long and only 1 to 2 km wide, will remind some visitors of a Scottish loch. It even has its own equivalent of the Loch Ness monster,

named "Memphre," sightings of which go back to 1798! The southern portion of the lake, which cannot be seen from Magog, is located in the United States. The name Memphrémagog, like Massawippi and Missisquoi, is an Abenaki word.

Sailing enthusiasts will be happy to learn that the lake is one of the best places in Québec to enjoy this sport.

Turn right on Rte. d'Austin, and right again on Chemin Fisher, which leads to the Abbaye de Saint-Benoît-du-Lac.

★★
Saint-Benoît-du-Lac

This municipality consists solely of the estate of the **Abbaye de Saint-Benoît-du-Lac**, an abbey founded in 1913 by Benedictine monks who were driven away from the Abbaye de Saint-Wandrille-de-Fontenelle in Normandy. Aside from the monastery, there are guest quarters, an abbey chapel and farm buildings. However, only the chapel and a few corridors are open to the public. Visitors will not want to miss the Gregorian chants sung at vespers at 5pm every day.

Anyone who needs to meditate may stay in the guest quarters, where men and women are separated. The monks also raise Charolais cattle, run a dairy (where they make Ermite and Mont-Saint-Benoît cheeses) and have two orchards, which are used for producing cider.

Make sure to stop in the abbey shop, in the basement of the main building, for a selection of up to 10 excellent cheeses, as well as apple products like hard cider, vinegar and sauce that rivals homemade *(Mon-Sat 9:30am to 11am and 11:45am to 5:30pm; ☎819-843-4336 or 877-343-4336).*

Backtracking along Chemin Fisher, a little road on the left leads to a handsome **round barn**, built in 1907 by Damase Amédée Dufresne. It is not open to the public, but its exterior qualifies it all the same as one of the province's best examples of this style of barn, developed in the United States to withstand strong winds (and also to prevent the devil from hiding in a corner).

Austin's **Église Saint-Augustin-de-Cantorbéry**, formerly an Anglican church, stands at the intersection, along with a monument honouring the hamlet's most famous citizen, Reginald Aubrey Fessenden, who worked out the principle behind the transmission of the human voice by radio waves.

Turn right on the road leading to Magog. Between the houses, there are some lovely views of the lake and the abbey. Turn right on Rte. 112.

★
Magog
(pop. 14,600)

Equipped with more facilities than any other town between Granby and Sherbrooke, Magog has a lot to offer sports enthusiasts. It is extremely well situated on the northern shore of Lac

Round barn

Memphrémagog, but has unfortunately been subjected to unbridled development for several years now. The town's cultural scene is worth noting. Visitors can go to the theatre or the music complex, set in the natural mountain surroundings. The textile industry, once of great importance in the lives of local residents, has declined, giving way to tourism. Visitors will enjoy strolling down Rue Principale, which is lined with shops and restaurants.

The **Théâtre du Vieux-Clocher**, see p 211.

The **Parc du Mont-Orford ★★**, see p 197.

The **Centre d'Arts Orford ★** see p 211.

To get to Georgeville, take Rte. 247 S., which runs along the east coast of Lac Memphrémagog.

★
Georgeville
(pop. 1,000)

Most of director Denys Arcand's *Le Déclin de l'Empire américain* (*The Decline of the American Empire, 1986*) was shot in the heart of this area's rolling countryside, synonymous with relaxing vacations. For a long time now, the little village of Georgeville has been a favourite resort area among English-speaking families. The Molsons, for example, own an island in the vicinity. Various celebrities in search of seclusion have also purchased houses on the lake. In the 19th century, ferryboats from Newport, on the southernmost American part of the lake, and from Knowlton's Landing, on the western shore, would all stop at Georgeville, where a number of large wooden hotels once stood. All of these unfortunately burned to the ground; only the extremely pleasant **Auberge Georgeville** remains.

The **Vieille École** (Old School), the **Centre Culturel** (Cultural Centre) and **St. George's Church** (1866) are other buildings of significant historical interest. The quay offers a lovely view of the Abbaye de Saint-Benoît-du-Lac.

Fitch Bay

The **Narrows Covered Bridge** lies further along on Rte. 247 *(turn right on Chemin Merri, then left on Chemin Ridgewood)*. Though more expensive to build, covered bridges lasted much longer because they were protected from bad weather. Consequently, there are a number of them in Québec. This particular one, built in 1881, spans 28m across Fitch Bay. Just next to it, there is a small park with picnic tables.

The surrounding roads are pleasant to explore, especially **Magoon Point Road**, which offers sweeping views of the lake, and **Route de Tomifobia**, which could be straight out of a painting by Grant Wood or one of his fellow American Regionalists. Rte. 247 S. leads to **Beebe Plain**, a town known for its granite quarries, which have enjoyed a revival in popularity in recent years, as granite, either bluish or pinkish, has been used for the facing of many postmodern skyscrapers all over North America.

★
Rock Island
(pop. 1,110)

Note that the villages of Rock Island, Stanstead Plain and Beebe Plain now form one municipality known as Stanstead. Straddling the American border, Rock Island is one of the strangest villages in the province. Walking down its streets, visitors will find themselves in the United States in certain spots and in Canada in others. Notices written in French give way

suddenly to signs in English. The flagpole on Monsieur Thériault's lawn flies the Canadian maple leaf, while the Stars and Stripes unfurls in a patriotic and peaceable manner right next door. Its many beautiful stone, brick and wooden buildings make Rock Island a pleasant place to explore on foot.

The **Haskell Free Library and Opera House ★** (*at the corner of Church and Caswell*), which dates from 1904, is both a library and a theatre. Straddling on the Canadian-American border, it was built as a symbol of the friendship between the two nations. The architect, James Ball, drew his inspiration from Boston's opera house, which is no longer standing. A black line running diagonally across the interior of the building marks the exact location of the border, which corresponds to the 45th parallel.

Head north to Stanstead Plain on Rte. 143 N. (Rue Main, then Rue Dufferin).

★
Stanstead Plain
(pop. 885)

Some of the most beautiful houses in the Eastern Townships are located in this prosperous community. The distilleries of the 1820s, and later, the granite quarries, enabled a number of the area's inhabitants to amass large fortunes in the 19th century. Particularly noteworthy is the Renaissance Revival **Maison Butters** (1866), in the style of a Tuscan villa, and the **Maison Colby**, which is described below. The **Collège de Stanstead** (1930), the **Couvent des Ursulines** (a French-Canadian order of nuns from Québec City and an unusual institution in these parts), and the Methodist and Anglican churches, all merit a leisurely visit.

The **Musée Colby-Curtis** ★ (*$4; mid-Jun to mid-Sep, Tue-Sun 11am to 5pm; rest of the year, Tue-Fri 10am to noon and 1pm to 5pm, Sat and Sun 12:30pm to 4:30pm; 535 Rue Dufferin;* ☎819-876-7322*),* located in a house complete with all of its original furnishings, provides an excellent indication of how the local bourgeoisie lived during the second half of the 19th century. The residence, which has a grey granite facade, was built in 1859 for a lawyer named James Carroll Colby, who called it Carrollcroft.

Continue on Rte. 143 N. To make an optional detour to Coaticook and Compton, continue east on the 141.

Coaticook
(pop. 6,930)

Coaticook, which means "River of the Land of Pines" in the language of the Abenakis, is a small industrial town. It is surrounded by a large number of dairy farms, making it Québec's dairy capital. Its old railroad station is quite interesting.

Located in the heart of Coaticook's residential area, the **Musée Beaulne** ★ *($5; mid-May to mid-Sep, Tue-Sun 10am to 5pm; mid-Sep to mid-May, Wed-Sun 1pm to 4pm; 96 Rue de l'Union;* ☎819-849-6560*)* is located in a large wooden mansion built in 1912 for the Norton family. The house was designed in a mixture of the Queen Anne and Shingle styles, then popular in the United States. It stands amidst a large English garden. Some of its rooms have been kept in the style typical of bourgeois homes at the dawn of the 20th century, while others contain textile and costume displays.

The **Parc de la Gorge de Coaticook** ★ see p 197.

Head back toward Compton on Route 147 N.

Compton
(pop. 3,000)

This village's main claim to fame is the fact that it is the birthplace of Louis-Stephen Saint-Laurent, Prime Minister of Canada from 1948 to 1957. He is remembered above all for his role in establishing NATO. There are also many orchards in the area.

Louis S. Saint-Laurent National Historic Site *($4; mid-May to late Sep, every day 10am to 5pm; 6790 Route Louis-S.-St-Laurent,* ☎819-835-5448*)* preserves the house where Saint-Laurent was born and the general store alongside it, which belonged to his father, providing a glimpse into early-20th-century rural life. Visitors can also listen to snatches of conversation around the stove and enjoy a multimedia show recounting the major achievements of Louis S. St-Laurent and the main events in the history of Canada and the world. A tour of the family home will allow you to discover the lifestyle of bygone days and admire over 2,500 objects that once belonged to the St-Laurent family. Plays and various special activities are offered throughout the summer. The Louis S. St-Laurent National Historic Site is located in a dynamic region with a charming setting that is the delight of many visitors. There is also a beautiful garden and gift shop on the premises.

To return to the main tour, take Rte. 208 to Massawippi, then turn right on Rte. 243, which leads to North Hatley.

★★
North Hatley
(pop. 800)

Attracted by North Hatley's enchanting countryside, wealthy American vacationers built luxurious villas here between 1890 and 1930. Most of these still line the northern part of Lac Massawippi, which, like Lac Memphrémagog, resembles a Scottish loch. Beautiful inns and gourmet restaurants add to the charm of the place, ensuring its reputation as a vacation spot of the utmost sophistication. In the centre of the village, visitors will notice the tiny Shingle-style **United Church**, which looks more Catholic than Protestant.

Hovey Manor ★ (*Chemin Hovey*), a large villa built in 1900, was modelled on Mount Vernon, George Washington's home in Virginia. It used to be the summer residence of an American named Henry Atkinson, who entertained American artists and politicians here every summer. The house has since been converted into an inn.

Continue on Route 108 to Lennoxville.

A former copper mine, the **Mine Capelton** (*$17.75; all the necessary equipment provided for the visit; guided tour every hour; mid-May to*

Hovey Manor

late Jun and Sep and Oct Sat and Sun 10am to 3pm, Jul and Aug every day 10am to 3pm; 800 Rte. 108, ☎819-346-9545) was, around the 1880s, one of the most impressive and technologically advanced mining complexes in Canada and in the Commonwealth. Dug by hand, it runs 135m below the surface of Capel mountain. Besides its geological interest, the 2hr tour reveals the fascinating way in which miners lived and aspects of the first industrial revolution. Temperatures hover around 9°C, so wear warm clothing. There is also a nice hiking trail offering lookouts and interpretive signs.

★
Lennoxville
(pop. 4,850)

This little town, whose population is still mainly English-speaking, is home to two prestigious English-language educational institutions: Bishop's University and Bishop's College. Established alongside the road linking Trois-Rivières to the U.S. border, the town was named after Charles Lennox, the fourth Duke of Richmond, who was governor of Upper and Lower Canada in 1818. Once off the main road (Rte. 143) explore the town's side streets to see the institutional buildings and lovely Second Empire and Queen Anne houses nestled in greenery.

Thanks to changes made to it between 1847 and 1896, **St. George's Anglican Church** (Rue Queen) is one of the most charming and picturesque churches in the Eastern Townships.

Jefferson Davis, President of the Confederacy and one of the leading figures behind the southern states' secession from the Union in 1861, enjoyed staying with his family in the **Maison Cummings** (33

Rue Belvedere), a brick house erected in 1864.

Since 1988, the Maison Speid, built in 1862, has housed the **Centre culturel et du Patrimoine Uplands** (free admission; late Jun to early Sep Tue-Sun 1pm to 4:30pm; early Sep to late Jun Thu, Fri and Sun 1pm to 4:30pm; closed in Jan; 9 Rue Speid, ☎819-564-0409), where visitors can see exhibits evoking the richness of the region's past.

Bishop's University ★ (College Road), one of three English-language universities in Québec, offers 1,300 students from all over Canada a personalized education in an enchanting setting. It was founded in 1843, through the efforts of a minister named Lucius Doolittle. Upon arriving at the university, visitors will see **McGreer Hall**, built in 1876 by architect James Nelson and later modified by Taylor and Gordon of Montréal to give it a medieval look. **St. Mark's Anglican Chapel**, which stands to its left, was rebuilt in 1891 after a fire. Its long, narrow interior has a lovely oak trim, as well as stained-glass windows by Spence and Sons of Montréal.

The **Bishop-Champlain Art Gallery** (free admission; Tue-Sun noon to 5pm; closed Jul and Aug; on campus, ☎819-822-9600, ext. 2687) has a permanent collection of over 150 works of art, including paintings by 19th-century Canadian landscape artists. It also organizes multidisciplinary exhibitions between September and April.

Head back towards Rte. 143, which leads to Sherbrooke.

★★
Sherbrooke
(pop. 78,125)

Sherbrooke, the Eastern Townships' main urban area,

is nicknamed the Queen of the Eastern Townships. It spreads over a series of hills on both sides of the Rivière Saint-François, accentuating its disorderly appearance. An industrial city, it nevertheless has a number of interesting buildings, the majority of which are located on the west bank.

Sherbrooke's origins date back to the beginning of the 19th century; like so many other villages in the region, it grew up around a mill and a small market. However, in 1823, it was designated as the site of a courthouse intended to serve the entire region, which set it apart from the neighbouring communities. The arrival of the railroad here in 1852, as well as the downtown concentration of institutions, such as the head office of the Eastern Township Bank, led to the construction of prestigious Victorian edifices which transformed Sherbrooke's appearance. Today, the city is home to a large French-language university, founded in 1952 in order to counterbalance Bishop's University in Lennoxville. Despite the city's name, chosen in honour of Sir John Coape Sherbrooke, governor of British North America at the time it was founded, the city's population has been almost entirely French-speaking (95%) for a long time.

Rte. 143 leads to Rue Queen, inside the Sherbrooke city limits. Turn left on Rue King Ouest, then right on Rue Wellington, where we recommend parking in order to continue the tour of the city on foot.

The **Hôtel de Ville** ★ (145 Rue Wellington Nord), or city hall, occupies the former Courthouse (the city's third), a granite building dating from 1904 that was designed by Elzéar Charest, head architect of the Department of Public Works. It is an

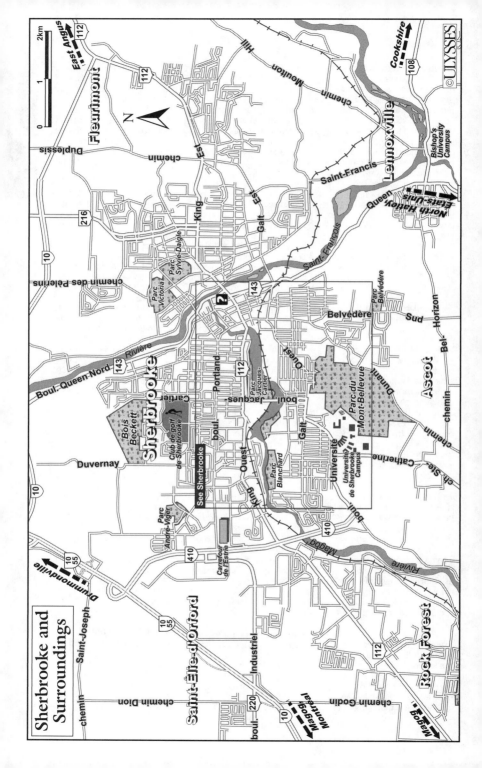

Sherbrooke and Surroundings

©ULYSSES

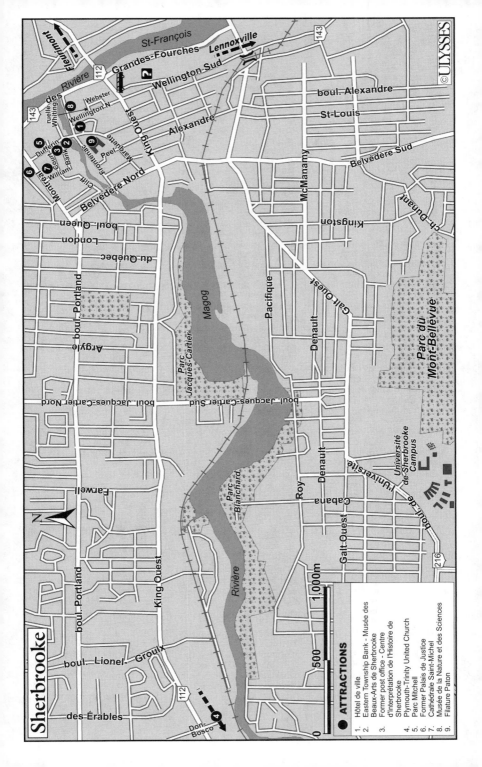

Sherbrooke

ATTRACTIONS

1. Hôtel de ville
2. Eastern Township Bank - Musée des Beaux-Arts de Sherbrooke
3. Former post office - Centre d'interprétation de l'Histoire de Sherbrooke
4. Plymouth-Trinity United Church
5. Parc Mitchell
6. Former Palais de Justice
7. Cathédrale Saint-Michel
8. Musée de la Nature et des Sciences
9. Filature Paton

© ULYSSES

example of Quebecers' enduring fondness for Second Empire architecture, with its French spirit. Visitors will recognize the segmental arches, the corner pavillions topped by false mansard roofs with wrought-iron cresting and the bull's-eye characteristic of the style. Strathcona Square, the garden in front of the Hôtel de Ville, marks the exact site of the market square that played such an important role in Sherbrooke's early development.

Turn left on Rue Frontenac, then right on Rue Dufferin, which crosses the frothy rapids of Rivière Magog, whose force was harnessed in the 19th century in order to provide power for the many mills located along the river.

An important financial institution in the 19th century, now merged with the CIBC (Canadian Imperial Bank of Commerce), the former **Eastern Townships Bank ★ ★** (*241 Rue Dufferin*) was established by the region's upper class, who were unable to obtain financing for local projects from the banks in Montréal. Its Sherbrooke head office, erected in 1877, was designed by Montréal architect James Nelson, involved at the time in building Bishop's University. It is considered the finest Second Empire building in Québec outside of Montréal and Québec City.

Following a donation from the Canadian Imperial Bank of Commerce (CIBC) and major renovations, the building now houses the **Musée des Beaux-Arts de Sherbrooke** (*$4; Tue-Sun 1pm to 5pm, Wed to 9pm; late Jun to early Sep 11am to 5pm, Wed to 9pm; 241 Rue Dufferin, ☎819-821-2115*). Gérard Gendron's work, which greets visitors in the main hall, reflects the building's former tenants and its present vocation. Besides the museum's

large collection of folk art, there are several works by local contemporary artists. Volunteers are available to answer questions on the exhibitions, which usually change every two months.

The bank and the **former post office** (*275 Rue Dufferin, ☎819-821-5406*) next door, designed by François-Xavier Berlinguet (1885), form a fine architectural ensemble. The post office houses the offices of the **Centre d'Interprétation de l'Histoire de Sherbrooke** (*$6; Tue-Fri 9am to noon and 1pm to 5pm; Jul and Aug, Tue-Fri 9am to 5pm, Sat and Sun 10am to 5pm; 275 Rue Dufferin, ☎819-821-5406*), an interpretive centre on Sherbrooke's history. The centre organizes architectural and historical tours of the city, and rents audio tapes (*$6*) for walking or driving tours.

Designed in 1851 by William Footner, the **Plymouth-Trinity United Church** (*380 Rue Dufferin*), seems to come straight out of a New England village, due to its size, as well as the building materials (red brick and wood painted white). Originally used by the Congregationalists, it was given its present name after several Protestant denominations united to form the United Church in 1925.

Continue on to Parc Mitchell.

Some of the loveliest houses in Sherbrooke are located on **Parc Mitchell ★ ★**, which is adorned with a fountain by sculptor George Hill (1921). **Maison Morey** (*not open to visitors; 428 Rue Dufferin*), is an example of the bourgeois Victorian style favoured by merchants and industrialists from the British Isles and the United States. It was built in 1873 for Thomas Morey.

Walk around the park, then down Rue Montréal, and turn left on Rue Williams.

Facing straight down the center of Rue Court, the **former Palais de Justice ★** (*Rue Williams*), Sherbrooke's second courthouse, was converted into a drill hall for the city's Hussards regiment at the end of the 19th century. Built in 1839 according to a design by William Footner, the edifice has a lovely neoclassical facade similar to another of his designs, the Marché Bonsecours (see p 87) in Montréal.

Head back toward Rue Dufferin on Rue Bank. Turn right on Rue Marquette and climb the hill in the direction of the seminary and the cathedral.

Seen from a certain distance, the **Cathédrale Saint-Michel** (*Rue Marquette*) looks like a European abbey church perched on a promontory. The cathedral's medieval air contrasts with the city's neoclassical past. Up close, however, it becomes apparent that the structure was built very recently and never completed. Begun by the architect Louis-Napoléon Audet in 1917, this Gothic Revival cathedral wasn't consecrated until 1958.

The Séminaire Saint-Charles, built in 1898, now houses the **Musée de la Nature et des Sciences ★** (*$7.50; Tue-Sun 10am to 5pm; 225 Rue Frontenac, ☎819-564-3200*), where visitors can see bird, plant and mineral collections, as well as interesting oil paintings, watercolours, sculptures and objects handmade by Aboriginal people.

Formerly a museum established by priests at the Séminaire de Sherbrooke, this brand new museum now focuses on the natural sciences and is primarily aimed at young people. In addition to travelling exhibits, the museum has a permanent collection of 65,000 objects collected by the priests and a permanent exhibit that explains the annual cycle of nature in southern Québec.

Continue on Rue Marquette towards the former Filature Paton, located on Rue Belvedere.

Sherbrooke's former textile industry started up in the second half of the 19th century, and was very profitable, as it was in many New England towns. The **Filature Paton ★** *(at the end of Rue Marquette)*, once the most important textile mill in the Eastern Townships, operated from 1866 to 1977. It was scheduled for demolition the year it closed, but after a few visits over the border, where many such factories have been converted into housing and businesses, the municipal authorities decided to preserve a number of the buildings for a multi-functional complex. Today, the mill is not only a model of how an area's industrial heritage may be preserved and such spaces transformed, but also a new focus for downtown Sherbrooke.

To return to Montréal, take Rte. 143 N. to Aut. 10 and head west.

Tour C: The Back Country

Duration of tour: two days

This most isolated part of the Eastern Townships is composed of an alternating series of mountains and plains. Long, deserted stretches of road link the local Loyalist villages. Far from the urban centres, these communities have in many cases remained primarily English-speaking and have retained their old-fashioned

charm. The area around Mont Mégantic was colonized in the early 19th century by Scottish settlers from the Hebrides, and Gaelic was commonly spoken here 100 years ago. French Canadians from the Rivière Chaudière valley (Beauce) began arriving at the end of the 19th century.

In Cookshire, pick up Rte. 212 E., which leads through the villages of Island Brook, West Ditton and La Patrie, offering beautiful views of Mont Mégantic. Continue on to Notre-Dame-des-Bois.

Notre-Dame-des-Bois (pop. 710)

Located in the heart of the Appalachians at an altitude of over 550m, this little community acts as a gateway to Mont Mégantic and its observatory, as well as Mont Saint-Joseph and its sanctuary.

From Notre-Dame-des-Bois, take the road in front of the church toward Val Racine. After 3.3km, turn left (after the Rivière aux Saumons). On the left, before the road starts heading upward, there is a tourist information booth. Several kilometres further, you will reach a junction. The road on the left leads to the observatory.

The **ASTROlab du Mont-Mégantic ★★** *(from $10; mid-May to mid-Jun Sat noon to 5pm and 8pm to 11pm, Sun noon to 5pm; late Jun to late Aug every day noon to 7:30pm and 8pm to 11pm; late Aug to mid-Oct Sat noon to 5pm andt 8pm to 11pm, Sun noon to 5pm; 189 Route du Parc, ☎866-888-2941)* is an interpretive centre focusing on astronomy. The interactive museum's various rooms and multime-

dia show reveal the beginnings of astronomy with the latest technology. A guided tour to the summit of Mont Mégantic, lasting approximately 1hr 15min, walks visitors through the facilities. Famous for its observatory, Mont Mégantic was chosen for its strategic location between the Universities of Montreal and Laval, as well as its distance from urban light sources. The second-highest summit in the Eastern Townships, it stands at 1,105m.

During the **Festival d'Astronomie Populaire du Mont Mégantic**, a local astronomy festival held the second week of July, astronomy buffs can observe the heavens through the most powerful telescope in eastern North America. Otherwise, the latter is only available to researchers. However, a new observatory with a 60cm telescope is now open to the public. In summer, basic celestial mechanics workshops are also given.

Head back to Rte. 212 E. At Woburn, take Rte. 161 N., which runs along beautiful Lac Mégantic.

A vast expanse of crystal-clear water stretching 17km, **Lac Mégantic ★★** is teeming with all sorts of fish, especially trout, and attracts a good many vacationers eager to go fishing or simply enjoy the local beaches. Five municipalities

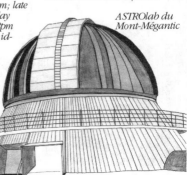

ASTROlab du Mont-Mégantic

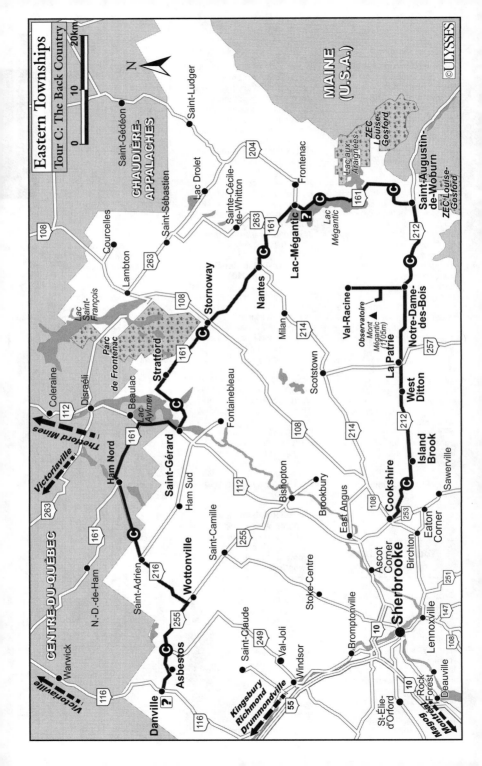

around the lake, Lac-Mégantic being the best-known, welcome visitors lured by the lovely mountainous countryside.

★ Lac-Mégantic (pop. 6,000)

The town of Lac-Mégantic was founded in 1885 by Scottish settlers from the Hebrides. Unable to make enough money from the relatively poor soil, the residents soon turned to forestry. Today, thousands of people come to the region every year to enjoy a wide variety of sporting activities. The town is beautifully located on the shores of Lac Mégantic.

In the **Église Sainte-Agnès** ★ (*4872 Rue Laval*), erected in 1913, visitors will discover a beautiful stained-glass window designed in 1849 for the Catholic Church of the Immaculate Conception in Mayfair, London.

*The road then leads through the villages of **Nantes** and **Stornoway**, **Stratford** and **Saint-Gérard**, passing alongside the Parc de Frontenac and skirting round Lac Aylmer before connecting with Route 216 and Route 255, which lead to Asbestos.*

The **Parc de Frontenac** ★ see p 387.

Asbestos (pop. 6,800)

Asbestos, as its name indicates, is one of the foremost asbestos-mining centres in the world. Asbestos releases harmful particles when improperly handled, which led to it being banned by the United States and a subsequent decline in mining activity in the town of Asbestos.

A bus excursion takes visitors to the **JM Asbestos Mine** (*$8;*

late May to late Jun and Sep Sun 1pm, early Jul to late Aug Wed-Sun 1pm; Boulevard St-Luc, ☎819-839-2911). The most spectacular attraction here is without a doubt the gargantuan fleet of 125-ton CAT 789 trucks, whose wheels measure 2m in diameter.

The **Musée Minéralogique et d'Histoire Minière** (*$1; late Jun to mid-Aug Wed-Sun 11am to 5pm; 345 Boulevard St-Luc, ☎819-879-6444 or 879-5308*), a museum outlining mineralogy and the history of mining, includes samples of asbestos from different mines both in Québec and abroad.

★ Danville (pop. 4,520)

This attractive, shady village has preserved a number of noteworthy Victorian and Edwardian residences, which bear witness to a time when wealthy Montréal families summered in Danville.

Parks

Tour A: The Orchards

The **Parc de de la Yamaska** (*$3.50; every day 8am until sundown; 1780 Boulevard David-Bouchard, Roxton Pond, ☎450-776-7182, www.sepaq.com*) was laid out around the Réservoir Choinière, now a pleasant swimming area. In winter, there are 40km of cross-country ski trails available for public use.

Just a few kilometres from downtown Granby, the **Centre d'Interprétation de la Nature du Lac Boivin** (*free admission; every day 8.30am to 4.30pm; 700 Rue Drum-*

mond, Granby, ☎450-375-3861) offers four trails along the marshy shores of the lake. An observation tower and blind offer good vantage points for aquatic plants and a variety of water birds. Mornings, when the trails are less busy, are the best time for birding. The paths are also open in the winter. There are temporary exhibits throughout the year in the information centre.

Tour B: The Lakes

The **Parc du Mont-Orford** ★★ (*$3.50; 3321 chemin du parc, Canton-d'Orford, ☎819-843-9855 or 877-843-9855, www.sepaq. com*) stretches over 58km² and includes—in addition to the mountain—the area around Lac Stukely. During the summer, visitors can enjoy the beach, the magnificent golf course (*$30 a round*), back-country campsites, and some 50km of hiking trails (the most beautiful path leads to Mont Chauve). The park also attracts winter sports lovers with its cross-country ski trails and 33 downhill ski runs.

The **Parc de la Gorge de Coaticook** ★ (*fee varies by activity; early May to late Jun, every day 10am to 5pm; late Jun to early Sep, every day 9am to 8pm; early Sep to late Oct, every day 10am to 5pm; Nov to May, Thu and Fri 6pm to 9pm, Sat 1pm to 4pm and 6pm to 9pm, Sun 11am to 5pm; 135 Rue Michaud and 400 Rue St-Marc, Coaticook, ☎888-524-6743*) protects the part of the impressive 50m gorge created by the Rivière Coaticook. Trails wind across the entire area, enabling visitors to see the gorge from different angles. Cross the suspension bridge over the gorge, if you dare!

Maple Syrup

By the time the first colonists arrived in America, the various indigenous cultures had already been enjoying maple syrup for a long time. In fact, it is impossible to determine when exactly the Aboriginals first discovered the sweet liquid. According to an Iroquois legend, it happened like this: Woksis, the Great Chief, headed out hunting one morning. The night had been cold, but the day promised to be warm. The day before, he had left his tomahawk stuck in a maple tree, and when he removed it, sap began to flow from the crack in the wood. The sap flowed into a bucket that happened to be sitting under the hole. Later, Woksis's wife needed water to prepare the evening meal. Upon seeing the bucket full of sap, she thought it would spare her a trip to the river. An intelligent and conscientious woman who hated waste, she tasted the water and found it a bit on the sweet side, but nevertheless good, and used it to make the meal. On his way home, Woksis smelled the sweet scent of maple from far away and knew something extra special was coo-

king. The sap had turned into syrup, making the meal positively succulent. And thus was born one of North America's sweetest traditions. Natives did not have the necessary materials to heat a cauldron at very high temperatures, so they used heated rocks, which they dropped into the water to make it boil. Another method was to let the maple water freeze overnight, then remove the layer of ice the following morning, repeating this process until nothing remained but a thick syrup. Maple syrup played a prominent role in the Aboriginal diet, culture and religion. The syrup-making methods used today were handed down by Europeans, who taught them to the natives.

Technological advances have led to great changes in the way maple products are made. The sugar season is in the spring, when nighttime temperatures are still below zero and days are warm, enabling the sap to flow more easily. The temperature thus plays a key role in the production of maple syrup. The first step is to carve a hole about 2.5cm deep in the maple trees, 1m from

the ground. A spout is then inserted in the hole and the sap flows either into a bucket or through a series of pipes leading to the sugar shack. In the case of the former, the sap must be collected every morning. Of course, the latter system is more common, and only small outfits still use the traditional bucket method.

Once it reaches the sugar shack, the sap is boiled to reduce it to syrup. When the liquid reaches 7°C above boiling, it becomes maple syrup. If it is boiled longer, until it reaches 14.5°C above boiling, it becomes maple taffy (*tire*), a real treat when poured onto the snow. It is also possible to make other products, such as maple sugar, maple butter and maple candy, but these all require more careful preparation.

Come springtime, Quebecers head off to the woods to go sugaring-off and enjoy those mainstays of the sugar shack menu, *oreilles de Christ* (literally Christ's ears, actually deep-fried lard), *œufs dans le sirop* (eggs in syrup) and *tire* (taffy) on snow.

Tour C: The Back Country

Known mainly for its famed observatory (see p 195), the **Parc du Mont-Mégantic** (*$3.50; every day 9am to 5pm, to 11pm during astronomy evenings; no pets allowed; 189 Route du Parc, Notre-Dame-des-Bois, ☎866-888-2941, www.sepaq.com*) covers an area of 58.8km². It displays the different types of mountainous vegetation characteristic of the Eastern Townships and contains the Mont St-Joseph and Mont Mégantic hills. Heavy infrastructure has not been able to disturb the tranquillity of this park, whose purpose is educational. Hikers and skiers can take advantage of the park's interpretive trails, cabins and campsites and, if lucky, observe up to 125 species of migrating birds. Snowshoeing in winter and mountain-biking in summer.

Outdoor Activities

Hiking

Tour A: The Orchards

The **Sentier de l'Estrie** (*☎450-297-0654*) is a network of more than 150km of trails through the Chapman, Kingsbury, Brompton, Orford, Bolton, Glen, Echo and Sutton areas. You can obtain a topographical map of the trail and the membership card necessary to walk it for $30. Keep in mind that most of the trail runs across private property. The various landowners have accorded an exclusive right of way to members.

Tour B: The Lakes

Parc d'Environnement Naturel de Sutton (*☎450-538-4085 or 800-565-8455*) is just as popular in the summer as in winter. The **Roundtop** hike, with its spectacular panoramas, attracts hikers from far and wide.

Parc du Mont-Orford (*☎819-843-9855 or 877-843-9855*) is a prized hiking spot in the Townships. Several sections of the **Sentier de l'Estrie** traverse it. It is an excellent choice for hikers as it contains a network of over 80km of trails of varying degrees of difficulty. The **Mont Chauve** and **Mont Orford** hikes are particularly interesting.

Tour C: The Back Country

Eight trails crisscross the **Parc du Mont-Mégantic**, totalling 60km of hiking trails. The latest one, traversing Mont Mégantic and the crests of Monts Victoria and St. Joseph, is certainly among the most beautiful in the region. Also, this network is now connected to the **Sentiers Frontaliers** (*☎819-549-2037 or 800-363-5515*), which encompass an area straddling the U.S. border.

Cycling

Tour A: The Orchards

The **Estriade** bicycle path runs along an old railway line. It covers 21km, linking Granby, Bromont and Waterloo.

La Station de Vélo de Montagne de Bromont (*150 Rue Champlain, Bromont, ☎450-534-2006, 450-534-2200 or 866-BROMONT*) has close to 100km of intermediate and expert level trails.

Bikers can also use the chairlift (*$13 for a lift, $27 for several*).

Tour B: The Lakes

The **parc du Mont-Orford** (*$3.50; Magog, ☎819-843-9855 or 877-843-9855*), may not be as popular as Bromont for mountain biking, but it nevertheless offers three trails for a total of 40km of easy, difficult and very difficult opportunities.

Horseback Riding

The **Centre Équestre de Bromont** (*100 Rue Laprairie, ☎450-534-3255*) hosted the 1976 Olympic equestrian events, for which a variety of stables and rings, both exterior and interior, were built. Some of these facilities are now used for riding classes.

Cruises

The **Croisières Memphrémagog** (*regular cruises $15, one-day cruises $55; mid-May to late Sep: regular cruises from 10am, reservations required for one-day cruises; Quai de Magog, ☎819-843-8068 or 888-842-8068*) offer 2hr cruises on magnificent Lac Memphrémagog, whose shores form part of both the Québec and U.S. borders. At around 9am, a second, one-day cruise leaves the wharf for Vermont where it makes a brief call at Newport. These cruises are all the more spectacular in the fall when the colours are at their brightest. Fares include a light snack. Reservations required.

Golf

Much valued for its quality green, the **Owl's Head** (*$45; 181 Chemin Owl's Head, Mansonville, ☎450-292-3666 or 800-363-3342*) golf course is easily the favourite amongst local golfers. Moreover, it is endowed with a very posh clubhouse and offers a superb view of the mountain after which it was named. Chances of teeing off are better on weekdays.

The **Dufferin Heights** (*$35; 4115 Route 143, Stanstead, ☎819-876-2113*) golf course, which recently celebrated its 75th anniversary, puts even the staunchest of golfers to the test. Its undulating terrain offers splendid views of the Appalachian Mountains and of lakes Massawippi and Memphrémagog.

Downhill Skiing

Tour A: The Orchards

The **Station de Ski Bromont** (*$39; 150 Rue Champlain, Bromont, ☎450-534-2200 or 866-BROMONT*) has 45 runs, 20 of which are lit for night-skiing (*Mon-Thu to 10pm, Fri and Sat to 10:30pm*). The mountain has a vertical drop of over 400m.

Tour B: The Lakes

The **Station de Ski du Mont Sutton** (*$41; 671 Chemin Maple, Sutton, ☎450-538-2545*) has 53 downhill ski runs and a vertical drop of 460m. It is known for its magnificent glade runs.

Mont Orford (*$36; Magog, ☎819-843-6548 or 800-567-*

2772), among the most attractive ski centres in Québec, offers 52 trails that will please everyone. It has a vertical drop of 540m.

Owl's Head (*$32; Chemin du Mont Owl's Head, Mansonville, ☎450-292-3342 or 800-363-3342*) is one of the most beautiful ski resorts in the Eastern Townships region, with sweeping views of Lac Memphrémagog and the surrounding mountains. Owl's Head will mainly please beginners and intermediate skiers, as there are no trails to challenge experts.

Cross-country Skiing

Tour B: The Lakes

The Sutton region is not only ideal for downhill skiing and hiking, but is also home to a superb network of cross-country ski trails. The **Sutton-en-Haut network** (*$6.95; 297 Rue Maple, Sutton-en-Haut, ☎450-538-2271*) includes 15 interconnected trails that allow skiers to switch tracks and levels of difficulty throughout the day.

Parc du Mont Orford (*$10; Magog-Orford, ☎819-843-9855*) also has a network of cross-country trails with a good reputation. Thirteen trails cover some 80km of terrain that will please all levels.

Tour C: The Back Country

The 82km-long **Centre de Ski de Fond Bellevue** (*$8; 70 Chemin Lay, Melbourne, ☎819-826-3869*) is a pleasant surprise. Fifteen trails for all levels.

Besides its famed observatory and excellent snow conditions, Parc du Mont-Mégantic has eight cross-country ski trails.

The **Sentiers du Mont-Mégantic** (*$8; Chemin de l'Observatoire, 189 Route du Parc, Notre-Dame-des-Bois, ☎866-888-2941*) offers one of the longest ski seasons in the province. Because of its altitude, skiing sometimes lasts into the month of May!

Adventure Packages

Tour B: The Lakes

A young and dynamic enterprise, the **Adrénaline** (*☎819-843-0045 or 888-475-3462*) outdoor-adventure school has an experienced staff and offers different activities, such as dogsledding expeditions, ice climbing, ice fishing and snowshoeing in winter and anything from beginners' rock climbing and river kayaking to panoramic rafting. In short, a host of activities for thrill-seekers! Prices include instructors and the required equipment. Personalized activities are also available upon request. Reservations required.

Accommodations

Tour A: The Orchards

Dunham

Le Temps des Mûres
$$
≈, pb/sb
202 Chemin Vail
☎(450) 266-1319
☎888-708-8050
≠(450) 266-1303
Located on a 160ha maple-tree farm on a scenic road lined by a tunnel of towering trees, Le Temps des Mûres could be just the spot you've dreamt of—that is, if you

dream of authentic country atmosphere at a very honest price. This handsome gabled brick farmhouse offers five cozy guest rooms, each with a planked wood floor and a duvet to snuggle under. A full breakfast is served at a long, communal wooden table. Children welcome.

Pom-Art B&B
$$ bkfst incl.
677 Chemin Hudon
☎*(450) 295-3514*
☎*888-537-6627*
Pom-Art, a blue-clapboard farmhouse built in 1820 and surrounded by orchards, is located near Lac Selby, just outside the village of Dunham. The decor is getting rather tired, particularly the shag carpeting, but the price is right, and hosts Denis and Lise offer guests a warm welcome, not to mention an exceptional breakfast where apples from the region figure prominently. The largest of the three rooms offers a view of the surrounding mountains.

Cowansville

Le Passe-Partout
$$ bkfst incl.
pb/sb
167 Route Pierre-Laporte
☎*(450) 260-1678*
www.passepartout.ca
Although you probably won't be spending much time in the industrial town of Cowansville, this bed and breakfast, with helpful, easygoing hosts and a casual atmosphere, has all the makings of a pleasant stay within easy reach of every point of interest on this tour. A former farmhouse built in 1865, each of its four smallish guest rooms has wide-plank wood floors, a ceiling fan and a unique decor, which ranges from a red-and-black Japanese-themed room to a cheery little blue-and-yellow number.

Bromont

Camping Parc Bromont
$
≈
24 Rue Lafontaine
☎*(450) 534-2712*
www.campingbromont.com
Camping Bromont has every convenience, including showers, laundry room, a swimming pool, hiking trails—even miniature golf! Most sections are wooded, providing campers with some privacy.

Casa Bromont
$$ bkfst incl.
1208 Rue Shefford
☎*(450) 534-2429*
www.casabromont.com
Enthusiastic young hosts Melanie and Sassan have transformed their *casa*, located on a tranquil 1ha property with access to their own swimming hole, into a welcoming B&B with three guest rooms. The burgundy Zen room has an in-room clawfoot tub and toilet (not for shy types), the Sahara has a big in-room tub and separate toilet, and the serene and cozy Green Dream has wide-plank wood floors and a private bathroom down the hall. Breakfasts may include eggs from their own hens, as well as home-baked goods, a hot dish and espresso.

Auberge Bromont
$$$
≡, ≈, ℜ
C.P. 510
95 Rue Montmorency
☎*(450) 554-3133*
☎*877-946-5325*
⇄*(450) 534-1700*
www.aubergebromont.com
Auberge Bromont is located near the town's golf course and ski hill. Purchased by the owners of the Château Bromont in 2002, Auberge Bromont is in the process of a renovation that its 50 dreary rooms had been needing for years. Although they were not yet completed when we visited, the place has loads of potential: it's beautifully set in

grounds surrounded by mature trees, and the reception is friendly.

Hôtel le Menhir
$$$
≡, ⊛, K, ℑ, ≈
125 Boulevard Bromont
☎*(450) 534-3790*
☎*800-461-3790*
⇄*(450) 534-1933*
www.hotellemenhir.com
Stretched out alongside the road leading to Mont Bromont, Hôtel Le Menhir, has some 40 decently furnished rooms. Package rates including breakfast and a day of skiing or golf are available.

Château Bromont
$$$$$
≡, ℑ, ☉, ≈, ℝ, ℜ, ◘, ☻, ♿, ⊛
90 Standstead
☎*(450) 534-3433*
☎*800-304-3433*
⇄*(450) 534-0514*
www.chateaubromont.com
Those looking for comfort and elegance should head to the Château Bromont. There is a variety of room configurations and styles, ranging from split-level rooms with the bed either at the top or bottom of a spiral staircase (unfortunately the decor of some of these is rather cold) to elegant suites and junior suites. The latter, featuring elegant neutral tones and balconies, are among the most attractive. All guest rooms feature robes and a pillow menu that allows you to choose the type that's just right for your noggin! The property is located alongside Mont Bromont, providing skiers with easy access to the slopes, via a shuttle bus.

Granby

Parc de la Yamaska
$
1780 Boulevard David-Bouchard
☎*450-776-7182*
Parc de la Yamaska has recently made campsites available to those with tents. Their arrangement doesn't offer much privacy, but they are located close to the pleasant

beach, an ideal spot for family relaxation.

Le Granbyen
$$-$$$
≡, ⊛, ≈, ℛ
700 Rue Principale
☎(450) 378-8406
☎800-267-8406

A typical roadside hotel for travellers on the move, Le Granbyen has decent but nondescript rooms.

Tour B: The Lakes

Around Lac Brome

Camping Domaine des Érables
$
688 Chemin Bondville, Rte. 215
☎(450) 242-8888
☎888-242-8888

Located on the shores of Lac Brome, the well-kept Camping Domaine des Érables offers all the comforts of life with its laundromat, showers, convenience store and other services. In short, those who swear by wilderness camping should give this place a miss.

Auberge Joli Vent
$$ bkfst incl.
≈, ℛ
667 Chemin Bondville, Foster
☎(450) 243-4272
⇄(450) 243-0202
www.aubergedujoli
vent.com

Auberge Joli Vent is a lovely inn with a pleasant setting, despite its roadside location. The modestly furnished rooms have a rustic charm.

Knowlton

La Venise Verte
$$ bkfst incl.
≈, pb/sb
58 Rue Victoria
☎(450) 243-1844
www.laveniseverte.com

This handsome brick home (1884) is a good alternative to its much pricier next-door neighbour, Auberge Lakeview Inn. Hosts Sylvie and Pierre have four guest rooms, three

of which have wide-planked wood floors. All are attractive and simply furnished with a mixture of antique and modern accessories; beds have cozy duvets and walls are painted soothing shades of blue, beige or ginger. Breakfasts feature organic products.

Auberge Knowlton
$$$ bkfst incl.
✖, ℛ
286 Chemin Knowlton
☎(450) 242-6886
⇄(450) 242-1055

A 12-room inn smack dab in the centre of town, Auberge Knowlton, built in 1849, has stood the test of time. Recently renovated, each room is different, but all have duvets, art posters, sparkling new bathroom tiles, individual heat control and ceiling fans, and are tastefully furnished with a mixture of antiques, reproductions and salvaged items, many of which are for sale. Guest rooms are on the small side, but large enough to open the hideabed provided in each. The main sour note is that the inn is situated on a busy road and trucks pass as of early morning; if you plan on sleeping until a reasonable hour, ask for a room at the rear, such as our favourite, no. 3, which has a high cathedral ceiling and sage-green walls.

Auberge Lakeview
$$$$$ ½b
⊗, ≈, ℛ, ⊛
50 Rue Victoria
☎(450) 243-6183
☎800-661-6183
⇄(450) 243-0602

Ideally located right in the village of Knowlton but off the main drag, Auberge Lakeview offers a thoroughly Victorian atmosphere. Indeed, renovations have restored some of the noble antiquity to this historic monument, built in the latter half of the 19th century. Cozy and romantic, the place is all oak and Victorian-style flowered wallpaper. Unfortunately, the standard guest rooms are absolutely

miniscule; the bathrooms are barely large enough to contain a shower stall. Though pricier, the studios, furnished with rustic, antique-style furniture, are a much better idea. There's a cozy pub on site, as well as a formal dining room.

Sutton

Auberge Le St-Amour
$$-$$$
K, ℛ
1 Rue Pleasant
☎(450) 538-6188
☎888-538-6188
www.auberge-st-amour.com

Occupying an imposing greenclapboard Second Empire residence (1902) right in the centre of town, Auberge Le St-Amour offers eight guest rooms and a two-bedroom suite with kitchenette, each decorated with murals honouring the French Impressionists. Unfortunately, most of the rooms are very dark and sombre, despite the flowery murals; most have cheap carpetting, others rough plywood floors. Room no. 8 is among the most attractive, with a Van Gogh–sun mural and a window seat; no. 9 and no. 7 are also good choices.

Dessine-Moi un Mouton
$$$ bkfst incl.
℥, ≈, ℛ
212 Chemin Maple
☎(450) 538-1515

If you don't mind paying a trifle more than for an average B&B after a day on (or off) the slopes, look no further. Dessine-Moi un Mouton ("draw me a sheep," a line from *The Little Prince*), a blue-and-white clapboard house on a large plot of land outside the village, is the perfect spot to spoil yourself. Chef Marc and artist Ginette (the latter is the painter of the B&B's whimsical sheep portraits) have created an elegant yet understated haven that is nothing like the bland ski condos along this road. The two romantic and cozy guest rooms and one studio are decorated with flair in cream and white and have their own private patios. All bathrooms feature a deep soaker tub, all beds lovely linens. Marc serves intimate dinners on Saturdays ($60/pers, bring your own wine) in an airy dining room with six tables. Children welcome, inquire about pets.

Auberge La Paimpolaise
$$$
≡, ≈, ℜ, ⊛
C. P. 548
615 Rue Maple
☎*(450) 538-3213*
☎*800-263-3213*
⇄*(450) 538-3970*
www.paimpolaise.com
Auberge La Paimpolaise is housed in two separate buildings. The reception area is located in a small, wooden, Swiss-chalet-style house, and the rooms are in a long concrete annex. This is a very plain hotel, with rather austere guest rooms, that caters mainly to skiers.

Vale Perkins (Knowlton's Landing)

Aubergine Relais de Campagne
$$ bkfst incl.
ℜ
160 Rue Cooledge
☎*(450) 292-3246*
www.laubergine.com
The Aubergine Relais de Campagne occupies a former post house dating from 1816. Built out of red brick, it has a long wooden veranda perfect for summer evenings. This inn is all the more pleasant for the gorgeous view it offers of Lac Memphrémagog.

Eastman

Spa Eastman
$$$$$ bkfst incl.
pb/sb, ✪, ≈, ℜ, ℨ
895 Chemin Des Diligences
☎*(450) 297-3009*
☎*800-665-5272*
⇄*297-3370*
www.spa-eastman.com
Nestled in the countryside, Spa Eastman is considered by some to be one of the best establishments of its kind on the planet. The whole gamet of body-care treatments is available here, either individually or in a package, by the day or during an extended stay, but always with the utmost in professionalism. And for the spirit, there's nothing better than a walk in the forest or cozying up with a book by the fire. Guests can also stay simply for the beauty and tranquility of the setting, without availing themselves of the spa. A large main wing and five smaller ones house 45 well-decorated guest rooms, ranging from the simple to the luxurious. The restaurant serves three healthy meals a day.

Bolton Centre

L'Iris Bleu
$$-$$$ bkfst incl.
ℜ
895 Chemin Missisquoi
☎*(450) 292-3530*
☎*877-292-3530*
Iris Bleue is a charming bed and breakfast. The lace curtains, flowered wallpaper and antique furniture decorating the rooms exude a warm atmosphere. You will be welcomed by the friendly owners, who go out of their way to make your stay a pleasant one. A Mediterranean-style evening meal *($$)* is served in the adorable dining room.

Magog

À Tout Venant
$$ bkfst incl.
624 Rue Bellevue Ouest
☎*(819) 868-0419*
☎*888-611-5577*
À Tout Venant was recently purchased by a couple from Lyon, France. Their five guest rooms are all located very close to one another, so soundproofing is not guaranteed. Our choice is the smallish and least expensive Soleil room, which has a wood floor and antiques. Abricot, with its own solarium, is also a pleasant option; the others, like the Rose, are entirely too froufrou to recommend. Lovely, sunny breakfast room.

Gîte de la Maison Hôte
$$ bkfst incl.
≈
2037 Chemin du Parc
☎*(819) 868-2604*
Christiane and Bernard skilfully transformed this clapboard house into a B&B in 1999 and have been the perfect hosts ever since. Their four impeccable guest rooms feature wood floors, attractive bedding and plenty of country cachet; some offer a view of Mont Orford. Guests rave about the absolutely sublime five-course breakfasts, which feature edible flowers and a seat on the patio (both in season, of course). An excellent place to base yourself in the Magog/Orford area and a definite step above many of the options in downtown Magog, which is just a short drive away.

Au Virage
$$
pb/sb
172 Rue Merry N.
☎*(819) 868-5828*
Situated in the heart of Magog and surrounded by many other B&Bs, Au Virage is a very acceptable option. Hosts Louise and Jean live in the attached house so there are no personal items cluttering the B&B, which retains a very

subdued, almost spartan decor. Their five guest rooms are rather small (those with pb are larger) and are decorated either with subdued colours or with burgundy and peach, the latter lending a rather dated look, and some strange art choices. However, a few antiques, wood floors and flowered fabrics warm them up. Rather elaborate breakfasts are served at a common table to encourage guests to socialize.

Motel de la Pente Douce
$$ bkfst incl.
K, ≈
1787 Chemin de la Rivière-aux-Cerises, R.R.2
☎(819) 843-1234
☎800-567-3530
***www.moteldelapente
douce.qbc.net***
The little Motel de la Pente Douce is plain-looking, but well-located near Mont Orford and offers decent rooms.

L'Ancestrale
$$-$$$
⊛, *pb/sb*
200 Rue Abott
☎(819) 847-5555
www.ancestrale.qc.ca
L'Ancestrale offers a simple, somewhat cluttered and very homey decor. The best of the four guest rooms is La Rêveuse, an intimate, ground-floor mini-suite with whirlpool bath and private patio. Simple, nutritious breakfasts are served, such as cereal with soy milk and scrambled eggs with vegetables. Very helpful and professional host.

Hôtel du Grand Lac
$$-$$$ bkfst incl.
⚒, ≡, ⊘, ℜ, ⌂
40 Rue Merry Sud
☎(819) 847-4039
☎800-267-4039
www.grandlac.com
Hôtel du Grand Lac is an uninspired brick and aluminum building. Guest rooms are nevertheless well-kept and modern.

L'Auberge L'Étoile-sur-le-Lac
$$$
≡, *K*, ≈, ℝ, ℜ, ⊛
1150 Rue Principale
☎(819) 843-6521
☎800-567-2727
www.etoile-sur-le-lac.com
Located on the highway just outside of Magog, this large hotel doesn't look like much from the outside, but its 50-odd guest rooms are entirely acceptable. Each of the new "luxury" rooms has a large patio overlooking the lake, as well as duvets, deep soaker tubs and new furniture—nice, but not quite luxurious. All standard rooms offer lake views.

Austin

Aux Jardins Champêtres
$$-$$$ bkfst incl.
≈, *sb*
1575 Chemin des Pères
☎(819) 868-0665
☎877-868-0665
***www.auxjardins
champetres.com***
Surrounded by wildflowers ans cats, Aux Jardins Champêtres recalls summers spent at grandma's. Located 10km from Magog toward l'Abbaye St-Benoit-du-Lac, this B&B owes its reputation to its excellent and varied country cooking. The five guest rooms are clearly an adjunct to the dining room—if you're not dining here, be aware that there will probably be noise until midnight. When we last visited, the country-style guest rooms, each with wood floors, were about to be renovated. Already small, they will surely be smaller once the private bathrooms are added.

Orford

Camping du Lac Stukely
$
3321 Chemin du Parc, Aut. 10 or 55, Exit 118, heading toward Parc du Mont Orford
☎(819) 843-9855
☎877-843-9855
www.sepaq.com
Located in Mont Orford park, Camping du Lac Stukely occupies a site on the lake of the same name. Dense forests surround the campground and mountain-biking trails are close by. At night, during summer, the community centre becomes a cinema. The campground also has a beach and rents small boats.

L'Auberge La Grande Fugue
$
May to Oct
3166 Chemin du Parc
☎(819) 843-8595
☎800-567-6155
Situated near the Centre d'Arts d'Orford, Auberge La Grande Fugue consists of a series of small shelters in a natural setting. A communal kitchen is available to guests.

Auberge Estrimont
$$$$
≡, ℜ, ⊘, *K*, ≈, ℜ, ⌂, ⊛
44 avenue de l'Auberge
☎(819) 843-1616
☎800-567-7320
⇝(819) 843-4180
www.estrimont.qc.ca
Located near Mont Orford, Auberge Estrimont has rooms and small condos. Made entirely of wood, the condos are equipped with balconies and fireplaces. Forest surrounds the property.

Manoir des Sables
$$$$-$$$$$
≡, ℜ, ⊘, *K*, ≈, ℜ, ⌂, ⊙, ⊛
90 avenue des Jardins
☎(819) 847-4747
☎800-567-3514
⇝(819) 847-3519
www.manoirdessables.com
In the shadow of Mont Orford is the very opulent and modern Manoir des Sables. The hotel features a multitude of

services and facilities such as indoor and outdoor swimming pools, an 18-hole golf course, tennis courts and a health spa. Guest rooms on the top floor offer magnificent views of the lake and of the 60ha property. Rooms in the "Privilège" wing come with exemplary service and include continental breakfasts. The rooms, standard (some are painted an attractive shade of blue) and deluxe (identical except that the latter have queen-size beds instead of doubles, and fireplaces), both offer very unattractive furniture, especially for a high-end establishment; the bathrooms, meanwhile, are spotless and rather appealing.

Village Mont Orford
$$$$$
K, ≈, ℝ
4969 Chemin du Parc
www.village-mont-orford.com
☎(819) 847-2662
☎800-567-3635
⇒(819) 847-2487
The Village Mont-Orford is comprised of several buildings, each containing a few lovely, fully equipped condos. Approximately 200m from there, a quadruple chair lift takes skiers up to Mont Orford's runs.

Georgeville

Auberge Georgeville
$$$$$ bkfst incl.
≡, ⊛, ℝ
71 Chemin Channel
☎(819) 843-8683
☎(819) 843-5045
www.aubergegeorgeville.com
Auberge Georgeville, situated in the tiny lakeside village of the same name, occupies an imposing pink-clapboard Victorian (1898) mansion. Its friendly welcome, wraparound verandah, wooden staircases, antiques and heavenly aromas emanating from the kitchen and cozy dining rooms create a warm atmosphere that oozes historic

cachet. Its 10 tiny guest rooms have wood floors and are decorated à la Laura Ashley; each has a private bathroom with shower. The inn's dining room has been much acclaimed over the years.

Ayer's Cliff

Auberge Ripplecove Inn
$$$$$
≡, ℛ, ≈, ℝ, ⊛
700 Rue Ripplecove
☎(819) 838-4296
☎800-668-4296
⇒(819) 838-5541
www.ripplecove.com
Located on 6ha property facing Lac Massawippi, the Ripplecove Inn is wonderfully peaceful. Its elegant Victorian-style dining room and tasteful guest rooms ensure comfort in unparalleled, intimate surroundings. Moreover, the more luxurious rooms have their own fireplaces and whirlpool baths. A variety of outdoor activities are offered. The place becomes absolutely magical in winter.

Coaticook

La Brise des Nuits
$$ bkfst incl.
142 Cutting
☎(819) 849-4667
La Brise des Nuits is a good bed and breakfast to keep in mind. The rooms are pleasantly decorated and the service is very friendly.

North Hatley

Le Chat Botté B&B
$$-$$$
⊛
550 Chemin de la Rivière
www.lechatbotte.ca
☎(819) 842-4626
Allergic types will have to give this lovely B&B a wide berth, as its very welcoming owner, Nico, is crazy about cats (the name of the B&B is French for "puss 'n' boots"). An artist in her spare time, she has adorned her Victorian home

with some of her striking canvases and has decorated her three guest rooms with character and originality. The smallest (and it is small) is successfully done up in terra cotta, while the largest is a romantic little number decorated in cream, with a gas fireplace and an in-room tub. All three have wood floors, sumptuous linens, feather beds and a sense of the romantic. Three-course breakfasts are served in a cozy, wainscoted breakfast room with individual tables for intimacy.

Auberge La Raveaudière
$$$ bkfst incl.
11 Hatley Centre
☎(819) 842-2554
⇒(819) 842-1304
www.laraveaudiere.com
La Raveaudière is a renovated farmhouse built around 1870 on a large plot of land, a short walk from the village centre. The grand yet inviting living room features burgundy walls and a Persian carpet on dark wood floors and large windows offering a view of the garden. Unfortunately, the seven guest rooms, which feature plenty of interesting angles and sunny colours, are starting to look a bit frayed around the edges and could use some freshening up. A full breakfast with homemade goodies can be enjoyed on the rear patio. Warm welcome.

Le Tapioca
$$$
680 Rue Sherbrooke
☎(819) 842-2743
www.tapioca.qc.ca
The moment you cross the threshold of this lovely white-clapboard mansion, you'll feel right at home, and that's due in large part to Marielle, your warm, easygoing host. She has simply but tastefully decorated her five guest rooms to make the most of their natural features, like wood floors and huge window frames. Two share a spacious patio, while a

third has its own Juliette balcony. Gentle hues and wicker give the place an airy, cheerful atmosphere. Each guest room has a full, ensuite bathroom, but some guests might be disappointed by the lack of bells and whistles (like whirlpool baths or soaker tubs). Elegant breakfasts are served at individual tables.

Auberge Hatley
$$$$
≡, ⚘, ≈, ℜ, ⊛
325 Chemin Virgin
☎*(819) 842-2451*
☎*800-336-2451*
⇌*(819) 842-2907*
www.aubergehatley.com
Auberge Hatley occupies a superb residence built in 1903. A member of the renowned Relais & Châteaux association, each of its 25 individually decorated guest rooms features a refined, country-style decor with flowery wallpaper, quilts, antiques and (sadly) wall-to-wall carpeting. The spacious living room looking out on the lake is furnished with beautiful antiques. A vast garden surrounds the inn and its pool. A magical, elegant place to escape to. Too rich for your budget? Come for lunch and a lovely view in the sunny formal dining room.

Manoir Hovey
$$$$$
⊛, ⊘, ⚘, ≈, ℜ
575 Chemin Hovey
☎*(819) 842-2421*
☎*800-661-2421*
⇌*(819) 842-2248*
www.manoirhovey.com
Built in 1900, Hovey Manor (see p 190) reflects the days when wealthy families spent their vacations in the beautiful country houses of the Townships. Converted into an inn 40 years ago, it is still extremely comfortable. The 40 rooms, some carpeted, some with wood floor, are decorated with lovely antique furniture and most offer a

magnificent view of Lac Massawippi. A wide expanse of lakeside lawn behind the property is perfect for carefree lounging in the summer months. In short, this lovely place has cachet to spare: it's perfect for a romantic weekend with your sweetie or for a special treat for grannie.

Lennoxville

Motel La Paysanne
$$
≡, ⚘, ≈
42 Rue Queen
☎*(819) 569-5585*
www.paysanne.com
Motel La Paysanne is easily accessible on the way into town. The rooms are spacious and simply decorated and the building's black and white exterior is attractive.

Sherbrooke

Charmes de Provence
$$ bkfst incl.
350 Rue du Québec, at the corner of boul. Portland
☎*(819) 348-1147*
www.charmesdeprovence.
com
True to form, the blue shutters and yellow walls of Charmes de Provence proudly display the colours of Provence, and the breakfasts also have a Mediterranean flavour. You can even play "pétanque" in the backyard of this friendly B&B!

Motel l'Ermitage
$$
≡, K, ⚘, ≈, ⊛
1888 Rue King Ouest
☎*(819) 569-5551*
☎*800-569-5551*
⇌*(819) 569-1446*
The Ermitage, a wood and brick motel located on the way into the city, is one of the most attractive lodgings in its category. The rooms are fairly comfortable, but starkly decorated. Parking available.

Hôtel Gouverneur Sherbrooke
$$-$$$
≡, ≈, ℜ
3131 Rue King Ouest
☎*(819) 565-0464*
☎*888-910-1111*
⇌*(819) 565-5505*
www.gouverneur.com
It is hard to miss the Hôtel des Gouverneurs on the way into town. Careful attention has been paid to the decor: pretty prints and flowers adorn the long hallways, and the rooms feature modern, elegant furniture.

Delta Sherbrooke Hôtel et Centre de Congrès
$$$$$
⚸, ≡, ⚘, ⊛, ⊘, ≈, ⊘, ℜ, ⌂
2685 Rue King Ouest
☎*(819) 822-1989*
☎*800-268-1133*
⇌*(819) 822-8990*
www.deltasherbrooke.com
The pinkish Delta Hotel is also on the way into town. It offers its guests a wide range of facilities, including an indoor pool, a whirlpool and an exercise room.

Tour C: The Back Country

Notre-Dame-des-Bois (Mont-Mégantic)

Camping Altitude
$
121 Route du Parc
☎*(819) 888-2206*
Situated less than 2km from Mont Mégantic, the quiet Camping Altitude offers nature lovers about 15 gravelled campsites at some distance from each other. Rudimentary facilities include outhouses and spring water taps.

Aux Berges de l'Aurore
$$ bkfst incl.
$$$$ ½b
closed winter
139 Route du Parc
☎*(819) 888-2715*
www.auberge-aurore.qc.ca
Aux Berges de l'Aurore is a charming little house in a

peaceful, natural setting, with four simple rooms.

Restaurants

Tour A: The Orchards

Frelighsburg

Aux Deux Clochers
$-$$
2 Rue de l'Église, corner Rue Principale
☎*(450) 298-5086*
Aux Deux Clochers is a bistro located in the centre of this attractive little village. Guests can enjoy consistently good classic cuisine or simply order a light meal. Breakfast is served on Saturdays and Sundays.

Dunham

La Rumeur Affamée
$
3809 Rue Principale
☎*(450) 295-2399*
They call this a "general specific food store" and while we don't have a clue what that means, that shouldn't stop anyone from partaking of the (pricey) cheese counter, patés, or home-baked goodies. Adjoining Bistrot Seeley (see below).

Le Tire-Bouchon de l'Orpailleur
$-$$
end Jun to mid Oct Wed-Sun
1086 route 202
☎*(450) 295-2763*
The restaurant at the L'Orpailleur vineyard, open only in the summer, has a short but high-quality menu. A pleasant patio looks out on the vineyard so guests can enjoy the lovely countryside while eating. The service is extremely friendly. Reservations required.

Picolletto
$$-$$$
Thu-Mon dinner
3698-A Rue Principale
☎*(450) 295-2664*
Picolletto, located along the Wine Route, occupies a cozy, rustic stone house where delicious French cuisine is served.

Bistrot Seeley
$$$
Tue-Sat (dinner),
Tue-Fri (lunch)
3809 Rue Principale
☎*(450) 295-1512*
Recently opened in a handsome red-brick 19th-century building that was originally a stagecoach stopover, Bistrot Seeley is an attractive restaurant of which its owners are justifiably proud. The interior has retained its brick walls, which serve as a backdrop for a changing roster of local artists. Pasta features heavily on the menu, as do a wide range of salads. Rear courtyard patio in season. Good selection of local microbrews.

Bedford

La Table Tournante
38 Rue Principale
☎*(450) 248-4664*
This inviting little spot, with wood floors and tables, brick walls and plenty of plants, is a recent addition to Bedford's main drag. For dinner, a daily four-course table d'hôte is offered, featuring seafood, lamb, duck, poultry, beef and veal; vegetarians, eat your heart out! Also open for lunch and weekend brunch.

Cowansville

McHaffy
$$$-$$$$
351 Rue Principale
☎*(450) 266-7700*
A must in the region, McHaffy, whose menu changes every two months, offers fine, international cuisine made with local ingredients and accompanied by a Blancs Coteaux wine chosen by Alain Bélanger, one

of Quebec's best wine waiters. At lunch, patrons enjoy lighter meals on a pleasant terrace. Not to be missed is the duck festival, from the end of September to mid-October, when chef Pierre Johnston creates excellent dishes for the occasion.

Bromont

Musée du Chocolat
$
679 Rue Shefford
☎*(450) 534-3893*
Chocolate for lunch? Not unless you insist: this little café in the museum of chocolate offers a lunch menu featuring quiches, sandwiches, and pâtés.

L'Étrier Rest-O-Bar
$$$
Tue-Sun dinner only
547 Rue Shefford
☎*(450) 534-3562*
L'Étrier Rest-O-Bar serves excellent cuisine to an established clientele. The restaurant is located a short distance outside the city in a pleasant, though little-visited spot.

La Jardinière
$$$
95 Rue Montmorency
☎*(450) 534-1199*
☎*888-276-6668*
The chef at the Jardinière prepares French cuisine with regional ingredients, such as duck from the poultry farms of Lac Brome and lamb from Saint-Grégoire. In the summer, guests can enjoy the terrace, the grill and the magnificent views of Mont Bromont. Sunday brunch is about $15.

Les Délices de la Table
$$$
641 Rue Shefford
☎*(450) 534-1646*
Les Délices de la Table is a small country-style caterer with bright yellow walls, lace curtains and tablecloths with floral and fruit motifs. It's the kind of place where you feel right at home as soon as you

open the door. Sample some tasty dishes, which are made with local products and carefully prepared by the chef/owner. Filled with regular customers, this tiny restaurant is becoming quite popular, so reservations are recommended.

Waterloo

Manoir Parmelee
$$$ (cash only)
bring your own wine
700 Rue Western
☎*(450) 539-2140*
Manoir Parmelee occupies the ground floor of a private Victorian home in a residential part of Waterloo. That, combined with the overfed feline wandering at will, the overly bright lighting and the not-quite-polished service, renders the experience not unlike dining at your slightly eccentric auntie's place. A fixed price of $23 (taxes included) gets you four courses, including seven main courses to choose from, such as a good seafood crepe or a generous plate of duck livers. As is common with French cuisine, vegetarians are out of luck. Despite (or because of) its slight eccentricities, this is definitely a good, reasonably priced spot for dinner with friends. Reservations required.

Granby

Ben la Bédaine
$
599 Rue Principale
☎*(450) 378-2921*
The name Ben la Bédaine, which means "Potbelly Ben," is certainly evocative; this place is a veritable shrine to French fries.

Casa du Spaghetti
$$
604 Rue Principale
☎*(450) 372-3848*
The Casa du Spaghetti is a good place for an inexpensive meal of pasta or pizza cooked in a wood-burning oven.

La Maison de Chez Nous
$$$-$$$$
Wed-Sun dinner only or by reservations
847 Rue Mountain
☎*(450) 372-2991*
The owner of Maison de Chez Nous gave up his wine cellar so that his customers, who may now bring their own wine, could save a little money. The menu offers Québec cuisine in its best and most refined form. Sunday brunch from 10:30am.

Tour B: The Lakes

Knowlton

Café Inn
$
264 Chemin. Knowlton
☎*(450) 243-0069*
Café Inn is a good spot for breakfast or lunch, especially in the summer when a patio seat will get you a pond view, a rare find in Knowlton. The specialty is *tartines*—open-face sandwiches—and thin-crust pizzas. Dinner served on Friday and Saturday nights.

Knowlton Pub
$
267 Knowlton Road
☎*(450) 242-6862*
The Knowlton Pub is without question one of the most popular spots in the Eastern Townships. The loud music hardly suits the rural setting, but it's a favourite nonetheless. During busy periods, the service is extremely slow. When business is slower, however, the English pub atmosphere and large terrace are pleasant.

Au Trois Canards
$$$
78 Lakeside
☎*(450) 242-5801*
It is gratifying to learn that the cuisine at Au Trois Canards is as appealing as the irresistible yellow-and-blue clapboard house it occupies. And nobody will be surprised to find

out that the specialty here is duck—the duck à l'orange is particularly sublime—but the menu also includes other French specialties. In addition to the nightly table d'hôte, there's also a very inexpensive *($-$$)* lunch and dinner bistro-style menu with comfort food like minced-duck pie. Excellent service.

Le Relais
$$$
286 Chemin Knowlton
☎*(450) 242-2232*
As is only proper in these parts, Brome Lake duck is the specialty at Le Relais, the restaurant at Auberge Knowlton: *confit, magret, brochettes* or an excellent warm-duck salad, for a light, refreshing change. Its casual, sunny dining room is encased in windows and decorated with a clutter of country bric-a-brac. There's also a huge selection of duckless mains, like burgers, quiches, steaks and vegetarian pastas, and local wines. A good bet.

Sutton

L'International Pâtisserie Café
$
10 Rue Principale South
☎*(450) 538-1717*
Ask anyone in town where to go for a bite and it's a good bet they'll send you here—so the uninviting decor, the noise and the cigarette smoke come as a disappointment. Nevertheless, the lunch offerings, such as soups, salads and sandwiches, are good and reasonably priced, and the service is pleasant.

Mocador
$$
17 Rue Principale Nord
☎*(450) 538-2426*
Mocador, located in a charming house with a picture window, serves simple fare and is a perfect place to enjoy a quiet meal.

Tartinizza
$$
Fri-Sun
19 Principale North
Owners Marie and Michel recently sold their popular French restaurant in Montréal for a simpler country life, and Tartinizza was part of the plan. Their focus is on thin-crust pizzas and sandwiches, served in a cozy little spot with planked wood floors and yellow walls. A selection of microbrews rounds out the offerings.

À la Fontaine
$$$
30 Rue Principale Sud
☎(450) 538-3045
At À la Fontaine visitors can enjoy succulent French cuisine while sitting on a pretty terrace.

Il Duetto
$$$
227 Académie-Élie
☎(450) 538-8239
Il Duetto serves fine Italian cuisine in a quiet country setting in the hills around Sutton. The pasta is home-made and the main dishes are inspired by the regional cuisines of Italy. The five-course menu **($$$$)** is a good sampling of the variety of Italian cooking.

Magog

La Grosse Pomme
$$
270 Rue Principale Ouest
☎(819) 843-9365
La Grosse Pomme is a friendly restaurant serving good bistro-style food. In the evening, the ambiance is livened up by chatty patrons both young and old. An old standby.

Le Saint-Tropez
$$$
211 Rue Merry South
☎(819) 843-2017
Located next to the marina on Lac Memphrémagog, Le Saint-Tropez offers the best in lakeside dining. In fact, the lake is such an attraction here,

particularly at sunset, that the owner has made sure that a seat in any of the three elegant, if somewhat sterile, dining rooms will provide a view. Its international-style cuisine is also popular, and the seasonal, four-course table d'hôte offers good value. Lakeside patio in season.

Les Toits Bleus
$$$
bring your own wine
1321 Gendron
☎(819) 847-0988
☎888-847-0988
If there's one restaurant that Townshippers are talking about, it's Les Toits Bleus. Run by a transplanted French couple—he from Orléans, she from Périgord—this 1880s farmhouse is the kind of place that whisks you in an instant to the French countryside. In summer, you can dine on the patio beneath the stars, while in winter, make sure to reserve a spot by the fireplace in the original dining room, which is much cozier than the recent annex. In true country style, patrons enter the dining room through the kitchen, where they are engulfed by the warmth and aromas. The table d'hôte can include three to six courses (*$24.75-$39.25*), which include a wonderful lamb, raised on site and served in succulent, lean slices, a *magret de canard* (chef Claude rejects Brome Lake duck in favour of its Outaouais cousin), and deer in red wine sauce. Children's menu available. This is a very popular spot so reserve well in advance—and don't forget your wine.

Ayer's Cliff

Auberge Ripplecove
$$$$
700 Rue Ripplecove
☎(819) 838-4296
☎800-668-4296
Recognized as a four-diamond establishment, the dining room at the Auberge Ripplecove offers fine gourmet

cuisine of great distinction. Its Victorian atmosphere and elegant decor make it an excellent place for a romantic meal.

North Hatley

Pilsen
$$
55 Rue Principale
☎(819) 842-2971
Take a reasonably priced, upgraded pub-style menu with something for everyone, add street-side tables with a lake view and a narrow patio on the lower level that literally floats above the river and you've got the formula for a long-standing favourite. Unfortunately, the lower-level pub is the smokers' domain but non-smokers might be willing to brave the haze for the extraordinary setting. Good salads and burgers.

Manoir Hovey
$$$$
575 Chemin Hovey
☎(819) 842-2421
☎800-661-2421
Graced with antique furniture and a fireplace, Manoir Hovey's lovely dining room exudes peace and quiet, which makes for a lovely evening. The cuisine, as refined as the Auberge Hatley's (see below), has also earned a lot of praise.

Auberge Hatley
$$$$
325 Chemin Virgin
☎(819) 842-2451
☎800-336-2451
The dining room at the Auberge Hatley, which has received numerous awards, is without question one of the region's best places to dine. The skillfully prepared gourmet meals will please even the most discerning palates—not to mention that the dining room is beautifully decorated and offers a magnificent view of Lac Massawippi. Reservations required.

Café Massawippi

$$$$

3050 Chemin Capelton

☎*(819) 842-4528*

This little house just beyond the centre of North Hatley is home to a real find. An inspired daily three-course table d'hôte introduces giant shrimp to passion fruit, medallions of caribou to cocoa and rabbit to fig marmelade, almost always with great success. Eclectic music and decor, with a *soupçon* of funkiness. Excellent wine list and service to match.

Lennoxville

Pub le Lion d'Or

$

2 Rue du Collège

☎*(819) 565-1015*

☎*(819) 562-4589*

The terrace at Pub le Lion d'Or is both lovely and noisy—especially when the students are celebrating! Three beers are brewed on site, a pale beer, a dark ale and a dark bitter. The food is simple, essentially the standard fare of English pubs.

Café Fine Gueule

$-$$

mid-Aug to late Jun

170 Rue Queen

☎*(819) 346-0031*

The Café Fine Gueule, located inside a superb stone house, serves simple fare in a relaxed atmosphere.

Sherbrooke

Presse Boutique Café

$-$$

4 Rue Wellington Nord

☎*(819) 822-2133*

A laid-back clientele frequents the Presse Boutique Café. In addition to visual-art exhibitions and shows by local and other musicians, patrons can enjoy a wide variety of imported beers, a simple menu (salads, *croque-monsieur*, sandwiches, etc.) and vegetarian dishes. Moreover, two Internet stations are available (*$6/hr, $1/10min*).

Le Cartier

$$

255 Boulevard Jacques-Cartier Sud

☎*(819) 821-3311*

It did not take long for Le Cartier to become a very popular restaurant. Overlooking Parc Jacques Cartier and only a short drive from the university, this small restaurant feels airy and comfortable because of its large bay windows. Its healthy and affordable food makes it a popular family spot; however, it is intimate enough for dinner with friends. There is a good selection of beers from Québec microbreweries.

Café Bla-Bla

$$

2 Rue Wellington Sud

☎*(819) 565-1366*

Café Bla-Bla has a varied menu and a wide selection of imported beers.

La Rose des Sables

$$

270 Rue Dufferin

☎*(819) 346-5571*

Good Moroccan food is in store at La Rose des Sables.

Le Sultan

$$

205 Rue Dufferin

☎*(819) 821-9156*

Le Sultan also specializes in Middle Eastern cuisine, in this case Lebanese food. The grilled meats are excellent.

Le Petit Sabot

$$-$$$

Mon-Sat

1410 Rue King Ouest

☎*(819) 563-0262*

The Petit Sabot is located inside an attractively decorated blue house with loads of character. The food is pleasantly different, game being the specialty.

Falaise Saint-Michel

$$$

100 Rue Webster

☎*(819) 346-6339*

Falaise Saint Michel is like a hidden treasure on a small, somewhat dreary street. Its specialty being refined regional cuisine, the restaurant serves a variety of excellent dishes, and also has a particularly well-stocked wine cellar.

Da Toni

$$$$

15 Belvédère Nord

☎*(819) 346-8441*

Located right in the heart of the new downtown area, the opulent Da Toni has a well-established reputation. Indeed, for 25 years now, patrons have been enjoying its fine French and Italian cuisine, served with a wide selection of wines in a classic decor. The table d'hôte features five excellent, reasonably priced main courses. Though somewhat noisy, the terrace allows guests to enjoy a drink outside during the summer.

Tour C: The Back Country

Danville

Le Temps des Cerises

$$$

79 Rue du Carmel

☎*(819) 839-2818*

☎*800-839-2818*

Le Temps des Cerises serves elegant, inventive cuisine in the distinctive and unique atmosphere of a former Protestant church.

Notre-Dame-des-Bois

Aux Berges de l'Aurore

$$$$

May to Oct

139 route du Parc

☎*(819) 888-2715*

Located close to lush Mont Mégantic, the intimate and very charming Aux Berges de l'Aurore serves excellent Québec cuisine. Seasoned with wild herbs gathered in the surrounding countryside, its dishes are most original. From the very first bite, guests will appreciate why it received the *Mérite de la Fine Cuisine Estrienne* award!

Entertainment

Bars and Nightclubs

Knowlton

Knowlton Pub
267 Knowlton Road
☎*(819) 242-6862*
The Knowlton Pub has earned
itself such a reputation that
even Montréalers in search of
a change of scenery go there
to while away an evening
among friends.

Magog

Microbrasserie Le Memphré
12 rue Merry S.
☎*(819) 843-3405*
This cozy, dimly lit brewpub,
with sofas arranged in front of
a roaring fire come the rigours
of winter, offers up rather
good pints of India Pale Ale
and Scotch Ale. When we
visited, the owners were
about to add a restaurant to
the mix.

Le Chat du Moulinier
101 rue du Moulin
☎*(819) 868-5678*
For jazz and a great atmosphere, look no further.

North Hatley

The Pilsen
55 Rue Principale
☎*(819) 842-2971*
The Pilsen is frequented by
vacationers who come to chat
and have a beer while gazing
out at Lac Massawippi.

Sherbrooke

Café du Palais
184 Wellington Nord
☎*(819) 566-8977*
The favourite dance bar with
vacationers is the Bar au Café

du Palais. Shows are pre-
sented on certain evenings.

King Hall
286 King Ouest
King Hall is a comfortable bar
with an interesting selection of
international beers.

Theatres

Sherbrooke

The Université de Sher-
brooke's cultural centre
houses the **Salle Maurice-
O'Bready** (*2500 Boulevard
Université,* ☎*819-820-1000 or
821-7742*), where concerts,
be they classical or rock, are
put on.

A former church converted to
a concert hall, the **Vieux
Clocher de Sherbrooke** (*1590
Galt Ouest,* ☎*819-822-2102*)
now welcomes music lovers
and entertainment-seekers.
Taking on the same role as its
predecessor in Magog, the
new hall, accommodating
approximately 500 spectators,
offers "discovery-shows" featuring young Quebecers and
well-established performers.
Performance listings can be
found in the Sherbrooke daily
La Tribune.

Orford

The **Centre d'Arts Orford**
(*3165 Chemin du Parc,*
☎*819-843-9871 or 800-567-
6155*) provides advanced
training courses to young
musicians during the summer.
An annual festival also takes
place at the centre, which is
made up of several buildings
designed in the 1960s by Paul-
Marie Côté. The exhibition
room that completes the
centre was originally the Man
and Music (*l'Homme et la
Musique*) pavilion at Expo 67,
and was designed by
Desgagné and Côté.

Magog

Located inside an old
Protestant church built in
1887, **Le Vieux-Clocher** (*64
Rue Merry Nord,* ☎*819-847-
0470*) staged many shows that
later became very successful in
both Québec and France.
Those interested in attending a
show should reserve their
seats well in advance. The
theatre is attractive, but small.

Festivals and Cultural Events

A few days of festivities are
organized as part of the
**Traversée Internationale du
Lac Memphrémagog** (*mid-Jul;*
☎*819-843-5000*), including
performances by Québec
theatrical artists, exhibits of all
kinds and shows by folk singers. The highlight of the celebrations (which celebrates its
25th anniversary in 2003) is
the arrival of swimmers from
Newport, U.S.A. The 42km
swim is undertaken by athletes
considered among the best in
the world.

For more than 50 years each
July and August, the **Festival
Orford** (*3165 Chemin du
Parc,* ☎*819-843-3981 or
888-310-3665*) offers a series
of concerts featuring ensem-
bles and world-famous virtuo-
sos. Several excellent free
concerts are also presented by
young musicians, who come
here for the summer to hone
their skills at the Centre d'Arts
Orford. This high-calibre
festival is an absolute must for
all music lovers.

The **Brome Fair** (☎*450-242-
3976*) has been drawing the
crowds each Labour Day
weekend (the weekend prior
to the first Monday in September) since 1856. A genuine
agricultural fair, complete with
local products, livestock exhibitions, contests and games.

Townshippers Day *(mid-Sep; Sherbrooke,* ☎*866-566-5717, www.townshippers.qc.ca)*, an annual celebration of the culture and heritage of English-speaking Townshippers, is an occasion for music, history, art, dance, children's activities and regional culinary delights.

Among the not-to-be-missed festivals in the Townships is **Le Canard en Fête** *(*☎*450-242-2982, www. cclacbrome.qc.ca)*, a duck festival held for several weekends from the end of September to mid October.

Shopping

Tour B: The Lakes

Knowlton

Polo Ralph Lauren Factory Outlet
45 Lakeside Rd.
☎*(450) 243-0052*
For a small village, Knowlton has a surprising number of shopping options, particularly for fashions. This shop offers discounts, sometimes substantial, on offerings by this popular American designer.

Brome Lake Ducks
Mon-Fri 8am to 5pm, Sat and Sun from 10am
40 Chemin Centre
☎*(450) 242-3825*
It's a little disillusioning to learn that the duck on the menu of the region's fine restaurants is not plucked out of Brome Lake by an intreped hunter and his pointer; instead of spending their days frolicking carelessly on Lac Brome, these ducks are raised by the thousand in a dozen aluminum barns just beyond the town centre. For duck sausage, foie gras, confit or freshly killed kritters, head to Brome Lake Ducks, where they process 1.7-million of them each year.

Sutton

Musée du Chocolate Belge
Tue-Sat
8 rue Principale S.
☎*(450) 538-0139*
Funny how every chocolatier worth his sugar is trying to make an educational experience out of what was once purely a sensual one. But if it helps to justify our indulgence, then why not? Here, Monsieur Henquin creates true works of art, like chocolate marquetry boxes that look almost too good to eat. Free demonstrations *(mid-Jun to mid-Oct Tue, Fri, Sat and Sun 1:30pm)*.

Magog

Les Trésors de la Grange
early May to early Nov, Fri 1pm to 5pm, Sat and Sun 10am to 5pm
790 Chemin des Pères
This 130-year-old barn outside Magog on the way to the abbey is a most atmospheric—and drafty— place to showcase local crafts. Reasonably priced woodwork, stained glass, jewellery and tasty tidbits, as well as paintings and antiques.

Lanaudière

The Lanaudière region

extends north of Montréal, from the plains of the St. Lawrence to the Laurentian plateau.

Except for the part of the region engulfed in the urban sprawl of Montréal, Lanaudière is a peaceful area of lakes, rivers, farmland, wild forests and huge open spaces. It is a great place to kick back and try your hand at the various sports and activities the area has to offer, like skiing, canoeing, snowmobiling, hiking, hunting and fishing. Your visit to this, one of the first colonized areas in New France, will most certainly also include a tour of the region's rich architectural heritage.

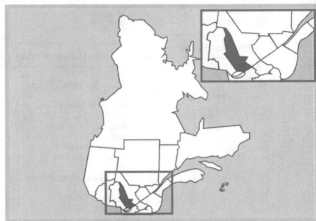

For more than 25 years the region has hosted an important event: le Festival International de Lanaudière. Music-lovers from across Québec converge on the region for classical and popular music concerts performed by artists from around the globe. Some concerts are given in the halls and churches of the region, while open-air concerts take place in a huge amphitheatre near Joliette. The city of Joliette is also home to one of Québec's most interesting regional museums, with an impressive collection of Québec art including many pieces of religious art.

Finding Your Way Around

Once a countryside of seigneurial manors and farmland that stretched from the shores of the St. Lawrence to the wild, mountainous land of the Aboriginals, the Lanaudière region has today been engulfed by the Montréal urban area. In keeping with this split personality we suggest two very different routes from Montréal: **Tour A: La Plaine ★ ★** and **Tour B: La Matawinie ★**.

Tour A: La Plaine

By Car

Aut. 25 is the extension of Boulevard Pie-IX and leads towards Terrebonne, the first stop on this tour. It continues east to Assomption on Rte. 344. Next take Rte. 343 N. to Joliette and Rte. 158 W. to Berthierville. To return to Montréal, follow lovely Rte. 138 W., also known as the Chemin du Roy, along the St. Lawrence River, with stops in Lanoraie, Saint-Sulpice and Repentigny.

Bus Stations

Terrebonne
Galeries de Terrebonne

Joliette
250 Rue Richard (at the Point
d'Arrêt restaurant)
☎*(450) 752-2255*

Repentigny
435 Boulevard Iberville (at the
hôtel de ville)
☎*(450) 654-2315*

Train Station

Joliette
380 Rue Champlain
☎*800-361-5390*

Tour B: Matawinie

By Car

Aut. 25 N., the extension of
Boulevard Pie-IX, joins Rte.
125 N., which leads to
Rawdon, Chertsey, Notre-
Dame-de-la-Merci and Saint-
Donat. From there Rte. 347
leads to Saint-Gabriel-de-
Brandon. Access to Saint-
Michel-des-Saints and the
Rouge-Matawin and
Mastigouche reserves is north
on Rte. 131.

Bus Stations

Rawdon
3228 1re Avenue (at the Patate à
Gogo)
☎*(450) 834-2000*

Saint-Donat
751 Rue Principale (Dépanneur
Boni-Soir)
☎*(819) 424-1361*

Practical Information

Most of this region falls within
the **450** area code. Note,
however, that the municipalities of Saint-Donat and Saint-
Michel-des-Saints use the **819**
area code.

Tourist Information

Regional Office

Tourisme Lanaudière
3645 Rue Queen, Rawdon, J0K 1S0
☎*834-2535 or 800-363-2788*
≈*834-8100*
*www.tourisme-
lanaudiere.qc.ca*

Tour A: La Plaine

Berthierville
760 Rue Gadoury
☎*836-1621*

Joliette
500 Rue Dollard
☎*759-5013 or 800-363-1775*

Terrebonne
1091 Boulevard Moody
☎*964-0681*

Tour B: La Matawinie

Rawdon
3590 Rue Metcalfe
☎*834-2282*

Saint-Donat
536 Rue Principale
☎*(819) 424-2883*
☎*888-783-6628*

Exploring

★★

Tour A: The Plain

Duration of tour: two days

In 1813, Marie-Charlotte
Tarieu Taillant de Lanaudière,
daughter of the seigneur of
Lavaltrie, married Barthélémy
Joliette. These two figures
were much more than a
couple of newlyweds how-
ever, for their union left behind a precious heritage to the
inhabitants of this region: the
name of the region,
Lanaudière, and the name of
its main city, Joliette. But far
beyond that, they also inspired
an enterprising spirit rarely
found amongst French Canadians at the time. This stimu-
lated the creation of a manufacturing base, locally controlled banks, and finally the
development of specialized
farming.

*Take Aut. 25, the extension of
Boulevard Pie-IX. Turn right
at the Terrebonne-Centreville
Exit (22). Turn right immediately on Boulevard Moody
then left on Rue Saint-Louis.
Park on Rue des Braves,
facing Île des Moulins.*

★★
**Terrebonne
(pop. 44,800)**

Located along the banks of the
rushing Rivière des Mille-Îles,

Names of New Merged Cities

Lavaltrie
Merger of Lavaltrie and
Saint-Antoine-de-
Lavaltrie.

Terrebonne
Merger of Terrebonne,
Lachenaie and La Plaine.

Repentigny
Merger of Repentigny
and Le Gardeur.

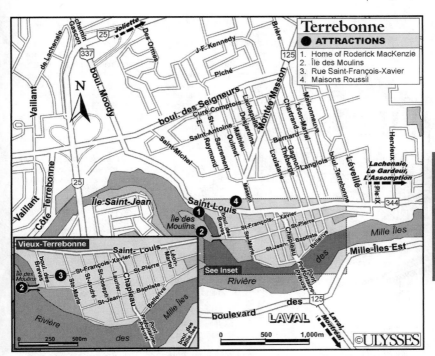

this municipality gets its name from the fertile soil (*terre* meaning earth, and *bonne* meaning good) from which it grew. Today, it is part of the ribbon of suburbia surrounding Montréal, yet the old town, divided into an *haute-ville* and *basse-ville* (upper and lower town), has preserved some of its residential and commercial buildings. Terrebonne is probably the best place in Québec to get an idea of what a prosperous 19th-century seigneury was really like.

The city was founded in 1707 and shortly thereafter the first flour and saw mills were built. In 1802 the seigneury of Terrebonne was purchased by Simon McTavish, director of the Northwest Company, which specialized in the fur trade. Terrebonne became a departure point for his lucrative commercial expeditions into northern Québec. Card-

ing mills for wool were soon added to those built under the French Regime, creating a veritable pre-industrial complex. In 1832 the Masson family took over the running of the seigneury and rebuilt most of the mills.

The 20th century began promisingly, until a large section of the lower town was destroyed by fire on December 1, 1922. Only the buildings on Rue Saint-François-Xavier and Rue Sainte-Marie were spared.

Rue Saint-Louis is the main artery of the upper-town bourgeois area. Besides the Manoir Masson, several other stately residences line the streets, in particular the **home of Roderick MacKenzie** (*906 Rue Saint-Louis*). Because he was one of the main shareholders in the Northwest Company, MacKenzie's home also served as the company's

headquarters at one time. Built of stone covered with stucco, it is adorned with an elegant Doric wood portico. A bit further along Rue Saint-Louis are some fine examples of Victorian architecture in wood (*number 938*) and in brick (*number 939*).

Return to Rue des Braves, heading towards l'Île des Moulins.

Île des Moulins ★★ (*free admission, $3 for the show Wed-Sun; late Jun to early Sep, every day 1pm to 9pm; at the end of Rue des Braves,* ☎471-0619) is an impressive concentration of mills and other pre-industrial equipment from the Terrebonne seigneury. Most of the buildings, located in a park, have been renovated and now serve as community and administrative buildings. Upon entering, the first building on the left is the

Île des Moulins

On your way back, follow the small Rue Saint-François-Xavier east of la Rue des Braves.

Along **Rue Saint-François-Xavier** are the picturesque homes that escaped the fire of 1922, now housing various restaurants and galleries. Some of these houses were built in the second half of the 18th century and have been painstakingly restored. They are similar to houses found on the outskirts of large Canadian cities at the beginning of the 19th century, made of wood and built low to the ground and close to the sidewalk.

Turn left onto Rue Saint-Louis.

old flour mill (1846), then the saw mill (restored in 1986), which houses the municipal library. Next is the Centre d'Accueil et d'Interprétation de l'Île des Moulins (information centre) in what used to be the seigneurial office. This cutstone building was constructed in 1848 according to plans by Pierre-Louis Morin.

The three-storey building on the left is the old bakery, built in 1803 for the Northwest Company, which used it to make cookies and *galettes* for the *voyageurs* collecting furs in the northern and western regions of the country. This bakery was one of the first large-scale bakeries in North America, and is also the oldest building left on the island. At the end of the walk is the new, larger mill, built in 1850 for Sophie Raymond. It produced wool fabrics sold throughout the region. The - Terrebonne cultural centre is now located there.

Th   e twin **Maisons Roussil** (*870 and 886 Rue Saint-Louis*) were built in 1825 by master carpenter Théodore Roussil. During the Rebellion of 1837-38, local rebels were held in the house before being transferred to the Pied-du-Courant prison in Montréal.

Leave Terrebonne on Rte. 344 E. (the continuation of Rue Saint-Louis) towards Lachenaie, then de Le Gardeur, to eventually arrive in L'Assomption.

★
L'Assomption
(pop. 16,200)

This small city owes its growth in part to a portage route established in 1717 by the Sulpician Pierre Le Sueur, who used to spend time paddling on the Rivière L'Assomption. The trail, used by voyageurs transporting their canoes from one river to the next, avoids a 5km detour by water. Origi-

nally simply called Le Portage, the settlement was a crossroads frequented by fur trappers and traders on the northern route. It was eventually included in the Saint-Sulpice seigneury, conceded to the Messieurs de Saint-Sulpice of Paris in 1647.

The proximity of the carding mills in Terrebonne, as well as the frequent visits by the *coureurs des bois*, prompted the women of L'Assomption to design a special wool sash to be worn by French Canadians, to distinguish them from the Scottish, many of whom were employees of the Northwest Company. Hence was born the famous *ceinture fléchée* (V-shaped sash), now a symbol of Québec. L'Assomption had the monopoly on sash production from about 1805 to 1825.

Enter L'Assomption by Rue Saint-Étienne. Parking is permitted opposite the church.

The monumental facade of the **Église de L'Assomption-de-la-Sainte-Vierge** ★ (*153 Rue du Portage*) was designed by Victor Bourgeau (1863). The chancel was undertaken in 1819 and contains the tabernacle, the altar and the Baroque pulpit by Urbain Brien dit Desrochers in 1834. The artistry of the vault is the work of Bourgeau, modelled after the one in La Prairie.

Take Rue du Portage, alongside the presbytery. This road follows Pierre le Sueur's original portage route. At the corner of Boulevard L'Ange-Gardien stand the old seigneurial office of the Sulpiciens (402 Boulevard L'Ange-Gardien) and the building that once housed the store known as the Magasin Le Roux, specializing in the sale of the "ceinture fléchée" (sashes) (195 Rue du Portage). Turn right on Boulevard L'Ange-Gardien.

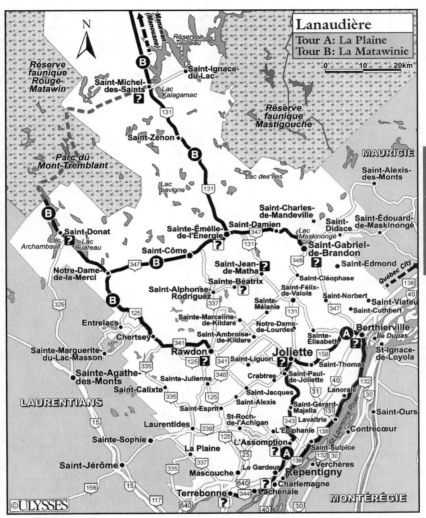

Lanaudière
Tour A: La Plaine
Tour B: La Matawinie

0   10   20km

The **Maison Archambault**
(*351 Boulevard L'Ange-Gardien*) is one of a few
examples left around Montréal
of this type of house, where
the main floor served as a
workshop and the second,
accessible by a long staircase,
was for the living quarters.
This particular example, built
in 1780, was the birthplace of
Francis Archambault (1880-1915), an opera star in

London, New York and
Boston a century ago.

The **Collège de
L'Assomption** ★
(*270 Boulevard L'Ange-Gardien*) for boys was
founded in 1832 by the town's
elite. The building is a fine
example of 19th-century
institutional architecture in
Québec, with its fieldstone
exterior (1869), mansard roof,
and superb silver dome,

added in 1882. The eclectic
wing to the east was built in
1892. Among the notable personalities who attended the
college is Sir Wilfrid Laurier,
Prime Minister of Canada
from 1896 to 1911.

The **Oasis du Vieux Palais de
Justice** (*free admission; year-
round, variable schedule;
reserve for guided tours;
255 Rue Saint-Étienne;* ☎ 589-
3266*), or old courthouse, was

originally three separate houses, constructed between 1811 and 1822. This rather long building housed a court of law and a registration office for many years. Victor Bourgeau, who designed the courtroom on the second floor, was not content with just modifying the openings; he also designed the furniture and woodwork. The courtroom remains intact, even though court has not been in session here since 1929.

The site of the first church in L'Assomption (1724), the remains of the seigneurial manor and the **Maison Séguin** *(284 Rue Saint-Étienne)*, a bourgeois residence in the Second Empire style built in 1880, are all located across from the old courthouse.

*Get back on Rue Saint-Étienne heading west (towards the church). At number 349 is the **Maison Le Sanche** (1812), an interesting example of a typical urban dwelling of the day with firebreak walls and built right up against the sidewalk.*

Follow Boulevard L'Ange-Gardien, then Rte. 343 N., which follows the Rivière L'Assomption. Alongside the road there are several houses with mansard roofs all oriented perpendicularly to the road to protect them from the prevailing winds. Continue along Rte. 343 N., which becomes Boulevard Manseau in Joliette, and passes some beautiful Victorian residences. Park the car near the large Place Bourget in order to explore the streets of Joliette on foot. The downtown area extends around Boulevard Manseau.

★
**Joliette
(pop. 18,000)**

At the beginning of the 19th century, notary Barthélémy Joliette (1789-1850) opened up logging camps in the northern section of the Lavaltrie seigneury, which was at the time still undeveloped land. In 1823 he founded "his" town around the sawmills and called it "L'Industrie," a name synonymous with progress and prosperity. The settlement grew so rapidly that in just a few years it had eclipsed its two rivals, Berthier and L'Assomption. In 1864 it was renamed Joliette in honour of its founder. Barthélémy Joliette completed many other ambitious projects, most notably the construction of the first railroad belonging to French Canadians, and a bank where money bearing the Joliette-Lanaudière name was printed.

Today, Joliette is an important regional centre. The city has a diocese, as well as two renowned cultural centres, the Musée d'Art de Joliette and the Amphithéâtre, where part of the famous music festival, the Festival International de Lanaudière, is held. The market building and the *hôtel de ville* (city hall), both donated by Monsieur Joliette, used to stand in the middle of **Place Bourget**. Since their demolition, shops have been built and the area has been turned into a pedestrian strip. The **Palais de Justice**, at the far end, follows the neoclassical model proposed by the Minister of Public Works at the time. Its construction in 1862 confirmed Joliette's status as capital of the region.

Follow Boulevard Manseau towards the cathedral.

The interesting white building at number 400 was built in 1858 and used to house the **Institut**, the first cultural centre in Québec to house a municipal library and a performance hall. The Greek Revival style of the facade was chosen as a display of defiance against the British colonial power.

The **Cathédrale Saint-Charles-Borromée** *(2 Rue Saint-Charles-Borromée N.)*, with its modest facade and single steeple, was originally just a simple parish church. The exterior of the church, constructed between 1888 and 1892, is plain yet impressive. The plans, drawn by architects Perrault and Mesnard, called for large proportions of the same scale as the Romanesque Revival churches built in Montréal at the time.

At the back of the cathedral is the **Palais Épiscopal**, an eloquent testament to the almighty power of the church in Québec before the Quiet Revolution. At 20 Rue Saint-Charles-Borromée Sud is the old seminary, now used as a CÉGEP (college).

Joliette owes its cultural vibrance to the clerics of Saint-Viateur who established themselves as the **Maison Provinciale des Clercs de Saint-Viateur** ★ *(132 Rue Saint-Charles-Borromée N.)* in the mid-19th century. In 1939, they undertook the construction of their new house. The plans, by Montréal architect René Charbonneau, were inspired by a sketch done by Père Wilfrid Corbeil. The building's massive Romanesque Revival arches and heavy stone tower are reminiscent of German monasteries of the Middle Ages. The chapel at the centre is often described as a modern version of the German church in Frielingsdorff. The magnificent stained-glass windows, designed by Marius Plamondon, the sculptures on the pews and the stations of the cross all create an ethereal atmosphere of mystery and contemplation.

Father Wilfrid Corbeil founded the exceptional **Musée d'Art de Joliette** ★★ *($4; summer Tue-Sun 11am to 5pm; rest of the year, Wed-Sun noon-5pm; 145 Rue Wilfrid-Corbeil,*

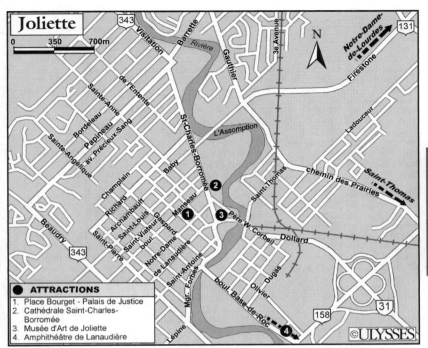

Joliette

0   350   700m

ATTRACTIONS
1. Place Bourget - Palais de Justice
2. Cathédrale Saint-Charles-Borromée
3. Musée d'Art de Joliette
4. Amphithéâtre de Lanaudière

©ULYSSES

Lanaudière

☎ 756-0311) with works collected during the 1940s by the clerics of Saint-Viateur that show Québec's place in the world. This is the most important regional museum in Québec. Since 1976 it has been located in a rather off-putting building on Rue Corbeil. On display are major pieces from Québec and Canadian artists like Marc-Aurèle de Foy Suzor-Côté, Jean-Paul Riopelle and Emily Carr, as well as works by European and American artists like Henry Moore and Karel Appel. One section of the museum is devoted to Québec religious art, while another contains religious art from the Middle Ages and Renaissance periods, with some excellent examples from France, Italy and Germany.

L'Amphithéâtre de Lanaudière is on the outskirts of town. To get there follow Rue Saint-Charles Borromée

Sud, then Rue Saint-Antoine, turn left on Chemin Base-de-Roc.

The Festival International de Lanaudière was begun by Father Fernand Lindsay. Each year during the months of July and August, a variety of music concerts and opera singers are presented as part of the festival. In 1989 the 2,000-seat open-air **Amphithéâtre de Lanaudière** *(1575 Base-de-Roc,* ☎ 759-7636*)* was constructed in order to increase the capacity and accessibility of the event, which up to that time was limited to the churches of the area. Artist Georges Dyens completed the interior design of the aisles and the exquisite sculptures. *Take the on-ramp to Rte. 158 E. close to the amphitheatre, and follow it toward Berthierville.*

★
Berthierville
(pop. 4,200)

The modest Autray Seigneury was conceded to Jean Bourdon, an engineer of the King of France, in 1637. The land corresponds to the sector Berthier-en-bas, or Berthierville, along the shores of the St. Lawrence. The Berthier Seigneury, which was much more extensive, was conceded to Sieur de Berthier in 1672 before passing through several hands. It corresponds in part to Berthier-en-haut, or Berthier. In 1765 both these tracts of land were acquired by James Cuthbert, an aide-de-camp of General Wolfe during the battle of the Plains of Abraham in Québec City, as well as a friend of the Duke of Kent. He developed the land mainly for use as a vacation spot.

The **Pont Couvert Grandchamps** *(on the right near Rte. 158)* crosses Rivière Bayonne. This covered wooden bridge was constructed in the Town style in 1883, making it one of the first of this kind of structure popularized in the United States in the 19th century. These bridges were built by town residents to reduce the cost, and were covered to avoid the deterioration of the structure supporting the road surface.

The **Église Sainte-Geneviève ★★** *(780 Montcalm)* is a Lanaudière treasure. Built in 1781, it is one of the oldest churches in the region. The interior's Louis-XVI styling was designed by Amable Gauthier and Alexis Millette between 1821 and 1830. Many elements in the decor combine to make this building truly exceptional. The decor has a richness rarely seen at that time, comprising elements such as the original high altar, crafted by Gilles Bolvin in 1759, the shell-shaped retable and the diamond-pattern ornamenting the vault. There are also several paintings, including one of Sainte-Geneviève (a French canvas from the 19th century hanging over the high altar), and six paintings by Louis Dulongré, painted in 1797.

The seigneurial **Chapelle des Cuthbert** *(free admission, every day early Jun to early Sep, 10am to 6pm; entrance on Rue de Bienville)*, which belonged to the Cuthbert family (1786) and was known officially as St. Andrew's, was the first Protestant church built in Québec. In the years following the British Conquest of 1760, French-inspired architecture remained the dominant style, as there were few British architects and workers. This explains the Catholic configuration of the church, designed by mason Antoine Selton and carpenter

Vadeboncœur. Many members of the Cuthbert family were buried in the chapel; however, their remains were moved in 1866. Since 1978, the building has served as a cultural centre for the residents of Berthierville.

Gilles Villeneuve, the championship race-car driver who was killed tragically during the qualifying trials for the 1982 Grand-Prix of Belgium, was from Berthierville. The **Musée Gilles-Villeneuve** *($6; every day 9am to 5pm; 960 Avenue Gilles-Villeneuve, ☎836-2714 or 800-639-0103)* is dedicated to the illustrious career of the Ferrari Formula I driver, his prizes, his souvenirs and his cars. In the last few years, Gilles's son Jacques has taken up where his father left off, becoming a top-ranked Formula I driver, at the heart of the British Williams-Renault team. The museum now devotes a new section to the career of Jacques Villeneuve.

Farther on, take Rte. 158 to Île Dupras and the village of **Saint-Ignace-de-Loyola**, from which a ferry leads to Sorel on the south shore of the St. Lawrence *(in summer, departures every half hour during the day, every hour in the evening, the crossing takes 10min; ☎836-4600)*.

Follow Rte. 138 W. towards Lanoraie, Lavaltrie and Saint-Sulpice.

Lanoraie
(pop. 2,012)

Rte. 138 follows the original Chemin du Roy, laid out in 1734 between Montréal and Québec City. Before then, people had to travel by canoe along the St. Lawrence. Several old houses still stand along the road between Berthierville and Lavaltrie.

Coteau-du-Sable, located to the northeast of the village of Lanoraie, has an important

Aboriginal archaeological site. The foundations of a longhouse built by Iroquois in the 19th century were discovered here. Numerous handcrafted artifacts have also been found at the site since the beginning of the 20th century.

Continue on Rte. 138 to Repentigny

Repentigny
(pop. 56,460)

The city of Repentigny was named after its first seigneur, Pierre Le Gardeur de Repentigny. It is pleasantly located at the confluence of the Rivière L'Assomption and the mighty St. Lawrence. Unfortunately, the three buildings of interest in Repentigny have almost been swallowed up by the urban chaos along Rue Notre-Dame. No longer in their original context, these buildings have to admired as individual examples of a bygone era.

Construction of the **Église de la Purification-de-la-Bienheureuse-Vierge-Marie ★** *(445 Rue Notre-Dame Est)* began in 1723, making it the oldest church in the diocese of Montréal. It has many characteristics of New France churches, such as the apse with the corners cut off and the orientation of the building parallel to the river. The facade was redone in 1850 with two towers instead of the original one steeple. The interior was restored to its original simplicity in 1984 following a fire which almost destroyed the whole church. The beautiful Louis-XV-style high altar was designed by Philippe Liébert in 1761.

The **Moulins à Vent** *(460 and 861 Rue Notre-Dame Est)* are quite a sight. These two windmills seem out of place amidst the gas stations and post-war bungalows of modern-day Repentigny. The Moulin du Sieur Antoine Jetté, at number

861, was built in 1823 and served as a grain mill until 1915. The Moulin de François Grenier was built in 1819, and is empty today. Both buildings have lost their mechanisms and sails.

To return to Montréal, follow Rue Notre-Dame de Repentigny, which is actually the continuation of the Montréal street of the same name.

Tour B: La Matawinie

Duration of tour: four days

The colonization of the hinterland of Lanaudière was undertaken around 1860 by Catholic missionaries concerned about the mass exodus of French Canadian farmers to the cotton textile mills of New England. Matawinie is not only well-supplied with forests but also has an abundance of lakes, mountains and rivers, which attract hunters, fishers and vacationers. The northern part of the region has long been inhabited by the Attikamekw Nation, a small Aboriginal group that used to be nomadic but is now settled around the village of Manawan.

This tour is long and rugged. A vehicle in good condition and camping equipment are strongly recommended since hotels and service stations are rare or nonexistent along the gravel roads around and beyond Saint-Michel-des-Saints.

★
Rawdon
(pop. 9,150)

After the Conquest of 1760, the British established a more familiar means of dividing the territory, namely the township. Governed by residents, townships were established to

accommodate American Loyalists and British immigrants. These townships were usually located on the periphery of land already conceded as seigneuries under the French Regime. The townships of Lanaudière were established in the foothills of the Laurentians, between the 19th-century seigneuries and the new territories opened up by the clergy after 1860. The township of Rawdon, at the centre of which is the town of Rawdon, was esyablished in 1799.

The **Centre d'Interprétation Multiethnique de Rawdon** *(free admission, donations welcome; Sat and Sun 1pm to 4pm; 3588 Rue Metcalfe, ☎834-3334)* describes the short history of the many ethnic groups that have settled in the region since the establishment of the township. The centre is located in a wood house painted in the typical style of the region. A stroll through the neighbouring streets to see the different community churches is a pleasant way of completing a tour of the centre. The Anglican Church and the Russian Orthodox Church are the most interesting.

The other spot of interest in the vicinity is **Parc des Cascades ★** *($6/car; mid-May to mid-Oct, every day; ☎834-4149)*, which can be reached on Rte. 341, the extension of Boulevard Pontbriand. Located on the bank of Rivière Ouareau, which runs in lovely cascades over the rocky riverbed here, this park includes a picnic area where sunbathers stretch out during the hot months of summer.

★
Saint-Donat
(pop. 3,530)

Minutes away from Mont-Tremblant, tucked between mountains reaching up to 900m and the shores of Lac

Archambault, the small town of Saint-Donat extends east to the shores of Lac Ouareau. Saint-Donat is also a departure point for the **Parc du Mont-Tremblant** (see p 238).

*Though Saint-Michel-des-Saints is accessible via a long trip through Parc du Mont-Tremblant, it is best to retrace your steps on Rte. 125 to **Notre-Dame-de-la-Merci**. Once there, follow Rte. 347 towards Sainte-Émilie-de-l'Énergie and then Rte. 131 N. towards Saint-Michel-des-Saints. Continue on Rte. 347 to reach Saint-Gabriel-de-Brandon.*

Saint-Gabriel-de-Brandon
(pop. 2,670)

The town of Saint-Gabriel-de-Brandon borders magnificent Lac Maskinongé. In fact, this 10km² lake is pretty much the town's only attraction; its beautiful **municipal beach**, which apparently can accommodate up to 5,000 swimmers, is very popular (see below).

Saint-Michel-des-Saints
(pop. 2,565)

Saint-Michel-des-Saints grew up along the shores of Lac Kaiagamac and is surrounded by the **Réserve Faunique Rouge-Matawin** (see p 238 and below) and the **Réserve Faunique Mastigouche** (see p 293).

Parks

Tour B: La Matawinie

The **Réserve Faunique Rouge-Matawin** *($3.50; 26km west of Saint-Michel-des-Saints; ☎833-5530 or 800-665-6527)* is 1,394km² of greenery, through which flow about

450 lakes and waterways. It is home to an abundant and fertile wildlife. There is no lack of things to do, from hiking, hunting, fishing, canoe-camping and wild-berry-picking, to snowmobiling in the winter.

Saint-Donat is one of the entry points to **Parc du Mont-Tremblant ★ ★** (see p 238), which is generally thought of as part of the Laurentians.

Outdoor Activities

Hiking

Tour B: La Matawinie

At the **parc des Sept-Chutes** (*$4.50; May to Nov every day 9am to 5pm; Rte. 131, ☎884-0484 or 833-1334*) in Saint-Zénon, some 12km of hiking trails, arranged so as to offer spectacular view points, line some scenic waterfalls.

The **Sentier de la Matawinie** (*about 5km from Sainte-Émélie-de-l'Énergie along Rte. 131 N., ☎886-3823 or 886-0688*) provides the opportunity to observe the Sept-Chutes from the Rivière Noire, as well as some of the other sights of the region. The trail zigzags between various lookout points and reaches an altitude of 565m before leading along a steep section of the trail to the Sept-Chutes in Saint-Zénon.

Parc Régional des Chutes-Monte-à-Peine-et-des-Dalles (*$5; accessible from Rtes. 131, 337 and 343, ☎883-6060*) is jointly managed by the municipalities of Saint-Jean-de-Matha, Sainte-Béatrix and Sainte-Mélanie. Many walking trails, totalling 12km, have been laid out in this 300ha park. Among the sights are three beautiful waterfalls on Rivière L'Assomption.

Swimming

Tour B: La Matawinie

The **Rawdon municipal beach** (*admission fee; ☎834-8121*), on the lake of the same name, is very popular during the summertime. Picnic area, fast-food stand, private parking, and pedal boats and kayaks are available for rent.

Blue jay

On the shores of superb Lac Maskinongé, the **Saint-Gabriel-de-Brandon municipal beach** (*free; ☎835-2105*) constitutes the main attraction in this little town. This large, beautiful beach can accommodate up to 5,000 bathers. Amenities include a picnic area, a fast-food stand, private parking, and pedal-boat, canoe, windsurfer and personal watercraft rentals.

Golf

Tour A: La Plaine

Terrebonne's **Centre de Golf Le Versant** (*$55; 2075 Côte Terrebonne, ☎964-2251*) has three 18-hole courses that are rated par 54, 71 and 72.

Club de Golf Base-de-Roc (*$39; 2870 Boulevard Base-de-Roc, ☎759-1818*) in Joliette offers a par-72, 18-hole course.

Tour B: La Matawinie

Among the many golf courses in the area, two that stand out are the 18-hole, par-73 course at **Club de Golf de Rawdon** (*$27; 3999 Lakeshore Dr., ☎834-2320*) and the 18-hole, par-72 course at **Club de Golf Saint-Jean-de-Matha** (*$32-$55; 945 Chemin Pain de Sucre., ☎886-9321*).

Cross-country Skiing

Tour B: La Matawinie

The **Station Touristique de la Montagne Coupée** (*$10; 204 Rue de la Montagne-Coupée, Saint-Jean-de-Matha, ☎886-3845*) offers outdoor activities year-round. In winter there are 80km of cross-country ski trails, with 43km of wider trails designed for practising "skating" techniques. Skis are available for rent on site. In the summer, there are trails for horseback riding and hiking.

There are many cross-country ski trails in the Saint-Donat area, in **Secteur La Donatienne** of **Parc des Pionniers** (*Chemin Hector-Bilodeau*), in **Montagne Noire**

and in **Secteur La Pimbina** of
Parc du Mont-Tremblant.

Downhill Skiing

Tour B: La Matawinie

**Station Touristique de Val
Saint-Côme** *($33; 501
Chemin Val St-Côme,* ☎*883-
0701 or 800-363-2766)* is
one of the largest downhill ski
centres in the Lanaudière
region. It has 21 runs, some of
which are lit for night skiing,
and a vertical drop of 300m.
Accommodations are also
available.

Snowmobiling

Tour B: La Matawinie

La Cuillère à Pot *(41 Rte.
329,* ☎*819-424-2252 or 800-
567-6704)*, in Saint-Donat, is
a favourite rest stop for snowmobilers; it offers various
packages and snowmobile
rental to its guests.

In Saint-Michel-des-Saints,
**Location de Motoneiges
Haute-Matawinie** *(Mon-Wed
8:30am to 6pm, Thu and Fri
8:30am to 8pm, Sat and Sun
8:30am to 3pm; 180 Rue
Brassard,* ☎*833-1355 or 800-
833-6015)* has a fleet of approximately 200 snowmobiles
for rent.

Accommodations

Tour A: La Plaine

Joliette

Château Joliette
$$$
≡, ℜ, ⊛
450 Rue St-Thomas
☎*752-2525 or 800-361-0572*
⇋*752-2520*
www.chateaujoliette.com
A large red-brick building by
the river, Château Joliette is
the largest hotel in town.
Though the long corridors are
cold and bare, the modern
rooms are large and comfort-
able.

Repentigny

La Villa des Fleurs
$-$$ bkfst incl.
≡, ✖, ≈, pb/sb
45 Rue Gaudreault
☎*654-9209*
⇋*654-1220*
Located on the outskirts of
Montréal, where a maple
grove once stood, La Villa des
Fleurs has four attractively
decorated rooms. Friendly
service and generous breakfasts.

Tour B: La Matawinie

Rawdon

Le Gîte du Catalpa
$$ bkfst incl.
ℜ, pb/sb
C.P. 1639
3730 Rue Queen
☎*834-5253*
The owners of this lovely
Victorian house on Rue
Queen have converted their
home into a five-room bed
and breakfast, Le Gîte du
Catalpa. In good weather, a
five-course breakfast is served
on the terrace or in the gar-
den.

Saint-Alphonse-Rodriguez

Auberge sur la Falaise
$$$-$$$$ bkfst incl.
≡, ⊛, ☉, ℜ, ≈, ☉, ℜ, △
324 Avenue du Lac Long Sud
☎*883-2269 or 888-325-2473*
⇋*883-0143*
www.aubergefalaise.com
Ten kilometres from the vil-
lage of Saint-Alphonse-Rodri-
guez, after a long climb past
peaceful Lac Long and into
what seems like another
world, is the marvellous
Auberge sur la Falaise. The
inn, perched on a promon-
tory, dominates this serene
landscape, reserving excep-
tional views for its guests. The
26 rooms in this modern
building are luxurious, and the
hotel does double duty as a
spa and also offers many
sports activities. Finally, the
cuisine served in the dining
room is among the best in the
area (see p 225).

Saint-Jean-de-Matha

**Auberge de la
Montagne Coupée**
$$$$$
≡, ℜ, ☉, ≈, ℜ, △, ☉, ⊛
1000 Chemin de la Montagne-
Coupée
☎*886-3891 or 800-363-8614*
⇋*886-5401*
www.montagnecoupee.com
Another exceptional establish-
ment, Auberge de la
Montagne Coupée appears
after what seems like an inter-
minable climb. Reward is at
hand though in this immense
white building with huge bay
windows. The hotel has
50 comfortable, modern
rooms bathed in natural light.
In the dining room and the
lounge, large windows reveal
a breathtaking panorama.
There is an equestrian centre
and a summer theatre at the
bottom of the grounds, and
the hotel has a remarkable
restaurant (see p 225).

Lanaudière

Saint-Donat

Parc du Mont-Tremblant
$
C.P. 1169
2951 Route 125 Nord
☎*(819) 424-7012*
The Pimbina section of Parc du Mont-Tremblant, near Saint-Donat and accessible via Rte. 125, offers 340 camp-sites.

Auberge Havre du Parc
$$
𝕽, K, 𝕽, ☻
2788 Rte. 125 Nord
☎*(819) 424-7686*
⊶*(819) 424-3432*
www.havreduparc.qc.ca
Located 10km just north of the village, the Auberge Havre du Parc is a haven of tranquil-lity. The magnificent location, on the shores of Lac Provost, and the comfort of the accom-modations, make it easy to relax and forget the daily grind.

Manoir des Laurentides
$$$
𝕽, K, ≈, 𝕽, ☻
290 Rue Principale
☎*(819) 424-2121*
☎*800-567-6717*
⊶*(819) 424-2621*
www.manoirdes laurentides.com
The Manoir des Laurentides, well located by the lakeside, offers good value for your money. The rooms in the three-storey main building are comfortable but ordinary, though each has its own bal-cony. There are also two rows of motel rooms that stretch to the lakefront and about 40 cottages equipped with kitchenettes. Since this spot is often quite lively, visi-tors who value peace and quiet should opt for motel rooms or cottages. A beach and a small marina are avail-able to guests.

Saint-Gabriel-de-Brandon

Auberge Aile-En-Ciel
$$-$$$
≡, 𝕽, ☻, K, 🐾, ≈, △, ☻, ☻
376 Rue Maskinongé, (Rte. 347)
☎*835-3775 or 877-367-3248*
⊶*835-1115*
www.aubergeaileenciel.com
Auberge Aile-En-Ciel is an inn in name only. It is actually more of a "condotel," offering about 20 apartments, each of which can accommodate two to six people. The rooms are large enough, though some of them are quite plain; the apartments feature fully equipped kitchenettes. Guests have access to an outdoor pool, a little beach on Lac Maskinongé, and a terrace with a grill.

Restaurants

Tour A: La Plaine

Terrebonne

Le Jardin des Fondues
$$-$$$$
186 Rue Ste-Marie
☎*492-2048*
Terrebonne's Le Jardin des Fondues, where the chic ambience adds to a delicious assortment of fondues and traditional French dishes, is sure to please fondue fans from far and wide.

L'Étang des Moulins
$$$
Wed-Sun
888 Rue St-Louis
☎*471-4018*
L'Étang des Moulins occupies a magnificent stone house that dominates Terrebonne's his-toric district. Inside, an inviting, romantic ambiance dominates, with tables draped in lace and French music wafting through the air. Large windows and a glassed-in terrace out back maximize the view of Ile des Moulins. On the menu are French classics successfully reinvented. Foodies will be happy to loosen the purse strings and splurge on the seven-course "menu inspira-tion." Service is attentive yet discreet. Without a doubt one of the best restaurants in Lanaudière.

Le Folichon
$$$-$$$$
Tue-Sun
804 Rue St-François-Xavier
☎*492-1863*
Le Folichon, which means playful and lighthearted, lives up to its name. Occupying a lovely, two-storey wood-framed house in the historic quarter of Terrebonne, the restaurant's warm atmosphere is powerful enough to make one forget the coldest days of winter. In the summer, the shaded terrace is the spot of choice. The five-course table d'hôte is generally memorable. The *feuilleté d'escargots* (snails in pastry) with tomatoes and leeks, the *magret de canard* (breast of duck) in a raspberry sauce, and the *contre-filet de chevreuil* (venison) in a honey and thyme sauce are particu-larly worth mentioning. Im-pressive wine list.

L'Assomption

Le Prieuré
$$$$
402 Boulevard L'Ange-Gardien
☎*589-6739*
Located in a historic 18th-century building, Le Prieuré has developed an excellent reputation over the years. The chef prepares savoury French cuisine with local products.

Joliette

L'Antre Jean
$$$
Wed-Sat
385 Boulevard St-Viateur
☎*756-0412*
Amongst the many fine restau-rants in town, L'Antre Jean seems to be the unofficial favourite with the locals.

French specialties, prepared as they are in France, are served as part of the table-d'hôte menu. The decor is warm and inviting and the atmosphere is unpretentious.

Chez Henri le Kentucky
$
30 Rue de La Visitation
☎759-1113
Chez Henri le Kentucky offers everything you would expectfrom a place open—come hell or high water—24 hours a day. A good place for travellers on a small budget.

Tour B: La Matawinie

Rawdon

Auberge Stewart
$-$$$
4333 Chemin du lac Brennen
☎834-8210
Auberge Steward occupies a rustic log building and serves succulent French and Québec cuisine. Escargots, Coquille Saint-Jacques, frog's legs, apple pie and other classics figure on the menu.

Saint-Alphonse-Rodriguez
 Auberge sur la Falaise
$$$$
324 Avenue du Lac Long Sud
☎883-2269
At the extraordinary Auberge sur la Falaise, meals are served in a setting of perfect tranquillity. Nestled deep in the forest, overlooking the calm surface of a lake, this establishment is the perfect retreat from the hectic pace of modern life (even if it is just for a meal). The chef skillfully adapts French cuisine to Québec flavours. The obvious choice for epicureans is the five-course gourmet menu—a memorable experience, indeed!

Saint-Jean-de-Matha
Auberge de la Montagne Coupée
$$$$
1000 Chemin de la Montagne-Coupée
☎886-3891
Auberge de la Montagne Coupée, another spot famous for its peaceful setting, offers an exciting menu of innovative Québec cuisine. The dining room is surrounded by two-storey bay windows that look out on an absolutely breathtaking scene. And this is just the beginning—the best part of the evening (the meal!) is yet to come. Imaginatively presented game dishes are enhanced by succulent treasures. The service is attentive; the wine list is excellent. Very copious breakfasts are also served.

Saint-Donat

La petite Michèle
$-$$$
327 Rue St-Donat
☎(819) 424-3131
La Petite Michèle is just the place for travellers looking for a good family restaurant. The atmosphere is relaxed, the service friendly and the menu traditional Québecois.

Maison Blanche
$$
515 Rue Principale
☎(819) 424-2222
The food is always delicious at the Maison Blanche. The house specialty, a divine, juicy, rare steak, is known far and wide.

Auberge Havre du Parc
$$$-$$$$
2788 Rte. 125 Nord, Lac-Provost
☎(819) 424-7686
Auberge Havre du Parc not only boasts an exceptionally peaceful setting, it also has an excellent selection of French specialties.

Entertainment

Theatres and Concert Halls

Terrebonne

Tiny but cozy, **Théâtre du Vieux-Terrebonne** (*867 St-Pierre*, ☎*492-4777*) has earned the respect of the Québec artistic community over the years and now draws some of the biggest names in song and comedy, who use it as a sort of testing ground before they bring their acts to Montréal. Touring theatre troupes also stop in regularly.

Joliette

There is nothing more pleasant than attending an open-air concert at the **Amphithéâtre de Lanaudière** (*1575 Bd. Base-de-Roc*, ☎*800-561-4343*), ideally located in a little, tree-ringed valley. The best of this acoustically privileged site's summer program is presented during the Festival International de Lanaudière.

Festivals and Cultural Events

Joliette

The most important event on the regional calendar is the **Festival International de Lanaudière** (☎ *759-7636 or 800-561-4343*). During the most beautiful weeks of the summer, dozens of classical, contemporary and popular music concerts are presented in the churches of the area and outdoors at the superb Amphithéâtre de Lanaudière.

The **Festival mémoire et racines** *(late Jul; St-Charles-Borromée, ☎752-6798 or 888-810-6798, www. memoireracines.qc.ca)* is a major festival of traditional music, dance and storytelling.

Repentigny

At the annual **Internationaux de Tennis Junior du Canada** *(end Aug; ☎654-2411)* tennis fans might discover tomorrow's Monica Selleses and John McEnroes.

Saint-Donat

When autumn arrives, the forests of the Saint-Donat region turn into a multicoloured natural extravaganza. To celebrate this spectacular burst of colour, various family activities are organized during **Week-ends des Couleurs** *(Sep and Oct; ☎819-424-2833 or 888-783-6628).*

Md.Pierson

The Laurentians

Without question the most renowned resort area in Québec, the beautiful Laurentides region, also called the Laurentians, attracts a great many visitors all year round.

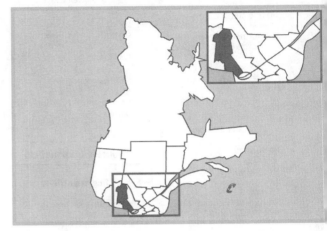

For generations now, people have been "going up north" to relax and enjoy the beauty of the Laurentian landscape. The lakes, mountains and forests provide a particularly good setting for a variety of physical activities or outings. As the region boasts the highest concentration of ski resorts in North America, skiing gets top billing here when winter rolls around. The villages scattered at the foot of the mountains are both charming and friendly.

The southern part of the region, known as the Basses-Laurentides (Lower Laurentians), was settled early on by French colonists, who came here to cultivate the rich farmland. A number of local villages reveal this history through their architectural heritage. The settling of the Laurentian plateau, initiated by the now-legendary Curé Labelle, began much later, toward the middle of the 19th century. The development of the Pays d'En Haut, or Upper Laurentians, was part of an ambitious plan to colonize the outlying areas of Québec in an effort to counter the exodus of French Canadians to industrial towns in the northeastern United States. Given the poor soil, farming here was hardly profitable, but Curé Labelle nevertheless succeeded in founding about 20 villages and attracting a good number of French Canadian colonists to the region.

Finding Your Way Around

Vacationers of all types have been coming to this region for a century, making tourism the most important local industry. The following two tours have been laid out to discover this vast area. **Tour A: Lac des** Deux-Montagnes ★ and **Tour B: Cottage Country ★★**.

Tour A: Lac des Deux-Montagnes

By Car

From Montréal follow Aut. 13 N. Take the exit for Rte. 344 W. towards Saint-Eustache. This road continues to Oka. A ferry from Oka leads to Hudson (see p 148) in the Montérégie region.

Bus Station

Saint-Eustache
550 Arthur Sauvé
☎ **(450) 472-9911**

Tour B: Cottage Country

By Car

From Montréal, take Aut. 15 (the *Autoroute des Laurentides*) to Saint-Jérôme (Exit 43). Landmarks along the way include the imposing Collège de Sainte-Thérèse (1881) and its church, on the right, and the only General Motors automobile assembly plant in Québec, on the left. A little further, before Saint-Jérôme, is Mirabel Airport. Hwy. 15 and then Rte. 117 lead to Saint-Jovite. Mont-Tremblant is north of here on Rte. 327. Continue on the 117 to reach Labelle and Mont-Laurier.

Bus Stations

Boisbriand
4117 Rue Lavoisier
☎*(450) 435-6767*

Piedmont
770 Boulevard de Laurentides
☎*(450) 227-2487*

Sainte-Adèle
1208 Rue Valiquette (Pharmacie Brunet)
☎*(450) 229-6609*

Lac-Mercier
1950 Ch. Principal
☎*(819) 425-8315*

Practical Information

Two **area codes** are used in the Laurentians; **450** up to Sainte-Adèle and **819** beyond.

Names of New Merged Cities

Sainte-Marguerite-Estérel
Merger of Estérel and Sainte-Marguerite-du-Lac-Masson.

Sainte-Agathe-des-Monts
Merger of Sainte-Agathe-des-Monts, Sainte-Agathe-Nord and Ivry-sur-le-Lac.

Grenville-sur-la-Rouge
Merger of Grenville and Calumet.

Saint-Sauveur
Merger of Saint-Sauveur-des-Monts and Saint-Sauveur.

Saint-Jérôme
Merger of Saint-Jérôme, Bellefeuille, Saint-Antoine and Lafontaine.

Mont-Tremblant
Merger of the ski resort of Tremblant, the village of Mont Tremblant, the city of Saint-Jovite, Mont Tremblant-Nord and the parish of Saint-Jovite.

Tourist Information

Regional Office

Maison du Tourisme des Laurentides
14142 Rue de la Chapelle
Mirabel, J7J 2C8
☎*(450) 436-8532*
☎*800-561-6693*
≈*(450) 436-5309*
www.laurentides.com

Tour A: Lac des Deux-Montagnes

Saint-Eustache
600 Rue Dubois, J7P 5L2
☎*(450) 491-4444*

Tour B: Cottage Country

Saint-Sauveur-des-Monts
605 chemin Des Frênes
☎*(450) 227-3417*

Sainte-Adèle
1490 rue Saint-Joseph
☎*(450) 229-3729*

Mont-Tremblant
1001 Montée Ryan
☎*(819) 425-2434*

Labelle
7404 Boulevard du Curé-Labelle
☎*(819) 686-2606*

Mont-Laurier
177 Boulevard Paquette
☎*(819) 623-4544*

Exploring

Tour A: Lac des Deux-Montagnes

Duration of tour: one day

The priests of the Sulpician order were instrumental to the colonization of this part of the Laurentians right from the early days of the French Regime. Vestiges of the seigneurial era may still be found on the shores of Lac des Deux-Montagnes, where nearly half the stops on this tour are located. Highlights of this short excursion through the lower Laurentians, just a half-hour from Montréal, are beautiful

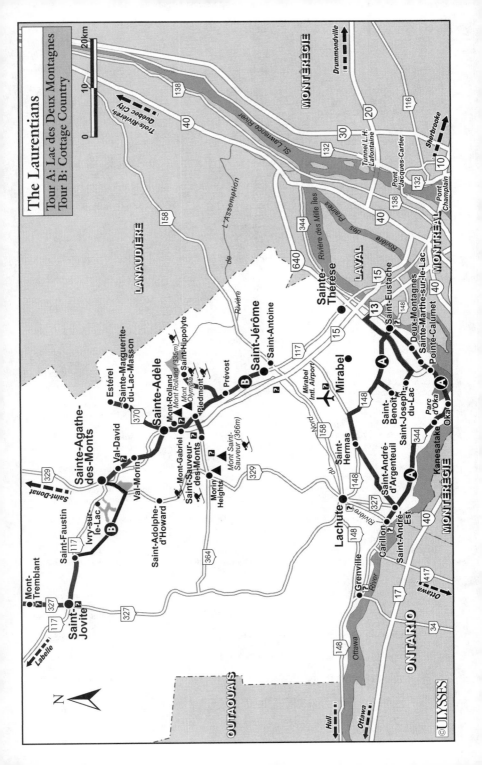

The Laurentians

Tour A: Lac Des Deux Montagnes
Tour B: Cottage Country

views of the lake and the opportunity to sample a wide variety of fresh produce at roadside stands along the way during the summer and fall.

Saint-Eustache (pop. 41,400)

In the early 19th century, Saint-Eustache was a prosperous farming community that had produced a French Canadian intellectual and political elite. These individuals played a major role in the Patriote Rebellion of 1837-38, making Saint-Eustache one of the main arenas of the tragic events that took place at the time. The village used to be the centre of the Mille-Îles seigneury, which was granted to Michel Sidrac du Gué of Boisbriand in 1683. It was the Lambert-Dumont family, however, that undertook the development of the seigneury in the middle of the 18th century. From 1960 on, Saint-Eustache became one of the most important suburbs on the Rive-Nord.

The **Église Saint-Eustache ★ ★** *(123 Rue Saint-Louis)* is remarkable mainly for its high Palladian facade built out of cut stone between 1831 and 1836. Its two belltowers bear witness to the prosperity of local residents in the years leading up to the rebellion. The church still bears traces of the fierce fighting that took place within its walls on December 14, 1837, when 150 Patriotes led by Jean-Olivier Chénier shut themselves up in the building to resist General Colborne's British troops. The British leader had his men bombard the church, and by the end of the battle, only its walls were left standing. The troops were then ordered to burn most of the houses in the village. It took Saint-Eustache more than 30 years to recover from these events.

Beside the church, visitors will find the presbytery, the convent (1898) and a monument to the Patriotes.

Take Rue Saint-Eustache, directly in line with the centre of the church, to Moulin Légaré.

Manoir Globensky *($3; Tue-Sun 9am to 5pm; 235 Rue Saint-Eustache, ☎450-974-5170)* is a large white house that once belonged to Charles-Auguste-Maximilien Globensky, husband of the heiress of the Saint-Eustache seigneury, Virginie Lambert-Dumont. Though it was built in 1862 after the abolition of the seigneurial system (1854), local residents have always referred to it as the "manor."

The stone walls of the **Moulin Légaré** *($3; year-round Mon-Fri 9am to 5pm, mid-May to mid-Oct also open Sat and Sun 9am to 5pm; 236 Rue St-Eustache, ☎450-974-5400)* date back to 1762. However, modifications made in the early 20th century have robbed the building of some of its character. This flour mill has been in continuous operation since it was built, making it the oldest water-powered mill still in use in Canada. Visitors can purchase wheat and buckwheat flour on the premises.

*Return to Rte. 344 W., which leads through Deux-Montagnes, **Sainte-Marthe-sur-le-Lac** and **Pointe-Calumet** before reaching Oka, the next stop on the tour.*

★ Oka (pop. 4,300)

The Sulpicians, like the Jesuits, established missions in the Montréal area with the goal of converting local natives to Catholicism. The disciples of Ignatius Loyola settled permanently in Kahnawake in 1716 (see p 171), and those of Jean-Jacques Olier followed in

their footsteps in 1721, settling on the shores of Lac des Deux-Montagnes in a lovely spot named Oka, which means "golden fish." Here, the Sulpicians welcomed Algonquins, Hurons and Mohawks, all allies of the French. While the Kahnawake mission was supposed to remain isolated from European-born inhabitants, a village of French colonists developed simultaneously around the Sulpician church.

At the end of the 18th century, a number of Iroquois from New York State supplanted the original Aboriginal inhabitants of the mission, giving an English character and, more recently, a new name (Kanesatake) to a whole section of territory located upriver from the village. Today, Oka is a centre for both recreational activities and tourism, as well as a distant suburb of Montréal. In 1990, during what has come to be known as the "Oka Crisis," the Mohawk Warriors of Kanesatake barricaded Rte. 344 at the western edge of Oka for several long months in an effort to affirm territorial rights and prevent a portion of the land from being turned into a golf course.

Abbaye Cistercienne d'Oka ★ *(1600 Chemin d'Oka, ☎450-479-8361)* is run by the Cistercian order, founded at the Abbaye de Citeaux by Robert de Molesme, Albéric and Étienne Harding at the end of the 11th century. It is a reformed branch of the Benedictine order. In 1881, a few Cistercian monks left the Abbaye de Bellefontaine in France in order to found a new abbey in Canada. The Sulpicians, who had already donated several pieces of their extensive territorial holdings in Montréal to various religious communities, granted the new arrivals a hillside in the seigneury of Deux-Montagnes. Within a few years, the monks had built the

Abbaye d'Oka, also known as La Trappe. The famous Oka cheese is still made here, and can be purchased in the cheese dairy adjoining the monastery. The Romanesque Revival–style chapel in the centre of the abbey is also worth a short visit.

Parc d'Oka ★, see p 238.

From the centre of Oka, turn left on Rue L'Annonciation to the church and the pier, which offers a beautiful view of Lac des Deux-Montagnes. The pier serves as the landing stage for the tiny private ferry-boat that links this tour to the Vaudreuil-Soulanges tour in Montérégie (see p 167).

The **Église d'Oka** ★ *(181 Rue des Anges)*, an eclectic church built in 1878 in the Romanesque Revival style, stands in front of the lake, on the same site once occupied by the church of the Sulpician mission (1733). It houses paintings belonging to the 18th-century French school, commissioned in Paris by Sulpician priests to adorn the stations of the cross (Calvaire) in Oka (1742). In 1776, these oil paintings were replaced by wooden bas-reliefs executed by François Guernon, which were better able to withstand the harsh Canadian climate. The bas-reliefs were severely damaged by vandals in 1970 before being removed from the oratories and chapels and hung in the Chapelle Kateri Tekakwitha, adjacent to the Église d'Oka.
Continue along Rue des Anges, then turn right on Rue Sainte-Anne before taking a left back on to Rte. 344 and heading towards Saint-André-d'Argenteuil.

The road then leads through **The Pines**, planted in 1886 to counter the erosion of the sandy soil. It was here, in this forest of 50,000 pine trees, that tensions peaked during the 1990 "Oka Crisis," when

the provincial police force, the Sûreté du Québec, and then the Canadian Army, faced the Mohawk Warriors in an armed stand-off.

On the edge of the village of Saint-Placide, further to the west, is the **Maison Routhier** *(3320 Rte. 344)*, childhood home of Basile Routhier, author of the lyrics to Canada's national anthem.

Turn left on Rue Saint-André which leads to Carillon (Rte. 344).

Carillon (pop. 300)

Charged with defending the colony against attacks from First Nations allied with the Dutch and later the English, Dollard des Ormeaux and 17 fellow soldiers were killed during a battle with the Iroquois in 1660. Their deaths prevented the Iroquois from taking Montréal. A plaque and a monument commemorate this bloody episode in the early history of New France. Known for many years as Long-Sault, Carillon is a peaceful village, which was populated by Loyalists in the early 19th century. Visitors will find a hydroelectric dam here, as well as a vast park with a pleasant picnic area. Every year, thousands of amateur sailors pass through Carillon's lock on their way to Ottawa.

The **Musée Regional d'Argenteuil** *($2.50; Jun to early Sep, Tue-Sun 10:30am to 4:30pm; early Sep to mid-Oct, Sat and Sun 10:30am to 4:30pm; 50 Rue Principale, ☎450-537-3861)* exhibits local antiques, as well as a collection of 19th-century clothing, in a handsome Georgian-style stone building erected in 1836. Originally intended to serve as an inn, it was converted the following year into a military barracks for the British troops who had come to put down the Patriote

Rebellion in the Saint-Eustache region.

To return to Montréal, take Rte. 640 E., then Rte. 13 S. and finally Rte. 20 E.

Tour B: Cottage Country

Duration of tour: one to three days

This part of the Laurentians has been the favourite playground of Montrealers since the 1930s. Located less than 1.5hrs from the big city, it encompasses a multitude of lakes, wooded mountains and villages equipped to accommodate visitors. Montréalers "go up north" to their cottages to relax, go canoeing—in short, to enjoy the natural surroundings. In winter, visitors from Ontario, New York and other parts of eastern North America join Montréalers in the charming local inns and luxury hotels. They come here not only to go downhill skiing, but also to snowshoe, cross-country ski or snowmobile across the snow-covered landscape, and spend pleasant evenings by the fireside. The Laurentians boast the largest concentration of ski hills in North America.

Saint-Jérôme (pop. 25,600)

This administrative and industrial town is nicknamed "La Porte du Nord" (The Gateway to the North), because it marks the passage from the St. Lawrence valley into the mountainous region that stretches north of Montréal and Québec City.

The Laurentians are one of the oldest mountain ranges on earth. Compressed by successive glaciations, the mountains are low, rounded, and composed of sandy soil. Colonization of this region began in the

The Laurentians

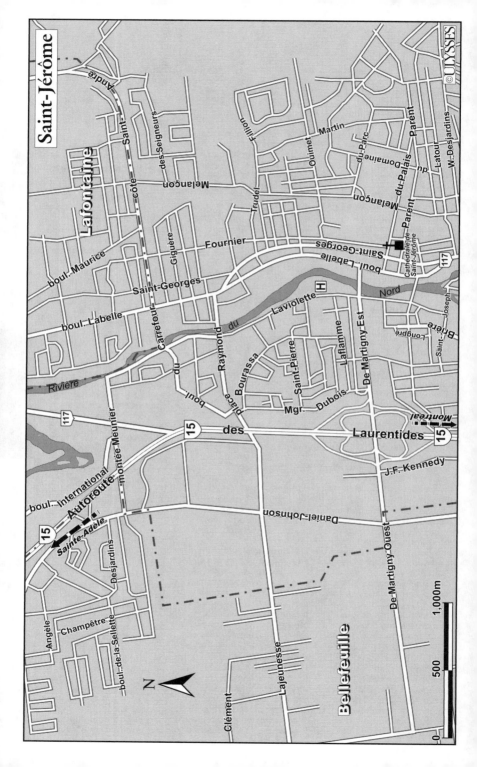
Saint-Jérôme

second half of the 19th century, with Saint-Jérôme as the starting point.

In the years following the rebellion of 1837-38, French Canadians began to feel cramped on their old, over-populated seigneuries. There was so little regional industry that families were forced to subdivide their farmlands in order to provide work for the new generations. These efforts, however, were decidedly insufficient. Thus began a mass exodus, during which several tens of thousands of Quebecers headed for the spinning mills of New England in the hopes of a better future. To this day, much of the population of the region around Saint-Jérôme is of French Canadian extraction. The all-powerful clergy of Québec tried a number of tactics to halt this exodus to the United States, the most important being the colonization of the upper Laurentians between 1880 and 1895, led by Curé Antoine Labelle of Saint-Jérôme. This unproductive land, hardly suitable for farming, was the source of many headaches for the colonists, who had to earn extra income cutting wood. Farmers became lumberjacks when winter rolled around. It was only thanks to sports-oriented tourism that the Upper Laurentians finally began to enjoy a certain degree of prosperity after 1945.

The **Cathédrale de Saint-Jérôme** ★ *(free admission; every day 7:30am to 4:30pm; facing Parc Labelle, 355 Rue St-Georges, ☎432-9741)*, a simple parish church when it was erected in 1899, is now a large Roman Byzantine–style edifice reflecting Saint-Jérôme's prestigious status as the "headquarters" of the colonization of the Laurentians. A bronze statue of Curé Labelle, sculpted by Alfred Laliberté, stands in front of the cathedral.

In 1997, an **open-air amphitheatre** was inaugurated in front of the church, in Parc Labelle. Behind it lies the **Promenade de la Rivière Nord** a pleasant riverside trail studded with information panels about the history of Saint-Jérôme.

Saint-Jérôme is also the starting point of the **Parc Linéaire le P'tit Train du Nord** ★ ★. This extraordinary bike path, which becomes a cross-country ski trail in winter, stretches 200km, from Saint-Jérôme to Mont-Laurier, along the same route once followed by the Laurentian railroad.

This railroad was built between 1891 and 1909 and played a crucial role in the colonization of the Laurentians. It came to be known as the P'tit Train du Nord or "Little Train of the North," a nickname immortalized in a song by Félix Leclerc. Later, right up until the 1940s, the railroad fostered the development of the region's tourist industry by providing access to all sorts of summer and winter resort areas.

Roads and then highways eventually made the Laurentians more and more accessible, rendering the P'tit Train du Nord obsolete by the 1980s. The railroad was dismantled in 1991, and the park was laid out a few years later. The park has since become one of the Laurentians' major attractions. It is punctuated from one end to the other with information panels, enabling visitors to learn more about the region's rich history, particularly the original train stations (Saint-Jérôme, Prévost, Mont-Rolland, Val-Morin, Sainte-Agathe-des-Monts, Saint-Faustin--Lac-Carré, Mont-Tremblant, Labelle, L'Annociation and Mont-Laurier), which are still standing. Some have even been restored, as is the case with the **Saint-Jérôme station**,

which was not only overhauled in 1997, but now has a pretty square next to it called **Place de la Gare**.

Continue along Aut. 15 N. toward Saint-Sauveur-des-Monts. On the way, the road runs alongside the village of Prévost, where the Laurentians' first downhill ski trails were opened in 1932. The following year, the first mechanical chairlift in North America was installed here. Take the Piedmont Exit (58).

Piedmont
(pop. 2,600)

Unlike other villages in the vicinity, Piedmont has not undergone much large-scale development. Mostly residential, it is a jumping-off point for fun waterslides and downhill skiing.

La Pente des Pays-d'en-Haut, see p 240

Station de Ski Mont-Olympia, see p 240

Station de Ski Mont-Avila, see p 240

Follow the signs for Rte. 364 and Saint-Sauveur-des-Monts, located right nearby, west of Aut. 15.

★
Saint-Sauveur-des-Monts (pop. 7,000)

Located perhaps a little too close to Montréal, Saint-Sauveur-des-Monts has been overdeveloped in recent years, and condominiums, restaurants and art galleries have sprung up like mushrooms. Rue Principale is very busy and is the best place in the Laurentians to mingle with the crowds. This resort is a favourite among entertainers, who own luxurious second homes on the mountainside. The Église Saint-Sauveur is also very popular with engaged couples, who have to

The Laurentians

put their names down on a long waiting list in order to be married there.

Station de Ski Mont-Saint-Sauveur, see p 240.

Station de Ski Mont-Habitant, see p 240.

Parc Aquatique du Mont-Saint-Sauveur, see p 240.

*From Saint-Sauveur-des-Monts, you can make a loop through charming **Morin-Heights**, with its two small white churches, one Catholic and the other Anglican, and pretty **Saint-Adolphe-d'Howard**. Rte. 364 O. and Rte. 329 N. lead ultimately to Saint-Agathe. Alternatively, get back on Aut. 15 N., then take the exit for Sainte-Adèle and Sainte-Margueritedu-Lac-Masson (69).*

★
Sainte-Adèle
(pop. 9,440)

The Laurentians were nicknamed the Pays-d'En-Haut (the Highlands) by 19th-century colonists heading for these northern lands, far from the St. Lawrence Valley. Writer and journalist Claude-Henri Grignon, born in Sainte-Adèle in 1894, used the region as the setting for his books. His famous novel, *Un homme et son péché* (A Man and his Sin), depicts the wretchedness of life in the Laurentians back in those days. Grignon asked his good friend, architect Lucien Parent, to design the village church, which graces Rue Principale to this day. On August 27, 1997, the villages of Mont-Rolland and Sainte-Adèle merged to form the new municipality of Sainte-Adèle.

Au Pays des Merveilles
($8.69; mid-Jun to late Aug, every day 10am to 6pm; 3595 Chemin de la Savane, ☎450-229-3141) is a small,

modest amusement park that will appeal mainly to young children. Slides, a wading pool, a miniature golf course, a maze, etc. have all been laid out in a setting reminiscent of Alice's Adventures in Wonderland *(Alice au Pays des Merveilles* in French). The admission fee (no discounts for children) is a bit steep.

Station de Ski Chanteclerc, see p 241.

Take Rte. 370 to Sainte-Marguerite-du-Lac-Masson. On the way, you'll see the charming Pavillon des Arts de Sainte-Adèle.

Sainte-Marguerite-du-Lac-Masson
(pop. 2,250)

All year round, vacationers come to the lovely rolling countryside of the Lac Masson area to unwind far from the hustle and bustle of Montréal. Two villages, have grown up on the shores of the lake, the elegant L'Estérel and the more modest, but more populated Sainte-Marguerite-du-Lac-Masson, which is located on the westernmost part of the lake. Those two villages have merged into one municipality.

Rte. 370 will take you to Sainte-Marguerite, on the shores of Lac Masson. A little square next to the church, in front of the renowned Bistro à Champlain (see p 248) offers a good view of the lake. The road then turns right, skirting around the lake on its way to Ville d'Estérel.

★
Ville d'Estérel
(pop. 95)

In Belgium, the name Empain is synonymous with financial success. Baron Louis Empain, who inherited the family fortune in the early 20th century, was an important builder, just like his father, who was

responsible for the construction of Heliopolis, a new section of Cairo (Egypt). During a trip to Canada in 1935, Baron Louis purchased Pointe Bleue, a strip of land that extends out into Lac Masson. In two years, from 1936 to 1938, he erected about 20 buildings on the site, all designed by Belgian architect Antoine Courtens, to whom we also owe the Palais de la Folle Chanson and the facade of the Église du Gésu in Brussels, as well as the Grande Poste in Kinshasa, Zaïre. Empain named this entire development **Domaine de l'Estérel**. The onset of World War II thwarted his plans, however, and after the war, the land was divided up. In 1958, a portion of it was purchased by a Québec businessman named Fridolin Simard, who began construction of the present **Hôtel L'Estérel** along Rte. 370, and then divided the rest of the property into lots. On these pieces of land, visitors will find lovely modern houses made of stone and wood designed by architect Roger D'Astou.

Val-Morin
(pop. 2,040)

Val-Morin is a modest village that has attracted cottage-goers who want to avoid the overdevelopment prevalent in some Laurentian villages. It is located in a mountainous region crisscrossed by cross-country ski trails, where a number of outdoor activities can be enjoyed.

Return to Rte. 117 N., and continue to Val-David.

Val-David
(pop. 3,225)

Val David attracts visitors not only because it is located near the Laurentian ski resorts, but also for its craft shops, where local artisans display their work. The village, made up of

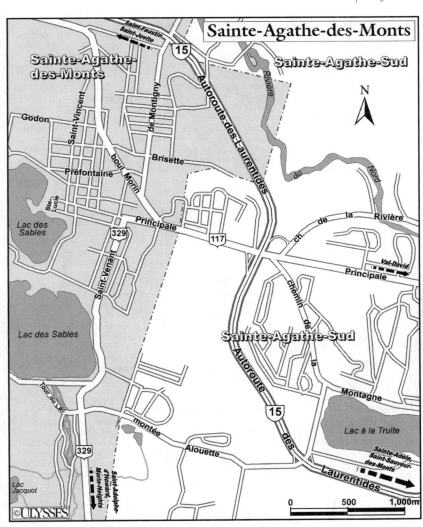

Sainte-Agathe-des-Monts

lovely houses, has managed to retain its own unique charm.

Every year, the **Village-du-Père-Noël** (*$9; early Jun to late Aug, every day 10am to 6pm; Rte. 117, 987 Rue Morin, ☎819-322-2146 or 800-287-NOEL*), or Santa's Village, attracts children eager to meet Saint Nicholas at his summer retreat. A number of activities are organized,

ensuring memorable days for the kids.

From Aut. 15 (Exit 86), turn right onto Rte. 117 N. Keep left and turn onto Rte. 329 S. (Rue Principale).

★
Sainte-Agathe-des-Monts (pop. 9,000)

Set in the heart of the Laurentians, this is a business-

and tourist-oriented town, which sprang up around a sawmill in 1849. When the railway was introduced to the region in 1892, Sainte-Agathe-des-Monts became the first resort area in the Laurentians. Located at the meeting point of two movements of coloni-zation, the British settling of the county of Argenteuil and the French Canadian settling of Saint-Jérôme, the town suc-ceeded in attracting wealthy vacationers, who, lured by Lac des Sables, built several beautiful villas around the lake and near the Anglican church. The region was once deemed a first-class resort by important Jewish families from Montréal and New York. In 1909, the Jewish community founded Mount Sinai Sanitarium (the present building was erected in 1930) and in the following years, built synagogues in Sainte-Agathe-des-Monts and Val-Morin.

Lac des Sables can be toured **by land or by water** ★. The Chemin du Lac (11km) can be followed by bicycle or by car.

Take the winding Rte. de Saint-Faustin through the mountains and around the lakes. Turn left on to Rte. 117 (caution: dangerous intersection), which leads to Saint-Jovite.

Whither Tremblant?

Because of the fusion fever that has hit Québec of late, many independent towns, villages and cities have merged. In keeping with the trend toward "bigger is better," St-Jovite, Mont-Tremblant village and the resort at the foot of the mountain are now part of "Ville de Mont-Tremblant." They are now known respectively as "Secteur St-Jovite," "Secteur du Village" and "Station Mont-Tremblant." We have adopted these names in our text.

Ville de Mont-Tremblant

Secteur Saint-Jovite (pop. 5,550)

Visitors will enjoy strolling down Rue Ouimet, which is lined with restaurants, tea rooms, antique shops and boutiques. Particularly notable buildings include a pretty little Victorian-style shopping centre and the village's original railway station, which has been moved to the side of the road and converted into a restaurant. At the end of a country road east of Saint-Jovite lies the enormous **Monastère des Apôtres de l'Amour Infini**. The monastery is crowned with a statue of the Sacred Heart. This schismatic sect has named its own pope, whose seat of power is Saint-Jovite.

Near the church, turn down Rue Limoges (327) in the direction of Mont Tremblant, which is already visible on the horizon. The road passes through Mont-Tremblant Village before reaching the Mont-Tremblant resort (open year-round).

★★★ Station Mont-Tremblant (Mont-Tremblant Resort)

Some of the largest resorts in the Laurentians were built by wealthy American families with a passion for downhill skiing. They chose this region for the beauty of the landscape, the province's French charm and above all for the northern climate, which makes for a longer ski season than in the United States. Station Mont-Tremblant was founded by Philadelphia millionaire Joseph Ryan in 1938. Since 1991, the resort has been owned by Intrawest, which also owns Whistler Resort in British Columbia, and which has invested $800 million in Tremblant over the past decade in order to put it on a par with the huge resorts of West-

ern Canada and the United States. At the height of the season, 74 trails, including several new ones, attract downhill skiers to Tremblant's slopes (914m). In the summer, the two magnificent golf courses are just as popular. Not only does this place have the longest and most difficult vertical drops in the region, it also boasts a brand-new resort complex set in an ersatz, yet extremely attractive, little village of traditional Quebec-style buildings at the base of the mountain.

Place Saint-Bernard is surrounded by the new hotel complexes as well as many shops, restaurants and bars. Vieux-Tremblant preserves a more authentic feel; several of the original and more traditional buildings have been renovated. No motor vehicles are permitted anywhere in the village, so you'll have to get around on foot, skis or snowshoes.

Charming **Chapelle Saint Bernard** (1942), a replica of Église Saint-Laurent, which once stood on Île d'Orléans, greets visitors on the way into the resort beside Lac Tremblant. The road on the right leads to the public parking lot, the **Panoramic Chairlift** and, 10km further north, to the entrance to **Parc du Mont-Tremblant** ★★ (see p 238).

This all-season resort area is still growing. Following the addition of new trails, Intrawest has been adding more accommodation units and conference centres.

★ Secteur du Village (pop. 764)

On the other side of Lac Tremblant lies charming Mont-Tremblant Village, not to be confused with the resort area. Here, in a more authentic setting, visitors will find

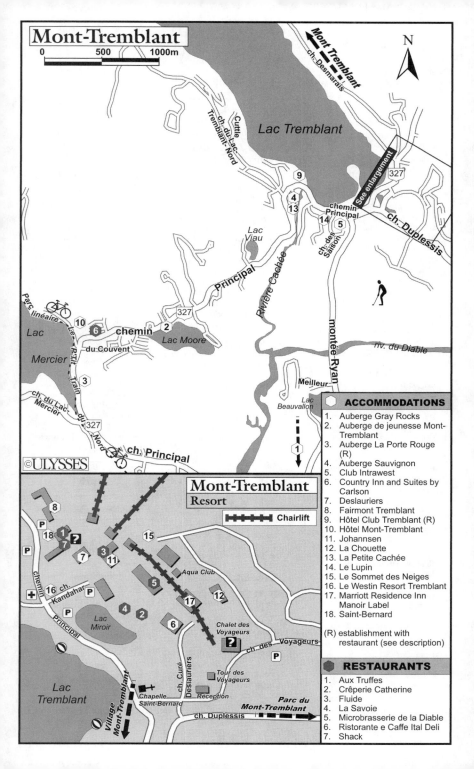

Mont-Tremblant

0   500   1000m

Lac Tremblant

Mont-Tremblant
ch. Desmarais

N

327

See enlargement

ch. Duplessis

chemin Principal

9

4
13

14

5

ch. des Saison

Lac Viau

Rivière Cachée

Principal

327

Lac Moore

chemin

du Couvent

Parc linéaire Le P'tit Train du Nord

Lac Mercier

10

6

3

ch. du Lac Mercier

327

ch. Principal

montée-Ryan

riv. du Diable

Meilleur

Lac Beauvallon

1

©ULYSSES

Mont-Tremblant
Resort

╋╋╋╋ Chairlift

8

P

18

1

7

?

7

3

11

15

Aqua Club

chemin Kandahar

16 ch.

P

P

5

17

12

P

4

2

6

Chalet des Voyageurs

?

ch. des Voyageurs

P

Lac Miroir

ch. Curé Deslauriers

Tour des Voyageurs

Lac Tremblant

Village Mont-Tremblant

Chapelle Saint-Bernard

Réception

Parc du Mont-Tremblant

ch. Duplessis

attractive shops and restaurants, as well as a number of other places to stay.

Note that the region has a new international airport in **La Macaza** *(www. tremblant.com)*.

Labelle (pop. 2,200)

Tourism in the densely forested northern portion of the Laurentians, commonly known as the Hautes-Laurentides (Upper Laurentians), is largely devoted to a wide range of outdoor activities (observing plant and animal life, hunting, fishing, camping, cross-country skiing, etc.). The traditional local industry, lumber, is currently on the decline. The region developed between 1870 and 1890, thanks to Saint-Jérôme's parish priest, Antoine Labelle, who did his utmost to open up new lands to attract farmers from the congested plain of the St. Lawrence to the Hautes-Laurentides. To do so, he converted the former lumberjack camps in the Rouge and Lièvre valleys, known as *fermes forestières* (forest farms), into villages for the colonists. This explains why certain municipalities in the Hautes-Laurentides still bear the name "ferme."

The town of Labelle is the main jumping-off point for the Parc du Mont-Tremblant.

Réserve Faunique Papineau-Labelle, see p 260

Réserve Faunique Rouge-Matawin, see below.

Parks

Tour A: Lac des Deux-Montagnes

The **Parc d'Oka and the Calvaire d'Oka** ★ *($3.50; 2020 Chemin d'Oka, ☎450-479-8365)* encompasses about 45km of trails for hikers in the summer and cross-country skiers in the winter. Most of the trails lie south of Rte. 344, crisscrossing a relatively flat area. North of Rte. 344, there are two other trails that lead to the top of the Colline d'Oka (168m), where visitors can drink in a view of the entire region. The longer trail (7.5km) ends at a panoramic viewing area, while the shorter one (5.5km) guides visitors past the oldest stations of the cross in the Americas. This calvary was set up by the Sulpicians back in 1740, in an effort to stimulate the faith of Aboriginals recently converted to Catholicism. Humble and dignified at the same time, the calvary is made up of four trapezoidal oratories and three rectangular chapels built of whitewashed stone. These little buildings, now empty, once housed wooden bas-reliefs depicting the Passion of Christ. The park also has campsites *($20/day, ☎450-479-8365)* and an information centre.

Tour B: Cottage Country

Parc du Mont-Tremblant ★★ *(Chemin du Lac Tremblant, ☎819-688-2281 or 877-688-2289)*, created in 1894, was originally known as Parc de la Montagne Tremblante (Trembling Mountain Park) in reference to an Algonquian legend. It covers an area of 1,250km², encompassing the mountain, seven rivers and about 500 lakes. The ski resort opened in 1938, and has been welcoming skiers ever since. A day of skiing costs $44. The park also offers nine cross-country ski trails, which stretch over 50km. The resort caters to sports enthusiasts all year round. Hikers can explore up to 100km of trails here. Two of these, La Roche and La Corniche, have been rated among the most beautiful in Québec. The park also has bicycle paths, mountain-bike circuits, and offers water sports like canoeing and windsurfing.

The **Réserve Faunique Rouge-Matawin** *(accessible via Rte. 117 and Rte. 321, l'Ascencion, ☎819-275-1811 or 800-665-6527)* is a wildlife reserve and home to a number of different species of animals, including the highest concentration of moose in the province. Bridle paths and hiking trails have been laid out. The rivers running through the park are suitable for canoeing.

Réserve Faunique Papineau-Labelle, see p 260.

Outdoor Activities

Hiking

Tour A: Lac des Deux-Montagnes

Parc d'Oka has 40km of hiking trails; see above.

Tour B: Cottage Country

The 0.4km **promenade** along the **Rivière du Nord** *(between Rue Martigny and Rue St-*

Joseph, St-Jérôme) is studded with thematic signposts, so visitors can learn about the region's history while enjoying a lovely view of the river.

Near Saint-Faustin, the **Centre touristique et éducatif des Laurentides** (*$5; late May late Oct, every day; 5000 chemin du Lac du Cordon,* ☎*819-326-1606*) has eight trails, which range in length from one to 10km, covering a total of 35km. Among these, Le Panoramique (3km) offers the loveliest views of the area. L'Aventurier, the longest trail (10km), leads to the top of a 530m-high mountain.

At Station Mont-Tremblant, the Tremblant Express chairlift will take you up to the new **ÉcoZone** (☎*877-873-6252 or 88T-REMBLANT*) centre, which has trails designed specifically for families (Le Manitou, Le 360°, Le Montagnard and Les Ruisseaux), as well as others for more seasoned hikers (Les Caps, Le Grand Brûlé, Les Sommets, Le Parben and Le Johannsen). All along the trails, there are markers containing information on the Laurentian wildlife.

Parc du Mont-Tremblant is an excellent place for hiking, as it has trails of all levels of difficulty. La Roche and La Corniche are both short, delightful hikes, while the 45km Diable trail is sure to satisfy even the most fanatical hiking buffs.

Rock-climbing

Tour B:
Cottage Country

The **Val-David** area is renowned for its rock faces. A number of mountains here are fully equipped to accommodate climbers' needs; **Mont King**, **Mont Condor** and **Mont**

Césaire are among the most popular. For more information, equipment rentals or guide services, contact **Passe Montagne** (*1760 Montée 2e Rang, Val-David;* ☎*819-322-2123 or 800-465-2123*), a trail-blazing rock-climbing outfit in the Val-David region. Their team of experts offer excellent advice.

Swimming

Tour A: Lac des Deux-Montagnes

The **Park d'Oka** (*$3.50; Jun to Sep;* ☎*450-479-8365*) has a very popular beach where canoes, sailboards and pedalboats are all available for rent. Picnic area, snack bar and restrooms.

Tour B:
Cottage Country

Among the region's other public beaches, we should mention those in **Sainte-Adèle** (*$4; Chemin Chanteclerc,* ☎*450-229-2921*), which is small but pleasant; in **Saint-Adophe-d'Howard** (*Chemin du Village,* ☎*819-327-2626*); in **Sainte-Agathe-des-Monts** (*$5; Lac des Sables*); in **Sainte-Marguerite-du-Lac-Masson** (*$5;* ☎*450-228-2545*) and the one in **Mont-Tremblant** (*$5; Chemin Principal,* ☎*819-425-8641*), as well as the **Club Plage et Tennis de la Station Touristique du Mont-Tremblant** (☎*819-681-5643*), which rents out canoes, kayaks, rowboats, sailboards and pedalboats.

Cycling

Tour B:
Cottage Country

The former railway line of the **P'tit Train du Nord** (☎*450-436-8532*), which carried Montréalers up north for many years, has been transformed into a superb 200km bike path from Saint-Jérôme to Mont-Laurier. It leads through a number of little villages where accommodations and restaurants in all price ranges can be found.

The **Station Touristique du Mont-Tremblant** (☎*877-TREMBLANT*) has a dozen mountain-bike trails. To reach them, you and your bike take a specially designed chairlift. There are several trails: La Cachée (*novice*); Le Labyrinthe (*intermediate*); La Nord-Sud, La Chouette and La Grand Nord (*advanced*); and La Sasquatch (*expert*).

Parc du Mont-Tremblant (☎*819-688-2281*) maintains some 100km of bike paths.

Rafting

Thanks to the thrilling Rivière Rouge, the Laurentians offer excellent conditions for whitewater rafting—among the best in Canada, according to some experts. Of course, there is no better time to enjoy this activity than during the spring thaw. Rafting during this period can prove quite a challenge, however, so previous experience is recommended. The best season for novices is summer, when the river is not too high and the weather is milder. For further information, contact **Nouveau Monde**,

Expéditions en Rivière *($79 per person on weekdays, $85 per person on weekends; 100 Chemin de la Rivière Rouge, Calumet; ☎819-242-7238 or 800-361-5033)*, which offers group outings every day.

Golf

Tour A: Lac des Deux-Montagnes

The **Club de Golf Carling Lake** *($70, $35 after 3pm; Rte. 327 N., 2235 Pine Hill, ☎450-533-5333)*, established near Lachute in 1961, is one of the most beautiful public golf courses in Canada, according to *Golf Digest* magazine. Furthermore, the elegant Hôtel du Lac Carling (see p 242) is located right nearby.

Tour B: Cottage Country

Among the dozens of golf courses scattered across the Laurentians, one of the more renowned is the **Club de Golf L'Estérel** *($52; Boulevard Fridolin-Simard, Estérel, ☎450-228-2571)*.

Mont-Tremblant resort also boasts a good golf course, **Le Diable** *(3005 Chemin Principal, Mont-Tremblant, ☎819-681-4653)*, which experts have ranked among the 10 best in Canada. Reservation required seven days in advance.

Club de Golf Gray Rocks *($55; 525 Chemin Principal, Mont-Tremblant, ☎819-425-2771 or 800-567-6767)*, which has one 18-hole course.

Waterslides and Tobogganing

Tour A: Lac des Deux-Montagnes

There are no fewer than 45 waterslides at the **Super Aqua Club** *($25; mid-Jun to late Aug, 10am to 7pm; 322 Montée de la Baie, ☎450-473-1013)* in Pointe-Calumet, as well as a wave pool and innertube "rivers." The water park is on the shores of Lac des Deux Montagnes and has a lovely sandy beach. Pedalboat and canoe rentals available.

Tour B: Cottage Country

During the winter, those who are interested in spending a pleasant day in the fresh air but don't want to ski can head over to **La Pente des Pays-d'en-Haut** *($27; mid-Dec to late Mar, Mon-Thu, 9am to 5pm, Fri and Sat 9am to 10pm; 440 Chemin Avila, ☎450-224-4014 or 800-668-7951)* and try the 19 different toboggan slides. In the summer, visitors can opt for the **Cascades d'Eau** *($21; mid-Jun to late Aug, every day 10am to 7pm; Exit 58 off Aut. 15; ☎450-227-3353)*, which has 17 waterslides.

Another waterslide option is the **Parc Aquatique du Mont-Saint-Sauveur** *($28; mid-Jun to early Sep, every day 10am to 7pm; Exit 60 off Aut. 15, 350 Rue St-Denis, ☎450-227-4671)*, with a wave pool and six slides, four of which are in a spiral, plus three more especially designed for children.

Downhill Skiing

Tour B: Cottage Country

There are two ski resorts in the mountains around Piedmont; **Station de ski Mont-Olympia** *($34; 330 Chemin de la Montagne, ☎450-227-3523 or 800-363-3696)* which has 23 trails and a total vertical drop of 200m, and **Station de ski Mont-Avila** *($32; Chemin Avila, ☎450-227-4671 or 800-363-2426)* where visitors will find about 10 trails, the longest of which is 1,050m.

A small mountain with a vertical drop of only 210m, **Station touristique Mont Saint-Sauveur** *($41; 350 Rue Saint Denis, St -Sauveur-des-Monts; ☎450-227-4671)* attracts lots of skiers because of its proximity to Montréal. It offers 34 downhill ski trails, a few of which are lit for night-skiing.

As Mont-Saint-Sauveur is often overcrowded, some might prefer the slopes of the neighbouring mountains, which have fewer trails but shorter lift lines. The **Station de Ski Mont-Habitant** *($32; 12 Boulevard des Skieurs, ☎450-227-2637)*, with 11 runs, is one of these.

We should also mention **Station de ski Morin-Heights** *($34; Chemin Bennett, ☎450-227-2020)*, which has 23 trails, 16 of which are lit for night-skiing; and the modest **L'Avalanche** *($25; 1657 Chemin de l'Avalanche, ☎450-327-3232)* ski centre, located near Saint-Adolphe-d'Howard.

The Sainte-Adèle region also attracts skiers with its two good-sized ski resorts. The **Station de Ski Mont-**

Gabriel ($25; 1501 Montée Gabriel, Ste-Adèle, ☎450-227-1100) has 18 trails (9 lit for night-skiing) for skiers of all different levels. The handsome Chanteclerc tourist complex was built near the **Station de ski Le Chanteclerc** ($33, 1474 Chemin Chanteclerc, ☎450-229-3555), with 24 trails, including 16 that are lit in the evening.

In Val-Morin, skiers can head to **Centre de ski Belle Neige** ($26; Rte. 117, ☎819-322-3311), which has 14 trails of all different levels of difficulty. In the Val-David area, you'll find **Mont-Alta** ($20; Rte. 117, ☎819-322-3206) and the **Station de ski Vallée-Bleue** ($24; 1418 Chemin Vallée-Bleue, ☎819-322-3427), with 22 and 17 trails, respectively.

The **Station de ski Mont-Blanc** ($35; Rte. 117, ☎819-688-2444 or 800-567-6715), in Saint-Faustin, has 36 runs and the second-highest vertical drop in the Laurentians (300m).

For several years now the **Station de ski Mont-Tremblant** (3005 Chemin Principal, Mont-Tremblant, ☎888-TREMBLANT) has been recognized as the number one vacation centre in North America. It now boasts a new slope: the Versant Soleil (the Sunny Side), with 15 runs facing due south and sheltered from the wind. This slope, along with the other sides of the mountain, forms a large ski area of 92 runs at an altitude of 649m, with snow parks and half-moons for lovers of glide sports. The 6km Nansen run will exhaust beginners, the challenging Zig Zag and Vertige runs will delight experts, and the 49ha of undergrowth will thrill the adventurous.

Gray Rocks ($30; 525 Chemin Principal, ☎819-425-2771 or 800-567-6767) is another resort in the region.

Jack Rabbit Johannsen

Born in Norway in 1875, Herman Smith-Johannsen immigrated to Canada in 1901. An engineer by profession, he started selling railroad equipment, which enabled him to visit a number of remote areas. He would ski to these places, meeting many Aboriginals along the way, who dubbed him "Wapoos," or Jack Rabbit. This nickname was then picked up by Smith-Johannsen's friends at the Montréal Ski Club.

Jack Rabbit Johannsen explored the Laurentians throughout the 1920s and 1930s. He even set up residence here and managed to develop an excellent network of cross-country ski trails.

It took him four years to clear a 128km trail known as the Maple Leaf, which stretches between the towns of Prévost and Labelle. Unfortunately, this lovely trail has since been interrupted by Autoroute 15 (Autoroute des Laurentides).

By founding a number of cross-country ski centres and opening numerous trails, Jack Rabbit Johannsen is remembered as a pioneer of sorts. This living legend hung up his skis, so to speak, at the age of 106 and passed away in 1987, at the age of 111. His legacy is the history of cross-country skiing in Québec.

It has 22 trails, with a vertical drop of 191m (much lower than at Mont-Tremblant).

Cross-country Skiing

Tour A: Lac des Deux-Montagnes

Park d'Oka ($7.50; Chemin d'Oka, ☎450-479-8365) has eight trails covering a total of about 50km. Three are ranked easy, three difficult and two very difficult. Those who prefer snowshoes to skis will be pleased to learn that the

park also has two snowshoe trails (5km in all).

Tour B: Cottage Country

The **Parc linéaire du P'tit Train du Nord** ($7; ☎450-436-8532), which stretches some 200km, becomes a wonderful cross-country ski and snowmobile trail in the winter. The section from Saint-Jérôme to Sainte-Agathe is reserved for skiers; the rest, as far as Mont-Laurier, is snowmobile territory.

The **Centre de ski de fond Morin-Heights** ($7; 612 Rue du Village, Morin-Heights,

The Laurentians

☎450-226-2417 or 450-226-1868) is one of the oldest cross-country ski resorts in Canada. It's the perfect place for "adventure skiing," that is, taking longer trips on ungroomed, back-country trails.

The **Centre de Ski de Fond L'Estérel** (*$8; 39 Boulevard Fridolin-Simard, Estérel*, ☎450-228-2571) is one of the best-organized cross-country resorts in the region. It is located at an altitude of 330m, so the snow conditions are excellent. Furthermore, this is truly a resort for skiers of all levels. Most of the trails are short, though not necessarily easy. There are 13 in all, four of which are easy, five difficult and four very difficult.

The **Centre Far Hills** (*$10; Chemin du Lac LaSalle, Val-Morin*, ☎819-322-2014, 514-990-4409 or 800-567-6636) maintains over 90km of cross-country trails. These run through a hilly, forested region, so skiers can drink in some lovely scenery. This is where you'll find the famous **Maple Leaf Trail**, cleared by none other than Jack Rabbit Johanssen (see p 241).

Parc du Mont-Tremblant, (see p 238)

Snowmobiling

Tour B: Cottage Country

Scores of snowmobile trails crisscross the Laurentians. Snowmobile rentals are available at the following places:

Randonneige
25 Rue Brisette
Sainte-Agathe-des-Monts
☎*(819) 326-0642*
☎*800-326-0642*

Location Constantineau
1117 Boulevard Albiny-Paquette
Mont-Laurier
☎*(819) 623-1724*

Hôtel L'Estérel
Chemin Fridolin-Simard
☎*(450) 228-2571*

Accommodations

Tour A: Lac des Deux-Montagnes

Oka

Parc d'Oka
$
May to Sep
☎*(450) 479-8365*
Park d'Oka has a magnificent campground with about 880 sites laid out in the middle of the forest.

La maison Dumoulin
$$ bkfst incl.
sb
C.P. 1072
53 Rue St-Sulpice
☎*(450) 479-6753*
La Maison Dumoulin has comfortable rooms, friendly service and a wonderful location on the shores of Lac des Deux-Montagnes.

Pine Hill

🏝 **Hôtel du Lac Carling**
$$$$ /pers ½b
≡, ⅀, ☉, ⚙, ≈, ℜ, △, ☯, ᕯ, ☉
2255 Rte 327 N.
☎*(450) 533-9211*
☎*800-661-9211*
⇰*(450) 533-4495*
www.laccarling.com
Hidden away on the shores of a lake just northwest of Lachute lies the remarkable but little-known Hôtel du Lac Carling. Made of stone and

pale wood, and graced with tall windows, this is a lovely, luxurious hotel. Inside, a sumptuous decor enhanced by numerous works of art and antiques awaits. The huge guest rooms are bathed in natural light. Some have a whirlpool bath, a patio or a fireplace. The hotel also has a sports centre complete with indoor tennis courts, a workout room, an indoor pool and a sauna. The renowned Club de Golf Carling Lake tops off the amenities (see p 240).

Tour B: Cottage Country

Saint-Sauveur-des-Monts

Le Bonnet d'Or
$$ bkfst incl.
⊛
405 Rue Principale
☎*(450) 227-9669*
☎*877-277-9669*
Le Bonnet d'Or features three guest rooms with wood-planked walls painted in deep colours and decorated in a Victorian style that is either cute or cloying, depending on your taste. Two suites, one with whirlpool bath, offer a more romantic setting. Friendly, pleasant proprietors but the main-street location may be bad news for light sleepers.

Motel Joli-Bourg
$$
≡, ⅀, ≈
60 Rue Principale
☎*(450) 227-4651*
From the outside, the Motel Joli-Bourg is fairly typical of motels in this category, with the parking lot occupying the place of honour. The management has, however, tried to make the rooms comfortable, equipping each of them with a fireplace.

Relais Saint-Denis
$$$
≡, ✖, ☉, ☾, ≈, ℝ, ℜ
61 Rue St-Denis
☎*(450) 227-4766*
☎*888-997-4766*
⇔*(450) 227-8504*
www.relaisst-denis.com
A small, friendly hotel, Relais Saint-Denis has rather ordinary-looking guest rooms, with a somewhat tired decor that lifts them just one step above a motel. Behind the building is a pleasant garden.

Manoir Saint-Sauveur
$$$$$ bkfst incl.
&, ≡, ☉, ≈, ℜ, ◠
246 Chemin du lac Millette
☎*(450) 227-1811*
☎*800-361-0505*
⇔*(450) 227-8512*
www.manoir-saint-sauveur.com
Manoir Saint-Sauveur, with some 300 rooms, focuses on athletic activities, offering lots of summer and winter packages with downhill skiing, golf or horseback riding, as well as a wide variety of facilities including tennis and squash courts. A new section was recently added with attractive new rooms sporting a warm beige hue and lovely duvets. Opt for these for a small extra charge (and ask for one on the mountain side). Manoir Saint-Sauveur manages to combine the coziness of a ski lodge and the elegance of a fine hotel. It is conveniently located within walking distance of the town of Saint-Sauveur.

Sainte-Adèle

Motel Chantolac
$$
≡, K, ☾, ≈, ℝ
156 Rue Morin
☎*(450) 229-3593*
☎*800-561-8875*
⇔*(450) 229-4393*
www.chantolac.com
The Motel Chantolac is a comfortable, well-located locale with reasonable rates. The rooms may not be spectacular, but they're a real bargain. Furthermore, the

place boasts a lovely location on the street leading to the Hôtel Le Chanteclerc, near lots of pleasant restaurants and just steps away from Lac Rond and its little beach.

Auberge de la Gare
$$ bkfst incl.
sb
1694 Chemin Pierre-Péladeau
☎*(450) 228-3140*
☎*888-825-4273*
www.aubergedelagare.com
Located a few kilometres outside Sainte-Adèle, Auberge de la Gare occupies a lovely Victorian house with elegant common areas and simple, country-style guest rooms decorated with pastel colours and a few antiques. There is a comfortable games room in the basement. Choice of sweet or savoury breakfast.

Le Chanteclerc
$$$$ bkfst incl.
≡, ☉, K, ≈, ℜ, ◠, ✪, ☻
1474 Chemin du Chanteclerc
☎*(450) 229-3555*
☎*800-363-2420*
⇔*(450) 229-5593*
www.lechanteclerc.com
At Hôtel Le Chanteclerc, whose name and emblem (a rooster) were inspired by Edmond Rostand's play, guests can enjoy a multitude of activities in an pristine lakeside setting at the foot of Mont Chanteclerc. The golf course is picturesque, with mountains on either side. The guest rooms themselves, however, are small and ultra-ordinary, the decor a dreary reminder of the 1980s. Avoid rooms on the fifth floor, as access to those at one end of this maze-like building require an unpleasant jaunt through the parking garage!

🚣 L'Eau à la Bouche
$$$$$
≡, ☉, ☾, ≈, ℜ
3003 boulevard Ste-Adèle
☎*(450) 229-2991*
☎*888-828-2991*
⇔*(450) 229-7573*
www.leaualabouche.com
A member of the prestigious Relais et Châteaux association, L'Eau à la Bouche is known for its excellent gourmet restaurant (see p 248) and extremely comfortable rooms. Don't be fooled by the building's rustic appearance; the rooms *are* elegantly furnished. The hotel itself dates from the mid-1980s and is set back from the road. It offers a splendid view of the ski slopes of Mont Chantecler. The restaurant is in a separate building. The complex is located on Rte. 117, a fair distance north of the village of Sainte-Adèle.

Ville d'Estérel

Hôtel l'Estérel
$$$$$
≡, ☉, ≈, ✪, ℜ, ◠
39 boulevard Fridolin-Simard
☎*(450) 228-2571*
☎*888-378-3735*
⇔*(450) 228-4977*
www.esterel.com
At the Hôtel l'Estérel, a large resort located on the shores of Lac Masson, guests can enjoy a variety of water sports and diverse athletic activities such as tennis, golf and cross-country skiing. The emphasis is placed on these activities; the rooms are dowdy and dreary and in desperate need of freshening up. Similarly, despite attempts to brighten them up, the dark corridors have a distinctly institutional feel to them, courtesy of cinderblock walls. And then there's that aroma of old motel...But then again, those who appreciate a lake view will be overjoyed by the lake-facing rooms, whose balconies literally overhang the lake—if you got any closer, you'd be swimming.

The Laurentians

Val-Morin

Far Hills Inn
$$$$
≡, ≈, ℜ, ◠
3399 Rue Far Hills Inn
☎(819) 322-2014
☎(514) 990-4409
☎800-567-6636
⇌(819) 322-1995
www.farhillsinn.com
Making the most of its extensive grounds, the Far Hills Inn has an extremely peaceful country setting. Its clientele includes cross-country skiers, who come to enjoy over 100km of trails.

Val-David

Chalet Beaumont
$
K, ℜ, ◠
1451 Beaumont
☎(819) 322-1972
☎800-461-8585
⇌(819) 322-3793
www.chaletbeaumont.com
Chalet Beaumont, located in a peaceful mountain setting, is one of only two youth hostels in the Laurentians. A log building with two fireplaces, it's a very appealing, comfortable place and an excellent option for outdoor enthusiasts on a tight budget. It is wise to ask who you'll be sharing a room with, as groups of young students often stay here on field trips to Val-David. From the bus stop, take Rue de l'Église across the village to Rue Beaumont and turn left; it's about a 2km walk

Le Temps des Cerises
$$ bkfst incl.
1347 Chemin de la Sapinière
☎(819) 322-1751
Le Temps des Cerises is a good choice in the B&B category. The people who run it are very friendly, which makes for a pleasant stay. The rooms are beautifully decorated, and each has a distinctive charm about it.

Auberge du Vieux Foyer
$$$$ ½b
≡, ℨ, K, ≈, ℜ, ⊛
3167 Rang 1er, Doncaster
☎(819) 322-2686
☎800-567-8327
⇌(819) 322-2687
www.aubergeduvieuxfoyer.com
The guest rooms in this tiny hotel are much cuter than one would imagine from its rather kitschy Swiss-style exterior. Each is unique and all are done up in pretty, deep colours, some with pine panelling, interesting art and attractive linens, with just a *soupçon* of the 80s look prevalent in Laurentian hotels. That said, claustrophobics should take note that they are closet-sized! Individual travellers should also beware that this place is popular with bus tours and conventions, so noise and a packed lobby are par for the course.

Hôtel La Sapinière
$$$$$
≡, ⊖, ℨ, ≈, ℜ
1244 Chemin de la Sapinière
☎(819) 322-2020
☎800-567-6635
⇌(819) 322-6510
www.sapiniere.com
La Sapinière is a rustic log building, dating from 1936 (and still under the original ownership). It's nothing luxurious at this price, and the faded yet cheery decor in each room features variations on the theme of pink carpeting, flowered wallpaper and lace curtains. Still, it makes for a comfortable place to stop during a tour of the region, especially for its beautiful location by a calm lake and surrounded by mountains and cross-country ski trails. Boats available for use.

Sainte-Agathe-des-Monts

Auberge Le Saint-Venant
$$ bkfst incl.
≡, K, ℝ
234 Rue St-Venant
☎(819) 326-7937
☎800-697-7937
⇌(819) 326-4848
www.st-venant.com
Auberge La Saint-Venant is one of the best-kept secrets in Sainte-Agathe. A big, beautiful, yellow house perched atop a hill, it has nine large, tastefully decorated rooms with big windows that let lots of light flood in. The service is friendly yet discreet.

Auberge La Caravelle
$$$ bkfst incl.
⊛, ≈, ℝ, ℜ
92 Rue Major
☎(819) 321-2444
☎800-661-4272
⇌(819) 326-0818
www.aubergelacaravelle.com
Auberge La Caravelle, a pretty blue-and-red house, defines itself as a "small, romantic inn". Appropriately, it is surrounded by a lovely garden full of flowers. Furthermore, half of its 16 rooms, including the bridal suite, are equipped with a whirlpool bath. The inn also has bicycles for its guests.

Lac-Supérieur

Base de Plein Air le P'tit Bonheur
$$$$ /pers
ℜ, sb
1400 Chemin du Lac Quenouille
☎(819) 326-4281
☎800-567-6788
⇌(819) 326-9516
www.ptitbonheur.com
The Base de Plein Air le P'tit Bonheur is nothing less than an institution in the Laurentians. Once a children's summer camp, it now caters to families looking for an "outdoor vacation." Set on a vast property on the shores of a lake, right in the heart of the forest, it has four buildings containing a total of nearly 430 beds, most in dormitories.

About 20 of the beds are in separate rooms, each equipped with a private bathroom and able to accommodate up to four people. Of course, this is the perfect place to enjoy all sorts of outdoor activities: sailing, hiking, cross-country skiing, skating, etc.

Auberge Caribou
$$$$$ ½b
ℜ
141 Tour du Lac
☎*(819) 688-5201*
☎*877-688-5201*
Keep this one under your hat: a rustic log chalet (built in 1945) within spitting distance of a lake with 14 cozy, affordably priced rooms (some with a lake view) and an excellent restaurant located in the Tremblant region. No two rooms are quite alike, but all feature knotty-wood panels, hand-painted leaf motifs and duvets. Most are cozy, rather than spacious, but there is a suite that can accommodate a small group or family. There are canoes available, and both a dock and a deck for lounging in summer. In the winter, the cross-country ski trails in Parc national du Mont-Tremblant are right nearby. Delicious breakfasts and fantastic dinners. A real gem.

Mont-Tremblant Resort

Station Mont-Tremblant
3005 Chemin Principal
☎*(819) 681-5555*
☎*800-461-5556*
⇌*(819) 681-5556*
www.tremblant.ca
The Station Mont-Tremblant directly manages a whole assortment of lodgings. Visitors may rent a room or an apartment in the **Country Inn and Suites by Carlson** (*$$$$$*; ≡, ≈, △, K) located near Lac Miroir in the "Vieux-Tremblant" area, or in the luxurious **Deslauriers**, **Saint-Bernard** and **Johanssen** (*$$$$$*; ≡, K) complexes, which face onto Place Saint-Bernard. Families will be better off with a fully equipped

condo in La Chouette (*$$$$$*). These units are small but flooded with natural light. What's more, they offer excellent value for the money, making them an option well worth considering in this area.

Club Intrawest
$$$$-$$$$$
⊘, K, ℜ, ≈, ⊙, △
200 Chemin des Saisons
☎*(819) 681-3535*
☎*800-799-3258*
⇌*(819) 681-3559*
www.clubintrawest.com
Primarily a time-share property, Club Intrawest also rents out studio (sleeps two) and one-bedroom apartments (sleeps four) in a number of low-rise buildings. Unfortunately, none offer much in the way of a view but inside, a pleasant surprise: an imaginative decor that is colourful and lighthearted. Reservations are a must.

🏊 Fairmont Tremblant
$$$$$
ⴲ, ≡, ⊛, ⊘, K, ℜ, ≈, ℜ, △
3045 Chemin Principal
☎*(819) 681-7000*
☎*800-441-1414*
⇌*(819) 681-7099*
www.fairmont.com
Overlooking station Mont-Tremblant resort, the Fairmont is one of only two additions to have been made to the prestigious Canadian Pacific hotel chain in a century, the other being located in Whistler, British Columbia. This imposing 316-room hotel manages to combine a genuine rustic warmth, well-suited to the surroundings, with all the comforts one expects from a top-flight establishment. It also houses a large convention centre and numerous conference rooms. The atmosphere and the decor are definitely more casual than that of the Westin, the newest Tremblant resort.

Sommet des Neiges
$$$$$
≡, ⊘, K, ℜ, ≈
Chemin de la Montagne
☎*800-461-8711*
Located right by the gondola, its silver dome unmistakable from anywhere in the resort, the Sommet des Neiges is the newest hotel to open in Tremblant under the Intrawest banner (2001). An all-suite hotel, each suite has a fully equipped kitchen, washer and drier, fireplace, balcony, glass walk-in shower and separate tub. There's plenty of woodwork in the decor, but its dark shade makes the rooms a little sombre. A good option for families.

🌴 Le Westin Resort Tremblant
$$$$$ bkfst incl.
≡, ℜ, ⊘, K, ≈, △
100 Chemin Kandahar
☎*(819) 681-8000*
⇌*(819) 81-8001*
www.westin.com
Opened in 2000, the Westin continues to set the bar high in terms of luxury and comfort. The lobby has the grandness and warmth of a country manor house, and the rooms, furnished with Westin's trademark "Heavenly Bed" and "Heavenly Bath," are boldly done up in red and gold and offer every comfort. Even the standard rooms are equipped with a kitchenette. While the service is generally excellent, it is unfortunately uneven.

Marriott Residence Inn - Manoir Labelle
$$$$$
ⴲ, ≡, ⊘, K, ℜ, ≈, ℜ
170 Chemin Curé-Deslauriers
☎*(819) 681-4000*
☎*888-272-4000*
⇌*(819) 681-4099*
www.marriott-tremblant.com
The prestigious, international Marriot chain has joined in the action at Tremblant, with its Manoir-Labelle Marriott Residence Inn, a large building located right at the start of the village. The place rents out

studios and one- or two-bedroom apartments, each equipped with a kitchenette. Some units even have a fireplace.

Mont-Tremblant Village

Parc du Mont-Tremblant
$
☎*(819) 688-2281*
☎*877-688-2289*
There are nearly 600 campsites in the Diable sector of Parc du Mont-Tremblant. Restrooms and showers.

Auberge de Jeunesse Internationale de Mont-Tremblant
$
ℜ
2213 Chemin Principal
☎*(819) 425-6008*
☎*800-461-8585*
⇒*(819) 425-3760*
www.hostelling tremblant.com
The Auberge de Jeunesse Internationale de Mont-Tremblant youth hostel has 84 beds, either in private rooms or dormitories. The common areas include a kitchen, a café/bar/restaurant and a living room with a fireplace.

Hôtel Mont-Tremblant
$$ bkfst incl.
≡, ℜ
1900 Rue Principale
☎*(819) 425-3232*
☎*888-887-1111*
⇒*(819) 425-9755*
botelmonttremblant.com
On the first floor of the Hôtel Mont Tremblant, visitors will find a bar; and on the second, rooms that are modest but satisfactory given the price and the location—all in the heart of the village, near the ski resort.

Auberge Sauvignon
$$$ bkfst incl.
≡, ⊛, ℜ
2723 Rue Principal
☎*(819) 425-5466*
☎*888-669-5466*
⇒*(819) 425-9260*
www.aubergesauvignon.com
The Auberge Sauvignon is a refreshing alternative to Mont-Tremblant's larger hotels. Francine's seven guest rooms are carefully decorated with country charm in neutral colours. Breakfast is continental, with homemade breads and fruit salad, and can be enjoyed in a cozy foyer with plenty of woodwork and dried flowers.

Auberge La Porte Rouge
$$$ ½b
≡, ⊛, K, ℑ, ≈, ℝ, ℜ
1874 Chemin Principal
☎*(819) 425-3505*
☎*800-665-3505*
⇒*(819) 425-6700*
www.aubergelaporte rouge.com
Auberge La Porte Rouge offers 14 standard rooms with balconies in its main, motel-style building, as well as "deluxe" rooms and chalets in separate buildings, some of which are converted old houses on the village's main street. Rooms are spacious and comfortable and have balconies, some facing the lake. Rates include breakfast and dinner in the hotel restaurant, **Le Saint-Louis** (see p 250).

La Petite Cachée
$$$ bkfst incl.
≡, ℑ, ≈
2681 Chemin Principal
☎*(819) 425-2654*
☎*866-425-2654*
⇒*(819) 425-6892*
www.petitecachee.com
La Petite Cachée, named after the nearby river, opened its doors in 1997. The rooms on the main floor have log walls and a cozy atmosphere, while those upstairs have a more elegant decor. All have wood floors and lovely linens and are impeccably decorated and

maintained by fastidious owners Manon and Normand. Some have balconies. But the best part about this B&B has to be its quality breakfasts. Normand gave up his cooking career to become an innkeeper, but every morning he returns to his first love and creates refined little dishes. Have a seat by one of the large mountain-facing windows in the dining room and let your taste buds come alive.

Le Lupin
$$$ bkfst incl.
≡, ℑ, ℜ
127 Pinoteau
☎*(819) 425-5474*
☎*877-425-5474*
⇒*(819) 425-6079*
www.lelupin.com
Built in 1945, this nine-room B&B has preserved the country atmosphere that reigned in Tremblant in the pre-Intrawest days. Country-style guest rooms range from the small, simply furnished standard and superior rooms, with wood floors, wood-planked walls and quilts, to a more romantic version, with deep soaker tubs, fireplace, CD player, wall-to-wall carpeting, and bubble bath. The smallest, simplest rooms are located in the basement, amidst ski memorabilia galore. Excellent, filling breakfasts (choice of sweet or savoury) and helpful hosts. Convenient location in a quiet spot just 1km from the ski hill, and the restaurants and bars of Station Mont-Tremblant. Allergy sufferers should note that there is a dog and two cats in residence.

Auberge Gray Rocks
$$$-$$$$ ½b
≡, ℑ, ⊘, K, ≈, ℝ, ℜ, ◻, ⅋, ⊛
525 Chemin Principal
☎*(819) 425-2771*
☎*800-567-6767*
⇒*(819) 425-3006*
www.grayrocks.com
The Auberge Gray Rocks, located 5km from Station Mont-Tremblant, toward St-Jovite, offers a range of activities and facilities, to satisfy

vacationers' every desire. Particular care has been taken to provide guests with the widest range of activities possible. The guest rooms, however, are small and rather dreary.

Hôtel Club Tremblant
$$$$$ ½b
≡, ⊘, K, 🕭, ≈, ℝ, ✪, 𝕽, △
121 Avenue Cuttle
☎ *(819) 425-8781*
☎ *800-567-8341*
= *(819) 425-9903*
www.clubtremblant.com

Hôtel Club Tremblant wins the prize for best view in Tremblant. Located just outside Station Mont-Tremblant, off the road leading to the village, its every room (120 in 10 buildings) offers a tremendous view of the lake and mountain as well as a balcony. Good thing, because the rooms themselves rather dreary and outdated, in the manner typical of ski condos built (or last renovated) in the 1980s. One of the earliest Tremblant inns, the current property grew out of a log house built in the early 1900s.

Restaurants

Tour A: Lac des Deux-Montagnes

Deux-Montagnes

Les Petits fils d'Alice
$$$$
Wed-Sun
1506 Chemin d'Oka
☎ *(450) 491-0653*

Les Petits Fils d'Alice serves fine French cuisine in a pleasant, intimate setting. During summer, you can eat outside on the terrace.

Oka

La petite Maison d'Oka
$$$-$$$$
Thu-Sun
bring your own wine
85 Rue Notre-Dame
☎ *(450) 479-6882*

La Petite Maison d'Oka is an excellent choice for anyone looking for fine French cuisine and an unpretentious atmosphere.

Pine Hill

Hôtel du Lac Carling
$$$$
2255 Rte 327 Nord
☎ *(450) 533-9211*
☎ *(514) 990-7733*

The splendid Hôtel du Lac Carling (see p 242) has a remarkable restaurant, L'lf, located in the rotunda of the main building, looking out onto the lake. Start off your gastronomic experience with a pheasant terrine *en croûte*, served with an apple and cranberry chutney, then continue with a vegetarian specialty like curried rice sauteed in olive oil, or boneless free-range quail stuffed with pears and green peppercorns. Luxurious decor. Romantic atmosphere.

Tour B: Cottage Country

Saint-Sauveur-des-Monts

Au Petit Café chez Denise
$-$$
338 Rue Principale

Had your fill of croissants and capuccino? Follow the locals to Denise's place for *la grosse bouffe*—eggs, bacon, ham, sausage, *fèves au lard* (pork and beans)... Breakfast is served until late, but if it's really late, tuck into a hot chicken sandwich, a club sandwich or a heaping plate of beef liver served with a dollop of mashed potatoes. Die-hard fashionistas might be gratified to find fruit crepes and the like, but they would do best to stick with the traditional fare.

Bistro Saint-Sauveur
$$-$$$
Tue-Sat
146 Rue Principale
☎ *(450) 227-1144*

The Bistro Saint-Sauveur offers its guests delicious French-bistro-style cuisine. The attractive decor creates a warm atmosphere perfect for a good meal among friends.

Moe's Deli & Bar
$$
21 Rue de la Gare
☎ *(450) 227-8803*

Moe's is a delicatessen-style restaurant with a varied menu. Big eaters will love the generous portions. The atmosphere is noisy, but extremely pleasant, making this a good place to enjoy a friendly get-together. The service is however occasionally brusque.

La Marmite
$$-$$$
314 Rue Principale
☎ *(450) 227-1554*

La Marmite serves succulent dishes in an extremely pleasant setting. It also has a lovely terrace, which you can enjoy during the summer.

Papa Luigi
$$-$$$
155 Rue Principale
☎ *(450) 227-5311*

The menu at Papa Luigi is made up of – you guessed it – Italian specialties, as well as seafood and grill dishes. Set up inside a lovely, wooden house, this restaurant draws big crowds, especially on weekends. Reservations strongly recommended.

Le Mousqueton
$$-$$$
Mon-Sat
120 Rue Principale
☎ *(450) 227-4330*

Innovative, contemporary Québec cuisine is served here in a warm, unpretentious atmosphere. Game, fish and even ostrich appear on the menu.

The Laurentians

Vieux Four
$$$
252 Rue Principale
☎*(450) 227-6060*
Always packed with regulars, the Vieux Four owes its popularity to its pasta dishes and delicious pizzas baked in a wood-burning oven. Its pleasant decor makes it a cozy place to go after a day of skiing.

Sainte-Adèle

La Chitarra
$$-$$$
140 Rue Morin, on the south side, at the corner of Rue Ouimet, at the top of the hill
☎*(450) 229-6904*
At La Chitarra, guests can savour French and Italian specialties. The pasta, meat and fish dishes are always excellent, but the desserts can be disappointing. This is a good restaurant to keep in mind when visiting Sainte-Adèle.

Le Chrysanthème
$$$
173 Rue Principale
☎*(450) 227-8888*
Le Chrysanthème has a beautiful, spacious outdoor seating area and is a wonderful place to dine on a fine summer evening. The restaurant serves authentic Szechuan cuisine, making for a nice change of pace in this area.

Clef des Champs
$$$-$$$$
closed Mon in winter
875 Chemin Pierre-Péladeau
☎*(450) 229-2857*
The Clef des Champs serves French cuisine fit for even the most discerning palates. The warmly decorated dining room is just right for an intimate dinner for two. The wine cellar is excellent.

Auberge La Biche au Bois
$$$$
Tue-Sun
100 boulevard Ste-Adèle
☎*(450) 229-8064*
The enchanting natural setting of Auberge La Biche au Bois is sure to stir up your appetite. The menu is made up of Québec and French specialties. Romantic ambiance.

L'Eau à la Bouche
$$$$
3003 boulevard Ste-Adèle
☎*(450) 229-2991*
One of the finest restaurants not only in the Laurentians but in all of Québec can be found at the hotel L'Eau à la Bouche (see p 243). Chef Anne Desjardins takes pride in outdoing herself day after day, serving her clientele outstanding French cuisine made with local ingredients. Two menus, one with three courses, the other with six, are offered each evening. Excellent wine list. An unforgettable gastronomic experience!

Sainte-Marguerite-du-Lac-Masson

Bistro à Champlain
$$$$
75 Chemin Masson
☎*(450) 228-4988*
⇔*(450) 228-4893*
Don't be put off by the uninspired exterior of the Bistro à Champlain. The place is actually one of the best restaurants in the Laurentians. It serves excellent nouvelle cuisine made with fresh local ingredients. The interior is extraordinary—a veritable art gallery where you can admire a number of paintings by the late Jean-Paul Riopelle, a close friend of the owner's, as well as works by other artists like Joan Mitchell and Louise Prescott. The restaurant also boasts one of the province's most highly reputed wine cellars, which may be toured by appointment. Everyone can sample some of the wines in this impressive stock, since even the finest are available by the glass. Reservations strongly recommended.

Val-Morin

Hôtel Far Hills
$$$$
3399 Rue Far Hills
☎*(819) 322-2014*
☎*(514) 990-4409 from Montréal*
The Hôtel Far Hills still has one of the finest restaurants in the Laurentians. The gourmet cuisine is positively world-class.

Val-David

La Vagabonde
$
Mer-Dim
1262 Chemin de la Rivière
☎*(819) 322-3953*
Primarily a bakery offering wholesome and delicious organic breads and treats, La Vagabonde is also a tiny café and tea room with a few tables and a patio in the conifers, where patrons wearing socks with their sandals sit around discussing yoga. A variety of unusual teas is lovingly served in Japanese tea sets. Très Zen...

Le Nouveau Continent
$
2301 Rue de l'Église
☎*(819) 322-6702*
Le Nouveau Continent serves simple, inexpensive food. The restaurant doubles as an exhibition space and a meeting place for artists, so the interior is decorated with works of art.

Le Grand Pa
$-$$
2481 Rue de l'Église
☎*(819) 322-3104*
The French restaurant Le Grand Pa is a very simple place with a homey atmosphere. On some evenings, the owner takes the time to play a few tunes on his guitar.

Hôtel La Sapinière
$$$$
1244 Chemin La Sapinière
☎(819) 322-2020
The restaurant in La Sapinière (see p 244) has been striving for over 60 years now to create innovative dishes inspired by the culinary repertoires of both Québec and France. Among the house specialties, the *lapereau* (young rabbit), *porcelet* (piglet) and the gingerbread are particularly noteworthy, and the *tarte au sucre à la crème* (sugar pie) is an absolute must. Very good wine list.

Sainte-Agathe-des-Monts

Le Havre des Poètes
$$
55 Rue St-Vincent
☎(819) 326-8731
At Le Havre des Poètes, singers perform French and Québec classics. The food is well-rated, but people come here mainly for the ambiance.

Chez Girard
$$-$$$
18 Rue Principale Ouest
☎(819) 326-0922
At the restaurant Chez Girard, set back a little from the road and not far from Lac des Sables, guests can enjoy delicious French cuisine in an extremely pleasant setting. It has two floors, the first being the noisiest.

Chatel Vienna
$$-$$$
Wed-Sun
6 Rue Ste-Lucie
☎(819) 326-1485
Chatel Vienna occupies a lovely period residence set on a little hill in front of Lac des Sables. While taking in the lovely view, guests savour Austrian dishes that are light and nourishing.

La Quimperlaise
$$-$$$
early Nov to early Jun Wed-Sun
11 Tour du Lac
☎(819) 326-1776
Installed in a little building, La Quimperlaise specializes in Breton dishes, especially crêpes filled with a wide variety of ingredients. The decor is charming, the atmosphere relaxed.

La Sauvagine
$$$$
1592 route 329 Nord
☎(819) 326-7673
Sauvagine is a French restaurant cleverly set up inside what used to be the chapel of a convent. Extremely well thought-out, it is decorated with large pieces of period furniture.

Saint-Jovite

Bagatelle Saloon
$$-$$$
Wed-Sun
852 Rue Ouimet
☎(819) 425-5323
The Bagatelle Saloon is the place to go in Saint-Jovite for a good steak or seafood. As you may have guessed by the name, the decor will transport you straight to the Far West.

Verre Bouteille
$$-$$$
888 Rue Ouimet
☎(819) 425-8776
This cute little bistro was a welcome addition to St-Jovite when it opened a few years back, but its reputation has suffered since the departure of its original chef. Still, it's worth a try for its reasonable three-course lunch specials ($), served until 2pm. *Rognons de veau* (veal kidneys), sweetbreads, mussels and pasta are included among the wide-ranging options.

Antipasto
$$-$$$
855 Rue Ouimet
☎(819) 425-7580
Antipasto, in the former train station, is a decent place to stop for a bite. The walls are adorned with pictures and signs that bear witness to the building's original purpose. Grab a seat by the cathedral window for the best atmosphere. The menu consists mainly of pizza, pasta and veal dishes. The best deal by far is the lunch special, which offers 12 choices ($) served in huge portions. Decent, though not outstanding, family fare, but a little pricey for dinner.

La Table Enchantée
$$-$$$
600 route 117 Nord
☎(819) 425-7113
La Table Enchantée, an inviting place with an understated decor, serves delectable Québec specialties. The chef does wonders with the *cipaille* and venison, among other produce.

Chez Roger
$$$
444 Rue St-Georges
☎(819) 429-6991
Located in an attractive old house just off Saint-Jovite's main drag, Chez Roger offers a short, changing menu of fine cuisine featuring such meaty items as *médaillons de cerf forestière* and osso buco *milanaise*. Outdoor seating on a cozy, covered terrace.

Cheval de Jade
$$$-$$$$
688 Rue Ouimet
☎(819) 425-5233
The Tremblant region's uncontested favourite spot for a splurge with your sweetie is certainly Cheval de Jade. Occupying a white shingled house just beyond Saint-Jovite's commercial centre, its simple yet elegant decor consists of brick and wood with dark-green walls and white-lace curtains. There is outside dining, beneath a canopy,

during the summer. The specialties of the house are fish (doré with lobster sauce, sole with truffled hollondaise sauce, bouillabaise) and flambées, and the service is attentive and friendly—no pretensions despite its star rating. A sure hit for a special night out.

Mont-Tremblant Resort

Fluide
$
☎*(819) 681-4681*
This juice bar, tucked into one of the sloping streets at the base of the mountain, is ideally located to restore the energy you spend skiing or walking. The fluids in question are delicious fresh juices and smoothies boosted with various natural ingredients known for their restorative properties.

Microbrasserie de la Diable
$
3005 Chemin Principal
☎*(819) 681-4546*
In the summer, you can take in the action on the pedestrian street from the lovely outdoor seating area of the Microbrasserie de la Diable. The interior, with tables set up on two floors, is a lot bigger than you'd think. Here, people tuck into spare ribs, sausages and smoked meats, washed down with one of the beers brewed on the premises, such as Extrême Onction, which has an 8.5% alcohol content.

Crêperie Catherine
$-$$
3005 Chemin Principal
☎*(819) 681-4888*
At Crêperie Catherine, you can savour an excellent selection of crêpes, which the chef prepares right before your eyes. During summer, you can sit outside on the pretty terrace.

Shack
$-$$
3035 Chemin Principal
☎*(819) 681-4700*
Le Shack's overloaded decor, which parodies a traditional sugar shack with its rustic furniture, artificial maple trees with the red leaves of an Indian summer, and wild geese hanging from the ceiling, is sure to bring a smile to your face. The place is located at the top of the village in the resort near the Fairmont Tremblant. Its big outdoor seating area, which is very popular in the summertime, looks out onto Place Saint-Bernard. The menu features simple fare like steak, roast chicken and burgers. Le Shack also has a morning buffet, where you can concoct a copious breakfast for yourself.

La Savoie
$$-$$$
☎*(819) 681-4573*
In an old *U*-shaped house in Vieux-Tremblant, slightly removed from all the hubbub, La Savoie serves *raclettes*, *pierrades*, fondues and other alpine specialties. Small outdoor seating area and a simple, pleasant atmosphere.

Aux Truffes
$$$$
3035 Chemin Principal
☎*(819) 681-4544*
Aux Truffes is the best restaurant in the Mont-Tremblant Resort. In an inviting modern decor, guests dine on succulent nouvelle cuisine. Truffles, foie gras and game are among the predominant ingredients.

Mont-Tremblant Village

Ristorante e Caffe Ital Delli
$$-$$$
1920A Chemin Principal
☎*(819) 425-3040*
Ask anyone in the know for an unpretentious eatery serving honest food at honest prices within close proximity to Tremblant, and chances are they'll send you here. A range of interesting pasta dishes (as well as veal and other meat dishes) is served in a simple decor of woodwork, brick and homey plaid tablecloths.

Club Tremblant
$$$-$$$$
avenue Cuttle
☎*(819) 425-2731*
The dining room at Club Tremblant (see p 247) offers a panoramic view of the lake and Mont Tremblant. The chef prepares traditional French gastronomic cuisine. On Thursday and Saturday nights, the restaurant serves a lavish buffet; the Sunday brunch is also very popular. Reservations strongly recommended.

Le Saint-Louis
$$$-$$$$
1874 Chemin Principal
☎*(819) 425-3505*
The dining room attached to the Auberge La Porte Rouge attracts many of its clients from the hotel's overnight guests, whose nightly rate includes dinner. And for a hotel restaurant, you could do much worse. Its short menu includes fish, lamb, duck and ostrich. There is a lake view from the tables, but the dining room is not particularly atmospheric and can be taken over by the arrival of a group. A decent choice for hotel guests, but not exciting enough to warrant a special trip.

Entertainment

Bars and Nightclubs

Saint-Sauveur-des-Monts

Les Vieilles Portes
Rue Principale
The bar Les Vieilles Portes is a nice place to get together with friends for a drink. It has a pleasant outdoor terrace open during the summer.

Bentley's
235 Rue Principale
Bentley's is often full of young people, who come here to have a drink before going out dancing.

Sainte-Adèle

Bourbon Street
Rte. 117, Mont-Rolland
Bourbon Street hosts good live music and is frequented by a relatively young clientele.

Mont-Tremblant Resort

Petit Caribou
The Petit Caribou is a young, energetic bar that really fills up after a good day of skiing.

Theatres

There is a strong tradition of summer theatre in the Laurentians. A number of well-known, well-loved theatres present quality French-language productions throughout the season. These include the **Théâtre Saint-Sauveur** (*22 Rue Claude*, ☎*450-227-8466*), the **Théâtre le Chanteclerc** (☎*450-229-3591*), **Le Patriote de Sainte-Agathe** (*Rue Saint-Venant*, ☎*819-326-3655*) and the **Théâtre Sainte-Adèle** (*1069 Boulevard Sainte-Adèle*, ☎*450-227-1389*).

Sainte-Adèle

The **Pavillon des Arts de Sainte-Adèle** (*1364 Chemin Pierre-Péladeau*, ☎*450-229-2586*) is a 210-seat concert hall in a former chapel. Twenty-five classical concerts are presented here annually. Each is followed by a music lover's wine and cheese in the adjoining gallery.

Festivals and Cultural Events

The **Festival des Couleurs** (☎*450-258-4924*) takes place from mid-September to early October, when the landscape is ablaze with flamboyant colours. Countless family activities are organized in Saint-Sauveur, Sainte-Adèle, Sainte-Marguerite-du-Lac-Masson, Sainte-Adolphe-d'Howard, Sainte-Agathe and Mont-Tremblant to celebrate this time of the year.

Val-Morin

Each year, on the third Sunday in September, the village of Val-Morin is closed off to automobile traffic, and cycling buffs flood into the area. This event, known as **Les Couleurs en Vélo** (*entry fees go up three weeks prior to the event*, ☎*819-322-3011*), offers a chance to explore this magnificent region while it's decked out in all its autumn finery. There are five routes ranging in length from 25 to 40km and covering various types of terrain, from flat stretches suitable for beginners and families to mountainous areas for more athletic types looking for a good challenge.

The cycling event itself starts at 12:30pm, but scores of other activities are held throughout the day.

Mont-Tremblant Resort

In mid-July, blues greats gather at the Mont-Tremblant resort for the **Festival de Blues de Tremblant** (☎*800-461-8711*). The shows are presented outdoors, as well as in local bars and restaurants.

The **Fête de la Musique** (☎*800-461-8711*), a classical music festival run by Angèle Dubeau (renowned violinist), is held at the Mont-Tremblant resort at the end of August. The concerts are held outdoors and in the Chapelle Saint-Bernard (see p 236).

Shopping

Tour B: Cottage Country

Saint-Sauveur-des-Monts

Visitors will find all sorts of treasures at **La Petite École** (*153 Rue Principale*), ranging from Christmas decorations to dried flowers, not to mention kitchen utensils and beauty products.

Those in search of all kinds of souvenirs will find just what they're looking for at **L'Art du Souvenir** (*191A Rue Principale*).

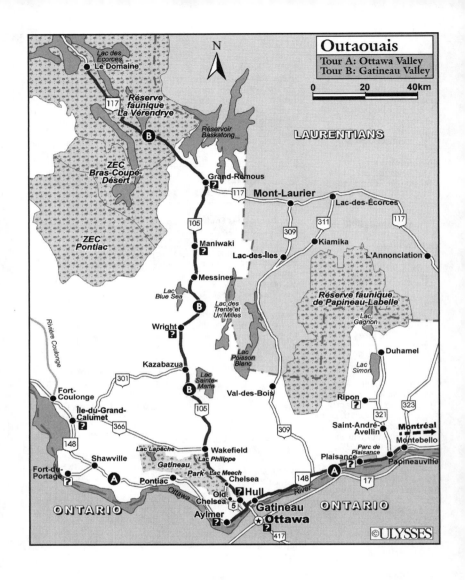

Outaouais
Tour A: Ottawa Valley
Tour B: Gatineau Valley

0   20   40km

N

Lac des Écorces
Le Domaine
Réserve faunique La Vérendrye
117
B
ZEC Bras-Coupé-Désert
Réservoir Baskatong
LAURENTIANS
Grand-Remous
117
Mont-Laurier
Lac-des-Écorces
105
311
117
309
Kiamika
Maniwaki
Lac-des-Îles
L'Annonciation
Messines
Lac Blue Sea
B
Lac des Trente et Un Milles
Réserve faunique de Papineau-Labelle
Lac Gagnon
Wright
Lac Poisson Blanc
Duhamel
Kazabazua
Lac Sainte-Marie
Lac Simon
ZEC Pontiac
Rivière Coulonge
301
B
Val-des-Bois
Ripon
323
Fort-Coulonge
105
321
Île-du-Grand-Calumet
366
309
Saint-André-Avellin
Montréal
Montebello
148
Lac Lapêche
Wakefield
Parc de Plaisance
Shawville
Lac Philippe
Papineauville
Fort-du-Portage
Gatineau
Park
Lac Meech
Plaisance
A
17
Pontiac
Chelsea
148
River
Ottawa
Old Chelsea
Hull
5
Aylmer
Gatineau
ONTARIO
ONTARIO
Ottawa
©ULYSSES
417

The Outaouais region,

discovered early on by explorers and trappers, was not settled by Europeans until the arrival of Loyalists from the United States in the early 19th century.

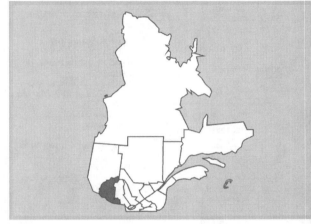

Forestry was long the region's main economic activity. Of particular importance to the industry were red and white pine, trees used for ship building. The logs were sent down the Ottawa River and the St. Lawrence to Québec City, where they were loaded onto ships headed for Great Britain. Forestry still plays an important role here, but service industries and government offices are also a major source of jobs, a situation resulting from the proximity of Canada's capital region.

Directly north of the cities of Hull, Gatineau and Aylmer, which recently merged, lies an expanse of rolling hills, lakes and rivers, which includes the magnificent Gatineau Park. The park is the location of the official summer residence of the Canadian Prime Minister and is a wonderful place for cycling, canoeing and cross-country skiing. The city of Hull, which borders Canada's capital city of Ottawa, has one of the best museums in the country: the Canadian Museum of Civilization. For its part, Ottawa, just across the river, is home to Canada's beautiful Parliament Buildings and a plethora of excellent museums.

Finding Your Way Around

Two tours of the region, following the Ottawa and Gatineau rivers, respectively are outlined in, **Tour A: The Ottawa Valley ★** and **Tour B: The Gatineau Valley ★**.

Tour A: The Ottawa Valley

By Car

From Montréal, there are two ways of reaching the departure point of the tour; one through the Ottawa River valley, and a faster way through Ontario.

1. Take Aut. 13 N., then Rte. 344 W., which corresponds to part of the **Lac des Deux-Montagnes ★** tour (see p 228). Finally take Rte. 148 W. toward Ottawa.

2. Take Aut. 40 W., which becomes Rte. 17 W. across the Ontario border. In Hawkesbury, cross the Ottawa River to return to Québec. Turn left on Rte. 148 W.,

toward Montebello and Ottawa.

Bus Stations

Montebello
535 Rue Notre-Dame
☎*(819) 423-6311*

Hull
238 Boulevard Saint-Joseph
☎*(819) 771-2442*

Ottawa (Ontario)
265 Catherine St.
☎*(613) 238-5900*

Train Station

Ottawa (Ontario)
200 Tremblay Road
☎*800-361-5390*

Tour B: The Gatineau Valley

By Car

Driving and cycling are the best ways to tour the whole valley. Follow Pormenade de la Gatineau from Boulevard Taché in Hull. You will almost immediately enter the Gatineau Park, created in 1938 by Canadian Prime Minister William Lyon Mackenzie King.

By Train

The small Hull-Chelsea-Wakefield steam train is a great way to see part of the rural Gatineau valley. The 32km trip takes approximately 5hrs and stops for two hours in Wakefield. In general, however, the best ways to explore the valley are by car or bicycle.

Practical Information

Area code: **819**

Name of New Merged City

Gatineau
Merger of Aylmer, Buckingham, Gatineau, Hull and Masson-Angers.

Tourist Information

Regional Office

Association Touristique de l'Outaouais
103 Rue Laurier, Hull, J8X 3V8
☎*778-2222 or 800-265-7822*
≠778-7758
www.tourisme-outaouais.org

Tour A: The Ottawa Valley

Montebello
502A Rue Notre-Dame
☎*423-5602*

Hull
103 Rue Laurier
☎*778-2222 or 800-265-7822*

Ottawa (Ontario)
90 Wellington Road
☎*(613) 239-5000*
☎*800-465-1867*

Tour B: The Gatineau Valley

Maniwaki
156 Rue Principale Sud
☎*449-6627*

Exploring

Tour A: The Ottawa Valley

Duration of tour: one to three days

All that remains of the Ottawa First Nation, slaughtered by the Iroquois in the 17th century, is their name. Ottawa, or in French, Outaouais, is used to denote the beautiful river that forms the border between Québec and Ontario, a vast region of lakes and forests, as well as Canada's capital city. The Ottawa River was once the main route of fur-trappers travelling to the Canadian Shield. These *voyageurs*, who worked for large trading companies, used this river each spring, returning in the fall with their precious cargo of pelts (beaver, seal, mink), which were then shipped to London and Paris from Montréal. This tour includes the "National Capital Region," most of which consists of the city of Ottawa, in Ontario.

★ Montebello (pop. 1,125)

The Outaouais region did not experience significant development under the French Regime. Located upstream from the Lachine Rapids, the area was not easily accessible by water, and was thus left to hunters and trappers until the early 19th century and the beginning of the forestry operations. The Petite-Nation seigneury, granted to Monseigneur de Laval in 1674, was the only attempt at colonization in this vast region. It was not until 1801, when the seigneury passed into the hands of notary Joseph Papineau, that the town of Montebello was established. Papineau's son, Louis-Joseph Papineau (1786-1871), head of the French Canadian nationalist movement in Montréal, inherited the Petite-Nation seigneury in 1817. Returning from an eight-year exile in the United States and France following the rebellion of 1837-38, disillusioned and disappointed by the stand taken by the Catholic clergy during the rebellion, Papineau retired to Montebello, where he built an impressive manor.

Manoir Papineau National Historic Site ★★ *($7; early May to early Sep, Thu-Sun 10am to 5pm; early Sep to mid-Oct Sat and Sun 10am to 5pm; 500 Rue Notre-Dame, ☎423-6965)* was erected between 1846 and 1849 in the monumental neoclassical villa style. The manor was designed by Louis Aubertin, a visiting French architect. The towers added in the 1850s give the house a medieval appearance. One of the towers houses a precious library that Papineau placed here to protect it from fire. The house has approximately 20 staterooms, through which visitors can now stroll, and features a rich Second Empire decor. It is located on lovely tree-shaded grounds. A small wooden walkway leads to the **Chapelle Funéraire des Papineau** (1855), where 11 members of the family are buried. Note that this is an Anglican chapel. Papineau's son joined the Church of England when his father died and was refused a Catholic burial. A bust of the elder Papineau, made from the funeral mask of the deceased by Napoléon Bourassa, is one of the interesting objects found in the chapel.

The **Château Montebello ★★** *(392 Rue Notre-Dame; ☎423-6341)* is a large resort hotel on the Papineau estate. It is the largest log building in the world. The hotel was erected in 1929 (Lawson and Little, architects) in a record 90 days. The impressive lobby has a central fireplace with six hearths, each facing one of the building's six wings.

The **Centre d'Interprétation de la Gare de Montebello** *(free admission; open all year round; 502 Rue Notre-Dame, ☎423-5602)* is an information centre in the former Montebello train station (1931). A display describes the role of the railway in the development of the Petite-Nation seigneury.

Spread over 600 ha, the **Parc Oméga ★** *($10; summer every day 9:30am to 6pm, winter 10am to 5pm; Rte. 323, ☎423-5487)* is home to many different animal species that can be watched from within one's vehicle, including bison, wild sheep, elk, wild goats, wild boar and deer.

*Rte. 321 heads north from Papineauville to Duhamel, providing access to the **Sentier d'Interprétation du Cerf de Virginie** (see p 260) and the **Réserve Faunique de Papineau-Labelle** (see p 260). Continuing east of*

*Papineauville on Rte. 148, you'll soon reach the **Parc de Plaisance** ★ (see p 260) and the **Chutes de Plaisance** (Rang Malo), (see p 260). Continue east on the 148 to Hull.*

Hull (Pop. 64,000)

Although the road leading into Hull is named after an important post-war town planner, the city is certainly not a model of enlightened urban development. Its architecture is very unlike that of Ottawa, just across the river. Hull is a mixture of old factories, typical working-class houses, tall, modern government office buildings, and barren land awaiting future government expansion. The town was founded by American Loyalist Philemon Wright, who introduced forestry operations to the Ottawa Valley. Wood from the region was cut, made into rafts and floated to Québec City, and eventually used in the construction of ships for the British Navy. By 1850, Hull was an important wood-processing centre. For many generations the Eddy Company, which is based in the area, has supplied matches to the entire world.

The modest wood-frame houses that line the streets of Hull are nicknamed "matchboxes" because they once housed many employees of the Eddy match factory, and because they have had more than their fair share of fires. In fact, Hull has burned so many times throughout its history that few of the town's historic buildings remain. The former town hall and beautiful Catholic church burned down in 1971 and 1972, respectively.

Ottawa has the reputation of being a quiet city, while Hull is considered more of a fun town, essentially because legal drinking age is a year

Manoir Papineau National Historic Site

Outaouais

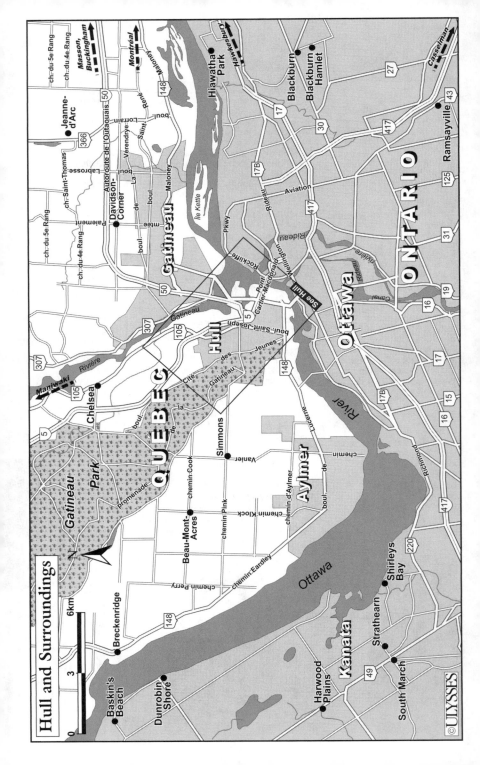

Hull and Surroundings

0   3   6km

© ULYSSES

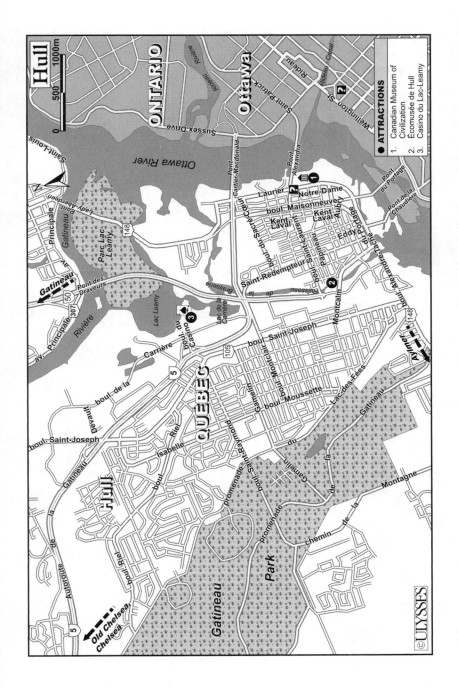

Hull

500 1000m

● ATTRACTIONS

1. Canadian Museum of Civilization
2. Écomusée de Hull
3. Casino du Lac-Leamy

ONTARIO

Ottawa

Rideau Canal

Wellington St.

Sussex Drive

Saint-Patrick

Rivière Rideau

Ottawa River

Saint-Louis

Pont Cartier-Macdonald

Pont Alexandra

Pont du Portage

Pont de la Chaudière

Laurier

Notre-Dame

boul. Maisonneuve

Kent

Laval

Kent

Laval

Eddy

du Portage

Papineau

boul. Sacré-Cœur

boul. Saint-Laurent

Saint-Redempteur

Saint-Redempteur

Tachè

boul. Alexandre-Tachè

Montcalm

Principale

Pont Lady-Aberdeen

Parc Lac-Leamy

148

Gatineau

Pont des Draveurs

50

307

Rivière

av. Principale

Lac Leamy

la Brasserie

le ruisseau de

Lac de la Carrière

Carrière

boul. du Casino

3

boul. Saint-Joseph

Montcalm

Ayimer

148

Carrière

105

5

QUÉBEC

Gamelin

boul. Montclair

boul. Moussette

Lac-des-Fées

Gatineau

Devault

boul. Devault

boul.-de-la

boul. Saint-Joseph

Isabelle

Riel

QUÉBEC

Gamelin

du

de la

Montagne

chemin de la

Hull

boul. Riel

de

la

promenade Saint-Raymond

promenade

Gatineau

Park

Old Chelsea, Chelsea

5

© ULYSSES

Canadian Museum of Civilization

others will gradually be replaced by various objects recounting the early days and growth of the Outaouais region's industries.

Take Aut. 50, then Rte. 5 north to the Boulevard du Casino Exit. Then take Rue Saint-Raymond, which becomes Boulevard du Casino.

younger and the bars stay open later in Québec. It is not uncommon to see crowds of Ontarians along the **Promenade du Portage** on Saturday nights.

Turn left onto Rue Papineau. The Canadian Museum of Civilization parking lot is at the end of this street.

The **Canadian Museum of Civilization** ★★★ *($10; early May to mid-Oct every day 9am to 6pm, Thu to 9pm; early Jul to early Sep also Fri to 9pm; mid-Oct to late Apr, Tue to Sun 9am to 5pm, Thu to 9pm, closed Mon; 100 Rue Laurier, ☎776-7000 or 800-555-5621, www.civilization. ca)* is one of many parks and museums that were established along this section of the Québec-Ontario border as part of a large redevelopment program in the National Capital Region between 1983 and 1989. Hull became the site of the magnificent Canadian Museum of Civilization, dedicated to the history of Canada's various cultural groups. If there is one museum that must be seen in Canada it is this one. In fact, it's the most frequented museum in the country. Douglas Cardinal, a First Nations architect from Alberta, drew up the plans for the museum's two striking curved buildings, one housing the administrative offices and restoration laboratories, and the other the museum's collections. Their undulating design brings to mind

rock formations of the Canadian Shield, shaped by wind and glaciers. There is a beautiful view of the Ottawa River and Parliament Hill from the grounds behind the museum.

The Grande Gallerie (Great Hall) houses the most extensive collection of totem poles in the world. Another collection brilliantly recreates different periods in Canadian history, from the arrival of the Vikings around 1000 CE to life in rural Ontario in the 19th century and French Acadia in the 17th century. Contemporary Aboriginal art, as well as popular arts and traditional crafts, are also on display. In 2003, the museum inaugurated its **First Peoples Hall**, dedicated to the First Nations of Canada. In the **Canadian Children's Museum**, young visitors choose a theme before being led through an extraordinary adventure. There is also an Imax cinema.

Continue south on Rue Laurier. At Rue Montcalm, turn right.

The **Écomusée de Hull** *($5; May to early Sep every day 10am to 4pm, early Sep to late Apr Tue-Sun 10am to 4pm; 170 Rue Montcalm, at Rue Papineau, ☎595-7790)*, which used to focus on educating the public about environmental issues, is now concentrating on the region's industrial history. Some elements of its collection will be part of the new exhibits, while

The **Casino du Lac-Leamy** ★★ *(11am to 3am; 1 Boulevard du Casino, ☎772-2100 or 800-665-2274)* has an impressive location between two lakes; Leamy Lake, in the park of the same name, and Lac de la Carrière, which is in the basin of an old limestone quarry. The theme of water is omnipresent around the superb building, completed in 1996. The magnificent walkway leading to the main entrance is dotted with towering fountains, and the harbour has 20 slips for boaters. The gambling area, which covers 6,563m^2, includes 1,800 slot machines and 64 playing tables spread around a simulated tropical forest. Attached to the casino is the Théâtre du Casino, a modern concert hall.

The opening of the casino also marked the first annual fireworks festival, **Les Grands Feux du Casino** *(☎771-FEUX or 800-771-FEUX)*, which takes place every year in August. The casino has excellent restaurants, including Baccara (see p 263), and two bars, as well as a heliport.

To go to Ottawa, turn right onto Rue Laurier, and head to the Alexandra Bridge, visible from the grounds of the Canadian Museum of Civilization.

Crossing the Ottawa River, visitors enter Ontario, the most populous province in Canada, with almost 11.5-million inhabitants.

★★★
Ottawa (Ontario)

Canada has one federal capital and 13 provincial or territorial capitals corresponding to 10 provinces and 3 territories. Ottawa, the federal capital, was founded in 1827 by Colonel By, who first named the city Bytown.

Following the 1849 Montréal riots and the lack of consensus on a location for a permanent capital for the British colony, Queen Victoria decided in 1857 to place the seat of the colonial government on the border of anglophone Upper Canada and francophone Lower Canada. Specifically, she chose the small Ontario city of Ottawa, on the Ottawa River. Ten years later, in 1867, the agreement that created the independent Dominion of Canada was finally signed, and the House of Commons sat for the first time in the new Parliament Buildings.

Ottawa has several interesting museums, including the **National Gallery of Canada**, located on the left when coming off the Alexandra Bridge. Also of interest in the city are the Gothic Revival buildings on **Parliament Hill** (*Wellington St.*), and the **Parliament Buildings**, dominated by the **Peace Tower**. For more detailed information, consult the *Ulysses Travel Guide Ontario* or the *Ulysses Travel Guide Ottawa-Hull*.

Return to Québec by crossing the Pont du Portage Bridge, a continuation of Wellington St. Turn left onto Boulevard Alexandre-Taché toward Aylmer (Rte. 148 W.). The Eddy factory can be seen on the left. Further down on the right is Promenade de la Gatineau, the starting point for the Gatineau Valley tour (see below).

★
Aylmer
(pop. 36,200)

Aylmer was once the administrative centre of the Outaouais region. The city was founded by Charles Symmes, an American from Boston who arrived in Canada in 1814. The Hudson's Bay Company, then a major player in the fur trade, centered its activities in this region. Today, Aylmer, with its residential streets lined with middle-class homes, is a suburb of Ottawa.

Prompted by his uncle, Philemon Wright, Charles Symmes settled in the Aylmer region in 1824. In 1830, he built the **old Symmes inn** ★ *(1 Rue Front, ☎685-5033)*, which became very popular with fur-trappers heading out to the Canadian Shield. The building, which has been completely restored and is now a performance hall, shows how widespread the urban architectural styles of the French Regime had become, even among Americans like Symmes. The inn thus features a raised ground floor, a covered porch, extended drip mouldings on the roof, imposing chimney stacks and the fieldstone walls and casement windows typical of traditional Québec houses. Perhaps Symmes had the inn built this way for purely commercial reasons, to appeal to a predominantly French Canadian clientele.

Tour B: The Gatineau Valley

Duration of tour: one day

The Gatineau Valley runs perpendicular to the Ottawa Valley. The Algonquins who once lived in the region were heavily involved in the fur trade with the French and later the English of the Hudson's Bay Company, before being driven out of the area by increasing development in the 19th century. Today the valley is a peaceful rural region dotted with villages founded by American Loyalists and Scottish settlers. The architecture, influenced by that of nearby Ontario, is characterized by simple neoclassical buildings built between 1830-1860. The forestry industry plays a significant role in the valley's economy, particularly farther north. At one time, wood was floated to Hull on the Rivière Gatineau.

★★
Gatineau Park

Gatineau Park (see p 260) is the starting point for this tour. The park, established in 1934, is an area of rolling hills, lakes and rivers that measures more than 35,000ha.

To get to the Gatineau Park Visitor Centre from Hull, take Aut. 5 N. to Exit 12. Turn left and follow the road signs. For the Domaine Mackenzie King. Take Chemin Kingsmere heading west, and turn left onto Rue Barnes.

The **Domaine Mackenzie-King** ★★ *($7, parking included; mid-May to mid-Oct Mon-Fri 11am to 5pm, Sat, Sun and holidays 10am to 6pm; closed Mon and Tue to mid-Jun; Rue Barnes in Kingsmere, Gatineau Park, ☎827-2020 or 800-465-1867).* William Lyon Mackenzie King was Prime Minister of Canada from 1921 to 1930, and again from 1935 to 1948. His love of art and horticulture rivalled his interest in politics and he was always happy to get away to his summer residence near Lac Kingsmere, which today is part of Gatineau Park. The estate consists of two houses (one of which is now a charming tea room), a landscaped garden and follies, false ruins that were popular at the time.

Outaouais

However, unlike most follies, which were designed to imitate ruins, those on the Mackenzie-King estate are authentic building fragments. Most were taken from the original Canadian House of Parliament, destroyed by fire in 1916, and from Westminister Palace, damaged by German bombs in 1941.

Return to Chemin Kingsmere and head east to Old Chelsea, where the Gatineau Park Visitor Centre is located.

Chelsea
(pop 6,580)

The town of Chelsea, on Rte. 105, was founded in 1819 by two Vermont merchants who purchased land here after refusing to pay $40 for the piece of land on which the Canadian Parliament now stands.

From the village of Chelsea, follow Chemin du Lac Meech. The road borders the lake and reaches the tip of Lac Mousseau, also known as Harrington Lake. The official summer residence of the Canadian Prime Minister is located nearby. Turn right on the unpaved road to reach Rte. 105 N. You will now head towards Wakefield, which is also called "La Pêche" since the merger of several villages located along the river of the same name.

★
Wakefield
(pop 5,500)

Founded around 1830 by Scottish, British and Irish settlers, Wakefield is a charming little town located at the mouth of Rivière La Pêche. It is quite pleasant to stroll down its main avenue, with shops and cafés on one side and the beautiful Gatineau River on the other. The Gendron covered bridge, painted a striking brick red, stands out in the distance, particularly in summer, when it is surrounded by

trees in foliage. Wakefield is also the arrival point of the popular **Hull-Chelsea-Wakefield Steam Train ★** (see p 254). Even if you don't take the trip, you can watch the train being manually turned around in the small park where the ride ends.

Wakefield is also the final resting place of Lester B. Pearson (1897-1972), former prime minister of Canada and a Nobel Peace Prize winner (1957) for his role in creating the United Nations peacekeeping force. Visitors leave pebbles on his grave in MacLaren Cemetery.

*Beyond Gatineau Park, Rte. 105 cuts a path through mountains and forests all the way to the 117 at Grand-Remous. The 117 leads eventually to the **Réserve Faunique La Vérendrye ★**, see p 273.*

Parks

Tour A: The
Ottawa Valley

The 26km long **Sentier d'Interprétation du Cerf de Virginie** (R.R.1, Duhamel, ☎428-7089) is a trail that crosses an area frequented by white-tailed deer, called *cerf de Virginie* or *chevreuil* in French, during the winter. The trails are open to hikers, snowshoers and cross-country skiers and allows visitors to observe these graceful animals. Fed by the inhabitants of Duhamel, the deer come here every year. The herd is estimated to number 3,000.

Located in both the Laurentians and Outaouais regions, the **Réserve Faunique de Papineau-Labelle** (mid-May to Nov; 443 Rte. 309, Val-des-Bois; accessible by Rte.

311 coming from Kiamika, by Rte. 321 coming from Lac-Nominingue, or by Rte. 117 coming from La Minerve; ☎454-2011, ext. 33, ☎428-7510 off season) stretches over almost 1,600km² of land and is home to a multitude of animals, including deer and moose. Hunting and fishing are permitted, and the hiking trails are well maintained. Canoe-camping enthusiasts can plan long trips here, though these usually require many portages. Long cross country ski trails (100km) are also maintained, and skiers can stay in the huts along the way (*$17.50 per person per day*). Approximately 120km of snowmobile trails crisscross the reserve.

The **Parc de Plaisance ★** (*$3.50; late Apr to mid-Oct every day all day; Route 138, Plaisance, ☎427-5334 or 877-752-4726, www.sepaq.com*) is one of the smallest parks in Québec. It borders the Ottawa River for some 27km and its goal is to introduce visitors to the animal and plant life of the region. To better observe birds and aquatic plants, wooden footbridges have been built above the marshes along the river. The park can also be explored by canoe, bicycle or hiking trails. Excursions guided by naturalists are organized.

During the 1980s, the former village of North Nation Mills was the site of several archaeological digs. Nearby are the magnificent **Chutes de Plaisance** (*$2.50; early Jun to mid-Oct, everyday 10am to 6pm, varying schedule off season; Rang Malo, ☎427-6400*). This is the perfect area for picnics and hikes.

Tour B: The
Gatineau Valley

Gatineau Park ★★ (*free admission, $7 parking for the Domaine Mackenzie-King*

---

and the beaches; 33 Chemin Scott, Chelsea, ☎827-2020 or 800-465-1867), a 35,000ha park, was founded during the Depression in 1934 to protect the forests from people looking for firewood. It is crossed by a 34km-long road dotted with panoramic lookout points, including **Belvédère Champlain**, which offer superb views of the lakes, rivers and hills of the region of Pontiac. Outdoor activities can be enjoyed here throughout the year. Hiking and mountain-biking trails are open during the summer. There are many lakes in the park, including Meech Lake, which was also the name of the Canadian constitutional agreement drawn up nearby but never ratified. Watersports such as windsurfing, canoeing and swimming are also very popular and the park rents small boats and camp sites. **Lusk Cave**, formed some 12,500 years ago by water flowing from melting glaciers, can be explored.

Outdoor Activities

Hiking

Gatineau Park *(☎827-2020 or 800-465-1867)* offers many hiking trails, over 125km in all, and just as many chances to discover its beauty. You can explore Lac Pink, a beautiful but polluted lake (you can't swim in it), on a 1.4km-trail. If you prefer splendid panoramic views, choose Mont-King, a 2.5km-long trail that leads to the summit and to gorgeous views of the Ottawa River Valley. And finally, if you have a bit more time and are interested in a fascinating excursion, the Lusk Cave trail is

10.5km long and leads to a 12,500-year-old marble cave.

At 1,628km², the immense **Réserve Faunique de Papineau-Labelle** *(443 Route 309, Val-des-Bois, ☎454-2011, ext. 33, ☎428-7510 off season)* is a veritable outdoor paradise. To appreciate the beauty of this untamed territory, there are hiking trails that lead into the depths of the forest.

Walking tours through marsh-lands have been arranged at the **Parc de Plaisance** (see p 260) to help people understand the significant role that these wetlands play in maintaining an ecological balance. The 1km-long path, La Zizanie des Marais, is fully accessible and particularly captivating. It leads to the heart of the marsh by way of wooden footbridges that pass over Baie de la Petite Presqu'île. Signs with a wealth of information on various aspects of the wildlife have been posted along the way. Many species of birds can be observed, including wild geese that stop here in great numbers during spring migration. Mammals, such as beavers and muskrats, also inhabit the region.

Canoeing

Canoeing is a unique and pleasant way to contemplate the magnificent landscape of the Outaouais. **Trailhead** *(1960 Rue Scott, ☎613-722-4229 or 800-574-8375)*, a company located in Ottawa, organizes single-day canoe trips and longer excursions in Gatineau Park. These tours are guided, allowing you to head deep into the forest in complete safety.

Expédition Eau Vive LAQS *(Hull, ☎827-4467 or 888-820-4467)* organizes trips on the rivers of the Outaouais for people who are completely inexperienced but still dream of canoe-tripping. More accomplished canoeists can choose a seven- to 15-day trip.

Downhill Skiing

Gatineau Park's Camp Fortune *(☎827-1717)* has 17 downhill ski runs, 13 of which are open at night. It costs between $21 and $36 during the day, between $15 and $24 at night, and $18 yo $29 for a half-day.

Cross-country Skiing

In winter, when there's a thick layer of snow, **Gatineau Park** *($7; ☎827-2020 or 800-465-1867)* maintains an impressive 200km of cross-country ski trails. These trails, 47 in all, are sure to delight skiers of all levels.

Bolder skiers who dream of going deep into the woods, far away from any signs of civilization, will find what they're looking for at the **Réserve Faunique de Papineau-Labelle** *($5/day; $20 for overnight cabins; ☎454-2011, ext. 33, www. sepaq.com)*, a 100km-long ski trail. There are heated cabins all along the route. Definitely a memorable adventure, but only for experienced skiers.

Accommodations

Tour A: The Ottawa Valley

Montebello

Château Montebello
$$$$$
≡, ☉, ≈, ℜ, △, ✪, ⅃, ⊛
392 Rue Notre-Dame
☎*423-6341 or 800-441-1414*
⇌*423-5283*
www.fairmont.com
This beautiful pine and cedar building stands next to Ottawa River. It is the largest log building in the world and is equipped with several facilities including an indoor and outdoor swimming pool, squash courts and a fitness center.

Hull

Auberge de la Gare
$$$-$$$$ bkfst incl.
≡, ⊛
205 Boulevard St-Joseph
☎*778-8085 or 800-361-6162*
⇌*595-2021*
www.aubergedelagare.ca
Auberge de la Gare is a simple, conventional hotel that offers good value. The service is both courteous and friendly, and the rooms are clean and well-kept, albeit nondescript.

Best Western Hôtel Jacques-Cartier
$$$$
≡, *K*, ≈, ℜ, ⊛
131 Rue Laurier
☎*770-8550 or 800-265-8550*
⇌*770-9705*
www.jacquescartier hotel.com
The small, austere lobby of the Best Western Hôtel Jacques-Cartier is hardly inviting. The rooms, decorated with modern furniture, are neither cozy nor luxurious but nonetheless comfortable.

Tour B: The Gatineau Valley

Gatineau Park

Philippe Lake Campground
$
Gatineau Park
☎*456-3016*
Without a doubt, one of the most beautiful places in the area to camp is Gatineau Park, which offers more than 300 campsites in three campgrounds: Philippe Lake, Taylor Lake and La Peche Lake. The former is the largest, and is equipped with facilities for RVs, while the other two offer wilderness or canoe-camping.

Wakefield

Wakefield Mill Inn
$$$$
⊛, ℑ, ≡, ℜ
60 Mill Rd.
☎*459-1838 or 888-567-1838*
⇌*459-1697*
www.wakefieldmill.com
This 19th-century mill, complete with river and roaring waterfall, is located on the edge of a large park offering a multitude of outdoor activities, a mere kilometre from a lovely village. Welcome to the Wakefield Mill Inn, a magnificent establishment where oldtime charm meets modern comfort. The historic aspect of the inn was well preserved during the renovations that transformed it into an inn a few years ago. The luxurious feel of the guest rooms, created with natural features such as wood, stone and brick, will please both leisure and business travellers. Each room and common area displays old photographs that capture the tumultuous history of the mill and the people who once used it. Today, its warm and courteous owners make the place come alive.

Restaurants

Tour A: The Ottawa Valley

Hull

Piz-za'za Restau Bar à Vin
$-$$
36 Rue Laval
☎*771-0565*
At Pi-za'za Restau Bar à Vin, you can sample an excellent variety of fine pizzas in a pleasant, relaxed atmosphere.

Café Les Quatre Jeudis
$-$$
44 Rue Laval
☎*771-9557*
A pleasant café/restaurant/bar/gallery/movie theatre/terrace with a very laid-back atmosphere, Les Quatre Jeudis is patronized by a young, slightly bohemian clientele. It shows movies, and its pretty terrace is very popular in the summertime.

Le Twist
$$
88 Rue Montcalm
☎*777-8886*
Le Twist provides a terrific setting in which to satisfy your cravings for a good burger and home-made fries. In the summer, you can sit outside on a large, completely private terrace. In short, this place has lots of atmosphere and attracts a fun crowd.

Le Tartuffe
$$$-$$$$
Mon-Sat
133 Rue Notre-Dame
☎*776-6424*
Le Tartuffe is a marvellous little gourmet French restaurant located just steps from the Canadian Museum of Civilization. With its friendly, courteous service and delightful, intimate ambiance, this place is sure to win your heart.

Le Sans-Pareil
$$$-$$$$
Mon-Sat
71 Boulevard St-Raymond
☎771-1471
Le Sans-Pareil is located 5min from Hull's casino, and right near the shopping centres. This is a Belgian restaurant, so it's only normal that chef Luc Gielen offers mussels (prepared in 12 different ways) on Tuesday nights. The sinfully good menu usually changes every three weeks, and the focus is on fresh products from various parts of Québec. The chef has a flair for combining ingredients in innovative ways, so don't hesitate to try the *menu gourmand*, which includes several courses, complete with the appropriate wines to wash them down. This place may be small, but it's truly charming. Check it out!

Le Panaché
$$$$
201 Rue Eddy
☎777-7771
A little restaurant specializing in French cuisine, Le Panaché has a relaxed, intimate ambiance.

Café Henry Burger
$$$$
69 Rue Laurier
☎777-5646
Stylish Café Henry Burger specializes in fine French cuisine. The menu changes according to the availability of the freshest ingredients, and always offers dishes to please the most discerning palate. The restaurant has long maintained an excellent reputation.

The casino has all the facilities for your gambling pleasure: two restaurants serve excellent meals away from all the betting: **Banco ($$)** offers a reasonably priced, quality buffet and various menu items, while the more chic and expensive **Baccara ($$$$**; *dinner only; 1 Boulevard du Casino*, **☎772-6210**) has won itself a place among the best

restaurants of the region. The set menu always consists of superb dishes that you can enjoy along with spectacular views of the lake. The well-stocked wine cellar and impeccable service round out this memorable culinary experience.

Chelsea

L'Orée du bois
$$$-$$$$
Tue-Sun, Tue-Sat in winter
15 Chemin Kingsmere
☎827-0332
It would be unheard of to visit the Outaouais without going to the Gatineau Park—if only for a meal. L'Orée du Bois occupies a rustic house in the country. The crocheted curtains and wood and brick interior add to the ambiance. This is the kind of family business that you find all over France. For years now, Manon has been welcoming guests and overseeing the dining rooms, while Guy focuses his expertise on the food. Guy has developed a French cuisine featuring ingredients from the various regions of Québec. The menu thus lists dishes made with wild mushrooms, fresh goat cheese, Lac Brome duck, venison and fish smoked on the premises, using maple wood. The prices are very reasonable, and the portions generous. A pleasant evening is guaranteed!

Wakefield

Chez Éric
$-$$
Wed-Mon
119 Valley Rd.
☎459-3747
Éric is the goldfish that sits imposingly on the counter of this friendly café... the place is so original and welcoming that it really does seem as though he is king! Local artists and poets decorate this small, two-storey establishment decorated with wood and colourful walls to sample tasty, creative

yet healthy dishes. Weather permitting, diners can leave Éric's side and have a seat under the trees in the garden, next to a stream, to enjoy coffee and dessert.

Café Pot-au-Feu
$$-$$$
794 River Rd.
☎459-2080
Located in the former village train station, Café Pot-au-Feu serves family-style cuisine as well as elaborate dishes. The elongated, old fashioned dining room is furnished with red armchairs on casters—relics from the days when travellers had to hurry not to miss their train, perhaps! When summer arrives, a lovely patio is set up near the railroad, which lines the river, making it a beautiful spot to enjoy a warm, sunny day.

Penstock
$$$$
60 Mill Rd.
☎459-1838 or 888-567-1838
The Wakefield Mill restaurant was named Penstock after the channel that brings water from the dam to the water wheel of a mill. In fact, it is located in the mill's former engine room. Quite a change from the old days! The place has managed to keep the mill's loveliest features, however, such as its stone walls and its opening onto the nearby falls, thanks to a terrace. The dining room offers an intimate atmosphere cozied up by the presence of a fireplace. The menu features fine cuisine with a hint of Canadian influences.

Papineauville

La Table de Pierre Delahaye
$$$
Wed-Sun
247 Rue Papineau
☎427-5027
La Table de Pierre Delahaye is worth a stop. This restaurant is sure to linger in your memory. It's run by a couple – Madame greets the guests and

Outaouais

Monsieur takes care of the food. The welcome is always warm and cordial, the Norman-style cuisine succulent. If the thought of sweetbreads makes your mouth water, look no further. The rooms in this historic house (1880) are oozing with atmosphere. Parties of eight or more can even have a room all to themselves.

Entertainment

Bars and Nightclubs

Hull

Café Les Quatre Jeudis
44 Rue Laval
☎771-9557
For many years now, Aux Quatre Jeudis has been the place for the café crowd. It has lots of atmosphere, and there's a big, attractive terrace to hang out on in the summer.

Le Bop Bar
5 Rue Aubry
☎777-3700
Le Bop Bar is a pleasant little place at Place Aubry. You can kick off your evening with a reasonably priced, decent meal. The music ranges from techno and disco to soft rock and even a little hard rock.

Le Fou du Roi
253 Boulevard St-Joseph
☎778-0516
Le Fou du Roi is where the thirty-something crowd hangs out. There's a dance floor, and the windows open onto a little terrace in the summertime. This place is also a popular after-work gathering place.

The **Casino du Lac-Leamy** (1 Boulevard du Casino) has two beautiful bars: the **777**

and **La Marina**, which serve no fewer than 70 Canadian microbrews.

Wakefield

In Wakefield, you will never be bored. There are several pubs for your entertainment, including the famous **Black Sheep Inn** (753 Riverside Dr., ☎459-3228), which stages a surprising variety of shows for such a small town; from Sunday-afternoon folk to African nights, a good time is always guaranteed. The artists who play here, whether local or internationally renowned, are usually quite worthwhile and entertain the entire village!

Theatres

Gatineau

Throughout the year, the **Maison de la Culture de Gatineau** (855 Boulevard de la Gappe, ☎243-2325) presents quality shows.

Hull

If you're interested in theatre, try the **Théâtre de l'Île** (1 Rue Wellington, ☎595-7455). In the summer, they offer dinner-theatre packages.

Festivals and Cultural Events

Hull-Ottawa

The **Ottawa-Hull International Jazz Festival** (late July; ☎613-291-2633) presents many shows in Hull and offers the chance to hear various contemporary jazz artists for a reasonable price (a pass costs less than $30 and allows entry to all performances).

Winterlude is the largest winter carnival in North America. Various activities are organized on the world's longest skating rink, the Rideau Canal, in Ottawa, as well as in other locations like Jacques-Cartier park. For further information: in Ottawa: ☎(613) 239-5000 in Hull: ☎595-7400 ☎800-465-1867

Aylmer

The **Fête de l'Été d'Aylmer** is centred around the Aylmer marina. For a few days in August, you can watch or take part in various competitions and activities out on the water. In the evening, well-known Québec singers take turns entertaining the crowd.

Gatineau

During the **Festival des Montgolfières** (☎243-2330 or 800-668-8383), held in Gatineau on Labour Day weekend, the sky is filled with colourful hot-air balloons, a real feast for the eyes. This well-organized event has earned itself an enviable reputation in just a few years and is the largest of its kind in Canada. A number of prominent singers perform here in the evening.

Casino

If you want to have fun and possibly win some money, the **Casino du Lac-Leamy** (9am to 4am; 1 Boulevard du Casino, ☎772-2100 or 800-665-2274) has what you're looking for. This huge casino has slot machines, Keno, blackjack and roulette tables, as well as two restaurants.

Shopping

Tour A: The Ottawa Valley

Hull

The **Canadian Museum of Civilization** gift shop (*100 Rue Laurier*) is, in a way, part of the exhibit. Although the craft pieces aren't of the same quality as those exhibited at the museum, you'll find all sorts of reasonably priced treasures and lots of great little curios. The museum also has a **bookstore** with a wonderful collection on the history of crafts in many different cultures.

Tour B: The Gatineau Valley

Wakefield

The small village of Wakefield has a few treats in store for those who wish to stroll down the avenue and visit a shop or two. The village is home to a community of artists and artisans and offers a good selection of shops. For example, the two **Jamboree** shops (*817 Riverside Rd.*, ☎*459-3453; 740 Riverside Rd.*, ☎*459-2537*) offer a wide array of local and not-so-local crafts, as well as homemade products, such as jam, chutney and relish (wild blueberry and zucchini).

Casino du Lac-Leamy

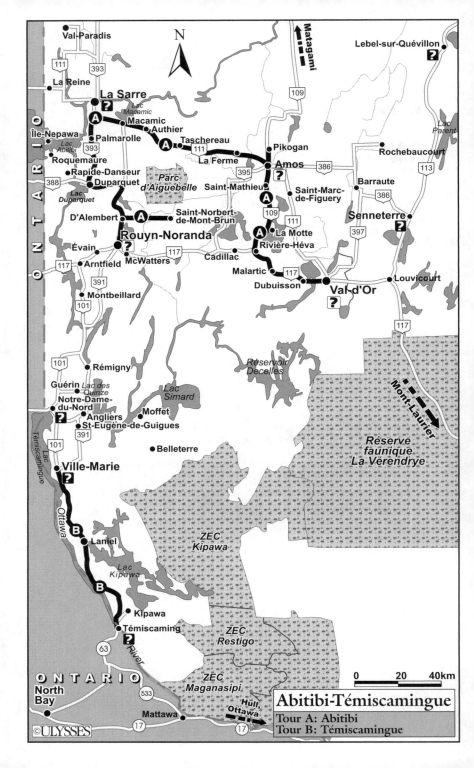

Abitibi-Témiscamingue

Tour A: Abitibi
Tour B: Témiscamingue

0   20   40km

Abitibi-Témiscamingue

A bitibi-Témiscamingue, together with Nord-du-Québec (Northern Québec), form the province's last frontier.

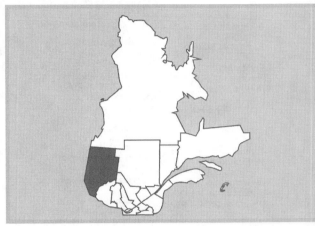

While the rich fertile land bordering Lac Témiscamingue and the Ottawa River was cleared in the 19th century, agricultural development in the rest of the region, where the soil is not as good, did not begin in earnest until the 1930s. The discovery of gold deposits in the 1920s provoked a second wave of migration, a true gold rush. The region has preserved its boomtown atmosphere as the mining industry still employs one fifth of the local workforce. Forestry and farming are also important to the regional economy.

Abitibi-Témiscamingue is traversed by a watershed which drains water into James Bay on one side and into the St. Lawrence on the other. The land is, however, quite flat. Nowadays, people come here to relive the great adventure of the gold rush, but most of all to enjoy the wide-open spaces and explore the huge forests and countless lakes, which are a hunter's, fisher's and snowmobiler's paradise.

Finding Your Way Around

Although Abitibi and Témiscamingue are considered part of the same general region, both are areas with unique identities. Thus, two separate tours are suggested: **Tour A: Abitibi ★** and **Tour B: Témiscamingue ★**.

Tour A: Abitibi

By Car

Since Abitibi is located approximately 500km from Montréal, it is best to plan an overnight stop along the way. Take Aut. 15 N. from Montréal, which turns into Rte. 117 at Sainte-Agathe. The Abitibi tour can be combined with the **Cottage Country** tour in the Laurentians tourist region (see p 231) and the **Témiscamingue** tour (see p 271).

Bus Stations

Val-d'Or
1420 4e Avenue
☎(819) 874-2200

Amos
132 10e Avenue Ouest
☎(819) 732-2821

Rouyn-Noranda
52 Rue Horne
☎(819) 762-2200

By Train

Senneterre
☎(819) 737-2979

Tour B: Témiscamingue

By Car

Témiscamingue can be reached from either Abitibi or various places in the province of Ontario. In the first case, follow Rte. 391 S. from Rouyn-Noranda. From Ontario, take Rtes. 17, 533 or 63 (on the south shore of the Ottawa River) to Témiscaming and follow the tour in reverse.

Bus Station

Ville-Marie
19 Rue Sainte-Anne (in Cagibi)
☎*(819) 629-2166*

By Boat

Another way to reach Témiscamingue is via the **Voie Navigable du Témiscamingue et de l'Outaouais**. This water route runs along the Ottawa River and ends at Lac Témiscamingue, the same route once used to float wood down to the sawmills and pulp and paper factories in Hull. For more information, contact the regional tourist information offices listed below.

Practical Information

Area code: *819*

Tourist Information

Regional Office

Association Touristique Régionale de L'Abitibi-Témiscamingue
170 Avenue Principale,
Bureau 103, Rouyn-Noranda
J9X 4P7
☎*762-8181 or 800-808-0706*
⇰*762-5212*
www.48nord.qc.ca

Names of New Merged Cities

Val-d'Or
Merger of Val-d'Or, Sullivan, Val-Senneville, Dubuisson and Vassan.

Rouyn-Noranda
Merger of Rouyn-Noranda, Cadillac, Évain,

Arntfield, Bellecombe, Cléricy, Cloutier, D'Alembert, Destor, McWatters, Mont-Brun, Montbeillard, Rollet, Lac-Montanier, Lac-Surimau and Rapides-des-Cèdres.

Tour A: Abitibi

Val-d'Or
1070, 3ᵉ Avenue,
C.P. 1543, J9P 5Y8
☎*824-9646*
☎*877-582-5367*
⇰*284-9648*
www.ville.valdor.qc.ca

Amos
892 Rte. 111 Est, J9T 2K4
☎*727-1242*
☎*800-670-0499*
⇰*727-3437*
www.ville.amos.qc.ca

Rouyn-Noranda
191 Avenue du Lac,
C.P. 242, J9X 5C3
☎*797-3195*
⇰*797-7134*
www.ville.rouyn-noranda.qc.ca

Tour B: Témiscamingue

Ville-Marie
7B Rue des Oblats Nord,
C.P. 1028, J0Z 3W0
☎*629-3355*
⇰*629-2793*
www.temiscamingue.net

Exploring

Tour A: Abitibi

Duration of tour: two days

The development of the Abitibi region began in 1912 with the arrival of the railroad. Because the region is isolated from the rest of Québec by the Cadillac fault (which demarcates the northern limit of the St. Lawrence River basin), it was virtually impossible to reach via water. At one time Abitibi was thought of as a promised land by the Catholic clergy, who began to draw farmers from the overdeveloped St. Lawrence Valley into the area to stop emigration to the United States. Discovery of copper and gold deposits in the early 1920s sped up the development of towns such as Val-d'Or, but the rest of the region has remained sparsely inhabited. During the Depression, developing Abitibi for agriculture became a way of reducing the desperate unemployment situation in large cities to the south. Measures taken by the Québec government between 1932 and 1939 resulted in a doubling of Abitibi's population and the creation of 40 new villages and towns.

The rolling countryside of Abitibi has countless lakes and rivers and is blanketed by extensive forests, making it ideal for hunting and fishing. In the Algonquin language, the word "Abitibi" means "area of high lands."

Val-d'Or
(pop. 32,000)

The search for gold in Québec under the French Regime

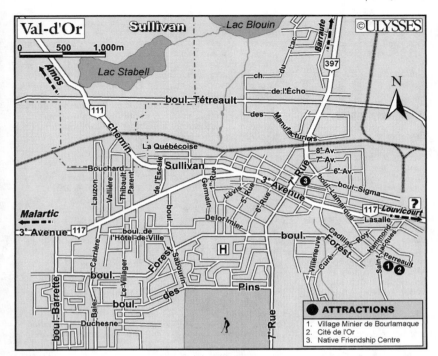

ATTRACTIONS
1. Village Minier de Bourlamaque
2. Cité de l'Or
3. Native Friendship Centre

ended after explorers who believed they had discovered the precious metal in the colony sent samples of their exciting find back to King François I. As it turned out, they had uncovered a worthless deposit of fool's gold. Following this embarrassing incident, further processing was abandoned as a waste of time. In 1922, however, prospectors discovered a tremendous gold deposit along the Cadillac fault. Shortly afterward, the town of Val-d'Or, literally "Valley of Gold," quickly sprang to life. Throughout the 1930s, Val-d'Or was the premier gold-mining town in the world, and today, it is still an important mining centre.

The Canadian-American company Teck-Hughes Gold Mines began exploiting the Lamaque mine in 1933, a welcome initiative during a period of high unemployment.

The **Village Minier de Bourlamaque** ★ *($3 guided tour; late Jun to early Sep, every day 9am to 6pm, rest of year by appointment; 90 Avenue Perreault, ☎825-7616)* was established in the spring of 1935 to accommodate the miners and their families. This gold-rush town has been preserved down to the smallest detail, first by the Lamaque company, which built it, and then by the town of Val-d'Or, which has had control of the town since 1965. This village is composed of authentic mining houses built from unhewn timber, which exemplify the typical rugged Canadian log cabin. The buildings are well maintained and still inhabited. The house at 123 Avenue Perreault has been converted into an information centre devoted to the history of Val-d'Or and the mining industry in Abitibi.

At **La Cité de l'Or** ★★ *($20; late Jun to early Sep, every day 9am to 6pm; Sep to May Mon-Wed 10am to 5pm, closed Thu and Fri, Sat 9am to 6pm, Sun 1pm to 6pm ; 123 Avenue Perreault, ☎825-7616)*, you head 80m underground into an old mine and learn about various gold-mining techniques. The tour, which lasts nearly 2hrs, offers a chance to see the incredible working conditions of the miners. Temperatures at the bottom of a mine are completely different from those outside, so bring along a warm sweater. After the tour, you can take a look at the above-ground facilities of the old Lamaque mine. A must see.

Native culture, including an annual Cree hockey tournament, is important in Val-d'Or and the **Native Friendship Centre** *(free admission; year-round; 1272, 7ᵉ Rue, ☎825-6857)* offers insights to the

Abitibi-Témiscamingue

history, legends and traditions of local First Nations. At the shop you can see works by Aboriginal craftspeople.

Continue along Rte. 117 to Malartic.

Malartic (pop. 3,850)

Gold mining is no longer an important economic activity in Malartic, but the buildings from the gold rush era have survived, giving the town an interesting Far West appearance.

The **Musée Minéralogique de Malartic** ★ *($4; Jun to Sep 9am to 5pm; 650 Rue de la Paix, ☎757-4677)* was founded by a group of miners who wanted to share their experiences with the public. Today, it is firmly planted in the 21st century, with very educational exhibits. The process that led to the creation of the Earth, and the uses of its minerals in our everyday lives, are dealt with. There is also a multimedia show.

At Rivière-Héva take Rte. 109 to Amos.

Amos (pop. 13,500)

After an exhausting voyage, the first settlers arrived in Abitibi in the summer of 1912. They set up camp along the banks of the Rivière Harricana, founding the village of Amos, named after the wife of Québec's Premier at the time, Sir Lomer Gouin. The original village, with its rustic cabins built from the trees that were cut to clear the site, quickly gave way to a modern town. Amos was the first settlement in Abitibi, and is still the administrative and religious centre of the region.

The **Cathédrale Sainte-Thérèse-d'Avila** ★

(11 Boulevard Mgr-Dudemaine, ☎732-2110), promoted to the rank of cathedral in 1939, was built in 1923 from a design by Montréal architect Aristide Beaugrand-Champagne. Its unusual circular structure, large dome and Roman Byzantine appearance are reminiscent of the Église Saint-Michel-Archange in Montréal, designed by the same architect. The interior is decorated with Italian marble, beautiful mosaics and French stained-glass windows.

The **Refuge Pageau** ★★ *($10; late Jun to late Aug Tue-Fri, late Aug to late Sep Sat and Sun; 3991 Chemin Croteau, ☎732-8999)* takes in wounded animals, treats their injuries, then sets them free again. Unfortunately, not all these animals can safely return to the wilderness, so they stay on the reserve, to the pleasure of visitors. In autumn, you can take in the magnificent spectacle presented by the migratory birds that stop here. You'll even see a barnacle goose protecting a cow! With a little luck, you'll spot Michel Pageau playing with these wild animals, which no other person can approach, in their cages. It is always impressive to see a man getting his face licked by a wolf or struggling with a bear! Aside from bears and wolves,

Cathédrale Sainte-Thérèse-d'Avila

there are foxes, raccoons, owls and various other members of Québec's animal population.

Rte. 109 then passes through Pikogan, and 620km farther, reaches James Bay and its massive hydroelectric installations (see Nord-du-Québec p 508). To continue the Abitibi tour, take Rte. 111 from Amos, then Rte. 393 N. to La Sarre.

La Sarre (pop. 8,100)

The village of La Sarre is located in a remote area crossed by long straight roads, where you must often drive 20km or more to buy a litre of milk. Forestry, an industry developed during the economic crisis of the 1930s, is still the main source of income in the region.

The **Centre d'Interprétation de la Foresterie** *(free admission; mid-Jun to late Aug 9:30am to 7:30pm; 600 Rue Principale, ☎333-3318),* at the local tourist information centre, describes the development of La Sarre's forestry industry.

There's more to La Sarre than wood. Cultural expression finds its home at the **Maison de la Culture** *(year-round, Mon-Fri 1pm to 4:30pm and 7pm to 9pm, Sat and Sun 1pm to 5pm; 195 Rue Principale; ☎333-2294),* where you'll find both the Richelieu municipal library and the Centre d'Art Rotary, which offer travelling and permanent exhibits by artists from the Abitibi-Témiscamingue region and elsewhere. Notice the **fresco** at the entrance of the Maison; if you look closer, you'll be able to read about 70 years of local history!

Retrace your steps south on Rte. 393 and continue to Duparquet, the site of an abandoned gold mine. Turn left onto Rte. 388 E., then right onto Rte. 101 S. to D'Alembert. At D'Alembert, turn left toward Saint-Norbert-de-Mont-Brun, where the entrance to Parc d'Aiguebelle ★ ★ is located (see p 273).

Take Rte. 101 S. to Rouyn-Noranda

Rouyn-Noranda (pop. 43,000)

Rouyn-Noranda was once two separate towns, Rouyn and Noranda, respectively located on the south and north shores of Lac Osisko (also called Trémoy). The town was established following the discovery of large gold and copper deposits in the region. In 1921 there was only forest and rock here. Five years later, however, a town, complete with churches, factories and houses, had developed. Historically, Rouyn has been the more commercial and industrial of the two cities. In contrast, the Noranda mining company carefully developed the village of Noranda as a predominately residential and institutional settlement. Even though the Rouyn-Noranda mines are now depleted, the town remains an important ore-processing centre.

The **Maison Dumulon** *($3; late Jun to early Sep, every day 9am to 8pm, early Sep to late Jun, Mon-Fri 9am to noon and 1pm to 5pm; 191 Avenue du Lac, ☎797-7125)* is a log house built by shopkeeper Joseph Dumulon in 1924; the property includes an adjoining general store. The Dumulon family played a

central role in the development of Rouyn by opening a store, an inn and a local post office. The building, made of spruce blocks, now houses a tourist information centre and a small information centre on the history of Rouyn-Noranda.

The **Russian Orthodox church** *($3; late Jun to early Sep, every day, 1pm to 6pm; 201 Rue Taschereau Ouest, ☎797-7125)* pays homage to the many Eastern European immigrants who played an important role in the development of Abitibi mining towns in the 1930s and 1940s. While the communities they established have declined in recent years, vestiges such as synagogues and other temples remain, though most are being used for other purposes.

"À Fleur d'eau" botanical park *(free admission; 250 Rue Dallaire, ☎797-8753).* A trail skirting Lac Édouard allows you to admire the aquatic flora and fauna of this enchanting park. Guided tours are offered *($2; late Jun to mid-Sep Mon-Thu; reservations required 24hrs in advance).* Ornithologists take note: the park is home to a great variety of birds.

The **Jardin Géologique** *(free admission; summer 9am to 10pm; Rue Pinder Est, in the botanical park)* of Rouyn-Noranda is one of the few of its kind in the world. The geological garden's 17 blocks of minerals acquaint visitors with the region's geology. Explanatory panels provide interesting information about Abitibi-Témiscamingue's mining and geological history.

Tour B: Témiscamingue

Duration of tour: 1½ days

Beautiful Lac Témiscamingue, the namesake of the entire

region, feeds the Ottawa River. Témiscamingue, which means "place of deep waters," was once the heart of Algonquin territory. For 200 years before the region started to become an important forestry area, the only non-Aboriginals in Témiscamingue were French trappers. By 1850, lumberjacks from the Outaouais region began travelling in the area to cut a seemingly endless supply of wood. In 1863, priests of the Oblate religious order settled in the region and helped found Ville-Marie in 1888, the first town in Témiscamingue.

Ville-Marie (pop. 3,000)

Due to its strategic location between southern Québec and Hudson Bay, Lac Témiscamingue entered regional colonial history in the 17th century. In 1686, the French Knight of Troyes stopped here briefly on an expedition to expel the British from the Hudson Bay region. During the same year, a trading post was set up along the lake. The opening of lumber camps in Témiscamingue during the 19th century brought a seasonal population to the area. Soon, permanent settlers and priests from an Oblate mission established the town of Ville-Marie. The town has a beautiful lakeside location that is highlighted by the surrounding parklands.

Located 8km south of Ville-Marie, the **Fort-Témiscamingue-Duhamel National Historic Site ★ ★** *($3 to $12; early Jun to early Sep; 834 Chemin du Vieux-Fort, ☎629-3222),* which was in service from 1720 to 1902, commemorates the important role the fur trade played in the Canadian economy. From the North West Company and the French regime to the Hudson's Bay Company, Fort-Témiscamingue was a meeting point for different cultures and

Abitibi-Témiscamingue

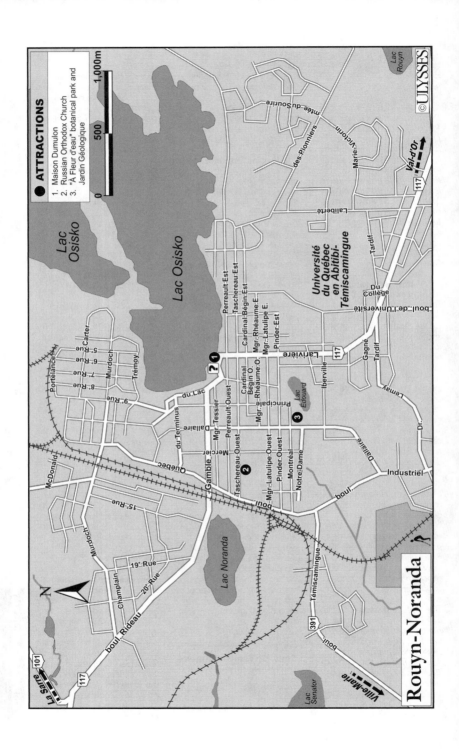

Rouyn-Noranda

religions— that is to say, between Westerners and First Nations peoples. The ancestral roots of the Ojibway in this region date back some 6,000 years.

An interpretive centre showcases a collection of regional archaeological artifacts, placing them within a historical framework, while an outdoor interpretive tour takes visitors to the site of various scenographies, which are scenic reproductions of the location and function of the former trading post's buildings. Right nearby stands the captivating "enchanted forest," studded with eastern thujas deformed by the harsh winters. Bordered by majestic Lac Témiscamingue, this coniferous forest has borne witness to several thousand years of history.

Follow Rte. 101 S. to Témiscaming.

Témiscaming (pop. 3,100)

This one-industry town was founded in 1917 by the Riordon paper company. The result was a "new town" along the lines of the British garden cities. The pretty homes are mostly Arts & Crafts in style; note the attractive, but somewhat out-of-place, marble fountain in the residential area.

Paper and carboard production are demystified at the **Tembec factory** ★ *(free admission; Mon-Fri 9am to 3pm, reservations required 24 hours in advance; 33 Rue Kipawa, ☎796-3305).*

Parks

Tour A: Abitibi

Parc d'Aiguebelle ★ ★ *($3.50; 1737 Rang Hudon, Mont-Brun, ☎637-7322 or 877-637-7344)* covers 243km². In addition to many lakes and rivers, the park has the region's highest hills. Several outdoor activities are possible, including canoeing, fishing, cycling and hiking during the summer, and cross-country skiing and snowshoeing during the winter.

The **Réserve Faunique La Vérendrye** ★ ★ *(reception at northern entrance; ☎736-7431; you can also get information from the Société des Établissement de Plein Air du Québec, C.P. 1330, 40 Place Hammond, Val-d'Or, J9P 4P8, ☎354-4392, www.sepaq.com).* At 13,615km², this wildlife reserve is the second-largest natural area in Québec. There are three entrances: the north entrance, which is 60km south of Val-d'Or, the Domaine, which is indicated on the TransCanada Highway, and an entrance to the south. At the Domaine there is a gas station, garage, convenience store, restaurant, and a place to rent boats and cottages. Picnic tables are set up by the lake. Every summer enthusiasts flock here canoeing, camping, fishing and cycling. This is one of Québec's most popular canoe-camping locations and a number of routes have been mapped out.

Outdoor Activities

In terms of tourism, Abitibi-Témiscamingue is still uncharted territory. Modern explorers will discover incredible richness, abundant unspoiled places and a seemingly infinite number of waterways! Although hunters and fishers have been coming to these fertile forests and waters for years, there's a lot more to this region than game and fish. Countless adventures await, from simple to extreme, in the untamed spaces and on the rivers and lakes.

Cross-country Skiing

Tour A: Abitibi

Camp Dudemaine *($6; every day, 10am to 5pm; Rte. 395, Amos; ☎732-8453)* has 22km of trails, a waxing room, ski rental and a restaurant. Both the skating and standard techniques are practised here. In the summer the trails are used for hiking and mountain-biking.

The **Club de Ski de Fond de Val-d'Or** *($7; Mon-Fri noon to 9pm, Sat and Sun 10am to 9pm; Chemin de l'Aéroport, Val-d'Or; ☎825-4398)* has 50km of trails including one international trail with lights! There's a waxing room, a rental shop, a heated hut and a snack bar.

Fishing and Hunting

Tour A: Abitibi

Hunting and fishing rule in this realm of lakes and rivers, wide-open spaces and endless forests. The outfitter **Pourvoirie du Balbuzard Sauvage** (☎737-8681) was awarded a Québec tourism prize for the excellence of its restaurant and the comfort of its facilities. The rates depend on the season and activity.

The **Pourvoirie Lac Faillon** (☎737-4429) is another very popular outfitter offering hunting and fishing. It also boasts a pretty beach.

Tour B: Témiscamingue

The internationally renowned **Réserve Beachêne** (☎627-3865 or 888-627-3855) offers sport fishing with a twist: the fish must be thrown back into the water. Superior quality fishing is therefore guaranted. The rooms, furthermore, are very comfortable, and the restaurant has an excellent reputation.

Aboriginal Adventure Packages

Société de Développement Économique AMIK
10 Rue Tom Rankin
Pikogan, J9T 3A3
☎732-3350
Winner of the 2000 award for outdoor and adventure tourism, the AMIK Economic Development Service offers customized excursion packages on the Harricana River. Aboriginal guides offer participants the chance to experience the Algonquin way of life as it was during the time of the great Aboriginal canoe expeditions. Excursionists will also get the opportunity to sample

traditional food and spend the night in a tipi or at a campsite. Reservations are required a week in advance. The excursion costs about $100 per person, but varies according to the package.

Association Faunique Kipawa
7C Rue des Oblats
Ville-Marie, J0Z 3W0
☎629-2002
The Kipawa wildlife association manages the ZEC (controlled zone of exploitation) in the Témiscamingue region (2,500km²) with regard to hunting, fishing, wilderness camping and outfitters. The ZEC's territory includes four outfitters that offer clients a range of activities depending on the season and the package chosen. For information on current rates, activities and regulations, contact the Kipawa association. Note that wilderness camping is free.

Adventure Packages

A few companies offer many different types of expeditions in Abitibi-Témiscamingue to challenge explorers, enthusiasts and beginners who want to experience some real wilderness.

Tour A: Abitibi

The **Conquérants du Nord** (46, 5e Avenue E.; ☎339-3300) promotes the nature capital of the north by organizing events like the Traversée du Lac Abitibi (seven-day lake crossing on skis) and the Raid des Conquérants (mountain-bike trek).

La Traversée de la Baie James
$2,750
Duration: 11 days
February
Distance: 160km

La Traversée du lac Abitibi
Coureur des bois: $310
Conquérant: $590
Duration: 5 days
early Mar
Distance: 100km

Wawatè (104 Avenue Perreault, Val-d'Or, ☎824-7652 or 825-9518) is an Algonquin word meaning "northern lights." This establishment is located at L'Orpailleur and offers all kinds of outdoor activities focusing on the natural and human riches of the Abitibi-Témiscamingue region.

Snowmobiling

This region is a veritable paradise for snowmobilers in winter. The 3,540km of snowbolilling trails cover the most beautiful areas of Abitibi-Témiscamingue. With the abundant snow, mild weather (cold but never damp) and the warm welcome from the people in the area, those who appreciate enchanting landscapes and nordic adventures are sure to be satisfied.

The routes in Abitibi join up with many other Québec tourist regions. Along the Trans-Québec trails you can reach Senneterre, Lebel-sur-Quévillon and Belleterre. From Ontario, trails pass through Temiscaming, Notre-Dame-du-Nord, Arntfield and La Reine. A number of businesses offer snowmobile and clothing rental. Be aware that certain companies impose restrictions such as a minimum age requirement and a valid driver's license.

Location Blais
280 Avenue Larivière
Rouyn-Noranda
☎797-9292

Moto Sport du Cuivre
175 Boulevard Évain Est
Évain
☎768-5611

Accommodations

Tour A: Abitibi

Amos

L'Aubergine
$
pb/sb
May to Oct
762 10e Avenue
☎732-4418
L'Aubergine is a large residence that has a sitting room with a fireplace and a lovely terrace.

Hôtel-Motel Amosphère
$$-$$$
&, ≡, ✖, ⊛, ℝ, ℜ, ◠
1031 Rte. 111 Est
☎732-7777
☎800-567-7777
≈732-5555
www.amosphere.com
Hôtel-Motel Amosphère is a hotel complex that provides high-class accommodation; in the evening the dining room offers house steak and seafood specialities. The Amosphère is also a stopover for snowmobilers in the winter, and offers heated garages for snowmobiles. It also has a lively dance club frequented by Abitibi-Témiscamingue's night owls.

La Sarre

Motel Le Bivouac
$$
≡, ✖, ℝ, ⊛
637 2e Rue E.
☎333-2241
≈333-2241
www.motelbivouac.com
Located on the way into La Sarre, the Motel Le Bivouac has an unusual character: the rooms are dedicated to the soldiers who served under Montcalm during the battle on the Plains of Abraham (1759), who have had townships and certain Abitibi-Temiscamingue municipalities named after them. Extremely pleasant.

Motel Villa Mon Repos
$$
≡, ✖, ℝ, ℜ, ⊛
32 Rte. 111 E.
☎333-2224 or 888-417-3767
≈333-9106
www.motelvillamon repos.qc.ca
The biggest hotel in the La Sarre area, the Motel Villa Mon Repos offers a variety of rooms close to the centre of town.

Rouyn-Noranda

Le Passant B&B
$-$$ bkfst incl.
pb/sb
489 Rue Perreault E.
☎762-9827
≈762-9827
www.lepassant.com
Four charming rooms (one with private bathroom and three with shared bathroom) await visitors at the friendly Le Passant Bed and Breakfast. Renowned for the quality of its meals, Mr. Michel Bellehumeur's establishment offers guests a fortifying breakfast made of products fresh from the garden.

Comfort Inn (Journey's End)
$$
≡, ✖, &
1295 Avenue Larivière
☎797-1313
≈797-9683
www.choicehotels.ca
There are a few motels along Avenue Larivière, including this Comfort Inn, a reliable old standby.

Hôtel-Motel de Ville
$$-$$$ bkfst incl.
≡, ✖, ℜ, ⊛
95 Rue Horne
☎762-0725 or 888-828-0725
≈762-7243
Adjacent to Hôtel Albert, the Motel De Ville offers comfortable, reasonably priced rooms. Moreover, the many facilities greatly improve the quality of this rather impersonal hotel. Every room also offers Internet access.

Hôtel Albert
$$-$$$
≡, ℜ, ⊛
84 Avenue Principale
☎762-3545 or 888-725-2378
≈762-7157
The Hôtel Albert, located downtown, is a real bargain. Its convenient location, impeccable service and simple yet comfortable rooms make this a reliable option in town.

Val-d'Or

Centre de plein air Arc-en-ciel
$
600 Chemin des Scouts
☎824-4152
≈824-4152
Set up in a forest of jackpine, eastern white pine, spruce, birch and poplar trees, the Arc-en-Ciel offers fishing in a pond stocked with rainbow trout, a nature trail, a domestic zoo (chickens, rabbits, cows, ponies), as well as tent rental (for four to 12 people, with reservations) on a daily, weekly or monthly basis.

Camping du lac Lemoyne
$
451 Chemin Plage Lemoyne
☎874-3066

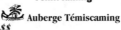 **Auberge de l'Orpailleur**
$$ bkfst incl.

104 Avenue Perreault
☎*825-9518*
⇄*824-7653*
The Auberge de l'Orpailleur, located in the mining village of Bourlamaque, was once a bunkhouse for unmarried miners. Not only is the place of historical interest, but its rooms are also attractively decorated, each in its own style. The warm welcome and generous breakfasts make for an unforgettable stay. The owner of the inn also runs an outfit that offers adventure packages (see Wawatè, p 274).

Hôtel Forestel Val-d'Or
$$
≡, 🐾, ≈, ℜ, ♿, ⊛
C.P. 967
1001 3e Avenue E.
☎*825-5660 or 800-567-6599*
⇄*825-8849*
www.forestel.ca
On the east edge of town is the Hôtel Forestel Val-d'Or. Forestel also houses the Centre des Congrès de Val-d'Or (conference centre). The restaurant serves regional and French cuisine and offers imported and Québec beers, as well as an elaborate wine list.

Motel l'Escale Hôtel Suite
$$-$$$
≡, 🐾, ℜ, ⊛
1100 Rue de l'Escale
☎*824-2711 or 800-567-6572*
⇄*825-2145*
www.lescale.qc.ca
L'Escale is a comfortable place with lots of atmosphere. Ask for one of the renovated rooms, which are considerably more attractive.

Tour B: Témiscamingue

Ville-Marie

Motel Caroline
$$
≡, 🐾, ℜ
2 Chemin de Fabre
☎*629-2965*
⇄*629-3363*
www.motelcaroline.zip411.net
The Motel Caroline has 16 simple rooms, some with a lovely view of Lac Témiscamingue. Good value.

Témiscaming

 Auberge Témiscaming
$$
≡, 🐾, ℜ, ⊛
1431 Chemin Kipawa
☎*627-3476 or 800-304-9469*
⇄*627-1367*
www.auberge-temis.com
The Auberge Témiscaming has a solid reputation in these parts. Its modern decor and courteous service have earned it regional prizes. Avoid the rooms near the staircases; they can be noisy.

Restaurants

Tour A: Abitibi

Amos

Restaurant Le Moulin
$$-$$$
100 1re Avenue O.
☎*732-8271*
The Au Moulin restaurant prepares refined French and local cuisine. Be sure to try the trout Saint-Mathieu, which will delight the most demanding of palates.

Rouyn-Noranda

OeufOrie
$
33 Rue Perreault E.
☎*797-4867*
Located in the town centre, this eatery has an original breakfast menu, offering lavish little dishes such as omelets, stuffed crepes and traditional eggs with home fries and choice meats. Modern, pleasant ambiance.

 Olive et Basil
$-$$
164A Rue Perreault E.
☎*797-6655*
A breath of fresh air for jaded palates, Olive et Basil offers a delicious, reasonably priced table d'hôte. The menu is composed of delectable Mediterranean specialties.

Val-d'Or

L'Amadeus
$$-$$$
166 Avenue Perreault
☎*825-7204*
L'Amadeus serves excellent French cuisine. The service is impeccable and the decor very pleasant.

La Grilladerie des Diplômés
$$-$$$$
1097 Rue de l'Escale
☎*824-2771*
At La Grilladerie des Diplômés you will be greeted by friendly staff and savour excellent food in a relaxed atmosphere.

Entertainment

Festivals and Cultural Events

Rouyn-Noranda

During the non-competitive **Festival du Cinéma International en Abitibi-Témiscamingue** *(late Oct; ☎762-6212)*, films from various countries make their North American (and sometimes even world) premiere.

Shopping

Val-d'Or

Boutique Wachiya
145 Rue Perreault
☎825-0434
The Wachiya shop offers a fine range of traditional Cree arts and crafts for all budgets. The dream-catchers and moccasins here are particularly refined.

Ville-Marie

Les Chocolats Martine
$2, guided tour (on reservation)
22 Rue Sainte-Anne
☎622-0146
The 30min guided tour of this small chocolate shop and adjacent small-scale factory offers chocoholics the opportunity to discover the many fascinating secrets behind the chocolate-making process. The tour ends on a high note with a sampling of one of their treats. Reservations 24hrs in advance.

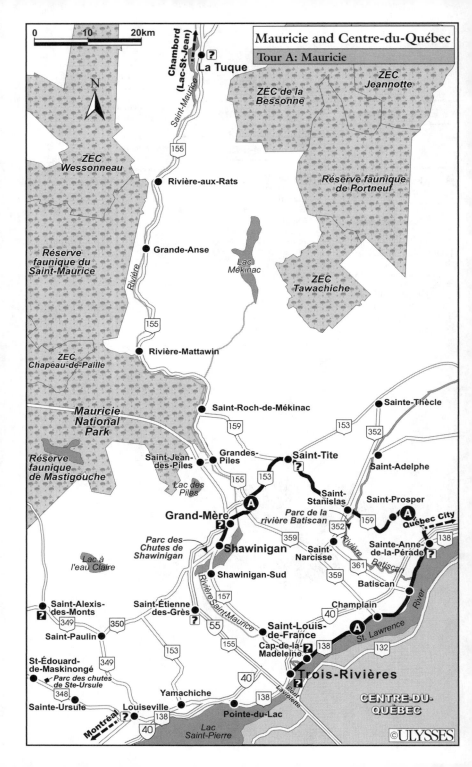

Mauricie and Centre-du-Québec

L a Mauricie

and the Centre-du-Québec are an amalgamation of diverse regions that were part of one huge tourism region until 2000. Since then, they have split in two, each with its own tourism infrastructure.

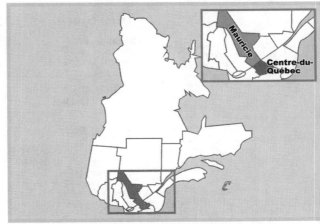

Located about halfway between Montréal and Québec City, these two regions forms a north-south axis that includes the three types of terrain that make up the province: the Canadian Shield, the St. Lawrence plains, and part of the Appalachian Mountain range.

The city of Trois-Rivières, the second city founded in New France (1634), is generally considered the heart of Mauricie. First a fur-trading post, it became an industrial centre with the founding of the Saint-Maurice ironworks in 1730. Since the end of the 19th century, the exploitation of the surrounding forests has made Trois-Rivières the hub of the provincial pulp and paper industry. Further up the Rivière Saint-Maurice, the towns of Shawinigan and Grand-Mère, also major industrial sites, serve as centres for the production of hydro-electric power, and for the

major industries that consume that power. To the north lies a vast untamed expanse of lakes, rivers and forests. This land of hunting and fishing also contains the magnificent La Mauricie National Park, reserved for outdoor activities such as canoeing and camping.

To the south of the St. Lawrence River lie the rural zones of Centre-du-Québec. Opened up very early to colonization, the land is still divided according to the old seigneurial system. In the extreme south of the region, the gently rolling hills of this countryside herald the Appala-

chian Mountains. There are interesting annual festivals in the region including the Festival International de Musique Actuelle, in Victoriaville, and the Mondial des Cultures, in Drummondville.

Finding Your Way Around

Two tours are suggested, one for the north shore of the St. Lawrence, the other for the south: **Tour A: Mauricie ★★ and Tour B: Centre-du-Québec ★**.

Tour A: Mauricie

By Car

From Montréal, take Aut. 40, followed by Aut. 55 S. for a short while, and then turn onto Rte. 138 E. as far as Trois-Rivières. Take Boulevard Royal and continue along Rue Notre-Dame to the downtown area. This part of town is best visited on foot. Next, you'll drive inland to Saint-Tite on Rte. 159 then head to Grand-Mère on Rte. 153. Once at Grand-Mère, those who want to explore the Haute-Mauricie (Upper Mauricie) can make a detour to La Tuque on the 155. To continue the main tour, stay on the 153, which leads through the Shawinigan region, among others. The portion of the tour between Trois-Rivières and Sainte-Anne-de-la-Pérade, which runs along Rte. 138 E., can be incorporated into an excursion along the St. Lawrence and up to Québec City.

From Montréal, it is also possible to get to Trois-Rivières via the south shore of the St. Lawrence on Aut. 20. You can also take the Chemin du Roy (Rte. 138), which leads to Québec City. The first road suitable for motor vehicles in Canada, the Chemin du Roy is the scenic route, with views of the countryside and the river. On the other hand, it takes quite a bit longer, so your decision will be based on how much time you have.

By Boat

There is a pleasant new and relatively fast way to get to Trois-Rivières from Montréal or Québec City: by boat with **Les Dauphins du Saint-Laurent**, *(☎514-288-4499 or 877-648-4499)*. The boat drop passengers off in the heart of Vieux-Trois-Rivières.

Bus Stations

Trois-Rivières
275 St. Georges
☎(819) 374-2944

Grand-Mère
800 6ᵉ Avenue
☎(819) 533-5565

Shawinigan
1563 Boulevard Saint-Sacrement
☎(819) 539-5144

By Train

La Tuque
550 Rue Saint-Louis
☎(819) 523-3257

Shawinigan
1560 Chemin du CN
☎(819) 537-9007

Tour B: Centre-du-Québec

By Car

This tour focuses on the St. Lawrence plains, where the main towns of the region are located. From Montréal or from Québec City, take Aut. 40 and then Aut. 55 S. Cross the Pont Laviolette at Trois-Rivières. Opened in 1967, this bridge is the only one that links the two shores between Montréal and Québec City. Once across, take Rte. 132 E. to Beschaillons. From there, follow Rte. 256 to Plessisville, then Rte. 116 to Victoriaville. Complete the loop by taking Rtes. 255, 226 and then 132 Est. Note that the region is easily accessible via Aut. 20, as well.

Bus Stations

Victoriaville
475 Boulevard Jutras E.
☎(819) 752-5400

Drummondville
330 Rue Heriot
☎(819) 477-2111
☎472-5252

By Train

Drummondville
330 Rue Heriot
☎(819) 472-5383

Practical Information

The area code is **819**, unless otherwise indicated.

Tourist Information

Tour A: Mauricie

Tourisme Mauricie
777 4ᵉ Rue, Shawinigan,
G9N 1H1
☎536-3334 or 800-567-7603
≈536-3373
www.icimauricie.com

Chambre de Commerce de Trois-Rivières
168 Rue Bonaventure, G9A 2B1
☎375-9628

Office de Tourisme et de Congrès de Trois-Rivières
1457 Rue Notre-Dame, G9A 4X4
☎375-1122 or 800-313-1123
≈375-0022

Chambre de Commerce du Cap-de-la-Madeleine
170 Rue des Chenaux
☎375-5346

Tour B: Centre-du-Québec

Tourisme Centre-du-Québec
20 Boulevatd Carignan O.,
Princeville, G6L 4M4
☎364-7177 or 888-816-4007
www.tourismecentre duquebec. com

Bécancour
3689 Boulevard Bécancour,
Bécancour, G9H 3W7
☎298-2070
www.cldbecancour.qc.ca

Names of New Merged Cities

Trois-Rivières
Merger of Trois-Rivières, Cap-de-la-Madeleine, Trois-Rivières-Ouest, Saint-Louis-de-France, Sainte-Marthe-du-Cap and Pointe-du-Lac.

Shawinigan
Merger of Shawinigan, Grand-Mère, Shawinigan-Sud, Lac-à-la-Tortue, Saint-Georges, Saint-Gérard-des-Laurentides, Saint-Jean-des-Piles, Lac-Wapizagonke and Lac-des-Cinq.

Bois-Francs
231-A Rue Notre-Dame E.,
Victoriaville, G6P 4A2
☎*758-9451 or 888 758-9451*
www.tourismebois
francs.com

Drummondville
1350 Rue Michaud, J2C 2Z5
☎*477-5529 or 877-235-9569*
www.tourisme-
drummond.com

Nicolet-Yamaska
420 Rte. Marie-Victorin,
Nicolet, J0G 1A0
☎*783-6363*
☎*866-279-0444*
www.tourismenicolet-
yamaska.net

Exploring

Tour A: Mauricie

Duration of tour: three days

The valley of the Rivière Saint-Maurice is located halfway between Montréal and Québec City, on the north shore of the St. Lawrence River. The cradle of Canada's first major industry, Mauricie has always been an industrial region. Its towns feature fine examples of architecture from Québec's industrial revolution. Nevertheless, the vast countryside surrounding the towns remains primarily an area of mountain wilderness covered in dense forest, perfect for hunting, fishing, camping and hiking.

★★
Trois-Rivières
(pop. 51,500)

The appearance of Trois-Rivière, once similar to Vieux-Québec, was completely changed by a fire in June 1908. Now, it resembles more a town of the American Midwest.

Often considered simply a place to stop for a break between Montréal and Québec, Trois-Rivières is unfortunately underestimated by most tourists.

However, Trois-Rivières remains a city redolent with Old World charm, with its many cafés, restaurants and bars on Rue des Forges, and the terrace overlooking the St. Lawrence River. Halfway between Montréal and Québec City, this urban centre is home to 100,000 people.

Located at the confluence of the St. Lawrence and Saint-Maurice rivers, where the latter divides into three branches, giving the town its name, Trois-Rivières was founded in 1634 by Sieur de Laviolette. From the outset, the town was surrounded by a stone wall that now marks the city's historic area. In the 17th century, there were three regional governments in

the St. Lawrence valley apart from the Governor of New France: that of Québec City, Montréal, and Trois-Rivières. More modest than its two sister cities, the latter boasted a population of a mere 600 and a total of 110 houses. The real boom took place in the middle of the 19th century with the advent of the pulp and paper industry. For a time, Trois-Rivières was the world's leading paper producer.

Park near the intersection of Notre-Dame and Laviolette. Walk up Rue Bonaventure (one street west of Laviolette) as far as the old Manoir de Boucher-de-Niverville, now the tourist information centre.

The **Manoir Boucher-de-Niverville** ★ *(free admission; Mon-Fri, 9am to 5pm; 168 Rue Bonaventure,* ☎*375-9628)* was fortunately spared in the 1908 fire. It is a unique example of 17th-century architecture, with few adaptations to the local environment. Inside the manor are a display of antique furniture and a diorama on local history.

A statue of Maurice Le Noblet Duplessis (1890-1959), Premier of Québec from 1936 to 1939, and from 1944 to 1959, stands in front of the manor. Duplessis was a conservative whose power was closely linked with the Catholic clergy of the time. His term of office is often referred to as the great darkness that preceded the Quiet Revolution.

Cross Rue Hart and walk along Parc Champlain to the cathedral.

The **Cathédrale de l'Assomption** ★ *(Mon-Sat 7am to 11:30am and 2pm to 5:30pm, Sun 8:30am to 11:30am and 2pm to 5pm, reservations required for guided tours; 363 Rue Bonaventure* ☎*374-2409)* was built in 1858 according to

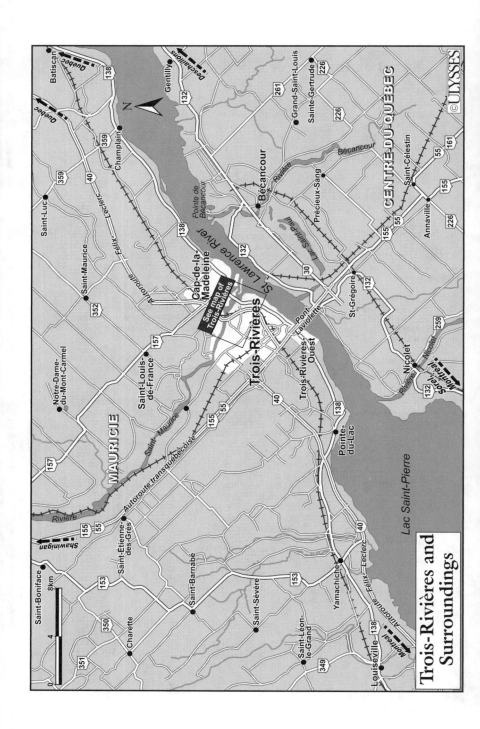

Trois-Rivières and Surroundings

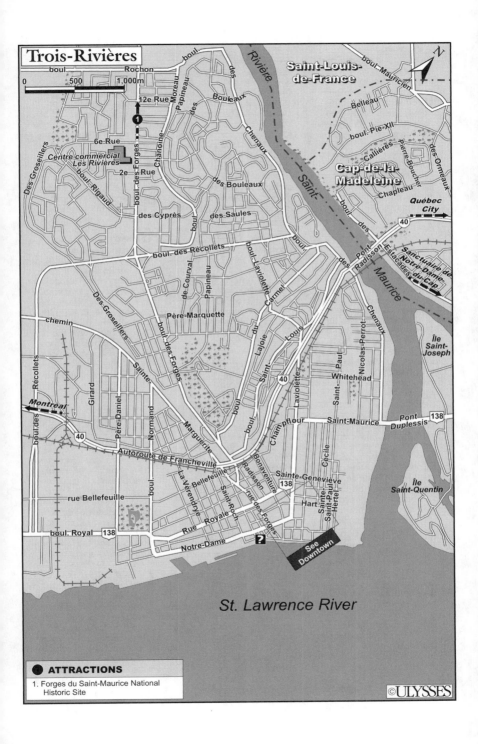

the plans of architect Victor Bourgeau, well known for the many churches he designed in the Montréal region. The cathedral's massive Gothic Revival style is vaguely reminiscent of London's Westminster Abbey, also designed in the mid-19th century. Guido Nincheri's stained-glass windows, executed between 1923 and 1934, are certainly the most interesting element in what is otherwise an austere interior.

Retrace your steps down Rue Bonaventure and turn left on Rue Hart.

South of Rue Hart is the new **Musée Québécois de Culture Populaire** ★★ (*$6.50; beg Jun to beg Sep every day 9:30am to 6:30pm, beg Sep to beg Jun, Tue-Sun 10am, to 5pm; seven exhibits and two sites to visit: the museum and the Vieille Prison de Trois-Rivières; 200 Rue Laviolette, ☎372-0406*). The general theme of the museum's new exhibits is food. The main exhibit, entitled "Québec all dressed," invites visitors to learn about the eating habits of the average Québec family. You will also learn why Québec is a top gastronomic destination in North America.
The **Vieille Prison de Trois-Rivières** ★ has been restored to welcome visitors and allow them to discover how prisoners lived here in the 1960s and 1970s.

Turn right on Rue Saint-Pierre and then left at Place Pierre-Boucher. Walk up Rue des Ursulines, the only street to have been spared from the fire of 1908.

Standing in Place Pierre-Boucher is the **Monument du Flambeau**, built in 1934 as part of the tricentennial celebrations of the town.

The **Manoir de Tonnancour** (*free admission; Tue-Fri 10am to noon and 1:30pm to*

5pm, Sat and Sun 1pm to 5pm, guided tours on reservation $2/pers.; 864 Rue des Ursulines, ☎374-2355*) was built in 1725 for René Godefroy de Tonnancour, Lord of Pointe-du-Lac and the King's prosecutor. After successive 19th-century incarnations as a fire station, a presbytery and a school, it is today an art gallery, the **Galerie d'art du Parc**. On the Place d'Armes, opposite the manoir, is a cannon from the Crimean war.

The former **Couvent des Récollets** ★ (*811 Rue des Ursulines*) is the only Récollet convent still standing in Québec. The building has been preserved thanks to its conversion into an Anglican church following the demise of the last member of the Trois-Rivières branch of the Récollet Order in 1776.

The **Monastère and Musée des Ursulines** ★ (*$2.50; Mar and Apr Wed-Sun 1:30pm to 5pm, May to early Nov Tue to Fri 9am to 5pm, Sat and Sun 1:30pm to 5pm; Nov to Feb by appointment only; 734 Rue des Ursulines, ☎375-7922*). The Ursulines first settled in 1697 in the house of Claude de Ramezay, who left Trois-Rivières after being named Governor of Montréal. The museum presents thematic displays featuring items from the collection of the Ursulines (paintings, liturgical garments, needlework, etc.). The displays are arranged so as to lead the visitor towards the chapel. It was redecorated and given a dome in 1897.

Walk across the pretty park in front of the Monastère des Ursulines to Terrasse Turcotte and Parc Portuaire.

In the port area, **Parc Portuaire** (*along the St. Lawrence River*), formerly known as Terrasse Turcotte was, until the 1920s, the favourite meeting place of the

local upper class. It later fell into disrepair, and was replaced by a new, tiered terrace between 1986 and 1990. Now the starting point for mini-cruises on the St. Lawrence, it also features a café and an exhibit on the pulp and paper industry.

The pulp and paper industry was the main economic activity in the Mauricie for many years and it still occupies a prominent place in the lives of the people of the region. It's not surprising, then, that the **Centre d'Exposition sur l'Industrie des Pâtes et Papiers** (*$3; early Jun to early Sep every day 9am to 6pm; Sep Mon-Fri 9am to 5pm, Sat and Sun 11am to 5pm; 800 Parc Portuaire, facing Rue des Forges; ☎372-4633*) is located here. Situated in the lovely harbour park, the centre has a permanent exposition describing all the facets of the pulp and paper industry, as well as the way in which it influenced the development of the region. A guided tour is recommended to get the most out of your visit, since the models are rather dull without any explanation.

The Forges Saint-Maurice are 10km from downtown along Boulevard des Forges.

The **Forges du Saint-Maurice National Historic Site** ★★ (*$4, guided tours; mid-May to Aug, every day 9:30am to 5pm; Sep and Oct 9:30am to 4pm; group reservations required; 10000 Boulevard des Forges, ☎378-5116*) is also called Lieu Historique National Les Forges du Saint-Maurice. These ironworks began in 1730, when Louis XV granted permission to François Poulin de Francheville to work the rich veins of iron-ore that lay under his land. The presence of dense wood lots from which charcoal is made, limestone, and a swift-running waterway, favoured the production of iron. The workers

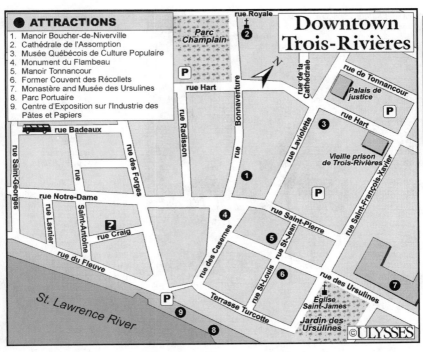

ATTRACTIONS
1. Manoir Boucher-de-Niverville
2. Cathédrale de l'Assomption
3. Musée Québécois de Culture Populaire
4. Monument du Flambeau
5. Manoir Tonnancour
6. Former Couvent des Récollets
7. Monastère and Musée des Ursulines
8. Parc Portuaire
9. Centre d'Exposition sur l'Industrie des Pâtes et Papiers

Downtown
Trois-Rivières

of this first Canadian iron-works mostly came Burgundy and Franche-Comté in France. They were kept busy making cannons for the king and wood-burning stoves for his subjects in New France.

After the British Conquest (1760), the plant passed into the hands of the British colonial government, who in turn ceded it to a private enterprise. The works were in use until 1883. At that time, the plant included the smelter and forges, as well as the Grande Maison, the foreman's house, at the centre of a worker's village. Following the 1908 fire, the residents of Trois-Rivières recuperated the material necessary to rebuild their town from the forge, leaving only the foundations of most buildings. In 1973, Parks Canada acquired the site and rebuilt the foreman's house to serve as an information centre. They set up a second,

very interesting centre on the site of the smelting forge.

The visit begins at the foreman's house, a huge white building said to have been inspired by the architecture of Burgundy. Various aspects of life at the ironworks are presented, as are the products of the works. On the second floor is a model depicting the layout of the works in 1845. The model is used as the basis of a sound and light show, after which the site can be perused by walking along various footpaths.

Trois-Rivières hosts the Festival Mondial de la Poésie (the World Poetry Festival) every fall, which has given it the well-deserved title of the poetry capital of Québec. The town had the brilliant idea of building a walkway, which it named "**Promenade de la Poésie**," with 300 plaques featuring excerpts from poets

across Québec

Go back toward Trois-Rivières along Boulevard des Forges. Turn left on Boulevard des Récollets, which then becomes Boulevard des Récollets. Turn left again on Rte. 138 E., cross the Rivière Saint-Maurice and turn right onto Rue Notre-Dame at Cap-de-la-Madeleine, one of the suburbs of Trois-Rivières.

Cap-de-la-Madeleine (pop. 35,070)

The heartland of Catholicism in North America, Québec is home to a number of major pilgrimage destinations visited every year by millions from all over the world. The **Sanctuaire Notre-Dame-du-Cap ★★** *(free admission, guided tours for groups on reservation; 626 Rue Notre-Dame, ☎374-2441)*, a shrine under the auspices of the Oblate Missionaries of the

Virgin Mary, is consecrated to the worship of the Virgin.

The history of this sanctuary began in 1879 when it was decided a new parish church was needed in Cap-de-la-Madeleine. It was the month of March, and the stones for the new church had to be transported from the south side of the river. Strangely, the river had not frozen over that winter.

Sanctuaire Notre-Dame-du-Cap

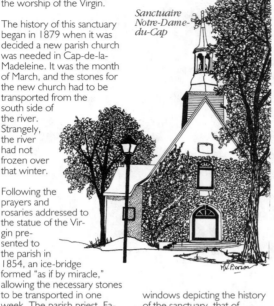

Following the prayers and rosaries addressed to the statue of the Virgin presented to the parish in 1854, an ice-bridge formed "as if by miracle," allowing the necessary stones to be transported in one week. The parish priest, Father Désilet, decided to preserve the old church and to turn it into a sanctuary devoted to the Virgin. Built between 1714 and 1717, the sanctuary is one of the oldest churches in Canada. Visitors meditate before the statue of the Virgin. It is recounted that in 1888, the statue opened its eyes in front of several witnesses.

Today, the miraculous ice-bridge is symbolized by the **Pont des Chapelets** (1924), visible in the garden of the sanctuary. A Stations of the Cross, a calvary, a holy sepulchre and a small lake complete this riverside garden. Surrounded by an expanse of asphalt and looking like something from the set of a Cecil B. DeMille movie is the enormous **Basilique Notre-Dame-du-Rosaire**. Work on the basilica was begun in 1955 by architect Adrien Dufresne, a disciple of Dom Bellot. The Dutch master glazier Jan Tillemans created three sets of

windows depicting the history of the sanctuary, that of Canada, and the mysteries of the rosary.

Take Notre-Dame Est to Rte. 138 (Boulevard Sainte-Madeleine). Along the way are the villages of Champlain, and then Batiscan, the site of an old presbytery.

Parc de l'Île de Saint-Quentin, see p 293.

★
Sainte-Anne-de-la-Pérade (pop. 2,300)

In the winter, this pretty farming village hosts a second village that springs up in the middle of the Rivière Sainte-Anne, which runs through the village. Hundreds of multicoloured shacks, heated and lit by electricity, shelter families that come from all over the world to fish for tomcod, also known as *petit poisson des chenaux*, which means "little channel fish." Ice-fishing in Sainte-Anne has become part of Québecois folklore over the

years, along with trips to sugar shacks and corn-roasts. The village is dominated by an imposing Gothic Revival church (1855) based on the basilica of Notre-Dame de Montréal.

Take Rte. 159 inland toward Saint-Prosper, Saint-Stanislas and Grand-Mère.

★
Grand-Mère (pop. 14,850)

The town was named after a rock bearing a strong resemblance to the profile of an old woman. Found on an island in the middle of the Saint-Maurice, the rock was transported piece by piece to a park in downtown Grand-Mère when the hydroelectric dam was constructed in 1913. The town and its neighbour Shawinigan are good examples of "company towns" where life revolves around one or two factories. The omnipresence of the factories extends to the residential patterns, the towns being divided into two distinct sections, one for management (mostly anglophone at first) and one for workers (almost exclusively francophone). The town features many well-thought-out industrial buildings designed by talented architects brought in from outside the area.

Grand-Mère came into being at the end of the 19th century as a result of the forestry industry. Pulp and paper factories processed trees cut down in the logging camps of Haute-Mauricie. The town was developed in 1897 by the Laurentide Pulp and Paper Company, the property of John Foreman, Sir William Van Horne and Russell Alger, hero of the American Civil War. After the 1929 stock market crash, the town's economy diversified and moved away from the pulp and paper industry that had helped it grow.

The **Pont de Grand-Mère** ★ was built in 1928 across the swift-running Rivière Saint-Maurice by American engineers Robinson and Steinman, who would become famous in the 1950s for their reconstruction of the Brooklyn Bridge in New York and the Mackinac Bridge in Michigan. On the left are the facilities of the Stone Consolidated Company, the descendant of the Laurentide Pulp and Paper. The hydroelectric centre of the vast industrial complex straddles the Saint-Maurice. It was designed in 1914 by New York architect George F. Hardy, who looked to the Cathedral of Albi in France for inspiration. To the right of the bridge is the Auberge Grand-Mère, a former inn designed by Edward Maxwell in 1897. The inn houses part of the splendid collection of Art Nouveau furniture from the Château Menier on the Île d'Anticosti.

Chemin Riverside leads to an exclusive residential neighbourhood and an attractive municipal golf course designed by Frederick de Peyster Townsend in 1912. The sod for the course was taken from the renowned St. Andrews golf course in Scotland. A left on 3ᵉ Avenue leads up a street with charming houses designed for the executives of the paper companies in the early 20th century. At the corner of 4ᵉ and 1ʳᵉ avenues is the handsome Anglican Church of St. Stephen by Le Boutillier and Ripley of Boston (1924). Standing opposite, between 5ᵉ and 6ᵉ avenues, is the Rocher de Grand-Mère with its famous profile of an old woman.

The **Église Catholique Saint-Paul de Grand-Mère** ★ *(on the corner of 6ᵉ Avenue and 4ᵉ Rue)* has an false Italianate facade put up in 1908. The colourful interior from the 1920s is adorned with both remounted paintings by Montréal artist Monty, and a Guido Nincheri fresco depicting the apotheosis of St. Paul. The high altar, as well as the side altars, is marble. Behind the church is an Ursuline convent affiliated with the one in Trois-Rivières.

La Mauricie National Park ★, see p 293.

Réserve Faunique Saint-Maurice ★, see p 293.

Shawinigan
(pop. 20,725)

In 1899, Shawinigan became the first city in Québec to be laid out according to the principles of urban planning, thanks to the powerful Shawinigan Water and Power Company, which supplied electricity to all of Montréal. The name of this hilly town means "portage at the peak" in Algonquian. The town itself was hard hit by the recession of 1989-93, which left indelible marks on its urban landscape: abandoned factories, burnt-out buildings, empty lots and so on. Nevertheless, Shawinigan boasts many architecturally interesting buildings from the first third of the 20th century. Some of its residential streets resemble those of interwar English suburbs.

Inaugurated in the spring of 1997, the **Cité de l'Énergie** ★ ★ *($14; mid-Jun to early Jul Tue-Sun 10am to 5pm, mid-Jul to early Sep every day 10am to 6pm, Sep to mid-Oct Tue-Sun 10am to 5pm; 1000 Avenue Melville, ☎536-8516 or 800-900-2483)* acquaints visitors, children and adults alike, with the history of industrial development in Québec in general and Mauricie in particular. The hub of this development is the town of Shawinigan, singled out by aluminum factories and electric companies a century ago thanks to the strong currents in the Rivière Saint-Maurice and the 50m-high falls nearby. A huge theme park, the Cité de l'Énergie, features several attractions: two hydroelectric power stations, one of which, the Centrale Shawinigan 2, is still in operation; a science pavilion and a 115m-high observation tower, which, needless to say, offers a sweeping view of the area, including the frothy Shawinigan Falls.

The Cité de l'Énergie provides transportation (by trolley, bus or boat) to make it easier to visit these attractions. A multimedia show is also presented. During your tour of the Cité, you will learn how various regional industries, such as hydroelectricity, pulp and paper, aluminum, etc., have evolved over the past 100 years. The development of innovations that led to scientific advances in these fields is explained step by step. Interactive exhibitions are presented in the Centre des Sciences, which also has a restaurant and a shop.

Réserve Faunique Mastigouche, see p 293.

Cité de l'Énergie

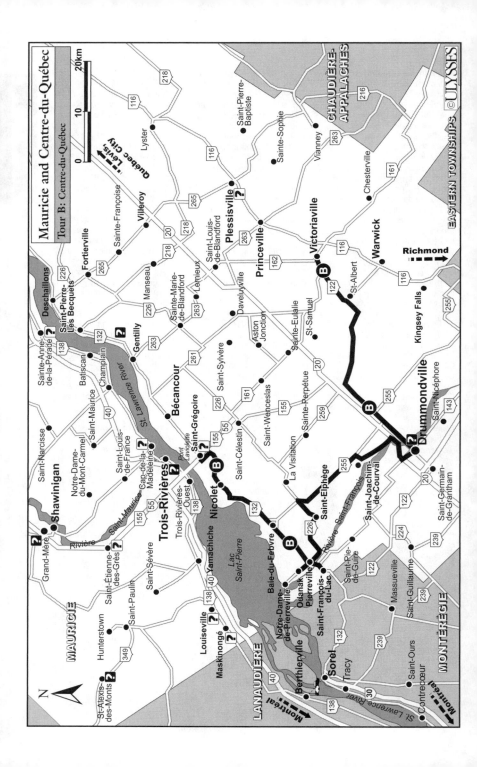

Mauricie and Centre-du-Québec
Tour B: Centre-du-Québec

Tour B:
Centre-du-Québec

Duration of tour: two days

The population of Centre-du-Québec is a mix of French, British, Acadian and Loyalist colonists. Up until the mid-19th century, there was not much going on here. However, the arrival of the Grand Trunk Railway began a process of industrialization that has yet to taper off. In the course of the last quarter century, some of Canada's largest and most modern factories have been built here. Paradoxically, nothing remains of the railway but the strip of land it occupied. The railbed is now a bike path.

Victoriaville
(pop. 40,000)

The economic heartland of the Centre-du-Québec, Victoriaville owes its development to the forestry and steel industries. Named after Queen Victoria, who reigned at the time of the town's establishment (1861), Victoriaville now incorporates the surrounding municipalities of Arthabaska and Sainte-Victoire-d'Arthabaska.

Arthabaska ★, the southern portion of Victoriaville, means "place of bulrushes and reeds" in the native language. It has produced or welcomed more than its share of prominent figures in the worlds of art and politics. Its residential sectors have always boasted a refined architecture, notably in the European and American styles. The town is especially known for its Victorian houses, particularly those along Avenue Laurier Ouest. In 1859, Arthabaska became the judicial district of the township. Construction of the courthouse, the prison and the registry office, which would make the

fortune of the town, followed. Arthabaska was superseded by Victoriaville at the turn of the 20th century, and though these buildings have now been demolished, it still retains a good part of its Belle Époque charm.

The **Maison Suzor-Coté** *(846 Boulevard des Bois-Francs Sud)* is the birthplace of landscape painter Marc-Aurèle de Foy Suzor-Coté (1869-1937). His father had built the humble home 10 years earlier. One of Canada's foremost artists, Suzor-Coté began his career decorating churches, including Arthabaska's, before leaving to study at the École des Beaux-Arts in Paris in 1891. After taking first prize at both the Julian and Colarossi academies, he worked in Paris before moving to Montréal in 1907. From then on, he returned annually to the family home, gradually turning it into a studio. His impressionist winter scenes and July sunsets are well-known. The house is still a private residence *(not open to the public)*.

Turn left on Rue Laurier Ouest (Rte. 161).

The **Sir Wilfrid Laurier National Historic Site** ★ *($3.50; Jul to Aug, Mon-Fri 9am to 5pm, Sat and Sun 1pm to 5pm; Sep to Jun, Tue-Fri 9am to noon and 1pm to 5pm, Sat and Sun 1pm to 5pm; 16 Rue Laurier Ouest, ☎357-8655)* occupies the house of the first French Canadian Prime Minister (1896 to 1911), Sir Wilfrid Laurier (1841-1919). Born in Saint-Lin in the Basses-Laurentides, Laurier moved to Arthabaska as soon as he finished his legal studies. His house was turned into a museum in 1929 by two admirers. The ground floor rooms retain their Victorian furniture, while the second floor is partly devoted to exhibits. Paintings and sculptures by Québec artists encouraged by the

Lauriers are on view throughout the house. Of particular interest are the portrait of Lady Laurier by Marc-Aurèle de Foy Suzor-Coté and the bust of Sir Wilfrid Laurier by Alfred Laliberté.

The **Église Saint-Christophe** ★ *(40 Rue Laurier Ouest, ☎357-2376)* was designed in 1871 by Joseph-Ferdinand Peachy from Québec City. It is best known for its polychromatic interior, completed by architects Perrault et Mesnard in 1887, and for its decoration by painters Marc-Aurèle de Foy Suzor-Coté and J. O. Rousseau from Saint-Hyacinthe. The church was declared a historic site in 2001.

Drummondville
(pop. 47,000)

Drummondville was founded in the wake of the War of 1812 by Frederick George Heriot, who gave it the name of the British Governor of the time, Sir Gordon Drummond. The colony was at first a military outpost on the Rivière Saint-François, but the building of mills and factories soon made it a major industrial centre.

Turn right on Rue Montplaisir.

The **Village Québécois d'Antan** ★★ *($16.95; early Jun to Sep, every day 10am to 6pm; 1425 Rue Montplaisir, ☎478-1441 or 877-710-0267)* traces 100 years of history. Some 70 colonial-era buildings have been reproduced to evoke the atmosphere of village life from 1810 to 1910. People in period costume make *ceintures fléchées* (arrow sashes), candles and bread. Many historical television shows are shot on location here.

Continue along Montplaisir following the signs for Parc des Voltigeurs.

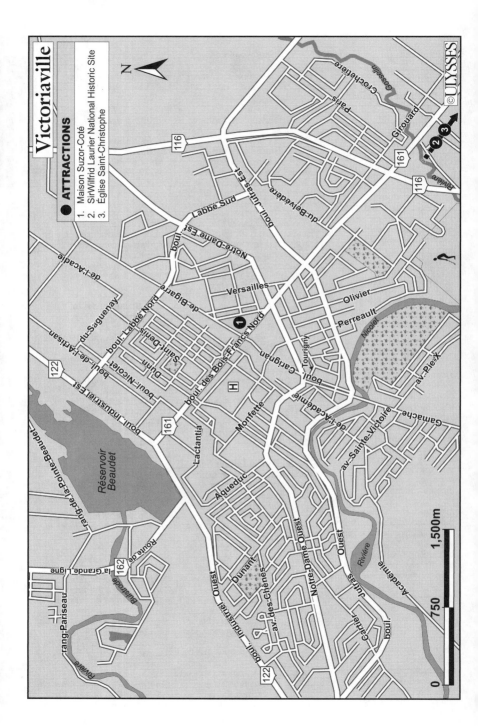

Victoriaville

ATTRACTIONS

1. Maison Suzor-Coté
2. SirWilfrid Laurier National Historic Site
3. Église Saint-Christophe

© ULYSSES

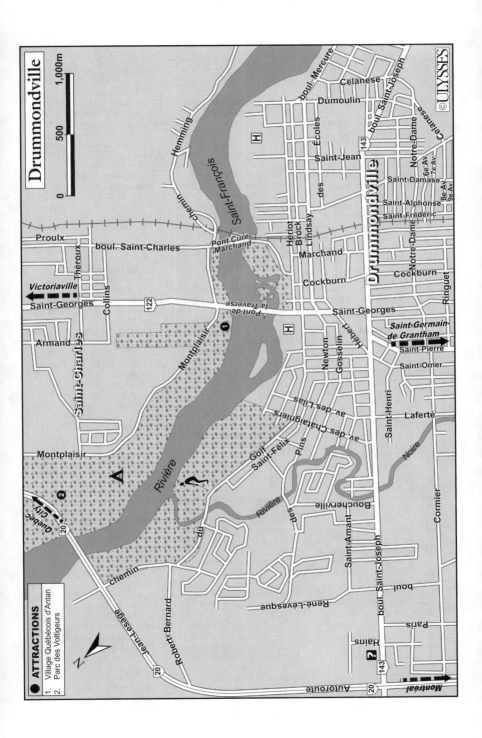

Drummondville

ATTRACTIONS
1. Village Québécois d'Antan
2. Parc des Voltigeurs

© ULYSSES

0   500   1,000m

The **Parc des Voltigeurs** ★ has recently been undergoing a facelift. The only heritage building between Montréal and Québec, which happens to be visible from Aut. 20, lies in the southern part of the park. The **Manoir Trent**, built in 1848 for retired British Navy officer George Norris Trent, is not really a manor, but a large farmhouse. It was acquired by the Compagnons de l'École Hotelière, a training school for hoteliers, which is also a reference centre that lets visitors sample its culinary attempts.

Continue along the east shore of Rivière Saint-François toward Saint-Joachim-de-Courval. Continue toward Pierreville and the nearby Odanak reserve.

Odanak
(pop. 390)

Marguerite Hertel, the owner of the Saint-François seigneury at the beginning of the 18th century, ceded a portion of her land on the east bank of the Saint-François to the government of Trois-Rivières for the creation of an Aboriginal village. The goal of resettling the Abenaki nation of Maine, who were allies of the French, was attained in 1700. Subsequently, at the time of the British conquest in 1759, the village was laid to waste by the British in reprisal. Odanak is still a reserve.

The **Musée des Abénaquis** ★ *($4.50; Mon-Fri 10am to 5pm, Sat and Sun 1pm to 5pm; Nov to Apr by appoinment only; 108 Waban-Aki / Rte. 132, ☎450-568-2600)* was founded in 1962, and allows visitors to explore Abenaki culture. A permanent exhibit depicts the ancestral way of life of the Abenakis and their relations with the French. The museum's animators bring to life the artifacts on display with traditional songs, legends and

dances. The **village church**, with its native carvings, is also well worth a visit.

Nicolet
(pop. 8,200)

The St. Lawrence valley shelters some towns and villages that were founded by the Acadians after their deportation from the Maritimes by the British army in 1755. Nicolet is one of these towns. It has been a bishopric since 1877. In 1955, a major landslide destroyed a part of the town's centre (the clay and marshy soil around Lac Saint-Pierre precludes settlement on its banks).

The **Cathédrale de Nicolet** ★ *(every day 9am to 4:30pm; May to Oct guided tours from 9:30am to 4:30pm; 671 Boulevard Louis-Fréchette, ☎293-5492)* replaced the church destroyed by the landslide of 1955. The curved shape of the reinforced concrete building, designed by Gérard Malouin in 1962, evokes a ship's sail. Jean-Paul Charland's gigantic stained-glass window (21m by 50m) for the church's facade is best appreciated from the inside.

Several religions are represented in Nicolet, a fact that surely influenced the founders of its **Musée des Religions** ★ *($4.50; every day 10am to 5pm; 900 Boulevard Louis-Fréchette, ☎293-6148)*. This museum presents interesting thematic exhibits on different religious traditions from around the world.

The **Ancien Séminaire** ★ *(350 Rue d'Youville)* of Nicolet was founded in 1803 by the Bishop of Québec, who wanted his future priests to receive their training far from the temptations of the city. The third-oldest seminary in Québec, Nicolet's seminary was also for a long time one of the province's most prestigious colleges. The imposing build-

ing was designed by Thomas Baillargé and built between 1827 and 1836. The seminary was closed during the Quiet Revolution and the building now houses the Institut de Police du Québec (police academy). Unfortunately, part of the building was damaged by fire in 1973.

The **Maison Rodolphe-Duguay** *($3.50; mid-May to mid-Oct, Tue-Sun 10am to 5pm; 195 Rang Saint-Alexis at Nicolet-Sud, ☎293-4103)* was the home of Québécois painter Rodolphe Duguay (1891-1973). He was devoted to his region's landscape and painted its rural scenes throughout his 60-year career. He began his studies at Montréal's Monument National, before spending seven years in Paris. When he returned to Québec, he moved back home to Nicolet and remained there for the rest of his life. In 1929, he set up a studio next to his house, the interior of which is similar to the one he had in Paris. This huge space is now open to the public and houses a retrospective of the artist's work.

Continue along Rte. 132 E. to the ancient village of Saint-Grégoire, now part of Nicolet.

The **Église Saint-Grégoire** ★★ *(4200 Boulevard Port-Royal)* is in the middle of the old village of Saint-Grégoire, founded in 1757 by a group of Acadians originally from Beaubassin. The parishioners began the construction of the present church in 1803. Since then the church has been touched up by two famous Québécois architects, Thomas Baillargé, who designed the 1851 neo-classical facade, and Victor Bourgeau, who remodelled the belltowers before decorating the arch of the nave.

In 1811, the church council acquired the precious retable and tabernacle from the

Récollet church in Montréal, which used to stand at the corner of Sainte-Hélène and Notre-Dame. Well-placed at Saint-Grégoire, the retable is the oldest in Québec, dating from 1713, and made by Jean-Jacques Bloem, known as Le Blond. The Louis-XIII style tabernacle is a major work executed by the carver Charles Chaboulié in 1703. The paintings by Parisian artist Joseph Uberti are much more recent (circa 1910).

Parks

Tour A: Mauricie

Situated at the mouth of the Rivière Saint-Maurice is the **Parc de l'Île Saint-Quentin** *($3; May to Oct 9am to 10pm, Nov to Apr 9am to 5pm; ☎373-8151).* This island of tranquillity and nature is ideal for strolling or swimming in summer and for skating and cross-country skiing in winter. There are also picnic grounds.

The **Parc de la Rivière-Batiscan** ★ *($4/pers., up to $14/car, free for children under five years old; early May to late Oct, every day 9am to 9pm; 200 Chemin du Barrage à Saint-Narcisse, ☎418-328-3599)* is devoted to wildlife conservation and the preservation of natural habitats. It is also a pleasant place for all kinds of activities, from walking and mountain-biking to camping and fishing. The park also offers nature and historical tours. In the middle of the park stands one of Québec's first hydroelectric plants. Constructed in 1897, the Saint-Narcisse station still provides power.

La **Mauricie National Park** ★★ *($3.50/person, $8/ family; ☎538-3232)* is also

known as Parc National de La Mauricie. It was created in 1970 to preserve a part of the Laurentians. It is the perfect setting for outdoor activities such as canoeing, walking, mountain biking, snowshoeing and cross-country skiing. Hidden among the woods are several lakes and rivers, as well as natural wonders of all kinds. Visitors can stay in dormitories year-round. Reservations can be made at ☎537-4555.

The **Réserve Faunique du Saint-Maurice** ★ *(3773 Rte. 155, ☎646-5687)* is accessible by a toll bridge *($12)* on the Rivière Saint-Maurice. Covering more than 750km², it includes several hiking trails equipped with huts. In the fall, moose- and game-hunting are allowed.

The **Réserve Faunique Mastigouche** *(Rte. 349, St-Alexis-des-Monts, ☎265-2098 or 800-665-6527)* covers 1,600km². Dotted with lakes and rivers, it is a prized canoe-camping spot. Hunting and fishing are also allowed. In winter, 180km of cross-country-ski trails and 130km of snowmobile trails are maintained. You can sleep in the shelters for $19/pers. *(reservations ☎265-3925).* Small chalets for four to eight people can also be rented for $25-$40/pers. *(reservations: SEPAQ ☎800-665-6527).*

Tour B: Centre-du-Québec

In 2000, Lac Saint-Pierre was declared a UNESCO Biosphere Reserve. It is now protected by the **Réserve de la Biosphère du Lac Saint-Pierre** *(☎800-474-9441).* The largest flood plain, largest rest stop for migrating wildfowl, first spring rest stop for migrating snow geese on the St. Lawrence and largest heron site in North America, Lac Saint-Pierre includes the

largest archipelago in the St. Lawrence River, (with some 100 islands), 20% of all its marshes and half its wetlands. Here, you can observe rare plants, nearly 300 bird species (over 100 of which are nesting species) and a dozen endangered species.

Outdoor Activities

Ice-fishing

From December to February, thousands of of **ice-fishing** enthusiasts converge on the Rivière Sainte-Anne to fish for tomcod. The river is covered with fishing huts in the winter. These can be rented, along with the necessary equipment, from the **Comité de Gestion de la Rivière Sainte-Anne** *(Ste-Anne-de-la-Pérade, ☎418-325-2475),* the river's management committee. The price is around $15/pers. per day (maximum four per cabin), and about $18 on weekends.

Cruises

Croisières M/S Jacques-Cartier—M/V Le Draveur $12
Departures from Parc Portuaire in Trois-Rivières, at 1pm and 8pm
☎375-3000 or 800-567-3737
Have a seat aboard a luxury 92-passenger catamaran and enjoy a cruise with commentary on the main points of interest in Trois-Rivières: the port, Laviolette bridge, Pointe des Ormes, Rivière St-Maurice and the archipelago of the Îles Saint-Quentin. Several

other longer cruises are also offered.

Canoeing

La Mauricie National Park is perfect for canoe trips. Strewn with lakes of all sizes, as well as a number of rivers, it has long been renowned among canoe-campers. Let yourself glide down narrow channels from one lake to another beneath luxuriant vegetation, accompanied by friendly water birds. You can rent a boat at the park and plan your own itinerary.

The region's two wildlife reserves, the **Réserve Faunique du Saint-Maurice** and the **Réserve Faunique Mastigouche**, are also good places to explore by canoe.

Cross-country Skiing

In winter, the **Réserve Faunique Mastigouche** has 200km of well-maintained trails. The **Réserve Faunique du Saint-Maurice** (see p 293) and **La Mauricie National Park** (see p 293) are also pleasant places to go cross-country skiing.

Cycling

In Québec, more and more bike paths are being laid out where railway lines used to be. One of these is the 77 km **Parc Linéaire des Bois-Francs** (*33 Pie-X, Victoriaville*, ☎*758-6414*), which runs between Tingwick and Lyster.

The **Circuit des Traditions de la MRC de Drummond** (*La Plaine rest stop, Aut. 20, Exit 179*; ☎*819-475-1164*) features 57.5 marked kilometres along the Route Verte, including 25km in the forest, along a former railroad track. Several tree species embellish this flat region. Don't miss the 7.5km crossing the Forêt Drummond, along the Saint-François river. A building with a large parking lot has been transformed into a rest area for cyclists.

Snowmobiling

In winter, the **Réserve Faunique de Mastigouche** (see p 293) is a playground for snowmobilers, with 130km of marked trails studded with heated shelters.

Dogsledding

At the **Réserve Faunique du Saint-Maurice**, you can experience the thrill of racing along a snowy trail with a team of dogs at your command. All winter long, this park maintains nearly 270km of marked trails laid out expressly for dogsledding.

Accommodations

Tour A: La Mauricie

Trois-Rivières

Stretching from the Ursuline convent to the Monument du Flambeau, Rue des Ursulines has about a half-dozen excep-

tionally charming bed and breakfasts that offer enchanting accommodations well within reach of activities in the town centre. Contact the local tourist office to make reservations, as rooms in these establishments fill up quickly.

Auberge de Jeunesse La Flottille
$
497 Rue Radisson
☎*378-8010*
The Auberge de Jeunesse La Flotille is a pleasant little youth hostel close to Trois Riviere's nightlife. There are some 40 beds in the summer season, 30 in the winter.

Gîte La Campanule
$$ bkfst incl.
⊛, *sb*
634 des Ursulines
☎*373-1133*
Adjacent to the Ursuline convent, Gîte La Campanule offers visitors an authentic bed-and-breakfast experience. A huge bathroom is shared among three upstairs rooms, two of which look out on the backyard's beautiful flowery garden. Of varying sizes, these rooms feature a comfortable country-style decor.

L'Émérillon
$$
890 terrasse Turcotte
☎*375-1010*
Housed in a colonial-style home built in the early 20th century, this elegant bed and breakfast overlooks the St. Lawrence River.

Hôtel Delta
$$$$
≡, ☉, ✖, ≈, ℜ, ⌂, ᶜᵇ, ⊛
1620 Notre-Dame
☎*376-1991 or 800-268-1133*
⇌*372-5975*
The high tower of the Hôtel Delta is easy to spot next to the downtown area. The rooms are spacious. The hotel also has sports facilities and a convention centre.

Grand-Mère

Auberge Le Florès
$$
≡, 🏋, ≈, ℜ, ◯, *sb*, ☯
4291 Avenue 50e
☎*538-9340 or 800-538-9340*
⇆*538-1884*
The Auberge Le Florès is a
superb period house. Though
not spectacular, the rooms are
quite comfortable.

L'Auberge Santé Lac des Neiges
$$-$$$
ℜ, ≈, ℜ, ◯, *pb/sb*, ☯, ⊛
100 Lac des Neiges, Ste-Flore de
Grand-Mère
☎*533-4518 or 800-757-4519*
⇆*533-4727*
*www.aubergesantelac
desneiges.qc.ca*
The stress of the daily grind
melts away immediately upon
reaching the Auberge Santé
Lac des Neiges. Nestled on a
peninsula, the building's mod-
ern architecture is tempered
by white stucco, wooden
beams and stairs, somewhat
reminiscent of the baroque
style. The common lounge is
particularly inviting, with its
many couches, windows with
a view of the lake and, above
all, a fire in the hearth. In this
relaxing setting, guests often
lounge about in their bath-
robes between treatments.
The inn's restaurant offers
elegantly presented French
cuisine. Many packages are
available in order to cater to
everyone's needs. In short,
the staff does everything possi-
ble to make you feel at home
and ensure that you leave
feeling like a new per-
son—completely refreshed
and invigorated.

Saint-Jean-des-Piles

Maison Cadorette
$$ bkfst incl.
1701 Rue Principale
☎*538-9883 or 888-538-9883*
The Maison Cadorette ac-
commodates guests just a few
minutes from the entrance to
La Mauricie National Park.
The rooms are attractively

decorated and the service is
impeccable.

Grandes-Piles

 Auberge Le Bôme
$$
ℜ, ◯, ⊛
720 2e Avenue
☎*538-2805 or 800-538-2805*
⇆*538-5879*
www.auberge-le-bome.qc.ca
The Auberge Le Bôme is an
excellent option in this region.
The rooms are beautifully
decorated, and the friendly
service makes for a very invit-
ing atmosphere. There is also
a superb sitting room, ideal for
fascinating discussions with
other travellers.

Shawinigan

Auberge l'Escapade
$$$
≡, ℜ, ⊛
3383 Rue Garnier
☎*539-6911 or 800-461-6911*
⇆*539-7669*
www.aubergeescapade.qc.ca
A well-kept place on the way
into town, the Auberge
l'Escapade has several different
personalities. The choice of
accommodations here ranges
from basic, inexpensive rooms
to luxurious rooms decorated
with period furniture. In between the two, there are
pretty, comfortable rooms
that offer good value for the
money. What's more, the
restaurant serves tasty food.

Gouverneur Shawinigan
$$$$
≡, ℜ, ≈, ℜ, ♿, ⊛
1100 promenade St-Maurice
☎*537-6000 or 888-922-1100*
⇆*537-6365*
*www.gouverneur
shawinigan.com*
Located right near
Shawinigan's town centre,
Gouverneur Shawinigan
meets the needs of both business and leisure travellers.

Saint-Élie-de-Caxton

La Station Touristique Floribell
$$
ℜ, *K*, ℜ
95 Chemin Lac Bell
☎*221-5731*
⇆*221-3347*
The Floribell holiday resort is
perfect for sociable travellers
or families on vacation. The
resort rents out campsites and
condos looking out on a lake
with crystal-clear waters,
where you can enjoy swim-
ming, boat rides or simply
building sand castles with your
family. What's more, right
nearby is a bike path that
winds through the surrounding
countryside leading right to the
gates of La Mauricie National
Park. In short, this place offers
the ambiance of a holiday
camp. The spotless, modern
condos, furnished with double
beds and sofa beds, can ac-
commodate up to four peo-
ple.

Saint-Paulin

Le Baluchon
$$$$
ℜ, ☉, *K*, ≈, ℜ, ◯, ☯, ⊛
3550 Chemin des Trembles
☎*268-2555 or 800-789-5968*
⇆*268-5234*
www.baluchon.com
Located alongside a river, Le
Baluchon is *the* place in the
area for active types. The vast
grounds highlight the beautiful
natural surroundings. There
are plenty of ways to occupy
your time here: hiking or
skiing along the river or
through the woods, kayaking,
canoeing, etc. Guests sleep in
one of two buildings, each
containing nearly 40 pleasant,
comfortable and modern
rooms. You can also relax at
the well-equipped spa or
tempt your palate in the dining
room (see p 297).

Saint-Alexis-des-Monts

Hôtel Sacacomie
$$$
ℑ, ℜ, △, ⊛
4000 Rang Sacacomie
☎*265-4444 or 888-265-4414*
⇌*265-4445*
www.sacacomie.com
Hôtel Sacacomie is a magnificent establishment with log cabins nestled in the middle of the forest near the Mastigouche reserve. Overhanging the majestic Lac Sacacomie, the facility has an idyllic location with a beach nearby. There's a great range of activities all year round.

Pointe-du-Lac

Auberge du Lac Saint-Pierre
$$$
≡, ≈, ℜ, △, ⊛
C.P. 10
1911 Rue Notre-Dame
☎*377-5971 or 888-377-5971*
⇌*377-5579*
www.aubergelacst-pierre.com
Auberge du Lac Saint-Pierre is located in Pointe-de-Lac, a small village at the north end of Lac Saint-Pierre, which is actually just a widening in the St. Lawrence. The flora and fauna that make their home in and around the «late» area are characteristic of marshy areas. Perched atop a promontory that slopes down to the shore, this large inn boasts an outstanding location. It has comfortable, modern rooms, some of which have a mezzanine for the beds, leaving more space in the main room. The dining room serves excellent food (see p 297). There are bicycles on hand if you feel like exploring the area.

Tour B: Centre-du-Québec

Bécancour

Auberge Godefroy
$$$$
≡, ℑ, ⊘, K, ≈, ℜ, △, ⊙, ⊛
17575 Boulevard Bécancour
☎*233-2200 or 800-361-1620*
⇌*233-2288*
www.aubergegodefroy.com
Auberge Godefroy is an imposing building with lots of windows. In winter, a crackling fire greets guests in the stately lobby. The 70 rooms are spacious and offer all the comforts one would expect from an establishment of this calibre. The hotel also has a spa and offers a variety of packages. Go ahead and indulge yourself in the dining room, as well (see p 297)!

Victoriaville

Le Suzor
$$
≡, ℜ, ⊛
1000 Boulevard Jutras
☎*357-1000*
⇌*357-5000*
www.hotelsuzor.com
The modern Le Suzor hotel is located in a quiet part of town. The pleasant, spacious rooms have new furniture.

Drummondville

Motel Blanchet
$$
≡, ℑ, K, ✗, ℝ, ℜ, ⊛
225 Boulevard St-Joseph Ouest
☎*477-0222 or 800-567-3823*
⇌*478-8706*
www.hotelblanchet.com
The Motel Blanchet has a good location and attractive, reasonably priced rooms.

Hôtel & Suites Le Dauphin
$$$
≡, ⊘, K, ≈, ℝ, ℜ, ⊛
600 Boulevard St-Joseph
☎*478-4141 or 800-567-0995*
⇌*478-7549*
www.le-dauphin.com
Hôtel & Suites Le Dauphin is located on a very busy street,

---

near a number of shopping centres. It has large, well-kept rooms with modern furnishings.

Restaurants

Tour A: La Mauricie

Trois-Rivières

Bolvert
$
1556 Rue Royale
☎*373-6161*
The Bolvert is an unpretentious little restaurant that serves delicious health-food dishes. The decor is a little bleak but the cuisine is simple and good.

Maison de cafés, Le Torréfacteur
$
1465 Rue Notre-Dame
☎*694-4484*
Coffee has now replaced alcohol as the social beverage of choice. It's therefore not surprising to see coffee houses popping up like mushrooms. Trois-Rivières is no exception; the locals' favourite place to meet is in a coffee house. In addition to a variety of hot beverages, this establishment also offers light fare and desserts.

Le Castel des Prés
$$-$$$$
5800 Boulevard Royal
☎*375-4921*
The Auberge Castel des Prés has two restaurants:
L'Étiquette ($$) serves bistro-style cuisine and **Chez Claude ($$$-$$$$)** offers traditional French cuisine and is an excellent choice in this area. The chef has won a number of culinary awards. The menu includes pasta, meat and fish dishes with rich, flavourful sauces. In warm weather,

Mauricie and Centre-du-Québec

guests can enjoy a sheltered outdoor terrace cooled by summer breezes.

Chez Gambrinus
$$
3160 Rue des Forges
☎*691-3371*
Located outside of town near the university, Chez Gambrinus restaurant and microbrewery attracts a clientele of regulars who are not shy to tell you how great the place is. It's one of those rare establishments where beer and oysters are elevated to unparalled heights. Game and hamburgers are also served. The place is located in an old home surrounded by a terrace. The atmosphere and welcome are warm, but the service is a little slow.

Au Four à Bois
$$
329 Laviolette
☎*373-3686*
Au Four à Bois, a regional institution, has been open for many years. The varied menu, which has evolved with time, offers pasta, seafood, grills and gourmet pizza at reasonable prices. Located in a large two-storey house with a wood stove in the middle of the main floor, the atmosphere is elegant but relaxed.

Angéline
$$
313 Rue des Forges
☎*372-0468*
There are several interesting restaurants on Rue Des Forges near the harbour park. Frequented by an eclectic crowd, Angéline's menu and audacious decor are inspired by Italy. There are scrumptious pasta dishes, a variety of pizzas and other Italian specialties. It isn't gourmet dining, but the place is unpretentious and has a large clientele.

Le Toscane
$$-$$$
901 Rue Royale
☎*378-1891*
Set up in an old house, this lovely restaurant is much appreciated by the locals for its excellent value. La Toscane serves refined Italian cuisine, which consists almost exclusively of fresh pasta and veal scaloppine, whose strength lies in its stove-top sauces. The chef pleasantly surprises with his choice of accompaniments by creating original preparations sometimes derived from other European cuisines (such as German). Moreover, the restaurant favours local produce and regional specialties. The service is friendly and attentive, which mitigates the stuffy atmosphere.

Le Lupin
$$$
Tue-Sat
376 Rue St-Georges
☎*370-4740*
Located in a charming ancestral home, Le Lupin serves some of the finest cuisine in the entire region. In addition to excellent *crêpes Bretonnes*, it offers game and perch, considered the region's specialities.

Grand-Mère

Crêperie de Flore
$$-$$$
3580 Avenue 50e
☎*533-2020*
The Crêperie de Flore has a simple, informal ambiance and specializes in Breton crêpes and veal.

Grandes-Piles

Auberge Le Bôme
$$$$
720 2e Avenue
☎*538-2805*
In addition to being charming and comfortable, the Auberge Le Bôme serves French cuisine combined with regional specialties like venison and

Arctic trout, with sensational results. An absolute must!

Pointe-du-Lac

Auberge du Lac Saint-Pierre
$$$-$$$$
1911 route 138
☎*377-5971 or 888-377-5971*
If you go to the Auberge du Lac Saint-Pierre (see p 296) for dinner, start your evening with a short walk on the shore to work up an appetite, or perhaps have an apéritif on the terrace, with its view of the river. The modern decor of the dining room is a bit cold, but there's nothing bland about the presentation of the dishes, much less their flavour. The menu, made up of French and Québec cuisine, includes trout, salmon, lamb and pheasant, all artfully prepared. Reservations required.

Saint-Paulin

Le Baluchon
$$$-$$$$
3550 Chemin des Trembles
☎*268-2555 or 800-789-5968*
Located on a magnificent estate, Le Baluchon (see p 295) offers choice French and Québec cuisine, as well as a "health-conscious" menu that will leave you feeling anything but deprived. The dining room has a soothing decor and a view of the river.

Tour B: Centre-du-Québec

Bécancour

Auberge Godefroy
$$$-$$$$
17575 Boulevard Bécancour
☎*233-2200 or 800-361-1620*
The spacious dining room at Auberge Godefroy (see p 296) looks out onto the river. The delicious French cuisine varies from classic to original creations made with regional produce. Succulent desserts!

Victoriaville

Shad Café
$
309 Notre-Dame Est
☎**751-0848**
The Shad Café is probably the only place in town where you can enjoy a light meal along with an imported beer or European coffee. The place is very pleasant both day and night, when it essentially turns into a bar whose clientele appreciates its unpretentious café ambiance.

Cactus Resto-bar
$$
139 Boulevard Bois-Francs Sud
☎**758-5311**
At Cactus, orange hues, brickwork and wainscotting create a warm, slightly intimate ambiance despite the high turnout. Generous portions of good Mexican food draw a mixed crowd. Like several establishments in Victoriaville, this restaurant turns into a laidback pub, complete with a pool table, at night.

Drummondville

Restaurant La Table d'Hôte Chez Mallet
$$-$$$
1320 Boulevard Mercure
☎**475-6965**
Though Drummondville initially seems devoid of good restaurants, visitors need only dig a little deeper. Located away from the town centre, this restaurant is a great gastronomic option for lovers of French cuisine. As its name indicates, this establishment offers tables d'hôte, ranging from lamb to poultry to ostrich.

Ristorante La Trattoria
$$-$$$
195 Rue Lindsay
☎**474-0020**
A local favourite, La Trattoria offers a choice menu of fine Italian cuisine. In season, the pretty tiered terrace looks out on bustling Rue Lindsay. The

welcome could be a little warmer, however.

Crêperie Bretonne
$$-$$$
131 Rue St-Georges
☎**477-9148**
Set up in the Mitchell house, Crêperie Bretonne is an attraction in itself. Indeed, this Victorian house was restored by its Breton-born owner, who put as much care into the renovations as she does into the preparation of her delicious crepes. The classy decor, which combines original wallpaper and tasteful innovations, exudes a muted ambiance. Moreover, patrons can browse through documents dealing with architectural influences and portfolios of photographs tracing the history of the house's restoration. And the crepes? Exquisite. Several types of menus are offered that introduce diners to a variety of flavours. Of particular note is the buckwheat crepe with seafood and cognac sauce—absolutely delicious. On a health note, all crepes are made with organic flour.

Entertainment

Bars and Nightclubs

Trois-Rivières

Downtown Trois-Rivières' reputation for its nightlife is well established and you need only stroll around to discover its captivating bars and nightclubs. This is particularly true in summer, when jam-packed terraces spill out onto the streets. For more information, consult *Le Sorteux*, a free monthly paper available at

several businesses in the region.

Café Bar Le Zénob
171 Rue Bonaventure
☎**378-9925**
Hot summer nights are very lively and enjoyable beneath the large trees of Zénob's front and rear terraces. This café-bar welcomes a fair share of local artists and regularly hosts exhibitions and art events.

Café Galerie l'Embuscade
1571 Badeaux
☎**374-0652**
Café Galerie l'Embuscade is a popular meeting place where artists, students and others gather to sip a beer or snack on a light meal. It also acts as a gallery to promote the works of many talented artists. Artistic events, such as live painting, are presented on the outdoor terrace in the summer.

Nord Ouest Café
1441 Rue Notre-Dame
☎**693-1151**
Nord Ouest Café is a laidback place with several floors, including a bar on the main floor, a private lounge, pool tables and games. It serves a variety of imported beer, as well as light fare.

Saint-Élie-de-Caxton

La Pierre Angulaire
cover charge for shows
reservations required
39 Chemin des Loisirs
☎**268-3393**
La Pierre Angulaire caféshowbar is run by a co-op that brings together several young local talents. The collective organizes shows, activities and entertainment of all kinds, but primarily devotes itself to the preservation of local traditions and folklore by hosting evenings of storytelling and traditional Quebecois music. Set in the middle of the woods, this café offers the warmest of ambiances where you are welcomed like one of the family.

Festivals and Cultural Events

Trois Rivières

The **Grand Prix de Trois-Rivières** (*early Aug; ☎373-9912, ticket sales: ☎380-9797 or 800-363-5051*), a Toyota Atlantic Championship race, is held in the city streets in early August. Now-famous drivers like Jacques Villeneuve have participated in this event in the past.

Drummondville

In mid-July, Drummondville hosts **Mondial des Cultures** (*☎472-1184 or 800-265-5412*). The goal of this festival is to encourage exchanges between the different traditions and cultures of the world.

Victoriaville

The **Festival de Musique Actuelle de Victoriaville** (*☎752-7912*) takes place each year in May. This festival is an exploration of new musical forms. Of course, this event won't appeal to everyone, but it is an adventure for musicians and spectators alike.

Shopping

Tour B: Centre-du-Québec

Bécancour

Chèvrerie l'Angélaine
12285 Boulevard Bécancour
(Rte. 132)
☎222-5702
The Chèvrerie l'Angélaine specializes in the breeding of Angora goats and makes a line of clothing called "La Molaire du Québec." The collection is made up of a great selection of sweaters, vests, shawls, jackets and fashion accessories.

Fromagerie L'Ancêtre
1615 Boulevard Port-Royal
☎233-9157
Both a shop and a restaurant, the Fromagerie L'Ancêtre makes delicious home-made dairy products, including three kinds of cheeses, butter and ice cream. All are made using natural manufacturing processes. The sampling of their products is accompanied by home-brewed wine and beer.

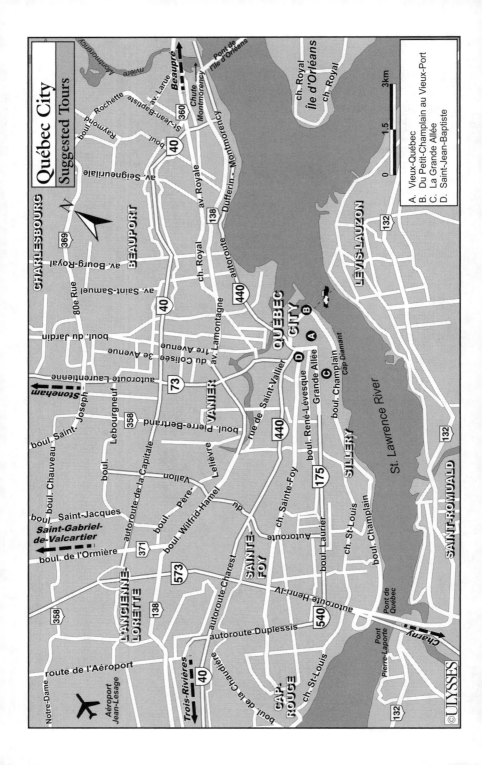

Québec City ★★★

Q uébec City ★★★ is a magical place whatever the season. Meandering through its winding streets on a winter evening is an enchanting experience: the snow sparkles under the light of the street lamps and the whole city looks like a scene from *A Christmas Carol.*

Diners savouring hearty fare appear through the window panes of a restaurant, illuminated by the light dancing from the hearth. They've come to join the carnival, or maybe they're setting off on an excursion to the ski slopes of Mont Sainte-Anne.

In the spring and summer, the terraces of Grande-Allée shelter their thirsty patrons under a sea of multicoloured parasols, while out on the Plains of Abraham an elderly woman performs her *Tai Chi* exercises. Fall keeps in reserve its own treasure of special moments to be shared with the inhabitants of the jewel of French America: the spectacular display of the leaves rustling in the fresh breeze; the sight of students dawdling to arrive just in time for the start of a geometry course at the university, while the politicians and civil servants

pursue their debates over one last coffee before returning to the Parliament buildings.

Québec City stands out as much for the stunning richness of its architectural heritage as for the beauty of its location. The Haute-Ville quarter covers a promontory more than 98m high, known as Cap Diamant, and juts out over the St. Lawrence River, which narrows here to a mere 1km. In fact, it is this narrowing of the river that gave the city its name: in Algonquian, *kebec* means "place where the river narrows." Affording an impregnable vantage point, the heights of Cap Diamant dominate the river and the surrounding countryside.

From the inception of New France, this rocky peak played a strategic role and was the site of major fortifications early on. Dubbed the "Gibraltar of North America," today Québec is the only walled city north of Mexico.

The cradle of New France, Québec City's atmosphere and architecture are more reminiscent of Europe than of America. The stone houses that flank its narrow streets and the many spires of its churches and religious institutions evoke the France of the Old Regime. In addition, the old fortifications of Haute-Ville, the Parliament and the grandiose administrative buildings attest eloquently to the importance of Québec City to the history of the country. Indeed, its historical and architectural richness are such that the city and its historic surroundings were recognized by UNESCO in 1985 as a World Heritage Site, the first in North America.

With over 95% of the population of French ancestry, the capital of Québec is home to an impressive number of excellent restaurants and cafés. It is a lively city all year round, distinguished in the fall by the changing colours of the leaves, in the winter by its famous carnival, in the spring by the musicians who take to the streets and the newly opened terraces, and in the summer by its summer festival. What's more, the region offers lovely mountainous landscapes within reach of the city.

This chapter contains suggestions for four different walking tours in the city, while the next chapter explores the surrounding area. For more information on Québec City, consult *Ulysses Travel Guide Québec City*.

A Short History of Québec City

During his second expedition in 1535, Jacques Cartier stopped at Stadacona, a native village located on land that would later become Québec City. Hoping to find precious stones, he christened the sheer and stony escarpment that overlooks the river Cap

Diamant, "Cape of Diamonds." At the time, Cartier was on a mission for the King of France, François I, to discover gold, as well as a passage to the Orient. After Cartier's three expeditions found neither of these, the King declined to finance further voyages to North America.

A few decades later, the significant profits to be made in the fur trade rekindled France's interest in this far-off land. After the failure of many trading posts both on the coast and in the interior, the area where Québec City now stands was chosen for the establishment of a permanent trading post. In 1608, Samuel de Champlain and his men erected and fortified a series of buildings at the foot of the cape. This first settlement was known as *Abitation*. Despite the extreme harshness of the first winter and the deaths of 20 of the 28 men from scurvy and malnutrition, 1608 marked the beginning of a permanent French presence in North America. Québec City was founded for the fur trade, therefore it initially attracted the interest of French merchants. Little by little, a few peasant families began to establish themselves. Basse-Ville became the centre of commercial activity and the residential area of the colonists. In fact, Québec's lower-town remained its urban and commercial centre until the middle of the 19th century, because the religious institutions of Haute-Ville opposed commercial development.

Early on, New France's capital became a prize in the rivalry that pitted France against England. Québec City was captured by the Kirke brothers in 1629, before being returned to France in 1632. Although the city held out against the English siege led by

Admiral Phipps in 1690, pressure from England continued to build throughout the 18th century. The outcome was decided in the famous battle of the Plains of Abraham in 1759, in which British troops led by General Wolfe defeated those of the Marquis de Montcalm. When New France was ceded to the British under the terms of the Treaty of Paris in 1763, the population of Québec City had reached almost 9,000.

Because of its geographic location, Québec City served as the entryway to the colony, as well as its principal economic centre.

The goods of the commercial triangle linking Canada, the West Indies and London were transhipped in the port of Québec City, which naturally developed an important shipyard. Nevertheless, Québec City began to lose ground rapidly with the growth of Montréal in the 19th century. Following the dredging of the St. Lawrence up to Montréal and the construction of a railway system with Montréal as its centre, Québec City was usurped as the focus of trade and as the foremost economic centre of Canada. Though Montréal became the Canadian metropolis, Québec City nonetheless retained an important role as the provincial capital and as a strategic military base. In the 1920s, it even enjoyed a certain prosperity based largely on the shoemaking industry.

The growth of Québec City in the 1960s paralleled that of the scope and power of Québec's provincial government. Today, the economy of the sole francophone capital of North America revolves around the civil service.

Finding Your Way Around

Four walking tours of Québec city are suggested: **Tour A: Vieux-Québec ★★★**, **Tour B: Du Petit-Champlain au Vieux-Port ★★★**, **Tour C: Grande-Allée ★★** and **Tour D: Saint-Jean-Baptiste ★**.

By Car

Québec City can be reached from Montréal along either shore of the St. Lawrence River. Aut. 40 East runs along the north shore, becoming the Rte. 440 on the outskirts of Québec City and then Boulevard Charest once you get downtown. On the south shore, Aut. 20 runs east until the Pierre-Laporte bridge. Across the bridge, Boulevard Laurier continues to Québec City, becoming Grande-Allée Est as you enter the downtown area.

Car Rental

Budget
Aéroport de Québec
☎*(418) 872-9885*
Vieux-Québec: 29 côte du Palais
☎*(418) 692-3660*
Sainte-Foy: 2481 ch. Ste-Foy
☎*(418) 651-6518*

Discount
Sainte-Foy (Centre Innovation): 2360 ch. Ste-Foy
☎*(418) 652-7289*

Hertz
Aéroport de Québec
☎*(418) 871-1571*
Québec: 580 Grande Allée
☎*(418) 647-4949*
Vieux-Québec: 44 côte du Palais
☎*(418) 694-1224*

National
Aéroport de Québec
☎*(418) 871-1224*
Québec: 295 rue St-Paul
☎*(418) 694-1727*

Via Route
2605 boul. Hamel O.
☎*(418) 682-2660*

By Plane

Aéroport International Jean-Lesage (see p 44), though smaller than Montréal's airports, does receive international flights.

By Boat

There is a pleasant new way to reach Québec City from Montréal or Trois-Rivières. **Les Dauphins du Saint-Laurent** (☎*514-288-4499 or 877-648-4499*) links these three cities on its daily summer runs by hydroplane, travelling at 65km/h. You can leave Montréal in the morning and be in Québec City 4½hrs later—a longer trip than it would be by car (about 2½hrs), but it makes for a pleasant, scenic trip.

By Bus

A network of bus routes covers the entire city. A $58.60 monthly pass allows unlimited travel. A single trip costs $2.25 (exact change only) or $1.90 with the purchase of tickets (sold at newspaper stands). Transfers, if needed, should be requested from the driver upon boarding. Take note that most bus routes are in operation between 6am and 12:30am. For more information: ☎*(418) 627-2511*.

Bus Station

320 Rue Abraham-Martin
Gare du Palais
☎*(418) 525-3000*

Train Station

Gare du Palais
450 Rue de la Gare-du-Palais
☎*800-835-3037*
www.viarail.ca

By Ferry

Even if you have no reason to go to Lévis on the south shore of the St. Lawrence River, you should take the ferry trip just for the view. The ferry dock is across from Place Royale; you should have no trouble finding it. The return trip from Lévis gives you a magnificent view of Québec City. A one-way trip costs $2 during winter and $2.50 in summer for an adult, and $8.50 for a car in winter and $9.85 during summer (maximum six passengers). The timetable varies from one season to the next so it is better to check directly for the times.

Société des Traversiers du Québec
10 Rue des Traversiers
☎*644-3704*
www.traversiers.gouv.qc.ca

Ride Sharing

Rides are organized to Québec City with **Allo-Stop Qué-**

Names of New Merged Cities

Québec City
Merger of Beauport, Cap-Rouge, Charlesbourg, Lac-Saint-Charles, L'Ancienne-Lorette, Loretteville, Québec City, Sainte-Foy, Saint-Émile, Sillery, Val-Bélair, Vanier and Saint-Augustin-de-Desmaures.

Québec City

bec *(655 Rue Saint-Jean,* ☎*418-522-0056)* (see p 49).

Taxis

Taxi Coop
☎*(418) 525-5191*

Taxi Québec
☎*(418) 525-8123*

Practical Information

Area code: *418*

Tourist Information Office

Bureau d'Information Touristique du Vieux-Québec
late Jun to early Sep every day 8:30am to 7:30pm, early Sep to mid-Oct every day 8:30am to 6:30pm, mid-Oct to late Jun Mon to Sat 9am to 5pm, Fri to 6pm, Sun 10am to 4pm
835 Avenue Wilfrid-Laurier, G1R 2L3
☎*649-2608*
≈*522-0830*
www.quebecregion.com

Centre Infotouriste de Québec
late Jun to early Sep every day 8:30am to 7pm, rest of year 9am to 5pm
12 Rue Sainte-Anne
(opposite the Château Frontenac), G1R 3X2
☎*877-266-5687*

Tourisme Québec
Case postale 979
Montréal, H3C 2W3
☎*877-266-5687*
≈*(514) 864-3838*
www.bonjourquebec.com

Post Office

300 Rue Saint-Paul
☎*694-6176*

Banks

Banque Royale
700 Place d'Youville
☎*692-6800*

Caisse Populaire Desjardins du Vieux-Québec
19 Rue des Jardins
☎*522-6806*

Banque Nationale
150 Boulevard René-Lévesque Est
☎*647-6100*

Guided Tours

Located in the tourist information office on Rue Sainte-Anne, **CD Tour** *($10, $15 for two people; 12 Rue Sainte-Anne,* ☎*654-1115)* rents out portable audio-tours for various parts of the city, including Vieux-Québec, the Cité Parlementaire, Parc-de-l'Artillerie and the Plaines d'Abraham. These tours are recorded on laser disc, so visitors can stop where and when they please. In the lively recordings, historic figures are brought back to life to tell visitors about the major events that shaped Québec City.

The **Société Historique de Québec** *($12; 72 Côte de la Montagne,* ☎*692-0556),* on Côte de la Montagne, offers guided tours of Vieux-Québec. There are a number of themes from which to choose. These walking tours usually last 1.5hrs to 2hrs and cover various aspects of the history of Québec City.

Exploring

Arriving in Québec City by car, the most common route is via Grande-Allée. After passing through a typical North American-style suburb, you come to a rather British-looking part of town with tree-lined streets. Next come the government buildings of the provincial capital, and finally, the imposing medieval-looking gates, and behind them the historic streets of the old city, Vieux-Québec.

Tour A: Vieux-Québec

Duration of tour: two days

Haute-Ville, or upper town, covers the plateau atop Cap Diamant. As the administrative and institutional centre, it is adorned with convents, chapels and public buildings whose construction dates back, in some cases, to the 17th century. The walls of Haute-Ville, dominated by the citadel, surround this section of Vieux-Québec and give it the characteristic look of a fortress. These same walls long contained the development of the town, yielding a densely built-up bourgeois and aristocratic milieu. With time, the picturesque urban planning of the 19th century contributed to the present-day image of Québec City through the construction of such fantastical buildings as the Château Frontenac and the creation of public spaces like Terrasse Dufferin, in the *belle époque* spirit.

The Haute-Ville walking tour begins at Porte Saint-Louis, near the parliament buildings.

The **Porte Saint-Louis** *(at the beginning of the street of the same name)* gateway is the result of Québec City merchants' pressuring the government between 1870 and 1875 to tear down the wall surrounding the city. The Governor General of Canada at the time, Lord Dufferin, was opposed to the idea and instead put forward a plan drafted by Irishman William H. Lynn to showcase the walls while improving traffic circulation. The design he submitted exhibits a Victorian romanticism in its use of grand gateways that bring to mind images of medieval castles and horsemen. The pepper-box tower of Porte Saint-Louis, built in 1878, makes for a striking first impression upon arriving in downtown Québec City.

On the right, once inside Porte Saint-Louis, is the **Club de la Garnison** *(97 Rue Saint-Louis)*, reserved for army officers, as well as the road leading to the citadel. As a visit to the citadel may require two or three hours, it is best to set aside a separate time to take a tour of the premises (see description at the end of the Haute-Ville walking tour, on p 316).

At the **Fortifications of Québec National Historic Site ★** *($3; early May to mid-Oct every day 10am to 5pm; 100 Rue St-Louis, ☎648-7016)*, you can visit the **Poudrière de l'Esplanade**, which houses the **Centre d'Initiation aux Fortifications et à la Poudrière de l'Esplanade**. This centre displays models and maps outlining the development of Québec City's defense system. Booklets are available with a complete tour of the city's fortifications, and there are also guided tours. Information plaques have been placed along the wall, providing another means of discovering the city's history. The walkway

on top of the wall can be reached by taking the stairs next to the city gates.

Québec City's first wall was built of earth and wooden posts. It was erected on the west side of the city in 1693, according to the plans of engineer Dubois Berthelot de Beaucours, to protect Québec City from the Iroquois. Work on much stronger stone fortifications began in 1745, designed by engineer Chaussegros de Léry, when England and France entered a new era of conflict. However, the wall was unfinished when the city was seized by the British in 1759. The British saw to the completion of the project at the end of the 18th century. Work on the citadel began in 1693 to a minor extent. However, the structure as we know it today was essentially built between 1820 and 1832. Nevertheless, the citadel is largely designed along the Vauban principles from the 17th century, principles that suit the location admirably.

Continue along Rue Saint-Louis and turn right on Rue Sainte-Ursule.

Chalmers-Wesley United Church *(78 Rue Sainte-Ursule, ☎692-2640)*. Until the end of the 19th century, Québec City had a small but influential community of Scottish Presbyterians, most of whom were involved in shipping and the lumber trade. This attractive Gothic Revival church is presently used by a variety of groups, testimony to the decline in the Scottish Presbyterian community. The church was built in 1852 and designed by John Wells, an architect known for a number of famous buildings, including the Bank of Montreal headquarters. The elegant Gothic Revival spire of the church contributes to the picturesque aspect of the city. The church's organ was restored in 1985.

Concerts are presented at the church every Sunday afternoon from the beginning of July until the middle of August. Donations are appreciated.

The **Sanctuaire Notre-Dame-du-Sacré-Coeur** *(free admission; every day 7am to 8pm; 71 Rue Sainte-Ursule, ☎692-3787)* faces Chalmers-Wesley United Church. The sanctuary was originally built for the Sacré Cœur missionaries. This place of worship, erected in 1910 and drafted by François-Xavier Berlinguet, is now open to everyone. The sanctuary has a Gothic Revival facade. Its two rather narrow steeples seem dwarfed by the size of the building. The interior of the structure, with its stained-glass windows and murals, is more attractive.

Turn left on Avenue Sainte-Geneviève.

A short detour down Rue Mont-Carmel (to the left) brings you to one of the remnants of Québec City's earliest fortifications, located in an out-of-the-way spot behind a row of houses. The **Cavalier du Moulin** was built in 1693 by engineer Dubois Bertholot de Beaucours. It is a redoubt set within the city walls from which it would be possible to destroy them in the event of a successful enemy invasion. The fortification is named for the windmill, or *moulin*, that used to sit on top of it.

Besides the city's major historic landmarks, Québec's appeal lies within its smaller, less imposing buildings, each of which has its own separate history. It is enjoyable to simply wander along the narrow streets of the old city, taking in the subtleties of architecture so atypical of North America. The **Maison Cirice-Têtu ★** *(25 Avenue Sainte-Geneviève)*, or Cirice-Têtu house, was built in 1852. It was designed by Charles Baillargé, a member of a celebrated family of architects who, beginning in the 18th century, left an important mark on the architecture of Québec City and its surroundings. The Greek Revival facade of the house, a masterpiece of the genre, is tastefully and discreetfully decorated with palmettes and laurel wreaths. The *piano nobile* has huge bay windows that open onto a single expansive living room in the London style. From the time of its construction, the house incorporated all the modern amenities: central heating, hot running water, and multiple bathrooms.

The charming square known as **Jardin des Gouverneurs ★** was originally the private garden of the governor of New France. The square was laid out in 1647 for Charles Huault de Montmagny to the west of Château Saint-Louis, the residence of the governor. A monument to opposing military leaders Wolfe and

Montcalm, both of whom died on the battlefields of the Plains of Abraham, was erected during the restoration of the garden in 1827.

Walking along **Terrasse Dufferin ★★★**, overlooking the St. Lawrence, provides an interesting sensation compared to the pavement we are used to. It was built in 1879 at the request of the governor general of the time, Lord Dufferin. The boardwalk's open-air pavilions and ornate streetlamps were designed by Charles Baillargé and were inspired by the style of French urban architecture common under Napoleon III. Terrasse Dufferin is one of Québec City's most popular sights and the preferred meeting place for young people. The view of the river, the south shore and Île d'Orléans is magnificent. During the winter months, a huge ice slide is set up at the western end of the boardwalk.

Terrasse Dufferin is located where the Château Saint-Louis, the long-destroyed elaborate residence of the governor of New France, used to stand. Built at the very edge of the escarpment, this three-storey building had a long, private stone terrace on the river side while the main entrance, consisting of a fortified facade, opened onto Place d'Armes and featured pavilions with imperial-type roofs. The château was built in the 17th century by architect François de la Joue and was enlarged in 1719 by engineer Chausegros de Léry. Its rooms, linked one to the other, were the scene of elegant receptions given for French nobility. Plans for the future of the entire continent were drawn up in this building. Château Saint-Louis was badly damaged during the British invasion of the city during the Conquest and was later remodelled according to British

● ATTRACTIONS

1. Fortifications of Québec National Historic Site	13. Musée d'Art Inuit Brousseau
2. Chalmers-Wesley United Church	14. Monastère des Ursulines
	15. Musée des Ursulines
3. Sanctuaire Notre-Dame-du-Sacré-Cœur	16. Anglican Cathedral of the Holy Trinity
4. Cavalier du Moulin	17. Édifice Price
5. Maison Cirice-Têtu	18. Place de l'Hôtel-de-Ville
6. Centre Infotouriste du Québec	19. Hôtel de ville et Centre d'Interprétation de la Vie Urbaine de la Ville de Québec
7. Musée du Fort	
8. Musée de Cire de Québec	20. Basilique-Cathédrale Notre-Dame-de-Québec
9. Ancien Palais de Justice	21. Séminaire de Québec
10. Maison Maillou	22. Musée de l'Amérique Française
11. Maison Kent	
12. Maison Jacquet	

23. Québec Expérience
24. Bureau de Poste and Parks Canada exhibition hall
25. Palais Archiépiscopal
26. Université Laval
27. Maison Montcalm
28. Musée Bon-Pasteur
29. Musée des Augustines de l'Hôtel-Dieu
30. Artillery Park National Historic Site
31. Église des Jésuites

◯ ACCOMMODATIONS

1. Au Jardin du Gouverneur	6. Centre international de séjour	11. Hôtel Clarendon
2. Auberge de la Chouette	7. Château Bellevue	12. Maison Acadienne
3. Auberge de la Paix	8. Château de Léry	13. Maison du Fort
4. Auberge du Trésor	9. Château de Pierre	14. Manoir LaSalle
5. Auberge Saint-Louis	10. Château Frontenac	15. Manoir Victoria
		16. Marquise de Bassano

● RESTAURANTS

1. À la Bastille Chez Bahüaud	8. Chez Temporel	14. Le Continental
2. Aux Anciens Canadiens	9. Guido Le Gourmet	15. Le Petit Coin Latin
3. Café de la Paix	10. L'Élysée-Mandarin	16. Le Saint-Amour
4. Café d'Europe	11. L'Entrecôte Saint-Jean	17. Les Frères de la Côte
5. Café Serge Bruyère	12. La Crémaillère	18. Portofino Bistro Italiano
6. Casse-Crêpe Breton	13. La Grande Table de Serge Bruyère	
7. Chez Livernois		

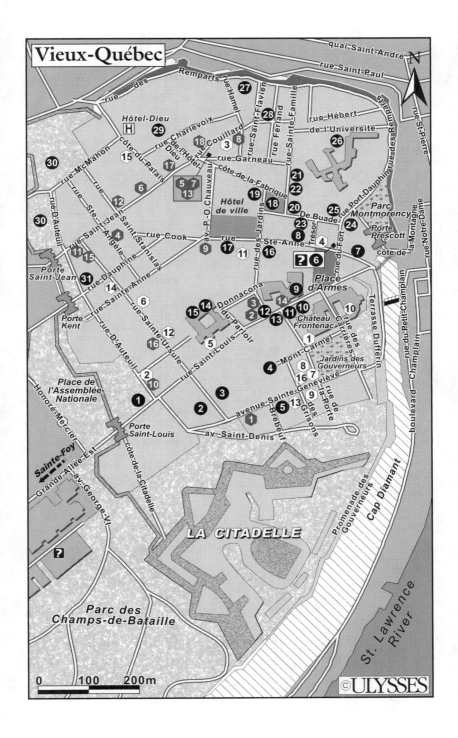

Vieux-Québec

N

quai-Saint-André

rue-Saint-Paul

Remparts-rue-Hamel

rue-des

27

28

rue-Saint-Flavien

rue-Ferland

rue-Sainte-Famille

rue-Hébert

de-l'Université

rue-St-Pierre

Hôtel-Dieu

H

29

côte-du-Palais

rue-Charlevoix

rue-de-l'Hôtel

Dieu

rue-Couillard

3

8

rue-Garneau

18

26

30

rue-McMahon

15

17

côte-de-la-Fabrique

21

22

rue-Port-Dauphin

rue-des-Remparts

rue-Saint-Stanislas

rue-Sainte-Jean

rue

6

5 7

13

Hôtel
de ville

19

18

20

De-Buade

25

24

Parc
Montmorency

Porte
Prescott

30

rue-D'Auteuil

rue-Sainte-Angèle

4

rue-Cook

9

17

11

23

8

rue-du-Trésor

rue-Ste-Anne

16

4

côte-de-

la-Montagne

rue-Notre-Dame

11

15

rue-Dauphine

14

?

6

Place
d'Armes

7

Porte
Saint-Jean

31

rue-Sainte-Anne

6

9

rue-des-Carrières

Terrasse-Dufferin

boulevard-Champlain

rue-du-Petit-Champlain

Porte
Kent

12

rue-Sainte-Ursule

16

Donnacona

15 14

3

2

12

14

11

10

Château
Frontenac

10

rue-du-Parloir

5

2

13

1

rue-de-la-Porte

Place de
l'Assemblée-
Nationale

2

10

rue-D'Auteuil

rue-Saint-Louis

3

Mont-Carmel

4

8

16

7

Jardins des
Gouverneurs

rue-des-Grisons

1

Honoré-Mercier

1

Porte
Saint-Louis

2

avenue-Sainte-Geneviève

5

13

9

Sainte-Foy

Grande-Allée-Est

côte-de-la-Citadelle

av.-Saint-Denis

1

rue-des-Brébeuf

Promenade-des-Gouverneurs

Cap-Diamant

av.-George-VI

?

LA CITADELLE

St. Lawrence
River

Parc des
Champs-de-Bataille

0   100   200m

©ULYSSES

tastes before being destroyed by fire in 1834.

There are two monuments at the far end of Terrasse Dufferin. One is dedicated to the memory of Samuel de Champlain, the founder of Québec City and father of New France. It was designed by Parisian sculptor Paul Chevré and erected in 1898. The second monument informs visitors that Vieux-Québec was recognized as a World Heritage Site by UNESCO in 1985. Québec City is the first city in North America to be included on this list. A staircase just to the left of the Champlain monument leads to the Place Royale quarter in Basse-Ville.

The first half of the 19th century saw the emergence of Québec City's tourism industry when the romantic European nature of the city began to attract growing numbers of American visitors. In 1890, the Canadian Pacific Railway company, under Cornelius Van Horne, decided to create a chain of distinguished hotels across Canada. The first of these hotels was the **Château Frontenac ★ ★ ★** *(1 Rue des Carrières)*, named in honour of one of the best-known governors of New France, Louis de Buade, Comte de Frontenac (1622-1698).

To visitors, the magnificent Château Frontenac, symbol of the provincial capital, is probably the most famous sight in Québec. Ironically, the hotel was

Château Frontenac

designed by an American architect, Bruce Price (1845-1903), known for his New York skyscrapers. The look of the hotel, which combines certain elements seen in Scottish manors and others seen in the chateaux of the Loire Valley in France, has come to be considered a national archetypal style called Château style.

Bruce Price, who also designed Montréal's Windsor train station and the famous Tuxedo Park development near New York City, was inspired by the picturesque location chosen for the hotel and by the mix of French and English cultures in Canada.

The Château Frontenac was built in stages. The first section was completed in 1893 and three sections were later added, the most important of these being the central tower (1923), the work of architects Edward and William Sutherland Maxwell. To fully appreciate the Château, go inside to the main hall, decorated in a style popular in 18th-century Parisian *hôtels particuliers*, and visit the Bar Maritime in the large main tower overlooking the river. The Château Frontenac has been the site of a number of important events in history. In 1944, the Québec Conference was held at the Château Frontenac. At this historic meeting, U.S. President Franklin D. Roosevelt, British Prime Minister Winston Churchill and Canadian Prime Minister Mackenzie King met to discuss

the future of post-war Europe. On the way out of the courtyard is a stone with the inscription of the Order of Malta, dated 1647, the only remaining piece of Château Saint-Louis.

Until the construction of the citadel, **Place d'Armes ★** was a military parade ground. It became a public square in 1832. In 1916, the *Monument de la Foi* (Monument of Faith) was erected in Place d'Armes to mark the tricentennial of the arrival of the Récollet religious order in Québec. Abbot Adolphe Garneau's statue rests on a base designed by David Ouellet.

At the other end of the square are the Centre Infotouriste de Québec and two museums. The back of the Anglican Cathedral of the Holy Trinity (see p 310) is also visible from here.

The **Centre Infotouriste de Québec** *(12 Rue Sainte-Anne)* is located in the former Union Hotel, a white building with a copper roof. A group of wealthy Quebecers saw the need for a luxury hotel in Québec City and commissioned British architect Edward Cannon to head the project, which was completed in 1803.

On either side of the Centre Infotouriste de Québec are two popular tourist attractions. Using an elaborate model of the city, along with a sound and light show, the **Musée du Fort** *($6.75; Jul to mid-Sep, every day 10am à 7pm; mid-Sep to late Oct and Apr to late Jun, every day 10am to 5pm, Feb and Mar Thu-Sun noon to 4pm; 10 Rue Sainte-Anne; ☎692-1759)* recreates the six sieges of Québec City, starting with the capture of the town by the Kirke brothers in 1629 and ending with the American invasion of 1775.

Musée de Cire de Québec *($3; May to Oct, every day 9am to 10pm, rest of the year every day 10am to 5pm; 22 Rue Sainte-Anne ☎692-2289)* displays wax likenesses of 60 individuals who played important roles in the history of Québec and North America, created by artists from the Grévin museum in Paris.

Return to Rue St-Louis

The **Ancien Palais de Justice** ★ *(12 Rue Saint-Louis)* is the city's original courthouse, built in 1883 by Eugène-Étienne Taché, architect of the parliament buildings. The courthouse resembles the parliament in a number of ways. Its French Renaissance Revival design preceded the Château style as the "official" style of the city's major building projects. The interior of the building was renovated between 1922 and 1930; it has several large rooms with attractive woodwork. Since 1987, the Ancien Palais de Justice building has been used by Québec's Ministry of Finance.

Maison Maillou *(17 Rue Saint-Louis)* is the location of the seat of Québec's chamber of commerce. This attractive French Regime house was built in 1736 by architect Jean Maillou. It was saved from destruction after the Stock Market Crash of 1929 led to the abandoning of plans to enlarge the Château Frontenac.

The history of **Maison Kent** *(25 Rue Saint-Louis)*, once a residence of Queen Victoria's father, the Duke of Kent, is somewhat clouded. There is some disagreement as to whether the house was built in the 17th or 18th century. It is clear, however, from its English sash windows and low-pitched roof, that the house underwent major renovations during the 19th century. The house was the site

Maison Jacquet

of the signing of the agreement that handed Québec over to the British following the Conquest of 1759. Ironically, the house is now occupied by the Consulate General of France.

Maison Jacquet ★ *(34 Rue Saint-Louis)*, a small, red-roofed building covered in white roughcast dating from 1690, is the oldest house in Haute-Ville; it is the only house in Vieux-Québec that still looks just as it did in the 17th century. The house is distinguished from those built during the following century by its high steep roof covering a living area with a very low ceiling. The house is named for François Jacquet, who once owned the land on which it stands. It was built by architect François de la Joue in 1690, for his own use. In 1815, the house was acquired by Philippe Aubert de Gaspé, author of the famous novel ***Les Anciens Canadiens*** (The Canadians of Old). The restaurant that now occupies the house takes its name from this book.

Well-known in Québec City for the quality of its works, La Galerie d'Art Inuit Brousseau now relies on a small museum to house the owner's private collection. The **Musée d'Art Inuit Brousseau** ★ *($6; every day 9:30am to 5:30pm; 39 Rue St-Louis, ☎694-1828)* is located in a renovated building on Rue Saint-Louis. Each of its

five rooms revolves around a specific theme, such as history, the materials used, and so forth. The works are thoughtfully divided up, and the visit is enhanced by the modern, spacious and well-lit rooms. The historical and cultural notes are thorough and interesting. At the end of the visit, there's a documentary about the artists, as well as a boutique where you can purchase some of their work.

Turn right on Rue du Parloir and right again at Rue Donnacona.

In 1535, Sainte Angèle Merici founded the first Ursuline community in Brescia, Italy. After the community had established itself in France, it became a cloistered order dedicated to teaching (1620). With the help of a benefactor, Madame de la Peltrie, the Ursulines arrived in Québec in 1639 and, in 1641, founded a monastery and convent where generations of young girls have received a good education. The **Monastère des Ursulines** ★★★ *(18 Rue Donnacona)*, or Ursuline convent, is the longest-operating girls' school in North America. Only the museum and chapel, a small part of the huge Ursuline complex, where several dozen nuns still live, are open to the public.

The Sainte-Ursuline chapel was rebuilt in 1901 on the site of the original 1722 chapel. Part of the magnificent interior decoration of the first chapel, created by Pierre-Nöel Levasseur between 1726 and 1736, survived and is present in the newer structure. The work includes a pulpit surmounted by a trumpeting angel and a beautiful altarpiece in the Louis XIV style. The tabernacle of the high altar is embellished with fine gilding applied by the Ursuline nuns. The Sacred Heart tabernacle, a masterpiece of the genre, is attributed to Jaques Leblond, also known as Latour, and dates from around 1770. Some of the paintings that decorate the church come from the collection of Father Jean-Louis Desjardins, a former chaplin of the Ursulines. In 1820, Desjardins bought several dozen paintings from an art dealer in Paris. The paintings had previously hung in Paris churches but were removed during the French Revolution. Works from this collection can still be seen in churches all over Québec. At the entrance hangs *Jésus chez Simon le Pharisien* (Jesus with Simon the Pharisee) by Philippe de Champaigne, and on the right of the nave hangs *La Parabole des Dix Vierges* (The Parable of the Ten Virgins), by Pierre de Cortone.

In an adjoining chapel is the tomb of Mère Marie de l'Incarnation, the founder of the Ursuline monastery in Québec. An opening provides a view of the nuns' chancel, rebuilt in 1902 by David Ouellet, who outfitted it with cupolas. An interesting painting by an unknown artist, *La France Apportant la Foi aux Indiens de la Nouvelle-France* (France bringing the faith to the Aboriginals of New France), also hangs in this section of the chapel.

The entrance to the **Musée des Ursulines** (*$5; May to Sep, Tue-Sat 10am to noon and 1pm to 5pm, Sun 1pm to 5pm; Oct to Dec and Feb to Apr, Tue-Sun 1pm to 4:30pm; 12 Rue Donnacona,* ☎*694-0694)* is across from the chapel. The museum outlines nearly four centuries of Ursuline history. On view are various works of art, Louis XIII furniture, impressive embroideries made of gold thread, and 18th-century altar cloths and church robes. Even the skull of Marquis de Montcalm is on display!

The **Holy Trinity Anglican Cathedral** ★★ *(31 Rue des Jardins)* was built following the British conquest of Québec, when a small group of British administrators and military officers established themselves in Québec City. These men wanted to distinguish their presence through the construction of prestigious buildings with typically British designs. However, their small numbers resulted in the slow progress of this vision until the beginning of the 19th century, when work began on an Anglican cathedral designed by Majors Robe and Hall, two military engineers. The Palladian-style church was completed in 1804. This significant example of non-French architecture changed the look of the city. The church was the first Anglican cathedral built outside Britain and, in its elegant simplicity, is a good example of British colonial architecture. The roof was made steeper in 1815 so that it would not be weighed down by snow.

The cathedral's interior, more sober than that of most Catholic churches, is adorned with various generous gifts from King George III, including several pieces of silverware and pews made of English oak from the forests of Windsor. The bishop's chair is said to have been carved from an elm tree under which Samuel de Champlain liked to sit.

Stained-glass windows and commemorative plaques have been added to the decor of the church over the years.

Continue along Rue des Jardins. To the right is a cobblestone section of Rue Sainte-Anne and on the left is the Hôtel Clarendon and the Price building.

The **Hôtel Clarendon** *(57 Rue Sainte-Anne)* began receiving guests in 1870 in the former Desbarats print shop (1858). It is the oldest hotel still operating in Québec. The Charles Baillargé-designed restaurant on the main floor is also the oldest restaurant in Canada. The Victorian charm of the somber woodwork evokes the *belle époque*. The Hôtel Clarendon was enlarged in 1929 by the addition of a brick tower featuring an Art Deco entrance hall designed by Raoul Chênevert.

The design of **Édifice Price** ★ *(65 Rue Sainte-Anne)* manages to adhere to traditional North American skyscraper architecture and yet does not look out of place among the historic buildings of Haute-Ville. Architects Ross and MacDonald of Montréal gave the building a tall yet discreet silhouette when they designed it in 1929. It features a copper roof typical of Château architecture. The main hall of the building, a fine example of Art Deco design, is covered in polished travertine and bronze bas-reliefs depicting the various activities of the Price company, which specialized in the production of paper.

Walk back up to Rue des Jardins.

The next stop is the quaint **Maison Antoine-Vanfelson** at 17 Rue des Jardins, built in 1780. A talented silversmith by the name of Laurent Amiot had a workshop here in the 19th century. The rooms on the second floor of this building feature wonderful Louis XV woodwork.

Place de l'Hôtel-de-Ville ★, a small square, was the location of the Notre-Dame market in the 18th century. A monument in honour of Cardinal Taschereau, created by André Vermare, was erected here in 1923.

The American Romanesque Revival influence seen in the **Hôtel de Ville** (*2 Rue des Jardins*) stands out in a city where French and British traditions have always predominated in the construction of public buildings. The building was completed in 1895 following disagreements among the mayor and the city councillors as to a building plan. Sadly, a Jesuit college dating from 1666 was demolished to make room for the city hall. Under the pleasant gardens outside the building, where popular events are held in the summer, is an underground parking lot, a much needed addition in this city of narrow streets.

The **Centre d'Interprétation de la Vie Urbaine de la Ville de Québec** (*$2; late Jun to early Sep, every day 10am to 5pm; rest of the year Tue-Sun 10am to 5pm; 43 Côte de la Fabrique, ☎691-4606*), an information centre on urban life in Québec City, is located in the basement of City Hall. It addresses questions of urban development and planning. An interesting model of the city provides an understanding of the layout of the area.

The history of Québec City's cathedral, the **Basilique-Cathédrale Notre-Dame-de-Québec ★★★** (*at the other end of Place de l'Hôtel-de-Ville*), underscores the problems faced by builders in New France and the determination of Quebecers in the

face of the worst circumstances. The cathedral as it exists today is the result of numerous phases of construction and a number of tragedies that left the church in ruins on two occasions. The first church on this site was built in 1632 under the orders of Samuel de Champlain, who was buried nearby four years later. This wooden church was replaced in 1647 by Église Notre-Dame-de-la-Paix, a stone church in the shape of a Roman cross that would later serve as the model for many rural parish churches. In 1674, New France was assigned its first bishop in residence, Monseigneur François-Xavier de Laval (1623-1708), who decided that this small church, after renovations befitting its status as the heart of such an enormous ministry, would become the seat of the Catholic Church in Québec. A grandiose plan was commissioned from architect Claude Baillif, which, despite personal financial contributions from Louis XIV, was eventually scaled down. Only the base of the west tower survives from this period. In 1742, the bishop had the church remodelled by engineer Gaspard Chaussegros de Léry, who is responsible for its present lay-

Basilique-Cathédrale Notre-Dame-de-Québec

out, featuring an extended nave illuminated from above. The cathedral resembles many urban churches built in France during the same period.

During the siege of Québec in 1759, the cathedral was bombarded and reduced to ruins. It was not rebuilt until the status of Catholics in Québec was settled by the British crown. The oldest Catholic parish north of Mexico was finally allowed to begin the reconstruction of its church in 1770, using the 1742 plans. The work was directed by Jean Baillargé (1726-1805), a member of a well-known family of architects and craftsmen. This marked the beginning of the Baillargé family's extended, fervent involvement in the reconstruction and renovation of the church. In 1789, the decoration of the church interior was entrusted to Jean Baillargé's son François (1759-1830), who had recently returned from three years of studying architecture in Paris at the Académie Royale. He designed the chancel's beautiful gilt baldaquin with winged caryatids four years later. The high altar, the first in Québec to be designed to look like the facade of a Basilica, was put into place in 1797. The addition of baroque pews and a plaster vault created an interesting contrast. Upon completion, the spectacular interior emphasized the use of gilding, wood and white plasterwork according to typically Québécois traditions.

In 1843, Thomas Baillargé (1791-1859), the son of François, created the present neoclassical facade and attempted to put up a steeple on the east side of the church. Work on the steeple was halted at the halfway point when it was discovered that the 17th-century foundations were not strong enough. Charles Baillargé (1826-1906), Thomas Baillargé's cousin, designed the wrought-iron gate around the front square in 1858. Between 1920 and 1922, the church was carefully restored, but just a few weeks after the work was completed, a fire seriously damaged the building. Raoul Chênevert and Maxime Roisin, who had already come to Québec from Paris to take on the reconstruction of the Basilica in Sainte-Anne-de-Beaupré, were put in charge of yet another restoration of the cathedral. In 1959, a mausoleum was put into place in the basement of the church. It holds the remains of Québec bishops and various governors (Frontenac, Vaudreuil, de Callière). In recent years, several masters' paintings hanging in the church have been stolen, leaving bare walls and an increased emphasis on ensuring the security of the remaining paintings, including the beautiful *Saint-Jérôme*, by Jacques-Louis David (1780), now at the Musée de l'Amérique Française.

Feux Sacrés *($7.50; early May to mid-Oct every day 1pm to 9pm; 20 Rue De Buade, ☎694-4000)*, a sound and light show, is set up inside the cathedral. It illustrates a page of Québec's history with the aid of 3D effects on three screens. Shows are in French and English simultaneously.

During the 17th century, the **Séminaire de Québec ★ ★ ★** *(1 Côte de la Fabrique, ☎692-3981)* was an oasis of European civilization in a rugged and hostile territory. To get an idea of how it must have appeared to students of the day, go through the old gate (decorated with the seminary's coat of arms) and into the courtyard before proceeding through the opposite entryway to the reception desk.

The seminary was founded in 1663 by Monseigneur

Francois de Laval, on orders from the Séminaire des Missions Étrangères de Paris (Seminary of Foreign Missions), with which it remained affiliated until 1763. As headquarters of the clergy throughout the colony, it was at the seminary that future priests studied, parochial funds were administered and ministerial appointments were made. Louis XIV's Minister, Colbert, further required the seminary to establish a smaller school devoted to the conversion and education of Aboriginals. Following the British conquest and the subsequent banishing of the Jesuits, the seminary became a college devoted to classical education. It also served as housing for the bishop of Québec after his palace was destroyed by the invasion. In 1852, the seminary founded the Université Laval, the first French-language university in North America. Today, most of Laval's campus is located in Sainte-Foy. The vast collection of seminary buildings is home to a priests' residence facing the river, a private school and the Faculty of Architecture of Université Laval, which returned to its former location in 1987.

Today's seminary is the result of rebuilding efforts following numerous fires and bombardments. Across from the old gate, the wing devoted to the offices of the Procurator, complete with sundial, can be seen. During Admiral Phipps's attack in 1690, it was in the vaulted cellars of this wing that the citizens of Québec City took refuge. It also contains the private chapel of Monsigneur Briand (1785), decorated with sculpted olive branches by Pierre Emond. Forming a right angle with the chapel is the beautiful parlor wing, constructed in 1696. The use of segmented arch windows in this attractive building is a direct influence of French models prior to their

adaptation to the climate of Québec.

The guided tours leaving from the reception centre at 2 Côte de la Fabrique include visits to the apartments of the seminary, the cellars, the chapel of Monseigneur Briand, and the exterior chapel built in 1890 to replace the original one from 1752 that burned down in 1888. In order to avoid any such recurrence, the interior, which is similar to that of Église de la Trinité in Paris, was covered over in tin and zinc and painted in *trompe-l'oeil*, following the design of Paul Alexandre de Cardonnel and Joseph-Ferdinand Peachy. The chapel contains the most significant collection of relics in North America, including relics of Saint-Augustine and Saint-Anselm, the martyrs of Tonkin, Saint Charles Borromé and Ignatius of Loyola. Some relics are both large and authentic while others are rather small and dubious. On the left is a funeral chapel housing a tomb containing the remains of Monseigneur de Laval, the first Bishop of North America.

To get to Musée de l'Amérique Française, follow Rue Sainte-Famille, which follows the seminary, and turn right on Rue de l'Université.

Musée de l'Amérique Française ★ ★ *($4; $8.50 for a package including admission to the Musée de la Civilisation and the Centre d'Interprétation de Place-Royale; late Jun to early Sep, every day 10am to 5:30pm; early Sep to late Jun, Tue-Sun, 10am to 5pm; 2 Côte de la Fabrique, ☎692-2843)* is a museum devoted to the history of French America. It contains a wealth of over 450,000 artifacts, including silverware, paintings, oriental art and numismatics, as well as scientific instruments, collected for educational purposes over the last three centuries by priests of the seminary. The museum occupies five floors of what used to be the residences of the Université Laval. The first Egyptian mummy brought to America is on view, as are several items that belonged to Monseigneur de Laval.

On returning to Place de l'Hôtel-de-Ville, turn left on Rue Buade

The old **Holt Renfrew** store *(43 Rue Buade)*, which opened in 1837, faces the cathedral. Originally concerned with the sale of furs, which they supply by appointment to Her Majesty the Queen, Holt's held the exclusive rights for the Canadian distribution of Christian Dior and Yves Saint-Laurent designs for a long time. Holt's is now closed, having given way to the boutiques of the **Promenades du Vieux-Québec**.

A little further on is the entrance to **Rue du Trésor**, which also leads to Place d'Armes and Rue Sainte-Anne. Artists come here to sell paintings, drawings and silkscreens, many of which depict views of Québec City.

Québec Expérience ($7.50; mid-May to mid-Oct every day 10am to 10pm; mid-Oct to mid-May every day 10am to 5pm; 8 Rue du Trésor, 2nd floor, ☎694-4000) is an elaborate show about the history of Québec City. This lively 3D multimedia presentation takes viewers back in time to relive the great moments in the city's history through its important historic figures. A wonderful way to learn about Québec City's past, these half-hour shows are a big hit with the kids. Presented in both French and English.

The **Bureau de Poste** ★ *(3 Rue De Buade)*, Canada's first post office, opened in Québec City in 1837. It was for a long time housed in the

old Hôtel du Chien d'Or, a solid dwelling built around 1753 for a wealthy Bordeaux merchant, who ordered a bas-relief depicting a dog gnawing a bone executed above the doorway. The following inscription appeared underneath the bas-relief, which was relocated to the pediment of the present post office in 1872: *Je suis un chien qui ronge l'os, en le rongeant je prends mon repos. Un temps viendra qui n'est pas venu où je mordrai qui m'aura mordu*, roughly, "I am a dog gnawing a bone, as I gnaw, I rest at home. Though it's not yet here there'll come a time when those who bit me will be paid in kind". It is said that the message was designated for Intendant Bigot, a swindler if ever there was one, who was so outraged he had the Bordeaux merchant killed.

The dome of the post office and the facade overlooking the river were added at the beginning of the 20th century. The building was renamed **Édifice Louis-S-Saint-Laurent**, in honour of the former Prime Minister of Canada. Besides the traditional post and philatelic services, a **Parks Canada exhibition hall** *(free admission; Mon-Fri 8am to 4:30pm, Sat and Sun 10am to 5pm; 3 Rue De Buade, ☎648-4177)* was added to illustrate Canada's natural and historical heritage.

Facing the post office stands a monument to Monseigneur François de Laval (1623-1708), the first Bishop of Québec, whose diocese covered two thirds of the North American continent. Designed by Philippe Hébert and erected in 1908, the monument boasts an attractive staircase leading to Côte de la Montagne and from there to Basse-Ville.

The Laval Bishop's monument is located directly in front of **Palais Archiépiscopal** *(2 Rue Port-Dauphin)* or archbishop-

ric, which was rebuilt by Thomas Baillargé in 1844. The first archbishopric stood in what is now Parc Montmorency. Designed by Claude Baillif and built between 1692 and 1700, the original palace was, by all accounts, one of the most gorgeous of its kind in New France. Drawings show an impressive building, complete with a recessed chapel, whose interior was reminiscent of Paris's Val de Grace. Though the chapel was destroyed in 1759, the rest of the building was restored and then occupied by the Legislative Assembly of Lower Canada from 1792 to 1840. It was demolished in 1848 to make room for the new parliamentary buildings, which went up in flames only four years later.

Parc Montmorency ★ was laid out in 1875 after the city walls were lowered along Rue des Remparts and the Governor General of Canada, Lord Dufferin, discovered the magnificent view from the promontory. George-Etienne Cartier, Prime Minister of the Dominion of Canada and one of the Fathers of Confederation, is honoured with a statue here, as are Louis Hébert, Guillaume Couillard and Marie Rollet, some of the original farmers of New France. These last three disembarked in 1617 and were granted the fiefdom of Sault-au-Matelot, on the future site of the seminary (1623). These attractive bronzes are the work of Montréal sculptor Alfred Laliberté.

Continue along the ramparts.

The halls of the old **Université Laval** ★ can be seen through a gap in the wall of the ramparts. Built in 1856 in the gardens of the seminary, they were completed in 1875 with the addition of an impressive mansard roof surmounted by three silver lanterns. When the spotlights shine on them at night, it creates the atmosphere of a royal gala. Note that Université Laval is now located on a large campus in Sainte-Foy.

Following Rue des Remparts, Basse-Ville, or lower town, comes into view. The patrician manors on the street along the ramparts provide a picturesque backdrop for the old Latin quarter extending behind them. The narrow streets and 18th-century houses of the quarter are well worth a detour.

Maison Montcalm *(45 to 51 Rue des Remparts)* was originally a very large residence constructed in 1727; it is now divided into three houses. The home of the Marquis de Montcalm during of the Battle of the Plains of Abraham, the building subsequently served to house the officers of the British Army before being subdivided and returned to private use. In the first half of the 19th century, many houses in Québec were covered in the sort of imitation stone boards that still protect the masonry of the Montcalm house. It was believed that the covering lent a more refined look to the houses.

Take Rue Saint-Flavien.

At the corner of Rue Couillard is **Maison François-Xavier-Garneau** *($5; Fri-Sun 1pm to 5pm, tours on the hour; 14 Rue St-Flavien, ☎692-2240)*. Québec City businessman Louis Garneau recently bought this neoclassical house (1862) where historian and poet François-Xavier-Garneau lived during the last years of his life. Throughout the summer, an actor dressed in period costume is on site to make the past come alive as you visit the rooms and admire the objects on display.

Near the corner of Rue Saint-Flavien and Rue Couillard is

the small Musée des Soeurs du Bon-Pasteur.

Musée Bon-Pasteur ★ *($2; Tue-Sun 1pm to 5pm; 14 Rue Couillard, ☎694-0243)*, founded in 1993, tells the story of the Bon Pasteur (meaning "Good Shepherd") community of nuns, which has been serving the poor of Québec City since 1850. The museum is located in the Béthanie house, an eclectic brick structure built around 1887 to shelter unwed mothers and their children. The museum occupies three floors of an 1878 addition and houses furniture as well as sacred objects manufactured or collected by the nuns.

Retrace your steps to Rue Couillard. Descend Rue Hamel until Rue Charlevoix, and turn left, continuing until the l'Hôtel-Dieu de Québec.

The Augustinian nurses founded their first convent in Québec in Sillery. Uneasy about the Iroquois, they relocated to Québec City in 1642 and began construction of the present complex, which includes a convent, a hospital and a chapel. Rebuilt several times, today's buildings mostly date from the 20th century. The oldest remaining part is the 1756 convent, built on the vaulted foundations from 1695, hidden behind the 1800 chapel. This chapel was erected using material from various French buildings destroyed during the Seven Years War. The stone was taken from the palace of the intendant, while its first ornaments came from the 17th-century Jesuit church. Today, only the iron balustrade of the bell tower bears witness to the original chapel. The present neoclassical facade was designed by Thomas Baillargé in 1839 after he completed the new interior in 1835. The nun's chancel can be seen to the right. Abbot Louis-Joseph

Desjardins used the chapel as an auction house in 1817 and again in 1821, after he purchased the collection of a bankrupt Parisian banker who had amassed works confiscated from Paris churches during the French Revolution. *La Vision de Sainte-Thérèse d'Avila* (Saint Theresa of Avila's Vision), a work by François-Guillaume Ménageot, which originally hung in the Carmel de Saint-Denis near Paris, can be seen in one of the side altars.

The **Musée des Augustines de l'Hôtel-Dieu** ★★ *($3; Tue-Sat, 9:30am to noon and 1:30pm to 5pm; Sun 1:30pm to 5pm; 32 Rue Charlevoix, ☎692-2492)* traces the history of the Augustinian community in New France through pieces of furniture, paintings and medical instruments. On display in the museum is the chest that contained the meagre belongings of the founders (pre-1639), as well as pieces from the Château Saint-Louis, the residence of the first governors under the French Regime, including portraits of Louis XIV and Cardinal Richelieu. Upon request, visitors can see the chapel and the vaulted cellars. The remains of Blessed Marie-Catherine de Saint-Augustin, the founder of the community in New France, are kept in an adjoining chapel, as is a beautiful gilded reliquary in the Louis XIV style, sculpted in 1717 by Noël Levasseur.

Follow the small street opposite the chapel (Rue Collins). At the corner of Rue Saint-Jean is a pleasant view of Côte de la Fabrique, with the Hôtel de Ville on the right and Cathédrale Notre-Dame in the background on the left. Turn right on Rue Saint-Jean, a pleasant commercial street in the heart of Vieux-Québec.

A short detour to the left down Rue Saint-Stanislas gives a view of the **old Methodist**

Church (*42 Rue Saint-Sta-nislas*), a beautiful Gothic Revival building built in 1850. Today it houses the **Institut Canadien**, a centre for literature and the arts. Before the Quiet Revolution of the 1960s, this centre was the focus of many a contentious dispute with the clergy over its "audacious" choice of books. The institute is home to a theatre and a branch of the municipal library.

The neighbouring building, number 44, is the **Ancienne Prison de Québec**, the old jail, built in 1808 by François Baillargé. In 1868, it was renovated to accommodate Morrin College, affiliated with Montréal's McGill University. This venerable institution of English-speaking Québec also houses the library of the **Québec Literary and Historical Society**, a learned society founded in 1824. The building on the corner of Rue Cook and Rue Dauphine surmounted by a palladian steeple is **St. Andrew's Presbyterian Church**, completed in 1811.

Return to Rue Saint-Jean and cross it. Turn left on Rue McMahon, and continue on to the reception and information centre of the Artillery Park.

Artillery Park National Historic Site ★ ★ (*$4; early May to mid-Oct every day 10am to 5pm, mid-Oct to late Mar hours vary, late Mar to early May Wed-Sun; 2 Rue D'Auteuil, ☎648-4205*), also called Lieu Historique National du Parc-de-l'Artillerie, takes up part of an enormous military emplacement running alongside the walls of the city. The reception and information centre is located in the old foundry, where munitions were manufactured until 1964. On display is a fascinating model of Québec City built between 1795 and 1810 by military engineer Jean-Bap-

tiste Duberger for strategic planning. The model has only recently been returned to Québec City, after having been sent to England in 1813. It is an unparalleled source of information on the layout of the city in the years following the British conquest.

The walk continues with a visit to the **Dauphine redoubt**, a beautiful white roughcast building near Rue McMahon. In 1712, military engineer Dubois Berthelot de Beaucours drafted plans for the redoubt, which was completed by Chaussegros de Léry in 1747. A redoubt is an independent fortified structure that serves as a retreat in case the troops are obliged to fall back. The redoubt was never really used for this purpose but rather as military barracks. Behind it can be seen several barracks and an old cartridge factory built by the British in the 19th century. The officers' barracks (1820), which has been converted into a children's centre for heritage interpretation, makes a pleasant end to the visit. You can take part in a 1hr guided tour led by characters in period costume or visit on your own with an audio-guide. There are also two other exhibits on the site: the first is a collection of antique toys and the second features dolls in an economuseum named **Les Dames de Soie** ("the silk ladies").

Walk back up Rue D'Auteuil.

The newest of Québec City's gates, **Porte Saint-Jean** actually has rather ancient origins. As of 1693 it was one of only three entrances to the city. It was reinforced by Chaussegros de Léry in 1757, and then rebuilt by the British. To satisfy merchants who were clamouring for the total destruction of the walls, a "modern" gate equipped with tandem carriage tunnels and corresponding pedestrian

passageways was erected in 1867. However, this structure did not fit in with Lord Dufferin's romantic vision of the city and was thus eliminated in 1898. The present gate did not replace it until 1936.

Number 29 on the left is an old Anglican orphanage built for the Society for Promoting Christian Knowledge in 1824, and was the first Gothic Revival–style building in Québec City. Its architecture was portentous, as it inaugurated the Romantic current that would eventually permeate the city.

The last of Québec's Jesuits died in 1800, his community having been banished by the British and then, in 1774, by the Pope himself. The community was resuscitated in 1814, however, and returned to Québec in 1840. Since its college and church on Place de l'Hôtel-de-Ville were no longer available, they were welcomed by the Congregationists, a brotherhood founded by the Jesuit Ponert in 1657 with a view of propagating the cult of the Virgin. These latter parishioners were able to erect the **Église des Jésuites ★** (*Rue D'Auteuil, at the corner of Rue Dauphine*).

François Baillargé designed the plans for the church which was completed in 1818. The facade was redone in 1930. The decoration of the interior began with the construction of the counterfeit vaulting. Its centrepiece is Pierre-Noël Levasseur's altar of 1770. Since 1925, the Jesuit church has been Québec's sanctuary for the worship of Canada's martyred saints.

Porte Kent, like Porte Saint-Louis, is the result of Lord Dufferin's romantic vision of the city. The plans for this gate, Vieux-Québec's prettiest, were drawn up in 1878 by Charles Baillargé, following the

Québec City

ideas of Irishman William H. Lynn.

Climb the stairway to the top of Porte Kent and walk along the wall towards Porte Saint-Louis.

On the other side of the walls is the Hôtel du Parlement (see p 324), and inside, several patrician homes along the Rue D'Auteuil. Number 69, the **Maison McGreevy** *(no visiting)* stands out by its sheer size. The house is the work of Thomas Fuller, the architect of the Parliament Buildings in Ottawa, and of New York's State Capitol. It was built in 1868 by McGreevy, a construction entrepreneur who also built Canada's first Parliament Buildings. Behind the rather commercial-looking facade of yellow Nepean sandstone is a perfectly preserved Victorian interior.

Climb down from the wall at Porte Saint-Louis. Côte de la Citadelle is on the other side of Rue Saint-Louis.

The Québec City's **Citadelle ★ ★ ★** *(at the far end of the Côte de la Citadelle)* represents three centuries of North American military history and is still in use. Since 1920, it has housed the Royal 22nd Regiment of the Canadian Army, a regiment distinguished for its bravery during World War II. Within the circumference of the enclosure are some 25 buildings including the officer's mess, the hospital, the prison, and the official residence of the Governor General of Canada, as well as the first observatory in Canada. The citadel's history began in 1693, when Engineer Dubois Berthelot de Beaucours had the Cap Diamant redoubt built at the highest point of Québec City's defensive system, some 100m above the level of the river. This solid construction is in-

cluded today inside the King's bastion.

Throughout the 18th century, French and then British engineers developed projects for a citadel that remained unfulfilled. Chaussegros de Léry's powderhouse of 1750, which now houses the Museum of the Royal 22nd Regiment, and the temporary excavation works to the west (1783) are the only works of any scope accomplished during this period. The citadel that appears today was built between 1820 and 1832 by Colonel Elias Walker Durnford. Dubbed the "Gibraltar of America," and built according to principles expounded by Vauban in the 17th century, the citadel has never borne the brunt of a single cannonball, though it has acted as an important element of dissuasion.

The **Musée du Royal 22ᵉ Régiment** *($6; Apr to mid-May every day 10am to 4pm; mid-May to mid-Jun every day 9am to 5pm, mid-Jun to early Sep every day 9am to 6pm, Sep every day 9am to 4pm, Oct every day 10am to 3pm; ☎694-2815)* is a museum that offers an interesting collection of arms, uniforms, insignia and military documents spanning almost 400 years. It is possible to go on a guided tour of the whole installation, to witness the changing of the guards, the retreat, and the firing of the cannon. The changing of the guards lasts 35min and takes place every day at 10am from late June to early September, weather permitting. The retreat lasts 30min and can be seen in July and August, on Tuesday, Thursday, Saturday and Sunday at 6pm, weather permitting.

Tour B: Petit-Champlain to Vieux-Port

Québec's port and commercial area is a narrow *U*-shaped piece of land wedged near the waters of the St. Lawrence. This area is sometimes called Basse-Ville of Vieux-Québec because of its location just at the foot of the Cap Diamant escarpment. The cradle of New France, Place-Royale is where, in 1608, Samuel de Champlain (1567-1635) founded the settlement he called "Abitation," which would become Québec City. In the summer of 1759, three quarters of the city was badly damaged by British bombardment. It took 20 years to repair and rebuild the houses. In the 19th century, the construction of multiple embankments allowed the expansion of the town and enabled the area around Place-Royale to be linked by road with the area around the intendant's palace. The port's decline at the beginning of the 20th century led to the gradual abandonment of Place-Royale; restoration work began in 1959. The Petit-Champlain district has been reclaimed by artisans who have set up shop here, especially on the Rue du Petit-Champlain. This area now caters mostly to tourists, who visit the numerous studios to watch the craftspeople at work and to buy their wares.

This walking tour begins at Porte Prescott, which straddles Côte de la Montagne. Those who do not enjoy walking would be well advised to take the funicular from Terrasse Dufferin and to begin the tour at the start of Rue Petit-Champlain.

The **Funiculaire (Funicular)** *($1.50; every day 7:30am to 11pm, sometimes later; ☎692-1132)* began operating in

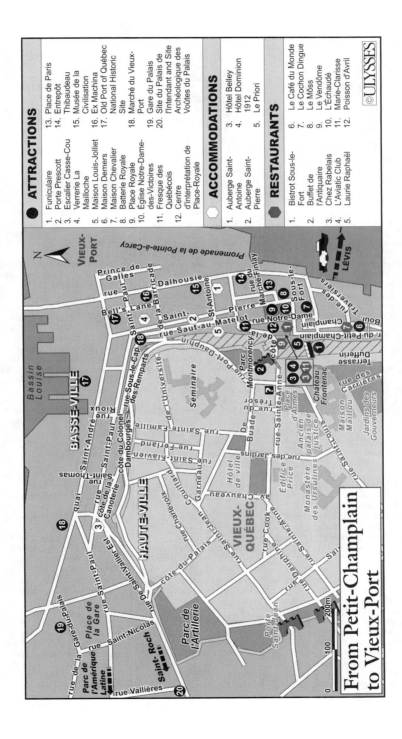

From Petit-Champlain to Vieux-Port

● ATTRACTIONS

1. Funiculaire
2. Porte Prescott
3. Escalier Casse-Cou
4. Verrerie La Mailloche
5. Maison Louis-Jolliet
6. Maison Demers
7. Maison Chevalier
8. Batterie Royale
9. Place Royale
10. Église Notre-Dame-des-Victoires
11. Fresque des Québécois
12. Centre d'interprétation de Place-Royale
13. Place de Paris
14. Entrepôt Thibaudeau
15. Musée de la Civilisation
16. Ex Machina
17. Old Port of Québec National Historic Site
18. Marché du Vieux-Port
19. Gare du Palais
20. Site du Palais de l'Intendant and Site Archéologique des Voûtes du Palais

◇ ACCOMMODATIONS

1. Auberge Saint-Antoine
2. Auberge Saint-Pierre
3. Hôtel Belley
4. Hôtel Dominion 1912
5. Le Priori

◆ RESTAURANTS

1. Bistrot Sous-le-Fort
2. Buffet de l'Antiquaire
3. Chez Rabelais
4. L'Aviatic Club
5. Laurie Raphaël
6. Le Café du Monde
7. Le Cochon Dingue
8. Le Môss
9. Le Vendôme
10. L'Échaudé
11. Marie-Clarisse
12. Poisson d'Avril

© ULYSSES

November 1879. It was put in place by entrepreneur W. A. Griffith in order to bring the lower and upper towns closer together. When the funicular was first built, water was transferred from one reservoir to another to make it function. It was converted to electricity in 1906, at the same time that Terrasse Dufferin was illuminated. The funicular is an outdoor elevator that eliminates the need to take the *Escalier Casse-Cou*, "breakneck stairway," or to go around Côte de la Montagne. The funicular was completely overhauled in 1998.

Porte Prescott *(Côte de la Montagne)* can be reached from Côte de la Montagne or from Terrasse Dufferin by means of a stairway and a charming footbridge on the left of the funicular's entryway. This discreetly postmodern structure was built in 1983 by the architectural firm of Gauthier, Guité, Roy, which sought to evoke the 1797 gate by Gother Mann. It allows pedestrians to cross directly from Terrasse Dufferin to Parc Montmorency.

Descend Côte de la Montagne and take the Escalier Casse-Cou on the right.

The **Escalier Casse-Cou** *(Côte de la Montagne)*, which literally means "the break-neck strairway," has been here since 1682. Until the beginning of the 20th century, it had been made of planks that were in constant need of repair or replacement. It connects the various businesses situated on different levels. At the foot of the stairway is **Rue du Petit-Champlain**, a narrow pedestrian street flanked by charming craft shops and pleasant cafés located in 17th and 18th century houses. Some of the houses at the foot of the stairway were destroyed by rockslides prior to the cliff's reinforcement in the 19th century.

At the foot of the Escalier Casse-Cou, a small *économusée* (economuseum) unveils the secrets of glass-blowing. At **Atelier Verrerie La Mailloche** *(free admission; end Jun to early Nov every day 9am to 10pm, rest of the year 9:30am to 5:30pm; 58 Rue Sous-le-Fort, ☎694-0445)*, visitors can observe the fascinating spectacle of artisans shaping molten glass according to traditional techniques. The finished products are sold in a shop on the second floor.

Maison Louis-Jolliet ★
(16 Rue du Petit-Champlain) is one of the earliest houses of Vieux-Québec (1683) and one of the few works of Claude Baillif still standing. The house was built after the great fire of 1682, which destroyed Basse-Ville. It was this tragedy that prompted the authorities to require that stone be used in all buildings. The fire also paved the way for some improvements in urban planning: roads were straightened and Place-Royale was created. Louis Jolliet (1645-1700) was the man who, along with Father Marquette, discovered the Mississippi and explored Hudson Bay. During the last years of his life, he taught hydrography at the Séminaire de Québec. The interior of the house was completely gutted and now contains the lower platform of the funicular (see above).

Follow Rue du Petit-Champlain until the end, where it meets Boulevard Champlain. You will see a colourful fresco on the façade of the last house.

You will probably need a few minutes to admire the many details that make up the beautiful **Fresque du Petit-Champlain** *(102 Rue du Petit-Champlain)*. Some 35 characters, both famous and unknown, who shaped the history of the province of Qué-

bec, and most particularly of Québec City and the Petit-Champlain district, come to life in six rooms. From the first floor to the attic, they are presented in various settings, such as artisan workshops and an inn. You'll feel as though the walls suddenly open up on different chapters in history!

Retrace your steps and take the stairway that leads to Boulevard Champlain. At the foot of the stairway, make sure to turn around and admire the exceptional view from below of the Château Frontenac.

Maison Demers ★ *(28 Boulevard Champlain)* was built in 1689 by mason Jean Lerouge. This impressive residence is an example of the bourgeois style of Québec's Basse-Ville. A two-storey residential facade looks on to Rue du Petit-Champlain while the rear, which was used as a warehouse, extends down another two storeys to open directly onto l'Anse du Cul-de-Sac.

The cove called l'**Anse du Cul-de-Sac**, also known as the Anse aux Barques, was Québec City's first port. In 1745, Intendant Gilles Hocquart ordered the construction of a major shipyard in the western part of the cove. Several French battleships were built there using Canadian lumber. In 1854, the terminus of the Grand Trunk railway was built on the embankments, and in 1858 the Marché Champlain went up, only to be destroyed by fire in 1899. Although it is now filled in and built-up, one can still distinguish traces of this natural harbour by examining the older urban arrangement. The location is presently occupied by administrative buildings and by the **terminus of the Québec-Lévis ferry**. A short return trip on the ferry provides a spectacular view of the ensemble of Vieux-Québec. Taking the ferry in the winter affords a rare chance to come face to face with the ice floes of the St. Lawrence.

Follow Boulevard Champlain east as far as Rue du Marché-Champlain. The ferry boards from the south end of this road.

Hôtel Jean-Baptiste-Chevalier ★★ *(60 Rue du Marché-Champlain)* is not a hotel but rather the townhouse of a wealthy family. The first building in the Place-Royale area to be restored, the hôtel is really three separate houses from three different periods: **Maison de l'Armateur Chevalier** (home of Chevalier the shipowner), built in a square in 1752; **Maison Frérot**, with a mansard roof (1683); and **Maison Dolbec**, dating from 1713. These houses were all repaired or partially rebuilt after the British Conquest. As a group, they were rescued from deterioration in 1955 by Gérard Morisset, the director of the Inventaire des Oeuvres d'Art, who suggested that they be purchased and restored by the government of Québec. This decision had a domino effect and prevented the demolition of Place-Royale.

Maison Chevalier *(free admission; end Jun to end Oct every day 10am to 5:30pm, May to end Jun Tue-Sun 10am to 5:30pm, Nov to May Sat and Sun 10am to 5pm; 60 Rue du Marché-Champlain, ☎643-2158)* harbours an annex of the Musée de la Civilisation, where an interesting exhibit, "Habiter au Passé" (Living in the Past) portrays the daily lives of the merchants of New France. The exhibit features furniture as well as everyday items. The original, stately Louis XV woodwork (circa 1764) can also be seen.

Take Rue Notre-Dame, and turn right onto Rue Sous-le-Fort.

With no walls to protect Basse-Ville, other means of defending it from the cannon-fire of ships in the river had to be found. Following the attack by Admiral Phipps in 1690, it was decided to set up the **Batterie Royale ★** *(at the far end of Rue Sous-le-Fort),* according to a plan drawn up by Claude Baillif. The strategic position of the battery allowed for the bombardment of any enemy ships foolhardy enough to venture into the narrows in front of the city. The ruins of the battery, long hidden under storehouses, were discovered in 1974. The crenellations, removed in the 19th century, were reconstructed, as was the wooden portal, discernible in a sketch from 1699.

The two rough stone houses on Rue Saint-Pierre, next to the battery, were built for Charles Guillemin in the early 18th century. The narrowness of the house on the left shows just how precious land was in Basse-Ville during the French Regime. Each lot, irregular or not, had to be used. A little further along, at number 25 Rue Saint-Pierre, is the Louis-Fornel house, where a number of artefacts are on display in vaults. This vaulted basement was built in the 17th century from the ruins of Champlain's stronghold, and extends right under the square.

Continue along Rue Saint-Pierre, and turn left on Rue de la Place to go up to Place-Royale.

Place-Royale ★★★ is the most European quarter of any city in North America. It resembles a village in northwestern France. Place-Royale is laden with symbolism, as it was on this very spot that New France was founded in 1608. After many unsuccessful attempts, this became the official departure point of French exploits in America. Under the French Regime,

Place-Royale was the only densely populated area in a vast, untamed colony. Today, it contains the most significant concentration of 17th- and 18th-century buildings in the Americas north of Mexico.

The square itself was laid out in 1673 by Governor Frontenac as a market. It replaced the garden of Champlain's Abitation, a stronghold that went up in flames in 1682, along with the rest of Basse-Ville. In 1686, Intendant Jean Bochart de Champigny erected a **bronze bust of Louis XIV** in the middle of the square, hence the name of the square, Place-Royale. In 1928, François Bokanowski, then the French Minister of Commerce and Communications, presented Québécois Athanase David with a bronze replica of the marble bust of Louis XIV in the Gallerie de Diane at Versailles to replace the missing statue. The bronze, by Alexis Rudier, was not set up until 1931, for fear of offending England.

Small, unpretentious **Église Notre-Dame-des-Victoires ★★** *(free admission; early May to mid-Oct every day 9:30am to 4:30pm, rest of the year 10am to 16:30pm, closed during weddings and christenings; 32 rue Sous-le-Fort, ☎692-1650)* is the oldest church in Canada. Designed by Claude Baillif, it dates from 1688. It was built on the foundations of Champlain's *Abitation* and incorporates some of its walls. Beside the church, black granite marks the foundation remains from the second Abitation de Champlain. These vestiges were discovered in 1976.

Initially dedicated to the Baby Jesus, it was rechristened Notre-Dame-de-la-Victoire after Admiral Phipp's attack of 1690 failed. It was later renamed Notre-Dame-des-Victoires (the plural) in memory of the misfortune of British

Admiral Walker, whose fleet ran aground on Île-aux-Oeufs during a storm in 1711. The bombardments of the Conquest left nothing standing but the walls of the church, spoiling the Levasseur's lovely interior. The church was restored in 1766, but was not fully rebuilt until the current steeple was added in 1861.

Raphaël Giroux is responsible for most of the present interior, which was undertaken between 1854 and 1857, but the strange "fortress" tabernacle of the main altar is a later work by David Ouellet (1878). Lastly, in 1888, Jean Tardivel painted the historical scenes on the vault and on the wall of the chancel. What are most striking, though, are the various pieces in the church: the *ex-voto* (an offering) that hangs from the centre of the vault depicting the *Brézé*, a ship that came to Canada in 1664 carrying soldiers of the Carignan Regiment; and the beautiful tabernacle in the Sainte-Geneviève chapel, attributed to Pierre-Noël Levasseur (circa 1730). Among the paintings are works by Boyermans and Van Loo, originally from the collection of Abbot Desjardins.

Under the French Regime, the square attracted many merchants and ship owners who commissioned the building of attractive residences. The tall house on the southwest corner of the square and on Rue de la Place, **Maison Barbel**, was built in 1754 for the formidable businesswoman Anne-Marie Barbel, widow of Louis Fornel. At the time, she owned a pottery factory on Rivière Saint-Charles and held the lease on the lucrative trading post at Tadoussac.

Maison Dumont *(1 Place-Royale)* was designed in 1689 by the tireless Claude Baillif for the vintner Eustache Lambert Dumont. The house incorporated elements of the old

store of the Compagnie des Habitants (1647). Visitors can see its huge vaulted basement now used, as it was in the past, to store casks and bottles of wine. Turned into an inn in the 19th century, the house was the favourite stopping place of U.S. President Howard Taft (1857-1930) on his way to his annual summer vacation in La Malbaie.

Maison Bruneau-Rageot-Drapeau, at number 3A, is a house built in 1763 using the walls of the old Nicolas Jérémie house. Jérémie was a Montagnais interpreter and a clerk at the fur-trading posts of Hudson Bay.

Maison Paradis, on Rue Notre-Dame, houses the **Atelier du Patrimoine Vivant** *(free admission; May to Sep every day 10am to 5pm, Sep to mid-Oct Wed-Sun 10am to 5pm; 42 Rue Notre-Dame, ☎647-1598)*. In these studios, various artisans hone their skills using traditional methods.

If you continue on Rue Notre-Dame towards Côte de la Montagne and then turn around, you will be surprised by the coloured spectacle. On the blind wall of Maison Soumande, in front of Parc de la Cetière, the colours of the **Fresque des Québécois ★ ★** are displayed. In fact, if they're not careful, passersby may actually miss the fresco: it is a *trompe l'œil*! A team of French and Québec artists created this fresco with the guidance of specialists (historians, geographers, etc.) who made sure the painting was realistic and instructive. On a surface area of 420m2 they brought together Québec City's architecture and famous sites such as Cap Diamant, the ramparts, a bookshop, houses of Vieux-Québec— in short, different places that the town's inhabitants encounter every day. Just like the crowd of admiring onlookers that gathers rain or shine, you can amuse yourself

for quite a while trying to identify the historical figures and the role they played. From top to bottom and from left to right, you will see Marie Guyart, Catherine de Longpré, François-Xavier Garneau, Louis-Joseph Papineau, Jean Talon, le Comte de Frontenac, Marie Fitzbach, Marcelle Mallet, Louis Jolliet, Alphonse Desjardins, Lord Dufferin, Félix Leclerc and finally, Samuel de Champlain, who started it all.

Return to Place-Royale and visit the **Centre d'Interprétation de Place-Royale ★ ★** *($3, free admission early Nov to end Mar and Tue early Apr to end Jun, $8.50 package with Musée de la Civilisation and Musée de l'Amérique Française; end Oct to end Jun Tue-Sun 10am to 5pm, end Jun to end Oct every day 9:30am to 5pm; 27 Rue Notre-Dame, ☎646-3167)*, which opened in 1999. To accommodate the centre, both the Hazeur and Smith houses, which had burned down, were rebuilt in a modern style while using a large portion of the original materials. The omnipresent glass lets you admire the exposed rooms as well as the buildings' architecture from all angles. Along by the glass walls between the two houses, a stairway goes down Côte de la Montagne to Place-Royale. From the staircase, you can see some of the centre's treasures. On each of the three levels, an exhibition presents chapters of Place-Royale's history. There are also artifacts that were discovered during archaeological digs under the square. Whether they are whole objects or tiny pieces that are difficult to identify, they are all instructive. You can also watch a multimedia show and admire scale models such as the one representing the second Abitation de Champlain in 1635.

You will learn, among other things, that the first inn to be established in Québec City was opened in 1648 by a Mr. Boidon. Coincidentally, his name in French (*Bois donc*) means "have a drink!". The hotel tradition continued on Place-Royale until the middle of the 20 century when the last hotel was destroyed by fire. Visitors had been welcomed, lodged and nourished there for 300 years. In the basement, the vaults of the house are transformed into a playroom where young and old can dress up as one of the former occupants. A great (and original) idea!

Continue along Rue de la Place until it opens onto Place de Paris.

Place de Paris ★ *(along Rue du Marché-Finlay)* is an elegant and sophisticated combination of contemporary art and traditional surroundings conceived by Québécois architect Jean Jobin in 1987. A large sculpture by French artist Jean-Pierre Raynault dominates the centre of the square. The work was presented by Jacques Chirac, who was then mayor of Paris, on behalf of his city, when he visited Québec City. Entitled *Dialogue avec l'Histoire* (Dialogue with History), the black granite and white marble work is said to evoke the first human presence in the area and forms a pair with the bust of Louis XIV, visible in the background. The Québécois have dubbed it the Colossus of Québec because of its imposing dimensions. From the square, which was once a market, there is a splendid view of the Batterie Royale, the Château Frontenac and the St. Lawrence River.

Entrepôt Thibaudeau *(215 Rue du Marché-Finlay)* is a huge building whose stone facade fronts onto Rue Dalhousie. It represents the last prosperous days of the

area before its decline at the end of the 19th century. The Second Empire building is distinguished by its mansard roof and by its segmental arch openings. It was built in 1880, following the plans of Joseph-Ferdinand Peachy, for Isidore Thibaudeau, president and founder of the Banque Nationale and importer of European novelties.

Head back up the street towards Rue Saint-Pierre and turn right.

Further along at number 92 is yet another imposing merchant's house, **Maison Estèbe** (1752). It is now part of the Musée de la Civilisation, whose smooth stone walls can be seen along the Rue Saint-Pierre. Guillaume Estèbe was a businessman and the director of the Saint-Maurice ironworks at Trois-Rivières. Having participated in a number of unsavoury schemes with Intendant Bigot during the Seven Years' War, he was locked-up in the Bastille for a few months on embezzlement charges. The house, where he lived for five years with his wife and 14 children, is built on an embankment that used to front onto a large private wharf which is now the courtyard of the museum. The courtyard is accessible through the gateway on the left. The 21-room interior escaped the bombardments of 1759. Some of the rooms feature handsome Louis XV woodwork. On the corner of Rue Saint-Jacques is the old **Banque de Québec** building (Edward Staveley, architect, 1861). Across the street, the old **Banque Molson** occupies an 18th-century house.

Turn right onto Rue Saint-Jacques. The entrance to the Musée de la Civilisation is on Rue Dalhousie, on the right.

The **Musée de la Civilisation** ★★ *($7, Tue free admission, except in*

summer, $8.50 package with Musée de l'Amérique Française and Centre d'Interprétation de la Place-Royale; end Jun to early Sep every day 10am to 7pm, early Sep to end Jun Tue-Sun 10am to 5pm; 85 Rue Dalhousie, ☎643-2158) is housed in a building that was completed in 1988 in the traditional architectural style of Québec City, with its stylized roof, dormer windows and a belltower like those common to the area. Architect Moshe Safdie, who also designed the revolutionary Habitat '67 in Montréal, Ottawa's National Gallery and Vancouver's Public Library, designed a sculptural building with a monumental exterior staircase at its centre. The lobby provides a charming view of Maison Estèbe and its wharf while preserving a contemporary look that is underlined by Astri Reuch's sculpture, **La Débâcle**.

The Musée de la Civilisation presents a great variety of temporary exhibitions. Themes such as humour, circus and song, for example, have been the object of very lively displays. Travelling exhibitions also recount the world's great civilizations, while permanent exhibitions provide a portrait of civilizations from the region. "Mémoires" recounts the history of the Québec people; "Nous les Premières Nations," developed in collaboration with First Nations peoples, is a large exhibition tracing the history of the 11 Aboriginal nations that originally inhabited Québec. You can view many objects as well as audiovisual materials such as the work of filmmaker Arthur Lamothe. Some of the more remarkable items are the Aboriginal artifacts, the large French Regime fishing craft unearthed during excavations for the museum itself, some highly ornate 19th-century horse-drawn hearses, and some Chinese *objets d'art* and pieces of furniture, including an imperial bed from the collection of the Jesuits. You can also visit the museum's vaulted cellar, which dates from the 18th century.

Head northeast, towards the Vieux Port, through Rue Dalhousie.

Beside the Musée de la Civilisation is a lavish *beaux-arts* fire station dating from 1912 that now houses **Ex Machina** (103 rue Dalhousie), a multi-disciplinary artistic production centre founded by Robert Lepage. Note the high tower with a copper dome rising on the southeast corner like a church spire, which was inspired by the tower of the Hôtel du Parlement. Firefighters used to hang up their hoses in the tower to dry and to prevent them from damage since in those days hoses were made out of fabric. The building has been expanded and in order to keep its character, a false wall similar to the original stone wall—but made of plastic—has been erected in front of the new part.

The **Vieux-Port** ★ *(160 Rue Dalhousie)* (old port) is often criticized for being overly American in a city with such a pronounced European sensibility. It was refurbished by the Canadian government on the occasion of the maritime celebration, "Québec 1534-1984."

There are various metallic structures designed to enliven the promenade, at the end of which is the handsome **Édifice de la Douane** *(2 Quai St-André)* (customs house). Its dome and columns are two features of its lovely neoclassical architecture. At the time the structure was built (1856-1857), the river actually flowed right next to it.

The entire port area between Place-Royale and the entrance

of **Bassin Louise** is known as **Pointe-à-Carcy**. At the beginning of the year 2000, the Commission du Vieux-Port started a new phase to completely renovate Pointe-à-Carcy and turn it into a veritable harbour for pleasure boats.

The **Économusée de la Bière** *(free admission; every day noon to 3pm; 37 Quai Saint-André, ☎692-2877)* (beer economuseum) has been set up in an established Vieux-Port bar, L'Inox. By reading the information panels on the walls, you will learn more about the long and glorious history of beer. You can also discover the secrets of beer-brewing by taking a guided tour. Since L'Inox is a microbrewery, it is possible to have the master brewer take you behind the scenes which are visible from the bar through a glass wall (reservations required). And not only will he explain how he makes the beer, he will offer you a taste of his work.

Take Rue Saint-Pierre on your left.

Place de la FAO is located at the intersection of Saint-Pierre, Saint-Paul and Sault-au-Matelot streets. This square honours the United Nations Food and Agriculture Organisation (FAO), whose first meeting was held at the Château Frontenac in 1945. The sculpture at the centre of the square represents the prow of a boat as it emerges from the waves, its female figurehead, *La Vivrière*, firmly grasping all kinds of fruit, vegetables and grains.

In the square at the corner of Rue Saint-Pierre stands an imposing building with a large round portico which formerly housed the **Imperial Bank of Commerce**.

Take Rue Sault-au-Matelot to Rue de la Barricade. This

street is named in honour of the barricade set up against invading revolutionaries coming from what was to become the United States. They attempted to take Québec City on December 31, 1775.

On the right, Rue de la Barricade leads to **Rue Sous-le-Cap**. This narrow passage was once wedged between the St. Lawrence and the Cap Diamant escarpment. At the end of the 19th century, the street housed working-class families of Irish origin. Today's inhabitants, finding the houses too small, have renovated the little cottages on the side of the cliff and connected them to their houses by walkways crossing the street at clothesline height. One almost enters Rue Sous-le-Cap on tiptoe because of the feeling that you're walking into another world. At the end of the street is Côte du Colonel-Dambourgès and then Rue Saint-Paul.

Rue Saint-Paul is a most pleasant street, lined with antique shops overflowing with beautiful Québec heritage furniture.

To get to the Centre d'Interprétation du Vieux-Port-de-Québec, take Rue Rioux or Rue des Navigateurs, which both meet up with Rue Quai Saint-André.

In the days of tall ships, Québec City was one of the most important gateways to America, since many vessels could not make their way any farther against the current. Its bustling port was surrounded by ship-yards that made great use of plentiful and high-quality Canadian lumber. The first royal shipyards appeared under the French Regime in the cove known as l'Anse du Cul-de-Sac. The Napoleonic blockade of 1806 forced the British to turn to their Canadian colony for wood and for the construction of battleships. This was a great boost for a number of shipyards and made fortunes for many of their owners. The **Old Port of Quebec Interpretation Centre** *($3; early May to early Sep every day 10am to 5pm; early Sep to mid-Oct 1pm to 5pm; 100 Rue Saint-André,* ☎*648-3300)* is a national historic site that concentrates on those flourishing days of navigation in Québec. You can also take part in guided tours *($8)* of the Vieux-Port accompanied by characters in period costume.

Take the promenade that runs along the basin to the Vieux-Port market.

Most of Québec City's public markets were shut down in the 1960s because they had become obsolete in an age of air-conditioned supermarkets and frozen food. However, people continued to want farm-fresh fruits and vegetables as well as contact with the farmers. Moreover, the market was one of the only non-aseptic places people could congregate. Thus, the markets gradually began to reappear at the beginning of the 1980s. **Marché du Vieux-Port ★** *(corner of Rue Saint-Thomas and Rue Saint-André)* was built in 1987 by the architectural partners Belzile, Brassard, Galienne and Lavoie. It is the successor to two other markets, Finlay and Champlain, that no longer exist. In the summer, the market is a pleasant place to stroll and take in the view of the Marina Bassin Louise at the edge of the market.

Continue along Rue Saint-Paul. Turn right on Rue Abraham-Martin and then left on Rue de la Gare-du-Palais until you reach the train station.

For over 50 years, the citizens of Québec City clamoured for a train station worthy of their city. Canadian Pacific finally

fulfilled their wish in 1915. Designed by New York architect Harry Edward Prindle in the same style as the Château Frontenac, the **Gare du Palais ★** *(Rue de la Gare-du-Palais)* gives visitors a taste of the romance and charm that await them in Québec City. The 18m-high arrival hall that extends behind the giant window of the facade is bathed in sunlight from the leaded glass skylight on the roof. The faïence tiles and multicoloured bricks in the walls lend a striking aspect to the entire ambiance. The station was closed for almost 10 years (from 1976 to 1985) at the time when railway companies were imitating airlines and moving their stations to the suburbs. Fortunately, it was reopened, with great pomp, and now houses the bus and train stations. Across from it, **Place de la Gare** offers a lovely spot where you can relax and admire an impressive fountain designed by Charles Daudelin.

The building on the right is Raoul Chênevert's 1938 **post office**. It illustrates the persistence of the Château style of architecture that is so emblematic of the city.

A little further on Boulevard Jean-Lesage is **Parc de l'Amérique-Latine**. There, two monuments honour the memory of two of the most important figures in Latin American history. The monuments to great liberators Simón Bolívar and José Martí were offered by the governments of Venezuela and Cuba respectively.

Return to to Rue Saint-Paul by Boulevard Jean-Lesage, which becomes Rue Vallière. At the corner of Rue Saint-Nicolas and Rue Saint-Paul, you are in the heart of the Quartier du Palais, so named because it surrounds the Palais de l'Intendant. To

reach it, head west on Rue De Saint-Vallier.

The block bordered by Ruelle de l'Ancien-Chantier, Rue Saint-Vallier Est, Rue Saint-Paul and Rue Saint-Nicolas is known as **L'Îlot Saint-Nicolas**. It was restored with verve by architects De Blois, Côté, Leahy.

The handsome stone building on the corner and the two others behind it on Rue Saint-Nicolas housed the famous **Cabaret Chez Gérard** from 1938 to 1978. It was here that Charles Trenet, Rina Ketty and many other famous French singers performed. Charles Aznavour actually got his start here. In the bohemian days of the 1950s, he sang here every night for many months for a mere pittance.

The big Scottish-brick building with the pinnacle inscribed "**Les Maisons Lecourt**" was erected across from l'Îlot Saint-Nicolas using the remnants of Intendant Bigot's "royal store." Nicknamed *La Fripone* (The Rogue's) because of the extortionary prices Bigot and his accomplices exacted from the miserable populace, the location was one of only two in the city during the French Regime where one could moor a boat (the other being l'Anse du Cul-de-Sac). In the 17th century, warehouses and wharfs were built along the estuary of the Saint-Charles, as was a shipyard with a drydock that bequeathed the street its name, Rue de l'Ancien-Chantier, meaning "old shipyard."

The **Site du Palais de l'Intendant ★** and the **Centre d'Interprétation Archéologique** are part of **l'Îlot des Palais** *($3; end Jun to early Sep every day 10am to 5pm, rest of the year with reservations only; 8 Rue Vallière,* ☎*691-6092)* and the **Site Archéologique des Voûtes du**

Palais, (the palace vaults archeological site). The intendant oversaw the day-to-day affairs of the colony. The royal stores, the few state enterprises and the prison were located near his residence. With so many opportunities to make himself rich, it was only natural that his should be the most splendid mansion in New France. The remains of one wing of the palace can still be seen in the shape of the segment of brown brick foundation wall that is now aboveground. The location was originally that of the brewery set up by the first intendant, Jean Talon (1625-1694). Talon took great effort to populate and develop the colony. For his trouble, he was made secretary of the king's cabinet upon his return to France. His brewery was replaced by a palace designed by engineer La Guer Morville in 1716. This elegant building had a classical entrance in cut stone that gave onto a horseshoe-shaped staircase. Twenty or so ceremonial rooms, arranged in a row one after the other, served for receptions and the meetings of the Conseil Supérieur.

The palace was spared British cannon-fire only to be burned to the ground during the American invasion of 1775-76. The arches of its cellars were used as the foundation of the Boswell brewery in 1872, bringing the site full circle. Visitors are free to inspect the cellars, where the archeological information centre is located. The centre displays artifacts and ruins of the site itself.

To return to Haute-Ville, climb Côte du Palais at the end of Rue Saint-Nicolas.

Tour C: Grande Allée

Duration of tour: one day

Riopelle

Jean-Paul Riopelle was one of Québec's most renowned painters, and its best-known internationally. Many of the impressive number of paintings he created are exhibited throughout the world. This legendary character, an abstract painter famous for his huge mosaics, left his mark on the world of contemporary art. He was born in Montréal in 1932, and his career took off with the Automatism movement in the 1940s. He was also a co-signatory of the Refus Global, an artistic manifesto. He lived in Paris for several years but returned to the province of Québec during the last years of his life. He died on March 12, 2002, in his manor on Île aux Grues, on the St. Lawrence River, in the migration path of the snow geese he held so dear to his heart.

Grande Allée appears on 17th-century maps, but it was not built up until the first half of the 19th century, when the city grew beyond its walls. Grande Allée was originally a country road linking the town to Chemin du Roi and thereby to Montréal. At that time, it was bordered by the large agricultural properties of the nobility and clergy of the French Regime. After the British Conquest, many of the domains were turned into country estates of English merchants who set their manors well back from the road. Then the neoclassical town spilled over into the area before the Victorian city had a chance to stamp the landscape with its distinctive style. Today's Grande Allée is the most pleasant route into the downtown area and the heart of extramural Haute-Ville. Despite the fact that it links the capital's various ministries, it is a lively street as many of the bourgeois houses that front Grande Allée appears on onto it have been converted into restaurants and bars.

This walking tour starts at Porte Saint-Louis and gradually works its way away from the walled city.

On the right is Paul Chevré's monument to the historian François-Xavier Garneau. In the background, against the ramparts and opposite the Parliament, is where the Carnaval's ice castle is sculpted each year and the site of the annual summer festival. On the right is the war memorial in front of which Remembrance Day ceremonies are held (November 11th).

The **Hôtel du Parlement** ★★★ *(free admission; guided tours late Jun to early Sep, Mon-Fri 9am and 4:30pm, Sat and Sun 10am to 4:30pm; early Sep to late Jun, Mon-Fri 9am to 4:30pm; at the corner of Avenue Honoré-Mercier and*

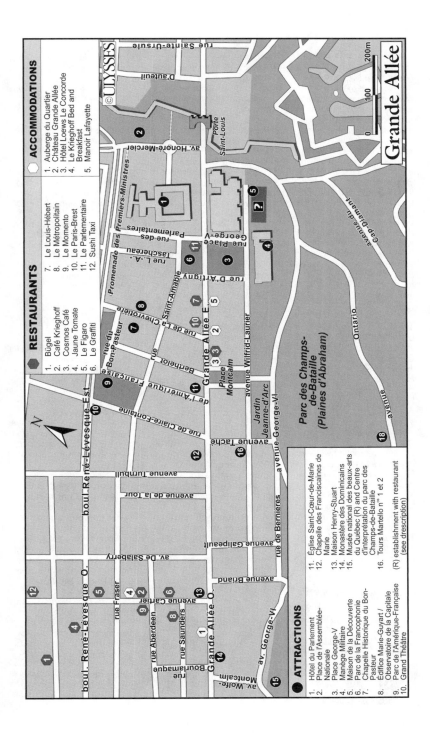

RESTAURANTS

1. Bügel
2. Café Krieghoff
3. Cosmos Café
4. Jaune Tomate
5. Le Figaro
6. Le Graffiti
7. Le Louis-Hébert
8. Le Métropolitain
9. Le Momento
10. Le Paris-Brest
11. Le Parlementaire
12. Sushi Taxi

ACCOMMODATIONS

1. Auberge du Quartier
2. Château Grande Allée
3. Hôtel Loews Le Concorde
4. Le Krieghoff Bed and Breakfast
5. Manoir Lafayette

ATTRACTIONS

1. Hôtel du Parlement
2. Place de l'Assemblée-Nationale
3. Manège Militaire
4. Place George-V
5. Maison de la Découverte
6. Parc de la Francophonie
7. Chapelle Historique du Bon-Pasteur
8. Édifice Marie-Guyart / Observatoire de la Capitale
9. Parc de l'Amérique-Française
10. Grand Théâtre
11. Église Saint-Cœur-de-Marie
12. Chapelle des Franciscaines de Marie
13. Maison Henry-Stuart
14. Monastère des Dominicains
15. Musée national des beaux-arts du Québec (R) and Centre d'interprétation du parc des Champs-de-Bataille
16. Tours Martello nº 1 et 2

(R) establishment with restaurant (see description)

Parc des Champs-de-Bataille
(Plaines d'Abraham)

Grande Allée

0   100   200m

© ULYSSES

Grande Allée, ☎*643-7239)* is known to Quebecers as l'Assemblée Nationale, the National Assembly. The seat of the government of Québec, this imposing building was erected between 1877 and 1886. It has a lavish French Renaissance exterior intended to reflect the unique cultural status of Québec in the North American context. Eugène-Étienne Taché (1836-1912) looked to the Louvre for his inspiration in both the plan of the quadrangular building and its decor. Originally destined to incorporate the two houses of parliament characteristic of the British system of government, as well as all of the ministries, it is today part of a group of buildings on either side of Grande Allée.

The numerous statues of the parliament's main facade constitute a sort of pantheon of Québec. The 22 bronzes of important figures in the history of the nation were cast by such well-known artists as Louis-Philippe Hébert and Alfred Laliberté. A raised inscription on the wall near the central passage identifies the statues. In front of the main entrance a bronze by Hébert entitled **La Halte dans la Forêt** (The Pause in the Forest) depicts an aboriginal family. The work, which is meant to honour the original inhabitants of Québec, was displayed at Paris's World's Fair in 1889. **Le Pêcheur à la Nigog** (Fisherman at the Nigog), by the same artist, hangs in the niche by the fountain.

Hôtel du Parlement

The building's interior is a veritable compendium of the icons of Québec's history. The handsome woodwork is in the tradition of religious architecture.

The members of parliament called *députés,* sit in the National Assembly, or Salon Bleu (Blue Chamber), where Charles Huot's painting, *La Première Séance de l'Assemblée Législative du Bas-Canada en 1792* (The First Session of the Legislative Assembly of Lower Canada in 1792) hangs over the chair of the president of the Assembly. A large work by the same artist covers the ceiling and evokes the motto of Québec, *Je me souviens* (I remember). The Salon Rouge (Red Chamber), intended for the Conseil Législatif, an unelected body eliminated in 1968, is now used for parliamentary commissions. A painting entitled *Le Conseil Souverain* (The Sovereign Council), a souvenir from the mode of government in the days of New France, graces this chamber. Several of the windows of the parliament building boast gorgeous Art-Nouveau stained glass by master glazier Henri Perdriau, a native of Saint-Pierre de Montélimar in Vendée, France. Undeniably, the most spectacular is the arch that adorns the entrance to the elegant Le restaurant Parlementaire (see p 341). This feature was designed by architect Omer Marchand in 1917. The debates of the National Assembly are open

to the public, but a pass must first be obtained.

Follow Grande Allée as far as Rue de la Chevrotière.

In the Parc de l'Hôtel du Parlement, there are three important monuments: one in honour of Honoré Mercier, premier of Québec from 1887 to 1891; another in honour of Maurice Duplessis, premier during the *grande noirceur* or "great darkness" (1936-1939 and 1944-1959), as well as the one representing René Lévesque, who holds a special place in the hearts of Quebecers and who was the premier from 1976 to 1985. Also, the **Promenade des Premiers-Ministres,** informs us with signs about the premieres that have led Québec since 1867.

In front of the Assemblée Nationale notice the beautiful **Place de l'Assemblée-Nationale,** divided in two by the handsome Avenue Honoré-Mercier. On the wall's side, many events are hosted throughout the year. In July, a stage is erected for the Summer Festival and in February, the Ice Palace, the focus of carnival festivities, is located here.

The dizzying growth of the civil service during the Quiet Revolution of the 1960s compelled the government to construct several modern buildings to house its various ministries. A row of beautiful Second Empire houses was demolished to make way for **Complexes H and J** *(on Grande Allée opposite the Hôtel du Parlement).* Dubbed "the bunker" by Quebecers, Pierre Saint-Gelais's 1970 building houses the office of the premier of the provincial government.

Place George V and the **Manège Militaire ★** *(Avenue Wilfrid-Laurier).* This expanse of lawn is used as the training area and parade ground of the military's equestrians. There are cannons and a statue in memory of the two soldiers who perished attempting to douse the flames of the 1889 fire in the suburb of Saint-Sauveur. Otherwise, the grounds serve mainly to highlight the amusing Château-style facade of the Manège Militaire, the Military Riding Academy, built in 1888 and designed by Eugène-Étienne Taché, the architect of the Hôtel du Parlement.

The Centre d'Interprétation du Parc des Champs-de-Bataille is on Avenue Wilfrid-Laurier behind the H and J Buildings, which border the Plains of Abraham. Occupying one of the Citadelle buildings, **Maison de la Découverte ★** *(835 Avenue Wilfrid-Laurier,* ☎*649-6157)* should please Québec City residents as much as visitors. Upstairs, at the Office du Tourisme de la région de Québec, travellers can get help finding their way around. On the ground floor, questions are answered about the Parc des Champs-de-Bataille, its history and the many activities that go on here. There are also a few services and an entrance to the Plains of Abraham. Various guided tours leave from here. One of them takes place on board the "Bus d'Abraham" guided by Abraham Martin in person!

Go back towards Grande Allée.

Parc de la Francophonie *(between Rue Saint-Augustin and Rue d'Artigny)* and **Complexe G**, which appears in the background, together occupy the site of the old Saint-Louis quarter, today almost entirely vanished. Parc de la Francophonie was laid out for open-air shows. It also takes the name Le Pigeonnier, which means dovecote, from the interesting concrete structure placed in the middle,

based on an idea by landscape architects Schreiber and Williams in 1973.

A little further to the west, the fabric of the old city is again in evidence. **Terrasse Stadacona** *(numbers 640 to 664)*, on the right, is a neoclassical row of townhouses on the English model: the multiple houses share a common facade. These houses date from 1847, and they have now been turned into bars and restaurants with terraces sheltered by multitudes of parasols. Opposite *(numbers 661 to 695)* is a group of Second Empire houses dating from 1882, a period when Grande Allée was the fashionable street in Québec City. These houses show the influence of the parliamentary buildings on the residential architecture of the quarter. Three other houses on Grande Allée are worth mentioning for the eclecticism of their facades: **Maison du Manufacturier de Chaussures W. A. Marsh** *(number 625)*, house of a prominent shoe manufacturer, designed in 1899 by Toronto architect Charles John Gibson; **Maison Garneau-Meredith** *(numbers 600 to 614)* of the same year; and **Maison William Price**, a real little Romeo-and-Juliet style place which is, unfortunately, dwarfed by the hotel **Le Concorde**. The revolving restaurant (see p 342) of this hotel affords a magnificent view of Haute-Ville and the Plains of Abraham.

In little **Parc Montcalm**, next to the hotel, is a statue commemorating the general's death on September 13, 1759, at the Battle of the Plains of Abraham. The **statue of French General Charles de Gaulle** (1890-1970), which faces away from Montcalm, created quite a controversy when it was erected in the spring of 1997. Farther along, at the entrance to the Plains of Abraham, **Jardin Jeanne-**

d'Arc ★★ boasts magnificent flowerbeds and a statue of Joan of Arc astride a spirited charger.

Turn right on Rue de la Chevrotière.

Behind the austere facade of the mother house of the Soeurs du Bon-Pasteur, a community devoted to the education of abandoned and delinquent girls, is the charming, Baroque Revival style **Chapelle Historique Bon-Pasteur ★★** *(free admission; Jul and Aug, Tue to Sat, 1:30pm to 4:30pm; 1080 Rue de la Chevrotière,* ☎*648-9710)*. Designed by Charles Baillargé in 1866, this tall, narrow chapel houses an authentic Baroque tabernacle dating from 1730. Pierre-Noël Levasseur's masterpiece of New France carving is surrounded by devotional miniatures hung on pilasters by the nuns.

Atop the 31 storeys of **Édifice Marie-Guyart**, the **Observatoire de la Capitale** *($4; late Jun to mid-Oct every day 10am to 5pm, mid-Oct to late Jun Tue to Sun 10am to 5pm; 1037 Rue De La Chevrotière,* ☎*644-9841 or 888-497-4322)*, provides a splendid view of Québec City and the surrounding area.

Go back to and take a right on Rue Saint-Amable. Walk up to the Parc de l'Amérique Française.

The **Parc de l'Amérique Française** is a recent creation dedicated to French America. It faces the head office of the Laurentien Insurance Company and is centered around a collection of flags of the various francophone communities of America.

The **Grand Théâtre** *(269 Boulevard René-Lévesque Est,* ☎*643-8131)* is located at the far end of the park. Inaugurated in 1971, the theatre of

Polish architect Victor Prus was to be a meeting place for the cream of Québec City society. There was quite a scandal, therefore, when Jordi Bonet's mural was unveiled and the assembled crowd could read the lines from a poem by Claude Péloquin: *Vous êtes pas tannés de mourir, bande de caves,* which roughly translates, "You bunch of straights ain't sick of dying." The theatre has two halls (Louis-Fréchette and Octave-Crémazie) and stages the concerts of the symphony orchestra as well as theatre, dance and variety shows.

Turn left on Rue Scott to return to the Grande Allée.

Église Saint-Cœur de Marie

(530 Grande Allée Est) was built for the Eudists in 1919 and designed by Ludger Robitaille. It looks more martial than devotional due to its bartizans, machicolations and towers, rather like a Mediterranean fortress with big archways knocked out of it. Across the way is the most outlandish row of Second Empire houses still standing in Québec City: **Terrasse Frontenac** *(455-555 Grande Allée Est)*. Its slender, fantastical peaks look like something from a fairy tale. They are the product of Joseph-Ferdinand Peachy's imagination (1895).

Chapelle des Franciscaines de Marie ★

is the chapel of a community of nuns devoted to the adoration of the Lord. They commissioned the Sanctuaire de l'Adoration Perpétuelle (Sanctuary of Perpetual Adoration) in 1901.

Musée National des Beaux-Arts du Québec

This exuberant Baroque Revival chapel invites the faithful to prayer and celebrates the everlasting presence of God. It features a small columned cupola supported by angels and a sumptuous marble baldaquin.

Several handsome, bourgeois houses dating from the early 20th century face the chapel. Among them, at numbers 433-435, is the residence of John Holt, proprietor of the Holt Renfrew stores. Both this and the neighbouring house, number 425, are styled after Scottish manors. Undeniably the most elegant in its mild Flemish and Oriental eclecticism is the house of Judge P. A. Choquette, designed by architect Georges-Émile Tanguay.

Maison Henry-Stuart *($5; late Jun to early Sep, every day 11am to 5pm; 82 Grande Allée Ouest, ☎647-4347),* on the corner of Cartier and Grande Allée, is one of the few remaining Regency-style Anglo-Norman cottages in Québec City. This type of colonial British architecture is distinguished by a large pavilion roof overhanging a low verandah surrounding the building. The house was built in 1849 and used to mark the border between city and country; its original garden still

surrounds it. The interior boasts several pieces of furniture from the Saint-Jean-Port-Joli manor and has been practically untouched since 1911. More or less closed to the public for a number of years, Maison Henry-Stuart and its garden, which belongs to the organisation "Jardins du Québec," now welcome visitors. The house is home to the Conseil des Monuments et Sites de Québec, which offers guided tours. Tea is now served here on summer afternoons. **Avenue Cartier**, visible on the right, regroups a large number of bars and restaurants that are popular with the locals.

In the area of the American-style **Maison Pollack** *(1 Grande Allée Ouest)* is the Renaissance Revival **Maison des Dames Protestantes** *(111 Grande Allée Ouest)*, built in 1862 by architect Michel Lecourt. Also nearby is **Maison Krieghoff** *(115 Grande-Allée Ouest)*, which was occupied in 1859 by the Dutch painter Cornelius Krieghoff.

Monastère des Dominicains ★

(175 Grande Allée Ouest, not open to the public) and its church are relatively recent realizations that testify to the persistence and historical exactitude of 20th-century Gothic Revival architecture. This sober building of British character incites reverence and meditation.

Turn left on Avenue Wolfe-Montcalm which is the entrance to both Parc Champs-de-Bataille and the Musée National des Beaux-Arts du Québec.

Located at the roundabout is the **Monument to General Wolfe**, victor of the decisive Battle of the Plains of Abraham. It is said to stand on the exact spot where he fell. The 1832 monument has been the object of countless demonstrations and acts of vandalism. Toppled again in 1963, it was rebuilt, this time with an inscription in French.

The **Musée National des Beaux-Arts du Québec** ★★★ *($10, free admission to permanent collection; early Jun to early Sep every day 10am to 6pm, Wed to 9pm; early Sep to end May Tue-Sun 10am to 5pm, Wed to 9pm; Parc des Champs de Bataille, ☎643-2150 or 866-220-2150, www.mdq.org)* previously called "Musée du Québec", was renovated and enlarged in 1992. The older, west-facing building is on the right. Parallel to Avenue Wolfe-Montcalm, the entrance is dominated by a glass tower similar to that of the Musée de la Civilisation. The 1933 neoclassical edifice is subterraneously linked with the old prison on the left. The latter has been cleverly restored to house exhibits, and has been rebaptized Édifice Baillargé in honour of its architect. Some of the cells have been preserved.

A visit to this important museum allows one to become acquainted with the painting, sculpture and silverwork of Québec from the time of New France to today. In 2000, the museum inaugurated a gallery (Salle 3) in honour of painter Jean-Paul Riopelle (who died in 2002) in which his huge mural (42m) *Hommage à Rosa Luxembourg* is displayed.

The collections of religious art gathered from rural parishes of Québec are particularly interesting. Also on display are official documents, including the original surrender of Qué-

bec (1759). The museum frequently hosts temporary exhibits from the United States and Europe.

On the first floor of the museum's Édifice Baillargé is the **Centre d'Interprétation du Parc des Champs-de-Bataille Nationaux (National Battlefield Park Interpretive Centre)** *($3.50; mid-May to early Sep every day 10am to 5:30pm, early Sep to mid-May Tue-Sun 10am to 5pm; Édifice Baillargé, level 1, ☎648-5641)*, which exhibits a reconstruction of the Battle of the Plains of Abraham and a model of the subsequent development of the area through a multi-media show.

Turn left on Avenue Georges VI and right on Avenue Garneau.

Parc des Champs-de-Bataille ★★★ *(free admission; ☎648-4071)* takes visitors back to July 1759: the British fleet, commanded by General Wolfe arrives in front of Québec City. The attack is launched almost immediately. In total, almost 40,000 cannonballs crash down on the besieged city. As the season grows short, the British must come to a decision before they are surprised by French reinforcements or trapped in the December freeze-up. On the 13th of September, under the cover of the night, British troops scale the Cap Diamant escarpment west of the fortifications. The ravines, which here and there cut into the otherwise uniform mass of the escarpment, allow them to climb and to remain hidden. By morning, the troops have taken position in the fields of **Abraham Martin**, hence the name of the battlefield and the park. The French are astonished, as they had anticipated a direct attack on the citadel. Their troops, with the aid of a few hundred Aboriginals warriors, throw themselves against the British. The gener-

als of both sides are slain, and the battle draws to a close in bloody chaos. New France is lost!

Parc des Champs-de-Bataille, where the battle took place, was created in 1908 to commemorate the event. At 101ha, the park is a superb recreational space. Previously occupied by a military training ground, the Ursulines and a few farms, the area of the park was laid out between 1929 and 1939 by landscape architect Frederick Todd. This project provided work for thousands of Québécois during the Depression. Today, the plains are a large green space crisscrossed by paths used for all kinds of winter and summer activities. You will find beautiful landscaping here as well as historical and cultural sites such as the **Kiosque Edwin-Bélanger**, which presents outdoor entertainment. At the park's eastern entrance, Maison de la Découverte (see p 327) presents a good introduction to the Plains, as various exhibitions and activities interpret its history and natural environment.

The **Martello Towers no.1 and no. 2** ★ are characteristic of British defenses at the beginning of the 19th century. Tower number 1 (1808) is visible on the edge of Avenue Ontario; number 2 (1815) blends into the surrounding buildings on the corner of Avenue Laurier and Avenue Taché. Inside the first tower, an exhibition recounts some of the military strategies used in the 19th century *($3.50; end Jun to early Sep every day 10am to 5:30pm)*. Renovated and illuminated at night, a third tower stands further north. It is located at the other extremity of the cape, in the Saint-Jean-Baptiste district, on Rue Latourelle.

This is the end of the Grande Allée walking tour. To return to the walled city, follow Ave-

nue Ontario east to Avenue Georges VI, or take Avenue du Cap-Diamant (in the hilly part of the park) to **Promenade des Gouverneurs**. *The promenade follows the citadel and overlooks the Cap Diamant escarpment, winding up at Terrasse Dufferin. This route affords stunning views of the city, the St. Lawrence River and the south shore.*

Tour D: Saint-Jean-Baptiste

Duration of tour: two hours

A hangout for young people, complete with bars, cafés and boutiques, the Saint-Jean-Baptiste quarter is perched on a hillside between Haute-Ville and Basse-Ville. The abundance of pitched and mansard roofs is reminiscent of parts of the old city, but the orthogonal layout of the streets is quintessentially North American. Despite a terrible fire in 1845, this old Québec City suburb retains several examples of wooden constructions, which were forbidden inside the city's walls.

The Saint-Jean-Baptiste tour begins at Porte Saint-Jean, on Place d'Youville. It threads along Rue Saint-Jean, the neighbourhood's main artery.

Place d'Youville, also called "carré d'Youville" (square), is the public space at the entrance of the old section of town. Formerly an important market square, it is today a bustling crossroads and cultural forum. A redevelopment has given the square a large promenade area with some trees and benches. The counterscarp wall, part of the fortifications removed in the 20th century, has been highlighted by the use of black granite blocks. In winter, part of the square is covered in ice, much to the delight of skaters

who twirl around to the sound of cheerful tunes.

At the beginning of the 20th century, Québec City was in dire need of a new auditorium, its Académie de Musique having burnt to the ground in March 1900. With the help of private enterprise, the mayor undertook the search for a new location. The Canadian government, owner of the fortifications, offered to furnish a strip of land along the walls of the city. Although narrow, the lot grew wider toward the back, permitting the construction of a fitting hall, the **Capitole de Québec** ★ *(972 Rue Saint-Jean)*. W. S. Painter, the ingenious Detroit architect already at work on the expansion of the Château Frontenac, devised a plan for a curved facade, giving the building a monumental air despite the limited size of the lot. Inaugurated in 1903 as the Auditorium de Québec, the building is one of the most impressive *beaux-arts* realizations in the country.

In 1927, the famous American cinema architect Thomas W. Lamb converted the auditorium into a sumptuous 1,700-seat cinema. Renamed the Théâtre Capitole, the auditorium nevertheless served as a venue for shows until the construction of the Grand Théâtre in 1971. Abandoned for a few years, the Capitole was entirely refurbished in 1992 by architect Denis Saint-Louis. The building now houses a dinner-theatre in the hall, a luxury hotel (see p 338) and a restaurant (see p 343) in the curved facade. The Capitole has recently acquired the adjoining cinema, on front of which is an imposing round sign. The cinema has been converted into a nightclub.

The Montcalm Market was levelled in 1932 in order to build the multifunctional space

called the **Palais Montcalm** *(995 Place d'Youville)*. Also known as the Monument National, this is the venue of choice for political rallies and demonstrations of all kinds. The auditorium has a sparse architecture which draws on both neoclassical and Art Deco schools. Today, visitors come here to see concerts or exhibitions.

Chapelle du Couvent des Soeurs de la Charité (1856) is visible on leaving Place d'Youville. Its delicate Gothic Revival facade is dwarfed by two huge towers.

Cross Avenue Dufferin, which was recently well restored. Higher up at the corner of Rue Saint-Joachim is a large network of buildings that includes the Centre des Congrès, the Place Québec shopping centre and the Hilton and Radisson Gouverneur hotels.

Centre des Congrès de Québec *(900 Boulevard René-Lévesque Est, ☎644-4000 or 888-679-4000)* was inaugurated in 1996 and is situated north of the Hôtel du Parlement. This large, modern building features glass walls that let the daylight stream in. It has an exhibition hall, several conference rooms and even a ballroom, and is connected to the Place Québec shopping centre and the Hilton and Radisson Gouverneur hotels (see p 337). Its creation has revived this previously dreary part of Boulevard René-Lévesque. Between the Hilton Québec hotel and the Centre des Congrès is the **Promenade Desjardins**, which recalls the life and work of Alphonse Desjardins, founder of the Caisses Populaires Desjardins credit union. At the end of the promenade is a great view of the city and the faraway mountains. At the entrance to the Centre des Congrès is the lively sculpture *Le Quatuor d'airain.*

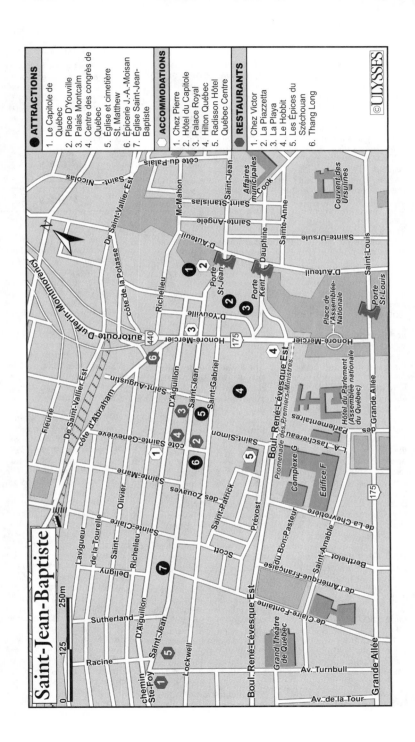

Saint-Jean-Baptiste

ATTRACTIONS

1. Le Capitole de Québec
2. Place D'Youville
3. Palais Montcalm
4. Centre des congrès de Québec
5. Église et cimetière St. Matthew
6. Épicerie J.-A.-Moisan
7. Église Saint-Jean-Baptiste

ACCOMMODATIONS

1. Chez Pierre
2. Hôtel du Capitole
3. Palace Royal
4. Hilton Québec
5. Radisson Hôtel Québec Centre

RESTAURANTS

1. Chez Victor
2. La Piazzetta
3. La Playa
4. Le Hobbit
5. Les Épices du Széchouan
6. Thang Long

© ULYSSES

From Rue Saint-Joachim, take Rue Saint-Augustin, which will lead you to Rue Saint-Jean, where you turn left.

There has been a cemetery on the site of the **Church and Cemetery of Saint Matthew ★** *(755 Rue Saint-Jean)* since 1771, when Protestants, whether French Hugenot, English Anglican or Scottish Presbyterian, banded together to found a Protestant grave-yard. Several 19th-century tombstones are still standing. The gravestones were care-fully restored recently, and the cemetery is now a public garden.

Located in the cemetery, along Rue Saint-Jean, is a lovely Anglican church. Its Gothic Revival architecture was influenced by the Ecclesiologists, an influential school of Anglican thought that sought to re-establish ties with the traditions of the Middle Ages. In its design, and even in its materials, it looks more like an ancient village church than a Victorian church with a Gothic decor. The nave was first erected in 1848; then, in 1870, William Tutin Thomas, the Montréal architect who designed the Canadian Centre for Architecture's Shaughnessy House, drafted an enlarge-ment, giving the church its present bell tower and inte-rior. Québec's Anglican com-munity dwindled in the 20th century, leading to the aban-donment of the church. In 1980, it was cleverly con-verted into a branch of the municipal library. Several of the adornments crafted by British artists have been re-tained: Percy Bacon's hand-some oak choir enclosure, Felix Morgan's alabaster pulpit, and Clutterbuck's beautiful stained glass. The sober vault with its exposed beams is also noteworthy.

Continue along Rue Saint-Jean.

At number 699, **Épicerie J.-A.-Moisan** *(699 Rue St-Jean)* was founded in 1871 and claims to be the "oldest gro-cery store in North America." It does in fact look like a gen-eral store from yesteryear, with its wooden floor and shelves, old advertisements and many tin cans.

The owner of the Érico choc-olate shop, a favourite among "chocoholics," had the great idea of adding a small choco-late museum to his shop. If this interests you, stop by the **Choco-Musée Érico** *(free admission; 634 Rue Saint-Jean, ☎524-2122)* to learn how the Mayans used cocoa, find out how this fruit grows, discover different recipes and more. Thanks to a window on the kitchen, you can even observe chocolate "artists" at work. And don't forget to sample!

The **Église Saint-Jean-Bap-tiste ★** *(Rue Saint-Jean on the corner of Rue de Ligny)* stands out as Joseph Ferdinand Peachy's masterpiece. A disci-ple of French eclecticism, Peachy was a whole hearted admirer of the Église de la Trinité in Paris. The resem-blance here is striking, as much in the portico as in the interior. Completed in 1885, the building caused the bank-ruptcy of its architect, who was, unfortunately for him, held responsible for cracks that appeared in the facade during construction. In front of the church there is now an attractive little square.

For a beautiful view of the city, take the Rue Claire-Fontaine stairs up to the corner of Rue Lockwell on the right. The climb is steep but the view is worth the effort, especially in the evening when the Basse-Ville lights dance at your feet behind the imposing church. When strolling through this neighbourhood's attractive streets, you will have many opportunities to catch a

glimpse of this great view. For example, you can go down Rue Sainte-Claire to the stairs leading to the Saint-Roch neighbourhood, which you will be able to see with the Laurentian mountains in the background.

Parks

Parc des Champs-de-Bataille ★ ★ ★ (see p 329), better known as the **Plains of Abraham**, is Québec City's undisputed park of parks. This immense green space covers about 100ha and stretches all the way to the Cap Diamant, which slopes down to the river. It is a magnificent place for local residents to enjoy all sorts of outdoor activities. Strollers and picnickers abound here during summer, but there is enough space for everyone to enjoy a little peace and quiet.

With its big trees and lawns, **Domaine Maizerets** *(free admission; 2000 Boulevard Montmorency, ☎691-2385)* is the perfect place for a leisurely stroll. Gardening buffs will love the arboretum *(☎660-6953)* and the landscaping; the Domaine also belongs to the Association des Jardins du Québec. In the heart of the arboretum is a butterfly aviary. Weather permitting (it is closed when it rains), visitors can walk into this world of butterflies, which features some 30 species from eastern Canada. Not only will you be amazed, but you will also learn about the different stages of their development. A num-ber of historic buildings can also be found here, including the château that houses a small exhibition on the history of the estate. All sorts of outdoor activities can be enjoyed here in both summer and winter. Outdoor concerts, plays and conferences on ornithology and other subjects are held at the Domaine Maizerets all year round.

Outdoor Activities

Cycling

Québec City is developing its cycling infrastructure. Today, more than 50km of cycling paths stretch out around the city. Consult the Ulysses Travel Guide *Le Québec cyclable* to obtain maps of those trails.

Certain paths are worth mentioning, such as the one leading from the Vieux-Port to Beauport and the one that follows part of the Rivière Saint-Charles. In addition, motorists have to make room for cyclists on some streets. Take note, however, that efforts are being made to develop a bike-path network in the city. Finally, parks like the Plains of Abraham are pleasant places for cycling and even have trails suitable for mountain bikes.

The Promo-Vélo association has a great deal of information on various kinds of tours available in the region. This organization also publishes a map of bike paths in the Québec City region.

Promo-Vélo
C. P. 700, succ. Haute-Ville
Québec, G1R 4S9
☎522-0087

Tourisme Saint-Raymond
☎*337-2900 or 800-409-2012*

Bicycle Rentals

You can rent mountain bikes at Station Mont-Sainte-Anne and in Parc de la Jacques-Cartier (see above).

Cyclo Services Voyages
$20/day
Marché du Vieux-Port
84 Rue Prince-de-Galles
☎*692-4052*
Cyclo Services Voyages also organizes excursions in the city and surrounding area.

Vélo Passe-Sport Plein air
$25/day
Côte du Palais
☎*692-3643*
This organization also organizes excursions in the city and surrounding area.

Vélotek
$25/day
463 Rue Saint-Jean
☎*648-6022*

Cruises

Croisières AML *(tickets sold at Quai Chouinard, ☎692-1159 or 800-563-4643)* offers cruises all summer, with a great view of Québec City and its surroundings from another angle. One of the ships owned by this company is the *M/V Louis-Jolliet ($24; departures 11:30am, 2pm, 4pm)* sailing from Québec City, its port of registry. The daytime cruises last 1.5hrs and take passengers to the foot of Montmorency Falls, while the evening cruises go to the tip of Île d'Orléans and include dinner in one of the boat's two dining rooms. These starlight cruises, which last several hours, always include live music, and you can dance the night away on the ship's deck!

Croisières de la Famille Dufour *(22 Quai St-André;*

☎*692-0222 or 800-463-5250)* take passengers to the lovely region of Charlevoix, to Pointe-au-Pic, to Île-aux-Coudres and even to the heart of the breathtaking Saguenay fjord aboard a big, modern catamaran.

In-Line Skating

On the **Plains of Abraham**, in front of the Musée du Québec, there is a big, paved rink for in-line skating. Scores of children and adults wearing protective helmets can be seen blading around the track on fine summer days. Equipment rentals are available at a small stand by the rink.

Jogging

Again, the place to go is the **Plains of Abraham**. The big, flat track in front of the Musée du Québec is good for a run, though people also go jogging on the paved streets and trails.

Ice Skating

From early fall to late spring, a small skating rink occupies the centre of **Place d'Youville**, complete with music-blaring loudspeakers. Skaters also have access to an indoor area equipped with restrooms *(every day noon to 10pm,* ☎*691-4685)*. In the heart of winter, snow-covered Place d'Youville takes on a magical air, as skaters glide around frost-covered Porte-Saint-Jean, the illuminated Capitole and lampposts draped with

Christmas decorations in the background.

Once it has iced over, **Rivière Saint-Charles** is turned into a natural skating rink that, weather permitting, winds 2 kilometres between the neighbourhoods of Limoilou and Saint-Roch, in Basse-Ville. There is a heated place to rest *(free admission; Mon-Fri noon to 10pm, Sat-Sun 10am to 10pm; 5 Rue de la Pointe-aux-Lièvres, ☎691-5488).*

Each winter, an ice rink is laid out on **Terrasse Dufferin**, so skaters can swirl about at the foot of the Château Frontenac, with a view of the icy river. You can put on your gear at the kiosk *(free admission; late Dec to mid-Mar, every day 11am to 11pm, ☎692-2955),* which also rents out skates *($5/hr).*

A lovely skating rink winds beneath the trees of **Domaine Maizerets** *(free admission; 2000 Boulevard Montmorency, ☎691-2385)* (see p 332). There is a small chalet nearby where you can take off your skates and warm up next to a wood stove. Skate rentals *($4; mid-Dec to mid-Mar, Mon-Fri 1pm to 4pm, Sat and Sun 10am to 4pm; every night 6pm to 9pm).*

Cross-country Skiing

The snow-covered **Plains of Abraham** provide an enchanting setting for cross-country skiing. Trails crisscross the park from one end to the other, threading their way through the trees or leading across a headland with views of the icy river. All right in the heart of the city!

Some extremely pleasant cross-country trails can also be found at **Domaine Maizerets** *(free admission; 2000 Boule-*

vard Montmorency, ☎691-2385) (see p 332). At the starting point, there is a little chalet heated with a wood-burning stove. Equipment rentals *($4; mid-Dec to mid-Mar, Mon to Fri 1pm to 4pm, Sat and Sun 10am to 4pm)* are available.

Tobogganing

The hills of the **Plains of Abraham** are wonderful for sledding. Bundle up well and follow the kids pulling toboggans to find the best spots!

During winter, a hill is created on **Terrasse Dufferin**. You can glide down it comfortably seated on a toboggan. First purchase your tickets at the little stand in the middle of the terrace *($2/ride; late Dec to mid-Mar, every day 11am to 11pm; 692-2955),* then grab a toboggan and climb to the top of the slide. Once you get there, make sure to take a look around: the view is magnificent!

Accommodations

Québec City has an abundance of hotels and accommodations of all kinds. In Vieux-Québec, many old historic houses have been converted into small hotels. They are often charming but can run a bit short on comfort. Many of the rooms in these establishments, for example, do not have private bathrooms. During the winter, many hotels offer special room rates on weekends. However, in the summer, it is best to reserve a room well in advance. The large influx of visitors to the winter carnival

in February can also make finding a room difficult.

Hospitalité Canada Tours is a free telephone service operated by the Maison du Tourisme de Québec *(12 Rue Ste-Anne; ☎800-665- 1528 or from Montreal ☎514 252-3117, www.hospitality-canada.com).* Depending on what kind of accommodations you're looking for, the staff will suggest various places belonging to the network and even make reservations for you.

Tour A: Vieux-Québec

Centre International de Séjour (Hostelling International)
$
19 Rue Ste-Ursule
☎694-0755 or 800-461-8585 from Montréal
☎(514) 252-3117
The Centre International de Séjour is a youth hostel with 240 beds for young people. The rooms can accommodate from three to six people, the dormitories from eight to 10, and there are also private double rooms.

Auberge de la Paix
$ bkfst incl.
plus $2 for bedding
if you don't have your own
sb, K
31 Rue Couillard
☎694-0735
Behind its lovely white facade in Vieux-Québec, Auberge de la Paix has a youth-hostel atmosphere. It has 60 beds in rooms able to accommodate from two to eight people, as well as a kitchenette and a living room. This inn lives up to its name by providing a friendly and fun place to relax. In the summer, a lovely garden is filled with flowers. Children are welcome!

Manoir LaSalle
$$
pb/sb, K
18 Rue Sainte-Ursule
☎*692-9953*
Manoir LaSalle is a small hotel
with 11 rooms, one of which
has a private bathroom. This
red-brick building is exemplary
of the architectural style of
some of the first homes built
in the city.

Au Jardin du Gouverneur
$$ bkfst incl.
≡
16 Rue Mont-Carmel
☎*692-1704*
≈*692-1713*
Au Jardin du Gouverneur is a
charming little hotel a in small
blue and white house opposite Parc des Gouverneurs.
Rooms are a good size but
there is nothing special about
the decor. No smoking.

Marquise de Bassano
$$ bkfst incl.
sb
15 Rue des Grisons
☎*692-0316*
www.total.net/~bassano
Vieux-Québec has been
home to some colourful char-
acters throughout its history.
At the corner of the Rue des
Grisons and Avenue Sainte-
Geneviève is a small Victorian
house which, it is said, was
built for one such character.
The dark panelling that deco-
rates the inside surely guards
some secrets of the Marquise
de Bassano. The house has
been transformed into a wel-
coming bed and breakfast,
with charming rooms and a
cheerful sitting room with a
piano and a fireplace. During
breakfast, which sometimes
lasts into the afternoon, the
young hosts take pleasure in
animating the discussions!

Maison du Fort
$$ bkfst incl.
≡, *K*
21 Avenue Ste-Geneviève
☎*692-4375*
≈*692-5257*
Maison du Fort is tucked away
in a quiet neighbourhood

around Parc des
Gouverneurs. This small residence offers adequate rooms,
and the service is quite welcoming.

Auberge Saint-Louis
$$ bkfst incl.
pb/sb, ℜ, ≡
48 Rue Saint-Louis
☎*692-2424 or 888-692-4105*
≈*692-3797*
Located on busy Rue Saint-
Louis, Auberge Saint-Louis is a
small, pleasant hotel. Room
prices vary according to ame-
nities offered. Less expensive
rooms do not have private
bathrooms. The hotel is well
maintained.

Maison Acadienne
$$-$$$
pb/sb, ⊛, ≡, ℝ
43 Rue Ste-Ursule
☎*694-0280*
A number of old houses on
Rue Sainte-Ursule have been
made into hotels. Among
these, Maison Acadienne
stands out with its large, white
facade. The rooms are rather
lacklustre, although some have
been renovated.

Auberge du Trésor
$$-$$$
ℜ, ≡
20 Rue Sainte-Anne
☎*694-1876 or 800-566-1876*
Auberge du Trésor was built
in 1676. Renovated many
times since then, it maintains
an impressive appearance.
Rooms are modern and com-
fortable. All rooms have pri-
vate bathrooms and colour
televisions.

Château de Léry
$$-$$$
≡, ⊛, *K*
8 Rue Laporte
☎*692-2692 or 800-363-0036*
≈*692-5231*
Located next to Parc des
Gouverneurs and overlooking
the river, the Château de Léry
has comfortable rooms.
Rooms facing the street offer a
good view. This hotel is in a
quiet neighbourhood in the
old part of the city, but is just a

few minutes' walk from the
bustle of downtown.

Le Clos Saint-Louis
$$-$$$ bkfst incl.
sb/pb, ⊛, ≡, ℑ
71 Rue St-Louis
☎*694-1311 or 800-461-1311*
≈*694-9411*
Le Clos Saint-Louis comprises
in two imposing Victorian
houses dating from 1844 on
Rue St-Louis. Located close to
Vieux-Québec and its attrac-
tions, this hotel has 25 rooms
spread out on four floors. The
rooms have all been arranged
to make their historic aspect
especially welcoming: some
have four-poster beds with
canopies, others old-fashioned
bookcases or fireplaces. The
rooms on the second floor are
particularly attractive with their
stone walls and exposed
wooden beams. Even if some
of the bathrooms must be
shared, they are all modern
and well equipped. In the
morning, coffee and croissants
are served in the basement.

Manoir Victoria
$$$
≡, ≈, ☺, △, ℜ, *K*, ⊛
44 Côte du Palais
☎*692-1030 or 800-463-6283*
≈*692-3822*
www.manoir-victoria.com
Manoir Victoria is a 145-room
hotel nestled on Côte du
Palais. Decorated in true Victorian style, it succeeds in
being both chic and very comfortable. The lobby, at the top
of a long flight of stairs, is inviting and contains both a bar
and a dining room. Manoir
Victoria offers well-equipped
suites and a number of cultural
and sports packages.

🏨 Hotel Clarendon
$$$
≡, ℜ, ⊛
57 Rue Ste-Anne
☎*692-4652 or 888-554-6001*
≈*692-4652*
www.hotelclarendon.com
Built in 1870, the Hotel Clar-
endon is one of the oldest
hotels in the city (see p 310).
The hotel has an unpreten-

tious exterior while the elegant interior is decorated in Art Deco style. The entrance hall is very attractive. The rooms in this hotel have been renovated many times over the years and are spacious and comfortable. This a very good place to stay in Vieux-Québec. Its restaurant, Le Charles-Baillargé (see p 339), serves elegant meals, and there is also a lively bar, L'Emprise (see p 343), which plays jazz music.

Château Bellevue
$$$

≡

16 Rue Laporte
☎*692-2473 or 800-463-2617*
⇒*692-4876*
The Château Bellevue has an impressive view of the river. The rooms are reasonable but equipped with rather sterile modern furniture.

Château de Pierre
$$$

≡

17 Avenue Ste-Geneviève
☎*694-0429 or 888-694-0429*
⇒*694-0153*
The Château de Pierre is housed in an old colonial-style house. The ostentatious entrance of this hotel is quite striking and somewhat flashy. The rooms are comfortable.

Château Frontenac
$$$$$
ℜ, ≡, ⎕, ⊛, ≈, ⊘
1 Rue des Carrières
☎*692-3861 or 800-268-9420*
⇒*692-1751*
www.fairmont.com
The Château Frontenac is by far the most prestigious hotel in Québec City. Enter its elegant lobby with its wood panelling and warm colours and let yourself be transported back in time. The Château Frontenac was built in 1893 and over the years has been the setting of several historic events. The decor exudes a classic, refined richness that is truly worthy of a castle. Its restaurant also offers a taste of luxury (see Le Champlain,

p 339). The sumptuous rooms provide the most comfortable environment possible, and although the size and benefits of the hotel's 618 rooms vary greatly, all are quite pleasant. The rooms overlooking the river have beautiful bay windows and, of course, the view is magnificent.

Tour B: Du Petit-Champlain au Vieux-Port

Hôtel Belley
$$
K
249 Rue St-Paul
☎*692-1694 or 888-692-1694*
⇒*692-1696*
The pleasant Hôtel Belley stands opposite the market at the Vieux-Port. A hotel since 1877, this handsome building will leave you with fond memories for years to come. It has eight simply decorated, cozy rooms, some with exposed brick walls, others with wooden beams and skylights. The ground floor is home to a bar called Taverne Belley (see p 343), whose breakfasts and lunches, served in two lovely rooms, are very popular with locals. A number of extremely comfortable and attractively decorated lodgings, some with terraces, are also available in another house across the street. These may be rented by the night, by the week or by the month.

Le Priori
$$$ bkfst incl.
⊛, ℜ, ℑ, K, ≡
15 Rue du Saul-au-Matelot
☎*522-8108 or 800-351-3992*
⇒*692-0883*
Le Priori is located on a quiet street in the Basse-Ville. The building is very old but has been renovated in a very modern style. The decor successfully contrasts the old stone walls of the building with up-to-date furnishings. Its appearance is striking and

even the elevator is distinctive. Le Priori is highly recommended.

Auberge Saint-Pierre
$$$$ bkfst incl.
K, ⊛, ≡
79 Rue St-Pierre
☎*694-7981 or 888-268-1017*
⇒*694-0406*
www.auberge.qc.ca
A lovely inn has recently opened in a building that had housed Canada's first insurance company since the end of the 19th century. The historic charm of the Auberge Saint-Pierre was conserved when the building was renovated. The rooms are similar to the neighbouring apartments, with their various landings and narrow hallways. Each room is beautiful, dark hardwood floors and sumptuously coloured walls. Those on the lower floors have lovely high ceilings, while those higher up provide a wonderful view.

Hôtel Dominion 1912
$$$$ bkfst incl.
≡, ⊛
126 Rue St-Pierre
☎*692-2224 or 888-833-5253*
⇒*692-4403*
www.hoteldominion.com
Dating from 1912 as its name implies, this beautiful buildings on Rue Saint-Pierre has been newly renovated into a hotel that charms its chic clientele. The luxurious Hôtel Dominion 1912 has a modern aspect with materials such as glass and wrought iron, but still maintains its original character. Elements of interior decoration such as cream-and-sand-coloured draperies and cushions, and luxuriously soft sofas and bedspreads add an extremely comfortable touch. Black-and-white photographs of the neighbourhood hang in each room, inviting you to go out and visit it. The upper floors have magnificent views of the river on one side and of the city on the other.

Ungava Caribou (Arctic reindeer)

This large species of deer can weigh up to 250kg when fully grown. It lives in the tundra, and its name comes from the Algonquian language.

White-tailed Deer

The white-tailed deer is the smallest species of deer in eastern North America, attaining a maximum weight of about 150kg. This graceful creature lives at the forest's edge and is one of the most commonly hunted animals in Québec. The male's antlers fall off each winter and grow back in the spring.

Moose

This is the largest member of the deer family in the world; it can measure more than 2m in height and weigh up to 600kg. The male is distinguished by its broad, flattened antlers, large head, rounded nose and by the hump on its back.

Black Bear

Most often found in forests, this is the most common species of bear in eastern Canada. It can weigh up to 150kg when fully grown, yet it is Canada's smallest bear. Be careful— the black bear is unpredictable and dangerous.

Wolf

This predator lives in packs. It measures between 67 and 95cm, and weighs no more than 50kg. Wolves attack their prey (often deer) in packs, and their viciousness makes them rather unsympathetic creatures. Wolves keep their distance from humans.

Red Fox

This small animal has striking auburn fur and is found throughout the forests of eastern Canada. A cunning creature, it keeps its distance from humans and is rarely seen. It hunts small animals and also feeds on nuts and berries.

Coyote

Smaller than the wolf, the coyote adapts easily to various surroundings; it can be spotted through southeastern Canada. If meat is unavailable, this carnivore can survive as a vegetarian.

Auberge Saint-Antoine
$$$$$ bkfst incl.

⊛, ≈, *K*, ℨ
10 Rue St-Antoine
☎*692-2211 or 888-692-2211*
⇌*692-1177*
www.saint-antoine.com
Auberge Sainte-Antoine is
located near the Musée de la
Civilisation. This lovely hotel is
divided into two buildings.
Guests enter through a tastefully renovated old stone
building. The entrance hall is
distinguished by exposed
wooden beams, stone walls
and a beautiful fireplace. Each
room is wonderfully deco-
rated according to a different
theme and has its own unique
charm.

Tour C: Grande Allée

Le Krieghoff B&B
$$ bkfst incl.
ℜ, ℝ, ≈
1091 Avenue Cartier
☎*522-3711*
⇌*647-1429*
www.cafekrieghoff.com
Café Krieghoff offers travellers
a bed and breakfast combination. The novelty, however, is
that breakfast is served in the
café itself (see p 341) which
guarantees both good food
and pleasant surroundings!
The friendly staff makes sure
that guests feel right at home
in the family-like atmosphere.
The five rooms nestled above
the restaurant are modest and
clean. Each one has access to
a private bathroom (even if it
is not connected to the
room), and they all share a
small sitting room and balcony
with a view of lively Avenue
Cartier.

Auberge du Quartier
$$-$$$ bkfst incl.
≡
170 Grande Allée O.
☎*525-9726 or 800-782-9441*
⇌*521-4891*
Looking for a charming little
neighbourhood inn? Situated
opposite the imposing Église
Saint-Dominique, just 5min
from the Plaines d'Abraham

and the Musée du Québec,
Auberge du Quartier should
please you. This large white
house has a dozen clean, well-
lit, attractive and modern
rooms. They are spread out
on three floors, with a suite in
the attic. Reception by the
owner and staff is very
friendly.

Château Grande Allée
$$$
≡
601 Grande Allée E.
☎*647-4433 or 800-263-1471*
⇌*646-7553*
The Château Grande Allée is a
recent addition to busy
Grande Allée. The well-kept
rooms are so large that they
look under-furnished. Making
up for this slight shortcoming
are various features, including
large bathrooms.

Manoir Lafayette
$$$
≡, ℜ
661 Grande Allée E.
☎*522-2652 or 800-363-8203*
⇌*522-4400*
Manoir Lafayette is attractive
and elegant. The hotel was
recently renovated and some
rooms are equipped with
comfortable antique furniture.
The Lafayette has an excellent
location.

Hôtel Loews
Le Concorde
$$$-$$$$
ᗺ, ≡, ≈, ☉, △, ℜ, ⊛
1225 Place Montcalm
☎*647-2222 or 800-463-5256*
⇌*647-4710*
Just outside Vieux-Québec is
the Hôtel Loews Le Con-
corde. It is part of the Loews
hotel chain and is spacious,
comfortable rooms with spectacular views of Québec City
and the surrounding area.
There is a revolving restaurant
on top of the hotel (see
L'Astral p 342).

Tour D:
Saint-Jean-Baptiste

Chez Pierre
$$ bkfst incl.
pb/sb, ℝ
636 Rue d'Aiguillon
☎*522-2173*
Chez Pierre is a bed and
breakfast with three rooms.
Two of them are situated in
the renovated basement, but
the third room is upstairs and
has all the charm of a faubourg
Saint-Jean-Baptiste apartment.
However, the bathroom of
the latter room is also situated
in the basement. Pierre, your
host, is a painter and his large
coloured canvases brighten up
the house. He serves a generous breakfast in the morning.

Hilton Québec
$$$
≡, ≈, ☉, △, ℜ, ᗺ
1100 Boulevard René-Lévesque E.
☎*647-2411 or 800-447-2411*
⇌*647-6488*
Located just outside Vieux-
Québec, the Québec Hilton
offers rooms with the kind of
comfort one expects of an
international hotel chain. The
Place Québec shopping mall is
located in the lobby, which is
connected to the new Centre
des Congres.

Radisson Hôtel Québec
Centre
$$$
≈, ≡, ☉, ᗺ, △, ℜ
690 Boulevard Rene-Lévesque E.
☎*647-1717 or 888-884-7777*
⇌*647-2146*
The Radisson Hôtel Québec
Centre is linked to the Centre
des Congrès. This hotel has
over 377 rooms, all nicely
decorated. Standard rooms
are furnished with slightly
rustic but elegant pine furniture. The hotel's heated
outdoor pool is open all year.

Hôtel du Théâtre Capitole
$$$$
℞, ≡, ⊛
972 Rue St-Jean
☎**694-9930 or 800-363-4040**
⇒**647-2146**
www.lecapitol.com
Adjoining the newly renovated theatre, the Hôtel du Théâtre Capitole is not luxurious, but the rooms are amusing, with a decor that resembles a stage set. At the entrance is the Il Teatro restaurant (see p 343).

Restaurants

Tour A: Vieux-Québec

Casse-Crêpe Breton
$
1136 Rue St-Jean
☎**692-0438**
Little Casse-Crêpe Breton is a popular spot that draws big crowds. Though it has been expanded, patrons still have to line up for a taste of its delicious crepes. Prepared right before your eyes, these delights are filled with your favourite ingredients by waitresses who manage to keep smiling in the midst of the hubbub. High-backed, upholstered seats help lend the place a warm atmosphere.

Chez Temporel
$
25 Rue Couillard
At Chez Temporel, the food is prepared right on the premises. Whether you opt for a rich butter croissant, a *croque-monsieur*, a salad or the special of the day, you can be sure it will be fresh and tasty. To top it all off, this establishment serves the best espresso in town! Tucked away on little Rue Couillard, the two-storey Temporel has been welcoming people of all ages and all stripes for over 20 years now.

Open early in the morning to late at night.

Le Petit Coin Latin
$
8½ Rue Sainte-Ursule
☎**692-2022**
Petit Coin Latin serves homestyle cooking in an ambiance reminiscent of a Parisian café. The decor is dominated by parlour chairs and mirrors, creating a relaxed, convivial atmosphere. The menu includes *croûtons au fromage*, quiche and salads. You can also snack on *raclette* (a swiss meal) served at the table on small burners with potatoes and cold cuts. Delicious! During summer, a lovely outdoor seating area enclosed by stone walls is open out back; to get there from the street, use the carriage entrance.

L'Entrecôte Saint-Jean
$$
1011 Rue Saint-Jean
☎**694-0234**
The Entrecôte Saint-Jean serves steaks prepared in a variety of ways accompanied by matchstick potatoes. Try the salad nuts and the chocolate profiteroles, which make a perfect ending to your meal. Great value for your money.

Les Frères de la Côte
$$-$$$
1190 Rue St-Jean
☎**692-5445**
Les Frères de la Côte serves delicious bistro fare, including pasta, grilled items, and thin-crust pizzas baked in a wood-burning oven and topped with delicious fresh ingredients. Unlimited mussels and fries are also available on certain evenings. The atmosphere is lively yet relaxed and the place is often packed, in keeping with the bustling activity on Rue St-Jean. Guests can take in the action through the restaurant's large windows.

Chez Livernois
$$-$$$
1200 Rue St-Jean
☎**694-0618**
Chez Livernois is a bistro located inside Maison Livernois now called Maison Serge-Bruyère. It is named after photographer Jules Livernois, who set up his studio in this imposing 19th-century house in 1889. The excellent cuisine consists mainly of pasta and dishes from the grill, and the atmosphere is a bit more relaxed than at La Grande Table (see p 339).

Portofino Bistro Italiano
$$-$$$
54 Rue Couillard
☎**692-8888**
Portofino was designed to resemble a typical Italian trattoria. A long bar, blue glasses, mirrors on the wall and soccer banners on the ceiling help create a warm, lively atmosphere. Don't be surprised if the owner greets you with a kiss! To top it all off, the mouth-watering Italian aromas will whet your appetite for the upcoming tourist season. During tourist season, the place is always full. Valet parking.

À la Bastille Chez Bahüaud
$$$
47 Avenue Ste-Geneviève
☎**692-2544**
À la Bastille Chez Bahüaud is located near the Plains of Abraham and is surrounded by trees. The wonderfully quiet terrace makes this the ideal spot for an intimate moonlit dinner. Inside, the decor is both elegant and comfortable and includes a billiard table. There is also a charming downstairs bar with a more intimate atmosphere. Fine French cuisine awaits you.

Café de la Paix
$$$
44 Rue des Jardins
☎**692-1430**
Café de la Paix occupies a narrow space a few steps from

the sidewalk on little Rue des Jardins. It has been around for years and enjoys a solid reputation among Québec City residents. The menu features traditional French cuisine such as frog's legs, beef Wellington, rabbit with mustard and grilled salmon.

L'Élysée-Mandarin
$$$
65 Rue d'Auteuil
☎692-0909
L'Élysée-Mandarin, which also boasts prime locations in Montréal and Paris, serves excellent Szechuan, Cantonese and Mandarin cuisine in a decor that features a small indoor garden and Chinese sculptures and vases. The food is always succulent and the service extremely courteous. If you are with a group, try the sampler menu: it would be a shame not to sample as many dishes as possible!

Le Charles-Baillargé
$$$-$$$$
57 Rue Sainte-Anne
☎692-2480
The Charles-Baillargé restaurant is located on the main floor of the beautiful Hôtel Clarendon (see p 335). Discriminating diners come here for excellent, traditional French cuisine served in comfortable surroundings.

Le Saint-Amour
$$$-$$$$
48 Rue Sainte-Ursule
☎694-0667
Chef and co-owner Jean-Luc Boulay creates succulent, innovative cuisine that is a feast for both the eyes and the palate. The desserts concocted in the *chocolaterie*, on the second floor, are absolutely divine. A truly gastronomic experience! To top it all off, the setting is beautiful and comfortable with a wonderful warm atmosphere. The solarium, open year-round and decorated with all sorts of flowers and plants, brightens up the decor. Valet parking.

Aux Anciens Canadiens
$$$-$$$$
34 Rue St-Louis
☎692-1627
Located in one of the oldest houses in Québec City (see Maison Jacquet p 309), the restaurant Aux Anciens Canadiens serves upscale versions of traditional Québecois specialties. Dishes include ham with maple syrup, pork and beans, and blueberry pie.

Café d'Europe
$$$-$$$$
27 Rue Sainte-Angèle
☎692-3835
Café d'Europe has a sober, slightly outdated decor. There is limited amount of space, and when the place is busy, the noise level gets pretty high. The service is courteous with a personal touch. Sophisticated French and Italian cuisine is presented in a traditional manner and served in generous portions. The flambée dishes are expertly prepared, and the smooth, flavourful sauces make this an unforgettable culinary experience.

Le Continental
$$$-$$$$
26 Rue St-Louis
☎694-9995
Le Continental, just steps away from the Château Frontenac, is one of the oldest restaurants in Québec City. The continental cuisine includes seafood, lamb and duck, among other dishes. Service is *au guéridon* (pedestal table) in a large, comfortable dining room.

La Crémaillère
$$$-$$$$
21 Rue St-Stanislas at the corner of Rue St-Jean
☎692-2216
Friendly service and exquisite cooking with a European flavour await you at La Crémaillère. A great deal of attention is given here to make your meal memorable. The attractive decor adds to the

charm of this inviting restaurant.

Guido Le Gourmet
$$$-$$$$
73 Rue Sainte-Anne
☎692-3856
Guido Le Gourmet will transport you to the world of fine dining. The menu, made up of French and Italian cuisine, includes quail, veal, salmon and other delicacies from both land and sea. The elegant decor and the large, lovely plates on the table provide a good indication of the pleasures that await you. Brunch is served on weekends.

Café de la Terrasse
$$$$
1 Rue des Carrières
☎692-3861
The Café de la Terrasse, in the Château Frontenac, has picture windows looking out onto Terrasse Dufferin. Attractive decor and delicious French cuisine.

Le Champlain
$$$$
1 Rue des Carrières
☎692-3861
Le Champlain is the Château Frontenac's own restaurant. Needless to say, its decor is extremely luxurious in keeping with the opulence of the rest of the hotel. The outstanding French cuisine also does justice to the Château's reputation. Chef Jean Soular, whose recipes have been published, adds a unique touch to the classic dishes. Impeccable service.

La Grande Table de Serge Bruyère
$$$$
1200 Rue St-Jean
☎694-0618
La Grande Table in Maison Serge-Bruyère has a solid reputation that extends far beyond the walls of the old city. First established by the late Serge Bruyère, an excellent cook who gave the place its name, this restaurant's reputation has been main-

tained from year to year thanks to the skills of various well-known chefs. Since the beginning of the year 2000, Serge Bruyère's former student, Martin Côté, has carried on the tradition after travelling all over the world perfecting his art. He creates magnificent French gastronomic dishes with the most exquisite, creamy sauces you will ever taste. La Grande Table is on the top floor of an historic house situated between Rue Garneau and Rue Couillard. The decor is attractive and paintings by Québec artists hang on the walls. Valet parking.

Tour B: Du Petit-Champlain au Vieux-Port

Buffet de l'Antiquaire
$
95 Rue St-Paul
☎692-2661
Buffet de l'Antiquaire is a pleasant snack bar that serves homestyle cooking. As indicated by its name, it is located in the heart of the antique dealers' quarter and is a good place to take a little break while treasure-hunting. It is also one of the first restaurants to open in the morning (6am).

Le Cochon Dingue
$$
46 Boulevard Champlain
☎692-2013
Cochon Dingue is a charming café-bistro located between Boulevard Champlain and Rue du Petit-Champlain. Mirrors and a checkerboard floor create a fun, attractive decor. The menu features bistro-style dishes such as *steak-frites* and *moules-frites* combos (steak and fries or mussels with fries). The desserts are heavenly!

Bistro Sous-le-Fort
$$-$$$
48 Rue Sous-le-Fort
☎694-0852
Bistro Sous le Fort has a somewhat stark decor and is frequented mainly by tourists. The restaurant serves delicious, reasonably priced Québécois cuisine.

🦀 Café du Monde
$$-$$$
57 Rue Dalhousie
☎692-4455
Café du Monde is a large Parisian-style brasserie that serves dishes one would expect from such a place, including *magret de canard* (duck filet), *tartare* (raw minced steak with herbs, etc.), *bavette* (beef steak) and of course, *moules-frites* (mussels and french fries). The lunch menu is interesting with its delicious *profiteroles* (cream puffs) served for dessert. On the weekend there are great brunches as well. The bright decor is condusive to relaxation and discussion: there are black-and-white tiles on the floor, leather seats, large windows overlooking the port and a long bar adorned with an imposing copper coffee machine. There is also a singles bar at the entrance. The waiters, dressed in long aprons, are quite helpful.

Le Môss
$$$
255 Rue St-Paul
☎692-0265
Le Môss is a Belgian bistro with a somewhat cold decor that includes black tables, brick walls, a stainless-steel counter and halogen lights. However, its *moules-frites* combo, dishes from the grill and desserts made with Belgian chocolate are delicious.

Poisson d'Avril
$$$
115 Rue St-André
☎692-1010
Poisson d'Avril is in an old house with stone walls and wooden beams that lend a

great deal of charm. The decor is enhanced by clever lighting and also by the shell-patterned fabric on the chairs. The menu includes well-prepared pasta, grilled dishes and seafood. Try the mussels!

L'Aviatic Club
$$$
450 de la Gare-du-Palais
☎522-3555
There are two restaurants in the magnificent Gare du Palais: a brand-new one with the evocative name of Charbon, which serves, as you might have guessed, food from the grill, and a second, which has been there for a number of years. The Aviatic Club takes you back in time with its mid-19th-century English-style decor featuring rattan armchairs, burgundy curtains, palm trees and a cosmopolitan menu.

Two good restaurants are perched on picturesque Escalier Casse-Cou, which leads to Rue du Petit-Champlain. On the top floor, **Chez Rabelais** (*$$$-$$$$; 2 Rue du Petit-Champlain, ☎694-9460)* serves French cuisine with an emphasis on seafood. A little lower down is **Marie-Clarisse** (*$$$$; 12 Rue du Petit-Champlain, ☎692-0857)*, where everything, except for the stone walls, is as blue as the sea—and with good reason: seafood is the house specialty. These divine dishes are served in a lovely dining room that has been very ornately decorated. When the cold weather sets in, a crackling fire warms you up.

Le Vendôme
$$$
36 Côte de la Montagne
☎692-0557
Le Vendôme is located halfway up Côte de la Montagne, and is one of the oldest restaurants in Québec City. It serves classic French dishes like Chateaubriand, *coq au*

vin and *duck à l'orange* in an intimate setting.

 L'Échaudé

$$$-$$$$

73 Rue Sault-au-Matelot

☎692-1299

L'Échaudé is an appealing restaurant with an Art Deco decor featuring a checkerboard floor and a mirrored wall. Relaxed atmosphere. Sophisticated cuisine prepared daily with fresh market ingredients.

Laurie Raphäel

$$$$

17 Rue Dalhousie

☎692-4555

Chef and co-owner Daniel Vézina is well known and one of the best chefs in Québec. When creating his mouth-watering dishes, Vézina draws inspiration from culinary traditions from all over the world, preparing giblets, sea food, meat, and other dishes. in innovative ways. It goes without saying, that the food at Laurie Raphaël is delicious! The restaurant is located in spacious quarters with a semi-circular exterior glass wall. The elegant decor includes creamy white curtains, sand and earth tones and a few decorative, wrought-iron objects.

Tour C: Grande Allée

Bügel

$

164 Rue Crémazie Ouest

☎523-7666

Craving a bagel? You'll find all different kinds at Bügel, a bagel bakery on pretty little Rue Crémazie. In a warm atmosphere enhanced by the aroma of a wood fire, you can snack on bagels with salami, cream cheese or veggie pâté and stock up on goodies to take back home.

Le Parlementaire

$-$$

Tue-Fri

at the corner of Ave. Honoré-Mercier and Grande Allée

☎643-6640

Visitors who might want to rub shoulders with members of Québec's National Assembly should have breakfast at Le Parlementaire. The menu features European and Québécois dishes. The restaurant is often packed, particularly at lunch, but the food is good. Open only for breakfast and lunch.

Cosmos Café

$$

575 Grande Allée Est

☎640-0606

The Cosmos Café promises a good time in a hip atmosphere, serving burgers, sandwiches and salads with a cosmopolitan flavour. Breakfasts here are quite good. A new Cosmos has opened in Sainte-Foy.

 Café Krieghoff

$$

1809 Avenue Cartier

☎521-3711

Named after the Dutch-born artist whose former home is located at the end of Avenue Cartier, Café Krieghoff occupies an old house on the same street. It serves tasty light meals (quiche, salads, etc.) and also has a good daily menu. The casual, convivial atmosphere is reminiscent of a Northern European café. During summer, its two outdoor seating areas are often packed.

Jaune Tomate

$$-$$$

120 Boulevard René-Lévesque Ouest

☎523-8777

This is a pretty yellow and red restaurant on Boulevard René-Lévesque near Avenue Cartier. It serves good Italian cuisine in a country-style decor. Come here on Saturday and Sunday mornings to sample the delicious and inventive brunches. The eggs benedic-

tine with hollandaise sauce flavoured with a zest of orange or teriyaki will make your weekend mornings a delight.

Café-Restaurant du Musée

$$-$$$

same hours as the museum

1 Avenue Wolfe-Montcalm

☎644-6780

Inside the Musée du Québec, you'll find the lovely Café-Restaurant du Musée. Run by a nearby hotel-management school, the restaurant's top priority is offering well-prepared food and outstanding service. Guests can gaze out at the Plains of Abraham and the river through large windows; in summer, the same view can be enjoyed from the patio.

Le Momento

$$-$$$

1144 Avenue Cartier

☎647-1313

Momento is decorated in modern fashion with warm colours and adorned with a fresco taken from a Boticelli painting. As you may have guessed, they serve refined, original Italian cuisine that is sure to offer some pleasant surprises. Prepared with basil, oregano, dried tomatoes, capers and olives, the sauces are rich, but not excessively, and they are quite savoury. The marinated salmon is perfectly prepared and will melt in your mouth.

Le Louis-Hébert

$$$

668 Grande Allée Est

☎525-7812

An elegant restaurant with a plush decor, Le Louis-Hébert serves French cuisine and delectable seafood. There is a plant-filled solarium at the back. Courteous, attentive service.

Voo Doo Grill

$$$

575 Grande Allée Est

☎647-2000

This old house was once the social club of the Union Nationale, the political party of the unforgettable Maurice Duplessis. Thus the name of the nightclub, Maurice, occupying the building's two upper floors (see p 344) where you can end the evening after a copious meal. Located on the second floor, the restaurant has kept some of the building's original architectural features and displays a most ingenious decor. A collection of African art work featuring masks, sculptures and dolls among other things, creates an entrancing effect. Unfortunately the music is not African, but *djumbé* players occasionally perform in the evening, adding a bit of rhythm to the already lively atmosphere. The Voo-Doo Grill menu has grilled food, of course—meat, fish and fowl as well as dishes cooked in a wok and served on spicy rice or satay with choice of sauce. All are tasty, creatively prepared and beautifully presented. The kitchen is open late.

Le Paris-Brest
$$$-$$$$
590 Grande Allée Est, corner De La Chevrotière
☎529-2243
At the Paris Brest, French cuisine is the specialty. Prepared with care, the food here will satisfy the most demanding gourmets. In summer, the restaurant opens its small terrace which looks onto Grande Allée.

Le Métropolitain
$$$-$$$$
1188 Avenue Cartier
☎649-1096
Le Métropolitain is *the* place for sushi in Québec City. These delicious Japanese morsels are a real feast, prepared before your very eyes by expert hands behind the glass counter. Other Oriental specialties, including fish and seafood dishes, are available here as well. The restaurant used to be located in the basement of another building and had a big sign at the entrance similar to those adorn-

ing certain métro stops in Paris. Its new, two-storey quarters are brighter.

L'Astral
$$$-$$$$
Hotel Loews Le Concorde
1225 Place Montcalm
☎647-2222
A rotating restaurant located atop one of the city's largest hotels, L'Astral serves excellent French food and provides a stunning view of the river, the Plains of Abraham, the Laurentian mountains and the city. It takes about one hour for the restaurant to make a complete rotation. This is a particularly good place for Sunday brunch.

Le Graffiti
$$$-$$$$
1191 Rue Cartier
☎529-4949
Le Graffiti's old-fashioned decor, is distinguished by exposed beams and brick walls, creating a warm ambience, where you can savour excellent French cuisine.

La Closerie
$$$$
966 Boulevard René-Lévesque Ouest
☎687-9975
La Closerie serves fine French cuisine. The chef, who has a well-established reputation, creates meals from fresh, prime quality ingredients. The exterior of this townhouse, located at a distance from tourist attractions, is no indication of what's inside—a gorgeous, intimate decor that guarantees pleasurable moments.

Tour D:
Saint-Jean-Baptiste

Chez Victor
$$
145 Rue St-Jean
☎529-7702
Located in a basement with a retro decor, Chez Victor serves salads and burgers—and not just any old burgers! The menu offers

several different kinds (including a delicious veggie burger), all big, juicy and served with fresh toppings. The homemade fries are sublime! Cordial service.

Thang Long
$$
869 Côte d'Abraham
☎524-0572
Thang Long, located on Côte d'Abraham, is tiny, but its menu will transport you to Vietnam, Thailand, China and even Japan! The decor of this neighbourhood restaurant is simple and unpretentious; the cuisine is truly up to the mark, and the service, very attentive. Try one of the meal-size soups— comfort food at bargain prices!

Le Hobbit
$$
700 Rue St-Jean
☎647-2677
Le Hobbit has occupied an old house in the Saint-Jean-Baptiste neighbourhood for years, and its stone walls, checkerboard floor and big windows overlooking bustling Rue St-Jean have not lost their appeal. There are two sections: the first is a café-style room where you can linger over an espresso and have a light meal; the second, a dining room with a delicious menu that changes daily and is never disappointing. Works by local artists are displayed here regularly.

La Piazzetta
$$
707 Rue St-Jean
☎529-7489
The layout of modern-looking Piazzetta is not really suitable for intimate dining. The restaurant is generally crowded but lively. An infinite variety of European-style pizzas is served. There are many franchises of this restaurant all over Québec; this one is the original, located in a house on Rue St-Jean.

Les Épices du Széchouan
$$-$$$
215 Rue St-Jean
☎648-6440
For exotic cuisine with succulent flavours and enticing aromas, try Les Épices du Széchouan, which occupies an old house in the Saint-Jean-Baptiste quarter. Its pretty decor is enhanced by a thousand and one Chinese trinkets. One table with a banquette is nestled beneath a corbelled wall. The house is a little ways from the street, so be careful not to miss it!

La Playa
$$$
780 Rue St-Jean
☎522-3989
La Playa, a small restaurant with a beautiful, cozy decor, offers Californian cuisine and dishes from other sunny spots. Top billing on the menu goes to pasta, which is served with flavourful sauces. The restaurant also has a *table d'hôte* featuring delicious meat and fish dishes. During summer, guests can dine on a charming little patio.

Il Teatro
$$$
972 Rue St-Jean
☎694-9996
Il Theatro, located inside the magnificent Théâtre Capitole, serves excellent Italian cuisine in a lovely dining room with a long bar and big, sparkling windows all around. The courteous service is on a par with the delicious food. During summer, guests can dine in a small outdoor seating area sheltered from the hustle and bustle of Place d'Youville.

Entertainment

Bars and Nightclubs

There is no cover charge at most bars and nightclubs in Québec City, except when they are hosting a special event or a show. During winter, most places require customers to check their coats, which costs a dollar or two.

Tour A: Vieux-Québec

Le Chanteuteuil
1001 Rue Saint-Jean
Le Chanteuteuil, at the foot of the hill on Rue D'Auteuil, is a pleasant bistro. People spend hours here chatting away, seated at bench-tables around bottles of wine or beers.

L'Emprise
Hôtel Clarendon
57 Rue Sainte-Anne
☎692-2480
The oldest hotel in the city (see p 335) houses the Emprise. This elegant bar is recommended to jazz fans.

Le Saint-Alexandre
1087 Rue Saint-Jean
☎694-0015
The Saint-Alexandre is an English-style pub that serves 175 types of beer, 19 of which are on tap. The decor is appealing and the ambiance pleasant.

Frankie's
48-C Côte de la Fabrique
At Frankie's nightclub, musicians of various musical persuassions are regularly invited to play. Neither of its two floors, which are decorated in lovely tones of red and black, features an actual dance floor, but patrons can "get down and boogie" pretty much wherever they want.

Tour B: Du Petit-Champlain au Vieux-Port

L'Inox
37 Quai Saint-André
☎692-2877
L'Inox is a big place at the Vieux-Port that brews good beer and serves other drinks. Its lager, *blanche* (white) and *rousse* (red) beers are all as delicious as can be. There is also a small beer-making museum on the premises.

Le Pape-Georges
8 Rue Cul-de-Sac
☎692-1320
Le Pape-Georges is a pleasant wine bar. Beneath the vaults of an old house in Petit Champlain, guests can sample a wide variety of wines while nibbling on snacks like cheese and *charcuteries*. The atmosphere is warm, especially when there's a *chansonnier* to heat things up.

Taverne Belley
249 Rue Saint-Paul
☎692-4595
Taverne Belley, in front of the Marché du Vieux-Port, has a few typical tavern features, such as a pool table and small, round, metal tables. The decor of its two rooms is both warm and fun, with colourful paintings hanging across exposed brick walls. A tiny fireplace warms the air nicely during winter.

Le Troubadour
29 Rue Saint-Pierre
☎694-9176
Le Troubadour, near Place Royale, is nestled beneath a vaulted ceiling. The place is made entirely of stone, which, combined with the long white candles stuck in bottles on the wooden tables, makes you feel as if you've stepped back in time to the Middle Ages. During winter, a crackling fire helps banish the cold.

Tour C: Grande Allée

Le Dagobert
600 Grande Allée Est
☎*522-0393*
Le Dagobert is a huge, popular nightclub located in an old stone house. There is always a crowd and no cover-charge.

Maurice
575 Grande Allée Est
☎*640-0711*
Maurice, is a big, chic, trendy nightclub that occupies the former residence of Maurice Duplessis, once premier of Québec. The place to go to see and be seen and dance to the latest hits. Chez Maurice hosts theme nights that also include a very popular disco night. On the top floor, a cigar room called **Charlotte** features a similar style decor. This is a room with sofas that serves its purpose well, later on you can get up and jive on a dance floor where live shows are sometimes presented. Sunday is Latino day. Cover charge.

Jules et Jim
1060 Avenue Cartier
☎*524-9570*
Little Jules et Jim has graced Avenue Cartier for several years now. It has a mellow ambiance, with booths and low tables reminiscent of Paris in the 1920s.

Le Turf
1175 avenue Cartier
On the lively Avenue Cartier, Le Turf (formerly known as the Merlin) is the place to be for the "beautiful" crowd (30 and over). In the basement, an English pub serves imported beer to the same type of clientele.

Tour D: Saint-Jean-Baptiste

Le Fou Bar
525 Rue Saint-Jean
☎*522-1987*
The Fou Bar is an appealing place with a regular clientele who come here to drink, chat with friends or check out the current works of art on display.

Gay and Lesbian Clubs

L'Amour Sorcier
789 Côte Sainte-Geneviève
☎*523-3395*
L'Amour Sorcier is a small bar in the Saint-Jean-Baptiste quarter. The atmosphere really heats up here sometimes. During summer, it has an attractive patio.

Le Drague
804 Rue St-Joachim
☎*649-7212*
This large gay nightclub has been completely renovated and today displays one of the most beautiful decors in Québec City. There is a spacious dance floor in the basement, and on Sunday evenings, outrageous drag-queen shows are presented.

Theatres and Performance Halls

The Québec City edition of French-language magazine *Voir* is distributed free of charge and provides information on the main events of the city.

Music

The **Orchestre Symphonique de Québec**, Canada's oldest symphony orchestra, performs regularly at the Grand Théâtre de Québec *(269 Boulevard René-Lévesque Est, ☎643-8131)*, where you can also catch the **Opéra de Québec**.

Theatres

Grand Théâtre de Québec
269 Boulevard René-Lévesque Est
☎*643-8131*
This theatre has two halls.

Le Palais Montcalm
995 Place d'Youville
☎*670-9011* (tickets)

Théâtre de la Bordée
315 rue St-Joseph Est
☎*694-9631*

Le Capitole de Québec
972 Rue Saint-Jean
☎*694-4444*

Le Périscope
2 Rue Crémazie Est
☎*529-2183*

Théâtre du Trident
at the Grand Théâtre de Québec
269 Boulevard René-Lévesque Est
☎*643-8131*

Cinema

Place Charest
500 Rue Dupont
☎*529-9745*

Festivals and Cultural Events

Carnaval de Québec
(☎626-3716 or 888-737-3789), Québec City's winter carnival, takes place annually during the first two weeks of February. It is an opportunity for visitors and residents of Québec City to celebrate the beauty of winter. It is also a good way to add a little life to a cold winter that often seems interminable. Various activities are organized. Some of the most popular include nighttime parades, canoe races over the partially frozen St. Lawrence River and the international ice and snow sculpture contests. This can be a bitterly cold period of the year, so dressing very warmly is essential.

The **Festival d'Été de Québec** *(mid-Jul; ☎1-888-992-5200)* is generally held for 10 days in early July when music, songs, dancing and other kinds of entertainment from all over the world liven up Québec City. The festival has everything it takes to be the city's most important cultural event. The outdoor shows are particularly popular. For most indoor shows, you must buy tickets. However, those presented outdoors are free.

In Parc de la Francophonie, **Plein Art Québec** (☎694-0260) displays, from late July to early August, all kinds of arts and crafts for sale.

People from the Québec City region have been enjoying themselves at **Expo-Québec** (*ExpoCité*, ☎691-7110) every August for 50 years now. This huge fair, complete with an amusement park, is held in front of the Colisée for about 10 days at the end of the month.

Shopping

Bookstores

La Maison Anglaise
Place de la Cité, Sainte-Foy
☎654-9523
The best selection of English books in Québec City.

CDs and Cassettes

Sillons Le Disquaire
1149 Avenue Cartier
☎524-8352

Archambault Musique
1095 Rue Saint-Jean
Vieux-Québec
☎694-2088

Craft Shops and Artisans' Studios

Atelier La Pomme
47 Rue Sous-le-Fort
☎692-2875
Leather goods.

Le Sachem
17 Rue Desjardins
☎692-3056
Aboriginal crafts.

Galerie-Boutique Métiers d'Art
29 Rue Notre-Dame
Place Royale
☎694-0267
Québec-made crafts.

Cinq Nations
25½ Rue du Petit-Champlain
and
20 Rue Cul-de-Sac
☎692-5476
Aboriginal crafts.

Les Trois Colombes
46 Rue Saint-Louis
☎694-1114
Handcrafted items and quality clothing.

L'Oiseau du Paradis
80 Rue du Petit-Champlain
☎692-2679
Paper and paper objects.

Pot-en-Ciel
27 Rue du Petit-Champlain
☎692-1743
Ceramics.

Verrerie La Mailloche
58 Rue Sous-le-Fort
Petit-Champlain
☎694-0445
Shop-made glass objects.

Ladieswear

La Cache
1150 Rue Saint-Jean
☎692-0398

Les Vêteries
33½ Rue du Petit-Champlain
☎694-1215

Simons
20 Côte de la Fabrique
☎692-3630

Menswear

Louis Laflamme
1192 Rue Saint-Jean
☎692-3774

Simons
20 Côte de la Fabrique
☎692-3630

Jewellery and Decorative Arts

Lazuli
774 Rue Saint-Jean
☎525-6528

Origines
54 Côte de la Fabrique
☎694-9257

Pierres Vives
23½ Rue du Petit-Champlain
☎692-5566

Louis Perrier Joaillier
48 Rue du Petit-Champlain
☎692-4633

Outdoor Clothing and Equipment

Azimut
1194 Avenue Cartier
☎648-9500
Clothing and accessories.

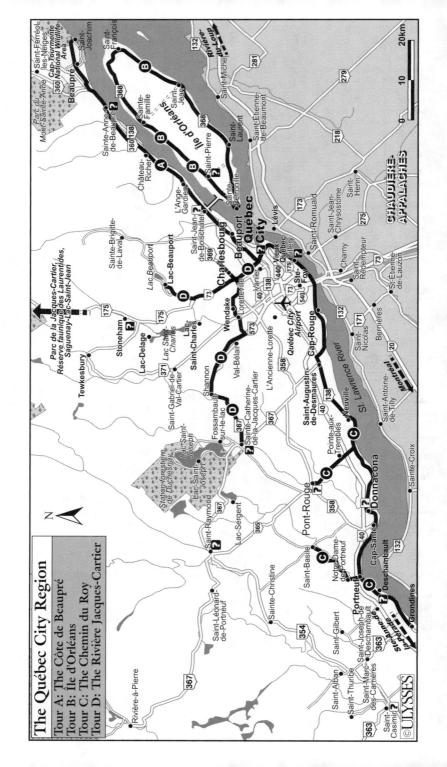

The Québec City Region

Tour A: The Côte de Beaupré
Tour B: Île d'Orléans
Tour C: The Chemin du Roy
Tour D: The Rivière Jacques-Cartier

© ULYSSES

The Québec City Region

U nder the French

Regime, Québec City was the main urban centre of New France and the seat of the colonial administration.

To supply produce to the city and its institutions, farms were introduced to the area in the middle of the 17th century. The farming region on the periphery of the city was the first populated rural zone in the St. Lawrence Valley. Traces of the first seigneuries granted to settlers in New France are still visible in this historically rich rural area. The farmhouses are the oldest of New France, and the descendants of their first residents are now scattered across the American continent.

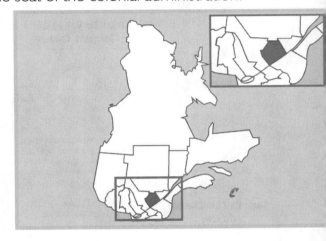

Finding Your Way Around

Four tours are suggested for the area surrounding Québec City: **Tour A: Côte de Beaupré ★★**, **Tour B: Île d'Orléans ★★**, **Tour C: Chemin du Roy ★★** and **Tour D: Vallée de la Jacques-Cartier ★**. With the exception of the Jacques-Cartier tour, which is longer and extends further into the wilderness, these excursions can all be done as day trips from Québec City.

Tour A: Côte de Beaupré

By Car

From Québec City, take the Autoroute Dufferin-Montmorency (Aut. 440) towards Beauport (Exit 24), then take Rue d'Estimauville. Turn right on Chemin Royal (Rte. 360), which becomes Avenue Royale, will lead you throughout the tour.

By Bus

Sainte-Anne-de-Beaupré *(9687 boul. Ste-Anne, Irving station, ☎418-827-5169)* is accessible by bus *(320 Rue Abraham-Martin, ☎418-525-3000)*.

If you do not have a car at your disposal, the only way to reach the Parc du Mont-Sainte-Anne, the Grand Canyon des Chutes Sainte-Anne and the Cap-Tourmente National Wildlife Area is by bus from Québec City to Sainte-Anne-de-Beaupré, and then taxi for the remaining 6km in each case.

Public Transportation

Bus no. 53 leaves from Place Jacques-Cartier *($2.25; Rue du Roi, at the corner of Rue de la Couronne)* and drops visitors near the Chute Montmorency.

Names of New Merged Cities

**Deschambault–
Grondines**
Merger of Deschambault
and Grondines.

Portneuf
Merger of Portneuf and
Notre-Dame-de-Portneuf.

Tour B: Île d'Orléans

By Car

From Québec, take Autoroute Dufferin-Montmorency (Rte. 440) to the Pont de l'Île. Cross the river and turn right on Rte. 368, also called Chemin Royal, which circles the island.

By Bus

There is no public transportation or bus service on or to Île d'Orléans. Some private companies organize tours of the island; to explore the island on your own and at your own pace, you will need a car or bicycle.

Tour C: The Chemin du Roy

By Car

From Québec City, head west on Grande-Allée, which eventually becomes Chemin Saint-Louis from Bagatelle to Sillery. After following Chemin St-Louis to Cap-Rouge, take Rte. 138, which you will follow for the rest of the tour. It is also possible to follow this tour in the opposite direction, in other words, starting in Montréal (Exit 236 off Rte. 40), or to add a visit to the village of La Pérade included in the Mauricie tour (see p 286).

Bus Station

Sainte-Foy
3001 Chemin des Quatre-Bourgeois
☎(418) 650-0087

By Train

Sainte-Foy
3255 Chemin de la Gare (corner Chemin St-Louis)
☎800-835-3037

Tour D: Vallée de la Jacques-Cartier

By Car

From Québec City, take Côte d'Abraham, turn right on Rue de la Couronne, then follow Autoroute Laurentienne (Aut. 73) to Exit 150. Turn right on 80e Rue Ouest, which leads to the heart of the Trait-Carré in Charlesbourg. Rte. 175 leads to Parc de la Jacques Cartier.

Public Transportation

To reach Charlesbourg from Québec City, take bus no. 801 (*métrobus*), whose stops are clearly indicated (for example, at Place d'Youville). From the Charlesbourg terminus, take bus no. 72 to Wendake. The historic village of Onhoüa Chetek8e is north of the reserve and accessible by taxi.

Practical Information

Area code: **418**

Tourist Information

Regional Office

Centre d'Information de l'Office du Tourisme et des Congrès de Québec
835 Avenue Wilfrid-Laurier,
G1R 2L3, Québec
☎649-2608
⇌522-0830
www.quebecregion.com

Tour A: Côté de Beaupré

Sainte-Anne-de-Beaupré
5490 Boulevard Ste-Anne
☎822-0122

Tour B: Île d'Orléans

Saint-Pierre
490 Côte du Pont
☎828-9411

Tour C: Chemin du Roy

Deschambault
12 Rue des Pins
☎286-3002

Tour D: Vallée de la Jacques-Cartier

Charlesbourg
7960 Boulevard Henri-Bourassa
☎624-7720

Exploring

Tour A: The Côte de Beaupré

Duration of tour: one day

This long, narrow strip of land, nestled between the St. Lawrence and the undeveloped wilderness of the Laurentian massif, is the ancestral home of many families whose roots go back to the beginning of the colony. It illustrates how the spread of the population was limited to the riverside in many regions of Québec and recalls the fragility of development in the era of New France. From Beauport to Saint-Joachim, the colony's first road, the Chemin du Roy, or king's road, built under orders from Monseigneur de Laval during the 17th century, follows the Beaupré shore. A typical style characterized by a raised main floor covered in stucco, long balconies with intricately carved wooden balusters and lace-curtained windows is repeated in houses along this road. Since about 1960, however, the suburbs of Québec City have gradually taken over the shore, marring the simple beauty of the area. Nevertheless, the Chemin du Roy is still an extremely pleasant route; whether rounding a cape, making one last jaunt in the Laurentians, or exploring the plains of the St. Lawrence, this route offers magnificent views of the mountains, fields, the river and Île d'Orléans.

★ Beauport (pop. 72,250)

Three types of urban development have shaped Beauport over the course of its history. Originally an agricultural settlement, in the 19th century, it became an important industrial town, finally evolving into one of the main suburbs of Québec City in the 1960s. In 1634, the Beauport seigneury, from which the present city grew, was granted to Robert Giffard, a doctor and surgeon from the Perche region of France. In the next few years, he enthusiastically set about building a manor house, a mill, and a small village, establishing one of the largest seigneuries in New France. Unfortunately, wars and fires have claimed several of these buildings, notably the huge fortified manor

house built in 1642, containing a chapel and a prison, which burned down in 1879.

The **Chemin Royal** ★ *(Route 360 Est)* corresponds to the original 17th-century Chemin du Roy, and follows both the upper and lower sections of the Côte de Beaupré. It traverses the former Beauport seigneury diagonally, which explains the angled placement of the buildings along the road. Many of these houses are ancestral homes, such as the **Maison Marcoux** constructed in the 18th century *(588 Avenue Royale)*.

Turn right on Rue du Couvent to find parking.

The **Bourg du Fargy** ★ district of Beauport was set up as a fortified village in the middle of the 17th century. In 1669, Seigneur Giffard drew up an ambitious plan for the town, which even included a market square. The **Maison Bellanger-Girardin** *(600 Avenue Royale, ☎666-2199)*, built in 1727 by the Marcoux family on land granted to Nicolas Bellanger of Normandy, is one of the last remaining vestiges of the original town. The house, designed for the harsh Canadian climate, has just a few small windows and thick doors. Since 1984, the building has housed a tourist information office, and the Centre d'Art et d'Histoire de Beauport. A group of Edwardian houses on Rue du Couvent (circa 1910) offers an interesting contrast to the French Regime–era style.

The large white house known as **Manoir Montmorency** *(2490 Avenue Royale, ☎663-3330)* was built in 1780 for British governor Sir John Haldimand. At the end of the 18th century, the house became famous as the residence of the Duke of Kent, son of George III and father of Queen Victoria. The manor, which was once a hotel, was severely damaged by fire in 1993. It has been restored according to the original plans and now hosts an information centre, a few shops and a restaurant (see p 367), that offers an exceptional view of the Montmorency Falls, the St. Lawrence and Île d'Orléans. The small Sainte-Marie chapel on the property and the gardens are open to the public.

The Manoir Montmorency is nestled in the **Parc de la Chute-Montmorency** ★★ *(free admission, parking $7.50, cablecar $5.50 one-way $7.50 return; accessible all year, check parking opening hours; ☎663-3330).* The Rivière Montmorency, which has its source in the Laurentians, flows along peacefully until it reaches a sudden 83m drop, at which point it tumbles into a void, creating one of the most impressive natural phenomena in Québec. One and a half times the height of Niagara Falls, the Montmorency Falls flow at a rate that can reach 125,000 litres-per-second during the spring thaw. Samuel de Champlain, the founder of Québec City, was impressed by the falls and named them after the viceroy of New France,

Manoir Montmorency

Charles, Duc de Montmorency. During the 19th century, the falls became a fashionable leisure area for the well-to-do of the region, who would arrive in horse-drawn carriages or sleighs.

A park has been created to preserve this magnificent spectacle for the public and tours of the falls are available. From the manor follow the beautiful cliff walk, location of the Baronne lookout. You'll soon reach two bridges, the Pont Au-dessus de la Chute and the Pont Au-dessus de la Faille, which pass the falls and the fault respectively, with spectacular views. Once in the park you'll find picnic tables and a playground. The bottom of the falls is reached by the 487-step panoramic staircase or the trail. The cable-car provides a relaxing and picturesque means of reaching the top. In winter, steam freezes into a cone of ice, called a sugar-loaf, making a good ice-wall that anyone feeling adventurous can climb.

The lower part of the park is also accessible by car, though a complicated detour is required: continue along Avenue Royale, turn right on Côte de l'Église, then right again on Aut. 40. The parking lot is on the right. To get back to Avenue Royale, take Boulevard Sainte-Anne west, Côte Saint-Grégoire and finally Boulevard des Chutes to the right.

Take Chemin Royal heading east.

The **Maison Laurent-dit-Lortie** ★ *(3200 Chemin Royal)* was originally constructed at the end of the 17th century. At the beginning of the following century, it was acquired by Jean Laurent-dit-Lortie. His descendants still live in the house. The imposing size of the building is the result of successive additions, while the steep slope of the roof is indicative of the age of

the original structure. The finely carved wood of the balcony, typical of the region, was probably installed around 1880.

Saint-Jean-de-Boischatel (pop. 3,660)

The municipality of Saint-Jean-de-Boischatel is located on former estate lands that were administered by the government and later granted to Jean Le Barbier in 1654. This land was set up as a fief in 1677 by Charles Aubert de la Chesnaye, who had recently acquired it. Dubbed "The Fief of Charleville," the district maintained its agricultural vocation until the beginning of the 1970s, when suburban development overtook the area.

The **Manoir de Charleville** ★ *(5580 Avenue Royale)* is one of the oldest standing buildings in Canada. It was built in 1670 for the farmer hired by the capital administration. The building's low profile, high gabled roof and small windows are typical of very old buildings in Québec. Unfortunately, the neighbouring property has recently been built up, partially obscuring this venerable site. The ancestor of the Trudel families of Québec moved into the building at the end of the 17th century. After 150 years, the house passed into the hands of the Huot family, who lived there until 1964.

L'Ange-Gardien (pop. 2,950)

Agriculture is still an important industry in Ange-Gardien, one of the oldest parishes on the Côte de Beaupré. The village boasts a number of century-old houses and has beautiful views of Île d'Orléans.

The **Chapelles de Procession** ★ built on either side of the village church *(6357 Avenue Royale)*, are

the oldest such chapels still standing in Québec, having been built during the French Regime (around 1750). These small, charming buildings served as altars of repose during the Corpus Christi Processions.

On small Rue de la Mairie stands the **Maison Laberge** *(24 Rue de la Mairie)*, the ancestral home of the Laberge family. Built in 1674, it has been enlarged many times since then. Twelve generations of this family, whose descendants now live all over Québec, inhabited this house until 1970.

★
Château-Richer (pop. 3,800)

Under the French Regime, Château-Richer was the nerve centre of the immense Beaupré seigneury, which extended from Saint-Jean-de-Boischatel to Baie-Saint-Paul in the Charlevoix region. Conceded in 1636 by the Compagnie des Cents Associés, this seigneury was granted to the Séminaire de Québec 30 years later, and stayed in their hands until the abolition of seigneurial tenure in 1854. In the 17th century, the directors of the seminary constructed Château Richer, a veritable castle endowed with a tower used as a prison. The building, which was bombarded during the British conquest, was practically in ruins when it was finally totally demolished around 1860.

The village's location is charming and picturesque, highlighted by the striking placement of the church on a promontory. Throughout the village, small wooden signs have been posted in front of historic buildings indicating any distinctive architectural features and when they were built.

The **Centre d'Interprétation de la Côte de Beaupré** ★ *($3; year-round; 7976 Avenue Royale, ☎824-3677)* is located in the Petit-Pré mill, which is visible from the curve in the road. An information centre, it has an interesting exhibition on the history and geography of the Côte de Beaupré. A model depicting the development of the region from pre-colonial times to the present day highlights the exhibition. The mill itself was rebuilt right after the British conquest, following a similar design used for the original mill built by the directors of the Séminaire de Québec in 1695.

Take Boulevard Sainte-Anne (Rte. 138), which runs parallel to the river, to Chemin Royal.

For those who are curious about bees and honey, here's an interesting little museum. The **Musée de l'Abeille** *(free admission; "bee safari" $3; late Jun to late Oct every day 9am to 6pm, late Oct to late Jun 9am to 5pm; 8862 Boulevard Ste-Anne, ☎824-4411)* offers a brief look into the lives of these tireless workers. Visitors can stroll through at their leisure or receive an introduction to the art of beekeeping by participating in a "bee safari." A beekeeper explains the steps involved in making honey and even mead (honey wine). There's also a pastry shop and a gift shop.

Continue on Chemin Royal

★
Sainte-Anne-de-Beaupré (pop. 3,300)

This long, narrow village is one of the largest pilgrimage sites in North America. In 1658, the first Catholic church on the site was dedicated to Saint Anne after sailors from Brittany, who had prayed to the Virgin Mary's mother, were saved from drowning during a storm on the

St. Lawrence. Soon, a great number of pilgrims began to visit the church. The second church, built in 1676, was replaced in 1872 by a huge temple, which was destroyed by fire in 1922. Finally work began on the present basilica, which stands at the centre of a virtual complex of chapels, monasteries and facilities as varied as they are unusual. They include the **Bureau des Bénédictions**, blessings office, and the Cyclorama. Each year, Sainte-Anne-de-Beaupré welcomes more than a million pilgrims, who stay in the hotels and visit the countless gift shops, many of which purvey items of a rather kitschy nature, along Avenue Royale.

To learn more about Québec folklore go to the **Atelier Paré** *(free admission; animated presentation $1; mid-May to mid-Oct, every day 9am to 5:30pm; mid-Oct to mid-May, Wed-Fri 1pm to 4pm, Sat and Sun 10am to 4pm; 9269 Avenue Royale, ☎827-3992)*. All the works presented at this wood-sculpting museum are inspired by the fascinating world of local legends.

The **Basilique Sainte-Anne-de-Beaupré** ★★★ *(every day 8:30am to 4:30pm; 10018 Avenue Royale, ☎827-3781)*, towering over the small, metal-roofed wooden houses that line the winding road, is surprising not only for its impressive size, but also for the feverish activity it inspires all summer long. The church's granite exterior, which takes on a different colour depending on the ambient light, was designed in the French Romanesque Revival style by Parisian architect Maxime Roisin, who was assisted by Quebecer Louis Napoléon Audet. Its spires rise 91m into the sky above the coast, while the nave is 129m long, and the transepts are over 60m wide. The wooden statue gilded with copper sitting atop the church's facade

was taken from the 1872 church. When the fire destroyed the former basilica, the statue stayed in place while everything collapsed around it.

The basilica's interior is divided into five naves supported by heavy columns with highly sculpted capitals. The vault of the main nave is adorned with sparkling mosaics designed by French artists Jean Gaudin and Auguste Labouret, recounting the life of Saint Anne. Labouret also created the magnificent stained glass, found all along the perimeter of the basilica. The left transept contains an extraordinary statue of Saint Anne cradling Mary in her right arm. Her tiara reminds the visitor that she is the patron saint of Québec. In a beautiful reliquary in the background, visitors can admire the Great Relic, part of Saint Anne's forearm sent over from the San Paolo Fuori le Mura in Rome. Finally, follow the ambulatory around the choir to see the 10 radiant chapels built in the 1930s, whose polychromatic architecture is Art Deco inspired.

Material retrieved after the demolition of the original church in 1676 was used to build the **Chapelle Commémorative** ★ *(free admission; May to mid-Sep, every day 8am to 4:30pm; alongside Avenue Royale, ☎827-3781)* in 1878. The steeple (1696) was designed by Claude Bailiff, an architect whose numerous other projects in 17th-century New France have all but disappeared, victims of wars and fires. Inside, the high altar comes from the original church built during the French Regime. It is the work of Jacques Leblond-dit-Latour (circa 1700). The chapel is adorned with 18th century paintings. The water from the Fontaine de Sainte-Anne, at the foot of the chapel, is said to have healing properties.

La Scala Santa ★ *(free admission; May to mid-Sep, every day 8am to 4:30pm; to the right of the Chapelle du Souvenir, ☎827-3781)*, a strange yellow and white wooden building (1891), houses a staircase, which pilgrims climb on their knees while reciting prayers. It is a replica of the Scala Santa, the sacred staircase conserved in Rome at San Giovanni in Laterano, which Christ climbed to get to the court of Pontius Pilate. An image of the Holy Land is inlaid in each riser.

The **Cyclorama de Jérusalem** ★ ★ *($6; late Apr to late Oct every day 9am to 6pm, Jul and Aug every day 9am to 8pm, 8 Rue Régina, near the parking lot, ☎827-3101)*, a circular building with oriental features, houses a 360° panorama of Jerusalem on the day of the crucifixion. This immense *trompe l'œuil* painting, measuring 14m by 100m, was created in Chicago around 1880 by French artist Paul Philippoteaux and his assistants. A specialist in panoramas, Philippoteaux produced a work of remarkable realism. It was first exhibited in Montréal before being moved to Sainte-Anne-de-Beaupré at the very end of the 19th century. Very few panoramas and cycloramas, so popular a century ago, have survived to the present day.

The **Musée de Sainte Anne** ★ *($2; Easter to mid-Oct, every day 10am to 5pm; 9803 Boulevard Ste-Anne, ☎827-6873)* is dedicated to sacred art honouring the mother of the Virgin Mary. These interestingly diverse pieces were acquired over many years from the basilica but have only recently been put on display for the public. Sculptures, paintings, mosaics, stained-glass windows and goldworks are dedicated to

the cult of Saint Anne, as well as written works expressing prayers or thanks for favours obtained. The history of pilgrimages to Sainte-Anne-de-Beaupré is also explained. The exhibition is attractively presented and spread over two floors.

Follow Avenue Royale to Saint-Joachim (Cap Tourmente). Cross Rte. 138, and go through the municipality of Beaupré. Turn right on Rue de l'Église in Saint-Joachim.

Other recommended destinations in the region include **Mont-Sainte-Anne** (see p 362) and the charming village of Saint-Ferréol-les-Neiges on Rte. 360 E., which branches off Avenue Royale at Beaupré.

Saint-Ferréol-les-Neiges (pop. 2,100)

At the east end of Saint-Ferréol-les-Neiges is **Les Sept Chutes** hydroelectric complex *($7; mid-May to late Jun every day 10am to 5pm; late Jun to early Sep every day 9am to 6pm; Sep to mid-Oct, every day 10am to 5pm; 4520 Avenue Royale, ☎826-3139 or 877-724-8837)*, which was active from 1916 to 1984 and has since been transformed into an information centre. You can learn about the stages of hydroelectric production and about the lives of people who worked in such powerstations. There are also paths along the Sainte-Anne-du-Nord river to the impressive, 130m-high falls.

Grand Canyon des Chutes Sainte-Anne, see p 362.

Saint-Joachim (pop. 1,500)

The village of Saint-Joachim was originally located on the banks of the river, near the farm belonging to the Séminaire du Québec. The town was burned to the

ground during the British conquest (1759). In the years that followed, it was rebuilt on its present site, safe from the line of cannon fire. Because of its isolation at the foot of Mont-Sainte-Anne, it has managed to keep some of its rural charm.

The first church in Saint Joachim, the **Église Saint-Joachim** ★ ★ *(free admission; mid-May to mid-Oct, every day 9am to 5pm; 165 Rue de l'Église, ☎827-4020)* (17th century) was burned by British troops in 1759. The present church, rebuilt inland along with the rest of the village, was completed in 1779. Unfortunately, the facade was redone in 1895, and has no aesthetic connection with the rest of the building. In fact, from the outside, this church is hardly worth nothing; the interior, however, remains a veritable masterpiece of religious art in Québec.

Once inside the church, your eye will be drawn to the chancel and its triumphal altarpiece composed of a high altar, older than the rest of the decor (1785) and above which hangs a painting by the Abbé Aide-Créquy entitled *Saint-Joachim et la Vierge* (Saint Joachim and the Virgin) (1779).

Beyond the church, turn left on Chemin du Cap.

★ ★
Cap-Tourmente

The pastoral and fertile land of Cap-Tourmente is the eastern-most section of the St. Lawrence plain, before the mountains of the Laurentian Massif reach the shores of the St. Lawrence. The colonization of this area at the beginning of the 17th century represented one of the first attempts to populate New France. Samuel de Champlain, the founder of Québec City, established a farm here in 1626, the ruins of which were recently unearthed. Cap-Tourmente was acquired by Monseigneur François de Laval in 1662, and was cultivated by the Société des Sieurs de Caen. Soon the land passed into the hands of the Séminaire de Québec, which eventually built a retreat for priests, a school, a summer camp and, most importantly, a huge farm that met the institution's dietary needs and brought in a substantial income. Following the British conquest, the seminary moved the seat of its Beaupré seigneury to Cap-Tourmente, leaving behind the ruins of the Château Richer. The **Château Bellevue** ★ was built between 1777 and 1781. This superb building is endowed with a neoclassical cut-stone portal. The property's Saint-Louis-de-Gonzague Chapel (1780) is well hidden in the trees.

Cap-Tourmente National Wildlife Area ★★ see p 362.

To return to Québec City, continue along the loop formed by the Cap-Tourmente road leading to Saint-Joachim, continue towards Beaupré before taking Rte. 138 W. It is possible to combine the Côte de Beaupré tour with the visit to Charlevoix described on p 466. To do this head to Rte. 138 E. via the steep, winding road northeast of the village of Saint-Joachim. Turn right towards Baie-St-Paul.

Tour B: Île d'Orléans

Duration of tour: one day

Located in the middle of the St. Lawrence River, downstream from Québec City, this 32km-by-5km island is famous for its old-world charm. Of all regions of Québec, the island

Typical Canadian house

is the most evocative of life in New France. When Jacques Cartier arrived in 1535, the island was covered in wild vines, which inspired its first name: Île Bacchus. However, it was soon renamed in homage to the Duc d'Orléans. With the exception of Sainte-Pétronille, the parishes on the island were established in the 17th century. The colonization of the entire island followed soon after. In 1970, the government of Québec designated Île d'Orléans a historic district. The move was made in part to slow down the development that threatened to turn the island into yet another suburb of Québec City, and also as part of a widespread movement among Quebecers to protect the roots of their French ancestry by preserving old churches and houses. Since 1936, the island has been linked to the mainland by a suspension bridge, the Pont de l'Île.

To get to the island from Québec City take the Autoroute Dufferin-Montmorency (Aut. 440) to the Pont de l'Île. Cross the river and turn right on Rte. 368, also called Chemin Royal, which circles the island.

★★
Sainte-Pétronille
(pop. 1,170)

Paradoxically, Saint-Pétronille was the site of the first French

settlement on Île d'Orléans and is also its most recent parish. In 1648, François de Chavigny de Berchereau and his wife Éléonore de Grandmaison established a farm and a Huron mission here. However, constant Iroquois attacks forced the colonists to move further east, to a spot facing Sainte-Anne-de-Beaupré. It was not until the middle of the 19th century that Sainte-Pétronille was consolidated as a village, as its beautiful location began attracting numerous summer visitors. Anglophone merchants from Québec City built beautiful second homes here, many of which are still line the road.

Turn right on Rue Horatio-Walker, which leads to the river banks and to a promenade.

The **Maison Horatio-Walker** ★ *(11 and 13 Rue Horatio-Walker)*. The red brick building and the stucco house beside it were, respectively, the workshop and residence of painter Horatio Walker from 1904 to 1938. The British-born artist liked the French culture and the meditative calm of Île d'Orléans. His workshop, designed by Harry Staveley, is a good example of English Arts and Crafts architecture.

The Porteous family, of English origin, settled in Québec City at the end of the 18th century. In 1900, they had the **Domaine Porteous ★** (*253 Chemin Royal*) built. This vast country house surrounded by superb gardens, was christened "La Groisardière." Designed by Toronto architects Darling and Pearson, the house revived certain aspects of traditional Québec architecture. The most notable of these are the Louis XV–inspired woodwork, and the general proportions used in the design of the house, which are similar to the Manoir Mauvide-Genest in Saint-Jean. Inside, there are many remounted paintings by William Brymner and Maurice Cullen depicting countryside scenes on Île d'Orléans. The building also incorporates art nouveau features. The property, which today belongs to the Foyer de Charité Notre-Dame-d'Orléans, a seniors' residence, was expanded between 1961 and 1964 when a new wing and a chapel were added.

Saint-Laurent (pop. 1,610)

Until 1950, Saint-Laurent's main industry was the manufacturing of *chaloupes*, boats and sailboats that were popular in the United States and Europe. Though production of these boats has ceased, some traces of the industry, such as abandoned boatyards, can still be seen off the road, near the banks of the river. The village was founded in 1679 and still has some older buildings, such as the beautiful **Maison Gendreau** built in 1720 (*2387 Chemin Royal, west of the village*) and the **Moulin Gosselin**, which now houses a restaurant (*758 Chemin Royal, east of the village*).

At the little **Forge à Pique-Assaut** (*Jun to Oct, everyday 9am to 5pm, Nov to May Mon-Fri 9am to noon and 1:30pm to 5pm; 2200 Chemin Royal, ☎828-9300*),

you can learn about the blacksmith trade by watching artisans at work in front of a large forge or by taking a guided tour. There's a shop on the second floor (see p 370).

★★ Saint-Jean (pop. 900)

In the mid-19th century, Saint-Jean was the preferred homebase of nautical pilots who made a living guiding ships through the difficult currents and rocks of the St. Lawrence. Some of their neoclassical or Second Empire houses remain along Chemin Royal and provide evidence of the privileged place held by these seamen, who were indispensable to the success of commercial navigation.

The most impressive remaining manor from the French Regime is in Saint-Jean. The **Manoir Mauvide-Genest ★★** (*$5; 1451 Chemin Royal, ☎829-2630*) was built in 1734 for Jean Mauvide, the Royal Doctor, and his wife, Marie-Anne Genest. This beautiful stone building has a rendering coat of white roughcast, in the traditional Norman architectural style. The property officially became a seigneurial manor in the middle of the 18th century, when Mauvide, who had become rich doing business in the Caribbean, bought the southern half of the Île d'Orléans seigneury.

In 1926, Camille Pouliot, descendant of the Genest family, bought the manor house. He then restored it, adding a summer kitchen and a chapel. He later transformed the house into a museum, displaying furniture and objects from traditional daily life. Pouliot was one of the first people to be actively interested in Québec's heritage. The manor still has a museum on the second floor devoted to antique furniture and everyday objects, while the main

floor is taken up by a restaurant. The manor rencently underwent intense historical restoration.

★ Saint-François (pop. 485)

Saint-François, the smallest village on Île d'Orléans, retains many heritage buildings. Some, however, are far from the Chemin Royal and are therefore difficult to see from Rte. 368. The surrounding countryside is charming and offers several pleasant panoramic views of the river, Charlevoix and the coast. The famous wild vine that gave the island its first name, Île Bacchus, can also be found in Saint-François.

On the roadside as you leave the village is an **observation tower ★★**, which offers excellent views to the north and east. Visible are the Îles Madame et au Ruau, which mark the meeting point of the fresh water of the St. Lawrence and the salt water of the gulf. Mont Sainte-Anne's ski slopes, Charlevoix on the north shore and the Côte-du-Sud seigneuries on the south shore can also be seen in the distance.

★ Sainte-Famille (pop. 1,025)

The oldest parish on Île d'Orléans was founded by Monseigneur de Laval in 1666 in order to establish a settlement across the river from Sainte-Anne-de-Beaupré for colonists who had previously settled around Sainte-Pétronille. Sainte-Famille has retained many buildings from the French Regime. Among them is the town's famous church, one of the greatest accomplishments of religious architecture in New France, and the oldest two-towered church in Québec.

The beautiful **Église Sainte-Famille** ★★ *(3915 Chemin Royal)* was built between 1743 and 1747, to replace the original church built in 1669. Inspired by the Église des Jésuites in Québec City, which has since been destroyed, Father Dufrost de la Jemmerais ordered the construction of two towers with imperial roofs. This explains the single steeple sitting atop the gable. Other unusual elements, such as five alcoves and a sun dial by the entrance (since destroyed), make the building even more original. In the 19th century, new statues were installed in the alcoves, and the imperial roofs gave way to two new steeples, bringing the total number of steeples to three.

Though modified several times, the interior decor retains many interesting elements. Sainte-Famille was a wealthy parish in the 18th century, thus allowing the decoration of the church to begin as soon as the frame of the building was finished. In 1748, Gabriel Gosselin installed the first pulpit, and in 1749 Pierre-Noël Levasseur completed construction of the present tabernacle

of the high altar. Louis-Basile David, inspired by the Quévillon school, designed the beautiful coffered vault in 1812. Many paintings adorn the church, among them are *La Sainte Famille* (The Holy Family) painted by Frère Luc during his stay in Canada in 1670, the *Dévotion au Sacré Coeur de Jésus* (Devotion to the Sacred Heart of Jesus, 1766) and *Le Christ en Croix* (Christ on the Cross) by François Baillargé (circa 1802). The church grounds offer a beautiful view of the coast.

Most of the French Regime farm homes on Île D'Orléans were built a distance from the road. Today, they are distinguished estates whose secluded character is jealously guarded by their owners, which means a visit is highly unlikely.

Église Sainte-Famille

Fortunately, thanks to a citizen's organization, **Maison Drouin** ★★ *($2; late Jun to early Sep, every day 10am to 6pm; early Sep to Oct Sat and Sun 10am to 6pm; ☎829-0330)* opens every summer, to the delight of curious visitors. Originally built in 1675 and later expanded in 1725, it is one of the oldest homes on the island and even in all of Québec. Located on a curve of Chemin Royal, it was built using large stones and wood beams. The guides, who are dressed in period costume, talk about the history of the home as they re-enact the everyday life of its former residents.

Situated far from its motherland across the Atlantic, this rustic house was not designed with the harsh climate in mind. The low, stone blocks are buried in snow in the wintertime. The entrances are small and the gables are covered with cedar shingles to protect the masonry. The three rooms on the main floor and the third floor exude the bygone era of the first settlers. The house is also full of antiques, furniture and tools, which clearly depict the life of the pioneers. A magnificent place to visit!

Saint-Pierre (pop. 2,075)

The most developed parish on Île d'Orléans had already lost some of its charm before the island was declared a historic site. Saint-Pierre is particularly important to the Quebecers, as the home for many years of the renowned poet and singer Félix Leclerc (1914-1988). The singer and songwriter, who penned *P'tit Bonheur*, was the first musician to introduce Quebec music to Europe. He is buried in the local cemetery.

At the end of the village there is a new site honouring the poet's memory. The **Espace**

Québec City Region

Félix-Leclerc *($3; mid-Feb to mid-Dec Tue-Sun 9am to 6pm; 682 Chemin Royal,* ☎828-1682) includes a wide array of interesting features: a building housing an exhibit on the life and work of Félix Leclerc, a *boîte à chansons* (a music venue for singer-songwriters) where young and old alike can belt out Leclerc's famous tunes or come up with some new ones of their own, and hiking trails to explore the heart of the island, as Leclerc did so many times. The site covers 50ha on both sides of the road, from the sand bars to the centre of the island, knows as the *mitan*. There is also a small café and picnic tables, so plan to stay a while!

The tour is now completed. Turn right to return to the mainland.

Tour C: Chemin du Roy

Duration of tour: one day

With the exception of Sillery, near Québec City, the towns and villages on this tour are all located along the Chemin du Roy, the first maintained road between Montréal and Québec City, built in 1734. This road, running along the St. Lawrence (some parts parallel to Rte. 138), and lined with beautiful 18th-century French-style houses, churches and windmills, is one of the most picturesque drives in Canada.

★★
Sillery
(pop. 13,100)

This well-to-do suburb of Québec City retains many traces of its varied history, influenced by the town's dramatic topography. There are actually two sections to Sillery, one at the base and the other at the top of a steep cliff that runs from Cap Diamant to

Cap-Rouge. In 1637, the Jesuits built a mission in Sillery on the shores of the river, with the idea of converting the Algonquins and Montagnais who came to fish in the coves upriver from Québec City. They named the fortified community for the mission's benefactor, Noël Brûlart de Sillery, an aristocrat who had recently been converted by Vincent de Paul.

By the following century, Sillery was already sought after for its beauty. The Jesuits converted their mission to a country house, and the bishop of Samos built Sillery's first villa (1732). Following the British Conquest, Sillery became the preferred town of administrators, military officers and British merchants, all of whom built themselves luxurious villas on the cliff, in architectural styles then fashionable in England. The splendour of these homes and their vast English gardens were in stark contrast to the simple houses lived in by workers and clustered at the base of the cliff. The occupants of these houses worked in the shipyards, where a fortune was being made building ships out of wood coming down the Outaouais region to supply the British navy during Napoleon's blockade, which began in 1806. The shipyards, set up in Sillery's sheltered coves, had all disappeared before Boulevard Champlain, now running along the river's edge, was built in 1960.

The **Siège Social de L'Industrielle-Alliance** *(1080 Chemin Saint-Louis)* looks like a modern villa, but was actually built as the headquarters for a large insurance company. It is one of the best examples of post-war architecture in Québec. The work of architects Pierre Rinfret and Maurice Bouchard (1950-52) was inspired by houses from the 19th century

and is accentuated by a beautiful garden.

The **Parc du Bois-de-Coulonge** ★ *(free admission; every day; 1215 Chemin St. Louis,* ☎528-0773) to the east borders Chemin Saint-Louis. This English park once surrounded the residence of the lieutenant-governor of Québec, the King or Queen's representative in Québec. The stately home was destroyed in a fire in 1966, though some of its outbuildings have survived, notably the guard's house and the stables. The Saint-Denys stream flows through the eastern end of the grounds at the bottom of a ravine. British troops gained access to the Plains of Abraham, where a historic battle decided the future of New France, by climbing through this ravine. Now Bois de Coulonge, member of the Jardins du Québec association, has magnificent gardens and a well-arranged arboretum to walk through.

Villa Bagatelle ★ *($3; Mar to Dec, every day 10am to 5pm; 1563 Chemin Saint-Louis* ☎688-8074 or 681-3010) was once home to an attaché of the British governor who lived on the neighbouring property of Bois-de-Coulonge. Built in 1848, the villa is a good example of 19th-century Gothic Revival residential architecture, as interpreted by American Alexander J. Davis. The house and its Victorian garden were impeccably restored in 1984, and they are now open to the public. On the grounds, there is an interesting information centre providing background on the villas and large estates of Sillery.

On Avenue Lemoine, which runs along the south side of Bagatelle, is the **Spencer Grange Villa** *(1321 Avenue Lemoine),* built in 1849 for Henry Atkinson. During the Second World War, the building was home to Zita de

Bourbon-Parme, the dethroned Empress of Austria.

The Gothic Revival **St. Michael's Church** *(1800 Chemin Saint-Louis)*, built in 1852, serves the Anglican congregation of Sillery. Nearby is the **Mount Hermon Protestant Cemetery** and the **Couvent des Soeurs de Sainte-Jeanne-d'Arc** (1917), a huge convent with the look of an imposing castle.

Turn left onto Côte de l'Église.

A short side trip leads to the **Cimetière de Sillery**, Sillery's Catholic cemetery, where René Lévesque, founder of the Parti Québecois and Premier of Québec from 1976 to 1984, is buried. To get there, turn right on Avenue Maguire, then left on Boulevard René-Lévesque Ouest.

The **Église Saint-Michel ★** *(at the corner of Chemin du Foulon and Côte de l'Église)*, Sillery's Catholic church, has many points in common with its Anglican counterpart St. Micheal's Church: its patron saint, its Gothic Revival style and the fact that both churches were built in the same year (1852). The Catholic church, designed by architect George Browne, is, however, much larger. Inside are five paintings from the famous Desjardins collection. These originally hung in Parisian churches until they were sold in 1792 following the French Revolution and brought to Québec by Abbé Desjardins.

The **Maison des Jésuites de Sillery ★★** *(donations accepted; closed Mon; Jun to Sep 11am to 5pm, Oct to May 1pm to 5pm; 2320 Chemin du Foulon, ☎654-0259)*, built of stone and covered with white plaster, occupies the former site of a Jesuit mission, a few ruins of which are still visible. In the 17th century, the mission included a fortified stone wall, a chapel, a priest's

residence and Aboriginal housing. As European illnesses, such as smallpox and measles, devastated the indigenous population, the mission was transformed into a hospice in 1702. At the same time, work began on the present house, a building with imposing chimney stacks. In 1763, the house was rented to John Brookes and his wife, writer Frances Moore Brookes, who immortalized it as the setting for her novel, *The History of Emily Montague*, published in London in 1769. It was also during this time that the structure was lowered and the windows were made smaller in size, in the New England saltbox tradition. The house now has two stories in front and one in back and is covered with a catslide roof.

By 1824, the main building was being used as a brewery and the chapel had been torn down. The house was later converted into offices for various shipyards. In 1929, the Maison des Jésuites became one of the first three buildings designated as historic by the government of Québec. Since 1948, it has housed a museum detailing the 350-year history of the property.

Continue along Chemin du Foulon, then take Côte à Gignac up the embankment on the right.

On the right at the end of Avenue Kilmarnock stands the villa of the same name. Today it is surrounded by suburban homes. This 1810 villa is one of the oldest in Sillery. On the left on Avenue de la Falaise is one of the first post-war suburbs. It was designed by French urban planner Jacques Gréber in 1948.

Turn right on Chemin Saint-Louis.

The **Domaine Cataraqui ★** *($5; Mar to mid-Dec every*

day 10am to 5pm, mid-Dec to Feb Tue to Sun 10am to 5pm; 2141 Chemin Saint-Louis, ☎681-3010) is the best-kept property of its kind still in existence in Sillery. It includes a large neoclassical residence, designed in 1851 by architect Henry Staveley, a winter garden and numerous outbuildings scattered across a beautiful, recently restored garden. The house was built for a wood merchant named Henry Burstall, whose business operated at the bottom of the cliff atop which the house stands. In 1935, Cataraqui became the residence of painter Henry Percival Tudor-Hart and his wife Catherine Rhodes. They sold the property to the Québec government to prevent it being divided up, as many others had been. Today the public can visit the house, a member of the Jardins du Québec association, and its superb gardens, where exhibits and concerts are regularly presented. In the early fall, many concerts are given during the **Festival de Musique Ancienne de Sillery**.

The very original, Gothic Revival interior of **Villa Benmore** *(2071 Chemin Saint-Louis)* was created in 1834 by architect George Browne, who had just arrived from Ireland. As with many former villas, the house now belongs to a religious community, and was enlarged many times.

Head west on Chemin Saint-Louis.

The **Maison Hamel-Bruneau** *(free admission; Tue-Sun 12:30pm to 5pm, Wed to 9pm; 2608 Chemin Saint-Louis, ☎654-4325)* is a beautiful example of Regency architecture, popular in British colonies at the beginning of the 19th century. This style is characterized by hip roofs with flared eaves covering low wraparound verandas. Graced with French windows, the Maison Hamel-Bruneau has been carefully restored and transformed into a cultural centre by the town of Sainte-Foy.

Turn left on Avenue du Parc to get to the Aquarium du Québec.

The **Parc Aquarium du Québec** *($24; Oct to Apr every day 10am to 4pm, May and Sep 10am to 5pm, Jun to Aug 10am to 7pm; 1675 Avenue des Hôtels, in Sainte-Foy,* ☎*659-5266)* had just re-opened following extensive renovations as this guidebook was going to press. The aquarium brings to life the ecosystems of the St. Lawrence River and that of the polar world by means of new technologies as well as the real thing: salt- and freshwater basins that are home to marine mammals such as seals, walruses and polar bears.

Take Chemin Saint-Louis west towards Cap-Rouge, then take Rue Louis-Francœur to the right before turing left down Côte de Cap-Rouge.

Cap-Rouge
(pop. 14,750)

Jacques Cartier and the Sieur de Roberval tried to establish a French colony at Cap-Rouge in 1541. They called their encampments Charlesbourg-Royal and France-Roy. The unfortunate souls who came with them, having no idea of how cold Canada could get in January, built frail wood buildings with paper windows! Most died during the winter, victims of the cold or of scurvy, a disease caused by a lack of vitamin C. The others returned to France in the spring.

A plaque has been placed at the **Site Historique de Cap-Rouge** *(at the end of Côte de Cap-Rouge),* an historic site commemorating the first French colony in America. Cartier and Roberval had

intended to make the site a base camp for expeditions heading out in search of a passage to the Orient.

Take Rue Saint-Félix heading west, turn left on Chemin du Lac, then left again on Rang de la Butte, which becomes Rte. Tessier. Turn left on Rte. 138 towards Saint-Augustin-de-Desmaures. Continue along Rte. 138 to Neuville.

★
Neuville
(pop. 1,125)

A vein of limestone, traversing the region from Neuville to Grondines, has been tapped for the construction of prestigious buildings across the province since the French Regime. This explains the large number of field-stone houses dotting the villages in the area. Today, most of the jobs related to the extraction and cutting of this grey stone are concentrated in the town of Saint-Marc-des-Carrières, west of Deschambault.

The village of Neuville was formerly part of the Pointe-aux-Trembles seigneury, granted to the royal engineer Jean Bourdon in 1653. The houses of Neuville are built into the hills at varying elevations so that most of them have a view of the St. Lawrence. This terraced layout lends this section of Chemin du Roy a certain charm.

The **"Château" de Neuville** *(205 Route 138),* on the left as you enter the village, is a fantastical home built between 1964 and 1972 with materials gathered from the demolition of about a hundred homes along the Grande-Allée in Québec City (see p 324).

The **Maison Darveau** *(50 Route 138)* was built in 1785 for one of the most important stonemasons in Neuville, which explains the

presence of the more elaborate stone frames around the windows and doors. In addition to these, the house has a classical portal, which, though common in France, was quite exceptional in Québec.

Turn right on Rue des Érables.

Rue des Érables ★★ *(guided visits,,* ☎*286-3002)* has one of the largest concentrations of old stone houses outside Québec's large urban centres. The abundance of the necessary raw material and the homowners' desire to make use of the talents of local builders and stonemasons explains this. Number 500 on Rue des Érables was built for Édouard Larue, who acquired the Neuville seigneury in 1828. The huge house is representative of traditional rural Québec architecture, with its raised stone foundation and gallery covered with flared eaves running the whole length of the facade.

In 1696, the villagers undertook the construction of the simple **Église Saint-François-de-Sales ★★** *(guided tours; 644 Rue des Érables,* ☎*286-3002).* It was added to and altered during the following centuries, to the point where the original elements of the building have all but disappeared. A newer chancel was built in 1761, the nave was expanded in 1854, and finally, a new facade was added in 1915. The present church is the result of these transformations. The interior of the church houses an impressive piece of baroque art from the period of the French Regime: a wooden baldaquin (a richly ornamented canopy over the altar) ordered in 1695 for the chapel of the episcopal palace in Québec City.

At the western end of Rue des Érables, take Rte. 138 to the right. Follow Rte. 138 W. to

*Pointe-aux-Trembles, then
Donnacona.*

*Turn right on Rue Notre-
Dame, to get to Donnacona,
then cross the bridge over the
Rivière Jacques-Cartier.*

★
Cap-Santé
(pop. 2,857)

This farming village enjoys an
enviable setting overlooking
the St. Lawrence. Formerly
part of the Portneuf seigneury,
Cap-Santé came into being at
the end of the 17th century
and grew slowly. If there is
such a thing as a typical
Québécois village, Cap-Santé
is probably it.

A plaque by the side of the
road indicates the **Site of Fort
Jacques-Cartier** *(close to
15 Rue Notre-Dame)*. Erected
hastily in 1759, at the peak of
the Seven Years War, the fort
was meant to slow down the
English on their march towards Montréal. The courageous Chevaliers de Lévis
tried desperately to save what
remained of New France with
these measures. The eventual
attack on the fort lasted barely
an hour, before the ill-
equipped French surrendered.
Only archaeological remains of
the wood fort have survived.
The **Cap-Santé seigneurial
manor**, built around 1740 on
the same site, is, however, still
standing, well concealed in the
woods.

Return to Rte. 138 on the left.

The construction of the **Église
Sainte-Famille ★ ★** *(guided
tours;* ☎*285-2311)* went on
between 1754 and 1764
under the auspices of curate
Joseph Filion, but was seriously disrupted by the British
conquest. In 1759, materials
intended for the finishing
touches on the building were
requisitioned for the construction of Fort Jacques-Cartier.
Nevertheless, the completed
church, with its two steeples

Vieux Presbytère

and its high nave lit by two
rows of windows, is an ambitious piece of work for its
time, and was possibly the
largest village church built
under the French Regime.
The three beautiful wooden
statues placed in the alcoves of
the facade in 1775 have miraculously survived Québec's
harsh climate. The imitation
cutstone done in wood covering the stone walls was added
in the 19th century. Before
stepping inside the church, be
sure to visit the wooded cemetery and presbytery built by
Thomas Baillargé in 1850.

Today the **Vieux Chemin ★**,
the old road, is nothing more
than a simple road passing in
front of the church, but it was
once part of the Chemin du
Roy, which linked Montréal
and Québec City. Numerous
well-preserved 18th-century
houses facing the river can still
be seen along the road, making it one of the most picturesque drives in Canada.

*Drive through Portneuf be-
fore stopping in
Deschambault.*

★ ★
Deschambault
(pop. 1,350)

The charming tranquillity of
this agricultural village on the
banks of the St. Lawrence was
a bit disturbed recently by the
development of an aluminum

smelter. Deschambault was
founded thanks to the efforts
of Seigneur Fleury de la
Gorgendière, who previously
had a church built in nearby
Cap Lauzon in 1720. Because
the village has grown slowly, it
retains its small-town charm.

The **Maison Deschambault**
(128 Route 138) is visible at
the end of a long tree-lined
lane. The stone building
equipped with fire-break walls
was probably built in the late
18th century. It was practically
in ruins in 1936, when the
Québec government, which
owned the building at the
time, undertook its restoration, a rarity in an era when
many elements of Québec's
heritage had already been lost.
The building now houses a
charming inn (see p 367), and
a fine French restaurant (see
p 369).

*Turn left on Rue de l'Église,
which leads to the village
square.*

With its large facade adorned
with two massive towers set
back slightly from the front of
the church, the **Église Saint-
Joseph** *(120 Rue St-Joseph)* is
unlike no other church in
Québec. Instead of the usual
gable, the roof of the church
has a hipped end adorned
with a statue. This solid building, erected between 1835
and 1841, is the work of architect Thomas Baillargé. The

original neoclassical steeples were destroyed and replaced during the 20th century with poor imitations of typical New France steeples.

The **Vieux Presbytère** *(donations accepted; Jun to Aug every day 9am to 5pm; May, Sep and Oct, Sat and Sun 10am to 5pm; 117 Rue Saint-Joseph, ☎286-6891)* occupies a prime location behind the church and offers a beautiful panoramic view of the river and the south shore. The small presbytery building, set apart in the centre of a large lawn, was built in 1815 to replace the first presbytery dating from 1735. The foundations of the original building are visible near the entrance. In 1955, an antique dealer saved the presbytery from destruction, then, in 1970, a residents' association began using the building as an exhibition centre, demonstrating a dynamic community commitment to preserving its heritage.

Get back on Rte. 138 W. This section of the Chemin du Roy is lined with many well-preserved traditional Québec homes. Turn right onto Rue de Chavigny.

The magnificent **Moulin de La Chevrotière ★** *(free admission; Jun to Sep, every day 10am to 6pm; 109 Rue de Chavigny, ☎286-6862)*, a former mill, now houses a facility where traditional building skills are taught. Every summer, young artisans from around Québec come to learn pre-industrial techniques of working with wood, iron and stone. The imposing building is located on a former section of the Chemin du Roy, renamed Rue de Chavigny in honour of Joseph de Chavigny de La Chevrotière, owner of the fief of the same name, who had this mill built in 1802. The roughcast structure just beside the mill, which houses

the forge, is in fact the original mill, built in 1766.

Get back on Rte. 138 heading towards Grondines.

★
Grondines
(pop. 675)

In the 18th century, the village of Grondines was situated on the banks of the St. Lawrence. In 1831, it was relocated inland to facilitate access and avoid flooding. Traces of the original village, found between the river and Rte. 138, show French architectural influences, whereas the core of the present village, centred around Rue Principale, displays decidedly more Victorian influences. The citizens of Grondines showed great concern for their environment during the 1980s, when they fought plans to run hydroelectric lines across the river. The people of Grondines finally won their case. The lines run under the river, keeping the picturesque countryside intact.

The remains of the first stone church in Grondines, the **Église Saint-Charles-Borromée ★** *(490 Route 138)* (1716), are visible near the mill. When the village was moved, a new church had to be built. Admired for the churches he designed in the neighbouring parishes, Thomas Baillargé was asked to design a magnificent church. However, funds became very scarce, so much so that the neoclassical structure begun in 1832 remained incomplete. The church steeples were not added until 1894, by which time neoclassicism was no longer in vogue, having given way to Victorian architecture. As a result, the towers, windows and doors were designed in the Gothic Revival style.

Inside, several interesting paintings are displayed, notably *La Madone du Rosaire*

(The Rosary Madonna) by Théophile Hamel (above the right lateral altar), and *Saint Charles-Borromée* by Jean-Baptiste Roy-Audy. The tabernacle of the high altar was sculpted in 1742 by Levasseur. Also of interest is the neoclassical presbytery from 1842, with its beautiful dormer-window-pediment.

Though it lost its imposing presence when it was converted into a lighthouse (a fate shared by many similar buildings) the **Moulin de Grondines** *(770 Rue du Moulin)* is still important for being the oldest building of its type still standing. The mill was built in 1672 for the Religieuses Hospitalières de l'Hôtel-Dieu, nuns working as nurses in the main hospital of Québec City, to whom the Grondines seigneury was granted in 1637.

The Chemin du Roy tour ends in Grondines, but could be combined with a visit to the Mauricie region in Sainte-Anne-de-la-Pérade, see p 286.

★
Tour D: Vallée de la Jacques-Cartier

Duration of tour: three days

After a quick tour through some of the first settlements of New France, this itinerary enters the resort regions of the Laurentides, before plunging into the wilderness of the Rivière Jacques-Cartier valley and the Réserve Faunique des Laurentides. Ideal for camping, river rafting and other outdoor activities, the virgin forest of the Rivière Jacques-Cartier is surprisingly close to the city.

★
Charlesbourg
(pop. 74,000)

The Notre-Dame-des-Anges seigneury was granted to the

Jesuits in 1626, making it one of the first permanent settlements inhabited by Europeans in Canada. Despite this early settlement and original seigneurial design, few buildings built before the 19th century remain in Charlesbourg. The fragility of early buildings and the push to modernize are possible explanations for this void. Since 1950, Charlesbourg has become one of the main suburbs of Québec City, and has lost much of its original character.

It is best to park near the church and explore the Trait-Carré on foot.

The **Église Saint-Charles-Borromée ★★** *(135 80° Rue Ouest)* revolutionized the art of building in rural Québec. Architect Thomas Baillargé, influenced by the Palladian movement, showed particular innovation in the way he arranged the windows and doors of the facade, to which he added a large pediment. Construction of the church began in 1828 and was uninterrupted. The original design has remained intact since. The magnificent interior decor by Baillargé was done in 1833.

At the corner of Boulevard Henri-Bourassa is the old Moulin des Jésuites.

The **Moulin des Jésuites ★** *(free admission; late Jun to mid-Aug, every day 10pm to 7pm; mid-Aug to mid-Jun, Sat and Sun 10am to 5pm; 7960 Boulevard Henri-Bourassa, ☎624-7720)*, a handsome mill, in roughcast fieldstone, is the oldest building in Charlesbourg. It was built in 1740 by the Jesuits, who were the landowners at the time. After several decades of neglect, the two-storey building was restored in 1990 and now houses the **Centre d'Interprétation du Trait-Carré** and a tourist bureau. Concerts and exhibits are also presented here.

A visit to the zoo is always guaranteed to fill both adults and children with wonder. The **Jardin Zoologique du Québec ★** *($24; Jun to Aug every day 10am to 8pm, Sep to May 10am to 5pm; 9300 Rue de la Faune, Charlesbourg, ☎622-0312)* is on an attractive site overrun by greenery and flowers. The zoo had been closed for extensive renovations and was scheduled to reopen just after this guidebook went to press. Call for more information.

Take Boulevard Saint-Joseph (the continuation of 80° Rue Ouest) which eventually becomes Boulevard Bastien.

★
Wendake
(pop. 1,035)

Forced off their land by the Iroquois in the 17th century, 300 Huron families moved to various places around Québec before settling in 1700 in Jeune-Lorette, today known as Wendake. Visitors will be charmed by the winding roads of the village in this native reserve located on the banks of the Rivière Saint-Charles. The museum and gift shop provide a lot of information on the culture of this peaceful and sedentary people.

The **Église Notre-Dame-de-Lorette ★** *(140 Boulevard Bastien)*, the Huron church, completed in 1730, is reminiscent of the first churches of New France. This humble building with a white plaster facade conceals unexpected treasures in its chancel and in the sacristy. Some of the objects on display were given to the Huron community by the Jesuits, and come from the first chapel in Ancienne-Lorette (late 17th century). Among the works to be seen are several statues by Noël Levasseur, created between 1730 and 1740, an altar-facing depicting an Aboriginal village, by the Huron sculptor

François Vincent (1790) and a beautiful *Vierge à l'Enfant* (Madonna and Child) sculpture, by a Parisian goldsmith (1717). In addition, the church has a reliquary made in 1676, 18th century chasubles and various liturgical objects by Paul Manis (circa 1715). However, the most interesting element is the small, Louis XIII–style gilded tabernacle on the high altar, sculpted by Levasseur in 1722.

Onhoüa Chetek8e *($8; late Apr to Oct every day 8:30am to 6pm, Nov to late Apr every day 9am to 5pm; 575 Rue Stanislas-Koska, ☎842-4308)* is a replica of a Huron village from the time of early colonization. The traditional design includes wooden longhouses and fences. Visitors are given an introduction to the lifestyle and social organization of the Huron nation. Various Aboriginal dishes are also served and worth a taste.

Parc de la Falaise et de la Chute Kabir Kouba, see p 363.

From Wendake, you can reach the **Lac Saint-Joseph** *region, to the northwest. This is a popular resort area for Québec City residents who swim and practice watersports in this lake all summer long and enjoy, among other things, its beach.*

Sainte-Catherine-de-la-Jacques-Cartier

Before reaching Lac Saint-Joseph, you'll pass Sainte-Catherine-de-la-Jacques-Cartier and the **Station Écotouristique Duchesnay ★** (see p 363), a lovely park that, come wintertime, features the famous **Ice Hotel ★** *(guided tour $12, in French everyday, every 2hrs from 10:30am to 8:30pm, in English from 11:30am to 7:30pm; ☎875-4522 or 877-505-0423, www.icehotel-canada.com).*

The Québec Ice Hotel (see p 367), a spectacular, Swedish-inspired structure, is unique in North America and definitely one of the region's "hottest" attractions. Its lifespan is obviously limited (early Jan to late Mar), but every year, builders return to the site to erect this stunning complex using several tonnes of ice and snow. And not only is the ice used for building, it also serves as decoration! The hotel houses an art gallery showcasing unusual snow and ice sculptures, as well as an exhibit room, a small movie theatre, a chapel and a bar where vodka is served in ice glasses. You'll simply be amazed!

Take Rte. 73, which becomes Rte. 175 and leads to Lac-Beauport.

Lac-Beauport (pop. 4,800)

The Lac-Beauport region is a popular year-round resort area. There are downhill ski centres in the region, including **Le Relais** (see p 365). Vacationers can also enjoy the lake's beautiful beaches.

The Jacques-Cartier tour ends here. To return to Québec City, follow Rte. 175 S. You could also continue north into the Saguenay - Lac-Saint-Jean tourist region (see p 457).

Parks

Tour A: Côte de Beaupré

Parc de la chute Montmorency, see p 349.

Mont-Sainte-Anne ★ *(2000 Blvd. Beau-Pré, Beaupré, ☎827-4561)* covers 77km² and includes a 800m-high

peak that is one of the most beautiful downhill-ski sites in Québec (see p 365). Various other outdoor activities are possible, as the park has 200km of mountain-bike trails, which become 200km of cross-country trails in winter. Access to these is $5 per day. Sports equipment can also be rented on site. There are a few hotels close to the ski hill and the park.

The **Grand Canyon des Chutes Sainte-Anne** *($7; early May to late Jun and early Sep to late Oct, every day 9am to 5:30pm; late Jun to early Sep 8:30am to 6:30pm; 40 Côte de la Miche or 206 Route 138, Beaupré, ☎827-4057)* was ceated by the rushing Rivière Sainte-Anne, which carves a deep path through the hills near Beaupré and plunges 74m into a large pothole 22m in width, formed by the resulting water current. Visitors can take in this impressive site from lookouts and a suspension bridge.

The **Cap-Tourmente National Wildlife Area ★★** *($5; 570 Chemin du Cap-Tourmente, Saint-Joachim, ☎827-4591)* is located on pastoral, fertile land. Each spring and autumn its sandbars are visited by countless snow geese, who stop to gather strength for their long migration. The reserve also has birdwatching facilities and naturalists on hand to answer your questions about the 250 species of birds and 45 species of mammals you might encounter on the hiking and walking trails that traverse the park.

Tour C: Chemin du Roy

Northwest of Quebec, the **Réserve Faunique de Portneuf** *(☎323-2021)* offers many kilometres of trails for various outdoor activities, including snowmobiling, cross-country skiing and snowshoeing. Lakes and rivers abound in

the area. Pleasant little chalets *(reservations ☎800-665-6527 or 890-6527)* well equipped for two to eight people, are available for rent.

Tour D: Vallée de la Jacques-Cartier

The **Réserve Faunique des Laurentides** *($3.50; Rte. 175 N., Mercier entrance, ☎848-2422 or 528-6868)* covers 8,000km². This huge wilderness is home to a diversified wildlife, including black bears and moose. Hunting and fishing (spotted trout) are permitted at certain times of the year; check with the information desk regarding permits. The reserve has beautiful cross-country ski trails, one-day and overnight hiking trails, small chalets for two to 17 people; rates for two are around $95 *(reservations ☎890-6527 or 800-665-6527)*. In the summer, canoeists can ply the waters of the Rivière Métabetchouane and the Rivière Écorces.

Throughout the year, hordes of visitors come to **Parc de la Jacques-Cartier ★★** *($3.50; Rte. 175 Nord, ☎848-3169 or 528-8787)*, located in the Réserve Faunique des Laurentides, 40km north of Quebec City. The area is called Vallée de la Jacques-Cartier, after the river of the same name that runs through it, winding between steep hills. Benefitting from the microclimate caused by the river being hemmed in on bothsides, the site is suitable for a number of outdoor activities. The vegetation and wildlife are abundant and diverse. The winding and well-laid-out paths sometimes lead to interesting surprises, like a moose and its offspring foraging for food in a marsh. Before heading out to discover all the riches the site has to offer, you can get information at the nature centre's reception area. Campsites (see p 367), chalets and equipment are all available for rent (see "Outdoor Activities" section).

At the park, specialists organize **Safaris d'Observation de l'Orignal** (moose observation safaris), from mid-September to mid-October as well as **Écoute des Appels Nocturnes des Loups**, nocturnal wolf-call-listening sessions at night from the beginning of July until mid-October, to familiarize people with these animals. Reservations are required for these educational excursions, which usually last 3hrs; it costs $15 for adults, and each of these activities requires that you walk through the forest.

About 45km from Québec City, on the shore of the region's largest lake, Lac Saint-Joseph, the **Station Écotouristique Duchesnay ★** *(143 Route Duchesnay, Ste-Catherine-de-la-Jacques-Cartier, ☎529-2911 or 875-2711, www.sepaq.com/ duchesnay)* allows visitors to familiarize themselves with the Laurentian forest. Located on an area of 90km2, this centre is dedicated to researching the fauna and flora of our forests and is now one of Sépaq's tourism and recreation centres. Long famous for its cross-country ski trails, it is also ideal for practicing all kinds of outdoor activities, such as hiking, on its 16km of maintained footpaths. There are also ample opportunities for watersports. The Jacques-Cartier–Portneuf bike path also traverses Duchesnay. In addition, you will find an interpretation centre that hosts educational and awareness-raising activities. The installations have been entirely renovated to offer visitors comfortable lodging and dining. In winter, the site is home to the **Ice Hotel** (see p 361).

The **Parc de la Chute et de la Falaise Kabir Kouba** (falls and cliff park) is in the Wendake Aboriginal village. A few small trails go along the edge of the

40m-cliff, at the bottom of which flows the Rivière Saint-Charles.

Outdoor Activities

Cycling

Located in the Vieux-Port de Québec, **Cyclo-Services** *(84 Dalhousie, Marché du Vieux-Port, ☎692-4052)* offers a series of cycling excursions around the city. They also offer bike rental *($7 per hour)*.

Tour A: Côte de Beaupré

A bicycle path runs from the Vieux-Port of Québec City to Parc de la Chute Montmorency, passing through Beauport on the way. Also, roads such as Chemin du Roy, on the Côte de Beaupré and Île d'Orléans *(bike rental at the Le Vieux-Presbytère guesthouse, see p 366)*, are meant to be shared between motorists and cyclists. Caution is always in order, but these trips are definitely worth the effort.

Tour D: Vallée de la Jacques-Cartier

In 1997, a brand new bicycle path was inaugurated in the Quebec region. Following the route of old railway lines, the **Piste Jacques-Cartier - Portneuf** *($5; 100 Rue St-Jacques, St-Raymond, ☎337-7525)* crosses through the Réserve Faunique Portneuf and the Station Forestière Duchesnay (where you can park your car and rent bicycles and runs alongside certain lakes in the area. Including the most recent additions, it is 63km in length, stretching from Rivière-à-Pierre to Shanon. Its magical setting and

safe conditions have already attracted many cyclists. In winter, the path is used for snowmobiling.

In **Parc de la Jacques-Cartier** *($3.50; Route 175 Nord, ☎848-3169, www.sepaq.com)* (see p 362), the trails are for both hikers and mountain-biking enthusiasts. Bike rental is available.

Hiking

Tour A: Côte de Beaupré

At **Cap-Tourmente** *(570 Chemin du Cap-Tourmente, St-Joachim, ☎827-4591 or 827-3776)* (see p 362), if your legs allow for it, you can take one of the trails up the cape, where you'll get a magnificent view of the river and surrounding countryside. You can also take an equally enjoyable stroll on wooden walkways along the shore, which are adapted for people with disabilities.

Tour D: Vallée de la Jacques-Cartier

The trails in **Parc de la Jacques-Cartier** *($3.50; Rte. 175 N., ☎848-3169)* (see p 362) are favoured by locals. Whether leisurely or steep, the trails lead you to lovely little spots in the forest and reveal magnificent views of the valley and its river.

The **Réserve Faunique de Portneuf** (see p 362), the **Station Écotouristique Duchesnay** *(Rte. 360, Beaupré, ☎827-4579 or 827-4561)*, and the **Station Touristique Stoneham** *(1420 Avenue du Hibou, Stoneham, ☎848-2144)* all offer many very pleasant hiking trails.

Québec City Region

Birdwatching

Tour A: Côte de Beaupré

One of the best places for birdwatching in the region is definitely the **Cap-Tourmente National Wildlife Area** *(St-Joachim, ☎827-4591 or 827-3776)* (see p 362). During spring and autumn, the thousands of migrating snow geese that overtake the area are a fascinating sight to behold. Any questions you might have after seeing these creatures up close and in such great numbers can be answered here. The reserve is also home to many other avian species. They are drawn here throughout the year by a number of bird houses and feeders.

Canoeing

Tour D: Vallée de la Jacques-Cartier

You can canoe on the rivers and lakes of the **Réserve Faunique de Portneuf** (p 362) and down the river at **Parc de la Jacques-Cartier** *(rental $36/day; Rte. 175 Nord, ☎848-3169)* (see p 362). Both have canoes for rent and Parc de la Jacques-Cartier also rents river kayaks.

Rafting

Tour D: Vallée de la Jacques-Cartier

In spring and summer the Rivière Jacques-Cartier gives adventurers a good run for their money. Two longstand-ing companies offer well-supervised rafting expeditions with all the necessary equipment. At **Village Vacances Valcartier** *(1860 Boulevard Valcartier, St-Gabriel-de-Valcartier, ☎844-2200 or 888-384-5524)*, they promise lots of excitement on an 8km ride. With **Excursions Jacques-Cartier** *(978 Avenue Jacques-Cartier Nord, Tewkesbury, ☎848-7238)*, you can also experience some very exciting runs. Rafting excursions are also offered on the Rivière Batiscan in the **Réserve Faunique de Portneuf** (see p 362).

Hunting and Fishing

In the Québec City area, you can hunt and fish at **Cap-Tourmente** *(☎827-3776)*, the **Réserve Faunique de Portneuf** *(☎323-2021)* and **Parc des Laurentides** *(☎848-2422)* among other places.

Golf

Tour A: Côte de Beaupré

The Station Mont-Sainte-Anne golf course, **Le Grand Vallon** *($65 Mon-Thu, $78 Fri-Sun; 200 Boulevard Beau Pré, Beaupré, ☎827-4561)* was entirely redesigned in 1999. Today, it offers a par-72 course with several sand traps and four lakes, and is known as one of the most interesting courses in eastern Canada.

Tobogganing and Waterslides

Tour D: Vallée de la Jacques-Cartier

You can zip down the hill in winter on an inner-tube at **Club Mont-Tourbillon** *(55 Montée du Golf, Lac-Beauport, ☎849-4418)*. They also offer all sorts of other activities, including cross-country skiing. There is a restaurant and a bar.

Winter or summer, the **Village des Sports** *(early Jun to Sep every day 10am to 5pm, Dec to Mar 10am à 10pm; 1860 Boulevard Valcartier, St-Gabriel-de-Valcartier, ☎844-2200 or 888-384-5524; from Québec City, take Rte. 371 Nord)* is the undisputed authority when it comes to slides. It is an outdoor-activity centre that offers every facility. In the summer, water slides and a wave pool draw huge crowds. In winter, ice slides will help you forget the cold for a little while. There is also snow rafting and skating on a 2.5km-long ice rink that snakes through the woods. There is a restaurant and a bar.

Cross-Country Skiing

Tour A: Côte de Beaupré

Mont-Sainte-Anne *($15; Mon-Fri 9am to 4pm, Sat and Sun 8:30am to 4pm; 2000 Boulevard Beau-Pré, Beaupré, ☎827-4561)* has 250km of well-maintained cross-country ski trails with some heated huts set up along the way. They rent ski equipment *($17/day)*.

Tour D: Vallée de la Jacques-Cartier

Nestled in the heart of the Réserve Faunique des Laurentides, **Camp Mercier** (*$6; every day 8:30am to 4pm; Route 175 N., Réserve Faunique des Laurentides, ☎848-2422 or 800-665-6527*) is criss-crossed by 192km of well-maintained trails in an extremely tranquil landscape. Given its ideal location, you can ski here from fall to spring. Long routes (up to 68km) with heated huts offer some interesting opportunities. There are also cottages for rent that can accommodate from two to 14 people (*$92/2ppl*).

In winter, **Station Écotouristique Duchesnay** (*$10; every day 8:30am to 4pm; Ste-Catherine-de-la-Jacques-Cartier, ☎875-2711*) is very popular with skiers in the area. There are 150km of well-maintained trails in this vast forest.

Downhill Skiing

Tour A: Côte de Beaupré

Mont-Sainte-Anne (*$52/day, $23/night; Mon 9am to 4pm, Tue-Fri 9am to 10pm, Sat 8:30am to 10pm, Sun 8:30pm to 10pm; 2000 Boulevard Beau-Pré, Beaupré, ☎827-4561*) is one of the biggest ski resorts in Québec. Among the 56 runs, some reach 625m in height and 15 are lit for night skiing. It's also a delight for snowboarders. Instead of buying a regular ticket, you can buy a pass worth a certain number of points, valid for two years, and each time you take the lift, points are deducted. Equipment rentals are also available (*skiing $25/day, snowboarding $35/day*).

Tour D: Vallée de la Jacques-Cartier

Le Relais (*$28/day, $19/ night; Mon-Thu 9am to 10pm, Fri 9am to 10:30pm, Sat 8:30am to 10:30pm, Sun 8:30am to 9pm; 1084 Boulevard du Lac, Lac-Beauport, ☎849-1851*) has 25 downhill-ski trails, all of which are lit for night skiing.

The **Station Touristique Stoneham** (*$41/day, $23/ night; Mon-Fri 9am to 10pm, Sat 8:30am to 10pm, Sun 8:30 to 9pm; Stoneham, ☎848-2411 or 800-463-6888*) welcomes visitors year-round. In the winter there are 30 runs, 16 of which are lit. For cross-country skiers there are 30km of maintained trails, which are at the disposal of hikers, mountain-bikers and horseback riders in the summer.

Dogsledding

Tour D: Vallée de la Jacques-Cartier

La Banquise des Chukchis (*228 Rang St-Georges, St-Basile, ☎329-3055*) is a company that offers various day or evening dogsledding packages where you lead the team yourself; one of the packages includes dinner. Friendly atmosphere.

The **Domaine de la Truite du Parc** (*$79/half-day; 4 Rue des Anémones, Stoneham, ☎848-3732*) is an outfitter that lets you drive your own dogsled team. In the summer you can fish for trout.

Accommodations

Tour A: The Côte de Beaupré

Beauport

Hôtel Ramada
$$$$
≡, ⊘, ℜ, &, ⊛
321 Boulevard Ste-Anne
☎666-2828 or 800-363-4619
≈666-2775
This hotel is on the outskirts of town, away from the sights. The rooms are large and pleasant, and there is a Chinese restaurant on the main floor.

Château-Richer

Auberge du Petit Pré
$$ bkfst incl.
sb
7126 Avenue Royale
☎824-3852
≈824-3098
At the Auberge du Petit Pré, which occupies an 18th-century house, you will be warmly received and well treated. Their four guest rooms are cozy and tastefully decorated. There is a large picture window, which is open when the weather is nice, two lounges, one with a T.V. and the other with a fireplace, as well as two bathrooms with clawfoot tubs. Breakfasts are generous and finely prepared. Also, if requested in advance, the owner will prepare one of his delicious dinners for you. The splendid aroma of the food fills the house and adds to its overall warmth.

Auberge du Sault-à-la-Puce
$$ bkfst incl.
⊛
8365 Avenue Royale
☎*824-5659*
≈*824-5669*
Marie-Thérèse Rousseau and Michel Panis left the city to settle in a beautiful 19th-century residence with a sloping roof on the Côte-de-Beaupré. They named the place Auberge du Sault-à-la-Puce for the tiny rapids in a nearby stream. Guests can pass their time on the Victorian veranda, relaxing on garden furniture and listening to the gentle lapping of the rapids. The hotel has five rooms that are decorated with elegant iron furniture making an interesting contrast with the rustic wood-panelling of the walls. All the rooms have their own bathrooms, although some have showers instead of bathtubs to save space.

Auberge Baker
$$ bkfst incl.
≡, ℑ, K, ℜ, ⊛
8790 Avenue Royale
☎*824-4478*
≈*824-4412*
www.auberge-baker.qc.ca
For over 50 years, The Auberge Baker has existed in this century old Côte-de-Beaupré house. Its stone walls, low ceilings, wood floors and wide-frame windows enchant visitors. The seven bedrooms are on the dimly lit upper floor but there is also a kitchenette, a bathroom and an adjoining terrace on the same floor. The rooms are meticulously decorated in authentic fashion and furnished with antiques. They serve delicious food (see p 368).

Beaupré
(Mont Sainte-Anne)

Camping Mont-Sainte-Anne
$
Rang St-Julien, St-Ferréol-les-Neiges
☎*826-2323 or 800-463-1568*
Camping Mont-Sainte-Anne has 166 campsites in a wooded area traversed by the Rivière Jean-Larose. Essential services are offered, and, because the campground is close to all the park's outdoor activities, the location is great.

Hôtel Val des Neiges
$$
≡, ℑ, ☉, ≈, ℜ, △, ⓬, ⊛
201 Val des Neiges
☎*827-5711 or 888-554-6005*
≈*827-5997*
www.familledufour.com
Many chalets have been built around the base of Mont Sainte-Anne, in newly developed areas. Among these is the Hôtel Val des Neiges. The decor is rustic and the rooms are comfortable. The complex also includes small, well-equipped condos. Cruise packages are also offered.

Château Mont-Sainte-Anne
$$$
≈, ☉, △, ℜ, K, ✪, ⓬, ≡, ℑ
500 Boulevard Beau-Pré
☎*827-5211 or 800-463-4467*
≈*827-3421*
www.chateaumontsaintean ne.com
Château Mont-Sainte-Anne is located at the foot of the slopes—you couldn't get much closer to the mountain. In the summer, this mountain becomes a beautiful park criss-crossed by hiking trails, at the base of which extends a large golf course. You can reserve one of the 240 guest rooms here for a short stay or rent a chalet or condo on site for longer family holidays. The comfort of the facilities will ensure you're cozy inside, while the many outdoor activities available will make sure you're kept busy outside, whatever the season.

La Camarine
$$$
≡, ℑ, ℜ, ⊛
10947 Boulevard Ste-Anne
☎*827-5703 or 800-567-3939*
≈*827-5430*
www.camarine.com
La Camarine faces the St. Lawrence River. This charming high-quality inn has 30 rooms. The decor successfully combines the rustic feel of the house with the more modern wooden furniture. A delightful spot.

Tour B: Île d'Orléans

There are about 50 bed and breakfasts on Île d'Orléans! A list can be obtained from the tourist office. There are also a few guesthouses with solid reputations and a campground. Therefore, there are plenty of options for getting the most out of your stay on this enchanting island.

Camping Orléans
$
≈
357 Chemin Royal, St-François
☎*829-2953*
≈*829-2563*
Camping Orléans has close to 80 campsites, most of which are shaded and offer a view of the river. Many services are offered. There is access to the river bank where you can go for a pleasant walk.

Le Vieux Presbytère
$$ bkfst incl.
pb/sb, ℜ,
1247 Avenue Monseigneur-d'Esgly, St-Pierre
☎*828-9723 or 888-828-9723*
≈*828-2189*
www.presbytere.com
At its name indicates, Le Vieux Presbytère guesthouse is located in an old presbytery just behind the village church. The structure is predominantly made out of wood and stone. Low ceilings with wide beams, wide-frame windows and antiques, such as woven bedcovers and braided rugs, take you back to the era of New France. The dining room and the lounge are inviting. This is a tranquil spot with rustic charm.

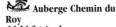 **Le Canard Huppé**
$$$ bkfst incl.
≡, ℜ, ≈, ℜ
2198 Chemin Royal, St-Laurent
☎*828-2292 or 800-838-2292*
≈*828-0966*
www.canard-huppe.qc.ca
Le Canard Huppée has enjoyed a very good reputation over the last few years. Their 11, clean, comfortable, country-style rooms are scattered with wooden ducks. The restaurant is also just as renowned and appealing (see p 368). The service is conscientious, and the surroundings, beautiful.

La Goéliche
$$$ bkfst incl.
≡, K, ≈, ℜ, ⊛
22 Chemin du Quai, Ste-Pétronille
☎*828-2248 or 888-511-2248*
≈*828-2745*
La Goéliche reopened in a new building after the former inn burned to the ground in 1996. The new establishment is slightly smaller and does not have the antique charm that made the original such a hit. Nevertheless, the modern setup still has a certain country-style appeal. The 16 rooms are comfortable and offer a lovely view of Québec City. There is a small living room with a fireplace and games. You can also rent a "chalet-condo" for the night, or for longer stays. The restaurant (see p 368) is worth the trip.

Tour C: The Chemin du Roy

Deschambault

 Auberge Chemin du Roy
$$ bkfst incl.
ℜ
106 Rue St-Laurent
☎*286-6958*
www.cheminduroy.com
The old Victorian house that has been reborn as Auberge Chemin du Roy is set on a beautiful property with waterfalls and gardens where good vegetables and lots of flowers grow. There are eight rooms, decorated with lace and antiques, along a narrow, winding hallway of the type often found in this type of old house. In the warmly decorated dining room, wonderful varied meals are served. The owners take great care of the property, the house and the guests, right down to the tiniest details.

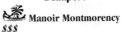 **Maison Deschambault**
$$$ bkfst incl.
ℜ
128 Chemin du Roy
☎*286-3386*
≈*286-4064*
Maison Deschambault offers five luxurious rooms, decorated with flower patterns and pastel colours. There is also a small bar, a dining room that serves fine cuisine (see p 369), a conference room, and a massage service all in an enchanting old manor house. Relaxing in this peaceful setting is no trouble at all.

Tour D: The Rivière Jacques-Cartier

Parc de la Jacques-Cartier

Camping Stoneham
$
101 St-Edmond
☎*848-2233*
Right in the heart of Parc de la Jacques-Cartier you can camp in magnificent surroundings. Along the river, there are numerous campsites, some rustic, others with some facilities. And, of course, there's no lack of things to do!

Sainte-Catherine-de-la-Jacques-Cartier

Ice Hotel
$$$$$
sb, ℝ
143 Route Duchesnay, Pavillon L'Aigle
☎*875-4522 or 877-505-0423*
≈*875-2833*
www.icehotel-canada.com
It's hard to believe that a hotel could actually be made of ice…but it really is (see p 361)! This magnificent structure is built from thousands of tonnes of ice and snow. Adventurous travellers come from all over the continent to spend the night in this chilly castle. Note, however, that because the ice provides natural insulation, the temperature always remains between 21°F and 28°F within the hotel walls. So you can snooze quite comfortably in one of its 31 rooms, all wrapped up in a thick sleeping bag laid atop deer pelts. And if you're new to winter camping, don't worry: the hotel staff is available day and night. Furthermore, the shared bathrooms are heated, and breakfast and dinner are served in a warm chalet. On site, guests can enjoy a multitude of outdoor activities. An unforgettable experience is guaranteed!

Québec City Region

Restaurants

Tour A: The Côte de Beaupré

Beauport

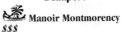 **Manoir Montmorency**
$$$
2490 Avenue Royale
☎*663-3330*
Manoir Montmorency (see p 349) enjoys a superb location above the Montmorency Falls. From the dining room surrounded by bay windows,

there is an absolutely magnificent view of the falls, the river and Île d'Orléans. Fine French cuisine, prepared with the best products in the region, is served in pleasant surroundings. A wonderful experience for the view and the food! The entrance fee to the Parc de la Chute Montmorency (where the restaurant is located) and the parking fees are waived upon presentation of your receipt or by mentioning your reservation.

Château-Richer

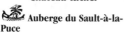 **Auberge du Sault-à-la-Puce**
$$$
8365 Avenue Royale
☎824-5659
The chef of the Auberge du Sault-à-la-Puce carefully prepares each meal with fresh fruit and vegetables from his garden. He also uses local products, such as meat and fowl from neighbouring villages. This establishment also has five guest rooms (see p 366) and offers a limited menu of three or four dishes inspired by French or Italian cuisine. The salmon tartare is delicious.

Auberge Baker
$$$-$$$$
8790 Avenue Royale
☎824-4852 or 824-4478
Auberge Baker (see p 366) has two dining rooms. One has stone walls and a fireplace, whereas the decor of the other is somewhat cold. They serve fine traditional Québec cuisine: game, meat and fowl are well prepared and presented with care.

Beaupré (Mont Sainte-Anne)

La Camarine
$$$$
10947 Boulevard Ste-Anne
☎827-1958
La Camarine also houses an excellent restaurant that serves Québec nouvelle cuisine. The dining room is peaceful, with a

simple decor. The innovative dishes are a feast for the senses. In the basement of the inn is another small restaurant, the **Bistro**, which offers the same menu and prices as upstairs but it is only open in the winter. Equipped with a fireplace, it is a cozy spot for an après-ski and open in the evening for drinks.

Tour B: Île d'Orléans

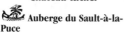 **La Goéliche**
$$$-$$$$
22 Chemin du Quai, Ste-Pétronille
☎828-2248
Although the dining room at La Goéliche is not whaat it waas once pleasant though, and it does offer one of the most beautiful views of Québec City. Fine French cuisine is served here, such as stuffed quail, nuggets of lamb and saddle of hare.

Canard Huppé
$$$-$$$$
2198 Chemin Royal, St-Laurent
☎828-2292
The dining room at the Canard Huppé serves fine regional cuisine. Prepared with fresh ingredients, locally abundant that abound in the area—island specialties such as duck, trout and maple products—these little dishes will delight the most demanding of palates. Although the room is somewhat dark, with forest green being the predominant colour, the country decor is, on the whole, pleasant. Reservations required.

Tour C: The Chemin du Roy

Sillery

Brynd
$
1360 Avenue Maguire
☎527-3844
Byrnd is the place to go to for smoked meat and has a variety for all tastes and appetites.

There are also items on the menu for those, and too bad for them, who don't want to try the house specialty. The meat is smoked and sliced in front of your eyes, just like at a real delicatessen!

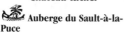 **Paparazzi**
$$-$$$
1363 Avenue Maguire
☎683-8111
Paparazzi serves Italian dishes. The salad with warm goat-cheese, spinach and caramelized walnuts is a true delight, as are other menu items. The decor is modern and pleasant with pretty tables covered in ceramic tiles set up on various levels.

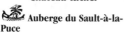 **Montego**
$$$
1460 Avenue Maguire
☎688-7991
In Sillery, the restaurant-club Montego promises a "sunny experience." The warmly decorated interior, the large colourful plates and the food presentation are a pleasure to behold. And the cooking will delight your tastebuds with sweet, hot and spicy flavours inspired by cuisine from California and from other sunny places!

Sainte-Foy

Mille-Feuilles
$$
1405 Chemin Ste-Foy
☎681-4520
Mille-Feuilles is a vegetarian restaurant where you can find good food that is healthy, delicious and carefully prepared. Located on a section of Chemin Ste-Foy that has a few shops and restaurants, the decor is a bit cool, but the ambiance is relaxed. There is a little bookstore that sells books on health.

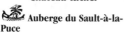 **La Fenouillère**
$$$-$$$$
3100 Chemin St-Louis
☎653-3886
At La Fenouillère, the menu of refined and creative French

cuisine promises a succulent dining experience. This restaurant is also proud to possess one of the best wine cellars in Québec. The decor is simple and comfortable.

Michelangelo
$$$-$$$$
3111 Chemin St-Louis
☎651-6262
Michelangelo serves fine Italian cuisine that both smells and tastes wonderful. The classically decorated dining room, although busy, is warm and intimate. The courteous and attentive service adds to the pleasure of the food.

Deschambault

Bistro Clan Destin
$$
109 Rue de l'Église
☎286-6647
Just in front of the village church is the Bistro Clan Destin, with its lovely flowery decor. The menu is varied, and good daily specials are served.

Maison Deschambault
$$$
128 route 138
☎286-3386
The restaurant in the Maison Deschambault Inn is well-known for its excellent menu, which consists mainly of fine French cuisine as well as various specialties of the region. The setting is particularly enchanting (see p 367).

Tour D: The Rivière Jacques-Cartier

Wendake

Nek8arre
$$-$$$
9am to 5pm, with reservations for dinner
575 Rue Stanislas-Kosca
☎842-4308
At the Huron Village (see p 361), there is a pleasant restaurant whose name means "the meal is ready to

serve." Nek8arre (pronounced "Nekwaray") introduces you to traditional Huron cooking. Wonderful dishes such as clay trout, caribou or venison brochettes with mushrooms accompanied by wild rice and corn, are some of the items on the menu. The wooden tables have little texts explaining the diet of Aboriginal peoples embedded in them. Numerous objects scattered here and there will arouse your curiosity, and luckily, the waitresses act as part-time "ethnologists" and can answer your questions. All this in a pleasant atmosphere. The entry fee to the village will be waived if you are only going to the restaurant.

Entertainment

Theatres

There are many good summer theatres in the area to liven up the beautiful evenings. Here are a few companies to look out for (consult local newspapers for listings).

Théâtre de la Fenière (*1500 Rue de la Fenière, L'Ancienne-Lorette, ☎872-1424*).

The **Moulin Marcoux** (*1 Boulevard Notre-Dame, Pont-Rouge, ☎873-3425*) presents various shows and exhibitions.

The **Salle Albert-Rousseau** in the Sainte-Foy Cegep (*2410 Chemin Ste-Foy, Ste-Foy, ☎659-6710*) presents excellent plays and shows throughout the year.

Festivals and Cultural Events

Beauport

On Wednesday and Saturday nights, throughout the summer, the Parc de la Chute Montmorency comes to life with the **Grands Feux Loto-Québec** (*☎523-3389 or 800-923-3389*). This magical fireworks display takes place over the falls. Fleets of small boats gather on the river to admire the show.

Shopping

Tour B: Île d'Orléans

Île d'Orléans has a handful of craft shops, antique dealers and cabinet-making studios. One of these, the **Corporation des Artisans de l'Île** (*☎828-2519*), is located in the Saint-Pierre church. There are also about half a dozen art galleries on the island, many in the village of Saint-Jean.

Québec City Region

The shop at the **Forge à Pique-Assaut** (*2200 Chemin Royal, St-Laurent, ☎828-9300*) (see p 354) sells various forged-metal objects, from candle holders to furniture. They also sell other crafts.

The **Chocolaterie de l'Île d'Orléans** (*150 Chemin Royal, Ste-Pétronille, ☎828-2252*) offers a whole range of little delectable treats. Their homemade ice-cream is also delicious.

In the former Saint-Jean presbytery (*2001 Chemin Royal*) in front of the church overlooking the river, there are two shops that deserve a visit: **Les Échoueries** sells a variety of crafts made by talented artists, and the **country-style bakery** bakes up home-made breads and pastries.

Chaudière-Appalaches

The Chaudière-

Appalaches region is made up of several small areas with very distinct geographical features.

Located opposite Québec City, on the south shore of the St. Lawrence River, it stretches across a vast fertile plain before slowly climbing into the foothills of the Appalachian Mountains, all the way to the U.S. border. The Rivière Chaudière, which originates in Lac Mégantic, runs through the centre of this region, then flows into the St. Lawrence across from Québec City.

A pretty, pastoral landscape unfolds along the river between Leclercville and Saint-Roch-des-Aulnaies, an area occupied very early on by the French. There are attractive villages, including Saint-Jean-Port-Joli, an important provincial craft centre. Out in the gulf, adventure awaits in the Archipel de l'Île-aux-Grues.

Farther south, the picturesque Beauce region extends along the banks of the Rivière Chaudière. The river rises dramatically in the spring, flooding some of the villages along its banks almost every year, lending muddied local inhabitants the nickname "*jarrets noirs*," which translates somewhat inelegantly as "black hamstrings." The dis-

covery of gold nuggets in the river bed attracted prospectors to the area in the 19th century. Farms have prospered in the rolling green hills of the Beauce for hundreds of years. Church steeples announce the presence of little villages, scattered evenly across the local countryside. The Beauce region is also home to Québec's largest concentration of maple groves, making it the true realm of the *cabane à sucre* or sugar shack. The spring thaw gets the sap flowing and signals the sugaring-off season. Local inhabitants, "Beaucerons," are also known for their sense of tradition and hospitality.

The "asbestos" region, located a little farther west of the Rivière Chaudière, around Thetford Mines, has a fairly varied landscape, punctuated with impressive open-cut mines.

Finding Your Way Around

Two tours have been laid out for the Chaudière-Appalaches region:

Tour A: The Seigneuries of the Côte-du-Sud ★★ runs along the St. Lawrence from Leclercville to Saint-Roch-des-Aulnaies, **Tour B: La**

Names of New Merged Cities

Saint-Georges
Merger of Saint-Georges, Saint-Georges-Est, Saint-Jean-de-la-Lande and Aubert-Gallion.

Sainte-Croix
Merger of the village and the parish of Sainte-Croix.

Lac-Etchemin
Merger of Lac-Etchemin and Sainte-Germaine-du-Lac-Etchemin.

Thetford Mines
Merger of Thetford Mines, Black Lake, Thetford-Partie-Sud, Robertsonville and Pontbriand.

Lévis
Merger of Charny, Lévis, Saint-Jean-Chrysostome, Saint-Nicolas, Saint-Rédempteur, Saint-Romuald, Pintendre, Saint-Étienne-de-Lauzon, Sainte-Hélène-de-Breakeyville and Saint-Joseph-de-la-Pointe-de-Lévy.

Beauce ★ leads through the valley of the Rivière Chaudière and the asbestos region.

Tour A: The Seigneuries of the Côte-du-Sud

By Car

From Montréal, take Hwy. 20 to Exit 253, then follow the 265 N. to Deschaillons, and turn right on Rte. 132 E. From Québec City, cross the river to take Rte. 132 in either direction.

Bus Stations

Lévis
5401 Blvd. Rive-Sud
☎837-5805

Montmagny
20 Blvd. Taché Est (Irving)
☎(418) 248-1850

Saint-Jean-Port-Joli
10 Ave. de Gaspé Est
☎598-6808

Train Stations

Montmagny
4 Rue de la Station
☎800-361-5390

By Ferry

The ferry between Québec City and Lévis (*$2.50 pedestrian or cyclist; $3.10 car plus charge for passengers,* ☎418-644-3704 *in Lévis*) takes only 15min. The schedule is subject to change, but there are frequent crossings.

The ferry to Île aux Grues, the **Grue des Îles** (*free;* ☎418-248-3549 *in Montmagny, 418-248-2968 in l'Isle-aux-Grues*), leaves from the Montmagny dock and takes about 20min. The schedule varies with the tide.

The following companies also ferry people to Île aux Grues or to Grosse Île. The boats of **Taxi des Îles** (*Île aux Grues $10 one way; Grosse Île $40 round-trip, 4.5hrs; 124 rue St. Louis, Montmagny;* ☎418-248-2818) is recognizable by the yellow-and-black colour scheme of its boats and frequently travels to the islands from the Montmagny dock. **Croisières Lachance** (*price varies by package, cruises to Grosse-île and the Montmagny archepelago; 110 de la Marina, Berthier-sur-Mer;* ☎418-259-2140 or 888-476-7734), offers daily cruises from Berthier-sur-Mer.

Tour B: La Beauce

By Car

From Québec City, take Hwy. 73 S. (use the Pont Pierre Laporte bridge). The Rivière Chaudière falls are on the right. Take Exit 101 to Rte. 173 and follow this to Vallée-Jonction.

Bus Stations

Saint-Georges
11655 promenade Chaudière
☎(418) 228-4040

Thetford Mines
127 Rue Saint-Alphonse Ouest
☎(4180 335-5120

Practical Information

Area Code: **418**

Tourist Information

Regional Office

Association Touristique Chaudière-Appalaches
800 Autoroute Jean-Lesage,
St Nicolas
☎831-4411 or 888-831-4411
⇥831-8442
www.chaudapp.qc.ca

Tour A: The Seigneuries of the Côte-du-Sud

Lévis
5995 Rue St. Laurent
☎838-6026

Montmagny
45 Avenue du Quai
☎248-9196 or 800-463-5643
⇥248-1436
www.montmagny.com

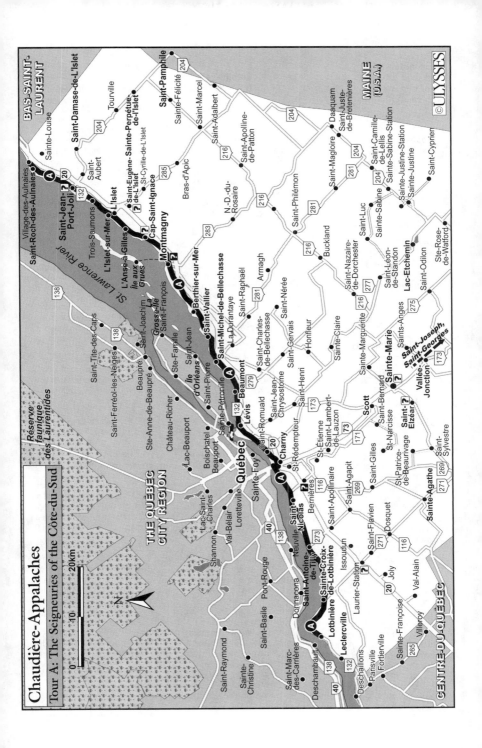

Cap-St-Ignace
100 Place del l'Église
☎*246-5390*
⇌*246-3350*

Saint-Jean-Port-Joli
7 Place de l'Église
☎*598-3747*
⇌*598-3085*

Tour B: La Beauce

Saint-Georges
11700 Boulevard Lacroix
☎*227-4642 or 877-923-2823*
⇌*228-2255*

Thetford Mines
682 Rue Monfette Nord
☎*335-7141 or 335-6511*
⇌*335-3008*
www.tourisme-amiante.com

Exploring

Tour A: The Seigneuries of the Côte-du-Sud

Duration of tour: two days

This tour is dotted with charming villages at regular intervals along the majestic St. Lawrence. It encompasses both the Rive-Sud of Québec City and the Côte-du-Sud (the southern shore and coast), gradually taking on a maritime flavour as the river widens. Visitors will enjoy stunning views of this vast stretch of water as its colour varies with the time of day and temperature, as well as Île d'Orléans and the mountains of Charlevoix. The tour also features some of the loveliest examples of traditional architecture in Québec, including churches, seigneurial manors, mills and old houses, whose windows open onto wide-open spaces. It is perhaps this region that best represents rural Québec.

★ Lotbinière (pop. 965)

Granted to René-Louis Chartier de Lotbinière in 1672, the seigneury of Lotbinière is one of the few estates to have always remained in the hands of the same family. Because he had a seat on the Conseil Souverain (sovereign council), the first seigneur did not actually live on the premises. Nevertheless, he saw to it that the land and the village of Lotbinière were developed. At the heart of Lotbinière, which quickly became one of the most important villages in the region, visitors will find a number of old houses made of stone and wood. This area is now protected by the provincial government.

Turn right on Route du Vieux-Moulin.

Moulin du Portage ★ (*Rang Saint-François*), a flour mill built in 1815 for Michel-Eustache-Gaspard-Alain Chartier de Lotbinière, lies in a pastoral setting on the banks of the Rivière du Chêne. Visitors can enjoy a pleasant walk or a picnic in the park surrounding the mill.

Along with its presbytery and former convent, the monumental **Église Saint-Louis ★ ★** (*7510 Rue Marie-Victorin*), set parallel to the St. Lawrence, provides a lovely setting from which to enjoy a view of the river. The present building is the fourth Catholic church to be built in the seigneury of Lotbinière. Designed by François Baillargé, it was begun in 1818. The spires, as well as the crown of the facade, are the result of modifications made in 1888. Its polychromatic exterior—white walls, blue steeples and red roof—creates a surprising (and very French) tricolour effect.

The decor of the church is a masterpiece of traditional religious art in Québec. Without question, the key piece is the neoclassical reredos shaped like a triumphal arch, sculpted by Thomas Baillargé in 1824. In the middle of it hang three paintings dating back to 1730, which are attributed to Frère François Brékenmacher, a Récollet monk from the Montréal monastery. The organ in the jube, originally intended for the Anglican cathedral in Québec City, was built in London by the Elliott Company in 1802. Too high for the Anglican church, it was put into storage before being acquired by Père Faucher, the parish priest, in 1846. A century later, it was restored and equipped for electric power by the Casavant Company of Saint-Hyacinthe.

Before reaching the village of Sainte-Croix, turn left on Route de la Pointe-Platon to the Domaine Joly de Lotbinière.

Sainte-Croix (pop. 1,675)

The Chartier de Lotbinière lineage dates back to the 11th century. In the service of French kings for many generations, the family preserved its contacts with the motherland even after it established itself in Canada, despite the British conquest and the distance between the two lands. In 1828, Julie-Christine Chartier de Lotbinière married Pierre-Gustave Joly, a rich Huguenot merchant from Montréal. In 1840, Joly purchased a part of the Sainte-Croix land from the Québec City Ursulines in order to build a seigneurial manor there, which would come to be known as the Manoir de la Pointe Platon, or the Domaine Joly de Lotbinière.

Domaine Joly-De Lotbinière ★ ★ (*$8; early*

May to late Oct 10am to 5pm; route de la Pointe-Platon, ☎926-2462) is part of the Jardins de Québec association. The main attraction here is the superb setting on the banks of the St. Lawrence. It is especially worthwhile to take the footpaths to the beach in order to gaze out at the river, the slate cliffs and the opposite shore, where the Église de Cap Santé is visible. Numerous rare century-old trees, floral arrangements and an aviary adorn the grounds of the estate. There is also a boutique and café with a patio. The manor, which was built in 1840 to overlook the river, is designed as a villa with wraparound verandas.

Inside is a small exhibition on the family of the Marquis de Lotbinière. Visitors will learn, for example, that Henri-Gustave, the son of Pierre-Gustave Joly, was born in Épernay (France), and later became Premier of Québec (1878-79), federal Revenue Minister and finally Lieutenant-Governor of British Columbia. The Domaine Joly de Lotbinière came under the care of the provincial government in 1967, when the last seigneur, Edmond Joly de Lotbinière, had to vacate the premises.

Upon leaving the parking lot, turn left on the road leading to Rte. 132 E.

Église Sainte-Croix *(alongside Rte. 132 E.)*. The Université Laval's agronomical centre is the economic mainspring for the village of Sainte-Croix. The village is dominated by its granite Baroque Revival church, built in 1911. The church has a coffered ceiling that is typical of the Belle Époque.

Continue along Rte. 132 E. Turn left on Chemin de Tilly, which leads to the centre of Saint-Antoine-de-Tilly.

★
Saint-Antoine-de-Tilly
(pop. 1,450)

In 1702, Noël Legardeur de Tilly acquired the seigneury of Auteuil, which now bears his name. The hamlet has evolved into the peaceful village looking over the river that visitors will find today. Saint-Antoine-de-Tilly still has a few small ship-building companies.

The present facade of **Église Saint-Antoine ★** *(3870 Chemin de Tilly)*, added in 1902, adorns the building erected at the end of the 18th century. The interior, decorated by André Pâquet between 1837 and 1840, highlights several beautiful paintings purchased at sales after the French Revolution, including *La Sainte Famille*

(The Holy Family), or *Intérieur de Nazareth* (Inside Nazareth), by Aubin Vouet, which once adorned the abbey church of Saint-Germain-des-Prés in Paris, and *La Visitation* (The Visitation), by A. Oudry. Other noteworthy works include *Jésus au Milieu des Docteurs* (Jesus Surrounded by Doctors) by Samuel Massé and *Saint François d'Assise* (St. Francis of Assisi), by Frère Luc. A stroll through the neighbouring cemetery offers a lovely view of the St. Lawrence and the church in silhouette.

Four generations of the Tilly family lived in the **Manoir de Tilly** *(3854 Chemin de Tilly)*, built at the end of the 18th century. The building, now an inn, has a low veranda with delicate wood trellises. A little farther along lies the Manoir Dionne, with a veranda decorated with wrought iron. This was the residence of Henriette de Tilly, wife of merchant Charles François Dionne, whose family owned a number of seigneuries on the Côte-du-Sud (south coast).

Continue along Rte. 132 E., through Saint-Nicolas, a former resort area. Follow the signs for Rte. 132 E. to Saint-Romuald, then Lévis. Drivers should pay particular attention near the Pont de Québec bridge, where the interchanges are frequent.

★★
Lévis
(pop. 41,500)

Founded by Henry Caldwell in 1826, Lévis developed rapidly during the second half of the 19th century, due to the introduction of the railroad (1854) and the establishment of several local shipyards, supplied with wood by sawmills owned by the Price and Hamilton families. Because there was no railway line on the north shore of the St. Lawrence at the

Domaine Joly-De Lotbinière

Chaudière-Appalaches

time, some of Québec City's shipping activities were transferred to Lévis. Originally known as Ville d'Aubigny, Lévis was given its present name in 1861, in memory of Chevalier François de Lévis, who defeated the British in the Battle of Sainte-Foy in 1760. The upper part of the city, consisting mostly of administrative buildings, offers some interesting views of Vieux-Québec, located on the opposite side of the river, while the very narrow lower part welcomes the trains and the ferry linking Lévis to the provincial capital. Lévis merged with its neighbour, **Lauzon**, in 1990.

Built during the stock market crash of 1929, the **Terrasse de Lévis ★★** *(Rue William-Tremblay)* offers spectacular views of downtown Lévis and Québec City. From here, you can take Vieux-Québec's Place Royale, located along the river, and the Château Frontenac and Haute-Ville above. A few modern skyscrapers stand out in the background, the tallest being the Édifice Marie-Guyart, located on Québec City's Parliament Hill.

Turn right on Rue Carrier. The Maison Alphonse-Desjardins, former home of the founder of the Mouvement Desjardins credit union, stands at the corner of Rue Mont-Marie and Rue Guénette.

Maison Alphonse-Desjardins *(free admission; Mon-Fri 10am to noon and 1pm to 4:30pm, Sat and Sun noon to 5pm; 6 Rue du Mont-Marie, ☎835-2090 or 800-463-4810 ext. 2090).* Alphonse Desjardins (1854-1920) was a stubborn man. Eager for the advancement of the French Canadian people, he struggled for many years to

promote the concept of the *caisse populaire* (credit union), a cooperative financial institution controlled by its members, and by all the small investors who hold accounts there. In the family kitchen of his house on Rue Mont-Marie, Desjardins and his wife Dorimène conceived the idea and set up the first *caisse populaire*. The Caisses Desjardins aroused suspicion at first, but eventually became an important economic lever. Today there are more than 1,200 branches across Québec, with more than 5 million members.

The Gothic Revival house where the Desjardins lived for nearly 40 years was built in 1882. It was beautifully restored on its 100th anniversary and converted into an information centre that focuses on Desjardins's career and achievements. Visitors can watch a video and see several restored rooms. The offices of the Société Historique Alphonse-Desjardins are located on the second floor.

Église Notre-Dame-de-la-Victoire ★ *(18 Rue Notre-Dame).* In 1851, a parish priest named Joseph Déziel proposed building a large Catholic church to

Maison Alphonse-Desjardins

serve the flourishing town. Thomas Baillargé, the architect of so many churches in the Québec City area, drew up the plans. His buildings express a complete mastery of the neoclassical vocabulary of Québec, where French and English styles converge. The interior, divided into three naves, has high-columned galleries. On the grounds of the church, there is a plaque marking the exact location of the English cannons that bombarded Québec City in 1759.

Those interested in visiting the Fort No.1 at Pointe de Lévy N.H.S. should take Rte. 132 E., then turn left on Chemin du Gouvernement. Otherwise, take Côte du Passage (away from the river) and turn left on Rue Saint-Georges, which becomes Rue Saint-Joseph in Vieux-Lauzon.

The **Fort No.1 at Pointe de Lévy National Historic Site ★** *($3; early May to late Aug every day 10am to 5pm, late Aug to late Sep Thu-Sun 1pm to 4pm; 41 Chemin du Gouvernement, ☎835-5182 or 800-463-6769)* is also called the Lieu Historique National du Fort-Numéro-Un. Fearing a surprise attack from the Americans at the end of the Civil War, the British (and later Canadian) government built three separate forts in Lévis, which were incorporated into Québec City's defence system. Only Fort No.1 remains intact. Made of earth and stone, it illustrates the evolution of fortified structures in the 19th century, when military techniques were advancing rapidly. Visitors will be particularly interested in the rifled bore, an imposing piece of artillery, as well as the vaulted pillboxes and the caponiers, masonry structures intended to protect the moat. The site also includes an exhibition on the history of the fort.

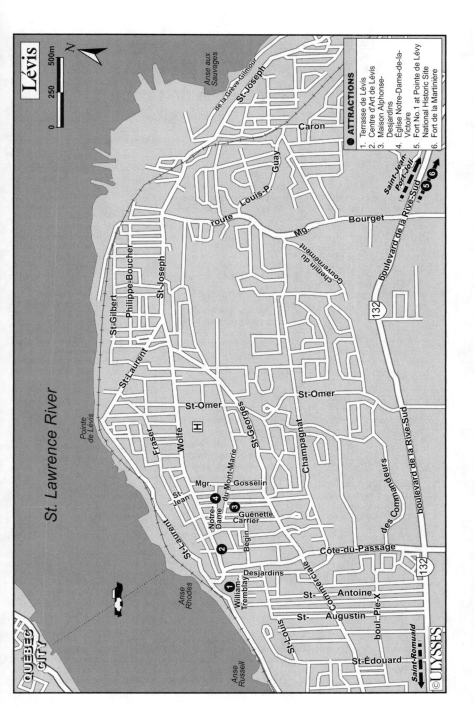

Lévis

St. Lawrence River

QUÉBEC CITY

Pointe de Lévis

Anse aux Sauvages

Anse Rhodes

Anse Russell

0   250   500m

N

ATTRACTIONS

1. Terrasse de Lévis
2. Centre d'Art de Lévis
3. Maison Alphonse-Desjardins
4. Église Notre-Dame-de-la-Victoire
5. Fort No.1 at Pointe de Lévy National Historic Site
6. Fort de la Martinière

St-Joseph
de la Grève-Gilmour

Caron

Louis-P.

Guay

route

Mgr.

Bourget

Chemin du Gouvernement

Saint-Jean-Port-Joli.

boulevard de la Rive-Sud

132

St-Gilbert

Philippe-Boucher

St-Joseph

St-Laurent

St-Omer

St-Omer

Fraser

Wolfe

St-Georges

Champagnat

des Commandeurs

H

St-Laurent

St-Jean

Mgr.

Notre-Dame-du-Mont-Marie

Gosselin

Carrier

Guénette

Côte-du-Passage

Bégin

Desjardins

William-Tremblay

Commerciale

St-Louis

St-Antoine

St-Augustin

boul.-Pie-X

St-Édouard

Saint-Romuald

132

© ULYSSES

Alphonse Desjardins (1854-1920)

Alphonse Desjardins was born in Lévis in 1854, where 46 years later he founded the Caisse Populaire de Lévis, the first in an important movement of credit unions, that has grown into the present-day Caisses Populaires Desjardins.

The injustice of the loan system of the day prompted Desjardins to create a savings organization that would meet the needs of small-scale investors. Credit unions already existed in Europe; by adapting their methods to the Québec situation, Desjardins realized his idea of a cooperative system in which community solidarity could benefit all of its members.

Desjardins spent three years refining his project when he took time off from his position as a House of Commons reporter in Ottawa. During parliamentary breaks, he returned to his home in Lévis. At the end of the year 1900, he convinced certain town notables that his project was viable and, on December 6, these men held a meeting during which the establishment of a new savings and loan company was proposed.

During the first years of this new institution, members came to deposit their nest eggs right at the Desjardins family home, on Rue du Mont-Marie, where Alphonse, or his wife Dorimène, would advise them and record their deposits.

Initially, the founders of the Caisses Populaires insisted that the credit union's activities be limited to the parish, but when they encouraged the creation of new unions, requests came in from all over the province. Since these were cooperatives, they were created by the demand of citizens who were inte-

rested in working together to get better savings and fairer credit.

Desjardins toured Québec for several years explaining his idea to volunteers. In 1909, 22 Caisses were active across the province; the 100th was inaugurated in 1912. Each credit union functioned independently under Desjardins's guidance. Three years later, the Québec government adopted a law permitting the Caisses Populaires to amalgamate into a larger movement that could help sustain struggling member branches.

At the end of his life, Alphonse Desjardins was as involved as ever in the activities of the Caisses Populaires. He who had so much faith in the human spirit of cooperation left behind a popular movement that today has close to five million members in 1,200 Caisses across Québec.

Finally, from the top of the wall, visitors can enjoy a lovely view of Québec City and Île d'Orléans. A little farther along are the remnants of **Fort de la Martinière** *($2; May to Oct, every day 9am to 4pm; Nov to Apr, Mon-Fri 9am to 4pm; 9805 Boul. de la Rive-Sud)* which also offers an exhibition

of various implements of war. The grounds have picnic areas.

Église Saint-Joseph-de-Lauzon ★ *(Rue Saint-Joseph)*. Lauzon was once the nucleus of the seigneury of the same name, granted to Jean de Lauzon, Governor of New

France, in 1636. The parish of Saint-Joseph, founded in 1673, is the oldest on Québec City's entire south shore. At the time, it encompassed the territory now occupied by Lévis, Saint-Romuald and Saint-Nicolas. The original church, destroyed by a fire in 1830, was replaced soon after by the present one, yet another design by the Baillargé family. Particularly notable are the two procession chapels located on either side of the church, the **Chapelle Sainte-Anne** (1789) and the **Chapelle Saint-François-Xavier** (1822). The **MIL Davie shipyard** lies opposite the latter.

Rue Saint-Joseph leads back to Rte. 132 E. (also known as Boulevard de la Rive-Sud). Continue on to Beaumont. A road on the left leads to the centre of the village.

★
Beaumont (pop. 2,070)

The Côte-du-Sud corresponds to the south coast (*côte sud*) of the St. Lawrence estuary and technically begins at Beaumont. With its silver-roofed churches, procession chapels for Corpus Christi and manors set in a landscape that seems larger than life, this is true French Canadian country. The seigneury of Beaumont (1672) is a fine example of the regional heritage.

The beautiful little **Église Saint-Étienne ★ ★** *(Chemin du Domaine)*, built in 1733, is one of the oldest churches still

standing in Québec. It looks straight down the axis of the main road, which curves inland just afterwards, forming a small triangular plaza in front of the church square. This formation is typical of classical 18th century French town planning. In 1759, during the British conquest, the British posted General Wolfe's proclamation decreeing the fall of New France on Beaumont's church. The villagers hastened to tear up the document. To punish them, General Moncton, who was responsible for the deportation of the Acadians in 1755, ordered his soldiers to set fire to the church. They held flaming torches to the door three times, but with no success. According to legend, each attempt was thwarted when a mysterious hand "miraculously" extinguished the flames.

Inside, the tabernacle of the high altar, sculpted around 1715, stands amidst a lovely Louis XV-style decor designed by Étienne Bercier in the early 19th century. In the middle of the retable is *Mort de Saint Étienne* by Antoine Plamondon (1826), and to the left, behind the pulpit, is a side

chapel that was added in 1894. On the right, as you leave the church, you will find both the present-day presbytery and the old stone presbytery-chapel that was built in 1721 and later converted to a library.

Two French Regime procession chapels, one at the village entrance (De Sainte-Anne, 1734) and the other at the exit (De la Vierge, around 1740), add to the old-fashioned charm of Beaumont.

Follow Chemin du Domaine east, until it intersects with Rte. 132 E. The Moulin de Beaumont lies a little farther on the left.

The **Moulin de Beaumont ★** *($6; early May to late Jun, Sat and Sun 10am to 4:30pm; late Jun to early Sep, Tue-Sun 10am to 4:30pm; early Sep to late Oct, Sat and Sun 10am to 4:30pm; 2 Rue du Fleuve, Rte. 132, ☎833-1867)* was built in 1821 on a plateau halfway down the waterfall in Maillou, and only its upper floors are visible from the road. The grounds of the mill, which include a picnic area, slope gradually down toward the St. Lawrence, offering lovely views of Île d'Orléans and the mountains on the opposite shore. There is even a staircase leading down to the tidal flats and the ruins of an older mill, the Moulin Péan. Visitors can purchase muffins and bread made with flour milled on the premises. Both are baked using traditional methods. A video relates the history of the mill as well as an account of the archaeological digs that have been carried out on the site.

★
Berthier-sur-Mer (pop. 1,265)

This village is aptly named (Berthier by the Sea) because on arriving here from the

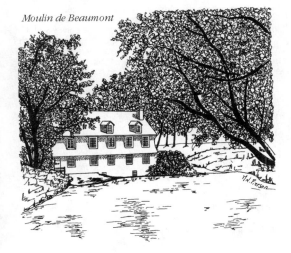
Moulin de Beaumont

Chaudière-Appalaches

west, visitors catch their first whiff of sea air. Here, Île d'Orléans has faded into the background, and the river, with its blue waves, starts to look like the ocean. On a clear day, typical sights include the mountains of Charlevoix, just opposite, and the fully equipped sailing harbour of this small summer resort founded back in the seigneurial era. Seigneur Dénéchaud's manor, built in the early 19th century, was destroyed by fire in 1992 after nearly 40 years of neglect.

From Berthier-sur-Mer, visitors can set off on a cruise of the St. Lawrence, around the Archipel de l'Isle-aux-Grues, also known as the Archipel de Montmagny. The trip includes a visit to the Grosse Île and the Irish Memorial National Historic Site and Île aux Grues itself (see descriptions below). Similar cruises also leave from Montmagny, 15km farther east.

Montmagny (pop. 11,885)

The **Centre Éducatif des Migrations** ★ *($4; Jun to Nov every day 9:30am to 5pm; 53 Rue du Bassin-Nord, ☎248-9334)* is located on the Pointe-aux-Oies campsite. This information centre on bird migrations deals with the *sauvagine*, or snow goose; it also has a theatre presenting a sound-and-light show about the colonization of the region and the arrival of immigrants at Grosse-Île. The sound-and-light show is an excellent way to begin your visit to Grosse-Île. Though the link between these two subjects seems somewhat tenuous, the exhibits and the show are extremely instructive.

Cross Boulevard Taché and pick up Rue du Bassin-Sud, which soon connects with Rue Saint-Ignace. After crossing one bridge, turn right on Rue de la Fabrique. Go over an-

other bridge, then just before the church, turn left on Rue Saint-Jean-Baptiste.

Visitors will notice that the centre of Montmagny, like that of most towns in Québec (as opposed to Europe), faces neither of the rivers that run alongside it. This is because waterways are a source of cold wind in the winter, and of flooding and ice-jams during the spring thaw. In the past, rivers were viewed from a strictly utilitarian angle and valued only for the purposes of transportation, industry and dumping waste. This means their banks were not graced with promenades.

Rue Saint-Jean-Baptiste and Rue Saint-Thomas meet at a point west of the church and are lined with a number of cafés, terraces and attractive shops in old houses. Avenue Sainte-Marie provides access to the beautiful and historic Taché house, hidden behind commercial buildings. The **Maison Historique Sir Étienne-Pascal-Taché** *($4; Jun to Sep, Mon-Fri 10am to 5pm, Sat and Sun 10am to 4pm; Sept to late Oct, Sat and Sun, 10am to 4pm; 37 Avenue Sainte-Marie, ☎248-9334)*, built in 1759, was the home of Sir Étienne Pascal Taché (1795-1865), who was Prime Minister of United Canada for a few years. He had the two picturesque towers looking out over the river added to the building.

Head back to Rue de la Fabrique and turn left, then take a right on Boulevard Taché, and another left on Avenue du Quai.

Before Avenue du Quai is the **Manoir Couillard de L'Espinay**, built in 1817 and now a luxury hotel (see p 389). The pier street runs along a beautifully landscaped walking path for the entire length of the Montmagny basin. This is a great spot to have

a picnic or simply to relax before departing on a boat trip. The **Montmagny pier** is an exceptional spot to see snow geese in spring and fall, and is one of the departure points to Grosse-Île and Île aux Grues. The harbour station is situated just before the pier.

Grosse Île and the Irish Memorial National Historic Site ★★ *(independent or guided visits; May to Oct; A catering service is available on site or bring your own lunch for a picnic by the shore; ☎248-8888 or 800-463-6769)* is also called the Lieu Historique National de la Grosse-Île-et-le-Mémorial-des-Irlandais. An excursion to Grosse Île is to step back into the sad history of North American immigration. Fleeing epidemics and famine, Irish emigrants to Canada were particularly numerous from the 1830s to the 1850s. In order to limit the spread of cholera and typhus, the New World, authorities required transatlantic passengers to submit to a quarantine before allowing them to disembark at the port of Québec. Grosse Île was the logical location for this isolation camp, far enough from the mainland to sequester its residents effectively, but close enough to be convenient. On this "Quarantine Island" each immigrant was inspected with a fine-tooth comb. Travellers in good health stayed in "hotels," the luxury of which depended on the class of the berths they had occupied on the ships. The sick were immediately hospitalized.

A total of four million immigrants from 42 different countries passed through the port of Québec between 1832 and 1937. It is impossible to ascertain how many of these spent time on Grosse Île, but close to 7,000 people perished there. In 1847, the year of the Great Potato Famine, a principle cause of Irish emigration, the typhus epidemic was particularly virulent and especially hard on Irish immigrants. Of the 7,000 deaths registered over 105 years, 5,434 were counted in this tragic year. In memory of this sad year, people of Irish descent have made pilgrimages to Grosse Île every year since 1909. A Celtic cross stands on the island, in memory of those who came here and of those unfortunates who did not survive. On March 17, 1997, Saint Patrick's Day, Minister of Canadian Heritage Sheila Copps remembered the tragedy, renaming the site Grosse Île and the Irish Memorial National Historic Site.

The guided tour of Grosse Île, part of which is made on a small motorized train, reveals the natural beauty of the island and its built structures. Among the 30 buildings still standing, a few are now open to the public: the disinfecting building, which has been open since the summer of 1997 and is presently being restored, informs visitors about Canadian technology at the end of the 19th century and gives them a glimpse inside a lazar house (a hospital for people with infectious diseases). This is where victims of the 1847 typhoid epidemic were quarantined. These precious remnants of a tragic page in Canadian history give the place a particular allure. Thanks to Parks Canada, history comes to life here. The barracks still stand, as does the imposing disinfection building, recently opened to the public for the first time. Together, these buildings recount a page from the history of this part of the continent.

Île aux Grues ★ ★ is the only island of the Isle-aux-Grues archipelago that is inhabited year round. It is an excellent spot for watching snow geese in the spring, for hunting in autumn, and for walking in

summer. In winter, the island is locked in by ice and residents can only access the mainland by airplane. A few rural inns dot this 10km-long agricultural island. A bicycle trip through its golden wheat fields along the river is one of the most pleasant ways to explore the area. The island is also accessible by car thanks to the *Grue des Îles* ferry (see p 372). At the centre of the island is the village of **Saint-Antoine-de-l'Isle-aux-Grues**, with its little church and its lovely houses. There is a craft shop, a cheese store that sells a delicious locally produced cheese, and a small museum that reveals past and present traditions of island life. To the east is the **Manoir Seigneurial McPherson-LeMoine**, which was rebuilt for Louis Liénard Villemonde Beaujeu after the island was sacked by the British army in 1759. This attractive house, fronted by a long gallery, was the summer home of historian James McPherson-LeMoine at the end of the 19th century. It later became the haven of painter Jean-Paul Riopelle until his death in 2002.

At the end of the dock there is a small tourist information stand that is staffed during high season. If you plan to spend a few days on the island, bring enough cash, since there is only one small bank on the island and it does not have an automatic teller machine.

Continue along Rte. 132 E. to Cap-Saint-Ignace. Turn right on the village road (Rue du Manoir).

Cap-Saint-Ignace (pop. 2,983)

The **Manoir Gamache ★** *(not open to visitors; 120 Rue du Manoir, on the right on the way into the village)* was built in 1744 as a chapel and presbytery. Miraculously spared during the British Conquest, it became the residence of

Seigneur Gamache shortly thereafter. The manor, with its thick, low square masonry and its high roof with dormer windows, is typical of rural architecture under the French Regime. The only unconventional element is the main door, which faces inland instead of the river. Its landscaping showcases this extremely well-restored manor.

Église Saint-Ignace ★ *(in the centre of the village)* was rebuilt between 1880 and 1894 as a replacement for the original church erected in 1772. Its long nave, lack of transepts, corner pinnacles and magnificent gilded interior with columned side galleries make it one of the most interesting buildings ever designed by David Ouellet. This Québec City architect did a great deal of work in the Beauce, the Bas-Saint-Laurent and Gaspésie regions.

Continue along the old village road, then turn left to get back on Rte. 132.

★ L'Islet-sur-Mer (pop. 1,800)

As its name ("Islet by the Sea") suggests, this village's activities centre on the sea. Since the 18th century, local residents have been handing down the occupations of sailor and captain on the St. Lawrence from father to son. Some have even become highly skilled captains and explorers on distant seas. In 1677, Governor Frontenac granted the seigneury of L'Islet to two families, the Bélangers and the Couillards, who quickly developed their lands. They turned both L'Islet-sur-Mer, on the banks of the St. Lawrence, and L'Islet, farther inland, into prosperous communities which still play an important role in the region.

The sea breeze, strong and mild at once, gives a good indication of the immensity of

Joseph-Elzéar Bernier (1852-1934)

Joseph-Elzéar Bernier, one of Québec's most famous sailors, was born into a long line of captains in 1852, in the lovely village of L'Islet-sur-Mer.

In 1869, at the age of 17, Joseph-Elzéar was named captain of a ship called the *Saint-Joseph*, which had been previously piloted by his father, making him the youngest captain in the world. During the following years, he navigated all of the oceans and seas on Earth, setting speed records along the way.

In 1904 he made the first of his exploratory voyages to the Arctic Ocean, financed by the Canadian government. A plaque on the Melville Peninsula commemorates his crowning achievement, the appropriation of this arctic territory in the name of the government of Canada.

Bernier then returned to commercial navigation in the Arctic and on the St. Lawrence River. Until the end of his life, at the age of 82, he maintained a close relationship with the sea.

the nearby river. A good place to breathe this sea air is from the front step of the **Église Notre-Dame-de-Bonsecours** ★★ (*15 Rue des Pionniers Est, Rte. 132*). The present church, begun in 1768, is a large stone building with no transepts. The interior decor, executed between 1782 and 1787, reflects the teachings of the Académie Royale d'Architecture in Paris, where the designer François Baillargé had recently been a student. Consequently, unlike earlier churches, the reredos mimics the shape of the semi-circular chancel, itself completely covered with gilded Louis XV and Louis XVI–style wood panelling. The coffered ceiling was added in the 19th century, as were the spires on the steeples, which were redone in 1882. The tabernacle was designed by Noël Levasseur and came from the

original church in 1728. Above it hangs *L'Annonciation* (The Annunciation), painted by Abbé Aide-Créquy in 1776. The glass doors on the left open onto the former congregationist chapel, added to the church in 1853, where occasional summer exhibitions with religious themes are put on.

With objects related to fishing, ship models, an interpretive centre and two real ships, the **Musée Maritime du Québec** ★★ (*$9; mid-May to late Jun and mid-Sep to mid-Oct, every day 9am to 5pm; late Jun to early Sep, every day 9am to 6pm; the rest of the year, Tue-Fri, 10am to noon and 1pm to 4pm; 55 Rue des Pionniers Est, ☎247-5001*) recounts the maritime history of the St. Lawrence from the 17th century to the present day. The

institution, founded by the Association des Marins du Saint-Laurent, occupies the former Couvent de l'Islet-sur-Mer (1877) and bears the name of one of the village's most illustrious citizens, Captain J. E. Bernier (1852-1934). Bernier was one of the first individuals to explore the Arctic, thus securing Canadian sovereignty in the Far North.

Heading towards Saint-Jean-Port-Joli, visitors will see the **Chapelle des Marins** (*Route des Pionniers*) of L'Islet (1835) on the left, along with the *Croix de Tempérance*, perched atop a hillock. These symbolic structures are used during the Corpus Christi procession, a tradition over three centuries old, revived a few years ago following the restoration of a number of chapels in villages along the Côte-du-Sud. This celebration takes place in the early evening on the second Sunday in June. It involves parish guards in costume, the penance of the Vatican and the Sacred Heart, and the monstrance and the Blessed Sacrament. The priest in all his finery is sheltered by a gold-embroidered baldaquin and followed by the congregation carrying candles, as he makes stops in front of the procession chapels. This event, dedicated to the Adoration of the Blessed Sacrament, is particularly spectacular in L'Islet-sur-Mer.

★
Saint-Jean-Port-Joli (pop. 3,400)

Saint-Jean-Port-Joli has become synonymous with handicrafts, specifically wood carving. The origins of this tradition go back to the Bourgault family, which made its living carving wood in the early 20th century. On the way into the town, Rte. 132 is lined with an impressive number of shops where visitors can purchase a wooden pipe-smoking grandfather or knitting woman. A museums exhibit the finest pieces. Though the handicraft business is flourishing now more than ever, the village is also known for its church, and for Philippe Aubert de Gaspé's novel *Les Anciens Canadiens* (Canadians of Old), written at the seigneurial manor.

On the way into the village, the **seigneurial mill** is visible on the right. Farther, on the left, the lovely **Maison Saint-Pierre**, built in 1765, precedes a lookout by the river.

The original manor of Saint-Jean-Port-Joli was destroyed during the British conquest. Another manor was built in 1764 on the same foundations and according to the same design as the first, but it unfortunately burned down in 1909. All that remains of **Philippe Aubert de Gaspé's Manor** *(710 de Gaspé Ouest)* is the bread oven by the side of the road. Philippe Aubert de Gaspé (1786-1871), Seigneur de Saint-Jean-Port-Joli, withdrew to his manor to write *Les Anciens Canadiens*, published in 1863. Considered the first French Canadian novel, the book's literary significance is as great as its ethnological interest, since it describes daily life at the end of the seigneurial era.

The **Musée des Anciens Canadiens** *($4; May, Jun, Sep, Oct every day 9am to 5:30pm; Jul and Aug, every day 8:30am to 9pm; 332 Avenue de Gaspé Ouest, ☎598-3392 or 598-6829)* exhibits a series of wood carvings depicting local traditions.

Maison Médard-Bourgault ★ *($4; mid-Jun to early Sep, every day 10am to 6pm; 322 Avenue de Gaspé Ouest, ☎598-3880)*. Médard Bourgault (1877-1967) was the first of a line of famous sculptors from Saint-Jean-Port-Joli. When he bought this

house in 1920, the master-mariner gave up navigating in order to devote himself entirely to woodcarving. As the years went by, he carved the walls and the furniture, producing a highly personal work of art. The house now belongs to his son, also a sculptor, who has his studio in the hose. If you want to see his work, and that of his father, just ask.

The **Économusée Les Bateaux Leclerc** *(guided tour $4; mid-May to Sep, every day 9am to 5pm, Oct to mid-May Mon-Fri 9am to noon and 1pm to 5pm; Jul and Aug every day 9am to 6pm; 307 Avenue de Gaspé Ouest, ☎598-3273)* exhibits the work of artisans who, for generations, have been creating miniature reproductions of boats that have navigated the St. Lawrence River. During the week, it is possible to watch the artists at work. The front of the house is adorned with a tall mural that seems to come right out of a fairy tale.

The charming **Église Saint-Jean-Baptiste** ★★ *(2 Avenue de Gaspé Ouest)*, built between 1779 and 1781, is recognizable by its bright red roof topped by two steeples, placed in a way altogether uncommon in Québec architecture: one in the front, the other in the back at the beginning of the apse. The church has a remarkable interior made of carved, gilded wood. Pierre Noël Levasseur's rocaille tabernacle, crowned with a wood shell supported by columns, comes from the original chapel and dates back to 1740. The side galleries added to the nave in order to increase the number of pews are also somewhat rare in Québec. Those in Saint-Jean-Port-Joli, dating back to 1845, are the only ones to have survived the waves of renovation and restoration of the past 40 years.

Continue along Rte. 132 to Saint-Roch-des-Aulnaies.

★★ Saint-Roch-des-Aulnaies (pop. 1,075)

This pretty village on the banks of the St. Lawrence is actually made up of two neighbourhoods. The one around the church is called Saint-Roch-des-Aulnaies, while the other, not far from the manor, is known as the Village des Aulnaies. The name "Aulnaies" refers to the abundance of alder trees *(aulnes)* that grow along the Rivière Ferrée, which powers the seigneurial mill. Nicolas Juchereau, the son of Jean Juchereau, Sieur de Maur from Perche, was granted the seigneury in 1656. Most of the old residences in Saint-Roch-des-Aulnaies are exceptionally large, a sign that local inhabitants enjoyed a certain degree of prosperity in the 19th century.

The manor and its mill are located on the right, after the bridge that spans the Rivière Ferrée.

Seigneurie des Aulnaies ★★ *($6; late May to early Sep every day 9am to 6pm; 525 Chemin de la Seigneurie, ☎354-2800 or 877-354-2800)*. The Dionne estate has been transformed into a fascinating information centre focusing on the seigneurial era. Visitors are greeted in the former miller's house, converted into a shop and café whose menu includes pancakes and muffins made with flour ground in the neighbouring mill, a large stone structure rebuilt in 1842 on the site of an older mill. Guided tours of the mill in operation enable visitors to understand its complex gearing system, set in motion by the Rivière Ferrée. Its main wheel is the largest in Québec.

The manor house, built on a promontory, is accessed by a

long stairway. Like the manor house at the **Domaine Joly-De Lotbinière** (see p 374), the Dionne home lacks austerity of typical seigneurial manors. It was designed by Charles Ballargé, a member of Québec's famous architectural dynasty, at the beginning of the Victorian era. His trademark is the Greek Revival ornamentation around the doorways (see **Maison Cirice-Têtu**, Québec City, p 305). In the basement, interactive displays explain in detail the principals of the seigneurial system and its impact on the landscape of rural Québec. The reception rooms on the main floor are plainly furnished in 19th-century style. A lovely garden, part of the Jardin du Québec association, as well as nature paths, surround the manor house. Guides and characters in period costume animate the site.

The Chaudière-Appalaches tourist area ends here, but the Côte-du-Sud continues all the way up to Rivière-du-Loup. We recommend combining this tour with one entitled **The Kamouraska Region ★★**, which leads through the Bas-Saint-Laurent region (see p 394).

To return to Québec City or Montréal quickly, head west on Hwy. 20, located just behind the village of Saint-Roch-des-Aulnaies.

Tour B: La Beauce

Duration of tour: two days

After the French Regime's timid attempts at colonization, Beauce, or Nouvelle-Beauce as it was frequently called in the 18th century, enjoyed a boom due to the opening of the Kennebec road (between 1810 and 1830), and then the railway (1870-1895). Both linked Québec and its capital to New England, passing through the valley of the Rivière Chaudière on the way. Agricultural hamlets all along this route flourished, becoming prosperous little industrial towns by the end of the 19th century. Known for their enterprising spirit and favoured by fortune, Beaucerons founded a number of businesses whose names, such as Vachon-Culinar and Canam-Manac, are now well-known in Québec.

Continue on Hwy. 73 and then Rte. 173, which runs alongside the Rivière Chaudière to the U.S. border. This road was named Route du Président-Kennedy in honour of the man whose memory is dear to the tens of thousands of Americans who take Rte. 173 each year to Québec City. Near Saint-Joseph, leave Rte. 173 in order to drive along the river to the centre of town.

★
Saint-Joseph-de-Beauce (pop. 4,430)

In Saint-Joseph, visitors will find a plaque commemorating **Route du Président-Kennedy**, which was renamed in 1970 *(347 Avenue du Palais)*. This major artery's modest origins date back to 1737, when the Beauce's first seigneurs were asked to open a road between the newly cleared lands and Lévis, located on the south shore of Québec City. In 1758, this original road was replaced by the wider, straighter Route Justinienne. It was not until 1830 that the road was extended across the border to Jackman, Maine.

Saint-Joseph is renowned for its extremely well-preserved group of religious buildings erected at the end of the 19th century on a hillock a good distance from the river, safe from floods. The first houses built along the Chaudière have long since been destroyed or, in some cases, moved to higher ground. This explains why the banks of the river are only slightly developed today.

The Romanesque Revival **Église Saint-Joseph** and its **Presbytery ★** *(Rue Sainte-Christine)*, built out of stone in 1865, are the work of François-Xavier Berlinguet and Joseph-Ferdinand Peachy, two architects from Québec City. The presbytery was designed by George-Émile Tanguay upon his return from a trip to France in the 1880s, an era marking the peak of the French Renaissance Revival style in the Paris region. Tanguay drew his inspiration from this style for the brick and stone presbytery, a veritable little palace for the parish priest and his curates.

The **Musée Marius-Barbeau ★** *($4; Mon-Fri 9am to 4:30pm; Sat and Sun 1pm to 4:30pm; 139 Rue Sainte-Christine, ☎397-4039)* focuses on the history of the Beauce region and explains the different stages of development in the Vallée de la Chaudière, from the first seigneuries, through the 19th-century gold rush, to the building of major communication routes. The arts and popular traditions studied by Beauceron ethnologist and folklorist Marius Barbeau are also prominently displayed. The building itself is the former convent of the Sisters of Charity (1887), a handsome polychromatic brick edifice built in the Second Empire style. Its neighbour to the south is the former orphanage, now used by social organizations.

Continue to Saint-Georges.

Saint-Georges (pop. 21,970)

Divided into Saint-Georges-Ouest and Saint-Georges-Est, on either side of the Rivière Chaudière, this industrial capital of the Beauce region is

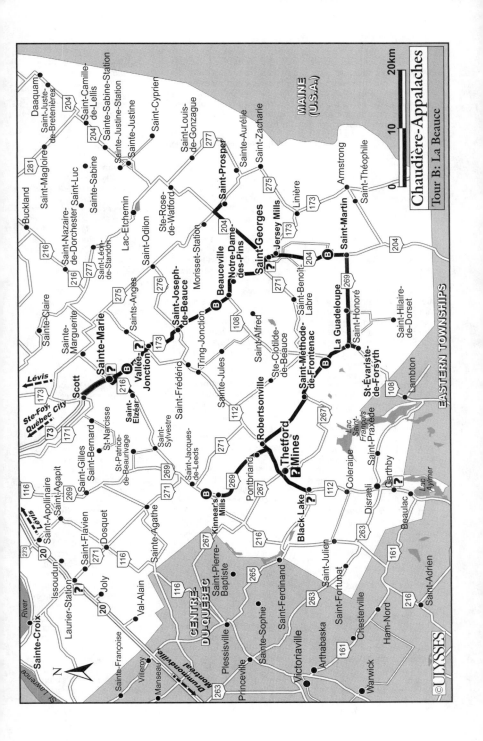

Chaudière-Appalaches
Tour B: La Beauce

reminiscent of a New England manufacturing town. A German-born merchant by the name of Georges Pfotzer is considered the true father of Saint-Georges for having taken advantage of the opening of the Lévis-Jackman route in 1830 in order to launch the forest industry here. In the early 20th century, the Dionne Spinning Mill and various shoe manufacturers established themselves in the region, leading to a significant increase in population. Today, Saint-Georges is a sprawling city. Though the outskirts are somewhat grim, there are a few treasures nestled in the centre of town.

The **Église Saint-Georges** ★★ *(1re Avenue, in Saint-Georges-Ouest)* stands on a promontory overlooking the Rivière Chaudière. Begun in 1900, it is unquestionably Québec City architect David Ouellet's masterpiece (built in collaboration with Pierre Lévesque). The art of the Belle Époque is beautifully represented here by the central steeple towering 75m and the magnificent three-level interior, which has been lavishly sculpted and gilded. In front of the church stands an imposing statue entitled **Saint Georges Terrassant le Dragon** *(St. George Slaying the Dragon)*. This is a fibreglass copy of the fragile original. Louis Jobin's original metal-covered wooden statue (1909) is now exhibited at the Musée du Québec in Québec City.

Parc des Sept-Chutes
see p 387.

The **Barrage Sartigan** *(on the way out of town)* was built in 1967 in order to regulate the flow of the Rivière Chaudière and limit spring flooding as much as possible.

Take Rte. 173 S. to Jersey Mills, and bear right on Rte. 204 to drive along the

Rivière Chaudière to Saint-Martin. Turn right on Rte. 269, which leads to La Guadeloupe and Saint-Évariste-de-Forsyth, and get back on Rte. 108, in the heart of Haute-Beauce.

Saint-Évariste-de-Forsyth (pop. 625)

Haute-Beauce is an isolated region, made up of high plateaus that were cultivated for the first time at the end of the 19th century. Its villages are new and sparsely populated, but residents are friendly and warm-hearted. Saint-Évariste looks out over the surrounding landscape, offering lovely views of neighbouring farms and maple groves.

Get back on Rte. 269 and head north toward Saint-Méthode-de-Frontenac. In Robertsonville, turn left onto Rte. 112 to visit the asbestos region.

Thetford Mines (pop. 17,300)

Asbestos is a strange ore with a whitish, fibrous appearance that is valued for its insulating properties and resistance to heat. It was discovered in the region in 1876, promoting the development of a portion of Québec that had previously been considered extremely remote. Large American and Canadian companies developed the mines in Asbestos, Black Lake and Thetford Mines (before the mines were nationalized in the early 1980s), building industrial empires which made Québec one of the highest-ranking producers of asbestos in the world.

The **Musée Minéralogique et Minier de la Région de Thetford Mines** *($6; late Jun to early Sep, every day 9.30am to 6pm; low season every day 1pm to 5pm; closed Jan and Feb; 711 Boulevard Smith Sud, ☎335-2123)* houses superb collections of

rocks and minerals from all over the world, including samples of asbestos taken from 25 different countries. There are also exhibits explaining the development of the mines and the different characteristics of rocks and minerals found in Québec.

Mine Tours ★★ *($12; reservations required; late Jun to early Sep every day departure at 1:30pm, Jul and Aug departures at 10:30am, 1:30pm and 3:30pm; 682 Rue Mofette N., ☎335-7141)* provide a unique opportunity to see an asbestos mine in operation. In addition to visiting extraction sites and going down into an open-cut mine, participants can attend an information session on asbestos-based products.

Parc de Frontenac ★, see p 387.

The neighbouring municipality of **Black Lake** *(8km southwest, along Rte. 112)* has one of the most impressive mining landscapes in America.

Return to Rte. 269 and head north toward Kinnear's Mills and Saint-Jacques-de-Leeds. The isolated hamlet of Kinnear's Mills, located off the main road, is worth a short visit.

Kinnear's Mills (pop. 360)

Between 1810 and 1830, the British colonial government established townships with English-sounding names on territory that hadn't yet been distributed under the seigneurial system. The village of Kinnear's Mills, located on the banks of the Rivière Osgoode, was founded by Scottish settlers in 1821. It is home to a surprising number of churches of different denominations reflecting the region's ethnic diversity – a Presbyterian church (1873), a Methodist church (1876), an Anglican church (1897), and a more recent Catholic church.

Continue on to Saint-Jacques-de-Leeds to visit a few more charming churches before heading back to Québec City.

Parks

Tour A: The Seigneuries of the Côte-du-Sud

Parc de la Chute de la Chaudière ★ *(Hwy. 73, Exit 130, Charny)*. Head out of Québec City via the Pont Pierre-Laporte. Once across the river, follow the signs for the Chutes (waterfalls). The Rivière Chaudière originates in Lac Mégantic. A length of 185km, it flows into the St. Lawrence just after the falls, which are the result of an unusual geological formation: a highly resistant layer of sandstone lies within a series of sedimentary rocks formed over 570 million years ago. The area around the falls was set aside as a park by the provincial government. From the footbridge stretching over the Rivière Chaudière, visitors can enjoy an impressive view of the falls. In the spring, the rate of flow reaches nearly 1,700,000 litres per second, 15 times more than usual, making this the most magnificent time to see the falls.

A road just next to Motel-Restaurant de la Plage leads to **Plage Berthier-sur-Mer**. Although not very large, this beach does offer beautiful sand and a peaceful atmosphere in which to enjoy the river. Facing the beach is a little island, and the view of the opposite bank is magnificent.

The western end of the beach is blocked off by rocks from the top of which the view is even more breathtaking.

Tour B: La Beauce

The **parc des Rapides du Diable** *(free admission; 173 Route du Président-Kennedy, Beauceville, to the west when leaving Beauceville; ☎774-6252)* is equipped with trails leading to the Chaudière and to the Diable rapids. You will have the opportunity to see the remains of a mill dating back to the Beauce gold rush.

The **Parc des Sept-Chutes** *(free admission; early Jun to early Sep, every day 9am to 9pm; 1er Avenue Ouest, ☎228-6070)*, not to be confused with the one in Saint-Féréol-les-Neiges, has hiking trails, an outdoor swimming pool, a miniature zoo and a number of other facilities for outdoor activities.

Located on the shores of Lac Saint-François, the **Parc de Frontenac** *(9 De la Plage Est, St-Daniel, ☎422-2136)* has a number of picnic areas, beaches and hiking trails. Visitors can also enjoy canoe-camping and a variety of other water sports here. Boats can be rented on site. Visitors can stay in cottages here.

Parc de la Chute Sainte-Agathe *($5/car, $15/camping; 342 rang Gosford Ouest, ☎599-2661)* is a wonderful place for swimming and hiking. In certain spots, you have to be pretty resourceful and hop from rock to rock to get to the water, but there is a little beach where everyone can enjoy the refreshing waterfalls and pools of Rivière Palmer. From the shore there is a charming view of a covered bridge across the falls.

Outdoor Activities

Hiking

Tour B: La Beauce

At **Parc de la Chute Sainte-Agathe** *(342 rang Gosford Ouest, Ste-Agathe, ☎599-2661)*, hikers can stroll along the banks of Rivière Palmer and through the surrounding woods.

Lovely forest walks and strolls on the shore of Lac Saint-François await at **Parc de Frontenac** *(599 ch. des Roys, St-Daniel-Lambton, ☎486-2300 or 877-696-7272)*.

Kayaking

Tour A: The Seigneuries of the Côte-du-Sud

The owners of **Maison Normand** *($30 for 3hrs with guide; 3894 Chemin de Tilly, St-Antoine-de-Tilly, ☎886-2218)* are dedicated kayakers who also own **Kayaks et Nature**. Every day, they accompany excursionists along the banks of the river, introducing them to its peaceful beauty. Here, safety is first (fun being a close second, of course), so supervision and initiation are done in the best possible conditions, at a pace that is comfortable for everyone.

Montmagny's bay is sheltered from the strong winds and currents of the river. It is the perfect spot for beginners to test the water and gradually familiarize themselves with their crafts before heading for deeper water, and it is the departure point for excursions along the banks of the river and to the islands of the Isle-aux-Grues archipelago offered by the team at **Kayak-Eau-Fleuve** (*$35/day; May to Oct, every day; 22 Av. des Canotiers*). River kayaks and canoes are also available for rent.

Cruises

Tour A: The Seigneuries of the Côte-du-Sud

Croisière Lachance (*$39, 5hr cruise; 110 Rue de la Marina, Berthier-sur-Mer,* ☎ *259-2140 or 888-476-7734*) offers cruises on a comfortable boat. Discover an archipelago rich in history (Archipel de l'Île-aux-Grues) with the Lachance family, members of which have been sailors for three generations. Their stories will take you back to island life as it was in the early 1900s.

Birdwatching

Tour A: The Seigneuries of the Côte-du-Sud

Ornitour is the only private company in Québec that offers bird-watching packages. There are various excursions depending upon the season: in the spring, trips to see the snow geese; from May to November, bird-watching excursions focusing on the history of the birds on Île-aux-Grues (departures from the Montmagny pier); in the winter, excursions on the Bombardier B-12 CS multi-passenger snowmobile, which allows you to go into the forest to watch and even feed the birds. (The blue tit will feed right out

of your hand!) The prices, which include binocular rental, transportation and a guide, vary depending upon the package. By reservation only. Individual or group visits.

Canoeing

Tour B: La Beauce

In Sainte-Marie, the tourist information kiosk is located at Manoir Taschereau and rents canoes (*$10/hour, $20/half-day, $30/day; Jun to late Aug*). Why not explore the area by paddling along the Chaudière river?

At Parc de Frontenac, visitors can enjoy great canoeing excursions on Lac Saint-François (boat rental available).

Cycling

Tour A: The Seigneuries of the Côte-du-Sud

Île aux Grues is ideal for cycling. Its small, flat roads follow the river and run through vast wheat fields, offering breathtaking views!

Tour B: La Beauce

A beautiful bicycle path begins in **Saint-Georges** and runs along the west and east sides of the Rivière Chaudière, all the way to Notre-Dame-les-Pins and Saint-Jean-de-la-Lande, uncovering hidden treasures of the Beauce that are well worth a pedal push or two! And if you run into a snag along the way, Saint-Georges is home to Procycle, the largest bicycle manufacturer in Canada!

Golf

Tour A: The Seigneuries of the Côte-du-Sud

Golf de l'Auberivière (*$30; 777 Rue Alexandre, Lévis,* ☎*835-0480*) is located a few minutes from the bridges to Quebec City in a lovely green space crisscrossed by two rivers and dotted with little lakes. This course is easily and quickly accessible.

Accommodations

Tour A: The Seigneuries of the Côte-du-Sud

Saint-Antoine-de-Tilly

Manoir de Tilly
$$$-$$$$ bkfst incl.
≡, ℜ, ⊙, ✖, ℜ, ☺, ⊛
3854 Chemin de Tilly
☎*886-2407 or 888-862-6647*
≈*886-2595*
www.manoirdetilly.com
Manoir de Tilly is a historic home that dates from 1786. The guest rooms are not, however, in the older part of the building, but in rather a modern wing that nonetheless offers all of the comfort and peace one could desire. Each room has a fireplace and a beautiful view. The service is attentive and the dining room offers fine cuisine (see p 390). The inn also has a spa and conference rooms.

Beaumont

Manoir de Beaumont
$$$ bkfst incl.
≈
485 Route du Fleuve
☎*833-5635*
⇄*833-7891*
www.manoirdebeaumont.
qbc.net
Perched high on a hill and surrounded by trees, the Manoir de Beaumont offers bed-and-breakfast accommodations in perfect peace and comfort. Its five rooms are attractively decorated in period style, matching the house itself. A large, sunny living room and a swimming pool are at guests' disposal.

Montmagny

Manoir des Érables
$$$-$$$$
≈, 𝔖, 🐾, ≈, 𝔑, ®
220 Boulevard Taché Est
☎*248-0100 or 800-563-0200*
⇄*248-9507*
www.manoirdeserables.com
The Manoir des Érables is an old, English-style seigneurial abode. The opulence of its period decor and the warm, courteous welcome make guests feel like royalty. The rooms are beautiful and comfortable, and many of them have fireplaces. On the ground floor there is pleasant cigar lounge decorated with hunting trophies where guests can choose from a wide variety of scotches and cigars. There is also a dining room (see p 390) and a bistro, both of which serve excellent cuisine. Also available are motel rooms under the maples, set off from the hotel, and a few rooms in a lodge that is just as inviting as the manor itself.

Île aux Grues

On Île aux Grues, two inns, a few campgrounds and some bed and breakfasts can accommodate visitors who want to stay overnight and witness the archipelago's magnificent sunsets.

Gîte Chez Bibiane
$ bkfst incl.
sb
270 Chemin du Roi
☎*248-6173*
Guests at Chez Bibiane receive a warm welcome from the live-in hosts who are discreet but not averse to conversation with guests who want to learn more about islanders and island life. The four small guestrooms are simply decorated. Breakfast, served in a room overlooking the river, includes fresh island cheese. The hosts also run a dairy farm on their land and, come autumn, a snow-goose hunting outfitter.

Saint-Eugène-de-L'Islet

Auberge des Glacis
$$/pers.
≈, 𝔑
46 Route de la Tortue
☎*247-7486 or 877-245-2247*
⇄*247-7182*
www.aubergedesglacis.com
Set in an old seigneurial mill at the end of a tree-lined lane, Auberge des Glacis has a special charm about it. Each of the comfortable rooms has a name and its own unique decor. Delicious French cuisine is featured in the dining room (see p 390). The stone walls and wood-framed windows of the mill have been preserved as part of the finery of the establishment, whose property includes a lake, birdwatching trails, a small terrace, and, of course, the river. This is an especially peaceful spot, perfect for relaxation.

L'Islet-sur-Mer

Auberge La Marguerite
$$-$$$ bkfst incl.
≈, ℝ, 𝔑
88 Chemin des Pionniers Est
☎*247-5454 or 877-788-5454*
www.aubergela
marguerite.com
A renovated house that dates back to 1754, the Auberge La Marguerite has managed to retain the charm of days gone

by. The eight rooms, named after the schooners that were once this region's claim to fame, are comfortable and tastefully decorated. Make sure not to miss breakfast!

Saint-Jean-Port-Joli

Camping de la Demi-Lieue
$
🐾, ≈
589 Avenue de Gaspé E.
☎*598-6108 or 800-463-9558*
⇄*598-9558*
La Demi-Lieue campground extends along the grounds of a former seigneury that is exactly one half-league long (a half league, the literal translation of the campground's name, is equivalent to about 2.4km or 1.5mi), providing ample space for all to enjoy this beautiful riverside spot. All necessary services are provided, including a security guard.

Maison de L'Ermitage
$$ bkfst incl.
pb/sb
56 Rue de l'Ermitage
☎*598-7553*
⇄*598-7667*
In an old, red-and-white house with four corner towers and a wraparound porch with a view of the river, the inn at Maison de L'Ermitage offers five cozy rooms and a tasty breakfast. The house is full of sunny spots furnished for reading and relaxing, and its yard slopes down to the river. The annual sculpture festival is held just next door (see p 391).

Tour B: La Beauce

Saint-Joseph-de-Beauce

Camping Municipal Saint-Joseph
$
🐾, ≈
221 Route 276
☎*397-5953 or 800-397-4358*
⇄*397-5715*
Near Saint-Joseph, Camping Municipal has 60 campsites

Chaudière-Appalaches

beside a river and its rapids. Swimming and many other activities are possible in this lovely setting.

Motel Bellevue
$-$$
≡, 🐾, ℜ, ⊛
1150 Avenue du Palais
☎*397-6132*
⌐*397-4779*
Motel Bellevue is located on the outskirts of town. Very ordinary looking, it has rooms decorated with plywood furniture. The adjacent restaurant serves good breakfasts.

Saint-Georges

Auberge-Motel Benedict-Arnold
$$
≡, 🐾, ≈, ℝ, ℜ, ⌂, ⊛
18255 Boulevard Lacroix
☎*228-5558 or 800-463-5057*
⌐*227-2941*
www.aubergearnold.qc.ca
Auberge-Motel Benedict-Arnold has been a well-known stopover near the United States border for many generations. The inn has more than 50 rooms, each of them decorated with privacy in mind. Motel rooms are also available. Two dining rooms offer quality fare . Obliging staff.

Restaurants

Tour A: The Seigneuries of the Côte-du-Sud

Lotbinière

La Romaine
$$
7406 Route Marie-Victorin
☎*796-2723*
Set in a Victorian house, La Romaine offers a good little menu for lunch and dinner, featuring fresh, locally produced ingredients. In the summertime, the set menu

always includes fish and seafood. Service is friendly and unpretentious.

Saint-Antoine-de-Tilly

🦞 **Manoir de Tilly**
$$$$
3854 Chemin de Tilly
☎*886-2407 or 888-862-6647*
Manoir de Tilly's dining room serves refined French cuisine based on local products such as lamb and duck or, for more imaginative dishes, ostrich and deer. The renovated dining room preserves not even a hint of the historic building, but is pleasant nonetheless. Here, diners savour carefully prepared and finely presented dishes, complemented by the view through the large windows on the north wall.

Lévis

La Piazzetta
$$-$$$
5410 Boulevard de la Rive-Sud
☎*835-5545*
Lévis is home to a branch of the popular Piazzeta restaurant chain; this one is unfortunately located in a rather commercial setting along Rte. 132, with none of the charm of Vieux-Lévis. Nonetheless, the ambiance is pleasant. Delicious, creatively garnished thin-crust pizza and tasty side dishes such as prosciutto and melon are served.

Beaumont

Jardins des Muses
$
57 du Domaine
Jardins des Muses is an altogether charming shop and café. Regional products are sold and tasted in a relaxed atmosphere.

Montmagny

🦞 **Manoir des Érables**
$$$$
220 Boulevard Taché E.
☎*248-0100 or 800-563-0200*
The dining room at Manoir des Érables (see p 389) fea-

tures fish and game. Goose, sturgeon, burbot, lamb and pheasant are lovingly prepared in traditional French style. Served in the inn's magnificent dining room, these local foods enchant guests, who, in fall and winter, dine in the warm glow of a fireplace. One of the finest restaurants in the region.

Île aux Grues

Visitors to Île aux Grues can replenish themselves either at the good fast-food stand near the dock or in the dining room of one of the island's two inns. On the west side of the island, the hull of a large, beached ship proclaims: "*Oh! que ma quille éclate, Oh! que j'aille à la mer*" ("Oh! my keel is bursting, Oh! I must go to sea"). The **Bateau Ivre**, literally the drunken ship, (*$$; May to early Sep; 118 Chemin Basse-Ville,* ☎*248-0129*) has been nourishing and entertaining islanders and visitors alike. Honest family cooking is served, and on some evenings a small band serenades diners. All of this takes place in the ship's interior, which has been left pretty much as it was when it sailed the seas. Needless to say, the place has a beautiful view of the river!

Saint-Eugène-de-L'Islet

🌴 **Auberge des Glacis**
$$$$
46 Route de la Tortue
☎*247-7486*
Auberge des Glacis serves fine French cuisine that is likely to become one of the best memories of any trip! The dining room, in a historic mill (see p 389), is bright and pleasantly laid out. Diners savour meat and fish dishes as easy on the eyes as they are on the taste buds. The restaurant also serves a light lunch, which may be enjoyed on a riverside terrace.

L'Islet-sur-Mer

La Paysanne
$$-$$$$
497 Chemin des Pionniers Est
☎*247-7276 or 877-660-7276*
La Paysanne is set right on the riverbank and offers a spectacular view of the St. Lawrence and the north shore. The fine French cuisine plays on regional flavours and is attractively presented.

Saint-Jean-Port-Joli

Café La Coureuse des Grèves
$$-$$$$
300 route de l'Église, (Rte 204)
☎*598-9111*
This café consistently offers visitors quality all around. Inside, enjoy memorable coffees in a warm ambiance, decorated with blond wood; in summer it's the terrace, which is decked out in flowers, that counts. Don't forget to ask about the legend of the coureuse des grèves.

Tour B: La Beauce

Saint-Georges

Il Mondo
$$-$$$
11615 Avenue 1re
☎*228-4133*
A restaurant-bar, Il Mondo is attractively decorated in the latest style, with ceramic, wood and wrought-iron elements. Internationally inspired cuisine, including nachos and panini, is featured, as is delicious coffee.

 **La Table du Père Nature**
$$$
10735 Avenue 1re
☎*227-0888*
La Table du Père Nature is definitely one of the best restaurants in town. Guests enjoy innovative French cuisine prepared with skill and sophistication. Just reading the menu is enough to make your mouth water. Game is occasionally served.

Entertainment

Bars and Nightclubs

Montmagny

L'Autre Bar
118 Rue Saint-Jean-Baptiste
L'Autre Bar is set in a former post office. This nightclub with a black and blue decor and terrace attracts an over-25 crowd on weekends. An attractive fresco on the bar's western wall brightens the terrace.

The Pub du Lys
135 St-Jean-Baptiste Est
☎*248-4088*
The Pub du Lys is a pleasant spot to sip a Guinness while chatting with friends. The cheerful owner, Hans, livens up the atmosphere every night with his special surprises. The terrace, a popular meeting place for a younger crowd, overflows during the summer season.

Saint-Georges

Vieux Saint-Georges
11655 1re Avenue
☎*228-3651*
The Vieux Saint-Georges is located inside a big, beautiful house. Its magnificent terrace is a great place to have a drink on a lovely summer evening.

Festivals and Cultural Events

Montmagny

In the fall, snow geese leave the northern breeding grounds where they have spent the summer and head south toward more clement climates. On the way, they stop on the banks of the St. Lawrence River, especially in spots that provide abundant food for them, like the sand bars of Montmagny. These avian visitors are the perfect excuse to celebrate the **Festival de l'Oie Blanche** *(12 days in mid-Oct, ☎248-3954)*, which features all sorts of activities related to watching and learning about these beautiful migratory birds.

Saint-Jean-Port-Joli

Every year at the end of June, Saint-Jean-Port-Joli welcomes sculptors from all over the world to the lively **Internationale de la Sculpture** *(☎598-7288)*. Renowned artists create works before your eyes, some of which are then exhibited throughout the summer.

Shopping

Tour A: The Seigneuries of the Côte-du-Sud

Lévis

Les chocolats Favoris / La Glacerie à l'Européenne
32 av. Bégin, vieux Lévis
☎*833-2287*
Here they make and sell delicious, irresistible chocolate treats and ice cream that can be enjoyed on their terrace.

Saint-Vallier

Artisanat Chamard *(mid-Mar to Dec every day 8am to 5pm, mid-Jun to mid-Sep every day 8am to 9pm; 601 Avenue de Gaspé E., ☎598-3425)* has enjoyed a great reputation for nearly half a century. Here, you can purchase woven pieces and ceramic objects, as

Chaudière-Appalaches

well as First Nations and Inuit art.

At the **"Village des Artisans"** (*mid-Jun to early Sep; 329 Avenue de Gaspé O.*, ☎598-6829), you will find a series of shops offering a good selection of crafts, such as pottery, wood toys, paintings, leather goods, woven pieces and sculptures.

Montmagny

Boutique Suzette-Couillard
70 rue St-Jean-Baptiste E.
☎*248-9642*
This is a good place to find all sorts of small items for your home, as well as antiques and jewellery.

Cap-Saint-Ignace

Les Créations du Berger
1008 ch. des Pionniers O.
☎*246-3400*
Les Créations du Berger offers a wide array of accessories made of sheepskin that are most welcome in wintertime!

Saint-Jean-Port-Joli

Saint-Jean-Port-Joli is renowned for its crafts and many of its shops sell the work of local artisans. If this sort of shopping interests you, this town has much to offer.

There are also a few second-hand stores here, to the delight of treasure hunters, many of them along Rte. 132.

Boutique Jacques-Bourgault (*326 Av. de Gaspé Ouest*), between Musée des Anciens Canadiens and Maison Médard-Bourgaut, sells contemporary and religious art.

Entr'Art (*812 av. de Gaspé O.*), which is both a gallery and a shop, offers a lovely selection of sculptures, paintings and stained glass.

Bas-Saint-Laurent

T**he picturesque**
Bas-Saint-Laurent region extends east along the
St. Lawrence River from the little town of La Pocatière to
the village of Sainte-
Luce and south to
the borders of the
United States and
New Brunswick.

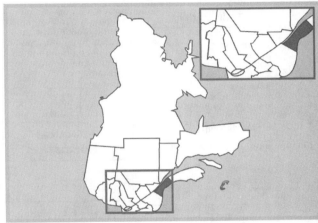

B esides the particularly
fertile agricultural land
next to the river, much of the
Bas-Saint-Laurent is com-
posed of farming and forestry
development areas covering
gently rolling hills sparkling
with lakes and streams.

A permanent European
presence in the Bas-Saint-
Laurent region began with the
founding of New France and
continued in stages that corresponded to the development
of different economic activities.
Before the end of the 17th
century, colonists attracted by
the fur trade founded trading
posts at Rivière-du-Loup, Bic,
Cabano and Notre-Dame-du-
Lac. Much of the fertile land
along the St. Lawrence River
Valley was cleared and cultivated at the beginning of the
following century. The layout
of farms in the region still
reflects the seigneurial system
originally used to divide land
among peasant farmers. Inland
areas, used for agriculture and
forestry, were first colonized
around 1850. There was a
final wave of settlers during

the Depression of the 1930s,
when unemployed city dwellers took refuge in the country.
The various periods of colonization are reflected in the
area's rich architectural heritage.

Finding Your
Way Around

The tour of **the Kamouraska
Region ★ ★**, follows the
St. Lawrence River from
La Pocatière to Sainte-Luce
and features sweeping views
of the river and the mountains
of the Charlevoix and
Saguenay regions.

By Car

Turn off Hwy. 20 and take
Rte. 132 East. Hwys. 232,
185 and 289 run through the
Bas-St-Laurent, taking you to
the heart of this region and
providing news of its spectacular forests and valleys.

Bus Stations

Rivière-du-Loup
83 Boulevard Cartier
☎*(418) 862-4884*

Rimouski
90 Rue Léonidas
☎*(418) 723-4923*

Names of New Merged Cities

Rimouski
Merger of Rimouski, Pointe-au-Père, Mont-Lebel, Rimouski-Est, Sainte-Blandine and Sainte-Odile-sur-Rimouski.

Sainte-Luce
Merger of Luceville and Sainte-Luce.

Exploring

★★

The Kamouraska Region

Train Stations

La Pocatière
95 Avenue de la Gare
☎*800-361-5390*

Rimouski
57 de l'Évêché Est
☎*800-361-5390*

Rivière-du-Loup
615 Rue Lafontaine
☎*800-361-5390*

Trois-Pistoles
231 Rue de la Gare ☎*800-361-5390*

By Ferry

Rivière-du-Loup
Cost: $11.50; bicycle $4.10, car $29.20
Duration: 1hr
☎*(418) 862-5094*
☎*(514) 849-4466 (from Montréal)*
☎*(418) 638-2856 (from St-Simeon)*
Links Rivière-du-Loup and Saint-Siméon in Charlevoix.

L'Isle-Verte
La Richardière **ferry**
($5; bicycle $6, car $30; May to Nov; ☎418-898-2843)
ferries passengers from L'Isle-Verte to Notre-Dame-des-Sept-Douleurs in 30min.

If you don't have a car, you can take a taxi-boat (*$6; ☎418-898-2199*).

Trois-Pistoles
A ferry runs between Trois-Pistoles and Les Escoumins (*$11.50; bicycle $4.10,*

car $29.95; Trois-Pistoles: ☎*418-851-4676, Escoumins:* ☎*418-233-4676*). The crossing takes 90min and, if you're lucky, you might see some whales. Reserve in advance for summer.

Practical Information

Area code: **418**

Tourist Information

Regional Office

Maison Touristique du Bas-Saint-Laurent
148 Rue Fraser, Rivière-du-Loup, G5R 1C8
☎*867-3015*
☎*800-563-5268*
≈*867-3245*
www.tourismebas-st-laurent.com

The Kamouraska Region

Rivière-du-Loup
189 Rue Hôtel-de-Ville
☎*862-1981 or 888-825-1981*

Saint-Fabien
33 Route 132 Ouest, G0L 2Z0
☎*869-3333*

Rimouski
50 Rue St-Germain Ouest, G5L 4B5
☎*723-2322*
☎*800-746-6875*

This tour begins near Kamouraska, but leads much further afield. However, since the region is best known as the setting of Anne Hébert's novel *Kamouraska*, this name also graces this tour, which is a logical extension of the Seigneuries of the Côte-du-Sud tour through the Chaudière-Appalaches region (see p 374). Together, these two tours give a good overall picture of the Côte-du-Sud region.

Take Rte. 132 E. to La Pocatière.

La Pocatière (pop. 5,000)

In 1672, the former La Pocatière seigneury was granted to Marie-Anne Juchereau, the widow of François Pollet de la Combe-Pocatière, an officer in the Carignan regiment. The land later fell into the hands of the d'Auteuil family, and still later the Dionne family. The opening of a college in La Pocatière in 1827, followed by the creation of Canada's first agricultural school in 1859, transformed the town into a centre of higher education, a role it still plays today. The main factory of the multinational Bombardier corporation is also located here. The subway cars used in Montréal, New York and several other big cities around the world are made here.

Take Avenue Painchaud to Rte. 132 E. to Rivière-Ouelle.

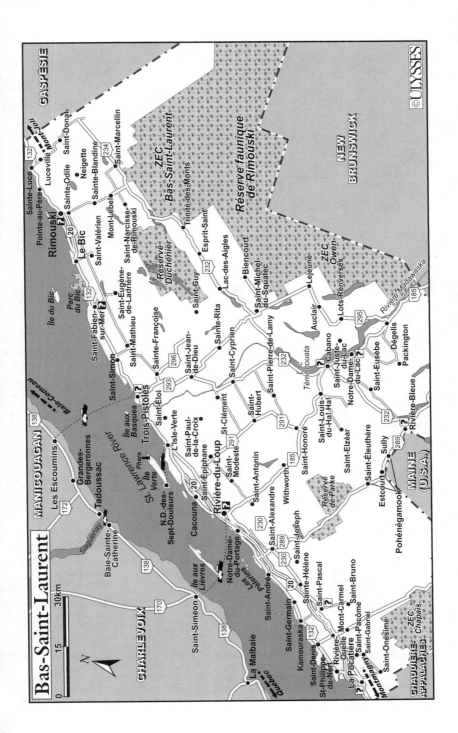

Rivière-Ouelle
(pop. 1,240)

This charming village, straddling the river after which it is
named, was founded in 1672
by Seigneur François de la
Souteillerie. In 1690, a naval
detachment under the com-
mand of British admiral William Phipps tried to land at
Rivière-Ouelle, and was immediately driven back by
about 40 colonists led by the
Abbé Pierre de Francheville.

*Take Rte. 132 E. to Saint-
Denis.*

Saint-Denis
(pop. 500)

A typical village in the heart of
the Kamouraska Region, Saint-
Denis is dominated by its
church. Next to the church
lies a monument honouring
Abbé Édouard Quertier
(1796-1872), the founder of
the "Croix Noire de la
Tempérance" (Black Cross of
Temperance). It was Monseigneur de Forbin-Janson's tour
of Canada in 1840-41 that led
him to found the movement.
He solemnly awarded a black
cross to each person who
promised to stop drinking.

★★
Kamouraska
(pop. 710)

On January 31, 1839, the
young Seigneur of
Kamouraska, Achille Taché,
was murdered by a former
friend, Doctor Holmes. The
Seigneur's wife had plotted
with Holmes, her lover, to do
in her husband and flee to
distant lands. The incident
inspired Anne Hébert's novel
Kamouraska, which was
made into a film by prominent
Québécois director Claude
Jutra. The novel, and later the
film, brought a level of fame to
the village. Kamouraska, an
Algonquin word meaning
"bulrushes by the water,"
earned a place in the colourful
history of rural Québec. For

many years, the village was
the eastern-most trading post
on the Côte-du-Sud.
Kamouraska stands on several
ranges of rocky hillocks that
provide a striking contrast to
the adjacent coastal plain. The
unusual rugged terrain is a
remnant of ancient mountains
long worn down by glaciers
and typical of the area.

The former **Palais de Justice**
(*$3; Jun to Sep, every day
9am to noon and 1pm to
5pm; 111 Avenue Morel,
☎492-9458*), designed by
architect Élzéar Charest, was
built in 1888 on the site of the
first courthouse in eastern
Québec. Its medieval-style
architecture sets it apart from
other North American courthouses, which are usually
neoclassical in style. The five
islands of the Kamouraska
archipelago can be seen in the
distance from the front steps
of the Palais.

*To fully appreciate the charm
of the village, head down the
street facing the Palais de
Justice and take narrow Avenue Leblanc to the pier.*

The **Musée de Kamouraska**
(*$4; early Jun to mid-Oct
every day 9am to 5pm, mid-
Oct to mid-Dec variable
schedule, mid-Dec to May
group reservations only; 69
Avenue Morel, ☎492-9783*),
which focuses on ethnology,
history and local traditions, is
housed in the former Couvent
de Kamouraska. A number of
historic artefacts from the
region are on display, including
a beautiful retable designed by
François-Noël Levasseur
(1734); it was taken from the
former village church. The
present **church**, facing the
museum, was built in 1914,
by Joseph-Pierre Ouellet.

Maison Amable-Dionne (*no
visitors allowed inside; located
east of the church*). Amable
Dionne was a merchant who
acquired a number of
seigneuries in the Côte-du-

Sud area during the first half of
the 19th century. His manor
house in La Pocatière is gone,
but his residence in
Kamouraska, built in 1802, is
still standing. Located east of
the church, it is a long building
with a neoclassical decor
added around 1850.

*For a look at the interior of
the region, take the road
between Kamouraska and
Saint-Pascal.*

Domaine Seigneurial Taché.
The Taché family acquired the
Kamouraska seigneury in
1790. Shortly thereafter, they
built his manor, the scene of
the now-famous local drama,
the murder of Achille Taché,
described in the introductin to
the town. The home is now a
bed and breakfast.

If you're interested in learning
about eels, stop by the **Site
d'Interprétation de l'Anguille**
(*$5; early Jun to mid-Oct,
every day 9am to 6pm; 205
Avenue Morel, ☎492-3935*),
which offers guided tours and
fishing trips. The tours last
about 30min. Eel fishing plays
an important role in the local
economy: 78% of the eels
fished in the Bas-Saint-Laurent
are caught in Kamouraska.
These snakelike fish account
for 97% of the local fishing
industry. The fishing season
runs from September to the
end of October.

*Head back to Rte. 132 and
turn right.*

★
Saint-Pascal
(pop. 2,500)

Berceau de Kamouraska
(*Rte. 132 E., 3km east of
Kamouraska*). A small chapel
marks the site of the original
village of Kamouraska,
founded in 1674 by Sieur
Morel de la Durantaye. In
1790, a powerful earthquake
destroyed the village, which
was rebuilt on the present site.
Just off Rte. 132 is Saint-

Germain-de-Kamouraska, and the ruins of the Manoir de la Pointe-Sèche (1835), one of the oldest and most elegant Regency cottages in Québec.

★
Saint-André
(pop. 600)

The countryside around Saint-André is a dramatic mix of steep hills plunging straight into the river and expansive fields. The tidal flats are typically lined with tall wooden fences strung with eel nets. The nearby rocky slopes of the Îles Pèlerins provide a striking backdrop. The islands are home to thousands of birds (including cormorants and black guillemots) and a penguin colony. If you are lucky, you might even catch a glimpse of a beluga whale or peregrine falcon.

The **Église Saint-André** ★★ (late Jun to early Sep, every day 9am to 11:30am and 1pm to 5pm; 128 Rue Principale, ☎493-2152), built between 1805 and 1811, is one of the oldest churches in the region. Its Récollet design, characterized by an absence of side chapels, a narrowing of the nave around the chancels and a flat caveat, differs from the Latin-cross design usually found in Québec churches.

Halte Écologique des Battures du Kamouraska, see p 400.

Falaises d'Escalade de Saint-André, see p 403.

★
Rivière-du-Loup
(pop. 17,800)

Rivière-du-Loup is set on several ranges of rolling hills. It has become one of the most important towns in the Bas-Saint-Laurent region. Its strategic location made it a marine communication centre for the Atlantic, the St. Lawrence, Lac Témiscouata and the St. John River in New Brunswick.

Later, it was an important railway centre, when the town was the eastern terminus of the Canadian train network. Rivière-du-Loup is the turn-off point for the road to New Brunswick and is linked by ferry to Saint-Siméon on the north shore of the river.

In order to fully enjoy your visit to Rivière-du-Loup, park your car on Rue Fraser and explore the town on foot. In addition to the tour suggested here, the local tourist office has put up a series of signs explaining the history of the town and its buildings.

Manoir Fraser ★ ($4; late Jun to mid-Oct, every day 10am to 5pm; 32 Rue Fraser, ☎867-3906). The Rivière du Loup seigneury was granted to a wealthy Québec merchant named Charles Aubert de la Chesnaye in 1673. It later passed through several owners, all of whom showed little interest in the remote region. The house, originally built for Timothy Donahue in 1830, became the Fraser family residence in 1835. In 1888, it was modified to suit contemporary tastes by Québec architect Georges-Émile Tanguay. The house was renovated in 1997 with the help of local residents, and is now open to the public with guided tours, as well as a multi-media presentation of an official dinner of the time.

Turn right on Rue du Domaine, then left on Rue Lafontaine.

Église Saint-Patrice ★ (121 Rue Lafontaine) was rebuilt in 1883 on the site of an earlier church erected in 1855. It houses several treasures, including a representation of the Stations of the Cross designed by Charles Huot, stained-glass windows created by the Castle company (1901) and statues by Louis Jobin. Rue de la Cour, in front of the church, leads to the **Palais de**

Justice (33 Rue de la Cour), the courthouse constructed in 1882 by architect Pierre Gauvreau. A number of judges and lawyers built beautiful houses on the shady streets nearby.

Head back toward Rue Fraser on Rue Deslauriers from the Palais de Justice.

The **Musée du Bas-Saint-Laurent** ★ ($5; early Jun to mid-Oct every day 10am to 6pm, off-season every day 1pm to 5pm, year-round Mon and Wed 6pm to 9pm; 300 Rue Saint-Pierre, ☎862-7547) displays objects characteristic of the region, and holds contemporary art exhibits (these are often more interesting). The building itself, made of concrete, is a perfect example of ugly modern architecture.

★
Cacouna
(pop. 1,350)

Cacouna is an Algonquin word meaning "land of the porcupine." The Victorian mansions scattered throughout the village are reminders of a golden age of vacationing in Québec, when Cacouna was a favourite summer resort among the Montréal elite. People began to spend summers in the village in 1840, drawn by the scenery and the saltwater of the St. Lawrence (which was said to have healing properties). While the grand hotels of the 19th century, such as St. Lawrence Hall, have disappeared, Cacouna is still geared towards tourism and recreational activities.

Built for shipowner Sir Hugh Montague Allan and his family, **Villa Montrose** ★ (no visitors allowed; 700 Rue Principale, ☎862-7889) is now a prayer house. Its American Colonial Revival architecture demonstrates the influence of New England's seaside resorts on their Canadian counterparts.

Bas-Saint-Laurent

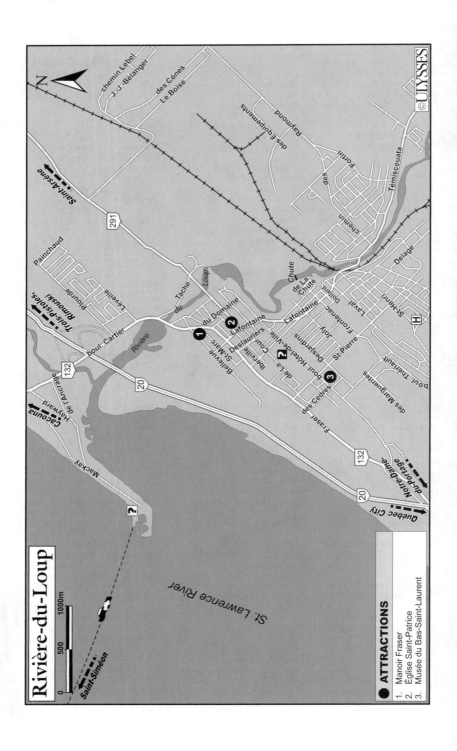

Rivière-du-Loup

ATTRACTIONS

1. Manoir Fraser
2. Église Saint-Patrice
3. Musée du Bas-Saint-Laurent

St. Lawrence River

© ULYSSES

Another of Cacouna's note-worthy houses is **Pine Cottage** (*no visitors allowed inside; 520 Rue Principale*), also known as Château Vert. It was built in 1867 for the Molsons (a family of brewers, bankers and entrepreneurs from Montréal), and is an excellent example of Gothic Revival residential architecture, little of which remains in Québec.

Église Saint-Georges and its Presbytery ★ (*455 Route de l'Église*, ☎862-4338). The architecture of the presbytery, built in 1838, is typical of farm-houses in the Montréal region, characterized by decorative firebreak walls, a roof with a fairly gentle pitch and straight eaves. The Église Saint-Georges, designed by Louis-Thomas Berlinguet, was built in 1845. The church repre-sents the culmination of a long architectural tradition in Qué-bec that disappeared when new building styles inspired by the past were introduced to rural parishes. Visitors won't want to miss its richly deco-rated interior containing a number of particularly inter-esting pieces, including gilded altars executed by François-Xavier Berlinguet in 1852 (when he was only 22 years old), stained-glass windows made by Maison Léonard of Québec City in 1897 and paintings by Italian artists Porta (over the high altar) and Pasqualoni (in the right cha-pel).

Site Ornithologique du Marais du Gros-Cacouna, see p 403.

★
**L'Isle-Verte
(pop. 1,040)**

The village of L'Isle-Verte was once an important centre of activity in the Bas-Saint-Laurent region; several build-ings remain from this period. Meanwhile, life in the sur-rounding countryside follows a traditional pattern that keeps

time with the continuing rhythm of the tides. Just off shore lies Île Verte, the island named by the explorer Jacques Cartier who, upon spotting the lush island, ex-claimed, "*Quelle île verte!*", literally "What a green island!". The only island in the Bas-Saint-Laurent inhabited year-round, Île Verte is more easily accessible than the other islands in the area (see below).

Île Verte ★★ (*$10 guided tour; mid-May to mid-Oct, every day 9am to noon and 1pm to 4pm; Route du Phare*, ☎898-2730). Though 12km long, only 40 people live on Île Verte. Its isolation and constant winds have discour-aged many would-be colonists over the years. Basque fishers (Île aux Basques lies nearby), however, made use of the island from very early on. French missionaries were also a presence on the island; they were there to convert the Malecite First Nation who came to the island every year to trade and fish. Around 1920, the island enjoyed an economic boom when the region became a source of a type of sea moss that was dried and used to stuff mat-tresses and carriage seats.

Visitors to the island have the opportunity to watch sturgeon and herring being salted in little smokehouses, taste ex-cellent local lamb, watch be-luga and blue whales and photograph the waterfowl, black ducks and herons. The **lighthouse**, located on the eastern tip of the island, is the oldest on the St. Lawrence (built in 1806). Five genera-tions of the Lindsay family tended the lighthouse from 1827 to 1964. From the top of the tower, the view can seem almost endless.

Baie de L'Isle-Verte National Wildlife Area ★, see p 402.

Continue on Rte. 132 E. to Trois-Pistoles.

**Trois-Pistoles
(pop. 3,810)**

According to legend, a French sailor passing through the region in the 17th century dropped his silver tumbler, worth three pistoles, in the nearby river, giving the river its unusual name. The name was adopted by the small industrial town that sprang up next to the river.

When the colossal **Église Notre-Dame-des-Neiges** ★★ (*late Jun to early Sep, every day 9am to 4:30pm; 30 Rue Notre-Dame Est*, ☎851-4949) was built in 1887, the citizens of Trois-Pistoles believed their church would soon be named the cathedral of the diocese. This explains the size and splendour of the building, topped by three silver stee-ples. The honour eventually fell to the Rimouski church, the masterpiece of architect David Ouellet, to the great dismay of the congregation of Notre-Dame-des-Neiges. An Ottawa canon by the name of Georges Bouillon decorated the elaborate Roman Byzantine interior.

Île aux Basques ★★, p 402.

Continue on Rte. 132 E. After Saint-Simon, turn left on Rte. de Saint-Fabien-sur-Mer to approach the water, or right on Rte. Saint-Fabien.

★★
**Saint-Fabien-sur-Mer
(pop. 1,910)
and Le Bic
(pop. 3,190)**

Here, the landscape suddenly becomes more rugged, giving visitors a taste of the Gaspé region farther east. In Saint-Fabien-sur-Mer, a line of cot-tages is wedged between the beach and a 200m-high cliff. An octagonally shaped barn built around 1888 is located inland in the village of Saint-Fabien. This type of farm building originated in the

Bas-Saint-Laurent

United States and, while interesting, proved relatively impractical and enjoyed limited popularity in Québec.

To get to the beautiful **Parc du Bic** ★★ *(see p 402), continue along Rte. 132 E., then turn left on Chemin de l'Orignal.*

The road skirts the village of Le Bic before reaching Rimouski, the largest urban centre in the Bas-Saint-Laurent.

★
Rimouski
(pop. 32,400)

At the end of the 17th century, a French merchant named René Lepage, originally from Auxerre, France, undertook the monumental task of clearing the Rimouski seigneury. The land thus became the easternmost area on the Gulf of St. Lawrence to be colonized under the French regime. In 1919, the Abitibi-Price company opened a factory here, turning the town into an important wood-processing centre. Today, Rimouski is considered the administrative capital of eastern Québec, and prides itself for being on the cutting edge of the arts. Rimouski means "land of the moose" in Micmac.

Musée Régional de Rimouski ★ *($4; Jun to Sep, Wed-Fri 9:30am to 8pm, Sat-Tue 10am to 6pm; the rest of the year, Wed-Sun noon to 5pm, Thu to 9pm; 35 Rue Saint-Germain Ouest, ☎724-2272)*. This museum of art and ethnology is housed in the former Église Saint-Germain, built between 1823 and 1827. The simple church, with its belltower set in the centre of the roof, is reminiscent of churches built under the French regime. The town's **Cathédrale St-Germain**, which houses a Casavant organ, and immense **Palais Épiscopal**,

built in 1901, are located nearby. In the neighbouring park is a monument honouring Seigneur Lepage.

Continue on Rte. 132 E., which is known by different names here, Boulevard Saint-Germain Ouest, then Boulevard René-Lepage, and finally Boulevard du Rivage.

The **Maison Lamontagne** ★ *($3; mid-May to mid-Oct, every day 9am to 6pm; 707 Boulevard du Rivage, ☎722-8388)* is one of the only buildings east of Kamouraska dating back to the French regime, and is one of the rare examples of half-timber architecture found in Canada. The left part of the house, an alternating sequence of posts and rough masonry filler made of stones and clay, dates from 1745, while the right part was added at the beginning of the 19th century. There is an exhibition on the architecture and antique furniture of the house inside.

The **Canyon des Portes de l'Enfer** *($6.50; mid-May to mid-Jun every day 9:30am to 5pm, mid-Jun to early Sep every day 8:30am to 6:30pm, early Sep to mid-Oct every day 9:30am to 5pm; 1280 Chemin Duchénier, Saint-Narcisse-de-Rimouski, 5.6km from Saint-Narcisse-de-Rimouski along a dirt road; ☎735-6063)* is a fascinating natural spectacle, especially in winter. Literally the "gates of hell," this canyon starts at the 18m Grand Saut falls, and stretches nearly 5km on either side of the Rivière Rimouski, with cliffs reaching as high as 90m in places. Guided boat tours are conducted in the canyon.

The next stop on the tour is Pointe-au-Père. Turn left on Rue Père Nouvel, then right on Rue du Phare.

Pointe-au-Père
(pop 5,000)

Musée de la Mer and the **Pointe-au-Père Lighthouse National Historic Site** ★★ *($9.50; early Jun to late Aug, every day 9am to 6pm; early Sep to mid-Oct, every day 9am to 5pm; off-season by reservation; 1034 Rue du Phare Ouest, ☎724-6214)* is also known as the Lieu Nationale Historique du Phare-Pointe-au-Père. It was off the shores of Pointe-au-Père that the *Empress of Ireland* sank in 1914, claiming the lives of 1,012 people. The Musée de la Mer houses a fascinating collection of objects recovered from the wreck and provides a detailed account of the tragedy. The nearby lighthouse, which is open to the public, marks the exact spot where the river officially becomes the Gulf of St. Lawrence.

The **monument to the *Empress of Ireland*** *(on the old road, by the shore)*. On the night of May 23, 1914, about 1,000 people perished when the *Empress of Ireland*, a Canadian Pacific ocean liner that provided service between Québec City and England, went down in the middle of the St. Lawrence. The liner had collided with a coal ship in the thick fog that occasionally blankets the river. This monument marks the burial place of just a few of the tragedy's many victims.

Parks

The Kamouraska Region

The **Halte Écologique des Battures du Kamouraska** *($5; early May to Jun 23 every day 10am to 6pm, Jun 24 to early*

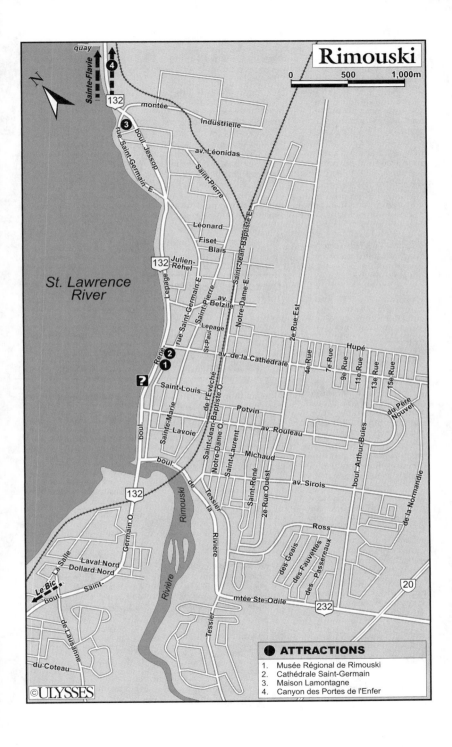

Sep every day 8am to 9pm, early Sep to late Oct every day 10am to 6pm; 273 Route 132 O., St-André de Kamouraska, ☎493-2604) explains the importance of the wetlands, or *battures*, along the river, which house many species of birds and a number of invertebrates. Visitors can have a picnic or explore the surroundings on foot to view the salt marshes and local plants and animals. There is a 65m-high lookout that commands an unobstructed view of the river.

The **Baie de L'Isle-Verte National Wildlife Area ★** *(mid-Jun to mid-Sep, by reservation guided tour approx. 2hrs; 371 Rte. 132, ☎898-2757).* It protects extensive grasslands that are ideal breeding grounds for black ducks, and marshes teeming with tiny aquatic animals. Trails provide an opportunity to better enjoy this exceptional site.

The Société Provencher offers excursions to **Île aux Basques ★★** *($15, 3hr guided tour; early Jun to early Sep every day according to tides Trois-Pistoles, ☎851-1202),* which it safeguards as an ornithological preserve. Birdwatchers will certainly enjoy a trip here. The island is also of historical interest. A few years ago, facilities used by Basque fishers were discovered. They came here on whaling expeditions in the 15th century, over 100 years before the explorer Jacques Cartier ever set foot on the island. The remains of ovens used to melt whale blubber are also visible at several places on the riverbanks. There are 2km of trails on the island.

Parc du Bic ★★ *($3.50; closed to cars in winter; for a schedule of summer activities, contact reception, Le Bic, ☎736-5035)* measures 33km² and features a jumble of coves, jutting shoreline, promontories, hills, escarpments and marshes, as well as deep bays teeming with a wide variety of plant and animal life. The park is a good place for hiking (26 km of trails), cross-country skiing and mountain biking, and also has an information centre *(Jun to mid-Oct every day 9am to 5pm).*

Outdoor Activities

Cruises and Whale-watching

The **Duvetnor** *(early Jun to mid-Sep, every day; 200 Rue Hayward, Rivière-du-Loup, ☎867-1660)* company offers a variety of cruises. You can visit the Îles du Bas-Saint-Laurent and see black guillemots, eider ducks and razorbills. The cruises start at the Rivière-du-Loup marina and last anywhere from 1.5 to 8hrs, depending on your destination. You can even stay overnight in a lighthouse on one of the islands.

Écomertours Nord-Sud *(mid-Jun to late Oct Mon-Fri 8:30am to 6pm, Sat and Sun 9am to 6pm, reservations necessary; 606 des Ardennes, Rimouski, ☎724-6227 or 888-*

724-8687) offers a variety of packages that showcase the river and the islands dotting it as far as the Gulf of St. Lawrence and the Basse-Côte-Nord. The boat used for these cruises, which range in length from two to eight days, is called the *Écho des Mers* (Echo of the Seas). It can carry up to 49 passengers and about 15 crew members and has comfortable cabins. These "ecotours" are led by specialists whose aim is to familiarize passengers with the region's flora and fauna. If you go all the way to the Basse-Côte-Nord, you'll have the opportunity to meet the locals. The company also offers more adventurous kayaking and scuba-diving packages. The cruises start at the Rimouski Est dock.

Cycling

The Kamouraska Region

The **Parc du Bic** *(Rte. 132, 21km west of downtown Rimouski, in Saint-Fabien and Bic, ☎736-5035)* is without question the most beautiful place in the region to go mountain biking. It has 14km of maintained trails. Unfortunately, it is no longer possible to bike up the Pic Champlain. You can hike up to take in the sunset, though.

The **Parc Beauséjour** *(Boulevard de la Rivière, Route 132, Rimouski, ☎724-3167)* has lots of bike paths. The **Sentier du Littoral** and the **Sentier de la Rivière Rimouski** *(less than 2km from downtown, ☎723-0480)* offer 7km of superb mountain-bike trails along the Rivière Rimouski and through a swamp.

Rock-climbing

There is a magnificent place to go climbing in Saint-André-de-Kamouraska. The climbing cliffs known as the **Falaises d'Escalade de Saint-André** *(for information contact the SEBKA:* ☎*493-2604)* are composed of an extremely hard stone that makes them safe to climb. Those daring enough to scale them will be rewarded with an extraordinary view of the area. Follow the signs to get there.

Kayaking

The Kamouraska Region

The **Société écologique des battures du Kamouraska (SEBKA)** *(St-André-de-Kamouraska;* ☎*493-2604)* offers sea kayaking expeditions in the Kamouraska archipelago with interpretive guides. Departures from the Kamouraska pier.

Rivi-Air Aventure *($36/half-day, $65/day with guide; mid-May to mid-Oct every day departures at 8pm, 1pm and 5:30pm; Le Bic marina, 3257 Route 132 Ouest,* ☎*732-5232)* arranges solo and group sea-kayaking excursions, helping visitors explore the Parc du Bic, its beaches, ponds and cliffs. Sunset outings take place from 5:30pm to 8:30pm. Add the $3.50 park entry fee to the price indicated above.

Birdwatching

The **Site Ornithologique du Marais du Gros-Cacouna** is a lovely place to go birding. Located at the port of Cacouna, the ornithological centre was created to harmonize local port activities with the natural riches of this marshy environment. If you'd like to take part in a 2hr guided tour of the area, contact the Société de Conservation de la Baie de l'Isle-Verte (☎898-2757). There are 2km of intermediate-level hiking paths.

Île Verte and its marshes are perfect for birdwatching. Thanks to the extraordinarily rich plant and animal life here, all sorts of pleasant surprises await visitors. The **Baie de L'Isle-Verte National Wildlife Area** (see p 402), crisscrossed by hiking trails, is particularly well-suited to wildlife observation.

The **Parc du Bic** (see p 402) is also frequented by several species of water and forest birds. You're sure to see some if you take a hike on the park's trails.

Fishing

The Kamouraska Area

The **Société d'Aménagement de la Rivière Ouelle** *(Route 230, at the bridge over the Rivière Ouelle,* ☎*852-3097)* has some 40 artificial pools. For a 40km stretch, the Rivière Ouelle is paradise for salmon fishing. The river has been stocked with thousands of young salmon (parr) over

the past few years, and its banks afford some splendid panoramic views. You can also enlist the services of a guide.

Cross-country Skiing

The Kamouraska Area

The **Station de Ski Val-Neigette** *($6; via Rte. 232, Sainte-Blandine, 8min from downtown Rimouski,* ☎*735-2800)* has 20km of cross-country trails.

The **Parc du Mont-Comi** *($5; R.R. 2, Saint-Donat-de-Rimouski, 31km southeast of downtown Rimouski,* ☎*739-4858)* has 18km of cross-country trails.

Accommodations

Kamouraska

Motel Cap Blanc
$$
K, 🐾
300 Avenue Morel
☎492-2919
≈492-2919
Motel Cap Blanc has simple, comfortable rooms with lovely views of the river.

Gîte chez Jean et Nicole
$$
pb/sb
81 Avenue Morel
☎492-2921
Jean and Nicole opened a four–room B&B in their lovingly maintained century home for the sheer pleasure of meeting people. They serve memorable breakfasts and they're located near the village and, more importantly, near the sea.

Saint-André

La Solaillerie
$$-$$$ bkfst incl.
ℜ
112 Rue Principale
☎493-2914
⇥493-2243
*www.aubergela
solaillerie.com*
A large house dating from the late 19th century, La Solaillerie has a magnificent white facade and a big wraparound porch on the second storey. Inside, the sumptuous decor evokes the era in which the house was built. The six guest rooms are cozy, comfortable and tastefully decorated in classic "old inn" tradition. As far as the food is concerned, gourmets can expect some delightful surprises (see p 405).

Rivière-du-Loup

**Auberge de Jeunesse
Internationale**
$ bkfst incl.
46 Boulevard de l'Hôtel-de-Ville
☎862-7566
⇥862-1843
The Auberge de Jeunesse Internationale in Rivière-du-Loup is a youth hostel that offers the most affordable accommodation in town. The rooms are dorm-style and simple but clean.

Auberge de la Pointe
$$-$$$
☺, K, 🐾, ≈, ℜ, △, ◐, ⊛
Closed Nov to Apr
10 Boulevard Cartier
☎862-3514 or 800-463-1222
⇥862-1882
*www.auberge-de-la-
pointe.qc.ca*
The Auberge de la Pointe is particularly well-located. In addition to comfortable rooms, guests can indulge in a hydrotherapy, algotherapy or massage-therapy session, and enjoy spectacular sunsets from the balcony. There is also a summer theatre.

Îles du Pot à L'Eau-de-Vie

**Phare de l'île du
Pot à l'Eau-de-Vie**
$$$$ fb
sb
200 Rue Hayward, Rivière-du-Loup
☎867-1660 or 877-867-1660
⇥867-3639
The Phare de l'Île du Pat à L'Eau-de-Vie, a lighthouse on an island in the middle of the St. Lawrence, exposes its white facade and red roof to the four winds. Owned by Duvetnor, a non-profit organization dedicated to protecting birds, the Pot à L'Eau-de-Vie archipelago is swarming with water birds. Duvetnor offers package rates that include accommodations, meals and a cruise on the river with a naturalist guide. The lighthouse, over a century old, has been carefully restored. It has three cozy guest rooms and delicious food is served. If you're looking for a peaceful atmosphere, this is the place to stay.

Saint-Antonin

Camping chez Jean
$
🐾, ≈
434 Rue Principale, Exit 499 off Aut. 20
☎862-3081
Camping Chez Jean is a campground with 73 sites, a swimming pool, laundry facilities and a snack bar.

*Phare de l'île du
Pot à l'Eau-de-Vie*

Île Verte

Les maisons du Phare
$$ bkfst incl
sb
28B Chemin du Phare
www.ileverte.net
☎898-2730
⇥898-4002
On lovely Île Verte, La Maison des Phares offers you the pleasure of staying in one of the two former lighthouse-keeper houses. Beach.

Trois-Pistoles

Camping Plage Trois-Pistoles
$
🐾, ≈
late May to late Sep
130 Rte 132 E.
☎851-2403
⇥851-4890
Camping Plage Trois-Pistoles is a 5min drive from Trois-Pistoles. Its unique setting on the banks of the St. Lawrence offers some of the most beautiful panoramic views of the region. You can go hiking along the beach or in the nearby woods. In August at low tide, you can see eel-catching nets stretched out along the river, adding a picturesque touch to the scenery. Laundry.

La Ferme Paysagée
$ bkfst incl.
sb
from Trois-Pistoles, turn right onto the Rte. 293 S. and continue 4km past the church of St-Jean de-Dieu
☎963-3315
*www.lafermepaysagee.
freeservers.com*
La Ferme Paysagée, a bed and breakfast on a farm, is popular with families and animal lovers. Deer, goats, sheep and even llamas are all kept on the farm.

Motel Trois-Pistoles

$$

≡, ✖, ℜ
64 Rte 132 O.
☎851-2563
✆851-0893

The Motel Trois-Pistoles has 29 comfortable rooms, some affording a lovely view of the river; the sunsets from this spot are absolutely magnificent.

Saint-Simon

Auberge Saint-Simon

$$

ℜ
early Jun to mid-Oct
18 Rue Principale, Rte. 132
☎738-2971

Built in 1830, charming Auberge Saint-Simon is a large house with a mansard roof typical of this period. The nine tastefully decorated rooms are rich in historical atmosphere.

Le Bic

Camping Bic

$

3382 route 132 Ouest, Parc du Bic
☎736-5035 or 800-665-6527

The Camping Bic has 100 campsites in magnificent Parc du Bic, where all kinds of outdoor activities are possible. Unfortunately, the noise from the highway can be heard at most of these campsites, even though the road is not visible from them.

Auberge du Mange Grenouille

$$-$$$ bkfst incl.

ℜ, ♦
148 Rue Ste-Cécile
☎736-5656
✆736-5657
www.aubergedumange grenouille.qc.ca

The Auberge du Mange Grenouille has a good reputation in Québec and beyond. Guests are warmly welcomed, served succulent food (see

p 406), and stay in 14 cozy rooms decorated with antiques. The inn also hosts murder-mystery evenings.

Rimouski

Hôtel Rimouski

$$-$$$

≡, ☉, ≈, ℝ, ℜ, ⊛
225 Boulevard René-Lepage Est
☎725-5000 or 800-463-0755
✆725-5725
www.hotelrimouski.com

Hôtel Rimouski has a unique design; its big staircase and long swimming pool in the lobby will appeal to many visitors. Children under 18 can stay in their parents' room for free.

Pointe-au-Père

Auberge La Marée Douce

$$-$$$ bkfst incl.

ℜ
1329 Boulevard Ste-Anne
☎722-0822
✆723-4512

The Auberge La Marée Douce is a riverside inn located in Pointe-au-Père, near the Musée de la Mer. Built in 1860, it has comfortable rooms, each with its own decor.

Sainte-Luce

Auberge Sainte-Luce

$$

K, ℜ
46 Route du Fleuve Ouest
☎739-4955
✆739-4923

Auberge Sainte-Luce is a converted century old house with simple but comfortable rooms. Guests also have access to a lookout and a beach.

Restaurants

The Kamouraska Region

Saint-André

La Solaillerie

$$$-$$$$

112 Rue Principale
☎493-2914

The dining room at La Solaillerie has been carefully decorated to highlight the historic character of the old house in which it is located. In this inviting setting, guests savour excellent cuisine lovingly prepared and served by the owners of the inn. Drawing his inspiration from a French culinary repertoire, the chef uses fresh regional ingredients like quail, lamb, and fresh and smoked salmon to create new dishes according to his fancy. Reservations required.

Notre-Dame-du-Portage

L'Estran Auberge sur Mer

$$$-$$$$

363 Rte. du Fleuve
☎862-0642 or 800-622-0642

The dining room at l'Estran Auberge sur Mer has a marvellous view of the river, which really does begin to resemble the sea here. The fine cuisine will enrapture the most exacting customers. Fish and seafood are served all summer long, accompanied by whatever is in season. In autumn, game is featured on the menu. Reservations required.

Rivière-du-Loup

La Terrasse, La Distinction

$$-$$$

171 Rue Fraser
☎862-6927

The restaurants in the Hôtel Lévesque, La Terrasse *($$)*

Bas-Saint-Laurent

and La Distinction *($$-$$$; closed Sun and Mon for dinner)* serve a variety of delicious Italian dishes, as well as smoked salmon prepared according to a traditional method in the hotel's smokehouse.

Saint-Patrice
$$$
169 Rue Fraser
☎862-9895
The Saint-Patrice is one of the best restaurants in town. Fish, seafood, rabbit and lamb are the specialities. At the same address, **Le Novelo** *($$)* serves pasta and thin-crust pizza in a bistro setting, and **La Romance** *($$$)* specializes in fondues.

Trois-Pistoles

L'ensoleillé
$$-$$$
138 Rue Notre-Dame Ouest
☎851-2889
The vegetarian café/restaurant L'ensolleillé has a very simple à-la-carte menu. The three-course lunch and dinner menus are a good deal.

Le Michalie
$$$
55 Rue Notre-Dame Est
☎851-4011
Le Michalie is a charming little restaurant serving some of the best regional cuisine, as well as gourmet Italian food.

Saint-Fabien

 **Auberge Saint-Simon**
$$$
18 Rue Principale
☎738-2971
In the warm, traditional atmosphere of the Auberge Saint-Simon, guests will enjoy another excellent Bas-Saint-Laurent dining experience. Rabbit, lamb, halibut and seafood are paired with fresh vegetables grown in the restaurant's garden.

Le Bic

 Auberge du Mange Grenouille
$$$-$$$$
148 Rue Ste-Cécile
☎736-5656
The Auberge du Mange Grenouille is one of the best restaurants in the Bas-Saint-Laurent. It was once a general store and is decorated with old furniture carefully chosen to complement the architecture. Guests are offered a choice of six daily tables d'hôte that include fowl, game, lamb and fish dishes. Everything served here is delicious, and the service is always attentive.

Rimouski

Le lotus
$$$
143 Rue Belzile
☎725-0822
If you're in the mood for Thai, Vietnamese or Cambodian food, head to Le Lotus, were delicious, very exotic and well-presented dishes are served. Every day, in addition to the à la carte menu, guests have the choice between a Mandarin dinner, a gastronomic dinner and a super gastronomic dinner, each of which includes four or five courses. Reservations recommended.

Café-bistro Le Saint-Louis
$$$
97 Rue St-Louis
☎723-7979
The Café-Bistro Le Saint-Louis looks just like its Parisian cousins, and is filled with all the same aromas. It offers a large selection of imported beer and microbrews. The menu, which changes daily, is delicious, and the dishes are served in a pleasant atmosphere.

Serge Poully
$$$-$$$$
284 Rue St-Germain Est
☎723-3038
Serge Poully serves game, seafood, steak and French specialties. The relaxed atmosphere and attentive service make this the perfect place for an intimate dinner for two.

Entertainment

Bars

Rimouski

Sens Unique
160 Avenue de la Cathédrale
The music and outdoor seating at the Sens Unique make this one of the most appealing places in Rimouski. The very diverse clientele ranges in age from 18 to 45.

Theatres

Le Bic

The **Théâtre Les Gens d'en Bas** *($18-$25; 50 Route du Golf, 16km west of downtown Rimouski,* ☎736-4141*)* puts on at least one play each summer. French-language performances are held from Tuesday to Saturday at 8:30pm *(summer only, schedules varies the rest of the year)* at the Grange-Théâtre du Bic, which boasts a magnificent natural setting.

Festivals and Cultural Events

Rimouski

The **Festi-Jazz** (*first weekend in Sep;* ☎ 724-7844) is a series of about 20 shows by jazz musicians from Québec and abroad. Some shows are presented in bars and theatres, others on the street. The festival lasts four days and is always held on Labour Day weekend (the first weekend of September).

The **Carrousel International du Film de Rimouski** (☎ 722-0103) is a film festival for the younger generation. It takes place the third week of September and lasts for seven days, during which about 40 films are shown. The screenings are held at the Centre Civique in the afternoon and evening.

Shopping

Rimouski

La Samare (*84 Rue St-Germain Ouest,* ☎ 723-0242) has a large array of articles made of fish skin, as well as a wide selection of carvings, vases and other objects, all handcrafted by Inuit artisans.

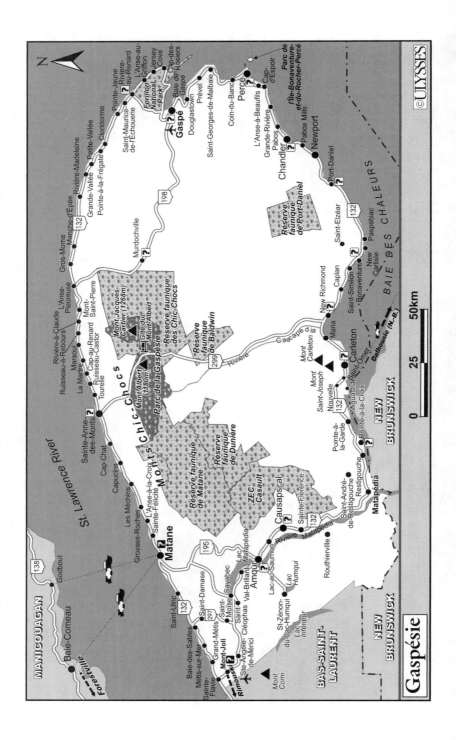

Gaspésie

© ULYSSES

Gaspésie

The shores of the vast

Gaspé peninsula are washed by the waters of Baie des Chaleurs, the St. Lawrence River and the Gulf of St. Lawrence.

Many Quebecers cherish unforgettable memories of their travels in this mythical land in the easternmost part of Québec. People dream of touring Gaspésie and discovering its magnificent coastal landscape, where the Chic-Chocs mountains plunge abruptly into the cold waters of the St. Lawrence. They dream of going all the way to the famous Percé rock, heading out to sea toward Île Bonaventure, visiting the extraordinary Forillon National Park, and then slowly returning along Baie des Chaleurs and through the valley of Rivière Matapédia in the hinterland.

This beautiful part of Québec, with its strikingly picturesque scenery, is inhabited by friendly, fascinating people, who still rely mainly on the sea for their living. The majority of Gaspesians live in small villages along the coast, leaving the centre of the peninsula covered with dense Boreal forest. The highest peak in southern Québec lies here, in the part of the Appalachians known as the Chic-Chocs.

The word *Gaspé* means "land's end" in the language of the Micmacs, who have been living in this region for thousands of years. Despite its isolation, the peninsula has attracted fishers from many different places over the centuries, particularly Acadians driven from their lands by the British in 1755. Its population is now primarily francophone.

Gaspésie's main attractions are its rugged, mountainous landscapes and the Gulf of St. Lawrence, which is so huge that it might as well be the ocean. The coastline is studded with a string of fishing villages, leaving the interior devoid of towns and roads,

much as it was when Jacques Cartier arrived in 1534.

Finding Your Way Around

The two tours in this chapter, **Tour A: The Peninsula ★★** and **Tour B: Baie des Chaleurs ★**, follow the coastline.

Tour A: The Peninsula

By Car

Take Rte. 132 E. The tour hugs the shore of the St. Lawrence River all the way to Percé, passing through

Names of New Merged Cities

Métis-sur-Mer
Merger of Les Boules and Métis-sur-Mer.

Port-Daniel-Gascons
Merger of Port-Daniel and Sainte-Germaine-de-l'Anse-aux-Gascons.

Mont-Joli
Merger of Mont-Joli and Saint-Jean-Baptiste.

Chandler
Merger of Chandler, Newport, Pabos Mills, Pabos and Saint-François-de-Pabos.

Matane
Merger of Matane, Petit-Matane, Saint-Luc-de-Matane and Saint-Jérôme-de-Matane.

Matane, Sainte-Anne-des-Monts and Gaspé. Once in L'Anse-Pleureuse, you can take a detour through Murdochville.

Bus Stations

Matane
521 Avenue du Phare E. (Irving station)
☎*(418) 562-4085*

Sainte-Anne-des-Monts
90 Boulevard Sainte-Anne
☎*(418) 763-3321*

Gaspé
20 Rue Adams
☎*(418) 368-1888*

Percé
L'Anse-à-Beaufils (Ultramar station)
☎*(418) 782-5417*

Train Stations

Gaspé
3 Boulevard Marina
☎*(418) 368-4313*

Percé
44 L'Anse-à-Beaufils
☎*800- 361-5390*

By Ferry

Baie-Comeau - Matane
(*$12.75, cars $29.95, motorcycles $22.45;* ☎*418-562-2500 or 877-562-6560):* the crossing takes 2hrs 30min. The schedule varies from year

to year so be sure to check when planning your trip. Reservations are a good idea during summer.

Godbout - Matane (*$12.75, cars $29.95, motorcycles $22.45;* ☎*418-562-2500 or 877-562-6560):* the crossing takes 2hrs 10min. Reservations are a good idea during summer.

Tour B: Baie des Chaleurs

By Car

This tour follows the road along the shore of the Baie des Chaleurs. In Matapédia, the tour heads inland to Causapscal.

Bus Stations

Bonaventure
118 Avenue Grand-Pré (Motel Grand-Pré)
☎*(418) 534-2053*

Carleton
561 Boulevard Perron
☎*(418) 364-7000*

Amqui
219 Boulevard Saint-Benoit E.
☎*(418) 629-6767*

Train Stations

Bonaventure
Rue de la Gare (near Avenue Grand-Pré)
☎*800-361-5390*

Carleton
Rue de la Gare
☎*800-361-5390*

Matapédia
10 Rue MacDonnell
☎*800-361-5390*

Practical Information

Area code: **418**

Tourist Information

Regional Office

Association Touristique de la Gaspésie
357 Rte de la Mer, Sainte-Flavie, G0J 2L0
☎*775-2223 or 800-463-0323*
≈*775-2234*
www.tourisme.gaspesie.com

Tour A: The Peninsula

Sainte-Flavie
357 Rte de la Mer, G0J 2L0
☎*775-2223*
≈*775-2234*

Matane
968 Avenue du Phare O., G4W 3P5
☎*562-1065*

Gaspé
27 Boulevard York E.
☎*368-6335*

Tour B: Baie des Chaleurs

Percé
142 Route 132 O.
☎*782-5448*

Carleton
629 Boulevard Perron, G0C 1J0
☎*364-3544*

Pointe-à-la-Croix
1830 Rue Principale, G0C 1L0
☎788-5670

Exploring

Tour A: The Peninsula

Duration of tour: 2 to 3 days

Europeans were fishing in the Gulf of the St. Lawrence before they even set foot on the North American continent. Today, not a trace remains of the camps they set up along the coast, but it is possible to imagine their reaction to this unknown continent and their encounters with the Aboriginal population. While touring the peninsula, visitors will pass alongside steep cliffs before reaching the hospitable areas where Jacques Cartier took possession of the land in the name of the king of France.

★
Grand-Métis
(pop. 270)

Grand-Métis is blessed with a micro-climate that once attracted wealthy summer visitors to the area, and also made it possible for horticulturist Elsie Reford to plant a landscape garden here. The garden is now the town's main attraction. It contains a number of species of trees and flowers that cannot be found anywhere else at this latitude in North America. The word "Métis" is derived from the Malecite name for the area, "Mitis" meaning "little poplar."

The **Jardins de Métis / Reford Gardens** ★ ★ ★ *($12; early Jul to late Aug, every day 8:30am to 6:30pm; Jun, Sep and Oct, every day 8:30am to*

5pm; 200 Route 132, ☎*775-2221, www.jardins metis.com)* are among Quebec's most beautiful gardens, and their name is world-renowned. The gardens are also a national historic site. In 1927, Elsie Stephen Meighen Reford inherited an estate from her uncle, Lord Mount Stephen, who had made his fortune by investing in the Canadian Pacific transcontinental railroad. The following year, she began laying out a landscape garden that she maintained and expanded until her death in 1954. Seven years later, the government of Québec purchased the estate and opened it to the public. The gardens are now owned by the grandson of their founder, Alexander Refort, who has endowed them with new energy, thanks to achievements like the International Garden Festival.

The garden is divided into eight distinct ornamental sections: the Floral Massif, the Rock Garden, the Rhododendron Garden, the Royal Walkway, the Primrose Garden, the Crab Apple Garden, the *Muret* (low wall) overlooking Baie de Mitis, and the Underbrush, which contains a collection of indigenous plants. The mosquitoes are voracious here, so don't forget your insect repellent.

The **Villa Reford** ★ ★ *(Jun to mid-Sep, every day 9am to 5pm; in the Jardins de Métis,* ☎*775-3165)*, a 37-room villa set in the midst of the Jardins de Métis, offers a glimpse of what life was like for turn-of-the-century Métissiens. Visitors can tour a number of rooms, the servants' quarters, the chapel, the general store, the school and the doctor's office. There is also a restaurant and gift shop.

Continue along Rte. 132 E. towards Matane. A brief detour through Métis-sur-Mer

provides an opportunity to get closer to the water.

★
Métis-sur-Mer
(pop. 250)

At the turn of the 20th century, this resort area, also known as Métis Beach, was a favourite among the professors of Montréal's McGill University, who rented elegant seaside cottages here for the summer vacation. Wealthy British families also built large New England–style homes in the area, attracted by the beauty of the landscape and the presence of a small Scottish community, established here in 1820 by John McNider, the seigneur of Métis. The village's harmonious appearance and high-quality wooden architecture set it apart from the surrounding municipalities.

Most Scots are members of the Presbyterian Church, the official church of Scotland, though a number of communities merged with the Methodists in the early 20th century to form the United Church; Métis-sur-Mer was one of these. Erected in 1874, the **Presbyterian Chapel** *(on the way into the village)* resembles a colonial Catholic church, due to the shape of its doors, windows and belltower.

The road then leads through Les Boules and the charming village of Baie-des-Sables before reaching Saint-Ulric.

Matane
(pop. 12,725)

The main attraction in Matane, whose name means "Beaver Pond" in Micmac, is the salmon and the famous local shrimp, which are celebrated at an annual festival. The town is the region's administrative centre and economic mainspring, due to its diversified industry based on fishing,

Gaspésie

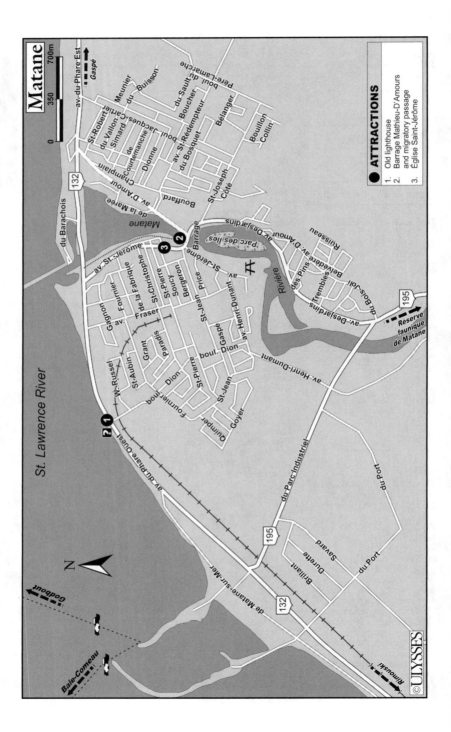

Matane

0 350 700m

St. Lawrence River

N

Godbout

Baie-Comeau

Rimouski

ATTRACTIONS

1. Old lighthouse
2. Barrage Mathieu-D'Amours and migratory passage
3. Église Saint-Jérôme

132

du Barachois

av. du Phare Ouest

de Matane-sur-Mer

Brillant

Durette

Savard

132

195

du Parc Industriel

du Port

du Port

Réserve faunique de Matane

195

av. Desjardins

du Bois-Joli

Bélvédère av. D'Amour

av. des Pins

des Trembles

Ruisseau

Rivière

parc des Îles

av. Henri-Dunant

boul. Dion

St-Jean

Goyer

Quimper

Fournier-mont

Dion

St-Pierre

St-Aubin

Grant

Paradis

W-Russel

av. Fraser

Gagnon

Fournier

de la Fabrique

St-Christophe

St-Pierre

Soucy

Bergeron

Price

St-Jean

av. St-Jérôme

St-Jérôme

Barrage

av. Desjardins

Côte

St-Joseph

du Bosquet

av. St-Redempteur

Boucher

boul. du Sault

Pére-Lamarche

Bélanger

Bouillon

Collin

Bouffard

Champlain

av. D'Amour

de la Marée

Matane

St-Robert

du Vallon

Simard

de Courtemanche

Dionne

boul. Jacques-Cartier

Meunier

du Buisson

av. du Phare Est

Gaspé

132

© ULYSSES

lumber, cement-making, oil refining and shipping. During World War II, German submarines came all the way to the town pier.

The **old lighthouse** *(968 Avenue du Phare)*, built in 1911 and no longer in use, greets visitors on their way into town. The lighthouse keeper's house now serves as a tourist office and miniature museum of local history.

The Rivière Matane runs through the centre of town. Here, visitors will find the **Barrage Mathieu-D'Amours ★** *(near Parc des Îles)*, a dam, along with a **migratory passage** *($2)* intended to help salmon swim upriver to spawn. From an observation area located below water level, visitors can take in the fascinating spectacle of the salmon struggling furiously against the current. At nearby **Parc des Îles**, there is a beach, a picnic area and an outdoor theatre.

Religious architecture in Québec was greatly influenced by a French monk and architect named Dom Bellot. However, before this man had even made his first trip to Canada in 1934, two architects by the name of Paul Rousseau and Philippe Côté had the **Église Saint-Jérôme ★** *(527 Rue Saint-Jérôme)* built, one of the precursors of modern religions art in Québec. The architect reused the walls of the town's former church, which was consumed by flames in 1932. As the ruins of the devastated church were too fragile to support the new structure, the full weight of the roof was placed on large, concrete parabolic arches. In the chancel, visitors will see a large mural by painter Lucien Martial.

Visitors can take an optional trip inland to the Réserve Faunique de Matane, a wild-life preserve located about an hour's drive from town. For information on the Réserve Faunique de Matane see p 421.

Return to Rte. 132 E. On the way to Cap-Chat and Sainte-Anne-des-Monts, the road runs alongside charming fishing villages with evocative names like Sainte-Félicité, L'Anse-à-la-Croix (Cross Cove), Grosses-Roches (Big Rocks), Les Méchins (a derivative of the French word for mean; "méchant") and Capucins (Capuchins).

Cap-Chat (pop. 3,000)

According to some, this little town owes its name to Champlain, who christened the area "Cap de Chatte" in honour of Commander de Chatte, the King's Lieutenant-General. Still others maintain that the name was inspired by a rock near the lighthouse, which is shaped like a crouching cat (*chat* is the French word for a cat). Erected in 1916, **Église Saint-Norbert** is the only sizable monument in the centre of town. Romanesque Revival in style, it is one of only a few churches east of Matane that is not built out of wood.

Electricity can be produced in a variety of ways. One of the most original and least employed methods is without question the wind turbine, or *éolienne* in French. The village of Cap-Chat is an ideal location for the production of wind energy and its many turbines create a somewhat supernatural landscape! The **Centre d'Interprétation de l'Énergie Éolienne Éole ★** *($8; early Jun to mid-Oct, every day 8:30am to 5pm; Rte 132, ☎786-5719)* is home to a 110m-high turbine, the tallest and strongest in the world,

as well as the largest concentration of turbines in eastern Canada.

The **Centre d'Interprétation du Vent et de la Mer Le Tryton** *($8; mid-Jun to mid-Sep, every day 8am to 6pm; 9 Route du Phare, near Cap-Chat, ☎786-5543)*, located alongside a lighthouse built in 1871, the centre traces the history of Cap-Chat and its ties to the wind and the Gulf of St. Lawrence. There are pleasant trails leading to the sea.

★ Sainte-Anne-des-Monts (pop. 7,200)

There are several interesting buildings in this town, including **Église Sainte-Anne**, built by Louis-Napoléon Audet in 1939, and the former Palais de Justice (courthouse), now the **Hôtel de Ville** (town hall), erected in 1885. Visitors will also find a number of lovely homes, built for various ship captains and industrialists. One of these is the historic Maison Lamontagne. Sainte-Anne-des-Monts is the point of departure for excursions to Rivière Sainte-Anne and the forests of Parc de la Gaspésie and the Réserve Faunique des Chic-Choc.

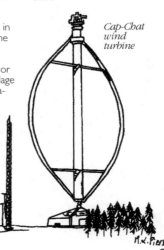

Cap-Chat wind turbine

At **Centre de Découverte Explorama** *(admission fee; Jun every day 9am to 6pm, Jul to Mid-Aug every day 9am to 8pm, mid-Aug to mid-Oct every day 9am to 6pm, rest of the year Mon-Fri 9am to 5pm, Sat and Sun 1pm to 5pm; 1 Rue du Quai, ☎ 763-2500)*, visitors can learn more about the Gaspé peninsula and its close links to the sea and the mountains through interpretive activities.

*From here, it is possible to set off on a side-trip into the heart of the peninsula. To do so, take Rte. 299, which leads to the entrance of **Parc de la Gaspésie** ★★★ (see p 421).*

Back on Rte. 132, visitors will pass through the villages of Tourelle, Ruisseau-Castor and Cap-au-Renard on the way to La Martre.

★★ From La Martre to L'Anse-Pleureuse

With its **wooden church** (1914) and **lighthouse** (1906), La Martre is a typical fishing village, located on the edge of the coastal plain. Beyond this point, the coast becomes much steeper and more jagged. The road zigzags into deep bays and out onto windswept capes. In a number of places, it passes so close to the sea that the waves lap at the asphalt in rough weather. It is worthwhile exploring some of the few roads leading inland from the villages, especially the gravel ones alongside Rivière à Claude and Rivière Mont-Saint-Pierre, to fully appreciate the ruggedness of the landscape and the mightiness of the rivers.

Musée des Phares et Balises ★ *($5; early Jun to late Sep, every day 9am to 5pm; 10 Avenue du Phare, ☎288-5698)*. In the red octagonal former lighthouse and the equally colourful lighthouse

keeper's house, there is an interesting exhibit on the history and operation of lighthouses in Gaspésie.

*The road then leads through Marsoui, Ruisseau-à-Rebours, Rivière-à-Claude, Mont-Saint-Pierre, where you will find launching pads for hanggliding, and finally, a village whose name is like something out of a ghost story, **L'Anse-Pleureuse** (Weeping Cove). From here, it is possible to take a side trip to **Murdochville**, the so-called "copper capital" of Québec, and the only sizable inland town in Gaspésie (Rte. 198).*

Murdochville (pop. 1,300)

Murdochville is located in the middle of the forest, 40km from civilization. It dates back only to 1951, when a company named Gaspésie Mines decided to mine the extensive copper deposits in this isolated region. The company built the town according to a relatively precise plan. In 1957, the Murdochville miners went on a difficult strike, demanding recognition of their right to form a union and thus marking one of the most important chapters in the history of trade unionism in Québec.

Unfortunately, a sad page in the history of the town was written in 2000, when the mine closed. After 50 years of working underground, the workers were laid off and mining of copper ceased.

Nevertheless, visitors can still take in the **Centre d'Interprétation du Cuivre** ★ *($10; early Jun to mid-Oct, every day 10am to 4pm; 345 Rte. 198, ☎784-3335 or 800-487-8601)*, an unusual experience because visitors are required to don a miner's uniform supplied by the centre before heading into a real underground gallery. The

objects on display illustrate the history of copper mining and the techniques involved in extracting the metal from the earth.

*Head back towards Anse-Pleureuse. Turn right onto Rte. 132, which leads through a number of other little villages with colourful names, such as **Gros-Morne** (Big Hill), **Manche-d'Épée** (Sword Handle), **Pointe-à-la-Frégate** (Frigate Point) and **L'Échouerie** (in French "echouer" means to run aground).*

★ L'Anse-au-Griffon (pop. 995)

Starting after the British conquest of New France in 1760, a small group of Anglo-Norman merchants took control of commercial fishing in the Gaspésie. One of these individuals, John LeBoutillier, built warehouses for salt, flour and dried cod in L'Anse-au-Griffon around 1840, and then began exporting cod to Spain, Italy and Brazil.

Maison LeBoutillier ★ *($4; early Jun to mid-Oct, every day 9am to 5pm; 578 Boulevard Griffon, ☎892-5150)*, a beautiful wooden house painted bright yellow, was built in 1840 to serve as a residence and office for the managers of LeBoutillier's company, which employed up to 2,500 people in the region 20 years later. Its roof has arched eaves, like those found on houses in Kamouraska (see p 396). Inside is a café, a craft shop and an information centre.

After passing through Jersey Cove, you'll reach Cap-des-Rosiers, gateway to the southern portion of Forillon National Park, where the landscape is more uneven, and the sea makes its existence ever more conspicuous.

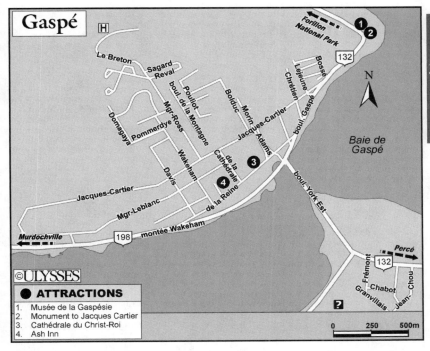

Gaspé

ATTRACTIONS

1. Musée de la Gaspésie
2. Monument to Jacques Cartier
3. Cathédrale du Christ-Roi
4. Ash Inn

©ULYSSES

0   250   500m

★
Cap-des-Rosiers
(pop. 525)

Located in a magnificent setting, Cap-des-Rosiers has been the scene of many shipwrecks. Two monuments have been erected in memory of one in particular—that of the sailing ship *Carriks*, which claimed the lives of 87 of the 200 or so Irish immigrants aboard. The victims were buried in the local cemetery, while most of the survivors settled in Cap-des-Rosiers, giving the community a surprising new character. Irish names, such as Kavanagh and Whalen, are still common in the area. It was also from atop this cape that the French spotted General Wolfe's fleet heading for Québec City in 1759.

Forillon National Park ★★★, see p 421.

The road skirts round Cap Gaspé, then leads to the bay of the same name, where jagged cliff suddenly give way to gentle valleys traversed by rivers.

★
Gaspé
(pop. 16,100)

It was here that Jacques Cartier claimed Canada for King Francis I of France in early July 1534. However, it was not until the beginning of the 18th century that the first fishing post was established in Gaspé, and the town itself did not develop until the end of that century.

Throughout the 19th century, the lives of an entire population of poorly educated, destitute French Canadian and Acadian fishers were regulated by the large fishing companies run by the merchants from the island of Jersey. During World

War II, Gaspé prepared to become the Royal Navy's main base in the event of a German invasion of Great Britain, which explains why there are a few military installations around the bay. Today, Gaspé is the most important town on the peninsula, as well as the region's administrative centre. The city follows the waterfront in a narrow ribbon of development.

In 1977, upon the initiative of the local historical society, the **Musée de la Gaspésie ★★** *($4; late Jun to early Sep, every day 9am to 6pm; early Sep to mid-Jun, Tue-Fri 9am to 5pm, Sat and Sun 1pm to 5pm; 80 Boulevard Gaspé, ☎368-1534)* was erected on Pointe Jacques Cartier, overlooking Baie de Gaspé. A museum of history and popular tradition, it houses a permanent exhibit entitled *Un Peuple de la Mer* (A People of the Sea), tracing life in

Gaspésie from the first Aboriginal inhabitants, members of the Micmac nation, all the way up to the present day. Temporary exhibits are also featured at the museum.

Next to the museum lies a superb **monument to Jacques Cartier**, executed by the Bourgault family of Saint-Jean-Port-Joli. The six bronze steles are inscribed with descriptions of Cartier arriving in Canada, taking possession of the land, and meeting the Aboriginal people for the first time.

Take Boulevard Gaspé to Rue Jacques-Cartier.

Cathédrale du Christ-Roi ★
(20 Rue de la Cathédrale), the only wooden cathedral in North America, has a contemporary design characteristic of Californian "shed" architecture, which is foreign to the east coast of the continent. Designed by Montréal architect Gérard Notebaert, it was erected in 1968 on the foundations of an earlier basilica, which was begun in 1932 to commemorate the 400th anniversary of Jacques Cartier's arrival in Canada, but was never completed due to a lack of funds. The interior is bathed in soft light from a lovely stained-glass window by Claude Théberge, who made it with antique glass. Visitors will also find a fresco showing Jacques Cartier taking possession of Canada. The fresco was received as a gift from France in 1934.

The Ash Inn ★ *(188 Rue de la Reine),* a former residence built in 1885 for Dr. William Wakeham, the famous Arctic explorer, is one of the only 19th-century stone houses in all of Gaspésie.

Heading out of Gaspé, visitors will get back on Rte. 132, leading to Percé. On the way, the road runs along the southern side of Baie de Gaspé, with its charming villages,

some of which were settled by small communities of American Loyalists, others by British immigrants. The British colonial government intentionally populated these distant regions with settlers who were staunchly loyal to the king of England, in the hopes of strengthening its position throughout Québec and promoting the rapid assimilation of the French Canadian population.

Continue along Rte. 132 to Percé.

★★
Percé
(pop. 3,800)

A famous tourist destination, Percé lies in a beautiful setting, which has unfortunately been somewhat marred by the booming hotel industry. The majestic scenery features several natural phenomena, the most important being the famous Rocher Percé, which is to Québec what the Sugar Loaf is to Brazil. Since the beginning of the 20th century, artists have been flocking to Percé every summer, charmed by the beautiful landscapes and the local inhabitants.

Percé was an important gathering place for the Aboriginals until the Denys family established a seasonal fishing camp here in the 17th century, attracting French and Basque fishers. In 1781, Charles Robin, a powerful merchant from the island of Jersey, founded a fishing business in L'Anse du Sud, at which point a number of Loyalists, Irish and immigrants from Guernsey joined the French Canadian population. At the time, the area's permanent population was still very small compared to the seasonal population working in Robin's flimsy buildings. Percé was also the main fishing port on Québec's coast throughout the 19th century. The tourist industry

took over in the 20th century, especially after Rte. 132 was built in 1929. Life in Percé nevertheless retains a precarious, seasonal quality.

Upon arriving in Percé, visitors are greeted by the arresting sight of the famous **Rocher Percé** ★★★, a wall of rock measuring 400m in length and 88m in height at its tallest point. Its name, which translates as pierced rock, comes from the two entirely natural arched openings at its base. Only one of these openings remains today, since the eastern part of the rock collapsed in the mid-19th century. At low tide, starting from Plage du Mont Joli, it is possible to walk to the rock and admire the majestic surroundings and the thousands of fossils trapped in the limestone (*inquire about the time of day and duration of the tides beforehand*).

The **Musée Le Chafaud** ★ *($5; Jun to early Sep every day 10am to 10pm, early Sep to early Oct every day 10am to 8pm; 145 Rte. 132, ☎782-5100)* occupies the largest building at Charles Robin's old plant in Percé. The *chafaud* is a building where fish was processed and stored. Today, it houses an exhibition on local heritage and is also used for various activities linked to the visual arts. The icehouse and salt shed still stand near the quay. On the other side of the street are the "Bell House," topped by a bell once used to call employees to work, the former company store, with its gabled roof and wood ornaments, and finally an old barn, which serves as the local arts centre.

At the Percé docks, there are a number of boats that take people out to **Île Bonaventure** (see p 422). During the high season, there are frequent departures from 8am to 5pm. Often, the crossing includes a short ride around the island

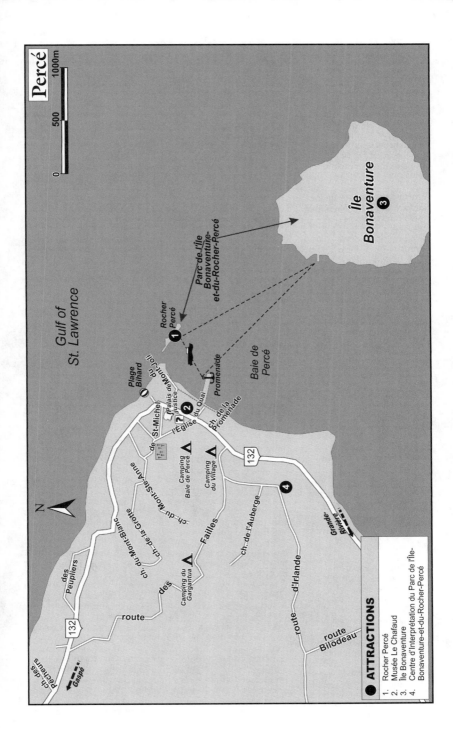

Percé

1000m

500

0

Gulf of
St. Lawrence

Plage
Bihard

Rocher
Percé

Parc de l'île-
Bonaventure-
et-du-Rocher-Percé

île
Bonaventure

③

①

N

du Mont-Joli

de St-Michel

l'Église

Palais de
Justice

②

du Quai

ch. de la
Promenade

Promenade

Baie de
Percé

ch.-du-Mont-Ste-Anne

Camping
Baie de Percé

Camping
du Village

132

ch.-de-la-Grotte

ch.-du-Mont-Blanc

Camping du
Gargantua

Failles

des

des
Peupliers

route

132

ch. des
Pêcheurs

Gaspé

ch. de l'Auberge

④

route
d'Irlande

route
Bilodeau

Grande
Rivière

● ATTRACTIONS

1. Rocher Percé
2. Musée Le Chafaud
3. Île Bonaventure
4. Centre d'Interprétation du Parc de l'île-
   Bonaventure-et-du-Rocher-Percé

and Rocher Percé, so that passengers can get a good look at the park's natural attractions. Most of these outfits let you spend as long as you want on the island and come back on any of their boats, which travel back and forth regularly between the island and the mainland. Note that pets are not permitted to accompany you to the island.

The **Centre d'Interprétation du Parc de l'Île-Bonaventure-et-du-Rocher-Percé** *(free admission; early Jun to mid-Oct, every day 9am to 5pm; 343 Route de l'Irlande, ☎782-2721)* shows a short film on the history of Île Bonaventure and the gannets that nest there. Visitors will also find an exhibition area, saltwater aquariums and two short footpaths. Finally, there is a shop run by local bird-watchers, which sells books and souvenirs.

The tour of the peninsula ends et Percé. To make a complete circle and return to Québec City or Montréal without having to double back, the most pleasant way is to combine the tour of the peninsula with the following tour of **Baie des Chaleurs.**

Tour B: Baie des Chaleurs

Duration of tour: two days

In 1604-06, Samuel de Champlain and Sieur de Monts founded the settlements of Île Sainte-Croix and Port-Royal, which were then populated by colonists from Poitou (France), thus marking the origins of Acadie (Acadia), a vast colony corresponding to the territory now occupied by Nova Scotia, Prince Edward Island and New Brunswick. In 1755, during the Seven Years War, the British captured the Acadians, whom they subse-

quently deported to faraway regions. A number of those who survived the trip attempted to return to their lands, which had been confiscated and then granted to new British colonists. Some settled in Louisiana, while others went to Québec and settled mostly in the Baie des Chaleurs area. Ironically, these Acadians were soon joined by Irish, Scottish and English immigrants, with whom they lived in relative peace, turning the area into a patchwork of French and English villages.

This tour leads through gentler landscapes and more farmlands than the tour of the peninsula. Visitors will also discover sandy beaches washed by calmer, warmer waters than those off Percé. The bay itself penetrates deep into the territory, creating a natural border between New Brunswick, to the south, and Québec, to the north. This route can serve as a springboard for a tour of the Îles-de-la-Madeleine or Canada's Atlantic provinces.

Take Rte. 132 to Paspébiac

Paspébiac
(pop. 3,550)

This little industrial town used to be the headquarters of the Robin company, which specialized in processing and exporting cod. The business was founded in 1766 by Charles Robin, a merchant from the island of Jersey, and then expanded to several spots along the coast of Gaspésie and even along the Côte-Nord. In 1791, Robin added a shipyard to his facilities in Paspébiac to build vessels to transport fish to Europe. Around 1840, the company began to face fierce competition from an enterprise owned by John LeBoutillier, one of Robin's former employees. Then, the failure of the Bank of Jersey in 1886 had a severe impact on fishing

enterprises in Gaspésie, which never regained their former power.

The **Site Historique du Banc-de-Pêche-de-Paspébiac** ★★ *($5; mid-Jun to mid-Sep, every day 9am to 6pm; mid-Sep to late Oct, every day 9am to 5pm; 3e Rue, Route du Quai, ☎752-6229)*. A *banc* is a strip of sand and gravel used for drying fish. Paspébiac's *banc,* along with the town's deep, well-protected natural port, lent itself to the development of a fishing industry. In 1964, there were still some 70 buildings from the Robin and LeBoutillier companies on the *banc.* That year, however, most of them were destroyed by a fire. The eight surviving buildings have been carefully restored in this historic site and are open to the public.

Most of these buildings were erected in the 19th century. Particularly noteworthy sights include the forge, the former carpenter's shop, the kitchens, the Robin company offices, a powder magazine and the 'B.B.' (1850), a structure with a high pointed roof used for storing cod. Some of the buildings house thematic exhibitions on shipbuilding, the international fish market and the history of the Jersey companies. The site also includes a shop and a restaurant with typical regional dishes.

★
New Carlisle
(pop. 1,500)

The New Carlisle region was settled by American Loyalists, who came here after the 1783 signing of the Treaty of Versailles, under which Great Britain recognized the independence of the United States. The charming village, with its four churches of different denominations, is not unlike those of New England. A visit to New Carlisle wouldn't be complete without a tour

Gaspésie

of its three Protestant churches, which are a great source of pride to the villagers. They are located along Rte. 132, which becomes Rue Principale, in the centre of the village.

Gothic Revival in style, **St. Andrew's Anglican Church** was built around 1890. Larger than most churches of its denomination in villages of comparable size, it bears witness to the importance of the Anglican community in New Carlisle. **Zion United Church**, which hardly has any members left, has a curious shape, while **Knox Presbyterian Church**, in the Scottish tradition, has a typical 1850s design.

There are only a few 19th-century bourgeois residences in Gaspésie, a region of fishers and forestry workers. **Maison Hamilton ★** *($3.50; mid-Jun to late Aug, every day 10am to noon and 1pm to 4:30pm; 115 Rue Principale, ☎752-6498)* is one of them. Its stone foundations make it even more remarkable. Its somewhat austere facade adheres to the neoclassical style of the period. Erected in 1852 for lawyer and deputy John Robinson Hamilton, the house is still occupied but the present owners have opened it to the public. Inside, visitors will discover a lovely assortment of Victorian furniture, including a piano dating back to 1840.

Much humbler than Maison Hamilton is the **birthplace of René Lévesque** (1922-1987) *(not open to visitors; 16 Mount Sorel)*. Premier of Québec from 1976 to 1985, Lévesque was the driving force behind the nationalisation of electricity in Québec, and the founder of the Parti Québécois. This house bears witness to the cultural intermingling between the French and the English that took place in the region during the 19th

century, when New Carlisle was the administrative centre of Baie des Chaleurs.

Continue along Rte. 132 to Bonaventure.

★
**Bonaventure
(pop. 3,000)**

This village was founded by Acadians taking refuge at the mouth of the Rivière Bonaventure (one of the best salmon rivers in North America) after Restigouche fell to the British in 1760. Today, Bonaventure is a bastion of Acadian culture in the Baie des Chaleurs area, as well as being home to a small seaside resort with a sandy beach and a deep water port. It is also one of the only places in the world where visitors will find goods made out of fish skin (wallets and purses).

An estimated one million Quebecers are of Acadian descent. The **Musée Acadien du Québec ★** *($5; late Jun to early Sep, every day 9am to 6pm; early Sep to mid-Oct, every day 9am to 5pm; rest of the year, Mon-Fri 9am to noon and 1pm to 5pm, Sat and Sun 1pm to 5pm; 95 Avenue Port-Royal, ☎534-4000)* recounts the odyssey of Acadians living in Québec and elsewhere in North America. The permanent collection includes 18th-century furniture, period paintings and photographs, and an audiovisual presentation of Acadian ethnography, which gives visitors an excellent idea of the spread of Acadian culture in North America. The museum occupies the village's old church hall, a large wooden building painted blue and white, dating back to 1914.

The construction of **Église Saint-Bonaventure ★** *(100 Avenue Port-Royal)* began in 1860, the same year the Catholic clergy finally started establishing parishes in

the Baie des Chaleurs region, considered very remote in those days. The building's facade was modified in 1919 according to a design by architect Pierre Lévesque. Its very colourful interior is decorated with remounted paintings by Georges S. Dorval of Québec City, as well as a number of wooden ornaments made to look like marble.

The **Bioparc de la Gaspésie** *($10; Jul and Aug every day 9am to 6pm; Jun, Sep and Oct 9am to 5pm; 123 Rue des Vieux-Ponts, ☎534-1997)* is an ideal spot for families. With the aid of multimedia presentations and guides, discover the secret world of Gaspésien animals: bears, seals, otters, lynx and caribou. Their natural habitats are recreated along a 1km path: tundra, river, *barachois*, forest and bay. The tour lasts 2hrs.

Grotte de Saint-Elzéar, see p 422.

Return to Rte. 132 and turn right, towards New Richmond. Take a left off the main road, onto Boulevard Perron Ouest.

★
**New Richmond
(pop. 4,000)**

The first English colonists in Gaspésie settled here after the Conquest of 1760. They were soon joined by Loyalists, and then Irish and Scottish immigrants. This strong British presence is evident in the architecture of New Richmond, with its tidy streets studded with little Protestant churches of various denominations.

Located on Pointe Duthie, on your way into the village, the **Village Gaspésien d'Héritage Britannique ★** *($7, including tour in shuttle; early Jun to early Sep, every day 9am to 6pm; early Sep to mid-Oct every day 9am to 5pm; 351*

Boulevard Perron O., ☎*392-4487)* is made up of buildings from the Baie des Chaleurs area, which were saved from demolition, transported to the grounds of the former Carswell estate and restored to house thematic exhibitions on Gaspesians of British extraction. Each structure illustrates a different group's arrival in the area: the vestiges of the Carswell residence are devoted to the British settlers; a Loyalist camp to those faithful subjects who came here in August 1784; a house and a grain warehouse to the Scottish immigrants, and another house to the Irish. Finally, in the last clearing, visitors will find the Willet house, which evokes the region's industrial development at the end of the 19th century.

St. Andrew's Presbyterian Church ★ *(211 Boulevard Perron Ouest)*, in the centre of New Richmond, is one of the oldest churches in the Baie des Chaleurs area, built in 1839 by Robert Bash. After a number of Protestant communities merged in the 20th century, St. Andrew's became part of the United Church of Canada.

★
Carleton
(pop. 2,900)

Carleton, like Bonaventure, is a stronghold of Acadian culture in Québec, and a seaside resort with a lovely sandy beach washed by calm waters that are warmer than elsewhere in Gaspésie and account for the name of the bay (*chaleur* means warmth). The mountains rising up behind the town give it a distinctive character. Carleton was founded in 1756 by Acadian refugees, who were joined by deportees returning from exile. Originally known as Tracadièche, the little town was renamed in the 19th century by the British elite, in honour of Sir Guy

Carleton, Canada's third governor.

Église Saint-Joseph ★ *(764 Boulevard Perron)* is one of the oldest Catholic churches in Gaspésie. Begun in 1849, it wasn't actually finished until 1917. It houses a tabernacle attributed to François Baillargé (1828), which was given to the parish at an undetermined date. The main vault is adorned with remounted paintings by Charles Huot.

Follow Rue du Quai (perpendicular to Rte. 132) toward the sea; after the Saint-Barnabé (a bar in a beached boat) take the gravel road and stop near the **observation tower**. Climb to the top of the tower, equipped with a telescope for bird watching. A guide is on hand to provide visitors with information on ornithology.

Nouvelle
(pop. 2,100)

Palaeontology buffs will surely be interested in **Parc de Miguasha ★★** *($3.50; early Jun to early Sep, every day 9am to 6pm; early Sep to mid-Oct, every day 9am to 5pm; 231 Miguasha O., ☎794-2475)*, a UNESCO World Heritage Site, and the second-largest fossil site in the world. The park's **palaeontology museum** displays fossils discovered in the surrounding cliffs, which formed the bottom of a lagoon 370 million years ago. The information centre houses a permanent collection of many interesting specimens. In the laboratory visitors can learn the methods used to remove fossils from the rock and identify them. The park also has an amphitheatre, used for audiovisual presentations.

West of Miguasha, Baie des Chaleurs narrows considerably as it approaches the mouth of the Rivière

Restigouche, which flows into it.

Pointe-à-la-Croix
(pop. 1,700)

On April 10, 1760, a French fleet set off from Bordeaux on its way to Canada, with the goal of liberating New France from the English. Only three ships reached Baie des Chaleurs, the others having fallen victim to English cannons as they headed out of the Gironde. The *Machault, Bienfaisant* and *Marquis-de-Malauze*, vessels weighing an average of 350 tonnes, survived, but the English troops caught up with the French at the mouth of the Restigouche in Baie des Chaleurs. A battle broke out, and the English defeated the French fleet within a few hours.

At the **Battle of Restigouche National Historic Site ★** *($4; early Jun to mid-Oct, every day 9am to 5pm; Route 132, ☎788-5676)*, also called the Lieu Historique National de la Bataille de la Restigouche, visitors can see a collection of objects recovered from the wreckage of the battle between these ships, as well as a few pieces of the frigate *Machault*. An interesting audiovisual presentation illustrates the different stages of the confrontation.

Between Pointe-à-la-Croix and Restigouche, there is a bridge that stretches across Baie des Chaleurs, linking Québec to New Brunswick.

Causapscal
(pop. 2,700)

The Matapédia, one of the best salmon rivers in North America, flows through the centre of Causapscal with its towering sawmills. Every year, fans of sportfishing come to the area. Salmon fishing and exclusive rights to the river have been a source of longstanding conflict between

Gaspésie

the local population and private clubs. Causapscal, whose name means Rocky Point in Micmac, was founded in 1839 after a post house known as La Fourche (The Fork) was opened at the junction of the Matapédia and the Causapscal.

Site Historique Matamajaw ★ *($3.90; early Jun to mid-Oct, every day 9am to 5pm; 53C Rue Saint-Jacques, ☎756-5999).* In 1873, Donald Smith, the future Lord Mount Stephen, acquired the fishing rights to the Matapédia. A few years later, he sold the rights to the Matamajaw Salmon Club. In general, members of clubs like this were American or English Canadian businessmen, who spent three or four days a year here in the middle of the woods, in a relaxing, holiday atmosphere. These individuals were offered the ultimate luxury of sending their catch home in refrigerated railway cars that waited for them at the Causapscal station. The club stopped operating around 1950, and the buildings on the Matamajaw property were listed as historic monuments and opened to the public in 1984. Here, visitors can see an exhibition on club life and the history of salmon fishing. Salmon can be observed on site, thanks to the addition of a pool. There are trails leading to **Parc Les Fourches**, where the Matapédia and Causapscal rivers meet and you can see fishers at work.

*The road then leads through **Mont-Joli**, which offers a lovely view of the St. Lawrence River, before coming full circle at the departure point of Tour A.*

Parks

Tour A: The Peninsula

The **Réserve Faunique de Matane** *(257 Rue Saint-Jérôme, ☎562-3700)* is a series of wooded hills and mountains, stretching over an area of 1,284km², and strewn with lakes and rivers excellent for salmon fishing.

Parc de la Gaspésie ★★★ *($3.50; early Jun to early Sep, every day 8am to 8pm; early Sep to mid-Oct limited hours; 124 1re Avenue O., Ste-Anne-des-Monts; also 900 Route du Parc; ☎763-7811or 866-727-2427)* covers an area of 800km² and encompasses the famous Monts Chic-Chocs. It was established in 1937, in an effort to heighten public awareness regarding nature conservation in the Gaspésie. The park is composed of conservation zones devoted to the protection of the region's natural riches, and an ambient zone, made up of a network of roads, trails and lodgings. The Chic-Chocs form the northernmost section of the Appalachian Mountains. They stretch over 90km, from Matane to the foot of Mont Albert. The McGerrigle Mountains lie perpendicular to the Chic-Chocs, covering an area of 100km². The park's trails run through three levels of terrain, leading all the way to the summits of the four highest mountains in the area, Mont Jacques-Cartier, Mont Richardson, Mont Albert and Mont Xalibu. This is the only place in Québec where white-tailed deer (in the rich vegetation of the first level), moose (in the Boreal forest) and caribou (in the tundra, at the top of the mountains) co-exist. Hikers are required to register before setting out.

The **Gîte du Mont-Albert** (see p 424) lies in the centre of the park. A very comfortable inn, it is known for its fine cuisine, delicate wooden architecture inspired by the French Regime, and stunning panoramic view. Erected in 1950, the main building houses the dining room and 17 rooms, while numerous little cottages in the same style are scattered across the hillside (☎800-463-0860).

The motto of **Forillon National Park** ★★★ *($4; $6 family; year round, every day; 122 Boulevard Gaspé, Gaspé, ☎368-5505)* is "harmony between man, land and sea." Many an outdoor enthusiast dreams about this series of forests, mountains and cliff-lined shores all crisscrossed by hiking trails. Home to a fairly wide range of animals, this national park abounds in foxes, bears, moose, porcupines and other mammals. Over 200 species of birds live here, including herring gulls, cormorants, finches, larks and gannets. Depending on the season, visitors might catch a glimpse of whales or seals from the paths along the coast. A variety of rare plants also lie hidden away in Forillon National Park, contributing to a greater understanding of the soil in which they grow. Visitors will find not only natural surroundings here in the park, but also traces of human activity. This vast area (245 km²) once included four little villages. The 200 families inhabiting them were relocated—not without a fight—when the park was established in 1970. The buildings of the greatest ethnological interest were kept and restored, namely the 10 or so **Maisons de Grande-Grave**, the **Phare de Cap-Gaspé** (the lighthouse), the **former Protestant Church** of Petit-Gaspé and the **Fort Péninsule**, part of the fortifications erected during World War II to protect Canada from attacks by German submarines.

Particularly notable buildings in Grande-Grave, originally populated by Anglo-Norman immigrants from the Island of Jersey in the English Channel, include the **Magasin Hyman** (1845). The store's interior has been carefully reconstructed to evoke the early 20th century, while the seaside **Ferme Blanchette** could easily grace a postcard. All of these are either fully or partly open to the public.

At **Parc de l'Île-Bonaventure-et-du-Rocher-Percé ★★** *($3.50 and transportation fee; early Jun to mid-Oct 9am to 5pm; 4 Rue du Quai, Percé, ☎782-2240)*, visitors will find large bird colonies, as well as numerous footpaths lined with rustic houses. The trails range from 2.8 to 4.9km in length, and cover a total of 15km. Due to the aridity of the surroundings, there are no stinging insects on the island. There is also no water along the trails, so be sure to bring a canteen. All trails end at an impressive bird sanctuary, where some 200,000 birds, including about 55,000 gannets, form a wildlife exhibition.

Created in 1953, the **Réserve Faunique de Port-Daniel** *(8km from Rte. 132 from Port-Daniel, ☎396-2789 or 396-2232)* is teeming with wildlife. Covering an area of 65km², it is laced with trails and strewn with lakes and cabins. To top it all off, there are some gorgeous views to drink in from some of its lookouts.

The **Grotte de Saint-Elzéar** *($37, children 8 and older only; early Jun to mid-Oct, first tour leaves at 8am; 198 Rue de l'Église Saint-Elzéar, ☎534-4335)* introduces visitors to 500,000 years of Gaspesian history. This speleological and geomorphological journey

offers participants the opportunity to visit the two largest caves in Québec. Warm clothing and a good pair of shoes are required, as the temperature is a steady 4°C.

Outdoor Activities

Hiking

Tour A: The Peninsula

Parc de la Gaspésie *($3.50; ☎763-3301)* has an outstanding network of hiking trails. On the same outing, you can pass through four different kinds of forests: a boreal forest, a coniferous forest, a subalpine forest made up of miniature trees, and finally, the tundra on the mountaintops. We especially recommend the Mont Jacques-Cartier (difficult) and Mont Albert (very difficult) trails. The Lac aux Américains trail is an excellent choice for novice hikers.

Forillon National Park *($4; $6 family; ☎368-5505)*, with its cliffs sculpted by the sea and its extraordinary landscapes, is a wonderful place to go hiking. Some of the trails are suitable for children.

Kayaking

Tour A: The Peninsula

Carrefour Aventure *($10/hr, $25/day; 106 Rue Cloutier, ☎797-5033)*, at Mont-Saint-Pierre, rents out sea kayaks (accessories included).

Tour B: Baie des Chaleurs

In Bonaventure, **Cime Aventure** *(200 Chemin Athanas-Arsenault, ☎534-2333 or 800-790-2463)* arranges kayak trips ranging in length from a few hours to six days.

Birdwatching

Tour A: The Peninsula

The **Jardins de Métis**, in Grand-Métis, are teeming with bird life—in the clearings, on the lawns, in the gardens, in the wooded area and near the river.

The **Baie des Capucins**, a saltwater marsh, is home to a multitude of birds that can be observed by taking a stroll along the path that follows its shores.

The **Parc de la Gaspésie** boasts over 150 avian species, who nest in different climates. You can observe them easily from the trails running through the park. Every Monday, Parc Ami Chic Chocs organizes a 4hr-bird watching excursion, which starts at 7am at the shop in the interpretive centre.

Île Bonaventure (see above), a protected nesting ground for cormorants and gannets, is a wonderful place to go birding.

Tour B: Baie des Chaleurs

The **Carleton *barachois*** is an excellent place to observe wildfowl, terns and great herons. There is a large colony of terns on the south end of the Carleton bank. A small observation tower, complete with information panels, makes it easy to get a good look at the birds.

Cruises and Whale-watching

Tour A: The Peninsula

Croisières Baie de Gaspé *($29; Grande-Grave,* ☎*368-8156)* offers whale-watching cruises on board a ship that plies the waters around Forillon National Park. Seals and dolphins also visit these waters so keep your eyes peeled.

Observation Littoral Percé *($40 for a 2½ to 3hr excursion, Jun to Oct; near the Hôtel Normandie; 240 Route 132, Percé,* ☎*782-5359)* hosts whale-watching excursions. With a little luck, you might also meet up with a school of white dolphins. Don't expect to see whale tails like those in photographs; usually, only the whale's back is visible, and often the animal is far away. The companies that organize these excursions must adhere to strict laws and have to pay large fines if they don't keep their distance. The outings start early in the morning. Make sure to bundle up and wear a good windbreaker.

Fishing

Tour A: The Peninsula

The **Réserve Faunique de Port-Daniel** *(8km from Rte. 132 from Port-Daniel,* ☎*396-2789 or 396-2232 off-season)* is strewn with about 20 lakes where you can go trout fishing. You have the choice between day-tripping it to the reserve or staying in

one of the lakeshore cabins, which must be reserved 48hrs in advance. In the latter case, you'll have a rowboat at your disposal.

In **Causapscal**, the visitor's welcome centre (☎*756-6174, for reservations:* 888-730-6174) in front of the Site Historique Matamajaw issues fishing permits for the Matapédia and Causapscal rivers.

Dogsledding

Tour A: The Peninsula

Dogsledding Expeditions *($550 and up; 38 Rang de la Coulée, St-Luc,* ☎*566-2176)*. These three- to five-day packages include transportation from the airport or the Mont-Joli train station, an excursion on horseback, a guide and team for each person, as well as all meals and sleeping arrangements. Groups are limited to six people. One-day and half-day excursions are also available for $125 and $70, respectively. These prices include one meal and a guide with a team of 10 to 12 dogs.

Cross-country Skiing

Tour A: The Peninsula

The **Station de Ski Val-d'Irène** *(prices varies; 115 Route Val-d'Irène,* ☎*629-3450)* boasts the best snow conditions in Québec. There are only 7km of maintained trails here, however. You can also take trail No. 3, which is not maintained.

Accommodations

Tour A: The Peninsula

Sainte-Flavie

Motel Gaspésiana
$$-$$$
≡, ❄, ℜ, ⊛
460 Rte de la Mer
☎**775-7233 or 800-404-8233**
⇋**775-9227**
Motel Gaspésiana has well-equipped, soundproofed rooms that are actually quite pleasant, thanks to their big windows.

Grand-Métis

Motel Métis
$$
❄, ≈
mid-Jun to mid-Oct
☎**775-6473**
The Motel Métis offers new, simple, modern rooms.

Métis-sur-Mer

Camping Annie
$
≈
1352 Rte 132
☎**936-3825**
⇋**936-3035**
www.campingannie.com
Camping Annie has 150 sites, 58 of which are equipped with RV hook-ups. There are hiking trails and bike paths right nearby. Located 8km from the Redford Gardens, this is a very friendly, welcoming place.

Au coin de la baie
$$-$$$
K, ℝ
mid-May to mid-Sep
1140 Rte 132
☎**936-3855**
⇋**936-3112**
Coin de la Baie is a motel with 14 lovely rooms.

Matane

Motel La Vigie
$$
≡, ℜ, ⊛
1600 Avenue du Phare O.
☎*562-3664 or 888-527-3664*
⇒*566-2930*
www.lavigie.com
Located near the snowmobile route, the Motel La Vigie offers simple rooms in a modern setting.

Auberge de La Seigneurie
$$ bkfst incl.
pb/sb
621 Rue St-Jérôme
☎*562-0021 or 877-783-4466*
⇒*562-4455*
*www.aubergela
seigneurie.com*
Visitors will find the perfect place to relax at the confluence of the St. Lawrence and Matane rivers: Auberge La Seigneurie. Located on the former site of the Fraser seigneury, this Inn has comfortable rooms.

Riotel Matane
$$-$$$
≡, ☉, ≈, ℜ, △, ⊛
250 avenue du Phare Est
☎*566-2651 or 888-427-7374*
⇒*562-7365*
www.riotel.qc.ca
The Riôtel Matane makes a charming first impression. Upon their arrival, visitors will notice the care that has been taken to make the place both attractive and comfortable. The wooden spiral staircase and leather armchairs are just a hint of what is to come. On their way through the restaurant and bar, guests will enjoy an exquisite view of the St. Lawrence. The rooms on the thirrd floor are among the newest in the hotel, which also has a tennis court and a golf course.

Parc de la Gaspésie

There are a number of different **campgrounds** *($; mid-Jun to late Sep)* in Parc de la Gaspésie, as well as 19 **cabins** *($$)* that can accommodate four, six or eight people *(☎763-2288 or 888-270-4483).*

Gîte du Mont-Albert
$$$
⌘, K, ≈, ℜ, △
☎*763-2288 or 866-727-2427*
⇒*763-7803*
For panoramic views, head to the Gîte du Mont-Albert, located in Parc de la Gaspésie. The building is *U*-shaped, so each comfortable room offers a sweeping view of Mont Albert and Mont McGerrigle.

Mont-Saint-Pierre

Auberge Nouvelle Vague
$
K, ℜ
84 Rue Prudent-Cloutier
☎*797-2851*
⇒*797-2851*
Auberge Nouvelle Vague offers very simple and inexpensive hostel accommodations.

Forillon National Park

There are four campgrounds in the park, with a total of 368 sites. To reserve one, call ☎*368-6050 (early Jun to mid-Oct, 122 Blvd. De Gaspé, G4X 1A9).* Only half the sites may be reserved; for the rest, the park follows a first-come, first-served policy so you'll want to arrive early in the morning to put your name on a waiting list. **Camping Des-Rosiers** *($; North Area),* a partially wooded area by the sea, has 155 tent and RV sites; **Camping Bon-Ami** *($; North Area)* has 135 tent and RV sites on a wooded stretch of land covered with fine gravel; **Petit Gaspé** *(South Area)* is a wooded area with 136 sites. The latter also has a campground reserved for groups of 10 or more.

Cap-aux-Os

Auberge de jeunesse de Cap-aux-Os
$
ℜ
2095 Boulevard Grande-Grève
☎*892-5153*
Located at the entrance to Forillon National Park, the Auberge de Jeunesse de Cap-aux-Os is the perfect hostel for visitors on a tight budget. The atmosphere is truly convivial in both the cafeteria and the large living room. Activities organized.

Gaspé

Résidence du Cégep de la Gaspésie et des Îles
$
K
94 Rue Jacques-Cartier
☎*368-2749*
www.cgaspesie.qc.ca
The residence hall of the CÉGEP de la Gaspésie et des Îles rents out its rooms between June 15 and August 15. Guests are provided with a kitchenette, bedding, towels and dishes.

Motel Fort Ramsay
$$
K, ✿, ℝ, ℜ
254 Boulevard Gaspé
☎*368-5094*
Situated between Forillon National Park and downtown Gaspé, the Motel Fort Ramseay offers simple rooms that are somewhat noisy, due to the proximity of the road.

Les Petits matins
$$ bkfst incl
129 Rue de la Reine
☎*368-1370*
Located near Le Brise Bise café (see p 426) in the centre of town, this B&B boasts three lovely, well-lit rooms. Hearty breakfasts are served. Nonsmoking only.

Hôtel des Commandants
$$$
≈, ℜ, ⊛
178 Rue de la Reine
☎*368-3355 or 800-462-3355*
⇒ *368-1702*
Formerly the Quality Inn, the Hôtel des Commandants is downtown, next to a shopping centre. The rooms are pleasant and comfortable.

Fort Prével

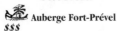 **Auberge Fort-Prével**
$$$
≈, ℜ
mid-Jun to mid-Sep
2053 Boulevard Douglas
☎*368-2281 or 888-377-3835*
⇒*368-1364*
Like the Gîte du Mont-Albert, the Auberge Fort-Prével is run by the Société des Établissements de Plein Air du Québec. The Fort Prével battery was used during the second World War, and an interpretive trail tells its story. There are 54 rooms and 13 equipped cottages (**$$$**). Great views of the ocean.

Percé

Camping du Gargantua
$
222 Rte des Failles
☎*782-2852*
Camping du Gargantua is definitely the most beautiful campground in the Percé area. It offers a view not only of Rocher Percé and the ocean, but also of the verdant surrounding mountains.

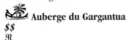 **Auberge du Gargantua**
$$
ℜ
Jun to mid-Oct
222 Rte des Failles
☎*782-2852*
⇒*782-5229*
L'Auberge du Gargantua has been looking out over Percé from atop its promontory for 30 years now, and it is well-known to anyone familiar with the Gaspé peninsula. Its restaurant (see p 427) is one of the best in the region, and its location and view are unfor-

gettable. The small, motel-style rooms are simply decorated but comfortable.

Chalets au Pic de l'Aurore
$$-$$$
ℜ, K, 🚗
mid-Jun to mid-Sep
1 Rte 132
☎*782-2166 or 800-463-4212*
⇒*782-5323*
www.resperce.com
The Chalets au Pic de l'Aurore are located above the coast north of Percé, overlooking the entire town. Each of the 17 cottage has an attractive terrace, a kitchenette, a bedroom and a living room with a fireplace.

Hôtel-Motel La Normandie
$$$
ℜ
221 Rte 132
☎*782-2337 or 800-463-0820*
⇒*782-2337*
www.normandieperce.com
The Hôtel-Motel La Normandie has a well–established reputation in Percé. During high season, this luxury establishment is full most of the time. Both the restaurant and the rooms offer a view of the famous Rocher Percé.

Tour B: Baie des Chaleurs

Paspébiac

Auberge du Parc
$$$
≈, ℜ, △, ✿, ⊛
early Feb to late Nov
68 Boulevard Gérard-D.-Lévesque O.
☎*752-3355 or 800-463-0890*
⇒*752-6406*
www.aubergeduparc.com
The Auberge du Parc occupies a 19th-century manor erected by the Robin company. It stands in the midst of a wooded area, providing a perfect place to relax. Whirlpools, body wraps, therapeutic massages, acupressure and a saltwater pool enhance the stay.

Carleton

Camping Carleton
$
mid-Jun to late Sep
Banc de Larocque
☎*782-3992*
www.carletonsurmer.com
Camping Carleton is located near the sea and the beach. Despite the lack of shady sites, this is a very quiet and pleasant place.

Hôtel-Motel Baie Bleue
$$-$$$
≈, ℜ, ⊛
482 Boulevard Perron
☎*364-3355 or 800-463-9099*
⇒*364-6165*
www.baiebleue.com
The Hotel-Motel Baie Bleue has 100 modern and well-maintained rooms.

Aqua-Mer Thalasso
$$$
$$$$$ bkfst incl.
≈, ✿
early May to late Oct
868 Boulevard Perron
☎*364-7055 or 800-463-0867*
⇒*364-7351*
www.aquamer.ca
Aqua-Mer Thalasso, located in an enchanting setting, offers a number of week-long thalassotherapy (sea-water treatment) packages.

Pointe-à-la-Garde

Auberge de jeunesse Château Bahia de Pointe-à-la-Garde
$ bkfst incl.
ℜ
152 Boulevard Perron
☎*788-2048*
⇒*788-2048*
Auberge de Jeunesse and Château Bahia de Pointe-à-la-Garde are set back from the road, halfway between Carleton and Matapédia. This youth hostel is a great place to relax. Guests are offered high-quality regional dishes such as fresh salmon and maple-flavoured ham, all at modest prices, and may sleep either in the hostel or in the château behind it.

Causapscal

Camping de Causapscal
$

≈

Jun to Aug
601 Rte 132 Ouest
☎**756-5621**
⇁**756-3344**
The Causapscal campground has 48 sites for tents and trailers.

Auberge la Coulée Douce
$$

≡, ℜ
21 Rue Boudreau
☎**756-5270 or 888-756-5270**
⇁**756-5271**
Auberge La Coulée Douce is open from spring to autumn, as well as during the winter, depending on demand. The former residence of a parish priest, this pleasant little family inn lies in the heart of the Matapédia valley. The rooms are cozily decorated with old furniture.

Restaurants

Tour A: The Peninsula

Matane

Pizzeria Italia
$-$$
toward downtown, at the corner of Rue Saint-Pierre and Rue Saint-Jérôme
☎**562-3646**
The Pizzeria Italia serves pizza made with fresh top-quality ingredients and an interesting choice of toppings.

Le Vieux Rafiot
$$-$$$
1415 avenue du Phare Ouest, alongside Rte. 132
☎**562-8080**
Le Vieux Rafiot attracts lots of visitors to its incredible dining room, which is divided into three sections by partitions with portholes and decorated

with paintings by local artists. In addition to the novel decor, guests can enjoy a variety of delicious dishes.

La Table du Capitaine Gourmand
$$-$$$
260 du Barachois
☎**562-3131**
La Table du Capitaine Gourmand serves up generous portions and attracts a clientele fond of fish and fresh seafood. It has a live lobster tank and is furnished with an assorted collection of objects, such as a treasure chest and a lobster pot. The seafood pizza is a real treat. Friendly service.

Cap-Chat

Fleur de Lys
$$-$$$
184 Rte 132 Est
☎**786-5518**
The Fleur de Lys invites visitors to savour dishes freshly prepared every day. Warm welcome.

Parc de la Gaspésie

🦌 **Gîte du Mont-Albert**
$$$$
☎**763-2288**
The Gîte du Mont-Albert offers innovative seafood dishes that are definitely worth a try. During the Game Festival in September you can sample more unusual meats like guinea hen, bison and partridge.

Gaspé

Café des Artistes
$-$$
249 Boulevard de Gaspé
☎**368-2255**
The owners of Café des Artistes, who are obviously artists, offer a completely original and attractive concept. In this art centre, you can linger over a delicious table d'hôte and then admire the works of various artists. The homemade ice creams (particularly the avocado) and sorbets are delightful, and the cheesecake

is truly original and absolutely delicious.

Bourlingueur
$-$$
39 montée de Sandy Beach
☎**368-4323**
Varnished wooden tables and chairs make the Bourlingueur look like an old English pub. This is a large place, where visitors can enjoy a relaxing meal of Canadian or Chinese food.

Brise Bise
$-$$
135 Rue de la Reine
☎**368-1456**
The bistro/bar Brise-Brise is probably the nicest café in Gaspé. The menu includes sausages, seafood, salads and sandwiches. The place also features an assortment of beer and coffee, an enjoyable happy hour, live shows all summer long, and dancing late into the evening.

Fort Prével

🦌 **Fort Prével**
$$$-$$$$
2053 Boulevard Douglas
☎**368-2281**
☎**888-377-3835**
At Fort Prével (see p 425), guests are plunged into a historic atmosphere and get to savour delicious French and Québec cuisine. These skillfully prepared and elegantly presented dishes are served in a huge dining room. The menu includes fish and seafood, of course, as well as all sorts of specialties that will satisfy any gourmet.

Percé

La Maison du Pêcheur
$$-$$$
155 place du Quai
☎**782-5331**
La Maison du Pêcheur lies right in the heart of the village. It is two restaurants in one; on the second floor, there is a *crêperie* which looks out on the sea and also serves breakfast, while the third floor is

reserved for dinner guests. The prices are a little high, but everything is first-rate.

La Normandie
$$$-$$$$
221 Rte 132 Ouest
☎782-2112
Regarded by many as one of the best restaurants in Percé, La Normandie serves delicious food in an altogether charming spot. Diners rave about the *feuilleté de homard au champagne* (lobster in puff pastry with champagne) and the *pétoncles à l'ail* (scallops with garlic). The restaurant also features an extensive wine list.

Auberge du Gargantua
$$$$
222 Rue des Failles
☎782-2852
The decor of the Auberge Gargantua is reminiscent of the French countryside where the owners were born. The dining room offers a splendid view of the surrounding mountains, so be sure to arrive early enough to enjoy it. The dishes are all gargantuan and delicious, and usually include an appetizer of periwinkle, a plate of raw vegetables, and soup. Guests choose their main dish from a long list, ranging from salmon to snow crab and a selection of game.

Tour B: Baie des Chaleurs

Bonaventure

Café Acadien
$$-$$$
early Jun to mid-Sep
168 Rue Beaubassin
☎534-4276
Café Acadien serves good food in a charming setting. Open throughout the summer season, this place is very popular with locals and tourists alike, which might explain why the prices are a little high.

New Richmond

Les Têtes Heureuses
$-$$
104 Chemin Cyr
☎392-6733
This café-bistro has both a charming atmosphere and an attractive menu with a vast selection of entrees, croissants, bagels, breads, pasta, quiches and rice. Everything is scrumptious, especially the home-made breads and desserts. A selection of imported and microbrewed beer is also available.

Carleton

La Seigneurie
$$-$$$$
482 Boulevard Perron
☎364-3355
La Seigneurie, the restaurant in the Hôtel-Motel Baie Bleue, serves a wide variety of delicious dishes based on game, fish and seafood. The view from the dining room is superb.

La Maison Monti
$$$-$$$$
840 Boulevard Perron
☎364-6181
La Maison Monti is the former residence of Honoré Bernard, known as Monti, a rich prospector who returned to Carleton after living out west for a while. The glassed-in dining room is comfortable, and the atmosphere pleasant. The menu is made of game, fish and seafood. The service is friendly and attentive.

Causapscal

Auberge La Coulée Douce
$$-$$$
21 Rue Boudreau
☎756-5270
The dining room at the Auberge La Coulée Douce serves delicious meals, such as *bouillabaisse gaspésienne* and fresh salmon prepared a number of different ways. Pleasant service.

Entertainment

Bars and Nightclubs

Gaspé

La Voûte
114 Rue de la Reine
☎368-1219
La Voûte caters mainly to students. The bar is busiest from 6pm to midnight. *Chansonniers* perform here regularly. On the second floor, there is a bar for people aged 25 and over.

Theatres

Petite-Vallée

The **Théâtre du Café de la Vieille Forge** (*Jun to late Aug, next to the Maison LeBreux; 4 Longue-Pointe,* **☎393-2222**) stages plays with a Gaspésian or Québécois flavour performed by local actors. Touring professional comedians and singers also perform here throughout the summer.

Carleton

The **Théâtre La Moluque** (*mid-Jul to late Aug, Tue to Sat 8:30pm; Rte 132, downtown; 586 Boulevard Perron,* **☎364-7151**) puts on professional stage productions. New and classic plays are both performed here.

Festivals and Cultural Events

Matane

Matane's famous shrimp is prized by seafood-lovers far beyond Gaspésie. The **Festival de la Crevette** (☎ *562-0404*) is held in its honour each year at the end of June.

Mont-Saint-Pierre

Mont-Saint-Pierre's **Fête du Vol Libre** (☎ *797-2222*) celebrates the town's vocation as a sky-diving centre. Sky-divers come here from all over to swoop over the bay all summer long, but at the end of July, when this activity-filled festival takes place, they really turn up in droves.

Shopping

Tour A: The Peninsula

Grand-Métis

Les Ateliers Plein Soleil (*Jardins de Métis,* ☎ *775-3165*), a group of artisans from Grand-Métis, runs the Maison Reford. They make all sorts of hand-woven table-cloths, doilies and napkins, which may be purchased in their shop, along with herbs, locally produced honey and home-made tomato ketchup.

Percé

Thanks to its central location, you can't miss the Place du Quai, a cluster of over 30 shops and restaurants, as well as a laundromat and an SAQ (liquor store).

Îles-de-la-Madeleine

T he Îles-de-la-Madeleine (sometimes referred to in English as the Magdalen Islands) rise from the middle of the Gulf of St. Lawrence more than 200km from the Gaspé Peninsula.

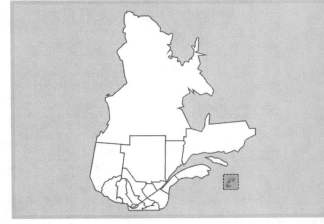

T hey constitute a 65km-long archipelago of about a dozen islands, many connected to one another by long sand dunes. Swept by winds from the open sea, these small islands offer superb, colourful scenery. The golden dunes and the long untouched beaches blend with the red sandstone cliffs and the blue sea. Villages with brightly painted houses, lighthouses and harbours add the finishing touches to the islands' beautiful scenery.

T he islands' 15,000 *Madelinots* (as residents are called) have always earned their livelihood from the sea, and continue to do so today by fishing for crab, bottom-feeding fish, mackerel and lobster. The population, mostly of French origin, live on seven islands of the archipelago: Île de la Grande Entrée, Grosse-Île, Île aux Loups, Île du Havre aux Maisons, Île du Cap aux Meules, Île du Havre Aubert and Île d'Entrée. Only Île d'Entrée, where a few families of Scottish ancestry live, is not linked by land to the rest of the archipelago.

T he Îles-de-la-Madeleine archipelago was first inhabited sporadically by Micmac peoples, also called the "Indians of the Sea." As of the 15th century, the islands were visited regularly by walrus and seal hunters, fishers and whalers, most of Breton or Basque descent. In 1534, Jacques Cartier came upon the islands during his first North American expedition. Permanent settlers did not arrive until after 1755, when Acadian families took refuge here after having escaped deportation. Following the British conquest, the Îles-de-la-Madeleine were annexed to Newfoundland before being integrated into Québec territory in 1774. A few years later, in 1798, King George III granted Admiral Isaac Coffin the title of seigneur of the Îles-de-la-Madeleine, ushering in a dismal period for the inhabitants of the archipelago. He and his family ruled the land despotically until 1895, when a Québec law allowed the Madelinots to buy back their land.

Finding Your Way Around

By Car

Of the seven inhabited islands of the Îles-de-la-Madeleine, six are linked together by Rte. 199. The proposed tour takes visitors to each island to discover some of the hidden treasures.

The seventh island, Île d'Éntrée, is only accessible by boat, and is a trip in itself. The **S.P. Bonaventure** *($16; ☎418-986-5705 or 986-8452)* leaves the Cap-aux-Meules pier from Monday to Saturday, and the trip takes approximately 1hr.

Car rentals are available for visitors who want to drive around the islands.

Cap-aux-Meules Honda
1090 Route 199, L'Étang-du-Nord
☎(418) 986-4085
They also rent motorcycles.

National Tilden
205 Chemin de l'Aéroport, Havre-aux-Maisons
☎(418) 969-4209
☎888-657-3036

Thrifty
188 Chemin de l'Aéroport, Havre-aux-Maisons
☎(418) 969-9006
☎800-367-2277

Location du Berceau
701 Chemin Principal, Havre-Aubert
☎(418) 937-5614

By Plane

Air Nova - Air Alliance (Air Canada) *(☎418-969-2888 or 800-630-3299)* offers daily flights to the Îles-de-la-Madeleine. Departures from Halifax, Québec City and Montréal. Most flights make stopovers in Québec City, Mont-Joli or Gaspé, so count on a 4hr trip. Considerable price reductions can be found by booking well in advance.

By Ferry

Le Madeleine **ferry** *($38, car $71.50, motorcycle $25.50, bicycle $9.25; ☎418-986-3278 or 888-986-3278)* leaves from Souris (Prince Edward Island) and reaches Cap-aux-Meules in about 5hrs. Try to reserve in advance if possible; if not, arrive at the pier a few hours before departure, or to be extra sure, go to Souris the day before your departure and reserve seats. Ask for the ferry-crossing schedule, as it changes from one season to the next.

CTMA Vacancier
☎(418) 986-3278
☎888-986-3278
This ferry departs weekly from Montréal on Friday afternoon, arriving on the islands on Sunday afternoon. On the way, there are stops in Québec City and Matane and opportunities for whale-watching in Tadoussac. The return trip arrives in Montréal Tuesday evening. Rates vary by package chosen.

By Bicycle

Bikes are definitely the best way to get around on the islands. Here is bike rental outfit:

Le Pédalier
365 Chemin Principal,
Cap-aux-Meules
☎(418) 986-2965

Practical Information

Area code: **418**

Tourist Information

Regional Office

Association Touristique des Îles-de-la-Madeleine
128 Chemin Débarcadère, Cap-aux-Meules
☎986-2245 or 888-624-4437
≈986-2327
www.ilesdela madeleine.com
mailing address: C.P. 1028, Cap-aux-Meules, G0B 1B0

Lodging reservation service
☎986-2245

Name of New Merged City

Îles de la Madeleine
Merger of L'Île-du-Havre-Aubert, L'Étang-du-Nord, Grande-Entrée, Havre-aux-Maisons, Fatima, Grosse-Île and Cap-aux-Meules.

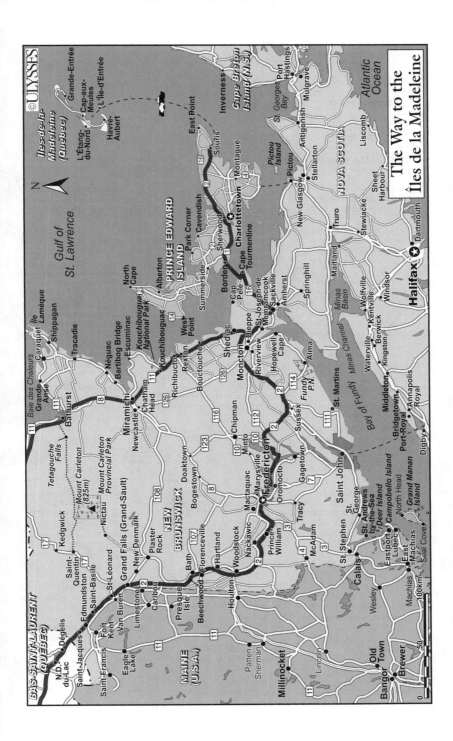

The Way to the Îles de la Madeleine

Exploring

Tour of the Islands

★
Île du Cap aux Meules
(pop. 1,600)

Our tour begins on Île du Cap aux Meules, since it is the archipelago's most populated island as well as the docking point for all the ferries (Cap-aux-Meules). Home to the region's major infrastructures, (hospital, high school, college), this island is the centre of local economic activity. This activity does not take away from the island's charm, however, with its brightly painted houses which some say allow sailors to see their homes from the sea.

Cap-aux-Meules, the only urban centre of the archipelago, has experienced major development over the past few years. Since many buildings were constructed quickly, aesthetics were not a primary consideration. A few of the traditional houses still stand.

A climb to the top of the **Butte du Vent ★ ★** reveals a superb panorama of the island and the gulf.

The beautiful **Chemin de Gros-Cap ★ ★**, south of Cap-aux-Meules, runs along the Baie de Plaisance and offers breathtaking scenery. If possible, stop at the **Pêcherie Gros-Cap**, where the employees can be seen at work in this fish-processing plant.

Head back and take Chemin de L'Étang-du-Nord to L'Étang-du-Nord.

For a long time, **L'Étang-du-Nord** was home to almost half the population of the Îles-de-la-Madeleine and constituted the largest fishing village. With the foundation of Cap-aux-Meules (1959) and Fatima (1954), however, it lost a significant part of its population, and now only has just over 3,000 inhabitants. The municipality, with its beautiful port, welcomes many visitors every year who come to take advantage of the region's tranquillity and natural beauty.

North of L'Étang-du-Nord, visitors can take in the splendid view by walking along the magnificent **Falaises de la Belle Anse ★ ★**. The violent waves crashing relentlessly along the coast are an impressive sight from the top of this rocky escarpment.

Return to L'Étang-du-Nord and take Chemin de L'Étang-du-Nord to the Aut. 199 junction; take this road toward Havre-Aubert, crossing the Dune du Havre aux Basques.

★★★
Île du Havre Aubert

Beautiful Île du Havre Aubert, dotted with beaches, hills and forests, has managed to keep its picturesque charm. From early on it was home to various colonies. Even today, buildings testify to these early colonial years. Prior to this, it was populated by Micmac communities, and relics have been discovered.

Havre-Aubert, the first stop on the island, stretches along the sea and benefits from a large bay ideal for fishing. Apart from the magnificent scenery, the most interesting attraction is without a doubt the **La Grave ★ ★ ★** area, which has developed along a pebbly beach and gets its charm from the traditional cedar-shingled houses. It lies at the heart of a lively area, and is home to

several cultural events. Boutiques and cafés line the streets, which are always enjoyable, even in bad weather. The few buildings along the sea were originally stores and warehouses that received the fish caught by locals.

For anyone interested in the fascinating world of marine life, the **Aquarium des Îles ★** *($5; early Jun to late Aug, every day 10am to 6pm, early Sep to mid-Oct, every day 10am to 5pm; 982 Route 199, La Grave, ☎937-2277)* is a real treat. Here, visitors can observe (and even touch) many different marine species, such as lobsters, crabs, sea urchins, eels, a ray, as well as a multitude of other fish and crustaceans. The second floor has more of an educational atmosphere with exhibits explaining the various fishing techniques used by the islands' fishers throughout the years.

The **Musée de la Mer ★** *($5; late Jun to late Aug, Mon-Fri 9am to 6pm, Sat and Sun 10am to 6pm; late Aug to late Jun, Mon-Fri 9am to noon and 1pm to 5pm, Sat and Sun 1pm to 5pm; 1023 Pointe Shea, at the end of Rte. 199, ☎937-5711)* recounts the history of the populating of the islands as well as the relationship that links Madelinots to the sea. Visitors also have the opportunity to explore the world of fishing and navigation, as well as discover some of the myths and legends that surround the sea.

When leaving Havre-Aubert, follow Chemin du Sable to Sandy Hook Dune.

Sandy Hook Dune ★ ★ ★
(see p 435)

Return along Chemin du Sable and take Chemin du Bassin to L'Étang-des-Caps.

The road that runs along the sea between the Pointe à

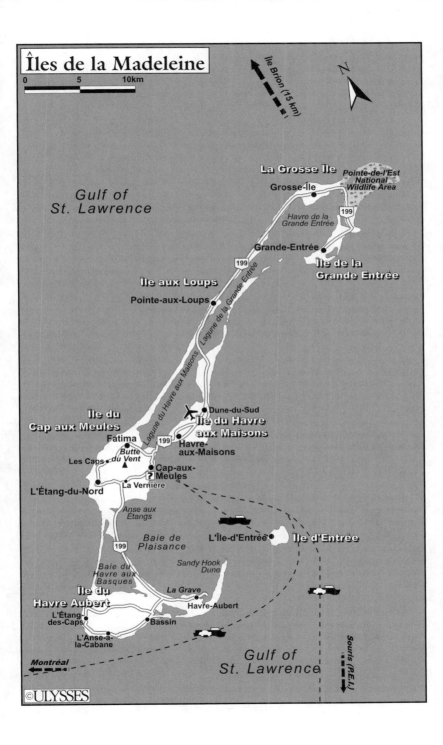

Marichite and L'Étang-des-Caps offers a magnificent **view ★ ★** of the Gulf of St. Lawrence. From the small village of **L'Étang-des-Caps**, the small Île Corps Mort is visible in the distance on clear days.

Return via Chemin de la Montagne, and follow Chemin du Bassin, then return towards Île du Cap aux Meules by taking Rte. 199, which leads to Île du Havre aux Maisons.

★★
Île du Havre aux Maisons (pop. 2,000)

Île du Havre aux Maisons is characterized by its bare landscape and its small, attractive villages with pretty little houses scattered along the winding roads. The steep cliffs at the southern end of the island overlook the gulf and offer a fascinating view of this immense stretch of water. The Dune du Nord and the Dune du Sud are two long strips of sand found at both extremities of the island and are home to beautiful beaches. In the centre of the village of **Havre-aux-Maisons** stand the Vieux Couvent (old convent) and the presbytery; the village is also the island's main centre of activity.

La Méduse ★ *(Mon-Sat 10am to 5pm; 37 Chemin de la Carrière, Havre-aux-Maisons, ☎969-4245)* glass-blowing factory opens its doors to visitors, allowing them to see the glass-blowers and work. Next to the workshop is a small shops that displays the items made there.

The scenic Chemin de la Pointe-Basse crosses the south of the island along the Baie de Plaisance and offers beautiful views. A small path along the road, between the Cap à Adrien and the Cap à Alfred, descends towards the

sea, revealing the charming natural haven of Pointe-Basse.

Don't miss the Fumoir d'antant (traditional smoke-house) and the **Économusée du Hareng Fumé** (smoked herring economuseum) *(27 ch. du Quai).*

Continue along Rte. 199, which leads to Grosse-Île, by crossing Île aux Loups.

Grosse-Île (pop. 575)

The rocky coasts of Grosse-Île have caused numerous shipwrecks, the survivors of which have settled here. A good number of these accidental colonists were Scottish, and approximately 500 of them still live here today. Most earn their living from fishing and agriculture; some also work in the Seleine saltworks, which opened in 1983.

Rte. 199 continues until the **Pointe-de-l'Est National Wildlife Area ★** (see below).

Follow Rte. 199 to Île de la Grande Entrée.

★
Île de la Grande Entrée (pop. 650)

Île de la Grande Entrée, colonized in 1870, was the last of the Îles-de-la-Madeleine to be inhabited. Upon arriving, cross Pointe Old-Harry to check out a striking view of the gulf. This tip of the island was named in honour of Harry Clark, who was the area's only inhabitant for many years. The island's main town, **Grande-Entrée**, has an active port that serves as a departure point for many brightly painted fishing boats, usually for lobster fishing.

The **Petite École Rouge** *(Jun to May Mon-Fri 9am to 4pm, Sat and Sun 11am to 4pm, Oct to May Mon-Thu 8am to 4pm; 787 Chemin Principal, Old Harry, ☎985-2116)* is a

reproduction of an old-fashioned British-style school-house. There is a permanent exhibit explaining the island's cultural heritage and the history of the English-speaking community. Next to the little schoolhouse, a commemorative park and a museum pay tribute to veterans.

To know more about the lives of seals, visit the **Centre d'interprétation du phoque ★** *(Jun to Aug, every day 11am to 6pm; 377 Rte. 199; ☎985-2833)* where various exhibits explain the lifestyle of these mammals.

To get to Île d'Entrée, which can be toured in one day, take the ferry from the Cap-aux-Meules dock.

★★
Île d'Entrée (pop. 200)

Île d'Entrée differs from the rest of the islands not only because of its geographic location (it is the only inhabited island that is not linked to the others), but also because of its population of some 200 residents, all of Scottish descent. This small community lives almost entirely from the sea, and has managed to settle on this land despite the waves and the wind. The island has its own infrastructure to meets the needs of its residents (electricity, roads, and telephone). An incredible serenity prevails here.

Parks

Grosse-Île

The eastern tip of Grosse-Île, made up of dunes and beaches, is home to the diverse bird life that is characteristic of these islands. It is

The *Blanchons*

The symbol of the eco-tourism industry in the Îles de la Madeleine, the *blanchon* is a young seal or "*loup-marin*" (sea-wolf), as the islanders call these mammals. During the first weeks of March, after a long journey along the shores of Labrador and through the Gulf of St. Lawrence, the seals give birth on the ice floes around the Îles de la Madeleine. Nearly three million seals make this trip each year. Once the young have been weaned, the animals head back up to the Arctic, where they spend the greater part of their lives.

The seals actually reach the islands in January, after swimming south along the shores of Labrador for about four months. They stay in the gulf for two or three months, building up their fatty tissue. The month of March is marked by the birth of thousands of these adorable little fur-balls, which have raised international awareness since the 1970s, when environmental groups demonstrated against the seal-hunt. The *blanchons* have to be a month and a half old before they can take their first dive, which makes them easy to observe. During this period, the *blanchons* grow at an astonishing rate; during the 12 days they are suckled by their mothers, their weight triples. Seal's milk is actually five times as rich as cow's milk.

The *blanchons* are no longer threatened by hunting, but adult seals are still hunted. Madelinots and Newfoundlanders kill nearly 50,000 seals a year. When it comes to fish, these animals are formidable predators. Some fishers even hold them responsible for the depleted fish stocks. Seals are far from being an endangered species, and in fact their population has grown considerably in recent years. In response to pressure from the fishers, the federal government has revived seal hunting by setting the quota at 200,000 a year.

one of the best sites for spotting various species, such as the rare piping plover (which only nests on the islands), the northern pintail, the betted kingfisher, the Atlantic puffin and the horned lark. Take care not to damage the nesting sites (generally clearly marked). This entire zone is protected by the **Pointe-de-l'Est National Wildlife Area ★**, also known as Réserve Nationale de Faune de la Pointe-de-l'Est.

Beaches

Île du Cap aux Meules

The **Plage de l'Hôpital**, located along the Dune du Nord, is a good place to go for a dip and watch the seals. It should be noted that the currents become dangerous toward Pointe-aux-Loups. The Anse, l'Hôpital, Cap de l'Hôpital, Plage de l'Hôpital and Étang-de-l'Hôpital are all named after a boat that came into the cove (*anse*) carrying passengers suffering from a contagious illness (typhus). The boat was quarantined, and only doctors and nurses were allowed on board.

Île du Havre Aubert

Like a long strip of sand stretching into the gulf, **Sandy Hook Dune ★ ★ ★** is several kilometres long and its beach is among the nicest on the islands.

The **Plage de l'Ouest ★** stretches from the northwest part of Île du Havre Aubert to the southwest part of Île du Cap aux Meules. Perfect for swimming and shell collecting, it is renowned for its magnificent sunsets.

Île du Havre aux Maisons

The **plage de la Dune du Sud** ★ offers several kilometres of beach, that is great for swimming.

Grosse-Île

One of the most beautiful beaches on the islands, the **Plage de la Grande Échouerie** ★★, stretches for about 10km in the Pointe-de-l'Est wildlife area.

Outdoor Activities

Scuba Diving

The waters around the islands make for great scuba diving. Encounters with schools of fish, lobsters and coral are guaranteed.

Le Repère du Plongeur
18 Allée Léo Leblanc, L'Étang-du-Nord
☎986-3962

Fishing

Visitors can take part in fishing trips organized by **Excursions en Mer** *(early Jun to mid-Sep; Quai de Cap-aux-Meules,* ☎986-4745*),* which also offers boat trips to Île d'Entrée and Île du Havre Aubert. All fishing equipment and instructions are provided on the boat.

Sailing and Windsurfing

L'Istorlet *(weekly rentals possible; 100 Chemin L'Istorlet, Havre-Aubert,* ☎937-5266 or 888-937-8166*)* offers sailing and windsurfing courses and rents out small boats. Its safe, sheltered location, near the Bassin, makes it the ideal spot for first-timers to try this sport. Expect to spend $30/hr for sailing and $25/hr for windsurfing. They also offer seal-watching excursions.

Cruises

A boat ride on the *Le Ponton Il* of the **Excursions de la Lagune** *($20; daily departures in the summer at 11am, 2pm, and 6pm; Île du Havre aux Maisons,* ☎969-2088*)* is an exciting 2hr trip on the waves, during which visitors can observe the sea floor and occasionally some shellfish through the boat's glass bottom.

Birdwatching

During the "échouerie" (two mornings per week) nature walks organized by the **Club Vacances "Les Iles"** *(Grande-Entrée,* ☎985-2833*),* you'll have a chance to see the nests of some whistling plovers, an endangered species. It is important that observers spend no more than 10 or 15min near the nests; to avoid disturbing the birds. At the beach, you'll see guillemots soaring through the air.

Hiking

The **Club Vacances "Les Îles"** *(Grande-Entrée,* ☎985-2833*)* organizes nature walks to help visitors discover the various ecosystems found on the Îles-de-la-Madeleine.

Horseback Riding

La Chevauchée des Îles *(year round 9am until dawn; L'Étang-des-Caps, Île du Havre Aubert,* ☎937-2368*)* organizes riding excursions in the forest and on the beach. Reservations required.

Les Calèches du Havre
784 Route 199, Havre-Aubert
☎*937-2586 or 937-2339*

Kayaking

L'Istorlet *(100 Chemin L'Istorlet, Havre-Aubert,* ☎937-5266*)* offers the chance to join kayaking excursions that take you to grottos and cliff bottoms. Other nautical activities are also offered.

Aérosport Carrefour d'Aventures *(1390 ch. La Vernière, L'Étang-du-Nord,* ☎986-6677*)* offers sea kayaking trips and training.

Accommodations

Île du Cap aux Meules

Camping Le Barachois
$
🐾
early May to late Oct
C.P. 117
87 Chemin du Rivage
☎*986-6065*
☎*986-5678*
Le Barachois campground can accommodate tents or campers in its 180 wind-sheltered sites. Located in the middle of a small wooded area along the sea, it has a peaceful atmosphere and a Beach.

🏚 Auberge chez Sam
$$
pb/sb
1767 Chemin de L'Étang-du-Nord
☎*986-5780*
The very warm welcome at the Auberge chez Sam will quickly make guests feel et home. The place has five attractive, well-kept rooms.

🏚 La Maison du Cap-Vert
$$ bkfst incl.
sb
202 Chemin L.-Aucoin, Fatima
☎*986-5331*
The Maison du Cap-Vert is a family inn with five absolutely charming rooms with comfy beds and a unique decor. This place has made a name for itself in just a short period of time. With its delicious, all-you-can-eat breakfasts, it is definitely a good deal.

Château Madelinot
$$$
K, ≈, ℝ, ℜ, △, ⊛
C.P. 44
323 Rte 199, Fatima
☎*986-3695 or 800-661-4537*
⇌*986-6437*
Visitors might first be surprised to find that the Château Madelinot is not a *château*, but rather a large house. But

the comfortable rooms and superb view of the sea make it easy to get over the disappointment. The place offers many services and is without a doubt the best-known accommodation on the islands.

Île du Havre Aubert

Camping Plage du Golfe
$
🐾
535 Chemin du Bassin
☎*937-5224*
⇌*937-5115*
The Plage du Golfe camground has more than 70 sites, some of which accommodate trailers.

La Marée Haute
$$-$$$ bkfst
ℑ., ℜ, *sb/pb*
25 Chemin des Fumoirs
☎*937-2492*
⇌*937-2492*
Located close to La Grave, La Marée Haute is a lovely little inn where guests are warmly welcomed. The rooms are cozy and attractively decorated. One of the owners also cooks; you won't regret trying one of these lovingly and meticulously prepared dishes. The view from the inn is absolutely awesome!

🏚 Auberge Havre sur Mer
$$-$$$ bkfst incl
⊛
May to Oct
1197 Chemin du Bassin
☎*937-5675*
⇌*937-2540*
www.demarque.qc.ca/havre
The Havre Sur Mer, near the cliff's edge, enjoys a magnificent location. The rooms have a communal terrace from which everybody can enjoy the beautiful view. The inn is furnished with antiques and attracts many visitors.

Île de la Grande Entrée

Camping Grande-Entrée du Club Vacances Les Îles
$
🐾, ℜ
377 Rte 199
☎*985-2833 or 888-537-4537*
⇌*985-2226*
www.clubiles.qc.ca
Grande-Entrée campground, at the Club Vacances Les Îles has 24 sites, eight of which are set up for trailers. A dormitory is available for visitors on rainy days.

Club Vacances Les Îles
$$$$ all inclusive
C.P. 59
377 Rte 199
☎*985-2833 or 888-537-4537*
www.clubiles.qc.ca
In addition to offering spacious, comfortable rooms, the Club Vacances "Les Îles" organizes several activities and excursions so that visitors can discover the area's natural riches. Guests can also take advantage of the cafeteria for their meals, where they are served generous portions.

Île d'Entrée

Chez McLean
$ bkfst incl.
sb
☎*986-4541*
Chez McLean was built over 60 years ago and has managed to keep its character of yesteryear.

Restaurants

Île du Cap aux Meules

P'tit Café
$$$
☎*986-2130*
Le P'tit Café, located in the Château Madelinot (see

p 437), serves Sunday brunch from 10am to 1:30pm. Those with a taste for novelty can order seafood, red meat or chicken cooked on a hot stone. The menu includes a large selection of appetizers, soups and charbroiled dishes. In addition to a view of the sea, the decor is enhanced by temporary exhibitions by artists from the islands and elsewhere in Québec.

La Table des Roy
$$$$
1188 Ch. La Vernière
☎986-3004
Since 1978, La Table des Roy has offered refined cuisine to delight every visitor's taste-buds. The tempting menu features seafood, prepared in a multitude of ways, such as grilled scallops and lobster with *coralline* sauce. The dining room is charming and adds a particular style to this excellent restaurant, which also offers dishes adorned with edible flowers and plants of the islands. Reservations recommended.

Île du Havre Aubert

Café de la Grave
$$
☎937-5765
Decorated like an old general store, the Café de la Grave has a very pleasant atmosphere. When the weather is bad, you can spend hours here chatting. In addition to muffins, croissants and a wide variety of coffees, the menu offers healthy and sometimes unusual dishes, such as *pâté de loup marin*, which are always good. This café is delightfully welcoming and will leave you with lasting memories.

La Saline
$$-$$$
1009 Rte. 199
☎937-2230
A former salting shed in La Grave, La Saline serves excellent regional cuisine. *Loup-marin*, cod, mussels, shrimp and other saltwater treats appear on the menu. Guests also have a splendid view of the sea.

La Marée Haute
$$$$
25 Chemin des Fumoirs, Havre-Aubert
☎937-2492
The chef and co-owner of La Marée Haute knows how to bring out the best in fish and seafood. In this lovely inn, you can sample sea perch, shark or mackerel while drinking in the magnificent view. You can taste the ocean in these dishes, whose expertly enhanced flavour will send you into raptures. The menu also includes a few equally well-prepared meat dishes and some succulent desserts.

Île du Havre aux Maisons

La P'tite Baie
$$$$
Tue-Mon
187 Rte 199
☎969-4073
La P'tite Baie serves well-prepared grilled foods, seafood and fish, as well as a number of beef, pork and chicken dishes. *Loup-marin* is served here in season. In addition to the à-la-carte menu, there is a table-d'hôte with a choice of two main dishes. The service is courteous, and a great deal of care has gone into the decor.

La Moulière
$$$
292 Rte 199
☎969-2233
There are two restaurants in the Hôtel Au Vieux Couvent. La Moulière, located on the main floor, occupies a large room that formerly served as a chapel. It serves excellent dishes in a lively atmosphere. **Rest-O-Bar** (**$$**) is found on the same floor, in the former parlour that extends onto a terrace overlooking the sea. Hamburgers and mussels are among the dishes served in this restaurant, which is as popular as La Moulière.

Grosse-Île

Chez B&J
$$
243 Rte 199
☎985-2926
Chez B&J serves fresh scallops, halibut, lobster salad and fresh fish.

Île de la Grande Entrée

Délice de la Mer
$$
907 Rte. 199, Quai de Grande-Entrée
☎985-2364
The Délice de la Mer specializes in simply prepared seafood dishes; the lobster is delicious. Affordable prices and home-made desserts.

Entertainment

Bars and Nightclubs

Île du Havre aux Maisons

The **Chez Gaspard** bar at the Hôtel Au Vieux Couvent occupies a former convent dining hall. Musicians play on some evenings, making the bar lively and noisy.

Theatre and Performance Hall

Festivals and Cultural Events

Shopping

Île du Havre Aubert

Located in **La Grave**, the **Vieux Treuil** *(Jul and Aug,* ☎*937-5138)* is a venue for theatre, jazz and classical music. Temporary exhibitions are also presented here.

The **Concours des Châteaux de Sable** takes place every August on the Havre-Aubert beach. Participants work for hours to build the best sand castle. Visitors wanting to put their talent to the test can register by calling Les Artisans du Sable at ☎**937-2917 or 986-6863**.

Les Artisans du Sable *(La Grave, Havre-Aubert,* ☎*937-2917)* sells items made of sand according to a special technique used only by Madelinot artisans. These items, which vary from decorations to lampshades, are wonderful souvenirs of the islands. You can also visit the **Économusée du Sable** to learn more about sand.

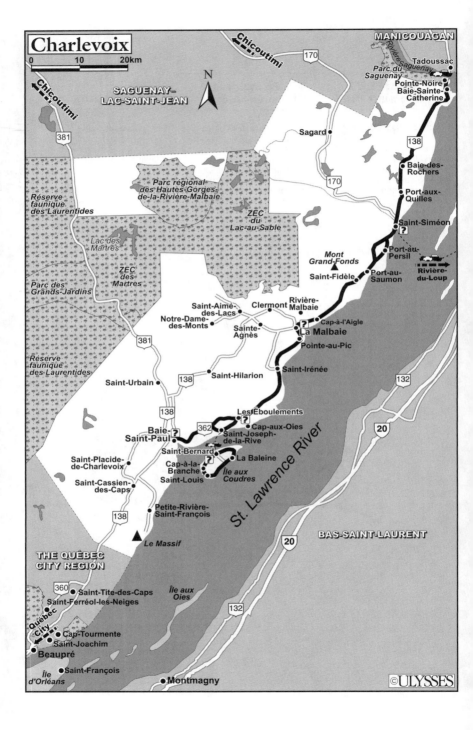

Charlevoix

For years, artists
have been captivated by the beauty of the Charlevoix region.

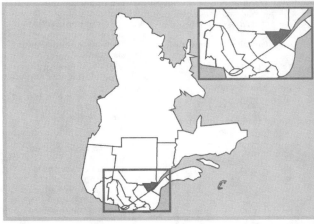

From the town of Saint-Joachim to the mouth of the Rivière Saguenay, dramatic mountainous countryside contrasts sharply with the expansive open water of the St. Lawrence. A scattering of charming villages and towns dot the coastline, dwarfed by mountains that recede into into the salt water of the river and steep-sided valleys. Away from the river, Charlevoix is a wild, rugged region where Boreal forest sometimes gives way to tundra. The old houses and churches found throughout the region are vestiges of Charlevoix's history as a French colony. In addition, the division of farmland in the area still reflects the seigneurial system of land grants used under the French Regime.

The rich architectural heritage and exceptional geography are complemented by a dazzling variety of flora and fauna. The Charlevoix region was declared a UNESCO World Biosphere Reserve in 1988 and it is home to many fascinating animal and plant species. A number of whale species feed at the mouth of the Rivière Saguenay during the summer. In the spring and fall, hundreds of thousands of snow geese make migratory stops in the region, creating a remarkable sight near Cap-Tourmente, farther west. Deep in the hinterland, the territory has all the properties of tundra, a remarkable occurrence at this latitude. This area is home to a variety of animal species such as caribou and the large Arctic wolf. Charlevoix also has many types of plants not found in other parts of eastern Canada.

Finding Your Way Around

The **Charlevoix ★★★** tour follows the St. Lawrence shoreline and includes some inland excursions. Before leaving, make sure your car is in good condition and remember to have the brakes checked: Charlevoix roads are often steep and winding.

By Car

To get to Charlevoix from Québec City, take Rte. 138, the main road in the region. For a more complete look at the region, consider combining this tour with the **Côte de Beaupré** tour (see p 348). After crossing a low-lying area close to the St. Lawrence, Rte. 138 veers into the rolling Charlevoix countryside. This is the southwest extremity of the Laurentians Mountains. The north side of the river valley is bordered by the Laurentians for hundreds of miles to the east. Île d'Orléans can be seen from here on clear days.

Bus Stations

Baie-Saint-Paul
2 Route de l'Équerre (Le Village
shopping centre)
☎*(418) 435-6569*

Saint-Hilarion
354 Route 138
☎*(418) 457-3855*

Clermont
83 Boulevard Notre-Dame
☎*(418) 439-3404*

La Malbaie–Pointe-au-Pic
46 Ste-Catherine
☎*(418) 665-2264*

Saint-Siméon
775 Rue Saint-Laurent
☎*(418) 638-2671*

By Ferry

The car ferry to **Île aux
Coudres** *(free;* ☎*418-438-
2743)* leaves from Saint-
Joseph-de-la-Rive. There is
usually a half-hour wait before
boarding during the summer
months. The crossing takes
approximately 15min. The
26km island tour takes about
half a day. The roads that run
along the river are ideal for
bike rides (bikes can be rented
on the island).

Saint-Siméon:
The ferry *($10, cars $29; Apr
to Jan;* ☎*638-2856)* from
Rivière-du-Loup travels to
Saint-Siméon in just over an
hour.

Baie-Sainte-Catherine:
The ferry *(free;* ☎*418-235-
4395)* travels between
Tadoussac and Baie-Sainte-
Catherine in approximately
10min.

Practical
Information

Area code: **418**

Tourist Information

Regional Office

**Association Touristique de
Charlevoix**
495 Boulevard de Comporté
C.P. 275, La Malbaie–Pointe-au-
Pic, G5A 1T8
☎*665-4454 or 800-667-2276*
⇤*665-3811*
*www.tourisme-
charlevoix.com*

Baie-Saint-Paul

**Bureau de Tourisme de
Charlevoix**
444 Boulevard Mgr-De Laval,
Route 138
(Maison du Tourisme de
Baie-Saint-Paul)
☎*435-4160*

Exploring

Charlevoix

Duration of tour: two days

The Charlevoix countryside
could have been created for
giants—the villages tucked into
bays or perched atop summits

look like dollhouses left behind
by a child. Rustic farmhouses
and luxurious summer houses
are scattered about, and some
have been converted into
inns. Although Charlevoix was
one of the first regions in
North America where tourism
flourished, the area further
inland is still a wilderness area
of valleys and tranquil lakes.

Le Massif ★ ★ ★ (see
p 450).

*Continue along Rte. 138 to
Baie-Saint-Paul.*

**★ ★
Baie-Saint-Paul
(pop. 7,380)**

Charlevoix's undulating geography has proved a challenge
to agricultural development.
Under the French Regime,
only a few attempts at colonisation were made in this vast
region which, along with parts
of the Beaupré coast, was
overseen by the Séminaire de
Québec. Baie-Saint-Paul, at
the mouth of the Rivière du
Gouffre valley, was home to a
few settlers.

Although Charlevoix has some
of the planet's oldest rock
formations, several major
earthquakes have rocked the
pastoral region since it was
first colonized. The following
description by Baptiste
Plamondon, then vicar of
Baie-Saint-Paul, appeared in
the October 22, 1870 edition
of the *Journal de Québec*:

"It was about half an hour
before noon...a tremendous
explosion stunned the population. Rather than simply trem-
ble, the earth seemed to boil,
such that it caused vertigo....
The houses could have been
on a volcano, the way they
were tossed about. Water
gushed fifteen feet into the air
through cracks in the
ground...."

Names of New Merged Cities

Saint-Siméon
Merger of the village and
the parish of Saint-
Siméon.

Les Éboulements
Merger of Les Éboule-
ments and Saint-Joseph-
de-la-Rive.

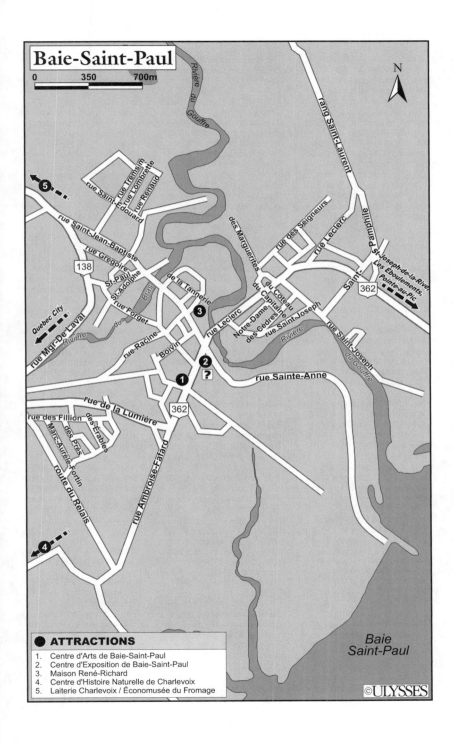

Baie-Saint-Paul

0   350   700m

N

ATTRACTIONS

1. Centre d'Arts de Baie-Saint-Paul
2. Centre d'Exposition de Baie-Saint-Paul
3. Maison René-Richard
4. Centre d'Histoire Naturelle de Charlevoix
5. Laiterie Charlevoix / Économusée du Fromage

©ULYSSES

A bend in the road reveals Baie-Saint-Paul in all its charm, and a slope leads to the heart of the village, which has maintained a quaint small-town atmosphere. Set out on foot along the pleasant Rue Saint-Jean-Baptiste, Rue Saint-Joseph, and Rue Sainte-Anne, where small wooden houses with mansard roofs now house boutiques and cafés. For over a century, Baie-Saint-Paul has attracted North American landscape artists, inspired by the mountains and a quality of light particular to Charlevoix. There are many art galleries and art centres in the area, which display and sell beautiful Canadian paintings and sculptures (see the art-gallery tour, p 456).

A selection of paintings by Charlevoix artists is displayed in the **Centre d'Art de Baie-Saint-Paul** ★ *(free admission; early Apr to late Jun, every day 10am to 5pm, late Jun to early Sep, every day 10am to 7pm, every day 10am to 5pm, mid-Nov to early Apr Thu to Sun 10am to 5pm; 4 Rue Ambroise-Fafard, ☎435-3681)*, designed in a modern-style in 1967 by architect Jacques DeBlois. A painting and sculpture symposium, where works by young artists are displayed, is held by the centre every August.

The **Centre d'Exposition de Baie-Saint-Paul** ★★ *($3; late Jun to early Sep, every day 10am to 7pm, early Sep to late Jun Thu-Sun 10am to 5pm; 23 Rue Ambroise-Fafard, ☎435-3681)* is a museum and gallery, completed in 1992 according to blueprints by architect Pierre Thibault. It houses travelling exhibits from around the world, as well as the René Richard gallery, where several paintings by this Swiss-born artist are on display (see below).

The **Maison René-Richard** ★ *($2.50; every day 10am to 6pm; 58 Rue Saint-Jean-Baptiste, ☎435-5571)*. In the early 20th century, François-Xavier Cimon inherited this house and grounds that extended to the Rivière du Gouffre. The portrait painter Frederick Porter Vinton struck up a friendship with the Cimon family, who let him set up a painting workshop on their property. The facility was later used by important artists, including Clarence Gagnon, A. Y. Jackson, Frank Johnston, Marc-Aurèle Fortin, and Arthur Lismer. These artists' works can be found in a number of Canadian museums. In 1942, painter René Richard took ownership of the house when he married one of the Cimon daughters. Since his death in 1983, the property and house have been open to the public. A tour of the grounds provides a fascinating glimpse into the Charlevoix of the 1940s, when artists and collectors from New York and Chicago congregated here during the summer.

The **Centre d'Histoire Naturelle de Charlevoix** ★ *(late Jun to early Sep, every day 9am to 5pm, Sep to late Jun Sat and Sun 10am to 4pm; 444 Boulevard Mgr-De Laval / Route 138, ☎435-6275)* explores geological history, flora, fauna, climate, and human history through a slide show. The centre is located at the Belvedere Baie St-Paul. The centre also offers a 2hr bus tour to the backcountry to discover the meteorological origins of Charlevoix.

Laiterie Charlevoix is home to the **Économusée du Fromage** ★★ *(free admission; late Jun to early Sep, every day 8am to 7pm; Sep to Jun Mon-Fri 8am to 5:30pm, Sat and Sun 10am to 4pm; 1167 Boulevard Mgr-De Laval, ☎435-2184)*, a museum dedicated to explaining

how cheese is produced. Founded in 1948, this dairy still makes its cheddar cheese the old-fashioned way—by hand. Every day before 11am, visitors can see cheesemakers in action and get a rudimentary grasp of how cheese is made and ripened. Since 1994, the Laiterie Charlevoix has been producing the delicious "Migneron de Charlevoix" cheese, winner of many prizes. They also produce a tasty blue cheese called "Ciel de Charlevoix."

Leave Baie-Saint-Paul by Rte. 362 (Rue Leclerc) toward Saint-Joseph-de-la-Rive, Les Éboulements and La Malbaie. A scenic lookout on a mountainside provides the opportunity to take in the view. A little farther, you will reach the entrance to **Domaine Charlevoix** (see p 449).

From Baie-Saint-Paul, you can take an optional excursion along Rtes. 138 and 381, in the direction of Saint-Urbain and the Charlevoix hinterland.

Parc des Grands-Jardins ★★ (see p 449).

Return toward Baie-Saint-Paul and take Rte. 362 heading east. A steep hill leads to the village of Saint-Joseph-de-la-Rive on the right, below Les Éboulements.

★
Saint-Joseph-de-la-Rive (pop. 200)

The rhythm of life in this village on the St. Lawrence followed the rhythm of the river for many generations, as the boats beached along the shore testify eloquently. In recent decades, however, tourism and handicrafts have replaced fishing and ship-building as the staples of the economy. East of the dock where the ferry to Île aux Coudres lands, a fine sandy beach tempts swimmers into the chilly saltwater. A little wooden building in front of the church is a reminder of the fragility of human endeavours within the immense marine landscape of Charlevoix.

The dimensions and white-painted wooden exterior of the **Église Catholique Saint-Joseph** ★ (*Chemin de l'Église*) are reminiscent of the Anglican churches found in Québec's Eastern Townships region. Its interior is decorated with various objects from the sea. For example, the altar is supported by anchors, and the baptismal fountain is actually an immense seashell, retrieved off the coast of Florida. A recorded presentation dealing with the church's liturgical ornaments is activated by a button on the right-hand side of the entrance.

The **Papeterie Saint-Gilles** ★ (*free admission for individuals; Mon-Fri 8am to 5pm, Sat and Sun 9am to 5pm; 304 Rue Félix-Antoine-Savard, ☎635-2430 ou 866-635-2430*) is a traditional papermaking workshop founded in 1966 by priest and poet Félix-Antoine Savard (1896-1982, author of *Menaud Maître-Draveur*) with the help of Mark Donohue, a member of a famous Canadian pulp and paper dynasty. Museum guides explain the different stages involved in making paper using 17th-century techniques. Saint-Gilles paper has a distinctive thick grain and flower or leaf patterns integrated into each piece, producing a high quality writing paper sold on site in various packages.

The **Musée Maritime de Charlevoix / Économusée de la Goélette** ★★ (*$3; mid-May to mid-Jun and early Sep to mid-Oct, Mon-Fri 9am to 4pm, Sat and Sun 11am to 4pm, late Jun to Sep every day 9am to 5pm; 305 Avenue de l'Église, ☎635-1131 or 635-2803*), located in a shipyard, recaptures the golden era of the schooner. Visitors are welcome to climb aboard the boats on the premises.

The **Santons de Charlevoix** (*free admission, except for groups: $1; May to Oct 10am to 5pm; 303 Rue de l'Église, ☎635-1362*). For a few years now, craftspeople in Saint-Joseph-de-la-Rive have been making *santons*, terracotta figurines representing the Christian nativity scene, including the villagers who gathered around the manger. Setting them apart from other figurines of this kind, the characters are dressed in traditional Québécois garb and the buildings are miniature representations of traditional houses typical of Charlevoix and Île aux Coudres.

★★
Île aux Coudres
(pop. 1,310)

Visitors are sometimes surprised to learn that a number of whale species live in the St. Lawrence River. For several generations the economic livelihood of Île aux Coudres centred around whale hunting, mainly belugas, and whale blubber was melted to produce lamp oil. Ship building, mainly small craft, was also an important regional industry.

L'Isle-aux-Coudres is the municipality that was formed when the villages of Saint-Bernard and Saint-Louis merged (*arrival and departure point on Île-aux-Coudres*). The ferry docks at the Quai de Saint-Bernard, where the following tour of the island begins. The dock is the best place from which to appreciate the view of the Charlevoix mountains. One of the last shipyards still in operation in the region can also be seen from here.

Follow Chemin Royal to Saint-Louis, where it becomes Chemin des Coudriers. Many old schooners are beached along the shore in the area, vestiges of a bygone era. Baie-Saint-Paul can be seen from Cap à Labranche on clear days. Île aux Coudres can be visited by bicycle but be aware that the sea breeze makes for challenging conditions.

The **Musée Les Voitures d'Eau** ★ (*$4; mid-May to mid-Jun Sat and Sun 10am to 5pm, mid-Jun to mid-Jul every day 10am to 5pm, mid-Jul to mid-Aug every day 9:30am to 6pm, mid-Aug to mid-Sep every day 10am to 5pm, mid-Sep to mid-Oct Sat and Sun 10am to 5pm; Chemin des Coudriers, St-Louis, ☎438-2208*) presents exhibits dealing with the history, construction and navigation of the small craft once built in the region. The museum was founded in 1973 by Captain Éloi Perron, who recovered the wreck of the schooner *Mont-Saint-Louis*, now on display.

Turn left onto Chemin du Moulin.

It is extremely rare to find a water mill and a windmill operating together. Indeed, the **Moulins Desgagné** ★★, or **Moulins de l'Île-aux-Coudres** (*$2.75; mid-May to late Jun every day 10am to 5pm; late Jun to late Aug every day 9am to 6:30pm, late Aug to mid-Oct every day 10am to 5pm; 247 Chemin du Moulin, St-Louis, ☎438-2184*), are a unique pair in Québec. Erected in 1825 and 1836 respectively, the mills complement one another by alternately generating power according to prevailing climatic conditions. Along with a forge and milling house, the mills were restored by the Québec government, which has also established on-site information centres. The machinery necessary for operation is still in perfect condition, and is now back at work grinding wheat and buckwheat into flour. Bread is made in an antique wood oven.

Near the end of the tour, visitors will notice posts sticking out of the water close to shore—these are strung with nets used to catch eels.

Take the ferry to Saint-Joseph-de-la-Rive and head to Les Éboulements.

★
Les Éboulements
(pop. 1,040)

In 1663, a violent earthquake in the region caused a gigantic landslide; it is said that half a small mountain sank into the river. The village of les Éboulements is named after the event (*éboulements* means landslide in English).

At the entrance to the grounds of the **Manoir de Sales-Laterrière** (*free admission; every day 9am to 11am and 2pm to 4pm; 159 Rue Principale,* ☎635-2666) and the **Moulin Banal ★ ★** (*$2; mid-Jun to early Sep, every day 10am to 5pm; 157 Rue Principale,* ☎635-2239) is a wooden processional chapel (circa 1840). Once located in the village of Saint-Nicolas on the south shore of the St. Lawrence, it stands beside the entrance to the grounds. The chapel was reconstructed in 1968, under the auspices of a heritage organization that also owns the nearby late-18th-century seigneurial mill. Visitors cannot enter the red-shuttered manor house, as it is currently used as a school by the Brothers of the Sacré-Coeur.

Head to the village, 1km to the east.

The name "Tremblay" has become to Québec what the name Dupont is to France, or

Smith to the United States. What is unique about the Tremblays in Québec is that they all have a common colonial ancestor: Pierre Tremblay from Perche, France, who arrived in Québec around 1650 and became seigneur of Les Éboulements. In the 19th century, various Tremblays moved from Charlevoix to the Saguenay and Lac-Saint-Jean regions, which continue to be associated with the family name. However, Les Éboulements still has the highest concentration of people with the last name "Tremblay" in Québec, and probably the world.

Return to Rte. 132. After a spectacular descent, the road leads to Saint-Irénée. Once at river level, the entrance to the Forget estate is ahead on the left.

★
Saint-Irénée
(pop. 640)

Saint-Irénée, or Saint-Irénée-les-Bains, as it was known during the Belle Époque, is the gateway to the part of Charlevoix usually considered the oldest vacation spot in North America. In the late 18th century, British sportsmen were the first Europeans to enjoy the pleasures of the simple life the wild region had to offer. They were followed by wealthy Americans escaping the heat of summer in the United States. Wealthy English and French Canadian families also had summer houses with lovely gardens built for them in Charlevoix. Saint-Irénée is renowned for its picture-perfect landscapes and classical music festival (see further below).

The **Domaine Forget ★** (*price and schedule vary according to activity; 5 Saint-Antoine,* ☎452-8111 or 888-336-7438) was home to Sir Rodolphe Forget (1861-1919), a prominent French

Canadian businessman in the early 20th century. The vast property had its own power plant in addition to a dozen interesting secondary buildings. Unfortunately, the main house, known as "Le Château," locally, was destroyed by fire in 1961. Inaugurated in the summer of 1996, the **Salle Françoys-Bernier** (*398 Chemin Les Bains,* ☎452-3535, ext. 820, or 888-DFORGET, ext. 820), at the Domaine Forget, can accommodate 600 music lovers, who are sure to be delighted with its wonderful acoustics.

Since 1977, the property has been home to the **Académie de Musique et de Danse de Saint-Irénée**, which holds summer sessions. Every summer a classical music festival is held here; it is a major social event in the lives of Charlevoix summer résidents.

Before arriving in Pointe-au-Pic, the road runs next to the **Club de Golf du Manoir Richelieu**, one of the highest rated golf resorts in the world. The club features an 18-hole course, a clubhouse and restaurants. Turn right onto Rue Principale at the bottom of Côte Bellevue.

★
La Malbaie–
Pointe-au-Pic
(pop. 9,460)

On his way to Québec City in 1608, Samuel de Champlain anchored in a Charlevoix bay for the night. To his surprise, he awoke the next morning to find his fleet resting on land and not in water. Champlain learned that day what many navigators would come to learn as well: the water recedes a great distance in this region and will trap any boat not moored in deep enough water. In exasperation, he exclaimed *"Ah! La malle baye!"* (Old French which

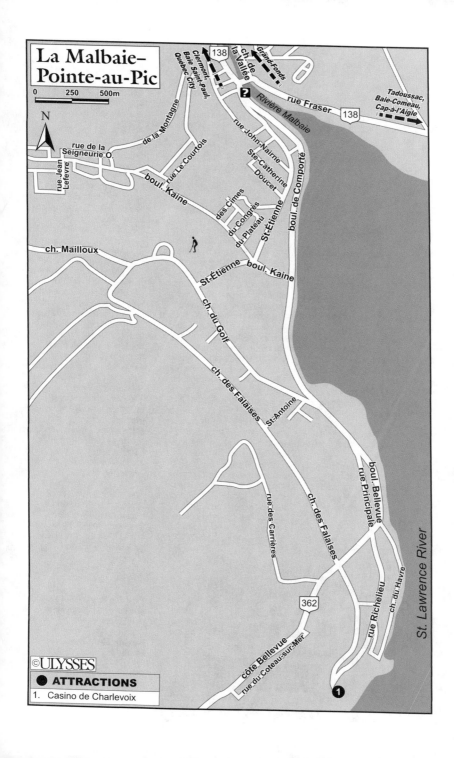

La Malbaie–Pointe-au-Pic

0   250   500m

N

Clermont,
Baie-Saint-Paul,
Québec City
138

ch. de
la Vallée

Grand-Fonds

?

Rivière Malbaie

rue Fraser

138

Tadoussac,
Baie-Comeau,
Cap-à-l'Aigle

rue de la
Seigneurie O.

de la Montagne

rue Jean
Lefevre

rue Le-Courtois

rue John-Nairne

Ste-Catherine

Ste-
Doucet

boul. Kaine

boul. de Comporté

des Cimes

du Congrès

du Plateau

St-Étienne

ch. Mailloux

St-Étienne   boul. Kaine

ch. du Golf

ch. des Falaises

St-Antoine

rue des Carrières

ch. des Falaises

boul. Bellevue

rue Principale

rue Richelieu

ch. du Havre

St. Lawrence River

362

côte Bellevue

rue du Coteau-sur-Mer

1

©ULYSSES

● **ATTRACTIONS**

1. Casino de Charlevoix

translates roughly to "Oh what a bad bay!"), inadvertently providing the name for many sites in the region. The towns of Pointe-au-Pic, La Malbaie, and Cap-à-l'Aigle now form a continuous web of streets and houses lining the bay.

The Malbaie seigneury passed through three seigneurs (lords) before being seriously developed. Jean Bourdon received the land for services rendered to the French crown in 1653. Too busy with his job as prosecutor for the king, he did nothing with it. The seigneury was then granted to Philippe Gaultier de Comporté, in 1672. Following his death, it was sold by his family to merchants Hazeur and Soumande, who harvested wood on the property for the construction of ships in France. The seigneury became crown property in 1724. Exceptionally, it was then granted, under English occupation, to Captain John Nairne and Officer Malcolm Fraser in 1762, who began colonizing it.

Seigneurs Nairne and Fraser initiated a longstanding tradition of hospitality in Charlevoix. They hosted, in their respective manors, friends and even strangers from Scotland and England. Following the example of these seigneurs, French Canadians began welcoming visitors from Montréal and Québec during the summer months. Eventually, larger inns had to be built to accommodate the increasing number of urban vacationers now arriving on steamships that moored at the dock in Pointe-au-Pic. Among the wealthy visitors was U.S. President Howard Taft and his family, who were very fond of Charlevoix.

In the early 20th century, a wave of wealthy Americans and English Canadians built summer houses along **Chemin des Falaises**, a street well worth exploring. The houses reflect popular architectural styles of the period, including the charming Shingle style characteristic of seaside resorts on the U.S. east coast, which is distinguished by a cedar shingle exterior. Another popular trend at the time was to build houses that resembled 17th-century French manor houses, complete with turrets and shuttered casement windows. Beginning in 1920, the architecture of summer residences started to incorporate traditional local building styles. La Malbaie architect Jean Charles Warren (1869-1929) became known for designing a style of rustic furniture, inspired by local traditions and the English Arts and Crafts movement. Owning one of his creations became a must among summer residents. The

Manoir Richelieu

most important and impressive building from the turn-of-the-century construction boom is the Manoir Richelieu, at the west end of Chemin des Falaises.

La Malbaie is now the regional administrative centre and, since its amalgamation with the neighbouring municipality of Pointe-au-Pic in 1995, has confirmed its position of strength within the region's tourist industry. It is henceforth officially known as "La Malbaie–Pointe-au-Pic".

The **Manoir Richelieu** ★★ (*181 Avenue Richelieu*), the only grand hotel in Charlevoix to survive, was built of wood in 1899. Destroyed in a fire, it was replaced by the current cement building in 1929. The hotel was designed by architect John Smith Archibald in the Château style. Many famous people have stayed at the hotel, from Charlie Chaplin to the King of Siam and the Vanderbilts of New York City. The casino is a reconstruction of the Château Ramezay in Montréal. Visitors not staying at the Manoir can nevertheless discreetly walk through its hallways, elegant salons and gardens overlooking the St. Lawrence.

The region's number-one attraction is the **Casino de Charlevoix** (*183 Rue Richelieu,* ☎*665-5300 or 800-665-2274*), an attractively designed European-style casino located next to the Manoir Richelieu. Proper dress required.

Parc des Hautes-Gorges-de-la-Rivière-Malbaie ★★ (see p 449).

Parc du Mont-Grand-Fonds ★ (see p 450).

Return to the main tour at Cap-à-l'Aigle.

Cap-à-l'Aigle
(pop. 760)

From Boulevard de Comporté in La Malbaie, visitors can catch a glimpse of a stately stone house sitting high on the Cap-à-l'Aigle escarpment. The building is the old manor house of the Malcolm Fraser seigneurs, a property also known as Mount Murray. It is matched to the east of Rivière Malbaie by the John Nairne seigneury, established west of the waterway and simply named Murray Bay in honour of James Murray, British Governor at the time. Cap-à-l'Aigle, whose tourism industry dates back to the 18th century, forms the heart of the Mount Murray seigneury.

Manoir Fraser ★ (*private property; Rte. 138*). Malcolm Fraser, like his compatriot John Nairne, belonged to the Fraser Highlanders, a Scottish regiment sent to Canada to help capture Louisbourg. After the signing of the Treaty of Paris in 1763, putting an end to the Seven Years' War, Nairne and Fraser settled in their seigneuries. Both spoke French; Nairne's family lived in exile in France because they sympathized with the Stuarts. Meanwhile, the Fraser family was of French origin, descendants of Jules de Berry, who served exquisite strawberries to Charles III, and so created their family name (in French, strawberries are called *fraises*, which later turned into Fraser). The Manoir Fraser was built for the son of Malcolm Fraser in 1827, according to plans by architect Jean-Baptiste Duléger. Damaged during a fire in 1975, the manor was restored by the Cabot family, which has held the title to the Cap-à-l'Aigle seigneury since 1902.

Turn right onto Chemin Saint-Raphaël and continue to the junction with Rte. 138 Est, which travels through Saint-Fidèle and Port-au-Saumon.

★
Port-au-Persil

This small but charming harbour town is set apart by its waterfall, Anglican chapel and winding road that leads through the beautiful mountain landscapes.

Saint-Siméon
(pop. 1,460)

From Saint-Siméon, roads lead to the Saguenay region, Côte-Nord, and Québec City. A ferry links the town of Rivière-du-Loup on the south shore of the St. Lawrence.

★
Baie-Sainte-Catherine
(pop. 290)

A tiny village on the north shore of the St. Lawrence, Baie-Sainte-Catherine borders a bay on the Saguenay estuary and has a picturesque sandy beach.

Parks

Domaine Charlevoix (*$10 including the shuttle to the river; early Jun to late Jun Sat and Sun, late Jun to early Sep, every day 10am to 5:30pm, early Sep to late Oct Sat and Sun; Route 362, Baie-Saint-Paul, ☎435-2626 or 877-435-2627*), just outside Baie-Saint-Paul, is a sports centre devoted to various outdoor activities such as cross-country skiing, hiking and mountain biking. Classical music is played along the short

trails, creating a lovely atmosphere. Its magnificent lookouts overhang the St. Lawrence and the Félix-Antoine-Savard terrace, from where you can admire beautiful Île aux Coudres. There is a good restaurant on the property.

Located at the eastern edge of the Réserve Faunique des Laurentides, the **Parc des Grands-Jardins ★★** (*$3.50; mid-May to late Jun and Aug to late Oct Mon, Wed, Fri 8am to 10pm, Sun, Tue, Thu, Sat 8am to 6pm; Jul every day 8am to 10pm; Centre d'Accueil Thomas-Fortin, Route 381, Km 31, ☎439-1227 or 866-702-9202*) is rich in flora and fauna characteristic of taiga and tundra, a very unusual occurrence this far south. Situated north of Saint-Urbain, this park covers 310km². Hikes led by naturalists are organized throughout the summer. Caribou have been spotted on some of the trails. The park's Mont du Lac des Cygnes (Swan Lake Mountain) trail is among the most beautiful in Québec. Visitors can also go on canoe-camping trips. Winter activities are also possible.

Parc des Hautes-Gorges-de-la-Rivière-Malbaie ★★ (*$3.50; late May to late Oct 8am to 7pm; from Baie-Saint-Paul, take Route 138 to Saint-Aimé-des-Lacs, ☎439-1227 or 866-702-9202*), which covers over 233km², was created to protect the area from commercial exploitation. Over 800 million years ago, a crack in the earth's crust formed the magnificent gorges after which the park is named; later, the terrain was shaped by glaciers. The park features an incredible diversity of vegetation, ranging from maple stands to alpine tundra. The rock faces, some of which are 800m high, tower over the river and are used for rock-climbing. The best known climb, "Pomme

Charlevoix

d'Or," is a 350m-high expert-level trail. Other park activities include snowmobiling, hiking (the Acropole trail is particularly scenic), and canoe-camping. The park's rental centre has mountain bikes (*$23/day*) and canoes (*$32/day*). **River boat cruises** (*$26; duration: 1hr 30min,* ☎*439-4402*) are also offered. A trip down the river is the best way to truly appreciate the park.

On the entrance road to the park, look for a sign on the right-hand side that says *"ZEC des Martres, secteur 7, Lac des Américains."* Nearby a suspension foot bridge spans Rivière Malbaie. There are some decent restaurants, as well as a pleasant tea room by a lake, which is inhabited by swans. An enchanting, pastoral setting!

Outdoor Activities

Downhill Skiing

Le Massif (*$42; 1350 rue Principale, Petite-Rivière-St-François,* ☎*632-5876*) is one of the finest ski centres in Québec. At 770m, it has the highest slopes in eastern Canada, and receives abundant snow each winter, which is enhanced with artificial snow to create ideal ski conditions. The mountain, which rises almost up from the river, has a breathtaking view from the summit. Since 2001, the Massif's infrastructure has been significantly upgraded without harming the skiing experience. It now offers some 30 trails for every level of expertise, and a comfortable chalet graces the summit.

Parc du Mont-Grand-Fonds (*$30; Mon-Fri 10am to 3:45pm, Sat and Sun 9am to 3:45pm; 1000 Chemin des Loisirs, La Malbaie,* ☎*665-0095 or 877-665-0095*) has 14 runs with a vertical drop of 355m. The longest one is 2,500m.

Cross Country Skiing

Parc du Mont-Grand-Fonds (*$11; Mon-Fri 10am to 3:45pm, Sat and Sun 9am to 3:45pm; 1000 Chemin des Loisirs, La Malbaie,* ☎*665-4405*) has some 160km of cross-country ski trails.

The **Génévrier activity centre** (*$4.35; 1175 Mgr-De Laval, Baie-Sainte-Paul,* ☎*435-6520 or 877-435-6520*) is located a few kilometres north of Baie-Saint-Paul. It has skating facilities, as well as approximately 40 cross-country skiing and snowshoeing trails. There are six runs: four beginners, one intermediate and one advanced. A skating rink and tobogganing hills have also been set up.

Parc des Grands-Jardins (*$3.50; see p 449*). During the winter, 60km-long hiking trails become cross-country skiing and snowshoeing trails. Chalets and shelters are available but must be reserved (☎*800-665-6527*).

Dogsledding

Le Chenil du Sportif (*$130/day per pers., $75/half-day per pers.; 65 Rang Ste-Marie, Les Éboulements,* ☎*635-2592*) organizes excursions that last from half a day to three days

and can include ice-fishing and snowshoeing expeditions. Le Chenil du Sportif lets dog-sledders lead their own team themselves through spectacular natural surroundings between Les Éboulements and Saint-Hilarion. Guides are experienced and friendly. Day packages include breakfast in a log cabin. There are cabins and trailers for longer stays.

Cycling

In La Baleine, on the east coast of the island, **Vélo-Coudres** (*743 Chemin des Coudriers,* ☎*438-2118*) rents out bikes of all kinds; **Roland Harvey Bicyclettes and Motel** (*27 Chemin Principal, La Baleine,* ☎*438-2343*) offers a smaller selection, but lower rates.

Hiking

In addition to the magnificent parks in the region (see p 449), hikers also flock to Charlevoix's beautiful **Sentier des Caps** (*$5/day; 1 Rue Leclerc, St-Tite-des-Caps,* ☎*823-1117 ou 866-823-1117*). The path stretches some 37km from Saint-Tite-des-Caps to Petite-Rivière-Saint-François, climbing 500 to 800m summits that drop off into the river. The mountain huts and campsites scattered along the trail let you take your time. Its 15- to 20-degree slopes will challenge even experienced hikers. The views of the river, especially from the lookouts, will literally take your breath away.

Accommodations

Baie-Saint-Paul

Le Balcon Vert
$
🛏, ℜ, *sb*
summer only
22 côte du Balcon Vert, Rte 362
☎*435-5587*
⇒*435-6669*
*www.balconvert.
charlevoix.net*
One of the least expensive places to stay in town is the Auberge de Jeunesse Le Balcon Vert. This youth hostel offers small chalets that sleep four people, as well as campsites.

Parc des Grands-Jardins
$
166 Boulevard de Comporté
The Parc des Grands-Jardins rents out small cottages and shelters. This park is a popular place for fishing, so if you want to stay here during summer, you'll have to reserve early. To do so, reserve with the ministry of the environment (Ministère de l'Environnement et de la Faune) at ☎800-665-6527.

Le Genévrier
$-$$$
🍳, K, ℜ
1175 Boulevard Mrg-De Laval, Rte 138
☎*435-6520 or 877-435-6520*
www.genevrier.com
Le Genévrier campground is a vast recreational-tourist complex in perfect harmony with its natural environment. Campers of all persuasions are sure to find what they are looking for here. The campground boasts 450 sites, mostly on forested land, for all types of lodging and shelter, from the biggest motorhomes to tents for wilderness camping. Several fully equipped, modern and comfortable

cottages are situated by the river or lake. In summer, two more rustic but fully equipped log cabins with bedding and showers are also for rent. Every day, an extensive program of sports and leisure activities is offered. Hiking and mountain-biking trails along the river.

Auberge La Pignoronde
$$
≡, ≈, ℜ
750 Boulevard Mgr-De Laval
☎*435-5505 or 888-554-6004*
*www.aubergelapignoronde
.com*
The strange circular building housing the Auberge la Pignoronde may be less than appealing from the outside, but the interior decor is quite charming, and the lobby features a welcoming fireplace. There is also an excellent view of the bay.

Auberge La Muse
$$$
ℜ, 🛏
39 Rue Saint-Jean-Baptiste
☎*435-6839 or 800-841-6839*
⇒*435-6289*
www.lamuse.com
Located at the heart of Baie-Saint-Paul, Auberge La Muse occupies both a period home beneath tall trees with a lovely balcony, and a former general store. The guest rooms are decorated in the Victorian style. Guests can sample the specialities that make this restaurant famous at the breakfast buffet.

Auberge Cap-aux-Corbeaux
$$$ bkfst incl.
⊛
2 Cap-aux-Corbeaux Sud
☎*435-5676 or 800-595-5676*
⇒*435-4125*
www.cap-aux-corbeaux.com
Nestled at the end of a little road along the cape overlooking Baie-Saint-Paul, Auberge Cap-aux-Corbeaux offers a breathtaking view. The inn itself is rather modern, but woodwork predominates. All the rooms are situated on the riverside so that guests can

fully enjoy the view. In one of the rooms, the double whirlpool tub is surrounded by windows, allowing for moments of absolute relaxation. On some summer evenings, the innkeepers serve their guests cocktails while a painter creates a canvas before their very eyes.

Auberge La Maison Otis
$$$$-$$$$$
≡, 🍳, ⊙, 🛏, ≈, ℜ, △, ◑, ⊛
23 Rue St-Jean-Baptiste
☎*435-2255 or 800-267-2254*
⇒*435-2464*
www.maisonotis.com
This former bank is an example of classic Québec architecture and is located in the heart of the city. Unfortunately, the interior is a real disappointment, with a mishmash decor straight out of the 1980s. The old section has small, snug rooms with bunk-beds, whereas the rooms in the new section are larger and cozy. The restaurant, however, is a delight (see p 453).

Saint-Hilarion

L'Aubergine
$$ bkfst incl.
🛏, ≈
179 Rang 6
☎*457-3018*
☎*877-457-3018*
www.aubergineinn.com
In addition to its beautiful name, L'Aubergine is the perfect place for tranquillity and the outdoors. The surrounding countryside is beautiful and offers numerous outdoor activities. Each of the six rooms has its own private entrance and bathroom, providing lots of privacy. The hosts prepare very good vegetarian evening meals, but reservations are required. Generous breakfasts.

Charlevoix

Île aux Coudres

Auberge La Coudrière et Motels
$$ ½b
≈, ℜ
280 Chemin La Baleine
La Baleine
☎*438-2838 or 888-438-2882*
The Auberge la Coudrière et Motels has very comfortable rooms. It is located near the river in a beautiful area perfect for quiet walks.

Hôtel-Motel Cap-aux-Pierres
$$$
☺, ≈, ℜ, △, ☼
246 Chemin La Baleine
La Baleine
☎*438-2711 or 888-554-6003*
www.hotelcapauxpierres.com
A long building with several skylights, the Hôtel-Motel Cap-aux-Pierres offers pleasant, rustic rooms.

Saint-Irénée

L'Eider Matinal
$$
310 Chemin des Bains
☎*452-8259*
⇌*452-8245*
L'Eider Matinal is as lovely inside as outside. This bed and breakfast occupies a beautiful century-old residence with a red roof, right in the middle of an attractively landscaped property facing the river. Its four guest rooms are tastefully decorated and offer modern comforts and antique furnishings. A charming front terrace embellishes the inn, and a pleasant sitting room is also available to guests. What's more, guests are greeted with a smile!

Auberge des Sablons
$$$
ℑ, ℜ, ☼, ⊛
290 Chemin des Bains
☎*452-3594 or 800-267-3594*
⇌*452-3240*
The charming Auberge des Sablons is a pretty white house with blue shutters,

located in a peaceful spot next to Domaine Forget. The rooms are pleasant.

La Malbaie– Pointe-au-Pic

Auberge La Romance
$$$-$$$$ bkfst incl.
⊛, ℑ, ✦
415 Chemin des Falaises
☎*665-4865*
⇌*665-4954*
www.aubergela romance.com
Auberge La Romance, as its name indicates, is focused from top to bottom on romantic getaways. Every detail has been planned in order to make guests feel as though they are on cloud nine. For example, each room features a double door for soundproofing and a speaker that plays romantic music day and night (guests have a remote control). This cedar-shingled home offers eight romantic rooms with Victorian decor and furnishings. Each one has a unique cachet, as well as several amenities that add an extra touch of romance, such as fireplace (gas or wood-burning), balcony, canopy bed or whirlpool tub.

Auberge des Falaises
$$$$ bkfst incl.
ℑ, ⊛, ≡, ≈, ℜ, K
250 Chemin des Falaises
☎*665-3731 ou 800-386-3731*
⇌*665-6194*
www.aubergedes falaises.com
Auberge des Falaises features several rooms with a spectacular view. The rooms are just the right size and quite comfortable, but guests will probably want to spend most of their time on their balcony if they stay in the most recent wing because all of its rooms overlook the cliff and the river, in the distance.

Auberge Des Trois Canards et Motels
$$$$-$$$$$ bkfst incl.
ℑ, K, ✦, ≈, ℜ, ⊛
115 Côte Bellevue
☎*665-3761 or 800-461-3761*
⇌*685-4727*
www.aubergedes 3canards.com
The Auberge Les Trois Canards et Motels has a magnificent view of the entire region. The inn offers nine rooms, each warmly decorated with a fireplace, thick carpets, and a whirlpool. The motel rooms are not as nice but still offer a great view of the water.

Manoir Richelieu–Hôtels Fairmont
$$$$$
≈, K, ℜ, ✦, ☺, ≡, ⊛, ℑ, ☼, △
181 Avenue Richelieu
☎*665-3703 or 800-441-1414*
⇌*665-3093*
www.fairmont.com
A veritable institution in Quebec, the Manoir Richelieu is a distinguished establishment that is still the choice holiday resort in Québec. What's more, $140 million was spent to renovate and expand the facility in 1999. Perched on a point overhanging the river, the century-old building is adorned with turrets, gables and a sloped roof. This jewel of Norman architecture has 405 rooms, 35 of which are suites. Some rooms are a little small, but all are comfortable. There are numerous boutiques on the main floor, as well as an underground passageway to the casino. Its refurbished decor includes works by local artists, whose creations are featured in the rooms, restaurant, health café and conference rooms. The woodwork, wrought iron and ceramics blend beautifully together.

Cap-à-l'Aigle

Auberge des Peupliers
$$$-$$$$
ℜ, ℜ, △, ✿
381 Rue St-Raphaël
☎*665-4423 or 888-282-3743*
⇒*665-3179*
*www.aubergedes
peupliers.com*
The Auberge des Peupliers sits on a hillside overlooking the St. Lawrence. The rooms are decorated with wooden furniture that creates a warm, charming atmosphere. The inn also has pleasant, quiet living rooms.

Auberge Fleurs de lune
$$$$ bkfst incl.
pb/sb, ⊛, K, ℜ, ♥
301 Rue Saint-Raphaël
☎*665-1090*
⇒*665-4458*
Auberge Fleurs de Lune offers a lovely bouquet indeed: each room is named after a flower and is decorated with flow-ered fabrics and accessories by Laura Ashley. In addition, they are all equipped with a bal-cony, allowing for a view of the river. The living room, complete with roaring fire in winter, is warm and welcom-ing.

La Pinsonnière
$$$$-$$$$$
≡, ℜ, ⊙, ≈, ℜ, △, ⊛
124 Rue St-Raphaël
☎*665-4431 or 800-387-4431*
⇒*665-7156*
www.lapinsonniere.com
The luxurious La Pinsonnière, member of the Relais & Châteaux, boasts a wonderful location on a headland over-hanging the river. The rooms are tastefully decorated, and each is different from the next. This is a very pleasant hotel and the restaurant is very popular (see p 455).

Restaurants

Baie-Saint-Paul

Auberge Le Balcon Vert
$
22 Côte du Balcon Vert
☎*435-5587*
Le Balcon Vert is a youth hostel with a small cafeteria that serves good, simple dishes, including several vege-tarian selections. Diners can also enjoy a terrace that offers a stunning view.

La Pâtisserie Les 2 Sœurs
$
mid-Jun to early Sep every day, from Labour Day to Thanksgiving Wed-Sun, Feb to Jun Sat and Sun
48 Rue St-Jean-Baptiste
☎*435-6591*
The Pâtisserie Les 2 Soeurs is a quiet, pleasant place that serves healthy food.

Café des Artistes
$-$$
25 Rue St-Jean-Baptiste
☎*435-5585*
The Café des Artistes has a beautiful mahogany bar and wicker armchairs. European pizzas and panini are served with delicious garnishings. On a hot summer day, the large windows in the front and the few tables on the gallery are great places to pass the time.

Al Dente
$$
30 rue Leclerc
☎*435-6695*
Behind the facade of this ordinary bungalow hides a lovely restaurant that is worth the detour for those who love fresh pasta. Al Dente, where you can also stock up on homemade pasta, sauce and other gourmet products, specializes in pasta, obviously, but also offers original dishes prepared with local products.

Saint-Pub
$$-$$$
2 Rue Racine, corner St-Jean-Bap-tiste
☎*240-2332*
The Saint-Pub is a charming restaurant that serves good bistro food. It is the flagship of the Charlevoix microbrewery, which makes excellent beers for all tastes. Saint-Pub is easy to spot on the charming Rue St-Jean-Baptiste, because of its colourful, original architecture and its lively terrace in sum-mer.

Le Mouton Noir
$$$
43 Rue Ste-Anne
☎*240-3030*
Le Mouton Noir is one of the revelations of Baie-Saint-Paul. Its cuisine is a product of the seasons, making use of the local bounty. The menu is inventive and the dishes are both refined and good. During the summer, a large terrace provides *al fresco* dining near the river.

L'Orange Bistro
$$$
29 Rue Ambroise-Fafard
☎*240-1197*
There are plenty of terraces along lovely Rue Fafard, but each one is unique. At L'Orange Bistro's terrace, just like in its cozy dining room, there is a menu that is mainly composed of meat and pasta, prepared with plenty of local products. If you enjoy burgers, don't miss the delicious veal hamburger.

L'Auberge la Maison Otis
$$$-$$$$
23 Rue St-Jean-Baptiste
☎*435-2255*
☎*800-267-2254*
The finest and most sophisti-cated cuisine is featured at L'Auberge la Maison Otis (see p 451) which has developed an avant-garde gourmet menu where regional flavours adopt new accents and com-positions. Guests are treated to a delightful culinary experi-

Charlevoix

ence and a relaxing evening in the oldest part of the inn, which used to be a bank. The service is impeccable, and several ingredients on the menu are home-made. Fine selection of wines.

Auberge La Pignoronde
$$$-$$$$
750 Boulevard Mgr-De Laval
☎*435-5505*
☎*888-554-6004*
Graced with an exceptional decor, the dining room of the Auberge La Pignoronde (see p 451) looks out on the Vallée du Gouffre and Île aux Coudres. The restaurant serves absolutely delicious fare, where meat, fish and seafood share the stage with panache. Service is particularly attentive.

Domaine Charlevoix
$$$$
Rte. 362
☎*435-2626*
If a breathtaking setting is what it takes to give you an appetite, then head to Domaine Charlevoix, where you can also enjoy a pleasant tour (see p 449). Whether you choose the Félix-Antoine-Savard terrace or the dining room with great big windows, the main attraction of your meal will be the extraordinary view unravelling before you: the cliff, the river below, Île aux Coudres... But your plate will also grab your attention; for both lunch (sandwiches and salads) and supper (an elaborate table d'hôte), local products get top billing.

Saint-Joseph-de-la-Rive

 **À la Mer Nature**
$$
598 Chemin du Quai
☎*635-1532*
Thanks to a cute sign along the road leading to the Île aux Coudres ferry, you can't miss the log structure housing this amusing restaurant. Run by a great team of friendly people, À la Mer Nature features a

warm, welcoming ambiance. Stop by for drinks and conversation, for dinner or for a simple snack on the terrace before boarding the ferry. Here, the chef is inspired by various types of cuisines throughout the world and adds a touch of creativity to everything, from Greek salad to broad-bean soup to souvlaki, pizza and grilled dishes. Delicious!

La Maison Sous les Pins
$$$
352 Rue F.-A.-Savard
☎*635-2583*
The warm and intimate dining rooms at the inn La Maison Sous les Pins can accommodate about 20 guests, who come here to discover the refined aromas emanating from a medley of regional and French dishes, with an emphasis on local ingredients. Friendly reception and romantic ambiance. Non-smoking.

Île aux Coudres

La Mer Veille
$$-$$$
160 Chemin des Coudriers
☎*438-2149*
La Mer Veille is a very popular restaurant that serves light meals and an appealing table d'hôte.

Les Éboulements

Les Saveurs Oubliées
$$$$
bring your own wine
350 Route 138
☎*635-9888*
Les Saveurs Oubliées, a restaurant owned by one of the founders of the "Route des Saveurs de Charlevoix," is described as a "Relais du terroir" (regional dining) establishment. And for good reason: the restaurant adjoins the Ferme Éboulmontaise, where lamb is raised and organic vegetables are grown. From the farm to your plate, literally! In a small, country-style room,

sample fine cuisine prepared by experienced chef Régis Hervé and made from quality products, to which are added other local products.

Saint-Irénée

Le St-Laurent Café
$$
128 Rue Principale
☎*452-3408*
In Saint-Irénée, the friendly St-Laurent Café is perched on a hill (one of many in Charlevoix), right next to the church. Inside, the establishment is most charming, inviting you to take a seat at a lovely, ceramic-topped table. Outside, the terrace overlooks the cape and reveals a beautiful view. The menu features colourful dishes, such as chicken-liver salad and sauté of chicken with maple syrup. A real treat!

Auberge des Sablons
$$$-$$$$
290 Chemin des Bains
☎*452-3594*
☎*800-267-3594*
Charm, romance and good taste combine with culinary quality at the Auberge des Sablons (see p 452) ensuring a delightful dining experience. Guests here can savour excellent French cuisine while admiring the ocean from the terrace or dining room.

La Malbaie–Pointe-au-Pic

Café de la Gare
$$
100 Chemin du Havre
☎*665-4272*
Despite its name (*gare* is French for "train station"), this establishment is not located near the train station but rather near the dock. Built with a rural architectural style, it stands next to the Quai de Pointe-au-Pic. Here, you can enjoy panini, hamburgers and other family-style

dishes in a large room with big windows.

Crêperie Le Passe Temps
$$-$$$
245 Boulevard De Comporté
☎665-7660
With its pleasant atmosphere, the crêperie Le Passe-Temps constitutes an excellent choice for both lunch and dinner. The menu features a great variety of buckwheat or whole-wheat-flour crêpes as main courses and desserts. The fresh pasta is exquisite, particularly the spaghetti with fresh tomatoes and Migneron cheese. The terrace is also a welcome treat.

Auberge Les Sources
$$$
8 Rue des Pins
☎665-6952
The dining room at Auberge Les Sources is filled with light, thanks to large windows overlooking the garden. Diners can sample very flavourful cuisine prepared with regional products.

Auberge Des Trois Canards
$$$$
115 côte Bellevue
☎665-3761 or 800-461-3761
The chefs at the Auberge des Trois Canards et Motels (see p 452) have always been daring and inventive in integrating local ingredients or game with their refined cuisine. Invariably succeeding, they have endowed the restaurant with an enviable nationwide reputation. The service is outstanding, and the staff is genuinely cordial and knowledgeable about the dishes served. Good wine list.

Le Saint-Laurent
$$$$
181 Rue Richelieu
☎665-441-1414
The dining room at the Manoir Richelieu has improved so much over the past few years that it it now one of the best restaurants in the region—and it offers unbeatable view of the river, to boot. The superb menu, generally composed of three meat choices and three fish choices, offers five courses. Sunday brunch here is a must, even if you aren't staying at the hotel.

Cap-à-l'Aigle

Auberge des Peupliers
$$$-$$$$
381 Rue St-Raphaël
☎665-4423 or 888-282-3743
The Auberge des Peupliers has many wonderful surprises in store for its guests, fruits of its chef's fertile imagination and audacity. Patrons have only to abandon themselves to these intoxicating French and regional flavours, sure to delight any palate.

La Pinsonnière
$$$$
124 Rue St-Raphaël
☎665-4431 or 800-387-4431
The food at La Pinsonnière (see p 453) has long been considered the height of gastronomic refinement in Charlevoix and, despite increasingly fierce competition, is still worthy of the title in many respects. La Pinsonnière offers a very upscale, classic gourmet menu that should be savoured at leisure. The wine cellar remains the best-stocked in the region and one of the finest in Québec.

Cap-à-l'Aigle

Petite Plaisance Inn
$$$
310 Rue Saint-Raphaël
☎665-2653 or 877-565-2653
Named after Marguerite Yourcenar's last residence,

Auberge Petite Plaisance offers good cuisine made from local products. The tastes of Charlevoix blend harmoniously, resulting in a very decent table d'hôte, while the setting features an old-fashioned touch, thanks to various objects, furnishings and walls steeped in history.

Entertainment

Bars and Nightclubs

Baie-Saint-Paul

Saint-Pub
2 Rue Racine
☎240-2332
A good spot for a taste of local microbrewed beer.

La Malbaie
On the road facing the Pointe-au-Pic dock are Le Bambochard and Le Jazz, two bars that have existed for several years. They are relatively lively during the weekend.

Festivals and Cultural Events

Baie-Saint-Paul

The **Symposium International de la Nouvelle Peinture au Canada** (**☎435-3681**) is held annually in Baie-Saint-Paul. Throughout the month of August, visitors can admire huge works based on a suggested theme and created here by approximately 15 artists from Québec, the rest of Canada and abroad.

Enjoying greater success every year, **Rêves d'Automne Charlevoix** (☎435-5150 or 800-761-5150, *www.reves automne.qc.ca*) takes place during the last week of September and the first week of October. This multi-disciplinary festival allows the public to fully appreciate the beauty of Indian summer in Charlevoix, offering a whole series of musical and theatrical performances, as well as irresistible gastronomic treats.

Saint-Irénée

Every summer, from mid-June to the end of August, the **Festival international du Domaine Forget** (☎452-3535, *www.domaine forget.com*) brings together many classical musicians and vocalists, famous both at home and abroad, who perform on the stage at the Salle Françoys-Bernier (hall), or during outdoor musical brunches every Sunday. You can request the programme by calling the number above. Season tickets available.

Casino

La Malbaie–Pointe-au-Pic

The **Casino de Charlevoix** (*183 Rue Richelieu,* ☎665-5300 or 800-665-2274), in Pointe-au-Pic, next to the Manoir Richelieu, is a European-style casino. Formal dress required.

Shopping

Baie-Saint-Paul

Baie-Saint-Paul is particularly noteworthy for its **art galleries**. There is a little of everything here, as each shop has its own specialty. Oils, pastels, watercolours, and etchings by big names and up and coming artists, originals and reproductions, sculpture and poetry—whatever your heart desires! Take an enjoyable

stroll along Rue St-Jean-Baptiste and the neighbouring streets, where you'll find countless beautiful galleries staffed by friendly and chatty art dealers.

Les Éboulements

Les Saveurs Oubliées
350 Route 138
☎**635-9888**
Adjoining the restaurant (see p 454) and the farm, a small shop offers the creations (meat dishes, jelly, jam, etc.) of Régis Hervé, which are made from fresh local products. A tour of the farm is also a pleasant experience.

Saint-Joseph-de-la-Rive

The wonderful paper made at the **Papeterie Saint-Gilles** (*304 Rue Félix-Antoine-Savard,* ☎635-2613 or 866-635-2430) is sold on the premises. The quality of the cotton paper is remarkable. Some of it is decorated with maple or fern leaves. You can also purchase a collection of narratives, stories and Québec songs printed on these fine sheets.

Saguenay–Lac-Saint-Jean

Lac Saint-Jean is a veritable inland sea with a diameter of over 35km; from it flows the Rivière Saguenay, the location of the south-ernmost fjord in the world.

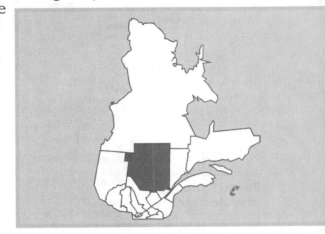

In a way, these two impressive bodies of water form the backbone of this magnificent region. Moving swiftly toward the St. Lawrence River, the Rivière Saguenay flows through a rugged landscape studded with cliffs and mountains. Aboard a cruise ship or from the banks of the river, visitors can enjoy a series of gorgeous panoramic views of this untouched natural setting. The Saguenay is navigable as far as Chicoutimi and governed by the eternal rhythm of the tides. Its rich marine-mammal life includes various species of whale in the summer. In the heart of the region, visitors will find the bustling city of Chicoutimi, the main urban centre in this part of Québec.

The region's first settlers came here in the 19th century, attracted by the beautiful fertile plains and excellent farmland around the lake. The hard life of these pioneers, who were farmers in the summer and lumberjacks in the winter, was immortalized in Louis Hémon's novel *Maria Chapdelaine.* Sweet, delicious blueberries abound in the area and have made the region of Lac Saint-Jean famous. The fruit is so closely identified with the region that Quebecers all over the province have adopted the term *bleuets*, blueberries, as an affectionate nickname for the local inhabitants. Residents of both the Saguenay and Lac Saint-Jean regions are renowned for their friendliness and spirit.

A considerable portion of the local work force is still involved in the same economic activities that brought the original settlers here towards the middle of the 20th century: forestry development in the Saguenay region and agriculture in the area around Lac Saint-Jean. Other industries have, however, developed since then, in particular aluminum smelters, because of the abundant supply of hydroelectric power.

Most settlers came from Charlevoix and the Côte-du-Sud regions in the middle of the 19th century, populating the twin regions of Saguenay and Lac-Saint-Jean, which were until then sporadically frequented by nomadic

Montagnais peoples, Jesuit missionaries and trappers. The latter were connected with small trading posts established back in the 17th century, which lay sprinkled across densely wooded territory. Everything is large scale in the Saguenay–Lac-Saint-Jean—not only the rivers and the lakes, but also the industrial complexes, which are often open to the public.

A few French Canadian families that originated in the Saguenay–Lac-Saint-Jean region actually became famous for their remarkable fertility. The Tremblays, for example, were so prolific that their surname is now closely linked with both areas.

Finding Your Way Around

Two tours have been laid-out for this region:

Tour A: The Saguenay Region ★★

Tour B: Circling Lac Saint-Jean ★★

Tour A: The Saguenay Region

By Car

From Québec City, take Rte. 138 E. to Saint-Siméon. Turn left onto Rte. 170, which passes through the village of Sagard on its way to the Parc du Saguenay. This road continues onto Chicoutimi. It is possible and even recommended to combine this tour with a tour of the Charlevoix

---

Names of New Merged Cities

Alma
Merger of Alma and Delisle.

Saguenay
Merger of Chicoutimi, Jonquière, La Baie, Laterrière, Shipshaw, Lac-Kénogami and Tremblay (part of).

---

region, farther south (see p 442).

Bus Stations

Chicoutimi
Autobus Tremblay et Tremblay
55 Rue Racine E
☎*(418) 543-1403*

Jonquière
Autocars Jasmin
2249 Rue Saint-Hubert
☎*(418) 547-2167*

Train Stations

Hébertville
15 Rue Saint-Louis
☎*800-361-5390*

Jonquière
2439 Rue Saint-Dominique
☎*800-361-5390*

Tour B: Circling Lac Saint-Jean

This tour can easily be done after the Saguenay tour. From Jonquière, take Rte. 170 W. to Saint-Bruno and then Rte. 169 around the lake.

Bus Stations

Alma
430 Rue du Sacré-Cœur (Coq-Rôti restaurant)
☎*(418) 662-5441*

Train Stations

Chambord
78 Rue de la Gare
☎*800-361-5390*

Practical Information

Area code: *418*

Tourist Information Offices

Regional Office

Fédération Touristique Régionale du Saguenay–Lac-Saint-Jean
198 Rue Racine E., Bureau 210
Chicoutimi, G7H 1R9
☎*543-9778 or 800-463-9651*
≠*543-1805*
www.tourismesaguenaylacs aintjean.qc.ca

Tour A: The Saguenay Region

La Baie
1171 7e Avenue
☎*697-5050 or 800-263-2243*
≠*697-5180*

Chicoutimi
295 Rue Racine Est
☎*698-3167 or 800-463-6565*
≠*693-0084*

Jonquière
2665 Boulevard du Royaume
☎*548-4004 or 800-561-9196*
≠*548-7348*

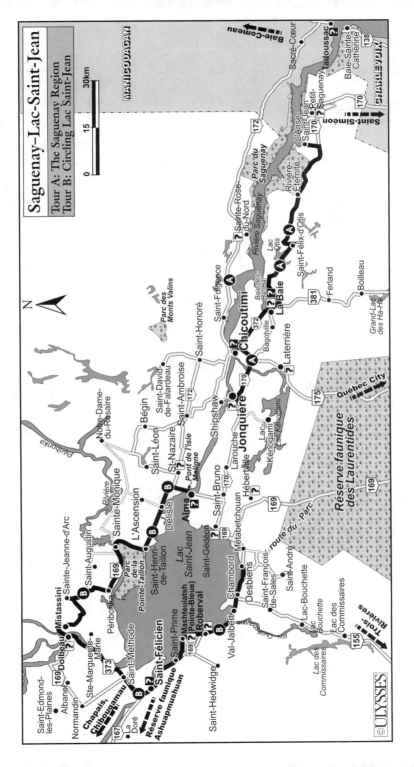

Saguenay-Lac-Saint-Jean

Tour A: The Saguenay Region
Tour B: Circling Lac Saint-Jean

Tour B: Circling Lac Saint-Jean

Alma
1671 Avenue du Pont Nord
☎*668-3611 or 888-668-3611*
≈*668-0031*

Saint-Félicien
1209 Boulevard du Sacré-Cœur
☎*679-9888*
≈*679-0562*

Exploring

Tour A: The Saguenay Region

Duration of tour: two days

The "realm of the Saguenay," as its inhabitants often refer to it, proudly and without an ounce of modesty, extends on both sides of the Rivière Saguenay and its gargantuan fjord. This region is characterized above all by its grandiose scenery and extraordinary flora and fauna. It was originally exploited for fur, and then wood, before eventually being permanently settled by such companies.

Since the beginning of the 20th century, the aluminum industry has flourished on the outskirts of local towns, taking advantage of the abundant supply of hydroelectric power provided by area rivers and the ports deep enough to accommodate the ships carrying bauxite, the mineral from which aluminum is extracted.

★ L'Anse-Saint-Jean (pop. 1,300)

In the spring of 1838, the first schooner chartered by the Société des Vingt-et-Un set off from the Charlevoix region to deposit settlers at various places along the banks of the Saguenay. The first stop was L'Anse-Saint-Jean, making this charming village with its many handcrafted bread ovens the oldest municipality in the Saguenay – Lac-Saint-Jean region. Noteworthy attractions include a stone **church**, designed by architect David Ouellet (1890) and a **covered bridge**, known as **Pont du Faubourg**, built in 1929. The village and its bridge were depicted on the back of the Canadian thousand-dollar bill. The **Belvédère de l'Anse de Tabatière**, with its a spectacular view of the sheer cliffs along the fjord, is also worth a visit. The village boasts a salmon river, a yacht club, and hiking and riding trails. It is also one of the many points of departure for river cruises of the Saguenay.

Return to Rte. 170, and head towards Rivière-Éternité.

★ Rivière-Éternité (pop. 555)

With a poetic name that translates as Eternity River, how could anyone resist being carried away by the stunning beauty of the Saguenay, especially because Rivière-Éternité is the gateway to **Parc du Saguenay ★★★** (see p 468) and the marvelous **Parc Marin du Saguenay– Saint-Laurent ★★★** (see p 482), where whales can be observed in their natural habitat.

On the first of the three cliffs that form Cap Trinité is a statue of the Virgin Mary, christened **Notre-Dame-du-Saguenay**. Carved out of pine by Louis Jobin, it was placed here in 1881 in thanks for a favour granted to a travelling salesman, who was saved from certain death when he fell near the cape. The statue is tall enough (8.5m) to be clearly visible from the deck of ships coming up the river.

Head back to Rte. 170. The road leads through Saint-Félix-d'Otis, along the shores of the lake of the same name, before reaching the town of La Baie.

★ La Baie (pop. 20,900)

La Baie is an industrial town occupying a beautiful site at the far end of the Baie des Ha! Ha! old French for *impasse* or dead-end. The colourful term "Ha!Ha!" was supposedly employed by the region's first explorers, who headed into the bay thinking it was a river. The town of La Baie is the result of the 1976 merging of three adjacent municipalities, Bagotville, Port-Alfred and Grande-Baie. The latter was founded in 1838 by the Société des Vingt-et-Un, making it the oldest of the three. At La Baie, the Saguenay is still influenced by the salt- water tides, giving the town a maritime feel. La Baie also has a large **sea port**, which is open to the public.

The **Musée du Fjord ★** (*3346 boul. de la Grande-Baie S.,* ☎*697-5077)* houses an interesting permanent exhibition describing the settling of the Saguenay region from an ethnographic angle. Temporary art and science exhibits are also presented here each year. The museum will re-open in 2004 after extensive renovations.

The Société des Vingt-et-Un was founded in La Malbaie (Charlevoix) in 1837 with the secret aim of finding new farmlands to ease overcrowding on the banks of the St. Lawrence. Under the pretext of cutting wood for the Hudson's Bay Company, the Société cleared the land around a number of coves along the Saguenay, and settled men, women and children there.

On June 11, 1838, Thomas Simard's schooner, with the first settlers on board, set anchor in the Baie des Ha! Ha! The colonists disembarked and, under the supervision of Alexis Tremblay, built the region's very first wood cabin (4m x 6m), thus marking the birth of the present town of La Baie.

At the **Palais Municipal ★** *($35; late Jun to mid-Aug, at 9pm; 591 5e Rue, ☎888-873-3333)*, visitors can see *La Fabuleuse Histoire d'un Royaume*, an elaborate historical pageant similar to those presented in some provincial French towns. Bringing this colourful extravaganza to life involves over 200 actors and 1,400 costumes, along with animals, carriages, lighting effects and sets.

The **Passe Migratoire à Saumon de la Rivière-à-Mars ★** *($2; mid-Jun to mid-Sep every day 10am to 6pm; 3232 Chemin St-Louis ☎697-5093)*, built on a part of the river located right in the heart of town, was designed to facilitate the salmons' upriver migration during their spawning period. From the pleasant park that has been laid out in the surrounding area, visitors can watch the salmon and occasionally fish for them *($30/pers.)*.

Take Rte. 372, west of La Baie, which leads into downtown Chicoutimi. As it is more pleasant to visit this part of the city on foot, we recommend parking in the area around the cathedral, located on Rue Racine.

★
Chicoutimi
(pop. 63,325)

In the language of the Montagnais, "Chicoutimi" means "there where it is

deep," a reference to the waters of the Saguenay, which are navigable as far as this city, the most important urban area in the entire Saguenay–Lac-Saint-Jean region. For over 1,000 years, nomadic Aboriginal peoples used this spot for meetings, festivities and trade. Starting in 1676, Chicoutimi became one of the most important fur-trading posts in New France. The post remained active up until the mid-19th century, when two industrialists, Peter McLeod and William Price, opened a sawmill nearby (1842). This finally enabled the development of a real town on the site, graced with the presence of three powerful rivers: the Moulin, the Chicoutimi and the Saguenay.

Religious and institutional buildings are predominant in downtown Chicoutimi, the main commercial thoroughfare of which is Rue Racine. Very little remained of the 19th-century Victorian town after most of Chicoutimi was destroyed by a raging fire in 1912; over the past 30 years, the rest has been "modernized" stripping it of its character. Along the streets, visitors will notice shop signs bearing typical Saguenay names, like Tremblay and Claveau, as well as English-sounding names, such as Harvey and Blackburn; this is indicative of a phenomenon found

only in this part of the country: the assimilation of English-speaking families into French-speaking society.

The **Cathédrale Saint-François-Xavier ★** *(514 Rue Racine E.)* was rebuilt on two different occasions, both times due to fire. The present building, erected between 1919 and 1922, was designed by architect Alfred Lamontagne. It is remarkable above all for its high facade, whose two towers, topped with silvered steeples, rise above the old port. In front of the cathedral, visitors will find the former post office, built of pink granite in the Second Empire style (1905).

Return to your car in order to visit other attractions located beyond the downtown area. Drive up Rue Bégin, west of the cathedral, then turn right on Rue Price E. Turn left on Boulevard Saint-Paul, then right on Rue Dubuc. The former home of folk artist Arthur Villeneuve lies on a small street by the name of Rue Taché, located on the left.

At the turn of the 20th century, several large-scale French Canadian enterprises were established in the Saguenay–Lac-Saint-Jean region, the largest being the pulp mills in Val-Jalbert and Chicoutimi. The **Pulperie de**

Pulperie de Chicoutimi

Saguenay–Lac-Saint-Jean

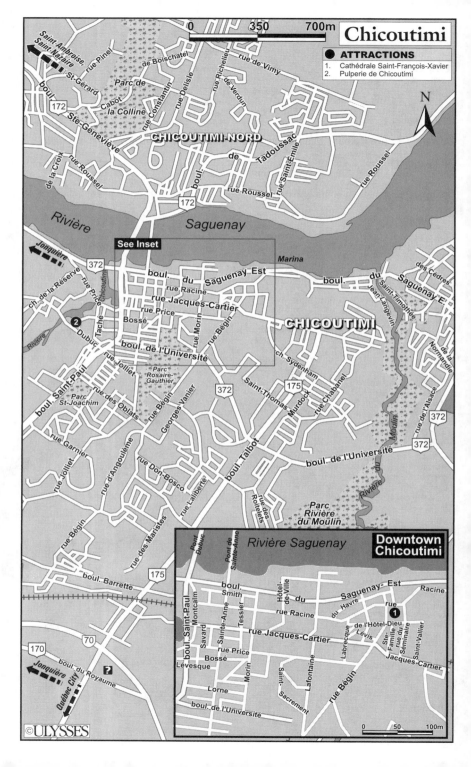

Chicoutimi ★ ★ *($12; late Jun to early Sep, every day, 9am to 6pm; early Sep to late Jun, Wed 5pm to 8pm, Thu-Fri 11am to 5pm, Sat and Sun 10am to 5pm; 300 Rue Dubuc, ☎698-3100 or 877-998-3100)* was founded in 1896 by Dominique Guay and then expanded several times by the powerful North American Pulp and Paper Company, directed by Alfred Dubuc. For 20 years, the company was the largest mechanical manufacturer of pulp and paper in Canada, supplying the French, American and British markets. This vast industrial complex, built alongside the turbulent Rivière Chicoutimi, included four pulp mills equipped with turbines and digesters, two hydroelectric stations, a smelter, a repair shop and a railway platform. The decline of pulp prices in 1921 and the crash of 1929 led to the closing of the pulp mill. It remained abandoned until 1980. In the meantime, most of the buildings were ravaged by fire, which, if nothing else, showed the strength of their thick stone walls. Since 1996, the whole complex has become a gigantic museum covering an area of over 1ha. In addition to stopping in at the Maison-Musée du Peintre Arthur-Villeneuve, visitors can go on a 12-stop self-guided tour of the site and take in a thematic exhibition.

Jonquière (pop. 57,000)

In 1847, the Société des Défricheurs (meaning land-clearers) du Saguenay received authorization to set up business alongside Rivière aux Sables. The name Jonquière was chosen in memory of one of the governors of New France, the Marquis de Jonquière. The town's early history is marked by the story of Marguerite Belley of La Malbaie, who escorted three of her sons to Jonquière on horseback to prevent them

from being tempted to emigrate to the United States. In 1870, the territory between Jonquière and Saint-Félicien, in the Lac-Saint-Jean region, was destroyed by a major forest fire. It took over 40 years for the region to recover. Today, Jonquière is regarded as an essentially modern town, whose economic mainspring is the Alcan aluminum smelter.

This multinational company owns several factories in the Saguenay–Lac-Saint-Jean region, replacing the Price brothers and their wood empire as the largest local employer. The towns of Arvida and Kénogami merged with Jonquière in 1975, forming a city large enough to rival nearby Chicoutimi. Jonquière is known for its industrial tours.

The **Centrale Hydroélectrique de Shipshaw** ★ ★ *(free admission; Jun to Aug, Mon-Fri 1:30pm to 14:30pm; 1471 Rte. du Pont, ☎699-1547)*, which began operating in 1931, is a striking example of Art Deco architecture. It supplies electricity to the local aluminum smelters.

Cross the Aluminum Bridge and turn left on Rue Price.

The **Aluminium Bridge**, opened in 1948, weighs about 160 tonnes, a third of the weight of an identical steel bridge. It was built as a means of promoting aluminum, which was rarely used in construction at the time.

The contemporary-style **Église Notre-Dame-de-Fatima** ★ *(3635 Rue Notre-Dame)* is renowned as one of the most famous white churches in the Saguenay region. Designed by Paul-Marie Côté and Léonce Gagné, it was erected in 1963. The stained-glass windows by artist Guy Barbeau produce a lovely play of light on the bare concrete interior.

The **Parc et Promenade de la Rivière-aux-Sables** *(2230 Rue de la Rivière-aux-Sables, ☎546-2177)* is the fruit of a major environmental restoration project carried out on the Rivière aux Sables, alongside the largest historic district in town. It links the Place des Nations de la Francité and Place Nikitoutagan to the immediate surroundings of the bridge on Boulevard Harvey. Here, visitors will find Les Halles, where many local market gardeners have stalls. There are a few places to eat in there as well, including an excellent crêpe restaurant. Both pedestrians and cyclists are permitted on the riverside promenade.

Tour B: Circling Lac Saint-Jean

Duration of tour: two days

Various Montagnais nations, including the Nation du Porc-Épic (Porcupine Nation), were once attracted to the vast expanse of water known today as Lac Saint-Jean (1,350km²). Europeans were unaware of the lake's existence for many years; it wasn't until 1647 that a Jesuit missionary named Jean de Ouen discovered it on his way to nurse some ailing local inhabitants. Long regarded as an inexhaustible source of fur, this region, with its rich farmlands, sandy beaches and relatively mild climate, was not actually settled until much later, in the second half of the 19th century. In 1926, Lac Saint-Jean's water level increased significantly when dams were built on the Saguenay, leading to the loss of several square kilometres of farmland. The following tour leads visitors around the lake in the same direction as the area was settled, coming almost full circle.

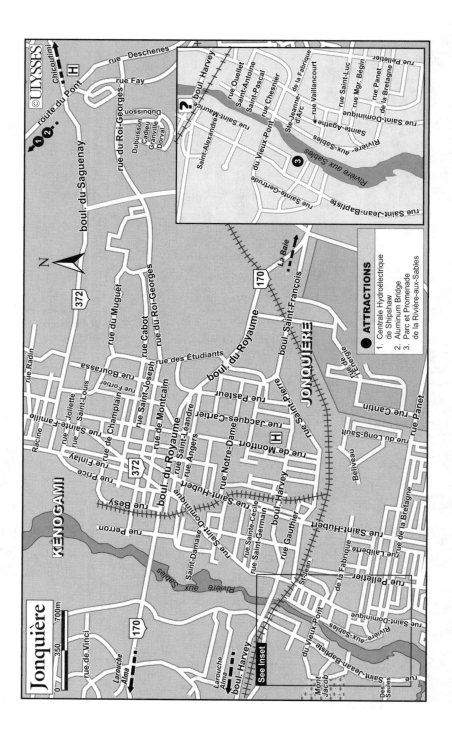

Jonquière

KÉNOGAMI

JONQUIÈRE

© ULYSSES

● **ATTRACTIONS**

1. Centrale Hydroélectrique de Shipshaw
2. Aluminum Bridge
3. Parc et Promenade de la Rivière-aux-Sables

See Inset

Desbiens
(pop. 1,175)

Located on either side of the Rivière Métabetchouane, this town is steeped in history. It was settled in 1652 by a Jesuit mission; a fur-trading post was added in 1676. The trading post consisted of a store, a chapel and several farm buildings. It prospered until 1880, when the buildings were dismantled and moved to Pointe-Bleue.

Many excavations have been conducted around the mouth of Rivière Métabetchouane, uncovering various archaeological traces of the Aboriginals' thousand-year-long habitation of the area, as well as remnants of the Jesuit mission and the fur-trading post. A number of the objects uncovered during these digs are on display at the **Centre d'Histoire et d'Archéologie de la Métabetchouane ★** *($4; late Jun to early Sep, every day 9am to 6pm; early Sep to late Jun, reservations only; 243 Rue Hébert, ☎346-5341).*

Guides lead visitors through the granite cave known as the **Trou de la Fée** *($8; mid-Jun to late Aug, every day 9am to 5:30pm; late Aug to early Sep, every day 10am to 4pm; Chemin du Trou de la Fée, ☎346-1242 or 346-5436);* the name means "the fairy's hideaway."

Continue along Rte. 169 toward Chambord.

Chambord
(pop. 1,660)

The **Village Historique de Val-Jalbert ★★** *($13; mid-May to mid-Jun and late Aug to mid-Oct, every day 9am to 5pm; mid-Jun to late Aug, every day 9am to 7pm; Rte. 169, ☎275-3132 or 888-675-3132)* began in 1901, when an industrialist by the name of Damase Jalbert built a pulp mill at the foot of the Rivière

Ouiatchouane fails. The enterprise prospered quickly, becoming the most important industrial company run entirely by French Canadians. The drop in pulp prices in 1921, followed by the shift to artificial pulp in the manufacture of paper, forced the mill to close down in 1927, at which point the village was completely deserted by its inhabitants.

Val-Jalbert is a rich slice of North America's industrial heritage. Part of the village still looks like a ghost town, while the rest has been carefully restored to provide visitors with accommodations and an extremely informative interpretation centre. Various viewing areas, linked by a gondola *($3.25),* have been built to enable visitors to appreciate fully the surroundings. There is a campground beside the village, and accommodations are available in some of the restored houses.

Continue along Rte. 169 to Roberval.

Roberval
(pop. 11,500)

This industrial town used to be the crossroads of the railway and the Lac Saint-Jean shipping routes. Today, it is the finishing point of the famous Traversée Internationale du Lac Saint-Jean, a swimming event held each year in July.

The **Centre Historique et Aquatique de Roberval ★** *($6; early Jun to mid-Jun and late Aug to mid-Sep, every day noon to 5pm; mid Jun to late Aug, 10am to 8pm; 700 Boulevard de la Traversée, ☎275-5550)* enables visitors to familiarize themselves with the history, wildlife and plant life of the Lac-Saint-Jean region. Particularly noteworthy is the aquarium, where various regional species of fish, including the famous *ouananiche,* a type of fresh-water salmon, have been collected. In a new

building with remarkable architecture, visitors can learn about the settlement of the lake's perimeter, as well as great moments in the history of the Traversée du Lac Saint-Jean.

Turn right on the little road that runs alongside the lake towards Mashteuiatsh (Pointe-Bleue).

★
Mashteuiatsh / Pointe-Bleue
(pop. 1,950)

The Montagnais lived in nomadic communities all around Lac Saint-Jean for over 1,000 years. Advancing colonisation and the forest industry eventually put an end to this way of life.

The **Musée Amérindien de Mashteuiatsh ★** *($6; mid-May to mid-Oct, every day 10am to 6pm, mid-Oct to May, Mon-Thu 9am to noon and 1pm to 4pm, Fri 9am to noon and 1pm to 3pm; 1787 Rue Amishk, ☎275-4842 or 888-875-4842)* focuses on the customs of the first inhabitants of the Saguenay–Lac-Saint-Jean region. Its temporary exhibitions help acquaint visitors with Canada's other Aboriginal peoples as well. Significant objects on permanent display include a set of chairs and a table used by the band council, different types of snowshoes and examples of traditional clothing. Artisans skilled in the techniques of their ancestors occasionally gather on the grounds of the museum to pass on their know-how.

Saint-Félicien
(pop. 11,050)

At the **Zoo Sauvage de Saint-Félicien ★★** *($18; Jun to Aug 9am to 6pm, Sep to mid-Oct 9am to 5pm, Jan to Mar Sat and Sun; 2230 Boulevard du Jardin, ☎679-0543 or 800-667-5687),* visitors can observe various species of Québec's indigenous wildlife in their natural habitat. What makes this zoo unusual is that the animals are not in cages, but roam about freely while visitors tour the zoo in small, screened buses. A lumber camp, a fur-trading post, a Montagnais encampment, and a settler's farm have all been reconstructed, and along with the authentic buildings onsite, add a historical feel to this unique zoo.

Dolbeau-Mistassini (15 400 hab.)

Mistassini and Dolbeau, which merged recently, are located on the banks of the Mistassini river, along Rte. 169. Be sure not to confuse Mistassini with the Cree village of Mistissini, located by Mistassini Lake some 300km away. Dolbeau-Mistassini is the self-declared blueberry capital of the world. Every year in late July and early August, the town hosts a blueberry festival, which is as much a reunion of the *Bleuets*, residents of the region, who have scattered across America, as it is a culinary event, featuring delicious chocolate-covered blueberries, among other goodies!

Continue along Rte. 169 toward Sainte-Jeanne-d'Arc and Péribonka.

★ Péribonka (pop. 560)

Louis Hémon was born in Brest (France) in 1880. After attending the Lycée Louis-LeGrand in Paris, he obtained his law degree from the Sorbonne. In 1903, he settled in London, where he started his career as a writer. His adventurous spirit eventually led him to Canada. He lived in Québec City, then in Montréal, where he met

some investors who wanted to build a railroad in the northern part of the Lac-Saint-Jean region. He headed off to scout out a location, but became fascinated instead by the local inhabitants' daily life. In June 1912, he met Samuel Bédard, who invited him to his home in Péribonka. Hémon helped out on the farm, secretly recording his impressions of the trip in a notebook. These impressions later formed the basis of his masterpiece, the novel *Maria Chapdelaine*.

Hémon did not, however, have time to enjoy his novel's tremendous success; on July 8, 1913, he was hit by a train while walking on the railroad tracks near Chapleau, Ontario, and died a few minutes later in the arms of his travelling companions.

Maria Chapdelaine was serialized in *Le Temps* in Paris, then published as a novel by Grasset in 1916, and finally translated into several languages. No other work of literature has done so much to make Québec known abroad. The novel was even adapted three times for the screen, by Jean Duvivier in 1934 (with Madeleine Renaud and Jean Gabin), Marc Allégret in 1949 (with Michèle Morgan in the title role) and Gilles Carle in 1983 (with Carole Laure in the title role). Péribonka is a charming village, which serves as the starting point for the swimming race, the Traversée Internationale du Lac Saint-Jean.

Musée Louis-Hémon – Complexe Touristique Maria-Chapdelaine ★ ★ *($5.50; Jun to Sep, every day 9am to 5pm; Sep to Jun, Mon-Fri 9am to 4pm; 700 Rte. 169, ☎374-2177)* is located in the house where Louis Hémon spent the summer of 1912 with Samuel Bédard and his

wife Eva (née Bouchard). It is still visible alongside Rte. 169 and is one of a few rare examples of colonial homes in the Lac-Saint-Jean region to have survived the improvements in the local standard of living. The extremely modest house that inspired Hémon was built in 1903. As it was converted into a museum in 1938, its furnishings have remained intact, and are still laid out in their original positions in the humble rooms. A large postmodern building was erected nearby in order to house Hémon's personal belongings, as well as various souvenirs of the villagers who inspired his work, and memorabilia relating to the success of *Maria Chapdelaine*.

The road then leads through the villages of Sainte-Monique, Saint-Henri-de-Taillon (access to Parc de la Pointe-Taillon) and Delisle. On the way to Alma, visitors will cross the Saguenay by the Pont de l'Isle Maligne, which overlooks the Alcan hydroelectric dam.

Alma (pop. 31,225)

This industrial town lies along the edge of the Lac-Saint-Jean region. It is home to a large aluminum smelter and a paper mill, all surrounded by working- and middle-class neighbourhoods. Parc Falaise serves as a reminder that Alma has been the twin town of Falaise, Normandy since 1969.

Tours of the facilities of the **Papeterie Alma ★** *(late Jun to early Sep, Tue-Thu 9.30am to 1.30pm; 1100 Rue Melançon, ☎668-9400, ext. 9348)* are also offered. The tour includes a visit to the pulp department and the machine room and an explanation of the manufacturing process.

The *Coureur des Bois*

The *coureur des bois* is a legendary figure in Québec culture. When the colony was first established, Champlain left a young man named Étienne Brûlé in this region. Brûlé learned the language of the Algonquins and travelled inland. In those days, men like him—who in some way illustrated the impact that the French had on the natives, be it positive or negative—were known as *truchements*.

Upon his return, Champlain found Brûlé dressed like the Aboriginals and completely adapted to their way of life. The *truchements* originally adopted the native lifestyle for economic reasons, as they did not want to offend their hosts and thus imperil the fur trade. However, as the months went by, they came to appreciate the Aboriginals' daily routines, which were in direct response to the environment. They thus learned to eat corn, wear snowshoes and use bark canoes. They also started using toboggans to carry their cargo.

Removed from church and state as they were, however, these *truchements* did have a tendancy to let themselves go altogether, and their unfettered liberty led to some rather dubious practices. This side of their life is clearly exemplified by Étienne Brûlé's death; he was killed and eaten by the Hurons, with whom he had lived for a long time.

With time, the *truchements'* reputation improved, thanks in large part to the wisdom of a number of men who played a crucial role in the development of the new colony. *Truchements* became *coureurs des bois*. The two most illustrious figures of this new generation were Médard Chouart, Sieur Des Groseillers, and Pierre-Esprit Radisson. Thanks to their bravery and ingenuity, these men established ties with the Aboriginals. Radisson learned the ropes by being captured, tortured and then finally adopted by the Iroquois. He even joined them on an expedition, wielding a tomahawk and returning with scalps and prisoners in the purest Iroquois tradition.

Des Groseilliers and Radisson extended the fur-trading routes as far as lakes Michigan and Superior, where they set up trading posts. In 1654, the governor established a permit system for the fur trade, thus putting an end to their plans to push on past the Great Lakes, where the Aboriginals hunted. In 1661, Des Groseilliers and Radisson were unable to reach an agreement with the governor and ran off without an official permit. They returned two years later with a sizeable load of furs, having learned of a land route to Hudson Bay. They were expecting to be welcomed as pioneers, but instead found themselves faced with a fine. Refusing to hang their heads, these two proud men switched over to the English camp and helped found the Hudson's Bay Company, a move that revived the negative image of the *coureurs des bois*.

Be that as it may, these *truchements*-turned-*coureurs-des-bois* were still the first Europeans to adopt and begin to understand the traditional native way of life. They chose this lifestyle because it corresponded to the geographic, climatic, economic and social conditions in the New World. Their behaviour may not always have been exemplary, but they nevertheless played a crucial role in Canada's development by serving as link between the European and Aboriginal cultures.

Saguenay–Lac-Saint-Jean

Parks

Tour A: The Saguenay Region

The **Parc du Saguenay** ★★★ *($3.50; 91 Chemin Notre-Dame, Rivière-Éternité, ☎272-1556 ou 877-272-5229)* extends across a portion of the shores of the Rivière Saguenay. It stretches from the banks of the estuary (located in the Manicouagan tourist region) to Sainte-Rose-du-Nord. In this area, steep cliffs plunge into the river, creating a magnificent landscape. The park has about 100km of hiking trails, providing visitors with an excellent opportunity to explore this fascinating region up close. A few of the more noteworthy trails include a short, relatively easy one along the banks of the Saguenay (1.7km), the Sentier de la Statue, which stretches 3.5km and includes a difficult uphill climb and the superb, 25km Sentier des Caps, which takes three days (registration required). During winter, the trails are used for cross-country skiing. Accommodation in the form of campsites and shelters is available. The park has three interpretive centres *(91 Chemin Notre-Dame, Rivière-Éternité; 1121 Route 172 Nord, Sacré-Cœur; 750 Chemin Moulin-Baude, Tadoussac).*

The **Parc des Monts-Valin** ★ *(accessible by Rte. 172, 27km from Chicoutimi, 17km from Saint-Fulgence, 360 Rang St-Louis, Accueil Petit-Séjour, ☎674-1200),* with its lofty summits, offers a whole slew of activities all year round. Hiking, mountain biking, canoeing, cabin stays and sport fishing are the summertime favourites.

During winter, snowfall reaches record levels of up to 5m. All this snow turns the trees into ghostlike figures, hence the legends of the "Vallée des Fantômes" (phantom valley) and the "Champs de Momies" (mummy fields). This wild and spectacular area, which looks out over the surrounding region, becomes a mecca for off-trail and cross-country skiing, snowshoeing and ice climbing.

Tour B: Circling Lac Saint-Jean

Parc de la Pointe-Taillon ★ *(fees depend on activities and services provided; 825 3e Rang Ouest, St-Henri-de-Taillon, ☎347-5371)* lies on the strip of land formed by the Rivière Péribonka, which extends into Lac Saint-Jean. It is an excellent place to enjoy water sports, such as canoeing and sailing, and also has magnificent sandy beaches. Bicycle paths and hiking trails provide access to the natural beauty of the park.

Outdoor Activities

Hiking

Tour A: The Saguenay Region

The **Sentier des Caps** *(after the Pont du Faubourg, turn right on Chemin Thomas Nord and continue for 3km, L'Anse-St-Jean, ☎272-2267 for reservations)* leads to the foot of one of the concrete pylons supporting Hydro-Québec's first 735 kw line. There are two lookouts, from which hikers can enjoy an

extraordinary view of the fjord.

Cruises

Tour A: The Saguenay Region

La Marjolaine *($35; Boulevard Saguenay, Port de Chicoutimi, ☎543-7630 or 800-363-7248)* organizes cruises on the Saguenay, one of the most enjoyable ways to take in the spectacular view of the fjord. The ship sets out from Chicoutimi, en route to Sainte-Rose-du-Nord. Passengers return by bus, except during June and September, when the return trip is by boat. Each cruise lasts an entire day. It is also possible to take the trip in the opposite direction, from Sainte-Rose-du-Nord to Chicoutimi.

See the Manicouagan chapter for more cruises on the Saguenay, p 483.

Ice-Fishing

Tour A: The Saguenay Region

Parc du Saguenay (see p 468) and the Rivière Saguenay attract hordes of ice-fishing enthusiasts. From December to mid-March, when the river is frozen, it is covered with fishers' colourful, little wooden shacks. The river is home to many species of fish, including cod, halibut and smelt. You can rent the necessary equipment in **Rivière-Éternité** *(only ice and seasonal fishing; free on charge when you rent a cabin)* and in **La Baie** *(1352 Anse-à-Benjamin, ☎544-4176).*

Downhill Skiing

Tour A: The Saguenay Region

The **Station Touristique du Mont-Édouard** ★ *($32; 67 Rue Dallaire, L'Anse-St-Jean, ☎272-2927)* has the highest vertical drop in the region (450m). There are 20 runs for skiers of all different ability levels.

In the Valin hills, where the park of the same name is located, there is also downhill skiing. **Le Valinouët** *($31; 200 Route du Valinouët, St-David-de-Falardeau, ☎673-6455 or 800-260-8254)* has 25 runs with a vertical drop of 350m. It is known for the quality of its snow.

Cross-Country Skiing

Tour A: The Saguenay Region

Located alongside the Rivière à Mars, 7km from La Baie, the **Centre de Plein Air Bec-Scie** *($6.50; 7400 Chemin des Chutes, ☎697-5132)* has a network of 10 trails, four of which are easy, four difficult and two very difficult.

The **Club de Ski le Norvégien** *($6; 4885 Chemin St-Benoît, Jonquière, ☎546-2344)* has 60km of trails for skiers of all levels.

Accommodations

Tour A: The Saguenay Region

L'Anse-Saint-Jean

Camping de L'Anse
$
🐕, ≈
325 Rue St-Jean-Baptiste
☎272-2554
☎272-2633 *(off season)*
≈272-3148
Camping de l'Anse not only faces the fjord, but also offers extremely well-equipped sites.

La Ferme des Trois Courts d'eau
$$ bkfst incl.
sb
6 Rue de L'Anse
☎272-2944
The three guest rooms in this little bed and breakfast occupy the second floor of a modest but superbly located farmhouse. The site is truly magnificent. Surrounded by pastures where cattles graze and crossed by a peaceful stream, the farm stands facing the bay where the Saint-Jean river meets the Saguenay river fjord. Guests have an unobstructed view of this meeting in a completely bucolic environment.

Auberge des Cévennes
$$
pb/sb, ℜ, ℝ, ≡, ℜ
294 Rue St-Jean-Baptiste
☎272-3180 or 877-272-3180
www.auberge-des-cevennes.qc.ca
Auberge des Cévennes has held court on Rue Saint-Jean-Baptiste for many years. This huge century-old property houses lovely well-decorated little guest rooms that look out over the long, wraparound verandah. In addition to these relaxing rooms, a common living room is available to

guests, who also have access to the spacious property around the house. The half-board option, which includes the evening table d'hôte (see p 471), is a good deal.

Les Gîtes du Fjord
$$$-$$$$$
ℜ, K, ≈, ℜ
344 Rue St-Jean-Baptiste
☎272-3430 or 800-561-8060
≈272-3480
Perched atop a cliff along the fjord, the Gîtes du Fjord rents out cottages and condominiums that are ideal for family vacations.

La Baie

🏮 **Auberge La Maison de la Rivière**
$$
≡, ℜ, ⊛
9122 Chemin de la Batture
☎544-2912 or 800-363-2078
≈544-2912
La Maison de la Rivière lies in an enchanting setting, surrounded by beautiful greenery. Its peaceful atmosphere makes it a daydreamers' paradise. Unique, specialized packages are offered that focus on regional and native gastronomy, wild plants, the outdoors, cultural activities, romanticism and alternative medicine. Comfortable, tastefully decorated rooms designated by names taken from nature. Ten of them have private balconies with stunning views of the fjord. Warm welcome. Guide service available.

Auberge des Battures
$$-$$$$
≡, ℜ, ⊛
6295 Boulevard de la Grande-Baie Sud
☎544-8234 or 800-668-8234
≈544-4351
www.battures.ca
L'Auberge des Battures not only offers a spectacular view of La Baie des Ha! Ha! it also has wonderful accommodations and refined cuisine.

Auberge des 21
$$$
≡, ⊛, ⊘, *K*, ℑ, ≈, ✪, ℜ, ○
621 Rue Mars
☎*697-2121 or 800-363-7298*
⇌*544-3360*
www.aubergedes21.com
The charming Auberge des 21 offers magnificent, comfortable rooms with a view of the Baie des Ha! Ha! There is a health club to help travellers relax as much as possible.

Chicoutimi

Hôtel du Fjord
$$-$$$ bkfst incl.
241 Morin
☎*543-1538 or 888-543-1538*
⇌*543-8253*
hoteldufjord.qc.ca
Hôtel du Fjord is located beyond the cluster of large hotels, near Parc Vieux-Port, Rivière Saguenay and the town centre.

Hôtel Gouverneur
$$-$$$$
≡, ≈, ℜ
1303 Boulevard Talbot
☎*549-6244 or 888-910-1111*
⇌*549-5527*
www.gouverneur.com
Located in the heart of town, the Hôtel Gouverneurs is a meeting place frequented by businesspeople looking for rooms with all the modern conveniences.

Jonquière

Auberge des Deux Tours
$ bkfst incl.
pb/sb, ≡
2522 Rue St-Dominique
☎*695-2022 ou 888 454-2022*
www.auberge
deuxtours.qc.ca
Facing the church on this busy street stands a house that doesn't easily go unnoticed. Its two towers inspired its owners to turn this house into an inn and its corridors, stairs and common rooms retain the memory of its former residents. The simple guest rooms have recently been brightened up with new colours. Guests are welcome to get fresh air on the verandah and on the balconies in the summer.

Cepal
$$ bkfst incl.
≡, ℜ, ≈
3350 Rue Saint-Dominique
☎*547-5728 or 800-361-5728*
⇌*547-4882*
www.cepalaventure.com
Surrounded by nature, by the shore of the Rivière aux Sables and not far from impressive Lac Kenogami, the Cepal resort offers outdoor holidays. There's something for the entire family to enjoy here, from snowmobiling to canoeing to fishing and hiking. The guest rooms are simple but comfortable. A variety of packages, including meals and activities, are available.

Auberge Villa Pachon
$$$ bkfst incl.
ℜ
1904 Rue Perron
☎*542-3568 or 888-922-3568*
⇌*542-9667*
www.aubergepachon.com
After it moved to Jonquière, the Chez Pachon restaurant (see p 472) became the Auberge Villa Pachon Restaurant, a restaurant-inn combination. It has five rooms and a suite in one of the loveliest historic houses in all of Saguenay-Lac-Saint-Jean, the ancestral home of the Price Brothers.

Hôtel Holiday Inn Saguenay
$$$$
≡, ⊘, ≈, ℜ, ♿
2675 Boulevard du Royaume
☎*548-3124 or 800-363-3124*
⇌*548-1638*
www.saguenay.holiday-inn.com
Though outside the centre of town, the Hôtel Holiday Inn Saguenay is nevertheless very well located on the road between Jonquière and Chicoutimi, and has nice rooms.

Tour B: Circling Lac Saint-Jean

Hébertville

Auberge Presbytère Mont-Lac-Vert
$$ bkfst incl.
ℜ
335 rang du Lac-Vert, Mont-Lac-Vert
☎*344-1548 or 800-818-1548*
⇌*344-1013*
www.aubergepresbytere.com
The Auberge Presbytère Mont-Lac-Vert enjoys a beautiful setting and has a warm, relaxing atmosphere. The food, furthermore, has received rave reviews from many guests.

Métabetchouan

Auberge La Maison Lamy
$$ bkfst incl.
pb/sb
56 Rue St-André
☎*349-3686 or 888-565-3686*
In a magnificent Bourgeois home in the heart of a quaint little town, Auberge La Maison Lamy has an irresistible charm, a meticulous decor and offers a warm welcome. Near Lac Saint-Jean and the Véloroute. Beach.

Val-Jalbert

This ghost town has an outstanding **campground** *($;* ☎*275-3132)*, a vast stretch of land, dotted with beautiful, natural sites that will delight those who enjoy rustic camping.

There are lodgings available in the historic village *($$$;* ☎*275-3132).*

Saint-Félicien

Camping de Saint-Félicien
$
♣, ≈, ℜ
2206 Boulevard du Jardin
☎*679-1719 or 866-679-1719*
⇌*679-5410*
As may be gathered from its name, the Camping de St-Félicien is located beside the

zoo, so you might be awakened by animal noises at night. It occupies a large property and is equipped with all the necessary facilities.

Hôtel du Jardin
$$-$$$
≡, ☺, 🏍, ≈, ℜ, ◐, ☯, ⊛
1400 Boulevard du Jardin
☎*679-8422 or 800-463-4927*
≈*679-4459*
www.hoteldujardin.com
The Hôtel du Jardin offers standard, confortable rooms near the zoo.

Péribonka
 Auberge de l'Île-du-Repos
$
K, ℜ
105 Rte Île-du-Repos
☎*347-5649 or 800-461-8585*
≈*347-4810*
Alone on an island, in the middle of the river, the Auberge de l'Île-du-Repos offers beautiful surroundings, an environment that stimulates conversation and a fascinating cultural programme. This is a large youth hostel that also has campsites available.

Alma
Complexe Touristique de la Dam-en-Terre
$$-$$$
≡, K, ≈, ℝ, ℜ
1385 Chemin de la Marina
☎*668-3016 or 888-289-3016*
≈*668-4599*
www.damenterre.qc.ca
The Complexe Touristique de la Dam-en-Terre rents out well designed cottages with a beautiful view of Lac Saint-Jean. Those with tents, can opt for the more economical campsites.

Restaurants

Tour A: The Saguenay Region

L'Anse-Saint-Jean

Bistro de l'Anse
$
319 Rue St-Jean-Baptiste
☎*272-4222*
Located in a former fishing camp, Bistro de l'Anse offers a warm ambiance. People come here to have a drink in the evening while enjoying musical performances, for an aperitif on the verandah or for a sandwich or a salad. The extensive property behind the house gives way to the Saint-Jean river estuary, into which many a fishing line has been dipped.

Le Maringouinfre
$$-$$$$
212 Rue St-Jean-Baptiste
☎*272-2385 or 877-272-2385*
The Maringouinfre is grill and seafood restaurant. Fresh ingredients and an intimate atmosphere are the highlights here.

Auberge des Cévennes
$$$
294 Rue St-Jean-Baptiste
☎*272-3180*
The restaurant at the Auberge des Cévennes (see p 469) offers a mouth-watering evening table d'hôte. On offer is classic French cuisine accented by local products, to enjoy inside or al fresco, weather permitting.

La Baie
 Le Doyen
$$$$
Auberge des 21
621 Rue Mars
☎*697-2121 or 800-363-7298*
With its succulent game dishes, Le Doyen boasts one of the region's best menus.

The dining room commands a remarkable, sweeping view of the Baie des Ha! Ha! The Sunday brunch is excellent. Run by renowned chef Marcel Bouchard, who has won numerous regional, national and international awards, Le Doyen is making a tangible contribution to the evolution and refinement of regional Québec cuisine.

 La Maison de la Rivière
$$$$
9122 Chemin de la Batture
☎*544-2912 or 800-363-2078*
The head chef at La Maison de la Rivière has developed a menu centred on Aboriginal traditions, regional dishes and international cuisine. This superb inn lies in an extremely pleasant setting, featuring a lovely view of the fjord.

Chicoutimi

La Bougresse
$$-$$$
260 Rue Riverin
☎*543-3178*
La Bougresse distinguishes itself by the variety and quality of its cuisine, which is always good. The confidence and loyalty of La Bougresse's Chicoutimi patrons are the best possible indication of the quality of the cuisine served here. The restaurant has regular all-the-mussels-you-can-eat nights.

La Cuisine
$$$-$$$$
387 Rue Racine Est
☎*698-2822*
The scent of freshly ground coffee permeates the air at La Cuisine. We especially recommend the steak tartare, mussels, rabbit, sweetbreads and *steak-frites* (steak and fries).

 Le Privilège
$$$$
1623 Boulevard St-Jean-Baptiste
☎*698-6262*
Le Privilège ranks among the finest restaurants in the region, offering a feast for the senses in a picturesque century-old

house. Intuitive cuisine with market-fresh ingredients is reserved for a lucky few at a time. Friendly, relaxed ambiance and service. Reservations required.

Jonquière

Le Bergerac
$$$-$$$$
Tue-Sat
3919 Rue St-Jean
☎542-6263
One of the finest restaurants in Jonquière, Le Bergerac has developed an excellent repertoire of dishes. Lunchtime menu du jour and evening table d'hôte.

Chez Pachon
$$$$
1904 Rue Perron
☎542-3568 or 888-922-3568
Chez Pachon, an institution in the town of Chicoutimi, moved to Jonquière in 1999. It now occupies the magnificent heritage home of the Price brothers, in a wonderful countryside setting. Its chef, who is already famous in the region, concocts a gourmet extravaganza of French-style cuisine with regional flavours. His specialities include *Cassoulet de Carcassonne* (a casserole dish from southwestern France), *confit de magret et foie de canard* (magret duck breast and liver confit), fillet and loin of lamb, calf sweetbreads, as well as fish and seafood. Dinner only. Reservations required.

L'Amandier
$$$$
Tue-Sun
5219 Chemin St-André
☎542-5395
L'Amandier has an astonishing dining room decorated with carved plaster and an overabundance of woodwork. The restaurant serves regional cuisine made with fresh

ingredients. Somewhat removed from town, however, it is not easy to find. Good food is joined here by a unique ambiance well-suited to dining among friends: the inviting decor and the hosts' hospitality create a festive mood. Reservations required.

Tour B: Circling Lac Saint-Jean

Saint-Félicien

Hôtel du Jardin
$$-$$$$
1400 Boulevard du Jardin
☎679-8422 or 800-463-4927
The fine regional cuisine served at the Hôtel du Jardin never disappoints.

Roberval

Château Roberval
$$-$$$$
1225 Boulevard St-Dominique
☎275-7511 or 800-661-7611
The Château Roberval is a renowned restaurant. The menu, made up of regional specialties, is full of pleasant surprises.

Alma

Bar restaurant chez Mario Tremblay
$$-$$$
534 Collard Ouest
☎668-7231
People don't come to the Bar Restaurant Chez Mario Tremblay to enjoy the meal of their life; they are attracted by the owner's reputation as a hockey player and coach, which earned him the nickname "*le bleuet bionique*" (the bionic blueberry). This brasserie-style restaurant is a popular gathering place for hockey fans.

Entertainment

Festivals and Cultural Events

Chicoutimi

The **Carnaval-Souvenir de Chicoutimi** *(mid-Feb; ☎543-4438 or 877-543-4439)* celebrates the customs of winter in days gone by with period costume and traditional activities.

Roberval

Since 1955, the last week in July has been devoted to the **Traversée Internationale du Lac Saint-Jean** *(☎275-2851)*. Swimmers cover the 40km between Péribonka and Roberval in eight hours, and some even make the return trip in 18 hours.

Shopping

Tour A: The Saguenay Region

Chicoutimi

If you're craving healthy, natural food, **Le Garde-Manger** *(at the corner of Ste-Famille and Hôtel-Dieu, behind the church, ☎696-1597)* is the perfect place to stock up for a picnic.

Blueberry Patches

Here in the land where three blueberries can just about fill a pie, you might want to check out one of the following blueberry patches:

Bleuetière Au Gros Bleuet
159 Rang 2, 3km from Falardeau
☎*673-3269*

Bleuetière de Saint-François-de-Sales Chemin du Moulin
15km west of the village of Saint-François-de-Sales
☎*348-6642*

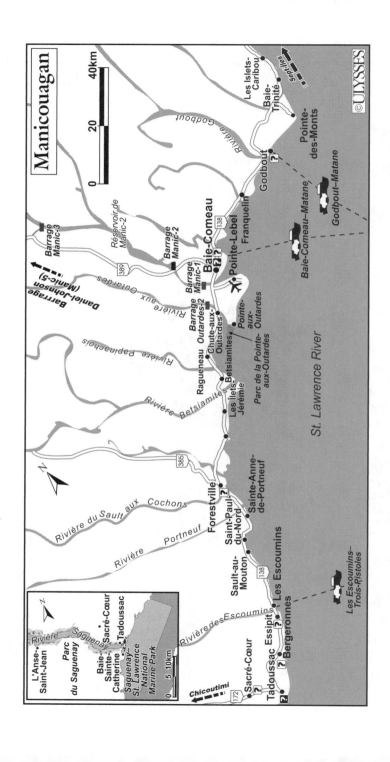

Manicouagan

Manicouagan

The Manicouagan region

borders the St. Lawrence for some 300km, extends north into the Laurentian plateau to include the Monts Groulx and the Réservoir Manicouagan, and is joined to the Duplessis region, forming what is called the Côte-Nord or north shore.

Covered by thick boreal forest, Manicouagan also has an extensive river system that powers the eight generating stations of the Manic-Outardes hydroelectric complex.

The history of Manicouagan has always been closely linked to the natural resources of the area. Even before the founding of Québec City, Europeans had set up outposts in the region to trade with Aboriginal communities. During the 19th century, forestry became the region's main industry. In 1959, the strong currents of the Rivière aux Outardes and the Rivière Manicouagan were put to use with the construction of eight large generating stations. Completed in 1989, the Manic Outardes complex now produces more than 6,500 megawatts of power and has helped to make Québec a

world leader in hydroelectric technology. The complex, which houses the largest arch and buttress dams in the world, is now open to visitors.

Rte. 138 stretches along the coast from the mouth of the Saguenay up to Baie-Trinité, and has beautiful views of steep cliffs and wild beaches. Birdwatchers and nature lovers will enjoy the Parc Régional de Pointe-aux-Outardes, home to a multitude of bird species, while more adventurous visitors may want to plan an expedition through the rugged and remote Monts Groulx area. One of the region's main attractions is the Parc Marin du Saguenay (marine park),

where a variety of whale species can be spotted during the summer months.

The Côte-Nord was historically an area common to Inuit and various other Aboriginal peoples, mainly because of its huge river system and sea-mammal-hunting potential. Before the "discovery" of Canada by Jacques Cartier in 1534, the region was visited by Basque and Breton fishers hunting for highly valued whale blubber that was melted down on the shore in large ovens. The blubber was later used to make candles and ointments. Although the Aboriginal presence in the area dates back thousands of years, there are few remaining traces of human habitation from before the 20th century. Today, the region is dotted with small fishing villages as well as pulp-and-paper and mining towns.

Tourism, based mainly on whale-watching, is playing an increasingly larger role in the region's economy, and the whales are now protected. Rte. 138, the backbone of the Côte-Nord tour, provides the opportunity to see long stretches of the immense St. Lawrence. A number of marked trails and minor roads branch off Rte. 132 along the way, providing access to several roaring rivers. In short, the Côte Nord is an exceptional wilderness area with an interesting history.

Finding Your Way Around

From Tadoussac, the Côte-Nord tour can be linked to the Charlevoix tour (see p 442) or to the Saguenay tour (see p 460). To get to Tadoussac, the first stop on the Côte-Nord tour, take the ferry across the mouth of the Saguenay which links Tadoussac to Baie-Sainte-Catherine. Since Tadoussac is small and easy to get around, explore it on foot. Cars can be left in the Parc du Saguenay parking lot, near the dock where the ferry pulls in.

By Car

From Beauport (near Québec), take Rte. 138, which runs along the north shore of the St. Lawrence River, to

Natashquan, in Duplessis. At Baie-Sainte-Catherine, a ferry crosses the Rivière Saguenay to Tadoussac. To follow the Manicouagan tour, continue on Rte. 138: You can't go wrong—there is only one highway!

Bus Stations

Tadoussac

443 Rue Bateau-Passeur (Petro-Canada station)
☎(418) 235-4653

Bergeronnes

138 Rte. 138 (Irving station)
☎(418) 232-6330

Baie-Comeau

212 Boulevard LaSalle
☎(418) 296-6921

By Ferry

Except for the Baie-Ste-Catherine—Tadoussac ferry, it is better to reserve a spot a few days in advance in the summer.

Baie-Sainte-Catherine/Tadoussac

The ferry ride from Baie-Sainte-Catherine to Tadoussac (*free; ☎418-235-4395*) takes only 10min. The schedule varies greatly from one season to the next, so make sure to double-check the times before planning a trip.

Baie-Comeau/Godbout/Matane

The ferry (*$12.75, car $29.95, motorcycle $22.45; ☎568-7575 Godbout, ☎294-8593 Baie-Comeau, ☎562-2500 Matane*) serving Godbout, Matane and Gaspésie leaves from Baie-Comeau and takes 2hrs 20min.

Les Escoumins

There is a ferry from Trois-Pistoles to Les Escoumins (*☎233-2266 or 233-4676 from Les Escoumins and 851-4676 from Trois Pistoles*) that lasts 1hr 30min.

Practical Information

Area code: *418*

Tourist Information

Regional Office

Association Touristique Régionale de Manicouagan
337 Boulevard Lasalle, suite 304
Baie-Comeau, G4Z 2Z1
☎*294-2876 or 888-463-5319*
⁼*294-2345*
www.tourismecote-nord.com

Tadoussac
197 Rue des Pionniers, G0T 2A0
☎*235-4744*
⁼*294-2345*

Baie-Comeau
3501 Boulevard Laflèche, G5C 1E4
☎*589-3610*

Exploring

La Côte-Nord

★★
**Tadoussac
(pop. 920)**

In 1600, eight years before Québec City was founded, Tadoussac was established as a trading post; it was chosen

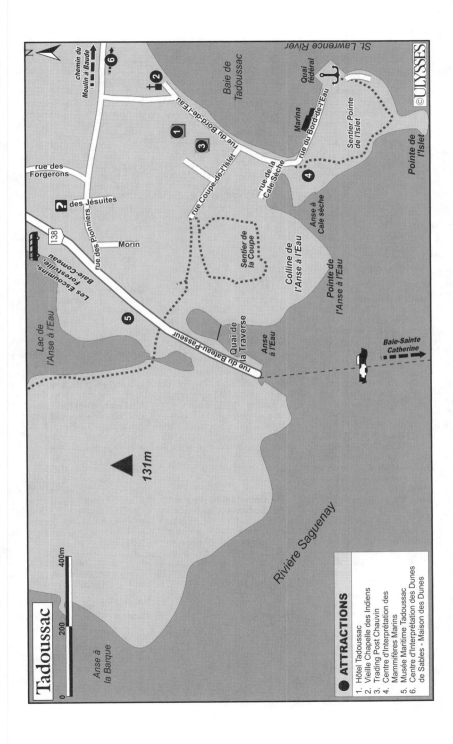

Tadoussac

N

0   200   400m

Anse à
la Barque

131m

Rivière Saguenay

Lac de
l'Anse à l'Eau

chemin du
Moulin à Baude

6 →

rue des
Forgerons

des Jésuites **7**

138

Morin

rue des Pionniers

Les Escoumins,
Baie-Comeau,
Baie-Comeau

5

rue Coupe-de-l'Islet

rue du Bord-de-l'Eau

2 †

1

3

Sentier de
la Coupe

rue de la
Cale Sèche

Quai de
la Traverse

rue du Bateau-Passeur

Anse
à l'Eau

Pointe de
l'Anse à l'Eau

Colline de
l'Anse à l'Eau

Anse à
Cale sèche

Marina

rue du Bord-de-l'Eau

4

Sentier Pointe
de l'Islet

Quai
fédéral

Baie de
Tadoussac

St. Lawrence River

Pointe de
l'Islet

Baie-Sainte
Catherine →

© ULYSSES

● ATTRACTIONS

1. Hôtel Tadoussac
2. Vieille Chapelle des Indiens
3. Trading Post Chauvin
4. Centre d'Interprétation des
   Mammifères Marins
5. Musée Maritime Tadoussac
6. Centre d'Interprétation des Dunes
   de Sables - Maison des Dunes

for its strategic location at the mouth of the Saguenay river. Tadoussac was the first permanent white settlement north of Mexico. In 1615, the Récollet religious order established a mission that operated until the mid-19th century. The town's tourism trade received a boost in 1864 when the original Tadoussac Hotel was built to better accommodate the growing number of visitors coming to the area to enjoy the sea air and breathtaking landscape. Although the town is old (by North American standards), it has a look of impermanence, as if a strong wind could sweep the entire town away.

Dominating the town, the **Hôtel Tadoussac ★** *(mid-May to mid-Oct; 165 Rue du Bord-de-l'Eau, ☎235-4421)* is to this community what the Château Frontenac is to Québec City: its symbol and landmark. The current hotel was built between 1942 and 1949 by the Canada Steamship Lines, following the destruction of the first hotel. Reminiscent of the resort hotels built in New England during the second half of the 19th century, Hôtel Tadoussac is long and low and its weathered wood-siding exterior contrasts sharply with the bright red roof. The polished wood panelling and antique furniture that characterize the interior decor reflect traditional rural French-Canadian tastes. The hotel was renovated in 2000.

In 1640 the Jesuits took over the Tadoussac mission from the Récollets. Several chapels were built successively on the same site. The one that remains, the **Vieille Chapelle des Indiens** *($2; late Jun to early Sep, every day 9am to 9pm; 169 Rue du Bord-de-l'Eau; ☎235-4324)*, also called Petite Chapelle de Tadoussac, was

built in 1747 under Father Claude-Godefroy Coquart of Melun, France. His was a vast ministry that included the parishes of Tadoussac, Saguenay, Lac-Saint-Jean and the rest of the Côte-Nord. The Tadoussac chapel is the oldest wooden chapel in Canada. Its plain interior contains an 18th-century tabernacle designed by Pierre Émond.

American William Hugh Coverdale, president of Canada Steamship Lines during the 1940s, had a passionate interest in history. In addition to rebuilding Hôtel Tadoussac (with 19th-century stylings) in 1942, he ordered the reconstruction of the town's first trading post (also North America's first), originally built in 1600. The **Trading Post Chauvin ★** *($3; late May to mid-Jun, every day 10am to 6pm, mid-Jun to mid-Sep, every day 9am to 8:30pm, mid-Sep to mid-Oct 10am to 6pm; 157 Rue du Bord-de-l'Eau, ☎235-4657)*, is open to visitors; take a look around and try to imagine a time when this was the only building on the continent lived in by Europeans. The building houses an interesting exhibit dealing with the fur trade between France and the Montagnais.

The **Centre d'Interprétation des Mammifères Marins ★** *($5.50; mid-May to mid-Jun every day noon to 5pm, mid-Jun to mid-Sep every day 9am to 8pm, mid-Sep to mid-Oct noon to 5pm; 108 Rue de la Cale-Sèche, ☎235-4701)* is an information centre that educates

Vieille Chapelle des Indiens

people about the whales that migrate to the region every summer. The centre features skeletons of various sea mammals, video presentations, and an aquarium with specimens of fish species that live in the St. Lawrence; naturalists are on hand to answer questions.

Life in Tadoussac has always centred around the sea. The **Musée Maritime Tadoussac** *($2.50; mid-Jun to early Sep 10am to 4pm; 145 Rue de Bateau-Passeur, ☎235-4446, ext. 242)* looks back on the high points in the evolution of the local shipping and shipbuilding industries.

The **Dunes** (sand dunes) and the **Maison des Dunes ★** are located approximately 5km north of Tadoussac. The dunes were formed thousands of years ago as glaciers receded. Although the government now protects the dunes, it is still possible to ski on them at certain times. For information and equipment rental contact the youth hostel or the **Centre d'interprétation des Dunes de Sable** *($3.50; Jun to early Sep every day 10am to 6pm, early Sep to mid-Oct every day 9am to 7pm; 750 Chemin du Moulin-à-Baude, ☎235-4238)*. Turn right onto Rue des Pionniers from Rte. 138. The dunes are 3.5km farther on. The Maison des Dunes parking lot is located 5.8km from Tadoussac, past the turnoff from Rte. 138.

★
Bergeronnes
(pop. 750)

The municipality of Bergeronnes is made up of the hamlets of Petites-Bergeronnes and Grandes-Bergeronnes, and is the site of an archaeological dig. Knives dating back to between 200 and 1100 CE—used by Aboriginals to cut seal and whale skins—have been uncovered here. Bergeronnes is also the best spot on land from which to observe some of the region's whale species; it is here that the blue whales come closest to shore.

The **Centre d'Interprétation Archéo-Topo** *($5.50; mid-May to mid-Oct, every day 9am to 5pm; 498 Rue de la Mer,* ☎*232-6286)* displays objects found during archeological digs carried out on the banks of the St. Lawrence since 1983. Most of these objects are of a certain ethnological interest, but may not fascinate all visitors.

The **Centre d'Interprétation et d'Observation de Cap-de-Bon-Désir** ★ *($5; early Jun to mid-Jun 9am to 6pm, mid-Jun to early Sep 8am to 8pm, early Sep to mid-Oct 9am to 6pm; 13 Chemin Du Cap-Bon-Désir,* ☎*232-6751)* is an information and observation centre located around the Cap Bon-Désir lighthouse (still in operation). It has an interesting exhibit on whales as well as a whale-observation point.

★
Les Escoumins
(pop. 2,150)

There are several nature trails in Les Escoumins that are perfect for fishing and birdwatching. The area is also known for its scuba diving. The town's metallic cross, planted on a headland jutting into the river, replaced the wooden cross erected by the Montagnais in 1664 to commemorate the arrival of missionary father Henri Nouvel. During the American Civil War, Southern officers, separated from their regiment, took refuge in Les Escoumins, while in the Second World War, a group of German soldiers left their submarine under the cover of darkness and went to shore to visit the local fair.

The **Centre des Loisirs Marins** *($5; early Jun to late*

Jun, every day 8:30am to 4:30pm, late Jun to early Sep every day 8:30am to 7pm; 41 Rue des Pilotes, ☎*233-2860)* caters mainly to a large clientele of divers, but you can also go there simply to watch the divers getting ready or the pilots setting out for the merchant ships. Footbridges provide access to dive sites and picnic areas. The centre also presents an exhibition on the sea bed. A lookout allows visitors to observe the sea mammals.

The Côte-Nord has long been inhabited by the Montagnais nation, a nomadic people that lived mainly by hunting and fishing. In the mid-19th century however, many white families from the Îles-de-la-Madeleine and Gaspésie settled in the region, disrupting this way of life and leading to the founding of the Essipit Native Reserve in 1903.

The reserve has nature trails, craft shops and a whale-watching tower.

Pointe-aux-Outardes
(pop. 1,540)

Magnificent **Parc Régional de Pointe-aux-Outardes** (see p 483) is at the end of the headland.

Return to Rte. 138 E. and continue to Baie-Comeau.

Baie-Comeau
(pop. 25,000)

In 1936, when Colonel Robert McCormick, publisher and senior editor of *The Chicago Tribune*, no longer wanted to be dependant upon foreign paper-making companies, he chose to build his own paper factory in Baie-Comeau, sparking the transformation of a quiet village into a bustling mill. Over the years, other large companies were attracted to Baie-Comeau by the abundance and low cost of

local hydroelectric power. The young town is named after Napoléon Comeau (1845-1923), famed trapper, geologist and naturalist of the Côte-Nord.

Baie-Comeau is divided into two distinct sections separated by a 4km-long rocky strip. The Mingan area, to the west, is the commercial and working-class part of town and is dominated by the Cathédrale Saint-Jean-Eudes (*987 Boulevard Joliet*). The Marquette area, to the east, is the sight of much of the town's heavy industry as well as a number of pleasant residential streets where many mill and factory executives have lived. A ferry regularly crosses the St. Lawrence between Baie-Comeau and Matane. The 2hr 30min crossing is a good way to appreciate the huge width of the river in this particular spot (it is over 30km wide here).

The first hydroelectric dams in Québec were built by private companies for industrial use and to provide electricity to nearby residents. Some of these companies held monopolies on the energy produced in large regions. Eventually, the Québec government nationalized most of the electric companies in 1964. From then on, Hydro-Québec took over and significantly expanded energy production to attract industries with large energy requirements and to export electricity to the United States.

The **Centre d'information d'Hydro-Québec** ★ *(135 Boulevard Comeau,* ☎*294-3923 or 800-ENERGIE)* is an information centre on hydro-electricity production in Québec and is a worthwhile stop to make before visiting the Manicouagan generating stations. The information presented gives an idea of how best to get around the sometimes overwhelmingly large facilities.

Manicouagan

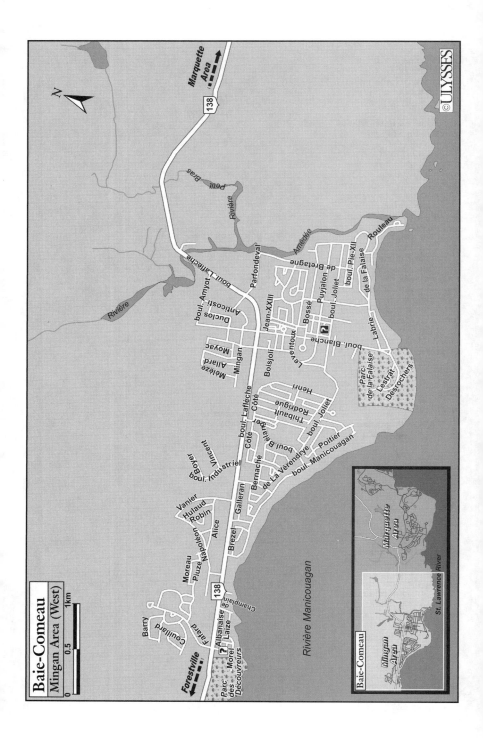

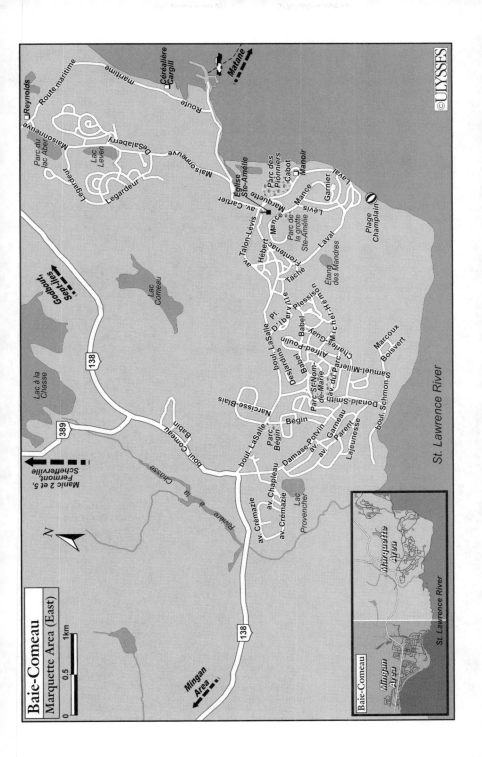

The **Centrales Manic 2 and Manic 5 (Barrage Daniel-Johnson)** ★★★ *(free admission; every day from late Jun to early Sep, 90min tour at 9am, 11am, 1:30pm and 3:30am; take Rte. 389: Manic 2 is at Km 21 and Manic 5 at Km 221; ☎294-3923 or 866-LAMANIC)*, the generating stations and dam, are located on the Rivière Manicouagan. A 30min drive through the beautiful Canadian Shield landscape leads to the first dam of the Manic 2 complex, the largest hollow-joint gravity dam in the world. A guided tour of the dam brings visitors inside the imposing structure. A 3hr drive farther north leads to the more impressive Manic 5 and the Daniel-Johnson dam. Built in 1968, the dam is named after a Québec premier who died on the morning the dam was officially declared completed. With a 214m central arch and measuring 1,314m in length, it is the largest multiple-arch structure in the world. The dam regulates the water supply to the generating stations of the Manic-Outardes complex. Visitors can walk to the foot of the dam as well as to the top, where there is a magnificent view of the Vallée de la Manicouagan and the reservoir, which measures 2,000km².

★
**Godbout
(pop. 390)**

The town of Godbout sits in a picturesque location on a bay. It is a marvellous spot for sport fishing, with both the salt water of the St. Lawrence and the rapids of Rivière Godbout offering good fishing opportunities. It is not surprising that local figure Napoléon Comeau chose to settle here to pursue his activities as fisherman, guide and naturalist. Comeau was familiar with traditional native medicines and identified many species of fish unknown to Canadian and

American scientists. A plaque in his memory, designed by sculptor Jean Bailleul, is on display near the church.

Most items displayed in the small, private **Musée Amérindien et Inuit** ★ *($3; late Jun to Oct every day 9am to 10pm; 134 Chemin Pascal-Comeau, ☎568-7306)* do not come from the Côte-Nord, but rather from the Canadian Yukon Territory and Nunavut. Nevertheless, these collections of Inuit art, gathered by the founder of the museum, Claude Grenier, are very interesting. Of particular note are the Inuit soapstone carvings.

Turn right onto the small road that leads to Pointe-des-Monts.

★
Pointe-des-Monts

At Pointe-des-Monts, the river widens to look like an ocean (it is almost 100km wide at Sept Îles). Winds continuously buffet the coastal towns located farther and farther apart as you travel eastward. Although the area was visited regularly by Europeans during the 16th century, its daunting weather conditions discouraged colonisation. Apart from a few fur-trading posts and one or two missions established under the French Regime, the first permanent residence in the area, a lighthouse, was built in the 19th century.

In 1805, after many ships were damaged or lost along the coast near Pointe-des-Monts, Québec port authorities decided to set up lighthouses along the river to reduce the risk of accidents. The Pointe-des-Monts lighthouse, built in 1829 and known as the **Phare de Pointe-des-Monts** ★ *($2.50; mid-Jun to mid-Sep, every day 9am to 6pm; 1830 Chemin du Vieux Phare;*

☎939-2400) was one of these. It has seven floors, circular rooms, a fireplace and recessed cupboards. Today, the building houses a bed and breakfast and an information centre dealing with the lives of lighthouse keepers.

Return to Rte. 138 and head east.

At this point the Manicouagan region gives way to the more rugged Duplessis region (see p 490), parts of which resemble the northern taiga forest region.

Parks

The **Parc du Saguenay** ★★★ *(Tadoussac area)* is located along the St. Lawrence between Tadoussac and Baie des Ha!-Ha! (see also Saguenay section, p 468), near the gulf of the Rivière Saguenay. The park has three hiking trails that wind through the hilly countryside: the Fjord trail, the Colline de l'Anse à l'Eau trail and the Pointe de l'Islet trail. The last of these offers a magnificent view of the St. Lawrence.

The **Parc Marin du Saguenay–Saint-Laurent** ★★★ *(182 Rue de l'Église, Tadoussac, ☎235-4703 or 800-463-6769)* features the Fjord du Saguenay, the southern-most fjord in the world and was created to protect the area's exceptional aquatic wildlife. The fjord was carved out by glaciers; it is 276m deep near Cap Éternité and just 10m deep at the mouth. The distinctive geography in the fjord, created by glacial deposits, includes a basin where fauna and flora indigenous to the Arctic can be found. The top 20m of water in the Saguenay is fresh and its temperature varies between 15°C and

New Regulations for Whale-Watching Boats

In the Saguenay–St. Lawrence Marine Park, priority is on the conservation of animal and plant life. Due to the growing popularity of whale-watching, there is concern over the effect that a great number of boats in close proximity might have on these marine mammals. In 2002, new regulations were introduced to ensure that the disturbance to the whales is minimized. Boats are prohibited from getting closer than 200m (400m for belugas, which are more vulnerable) to whales and are obliged to adopt safe behaviour when they are within one nautical mile from a whale. These regulations are strictly enforced. If you will be operating a boat in the park, make sure you familiarize yourself with them.

18°C, whereas the deeper water is saline and maintains a temperature of approximately 1.5°C. This environment, a remainder of the ancient Goldthwait sea, supports wildlife such as the arctic shark and the beluga, creatures otherwise seen farther north.

A number of whale species frequent the region to feed on the marine organisms that proliferate here due to the constant oxygenation in the water. One of these, the blue whale, reaches lengths of 30m and is the largest mammal in the world. Seals and occasionally dolphins can be seen in the park as well.

From early on, European fishers took advantage of the abundance of marine life, with the result that some species were overhunted. Today, visitors can venture out on the river to observe the whales at close range. However, strict rules have been set to protect the animals from being mistreated, and boats must maintain a certain distance.

The **Parc Nature de Pointe-aux-Outardes ★** *($4; early Jun to early Sep, every day 8am to 6pm, Sep and Oct 8am to 5pm; 4 Rue Labrie Ouest, Pointe-aux-Outardes,* ☎*567-4226)* follows the river and has beautiful beaches. It is primarily known as one of the largest bird migration and nesting sites in Québec. More than 175 species of birds have been identified here. The park also has walking trails, a salt marsh, sand dunes, and stands of red pine.

Outdoor Activities

Cruises and Whale-Watching

Many agencies near the dock organize boat trips on the river:

Croisières AML *($45; early May to late Oct, 2 departures a day; 177 Rue des Pionniers, Tadoussac, departure from the Pier of Tadoussac and from Baie-Sainte-Catherine* ☎*235-4262 or 800-463-1292)*, offers whale-watching trips in large, comfortable boats that accommodate up to 300 people. The expedition lasts approximately 3hrs, with a selection of large, comfortable boats or rubber dinghies, which are very safe. Nature guides accompany the passengers. Departures from the Tadoussac and Baie-Sainte-Catherine piers. Cruises on the Saguenay are also offered.

Groupe Dufour *($40; May to Oct, 3 departures a day; 165 Rue du Bord-de-l'Eau, Tadoussac;* ☎*235-4421 or 800-561-0718)* offers excursions on large, comfortable boats such as the wonderful *Famille-Dufour II* catamaran. If you want to be closer to the action, the company also has a few large, powerful dinghies. Whale-watching excursions as well as cruises on the Saguenay are offered and have nature guides on board.

The **Croisières Neptune** *($36; mid-May to mid-Oct; 2hr tour at 6:30am, 9am, 11:30am, 2pm and 4:30pm; 507 Rue du Boisé, Bergeronnes,* ☎*232-6716)* whisks thrill-seekers into the heart of the fjord aboard 8m-long, well-equipped rubber dingies to watch the magnificent sea mammals frolicking about.

The Ross clan of Les Escoumins truly deserve the title **Les Pionniers des Baleines** (*$32.50; mid-May to mid-Oct three departures a day 2hr 15min cruise; 41 Rue des Pilotes, Les Escoumins,* ☎*233-3274*), or the "whale pioneers." They have two inflatable dinghies, each able to accommodate 12 passengers.

The **Gîte du Phare de Pointe-des-Monts** (*late Jun to early Sep; 2.5hr cruise: $25, 5hr cruise: $50; 1830 Chemin du Vieux Phare, Pointe-des-Monts,* ☎*939-2332*) organizes several fascinating excursions, which are a wonderful way to wind up a stay in this extraordinary place. Aboard a rubber dinghy or a small fishing boat, passengers can contemplate the seascape at the beginning of the Gulf of St. Lawrence and observe the sea mammals that live there.

Kayaking

Sea kayaks are completely different from river kayaks. They are stable enough to be taken out onto the ocean, giving kayakers, alone or in pairs, the freedom to observe whales and seals at very close range. Of course, you'll also need a little luck!

Remember that the mouth of the fjord du Saguenay is subject to very strong wind and waves. Inexperienced kayakers should go with a professional guide, and are advised to choose their guide carefully—not all in the Tadoussac area are recommended. Some bad experiences have been reported.

The following outfits provide kayak rentals and introductory

courses for this kind of adventure, and offer one- to five-day guided trips. The rates vary depending on the package: **Tayaout Plein Air** (*148 Rue du Bord-de-l'Eau, Tadoussac,* ☎*235-1056 or 888-766-1056*) and **Mer et Monde** (*53 Rue Principale, Bergeronnes,* ☎*232-6779 or 866-637-6663*).

Scuba Diving

Located within the Parc Marin du Saguenay et du Saint-Laurent, the Escoumins area attracts scuba divers year round. Four sites are accessible by land, about 20 others by boat. Divers who venture farther offshore should bear in mind that the strong currents, combined with the movement of the tides, can sweep them away in no time at all. The underwater scenery at the Quai des Pilotes in Les Escoumins is amazing. Huge numbers of anemones, starfish and sea urchins can be seen all along the steep wall.

A network of footbridges provides access to the sites and facilities, while the **Centre des Loisirs Marins des Escoumins** (*mid-May to mid-Oct; 41 Rue des Pilotes, Les Escoumins,* ☎*233-2860*) provides information and has changing rooms, showers where you can rinse off your gear, carts and a shop.

The underwater Pointe-des-Monts area is known for its "ship cemetery," as many a boat has gone down in this strategic spot at the base of the gulf since Europeans first arrived in the New World.

Hiking

The numerous short and medium-length trails that lace the Tadoussac area are fantastic, since they lead through radically different ecosystems.

Tadoussac is also the starting point of one of the most remarkable long trails in Québec: the strikingly beautiful **Sentier du Fjord** (☎*235-4238, ☎877-272-5229 for camping reservation, www.sepaq.com*). This 43km, intermediate trail starts near the Baie Sainte-Margerite. For almost its entire length, it offers a view of the mouth of the Saguenay, the cliffs, the capes, the river and the village. There is a rudimentary campground about 9km from the start. When you reach the end of the trail, you can continue hiking to Passe-Pierre, where you'll find another campground superbly laid out in an idyllic spot.

Birdwatching

The Tadoussac area is one of the best places in Québec to observe birds of prey. It is a potential migratory corridor. Specialists have counted phenomenal numbers of these creatures here. Keep your eyes peeled!

By entering the village on the left-hand access road, before the viaduct, you'll pass the back of the church. Take Rue de la Mer to the little park at **Pointe-à-John**, an excellent vantage point from which to view whales and scores of sea and shore birds on the sand bar. Winter is the most active time of year here.

Most people come to the **Cap-de-Bon-Désir park**

(Bergeronnes) to watch the whales from the shore, but birdwatchers will find a trail leading to a lookout that offers a magnificent view of the Baie de Bon-Désir, west of the cape.

If you plan on going to the edge of the **marsh in Saint-Paul-du-Nord** to observe the abundant bird life there, the first thing you should do is stop by the **Centre d'Interprétation des Marais Salés** *(741 Route 138, Longue-Rive, ☎231-1077)*, which is of invaluable assistance in planning any birdwatching activity in the area. The centre has a self-guided nature trail that makes it easier to tour the salt marsh and helps familiarize visitors with this captivating ecosystem.

Sainte-Anne-de-Portneuf boasts one of the best birdwatching areas in Québec: the **Barre de Portneuf**, also known as the Banc de Portneuf. This 4km-long sandy point, visible from the mainland, is very easy to get to. As many as 15,000 birds have been counted here in one day during the migratory season. The best time to go birdwatching here is from the end of July to the end of September, preferably when the tide is in and the birds are gathered on the inner shore. Access to the sandbank is gained by the parking lot at the north end.

Wide, sandy, wooded Manicouagan peninsula features several attractions: the Baie Henri-Grenier, Pointe-Lebel, Pointe-aux-Outardes and Pointe-Paradis beach, all of which are teeming with shore birds. There is some interesting birdwatching to be done here from mid-April to the end of September.

The area around the **Pointe-des-Monts lighthouse** is known as an excellent place to

observe numerous species of sea birds. Because they are so isolated and located so far out into the river, Pointe-des-Monts and its old lighthouse attract scores of red-tailed loons and other divers.

Dogsledding

The **Maison Majorique** youth hostel organizes guided dogsled rides *($55 for a half-day, 18km or 20km tour; ☎235-4372)*. Clients are accompanied by a guide and get to "drive."

Accommodations

Tadoussac

Camping Tadoussac
$
428 Rue du Bateau-Passeur
☎*235-4501 or 888-868-6666*
⇒*235-4902*
www.essipit.com
No place offers a more stunning panoramic view than Camping Tadoussac, which looks out over the bay and the village.

Maison Majorique
$
sb
158 Rue du Bateau-Passeur
☎*235-4372 or 800-461-8585*
⇒*235-4608*
The Maison Majorique is Tadoussac's youth hostel. It has dormitories, private rooms, even campsites in summer, and they offer a whole variety of outdoor activities as well as reasonably priced cafeteria meals. Beach.

La Mer Veilleuse
$$ bkfst incl.
⊗, ℜ, *sb*
113 de la Coupe-de-L'Islet
☎*235-4396*
⇒*235-1142*
A small, tastefully decorated hotel, La Mer Veilleuse has a lovely view of the river. The hotel offers excellent breakfasts, and the service is efficient and courteous. Beach.

Gîte Vue du Perron
$$ bkfst incl.
K, 🐾, sb
261 Rue Champlain
☎*235-4929*
⇒*235-1173*
Perched on a hill in the village, Le Gîte Vue du Perron is a great place for families or groups of four since it offers an apartment with two rooms.

Maison Hovington
$$ bkfst incl.
May to Oct
285 Rue des Pionniers
☎*235-4466*
☎*(514) 671-4656 (off-season)*
⇒*235-4897*
Set up in an old, beautiful home facing the river, the Maison Hovington offers a superb view. The rooms are well-maintained.

Maison Clauphi
$$ bkfst incl.
sb
mid-May to mid-Oct
188 Rue des Pionniers
☎*235-4303*
⇒*235-4303*
www.clauphi.com
The Maison Clauphi has an inn, a motel with small rooms, and a few little cabins. It is well-located in the village and offers all sorts of outdoor activities as well as bike rentals.

🦞 La Galouïne
$$ bkfst incl.
pb/sb, K
251 Rue des Pionniers
☎*235-4380*
"Galouïne" is an Acadian word meaning a storm wind. Not to

Manicougan

worry though—you'll be protected from the elements under the roof of this pleasant little B&B! This isn't Acadia, but the Madelinot (from the Iles de la Madeleine) origins of the kindly hosts explains the name given to this huge house made even bigger by long balconies. Marie-Line, who decorated the inviting guest rooms, gave them a creative, personal touch. The warm or bright colours that dominate inside and out add loads of charm. There are two guest rooms in the attic, for even more country cachet! A well equipped kitchen is available to guests who want to prepare their own simple meals.

Maison Harvey-Lessard
$$
≡, ✪, ⊛
early Jun to early Nov
16 Rue Bellevue
☎*235-4802 or 827-5505*
⇋*827-6926*
harveylessard.com
The balconies of La Maison Harvey-Lessard have some of the most spectacular views in Tadoussac. Pleasant, tastefully decorated rooms.

Le Béluga
$$
ℜ
191 Rue des Pionniers
☎*235-4784*
⇋*235-4295*
www.le-beluga.qc.ca
Conveniently located in the town, Le Béluga hotel-motel has spacious, comfortable rooms.

Hôtel Tadoussac
$$$$$
≈, ℜ
mid-May to mid-Oct
165 Rue du Bord-de-l'Eau
☎*235-4421 or 800-561-0718*
⇋*235-4607*
www.familledufour.com
Located by the river, the Hôtel Tadoussac (see p 478) resembles a late 19th-century manor house and is distinguished by its bright red roof. The hotel, made famous as the backdrop for the movie

Hotel New Hampshire, is not as comfortable as one might expect.

Bergeronnes

Camping Bon Désir
$
🐕
198 route 138
☎*232-6297*
☎*232-6326 (off-season)*
⇋*232-1019*
Located by the river, the Camping Bon Désir offers an outstanding panoramic view and direct access to the sea for kayakers. You can also enjoy some whale-watching while you're here.

Auberge La Rosepierre
$$ bkfst incl.
pb/sb, ℜ, ⊛
66 Rue Principale
☎*232-6543 or 888-264-6543*
⇋*232-6215*
www.rosepierre.com
Auberge La Rosepierre is a superb inn with comfortable, elegant rooms. Various kinds of Québec granite have been incorporated into the structure, a subject the owners are passionate about. The granite does not create a chilly atmosphere; on the contrary, you'll feel right at home as soon as you arrive. Bike rentals.

Pointe-Lebel

Le Camping de la Mer
$
🐕, ≈, ℜ
72 Rue Chouinard
☎*589-6576*
⇋*295-2670*
There is a place on the Manicougan peninsula that will seem like heaven on earth to anyone who likes powdery beaches. Camping de la Mer is for people who want to enjoy everything the sea and the shore have to offer. Hiking trails, horseback riding, birdwatching and, to top it all off, one of the longest beaches in Québec.

Les Tourne-Pierres
$$ bkfst incl.
18 Rue Chouinard
☎*589-5432*
⇋*589-1430*
Les Tourne-Pierres, a pleasant house with a family atmosphere, is an outstanding bed and breakfast. The hosts are as hospitable as can be and have a passion for their part of the province. Furthermore, the place is located near a unique natural area where you can enjoy a whole slew of outdoor activities.

Baie-Comeau

La Caravelle
$$
ℜ, 🐕, ≈, ℜ, △
202 Boulevard LaSalle
☎*296-4986 or 800-463-4986*
⇋*296-4622*
Anyone who visits Baie-Comeau regularly knows about La Caravelle, a hotel-motel that looks out over the town from atop a hill. It has 70 rooms, a number of which are available at low rates. Some rooms are equipped with a water bed and all with a fireplace.

Le Petit Château
$$-$$$ bkfst incl.
≡
2370 Boulevard Laflèche
☎*295-3100*
⇋*295-3225*
What, you might ask, is that splendid house in its own little Garden of Eden right in the middle of town? Le Petit Château, a bed and breakfast, has a simple, country atmosphere but is nonetheless inviting.

Hôtel le Manoir
$$-$$$$
≡, ℜ, ☉, ℜ, ✪, ⊛
8 Rue Cabot
☎*296-3391 or 800-463-8567*
⇋*296-1435*
The beautiful stone building next to the water is L'Hôtel le Manoir. The hotel offers spacious and bright rooms.

Ask for a room overlooking the river. Beach.

Godbout

 **Gîte Aux Berges**
$
ℜ, sb
Apr to Sep
180 Rue Pascal-Comeau
☎*568-7816*
⇢*568-7833*
www.maisonnette-chalet-quebec.com
Any way you look at it, Aux Berges is one of the best bed and breakfast on the Côte-Nord. The rooms are simple and the place is far from luxurious, but the graciousness of the hosts, the tourist services available to guests and the sophisticated regional cuisine make all the difference. This is a place to kick back and relax in the heart of a fascinating village. Aux Berges also rents out log cabins, located near the main building. Beach.

Pointe-des-Monts

Gîte du Phare de Pointe-des-Monts
$$ bkfst incl.
✗*, pb/sb*
mid-Jun to mid-Sep
Rte du Vieux Fort
☎*939-2332*
☎*598-8408 (off season)*
www.pointe-des-monts.com
The Gîte du Phare de Pointe-des-Monts offer five comfortable rooms in a setting that has been declared a historic monument. The location, on the banks of the St. Lawrence, makes for an unforgettable stay.

Restaurants

Tadoussac

Le Gibard
$
early May to late Oct
137 Rue du Bord-de-l'Eau
☎*235-4534*
Le Gibard is a small café-bar where you can leisurely sip a bowl of delicious café au lait in the morning or a glass of cold beer in the afternoon. Simple meals are also prepared. The place is attractive, with its large windows overlooking the port and the river.

Café Bohème
$
239 Rue des Pionniers
☎*235-1180*
Tadoussac's old general store has been reborn as Café Bohème, an inviting place for a taste of the bohemian lifestyle. Comfortably ensconced on the terrace with a view of the comings and goings, or within its wood-panelled walls adorned with attractive photographs, this is a choice spot to enjoy an espresso, a sandwich, a salad, or a decadent dessert.

Au Père Coquart Café
$-$$
early Jun to Oct
115 Rue de la Coupe-de-L'Islet
☎*235-1170*
On a small street perpendicular to Rue Bord-de-l'Eau is an inviting café named in honour of the Jesuit Father who built the old Tadoussac chapel. Au Père Coquart Café serves standard food and regional specialities in the same relaxed atmosphere that you find just about everywhere in this village.

Café du Fjord
$$
154 Rue du Bateau-Passeur
☎*235-4626*
The Café du Fjord is very popular. A seafood buffet is offered for lunch, and nights are livened up with shows or with dance music.

Restaurant la Bolée
$$$-$$$$
164 Rue Morin
☎*235-4750*
Try Restaurant la Bolée for simple but tasty meals like stuffed crepes. It is also a good place to come later on in the evening for a drink. There is a bakery below the restaurant.

Bergeronnes

 **Auberge La Rosepierre**
$$-$$$
66 Rue Principale
☎*232-6543*
An inn with a unique charm about it, Auberge La Rosepierre (see p 486) has a tastefully decorated dining room with a table d'hôte featuring regional flavours and cooking methods. Naturally, fish and seafood dishes occupy a large part of the menu and are always prepared with flair.

Les Escoumins

Restaurant Le Bouleau
$$$-$$$$
Complexe Hôtelier Pelchat
445 Rte 138
☎*233-2401*
In addition to its spectacular view, Restaurant Le Bouleau at the Complexe Hôtelier Pelchat offers a wide range of local seafood dishes, all well prepared.

Manicouagan

Baie-Comeau

Les 3 Barils
$$-$$$
200 Boulevard LaSalle
☎**296-3681**
Les 3 Barils is an unpretentious place serving simple fare.

 Le Manoir
$$$
8 Rue Cabot
☎**296-3391**
The hotel restaurant at Le Manoir (see p 486) has a well-established reputation. In an extremely inviting and luxurious decor, guests dine on expertly prepared cuisine worthy of the most elaborate praise. A meeting place for businesspeople and industrialists, it will also appeal to tourists, who will enjoy the unique view of the bay and the holiday atmosphere that pervades the outdoor seating area. Outstanding wine list.

Pointe-des-Monts

Phare de Pointe-des-Monts
$$$
route du Vieux Fort
☎**939-2332**
Phare de Pointe-des-Monts, located in a quiet little bay, specializes in fresh seafood dishes. The cuisine is excellent and the service, impeccable.

Entertainment

Bars and Nightclubs

Tadoussac

Find out what acts are booked at the **Café du Fjord** *(154 Rue du Bateau-Passeur,* ☎*235-4626)*, where big names in rock, jazz and blues perform from June to the end of August.

Festivals and Cultural Events

Tadoussac

In the middle of June, the **Festival de la Chanson de Tadoussac** *(*☎*235-4108, www.chansontadoussac.com)* is held in various local bars. This string of shows spotlights well-known singers and up-and-coming artists.

Shopping

Tadoussac

In a village where you can find every kind of souvenir imaginable, the **Boutique Nima** *(231 Rue des Pionniers,* ☎*235-4858)* stands out for quality, selling magnificent Aboriginal art.

Métiers d'Art du Rivage
251 Rue des Pionniers
☎**235-4380**
Located on the ground floor of La Galouïne bed and breakfast (see p 485), this lovely shop

carries original items, most of which hand crafted with sand on the Îles de la Madeleine. Made of sand, the pitchers, vases, knick-knacks, book ends and plenty of other items are truly impressive. You'll also find jewellery and assorted objects inspired by a whole host of items that have washed up on the beaches on the islands. Marie-Line, the pleasant proprietor, will giftwrap your purchases with flair.

La Boutique du Photographe
239 Rue des Pionniers
☎**235-1180**
Occupying one end of Café Bohème (see p 487), which also provides wall space for photo exhibitions, La Boutique du Photographe (the photography shop) provides as much pleasure to those who enjoy taking pictures as to those who simply like to look at them.

Duplessis is a vast,

remote region bordered to the south for almost 1,000km by the Gulf of St. Lawrence and to the north by Labrador.

Its small population of francophones, anglophones and the Montagnais First Nation is concentrated along the St. Lawrence coast and in a few inland mining towns. The region is far from any large urban centres, and its economy has always been based on natural resources. Aboriginals have lived in the region for thousands of years. In the 16th century, Basque and Breton fishers and whalers set up seasonal posts in the region. Today, the important economic activities are fishing, forestry, and iron and titanium mining. Additional jobs are provided by a large aluminum smelter, which was built in Sept-Îles to take advantage of the availability of hydroelectricity.

The region's most celebrated son is popular Québec singer Gilles Vigneault, who has written songs that describe life in this corner of the province. From Natashquan eastward, the small towns that dot the coast are not linked to the rest of Québec by road. Duplessis is an area of expansive wilderness rich in a variety of flora and fauna. With the added attraction of its remoteness, the region offers excellent hunting and fishing opportunities. Of particular interest to some visitors are the magnificent Île d'Anticosti and the beautiful Mingan archipelago.

The Duplessis region encompasses the middle and lower half of Côte-Nord. To explore this isolated part of Québec, we have suggested two tours:

Tour A: Minganie ★

Tour B: Gilles Vigneault Country ★★

Finding Your Way Around

Tour A: Minganie

This tour can be linked to the Côte-Nord tour (see p 476) of the Manicouagan region. The first town on the tour is Pointe-aux-Anglais, which has been part of the municipality of Rivière-Pentecôte for several years now. The town of Rivière-Pentecôte itself is located 12km north. This tour ends at Havre-St-Pierre.

By Car

Route 138 provides access to much of this region before ending at Havre-Saint-Pierre.

By Plane

Les Ailes de Gaspé (☎418-368-1995) offers charter flights in this region.

During the summer and the Christmas season, **Air Satellite** (☎418-589-8923) offers daily flights from Rimouski, Sept-Îles, Baie-Comeau, Havre-Saint-Pierre and Longue-Pointe-de-Mingan.

Confortair (☎418-968-4660 or 800-353-4660) offers charter flights to Île d'Anticosti.

Bus Stations

Sept-Îles
126 Rue Monseigneur Blanche
☎(418) 962-2126

Havre-Saint-Pierre
843 Boulevard de l'Escale
☎(418) 538-2033

By Train

QNS&L
☎(418) 968-7803
The train links Sept-Îles to Schefferville and runs three times a week in summer and twice times a week in winter. The trip lasts from 10 to 12hrs and crosses the Canadian Shield to the outlying tundra.

By Boat

The **Relais Nordik** cargo boat (Apr to Jan; reservations required; ☎418-723-8787 or 800-463-0680) leaves from Sept-Îles and travels to Port-Menier, Havre-Saint-Pierre, Natashquan, Kegaska, La Romaine, Harrington Harbour, Tête-à-la-Baleine, La Tabatière, Saint-Augustin, Vieux-Fort and Blanc-Sablon. There is only one departure a week, so check the schedule before planning a trip.

Tour B: Gilles Vigneault Country

In 1996, Route 138 was extend to reach Natashquan. However, during the summer, only hydroplanes and weekly supply boats from Havre-Saint-Pierre link the inhabitants of the scattered villages farther east to the rest of Québec. In the winter, snow and ice provide a natural route for snowmobiles between villages. The following tour will be of particular interest to those who really love the outdoors and want to get away from the stress and bustle of the city.

Practical Information

Area code: **418**

Tourist Information

Regional Office

Association Touristique Régionale de Duplessis
312 Avenue Brochu, Sept-Îles
G4R 2W6
☎962-0808 or 888-463-0808
≈962-6518
www.tourismecote-nord.com

Tour A: La Minganie

Corporation touristique de Sept-Îles
1401 Boulevard Laure Ouest,
G4R 4K1
☎962-1238 or 888-880-1238
≈968-0022

Havre-Saint-Pierre
957 Rue de la Berge
☎538-2512

Tour B: Gilles Vigneault Country

Natashquan
33 Allée des Galets
☎726-3756

Exploring

Tour A: Minganie

Duration of tour: four days

Beyond Pointe-des-Monts (in Manicouagan) the region quickly becomes deserted as forests and cliffs give way to windswept coastal plains. Just north of the main road, an uninhabited region begins that stretches to the North Pole and beyond.

Minganie takes its name from the islands of the Mingan archipelago and is known for its rushing salmon-filled rivers. Whale hunting attracted the first settlers to the Côte-Nord, but has now been replaced by whale-watching, an activity that can be enjoyed all along the coast.

Few vestiges of Minganie's colonial past have survived. The long-ago presence of Basque fishers and French settlers can be confirmed only by archaeologists.

During the Second World War, German submarines ventured close to the coast of Minganie, using the same passage as European supply ships and cargo boats. Local residents reported seeing submarines surface not far from their homes. Apparently, German soldiers even secretly left their boats to purchase food and liquor.

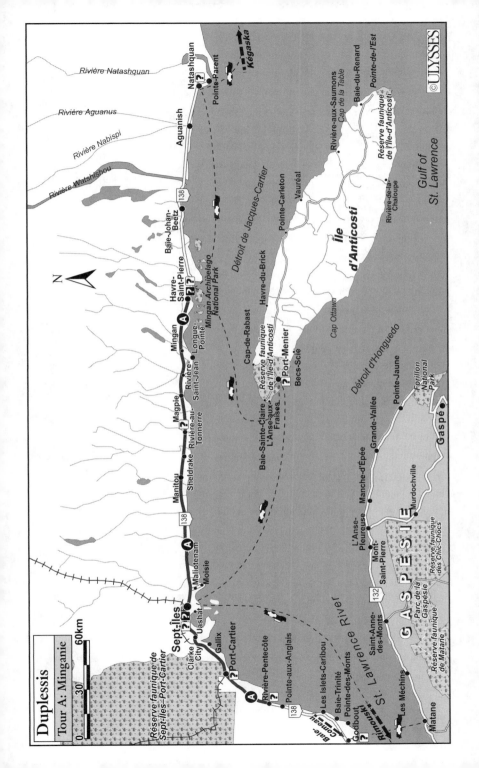

Rivière-Pentecôte
(pop. 640)

The British army attempted to take New France by force on several occasions. In 1711, during the Spanish Civil War, a large fleet commanded by Admiral Walker was sent from England to take Québec. However, due to fog on the St. Lawrence, the British ships ran aground on the Île-aux-Œufs reefs. The point of land just across the reefs was thereby named Pointe-aux-Anglais, in honour the ill-fated expedition; it is now part of Rivière-Pentecôte.

The **Musée Louis-Langlois** ★ *($2; end of Jun to early Sep, every day 10am to 5pm; 2088 Route Mgr-Labrie in Pointe-aux-Anglais,* ☎*799-2262 or 799-2212)* features an exhibit on the shipwreck of Admiral Walker's fleet in 1711. Vestiges retrieved from the sunken ships help tell the story of this maritime catastrophe that, thankfully, was followed by many decades of peace.

Réserve Faunique de Sept-Îles–Port-Cartier ★ see p 498.

Continue along Rte. 138 to Sept-Îles.

Sept-Îles
(pop. 26,000)

This town, which extends along the vast Baie de Sept-Îles (45km²), is the administrative centre of the Côte Nord. A fur-trading post under the French Regime, Sept-Îles experienced an industrial boom in the early 20th century sparked by the development of the forestry industry. By about 1950, Sept-Îles had become an important relay point in the transport of iron and coal, resources extracted from the Schefferville and Fermont mines and sent to Sept-Îles by railroad. The town's deep-water port is ice-free during the winter and ranks second in Canada after Montréal in terms of tonnage handled annually. Sept-Îles is named after the archipelago of seven islands in the entrance to the bay. The town is a good starting point for exploring the northern regions of Labrador and Nord-du-Québec.

The **Vieux-Poste** ★ *($3.25; late Jun to late Aug, every day 9am to 5pm; Boulevard des Montagnais,* ☎*968-2070)* is a reconstruction of the important Sept-Îles fur-trading post established during the French Regime. Based on archaeological excavations and documents from the period, the compound appears as it would have in the mid-18th century, complete with a chapel, stores, houses and protective wooden fences. Montagnais culture is explored through exhibits and various outdoor activities that vary by season.

The **Musée Régional de la Côte-Nord** ★ *($4; summer, every day 9am to 5pm; rest of the year, Mon-Fri 9am to noon, 1pm to 5pm, Sat and Sun 1pm to 5pm; 500 Boulevard Laure,* ☎*968-2070),* displays some 40,000 objects of anthropological and artistic importance found during the many archaeological excavations carried out along the Côte-Nord, as well as mounted wildlife, Aboriginal objects and contemporary artistic works (paintings, sculptures and photographs) from various regions of Québec.

The **Musée Innu Shaputuan** *($3; 290 Boulevard des Montagnais,* ☎*962-4000)* has a captivating exhibit on the history and culture of the Montagnais of the Côte-Nord. The museum is connected to an excellent restaurant whose menu offers delicious local cuisine with impeccable service. A remarkable and promising initiative.

The **Parc du Vieux-Quai**, on Baie des Sept-Îles, is the most popular summer recreation spot in the area. The park has many points from which visitors can enjoy the magnificent view of the distant islands. Several local artists also display their work here.

Parc de l'Archipel des Sept-Îles ★ ★ see p 498.

Return to Route 138 E.. After De Grasse, turn right and head to Maliotenam and Moisie.

Mingan
(pop. 400)

Montagnais and non-Aboriginals live together in this village located on the mainland opposite the Îles de Mingan. The name Mingan, of Celtic origin *(Maen Cam),* means "curved stone," and refers to rock formations on the islands. The formations made an impression on early visitors from Brittany, reminding them of ancient stones and dolmens. Mingan is also a major salmon-fishing location.

★
Havre-Saint-Pierre
(pop. 3,520)

This small picturesque town was founded in 1857 by fishers from the Îles-de-la-Madeleine. In 1948, following the discovery of large titanium deposits 43km inland, the town's economy was transformed overnight by the QIT-Feret-Titarle company. It became an active industrial centre and port. Since the opening of the Mingan Archipelago National Park Reserve in 1983, Havre-Saint-Pierre has also developed a significant tourism industry. The town is an excellent starting point for visitors who want to explore the Îles de Mingan and the large Île d'Anticosti.

The **Centre Culturel et d'Interprétation de Havre-**

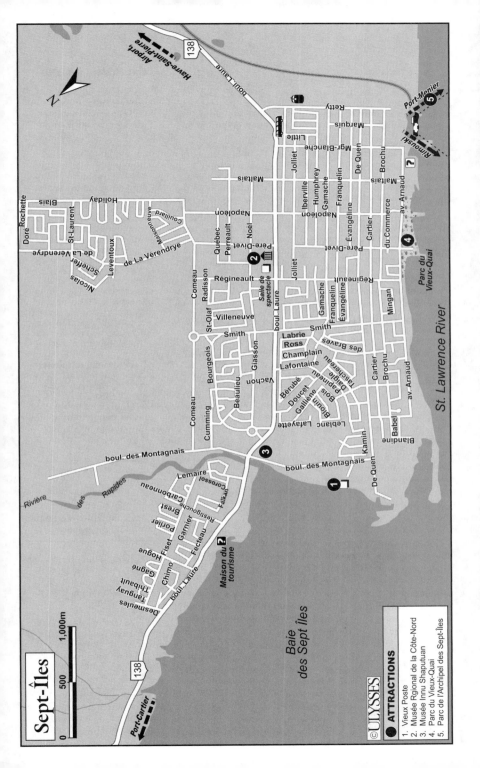

Sept-Îles

0   500   1,000m

138 Port-Cartier
138 Havre-Saint-Pierre
Airport

N

Baie des Sept Îles

St. Lawrence River

Port-Menier
Rimouski

© ULYSSES

ATTRACTIONS

1. Vieux Poste
2. Musée Rgional de la Côte-Nord
3. Musée Innu Shaputuan
4. Parc du Vieux-Quai
5. Parc de l'Archipel des Sept-Îles

Rivière des Rapides
boul. des Montagnais
boul. des Montagnais
boul. Laure
Maison du tourisme
Desmeules
Thibault
Tanguay
Gagne
Hogue
Chimo
Fiser
Garnier
Portier
Brest
Carbonneau
Restigouche
Corossol
Falkan
Fecteau
Lemaire
De Quen
Kamin
Leblanc
Lafayette
Bois
Blouin
Doucet
Papineau
Gallienne
Béruge
Tischereau
Daigle
Lafontaine
Champlain
Ross
Labrie
des Braves
Smith
Gamache
Franquelin
Régineault
Évangéline
Mingan
Cartier
Brochu
av. Arnaud
Babel
Blandine
Père-Divet
du Commerce
De Quen
Évangéline
Franquelin
Gamache
Humphrey
Iberville
Jolliet
Napoléon
Marquis
Mgr-Blanche
Retry
Little
Mallais
Napoléon
Noël
Quebec
Perreault
Père-Divet
Régineault
Salle de spectacle
Smith
Villeneuve
Giasson
Beaulieu
Vachon
Comeau
Cumming
Bourgeois
St-Olaf
Radisson
Comeau
Gouillard
Maisonneuve
Holiday
Blais
Doré Rochette
St-Laurent
de La Vérendrye
Leventoux
Scheffer
Nicolas
de La Vérendrye
Jolliet
Mallais
Cartier
av. Arnaud
Brochu
Parc du Vieux-Quai

Saint-Pierre ★ *($2; early Jul to early Sep, every day 10am to 10pm; 957 Rue de la Berge,* ☎*538-2512 or 538-2450)* is an information centre in the Clark family's former general store, which has been skilfully restored. Local history is recounted with an exhibit and slide show.

Centre d'Accueil et d'Inter-prétation, Réserve de Parc National de l'Archipel-de-Mingan *(free admission; mid-Jun to late Aug; 975 Rue de l'Escale,* ☎*538-5264)* is the information centre for the Mingan Archipelago park. Here, visitors will find a photo exhibit as well as information concerning the flora, fauna and geology of the Mingan islands.

Mingan Archipelago National Park Reserve ★★ see p 498.

Île d'Anticosti is accessible by the Nordik Express cargo boat, or by plane with Inter-Cana-dian.

★★ Île d'Anticosti (pop. 340)

The presence of Aboriginals on Île d'Anticosti goes back many years. The Montagnais made sporadic visits to the island, but the harsh climate discouraged

permanent settlement. In 1542, Basque fishers named the island "Anti Costa," which roughly means "anti-coast," or "after travelling all this way across the Atlantic, we still haven't reached the mainland!" In 1679, Louis Jolliet was given the island by the King of France for leading important expeditions into the middle of the North American conti-nent. Jolliet's efforts to settle Anticosti were limited by the island's isolation, poor soil and high winds. To make matters much worse, British troops returning from a failed bid to take Québec City in 1690 were shipwrecked on the island and slaughtered most of the settlers living there. Anticosti is feared by sailors, because more than 400 ships have run aground here since the 17th century.

In 1895, Île d'Anticosti became the exclusive property of Henri Menier, a French choc-olate tycoon. The "Cocoa Baron" introduced white-tailed deer and foxes to the island to create a personal hunting preserve. In addition, he es-tablished the villages of Baie-Sainte-Claire (later aban-doned) and Port-Menier, now the only settlement on the island. Menier governed the island like an absolute mon-arch reigning over his subjects. He established forestry opera-tions on the island and com-missioned a cod-fishing fleet. In 1926, his heirs sold Anticosti to a consortium of Canadian forestry companies named Wayagamack, which continued operations until 1974, when the island was sold to the Québec govern-ment and became a wildlife reserve. Not until 1983 were residents given the right to purchase land and houses on the island. Anticosti, still unexplored in parts, holds many surprises, such as the **Grotte à la Patate** cave (see p 499), discovered in 1982.

Port-Menier (pop. 280)

Port-Menier, where the ferry from Havre-Saint-Pierre docks, is the only inhabited village on the island. Most village houses were built dur-ing the Menier era, giving the village a certain architectural uniformity.

Foundations of the **Château Menier** (1899), an elaborate wooden villa built in the American Shingle style, can be seen from Route de Baie-Sainte-Claire. Because the villagers could not adequately maintain the spectacular es-tate, they set fire to it in 1954, reducing an irreplaceable historic building to ashes. In **Baie-Sainte-Claire**, visitors can see the remains of a lime kiln built in 1897, the only vestige of the short-lived village that once stood on this site.

The **Écomusée d'Anticosti ★** *(free admission; late Jun to late Aug, every day 10am to 8pm;* ☎*535-0250 or 535-0311)* displays photographs taken around the turn of the 20th century, when Henri Menier owned Île d'Anticosti.

Réserve Faunique de l'Île d'Anticosti ★★ see p 499.

Tour B: Gilles Vigneault Country

Duration of tour: three to five days

"Mon pays, ce n'est pas un pays, c'est l'hiver," ("My coun-try is not a country, it is win-ter"), is how Gilles Vigneault describes this subarctic part of the world, where icebergs can be seen in the distance in mid-July. Animals such as bears, moose, walrus, seals, and whales can be spotted throughout the region. The area was colonized in the mid-19th century; previously it was visited for some time by fur

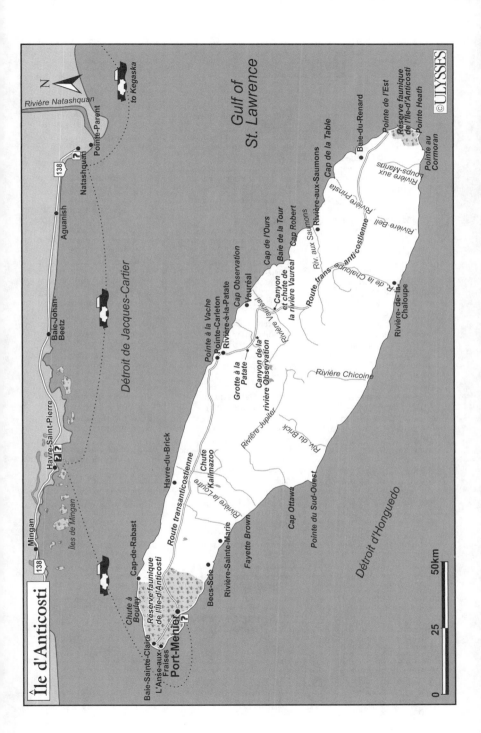

Île d'Anticosti

© ULYSSES

traders and cod-fishing vessels. Francophone, Montagnais and anglophone villages dot the coast. Some of the anglophone villages, originally inhabited by fishers from the Isle of Jersey (in the English Channel), have very little geographical or sentimental attachment to Québec. The lower Côte-Nord, with its wooden fishing cabins and old docks, has retained much of its original character.

Baie-Johan-Beetz
(pop. 100)

Originally known as "Piastrebaie," due to its location at the mouth of the Rivière Piashti, this village was renamed after the learned Belgian naturalist Johan Beetz in 1918. Piastrebaie was founded around 1860 by Joseph Tanguay, who, along with his wife, Marguerite Murdock, earned a living here fishing salmon. Over the following years, a number of immigrants from the Îles-de-la-Madeleine arrived. These included the Bourque, Loyseau, Desjardins and Devost families, whose descendants still live mainly on hunting and fishing.

Maison Johan-Beetz ★ *($3; early Jun to mid-Sep, every day 9am to 5pm; reservations recommended; 15 Rue Johan-Beetz,* ☎*539-0137).* Johan Beetz was born in 1874 at the Oudenhouven castle in Brabant, Belgium. Grief-stricken over the death of his fiancée, he wanted to take off for the Congo, but a friend convinced him to emigrate to Canada instead. A hunting and fishing fanatic, he visited the Côte-Nord, and soon set up residence there. In 1898, he married a Canadian and built this charming Second Empire–style house, which can be visited by appointment. Beetz painted lovely still-lifes on the doors inside. In 1903, he became something of a pioneer in the fur industry

when he started breeding animals for their pelts, which he sold to the Maison Revillon in Paris.

Johan Beetz contributed greatly his neighbours' quality of life. Thanks to his university studies, he had learned the rudiments of medicine and became the man of science in whom the villagers placed their trust. Equipped with books and makeshift instruments, he treated the ills of the inhabitants of the Côte-Nord as best he could. He even managed to save the village from Spanish influenza with a skilfully monitored quarantine. If you ask the elderly people here to tell you about Monsieur Beetz, you'll hear nothing but praise.

The **Refuge d'Oiseaux de Watshishou** ★ *(east of the village)* is a bird sanctuary that houses several colonies of aquatic birds.

★
Natashquan
(pop. 400)

This small fishing village, with its wooden houses buffeted by the wind, is where the famous poet and songwriter Gilles Vigneault was born in 1928. Many of his songs describe the people and scenery of the Côte-Nord. He periodically returns to Natashquan for inspiration and still owns a house here. In the Montagnais language, Natashquan means "place where bears are hunted." The neighbouring village of Pointe-Parent is inhabited by Montagnais.

★
Harrington Harbour
(pop. 315)

Set apart by its makeshift wooden sidewalks, the modest anglophone fishing village of Harrington Harbour is located on a small island. The rocky terrain ruled out a conventional village layout, leading

inhabitants to link their houses by slightly elevated wooden footbridges.

Heading east, supply boats wind through a multitude of striking bare and rocky islands that look like something from another planet.

★
Tête-à-la-Baleine
(pop. 350)

Tête-à-la-Baleine, the sixth stop on the supply-boat route, is a picturesque village where seals are still hunted. Fishers from Tête-à-la-Baleine move to Île Providence during the summer in order to get closer to good fishing sites. However this tradition is quickly falling out of favour, and many of the island homes have been abandoned in the past few years. Some of the cedar-shingled houses can now be rented by visitors. There is also a pretty chapel, built in 1895, on Île Providence.

The boat makes stops at Baie-des-Moutons and La Tabatière before reaching Saint-Augustin.

Saint-Augustin
(pop. 930)

Located about 12km upstream on the Rivière Saint-Augustin, the town of Saint-Augustin is the most populous on the lower north shore. To reach Saint-Augustin, boats pass through a beautiful estuary, protected to the west by the Kécarpoui archipelago and to the east by the Saint-Augustin archipelago. The Pakuashipi Montagnais community is situated near the village.

The boat stops at Vieux-Fort before ending its voyage in Blanc-Sablon.

Québec Architecture

Québec architecture is at once the result of a
population adapting to a difficult climate and
a synthesis of French, British and American
influences. The photos in this section illustrate the evolution of Québec architecture,
including both simple buildings erected by
farmers and elaborate works designed by
world-renowned architects.

This mansion is a good example of how architectural styles from the French regime in Québec remained well
after the British conquest of 1760. Its dutch windows with small panes, thick fieldstone walls and sloping roof
with dormer windows are typical of the architecture found in New France in the 17th and 18th centuries.

For many years, Québec invested all of its creative energies in the interior decors of its churches, which resulted in veritable woodworking masterpieces. The choir of Église de la Visitation du Sault-au-Récollet (Montréal), designed by Philippe Liébert and David-Fleury David between 1764 and 1818, skillfully combines Louis XV and Louis XVI styles. The traditional combination of white and gold is embellished with bright colours.

Marché Bonsecours, erected between 1845 and 1850, reflects mid-19th-century British colonial ambitions in Montréal. Its metallic dome, formidable portico, Tuscan pillars and sash windows are typically neoclassical—a very popular style throughout the British Empire during the first half of the 19th century.

The inhabitants' sense of insecurity, along with the king's desire to better protect his colony, resulted in the towns and villages of New France being surrounded by wood or stone fortresses. A number of forts designed to slow down the enemy were also established. Indeed, the fortresses had to resist both the surprise attacks of hostile Aboriginal peoples as well as the British army, which would arrive by sea on war ships.

Throughout the 19th century, Quebecers endeavored to adapt to the climatic extremes of the St. Lawrence Valley by developing what was to become a traditional Québec architecture. For example, they raised the masonry foundation and adorned their houses with long verandas to prevent snow from piling on window sills. The decreased pitch of the roof kept snow from falling off, so it could serve as insulation.

What makes Vieux Québec so charming is not only its great monuments but also its houses, each of which has its own story to tell. It is enjoyable to stroll through its narrow streets and observe the minute details of this compact architecture, losing oneself in an urban landscape that is quite unusual to most North Americans.

Colourful Victorian homes such as these, with impossibly steep or contorted exterior staircases, have become emblematic of Montreal.
- *Patrick Escudero*

In 1851, Father Joseph Déziel decided to build a large Catholic church for his rapidly expanding city. It was Thomas Baillargé, the architect who designed many of Québec City's churches, who drew up the plans. The architecture featured at the Notre-Dame de Lévis church is a beautiful example of the Québécois neoclassical tendency, combining the French and English styles. The interior, divided into three naves, features high galleries with columns, and outside, a plaque marks the place where English cannons bombarded Québec City in 1759.

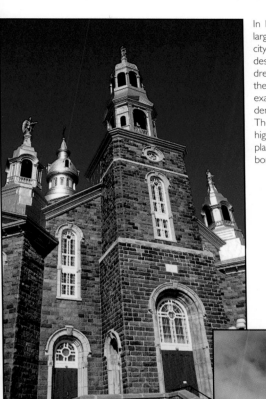

The Château Frontenac, a magnificent hotel, symbolizes Québec City. Designed by American architect Bruce Price, its style was influenced both by the castles of Scotland and those of the Loire region of France.

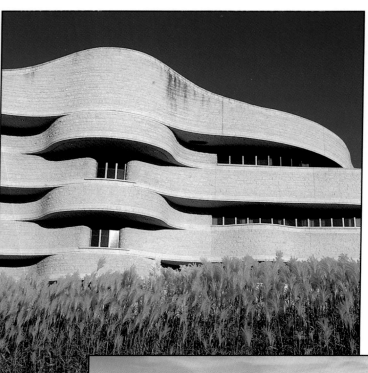

The unique architecture of the Canadian Museum of Civilization in Hull was designed by Douglas Cardinal, an Aboriginal architect from Alberta. This museum is composed of two unusual, organically shaped structures.

The unique architecture of Habitat '67 in Montréal makes these posh condominiums resemble a pile of blocks.

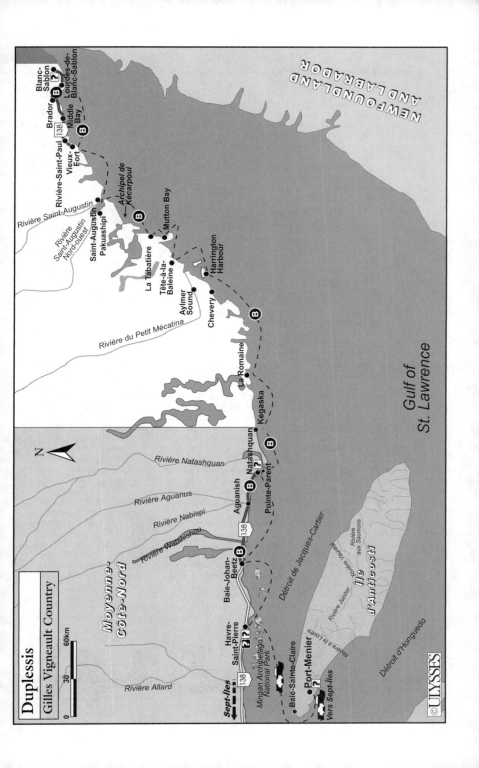

Duplessis
Gilles Vigneault Country

©ULYSSES

Lourdes-de-Blanc-Sablon (pop. 750)

This small fishing village has administrative offices and a health-care centre that serve this part of the lower north shore.

The lower north shore is still served by missionary priests, just as it was during the colonial era. In 1946, Monseigneur Scheffer was named first vicar of the Schefferville-Labrador region. The **Musée Scheffer** (*free admission; every day 8am to 9pm; in the Église de Lourdes-de-Blanc-Sablon,* ☎461-2000) outlines the history of the Blanc-Sablon region.

Blanc-Sablon (pop. 330)

This isolated region was visited as early as the 16th century by Basque and Portuguese fishers. They established camps where they melted seal blubber and salted cod before shipping it to Europe. It has been suggested that Vikings, who are known to have established a settlement on the nearby island of Newfoundland, might have set up a village near Blanc-Sablon around the year 1000. However, archaeological digs have only just begun. Brador, a fishing camp used by French fishers from Courtemanche, has recently been reconstructed.

Blanc-Sablon is only 4km from Labrador, a large, mostly Arctic territory. Much of Labrador was once part of the province of Québec; it is now the mainland half of the province of Newfoundland and Labrador. It is accessible by road from Blanc-Sablon. The former British colony of Newfoundland did not become a part of Canada until 1949. A ferry links Blanc-Sablon and the island of Newfoundland.

Parks

Tour A: Minganie

The **Réserve Faunique de Sept-Îles Port-Cartier** ★ (*24 Boulevard des Îles, Port-Cartier;* ☎766-2524) stretches over 6,423km², and is visited mostly by hunters and anglers. In addition, the Rivière aux Rochers rapids are popular with experienced canoeists.

The **Parc Régional de l'Archipel des Sept-Îles** ★★ is made up of several islands: Petite Boule, Grande Boule, Dequen, Manowin, Corossol, Grande Basque and Petite Basque. There is also an abundance of cod in the area, making fishing a popular activity. Trails and campsites have been set up on Île Grande Basque. For cruises around the archipelago, see p 499.

A series of islands and islets stretching over a 95km-long area, the **Mingan Archipelago National Park Reserve** ★★ (*1303 Rue de la Digue, Havre-St-Pierre,* ☎538-3331 or 538-3285) boasts incredible natural riches. The islands are characterized by distinctive rock formations, made up of very soft stratified limestone that has been sculpted by the waves. The formations are composed of marine sediment that was swept into the area some 250 million years ago from equatorial regions before being washed up on land and covered by a mantle of ice several kilometres thick. As the ice melted some 7,000 years ago, the islands re-emerged with their impressive stone monoliths. In addition to this fascinating element, the marine environment encouraged the development of varied and unusual plant life. Approximately 200 species of birds nest here, including the Atlantic puffin, the gannet, and the Arctic tern. The river is also home to several whale species, including the blue whale.

There are two **visitor information centres**, one in Longue-Pointe-de-Mingan (*625 Rue du Centre,* ☎949-2126) and the other in Havre-Saint-Pierre (*975 Boulevard de l'Escale,* ☎538-5264). Both are open only in the summer. There are campsites on the island (see p 501). Some of the islands have hiking trails.

In addition to natural attractions, the park also contains the vestiges of a very old Aboriginal settlement dating back over 4,000 years. Montagnais from the village of Mingan were the first to visit this spot regularly, to hunt for whales and gather berries.

Apart from the Viking explorers, who are known to have

visited the island of New-foundland, the first Europeans to set foot on Canadian soil are believed to have been Basque and Breton whale hunters, who left evidence of their presence on Mingan islands. Archaeologists have found remnants of the circular ovens made of stone and red tile (16th century) in which they used to melt the whale blubber before exporting it to Europe, where it was used to make candles. In 1679, Frenchmen Louis Jolliet and Jacques de Lalande purchased the archipelago for use as a fur-trading post and cod-salting site. The related installations were destroyed by the British during the Conquest (1760).

Measuring 222km in length and 56km in width, the **Parc d'Anticosti ★ ★** is big enough to accommodate a number of activities, including walking, swimming and fishing. The island has belonged to the Québec government since 1974, but was not open to hikers until 1986. Contributing to the magnificent scenery are breathtaking panoramas, long beaches, waterfalls, caves, cliffs, and rivers.

It is possible to visit the park's many natural attractions by car, provided that your vehicle is in good shape, but you'll need a few days. Sixty-five kilometres from Port-Menier, you'll find a waterfall called **Chute Kalimazoo** (*Île d'Anticosti*). A little farther lies **Baie-MacDonald**, named after Peter MacDonald, a fisher from Nova Scotia, who lived here as a hermit for a number of years. It is said that after falling ill and being treated in Baie-Sainte-Catherine, he walked nearly 120km in showshoes to get back home. The bay is a magnificent spot, trimmed with a long strip of fine sand. If you continue on the road that runs alongside these magnificent beaches, you'll come to **Pointe**

Carleton, whose lighthouse dates from 1918. Nearby, you can see the wreckage of the **M.V. Wilcox**, a minesweeper that ran aground in 1954.

About 12km from Pointe Carleton, you'll find the road leading to the **Caverne de la Rivière à la Patate**. If your car has four-wheel drive, you can follow the road for 2km, then you'll have to walk two more. This cave, which stretches nearly 625m, was discovered in 1981 and examined by a team of geographers in 1982.

The **Chute and Canyon de la Vauréal ★ ★** are two of the major natural sites on Île Anticosti. The waterfall (*chute*) flows into the canyon from a height of 70m, offering a truly breathtaking spectacle. You can take a short (1hr) hike along the river, inside the canyon, to the base of the falls. This will give you a chance to see some magnificent grey limestone cliffs streaked with red and green shale. If you continue 10km on the main road, you'll come to the turn-off for **Baie de la Tour ★ ★**, which lies another 14km away. There, you'll find a long beach with majestic limestone cliffs rising up behind it.

Outdoor Activities

Cruises and Whale-watching

Tour A: Minganie

The **Tournée des îles** (*$35; Marina Havre-Saint-Pierre, kiosk #2, ☎538-2547*), a 4hr cruise through the Archipel des Sept-Îles, offers a glimpse of the rich marine life of the St. Lawrence, home to many

kinds of aquatic mammals, particularly whales. The boat goes to Île Corossol, a large bird sanctuary.

For whale-lovers, the most wonderful experience the Côte-Nord has to offer is to set out with the biologists of the **Station de Recherche des Iles de Mingan** (*$75/person; 378 Rue du Bord-de-la-Mer, Longue-Pointe, ☎949-2845*) for a close encounter with some **humpback whales**. Seated aboard 7m dinghies, passengers take part in a day of research, which involves identifying the animals by the markings under their tails. Biopsies are occasionally carried out as well, and useful data is compiled. These outings are not recommended for anyone prone to seasickness, however, as they start at the research station at 7am and last a minimum of 6hrs (sometimes much longer) in turbulent waters.

Birdwatching

Tour A: Minganie

Amateur ornithologists can observe all sorts of shorebirds, swamp birds and ducks throughout the **Baie de Sept-Iles**. Particularly good spots for birdwatching along the shore include Pointe du Poste, at the end of Rue De Quen, the Vieux Quai (the old quay) and two stopping places along the 138, west of town. Île Corossol is home to various colonies of seabirds, which can be seen during a cruise around the islands in the bay.

The **Mingan Archipelago Natural Park Reserve** boasts many natural wonders found nowhere else in Québec or elsewhere on the eastern part of the continent. This is true of its avian inhabitants. For example, the sanctuary is home to one of the few colonies of puffins in the gulf, on Île aux Perroquets, at the western tip of the archipelago. These birds can be observed during a cruise from Havre-Saint-Pierre, Mingan or Longue-Pointe.

Tour B: Gilles Vigneault Country

At the **Refuge d'Oiseaux de Watshishou** in Baie-Johan-Beetz, feathered fauna can be observed while strolling along wooden walkways.

Scuba Diving

Tour A: Minganie

Protected by the surrounding islands, the Baie de Sept-Îles is well-suited to scuba diving. Over 75 dive sites of all different levels of difficulty are found here. Two artificial shipwrecks were even added in 1995. The underwater scenery of the bay is distinguished by its rock walls covered with colourful anemones, which are flamboyant in the clear water.

Kayaking

Tour A: Minganie

Excursions Vie à Nature runs the **Centre d'Information sur le Kayak de Mer** in Minganie, which can offer advice to kayakers travelling with their own boat and provide them with a special kayaker's map of the Archipel-de-Mingan, as well as various equipment and other items related to sea kayaking.

For those without their own kayak, **Expéditions Agaguk** *(1062 Rue Boréale, Havre-St-Pierre, ☎538-1588)* organizes safe, guided trips in one of their kayaks.

Downhill Skiing

Tour A: Minganie

The **Station de Ski Gallix** *(\$24.50; Dec to Apr, Mon-Fri 10am to 3pm, Sat and Sun 9am to 3:30pm, 1 Chemin du Centre se Ski Gallix, ☎766-7547 ou 766-5900)* offers downhill skiers a vertical drop of 185m and 22 runs, seven of which are lit for night-skiing.

Snowmobiling

Tour A: Minganie

For first-timers, a map of the region's snowmobile trails can be obtained from the Association Touristique de Duplessis, where the following organization is located:

Association des clubs de motoneige de la Côte-Nord
312 Avenue Brochu, Sept-Îles, G4R 2W6
☎296-8967

Tour B: Gilles Vigneault Country

The **Innu community of Pakuashipi** *(Conseil des Innus de Pakuashipi, Pakuashipi/Saint-Augustin, ☎947-2253)* offers several activities to familiarize visitors with Aboriginal culture, such as snowmobile excursions (within an 80km radius) with hunting and fishing, as well as stays in wood cabins. Pakuashipi is only accessible by plane or snowmobile from Natashquan.

Accommodations

Tour A: Minganie

Sept-Îles

Camping Sauvage de l'Île Grande-Basque
\$
late May to mid-Sep
Corporation Touristique de Sept-Îles,
1401 Boulevard Laure Ouest
☎962-1238
☎968-1818 *(summer)*
≈968-0022
Many city-dwellers dream of camping on an unspoiled island in the wilderness. Camping Sauvage de l'Île Grande-Basque can make such dreams a reality in the magnificent setting of the Baie de Sept-Îles. This island is the closest to the shore, making it a good stopping place for kayakers and canoeists. Firepits and firewood available. No drinking water.

Auberge Internationale Le Tangon
\$
sb
555 Avenue Jacques-Cartier
☎962-8180
≈961-2965
The Auberge Internationale Le Tangon, the Sept-Îles youth hostel, offers travellers on tight budgets an inexpensive place to spend the night, a cozy atmosphere and the opportunity to make some new acquaintances.

Hôtel Sept-Îles
\$-\$\$
ℝ, ℜ, ⊛
451 avenue Arnaud
☎962-2581 or 800-463-1753
≈962-6918
www.hotelseptiles.com
The Hôtel Sept-Îles stands alongside the river and has a lovely view. The rooms are

simply decorated but quite comfortable.

Havre-Saint-Pierre

Mingan Archipelago National Park Reserve
$
May to Sep
☎*538-3285 (in season)*
☎*538-3331 (off season)*
⇄*538-3595*
www.parcscanada.qc.ca
The Mingan Archipelago National Park Reserve has 34 rudimentary campsites scattered across six islands in the archipelago. Each island has its own distinctive characteristics. Campers looking for solitude and complete tranquillity in a dazzling seascape will find all their wishes fulfilled here. Independence and excellent organizational skills are a must, however. The only amenities on the islands are a platform for tents, restrooms with no running water, tables, cooking grills, firewood and woodsheds. During the tourist season, it is possible to make individual reservations up to seven days in advance and group reservations up to six months in advance. Campers can also try their luck at the auction, held at the visitor information centre in Havre-Saint-Pierre every day at 2:45pm, at which time reserved sites that have not been claimed are re-assigned on a first-come, first-served basis. The maximum stay permitted on one island is six days. There is a water-taxi service for those without their own boat (extra charge). As the temperature is extremely variable, campers are advised to pack plenty of warm, dry clothing. It is also necessary to bring along enough potable water and food for two days more than your scheduled stay, even if you plan to be here for only one day, since boat transportation can be suspended due to bad

weather and fog. A wonderful place for sea kayaking. Beach.

Auberge de la Minganie
$
K, sb
May to Oct
3980 route 138
☎*538-1538*
The friendly Auberge de la Minganie youth hostel is located on the outskirts of town, beside the Mingan Archipelago National Park Reserve. Visitors arriving by bus can ask the driver to let them off here. Many cultural and outdoor activities are offered.

Hôtel-Motel du Havre
$$-$$$
≡
970 Boulevard de l'Escale
☎*538-2800 or 888-797-2800*
⇄*538-3438*
You can't miss the Hôtel-Motel du Havre, located at the intersection of the main road and Rue de l'Escale, which runs through town to the docks. This place is definitely the big hotel in town. Though some rooms have benefited from recent attempts at renovation, others remain drab and a bit depressing. Friendly service.

Île d'Anticosti

Auberge Au Vieux Menier
$ bkfst incl. in the B&B
sb
Jun to Sep
C.P. 112
26 Chemin de la Ferme,
Port-Menier
☎*535-0111*
The Auberge Au Vieux Menier falls somewhere between a bed and breakfast and a youth hostel. Located on the site of the former Saint-Georges farm. Exhibitions. Low rates.

Auberge Port-Menier
$$$
ℜ
rue des Menier, Port-Menier
☎*535-0122*
⇄*535-0204*
The Auberge Port-Menier, a venerable institution on the

island, offers clean rooms in a modest setting. The lobby is decorated with magnificent wooden reliefs from the Château Meunier. The inn serves as the starting point for a number of guided tours. Bicycle rentals.

Tour B: Gilles Vigneault Country

Baie-Johan-Beetz

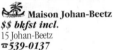 **Maison Johan-Beetz**
$$ bkfst incl.
15 Johan-Beetz
☎*539-0137*
The historic Maison Johan-Beetz is a truly exceptional hotel and a veritable monument decorated with Beetz's own artwork. The rooms are comfortable but basic.

Natashquan

Auberge La Cache
$$
K
183 Chemin d'En Haut
☎*726-3347 or 888-726-3347*
⇄*726-3508*
The Auberge La Cache has about 10 pleasant rooms.

Kégaska

 Gîte le Brion
$$
sb
Avenue Kegaska
☎*726-3738*
⇄*726-3738*
www.kegaska.com
A warm welcome in either French or English and a good meal await you at the Auberge Brion, a truly delightful little family inn. Relaxed atmosphere and attentive service. Open year-round. Beach.

Restaurants

Tour A: Minganie

Sept-Îles

Café du Port
$$-$$$
495 Avenue Brochu
☎962-9311
The charming Café du Port prepares simple, delicious dishes. It is one of the area's most popular restaurants.

Havre-Saint-Pierre

 Chez Julie
$-$$$$
1023 Rue Dulcinée
☎538-3070
Chez Julie has an excellent reputation for seafood. The coffee shop decor, including vinyl seat covers, does not seem to discourage the customers, who flock to the restaurant for seafood and smoked-salmon pizzas.

Île d'Anticosti

 Pointe-Carleton
$-$$
The dining room of the Pointe-Carleton is the best and most pleasant place to eat on the island. Whether you're sitting in the bright dining room or outside on the terrace, the view is spectacular

and the cuisine succulent. A different specialty is featured every evening. If you happen to come on a "Bacchante" night (fisherman's platter), don't miss it.

Auberge Place de l'Île
$
☎535-0279
Auberge Place de l'Île offers excellent family-style cuisine with a different lunch menu every day. Located in the heart of town, the inn has seven clean, comfortable rooms.

Entertainment

Bars and Nightclubs

Port-Cartier

With its shows, exhibitions, bar and restaurant, the **Graffitti** (☎766-3513) dinner theatre is one of the liveliest and most popular places in town.

Sept-Îles

In the heart of town, right alongside the Parc du Vieux-Quai's magnificent promenade, the **Matamek** (*451 Avenue Arnaud, Hôtel Sept-Îles, back entrance*) is where locals and visitors go for happy

hour and lively nights out. The atmosphere is conducive to talking, camaraderie and making new friends. Thirty-something crowd.

Shopping

Sept-Îles

Local artists and craftspeople sell their creations at the **Boutique de Souvenirs de la Terrasse du Vieux-Quai** (*during the tourist season;* ☎962-4174) and Les Abris de la Promenade du Vieux-Quai, located at the west end of the promenade. **Les Artisans du Platin** (*451 Avenue Arnaud,* ☎968-6115) is another place to check out.

The **Musée Régional de la Côte-Nord** (*500 Boulevard Laure,* ☎968-2070) has a shop with an interesting selection of typical Montagnais crafts.

Île d'Anticosti

Port-Menier

Les Artisans d'Anticosti (*mid-Jun to late Dec every day 8am to 6pm;* ☎535-0270) boast a superb assortment of crafts and deerskin clothing, as well as jewellery made from antlers. T-shirts and maps are also sold here.

Nord-du-Québec

The geographic area

encompassing the tourist region of Nord-du-Québec (Northern Québec) is a gigantic northern territory stretching north from the 49th parallel to the 62nd parallel.

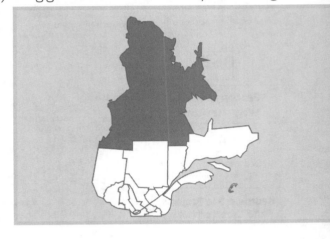

It covers more than half of Québec's total area. The rough beauty of this barren landscape, its harsh winter climate and its unique tundra vegetation giving way to taiga and then boreal forest, create a region completely different from the rest of Québec, leading many southern Quebecers to imagine it as an inhospitable environment. After all, all roads and railways stop about halfway into the region and almost 2,000km separate Montréal and the village of Ivujivik, the northernmost village in Québec. Some travellers do venture north, but for the most part this vast territory remains the land of northern Aboriginal peoples.

The 14 communities along the shores of Hudson Bay, Hudson Strait and Ungava Bay are home to some 9,500 people, 90% of whom are Inuit. In Inuktitut, the language of the Inuit, this territory is known as **Nunavik**. This territory is largely administered by the Inuit. The Cree, who number 12,000, live in nine villages on the taiga, mostly along the shores of James Bay

(see "Portrait", Aboriginal Peoples, p 25), in an administrative territory known as **Baie-James**.

From the first days of North American colonization, English and French forces fought for the control of the fur trade in this vast region. Today, and for the last 30 years, it is the government of Québec that has taken a keen interest in the resources of these lands, namely the massive potential for hydroelectric power contained in certain rivers. Huge hydroelectric dams were constructed in the James Bay region, now capable of putting out 10,282 megawatts of power.

The North is an important part of the Canadian conscience. And yet, although Canadians consider themselves "northerners," the vast majority of Canadians live along a narrow strip of land along the Canada – U.S. border; most will never venture this far north. Yet the mystique of the North has long drawn adventurous visitors, many of whom have come to fish in its crystal-clear waters or hunt its abundant wildlife.

Increasingly, though, Northern Québec has been attracting another kind of tourist: its vast wilderness and wildlife are attracting nature and adventure lovers in growing numbers from all corners of the world. Similarly, "southern" city dwellers, who want to experience a way of life that they consider to be closer to nature, are fascinated by the culture of Québec's Cree and Inuit peoples, who are finding creative and exciting ways to respond to this demand. How about a dog sledding expedition across the tundra or a night in a teepee?

Finding Your Way Around

This immense region is divided into two sections: **Hydroelectric Projects and Cree Territory**, and **Nunavik**.

Hydroelectric Projects and Cree Territory

By Car

The region of Nord-du-Québec constitutes 51% of the territory of Québec but has only about 40,000 inhabitants (Inuit, Cree and non-Aboriginal). Rte. 109 penetrates part of this immense territory, travelling from Amos in Abitibi-Témiscamingue to Radisson. This 600km route is entirely paved and practically deserted. There is only one rest stop on this highway where you can fill up on food and gas, at Km 381. It is crucial to be prepared on this leg. In fact, although it is a long one, we recommend that you complete this trip in one day.

Another road heads east-west and accesses the hydroelectric installations of La Grande—LG-2, LG-3, LG-4, Brisay and Caniapiscau—but it is impossible to travel past Km

323 without authorization from Hydro-Québec. The section of the road from LG-2 to LG-4 is gravel. There is also a road linking Radisson to Chisasibi and LG-1.

The 437km-long Route du Nord runs east from Rte. 109, linking Chibougamau, Nemiscau, and, at the latitude of Rivière Rupert, Route de la Baie-James. Gasoline is available at the **Nemiscau Cree Construction station** *(Mon-Sat 7am to 9am and 3pm to 6pm)* and at a gas station at the entrance to the village of **Nemiscau** *(every day 9am to 3pm)*.

The Route du Nord is an earth-and-stone road that is especially difficult in summer and on which it is preferable to drive an all-terrain vehicle. There is constant traffic from heavy-weight trucks on this road, and they are not inclined to cede passage—drive defensively and keep to the right. When a truck comes barrelling down the middle of the road, pull over to the right and let it pass. Conditions on the Route du Nord are better in winter when the road surface, although icy, is harder and smoother.

Car Rental

Location Aubé
La Grande airport
☎*(819) 638-8353*
=*(819) 638-7294*

By Plane

Because of the current restructuring of the Canadian airline industry, airline routes and carriers for these destinations are subject to change and the following information should be used for reference only.

Air Alma
☎*800-463-9660*
Air Alma offers flights to Chibougamau from Montréal. The lowest round-trip fare,

about $500, is available three days prior to departure.

Air Creebec
☎*800-567-6567*
www.aircreebec.ca
Air Creebec is the only airline that serves all of the Cree villages of Northern Québec, from Montréal and Val-d'Or. Mistissini, Oujé-Bougoumou and Waswanipi can be reached by taxi or rental car from the airport at Chibougamau. Air Creebec also offers flights to La Grande/ Radisson. By reserving seven days in advance, you can get up to 50% off regular fares. Discounted round-trip fares from Montreal range from about $350 (Chibougamau) to $800 (Chisasibi).

Air Inuit
☎*800-361-2965*
This airline offers service to the Radisson/La Grande hydroelectric facility.

By Bus

Guided tours of the Radisson region are another travel option. **Tours Chanteclerc** *(152 Rue Notre-Dame Est,* ☎*514-398-9009 or 800-361-8415)* organizes bus tours from Québec City to James Bay and the LG-2 hydroelectric dam. The trip usually takes a week and covers a distance of over 1,600km between Québec and Radisson.

Nunavik

No roads or railroads link the Inuit communities of Nunavik. Car and train travel are out of the question. Flying is the only way to travel between villages in this area.

A small, unpaved road links the Naskapi village of Kawawachikamach to Schefferville, which is accessible by train or by plane.

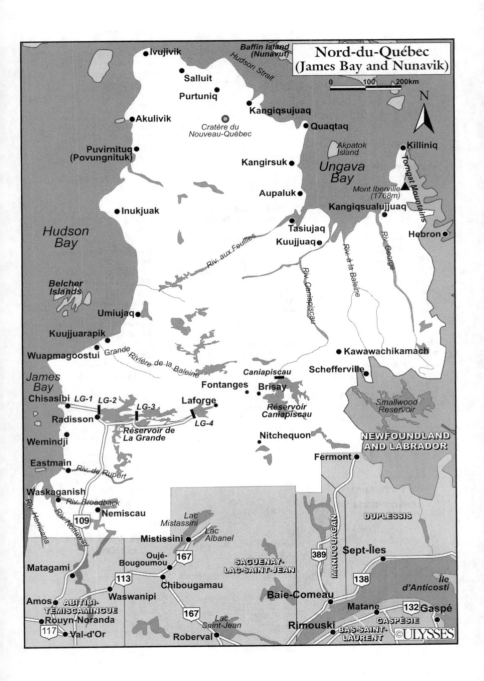

By Plane

Air Inuit
☎*800-361-2965*
This airline serves all the Inuit villages of Northern Québec and Canada. There is a significant discount for travellers who make reservations seven days in advance.

Air Creebec
☎*800-567-6567*
www.aircreebec.ca
Air Creebec serves Kuujjuarapik only from Montréal. A round-trip fare of about $800 is available seven days prior to departure.

Air Canada
☎*(514) 393-3333*
☎*888-247-2262*
There are no direct flights to Schefferville but Air Canada offers a flight to Sept Isles with a connecting flight to Schefferville with Aviation Québec-Labrador.

First Air
☎*800-267-1247*
www.firstair.com
First Air links Montreal and Kuujjuaq. Significant discounts on the $1,500-$2,000 return fare are available for flights booked seven days in advance.

Practical Information

The **area code** for Nord-du-Québec is **819** except in Mistissini and Oujé-Bougoumou, where it is **418**.

Tourist Information

The tourism infrastructure in this region is relatively undeveloped. It is difficult to travel around the area, so it is recommended to make all reservations for both hotels and

excursions in advance. For exploring this isolated territory, as well as for hunting and fishing trips, it is strongly recommended to hire the services of an outfitter.

Be aware that prices for goods and services are significantly higher in the North than they are in southern Quebec. The vast majority of consumer goods have to be air freighted up to the North and the cost of living is relatively high, hence the price difference.

Hydroelectric Projects and Cree Territory

Hydroelectric Projects

James Bay Tourism
Mon-Fri 8:30am to 4pm 166, Boulevard Springer, C.P. 1270, Chapais, G0W 1H0
☎*(418) 745-3969*
☎*888-745-3969*
⇒*(418) 745-3970*

Municipality of James Bay
All visitors travelling by road must stop and register (☎*819-739-4473*, ⇒*819-739-2088*, *www.municipalite. baie-james.qc.ca)* at the small office at Km 6 of the road between Matagami and Radisson. Reservations for tours of hydroelectric dams can also be made here.

Chibougamau
600 3e Rue, Bureau 2, Chibougamau, G8P 1P1
☎*(418) 748-6060*
⇒*(418) 748-4020*

Service de Sécurité Civile et Tourisme de la Municipalité de la Baie-James
(Municipality of James Bay Tourism and Civil Security Service)
110 Boulevard Matagami, C.P. 500, Matagami, J0Y 2A0
☎*739-2030*
⇒*739-2713*
www.municipalite.baie-james. qc.ca

Cree Territory

There are plans in the works to create a central Cree tourism information office. For the moment though, the following is a good source of information:

Cree Regional Authority
☎*(514) 861-5837*
⇒*(514) 861-0760*
www.gcc.ca

Nunavik

The three organizations listed below are good contacts for information on the Nunavik region:

Association Touristique du Nunavik
C.P. 779, Kuujjuaq, J0M 1C0
☎*888-594-3424*
⇒*(819) 964-2002*
www.nunavik-tourism.com

Fédération des Coopératives du Nouveau-Québec
19950 Clark Graham, Baie-d'Urfé, H9X 3R8
☎*(514) 457-9371*
⇒*(514) 457-4626*

Naskapi Band of Québec
C.P. 5111, Kawawachikamach, G0G 2Z0
☎*(418) 585-2686*
⇒*(418) 585-3130*

Exploring

Hydroelectric Projects and Cree Territory

Whether it's called Moyen Nord, Radissonnie, Baie-James or Cree land, this region, as difficult to define as it is to name, represents the most northerly region of Québec accessible by road. These roads, laid out by dam builders and mine operators, truly opened up the heart of Québec to its southern population while simultaneously giving the native peoples of the north an entry, for better or for worse, to the world down south.

A whole universe opens up here to adventurous travellers who seek authenticity and a radical change of scene. Everything is different here: time, climate, wildlife, flora, space, people... No aspect of life here resembles anything found anywhere else.

Matagami
(pop. 2,300)

Matagami is a small mining town that was established in 1963. Rich zinc and copper mines attracted residents to this area, which is the overland entrance way to the James Bay region.

The Road from Matagami to Radisson

It took 450 days in 1972-73 for Québec labourers to meet the challenge of opening up the 740km Route de la Baie-James to Chisasibi. The size of the rivers that had to be bridged and the incredible number of lakes that had to be skirted made it a considerable accomplishment, indeed. As the road winds northward the landscape changes subtly as black spruce gradually diminish in size and become frail and stunted.

★
Nemiscau
(pop. 550)

The French began trading furs as early as 1661 in this historic crossroads, and commerce continued to play a determining role in the history of Nemiscau, mainly thanks to the Hudson's Bay Company, which maintained a post here until 1970. At that point, this centre of economic activity disappeared and the Cree dispersed to found a beautiful, brand-new village on the

shores of marvellous Lac Champion in 1979. This relatively new, well-equipped village has become the administrative centre of the Grand Council of the Cree.

★★
Radisson
(pop. 350)

This town was built in 1974 to accommodate the workers from the south who were arriving as part of the James Bay hydroelectric project. During the boom years of construction on the hydro project, the population of Radisson was more than 3,000.

If this area interests you, **Voyages Jamésiens** (*96 Rue Albanel, ☎819-638-6673*) offers a weekend trip to James Bay for a little under $700 per person, including transportation from Québec City or Montréal, accommodation and activities. In addition to visits to dams, the tour includes motorized canoe trips on the La Grande river in summer, or afternoons of cross-country skiing in winter.

Radisson's main draw is its impressive hydroelectric complex. Visitors can tour the **Centrale Robert-Bourassa ★★★** formerly known as La Grande 2 or LG-2 (*free admission, year-round Wed, Fri and Sun at 1pm, summer every day at 1pm, reservations required 48hrs in advance; from anywhere in Québec ☎800-291-8486, in the region or outside of Québec ☎638-8486*). Visits to **La Grande-1** are also available (*year-round on availability, reserve 48hrs in advance; summer every day except Wed-Mon at 8am*). The tour lasts 4hrs and includes a tour of the exterior facilities and an information session.

During the 1960s, the Québec government envisioned a plan to tap the hydroelectric

potential of the James Bay region by constructing dams along its rivers. It was not until the 1970s that a development project for the damming of the Rivière La Grande (Chisasibi, in Cree), which runs 800km from east to west before flowing into James Bay, was proposed by then Québec premier, Robert Bourassa. The project was divided into two phases, the first being the construction of three powerful damming centres along the river, namely La Grande-2 (LG-2), recently renamed Robert-Bourassa, La Grande-3 (LG-3) and La Grande-4 (LG-4). Construction began in 1973 and spanned several years, since damming the river was an intense and complex project. To increase the flow of the Rivière La Grande, various waterways were diverted, namely the Eastmain and the Opinaca, as well as the Caniapiscau in the east. The source of the Rivière Caniapiscau was used to create the largest artificial lake in Québec, a reservoir covering more than $4,275km^2$.

The La Grande Hydroelectric complex required the construction of dams and dykes. The former were used to close off the river beds and raise the water level, thereby creating falls; the latter were used to stop the rising waters from flowing out via secondary valleys. All of the water is contained and swept up into the intakes, then it is directed along a series of pipes leading to the turbines, which it activates.

On October 27, 1979 the LG-2 (Robert-Bourassa) generating station started producing electricity. The other two, the LG-3 and LG-4 generating stations, became operational in 1982 and 1984, respectively. In 1990, these three generating stations were responsible for almost half of Hydro-Québec's total production of electricity. The second

Nord-du-Québec

The Hudson Bay Meteorite

If you look at a map of Québec, you will see that the east of Hudson Bay forms a perfect arc. You will also see the Belcher Islands in the centre of the bay. Some scientists attribute this geological formation to the impact of a meteorite. When a meteorite lands, it forms a perfectly round crater. In addition, the force of the impact creates a phenomenon of centrifugal and centripetal waves—a little like what happens when you throw a rock into the water. As these three elements are all present, it is possible to hypothesize that a meteorite hit the middle north of Québec. There are actually a number of sizeable meteoritic craters in Québec: the Cratère du Nouveau-Québec, the semi-crater in Charlevoix, which you can visit, and the largest crater in the province, the Réservoir Manicouagan.

If this hypothesis is accurate, the Hudson Bay meteorite was the largest ever to hit the face of the Earth. The impact would have been powerful enough to alter the planet's axis and thus cause major climatic changes. In fact, given all the potential repercussions, it could have led to the disappearance of the dinosaurs!

There is insufficient evidence, however, to say for certain that this gigantic hollow was created by meteoritic impact. The presence of rocks similar to those collected on lunar expeditions made it possible to identify the meteorite responsible for the Réservoir Manicouagan. Yet various studies contradict each other when it comes to the Hudson Bay meteorite. Consequently, Québec cannot yet claim the largest meteoritic crater on earth, which is officially in the Gulf of Mexico, around the Yucatan Peninsula. Some scientists attribute Hudson Bay's geological formation to the movement of tectonic plates. Again, though, they have found no proof in the sea bed to support their theory. Perhaps it was caused by the glacier that raged its way through Québec 20,000 years ago. The mystery has yet to be solved.

phase of the project involved the upgrading of the LG-2 (thereby creating the LG-2A generating station, which was completed in 1992), and the construction of four other generating stations, including three on the Rivière Laforge. The Laforge-1 and Brisay stations, or *centrales*, started operating in 1993; La Grande-1 was completed in 1995 and Laforge-2 in 1996.

The La Grande-2 generating station is the third- most powerful in the world (with an installed capacity of 7,634 megawatts), after Itaipu in Brazil, on the border of Para-guay (installed capacity of 12,600 megawatts), and Guri in Venezuela (installed capacity of 10,000 megawatts). Built 137m below the ground, La Grande-2 is the largest underground generating station in the world. The dam is 2.8km long and 162m-high, supplied by a 2,835km² reservoir. In years when the annual rainfall is very high, a drainage system of floodgates is necessary. The engineering of such a system involves eight 12-by-20m containers, and a 1,500m-long by 110m-deep collection canal. It has been nicknamed the *escalier des géants* (giant's staircase), since it represents 10 "steps," each about 10m high and carved in the rock. When water levels are exceptionally high, the system can drain 16,280m² of water per second, the equivalent of the average flow of the St. Lawrence River. So far, the system has rarely been put to use; only between 1979 and 1981 until the turbines inside the generating station were completed, and on August 30, 1987, for a couple of hours during a visit by French Prime Minister Jacques Chirac. With the opening of LG-2A, La Grande-2 will probably be used only once every 75 years.

The power station consists of four levels: the first level houses the machine room, the second the alternators, the third provides access to the spiral containers (inside which are the turbines) and the last level houses the drainage gallery. To absorb the high and low pressure, which builds up when the machines are turned on and off, an equilibrium chamber was built.

The construction of this hydroelectric complex has had very serious repercussions not only for the environment but also for the Aboriginal populations living off the land in this region. To create the reservoirs, some 11,505km² of land was flooded, representing 6.5% of the hydrographic basin of the Rivière La Grande and 2.9% of Cree hunting grounds. During the whole construction of this hydroelectric mega-project, Hydro-Québec and its subsidiary SEBJ (Société d'Énergie de la Baie James), which administers all hydroelectric projects in the area, both carried out environmental-impact studies on this project, and they continue to follow up on their findings. Part of the flooded land was Aboriginal hunting ground, and the Inuit and Cree who used these lands contested the provincial government's use of their ancestral lands. The negotiations between all the parties involved continued right up to November 11, 1975, the signing day of the James Bay and Northern Québec Agreements, which established the rights and obligations of the Inuit and Cree, as well as the plan of action of the hydroelectric project. According to the agreement signed by all those concerned (the Cree, the Inuit, the Québec and Canadian governments, Hydro-Québec, the SEBJ and the SDBJ), the Cree and Inuit were guaranteed exclusive use of certain lands, as well as guarantees of exclusive hunt-

ing, fishing and trapping rights on the land, especially for certain species of animals. Those involved also received greater administrative powers over their lands, as well as monetary compensation. Since 1975, 11 supplementary agreements and eight specific accords have been signed to better define each party's rights.

The entrance to the complex is like a terrifying descent into the belly of the earth. The cathedral-sized turbine room is surreal. Megalomaniacs will thrill to the sheer size of this place.

Radisson – Brisay

The Route de la Baie-James does not end in Radisson. From Lac Yasinski (Km 544), the long gravel road continues to Réservoir Caniapiscau and the Brisay dam, the exact geographic centre of Québec.

Chisasibi
(pop. 3,250)

A Cree word meaning "the big river," Chisasibi is a modern village that was built in 1981, after the Cree left Île de Fort George. This little village was laid out in keeping with the Cree's matriarchal society, so that the houses stand in small groups, with the mother's house surrounded by those of her daughters. The two-storey wooden houses are often accompanied by a tepee that serves as the kitchen, since the Cree prefer to cook their food over a fire rather than on an electric stove. You'll notice that the streets have no names, and that many are dead ends. Don't let this discourage you—the Cree are very friendly and quick to help out. The cemetery is also interesting, as it contains examples of two different burial traditions. The Cree buried their dead where they passed away, facing the rising sun. Because many people died in

the forest, the Cree would build a small fence around the tomb to make it easier to locate. Today, due to the influence of European religions, they bury the dead in a communal cemetery, but the fence tradition has endured. Chisasibi is a dry community, so don't bring any alcohol with you when you visit, and don't be surprised to see a roadblock a few kilometres before the village; it's a checkpoint.

Île de Fort George

With the increased flow of the Rivière La Grande, the shores of the island are eroding faster than normal. The Cree therefore agreed to move their village to the present site of Chisasibi. The island is still of great symbolic importance to them, however. In fact, all the Cree in Canada and their non-Aboriginal brothers and sisters get together here every August for the **Grand Pow Wow**. Visitors to the island can take the opportunity to sample the traditional Cree lifestyle. You'll sleep on a layer of spruce branches in a tepee and eat as the Cree have for thousands of years. For more information, contact the **Chisasibi Mandow Agency** (☎800-771-2733).

Waskaganish
(pop. 1,600)

Founded in 1668 by Médard Couart Des Groseillers, this village was first called Rupert, then Rupert's House and Fort Rupert, in honour of the first governor of the Hudson's Bay Company. Changing hands between the French and the English, this important trading post remained one of the most active up until 1942, the same year the village's infrastructure was put in place.

The traditional campsite **Nuutimesaanaan** (Smokey Hill), where fish and fish eggs (*waakuuch*) were smoked, can be visited.

Eastmain
(pop. 550)

Eastmain enjoys a striking view of the mouth of the river and exudes the warmth and welcome of an isolated community.

Wemindji
(pop. 1,000)

The Cree did not establish this community, on the shores of James Bay at the mouth of the Maquatua river, until 1959 when they left Vieux-Comptoir, 45km to the south. While a large proportion of the population still occupies itself with traditional activities, the Cree have also developed new economic sectors with the creation of Wemindji Cree Fur Ranch, a large fox and lynx farm. The name Wemindji means "ochre mountain," and the hills surrounding the village contain rich deposits of this mineral, which is mixed with grease to make paint.

Chibougamau
(pop. 8,700)

Chibougamau? This name derived from an Aboriginal language has managed to retain its mystery over the years, as there is still no consensus as to its meaning. Located 250km northwest of Lac Saint-Jean, Chibougamau is the largest city in Northern Québec, with 25% of the region's population. It is also situated at the crossroads of major roads between Abitibi-Témiscaminque and Saguenay–Lac-Saint-Jean, and since the opening of the Route du Nord in 1993, it is the gateway to Northern Québec. It is also a major entry point by air. A young city, it developed as a result of the opening of mining operations at the beginning of the 20th century. Several mining companies moved in over the following years, with more or less success. Today, it is an established mining and forestry

town; a new open-pit mine started operation in 1997. And while the town itself isn't likely to draw tourists, the surrounding land and the services offered in Chibougamau make it an important gateway into Northern Québec.

★★
Oujé-Bougoumou
(pop. 650)

This most recently established Cree village is in many ways also the most remarkable one. After a long, meandering journey from Mistissini to Chibougamau, Lac aux Dorés, Chapais and onward, a group of Cree chose Lac Opémiska for their permanent settlement. Through their determination they gained reservation status and were permitted to draw up plans for a unique and fascinating village. Architect Douglas Cardinal, the creative mind behind the Museum of Civilization in Hull, was entrusted with the task of designing the settlement. Oujé-Bougoumou's architecture is profoundly traditional despite the prevalence of symbolism and the emphasis on vanishing lines. Each residence evokes an ancient teepee, particularly in the slope of its roof. The main buildings are especially impressive. The village as a whole is laid out in the shape of a goose, at one end of which stands a reconstructed traditional village that is used for important community events and to accommodate tourists.

In 1995, Oujé-Bougoumou earned official recognition from the United Nations as one of the 50 villages in the world that best represents the goals of social cooperation, respect for the environment and sustainable development, all which the UN seeks to promote.

At the village entrance, you will notice a unique building from which a column of

smoke rises. This is the **cogeneration plant**, which provides heat to every building in the village with a hot water system fuelled by the waste shavings from the Barrette de Chapais sawmill 26km away.

★
Mistissini
(pop. 3,200)

At the heart of what was known as Le Domaine du Roi (the king's domain) during the fur trade, halfway between the St. Lawrence Valley and Hudson Bay, Mistissini, along with its immense lake, has been a tremendously important cultural crossroads for centuries. Mistissini is on the southwest tip of Lac Mistassini, on Presqu'île Watson (peninsula), between Baie du Poste and Baie Abatagouche.

With an area of 2,336km^2, **Lac Mistassini** was the largest expanse of water in Québec before the creation of the great reservoirs. It is 161km long, 19km wide and up to 180m deep in places. It is the main source of Rivière Rupert. Champlain knew of the lake's existence as early as 1603, but French explorers did not reach it until 1663, when Guillaume Couture accomplished that feat. The Jesuit Charles Albanel crossed it in 1672 during an expedition from Lac Saint-Jean to James Bay.

★★
Whapmagoostui
(pop. 600)
and
★
Kuujjuarapik
(pop. 1,300)

Here is a truly unique community, as much for its history and geographic location as for its social makeup. The Cree village of Whapmagoostui sits across from the Inuit village of Kuujjuarapik at the mouth of Grande Rivière de la Baleine on Hudson Bay. This coexistence has lasted for about two centuries around the trading post known as Great Whale or Poste-de-la-Baleine. These villages are actually only one agglomeration divided by what some locals call an imaginary border, which visitors cross completely obliviously. A closer look, however, reveals that the two communities share no public services whatsoever, regardless of the harmony between them. Even the new medical clinic (CLSC), which was built right on the boundary line, is partisan. The Inuit are cared for on one side of the corridor, the Cree on the other, and each group on a different day. The best example of integration is the bar, on the Inuit side of town, which is frequented by both communities simultaneously, although each has its own section.

Whapmagoostui is the northernmost Cree village, at the very edge of Cree territory and on the fringes of Inuit territory, which historically has extended all the way to the shores of extraordinary Lac Guillaume-Delisle.

The villages are bordered by a large sandy beach that forms dunes from atop which the magnificent **Îles Manitounuk** are visible. These formations are called **Hudson cuestas**, which are characterized by sandy beaches and dunes facing the open water of the bay and spectacular towering cliffs facing the continent. They are refuges for countless **birds**, **seals**, **whales** and **belugas**.

Nunavik

Kuujjuarapik (pop. 1,300)

See Whapmagoostui, above.

★ Umiujaq (pop. 350)

Situated 160km north of Kuujjuarapik, the village of Umiujaq was inaugurated in December 1986. The James Bay and Northern Québec Agreements offered the Inuit of Kuujjuarapik the option of moving to the region of Lac Guillaume-Delisle, in the eventuality of the completion of the Great Whale hydroelectric project. A portion of the residents, fearing the harmful effects of the dam project, voted in favour of a plan to create a new community further north, which became the little village of Umiujaq, after a referendum in October 1982. After numerous archaeological, ecological and land-use studies, construction of the village began in the summer of 1985 and was completed a year and a half later.Sitting at the foot of a hill that resembles an umiak (a large sealskin boat), Umiujaq looks out onto Hudson Bay.

★ Inukjuak (pop. 1,200)

Nunavik's second-largest village, Inukjuak is set 360km north of Kuujjuarapik, at the mouth of the Innuksuac river, facing the Hopewell Islands.

The lives of the residents of Inukjuak remain strongly tied to traditional activities. Discovery of a steatite deposit has promoted sculpture-making; many of the most renowned sculptors in Nunavik live and work in the small studios here.

The oldest buildings in the village are the old Anglican mission and the former trading post, both of them located behind the Northern store and the cooperative that was founded in 1967.

The **Hopewell Islands**, with their steep cliffs, are worth

closer examination, especially in the springtime when ice floes, driven by tides and currents, form an immense field of gigantic, interlocking ice blocks.

Puvirnituq (pop. 1,200)

This community is located on the east shore of the Puvirnituq river, about 4km from the bay of the same name and 180km north of Inukjuak. The land surrounding the village forms a plateau at an altitude of about 65m.

For the last few years, in an effort to be true to the original pronunciation, the name "Povungnituk" has been written "Puvirnituq." This is an Inuktitut word that means "the place with an odour of high meat," a rather original name that refers to a period when the river was higher than usual and many animals drowned trying to cross it. The odour of the animals' decomposing carcasses on the beach inspired this appellation. Another story tells that an epidemic ravaged a camp here, killing every inhabitant and sparing no one to bury the dead, so that when family and friends arrived from neighbouring camps in the spring, the air was foul with the odour of decaying bodies.

Puvirnituq is home to the Inuulitsivik Health Centre, one of two hospitals in Nunavik, the other being that of Kuujjuaq, on Ungava Bay. This centre is known, among other things, for its midwifery pilot project, which has provided front-line obstetric services for years. Puvirnituq is also known for its sculptors, who founded one of Nunavik's most dynamic cooperatives.

Akulivik (pop. 450)

The village of Akulivik is 100km north of Puvirnituq, its

closest neighbour, and 650km north of Kuujjuarapik. It is built on a peninsula that juts into Hudson Bay facing Smith Island. The community is bordered to the south by the mouth of the Illukotat river and to the north by a deep bay that forms a natural harbour, sheltering the village from the wind. This geographic configuration encourages early spring thaws and makes the area prime hunting ground. Fossilized shells, vestiges of the last ice age, have eroded into crumbs, so the ground has an unusual, sandy quality.

Smith Island, which is part of the Northwest Territories, lies across from the village a few minutes away by boat or snowmobile. This mountainous island, which offers scenery of fascinating beauty, is a springtime habitat for thousands of **snow** and **Canada geese**.

Ivujivik
(pop. 275)

The most northerly village in Québec, Ivujivik is situated 150km from Akulivik and 2,140km from Québec City. It is nestled in a little cove south of Digges Strait and Digges Islands, in a mountainous region near Cap Wolstenholme. Ivujivik is the site of battling ocean currents at every tide since Hudson Bay and Hudson Strait meet here. Even the name Ivujivik refers to this phenomenon; in Inuktitut it means, "place where strong currents make the ice accumulate."

★★
Salluit
(pop. 1,200)

Situated 250km north of Puvirnituq, 115km east of Ivujivik and 2,125km from Québec City, Salluit is nestled in a valley formed by steep mountains, about 10km from

the mouth of the fjord of the same name.

The actual site of Salluit, dominated by jagged mountains and steep hills, is absolutely spectacular. Located between the sea and the mountains on a magnificent **fjord ★★**, it is one of the most picturesque villages in Nunavik. **Deception Bay**, which the Inuit call Pangaligiak, is famous for its hunting, its excellent fishing and the year-round richness of its wildlife and vegetation.

★★
Kangiqsujuaq
(pop. 500)

Surrounded by majestic mountains at the bottom of a superb valley, Kangiqsujuaq, an Inuktitut word that means "the large bay," stands proudly over the fjord of immense Wakeham Bay.

The most impressive natural tourist attraction of the area, and of Nunavik generally, is without question the **Cratère du Nouveau-Québec ★★**, which the Inuit call Pingualuit. Less than 100km from the village, this gigantic crater has imposing dimensions: its diameter measures 3,770m and it is 446m deep. Discovered by Chubb, an aviator who was intrigued by its perfectly round shape, the crater was formed by the fall of an enormous meteorite. A research team from the Université de Montréal solved the mystery of its water source when they discovered a subterranean spring in the crater's depths.

On the coastal islands east of the village, there are remains of ancient campsites that date from the Thule era.

Quaqtaq
(pop. 275)

Quaqtaq is delimited to the north by mountainous relief and to the south and east by low rocky hills. Located

157km from its nearest neighbour, Kangiqsujjuaq, and 350km north of Kuujjuaq, the village stretches over a peninsula that juts into Hudson Strait and forms the coast of Diana Bay, known as Tuvaaluk, "the large ice floe," among the Inuit. This point of land also marks the convergence of Hudson Strait and Ungava Bay.

Because the Inuit and their ancestors have occupied this region for almost 2,000 years, many **archaeological sites** can be found in the area. The surroundings of **Diana Bay**, an area renowned for its hunting, fishing and wildlife observation, is the habitat of about 1,000 **musk oxen ★**. The luckiest visitors to the area occasionally spot **snowy owls**.

Kangirsuk
(pop. 400)

This little community is located on the north shore of Rivière Arnauk, 13km upstream from Ungava Bay. Once known as Payne Bay and Bellin, the village is 118km south of Quaqtaq, 230km north of Kuujjuaq and 1,536km from Québec City.

A few archaeological sites are located near the village, including a large one on **Pamiok Island**. These sites, which are of exceptional quality, open a window on the distant past of the region's first inhabitants. The Vikings visited the Lac Payne area as early as the 11th century. Artifacts from this era can be found around the outskirts of Kangirsuk.

★
Kuujjuaq
(pop. 2,100)

Situated 1,304km north of Québec City, the administrative, economic and political capital of Nunavik stretches over flat sandy ground on the western shore of Rivière Koksoak, 50km upstream from its mouth on Ungava Bay. With a population of over 1,400 residents, including a good number of non-natives, Kuujjuaq is the largest Inuit community in Québec.

Today, Kuujjuaq (Inuktitut for "big river") is the administrative centre of the territory of Nunavik and the headquarters of the Administration Régionale de Kativik. Various governmental and regional organizations have offices here, as well. The town's two large landing strips are part of the DEW (Distant Early Warning) line, and the village is the hub of air transport in Northern Québec and home to the head offices of many charter airlines.

Kuujjuaq is also known as Fort Chimo. In the 19th and early 20th centuries, it was a prosperous Hudson Bay Company (HBC) fur-trading post. Since then, the village was moved to the other bank of the Koksoak river, where it was easier to build the landing strip that the Americans needed for the military base that they operated here in the 1940s. Today, you can visit "Old Chimo," where buildings dating from the HBC era still stand, now used for a children's summer camp.

Kuujjuaq has hotels, restaurants, stores, a bank and craft shops. It offers most of the services that are available in regional capitals of the south. Tulattavik Hospital provides top-of-the-line health-care services and constitutes the principal medical resource of the Ungava region. Kuujjuaq also has its own convention centre, which opened for the occasion of the 2002 General Assembly of the Inuit Circumpolar Conference, which united Inuit living in Canada, Alaska, Greenland and

Russia to discuss politics, culture and society.

Majestic **Rivière Koksoak ★** is one of the marvels of the area. It adds a unique and very picturesque dimension to Kuujjuaq's setting, and its tides shape landscapes of fascinating beauty.

★★★
Kangiqsualujjuaq
(pop. 650)

Located 160km northeast of Kuujjuaq on the east coast of Ungava Bay, Kangiqsuialujjuaq (Inuktitut for "the long bay") was once known as George River, a name more readily pronounced by non-Inuit. Up until 1959 there was no real village here; summer camps were established on the coast and winter camps were about 50km into the interior. The hamlet was created on the initiative of local Inuit who founded the first cooperative in Nouveau-Québec here with the goal of creating a commercial char fishery. Construction of the village began at the very beginning of the 1960s, and the first public services were organized here at that time.

Kangiqsualujjuaq made headlines around the world as a result of a tragedy that occurred on January 1, 1999. While nearly the entire village was gathered in the school gymnasium for New Year's celebrations, an avalanche suddenly

Polar bear

crushed the building, which was situated at the foot of a steep hill. Fourteen inhabitants lost their lives, marking forever the tiny community.

The region attracts one of the largest herds of caribou in the world. In fact, the **Rivière George herd** is the most imposing in Nunavik, with approximately 600,000 heads. Kangiqsualujjuaq hunters supply Les Aliments Arctiques du Nunavik with a large proportion of the 3,000 kilograms of caribou meat that it puts on the market annually, both locally and in the south.

The **Torngat Mountains ★★★**, whose name means "mountains of bad spirits" in Inuktitut, are situated about 100km east of the village, between Ungava Bay and the Atlantic Ocean, at the Québec-Labrador border. At over 220km long and 100km wide, they are the tallest mountains in Québec, making the chain as important as the Alps. Many of the summits reach altitudes of 1,700m, including majestic **Mont d'Iberville ★** (the highest summit in Québec), which dominates the range with its height of 1,768m.

Kawawachikamach
(pop. 600)

Situated 15km from Schefferville, some 1,000km north of Montréal and right next to the Labrador border, Kawawachi-kamach is the only Naskapi community in Québec. Related to the Cree and the Montagnais, the Naskapi are also part of the Algonkian language family. Kawawachi-kamach, a Naskapi word that means "the place where the sinuous river becomes a great lake," is located in a region of exceptional natural beauty and innumerable lakes and rivers.

Nord-du-Québec

A nomadic people of great hunters, the Naskapi followed the migration route of the caribou, on which they depended for survival. Following the near-disappearance of the caribou from their territory and their increased dependence on trading posts, the Naskapi experienced years of hardship marked by famine starting in 1893. Fleeing hunger and sickness, and assisted by the federal government, a number of families settled near Fort Chimo in 1949. Seven years later, the Naskapi decided to move to the Montagnais community of Matimekosh, near Schefferville, in the hope of bettering their living conditions.

In 1978, the Naskapi, encouraged by the treaty signed three years earlier with the Inuit and the Cree, signed the Northeastern Québec Agreement with the federal and provincial governments. The Naskapi thereby abandoned title to their ancestral lands and in return obtained financial compensation, inalienable rights over certain territories and new fishing, hunting and trapping rights. In addition, they decided to establish a community on the shores of Lake Matemace, 15km northeast of Schefferville. Inaugurated in 1984, the village of Kawawachikamach has modern equipment for collective use, a dispensary and a shopping centre.

The 1982 closure of the Iron Ore factory, the main employer of Naskapi men, dealt a hard blow to the young community. The Naskapi then turned toward adventure tourism and outfitting to make a living. In 1989, they took over the well-reputed Tuktu hunting and fishing club.

Outdoor Activities

Aboriginal Adventure Packages

Hydroelectric Projects and Cree Territory

Radisson

Some dream of catching giant fish in untamed wilderness. Others want to hunt caribou in the taiga or simply observe these animals on snowmobile photo-safaris. Still others hope to have the family vacation of a lifetime in a comfortable cottage at the end of the world. **La Pourvoirie Mirage** (☎*819-339-3150)* has put together very attractive packages that can make any of these dreams come true.

Chisasibi

The **Chisasibi Mandow Agency** (☎*819-855-3373)* is the best organized and the most reliable tourism organization in the Cree territory, and it offers the greatest variety of outings. Under the aegis of the band council, Mandow offers fishing trips, photo-safaris, wildlife observation trips, and snowmobiling, cross-country skiing and canoeing excursions.

Nadockmi (☎*819-855-3000)*, an outfitter located on the Kapsaouis river, organizes hunting (caribou and black bear) and fishing trips and arranges for cultural visits with the Cree (see p 28).

As noted earlier, Cree communities are becoming increasingly involved in tourism. Below are just a few of the companies and communities offering outdoor activities in the region. Should you have a particular community in mind

that is not mentioned below, contact one of the sources listed under Tourist Information.

Oujé-Bougoumou

The tourism office conducts 90min tours of this award-winning community and its cultural village. It will also help you plan lengthier tours and packages, such as those organized by the following companies:

Nuuhchimi Wiinuu Tours
74 Opataca St.
Oujé-Bougoumou, G0W 3C0
☎*800-745-2045*
≈*(418) 745-3500*
www.ouje.ca/tourism
David and Anna Bosum provide visitors with a first-hand experience of Cree culture. Snowshoeing trips in the bush, Cree cultural teaching, "country foods" like moose, beaver and ptarmigan, traditional handicrafts and storytelling, are part of the experience.

Nunavik

Québec law requires that anyone hunting in Nunavik must hire a guide. For more information, contact the **Société de la faune et des parcs du Québec** (see Tourist Information). The **Association Touristique du Nunavik** (see Tourist Information) can provide further information on packages and rates. Note that most of the outfitters described below have their offices outside the region; make sure to contact them prior to your arrival.

Arctic Adventures / Inuit Adventures
☎*(514) 457-9371*
☎*800-465-9474*
Tour divisions of the **Fédération des Coopératives du Nouveau-Québec**, which is entirely owned by the Inuit of Nunavik, Arctic Adventures and Inuit Adventures have been offering excursions to Nunavik since 1969 and 1990,

respectively. While Arctic Adventures handles hunting and fishing expeditions, Inuit Adventures offers cultural-adventure tours in locations all across Nunavut, including Inukjuak, Puvirnituq, Ivujivik, Kangiqsujuaq and Kangirsuk.

Fédération des coopératives du Nouveau-Québec *(☎514-457-9371 or 800-363-7610)* offers adventure-tourism packages in the region of Inukjuak, including observing caribou and ptarmigans in their natural habitat, ice-fishing for trout and spending an unforgettable night in an igloo.

Kangiqsujuaq

Inuit Adventures *(see above)* offers exploratory snowmobile journeys to the giant Cratère du Nouveau-Québec.

Aventures Ammuumaajjuq *(☎819-338-3368 or 338-3377)* specializes in adventure tourism, ecotourism, hunting and fishing.

Quaqtaq

Tommy Angnatuk *(☎819-492-9071)* owns two sea kayaks and organizes expeditions from Diana Bay to the islands of Ungava Bay.

Tasiujaq

Safari Nordik
☎(450) 971-1800
☎800-361-3748
Safari Nordik is an outfitter specialized in trout, salmon and char fishing. In summer they also organize trips down Rivière aux Feuilles in inflatable or standard canoes.

Kuujjuaq

Ungava Adventures
☎(514) 694-4424
☎866-444-3445
Many outfitters, like Ungava Adventures, organize trips in the Kuujjuaq area that feature caribou hunting, salmon and

char fishing, and extraordinary photo-safaris.

Arctic Aventures *(see above)* organizes ptarmigan-hunting and ice-fishing excursions, as well as packages, with or without guides, that include caribou hunting or salmon and char fishing with nights in a camp.

Qimutsik Eco-Tours
☎(514) 694-8264
☎888-297-3467
Qimutsik Eco-Tours is the dream-child of two young Inuit men from Nunavik, who, along with their Montreal-based partner, offer week-long dogsledding tours from Kuujjuaq during the winter and spring. Participants sleep in prospectors' tents and igloos, which they build with help from their guides.

Accommodations

Hydroelectric Projects and Cree Territory

Radisson

Two campgrounds are open for the summer in the Radisson region: **Camping Municipal** *($$;* *☎418-276-5675)* and **Camping Saint-Louis** *($$;* *☎418-276-4670)*, both in Mistissini.

Hôtel-Motel Le carrefour La Grande
$$
꓿, *K, pb/sb*
53 Avenue Des Groseillers
☎(819) 638-6005
≈(819) 638-7497
Hôtel-Motel Le Carrefour La Grande offers acceptable rooms, all of them equipped with kitchenettes.

Auberge Radisson
$$
ℛ, ℜ
66 Avenue Des Groseillers
☎(819) 638-7201
☎888-638-7201
≈(819) 638-7785
www.municipalite.baie-james.qc.ca
Auberge Radisson rents modern, comfortable rooms. All have televisions and private bathrooms.

Chisasibi

Motel Chisasibi
$$$
above the shopping centre
☎819-855-2838
≈819-855-2735
The Motel Chisasibi offers 20 comfortable rooms with private washrooms and televisions. No food service.

Chibougamau

Hôtel-Motel Harricana
$$-$$$
ℜ, ℝ, ≡, ⊛
1000 3ᵉ Rue
☎748-7771
≈748-2887
Hôtel-Motel Harricana offers about 100 guest rooms done up in 1980s-style pastel tones. Nevertheless, it's quite comfortable, and there are conference rooms that are handy for business meetings. The hotel organizes snowmobile tours and dogsledding trips.

Oujé-Bougoumou

Capissisit Lodge
$$
ℜ
☎(418) 745-3944
Twelve comfortable rooms are available at the Capissisit Lodge. The furniture in the main room, the work of Native American artisans from the southern United States, is particularly attractive.

Nord-du-Québec

Kuujjuarapik

Kuujjuaraapik Inn
$$$$
℞
☎*819-929-3374*
⇄*819-929-3062*
The Kuujjuaraapik Inn offers
17 double rooms. And also
rents snowmobiles.

Nunavik

The **Fédération des
Coopératives du Nouveau-
Québec (FCNQ)** operates
most of the hotel establishments in Inuit communities.
Reservations for FCNQ hotels
should be made through the
central number (☎*800 363-
7610*). The telephone numbers of individual hotels are
also provided below.

Inukjuak

Hôtel Inukjuak
☎*(819) 254-8306*
Inukjuak Hotel can accommodate 21 people and offers
the following rates: *$$$$* plus
tax for a double occupancy
room with two single beds,
$$$$ for a double occupancy
room with one large bed and
a television, and *$$$* for one
person. The manager is **Myna
Weetaluktuk** (☎*254-8306 or
254-8138 at the co-op*).

Akulivik

Danielly Qinuajuak
$$$
☎*(819) 496-2526*
☎*(819) 496-2002*
(coopérative)
☎*800-363-7610 FCNQ*

Salluit

Qavvik Hotel
$$$$$
☎*(819) 255-8501*
⇄*(819) 255-8504*
The **Fédération des
Coopératives du Nouveau-
Québec** does not operate any
hotels here, but there is one
private establishment where
you can stay. The **Qavvik**

Hotel offers 10 rooms, each
with two small beds.

Kangiqsujuaq

Lukasi Napaaluk
$$$$$
☎*(819) 338-3252*
The only hotel in the village is
managed by **Lukasi Napaaluk**
and can accommodate 14
people.

Quaqtaq

The **FCNQ** runs the only place
to stay in Quaqtaq. The manager can be contacted at
☎*492-9206*. The house
lodges up to seven guests at a
flat, per-person rate *($$)*.

Kangirsuk

The only hotel in the commu-
nity is operated by the **FCNQ**.
Its manager can be contacted
at ☎*935-4382*. The house
accommodates up to seven
guests at a flat, per-person
rate *($$)*.

Aupalu

There is but one hotel in this
small village, operated by the
FCNQ. Its manager can be
reached at ☎*491-7060*. Lodgings consist of a house that can
only accommodate six guests,
at a flat per-person rate *($$)*,
which sometimes means
sharing a room with other
travellers. Reservations are
strongly recommended.

Kuujjuaq

The **FCNQ** manages one of the
two hotels in the village. The
manager can be contacted at
☎*964-2272*. It can accommo-
date 20 people.

Kuujjuaq Inn
$$$$$
🐾, ℞
☎*(819) 964-2903*
⇄*(819) 964-2031*
The Auberge Kuujjuaq Inn has
22 double rooms with televi-
sions and private bathrooms.

Count on spending $225 for
two people.

Kangiqsualujjuaq

The only hotel establishment
in the community is operated
by the **FCNQ**. The manager
can be reached at
☎*337-5241*. The house can
accommodate seven people
and offers a flat per-person
rate *($$)*. The rooms can hold
receive two to four guests and
sometimes must be shared
with other travellers.

Restaurants

Hydroelectric Projects
and Cree Territory

Nemiscau

Hôtel Nemaska
$$$
2 Lakeshore
☎*(819) 673-2615*
Nemiscau has modern and
comfortable lodgings at **Hôtel
Nemaska**, in the Cree council
building.

Radisson

Radis-Nord
57 Avenue Des Groseillers
☎*819-638-7255*
☎*638-7242*
Le Radis-Nord is a general
store that sells foodstuffs and
provisions. It is a good spot to
keep in mind for those plan-
ning excursions into the sur-
rounding wilderness.

Restaurant Radisson
$-$$$
61 Avenue Des Groseillers
☎*819-638-7387*
Restaurant Radisson offers
simple but tasty cuisine and
has a liquor license.

Auberge Radisson
$$$-$$$$
66 Avenue Des Groseillers
☎819-638-7201
The restaurant at Auberge Radisson features an excellent menu and courteous and congenial service.

Nunavik

Puvirnituq

Allie's Coffee Shop
$
☎819-988-2600
Allie's Coffee Shop serves fast-food-style meals.

Kuujjuaq

Kuujjuaq Inn
$$-$$$
☎819-964-2903
⇌819-964-2031
The Kuujjuaq Inn offers restaurant service. The chef often prepares freshly caught fish or game.

Entertainment

Bars

Nunavik

Kuujjuaq

Adjoining the Kuujjuaq Inn is the **Lounge**, a café where Kuujjuamiut gather after work or after a meal in the hotel restaurant.

Ikkaqivvik Bar
The music here is as eclectic as it gets, ranging from Inuktitut country, to techno to throatsinging to disco. They even give weekly salsa and merengue classes!

Kuujjuarapik

Kuujjuarapik has a **bar**, open from noon to midnight, that has dancing and serves alcohol.

Movie Theatre

Nunavik

Kuujjuaq

Conference Centre
The new conference centre is now used as a **cinema**—the northernmost cinema in Québec.

Festivals and Cultural Events

Nunavik

Snow Festival
(Early Apr, biennially: 2003, 2005, etc.; Puvirnituq)
This festival is an occasion for villagers to participate in traditional Inuit games on the ice facing the village. The most spectacular part of the festival is the ice sculpture competition.

Easter Games
(Mid-Apr)
Like at Puvirnituq's Snow Festival, this festival is an occasion to participate in traditional Inuit games. The activities generally take place at the "Forum," the village sports centre, and at Stewart Lake, 5km north of the village. A snowmobile race between Kuujjuaq and Tasiuaq is one of the most popular parts of the festival.

Aqpik Jam
(Mid-Aug; Kuujjuaq)
Named after the cloudberry *(aqpik)*, an edible, bitter-tasting amber fruit harvested in autumn, this annual music festival unites Inuit from Canada, Alaska and Greenland.

Shopping

It would be a shame to return from a trip to the North without a handcrafted souvenir of your visit. A trip to Cree territory would not be complete without a tamarack goose—a decoy still made in the traditional way with aromatic tamarack pine twigs. A trip to Nunavik, on the other hand, demands a soapstone carving or a piece of caribou-antler jewellery.

Hydroelectric Projects and Cree Territory

Radisson

Inouis *(65 Avenue Des Groseillers, ☎819-638-6969)*, a shop that specializes in Aboriginal art, sells magnificent carvings and lovely pendants.

Chisasibi

A small, extremely interesting shop is set up in the large teepee. It has an excellent selection of products created by local artisans.

Nunavik

Kuujjuarapik

The great interest expressed by members in the village's well-established cooperative movement is evident in the quantity and quality of sculptures produced in Puvirnituq. Credit and debit (ATM) cards

Nord-du-Québec

are accepted at the Northern store and at the co-op store.

Kuujjuaq

In addition to the cooperative, two other establishments exhibit the talents of Inuit artists here: **Innivik Arts and Crafts Shop** (☎819-964-2780 or *964-2590*) and **Tivi Galleries** (*844A Airport Road*, ☎*819-964-2465 or 800-964-2465*).

Kangiqsualujjuaq

Artisans create all sorts of crafts with caribou skin. They have preserved the ancestral art of making mittens and export a portion of their products to other Inuit villages. Other items of clothing are also made here, like *kamiks*, slippers, coats, and *nasaks*, as well as caribou-antler jewellery.

Index

Index

Index

Index

Index

Order Form

Ulysses Travel Guides

☐ Acapulco .... $14.95 CAN
$9.95 US
☐ Alberta's Best Hotels . $14.95 CAN
and Restaurants $12.95 US
☐ Arizona–Grand ..... $24.95 CAN
Canyon $17.95 US
☐ Atlantic Canada .... $24.95 CAN
$17.95 US
☐ Beaches of Maine ... $12.95 CAN
$9.95 US
☐ Bed and Breakfasts .. $17.95 CAN
In Ontario $12.95 US
☐ Belize .... $16.95 CAN
$12.95 US
☐ Boston .... $17.95 CAN
$12.95 US
☐ British Columbia's Best $14.95 CAN
Hotels and Restaurants $9.95 US
☐ Calgary .... $17.95 CAN
$12.95 US
☐ California .... $29.95 CAN
$21.95 US
☐ Canada .... $29.95 CAN
$21.95 US
☐ Cancún & .... $19.95 CAN
Riviera Maya $14.95 US
☐ Cape Cod, Nantucket $17.95 CAN
and Martha's Vineyard $12.95 US
☐ Cartagena .... $12.95 CAN
(Colombia) $9.95 US
☐ Chicago .... $19.95 CAN
$14.95 US
☐ Chile .... $27.95 CAN
$17.95 US
☐ Colombia .... $29.95 CAN
$21.95 US
☐ Costa Rica .... $27.95 CAN
$19.95 US
☐ Cuba .... $24.95 CAN
$17.95 US
☐ Dominican .... $24.95 CAN
Republic $17.95 US
☐ Ecuador and ...... $24.95 CAN
Galápagos Islands $17.95 US
☐ El Salvador .... $22.95 CAN
$14.95 US
☐ Guadalajara .... $17.95 CAN
$12.95 US
☐ Guadeloupe .... $24.95 CAN
$17.95 US
☐ Guatemala .... $24.95 CAN
$17.95 US

☐ Havana .... $16.95 CAN
$12.95 US
☐ Hawaii .... $29.95 CAN
$21.95 US
☐ Honduras .... $24.95 CAN
$17.95 US
☐ Huatulco– .... $17.95 CAN
Puerto Escondido $12.95 US
☐ Inns and Bed & .... $17.95 CAN
Breakfasts in Québec $12.95 US
☐ Jamaica .... $24.95 CAN
$17.95 US
☐ Las Vegas .... $17.95 CAN
$12.95 US
☐ Lisbon .... $18.95 CAN
$13.95 US
☐ Los Angeles .... $19.95 CAN
$14.95 US
☐ Los Cabos and La Paz $14.95 CAN
$7.99 US
☐ Louisiana .... $29.95 CAN
$21.95 US
☐ Martinique .... $24.95 CAN
$17.95 US
☐ Miami .... $17.95 CAN
$12.95 US
☐ Montréal .... $19.95 CAN
$14.95 US
☐ New England ...... $29.95 CAN
$21.95 US
☐ New Orleans ...... $17.95 CAN
$12.95 US
☐ New York City ..... $19.95 CAN
$14.95 US
☐ Nicaragua .... $24.95 CAN
$16.95 US
☐ Ontario's Best Hotels $16.95 CAN
and Restaurants $12.95US
☐ Ontario .... $27.95 CAN
$19.95US
☐ Ottawa–Hull .... $17.95 CAN
$12.95 US
☐ Panamá .... $27.95 CAN
$17.95 US
☐ Peru .... $27.95 CAN
$19.95 US
☐ Phoenix .... $16.95 CAN
$12.95 US
☐ Portugal .... $24.95 CAN
$16.95 US

Ulysses Travel Guides (continued)

☐ Provence & . . . . the Côte d'Azur	$29.95 CAN $21.95US	☐ Seattle	$17.95 CAN $12.95 US
☐ Puerto Plata–Sosua .	$14.95 CAN $9.95 US	☐ St. Lucia	$17.95 CAN $12.95 US
☐ Puerto Rico	$24.95 CAN $17.95 US	☐ St. Martin– . . . . St. Barts	$17.95 CAN $12.95 US
☐ Puerto Vallarta	$14.95 CAN $10.95 US	☐ Toronto	$19.95 CAN $14.95 US
☐ Québec	$29.95 CAN $21.95 US	☐ Tunisia	$27.95 CAN $19.95 US
☐ Québec City	$17.95 CAN $12.95 US	☐ Vancouver	$17.95 CAN $12.95 US
☐ San Diego	$17.95 CAN $12.95 US	☐ Washington D.C. . . .	$18.95 CAN $13.95 US
☐ San Francisco	$17.95 CAN $12.95 US	☐ Western Canada . . .	$29.95 CAN $21.95 US

budget.zone

☐ Central America	$14.95 CAN $10.95 US	☐ Western Canada . . .	$14.95 CAN $10.95 US

Ulysses Travel Journals

☐ Ulysses Travel Journal (Blue, Red, Green, Yellow, Sextant)	$9.95 CAN $7.95 US	☐ Ulysses Travel Journal (80 Days)	$14.95 CAN $9.95 US

Ulysses Green Escapes

☐ Cross-Country Skiing and Snowshoeing in Ontario	$22.95 CAN $16.95 US	☐ Ontario's Bike Paths . and Rail Trails	$19.95 CAN $14.95 US
☐ Cycling in France . . .	$22.95 CAN $16.95 US	☐ Hiking in the . . . . Northeastern U.S.	$19.95 CAN $13.95 US
☐ Cycling in Ontario . . .	$22.95 CAN $16.95 US	☐ Hiking in Québec . . .	$22.95 CAN $16.95 US
		☐ Hiking in Ontario . . .	$22.95 CAN $16.95 US

Ulysses Conversation Guides

☐ Canadian French . . . for Better Travel	$12.95 CAN $9.95 US	☐ Portuguese for . . . . . . Better Travel	$9.95 CAN $6.95 US
☐ French for . . . . Better Travel	$9.95 CAN $6.95 US	☐ Spanish for Better . . . Travel in Spain	$9.95 CAN $6.95 US
☐ Italian for . . . . Better Travel	$9.95 CAN $6.95 US	☐ Spanish for Better . . . Travel in Latin America	$9.95 CAN $6.95 US

Title	Qty	Price	Total

Name:	Subtotal	
	Shipping	$4.75 CAN $5.75 US
Address:	Subtotal	
	GST in Canada 7%	
	Total	

Tel: Fax:

E-mail:

Payment: ☐ Cheque   ☐ Visa   ☐ MasterCard

Card number_____ Expiry date_____

Signature_____

Ulysses Travel Guides

4176 St. Denis Street,
Montréal, Québec, H2W 2M5
☎ *(514) 843-9447*
fax: *(514) 843-9448*

305 Madison Avenue,
Suite 1166,
New York, NY 10165
Toll-free: *1-877-542-7247*

www.ulyssesguides.com
info@ulysses.ca